CRIME
IN THE
UNITED STATES

SECOND EDITION

2008

CRIME
IN THE
UNITED STATES

SECOND EDITION

2008

Published in the United States of America
by Bernan Press, a wholly owned subsidiary of
The Rowman & Littlefield Publishing Group, Inc.
4501 Forbes Boulevard, Suite 200
Lanham, Maryland 20706

Bernan Press
800-865-3457
info@bernan.com
www.bernan.com

ISBN 10: 1-59888-266-X
ISBN 13: 978-1-59888-266-7
eISBN 10: 1-59888-288-0
eISBN 13: 978-1-59888-288-9

♾™ The paper used in this publication meets the minimum requirements of
American National Standard for Information Sciences—Permanence of
Paper for Printed Library Materials, ANSI/NISO Z39.48-1992.
Manufactured in the United States of America.

CONTENTS

SECTION I:
SUMMARY OF THE UNIFORM CRIME REPORTING (UCR) PROGRAM

SUMMARY OF THE UNIFORM CRIME REPORTING (UCR) PROGRAM

Bernan Press is proud to present its second edition of *Crime in the United States*. This title was formerly published by the Federal Bureau of Investigation (FBI), but is no longer available in printed form from the government.

This section examines the best way of using the publication's data and discusses the history of the UCR Program, which collects the data used in *Crime in the United States*.

About the UCR Program

The UCR Program's primary objective is to generate reliable information for use in law enforcement administration, operation, and management; however, over the course of the program, its data have become one of the country's leading social indicators.

The UCR Program is a nationwide, cooperative statistical effort of more than 17,000 city, university and college, county, state, tribal, and federal law enforcement agencies who voluntarily report data on crimes brought to their attention. During 2006, the law enforcement agencies that were active in the UCR Program represented 94.2 percent of the total population. This coverage included 95.6 percent of the nation's population in metropolitan statistical areas (MSAs), 86.3 percent of the population in cities outside metropolitan areas, and 88.1 percent of the population in nonmetropolitan counties.

Note for Users

It is important for UCR data users to remember that the FBI's primary objective is to generate a reliable set of crime statistics for use in law enforcement administration, operation, and management. The FBI does not provide a ranking of agencies; instead, it provides alphabetical tabulations of states, metropolitan statistical areas, cities with over 10,000 inhabitants, suburban and rural counties, and colleges and universities. Law enforcement officials use these data for their designed purposes. Additionally, the public relies on these data for information about the fluctuations in levels of crime from year to year, while criminologists, sociologists, legislators, city planners, media outlets, and other students of criminal justice use them for a variety of research and planning purposes. Since crime is a sociological phenomenon influenced by a variety of factors, the FBI discourages data users from ranking agencies and using the data as a measurement of the effectiveness of law enforcement.

To ensure that data are uniformly reported, the FBI provides contributing law enforcement agencies with a handbook that explains how to classify and score offenses and provides uniform crime offense definitions. Acknowledging that offense definitions may vary from state to state, the FBI cautions agencies to report offenses according to the guidelines provided in the handbook, rather than by local or state statutes. Most agencies make a good faith effort to comply with established guidelines.

Nearly 17,000 agencies contribute data to the FBI in any given year; however, because of computer problems, changes in record management systems, personnel shortages, or other reasons, some agencies cannot provide data for publication.

The UCR Program publishes the statistics most commonly requested by data users. More information regarding the availability of UCR Program data is available by telephone at (304) 625-4995, by fax at (304) 625-5394, or by e-mail at <cjis_comm@leo.gov>. E-mail data requests cannot be processed without the requester's full name, mailing address, and contact telephone number.

Variables Affecting Crime

Until data users examine all the variables that affect crime in a town, city, county, state, region, or college or university, they can make no meaningful comparisons.

Caution Against Ranking

In each edition of *Crime in the United States*, many entities—including news media, tourism agencies, and other organizations with an interest in crime in the nation—use reported figures to compile rankings of cities and counties. However, these rankings are merely a quick choice made by that data user; they provide no insight into the many variables that mold the crime in a particular town, city, county, state, or region. Consequently, these rankings may lead to simplistic and/or incomplete analyses, which can create misleading perceptions and thus adversely affect cities and counties, along with their residents.

Considering Other Characteristics of a Jurisdiction

To assess criminality and law enforcement's response from jurisdiction to jurisdiction, data users must consider many variables, some of which (despite having significant impact on crime) are not readily measurable or applicable among all locales. Geographic and demographic factors specific to each jurisdiction must be considered and applied in order to make an accurate and complete assessment of crime in that jurisdiction. Several sources of information are available to help the researcher explore the variables that affect crime in a particular locale. U.S. Census Bureau data, for example, can help the user better understand the makeup of a locale's population. The transience of the population, its racial and ethnic makeup, and its composition by age and gender, educational levels, and prevalent family structures are all key factors in assessing and understanding crime.

Local chambers of commerce, planning offices, and similar entities provide information regarding the economic and cultural makeup of cities and counties. Understanding a jurisdiction's industrial/economic base, its dependence upon neighboring jurisdictions, its transportation system, its economic dependence on nonresidents (such as tourists and convention attendees), and its proximity to military installations, correctional institutions, and other types of facilities all contribute to accurately gauging and interpreting the crime known to and reported by law enforcement.

The strength (including personnel and other resources) and aggressiveness of a jurisdiction's law enforcement agency are also key factors in understanding the nature and extent of crime occurring in that area. Although information pertaining to the number of sworn and civilian employees can be found in this publication, it cannot be used alone as an assessment of the emphasis that a community places on enforcing the law. For example, one city may report more crime than another comparable city because its law enforcement agency identifies more offenses. Attitudes of citizens toward crime and their crime reporting practices—especially for minor offenses—also have an impact on the volume of crimes known to police.

Make Valid Assessments of Crime

It is essential for all data users to become as well educated as possible about understanding and quantifying the nature and extent of crime in the United States and in the more than 17,000 jurisdictions represented by law enforcement contributors to the UCR Program. Valid assessments are possible only with careful study and analysis of the various unique conditions that affect each local law enforcement jurisdiction.

Some factors that are known to affect the volume and type of crime occurring from place to place are:

- Population density and degree of urbanization

- Variations in composition of population, particularly in the concentration of youth

- Stability of the population with respect to residents' mobility, commuting patterns, and transient factors

- Modes of transportation and highway systems

- Economic conditions, including median income, poverty level, and job availability

- Cultural factors and educational, recreational, and religious characteristics

- Family conditions, with respect to divorce and family cohesiveness

- Climate

- Effective strength of law enforcement agencies

- Administrative and investigative emphases of law enforcement

- Policies of other components of the criminal justice system (i.e., prosecutorial, judicial, correctional, and probational policies)

- Residents' attitudes toward crime

- Crime reporting practices of residents

Although many of the listed factors equally affect the crime of a particular area, the UCR Program makes no attempt to relate them to the data presented. **The data user is therefore cautioned against comparing statistical data of individual reporting units from cities, counties, metropolitan areas, states, or colleges or universities solely on the basis on their population coverage or student enrollment.** Until data users examine all the variables that affect crime in a town, city, county, state, region, or college or university, they can make no meaningful comparisons.

Historical Background

Since 1930, the FBI has administered the UCR Program; the agency continues to assess and monitor the nature and type of crime in the nation. Data users look to the UCR Program for various research and planning purposes.

Recognizing a need for national crime statistics, the International Association of Chiefs of Police (IACP) formed the Committee on Uniform Crime Records in the 1920s to develop a system of uniform crime statistics. Establishing offenses known to law enforcement as the appropriate measure, the committee evaluated various crimes on the basis of their seriousness, frequency of occurrence, pervasiveness in all geographic areas of the country, and likelihood of being reported to law enforcement. After studying state criminal codes and making an evaluation of the record-keeping practices in use, the committee completed a plan for crime reporting that became the foundation of the UCR Program in 1929.

Seven main offense classifications, known as Part I crimes, were chosen to gauge the state of crime in the nation. These seven offense classifications included the violent crimes of murder and nonnegligent manslaughter, forcible rape, robbery, and aggravated assault; also included were the property crimes of burglary, larceny-theft, and motor vehicle theft. By congressional mandate, arson was added as the eighth Part I offense category. Data collection for arson began in 1979. Agencies classify and score offenses according to a Hierarchy Rule (with the exception of justifiable homicide, motor vehicle theft, and arson) and report their data to the FBI.

During the early planning of the program, it was recognized that the differences among criminal codes precluded a mere aggregation of state statistics to arrive at a national total. Also, because of the variances in punishment for the same offenses in different states, no distinction between felony and misdemeanor crimes was possible. To avoid these problems and provide nationwide uniformity in crime reporting, standardized offense definitions were developed. Law enforcement agencies use these to submit data without regard for local statutes. The definitions used by the program can be found in Appendix II.

In January 1930, 400 cities (representing 20 million inhabitants in 43 states) began participating in the UCR Program. Congress enacted Title 28, Section 534, of the *United States Code* that same year, which authorized the attorney general to gather crime information. The attorney general, in turn, designated the FBI to serve as the national clearinghouse for the collected crime data. Since then, data based on uniform classifications and procedures for reporting have been obtained annually from the nation's law enforcement agencies.

Advisory Groups

Providing vital links between local law enforcement and the FBI for the UCR Program are the Criminal Justice Information Systems Committees of the IACP and the National Sheriffs' Association (NSA). The IACP represents the thousands of police departments nationwide, as it has since the program began. The NSA encourages sheriffs throughout the country to participate fully in the program. Both committees serve the program in advisory capacities.

In 1988, a Data Providers' Advisory Policy Board was established. This board operated until 1993, when it combined with the National Crime Information Center Advisory Policy Board to form a single Advisory Policy Board (APB) to address all FBI criminal justice information services. The current APB works to ensure continuing emphasis on UCR-related issues. The Association of State Uniform Crime Reporting Programs (ASUCRP) focuses on UCR issues within individual state law enforcement associations and also promotes interest in the UCR Program. These organizations foster widespread and responsible use of uniform crime statistics and lend assistance to data contributors.

Redesign of UCR

Although UCR data collection was originally conceived as a tool for law enforcement administration, the data were widely used by other entities involved in various forms of social planning by the 1980s. Recognizing the need for more detailed crime statistics, law enforcement called for a thorough evaluative study to modernize the UCR Program. The FBI formulated a comprehensive three-phase redesign effort. The Bureau of Justice Statistics (BJS), the agency in the Department of Justice responsible for funding criminal justice information projects, agreed to underwrite the first two phases. These phases were conducted by an independent contractor and structured to determine what, if any, changes should be made to the current program. The third phase would involve implementation of the changes identified.

During the first phase, which began in 1982, the historical evolution of the UCR Program was examined. All aspects of the program, including its objectives and intended user audience, data items, reporting mechanisms, quality control issues, publications and user services, and relationships with other criminal justice data systems, were studied.

Early in 1984, a conference on the future of UCR Program launched the second phase of the study that examined the program's potential and concluded with a set of recommended changes. Phase two ended in early 1985 with the production of a report, *Blueprint for the Future of the Uniform Crime Reporting Program.* The study's Steering Committee reviewed the draft report at a March 1985 meeting and made various recommendations for revision.

The committee members, however, endorsed the report's concepts.

In April 1985, the phase two recommendations were presented at the eighth National UCR Conference. Various considerations for the final report were set forth, and the overall concept for the revised UCR Program was unanimously approved. The joint IACP/NSA Committee on UCR also issued a resolution endorsing the *Blueprint.*

The final report, the *Blueprint for the Future of the Uniform Crime Reporting Program,* was released in the summer of 1985. It specifically outlined recommendations for an expanded, improved UCR Program to meet future informational needs. There were three recommended areas of enhancement to the UCR Program:

- Offenses and arrests would be reported using an incident-based system.

- Data would be collected on two levels. Agencies in level one would report important details about those offenses comprising the Part I crimes, their victims, and arrestees. Level two would consist of law enforcement agencies covering populations of more than 100,000 and a sampling of smaller agencies that would collect expanded detail on all significant offenses.

- A quality assurance program would be introduced.

To begin implementation, the FBI awarded a contract to develop new offense definitions and data elements for the redesigned system. The work involved (a) revising the definitions of certain Part I offenses, (b) identifying additional significant offenses to be reported, (c) refining definitions for both, and (d) developing data elements (incident details) for all UCR Program offenses in order to fulfill the requirements of incident-based reporting versus the current summary system.

Concurrent with the preparation of the data elements, the FBI studied the various state systems to select an experimental site for implementing the redesigned program. In view of its long-standing incident-based program and well-established staff dedicated solely to UCR, the South Carolina Law Enforcement Division (SLED) was chosen. The SLED agreed to adapt its existing system to meet the requirements of the redesigned program and to collect data on both offenses and arrests relating to the newly defined offenses.

Following the completion of the pilot project conducted by the SLED, the FBI produced a draft of guidelines for an enhanced UCR Program. Law enforcement executives from around the country were then invited to a conference where the guidelines were presented for final review.

During the conference, three overall recommendations were passed without dissent: the establishment of a new, incident-based national crime reporting system; the FBI as the managing agency for the program; and the creation of an Advisory Policy Board composed of law enforcement executives to assist in directing and implementing the new program.

Information about the redesigned UCR Program, called the National Incident-Based Reporting System, or NIBRS, is contained in several documents. The *Data Collection Guidelines* publication (August 2000) contains a system overview and descriptions of the offense codes, reports, data elements, and data values used in the system. The *Error Message Manual* (December 1999) contains designations of mandatory and optional data elements, data element edits, and error messages. The *Data Submission Specifications* publication is for the use of local and state systems personnel who are responsible for preparing magnetic media for submission to the FBI. The document is available on the FBI's Web site at <www.fbi.gov/ucr/ucr.htm>. Another publication, *Handbook for Acquiring a Records Management System (RMS) That Is Compatible with NIBRS,* is also available on that site.

A NIBRS edition of the *UCR Handbook* was published in 1992 to assist law enforcement agency data contributors implementing the NIBRS within their departments. This document is geared toward familiarizing local and state law enforcement personnel with the definitions, policies, and procedures of the NIBRS. It does not contain the technical coding and data transmission requirements presented in the other NIBRS publications.

The NIBRS collects data on each single incident and arrest within 22 crime categories. For each offense known to police within these categories, incident, victim, property, offender, and arrestee information are gathered when available. The goal of the redesign is to modernize crime information by collecting data currently maintained law enforcement records, making the enhanced UCR Program a by-product of current records systems while maintaining the integrity of the program's long-running statistical series.

Implementation of the NIBRS is occurring at a pace commensurate with the resources, abilities, and limitations of the contributing law enforcement agencies. The FBI was able to accept NIBRS data as of January 1989, and to date, the following 31 state programs have been certified for NIBRS participation: Arizona, Arkansas, Colorado, Connecticut, Delaware, Idaho, Iowa, Kansas, Kentucky, Louisiana, Maine, Massachusetts, Michigan, Missouri, Montana, Nebraska, New Hampshire, North

Dakota, Ohio, Oregon, Rhode Island, South Carolina, South Dakota, Tennessee, Texas, Utah, Vermont, Virginia, Washington, West Virginia, and Wisconsin. Among those that submit NIBRS data, 10 states (Delaware, Idaho, Iowa, Michigan, Montana, South Carolina, Tennessee, Vermont, Virginia, and West Virginia) submit all their data via the NIBRS.

Ten state programs are in various stages of testing the NIBRS. Six other state agencies, as well as agencies in the District of Columbia, are in various stages of planning and developing NIBRS.

Suspension of the Crime Index and Modified Crime Index

In June 2004, the Criminal Justice Information Services Advisory Policy Board (CJIS APB) approved discontinuing the use of the Crime Index in the UCR Program and its publications and directed the FBI to publish a violent crime total and a property crime total until a more viable index is developed. The Crime Index was first published in *Crime in the United States* in 1960. Congress designated arson as a Part I offense in October 1978, and the UCR Program began collecting arson data in 1979. The FBI adopted the term Modified Crime Index to reflect the addition of arson as a Part I offense. The Modified Crime Index was the number of Crime Index offenses plus arson. However, in recent years, the Crime Index (and subsequently the Modified Crime Index) has not been a true indicator of the degree of criminality. The Crime Index was simply the title used for an aggregation of the seven main offense classifications (Part I offenses) for which data has been collected since the program's implementation.

The Crime Index and Modified Crime Index were driven upward by the offense with the highest number, creating a bias against a jurisdiction with a high number of larceny-thefts but a low number of other serious crimes such as murder and forcible rape. Thus, the sheer volume of those offenses overshadows more serious but less frequently committed offenses. CJIS studied the appropriateness and usefulness of the Crime Index and Modified Crime Index for several years and brought the matter before many advisory groups affiliated with the UCR Program. The consensus was that the Crime Index and Modified Crime Index no longer served their original purpose, and that the UCR Program should suspend their use and develop a more robust index of crime.

SECTION II:
OFFENSES REPORTED

VIOLENT CRIME

- Murder
- Forcible Rape
- Robbery
- Aggravated Assault

PROPERTY CRIME

- Burglary
- Larceny-Theft
- Motor Vehicle Theft
- Arson

VIOLENT CRIME

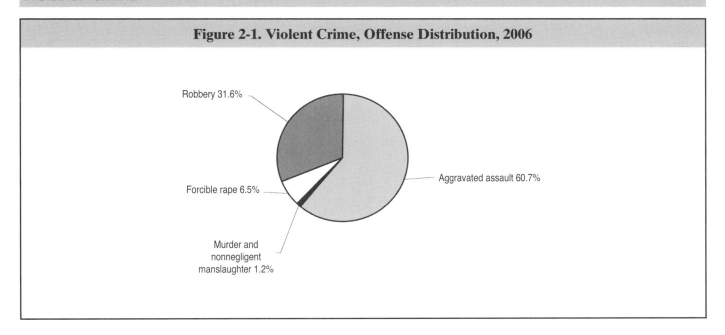

Figure 2-1. Violent Crime, Offense Distribution, 2006

Robbery 31.6%

Forcible rape 6.5%

Murder and nonnegligent manslaughter 1.2%

Aggravated assault 60.7%

Definition

Violent crime consists of four offenses: murder and nonnegligent manslaughter, forcible rape, robbery, and aggravated assault. According to the Uniform Crime Reporting (UCR) Program, run by the Federal Bureau of Investigation (FBI), violent crimes involve either the use of force or the threat of force.

Data Collection

The data presented in *Crime in the United States* reflect the Hierarchy Rule, which counts only the most serious offense in a multiple-offense criminal incident. In descending order of severity, the violent crimes are murder and nonnegligent manslaughter, forcible rape, robbery, and aggravated assault; these are followed by the property crimes of burglary, larceny-theft, and motor vehicle theft. More information on the expanded violent crime tables (which are available online but not included in this publication) can be found in Appendix I.

National Volume, Trends, and Rate

In 2006, an estimated 1,417,745 violent crimes occurred in the United States. Aggravated assault accounted for 60.7 percent of these crimes, followed by robbery (31.6 percent), forcible rape (6.5 percent), and murder (1.2 percent). (Table 1)

The UCR Program reports data in 2-year, 5-year, and 10-year increments to formulate trend information. From 2005 to 2006, the estimated volume of violent crime in the United States increased 1.9 percent. (The estimated number of property crimes fell 1.9 percent during the same period.) The 5-year and 10-year trend data showed that the estimated number of violent crimes decreased 0.4 percent between 2002 and 2006 and decreased 13.3 percent between

1997 and 2006. The rate of violent crime in 2006 was 473.5 per 100,000 inhabitants, the second consecutive increase after 13 years of decreasing rates. (Tables 1 and 1A)

An examination of the volume of individual offenses within the violent crime category showed that in a year-to-year comparison of data from 2005 and 2006, the estimated number of aggravated assaults decreased 0.2 percent, the estimated number of robberies increased 7.2 percent, and the estimated number of murders increased 1.8 percent. Forcible rape showed its second consecutive decline, by dropping 2.0 percent from 2005 to 2006. (Tables 1 and 1A)

Among each of the four violent crimes categories, aggravated assault had the highest rate of occurrence. There were an estimated 287.5 aggravated assaults, 149.4 robberies, 30.9 forcible rapes, and 5.7 murders per 100,000 inhabitants in the United States in 2006. (Table 1)

Regional Offense Trends and Rate

The UCR Program divides the United States into four regions: the Northeast, the South, the Midwest, and the West. (More details concerning geographic regions are provided in Appendix III.) The population distribution of the regions is provided in Table 3, and the estimated volume and rate of violent crime by region can be found in Table 4.

The Northeast

The Northeast accounted for an estimated 18.3 percent of the nation's population in 2006 and an estimated 15.1 percent of its violent crimes. (Table 3) Of the four regions, the Northeast had the only decrease (down 0.4 percent) in the estimated number of violent crimes from 2005 to 2006. The region's population grew by 0.1 percent during this period. In the Northeast, the estimated number of rob-

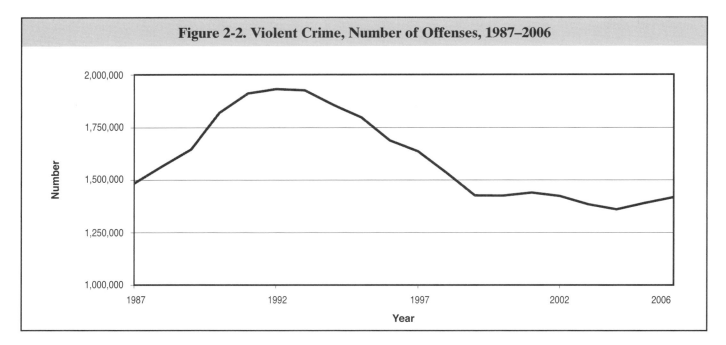

Figure 2-2. Violent Crime, Number of Offenses, 1987–2006

beries increased 2.3 percent and the estimated number of murders increased 1.9 percent, while the estimated number of aggravated assaults decreased 1.6 percent and the estimated number of forcible rapes decreased 6.6 percent. (Table 4)

In 2006, there were an estimated 391.9 violent crimes per 100,000 inhabitants in the Northeast, a 0.5 percent decrease from 2005 figure. By offense, rates were estimated at 215.6 aggravated assaults, 151.2 robberies, 20.6 forcible rapes, and 4.5 murders per 100,000 inhabitants. (Table 4)

The Midwest

With an estimated 22.1 percent of the total population of the United States, the Midwest accounted for 23.2 percent of the nation's estimated number of violent crimes in 2006. (Table 3) The region had a 1.8 percent increase in violent crime and a 0.4 percent growth in population from 2005 to 2006. The estimated number of aggravated assaults in the Midwest increased 0.6 percent, the estimated number of robberies increased 5.3 percent, and the estimated number of murders grew 0.7 percent from 2005 to 2006, while the estimated number of forcible rapes fell 3.0 percent. (Table 4)

The rate of violent crime in the Midwest was estimated at 419.1 incidents per 100,000 inhabitants in 2006, a 1.4 percent increase from the 2005 rate. In 2006, there were 246.6 aggravated assaults, 132.1 robberies, 35.4 forcible rapes, and 5.0 murders per 100,000 inhabitants in the region. The forcible rape rate, with a 3.4 percent decline from the 2005 figure, was the only rate to decrease for the Midwest in 2006. (Table 4)

The South

The South, the nation's most populous region, accounted for an estimated 36.4 percent of the nation's population

in 2006. An estimated 42.1 percent of the nation's violent crimes took place in this region in 2006. (Table 3) Violent crime in the South increased 2.3 percent from 2005 to 2006, and the region's population grew 1.4 percent during this period. The estimated number of aggravated assaults increased 0.4 percent from 2005 to 2006, while the estimated number of robberies increased 7.4 percent and the estimated number of murders grew 3.6 percent. The estimated number of forcible rapes showed the region's only decline, dropping 0.2 percent from 2005 to 2006. (Table 4)

The estimated rate of violent crime in the South was 547.5 incidents per 100,000 inhabitants in 2006. There were 351.0 aggravated assaults, 157.1 robberies, 32.7 forcible rapes, and 6.8 murders per 100,000 inhabitants. The forcible rape and aggravated assault rates both showed declines between 2005 and 2006, dropping 1.6 percent and 1.0 percent, respectively. (Table 4)

The West

With an estimated 23.2 percent of the nation's population in 2006, the West also accounted for an estimated 23.2 percent of the nation's violent crime. (Table 3) Violent crime increased 3.0 percent in this region from 2005 to 2006, while its population grew 1.5 percent. Three of the four violent offense categories decreased in number from 2005 to 2006: aggravated assault dropped 0.9 percent, forcible rape declined 1.3 percent, and murder decreased 0.8 percent. Only robbery showed an increase, rising 12.3 percent. (Table 4)

The estimated rate of violent crime in the West in 2006 was 473.5 incidents per 100,000 inhabitants, a 1.5 percent increase from the 2005 rate. There were 283.6 aggravated assaults, 152.5 robberies (up over 10 percent from 2005), 31.8 forcible rapes, and 5.6 murders per 100,000 inhabitants in this region in 2006. (Table 4)

Community Types

The UCR Program aggregates crime data into three community types: metropolitan statistical areas (MSAs), cities outside MSAs, and nonmetropolitan counties outside MSAs. Appendix III provides additional information regarding community types. Just over 83 percent of the nation's population lived in MSAs in 2006. Residents of cities outside MSAs accounted for 6.7 percent of the country's population, while 10.2 percent of the population lived in nonmetropolitan counties. (Table 2)

An examination of the volume of violent crime by community type showed that 90.3 percent of the estimated number of violent crimes in the United States occurred in MSAs, 5.3 percent occurred in cities outside MSAs, and 4.3 percent occurred in nonmetropolitan counties. By community type, the violent crime rates were estimated at 514.6 incidents per 100,000 inhabitants in MSAs, 382.4 incidents per 100,000 inhabitants in cities outside MSAs, and 199.2 incidents per 100,000 inhabitants in nonmetropolitan counties. (Table 2)

Population Groups: Trends and Rates

In the UCR Program, data are also aggregated into population groups; these groups are described in more detail in Appendix III. The nation's cities had an overall increase of 2.0 percent in the estimated number of violent crimes from 2005 to 2006. By city population group, cities with over 250,000 inhabitants had the smallest percentage increase in the estimated number of violent crimes (1.0 percent), while cities with 25,000 to 49,999 inhabitants posted the greatest increase (3.8 percent). (Table 12)

The law enforcement agencies in the nation's cities collectively reported a rate of 589.0 violent crimes per 100,000 inhabitants in 2006. Law enforcement agencies in cities subset of 250,000 to 499,999 inhabitants reported the highest violent crime rate, with 995.6 violent crimes per 100,000 inhabitants; the violent crime rate for all cities with 250,000 or more inhabitants was 936.7. Agencies in cities with 10,000 to 24,999 inhabitants reported the lowest violent crime rate (311.7 incidents per 100,000 inhabitants). Law enforcement agencies in the nation's metropolitan counties reported a collective violent crime rate of 343.2 per 100,000 inhabitants, while agencies in nonmetropolitan counties reported a collective rate of 206.2 violent crimes per 100,000 inhabitants. (Table 16)

Weapons Distribution

The UCR Program collects weapons data for murder, robbery, and aggravated assault offenses. In 2006, firearms were used in 67.9 percent of murders, in 42.2 percent of the robbery offenses, and in 21.9 percent of the aggravated assaults. Of the homicides for which the type of weapon was specified, firearms were used in 73.4 percent of the offenses. Handguns made up 88.4 percent of identified firearms used. (Tables 1 and 19 and Expanded Homicide Table 7)

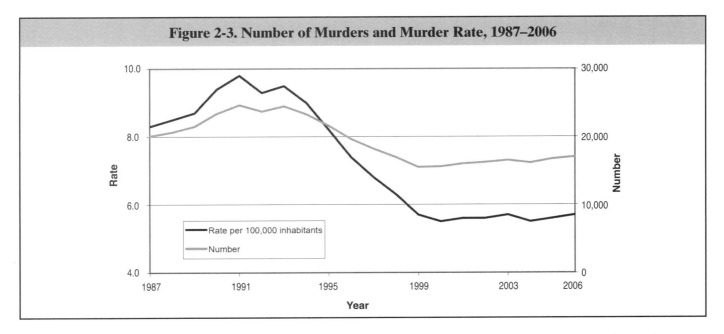

Figure 2-3. Number of Murders and Murder Rate, 1987–2006

MURDER

Definition

The UCR Program defines murder and nonnegligent manslaughter as the willful (nonnegligent) killing of one human being by another. The classification of this offense is based solely on police investigation, rather than on the determination of a court, medical examiner, coroner, jury, or other judicial body. The UCR Program does not include the following situations under this offense classification: deaths caused by negligence, suicide, or accident; justifiable homicides; and attempts to murder or assaults to murder, which are considered aggravated assaults.

Data Collection

The UCR Program's *Supplementary Homicide Report* (SHR) provides information about murder victims and offenders by age, sex, and race; the types of weapons used in the murders; the relationships of the victims to the offenders; and the circumstances surrounding the incident. Law enforcement agencies are asked to complete an SHR for each murder reported to the UCR Program.

National Volume, Trends, and Rates

The UCR Program's homicide data for 2006 topped 17,000 for the first time since 1997. An estimated 17,034 persons were murdered nationwide in 2006, an increase of 1.8 percent from the 2005 estimate. An analysis of 5-year and 10-year trend data showed that the 2006 estimate increased 5.0 percent from the 2002 (5-year) estimate, but decreased 6.4 percent from the 1997 (10-year) estimate. Murder accounted for 1.2 percent of the overall estimated number of violent crimes in 2006.

The 2006 data yielded an estimated rate of 5.7 murders per 100,000 inhabitants, a 0.8 percent increase from the 2005 rate. The 2006 rate is 1.0 percent higher than the rate

from 2002, but represents a 16.3 percent decline from the 1997 rate. (Tables 1 and 1A)

Regional Offense Trends and Rates

The UCR Program divides the United States into four regions: the Northeast, the South, the Midwest, and the West. (More details concerning geographic regions are provided in Appendix III.) The estimated number of murders increased in three of the four regions, with the highest increase, 3.6 percent, in the South.

The Northeast

In 2006, the Northeast accounted for an estimated 18.3 percent of the nation's population and 14.4 percent of its estimated number of murders. With an estimated 2,455 murders, the Northeast saw a 1.9 percent increase compared with the 2005 figure. The region's population grew 0.1 percent from 2005 to 2006. The offense rate for the Northeast was 4.5 murders per 100,000 inhabitants, up from 4.4 murders per 100,000 inhabitants in 2005. (Tables 3 and 4)

The Midwest

The Midwest accounted for an estimated 22.1 percent of the nation's total population (the region's population having grown 0.4 percent from 2005 to 2006) and 19.4 percent of the country's estimated number of murders in 2006. There were an estimated 3,307 murders in the Midwest in 2006, a 0.7 percent increase from the estimated figure for 2005. The Midwest experienced a rate of 5.0 murders per 100,000 inhabitants in 2006, equaling the estimated rate for 2005. (Tables 3 and 4)

The South

The South, the nation's most populous region, experienced a 1.4 percent growth in population from 2005 to 2006. The region accounted for an estimated 36.4 percent of the nation's population in 2005 and the nation's highest proportion of murders (43.2 percent). The estimated 7,367 murders represented a 3.6 percent increase in the estimated number of murders from 2005 to 2006. The region's estimated rate of 6.8 murders per 100,000 inhabitants represented an increase of 2.1 percent from the estimated rate for 2005. (Tables 3 and 4)

The West

The West accounted for an estimated 23.2 percent of the nation's population and 22.9 percent of the estimated number of murders in 2006. Its population grew 1.5 percent from 2005 to 2006. The West experienced an estimated 3,905 murders, a 0.8 percent decrease from the 2005 estimate. The region's murder rate was 5.6 per 100,000 inhabitants, a decrease from the 2005 rate of 5.8. (Tables 3 and 4)

Community Types

The UCR Program aggregates data for three community types: metropolitan statistical areas (MSAs), cities outside MSAs, and nonmetropolitan counties outside MSAs. (See Appendix III for definitions.) In 2006, MSAs accounted for 83.1 percent of the nation's population and 85.5 percent of the estimated total number of murders. With 15,429 estimated homicides, MSAs experienced a rate of 6.2 murders per 100,000 inhabitants in 2006. Cities outside MSAs accounted for 6.7 percent of the U.S. population and (with an estimated 653 murders) accounted for 3.8 percent of the estimated murders in the nation. The murder rate for cities outside MSAs was 3.3 per 100,000 inhabitants. (Table 2)

In 2006, 10.2 percent of the nation's population lived in nonmetropolitan counties outside MSAs. An estimated 952 murders took place in these counties, accounting for 5.6 percent of the nation's estimated total. The murder rate for nonmetropolitan counties outside MSAs was 3.1 murders per 100,000 inhabitants. (Table 2)

Population Groups: Trends and Rates

The UCR Program uses the following population group designations in its data presentations: cities (grouped according to population size) and counties (classified as either metropolitan or nonmetropolitan). A breakdown of these classifications is provided in Appendix III.

From 2005 to 2006, the nation's cities experienced a 1.9 percent increase in homicides. The city groups with 100,000 to 249,999 inhabitants, 50,000 to 99,999 inhabitants, and 25,000 to 49,999 inhabitants all experienced decreases in homicides from 2005 to 2006. The city group of 10,000 to 24,999 inhabitants had the largest increase in murders (7.8 percent). Metropolitan counties experienced an increase in homicides of 6.1 percent from 2005 to 2006, while nonmetropolitan counties experienced a decrease of 10.8 percent. (Table 12)

In 2006, cities collectively had a rate of 7.1 murders per 100,000 inhabitants. Cities with 500,000 to 999,999 inhabitants had the highest murder rate (13.9 murders per 100,000

inhabitants) among city population groups, while cities with fewer than 10,000 inhabitants had the lowest murder rate (2.5 murders per 100,000 inhabitants). The homicide rates for metropolitan and nonmetropolitan counties were 4.2 and 3.2 per 100,000 inhabitants, respectively. Suburban areas had a homicide rate of 3.5 per 100,000 inhabitants. (Table 16)

Offense Analysis

Supplementary Homicide Reports

The UCR Program's *Supplementary Homicide Report* (SHR) provides information regarding the age, sex, and race of both the murder victim and the offender; the type of weapon used in the offense; the relationship of the victim to the offender; and the circumstances surrounding the offense. Of the estimated 17,034 murders that were committed in the United States in 2006, law enforcement agencies contributed data to the UCR Program through SHRs for 14,990 of the incidents. More information on these reports and the expanded homicide tables (which are available online but not included in this publication) can be found in Appendix I. Highlights from these tables have been included below.

Victims

Based on 2006 supplemental homicide data (where the ages, sexes, or races of the murder victims were *known*), 87.9 percent of victims were over 18 years of age, 10.3 percent were under 18 years of age, and the age of 1.8 percent of the victims was unknown. Black victims accounted for 49.5 percent of the victims for whom race was known, followed by White victims (46.4 percent). Male victims made up 78.7 percent of victims for whom sex was known. (Expanded Homicide Tables 1 and 2)

Offenders

The data for 2006 concerning murders for which the offenders were known showed that 93.8 percent of offenders were adults. For murders where the gender of the offender was known, 90.9 percent were male. Black offenders accounted for 54.8 percent of offenders for whom race was known, followed by White offenders (42.8 percent) and offenders of other races (2.4 percent); 82.9 percent of White victims were murdered by White offenders and 93.2 percent of Black victims were murdered by Black offenders. (Expanded Homicide Tables 3 and 5)

Victim-Offender Relationships

For incidents in which the victim-offender relationship was known, 21.6 percent of victims were slain by family members, 23.1 percent were murdered by strangers, and 55.3 percent were killed by someone with whom they were acquainted (neighbor, friend, boyfriend, etc.). The 2006 data also showed that 32.2 percent of female victims were killed by their husbands or boyfriends. (Expanded Homicide Tables 2 and 9)

Weapons

For incidents in 2006 in which the murder weapon was specified, 73.4 percent were committed with firearms. Of murders committed with firearms, 76.6 percent involved handguns, 4.7 percent involved shotguns, and 4.3 percent involved rifles. Knives or cutting instruments were used in 12.2 percent of the murders; personal weapons, such as hands, fists, and feet, were used in 5.6 percent of the murders. Blunt objects, such as clubs and hammers, were used in 4.0 percent of the incidents. Other weapons, such as poisons, narcotics, explosives, etc., were used in 10.3 percent of the murders. (Expanded Homicide Table 7)

Circumstances

For murders for which circumstances were known, 26.1 percent of the victims were slain during arguments (including romantic triangles), and 16.3 percent were killed in conjunction with a felony (i.e., the victim was slain while being raped, robbed, etc.). Circumstances were unknown for 34.8 percent of reported homicides. Another 5.8 percent of murders with known circumstances involved juvenile gangland killing. (Expanded Homicide Table 9)

Justifiable Homicide

Certain willful killings must be reported as justifiable, or excusable, homicide. In the UCR Program, justifiable homicide is defined as, and is limited to, the following:

- The killing of a felon by a peace officer in the line of duty.

- The killing of a felon, during the commission of a felony, by a private citizen.

Because these killings are determined by law enforcement investigation to be justifiable, they are tabulated separately from murder and nonnegligent manslaughter.

During 2006, law enforcement agencies provided supplemental data for 617 justifiable homicides. A breakdown of those figures revealed that law enforcement officers justifiably killed 376 felons and private citizens justifiably killed 241 felons. Expanded Homicide Tables 13 and 14 provide further details about justifiable homicide but are not published in this text; see Appendix I for more information.

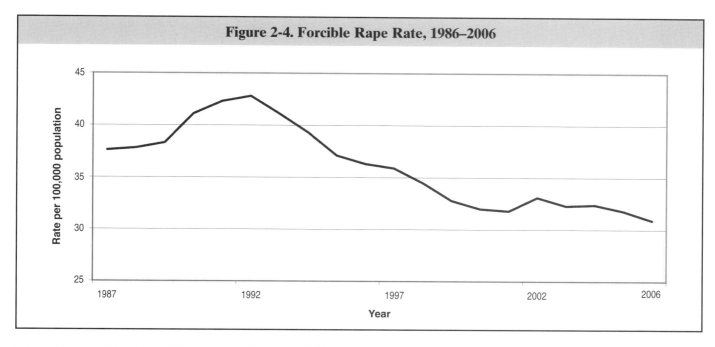

Figure 2-4. Forcible Rape Rate, 1986–2006

FORCIBLE RAPE

Definition

Forcible rape is the carnal knowledge of a female forcibly and against her will. Assaults and attempts to commit rape by force or threat of force are included; however, statutory rape (without force) and other sex offenses are excluded.

Data Collection

The UCR Program counts one offense for each female victim of a forcible rape, attempted forcible rape, or assault with intent to rape, regardless of the victim's age. A rape by force involving a female victim and a familial offender is counted as a forcible rape not an act of incest. The Program collects only arrest statistics concerning all other crimes of a sexual nature. The offense of statutory rape, in which no force is used but the female victim is under the age of consent, is included in the arrest total for the sex offenses category. Sexual attacks on males are counted as aggravated assaults or sex offenses, depending on the circumstances and the extent of any injuries.

For this overview only, the FBI deviated from standard procedure and manually calculated the 2006 rate of female rapes based upon the national female population provided by the U.S. Census Bureau.

National Volume, Trends, and Rates

During 2006, approximately 92,455 females nationwide were victims of forcible rape. This estimate represents a 2.0 percent decrease from the 2005 figure and a 2.9 percent decrease from the 2002 figure. The data also showed a 3.8 percent decrease from the 1997 estimated figure. (Tables 1 and 1A)

In preparing rate tables, the UCR Program's computer system automatically calculates offense rates per 100,000 inhabitants for all Part I crimes, which include murder and nonnegligent manslaughter, forcible rape, robbery, aggravated assault, burglary, larceny-theft, motor vehicle theft, and arson. (See Appendix II for more information.) Thus, the rate data are based upon the total U.S. population. However, for this overview, the 2006 rate of female rapes has been recalculated based upon the national female population provided by the Census Bureau. The recalculation resulted in a rate of 60.9 rape victims per 100,000 females, which was down 2.9 percent from the 2005 rate of 62.7.

Of the forcible rapes known to law enforcement agencies in 2006, rapes by force made up 91.9 percent of reported rape offenses, and assaults to rape attempts accounted for 8.1 percent of reported rape offenses. This equated to 56.0 rapes by force per 100,000 female inhabitants and 4.9 assaults to rape attempts per 100,000 females in 2006. (Tables 1 and 19.)

Regional Offense Trends and Rates

The UCR Program divides the United States into four regions: the Northeast, the South, the Midwest, and the West. (More details concerning geographic regions are provided in Appendix III.) Regional analysis offers estimates of the volume of female rapes, the percent change from the previous year's estimate, and the rate of rape per 100,000 female inhabitants in each region. (Tables 3 and 4)

The Northeast

The Northeast made up 18.3 percent of the U.S. population in 2006 and experienced a 0.1 percent growth in population from 2005 to 2006. In 2006, an estimated 11,303 forcible rapes of females—12.2 percent of the national total—occurred in the Northeast. This was a decline of 6.6 percent from the 2005 estimated figure. (Tables 3 and 4)

The Midwest

The Midwest, which accounted for 22.1 percent of the U.S. population in 2006, experienced a 0.4 percent increase in population from 2005 to 2006. Over one-quarter (25.3 percent) of all forcible rapes in the nation occurred in the Midwest in 2006. However, the 2006 estimate (23,413 forcible rapes) represented a slight decline from the 2005 estimate. (Tables 3 and 4)

The South

The South, the nation's most populous region, accounted for an estimated 36.4 percent of the nation's population in 2006 (and experienced a population growth of 1.4 percent from 2005 to 2006); the region also accounted for an estimated 38.6 percent of the nation's estimated number of forcible rapes. There were an estimated 35,667 female victims of forcible rape in the South in 2006, down slightly from 35,747 in 2005. (Tables 3 and 4)

The West

The West, which experienced a population growth of 1.5 percent from 2005 to 2006, accounted for 23.2 percent of the nation's population in 2006. The region also accounted for 23.9 percent of the nation's total number of estimated forcible rapes with an estimated 22,072 offenses. The West saw a decline in forcible rapes from 2005 to 2006. (Tables 3 and 4)

Community Types

Using the U.S. Office of Management and Budget's designations, the UCR Program aggregates crime data by type of community in which the offenses occur: metropolitan statistical areas (MSAs), cities outside MSAs, and nonmetropolitan counties outside MSAs. (Appendix III provides more detailed information about community types.) In 2006, MSAs accounted for 83.1 percent of the nation's population 83.7 percent of the nation's estimated number of forcible rapes. An estimated 77,384 females were forcibly raped in metropolitan areas. (Table 2) Cities outside MSAs are mostly incorporated areas served by city law enforcement agencies. Though accounting for only 6.7 percent of the U.S. population in 2006, cities outside MSAs accounted for 8.4 percent of the nation's estimated forcible rapes (7,720 offenses). (Table 2) In 2006, approximately 10.2 percent of the nation's population lived in nonmetropolitan counties outside MSAs (counties made up of mostly nonincorporated areas served by noncity law enforcement agencies). Collectively, these areas had an estimated 7,351 forcible rapes, representing 8.0 percent of the nation's estimated total. (Table 2)

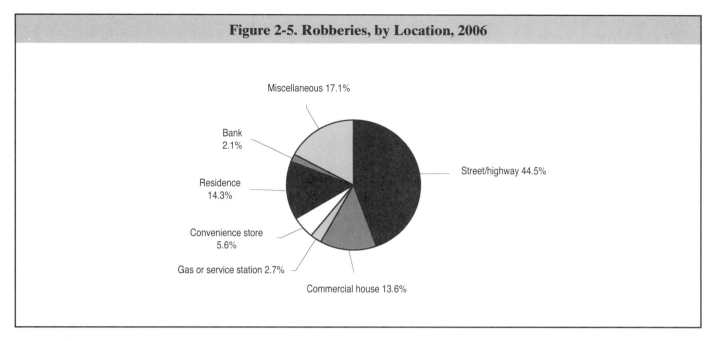

Figure 2-5. Robberies, by Location, 2006

Miscellaneous 17.1%

Bank 2.1%

Residence 14.3%

Convenience store 5.6%

Gas or service station 2.7%

Commercial house 13.6%

Street/highway 44.5%

ROBBERY

Definition

The UCR Program defines robbery as the taking or attempting to take anything of value from the care, custody, or control of a person or persons by force or threat of force or violence and/or by putting the victim in fear.

National Volume, Trends, and Rates

Reversing its 3-year trend of decline, the number of robberies nationwide increased in 2006. Estimated offenses totaled 447,403 in 2006, a 7.2 percent increase from the 2005 estimate. However, the estimated number of offenses declined 10.3 percent in a comparison with the data from 10 years earlier.

Regional Offense Trends and Rates

The UCR Program divides the United States into four regions: the Northeast, the South, the Midwest, and the West. (More details concerning geographic regions are provided in Appendix III.)

The Northeast

The Northeast, with an estimated 18.3 percent of the nation's population in 2006 (and a 0.1 percent growth in population from 2005 to 2006), accounted for 18.5 percent of its estimated number of robberies. (Table 3) The estimated number of robberies increased 2.3 percent from the 2005 estimate. The rate for this region was 151.2 robberies per 100,000 inhabitants, a 2.2 percent increase from the 2005 rate. (Table 4)

The Midwest

The Midwest accounted for 22.1 percent of the total population of the United States, and 19.5 percent of its

estimated number of robberies, in 2006. The region experienced a 0.4 percent growth in population from 2005 to 2006. (Table 3) There were an estimated 87,464 robberies in the Midwest in 2006, a 5.7 percent increase from the estimated figure from 2005. The region's robbery rate was 132.1 robberies per 100,000 inhabitants in 2006, a 5.3 percent increase from the estimated rate for 2005. (Table 4)

The South

The South, the nation's most highly populated region, experienced a 1.4 percent growth in population from 2005 to 2006; in 2006, it accounted for an estimated 36.4 percent of the nation's population in 2006 and 38.3 percent of the nation's estimated number of robberies. (Table 3) This figure represented a 7.4 percent increase from the 2005 figure. The region experienced the highest rate of robberies per 100,000 inhabitants (157.1), a 5.9 percent increase from the 2005 rate. (Table 4)

The West

The West, having experienced a population growth of 1.5 percent from 2005 to 2006, was home to an estimated 23.2 percent of the nation's population and accounted for 23.6 percent of the nation's estimated number of robberies in 2006. (Table 3) The estimated number of robberies in the region in 2006 represented a 12.3 percent increase from the 2005 figure. Of all four regions, the Midwest experienced the highest increase in robberies from 2005 to 2006. The rate of robberies per 100,000 inhabitants in the West was 152.5, a 10.7 percent increase from the 2005 rate. This was the second highest rate among the four regions. (Table 4)

Community Types

The UCR Program aggregates data for three community types: metropolitan statistical areas (MSAs), cities outside MSAs, and nonmetropolitan counties outside MSAs. MSAs include a central city or urbanized area with at least 50,000 inhabitants, as well as the county that contains the principal city and other adjacent counties that have, as defined by the U.S. Office of Management and Budget, a high degree of social and economic integration as measured through commuting. Cities outside MSAs are mostly incorporated areas, and nonmetropolitan counties are made up of mostly unincorporated areas served by noncity law enforcement.

In 2006, MSAs were home to an estimated 83.1 percent of the nation's population, and 96.1 percent of the nation's estimated number of robberies took place in these areas. Robberies in MSAs occurred at a rate of 172.8 per 100,000 inhabitants. Cities outside MSAs accounted for 6.7 percent of the U.S. population and accounted for 2.8 percent of the estimated number of robberies in the nation. The robbery rate for cities outside MSAs was 62.3 per 100,000 inhabitants. Nonmetropolitan counties made up 10.2 percent of the nation's estimated population and 1.1 percent of the nation's estimated robberies, at a rate of 16.1 robberies per 100,000 inhabitants. (Table 2)

Population Groups: Trends and Rates

The national UCR Program aggregates data by various population groups, which include cities, metropolitan counties, and nonmetropolitan counties. A definition of these groups can be found in Appendix III. All of the population groups experienced increases in the estimated number of robberies in 2006, compared with the figure for 2005. Robberies in cities as a whole increased 6.5 percent. Among the population groups labeled *city*, those cities with 25,000 to 49,999 inhabitants had the greatest increase in the number of robberies (10.4 percent), while cities with 1,000,000 or more inhabitants had the smallest increase in number of robberies (3.1 percent). Nonmetropolitan counties had a 2.9 percent increase in the estimated number of robberies, and metropolitan counties showed a 9.1 percent increase. The number of robberies in suburban areas increased 9.7 percent. (Table 12)

Among the population groups, the nation's cities collectively had a rate of 207.5 robberies per 100,000 inhabitants. Of the population groups designated *city*, those with 1,000,000 or more inhabitants had the highest rate (387.6 per 100,000 inhabitants), while those with fewer than 10,000 inhabitants had the lowest rate (55.8 per 100,000 inhabitants). Of the two county groups, metropolitan counties had a rate of 79.6 robberies per 100,000 inhabitants, while nonmetropolitan counties had a rate of 15.9

robberies per 100,000 inhabitants. Suburban areas had a robbery rate of 80.9. (Table 16)

Offense Analysis

The UCR Program collects supplemental data about robberies to document the use of weapons, the dollar loss associated with the offense, and the location types.

Robbery by Weapon

An examination of the 2006 supplemental data regarding the type of weapons offenders used in the commission of the robbery revealed that assailants relied on strong-arm tactics in 39.9 percent of all robberies; they employed firearms in 42.2 percent of robberies. Offenders used knives or other cutting instruments in 8.6 percent of these crimes. In the remainder of the robberies, the offenders used other types of weapons. (Expanded Robbery Table 3)

Loss by Dollar Value

Based on the supplemental reports from law enforcement agencies, robberies cost victims, collectively, an estimated $567 million in 2005. (Tables 1 and 23) The average loss per robbery was $1,268. Average dollar losses were the highest for banks, which suffered an average loss of $4,330 per offense. Gas and service stations lost an average $1,169 per offense. Commercial houses, which include supermarkets, department stores, and restaurants, had average losses of $1,589. An average of $1,469 was taken from residences; individuals lost $980, on average, from street and highway robberies. An average of $761 was lost in each offense against convenience stores. (Table 23)

Robbery Trends by Location

Among the location types, robberies from banks increased 10.5 percent from 2005 to 2006. Robberies that occurred at residences increased 8.0 percent, and those at commercial houses rose 3.5 percent. The number of robberies on streets and highways increased 10.5 percent, and robberies at convenience stores increased 6.1 percent. (Table 23)

Percent Distribution

By location type, the greatest proportion of robberies in 2006 occurred on streets and highways (44.5 percent). Robbers targeted commercial houses in 13.6 percent of offenses and residences in 14.3 percent of offenses. Convenience stores accounted for 5.6 percent of robberies, followed by gas and service stations (2.7 percent) and banks (2.1 percent). (Table 23)

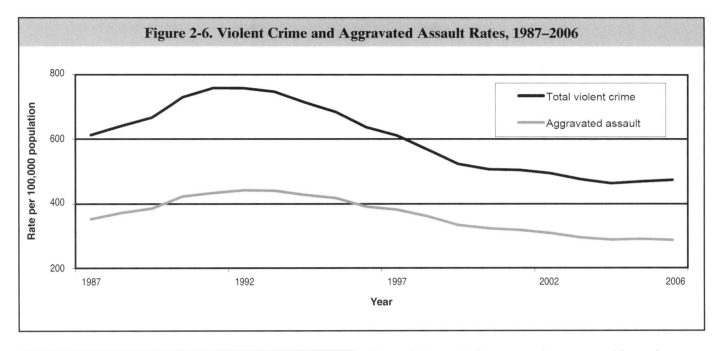

Figure 2-6. Violent Crime and Aggravated Assault Rates, 1987–2006

AGGRAVATED ASSAULT

Definition

The UCR Program defines aggravated assault as an unlawful attack by one person upon another for the purpose of inflicting severe or aggravated bodily injury. This type of assault is usually accompanied by the use of a weapon or by other means likely to produce death or great bodily harm. Attempted aggravated assaults that involve the display or threat of a gun, knife, or other weapon are included in this crime category because serious personal injury would likely result if these assaults were completed. When aggravated assault and larceny-theft occur together, the offense falls under the category of robbery.

National Volume, Trends, and Rates

In 2006, estimated occurrences of aggravated assault totaled 860,853, a 1.1 percent decrease from the 2005 figure. The 5-year and 10-year trend data show a 3.4 percent decrease and a 15.9 percent decrease, respectively. The 2006 data also show a decrease in the rate of aggravated assault per 100,000 U.S. inhabitants. This rate, estimated at 287.5, represents a 1.1 percent decrease from the 2005 rate. However, it also represents a 7.1 percent decrease from the 2002 (5-year trend) rate and a 24.8 percent decrease from the 1997 (10-year trend) rate. (Table 1)

Among the four types of violent crime offenses (murder, forcible rape, robbery, and aggravated assault), aggravated assault typically has the highest rate of occurrence. This trend continued in 2006 with aggravated assault accounting for 60.7 percent of all violent crime. (Table 1)

Regional Offense Trends and Rates

The UCR Program divides the United States into four regions: the Northeast, the South, the Midwest, and the

West. (More details concerning geographic regions are provided in Appendix III.) In the Midwest and the South, the estimated number of aggravated assaults increased from 2005 to 2006; while the Northeast and West both had declines in the number of aggravated assaults. (Table 4)

The Northeast

The region with the smallest proportion of the nation's population (an estimated 18.3 percent in 2006, representing a 0.1 percent population growth from 2005 to 2006) also accounted for the smallest proportion of the nation's estimated number of aggravated assaults (13.7 percent). (Table 3) Occurrences of aggravated assault decreased 1.6 percent from 2005 to 2006, down to an estimated 118,032. The region also had the lowest aggravated assault rate in the nation, at 215.6 incidents per 100,000 inhabitants, a 1.8 percent decline from the 2005 rate. (Table 4)

The Midwest

With 22.1 percent of the nation's total population in 2006—and with a 0.4 percent growth in population from 2005 to 2006—the Midwest accounted for approximately 19.0 percent of the nation's estimated number of aggravated assaults. (Table 3) Occurrences of this offense increased 0.6 percent from the estimated total for 2005, rising to an estimated 163,302 incidents. The region's aggravated assault rate, at 246.6 incidents per 100,000 inhabitants, represented a 0.2 percent increase from the 2005 rate. (Table 4)

The South

The South, the nation's most highly populated region, accounted for an estimated 36.4 percent of the nation's population in 2006. (Table 3) From 2005 to 2006, the estimated number of aggravated assaults increased 0.4 percent, reaching a total of 382,853 incidents. However, the region experienced population growth of 1.4 percent during this period, resulting in a slight decline (1.0 percent) in the rate of aggravated assaults, to 351.0 per 100,000 inhabitants. (Table 4)

The West

In 2006, the West was home to an estimated 23.2 percent of the nation's population and experienced a 1.5 percent growth in population from 2005 to 2006. The region accounted for 22.8 percent of the nation's estimated number of aggravated assaults. (Table 3) From 2005 to 2006, the estimated number of offenses decreased 0.9 percent to 196,666 incidents. The rate, estimated at 283.6 offenses per 100,000 inhabitants, decreased 2.4 percent from 2005. (Table 4)

Community Types

The UCR Program aggregates data for three community types: metropolitan statistical areas (MSAs), cities outside MSAs, and nonmetropolitan counties outside MSAs. MSAs include a central city or urbanized area with at least 50,000 inhabitants, as well as the county that contains the principal city and other adjacent counties that have a high degree of social and economic integration as measured through commuting. Cities outside MSAs are mostly incorporated areas, and nonmetropolitan counties are made up of mostly unincorporated areas. (For additional information about community types, see Appendix III.)

In 2006, 83.1 percent of the nation's population lived in MSAs, where the rate of aggravated assault was an estimated 304.4 per 100,000 inhabitants. Cities outside MSAs (with 6.7 percent of the U.S. population) had the next-highest rate of aggravated assault at 278.4 offenses per 100,000 inhabitants. Nonmetropolitan counties accounted for 10.2 percent of the U.S. population and had an offense rate of 155.9 aggravated assaults per 100,000 inhabitants. (Table 2)

Population Groups: Trends and Rates

To calculate 2-year trend data for population groups, the UCR Program staff reviewed reports from all agencies that submitted statistics on aggravated assaults for at least 6 common months in 2004 and 2005. (For an explanation of population-group designations and the number of agencies contributing to the UCR Program, see Appendix III; for the methodology used in tabular presentations, see Appendix I.)

From 2005 to 2006, the number of aggravated assaults in four of the six city groups increased. Cities with 25,000 to 49,999 inhabitants and cities with 50,000 to 99,999 inhabitants experienced the greatest increase (both at 1.8 percent). Cities with populations of 250,000 or more experienced a decline of 1.4 percent. In metropolitan counties, the number of aggravated assaults rose 1.4 percent; in nonmetropolitan counties, this number decreased 4.3 percent. Aggravated assaults in suburban areas increased 1.1 percent from 2005 to 2006. (Table 12)

Based on reports from agencies submitting 12 months of complete data for 2006, aggravated assault occurred at an estimated rate of 299.3 offenses per 100,000 inhabitants nationwide. The collective rate for cities was 339.7 aggravated assaults per 100,000 inhabitants. Among city population groups, rates ranged from a high of 501.3 offenses per 100,000 inhabitants (in cities with 250,000 or more inhabitants) to a low of 202.0 offenses per 100,000 inhabitants (in cities with 10,000 to 24,999 inhabitants). The aggravated assault rate was 235.1 in metropolitan counties and 162.7 in nonmetropolitan counties. (Table 16)

Offense Analysis

Aggravated Assault by Weapon

The UCR Program collects data about the type of weapons used in aggravated assaults. In 2006, personal weapons (such as hands, feet, fists, etc.) were used in 25.0 percent of aggravated assaults for which weapons information was known, firearms were used in 21.9 percent of aggravated assaults, and knives and other cutting instruments were used in 18.7 percent of aggravated assaults. Weapons classified in the "other" category were used in the remaining 34.4 percent of offenses. (Table 19)

An analysis by weapon type showed that the rate of aggravated assaults per 100,000 inhabitants was 72.7 with personal weapons, 64.2 with firearms, 55.0 with knives and other cutting instruments, and 101.0 with weapons in the "other" category.

PROPERTY CRIME

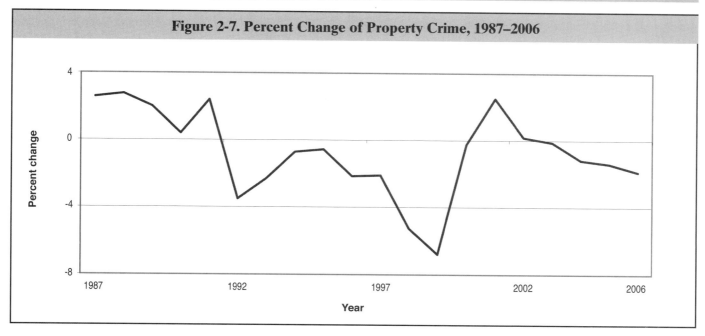

Figure 2-7. Percent Change of Property Crime, 1987–2006

Definition

The Uniform Crime Reporting (UCR) Program's definition of property crime includes the offenses of burglary, larceny-theft, motor vehicle theft, and arson. The object of theft-type offenses is the taking of money or property without the use of force or threat of force against the victims. Property crime includes arson because the offense involves the destruction of property; however, arson victims may be subjected to force. Because of limited participation and the varying collection procedures conducted by local law enforcement agencies, only limited data are available for arson. Arson statistics are included in the trend, clearance, and arrest tables in *Crime in the United States*, but they are not included in any estimated volume data. More information on the expanded arson tables (which are available online but not included in this publication) can be found in Appendix I.

Data Collection

The data presented in *Crime in the United States* reflect the Hierarchy Rule, which counts only the most serious offense in a multiple-offense criminal incident. In descending order of severity, the violent crimes are murder and nonnegligent manslaughter, forcible rape, robbery, aggravated assault; these are followed by the property crimes of burglary, larceny-theft, and motor vehicle theft.

National Volume, Trends, and Rates

An estimated 9,983,568 property crimes were committed in the United States in 2006, representing a 1.9 percent decrease from the 2005 (2-year trend) estimate, a 4.5 percent decrease from the 2002 (5-year trend) estimate, and a 13.6 percent decrease from the 1997 (10-year trend) estimate. (Tables 1 and 1A)

In 2006, larceny-theft and motor vehicle theft incidents showed a decline from their 2005 estimates; however, the number of estimated incidents of burglary showed an increase during this period. The number of larceny-thefts was down 2.6 percent and the number of motor vehicle thefts was down 3.5 percent. The number of burglaries increased 1.3 percent. (Tables 1 and 1A)

The estimated property crime rate per 100,000 inhabitants in 2006 was 3,334.5, a 2.8 percent decrease from the 2005 rate, an 8.2 percent decrease from the 2002 rate, and a 13.6 percent decrease from the 1997 rate. (Tables 1 and 1A)

Regional Offense Trends and Rates

The UCR Program separates the United States into four regions: the Northeast, the Midwest, the South, and the West. (Geographic breakdowns can be found in Appendix III.) Property crime data collected by the UCR Program and aggregated by region reflected the following results.

The Northeast

The Northeast region accounted for 18.3 percent of the nation's population and experienced a 0.1 percent growth in population from 2005 to 2006. The region also accounted for 12.4 of the nation's estimated number of property crimes in 2006. (Table 3) Law enforcement in the Northeast saw a 0.8 percent decrease in the estimated number of property crimes from 2005 to 2006. The property crime rate for the Northeast, estimated at 2,268.6 incidents per 100,000 inhabitants, was 0.9 percent lower than the 2005 rate. (Table 4)

The Midwest

The Midwest, with 22.1 percent of the U.S. population in 2006 and a 0.4 percent growth in population from 2005 to

2006, accounted for 21.7 percent of the nation's estimated number of property crimes. (Table 3) Law enforcement in the Midwest saw a 0.5 percent increase in the estimated number of property crimes in the Midwest from 2005 to 2006. The rate of property crime in the Midwest in 2006, estimated at 3,271.2 incidents per 100,000 inhabitants, represented a 0.1 percent decrease from the 2005 rate. (Table 4)

The South

The South, the nation's most populous region, accounted for 36.4 percent of the U.S. population in 2006 and experienced a 1.4 percent growth in population from 2005 to 2006. The region also accounted for an estimated 41.3 percent of the nation's property crimes. (Table 3) The South experienced a 1.3 percent decrease in its estimated number of property crimes from 2005 to 2006. The 2006 property crime rate, an estimated 3,780.8 incidents per 100,000 inhabitants, was 2.7 percent lower than the 2005 rate. (Table 4)

The West

In 2006, the West accounted for 23.2 percent of the nation's population; the region experienced a 1.5 percent growth in population from 2005 to 2006. The West also accounted for 24.6 percent of the nation's estimated number of property crimes. (Table 3) From 2005 to 2006, the estimated number of property crimes in this region decreased 5.4 percent. The estimated property crime rate in the West in 2006, 3,534.4 incidents per 100,000 inhabitants, was 6.8 percent lower than the 2005 rate. (Table 4)

Community Types

The UCR Program aggregates data by three community types: metropolitan statistical areas (MSAs), cities outside metropolitan areas, and nonmetropolitan counties. (Additional in-depth information regarding community types can be found in Appendix III.) In 2006, 83.1 percent of the U.S. population lived in MSAs. The property crime rate for MSAs was 3,499.7 per 100,000 inhabitants. Cities outside metropolitan areas, which accounted for 6.7 percent of the total population in 2006, had a property crime rate of 3,849.3 per 100,000 inhabitants. Nonmetropolitan counties, with 10.2 percent of the nation's population in 2006, had a property crime rate of 1,653.5 per 100,000 inhabitants. (Table 2)

Population Groups: Trends and Rates

The UCR Program organizes the agencies that contribute data into population groups, which include cities, metropolitan counties, and nonmetropolitan counties. (Appendix III provides further details about these groups.) From 2005 to 2006, law enforcement in the nation's cities collectively reported a 2.6 percent decrease in the number of property crimes. All city groups experienced decreased in the number of property crimes; cities with 100,000 to 249,000 inhabitants had the largest declines at 3.4 percent. Metropolitan and nonmetropolitan counties experienced declines of 0.3 and 2.3 percent, respectively. (Table 12)

The nation's cities collectively had a property crime rate of 3,991.2 incidents per 100,000 inhabitants in 2006. Nonmetropolitan counties had a rate of 1,667.6 incidents per 100,000 inhabitants, and metropolitan counties had a rate of 2,478.2 incidents per 100,000 inhabitants. Property crime rates for each population group can be found in Table 16.

Offense Analysis

The estimated dollar loss attributing to property crimes (excluding arson) in 2006 was $17.6 billion, representing a 6.7 percent increase from the 2005 figure. Among the individual property crime categories, the dollar losses were an estimated $4 billion for burglary, $5.6 billion for larceny-theft, and $7.9 billion for motor vehicle theft. (Tables 1 and 23) Arson had an average dollar loss of $13,325 for the 61,304 incidents for which monetary figures were reported. (Expanded Arson Table 2)

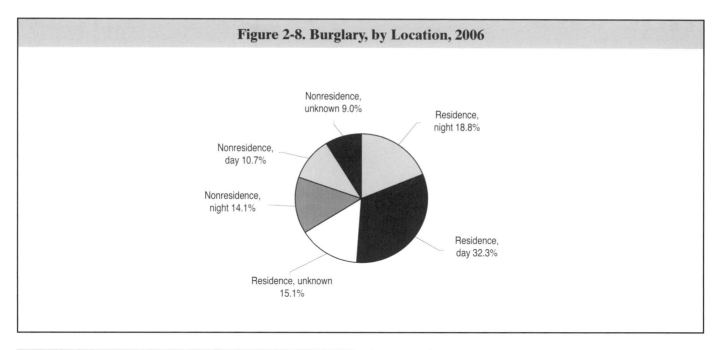

Figure 2-8. Burglary, by Location, 2006

- Nonresidence, unknown 9.0%
- Residence, night 18.8%
- Nonresidence, day 10.7%
- Nonresidence, night 14.1%
- Residence, day 32.3%
- Residence, unknown 15.1%

BURGLARY

Definition

The UCR Program defines burglary as the unlawful entry of a structure to commit a felony or theft. To classify an offense as a burglary, the use of force to gain entry need not have occurred. The program has three subclassifications for burglary: forcible entry, unlawful entry where no force is used, and attempted forcible entry. The UCR definition of "structure" includes, but is not limited to, apartments, barns, house trailers or houseboats (when used as permanent dwellings), offices, railroad cars (but not automobiles), stables, and vessels (i.e., ships).

National Volume, Trends, and Rate

In 2006, an estimated 2,183,746 burglary offenses occurred in the United States. This figure represented a 1.3 percent increase from the 2005 figure. An examination of 5-year and 10-year trends demonstrated a 1.5 percent increase from the 2002 estimate and an 11.2 percent decrease from 1997 estimate. However, the burglary rate for the United States in 2006 was 729.4 incidents per 100,000 inhabitants, a 0.3 percent decrease from the 2005 rate. Burglary accounted for 21.9 percent of the estimated number of property crimes committed in 2006. (Tables 1 and 1A)

Regional Offense Trends and Rates

The UCR Program divides the United States into four regions: the Northeast, the Midwest, the South, and the West. (Details regarding these regions can be found in Appendix III.) An analysis of burglary data by region showed the following details.

The Northeast

In 2006, 18.3 percent of the nation's population lived in the Northeast, which experienced a 0.1 percent growth in population from 2005 to 2006. This region accounted for 10.8 percent of the estimated total number of burglary offenses in the nation. This figure represented a 1.4 percent increase from the 2005 estimate. The region's burglary rate, an estimated 429.9 offenses per 100,000 inhabitants, represented an increase of 1.3 percent from the 2005 rate. (Tables 3 and 4)

The Midwest

The Midwest accounted for 22.1 percent of the nation's population in 2006 and experienced a 0.4 percent growth in population from 2005 to 2006. This region also accounted for 21.0 percent of the nation's estimated number of burglaries. The estimated number of burglaries in this region increased 4.1 percent from 2005 to 2006. The Midwest had a burglary rate of 692.1 offenses per 100,000 inhabitants, a 3.7 percent increase from the 2005 rate. (Tables 3 and 4)

The South

The South, the nation's most highly populated region, had the most burglaries in 2006 (an estimated 985,937). With 36.4 percent of the nation's population (and having experienced a 1.4 percent growth in population from 2005 to 2006), this region accounted for 45.1 percent of all burglaries in the United States. The estimated rate of burglary in the South was 903.8 incidents per 100,000 inhabitants, a 0.6 percent decrease from the 2005 rate. (Tables 3 and 4)

The West

The West accounted for 23.2 percent of the nation's population in 2006 and experienced a 1.5 percent growth in population from 2005 to 2006. In 2006, this region also accounted for an estimated 23.1 percent of the nation's burglaries. The region's burglary rate was 727.0, a 3.9 percent decrease from the 2005 rate. The total number of burglaries (504,183) represented a 2.5 percent decrease from the 2005 figure. (Tables 3 and 4)

Community Types

The UCR Program aggregates data by three community types: metropolitan statistical areas (MSAs), cities outside MSAs, and nonmetropolitan counties. (See Appendix III for more information regarding community types.) In 2006, 83.1 percent of the U.S. population lived in MSAs, and an estimated 87.2 percent of all burglaries occurred in this type of community. Inhabitants of cities outside MSAs accounted for 6.7 percent of the total population in 2006 and 7.7 percent of the estimated number of burglaries; nonmetropolitan counties, with 10.2 percent of the U.S. population, accounted for 5.1 percent of all burglaries. The burglary rates per 100,000 inhabitants were 748.6 in MSAs, 797.9 in cities outside MSAs, and 528.4 in nonmetropolitan counties. (Table 2)

Population Groups: Trends and Rates

In addition to analyzing data by region and community type, the UCR Program aggregates crime statistics by population groups. Cities are categorized into six groups based on the number of inhabitants; counties are categorized into two groups, metropolitan and nonmetropolitan. (Appendix III offers further details regarding these population groups.)

An examination of data from law enforcement agencies that provided statistics for at least 6 common months in 2005 and 2006 showed that the nation's cities experienced a collective 0.8 percent increase in burglaries from 2005 to 2006. Burglaries increased in every city group. Cities with 10,000 to 24,999 inhabitants and those with 25,000 to 49,999 inhabitants experienced the largest increase (1.5 percent) and cities with under 10,000 inhabitants experienced the smallest increase (0.4 percent). However, cities with 1,000,000 inhabitants or more—a subset of the city group of cities with 250,000 inhabitants or more—experienced a 2.3 percent decline in the number of burglaries, though the number for the overall group increased 0.6 percent. The volume of burglaries increased 2.4 percent in metropolitan counties, but decreased 2.8 percent in nonmetropolitan counties. (Table 12)

The UCR Program calculates burglary rates for population groups from the information provided by participating agencies that submitted all 12 months of offense data for the year. In 2006, the nation's cities had 820.4 offenses per 100,000 inhabitants. The largest cities (those with 250,000 or more inhabitants) had the highest burglary rate at 975.2 incidents per 100,000 inhabitants. Cities with 10,000 to 24,999 inhabitants had the lowest burglary rate— 631.3 incidents per 100,000 inhabitants. Metropolitan counties had a rate of 622.4 per 100,000 inhabitants, and nonmetropolitan counties had a rate of 537.9 per 100,000 inhabitants. (Table 16)

Offense Analysis

The UCR Program requests that participating law enforcement agencies provide details regarding the nature of burglaries in their jurisdictions, such as type of entry, type of structure, time of day, and dollar loss associated with each offense.

An examination of data from agencies that provided burglary data for all 12 months of 2006 revealed that 60.9 percent of all burglaries involved forcible entry. Unlawful entry accounted for 32.5 percent of offenses, and attempted forcible entry accounted for 6.6 percent of burglaries reported to the UCR Program in 2006. (Table 19)

As in the past, burglars targeted residences more often than nonresidential structures. An analysis of data from agencies that provided supplemental burglary data for at least 6 months of 2006 showed that 66.2 percent of burglaries occurred at residences, while 34.2 percent of burglaries occurred at nonresidential structures. (Table 23)

Law enforcement agencies were unable to determine the time of day for 24.1 percent of all reported burglaries. However, of the burglaries for which time of day could be established, most burglaries of residences (63.1 percent) occurred during the day (between 6 a.m. and 6 p.m.). Nonresidential structures were targeted more often at night, with 56.7 percent of all nonresidential burglaries occurring between 6 p.m. and 6 a.m. The average dollar loss per burglary was $1,834. (Table 23)

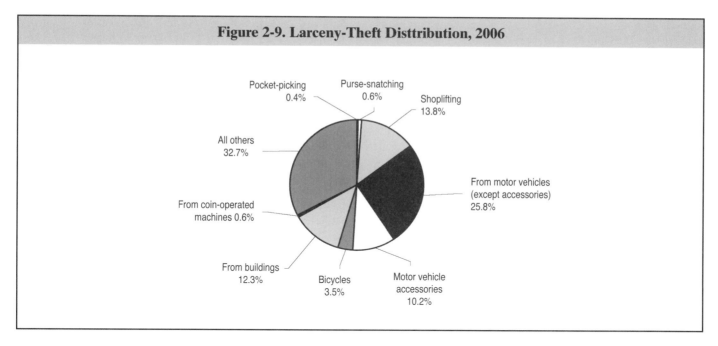

Figure 2-9. Larceny-Theft Disttribution, 2006

LARCENY-THEFT

Definition

The UCR Program defines larceny-theft as the unlawful taking, carrying, leading, or riding away of property from the possession or constructive possession of another. Examples are thefts of bicycles, motor vehicle parts and accessories, shoplifting, pocket picking, or the stealing of any property or article not taken by force and violence or by fraud. Attempted larcenies are included. Embezzlement, confidence games, forgery, check fraud, etc., are excluded from this category.

National Volume, Trends, and Rates

In 2006, larceny-theft accounted for an estimated 66.2 percent of the nation's property crimes. (Table 1) Trend data showed that the number of larceny-thefts decreased 2.6 percent from 2005 to 2006 (2-year trend data), decreased 6.4 percent from 2002 to 2006 (5-year trend data), and decreased 14.7 percent from 1997 to 2006 (10-year trend data). The trend data also showed decreases in the larceny-theft rates per 100,000 inhabitants during these periods. The larceny-theft rate decreased 3.5 percent between 2005 and 2006, 10.0 percent between 2002 and 2006, and 23.7 percent between 1997 and 2006. (Table 1)

Regional Offense Trends and Rates

The UCR Program defines four regions within the United States: the Northeast, the Midwest, the South, and the West. (See Appendix III for a geographical description of each region.) A comparison of 2005 and 2006 data showed that both the estimated number and the estimate rate of larceny-theft declined across all regions. (Tables 3 and 4) The following paragraphs provide a region overview of larceny-theft.

The Northeast

The region with the smallest proportion (18.3 percent) of the U.S. population in 2006, the Northeast experienced the smallest growth in population in the nation from 2005 to 2006 (0.1 percent). The region also experienced the fewest larceny-thefts in the country, accounting for only 13.4 percent of all larceny-thefts. (Table 3) The estimated number of offenses in 2006—884,825—represented a 0.5 percent decline from 2005, and the estimated rate—1,616.4 incidents per 100,000 inhabitants—represented a 0.6 percent decline. (Table 4)

The Midwest

With 22.1 percent of the U.S. population in 2006, and a 0.4 percent growth in population from 2005 to 2006, the Midwest accounted for an estimated 22.5 percent of the nation's larceny-thefts. (Table 3) The estimated number of offenses (1,487,599) declined 0.1 percent compared with the 2005 data, and the estimated rate of occurrences (2,246.5 incidents per 100,000 inhabitants) declined 0.5 percent. (Table 4)

The South

With more than one-third of the U.S. population in 2006 (36.4 percent), the South experienced a 1.4 percent growth in population from 2005 to 2006. The region had the nation's highest percentage of larceny-theft offenses: an estimated 41.3 percent. (Table 3) Estimated offenses in this region totaled 2,725,921, a 2.6 percent decrease from the 2005 estimate. The South's larceny-theft rate—estimated at 2,498.9 offenses per 100,000 inhabitants—decreased 4.0 percent from the 2005 estimate. (Table 4)

The West

In 2006, an estimated 23.1 percent of the U.S. population lived in the West, which experienced a 1.5 percent growth in population from 2005 to 2006. This region was also where 22.8 percent of the nation's estimated number of larceny-thefts took place. (Table 3) Occurrences of larceny-theft declined 6.1 percent from 2005 to 2006, dropping to an estimated total of 1,508,668 offenses. The region's larceny-theft rate, estimated at 2,175.3 offenses per 100,000 inhabitants, declined 7.4 percent from the 2005 rate. (Table 4)

Community Types

The UCR Program aggregates data for three community types: metropolitan statistical areas (MSAs), cities outside MSAs, and nonmetropolitan counties outside MSAs. MSAs include a central city or urbanized area with at least 50,000 inhabitants, as well as the county that contains the principal city and other adjacent counties that share a high degree of social and economic integration as measured through commuting. Cities outside MSAs are mostly incorporated areas, and nonmetropolitan counties are composed of unincorporated areas. (See Appendix III for more information regarding community types.)

In 2006, MSAs were home to an estimated 83.1 percent of the nation's population and experienced 86.7 percent of the nation's larceny-theft incidents. Cities outside MSAs accounted for 6.7 percent of the U.S. population and 8.7 percent of larceny-theft offenses. Nonmetropolitan counties, which were home to 10.2 percent of the nation's population, accounted for 4.6 percent of the estimated number of larceny-theft offenses. (Table 2)

Population Groups: Trends and Rates

To calculate 2-year trend data for population groups, the UCR Program reviewed reports from all agencies that submitted statistics on larceny-theft offenses for at least 6 common months in 2005 and 2006. (For an explanation of population groups and the number of agencies contributing to the UCR Program, see Appendix III; for the methodology used in tabular presentations, see Appendix I.)

In cities, collectively, occurrences of larceny-theft declined 3.4 percent between 2005 and 2006; all city groups, along with both metropolitan and nonmetropolitan counties, experienced declines in occurrences of larceny-theft during this time period. Among the city groups, cities with 100,000 to 249,999 inhabitants experienced the greatest decrease (4.1 percent). Cities with

25,000 to 49,999 inhabitants had the smallest decrease (3.0 percent). In metropolitan and nonmetropolitan counties, the declines were 0.9 percent and 1.9 percent, respectively. (Table 12)

Based on reports of larceny-theft offenses from U.S. law enforcement agencies that submitted 12 months of complete data for 2006, this offense occurred at a rate of 2,255.6 offenses per 100,000 inhabitants. The collective rate for cities was 2,664.6 offenses per 100,000 inhabitants. Among city population groups, cities with 100,000 to 249,000 inhabitants had the highest larceny-theft rate, 2,921.0 incidents per 100,000 inhabitants. Cities with 10,000 to 24,999 inhabitants had the lowest rate at 2,335.3 incidents per 100,000 inhabitants. In metropolitan counties, the rate was 1,556.5 incidents per 100,000 inhabitants; in nonmetropolitan counties, the rate was 995.2 incidents per 100,000 inhabitants. (Table 16)

Offense Analysis

Distribution

Thefts from motor vehicles accounted for the majority of larceny-theft offenses in 2006 (26.5 percent). Table 23 provides a further breakdown of larceny-theft offenses, including shoplifting, thefts from buildings, thefts of motor vehicle accessories, thefts of bicycles, thefts from coin-operated machines, purse snatching, and pocket picking. The "all other" category, which includes the less-defined types of larceny-theft, accounted for 33.0 percent of all offenses. (Table 23)

Loss by Dollar Value

Larceny-theft offenses cost victims an estimated $5.6 billion dollars in 2006, up from $5.2 billion in 2005. (Tables 1 and 23) The average value of property stolen was $855 per offense, up from $764 in 2005. Larceny-theft from buildings had the highest average dollar loss per offense at $1,170. Thefts from motor vehicles had an average dollar loss of $734 per offense; thefts of motor vehicle accessories, $522; purse snatching, $440; pocket picking, $443; thefts from coin-operated machines, $317; thefts of bicycles, $263; and shoplifting, $194. (Table 23)

Offenses in which the stolen property was valued at more than $200 accounted for 42.5 percent of all larceny-thefts. Table 23 provides further analysis, including the average dollar value per offense, of all offenses in the overall category of property crime.

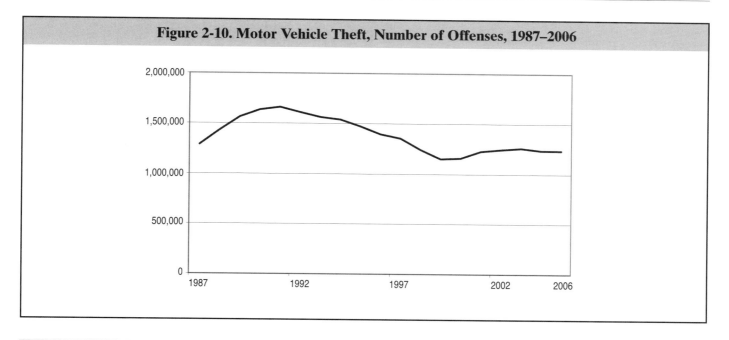

Figure 2-10. Motor Vehicle Theft, Number of Offenses, 1987–2006

MOTOR VEHICLE THEFT

Definition

The UCR Program defines motor vehicle theft as the theft or attempted theft of a motor vehicle. The offense includes the stealing of automobiles, trucks, buses, motorcycles, snowmobiles, etc. The taking of a motor vehicle for temporary use by a person or persons with lawful access is excluded.

National Volume, Trends, and Rates

In 2006, an estimated 1,192,809 motor vehicle thefts took place in the United States. The number of motor vehicles estimated to have been stolen decreased 3.5 percent between 2005 and 2006, decreased 4.3 percent between 2002 and 2006, and decreased 11.9 percent between 1997 and 2006. (Table 1)

The estimated rate of motor vehicle theft in 2006 was 398.4 incidents per 100,000 inhabitants. In the 2-year, 5-year, and 10-year trend data, this rate showed decline: the 2006 rate was 4.4 percent lower than the 2005 rate, 8.0 percent lower than the 2002 rate, and 21.2 percent lower than the 1997 rate. (Table 1)

Regional Offense Trends and Rates

In order to analyze crime by geographic area, the UCR Program divides the United States into four regions: the Northeast, the Midwest, the South, and the West. (See Appendix III for a geographical description of each region.) This section provides a regional overview of motor vehicle theft.

The Northeast

The Northeast accounted for an estimated 18.3 percent of the nation's population in 2006 and experienced a 0.1 per-

cent growth in population from 2005 to 2006. The region also accounted for an estimated 10.2 percent of its motor vehicle thefts. (Table 3) An estimated 121,679 motor vehicle thefts occurred in the Northeast in 2006, representing a 6.5 percent decrease from the 2005 estimate. This was the largest decline among the regions. The estimated rate of 222.3 motor vehicle thefts per 100,000 inhabitants in the Northeast in 2006 represented a 6.6 percent decline from the 2005 rate. (Table 4)

The Midwest

An estimated 22.1 percent of the country's population resided in the Midwest in 2006, and the region experienced a 0.4 growth in population from 2005 to 2006. The region accounted for 18.5 percent of the nation's motor vehicle thefts. (Table 3) The Midwest had an estimated 220,269 motor vehicle thefts in 2006, a 2.4 percent decrease from the previous year's total. The motor vehicle theft rate was estimated at 332.6 motor vehicles stolen per 100,000 inhabitants, a 2.8 percent decrease from the 2005 rate. (Table 4)

The South

The South, the nation's most populous region, was home to an estimated 36.4 percent of the U.S. population in 2006 and experienced a 1.4 percent growth in population from 2005 to 2006. This region accounted for 34.6 percent of the nation's motor vehicle thefts. (Table 3) The estimated 412,435 motor vehicle thefts in the South decreased 0.1 percent from the 2005 estimate. Motor vehicles in the South were stolen at an estimated rate of 378.1 per 100,000 inhabitants in 2006, a rate that was 1.4 percent lower than the 2005 rate. (Table 4)

The West

With approximately 23.2 percent of the U.S. population in 2006, the West experienced a 1.5 percent growth in population from 2005 to 2006. This region accounted for 36.8 percent of all motor vehicle thefts in the nation in 2006. (Table 3) By volume, the largest number of motor vehicle thefts, an estimated 438,426, occurred in this region. This number represented a 6.3 percent decrease from the previous year's estimate. The motor vehicle theft rate for the West was also lower in 2006 than in 2005: the 2006 rate of 632.1 motor vehicles stolen per 100,000 inhabitants was 7.6 percent lower than the 2005 rate. (Table 4)

Community Types

The UCR Program aggregates data by three community types: metropolitan statistical areas (MSAs), cities outside MSAs, and nonmetropolitan counties. MSAs are areas that include a principal city or urbanized area with at least 50,000 inhabitants and the county that contains the principal city and other adjacent counties that have, as defined by the U.S. Office of Management and Budget, a high degree of economic and social integration.

The vast majority (83.1 percent) of the U.S. population resided in MSAs during 2006, where approximately 93.5 percent of motor vehicle thefts occurred. For 2006, the UCR Program estimated an overall rate of 448.0 motor vehicles stolen per 100,000 MSA inhabitants. Cities outside MSAs and nonmetropolitan counties made up 6.7 and 10.2 percent of the nation's population, respectively. Cities outside MSAs accounted for 3.1 percent of motor vehicle thefts, and nonmetropolitan counties accounted for 3.4 percent of motor vehicle thefts. The UCR Program estimated a 2006 rate of 186.8 motor vehicles stolen for every 100,000 inhabitants in cities outside MSAs and a rate of 133.1 motor vehicles stolen per 100,000 inhabitants in nonmetropolitan counties. (Table 2)

Population Groups: Trends and Rates

The UCR Program aggregates data by various population groups, which include cities, metropolitan counties, and nonmetropolitan counties. (A definition of these groups can be found in Appendix III.)

In cities, collectively, the number of motor vehicle thefts decreased 4.1 percent in from 2005 to 2006. Cities with 1,000,000 or more inhabitants and cities with 100,000 to 249,999 inhabitants experienced the greatest declines—5.8 percent. Both metropolitan and nonmetropolitan counties experienced decreases, at 2.8 percent and 4.1 percent, respectively. (Table 12)

Among the population groups, in 2006 cities had a collective motor vehicle theft rate of 506.2 per 100,000 inhabitants. The largest cities, those with 250,000 or more inhabitants, experienced the highest rate of motor vehicle thefts with 827.2 motor vehicle thefts per 100,000 inhabitants. (Within this city group, cities with 500,000 to 999,999 inhabitants had the highest motor vehicle theft rate at 971.1 incidents per 100,000 inhabitants.) Conversely, the nation's smallest cities, those with populations under 10,000, had the lowest rate of motor vehicle theft with 201.9 incidents per 100,000 in population. Within the county groups, metropolitan counties had a rate of 299.3 motor vehicles stolen per 100,000 inhabitants, while nonmetropolitan counties had a rate of 134.5 incident per 100,000 inhabitants. (Table 16)

Offense Analysis

Based on the reports of law enforcement agencies, the UCR Program estimated the combined value of motor vehicles stolen nationwide in 2006 at approximately $7.9 billion. (Tables 1 and 23) Automobiles were, by far, the most frequently stolen vehicle, accounting for 73.5 percent of all vehicles stolen. Trucks and buses accounted for 17.8 percent of stolen vehicles, and other vehicles accounted for 8.6 percent of stolen vehicles. (Table 19)

By type of vehicle, automobiles were stolen at a rate of 311.6 cars per 100,000 inhabitants in 2006. Trucks and buses were stolen at a rate of 75.5 vehicles per 100,000 in population, and other types of vehicles were stolen at a rate of 36.6 vehicles per 100,000 inhabitants. (Table 19)

ARSON

Definition

The UCR Program defines arson as any willful or malicious burning or attempt to burn (with or without intent to defraud) a dwelling house, public building, motor vehicle, aircraft, personal property of another, etc.

Data Collection

Only fires that investigators determined were willfully set (not fires labeled as "suspicious" or "of unknown origin") are included in this arson data collection. Points to consider regarding arson statistics include:

National offense rates per 100,000 inhabitants (found in Tables 1 through 4) do not include arson data; the FBI presents rates for arson separately. Arson rates are calculated based upon data received from all law enforcement agencies that provide the UCR Program with data for 12 complete months.

Arson data collection does not include estimates for arson, because the degree of reporting arson offenses varies from agency to agency. Because of this unevenness of reporting, arson offenses are excluded from Tables 1 through 7, all of which contain offense estimations.

The number of arsons reported by individual law enforcement agencies is available in Tables 8 through 11. Arson trend data (which indicate year-to-year changes) can be found in Tables 12 through 15, and arson clearance data (crimes solved) can be found in Tables 25 through 28.

National Coverage

In 2006, 13,943 agencies (providing 1 to 12 months of data) reported 69,055 arson offenses. Supplemental data, such as the type of structure burned and the estimated dollar loss, were received for 61,304 arsons. (Unpublished Expanded Arson Table 2; see Appendix I for more information.) The UCR Program received 12 complete months of arson data from 11,223 agencies, representing 80.6 percent of the U.S. population. (See Appendix I for more information.)

Population Groups: Trends and Rates

The number of arsons reported in 2006 increased 2.1 percent from the 2005 figure. Law enforcement agencies in the nation's cities collectively reported a 2.2 percent decline in the number of arsons from the 2005 figure. Among the population groups labeled *city,* those with 50,000 to 99,999 inhabitants had the largest year-to-year increase in reported arsons, 10.6 percent; arsons in cities with 250,000 or more inhabitants had the greatest decline, 0.9 percent. Agencies in the nation's metropolitan counties reported a 2.7 percent increase in the number of arsons, and those in nonmetropolitan counties reported a 2.1 percent decline. (Table 12)

Arson rates were based on information received from 11,223 agencies that provided 12 months of complete arson data to the UCR Program. An examination of data from those agencies indicated that in 2006, the highest rate—48.5 arsons per 100,000 inhabitants—was reported in cities with 250,000 to 499,999 inhabitants; cities with 250,000 or more inhabitants had a collective arson rate of 45.4. Cities with 10,000 to 24,999 residents had the lowest arson rate of all the city groups, 18.9 per 100,000 inhabitants. Metropolitan counties had 22.4 arsons per 100,000 inhabitants, and nonmetropolitan counties had 16.1 arsons per 100,000 inhabitants, the lowest of all the population groups. (Expanded Arson Table 1)

Offense Analysis

The UCR Program breaks down arson offenses into three property categories: structural, mobile, and other. In addition, the structural property type is broken down into seven types of structures, and the mobile property type consists of two subgroupings. The program also collects information on the estimated dollar value of the damaged property.

Property Type

The number of arsons decreased for structural property types, but increased for mobile and other property types in 2006. Arsons for the structural property type decreased 0.3 percent while arsons for the mobile property type increased 0.7 percent and arsons of other property types increased 8.4 percent. (Table 15)

Distributions by Property Type

In 2006, arsons of structures accounted for 42.3 percent of all arsons. Of these arsons, 60.3 percent involved residential properties. Of the residential arsons, most (44.2 percent) were single-occupancy residences, such as houses, townhouses, duplexes, etc. Mobile arsons accounted for 28.2 percent of all arsons. Within this category, 94.3 percent of offenses involved the burning of motor vehicles. Other types of property, such as crops, timber, fences, etc., accounted for 29.6 percent of reported arson offenses. (Expanded Arson Table 2)

Dollar Loss

In monetary terms, the average dollar loss in 2006 for arson was $13,325. The average dollar loss for a structural arson was $25,327. Mobile property had an average dollar loss of $7,209. Other property types had an average dollar loss of $1,988. (Expanded Arson Table 2)

Within the structural arson category, the industrial/manufacturing subcategory had the highest average dollar loss at $66,856. Within that same category, single-occupancy dwellings had an average dollar loss of $25,117. Other residential dwellings had an average dollar loss of $21,265. (Expanded Arson Table 2)

Table 1. Crime in the United States, by Volume and Rate per 100,000 Inhabitants, 1987–2006

(Number, rate per 100,000 population, percent.)

Year	Population[1]	Violent crime		Murder and nonnegligent manslaughter		Forcible rape		Robbery		Aggravated assault	
		Number	Rate	Number	Rate	Number	Rate	Number	Rate	Number	Rate
1987	242,288,918	1,483,999	612.5	20,096	8.3	91,111	37.6	517,704	213.7	855,088	352.9
1988	244,498,982	1,566,221	640.6	20,675	8.5	92,486	37.8	542,968	222.1	910,092	372.2
1989	246,819,230	1,646,037	666.9	21,500	8.7	94,504	38.3	578,326	234.3	951,707	385.6
1990	249,464,396	1,820,127	729.6	23,438	9.4	102,555	41.1	639,271	256.3	1,054,863	422.9
1991	252,153,092	1,911,767	758.2	24,703	9.8	106,593	42.3	687,732	272.7	1,092,739	433.4
1992	255,029,699	1,932,274	757.7	23,760	9.3	109,062	42.8	672,478	263.7	1,126,974	441.9
1993	257,782,608	1,926,017	747.1	24,526	9.5	106,014	41.1	659,870	256.0	1,135,607	440.5
1994	260,327,021	1,857,670	713.6	23,326	9.0	102,216	39.3	618,949	237.8	1,113,179	427.6
1995	262,803,276	1,798,792	684.5	21,606	8.2	97,470	37.1	580,509	220.9	1,099,207	418.3
1996	265,228,572	1,688,540	636.6	19,645	7.4	96,252	36.3	535,594	201.9	1,037,049	391.0
1997	267,783,607	1,636,096	611.0	18,208	6.8	96,153	35.9	498,534	186.2	1,023,201	382.1
1998	270,248,003	1,533,887	567.6	16,974	6.3	93,144	34.5	447,186	165.5	976,583	361.4
1999	272,690,813	1,426,044	523.0	15,522	5.7	89,411	32.8	409,371	150.1	911,740	334.3
2000	281,421,906	1,425,486	506.5	15,586	5.5	90,178	32.0	408,016	145.0	911,706	324.0
2001[2]	285,317,559	1,439,480	504.5	16,037	5.6	90,863	31.8	423,557	148.5	909,023	318.6
2002	287,973,924	1,423,677	494.4	16,229	5.6	95,235	33.1	420,806	146.1	891,407	309.5
2003	290,788,976	1,383,676	475.8	16,528	5.7	93,883	32.3	414,235	142.5	859,030	295.4
2004	293,656,842	1,360,088	463.2	16,148	5.5	95,089	32.4	401,470	136.7	847,381	288.6
2005[3]	296,507,061	1,390,745	469.0	16,740	5.6	94,347	31.8	417,438	140.8	862,220	290.8
2006	299,398,484	1,417,745	473.5	17,034	5.7	92,455	30.9	447,403	149.4	860,853	287.5

Year	Property crime		Burglary		Larceny-theft		Motor vehicle theft	
	Number	Rate	Number	Rate	Number	Rate	Number	Rate
1987	12,024,709	4,963.0	3,236,184	1,335.7	7,499,851	3,095.4	1,288,674	531.9
1988	12,356,865	5,054.0	3,218,077	1,316.2	7,705,872	3,151.7	1,432,916	586.1
1989	12,605,412	5,107.1	3,168,170	1,283.6	7,872,442	3,189.6	1,564,800	634.0
1990	12,655,486	5,073.1	3,073,909	1,232.2	7,945,670	3,185.1	1,635,907	655.8
1991	12,961,116	5,140.2	3,157,150	1,252.1	8,142,228	3,229.1	1,661,738	659.0
1992	12,505,917	4,903.7	2,979,884	1,168.4	7,915,199	3,103.6	1,610,834	631.6
1993	12,218,777	4,740.0	2,834,808	1,099.7	7,820,909	3,033.9	1,563,060	606.3
1994	12,131,873	4,660.2	2,712,774	1,042.1	7,879,812	3,026.9	1,539,287	591.3
1995	12,063,935	4,590.5	2,593,784	987.0	7,997,710	3,043.2	1,472,441	560.3
1996	11,805,323	4,451.0	2,506,400	945.0	7,904,685	2,980.3	1,394,238	525.7
1997	11,558,475	4,316.3	2,460,526	918.8	7,743,760	2,891.8	1,354,189	505.7
1998	10,951,827	4,052.5	2,332,735	863.2	7,376,311	2,729.5	1,242,781	459.9
1999	10,208,334	3,743.6	2,100,739	770.4	6,955,520	2,550.7	1,152,075	422.5
2000	10,182,584	3,618.3	2,050,992	728.8	6,971,590	2,477.3	1,160,002	412.2
2001[2]	10,437,189	3,658.1	2,116,531	741.8	7,092,267	2,485.7	1,228,391	430.5
2002	10,455,277	3,630.6	2,151,252	747.0	7,057,379	2,450.7	1,246,646	432.9
2003	10,442,862	3,591.2	2,154,834	741.0	7,026,802	2,416.5	1,261,226	433.7
2004	10,319,386	3,514.1	2,144,446	730.3	6,937,089	2,362.3	1,237,851	421.5
2005[3]	10,174,754	3,431.5	2,155,448	726.9	6,783,447	2,287.8	1,235,859	416.8
2006	9,983,568	3,334.5	2,183,746	729.4	6,607,013	2,206.8	1,192,809	398.4

Note: Although arson data are included in the trend and clearance tables, sufficient data are not available to estimate totals for this offense.
[1] Populations are U.S. Census Bureau provisional estimates as of July 1 for each year except 1990 and 2000, which are decennial census counts.
[2] The murder and nonnegligent homicides that occurred as a result of the events of September 11, 2001, are not included in this table.
[3] The 2005 crime figures have been adjusted.

Table 1a. Crime in the United States Percent Change in Volume and Rate per 100,000 Inhabitants for 2 Years, 5 Years, and 10 Years

(Percent change.)

Year	Violent crime		Murder and nonnegligent manslaughter		Forcible rape		Robbery		Aggravated assault	
	Number	Rate	Number	Rate	Number	Rate	Number	Rate	Number	Rate
2005–2006	+1.9	+1.0	+1.8	+0.8	-2.0	-3.0	+7.2	+6.1	-0.2	-1.1
2002–2006	-0.4	-4.2	+5.0	+1.0	-2.9	-6.6	+6.3	+2.3	-3.4	-7.1
1997–2006	-13.3	-22.5	-6.4	-16.3	-3.8	-14.0	-10.3	-19.7	-15.9	-24.8

Year	Property crime		Burglary		Larceny-theft		Motor vehicle theft	
	Number	Rate	Number	Rate	Number	Rate	Number	Rate
2005–2006	-1.9	-2.8	+1.3	+0.3	-2.6	-3.5	-3.5	-4.4
2002–2006	-4.5	-8.2	+1.5	-2.4	-6.4	-10.0	-4.3	-8.0
1997–2006	-13.6	-22.7	-11.2	-20.6	-14.7	-23.7	-11.9	-21.2

Note: Although arson data are included in the trend and clearance tables, sufficient data are not available to estimate totals for this offense.

Table 2. Crime in the United States by Community Type, 2006

(Number, percent, rate per 100,000 population.)

Area	Population[1]	Violent crime	Murder and non-negligent man-slaughter	Forcible rape	Robbery	Aggravat-ed assault	Property crime	Burglary	Larceny-theft	Motor vehicle theft
United States Total.............................	299,398,484	1,417,745	17,034	92,455	447,403	860,853	9,983,568	2,183,746	6,607,013	1,192,809
Rate per 100,000 inhabitants...............		473.5	5.7	30.9	149.4	287.5	3,334.5	729.4	2,206.8	398.4
Metropolitan Statistical Areas............	248,798,842									
Area actually reporting[2]......................	95.6%	1,202,186	14,572	72,878	403,380	711,356	8,226,522	1,766,498	5,392,106	1,067,918
Estimated total......................................	100.0%	1,280,264	15,429	77,384	430,003	757,448	8,707,148	1,862,416	5,730,014	1,114,718
Rate per 100,000 inhabitants...............		514.6	6.2	31.1	172.8	304.4	3,499.7	748.6	2,303.1	448.0
Cities Outside Metropolitan Areas.....	20,027,212									
Area actually reporting[2]......................	86.3%	67,421	561	6,665	10,770	49,425	669,526	139,065	497,254	33,207
Estimated total......................................	100.0%	76,594	653	7,720	12,470	55,751	770,898	159,800	573,692	37,406
Rate per 100,000 inhabitants...............		382.4	3.3	38.5	62.3	278.4	3,849.3	797.9	2,864.6	186.8
Nonmetropolitan Counties	30,572,430									
Area actually reporting[2]......................	88.1%	55,924	850	6,483	4,446	44,145	456,828	145,329	274,342	37,157
Estimated total......................................	100.0%	60,887	952	7,351	4,930	47,654	505,522	161,530	303,307	40,685
Rate per 100,000 inhabitants...............		199.2	3.1	24.0	16.1	155.9	1,653.5	528.4	992.1	133.1

Note: Although arson data are included in the trend and clearance tables, sufficient data are not available to estimate totals for this offense. Therefore, no arson data are published in this table.

[1] Populations are U.S. Census Bureau provisional estimates as of July 1, 2006.

[2] The percentage reported under "Area actually reporting" is based on the population covered by agencies providing 3 months or more of crime reports to the FBI.

Table 3. Population and Offense Distribution, by Region, 2006

(Percent distribution.)

Region	Population	Violent crime	Murder and nonnegli-gent man-slaughter	Forcible rape	Robbery	Aggravated assault	Property crime	Burglary	Larceny-theft	Motor vehicle theft
United States Total[1]	100.0	100.0	100.0	100.0	100.0	100.0	100.0	100.0	100.0	100.0
Northeast	18.3	15.1	14.4	12.2	18.5	13.7	12.4	10.8	13.4	10.2
Midwest.................................	22.1	19.6	19.4	25.3	19.5	19.0	21.7	21.0	22.5	18.5
South	36.4	42.1	43.2	38.6	38.3	44.5	41.3	45.1	41.3	34.6
West..	23.2	23.2	22.9	23.9	23.6	22.8	24.6	23.1	22.8	36.8

Note: Although arson data are included in the trend and clearance tables, sufficient data are not available to estimate totals for this offense. Therefore, no arson data are published in this table.

[1] Because of rounding, the percentages may not add to 100.0.

Table 4. Crime, by Region, Geographic Division, and State, 2005–2006

(Number, rate per 100,000 population, percent.)

Area	Year	Population[1]	Violent crime		Murder and nonnegligent manslaughter		Forcible rape		Robbery	
			Number	Rate	Number	Rate	Number	Rate	Number	Rate
UNITED STATES TOTAL[2,3,4,5]	2005............	296,507,061	1,390,745	469.0	16,740	5.6	94,347	31.8	417,438	140.8
	2006............	299,398,484	1,417,745	473.5	17,034	5.7	92,455	30.9	447,403	149.4
	Percent change........		+1.9	+1.0	+1.8	+0.8	-2.0	-3.0	+7.2	+6.1
Northeast[2]	2005............	54,679,292	215,441	394.0	2,410	4.4	12,101	22.1	80,918	148.0
	2006............	54,741,353	214,550	391.9	2,455	4.5	11,303	20.6	82,760	151.2
	Percent change........		-0.4	-0.5	+1.9	+1.8	-6.6	-6.7	+2.3	+2.2
New England[2]	2005............	14,255,073	45,922	322.1	363	2.5	3,671	25.8	13,310	93.4
	2006............	14,269,989	45,247	317.1	370	2.6	3,496	24.5	13,940	97.7
	Percent change........		-1.5	-1.6	+1.9	+1.8	-4.8	-4.9	+4.7	+4.6
Connecticut[2]	2005............	3,500,701	9,542	272.6	105	3.0	712	20.3	3,933	112.3
	2006............	3,504,809	9,841	280.8	108	3.1	636	18.1	4,241	121.0
	Percent change........		+3.1	+3.0	+2.9	+2.7	-10.7	-10.8	+7.8	+7.7
Maine	2005............	1,318,220	1,483	112.5	19	1.4	326	24.7	323	24.5
	2006............	1,321,574	1,526	115.5	23	1.7	339	25.7	384	29.1
	Percent change........		+2.9	+2.6	+21.1	+20.7	+4.0	+3.7	+18.9	+18.6
Massachusetts[2]	2005............	6,433,367	29,644	460.8	178	2.8	1,751	27.2	7,837	121.8
	2006............	6,437,193	28,775	447.0	186	2.9	1,742	27.1	8,047	125.0
	Percent change........		-2.9	-3.0	+4.5	+4.4	-0.5	-0.6	+2.7	+2.6
New Hampshire[2]	2005............	1,306,819	1,761	134.8	19	1.5	406	31.1	365	27.9
	2006............	1,314,895	1,824	138.7	13	1.0	344	26.2	423	32.2
	Percent change........		+3.6	+2.9	-31.6	-32.0	-15.3	-15.8	+15.9	+15.2
Rhode Island[2]	2005............	1,073,579	2,710	252.4	34	3.2	323	30.1	776	72.3
	2006............	1,067,610	2,429	227.5	28	2.6	285	26.7	735	68.8
	Percent change........		-10.4	-9.9	-17.6	-17.2	-11.8	-11.3	-5.3	-4.8
Vermont[2]	2005............	622,387	782	125.6	8	1.3	153	24.6	76	12.2
	2006............	623,908	852	136.6	12	1.9	150	24.0	110	17.6
	Percent change........		+9.0	+8.7	+50.0	+49.6	-2.0	-2.2	+44.7	+44.4
Middle Atlantic	2005............	40,424,219	169,519	419.4	2,047	5.1	8,430	20.9	67,608	167.2
	2006............	40,471,364	169,303	418.3	2,085	5.2	7,807	19.3	68,820	170.0
	Percent change........		-0.1	-0.2	+1.9	+1.7	-7.4	-7.5	+1.8	+1.7
New Jersey	2005............	8,703,150	30,919	355.3	417	4.8	1,208	13.9	13,215	151.8
	2006............	8,724,560	30,672	351.6	428	4.9	1,237	14.2	13,357	153.1
	Percent change........		-0.8	-1.0	+2.6	+2.4	+2.4	+2.1	+1.1	+0.8
New York	2005............	19,315,721	85,839	444.4	874	4.5	3,636	18.8	35,179	182.1
	2006............	19,306,183	83,966	434.9	921	4.8	3,169	16.4	34,489	178.6
	Percent change........		-2.2	-2.1	+5.4	+5.4	-12.8	-12.8	-2.0	-1.9
Pennsylvania	2005............	12,405,348	52,761	425.3	756	6.1	3,586	28.9	19,214	154.9
	2006............	12,440,621	54,665	439.4	736	5.9	3,401	27.3	20,974	168.6
	Percent change........		+3.6	+3.3	-2.6	-2.9	-5.2	-5.4	+9.2	+8.9
Midwest[2,3,4]	2005............	65,936,397	272,526	413.3	3,283	5.0	24,140	36.6	82,747	125.5
	2006............	66,217,736	277,486	419.1	3,307	5.0	23,413	35.4	87,464	132.1
	Percent change........		+1.8	+1.4	+0.7	+0.3	-3.0	-3.4	+5.7	+5.3
East North Central[2,3,4]	2005............	46,130,608	200,263	434.1	2,551	5.5	17,174	37.2	66,640	144.5
	2006............	46,275,645	202,144	436.8	2,565	5.5	16,861	36.4	69,949	151.2
	Percent change........		+0.9	+0.6	+0.5	+0.2	-1.8	-2.1	+5.0	+4.6
Illinois[2,3,4]	2005............	12,765,427	70,496	552.2	770	6.0	4,313	33.8	23,255	182.2
	2006............	12,831,970	69,498	541.6	780	6.1	4,078	31.8	23,782	185.3
	Percent change........		-1.4	-1.9	+1.3	+0.8	-5.4	-5.9	+2.3	+1.7
Indiana	2005............	6,266,019	20,302	324.0	356	5.7	1,856	29.6	6,809	108.7
	2006............	6,313,520	19,876	314.8	369	5.8	1,835	29.1	7,243	114.7
	Percent change........		-2.1	-2.8	+3.7	+2.9	-1.1	-1.9	+6.4	+5.6
Michigan[2]	2005............	10,100,833	55,936	553.8	629	6.2	5,199	51.5	13,348	132.1
	2006............	10,095,643	56,778	562.4	713	7.1	5,269	52.2	14,208	140.7
	Percent change........		+1.5	+1.6	+13.4	+13.4	+1.3	+1.4	+6.4	+6.5
Ohio[2]	2005............	11,470,685	40,162	350.1	590	5.1	4,671	40.7	18,673	162.8
	2006............	11,478,006	40,209	350.3	539	4.7	4,548	39.6	19,149	166.8
	Percent change........		+0.1	+0.1	-8.6	-8.7	-2.6	-2.7	+2.5	+2.5
Wisconsin[2]	2005............	5,527,644	13,367	241.8	206	3.7	1,135	20.5	4,555	82.4
	2006............	5,556,506	15,783	284.0	164	3.0	1,131	20.4	5,567	100.2
	Percent change........		+18.1	+17.5	-20.4	-20.8	-0.4	-0.9	+22.2	+21.6

Note: Although arson data are included in the trend and clearance tables, sufficient data are not available to estimate totals for this offense. Therefore, no arson data are published in this table.

[1] Populations are U.S. Census Bureau provisional estimates as of July 1, 2006, and July 1, 2005.
[2] The 2005 crime figures have been adjusted.
[3] Limited data for 2005 and 2006 were available for Illinois.
[4] The data collection methodology for the offense of forcible rape used by the Illinois (with the exception of Rockford, Illinois) and the Minnesota state (2006 data only) Uniform Crime Reporting (UCR) Programs do not comply with national UCR Program guidelines. Consequently, their figures for forcible rape were estimated for inclusion in this table.
[5] Includes offenses reported by the Zoological Police and the Metro Transit Police.

Table 4. Crime, by Region, Geographic Division, and State, 2005–2006 (*Contd.*)

(Number, rate per 100,000 population, percent.)

Area	Year	Aggravated assault		Property crime		Burglary		Larceny-theft		Motor vehicle theft	
		Number	Rate	Number	Rate	Number	Rate	Number	Rate	Number	Rate
UNITED STATES TOTAL[2, 3, 4, 5]	2005	862,220	290.8	10,174,754	3,431.5	2,155,448	726.9	6,783,447	2,287.8	1,235,859	416.8
	2006	860,853	287.5	9,983,568	3,334.5	2,183,746	729.4	6,607,013	2,206.8	1,192,809	398.4
	Percent change	-0.2	-1.1	-1.9	-2.8	+1.3	+0.3	-2.6	-3.5	-3.5	-4.4
Northeast[2]	2005	120,012	219.5	1,251,778	2,289.3	232,140	424.5	889,531	1,626.8	130,107	237.9
	2006	118,032	215.6	1,241,852	2,268.6	235,348	429.9	884,825	1,616.4	121,679	222.3
	Percent change	-1.6	-1.8	-0.8	-0.9	+1.4	+1.3	-0.5	-0.6	-6.5	-6.6
New England[2]	2005	28,578	200.5	341,953	2,398.8	68,992	484.0	235,667	1,653.2	37,294	261.6
	2006	27,441	192.3	341,602	2,393.8	69,727	488.6	236,594	1,658.0	35,281	247.2
	Percent change	-4.0	-4.1	-0.1	-0.2	+1.1	+1.0	+0.4	+0.3	-5.4	-5.5
Connecticut[2]	2005	4,792	136.9	90,270	2,578.6	15,245	435.5	64,416	1,840.1	10,609	303.1
	2006	4,856	138.6	87,764	2,504.1	14,694	419.3	62,680	1,788.4	10,390	296.4
	Percent change	+1.3	+1.2	-2.8	-2.9	-3.6	-3.7	-2.7	-2.8	-2.1	-2.2
Maine	2005	815	61.8	31,889	2,419.1	6,323	479.7	24,218	1,837.2	1,348	102.3
	2006	780	59.0	33,286	2,518.7	6,779	512.9	25,167	1,904.3	1,340	101.4
	Percent change	-4.3	-4.5	+4.4	+4.1	+7.2	+6.9	+3.9	+3.7	-0.6	-0.8
Massachusetts[2]	2005	19,878	309.0	151,727	2,358.4	34,728	539.8	98,079	1,524.5	18,920	294.1
	2006	18,800	292.1	153,913	2,391.0	35,181	546.5	100,771	1,565.4	17,961	279.0
	Percent change	-5.4	-5.5	+1.4	+1.4	+1.3	+1.2	+2.7	+2.7	-5.1	-5.1
New Hampshire[2]	2005	971	74.3	24,031	1,838.9	4,192	320.8	18,493	1,415.1	1,346	103.0
	2006	1,044	79.4	24,642	1,874.1	4,358	331.4	18,862	1,434.5	1,422	108.1
	Percent change	+7.5	+6.9	+2.5	+1.9	+4.0	+3.3	+2.0	+1.4	+5.6	+5.0
Rhode Island[2]	2005	1,577	146.9	29,287	2,728.0	5,319	495.4	19,567	1,822.6	4,401	409.9
	2006	1,381	129.4	27,618	2,586.9	5,415	507.2	18,621	1,744.2	3,582	335.5
	Percent change	-12.4	-11.9	-5.7	-5.2	+1.8	+2.4	-4.8	-4.3	-18.6	-18.2
Vermont[2]	2005	545	87.6	14,749	2,369.7	3,185	511.7	10,894	1,750.4	670	107.7
	2006	580	93.0	14,379	2,304.7	3,300	528.9	10,493	1,681.8	586	93.9
	Percent change	+6.4	+6.2	-2.5	-2.7	+3.6	+3.4	-3.7	-3.9	-12.5	-12.8
Middle Atlantic	2005	91,434	226.2	909,825	2,250.7	163,148	403.6	653,864	1,617.5	92,813	229.6
	2006	90,591	223.8	900,250	2,224.4	165,621	409.2	648,231	1,601.7	86,398	213.5
	Percent change	-0.9	-1.0	-1.1	-1.2	+1.5	+1.4	-0.9	-1.0	-6.9	-7.0
New Jersey	2005	16,079	184.7	203,391	2,337.0	38,980	447.9	136,728	1,571.0	27,683	318.1
	2006	15,650	179.4	199,958	2,291.9	39,433	452.0	135,801	1,556.5	24,724	283.4
	Percent change	-2.7	-2.9	-1.7	-1.9	+1.2	+0.9	-0.7	-0.9	-10.7	-10.9
New York	2005	46,150	238.9	405,990	2,101.9	68,034	352.2	302,220	1,564.6	35,736	185.0
	2006	45,387	235.1	396,304	2,052.7	68,565	355.1	295,605	1,531.1	32,134	166.4
	Percent change	-1.7	-1.6	-2.4	-2.3	+0.8	+0.8	-2.2	-2.1	-10.1	-10.0
Pennsylvania	2005	29,205	235.4	300,444	2,421.9	56,134	452.5	214,916	1,732.4	29,394	236.9
	2006	29,554	237.6	303,988	2,443.5	57,623	463.2	216,825	1,742.9	29,540	237.4
	Percent change	+1.2	+0.9	+1.2	+0.9	+2.7	+2.4	+0.9	+0.6	+0.5	+0.2
Midwest[2, 3, 4]	2005	162,356	246.2	2,154,559	3,267.6	440,218	667.6	1,488,590	2,257.6	225,751	342.4
	2006	163,302	246.6	2,166,146	3,271.2	458,278	692.1	1,487,599	2,246.5	220,269	332.6
	Percent change	+0.6	+0.2	+0.5	+0.1	+4.1	+3.7	-0.1	-0.5	-2.4	-2.8
East North Central[2, 3, 4]	2005	113,898	246.9	1,492,601	3,235.6	316,549	686.2	1,012,612	2,195.1	163,440	354.3
	2006	112,769	243.7	1,511,762	3,266.9	330,954	715.2	1,019,828	2,203.8	160,980	347.9
	Percent change	-1.0	-1.3	+1.3	+1.0	+4.6	+4.2	+0.7	+0.4	-1.5	-1.8
Illinois[2, 3, 4]	2005	42,158	330.3	394,670	3,091.7	77,635	608.2	277,662	2,175.1	39,373	308.4
	2006	40,858	318.4	387,478	3,019.6	77,259	602.1	272,578	2,124.2	37,641	293.3
	Percent change	-3.1	-3.6	-1.8	-2.3	-0.5	-1.0	-1.8	-2.3	-4.4	-4.9
Indiana	2005	11,281	180.0	216,778	3,459.6	43,756	698.3	151,278	2,414.3	21,744	347.0
	2006	10,429	165.2	221,127	3,502.4	46,168	731.3	153,093	2,424.8	21,866	346.3
	Percent change	-7.6	-8.2	+2.0	+1.2	+5.5	+4.7	+1.2	+0.4	+0.6	-0.2
Michigan[2]	2005	36,760	363.9	312,892	3,097.7	70,527	698.2	194,090	1,921.5	48,275	477.9
	2006	36,588	362.4	324,351	3,212.8	76,107	753.9	198,227	1,963.5	50,017	495.4
	Percent change	-0.5	-0.4	+3.7	+3.7	+7.9	+8.0	+2.1	+2.2	+3.6	+3.7
Ohio[2]	2005	16,228	141.5	420,705	3,667.7	100,183	873.4	279,051	2,432.7	41,471	361.5
	2006	15,973	139.2	422,235	3,678.6	104,426	909.8	280,384	2,442.8	37,425	326.1
	Percent change	-1.6	-1.6	+0.4	+0.3	+4.2	+4.2	+0.5	+0.4	-9.8	-9.8
Wisconsin[2]	2005	7,471	135.2	147,556	2,669.4	24,448	442.3	110,531	1,999.6	12,577	227.5
	2006	8,921	160.6	156,571	2,817.8	26,994	485.8	115,546	2,079.5	14,031	252.5
	Percent change	+19.4	+18.8	+6.1	+5.6	+10.4	+9.8	+4.5	+4.0	+11.6	+11.0

Note: Although arson data are included in the trend and clearance tables, sufficient data are not available to estimate totals for this offense. Therefore, no arson data are published in this table.

[2] The 2005 crime figures have been adjusted.

[3] Limited data for 2005 and 2006 were available for Illinois.

[4] The data collection methodology for the offense of forcible rape used by the Illinois (with the exception of Rockford, Illinois) and the Minnesota state (2006 data only) Uniform Crime Reporting (UCR) Programs do not comply with national UCR Program guidelines. Consequently, their figures for forcible rape were estimated for inclusion in this table.

[5] Includes offenses reported by the Zoological Police and the Metro Transit Police.

Table 4. Crime, by Region, Geographic Division, and State, 2005–2006 (*Contd.*)

(Number, rate per 100,000 population, percent.)

Area	Year	Population[1]	Violent crime		Murder and nonnegligent manslaughter		Forcible rape		Robbery	
			Number	Rate	Number	Rate	Number	Rate	Number	Rate
West North Central[2, 4]	2005	19,805,789	72,263	364.9	732	3.7	6,966	35.2	16,107	81.3
	2006	19,942,091	75,342	377.8	742	3.7	6,552	32.9	17,515	87.8
	Percent change		+4.3	+3.5	+1.4	+0.7	-5.9	-6.6	+8.7	+8.0
Iowa[2]	2005	2,965,524	8,697	293.3	40	1.3	847	28.6	1,153	38.9
	2006	2,982,085	8,455	283.5	55	1.8	828	27.8	1,298	43.5
	Percent change		-2.8	-3.3	+37.5	+36.7	-2.2	-2.8	+12.6	+12.0
Kansas[2]	2005	2,748,172	10,701	389.4	101	3.7	1,098	40.0	1,795	65.3
	2006	2,764,075	11,748	425.0	127	4.6	1,238	44.8	1,877	67.9
	Percent change		+9.8	+9.2	+25.7	+25.0	+12.8	+12.1	+4.6	+4.0
Minnesota[4]	2005	5,126,739	15,243	297.3	115	2.2	2,258	44.0	4,724	92.1
	2006	5,167,101	16,123	312.0	125	2.4	1,645	31.8	5,433	105.1
	Percent change		+5.8	+4.9	+8.7	+7.8	-27.1	-27.7	+15.0	+14.1
Missouri	2005	5,797,703	30,477	525.7	402	6.9	1,625	28.0	7,196	124.1
	2006	5,842,713	31,880	545.6	368	6.3	1,764	30.2	7,587	129.9
	Percent change		+4.6	+3.8	-8.5	-9.2	+8.6	+7.7	+5.4	+4.6
Nebraska[2]	2005	1,758,163	5,052	287.3	44	2.5	581	33.0	1,040	59.2
	2006	1,768,331	4,983	281.8	50	2.8	548	31.0	1,129	63.8
	Percent change		-1.4	-1.9	+13.6	+13.0	-5.7	-6.2	+8.6	+7.9
North Dakota[2]	2005	634,605	706	111.3	12	1.9	180	28.4	54	8.5
	2006	635,867	813	127.9	8	1.3	193	30.4	72	11.3
	Percent change		+15.2	+14.9	-33.3	-33.5	+7.2	+7.0	+33.3	+33.1
South Dakota[2]	2005	774,883	1,387	179.0	18	2.3	377	48.7	145	18.7
	2006	781,919	1,340	171.4	9	1.2	336	43.0	119	15.2
	Percent change		-3.4	-4.3	-50.0	-50.4	-10.9	-11.7	-17.9	-18.7
South[2, 5]	2005	107,552,100	583,798	542.8	7,112	6.6	35,747	33.2	159,609	148.4
	2006	109,083,752	597,281	547.5	7,367	6.8	35,667	32.7	171,394	157.1
	Percent change		+2.3	+0.9	+3.6	+2.1	-0.2	-1.6	+7.4	+5.9
South Atlantic[2, 5]	2005	56,211,935	319,057	567.6	3,670	6.5	16,806	29.9	90,169	160.4
	2006	57,143,670	327,457	573.0	3,859	6.8	16,849	29.5	97,580	170.8
	Percent change		+2.6	+1.0	+5.1	+3.4	+0.3	-1.4	+8.2	+6.5
Delaware	2005	841,741	5,332	633.4	37	4.4	377	44.8	1,306	155.2
	2006	853,476	5,817	681.6	42	4.9	400	46.9	1,735	203.3
	Percent change		+9.1	+7.6	+13.5	+12.0	+6.1	+4.6	+32.8	+31.0
District of Columbia[5]	2005	582,049	8,032	1,380.0	195	33.5	166	28.5	3,700	635.7
	2006	581,530	8,772	1,508.4	169	29.1	185	31.8	3,829	658.4
	Percent change		+9.2	+9.3	-13.3	-13.3	+11.4	+11.5	+3.5	+3.6
Florida	2005	17,768,191	125,957	708.9	883	5.0	6,592	37.1	30,141	169.6
	2006	18,089,888	128,795	712.0	1,129	6.2	6,475	35.8	34,147	188.8
	Percent change		+2.3	+0.4	+27.9	+25.6	-1.8	-3.5	+13.3	+11.3
Georgia	2005	9,132,553	40,725	445.9	564	6.2	2,143	23.5	14,041	153.7
	2006	9,363,941	44,106	471.0	600	6.4	2,173	23.2	15,509	165.6
	Percent change		+8.3	+5.6	+6.4	+3.8	+1.4	-1.1	+10.5	+7.7
Maryland	2005	5,589,599	39,369	704.3	552	9.9	1,266	22.6	14,378	257.2
	2006	5,615,727	38,110	678.6	546	9.7	1,178	21.0	14,375	256.0
	Percent change		-3.2	-3.6	-1.1	-1.5	-7.0	-7.4	*	-0.5
North Carolina	2005	8,672,459	40,650	468.7	585	6.7	2,302	26.5	12,635	145.7
	2006	8,856,505	42,124	475.6	540	6.1	2,495	28.2	13,484	152.2
	Percent change		+3.6	+1.5	-7.7	-9.6	+8.4	+6.1	+6.7	+4.5
South Carolina[2]	2005	4,246,933	32,590	767.4	314	7.4	1,862	43.8	5,657	133.2
	2006	4,321,249	33,078	765.5	359	8.3	1,762	40.8	5,899	136.5
	Percent change		+1.5	-0.2	+14.3	+12.4	-5.4	-7.0	+4.3	+2.5
Virginia[2]	2005	7,564,327	21,434	283.4	458	6.1	1,763	23.3	7,495	99.1
	2006	7,642,884	21,568	282.2	399	5.2	1,792	23.4	7,749	101.4
	Percent change		+0.6	-0.4	-12.9	-13.8	+1.6	+0.6	+3.4	+2.3
West Virginia[2]	2005	1,814,083	4,968	273.9	82	4.5	335	18.5	816	45.0
	2006	1,818,470	5,087	279.7	75	4.1	389	21.4	853	46.9
	Percent change		+2.4	+2.1	-8.5	-8.8	+16.1	+15.8	+4.5	+4.3
East South Central[2]	2005	17,585,176	84,047	477.9	1,209	6.9	6,326	36.0	22,551	128.2
	2006	17,754,447	85,218	480.0	1,182	6.7	6,088	34.3	24,932	140.4
	Percent change		+1.4	+0.4	-2.2	-3.2	-3.8	-4.7	+10.6	+9.5

Note: Although arson data are included in the trend and clearance tables, sufficient data are not available to estimate totals for this offense. Therefore, no arson data are published in this table.

[1] Populations are U.S. Census Bureau provisional estimates as of July 1, 2006, and July 1, 2005.
[2] The 2005 crime figures have been adjusted.
[4] The data collection methodology for the offense of forcible rape used by the Illinois (with the exception of Rockford, Illinois) and the Minnesota state (2006 data only) Uniform Crime Reporting (UCR) Programs do not comply with national UCR Program guidelines. Consequently, their figures for forcible rape were estimated for inclusion in this table.
[5] Includes offenses reported by the Zoological Police and the Metro Transit Police.
* Less than one-tenth of 1 percent.

Table 4. Crime, by Region, Geographic Division, and State, 2005–2006 (*Contd.*)

(Number, rate per 100,000 population, percent.)

Area	Year	Aggravated assault		Property crime		Burglary		Larceny-theft		Motor vehicle theft	
		Number	Rate	Number	Rate	Number	Rate	Number	Rate	Number	Rate
West North Central[2,4]	2005	48,458	244.7	661,958	3,342.2	123,669	624.4	475,978	2,403.2	62,311	314.6
	2006	50,533	253.4	654,384	3,281.4	127,324	638.5	467,771	2,345.6	59,289	297.3
	Percent change	+4.3	+3.6	-1.1	-1.8	+3.0	+2.3	-1.7	-2.4	-4.8	-5.5
Iowa[2]	2005	6,657	224.5	84,370	2,845.0	18,147	611.9	60,723	2,047.6	5,500	185.5
	2006	6,274	210.4	83,579	2,802.7	18,017	604.2	60,556	2,030.7	5,006	167.9
	Percent change	-5.8	-6.3	-0.9	-1.5	-0.7	-1.3	-0.3	-0.8	-9.0	-9.5
Kansas[2]	2005	7,707	280.4	104,588	3,805.7	19,028	692.4	76,222	2,773.6	9,338	339.8
	2006	8,506	307.7	103,658	3,750.2	19,992	723.3	74,963	2,712.0	8,703	314.9
	Percent change	+10.4	+9.7	-0.9	-1.5	+5.1	+4.5	-1.7	-2.2	-6.8	-7.3
Minnesota[4]	2005	8,146	158.9	158,301	3,087.8	29,716	579.6	114,304	2,229.6	14,281	278.6
	2006	8,920	172.6	159,119	3,079.5	30,173	583.9	115,567	2,236.6	13,379	258.9
	Percent change	+9.5	+8.6	+0.5	-0.3	+1.5	+0.7	+1.1	+0.3	-6.3	-7.0
Missouri	2005	21,254	366.6	227,809	3,929.3	42,822	738.6	159,288	2,747.4	25,699	443.3
	2006	22,161	379.3	223,570	3,826.5	44,647	764.1	153,490	2,627.0	25,433	435.3
	Percent change	+4.3	+3.5	-1.9	-2.6	+4.3	+3.5	-3.6	-4.4	-1.0	-1.8
Nebraska[2]	2005	3,387	192.6	60,348	3,432.4	9,408	535.1	45,359	2,579.9	5,581	317.4
	2006	3,256	184.1	59,075	3,340.7	9,452	534.5	44,585	2,521.3	5,038	284.9
	Percent change	-3.9	-4.4	-2.1	-2.7	+0.5	-0.1	-1.7	-2.3	-9.7	-10.2
North Dakota[2]	2005	460	72.5	12,848	2,024.6	2,043	321.9	9,732	1,533.6	1,073	169.1
	2006	540	84.9	12,719	2,000.3	2,393	376.3	9,314	1,464.8	1,012	159.2
	Percent change	+17.4	+17.2	-1.0	-1.2	+17.1	+16.9	-4.3	-4.5	-5.7	-5.9
South Dakota[2]	2005	847	109.3	13,694	1,767.2	2,505	323.3	10,350	1,335.7	839	108.3
	2006	876	112.0	12,664	1,619.6	2,650	338.9	9,296	1,188.9	718	91.8
	Percent change	+3.4	+2.5	-7.5	-8.4	+5.8	+4.8	-10.2	-11.0	-14.4	-15.2
South[2,5]	2005	381,330	354.6	4,177,564	3,884.2	966,083	898.2	2,799,255	2,602.7	412,226	383.3
	2006	382,853	351.0	4,124,293	3,780.8	985,937	903.8	2,725,921	2,498.9	412,435	378.1
	Percent change	+0.4	-1.0	-1.3	-2.7	+2.1	+0.6	-2.6	-4.0	+0.1	-1.4
South Atlantic[2,5]	2005	208,412	370.8	2,130,015	3,789.3	482,758	858.8	1,418,685	2,523.8	228,572	406.6
	2006	209,169	366.0	2,122,337	3,714.0	497,094	869.9	1,399,721	2,449.5	225,522	394.7
	Percent change	+0.4	-1.3	-0.4	-2.0	+3.0	+1.3	-1.3	-2.9	-1.3	-2.9
Delaware	2005	3,612	429.1	26,245	3,117.9	5,811	690.4	18,085	2,148.5	2,349	279.1
	2006	3,640	426.5	29,171	3,417.9	6,189	725.2	20,166	2,362.8	2,816	329.9
	Percent change	+0.8	-0.6	+11.1	+9.6	+6.5	+5.0	+11.5	+10.0	+19.9	+18.2
District of Columbia[5]	2005	3,971	682.2	26,133	4,489.8	3,577	614.6	14,836	2,548.9	7,720	1,326.3
	2006	4,589	789.1	27,063	4,653.8	3,835	659.5	15,907	2,735.4	7,321	1,258.9
	Percent change	+15.6	+15.7	+3.6	+3.7	+7.2	+7.3	+7.2	+7.3	-5.2	-5.1
Florida	2005	88,341	497.2	712,998	4,012.8	164,783	927.4	472,912	2,661.6	75,303	423.8
	2006	87,044	481.2	721,084	3,986.1	170,873	944.6	473,774	2,619.0	76,437	422.5
	Percent change	-1.5	-3.2	+1.1	-0.7	+3.7	+1.9	+0.2	-1.6	+1.5	-0.3
Georgia	2005	23,977	262.5	378,534	4,144.9	84,463	924.9	249,594	2,733.0	44,477	487.0
	2006	25,824	275.8	364,183	3,889.2	85,117	909.0	235,903	2,519.3	43,163	460.9
	Percent change	+7.7	+5.0	-3.8	-6.2	+0.8	-1.7	-5.5	-7.8	-3.0	-5.4
Maryland	2005	23,173	414.6	198,483	3,550.9	35,922	642.7	128,491	2,298.8	34,070	609.5
	2006	22,011	392.0	195,476	3,480.9	37,457	667.0	127,497	2,270.4	30,522	543.5
	Percent change	-5.0	-5.5	-1.5	-2.0	+4.3	+3.8	-0.8	-1.2	-10.4	-10.8
North Carolina	2005	25,128	289.7	353,855	4,080.2	104,298	1,202.6	221,091	2,549.3	28,466	328.2
	2006	25,605	289.1	364,960	4,120.8	107,407	1,212.7	227,427	2,567.9	30,126	340.2
	Percent change	+1.9	-0.2	+3.1	+1.0	+3.0	+0.8	+2.9	+0.7	+5.8	+3.6
South Carolina[2]	2005	24,757	582.9	185,606	4,370.4	42,741	1,006.4	126,489	2,978.4	16,376	385.6
	2006	25,058	579.9	183,322	4,242.3	42,772	989.8	124,148	2,873.0	16,402	379.6
	Percent change	+1.2	-0.5	-1.2	-2.9	+0.1	-1.6	-1.9	-3.5	+0.2	-1.6
Virginia[2]	2005	11,718	154.9	200,404	2,649.3	29,829	394.3	154,584	2,043.6	15,991	211.4
	2006	11,628	152.1	189,406	2,478.2	31,913	417.6	142,679	1,866.8	14,814	193.8
	Percent change	-0.8	-1.8	-5.5	-6.5	+7.0	+5.9	-7.7	-8.7	-7.4	-8.3
West Virginia[2]	2005	3,735	205.9	47,757	2,632.6	11,334	624.8	32,603	1,797.2	3,820	210.6
	2006	3,770	207.3	47,672	2,621.5	11,531	634.1	32,220	1,771.8	3,921	215.6
	Percent change	+0.9	+0.7	-0.2	-0.4	+1.7	+1.5	-1.2	-1.4	+2.6	+2.4
East South Central[2]	2005	53,961	306.9	634,325	3,607.2	158,305	900.2	421,364	2,396.1	54,656	310.8
	2006	53,016	298.6	630,734	3,552.5	161,791	911.3	413,920	2,331.4	55,023	309.9
	Percent change	-1.8	-2.7	-0.6	-1.5	+2.2	+1.2	-1.8	-2.7	+0.7	-0.3

Note: Although arson data are included in the trend and clearance tables, sufficient data are not available to estimate totals for this offense. Therefore, no arson data are published in this table.

[2] The 2005 crime figures have been adjusted.

[4] The data collection methodology for the offense of forcible rape used by the Illinois (with the exception of Rockford, Illinois) and the Minnesota state (2006 data only) Uniform Crime Reporting (UCR) Programs do not comply with national UCR Program guidelines. Consequently, their figures for forcible rape were estimated for inclusion in this table.

[5] Includes offenses reported by the Zoological Police and the Metro Transit Police.

Table 4. Crime, by Region, Geographic Division, and State, 2005–2006 (*Contd.*)

(Number, rate per 100,000 population, percent.)

Area	Year	Population[1]	Violent crime		Murder and nonnegligent manslaughter		Forcible rape		Robbery	
			Number	Rate	Number	Rate	Number	Rate	Number	Rate
Alabama	2005	4,548,327	19,678	432.6	374	8.2	1,564	34.4	6,447	141.7
	2006	4,599,030	19,557	425.2	382	8.3	1,649	35.9	7,059	153.5
	Percent change		-0.6	-1.7	+2.1	+1.0	+5.4	+4.3	+9.5	+8.3
Kentucky	2005	4,172,608	11,134	266.8	190	4.6	1,421	34.1	3,690	88.4
	2006	4,206,074	11,063	263.0	168	4.0	1,297	30.8	3,626	86.2
	Percent change		-0.6	-1.4	-11.6	-12.3	-8.7	-9.5	-1.7	-2.5
Mississippi	2005	2,908,496	8,131	279.6	214	7.4	1,147	39.4	2,405	82.7
	2006	2,910,540	8,691	298.6	223	7.7	1,000	34.4	3,118	107.1
	Percent change		+6.9	+6.8	+4.2	+4.1	-12.8	-12.9	+29.6	+29.6
Tennessee[2]	2005	5,955,745	45,104	757.3	431	7.2	2,194	36.8	10,009	168.1
	2006	6,038,803	45,907	760.2	409	6.8	2,142	35.5	11,129	184.3
	Percent change		+1.8	+0.4	-5.1	-6.4	-2.4	-3.7	+11.2	+9.7
West South Central[2]	2005	33,754,989	180,694	535.3	2,233	6.6	12,615	37.4	46,889	138.9
	2006	34,185,635	184,606	540.0	2,326	6.8	12,730	37.2	48,882	143.0
	Percent change		+2.2	+0.9	+4.2	+2.9	+0.9	-0.4	+4.3	+2.9
Arkansas[2]	2005	2,775,708	14,670	528.5	189	6.8	1,202	43.3	2,532	91.2
	2006	2,810,872	15,506	551.6	205	7.3	1,308	46.5	2,766	98.4
	Percent change		+5.7	+4.4	+8.5	+7.1	+8.8	+7.5	+9.2	+7.9
Louisiana	2005	4,507,331	26,889	596.6	450	10.0	1,421	31.5	5,337	118.4
	2006	4,287,768	29,919	697.8	530	12.4	1,562	36.4	5,729	133.6
	Percent change		+11.3	+17.0	+17.8	+23.8	+9.9	+15.6	+7.3	+12.8
Oklahoma	2005	3,543,442	18,044	509.2	187	5.3	1,481	41.8	3,230	91.2
	2006	3,579,212	17,803	497.4	207	5.8	1,488	41.6	3,133	87.5
	Percent change		-1.3	-2.3	+10.7	+9.6	+0.5	-0.5	-3.0	-4.0
Texas	2005	22,928,508	121,091	528.1	1,407	6.1	8,511	37.1	35,790	156.1
	2006	23,507,783	121,378	516.3	1,384	5.9	8,372	35.6	37,254	158.5
	Percent change		+0.2	-2.2	-1.6	-4.1	-1.6	-4.1	+4.1	+1.5
West[2]	2005	68,339,272	318,980	466.8	3,935	5.8	22,359	32.7	94,164	137.8
	2006	69,355,643	328,428	473.5	3,905	5.6	22,072	31.8	105,785	152.5
	Percent change		+3.0	+1.5	-0.8	-2.2	-1.3	-2.7	+12.3	+10.7
Mountain[2]	2005	20,317,824	89,166	438.9	1,091	5.4	8,009	39.4	20,738	102.1
	2006	20,845,987	93,590	449.0	1,087	5.2	8,055	38.6	23,975	115.0
	Percent change		+5.0	+2.3	-0.4	-2.9	+0.6	-2.0	+15.6	+12.7
Arizona	2005	5,953,007	30,478	512.0	445	7.5	2,006	33.7	8,579	144.1
	2006	6,166,318	30,916	501.4	465	7.5	1,941	31.5	9,226	149.6
	Percent change		+1.4	-2.1	+4.5	+0.9	-3.2	-6.6	+7.5	+3.8
Colorado	2005	4,663,295	18,498	396.7	173	3.7	2,026	43.4	3,948	84.7
	2006	4,753,377	18,616	391.6	158	3.3	2,076	43.7	3,835	80.7
	Percent change		+0.6	-1.3	-8.7	-10.4	+2.5	+0.5	-2.9	-4.7
Idaho	2005	1,429,367	3,670	256.8	35	2.4	577	40.4	266	18.6
	2006	1,466,465	3,625	247.2	36	2.5	587	40.0	301	20.5
	Percent change		-1.2	-3.7	+2.9	+0.3	+1.7	-0.8	+13.2	+10.3
Montana	2005	934,737	2,634	281.8	18	1.9	301	32.2	177	18.9
	2006	944,632	2,397	253.7	17	1.8	269	28.5	164	17.4
	Percent change		-9.0	-10.0	-5.6	-6.5	-10.6	-11.6	-7.3	-8.3
Nevada	2005	2,412,301	14,654	607.5	206	8.5	1,016	42.1	4,702	194.9
	2006	2,495,529	18,508	741.6	224	9.0	1,079	43.2	7,027	281.6
	Percent change		+26.3	+22.1	+8.7	+5.1	+6.2	+2.7	+49.4	+44.5
New Mexico[2]	2005	1,925,985	12,448	646.3	144	7.5	1,041	54.1	1,893	98.3
	2006	1,954,599	12,572	643.2	132	6.8	1,094	56.0	2,105	107.7
	Percent change		+1.0	-0.5	-8.3	-9.7	+5.1	+3.6	+11.2	+9.6
Utah	2005	2,490,334	5,612	225.4	56	2.2	920	36.9	1,095	44.0
	2006	2,550,063	5,722	224.4	46	1.8	869	34.1	1,245	48.8
	Percent change		+2.0	-0.4	-17.9	-19.8	-5.5	-7.8	+13.7	+11.0
Wyoming	2005	508,798	1,172	230.3	14	2.8	122	24.0	78	15.3
	2006	515,004	1,234	239.6	9	1.7	140	27.2	72	14.0
	Percent change		+5.3	+4.0	-35.7	-36.5	+14.8	+13.4	-7.7	-8.8
Pacific	2005	48,021,448	229,814	478.6	2,844	5.9	14,350	29.9	73,426	152.9
	2006	48,509,656	234,838	484.1	2,818	5.8	14,017	28.9	81,810	168.6
	Percent change		+2.2	+1.2	-0.9	-1.9	-2.3	-3.3	+11.4	+10.3
Alaska	2005	663,253	4,194	632.3	32	4.8	538	81.1	537	81.0
	2006	670,053	4,610	688.0	36	5.4	509	76.0	605	90.3
	Percent change		+9.9	+8.8	+12.5	+11.4	-5.4	-6.4	+12.7	+11.5

Note: Although arson data are included in the trend and clearance tables, sufficient data are not available to estimate totals for this offense. Therefore, no arson data are published in this table.
[1] Populations are U.S. Census Bureau provisional estimates as of July 1, 2006, and July 1, 2005.
[2] The 2005 crime figures have been adjusted.

Table 4. Crime, by Region, Geographic Division, and State, 2005–2006 (*Contd.*)

(Number, rate per 100,000 population, percent.)

Area	Year	Aggravated assault		Property crime		Burglary		Larceny-theft		Motor vehicle theft	
		Number	Rate	Number	Rate	Number	Rate	Number	Rate	Number	Rate
Alabama	2005	11,293	248.3	177,393	3,900.2	43,473	955.8	120,780	2,655.5	13,140	288.9
	2006	10,467	227.6	181,021	3,936.1	44,571	969.1	121,610	2,644.3	14,840	322.7
	Percent change	-7.3	-8.3	+2.0	+0.9	+2.5	+1.4	+0.7	-0.4	+12.9	+11.7
Kentucky	2005	5,833	139.8	105,608	2,531.0	26,458	634.1	70,354	1,686.1	8,796	210.8
	2006	5,972	142.0	107,023	2,544.5	27,122	644.8	70,658	1,679.9	9,243	219.8
	Percent change	+2.4	+1.6	+1.3	+0.5	+2.5	+1.7	+0.4	-0.4	+5.1	+4.2
Mississippi	2005	4,365	150.1	95,231	3,274.2	26,866	923.7	60,873	2,092.9	7,492	257.6
	2006	4,350	149.5	93,393	3,208.8	27,239	935.9	57,807	1,986.1	8,347	286.8
	Percent change	-0.3	-0.4	-1.9	-2.0	+1.4	+1.3	-5.0	-5.1	+11.4	+11.3
Tennessee[2]	2005	32,470	545.2	256,093	4,299.9	61,508	1,032.8	169,357	2,843.6	25,228	423.6
	2006	32,227	533.7	249,297	4,128.3	62,859	1,040.9	163,845	2,713.2	22,593	374.1
	Percent change	-0.7	-2.1	-2.7	-4.0	+2.2	+0.8	-3.3	-4.6	-10.4	-11.7
West South Central[2]	2005	118,957	352.4	1,413,224	4,186.7	325,020	962.9	959,206	2,841.7	128,998	382.2
	2006	120,668	353.0	1,371,222	4,011.1	327,052	956.7	912,280	2,668.6	131,890	385.8
	Percent change	+1.4	+0.2	-3.0	-4.2	+0.6	-0.6	-4.9	-6.1	+2.2	+1.0
Arkansas[2]	2005	10,747	387.2	112,914	4,067.9	30,118	1,085.1	75,510	2,720.4	7,286	262.5
	2006	11,227	399.4	111,521	3,967.5	32,042	1,139.9	72,016	2,562.1	7,463	265.5
	Percent change	+4.5	+3.2	-1.2	-2.5	+6.4	+5.1	-4.6	-5.8	+2.4	+1.1
Louisiana	2005	19,681	436.6	166,611	3,696.4	39,382	873.7	112,840	2,503.5	14,389	319.2
	2006	22,098	515.4	171,239	3,993.7	44,986	1,049.2	110,613	2,579.7	15,640	364.8
	Percent change	+12.3	+18.0	+2.8	+8.0	+14.2	+20.1	-2.0	+3.0	+8.7	+14.3
Oklahoma	2005	13,146	371.0	143,406	4,047.1	35,692	1,007.3	93,814	2,647.5	13,900	392.3
	2006	12,975	362.5	129,002	3,604.2	34,377	960.5	81,267	2,270.5	13,358	373.2
	Percent change	-1.3	-2.3	-10.0	-10.9	-3.7	-4.6	-13.4	-14.2	-3.9	-4.9
Texas	2005	75,383	328.8	990,293	4,319.0	219,828	958.8	677,042	2,952.8	93,423	407.5
	2006	74,368	316.4	959,460	4,081.5	215,647	917.3	648,384	2,758.2	95,429	405.9
	Percent change	-1.3	-3.8	-3.1	-5.5	-1.9	-4.3	-4.2	-6.6	+2.1	-0.4
West[2]	2005	198,522	290.5	2,590,853	3,791.2	517,007	756.5	1,606,071	2,350.1	467,775	684.5
	2006	196,666	283.6	2,451,277	3,534.4	504,183	727.0	1,508,668	2,175.3	438,426	632.1
	Percent change	-0.9	-2.4	-5.4	-6.8	-2.5	-3.9	-6.1	-7.4	-6.3	-7.6
Mountain[2]	2005	59,328	292.0	837,372	4,121.4	164,599	810.1	542,820	2,671.6	129,953	639.6
	2006	60,473	290.1	794,295	3,810.3	162,688	780.4	506,525	2,429.8	125,082	600.0
	Percent change	+1.9	-0.7	-5.1	-7.5	-1.2	-3.7	-6.7	-9.1	-3.7	-6.2
Arizona	2005	19,448	326.7	287,345	4,826.9	56,328	946.2	176,112	2,958.4	54,905	922.3
	2006	19,284	312.7	285,370	4,627.9	57,055	925.3	173,466	2,813.1	54,849	889.5
	Percent change	-0.8	-4.3	-0.7	-4.1	+1.3	-2.2	-1.5	-4.9	-0.1	-3.6
Colorado	2005	12,351	264.9	188,449	4,041.1	34,746	745.1	127,602	2,736.3	26,101	559.7
	2006	12,547	264.0	164,054	3,451.3	32,422	682.1	110,837	2,331.8	20,795	437.5
	Percent change	+1.6	-0.3	-12.9	-14.6	-6.7	-8.5	-13.1	-14.8	-20.3	-21.8
Idaho	2005	2,792	195.3	38,556	2,697.4	8,066	564.3	27,606	1,931.3	2,884	201.8
	2006	2,701	184.2	35,471	2,418.8	7,526	513.2	25,516	1,740.0	2,429	165.6
	Percent change	-3.3	-5.7	-8.0	-10.3	-6.7	-9.1	-7.6	-9.9	-15.8	-17.9
Montana	2005	2,138	228.7	29,407	3,146.0	3,642	389.6	23,794	2,545.5	1,971	210.9
	2006	1,947	206.1	25,387	2,687.5	2,935	310.7	20,704	2,191.8	1,748	185.0
	Percent change	-8.9	-9.9	-13.7	-14.6	-19.4	-20.3	-13.0	-13.9	-11.3	-12.2
Nevada	2005	8,730	361.9	102,424	4,245.9	23,481	973.4	52,012	2,156.1	26,931	1,116.4
	2006	10,178	407.8	102,036	4,088.8	24,820	994.6	50,255	2,013.8	26,961	1,080.4
	Percent change	+16.6	+12.7	-0.4	-3.7	+5.7	+2.2	-3.4	-6.6	+0.1	-3.2
New Mexico[2]	2005	9,370	486.5	79,575	4,131.7	20,939	1,087.2	50,707	2,632.8	7,929	411.7
	2006	9,241	472.8	76,956	3,937.2	20,909	1,069.7	46,822	2,395.5	9,225	472.0
	Percent change	-1.4	-2.8	-3.3	-4.7	-0.1	-1.6	-7.7	-9.0	+16.3	+14.6
Utah	2005	3,541	142.2	95,546	3,836.7	14,971	601.2	72,082	2,894.5	8,493	341.0
	2006	3,562	139.7	89,671	3,516.4	14,701	576.5	66,671	2,614.5	8,299	325.4
	Percent change	+0.6	-1.8	-6.1	-8.3	-1.8	-4.1	-7.5	-9.7	-2.3	-4.6
Wyoming	2005	958	188.3	16,070	3,158.4	2,426	476.8	12,905	2,536.4	739	145.2
	2006	1,013	196.7	15,350	2,980.6	2,320	450.5	12,254	2,379.4	776	150.7
	Percent change	+5.7	+4.5	-4.5	-5.6	-4.4	-5.5	-5.0	-6.2	+5.0	+3.7
Pacific	2005	139,194	289.9	1,753,481	3,651.5	352,408	733.9	1,063,251	2,214.1	337,822	703.5
	2006	136,193	280.8	1,656,982	3,415.8	341,495	704.0	1,002,143	2,065.9	313,344	645.9
	Percent change	-2.2	-3.1	-5.5	-6.5	-3.1	-4.1	-5.7	-6.7	-7.2	-8.2
Alaska	2005	3,087	465.4	23,975	3,614.8	4,131	622.8	17,249	2,600.7	2,595	391.3
	2006	3,460	516.4	24,155	3,604.9	4,136	617.3	17,490	2,610.2	2,529	377.4
	Percent change	+12.1	+10.9	+0.8	-0.3	+0.1	-0.9	+1.4	+0.4	-2.5	-3.5

Note: Although arson data are included in the trend and clearance tables, sufficient data are not available to estimate totals for this offense. Therefore, no arson data are published in this table.

[2] The 2005 crime figures have been adjusted.

Table 4. Crime, by Region, Geographic Division, and State, 2005–2006 (*Contd.*)

(Number, rate per 100,000 population, percent.)

Area	Year	Population[1]	Violent crime		Murder and nonnegligent manslaughter		Forcible rape		Robbery	
			Number	Rate	Number	Rate	Number	Rate	Number	Rate
California	2005..........................	36,154,147	190,178	526.0	2,503	6.9	9,392	26.0	63,622	176.0
	2006..........................	36,457,549	194,120	532.5	2,485	6.8	9,212	25.3	70,968	194.7
	Percent change		+2.1	+1.2	-0.7	-1.5	-1.9	-2.7	+11.5	+10.6
Hawaii	2005..........................	1,273,278	3,253	255.5	24	1.9	343	26.9	1,001	78.6
	2006..........................	1,285,498	3,615	281.2	21	1.6	355	27.6	1,143	88.9
	Percent change		+11.1	+10.1	-12.5	-13.3	+3.5	+2.5	+14.2	+13.1
Oregon	2005..........................	3,638,871	10,444	287.0	80	2.2	1,266	34.8	2,478	68.1
	2006..........................	3,700,758	10,373	280.3	86	2.3	1,195	32.3	2,689	72.7
	Percent change		-0.7	-2.3	+7.5	+5.7	-5.6	-7.2	+8.5	+6.7
Washington	2005..........................	6,291,899	21,745	345.6	205	3.3	2,811	44.7	5,788	92.0
	2006..........................	6,395,798	22,120	345.9	190	3.0	2,746	42.9	6,405	100.1
	Percent change		+1.7	+0.1	-7.3	-8.8	-2.3	-3.9	+10.7	+8.9
Puerto Rico	2005..........................	3,911,810	9,579	244.9	766	19.6	169	4.3	5,550	141.9
	2006..........................	3,927,776	8,929	227.3	739	18.8	118	3.0	5,245	133.5
	Percent change		-6.8	-7.2	-3.5	-3.9	-30.2	-30.5	-5.5	-5.9

Note: Although arson data are included in the trend and clearance tables, sufficient data are not available to estimate totals for this offense. Therefore, no arson data are published in this table.

[1] Populations are U.S. Census Bureau provisional estimates as of July 1, 2006, and July 1, 2005.

Table 4. Crime, by Region, Geographic Division, and State, 2005–2006

(Number, rate per 100,000 population, percent.)

Area	Year	Aggravated assault		Property crime		Burglary		Larceny-theft		Motor vehicle theft	
		Number	Rate	Number	Rate	Number	Rate	Number	Rate	Number	Rate
California	2005............................	114,661	317.1	1,200,531	3,320.6	250,521	692.9	692,467	1,915.3	257,543	712.3
	2006............................	111,455	305.7	1,156,017	3,170.9	246,464	676.0	666,860	1,829.1	242,693	665.7
	Percent change	-2.8	-3.6	-3.7	-4.5	-1.6	-2.4	-3.7	-4.5	-5.8	-6.6
Hawaii	2005............................	1,885	148.0	61,115	4,799.8	9,792	769.0	42,188	3,313.3	9,135	717.4
	2006............................	2,096	163.0	54,382	4,230.4	8,709	677.5	37,910	2,949.1	7,763	603.9
	Percent change	+11.2	+10.1	-11.0	-11.9	-11.1	-11.9	-10.1	-11.0	-15.0	-15.8
Oregon	2005............................	6,620	181.9	160,199	4,402.4	27,621	759.1	113,316	3,114.0	19,262	529.3
	2006............................	6,403	173.0	135,895	3,672.1	23,879	645.2	97,556	2,636.1	14,460	390.7
	Percent change	-3.3	-4.9	-15.2	-16.6	-13.5	-15.0	-13.9	-15.3	-24.9	-26.2
Washington	2005............................	12,941	205.7	307,661	4,889.8	60,343	959.1	198,031	3,147.4	49,287	783.3
	2006............................	12,779	199.8	286,533	4,480.0	58,307	911.6	182,327	2,850.7	45,899	717.6
	Percent change	-1.3	-2.9	-6.9	-8.4	-3.4	-4.9	-7.9	-9.4	-6.9	-8.4
Puerto Rico	2005............................	3,094	79.1	55,466	1,417.9	17,191	439.5	28,976	740.7	9,299	237.7
	2006............................	2,827	72.0	53,197	1,354.4	16,668	424.4	27,936	711.2	8,593	218.8
	Percent change	-8.6	-9.0	-4.1	-4.5	-3.0	-3.4	-3.6	-4.0	-7.6	-8.0

Table 5. Crime, by State and Territory, 2006

(Number, percent, rate per 100,000 population.)

State	Area	Popula-tion	Violent crime	Murder and non-negligent man-slaughter	Forcible rape	Robbery	Aggra-vated assault	Property crime	Burglary	Larceny-theft	Motor vehicle theft
ALABAMA	Metropolitan Statistical Area..........	3,258,752									
	Area actually reporting...................	88.0%	14,007	300	1,144	5,824	6,739	129,240	32,168	85,756	11,316
	Estimated total.................................	100.0%	15,414	318	1,256	6,313	7,527	142,577	35,249	94,969	12,359
	Cities outside metropolitan areas ...	587,537									
	Area actually reporting...................	55.8%	1,641	23	141	379	1,098	16,020	3,263	11,846	911
	Estimated total.................................	100.0%	2,920	41	249	670	1,960	28,509	5,803	21,091	1,615
	Nonmetropolitan counties...............	752,741									
	Area actually reporting...................	60.6%	741	14	87	46	594	6,022	2,133	3,364	525
	Estimated total.................................	100.0%	1,223	23	144	76	980	9,935	3,519	5,550	866
	State Total...	4,599,030	19,557	382	1,649	7,059	10,467	181,021	44,571	121,610	14,840
	Rate per 100,000 inhabitants...........		425.2	8.3	35.9	153.5	227.6	3,936.1	969.1	2,644.3	322.7
ALASKA	Metropolitan Statistical Area..........	328,283									
	Area actually reporting...................	97.4%	2,949	18	320	526	2,085	14,143	2,108	10,385	1,650
	Estimated total.................................	100.0%	3,023	18	324	538	2,143	14,804	2,172	10,943	1,689
	Cities outside metropolitan areas ...	124,198									
	Area actually reporting...................	89.6%	543	8	90	35	410	4,224	561	3,365	298
	Estimated total.................................	100.0%	606	9	100	39	458	4,716	626	3,757	333
	Nonmetropolitan counties...............	217,572									
	Area actually reporting...................	100.0%	981	9	85	28	859	4,635	1,338	2,790	507
	State Total...	670,053	4,610	36	509	605	3,460	24,155	4,136	17,490	2,529
	Rate per 100,000 inhabitants...........		688.0	5.4	76.0	90.3	516.4	3,604.9	617.3	2,610.2	377.4
ARIZONA	Metropolitan Statistical Area..........	5,690,411									
	Area actually reporting...................	98.4%	28,822	455	1,830	9,016	17,521	268,052	52,408	162,733	52,911
	Estimated total.................................	100.0%	29,177	458	1,854	9,099	17,766	272,056	53,391	165,184	53,481
	Cities outside metropolitan areas ...	202,701									
	Area actually reporting...................	91.4%	839	4	38	70	727	7,656	1,594	5,375	687
	Estimated total.................................	100.0%	918	4	42	77	795	8,376	1,744	5,880	752
	Nonmetropolitan counties...............	273,206									
	Area actually reporting...................	77.3%	635	2	35	39	559	3,817	1,484	1,857	476
	Estimated total.................................	100.0%	821	3	45	50	723	4,938	1,920	2,402	616
	State Total...	6,166,318	30,916	465	1,941	9,226	19,284	285,370	57,055	173,466	54,849
	Rate per 100,000 inhabitants...........		501.4	7.5	31.5	149.6	312.7	4,627.9	925.3	2,813.1	889.5
ARKANSAS	Metropolitan Statistical Area..........	1,644,224									
	Area actually reporting...................	96.8%	11,484	156	933	2,267	8,128	77,898	21,416	50,895	5,587
	Estimated total.................................	100.0%	11,683	158	953	2,289	8,283	79,512	21,965	51,848	5,699
	Cities outside metropolitan areas ...	496,029									
	Area actually reporting...................	97.0%	2,652	27	216	402	2,007	21,602	6,619	14,004	979
	Estimated total.................................	100.0%	2,733	28	223	414	2,068	22,262	6,821	14,432	1,009
	Nonmetropolitan counties...............	670,619									
	Area actually reporting...................	92.5%	1,009	18	122	58	811	9,020	3,013	5,308	699
	Estimated total.................................	100.0%	1,090	19	132	63	876	9,747	3,256	5,736	755
	State Total...	2,810,872	15,506	205	1,308	2,766	11,227	111,521	32,042	72,016	7,463
	Rate per 100,000 inhabitants...........		551.6	7.3	46.5	98.4	399.4	3,967.5	1,139.9	2,562.1	265.5
CALIFORNIA	Metropolitan Statistical Area..........	35,608,453									
	Area actually reporting...................	100.0%	191,037	2,453	8,921	70,670	108,993	1,136,833	240,629	655,694	240,510
	Cities outside metropolitan areas ...	271,190									
	Area actually reporting...................	100.0%	1,335	12	133	182	1,008	9,689	2,480	6,291	918
	Nonmetropolitan counties...............	577,906									
	Area actually reporting...................	100.0%	1,748	20	158	116	1,454	9,495	3,355	4,875	1,265
	State Total...	36,457,549	194,120	2,485	9,212	70,968	111,455	1,156,017	246,464	666,860	242,693
	Rate per 100,000 inhabitants...........		532.5	6.8	25.3	194.7	305.7	3,170.9	676.0	1,829.1	665.7
COLORADO	Metropolitan Statistical Area..........	4,085,808									
	Area actually reporting...................	97.9%	16,588	147	1,835	3,696	10,910	145,204	29,247	96,447	19,510
	Estimated total.................................	100.0%	16,843	149	1,870	3,743	11,081	148,489	29,801	98,778	19,910
	Cities outside metropolitan areas ...	303,195									
	Area actually reporting...................	94.0%	1,152	6	146	77	923	10,768	1,686	8,528	554
	Estimated total.................................	100.0%	1,225	6	155	82	982	11,456	1,794	9,073	589
	Nonmetropolitan counties...............	364,374									
	Area actually reporting...................	96.2%	527	3	49	10	465	3,951	795	2,871	285
	Estimated total.................................	100.0%	548	3	51	10	484	4,109	827	2,986	296
	State Total...	4,753,377	18,616	158	2,076	3,835	12,547	164,054	32,422	110,837	20,795
	Rate per 100,000 inhabitants...........		391.6	3.3	43.7	80.7	264.0	3,451.3	682.1	2,331.8	437.5

Note: Although arson data are included in the trend and clearance tables, sufficient data are not available to estimate totals for this offense. Therefore, no arson data are published in this table.

Table 5. Crime, by State and Territory, 2006 *(Contd.)*

(Number, percent, rate per 100,000 population.)

State	Area	Popula-tion	Violent crime	Murder and non-negligent man-slaughter	Forcible rape	Robbery	Aggra-vated assault	Property crime	Burglary	Larceny-theft	Motor vehicle theft
CONNECTICUT	Metropolitan Statistical Area..........	2,819,925									
	Area actually reporting...................	99.3%	9,176	104	538	4,117	4,417	80,280	12,956	57,590	9,734
	Estimated total................................	100.0%	9,203	104	541	4,129	4,429	80,713	13,027	57,914	9,772
	Cities outside metropolitan areas...	158,762									
	Area actually reporting...................	100.0%	300	1	27	45	227	3,171	647	2,295	229
	Nonmetropolitan counties...............	526,122									
	Area actually reporting...................	100.0%	338	3	68	67	200	3,880	1,020	2,471	389
	State Total.......................................	3,504,809	9,841	108	636	4,241	4,856	87,764	14,694	62,680	10,390
	Rate per 100,000 inhabitants...........		280.8	3.1	18.1	121.0	138.6	2,504.1	419.3	1,788.4	296.4
DELAWARE	Metropolitan Statistical Area..........	674,845									
	Area actually reporting...................	100.0%	4,795	40	305	1,577	2,873	23,513	4,643	16,335	2,535
	Cities outside metropolitan areas...	40,072									
	Area actually reporting...................	100.0%	385	2	33	94	256	2,238	486	1,679	73
	Nonmetropolitan counties...............	138,559									
	Area actually reporting...................	100.0%	637	0	62	64	511	3,420	1,060	2,152	208
	State Total.......................................	853,476	5,817	42	400	1,735	3,640	29,171	6,189	20,166	2,816
	Rate per 100,000 inhabitants...........		681.6	4.9	46.9	203.3	426.5	3,417.9	725.2	2,362.8	329.9
DISTRICT OF COLUMBIA[1]	Metropolitan Statistical Area..........	581,530									
	Area actually reporting...................	100.0%	8,772	169	185	3,829	4,589	27,063	3,835	15,907	7,321
	Cities outside metropolitan areas...	None									
	Nonmetropolitan counties...............	None									
	Total...	581,530	8,772	169	185	3,829	4,589	27,063	3,835	15,907	7,321
	Rate per 100,000 inhabitants...........		1,508.4	29.1	31.8	658.4	789.1	4,653.8	659.5	2,735.4	1,258.9
FLORIDA	Metropolitan Statistical Area..........	17,028,925									
	Area actually reporting...................	99.9%	123,064	1,091	6,135	33,444	82,394	692,520	162,335	455,797	74,388
	Estimated total................................	100.0%	123,126	1,091	6,138	33,462	82,435	692,936	162,428	456,079	74,429
	Cities outside metropolitan areas...	185,034									
	Area actually reporting...................	94.2%	1,738	9	89	323	1,317	8,569	2,075	5,936	558
	Estimated total................................	100.0%	1,845	10	94	343	1,398	9,095	2,202	6,301	592
	Nonmetropolitan counties...............	875,929									
	Area actually reporting...................	100.0%	3,824	28	243	342	3,211	19,053	6,243	11,394	1,416
	State Total.......................................	18,089,888	128,795	1,129	6,475	34,147	87,044	721,084	170,873	473,774	76,437
	Rate per 100,000 inhabitants...........		712.0	6.2	35.8	188.8	481.2	3,986.1	944.6	2,619.0	422.5
GEORGIA	Metropolitan Statistical Area..........	7,562,594									
	Area actually reporting...................	97.6%	36,773	505	1,785	14,073	20,410	298,615	70,253	189,481	38,881
	Estimated total................................	100.0%	37,540	514	1,824	14,354	20,848	305,654	71,816	194,121	39,717
	Cities outside metropolitan areas...	665,603									
	Area actually reporting...................	76.8%	3,066	36	164	697	2,169	27,315	5,419	20,765	1,131
	Estimated total................................	100.0%	3,991	47	214	907	2,823	35,542	7,051	27,019	1,472
	Nonmetropolitan counties...............	1,135,744									
	Area actually reporting...................	81.4%	2,096	32	110	202	1,752	18,702	5,085	12,011	1,606
	Estimated total................................	100.0%	2,575	39	135	248	2,153	22,987	6,250	14,763	1,974
	State Total.......................................	9,363,941	44,106	600	2,173	15,509	25,824	364,183	85,117	235,903	43,163
	Rate per 100,000 inhabitants...........		471.0	6.4	23.2	165.6	275.8	3,889.2	909.0	2,519.3	460.9
HAWAII	Metropolitan Statistical Area..........	912,693									
	Area actually reporting...................	100.0%	2,745	17	229	956	1,543	38,310	5,482	26,540	6,288
	Cities outside metropolitan areas...	None									
	Nonmetropolitan counties...............	372,805									
	Area actually reporting...................	100.0%	870	4	126	187	553	16,072	3,227	11,370	1,475
	State Total.......................................	1,285,498	3,615	21	355	1,143	2,096	54,382	8,709	37,910	7,763
	Rate per 100,000 inhabitants...........		281.2	1.6	27.6	88.9	163.0	4,230.4	677.5	2,949.1	603.9
IDAHO	Metropolitan Statistical Area..........	945,612									
	Area actually reporting...................	99.7%	2,678	21	455	252	1,950	26,110	5,460	18,806	1,844
	Estimated total................................	100.0%	2,687	21	456	253	1,957	26,193	5,478	18,865	1,850
	Cities outside metropolitan areas...	230,284									
	Area actually reporting...................	98.9%	455	4	60	39	352	5,789	1,079	4,406	304
	Estimated total................................	100.0%	460	4	61	39	356	5,852	1,091	4,454	307
	Nonmetropolitan counties...............	290,569									
	Area actually reporting...................	98.9%	473	11	69	9	384	3,387	946	2,172	269
	Estimated total................................	100.0%	478	11	70	9	388	3,426	957	2,197	272
	State Total.......................................	1,466,465	3,625	36	587	301	2,701	35,471	7,526	25,516	2,429
	Rate per 100,000 inhabitants...........		247.2	2.5	40.0	20.5	184.2	2,418.8	513.2	1,740.0	165.6

Note: Although arson data are included in the trend and clearance tables, sufficient data are not available to estimate totals for this offense. Therefore, no arson data are published in this table.

[1] Includes offenses reported by the Zoological Police and the Metro Transit Police.

Table 5. Crime, by State and Territory, 2006 *(Contd.)*

(Number, percent, rate per 100,000 population.)

State	Area	Population	Violent crime	Murder and non-negligent man-slaughter	Forcible rape	Robbery	Aggra-vated assault	Property crime	Burglary	Larceny-theft	Motor vehicle theft
ILLINOIS[2, 3]	State Total...............	12,831,970	69,498	780	4,078	23,782	40,858	387,478	77,259	272,578	37,641
	Rate per 100,000 inhabitants...........		541.6	6.1	31.8	185.3	318.4	3,019.6	602.1	2,124.2	293.3
INDIANA	Metropolitan Statistical Area..........	4,903,644									
	Area actually reporting...................	85.1%	17,075	316	1,478	6,658	8,623	172,191	36,019	117,501	18,671
	Estimated total...............................	100.0%	18,120	328	1,578	6,877	9,337	186,973	39,081	127,955	19,937
	Cities outside metropolitan areas...	507,489									
	Area actually reporting...................	81.9%	885	6	102	239	538	18,715	3,359	14,451	905
	Estimated total...............................	100.0%	1,080	7	124	292	657	22,838	4,099	17,635	1,104
	Nonmetropolitan counties...............	902,387									
	Area actually reporting...................	52.9%	357	18	70	39	230	5,981	1,579	3,966	436
	Estimated total...............................	100.0%	676	34	133	74	435	11,316	2,988	7,503	825
	State Total...............................	6,313,520	19,876	369	1,835	7,243	10,429	221,127	46,168	153,093	21,866
	Rate per 100,000 inhabitants...........		314.8	5.8	29.1	114.7	165.2	3,502.4	731.3	2,424.8	346.3
IOWA	Metropolitan Statistical Area..........	1,634,007									
	Area actually reporting...................	98.8%	5,996	30	572	1,155	4,239	58,078	11,518	42,938	3,622
	Estimated total...............................	100.0%	6,036	30	577	1,160	4,269	58,594	11,603	43,346	3,645
	Cities outside metropolitan areas...	595,689									
	Area actually reporting...................	92.8%	1,720	10	174	115	1,421	18,230	4,132	13,210	888
	Estimated total...............................	100.0%	1,854	11	188	124	1,531	19,647	4,453	14,237	957
	Nonmetropolitan counties...............	752,389									
	Area actually reporting...................	98.6%	557	14	62	14	467	5,261	1,933	2,930	398
	Estimated total...............................	100.0%	565	14	63	14	474	5,338	1,961	2,973	404
	State Total...............................	2,982,085	8,455	55	828	1,298	6,274	83,579	18,017	60,556	5,006
	Rate per 100,000 inhabitants...........		283.5	1.8	27.8	43.5	210.4	2,802.7	604.2	2,030.7	167.9
KANSAS	Metropolitan Statistical Area..........	1,741,155									
	Area actually reporting...................	99.6%	8,446	99	785	1,634	5,928	70,874	13,033	50,705	7,136
	Estimated total...............................	100.0%	8,465	99	787	1,636	5,943	71,073	13,064	50,858	7,151
	Cities outside metropolitan areas...	603,197									
	Area actually reporting...................	96.5%	2,234	18	322	189	1,705	24,070	4,657	18,397	1,016
	Estimated total...............................	100.0%	2,315	19	334	196	1,766	24,933	4,824	19,057	1,052
	Nonmetropolitan counties...............	419,723									
	Area actually reporting...................	98.8%	957	9	116	44	788	7,563	2,080	4,989	494
	Estimated total...............................	100.0%	968	9	117	45	797	7,652	2,104	5,048	500
	State Total...............................	2,764,075	11,748	127	1,238	1,877	8,506	103,658	19,992	74,963	8,703
	Rate per 100,000 inhabitants...........		425.0	4.6	44.8	67.9	307.7	3,750.2	723.3	2,712.0	314.9
KENTUCKY	Metropolitan Statistical Area...........	2,385,538									
	Area actually reporting...................	94.2%	7,878	85	629	3,000	4,164	70,770	16,675	47,647	6,448
	Estimated total...............................	100.0%	8,165	87	668	3,106	4,304	74,756	17,494	50,537	6,725
	Cities outside metropolitan areas...	522,702									
	Area actually reporting...................	79.7%	1,040	10	146	262	622	13,019	2,785	9,438	796
	Estimated total...............................	100.0%	1,305	13	183	329	780	16,328	3,493	11,837	998
	Nonmetropolitan counties...............	1,297,834									
	Area actually reporting...................	87.0%	1,386	59	388	166	773	13,872	5,339	7,210	1,323
	Estimated total...............................	100.0%	1,593	68	446	191	888	15,939	6,135	8,284	1,520
	State Total...............................	4,206,074	11,063	168	1,297	3,626	5,972	107,023	27,122	70,658	9,243
	Rate per 100,000 inhabitants...........		263.0	4.0	30.8	86.2	142.0	2,544.5	644.8	1,679.9	219.8
LOUISIANA	Metropolitan Statistical Area..........	3,220,811									
	Area actually reporting...................	93.4%	22,291	456	1,154	4,860	15,821	129,567	33,446	82,906	13,215
	Estimated total...............................	100.0%	23,381	468	1,202	5,045	16,666	137,004	34,968	88,228	13,808
	Cities outside metropolitan areas...	362,920									
	Area actually reporting...................	57.9%	1,960	18	97	289	1,556	11,450	3,296	7,616	538
	Estimated total...............................	100.0%	3,248	30	160	468	2,590	19,297	5,485	12,920	892
	Nonmetropolitan counties...............	704,037									
	Area actually reporting...................	85.5%	2,814	27	171	185	2,431	12,779	3,878	8,097	804
	Estimated total...............................	100.0%	3,290	32	200	216	2,842	14,938	4,533	9,465	940
	State Total...............................	4,287,768	29,919	530	1,562	5,729	22,098	171,239	44,986	110,613	15,640
	Rate per 100,000 inhabitants...........		697.8	12.4	36.4	133.6	515.4	3,993.7	1,049.2	2,579.7	364.8

Note: Although arson data are included in the trend and clearance tables, sufficient data are not available to estimate totals for this offense. Therefore, no arson data are published in this table.

[2] Limited data for 2006 were available for Illinois.

[3] The data collection methodology for the offense of forcible rape used by the Illinois (with the exception of Rockford, Illinois) and the Minnesota state UCR Programs do not comply with national UCR guidelines. Consequently, their figures for forcible rape (with the exception of Rockford, Illinois) have been estimated for inclusion in this table. Table 8, Offenses Known to Law Enforcement, provides the reported female forcible rape crime figure.

Table 5. Crime, by State and Territory, 2006 *(Contd.)*

(Number, percent, rate per 100,000 population.)

State	Area	Popula-tion	Violent crime	Murder and non-negligent man-slaughter	Forcible rape	Robbery	Aggra-vated assault	Property crime	Burglary	Larceny-theft	Motor vehicle theft
MAINE	Metropolitan Statistical Area...........	769,373									
	Area actually reporting..................	100.0%	971	9	193	332	437	20,913	4,022	16,018	873
	Cities outside metropolitan areas ...	276,904									
	Area actually reporting..................	100.0%	400	3	106	39	252	8,418	1,419	6,749	250
	Nonmetropolitan counties...............	275,297									
	Area actually reporting..................	100.0%	155	11	40	13	91	3,955	1,338	2,400	217
	State Total..	1,321,574	1,526	23	339	384	780	33,286	6,779	25,167	1,340
	Rate per 100,000 inhabitants...........		115.5	1.7	25.7	29.1	59.0	2,518.7	512.9	1,904.3	101.4
MARYLAND	Metropolitan Statistical Area...........	5,320,939									
	Area actually reporting..................	100.0%	36,857	536	1,111	14,173	21,037	186,630	35,380	121,218	30,032
	Cities outside metropolitan areas ...	75,606									
	Area actually reporting..................	100.0%	553	2	27	118	406	4,398	825	3,416	157
	Nonmetropolitan counties...............	219,182									
	Area actually reporting..................	100.0%	700	8	40	84	568	4,448	1,252	2,863	333
	State Total..	5,615,727	38,110	546	1,178	14,375	22,011	195,476	37,457	127,497	30,522
	Rate per 100,000 inhabitants...........		678.6	9.7	21.0	256.0	392.0	3,480.9	667.0	2,270.4	543.5
MASSACHU-SETTS	Metropolitan Statistical Area...........	6,411,278									
	Area actually reporting..................	97.7%	28,293	185	1,708	7,953	18,447	150,511	34,341	98,517	17,653
	Estimated total.................................	100.0%	28,701	186	1,738	8,047	18,730	153,418	35,054	100,430	17,934
	Cities outside metropolitan areas ...	24,878									
	Area actually reporting..................	98.6%	73	0	4	0	69	488	125	336	27
	Estimated total.................................	100.0%	74	0	4	0	70	495	127	341	27
	Nonmetropolitan counties...............	1,037									
	Area actually reporting..................	100.0%	0	0	0	0	0	0	0	0	0
	State Total..	6,437,193	28,775	186	1,742	8,047	18,800	153,913	35,181	100,771	17,961
	Rate per 100,000 inhabitants...........		447.0	2.9	27.1	125.0	292.1	2,391.0	546.5	1,565.4	279.0
MICHIGAN	Metropolitan Statistical Area...........	8,219,091									
	Area actually reporting..................	99.3%	52,561	687	3,990	13,959	33,925	282,428	65,703	168,868	47,857
	Estimated total.................................	100.0%	52,753	688	4,014	14,005	34,046	284,315	66,036	170,199	48,080
	Cities outside metropolitan areas ...	644,856									
	Area actually reporting..................	91.3%	1,529	2	389	127	1,011	17,366	2,682	14,030	654
	Estimated total.................................	100.0%	1,639	2	415	136	1,086	18,735	2,890	15,137	708
	Nonmetropolitan counties...............	1,231,696									
	Area actually reporting..................	98.8%	2,358	23	830	66	1,439	21,045	7,095	12,736	1,214
	Estimated total.................................	100.0%	2,386	23	840	67	1,456	21,301	7,181	12,891	1,229
	State Total..	10,095,643	56,778	713	5,269	14,208	36,588	324,351	76,107	198,227	50,017
	Rate per 100,000 inhabitants...........		562.4	7.1	52.2	140.7	362.4	3,212.8	753.9	1,963.5	495.4
MINNESOTA[3]	Metropolitan Statistical Area...........	3,745,658									
	Area actually reporting..................	98.3%		111		5,239	7,295	125,456	23,113	90,896	11,447
	Estimated total.................................	100.0%		112		5,273	7,362	127,647	23,430	92,629	11,588
	Cities outside metropolitan areas ...	564,999									
	Area actually reporting..................	98.7%		4		125	827	18,912	2,954	15,093	865
	Estimated total.................................	100.0%		4		127	840	19,215	3,001	15,335	879
	Nonmetropolitan counties...............	856,444									
	Area actually reporting..................	98.7%		9		33	709	12,103	3,695	7,507	901
	Estimated total.................................	100.0%		9		33	718	12,257	3,742	7,603	912
	State Total..	5,167,101	16,123	125	1,645	5,433	8,920	159,119	30,173	115,567	13,379
	Rate per 100,000 inhabitants...........		312.0	2.4	31.8	105.1	172.6	3,079.5	583.9	2,236.6	258.9
MISSISSIPPI	Metropolitan Statistical Area...........	1,271,958									
	Area actually reporting..................	80.5%	3,984	107	453	1,845	1,579	45,295	12,165	27,939	5,191
	Estimated total.................................	100.0%	4,387	118	514	1,965	1,790	51,076	13,576	31,710	5,790
	Cities outside metropolitan areas ...	594,750									
	Area actually reporting..................	80.3%	2,009	43	226	674	1,066	22,051	6,106	14,885	1,060
	Estimated total.................................	100.0%	2,501	54	281	839	1,327	27,450	7,601	18,529	1,320
	Nonmetropolitan counties...............	1,043,832									
	Area actually reporting..................	45.8%	834	24	93	146	571	6,855	2,785	3,498	572
	Estimated total.................................	100.0%	1,803	51	205	314	1,233	14,867	6,062	7,568	1,237
	State Total..	2,910,540	8,691	223	1,000	3,118	4,350	93,393	27,239	57,807	8,347
	Rate per 100,000 inhabitants...........		298.6	7.7	34.4	107.1	149.5	3,208.8	935.9	1,986.1	286.8

Note: Although arson data are included in the trend and clearance tables, sufficient data are not available to estimate totals for this offense. Therefore, no arson data are published in this table.

[3] The data collection methodology for the offense of forcible rape used by the Illinois (with the exception of Rockford, Illinois) and the Minnesota state UCR Programs do not comply with national UCR guidelines. Consequently, their figures for forcible rape (with the exception of Rockford, Illinois) have been estimated for inclusion in this table. Table 8, Offenses Known to Law Enforcement, provides the reported female forcible rape crime figure.

Table 5. Crime, by State and Territory, 2006 *(Contd.)*

(Number, percent, rate per 100,000 population.)

State	Area	Popula-tion	Violent crime	Murder and non-negligent man-slaughter	Forcible rape	Robbery	Aggra-vated assault	Property crime	Burglary	Larceny-theft	Motor vehicle theft
MISSOURI	**Metropolitan Statistical Area**	4,268,725									
	Area actually reporting	99.9%	26,738	316	1,479	7,261	17,682	183,778	35,361	125,192	23,225
	Estimated total	100.0%	26,747	316	1,480	7,263	17,688	183,866	35,375	125,259	23,232
	Cities outside metropolitan areas	686,656									
	Area actually reporting	100.0%	2,934	29	155	272	2,478	26,877	4,885	20,810	1,182
	Nonmetropolitan counties	887,332									
	Area actually reporting	100.0%	2,199	23	129	52	1,995	12,827	4,387	7,421	1,019
	State Total	5,842,713	31,880	368	1,764	7,587	22,161	223,570	44,647	153,490	25,433
	Rate per 100,000 inhabitants		545.6	6.3	30.2	129.9	379.3	3,826.5	764.1	2,627.0	435.3
MONTANA	**Metropolitan Statistical Area**	329,373									
	Area actually reporting	99.6%	753	5	98	109	541	12,049	1,304	10,006	739
	Estimated total	100.0%	757	5	99	109	544	12,092	1,308	10,042	742
	Cities outside metropolitan areas	199,268									
	Area actually reporting	92.5%	592	5	74	32	481	6,833	670	5,746	417
	Estimated total	100.0%	640	5	80	35	520	7,390	725	6,214	451
	Nonmetropolitan counties	415,991									
	Area actually reporting	95.8%	958	7	86	19	846	5,658	864	4,262	532
	Estimated total	100.0%	1,000	7	90	20	883	5,905	902	4,448	555
	State Total	944,632	2,397	17	269	164	1,947	25,387	2,935	20,704	1,748
	Rate per 100,000 inhabitants		253.7	1.8	28.5	17.4	206.1	2,687.5	310.7	2,191.8	185.0
NEBRASKA	**Metropolitan Statistical Area**	1,005,748									
	Area actually reporting	99.8%	4,081	40	340	1,056	2,645	40,975	6,165	30,519	4,291
	Estimated total	100.0%	4,083	40	341	1,056	2,646	41,025	6,171	30,560	4,294
	Cities outside metropolitan areas	399,057									
	Area actually reporting	92.3%	634	3	150	58	423	12,913	2,078	10,360	475
	Estimated total	100.0%	687	3	163	63	458	13,990	2,251	11,224	515
	Nonmetropolitan counties	363,526									
	Area actually reporting	81.1%	173	6	36	8	123	3,293	835	2,272	186
	Estimated total	100.0%	213	7	44	10	152	4,060	1,030	2,801	229
	State Total	1,768,331	4,983	50	548	1,129	3,256	59,075	9,452	44,585	5,038
	Rate per 100,000 inhabitants		281.8	2.8	31.0	63.8	184.1	3,340.7	534.5	2,521.3	284.9
NEVADA	**Metropolitan Statistical Area**	2,232,781									
	Area actually reporting	100.0%	17,776	213	988	6,986	9,589	96,861	23,388	47,063	26,410
	Cities outside metropolitan areas	46,430									
	Area actually reporting	100.0%	139	2	11	19	107	1,475	348	1,008	119
	Nonmetropolitan counties	216,318									
	Area actually reporting	100.0%	593	9	80	22	482	3,700	1,084	2,184	432
	State Total	2,495,529	18,508	224	1,079	7,027	10,178	102,036	24,820	50,255	26,961
	Rate per 100,000 inhabitants		741.6	9.0	43.2	281.6	407.8	4,088.8	994.6	2,013.8	1,080.4
NEW HAMPSHIRE	**Metropolitan Statistical Area**	818,467									
	Area actually reporting	87.7%	1,124	7	187	315	615	13,846	2,436	10,519	891
	Estimated total	100.0%	1,219	7	206	333	673	15,132	2,645	11,511	976
	Cities outside metropolitan areas	443,220									
	Area actually reporting	85.3%	481	5	105	76	295	7,863	1,330	6,169	364
	Estimated total	100.0%	564	6	123	89	346	9,221	1,560	7,234	427
	Nonmetropolitan counties	53,208									
	Area actually reporting	2.8%	13	0	7	1	5	49	17	30	2
	Estimated total	100.0%	41	0	15	1	25	289	153	117	19
	State Total	1,314,895	1,824	13	344	423	1,044	24,642	4,358	18,862	1,422
	Rate per 100,000 inhabitants		138.7	1.0	26.2	32.2	79.4	1,874.1	331.4	1,434.5	108.1
NEW JERSEY	**Metropolitan Statistical Area**	8,724,560									
	Area actually reporting	100.0%	30,672	428	1,237	13,357	15,650	199,958	39,433	135,801	24,724
	Cities outside metropolitan areas	None									
	Nonmetropolitan counties	None									
	State Total	8,724,560	30,672	428	1,237	13,357	15,650	199,958	39,433	135,801	24,724
	Rate per 100,000 inhabitants		351.6	4.9	14.2	153.1	179.4	2,291.9	452.0	1,556.5	283.4

Note: Although arson data are included in the trend and clearance tables, sufficient data are not available to estimate totals for this offense. Therefore, no arson data are published in this table.

Table 5. Crime, by State and Territory, 2006 *(Contd.)*

(Number, percent, rate per 100,000 population.)

State	Area	Population	Violent crime	Murder and non-negligent manslaughter	Forcible rape	Robbery	Aggravated assault	Property crime	Burglary	Larceny-theft	Motor vehicle theft
NEW MEXICO	Metropolitan Statistical Area...........	1,271,503									
	Area actually reporting..................	99.5%	8,541	90	717	1,682	6,052	53,123	13,950	31,513	7,660
	Estimated total..............................	100.0%	8,583	90	721	1,687	6,085	53,314	14,000	31,631	7,683
	Cities outside metropolitan areas ...	403,133									
	Area actually reporting..................	85.7%	2,521	19	192	303	2,007	15,947	4,001	11,105	841
	Estimated total..............................	100.0%	2,942	22	224	354	2,342	18,606	4,668	12,957	981
	Nonmetropolitan counties...............	279,963									
	Area actually reporting..................	84.3%	884	17	126	54	687	4,247	1,890	1,884	473
	Estimated total..............................	100.0%	1,047	20	149	64	814	5,036	2,241	2,234	561
	State Total...................................	1,954,599	12,572	132	1,094	2,105	9,241	76,956	20,909	46,822	9,225
	Rate per 100,000 inhabitants...........		643.2	6.8	56.0	107.7	472.8	3,937.2	1,069.7	2,395.5	472.0
NEW YORK	Metropolitan Statistical Area...........	17,735,074									
	Area actually reporting..................	99.5%	80,396	896	2,667	34,105	42,728	363,341	61,166	271,113	31,062
	Estimated total..............................	100.0%	80,557	896	2,675	34,166	42,820	365,023	61,421	272,461	31,141
	Cities outside metropolitan areas ...	578,364									
	Area actually reporting..................	96.8%	1,581	12	171	236	1,162	16,360	2,956	12,941	463
NEW YORK	Estimated total..............................	100.0%	1,633	12	177	244	1,200	16,895	3,053	13,364	478
	Nonmetropolitan counties...............	992,745									
	Area actually reporting..................	100.0%	1,776	13	317	79	1,367	14,386	4,091	9,780	515
	State Total...................................	19,306,183	83,966	921	3,169	34,489	45,387	396,304	68,565	295,605	32,134
	Rate per 100,000 inhabitants...........		434.9	4.8	16.4	178.6	235.1	2,052.7	355.1	1,531.1	166.4
NORTH CAROLINA	Metropolitan Statistical Area...........	6,127,860									
	Area actually reporting..................	99.1%	31,796	370	1,796	11,070	18,560	265,922	75,958	166,556	23,408
	Estimated total..............................	100.0%	32,072	371	1,816	11,147	18,738	269,017	76,701	168,742	23,574
	Cities outside metropolitan areas ...	845,280									
	Area actually reporting..................	95.8%	5,314	69	296	1,602	3,347	48,292	12,472	33,216	2,604
	Estimated total..............................	100.0%	5,536	72	308	1,668	3,488	50,326	12,994	34,622	2,710
	Nonmetropolitan counties...............	1,883,365									
	Area actually reporting..................	96.1%	4,338	93	356	643	3,246	43,825	17,016	23,118	3,691
	Estimated total..............................	100.0%	4,516	97	371	669	3,379	45,617	17,712	24,063	3,842
	State Total...................................	8,856,505	42,124	540	2,495	13,484	25,605	364,960	107,407	227,427	30,126
	Rate per 100,000 inhabitants...........		475.6	6.1	28.2	152.2	289.1	4,120.8	1,212.7	2,567.9	340.2
NORTH DAKOTA	Metropolitan Statistical Area...........	295,930									
	Area actually reporting..................	99.6%	566	6	130	46	384	7,683	1,408	5,691	584
	Estimated total..............................	100.0%	567	6	130	46	385	7,719	1,415	5,718	586
	Cities outside metropolitan areas ...	135,705									
	Area actually reporting..................	88.6%	155	1	39	18	97	3,020	480	2,314	226
	Estimated total..............................	100.0%	174	1	44	20	109	3,409	542	2,612	255
	Nonmetropolitan counties...............	204,232									
	Area actually reporting..................	89.5%	64	1	17	5	41	1,424	390	881	153
	Estimated total..............................	100.0%	72	1	19	6	46	1,591	436	984	171
	State Total...................................	635,867	813	8	193	72	540	12,719	2,393	9,314	1,012
	Rate per 100,000 inhabitants...........		127.9	1.3	30.4	11.3	84.9	2,000.3	376.3	1,464.8	159.2
OHIO	Metropolitan Statistical Area...........	9,241,305									
	Area actually reporting..................	85.5%	35,300	495	3,530	17,694	13,581	326,493	83,224	210,645	32,624
	Estimated total..............................	100.0%	37,246	509	3,872	18,412	14,453	361,049	90,352	236,059	34,638
	Cities outside metropolitan areas ...	895,757									
	Area actually reporting..................	77.0%	1,383	9	324	432	618	29,645	5,422	23,196	1,027
	Estimated total..............................	100.0%	1,797	12	421	561	803	38,513	7,044	30,135	1,334
	Nonmetropolitan counties...............	1,340,944									
	Area actually reporting..................	72.7%	847	13	185	128	521	16,477	5,109	10,312	1,056
	Estimated total..............................	100.0%	1,166	18	255	176	717	22,673	7,030	14,190	1,453
	State Total...................................	11,478,006	40,209	539	4,548	19,149	15,973	422,235	104,426	280,384	37,425
	Rate per 100,000 inhabitants...........		350.3	4.7	39.6	166.8	139.2	3,678.6	909.8	2,442.8	326.1
OKLAHOMA	Metropolitan Statistical Area...........	2,267,196									
	Area actually reporting..................	100.0%	13,484	158	1,073	2,756	9,497	94,550	25,200	58,450	10,900
	Cities outside metropolitan areas ...	697,754									
	Area actually reporting..................	100.0%	3,045	15	286	333	2,411	26,399	6,422	18,338	1,639
	Nonmetropolitan counties...............	614,262									
	Area actually reporting..................	100.0%	1,274	34	129	44	1,067	8,053	2,755	4,479	819
	State Total...................................	3,579,212	17,803	207	1,488	3,133	12,975	129,002	34,377	81,267	13,358
	Rate per 100,000 inhabitants...........		497.4	5.8	41.6	87.5	362.5	3,604.2	960.5	2,270.5	373.2

Note: Although arson data are included in the trend and clearance tables, sufficient data are not available to estimate totals for this offense. Therefore, no arson data are published in this table.

Table 5. Crime, by State and Territory, 2006 *(Contd.)*

(Number, percent, rate per 100,000 population.)

State	Area	Population	Violent crime	Murder and non-negligent man-slaughter	Forcible rape	Robbery	Aggravated assault	Property crime	Burglary	Larceny-theft	Motor vehicle theft
OREGON	**Metropolitan Statistical Area**...........	2,853,550									
	Area actually reporting..................	99.2%	8,838	70	957	2,455	5,356	108,681	18,428	77,967	12,286
	Estimated total................................	100.0%	8,873	70	962	2,462	5,379	109,221	18,544	78,337	12,340
	Cities outside metropolitan areas ...	390,157									
	Area actually reporting..................	98.0%	986	7	146	178	655	17,427	2,845	13,403	1,179
	Estimated total................................	100.0%	1,006	7	149	182	668	17,782	2,903	13,676	1,203
	Nonmetropolitan counties...............	457,051									
	Area actually reporting..................	93.6%	462	8	79	42	333	8,326	2,277	5,190	859
	Estimated total................................	100.0%	494	9	84	45	356	8,892	2,432	5,543	917
	State Total..	3,700,758	10,373	86	1,195	2,689	6,403	135,895	23,879	97,556	14,460
	Rate per 100,000 inhabitants...........		280.3	2.3	32.3	72.7	173.0	3,672.1	645.2	2,636.1	390.7
PENNSYLVANIA	**Metropolitan Statistical Area**	10,449,475									
	Area actually reporting..................	94.3%	49,071	686	2,748	19,995	25,642	256,011	47,258	182,019	26,734
	Estimated total................................	100.0%	50,510	697	2,839	20,400	26,574	268,751	49,152	192,026	27,573
	Cities outside metropolitan areas ...	880,121									
	Area actually reporting..................	84.9%	2,240	16	231	345	1,648	16,996	3,165	13,120	711
	Estimated total................................	100.0%	2,637	19	272	406	1,940	20,008	3,726	15,445	837
	Nonmetropolitan counties...............	1,111,025									
	Area actually reporting..................	100.0%	1,518	20	290	168	1,040	15,229	4,745	9,354	1,130
	State Total..	12,440,621	54,665	736	3,401	20,974	29,554	303,988	57,623	216,825	29,540
	Rate per 100,000 inhabitants...........		439.4	5.9	27.3	168.6	237.6	2,443.5	463.2	1,742.9	237.4
PUERTO RICO	**Metropolitan Statistical Area**...........	3,730,638									
	Area actually reporting..................	100.0%	8,648	720	113	5,129	2,686	51,273	15,783	27,139	8,351
	Cities outside metropolitan areas ...	197,138									
	Area actually reporting..................	100.0%	281	19	5	116	141	1,924	885	797	242
	Total	3,927,776	8,929	739	118	5,245	2,827	53,197	16,668	27,936	8,593
	Rate per 100,000 inhabitants...........		227.3	18.8	3.0	133.5	72.0	1,354.4	424.4	711.2	218.8
RHODE ISLAND	**Metropolitan Statistical Area**...........	1,067,610									
	Area actually reporting..................	100.0%	2,414	27	283	735	1,369	27,572	5,414	18,604	3,554
	Cities outside metropolitan areas ...	None									
	Nonmetropolitan counties...............	None									
	Area actually reporting..................	100.0%	15	1	2	0	12	46	1	17	28
	State Total..	1,067,610	2,429	28	285	735	1,381	27,618	5,415	18,621	3,582
	Rate per 100,000 inhabitants...........		227.5	2.6	26.7	68.8	129.4	2,586.9	507.2	1,744.2	335.5
SOUTH CAROLINA	**Metropolitan Statistical Area**...........	3,265,103									
	Area actually reporting..................	99.9%	25,185	282	1,351	4,816	18,736	141,611	31,866	96,260	13,485
	Estimated total................................	100.0%	25,190	282	1,351	4,817	18,740	141,650	31,873	96,290	13,487
	Cities outside metropolitan areas ...	274,152									
	Area actually reporting..................	98.7%	3,374	22	126	556	2,670	16,750	3,754	12,268	728
	Estimated total................................	100.0%	3,420	22	128	564	2,706	16,978	3,805	12,435	738
	Nonmetropolitan counties...............	781,994									
	Area actually reporting..................	100.0%	4,468	55	283	518	3,612	24,694	7,094	15,423	2,177
	State Total..	4,321,249	33,078	359	1,762	5,899	25,058	183,322	42,772	124,148	16,402
	Rate per 100,000 inhabitants...........		765.5	8.3	40.8	136.5	579.9	4,242.3	989.8	2,873.0	379.6
SOUTH DAKOTA	**Metropolitan Statistical Area**...........	342,204									
	Area actually reporting..................	97.0%	798	7	221	72	498	7,050	1,554	5,101	395
	Estimated total................................	100.0%	808	7	223	72	506	7,166	1,579	5,185	402
	Cities outside metropolitan areas ...	210,633									
	Area actually reporting..................	63.9%	230	1	50	24	155	2,731	434	2,153	144
	Estimated total................................	100.0%	360	2	78	38	242	4,272	679	3,368	225
	Nonmetropolitan counties...............	229,082									
	Area actually reporting..................	66.7%	114	0	23	6	85	817	261	495	61
	Estimated total................................	100.0%	172	0	35	9	128	1,226	392	743	91
	State Total..	781,919	1,340	9	336	119	876	12,664	2,650	9,296	718
	Rate per 100,000 inhabitants...........		171.4	1.2	43.0	15.2	112.0	1,619.6	338.9	1,188.9	91.8
TENNESSEE	**Metropolitan Statistical Area**...........	4,391,468									
	Area actually reporting..................	100.0%	38,655	353	1,741	10,529	26,032	196,352	47,837	129,976	18,539
	Cities outside metropolitan areas ...	598,898									
	Area actually reporting..................	99.7%	3,904	19	230	458	3197	30,134	6920	21458	1756
	Estimated total................................	100.0%	3,916	19	231	459	3,207	30,231	6,942	21,527	1,762
	Nonmetropolitan counties...............	1,048,437									
	Area actually reporting..................	100.0%	3,336	37	170	141	2,988	22,714	8,080	12,342	2,292
	State Total..	6,038,803	45,907	409	2,142	11,129	32,227	249,297	62,859	163,845	22,593
	Rate per 100,000 inhabitants...........		760.2	6.8	35.5	184.3	533.7	4,128.3	1,040.9	2,713.2	374.1

Note: Although arson data are included in the trend and clearance tables, sufficient data are not available to estimate totals for this offense. Therefore, no arson data are published in this table.

Table 5. Crime, by State and Territory, 2006 (Contd.)

(Number, percent, rate per 100,000 population.)

State	Area	Population	Violent crime	Murder and non-negligent man-slaughter	Forcible rape	Robbery	Aggravated assault	Property crime	Burglary	Larceny-theft	Motor vehicle theft
TEXAS	Metropolitan Statistical Area	20,438,199									
	Area actually reporting	99.9%	111,939	1,270	7,454	36,324	66,891	885,259	194,612	599,405	91,242
	Estimated total	100.0%	111,966	1,270	7,456	36,330	66,910	885,622	194,685	599,669	91,268
	Cities outside metropolitan areas	1,415,994									
	Area actually reporting	98.8%	5,730	41	570	745	4,374	49,268	12,021	34,866	2,381
	Estimated total	100.0%	5,786	42	576	751	4,417	49,774	12,147	35,227	2,400
	Nonmetropolitan counties	1,653,590									
	Area actually reporting	100.0%	3,626	72	340	173	3,041	24,064	8,815	13,488	1,761
	State Total	23,507,783	121,378	1,384	8,372	37,254	74,368	959,460	215,647	648,384	95,429
	Rate per 100,000 inhabitants		516.3	5.9	35.6	158.5	316.4	4,081.5	917.3	2,758.2	405.9
UTAH	Metropolitan Statistical Area	2,262,521									
	Area actually reporting	99.3%	5,263	39	778	1,211	3,235	82,590	13,419	61,286	7,885
	Estimated total	100.0%	5,288	39	782	1,215	3,252	83,013	13,499	61,589	7,925
	Cities outside metropolitan areas	135,855									
	Area actually reporting	89.6%	199	4	42	19	134	3,720	591	2,940	189
	Estimated total	100.0%	222	4	47	21	150	4,151	659	3,281	211
	Nonmetropolitan counties	151,687									
	Area actually reporting	88.4%	187	3	35	8	141	2,216	480	1,592	144
	Estimated total	100.0%	212	3	40	9	160	2,507	543	1,801	163
	State Total	2,550,063	5,722	46	869	1,245	3,562	89,671	14,701	66,671	8,299
	Rate per 100,000 inhabitants		224.4	1.8	34.1	48.8	139.7	3,516.4	576.5	2,614.5	325.4
VERMONT	Metropolitan Statistical Area	205,512									
	Area actually reporting	100.0%	417	4	72	64	277	6,145	1,246	4,669	230
	Cities outside metropolitan areas	198,565									
	Area actually reporting	100.0%	265	0	47	32	186	5,161	917	4,070	174
	Nonmetropolitan counties	219,831									
	Area actually reporting	97.0%	165	8	30	14	113	2,981	1,103	1,701	177
	Estimated total	100.0%	170	8	31	14	117	3,073	1,137	1,754	182
	State Total	623,908	852	12	150	110	580	14,379	3,300	10,493	586
	Rate per 100,000 inhabitants		136.6	1.9	24.0	17.6	93.0	2,304.7	528.9	1,681.8	93.9
VIRGINIA	Metropolitan Statistical Area	6,533,826									
	Area actually reporting	99.7%	19,427	346	1,536	7,384	10,161	168,414	27,548	127,482	13,384
	Estimated total	100.0%	19,514	347	1,544	7,411	10,212	169,152	27,658	128,060	13,434
	Cities outside metropolitan areas	269,141									
	Area actually reporting	99.2%	834	11	90	165	568	8,187	1,184	6,564	439
	Estimated total	100.0%	840	11	91	166	572	8,250	1,193	6,615	442
	Nonmetropolitan counties	839,917									
	Area actually reporting	100.0%	1,214	41	157	172	844	12,004	3,062	8,004	938
	State Total	7,642,884	21,568	399	1,792	7,749	11,628	189,406	31,913	142,679	14,814
	Rate per 100,000 inhabitants		282.2	5.2	23.4	101.4	152.1	2,478.2	417.6	1,866.8	193.8
WASHINGTON	Metropolitan Statistical Area	5,594,948									
	Area actually reporting	99.9%	20,529	174	2,393	6,177	11,785	256,367	51,004	161,718	43,645
	Estimated total	100.0%	20,530	174	2,393	6,177	11,786	256,388	51,008	161,732	43,648
	Cities outside metropolitan areas	333,641									
	Area actually reporting	93.5%	880	8	197	142	533	16,433	3,056	12,342	1,035
	Estimated total	100.0%	942	9	211	152	570	17,569	3,267	13,195	1,107
	Nonmetropolitan counties	467,209									
	Area actually reporting	100.0%	648	7	142	76	423	12,576	4,032	7,400	1,144
	State Total	6,395,798	22,120	190	2,746	6,405	12,779	286,533	58,307	182,327	45,899
	Rate per 100,000 inhabitants		345.9	3.0	42.9	100.1	199.8	4,480.0	911.6	2,850.7	717.6
WEST VIRGINIA	Metropolitan Statistical Area	1,001,255									
	Area actually reporting	94.9%	2,992	38	257	621	2,076	29,528	7,095	20,007	2,426
	Estimated total	100.0%	3,112	39	266	640	2,167	30,859	7,399	20,922	2,538
	Cities outside metropolitan areas	224,905									
	Area actually reporting	84.1%	650	8	30	112	500	5,732	1,165	4,238	329
	Estimated total	100.0%	772	9	36	133	594	6,813	1,385	5,037	391
	Nonmetropolitan counties	592,310									
	Area actually reporting	93.3%	1,123	25	81	75	942	9,333	2,564	5,843	926
	Estimated total	100.0%	1,203	27	87	80	1,009	10,000	2,747	6,261	992
	State Total	1,818,470	5,087	75	389	853	3,770	47,672	11,531	32,220	3,921
	Rate per 100,000 inhabitants		279.7	4.1	21.4	46.9	207.3	2,621.5	634.1	1,771.8	215.6

Note: Although arson data are included in the trend and clearance tables, sufficient data are not available to estimate totals for this offense. Therefore, no arson data are published in this table.

Table 5. Crime, by State and Territory, 2006 *(Contd.)*

(Number, percent, rate per 100,000 population.)

State	Area	Popula-tion	Violent crime	Murder and non-negligent man-slaughter	Forcible rape	Robbery	Aggra-vated assault	Property crime	Burglary	Larceny-theft	Motor vehicle theft
WISCONSIN	**Metropolitan Statistical Area**.........	4,016,819									
	Area actually reporting..................	100.0%	13,947	151	838	5,460	7,498	125,769	20,876	92,218	12,675
	Cities outside metropolitan areas ...	626,116									
	Area actually reporting..................	100.0%	1,112	4	171	72	865	20,157	2,791	16,705	661
	Nonmetropolitan counties............	913,571									
	Area actually reporting..................	100.0%	724	9	122	35	558	10,645	3,327	6,623	695
	State Total...........................	5,556,506	15,783	164	1,131	5,567	8,921	156,571	26,994	115,546	14,031
	Rate per 100,000 inhabitants...........		284.0	3.0	20.4	100.2	160.6	2,817.8	485.8	2,079.5	252.5
WYOMING	**Metropolitan Statistical Area**.........	156,699									
	Area actually reporting..................	100.0%	337	4	59	45	229	6,100	993	4,807	300
	Cities outside metropolitan areas ...	212,064									
	Area actually reporting..................	97.4%	633	3	62	21	547	7,048	909	5,813	326
	Estimated total................................	100.0%	651	3	64	22	562	7,237	933	5,969	335
	Nonmetropolitan counties............	146,241									
	Area actually reporting..................	95.8%	236	2	16	5	213	1,928	377	1,416	135
	Estimated total................................	100.0%	246	2	17	5	222	2,013	394	1,478	141
	State Total...........................	515,004	1,234	9	140	72	1,013	15,350	2,320	12,254	776
	Rate per 100,000 inhabitants...........		239.6	1.7	27.2	14.0	196.7	2,980.6	450.5	2,379.4	150.7

Note: Although arson data are included in the trend and clearance tables, sufficient data are not available to estimate totals for this offense. Therefore, no arson data are published in this table.

Table 6. Crime, by Metropolitan Statistical Area, 2006

(Number, percent, rate per 100,000 population.)

Metropolitan statistical area	Counties/principal cities	Popula-tion	Violent crime	Murder and non-negligent man-slaughter	Forcible rape	Robbery	Aggra-vated assault	Property crime	Burglary	Larceny-theft	Motor vehicle theft
Abilene, TX M.S.A.[1]											
	Includes Callahan,[1] Jones, and Taylor Counties	162,776									
	City of Abilene..................................	118,009	554	5	67	107	375	5,045	1,282	3,460	303
	Total area actually reporting	100.0%	638	6	75	109	448	5,741	1,531	3,852	358
	Rate per 100,000 inhabitants		391.9	3.7	46.1	67.0	275.2	3,526.9	940.6	2,366.4	219.9
Albany, GA M.S.A.											
	Includes Baker, Dougherty, Lee, Terrell, and Worth Counties..............	168,071									
	City of Albany....................................	77,815	553	8	31	243	271	5,279	1,645	3,235	399
	Total area actually reporting	99.2%	669	11	37	262	359	7,100	2,149	4,443	508
	Estimated total..................................	100.0%	676	11	37	265	363	7,171	2,162	4,494	515
	Rate per 100,000 inhabitants		402.2	6.5	22.0	157.7	216.0	4,266.6	1,286.4	2,673.9	306.4
Albany-Schenectady-Troy, NY M.S.A.											
	Includes Albany, Rensselaer, Saratoga, Schenectady, and Schoharie Counties...........................	851,151									
	City of Albany....................................	93,773	1,217	5	50	388	774	4,820	1,058	3,521	241
	City of Schenectady	61,444	712	6	52	309	345	3,449	1,119	1,994	336
	City of Troy.......................................	48,439	373	1	18	120	234	2,279	614	1,482	183
	Total area actually reporting	100.0%	3,165	18	207	964	1,976	23,349	4,849	17,314	1,186
	Rate per 100,000 inhabitants		371.8	2.1	24.3	113.3	232.2	2,743.2	569.7	2,034.2	139.3
Albuquerque, NM M.S.A.											
	Includes Bernalillo, Sandoval, Torrance, and Valencia Counties.......	808,790									
	City of Albuquerque	500,955	4,550	34	286	1,171	3,059	31,757	6,352	19,890	5,515
	Total area actually reporting	99.8%	6,281	72	419	1,409	4,381	38,978	8,960	23,308	6,710
	Estimated total..................................	100.0%	6,291	72	420	1,410	4,389	39,023	8,972	23,336	6,715
	Rate per 100,000 inhabitants		777.8	8.9	51.9	174.3	542.7	4,824.9	1,109.3	2,885.3	830.3
Alexandria, LA M.S.A.											
	Includes Grant and Rapides Parishes................................	140,250									
	City of Alexandria	43,311	1,054	4	29	185	836	4,494	1,299	2,937	258
	Total area actually reporting	94.2%	1,434	10	70	205	1,149	6,895	2,068	4,319	508
	Estimated total..................................	100.0%	1,497	10	73	216	1,198	7,358	2,151	4,669	538
	Rate per 100,000 inhabitants		1,067.4	7.1	52.0	154.0	854.2	5,246.3	1,533.7	3,329.1	383.6
Altoona, PA M.S.A.											
	Includes Blair County	126,907									
	City of Altoona	47,218	245	0	32	84	129	1,502	439	976	87
	Total area actually reporting	94.8%	371	1	48	108	214	3,051	762	2,126	163
	Estimated total..................................	100.0%	386	1	49	112	224	3,192	783	2,237	172
	Rate per 100,000 inhabitants		304.2	0.8	38.6	88.3	176.5	2,515.2	617.0	1,762.7	135.5
Amarillo, TX M.S.A.											
	Includes Armstrong, Carson, Potter, and Randall Counties	245,428									
	City of Amarillo	188,208	1,623	5	98	401	1,119	11,080	2,412	7,617	1,051
	Total area actually reporting	100.0%	1,722	7	103	406	1,206	11,879	2,591	8,182	1,106
	Rate per 100,000 inhabitants		701.6	2.9	42.0	165.4	491.4	4,840.1	1,055.7	3,333.8	450.6
Ames, IA M.S.A.											
	Includes Story County	80,377									
	City of Ames	52,541	147	0	24	17	106	1,465	363	1,061	41
	Total area actually reporting	100.0%	205	0	35	19	151	2,140	512	1,559	69
	Rate per 100,000 inhabitants		255.0	0.0	43.5	23.6	187.9	2,662.5	637.0	1,939.6	85.8
Anchorage, AK M.S.A.											
	Includes Anchorage Municipality and Matanuska-Susitna Borough	294,862									
	City of Anchorage	277,692	2,592	17	248	465	1,862	11,721	1,733	8,543	1,445
	Total area actually reporting	97.1%	2,675	17	252	478	1,928	12,214	1,771	8,966	1,477
	Estimated total..................................	100.0%	2,749	17	256	490	1,986	12,875	1,835	9,524	1,516
	Rate per 100,000 inhabitants		932.3	5.8	86.8	166.2	673.5	4,366.4	622.3	3,230.0	514.1

[1] Because of changes in the state/local agency's reporting practices, figures are not comparable to previous years' data.

Table 6. Crime, by Metropolitan Statistical Area, 2006 (*Contd.*)

(Number, percent, rate per 100,000 population.)

Metropolitan statistical area	Counties/principal cities	Population	Violent crime	Murder and non-negligent man-slaughter	Forcible rape	Robbery	Aggravated assault	Property crime	Burglary	Larceny-theft	Motor vehicle theft
Anderson, SC M.S.A.											
	Includes Anderson County.................	178,243									
	City of Anderson	26,302	256	4	22	39	191	1,601	324	1,144	133
	Total area actually reporting	100.0%	1,163	18	90	159	896	8,213	1,952	5,486	775
	Rate per 100,000 inhabitants..............		652.5	10.1	50.5	89.2	502.7	4,607.8	1,095.1	3,077.8	434.8
Ann Arbor, MI M.S.A.											
	Includes Washtenaw County..............	340,995									
	City of Ann Arbor..............................	112,989	344	0	32	85	227	2,923	631	2,119	173
	Total area actually reporting	100.0%	1,060	9	114	268	669	9,542	2,061	6,691	790
	Rate per 100,000 inhabitants..............		310.9	2.6	33.4	78.6	196.2	2,798.3	604.4	1,962.2	231.7
Appleton, WI M.S.A.											
	Includes Calumet and Outagamie Counties..........................	215,932									
	City of Appleton	70,475	188	1	26	26	135	2,135	381	1,690	64
	Total area actually reporting	100.0%	273	2	54	39	178	4,928	696	4,067	165
	Rate per 100,000 inhabitants..............		126.4	0.9	25.0	18.1	82.4	2,282.2	322.3	1,883.5	76.4
Asheville, NC M.S.A.											
	Includes Buncombe, Haywood, Henderson, and Madison Counties	400,669									
	City of Asheville	73,672	473	4	49	206	214	4,099	793	2,834	472
	Total area actually reporting	99.5%	1,135	11	104	313	707	11,846	3,482	7,193	1,171
	Estimated total....................................	100.0%	1,146	11	105	316	714	11,962	3,510	7,275	1,177
	Rate per 100,000 inhabitants..............		286.0	2.7	26.2	78.9	178.2	2,985.5	876.0	1,815.7	293.8
Athens-Clarke County, GA M.S.A.											
	Includes Clarke, Madison, Oconee, and Oglethorpe Counties..	180,707									
	City of Athens-Clarke County	106,700	373	5	53	125	190	5,634	1,116	4,154	364
	Total area actually reporting	84.2%	494	7	62	135	290	6,961	1,302	5,197	462
	Estimated total....................................	100.0%	596	9	68	172	347	7,856	1,536	5,731	589
	Rate per 100,000 inhabitants..............		329.8	5.0	37.6	95.2	192.0	4,347.4	850.0	3,171.4	325.9
Atlanta-Sandy Springs-Marietta, GA M.S.A.[2]											
	Includes Barrow,[2] Bartow, Butts, Carroll, Cherokee, Clayton, Cobb, Coweta, Dawson, DeKalb, Douglas, Fayette, Forsyth, Fulton, Gwinnett, Haralson, Heard, Henry, Jasper, Lamar, Meriwether, Newton, Paulding, Pickens, Pike, Rockdale, Spalding, and Walton Counties..........................	5,075,647									
	City of Atlanta	485,804	7,548	110	171	2,959	4,308	32,231	7,401	18,952	5,878
	City of Marietta...................................	63,228	400	1	19	235	145	2,622	548	1,626	448
	Total area actually reporting	98.0%	26,298	372	1,074	10,451	14,401			115,927	28,114
	Estimated total....................................	100.0%	26,762	377	1,098	10,620	14,667			118,849	28,594
	Rate per 100,000 inhabitants..............		527.3	7.4	21.6	209.2	289.0			2,341.6	563.4
Atlantic City, NJ M.S.A.											
	Includes Atlantic County....................	271,221									
	City of Atlantic City	40,399	842	18	46	355	423	3,859	507	3,148	204
	Total area actually reporting	100.0%	1,519	30	79	599	811	10,534	1,985	8,072	477
	Rate per 100,000 inhabitants..............		560.1	11.1	29.1	220.9	299.0	3,883.9	731.9	2,976.2	175.9
Augusta-Richmond County, GA-SC M.S.A.											
	Includes Burke, Columbia, McDuffie, and Richmond Counties, GA and Aiken and Edgefield Counties, SC....	534,131									
	Total area actually reporting	96.3%	1,966	31	222	838	875	23,593	4,952	15,972	2,669
	Estimated total....................................	100.0%	2,041	32	226	866	917	24,274	5,117	16,399	2,758
	Rate per 100,000 inhabitants..............		382.1	6.0	42.3	162.1	171.7	4,544.6	958.0	3,070.2	516.4

[2] The FBI determined that the agency's data were underreported. Consequently, affected data are not included in this table.

Table 6. Crime, by Metropolitan Statistical Area, 2006 *(Contd.)*

(Number, percent, rate per 100,000 population.)

Metropolitan statistical area	Counties/principal cities	Population	Violent crime	Murder and non-negligent manslaughter	Forcible rape	Robbery	Aggravated assault	Property crime	Burglary	Larceny-theft	Motor vehicle theft
Austin-Round Rock, TX M.S.A.											
	Includes Bastrop, Caldwell, Hays, Travis, and Williamson Counties	1,493,692									
	City of Austin..................................	709,813	3,658	20	319	1,358	1,961	41,573	7,467	31,562	2,544
	City of Round Rock	88,762	104	0	23	31	50	1,968	277	1,642	49
	Total area actually reporting	99.9%	5,154	29	523	1,565	3,037	58,857	11,422	44,064	3,371
	Estimated total...................................	100.0%	5,157	29	523	1,566	3,039	58,892	11,429	44,089	3,374
	Rate per 100,000 inhabitants..............		345.3	1.9	35.0	104.8	203.5	3,942.7	765.2	2,951.7	225.9
Bakersfield, CA M.S.A.											
	Includes Kern County	763,641									
	City of Bakersfield.............................	298,198	1,575	24	43	549	959	15,915	3,729	9,623	2,563
	Total area actually reporting	100.0%	4,189	65	201	1,059	2,864	33,464	8,712	18,991	5,761
	Rate per 100,000 inhabitants..............		548.6	8.5	26.3	138.7	375.0	4,382.2	1,140.9	2,486.9	754.4
Baltimore-Towson, MD M.S.A.											
	Includes Anne Arundel, Baltimore, Carroll, Harford, Howard, and Queen Anne's Counties and Baltimore City	2,662,948									
	City of Baltimore	637,556	10,816	276	138	4,229	6,173	32,321	7,608	18,451	6,262
	Total area actually reporting	100.0%	21,937	355	501	7,842	13,239	92,748	19,052	60,997	12,699
	Rate per 100,000 inhabitants..............		823.8	13.3	18.8	294.5	497.2	3,482.9	715.4	2,290.6	476.9
Bangor, ME M.S.A.											
	Includes Penobscot County................	147,076									
	City of Bangor....................................	31,076	52	2	1	24	25	1,897	216	1,633	48
	Total area actually reporting	100.0%	111	3	14	33	61	4,626	784	3,699	143
	Rate per 100,000 inhabitants..............		75.5	2.0	9.5	22.4	41.5	3,145.3	533.1	2,515.0	97.2
Barnstable Town, MA M.S.A.[3]											
	Includes Barnstable County	227,875									
	City of Barnstable	48,113	330	1	33	32	264	1,320	508	725	87
	Total area actually reporting	97.5%		4	61	85		6,006	2,186	3,497	323
	Estimated total...................................	100.0%		4	62	89		6,116	2,213	3,569	334
	Rate per 100,000 inhabitants..............			1.8	27.2	39.1		2,683.9	971.1	1,566.2	146.6
Baton Rouge, LA M.S.A.											
	Includes Ascension, East Baton Rouge, East Feliciana, Iberville, Livingston, Pointe Coupee, St. Helena, West Baton Rouge, and West Feliciana Parishes	695,541									
	City of Baton Rouge	210,486	2,954	57	93	1,049	1,755	14,684	4,021	9,209	1,454
	Total area actually reporting	92.4%	5,411	95	219	1,461	3,636	32,566	7,971	21,781	2,814
	Estimated total...................................	100.0%	5,711	100	236	1,509	3,866	34,601	8,443	23,173	2,985
	Rate per 100,000 inhabitants..............		821.1	14.4	33.9	217.0	555.8	4,974.7	1,213.9	3,331.7	429.2
Battle Creek, MI M.S.A.											
	Includes Calhoun County	138,844									
	City of Battle Creek	62,628	781	7	67	116	591	3,477	831	2,428	218
	Total area actually reporting	100.0%	1,104	11	103	153	837	5,707	1,366	4,011	330
	Rate per 100,000 inhabitants..............		795.1	7.9	74.2	110.2	602.8	4,110.4	983.8	2,888.9	237.7
Bay City, MI M.S.A.											
	Includes Bay County	108,757									
	City of Bay City	34,792	145	0	29	32	84	1,340	340	880	120
	Total area actually reporting	100.0%	280	2	64	50	164	2,819	662	1,940	217
	Rate per 100,000 inhabitants..............		257.5	1.8	58.8	46.0	150.8	2,592.0	608.7	1,783.8	199.5
Beaumont-Port Arthur, TX M.S.A.											
	Includes Hardin, Jefferson, and Orange Counties.................................	394,399									
	City of Beaumont	114,967	1,155	10	75	344	726	6,962	1,887	4,525	550
	City of Port Arthur.............................	58,290	394	2	12	140	240	2,075	814	1,014	247
	Total area actually reporting	100.0%	2,228	18	162	618	1,430	15,678	4,531	9,750	1,397
	Rate per 100,000 inhabitants..............		564.9	4.6	41.1	156.7	362.6	3,975.2	1,148.8	2,472.1	354.2

[3] The data collection methodology for the offense of aggravated assault used by this agency does not comply with national Uniform Crime Reporting (UCR) Program guidelines. Consequently, the figures for aggravated assault and violent crime (of which aggravated assault is a part) are not included in this table.

Table 6. Crime, by Metropolitan Statistical Area, 2006 (*Contd.*)

(Number, percent, rate per 100,000 population.)

Metropolitan statistical area	Counties/principal cities	Population	Violent crime	Murder and non-negligent man-slaughter	Forcible rape	Robbery	Aggravated assault	Property crime	Burglary	Larceny-theft	Motor vehicle theft
Bellingham, WA M.S.A.											
	Includes Whatcom County	186,623									
	City of Bellingham..............................	75,828	196	0	33	76	87	5,334	791	4,267	276
	Total area actually reporting	100.0%	432	1	76	98	257	8,840	1,818	6,504	518
	Rate per 100,000 inhabitants..............		231.5	0.5	40.7	52.5	137.7	4,736.8	974.2	3,485.1	277.6
Bend, OR M.S.A.											
	Includes Deschutes County	143,700									
	City of Bend	68,253	149	1	22	32	94	2,912	489	2,193	230
	Total area actually reporting	100.0%	313	2	43	48	220	5,111	964	3,771	376
	Rate per 100,000 inhabitants..............		217.8	1.4	29.9	33.4	153.1	3,556.7	670.8	2,624.2	261.7
Billings, MT M.S.A.											
	Includes Carbon and Yellowstone Counties........................	147,997									
	City of Billings....................................	99,667	209	2	28	44	135	4,304	465	3,518	321
	Total area actually reporting	99.1%	268	3	37	48	180	5,284	605	4,288	391
	Estimated total....................................	100.0%	272	3	38	48	183	5,327	609	4,324	394
	Rate per 100,000 inhabitants..............		183.8	2.0	25.7	32.4	123.7	3,599.4	411.5	2,921.7	266.2
Binghamton, NY M.S.A.											
	Includes Broome and Tioga Counties	249,087									
	City of Binghamton	45,614	206	2	9	63	132	2,353	288	2,016	49
	Total area actually reporting	100.0%	529	6	68	117	338	6,438	983	5,307	148
	Rate per 100,000 inhabitants..............		212.4	2.4	27.3	47.0	135.7	2,584.6	394.6	2,130.6	59.4
Birmingham-Hoover, AL M.S.A.											
	Includes Bibb, Blount, Chilton, Jefferson, St. Clair, Shelby, and Walker Counties..............	1,099,986									
	City of Birmingham	233,577	3,175	104	220	1,429	1,422	19,007	4,813	12,113	2,081
	City of Hoover	68,079	129	2	17	81	29	2,387	312	1,917	158
	Total area actually reporting	89.1%	5,742	132	451	2,413	2,746	43,189	10,618	28,457	4,114
	Estimated total....................................	100.0%	6,187	138	487	2,572	2,990	47,475	11,565	31,463	4,447
	Rate per 100,000 inhabitants..............		562.5	12.5	44.3	233.8	271.8	4,316.0	1,051.4	2,860.3	404.3
Bismarck, ND M.S.A.											
	Includes Burleigh and Morton Counties............................	99,220									
	City of Bismarck	57,304	138	1	15	10	112	1,590	256	1,242	92
	Total area actually reporting	100.0%	191	2	29	11	149	2,224	412	1,678	134
	Rate per 100,000 inhabitants..............		192.5	2.0	29.2	11.1	150.2	2,241.5	415.2	1,691.2	135.1
Blacksburg-Christiansburg-Radford, VA M.S.A.											
	Includes Giles, Montgomery, and Pulaski Counties and Radford City...	152,562									
	City of Blacksburg..............................	39,520	76	1	17	10	48	634	117	477	40
	City of Christiansburg	18,105	29	0	7	9	13	631	98	509	24
	City of Radford....................................	14,720	55	1	8	7	39	540	111	401	28
	Total area actually reporting	99.5%	321	8	64	50	199	3,971	743	3,013	215
	Estimated total....................................	100.0%	324	8	64	51	201	3,997	747	3,033	217
	Rate per 100,000 inhabitants..............		212.4	5.2	42.0	33.4	131.7	2,619.9	489.6	1,988.0	142.2
Bloomington, IN M.S.A.											
	Includes Greene, Monroe, and Owen Counties.........................	178,886									
	City of Bloomington............................	69,474	238	1	26	65	146	2,884	663	2,077	144
	Total area actually reporting	95.3%	400	4	45	79	272	4,972	1,282	3,452	238
	Estimated total....................................	100.0%	425	4	47	87	287	5,293	1,334	3,694	265
	Rate per 100,000 inhabitants..............		237.6	2.2	26.3	48.6	160.4	2,958.9	745.7	2,065.0	148.1
Boise City-Nampa, ID M.S.A.											
	Includes Ada, Boise, Canyon, Gem, and Owyhee Counties	558,432									
	City of Boise..	198,212	772	6	127	111	528	6,616	1,165	5,074	377
	City of Nampa	73,588	240	3	41	31	165	2,488	538	1,658	292
	Total area actually reporting	99.5%	1,601	15	259	185	1,142	15,110	3,274	10,645	1,191
	Estimated total....................................	100.0%	1,610	15	260	186	1,149	15,193	3,292	10,704	1,197
	Rate per 100,000 inhabitants..............		288.3	2.7	46.6	33.3	205.8	2,720.7	589.5	1,916.8	214.4

Table 6. Crime, by Metropolitan Statistical Area, 2006 (*Contd.*)

(Number, percent, rate per 100,000 population.)

Metropolitan statistical area	Counties/principal cities	Population	Violent crime	Murder and non-negligent man-slaughter	Forcible rape	Robbery	Aggra-vated assault	Property crime	Burglary	Larceny-theft	Motor vehicle theft
Bowling Green, KY M.S.A.											
	Includes Edmonson and Warren Counties	111,859									
	City of Bowling Green	52,681	369	5	59	103	202	2,735	559	2,033	143
	Total area actually reporting	100.0%	393	5	60	108	220	3,655	783	2,679	193
	Rate per 100,000 inhabitants		351.3	4.5	53.6	96.6	196.7	3,267.5	700.0	2,395.0	172.5
Bremerton-Silver-dale, WA M.S.A.											
	Includes Kitsap County	244,796									
	City of Bremerton	38,478	346	1	70	76	199	1,687	407	1,102	178
	Total area actually reporting	100.0%	1,014	3	231	125	655	6,521	1,742	4,178	601
	Rate per 100,000 inhabitants		414.2	1.2	94.4	51.1	267.6	2,663.9	711.6	1,706.7	245.5
Brownsville-Harlin-gen, TX M.S.A.											
	Includes Cameron County	389,032									
	City of Brownsville	172,239	867	5	46	168	648	8,385	1,377	6,483	525
	City of Harlingen	64,084	353	3	22	67	261	4,570	1,043	3,255	272
	Total area actually reporting	100.0%	1,678	12	125	277	1,264	18,292	3,882	13,316	1,094
	Rate per 100,000 inhabitants		431.3	3.1	32.1	71.2	324.9	4,701.9	997.9	3,422.9	281.2
Brunswick, GA M.S.A.											
	Includes Brantley, Glynn, and McIntosh Counties	101,593									
	City of Brunswick	16,468	449	2	8	89	350	1,343	345	930	68
	Total area actually reporting	90.5%	768	4	32	163	569	4,136	990	2,904	242
	Estimated total	100.0%	803	5	34	176	588	4,435	1,069	3,081	285
	Rate per 100,000 inhabitants		790.4	4.9	33.5	173.2	578.8	4,365.5	1,052.2	3,032.7	280.5
Buffalo-Niagara Falls, NY M.S.A.											
	Includes Erie and Niagara Counties	1,150,784									
	City of Buffalo	280,494	3,957	74	174	1,708	2,001	15,436	4,447	8,864	2,125
	City of Cheektowaga Town	80,995	221	2	14	75	130	2,419	415	1,867	137
	City of Tonawanda	15,376	49	0	5	12	32	425	42	367	16
	City of Niagara Falls	53,008	643	4	35	201	403	2,788	791	1,802	195
	Total area actually reporting	100.0%	5,899	86	331	2,249	3,233	33,709	8,261	22,475	2,973
	Rate per 100,000 inhabitants		512.6	7.5	28.8	195.4	280.9	2,929.2	717.9	1,953.0	258.3
Burlington, NC M.S.A.											
	Includes Alamance County	143,337									
	City of Burlington	48,542	445	4	17	110	314	3,118	692	2,251	175
	Total area actually reporting	98.6%	749	6	30	144	569	5,670	1,425	3,885	360
	Estimated total	100.0%	759	6	31	147	575	5,778	1,451	3,961	366
	Rate per 100,000 inhabitants		529.5	4.2	21.6	102.6	401.2	4,031.1	1,012.3	2,763.4	255.3
Cape Coral-Fort Myers, FL M.S.A.											
	Includes Lee County	553,945									
	City of Cape Coral	142,371	406	6	52	83	265	4,908	1,462	3,115	331
	City of Fort Myers	59,413	937	15	38	327	557	2,910	561	1,691	658
	Total area actually reporting	100.0%	3,157	48	196	866	2,047	20,043	5,736	11,998	2,309
	Rate per 100,000 inhabitants		569.9	8.7	35.4	156.3	369.5	3,618.2	1,035.5	2,165.9	416.8
Carson City, NV M.S.A.											
	Includes Carson City	57,936									
	Total area actually reporting	100.0%	195	2	2	22	169	1,247	291	819	137
	Rate per 100,000 inhabitants		336.6	3.5	3.5	38.0	291.7	2,152.4	502.3	1,413.6	236.5
Casper, WY M.S.A.											
	Includes Natrona County	70,582									
	City of Casper	52,318	130	0	20	12	98	2,581	441	2,023	117
	Total area actually reporting	100.0%	169	2	21	16	130	3,186	592	2,451	143
	Rate per 100,000 inhabitants		239.4	2.8	29.8	22.7	184.2	4,513.9	838.7	3,472.6	202.6
Cedar Rapids, IA M.S.A.											
	Includes Benton, Jones, and Linn Counties	247,720									
	City of Cedar Rapids	123,773	401	6	39	136	220	5,872	1,114	4,460	298
	Total area actually reporting	96.1%	513	7	57	139	310	7,193	1,443	5,375	375
	Estimated total	100.0%	531	7	59	141	324	7,441	1,484	5,571	386
	Rate per 100,000 inhabitants		214.4	2.8	23.8	56.9	130.8	3,003.8	599.1	2,248.9	155.8

Table 6. Crime, by Metropolitan Statistical Area, 2006 (*Contd.*)

(Number, percent, rate per 100,000 population.)

Metropolitan statistical area	Counties/principal cities	Population	Violent crime	Murder and non-negligent man-slaughter	Forcible rape	Robbery	Aggra-vated assault	Property crime	Burglary	Larceny-theft	Motor vehicle theft
Charleston, WV M.S.A.											
	Includes Boone, Clay, Kanawha, Lincoln, and Putnam Counties...........	306,706									
	City of Charleston..............................	51,221	508	2	19	112	375	3,559	729	2,603	227
	Total area actually reporting..............	87.5%	1,131	22	75	207	827	10,414	2,403	7,040	971
	Estimated total..................................	100.0%	1,220	23	82	218	897	11,336	2,627	7,653	1,056
	Rate per 100,000 inhabitants..............		397.8	7.5	26.7	71.1	292.5	3,696.0	856.5	2,495.2	344.3
Charleston-North Charleston, SC M.S.A.											
	Includes Berkeley, Charleston, and Dorchester Counties...................	604,149									
	City of Charleston..............................	108,371	960	23	45	245	647	4,358	707	3,108	543
	City of North Charleston	87,655	1,481	28	81	544	828	7,470	1,331	5,040	1,099
	Total area actually reporting..............	100.0%	5,017	76	291	1,226	3,424	26,263	5,390	17,713	3,160
	Rate per 100,000 inhabitants..............		830.4	12.6	48.2	202.9	566.7	4,347.1	892.2	2,931.9	523.0
Charlotte-Gastonia-Concord, NC-SC M.S.A.[2]											
	Includes Anson, Cabarrus, Gaston, Mecklenburg, and Union[2] Counties, NC and York County, SC....................	1,550,796									
	City of Charlotte-Mecklenburg, NC	699,398	7,532	83	346	3,207	3,896	48,886	13,582	28,154	7,150
	City of Gastonia, NC...........................	70,340	710	4	30	220	456	5,816	1,271	4,056	489
	City of Concord, NC...........................	62,311	280	3	14	98	165	2,924	459	2,149	316
	City of Rock Hill, SC...........................	60,480	747	6	32	113	596	2,716	484	2,015	217
	Total area actually reporting..............	97.6%		127	557	4,131		79,394	21,319	48,536	9,539
	Estimated total..................................	100.0%		128	569	4,180		81,387	21,797	49,944	9,646
	Rate per 100,000 inhabitants..............			8.3	36.7	269.5		5,248.1	1,405.5	3,220.5	622.0
Charlottesville, VA M.S.A.											
	Includes Albemarle, Fluvanna, Greene, and Nelson Counties and Charlottesville City........................	190,302									
	City of Charlottesville	40,840	322	3	30	77	212	2,174	316	1,675	183
	Total area actually reporting..............	100.0%	539	4	61	129	345	5,517	853	4,230	434
	Rate per 100,000 inhabitants..............		283.2	2.1	32.1	67.8	181.3	2,899.1	448.2	2,222.8	228.1
Chattanooga, TN-GA M.S.A.											
	Includes Catoosa, Dade, and Walker Counties, GA and Hamilton, Marion, and Sequatchie Counties, TN............	501,115									
	City of Chattanooga, TN	156,730	1,935	17	118	532	1,268	12,275	2,273	8,876	1,126
	Total area actually reporting..............	100.0%	3,004	26	187	646	2,145	21,287	4,307	15,132	1,848
	Rate per 100,000 inhabitants..............		599.5	5.2	37.3	128.9	428.0	4,247.9	859.5	3,019.7	368.8
Cheyenne, WY M.S.A.											
	Includes Laramie County	86,117									
	City of Cheyenne	56,356	117	2	29	23	63	2,364	266	1,975	123
	Total area actually reporting..............	100.0%	168	2	38	29	99	2,914	401	2,356	157
	Rate per 100,000 inhabitants..............		195.1	2.3	44.1	33.7	115.0	3,383.8	465.6	2,735.8	182.3
Chico, CA M.S.A.											
	Includes Butte County	216,114									
	City of Chico.....................................	72,070	337	1	66	92	178	2,658	741	1,559	358
	Total area actually reporting..............	100.0%	787	11	113	144	519	7,107	2,085	4,012	1,010
	Rate per 100,000 inhabitants..............		364.2	5.1	52.3	66.6	240.2	3,288.5	964.8	1,856.4	467.3
Cincinnati-Middletown, OH-KY-IN M.S.A.											
	Includes Dearborn, Franklin, and Ohio Counties, IN; Boone, Bracken, Campbell, Gallatin, Grant, Kenton, and Pendleton Counties, KY; and Brown, Butler, Clermont, Hamilton, and Warren Counties, OH	2,076,054									
	City of Cincinnati, OH.......................	309,104	3,766	89	291	2,339	1,047	22,107	6,009	13,523	2,575
	City of Middletown, OH.....................	51,535	213	1	37	80	95	4,021	860	3,009	152
	Total area actually reporting..............	81.5%	6,974	117	811	3,419	2,627	66,644	13,910	47,614	5,120
	Estimated total..................................	100.0%	7,572	122	907	3,627	2,916	76,619	16,008	54,862	5,749
	Rate per 100,000 inhabitants..............		364.7	5.9	43.7	174.7	140.5	3,690.6	771.1	2,642.6	276.9

2 The FBI determined that the agency's data were underreported. Consequently, affected data are not included in this table.

Table 6. Crime, by Metropolitan Statistical Area, 2006 (*Contd.*)

(Number, percent, rate per 100,000 population.)

Metropolitan statistical area	Counties/principal cities	Popula-tion	Violent crime	Murder and non-negligent man-slaughter	Forcible rape	Robbery	Aggra-vated assault	Property crime	Burglary	Larceny-theft	Motor vehicle theft
Clarksville, TN-KY M.S.A.											
	Includes Christian and Trigg Counties, KY and Montgomery and Stewart Counties, TN..........................	246,355									
	City of Clarksville, TN	114,314	1,023	6	50	195	772	4,242	1,348	2,611	283
	Total area actually reporting	99.7%	1,390	12	95	266	1,017	7,626	2,249	4,839	538
	Estimated total....................................	100.0%	1,392	12	95	267	1,018	7,653	2,254	4,859	540
	Rate per 100,000 inhabitants..............		565.0	4.9	38.6	108.4	413.2	3,106.5	914.9	1,972.4	219.2
Cleveland, TN M.S.A.											
	Includes Bradley and Polk Counties.....................................	109,410									
	City of Cleveland..............................	38,672	361	1	26	34	300	2,122	456	1,523	143
	Total area actually reporting	100.0%	694	1	39	38	616	3,456	845	2,343	268
	Rate per 100,000 inhabitants..............		634.3	0.9	35.6	34.7	563.0	3,158.8	772.3	2,141.5	245.0
Cleveland-Elyria-Mentor, OH M.S.A.											
	Includes Cuyahoga, Geauga, Lake, Lorain, and Medina Counties	2,128,904									
	City of Cleveland..............................	452,759	7,004	75	445	4,288	2,196	28,220	9,650	12,036	6,534
	City of Elyria...................................	56,129	232	4	24	89	115	2,718	745	1,807	166
	City of Mentor..................................	51,548	42	0	5	15	22	1,167	154	948	65
	Total area actually reporting	80.2%	9,016	93	645	5,166	3,112	54,002	15,829	29,709	8,464
	Estimated total....................................	100.0%	9,786	99	766	5,461	3,460	66,651	18,242	39,190	9,219
	Rate per 100,000 inhabitants..............		459.7	4.7	36.0	256.5	162.5	3,130.8	856.9	1,840.9	433.0
Coeur d'Alene, ID M.S.A.											
	Includes Kootenai County.................	131,006									
	City of Coeur d'Alene.......................	41,106	269	0	35	17	217	1,911	369	1,428	114
	Total area actually reporting	100.0%	451	1	77	27	346	3,801	874	2,673	254
	Rate per 100,000 inhabitants..............		344.3	0.8	58.8	20.6	264.1	2,901.4	667.1	2,040.4	193.9
College Station-Bryan, TX M.S.A.											
	Includes Brazos, Burleson, and Robertson Counties.....................	195,111									
	City of College Station.......................	74,439	210	0	39	33	138	2,860	549	2,192	119
	City of Bryan....................................	68,185	589	6	31	100	452	3,760	1,004	2,570	186
	Total area actually reporting	100.0%	950	8	90	144	708	8,284	1,944	5,941	399
	Rate per 100,000 inhabitants..............		486.9	4.1	46.1	73.8	362.9	4,245.8	996.4	3,044.9	204.5
Colorado Springs, CO M.S.A.											
	Includes El Paso and Teller Counties....................................	598,605									
	City of Colorado Springs	376,807	2,145	15	251	612	1,267	18,076	3,347	12,940	1,789
	Total area actually reporting	99.9%	3,296	18	326	665	2,287	22,325	4,463	15,618	2,244
	Estimated total....................................	100.0%	3,298	18	326	665	2,289	22,359	4,469	15,642	2,248
	Rate per 100,000 inhabitants..............		550.9	3.0	54.5	111.1	382.4	3,735.2	746.6	2,613.1	375.5
Columbia, MO M.S.A.											
	Includes Boone and Howard Counties...	154,404									
	City of Columbia................................	92,485	460	2	23	113	322	3,105	544	2,335	226
	Total area actually reporting	100.0%	679	3	33	134	509	4,632	847	3,447	338
	Rate per 100,000 inhabitants..............		439.8	1.9	21.4	86.8	329.7	2,999.9	548.6	2,232.5	218.9
Columbia, SC M.S.A.											
	Includes Calhoun, Fairfield, Kershaw, Lexington, Richland, and Saluda Counties...........................	700,605									
	City of Columbia................................	118,909	1,290	7	56	375	852	6,994	1,254	5,086	654
	Total area actually reporting	99.9%	5,090	59	250	942	3,839	26,976	5,480	19,121	2,375
	Estimated total....................................	100.0%	5,092	59	250	942	3,841	26,993	5,483	19,134	2,376
	Rate per 100,000 inhabitants..............		726.8	8.4	35.7	134.5	548.2	3,852.8	782.6	2,731.1	339.1

Table 6. Crime, by Metropolitan Statistical Area, 2006 (*Contd.*)

(Number, percent, rate per 100,000 population.)

Metropolitan statistical area	Counties/principal cities	Popula-tion	Violent crime	Murder and non-negligent man-slaughter	Forcible rape	Robbery	Aggra-vated assault	Property crime	Burglary	Larceny-theft	Motor vehicle theft
Columbus, GA-AL M.S.A.											
	Includes Russell County, AL and Chattahoochee, Harris, Marion, and Muscogee Counties, GA	292,291									
	City of Columbus, GA	191,221	1,187	17	19	582	569	13,825	2,773	9,202	1,850
	Total area actually reporting	90.2%	1,363	19	30	630	684	15,473	3,123	10,395	1,955
	Estimated total..................................	100.0%	1,435	20	36	651	728	16,186	3,340	10,816	2,030
	Rate per 100,000 inhabitants		490.9	6.8	12.3	222.7	249.1	5,537.6	1,142.7	3,700.4	694.5
Columbus, IN M.S.A.											
	Includes Bartholomew County	74,027									
	City of Columbus................................	39,641	76	2	12	15	47	2,554	277	2,153	124
	Total area actually reporting	99.6%	151	3	16	17	115	3,056	380	2,547	129
	Estimated total..................................	100.0%	152	3	16	17	116	3,068	382	2,556	130
	Rate per 100,000 inhabitants		205.3	4.1	21.6	23.0	156.7	4,144.4	516.0	3,452.8	175.6
Columbus, OH M.S.A.											
	Includes Delaware, Fairfield, Franklin, Licking, Madison, Morrow, Pickaway, and Union Counties	1,710,708									
	City of Columbus	731,547	5,948	104	586	3,646	1,612	52,098	14,816	30,882	6,400
	Total area actually reporting	88.4%	7,105	111	829	4,156	2,009	76,228	20,395	48,234	7,599
	Estimated total..................................	100.0%	7,292	113	874	4,215	2,090	80,395	21,420	51,149	7,826
	Rate per 100,000 inhabitants		426.3	6.6	51.1	246.4	122.2	4,699.5	1,252.1	2,989.9	457.5
Corpus Christi, TX M.S.A.											
	Includes Aransas, Nueces, and San Patricio Counties	425,272									
	City of Corpus Christi	291,507	2,070	21	167	468	1,414	19,138	3,005	15,261	872
	Total area actually reporting	100.0%	2,449	25	247	508	1,669	24,932	4,352	19,508	1,072
	Rate per 100,000 inhabitants		575.9	5.9	58.1	119.5	392.5	5,862.6	1,023.3	4,587.2	252.1
Cumberland, MD-WV M.S.A.											
	Includes Allegany County, MD and Mineral County, WV	100,893									
	City of Cumberland, MD....................	20,972	188	1	20	25	142	1,284	311	936	37
	Total area actually reporting	99.3%	372	1	38	46	287	2,705	690	1,898	117
	Estimated total..................................	100.0%	373	1	38	46	288	2,727	694	1,915	118
	Rate per 100,000 inhabitants		369.7	1.0	37.7	45.6	285.5	2,702.9	687.9	1,898.1	117.0
Dallas-Fort Worth-Arlington, TX M.S.A.											
	Includes Metropolitan Divisions of Dallas-Plano-Irving and Fort Worth-Arlington	5,984,390									
	City of Dallas....................................	1,248,223	15,058	187	665	6,914	7,292	85,592	21,653	50,009	13,930
	City of Fort Worth	641,752	4,209	49	247	1,417	2,496	36,473	8,998	24,128	3,347
	City of Arlington...............................	373,086	2,728	14	192	890	1,632	19,666	4,042	13,905	1,719
	City of Plano....................................	257,183	743	4	42	154	543	8,618	1,394	6,642	582
	City of Irving...................................	199,137	850	3	48	264	535	9,644	1,674	6,728	1,242
	City of Carrollton	122,239	229	5	6	87	131	3,782	815	2,489	478
	City of Denton	107,105	329	0	60	65	204	3,168	664	2,295	209
	City of Richardson............................	101,998	234	3	11	98	122	3,118	685	2,121	312
	City of McKinney	99,318	264	2	41	37	184	2,217	490	1,616	111
	Total area actually reporting	99.9%	31,975	336	2,036	11,622	17,981	264,433	60,534	173,933	29,966
	Estimated total..................................	100.0%	31,976	336	2,036	11,622	17,982	264,451	60,538	173,946	29,967
	Rate per 100,000 inhabitants		534.3	5.6	34.0	194.2	300.5	4,419.0	1,011.6	2,906.7	500.8
Dallas-Plano-Irving, TX M.D.											
	Includes Collin, Dallas, Delta, enton, Ellis, Hunt, Kaufman, and Rockwall Counties	4,003,448									
	Total area actually reporting	99.9%	22,399	255	1,313	8,790	12,041	176,664	41,033	113,191	22,440
	Estimated total..................................	100.0%	22,400	255	1,313	8,790	12,042	176,682	41,037	113,204	22,441
	Rate per 100,000 inhabitants		559.5	6.4	32.8	219.6	300.8	4,413.2	1,025.0	2,827.7	560.5
Fort Worth-Arlington, TX M.D.											
	Includes Johnson, Parker, Tarrant, and Wise Counties.............................	1,980,942									
	Total area actually reporting	100.0%	9,576	81	723	2,832	5,940	87,769	19,501	60,742	7,526
	Rate per 100,000 inhabitants		483.4	4.1	36.5	143.0	299.9	4,430.7	984.4	3,066.3	379.9

Table 6. Crime, by Metropolitan Statistical Area, 2006 *(Contd.)*

(Number, percent, rate per 100,000 population.)

Metropolitan statistical area	Counties/principal cities	Popula-tion	Violent crime	Murder and non-negligent man-slaughter	Forcible rape	Robbery	Aggra-vated assault	Property crime	Burglary	Larceny-theft	Motor vehicle theft
Dalton, GA M.S.A.	Includes Murray and Whitfield Counties................	135,931									
	City of Dalton	33,172	148	1	10	32	105	1,390	209	1,065	116
	Total area actually reporting	99.5%	437	2	31	44	360	4,408	982	3,039	387
	Estimated total....................................	100.0%	440	2	31	45	362	4,440	988	3,062	390
	Rate per 100,000 inhabitants..............		323.7	1.5	22.8	33.1	266.3	3,266.4	726.8	2,252.6	286.9
Danville, VA M.S.A.	Includes Pittsylvania County and Danville City	109,073									
	City of Danville.................................	46,603	193	4	5	75	109	2,105	426	1,569	110
	Total area actually reporting	100.0%	270	5	19	89	157	2,772	673	1,920	179
	Rate per 100,000 inhabitants..............		247.5	4.6	17.4	81.6	143.9	2,541.4	617.0	1,760.3	164.1
Dayton, OH M.S.A.	Includes Greene, Miami, Montgom-ery, and Preble Counties....................	844,605									
	City of Dayton....................................	159,067	1,721	37	120	810	754	11,759	3,525	6,037	2,197
	Total area actually reporting	77.8%	2,491	43	319	1,061	1,068	26,894	6,307	17,332	3,255
	Estimated total....................................	100.0%	2,747	45	367	1,153	1,182	31,625	7,323	20,775	3,527
	Rate per 100,000 inhabitants..............		325.2	5.3	43.5	136.5	139.9	3,744.4	867.0	2,459.7	417.6
Decatur, AL M.S.A.	Includes Lawrence and Morgan Counties...	149,687									
	City of Decatur	55,406	249	2	25	80	142	3,629	716	2,630	283
	Total area actually reporting	97.4%	396	7	45	109	235	5,507	1,244	3,852	411
	Estimated total....................................	100.0%	412	7	46	115	244	5,662	1,275	3,964	423
	Rate per 100,000 inhabitants..............		275.2	4.7	30.7	76.8	163.0	3,782.6	851.8	2,648.2	282.6
Deltona-Daytona Beach-Ormond Beach, FL M.S.A.	Includes Volusia County	498,320									
	City of Daytona Beach.......................	65,507	896	4	55	302	535	5,132	1,615	2,873	644
	City of Ormond Beach........................	39,264	123	1	7	20	95	1,160	236	872	52
	Total area actually reporting	100.0%	2,716	21	162	636	1,897	19,139	5,407	11,877	1,855
	Rate per 100,000 inhabitants..............		545.0	4.2	32.5	127.6	380.7	3,840.7	1,085.0	2,383.4	372.3
Denver-Aurora, CO M.S.A.	Includes Adams, Arapahoe, Broom-field, Clear Creek, Denver, Douglas, Elbert, Gilpin, Jefferson, and Park Counties...	2,404,612									
	City of Denver....................................	568,465	4,325	51	342	1,280	2,652	26,266	6,543	13,376	6,347
	City of Aurora....................................	302,855	1,858	17	217	600	1,024	12,805	2,470	8,292	2,043
	Total area actually reporting	99.9%	10,279	106	1,152	2,627	6,394	88,506	17,912	55,823	14,771
	Estimated total....................................	100.0%	10,285	106	1,153	2,628	6,398	88,575	17,924	55,872	14,779
	Rate per 100,000 inhabitants..............		427.7	4.4	47.9	109.3	266.1	3,683.5	745.4	2,323.5	614.6
Des Moines-West Des Moines, IA M.S.A.[1]	Includes Dallas, Guthrie, Madison, Polk, and Warren Counties.................	525,225									
	City of Des Moines[1]	195,194	1,306	6	62	374	864	13,505	2,189	10,331	985
	City of West Des Moines	53,048	98	0	20	9	69	1,847	241	1,538	68
	Total area actually reporting	100.0%	1,829	8	122	435	1,264	21,169	3,549	16,249	1,371
	Rate per 100,000 inhabitants..............		348.2	1.5	23.2	82.8	240.7	4,030.5	675.7	3,093.7	261.0

[1] Because of changes in the state/local agency's reporting practices, figures are not comparable to previous years' data.

Table 6. Crime, by Metropolitan Statistical Area, 2006 (*Contd.*)

(Number, percent, rate per 100,000 population.)

Metropolitan statistical area	Counties/principal cities	Population	Violent crime	Murder and non-negligent man-slaughter	Forcible rape	Robbery	Aggra-vated assault	Property crime	Burglary	Larceny-theft	Motor vehicle theft
Detroit-Warren-Livonia, MI M.S.A.											
	Includes Metropolitan Divisions of Detroit-Livonia-Dearborn and Warren-Troy-Farmington Hills	4,477,154									
	City of Detroit	884,462	21,394	418	593	7,240	13,143	62,338	18,134	21,287	22,917
	City of Warren	134,974	842	5	75	241	521	4,883	790	2,288	1,805
	City of Livonia	97,733	167	0	19	65	83	2,318	366	1,639	313
	City of Dearborn	93,856	456	2	21	164	269	4,947	670	3,242	1,035
	City of Troy	80,966	93	2	10	26	55	2,018	321	1,550	147
	City of Farmington Hills	80,023	134	0	14	32	88	1,553	325	1,060	168
	City of Southfield	76,627	1,041	1	36	164	840	3,604	894	2,003	707
	City of Pontiac	67,163	1,221	8	86	276	851	3,425	1,566	1,294	565
	City of Taylor	64,800	234	4	33	78	119	2,736	382	1,983	371
	City of Novi	52,983	50	0	5	11	34	1,208	106	1,056	46
	Total area actually reporting	99.5%	33,819	506	1,813	10,178	21,322	160,161	36,384	85,349	38,428
	Estimated total	100.0%	33,894	507	1,822	10,196	21,369	160,892	36,513	85,864	38,515
	Rate per 100,000 inhabitants		757.0	11.3	40.7	227.7	477.3	3,593.6	815.5	1,917.8	860.3
Detroit-Livonia-Dearborn, MI M.D.											
	Includes Wayne County	1,993,241									
	Total area actually reporting	98.8%	25,384	458	955	8,481	15,490	97,643	24,378	43,669	29,596
	Estimated total	100.0%	25,459	459	964	8,499	15,537	98,374	24,507	44,184	29,683
	Rate per 100,000 inhabitants		1,277.3	23.0	48.4	426.4	779.5	4,935.4	1,229.5	2,216.7	1,489.2
Warren-Troy-Farmington Hills, MI M.D.											
	Includes Lapeer, Livingston, Macomb, Oakland, and St. Clair Counties	2,483,913									
	Total area actually reporting	100.0%	8,435	48	858	1,697	5,832	62,518	12,006	41,680	8,832
	Rate per 100,000 inhabitants		339.6	1.9	34.5	68.3	234.8	2,516.9	483.4	1,678.0	355.6
Dothan, AL M.S.A.											
	Includes Geneva, Henry, and Houston Counties	137,829									
	City of Dothan	62,410	375	7	57	186	125	3,303	869	2,234	200
	Total area actually reporting	88.5%	442	7	58	194	183	4,268	1,164	2,809	295
	Estimated total	100.0%	508	8	63	219	218	4,898	1,291	3,265	342
	Rate per 100,000 inhabitants		368.6	5.8	45.7	158.9	158.2	3,553.7	936.7	2,368.9	248.1
Dover, DE M.S.A.											
	Includes Kent County	145,667									
	City of Dover	34,693	289	2	17	47	223	1,702	142	1,435	125
	Total area actually reporting	100.0%	881	8	92	140	641	4,523	901	3,289	333
	Rate per 100,000 inhabitants		604.8	5.5	63.2	96.1	440.0	3,105.0	618.5	2,257.9	228.6
Dubuque, IA M.S.A.											
	Includes Dubuque County	92,118									
	City of Dubuque	58,105	354	0	21	16	317	1,694	436	1,179	79
	Total area actually reporting	100.0%	403	0	23	16	364	1,945	533	1,305	107
	Rate per 100,000 inhabitants		437.5	0.0	25.0	17.4	395.1	2,111.4	578.6	1,416.7	116.2
Duluth, MN-WI M.S.A.[4]											
	Includes Carlton and St. Louis Counties, MN[4] and Douglas County, WI	277,120									
	City of Duluth, MN[4]	85,463		1		116	224	4,057	630	3,214	213
	Total area actually reporting	97.6%		4		153	431	8,910	1,705	6,710	495
	Estimated total	100.0%		4		156	438	9,138	1,738	6,890	510
	Rate per 100,000 inhabitants			1.4		56.3	158.1	3,297.5	627.2	2,486.3	184.0
Durham, NC M.S.A.[1]											
	Includes Chatham, Durham, Orange, and Person Counties	465,289									
	City of Durham[1]	208,932	1,957	13	98	977	869	11,866	3,098	7,617	1,151
	Total area actually reporting	100.0%	2,824	22	157	1,185	1,460	21,041	5,567	13,859	1,615
	Rate per 100,000 inhabitants		606.9	4.7	33.7	254.7	313.8	4,522.1	1,196.5	2,978.6	347.1

[1] Because of changes in the state/local agency's reporting practices, figures are not comparable to previous years' data.
[4] The data collection methodology for the offense of forcible rape used by the Minnesota state UCR Program does not comply with national UCR Program guidelines. Consequently, their figures for forcible rape and violent crime (of which forcible rape is a part) are not published in this table.

Table 6. Crime, by Metropolitan Statistical Area, 2006 (*Contd.*)

(Number, percent, rate per 100,000 population.)

Metropolitan statistical area	Counties/principal cities	Popula-tion	Violent crime	Murder and non-negligent man-slaughter	Forcible rape	Robbery	Aggra-vated assault	Property crime	Burglary	Larceny-theft	Motor vehicle theft
Eau Claire, WI M.S.A.											
	Includes Chippewa and Eau Claire Counties	154,604									
	City of Eau Claire	62,799	100	0	8	13	79	2,191	390	1,707	94
	Total area actually reporting	100.0%	201	0	18	21	162	3,854	708	2,975	171
	Rate per 100,000 inhabitants		130.0	0.0	11.6	13.6	104.8	2,492.8	457.9	1,924.3	110.6
El Centro, CA M.S.A.											
	Includes Imperial County	157,226									
	City of El Centro	39,993	328	0	6	59	263	1,973	721	986	266
	Total area actually reporting	100.0%	663	3	18	139	503	6,388	2,192	3,054	1,142
	Rate per 100,000 inhabitants		421.7	1.9	11.4	88.4	319.9	4,062.9	1,394.2	1,942.4	726.3
Elizabethtown, KY M.S.A.											
	Includes Hardin and Larue Counties	111,512									
	City of Elizabethtown	23,634	85	0	12	36	37	1,088	218	821	49
	Total area actually reporting	100.0%	175	0	27	56	92	1,913	434	1,383	96
	Rate per 100,000 inhabitants		156.9	0.0	24.2	50.2	82.5	1,715.5	389.2	1,240.2	86.1
Elkhart-Goshen, IN M.S.A.											
	Includes Elkhart County	196,656									
	City of Elkhart	52,616	284	12	26	230	16	4,069	936	2,857	276
	City of Goshen	31,476	77	2	18	22	35	1,301	199	1,047	55
	Total area actually reporting	100.0%	420	15	58	281	66	7,144	1,538	5,136	470
	Rate per 100,000 inhabitants		213.6	7.6	29.5	142.9	33.6	3,632.7	782.1	2,611.7	239.0
Elmira, NY M.S.A. City of Elmira											
	Includes Chemung County	89,752									
	City of Elmira	30,008	113	1	2	45	65	1,457	281	1,146	30
	Total area actually reporting	100.0%	193	2	20	56	115	2,387	422	1,902	63
	Rate per 100,000 inhabitants		215.0	2.2	22.3	62.4	128.1	2,659.6	470.2	2,119.2	70.2
El Paso, TX M.S.A.											
	Includes El Paso County	742,047									
	City of El Paso	615,553	2,413	13	291	503	1,606	20,576	2,212	14,845	3,519
	Total area actually reporting	100.0%	2,804	22	322	546	1,914	23,656	2,771	17,096	3,789
	Rate per 100,000 inhabitants		377.9	3.0	43.4	73.6	257.9	3,187.9	373.4	2,303.9	510.6
Erie, PA M.S.A.											
	Includes Erie County	280,694									
	City of Erie	102,703	554	2	69	275	208	2,987	740	2,106	141
	Total area actually reporting	100.0%	824	4	113	309	398	5,795	1,411	4,080	304
	Rate per 100,000 inhabitants		293.6	1.4	40.3	110.1	141.8	2,064.5	502.7	1,453.5	108.3
Eugene-Springfield, OR M.S.A.											
	Includes Lane County	340,676									
	City of Eugene	146,885	370	3	44	155	168	8,113	1,561	5,386	1,166
	City of Springfield	56,553	182	2	11	29	140	3,969	651	2,785	533
	Total area actually reporting	100.0%	910	8	95	219	588	15,287	3,280	9,952	2,055
	Rate per 100,000 inhabitants		267.1	2.3	27.9	64.3	172.6	4,487.3	962.8	2,921.3	603.2
Evansville, IN-KY M.S.A.											
	Includes Gibson, Posey, Vanderburgh, and Warrick Counties, IN and Henderson and Webster Counties, KY	351,930									
	City of Evansville, IN	116,686	540	6	61	185	288	5,307	1,131	3,933	243
	Total area actually reporting	76.1%	756	8	83	201	464	7,867	1,532	5,958	377
	Estimated total	100.0%	912	10	100	248	554	10,043	1,970	7,528	545
	Rate per 100,000 inhabitants		259.1	2.8	28.4	70.5	157.4	2,853.7	559.8	2,139.1	154.9
Fairbanks, AK M.S.A.											
	Includes Fairbanks North Star Borough	33,421									
	City of Fairbanks	31,626	268	1	67	47	153	1,617	297	1,163	157
	Total area actually reporting	100.0%	274	1	68	48	157	1,929	337	1,419	173
	Rate per 100,000 inhabitants		819.8	3.0	203.5	143.6	469.8	5,771.8	1,008.3	4,245.8	517.6

Table 6. Crime, by Metropolitan Statistical Area, 2006 (Contd.)

(Number, percent, rate per 100,000 population.)

Metropolitan statistical area	Counties/principal cities	Population	Violent crime	Murder and non-negligent man-slaughter	Forcible rape	Robbery	Aggra-vated assault	Property crime	Burglary	Larceny-theft	Motor vehicle theft
Fargo, ND-MN M.S.A.[4]											
	Includes Clay County, MN[4] and Cass County, ND	185,052									
	City of Fargo, ND	90,818	231	2	69	19	141	2,679	525	1,930	224
	Total area actually reporting	100.0%		2		30	215	4,369	818	3,206	345
	Rate per 100,000 inhabitants			1.1		16.2	116.2	2,361.0	442.0	1,732.5	186.4
Farmington, NM M.S.A.											
	Includes San Juan County	127,924									
	City of Farmington	43,748	300	1	56	31	212	1,406	378	897	131
	Total area actually reporting	100.0%	763	4	100	46	613	2,948	709	2,001	238
	Rate per 100,000 inhabitants		596.4	3.1	78.2	36.0	479.2	2,304.5	554.2	1,564.2	186.0
Fayetteville, NC M.S.A.											
	Includes Cumberland and Hoke Counties	352,430									
	City of Fayetteville	132,521	1,299	15	61	510	713	13,091	3,519	8,549	1,023
	Total area actually reporting	100.0%	2,139	30	105	696	1,308	21,198	6,362	13,281	1,555
	Rate per 100,000 inhabitants		606.9	8.5	29.8	197.5	371.1	6,014.8	1,805.2	3,768.4	441.2
Fayetteville-Springdale-Rogers, AR-MO M.S.A.											
	Includes Benton, Madison, and Washington Counties, AR and McDonald County, MO	409,630									
	City of Fayetteville, AR	67,416	357	0	41	35	281	3,229	602	2,455	172
	City of Springdale, AR	60,782	281	2	61	36	182	2,617	471	1,942	204
	City of Rogers, AR	48,905	101	0	44	13	44	2,520	292	2,147	81
	City of Bentonville, AR	29,875	72	0	19	9	44	802	118	642	42
	Total area actually reporting	100.0%	1,308	9	260	114	925	12,918	2,731	9,403	784
	Rate per 100,000 inhabitants		319.3	2.2	63.5	27.8	225.8	3,153.6	666.7	2,295.5	191.4
Flagstaff, AZ M.S.A.											
	Includes Coconino County	128,601									
	City of Flagstaff	59,585	428	3	46	89	290	4,024	497	3,340	187
	Total area actually reporting	100.0%	690	3	65	109	513	5,660	786	4,623	251
	Rate per 100,000 inhabitants		536.5	2.3	50.5	84.8	398.9	4,401.2	611.2	3,594.8	195.2
Flint, MI M.S.A.											
	Includes Genesee County	442,777									
	City of Flint	118,256	3,070	54	143	627	2,246	8,117	3,058	3,538	1,521
	Total area actually reporting	99.9%	4,115	68	310	864	2,873	18,356	5,573	10,202	2,581
	Estimated total	100.0%	4,116	68	310	864	2,874	18,367	5,575	10,210	2,582
	Rate per 100,000 inhabitants		929.6	15.4	70.0	195.1	649.1	4,148.1	1,259.1	2,305.9	583.1
Florence, SC M.S.A.											
	Includes Darlington and Florence Counties	201,529									
	City of Florence	31,755	523	4	17	155	347	3,226	461	2,542	223
	Total area actually reporting	100.0%	2,339	12	79	395	1,853	11,518	2,447	8,200	871
	Rate per 100,000 inhabitants		1,160.6	6.0	39.2	196.0	919.5	5,715.3	1,214.2	4,068.9	432.2
Fond du Lac, WI M.S.A.											
	Includes Fond du Lac County	99,701									
	City of Fond du Lac	42,591	124	0	23	16	85	1,182	162	986	34
	Total area actually reporting	100.0%	188	1	41	17	129	1,853	290	1,487	76
	Rate per 100,000 inhabitants		188.6	1.0	41.1	17.1	129.4	1,858.6	290.9	1,491.5	76.2
Fort Collins-Loveland, CO M.S.A.											
	Includes Larimer County	277,068									
	City of Fort Collins	130,446	493	0	76	36	381	4,570	701	3,585	284
	City of Loveland	60,689	98	0	9	18	71	1,807	242	1,465	100
	Total area actually reporting	100.0%	718	5	113	61	539	8,433	1,386	6,532	515
	Rate per 100,000 inhabitants		259.1	1.8	40.8	22.0	194.5	3,043.7	500.2	2,357.5	185.9

[4] The data collection methodology for the offense of forcible rape used by the Minnesota state UCR Program does not comply with national UCR Program guidelines. Consequently, their figures for forcible rape and violent crime (of which forcible rape is a part) are not published in this table.

Table 6. Crime, by Metropolitan Statistical Area, 2006 (Contd.)

(Number, percent, rate per 100,000 population.)

Metropolitan statistical area	Counties/principal cities	Popula-tion	Violent crime	Murder and non-negligent man-slaughter	Forcible rape	Robbery	Aggra-vated assault	Property crime	Burglary	Larceny-theft	Motor vehicle theft
Fort Smith, AR-OK M.S.A.											
	Includes Crawford, Franklin, and Sebastian Counties, AR and Le Flore and Sequoyah Counties, OK....	288,013									
	City of Fort Smith, AR	83,422	876	11	83	131	651	5,491	1,089	4,039	363
	Total area actually reporting	87.2%	1,383	16	146	150	1,071	8,789	2,073	6,158	558
	Estimated total....................................	100.0%	1,505	17	159	160	1,169	9,762	2,435	6,690	637
	Rate per 100,000 inhabitants..............		522.5	5.9	55.2	55.6	405.9	3,389.4	845.4	2,322.8	221.2
Fort Walton Beach-Crestview-Destin, FL M.S.A.											
	Includes Okaloosa County	185,244									
	City of Fort Walton Beach.................	20,151	138	1	15	32	90	844	163	608	73
	City of Crestview	18,006	98	1	11	16	70	714	70	599	45
	Total area actually reporting	99.6%	706	5	57	106	538	5,333	1,037	3,863	433
	Estimated total....................................	100.0%	710	5	57	107	541	5,364	1,044	3,884	436
	Rate per 100,000 inhabitants..............		383.3	2.7	30.8	57.8	292.0	2,895.6	563.6	2,096.7	235.4
Fort Wayne, IN M.S.A.[5]											
	Includes Allen,[5] Wells, and Whitley Counties	407,093									
	City of Fort Wayne[5]...........................	224,820	708	18	80	404	206	10,767	2,128	7,934	705
	Total area actually reporting	91.1%	810	18	96	425	271	12,447	2,538	9,043	866
	Estimated total....................................	100.0%	877	19	102	442	314	13,337	2,707	9,688	942
	Rate per 100,000 inhabitants..............		215.4	4.7	25.1	108.6	77.1	3,276.2	665.0	2,379.8	231.4
Fresno, CA M.S.A.											
	Includes Fresno County	885,487									
	City of Fresno.....................................	465,269	3,524	52	133	1,282	2,057	23,407	4,366	14,097	4,944
	Total area actually reporting	100.0%	4,895	74	214	1,621	2,986	39,437	7,761	23,728	7,948
	Rate per 100,000 inhabitants..............		552.8	8.4	24.2	183.1	337.2	4,453.7	876.5	2,679.7	897.6
Gadsden, AL M.S.A.											
	Includes Etowah County	104,122									
	City of Gadsden	37,743	326	2	41	195	88	3,251	829	2,174	248
	Total area actually reporting	80.0%	411	5	48	211	147	4,267	1,138	2,801	328
	Estimated total....................................	100.0%	499	6	55	244	194	5,096	1,306	3,400	390
	Rate per 100,000 inhabitants..............		479.2	5.8	52.8	234.3	186.3	4,894.3	1,254.3	3,265.4	374.6
Gainesville, FL M.S.A.											
	Includes Alachua and Gilchrist Counties	244,306									
	City of Gainesville	110,009	1,090	7	96	250	737	5,763	1,420	3,877	466
	Total area actually reporting	100.0%	2,282	14	181	382	1,705	11,359	2,880	7,655	824
	Rate per 100,000 inhabitants..............		934.1	5.7	74.1	156.4	697.9	4,649.5	1,178.8	3,133.4	337.3
Gainesville, GA M.S.A.											
	Includes Hall County	171,095									
	City of Gainesville	33,486	217	2	17	77	121	1,959	228	1,584	147
	Total area actually reporting	99.8%	431	3	36	94	298	5,074	962	3,457	655
	Estimated total....................................	100.0%	433	3	36	95	299	5,088	965	3,467	656
	Rate per 100,000 inhabitants..............		253.1	1.8	21.0	55.5	174.8	2,973.8	564.0	2,026.4	383.4
Glens Falls, NY M.S.A.											
	Includes Warren and Washington Counties	128,917									
	City of Glens Falls	14,146	26	0	2	8	16	616	79	529	8
	Total area actually reporting	100.0%	205	2	38	14	151	2,666	576	2,018	72
	Rate per 100,000 inhabitants..............		159.0	1.6	29.5	10.9	117.1	2,068.0	446.8	1,565.3	55.8
Goldsboro, NC M.S.A.											
	Includes Wayne County	116,732									
	City of Goldsboro	39,442	328	4	3	95	226	2,435	633	1,650	152
	Total area actually reporting	98.1%	591	7	8	141	435	4,830	1,533	3,010	287
	Estimated total....................................	100.0%	602	7	9	144	442	4,946	1,561	3,092	293
	Rate per 100,000 inhabitants..............		515.7	6.0	7.7	123.4	378.6	4,237.1	1,337.3	2,648.8	251.0

[5] Due to an annexation, population and figures may not be comparable to previous years' data.

Table 6. Crime, by Metropolitan Statistical Area, 2006 (*Contd.*)

(Number, percent, rate per 100,000 population.)

Metropolitan statistical area	Counties/principal cities	Popula-tion	Violent crime	Murder and non-negligent man-slaughter	Forcible rape	Robbery	Aggra-vated assault	Property crime	Burglary	Larceny-theft	Motor vehicle theft
Grand Forks, ND-MN M.S.A.[4,6]											
	Includes Polk County, MN[4] and Grand Forks County, ND[6].................	97,197									
	City of Grand Forks, ND..................	50,239	91	1	19	12	59	1,800	281	1,370	149
	Total area actually reporting............	98.6%		2		15	112			1,949	209
	Estimated total................................	100.0%		2		15	113			1,976	211
	Rate per 100,000 inhabitants.............			2.1		15.4	116.3			2,033.0	217.1
Grand Junction, CO M.S.A.											
	Includes Mesa County........................	132,327									
	City of Grand Junction	46,155	288	3	37	39	209	2,850	440	2,176	234
	Total area actually reporting.............	100.0%	368	6	43	48	271	4,654	852	3,379	423
	Rate per 100,000 inhabitants.............		278.1	4.5	32.5	36.3	204.8	3,517.0	643.9	2,553.5	319.7
Grand Rapids-Wyoming, MI M.S.A.											
	Includes Barry, Ionia, Kent, and Newaygo Counties.............................	769,263									
	City of Grand Rapids.........................	193,297	1,923	22	65	700	1,136	10,103	2,484	6,922	697
	City of Wyoming................................	69,947	325	0	60	64	201	2,207	603	1,346	258
	Total area actually reporting.............	99.1%	3,272	26	393	855	1,998	24,808	5,777	17,517	1,514
	Estimated total................................	100.0%	3,293	26	396	860	2,011	25,013	5,813	17,662	1,538
	Rate per 100,000 inhabitants.............		428.1	3.4	51.5	111.8	261.4	3,251.6	755.7	2,296.0	199.9
Great Falls, MT M.S.A.											
	Includes Cascade County....................	80,331									
	City of Great Falls	56,878	186	2	11	29	144	2,772	224	2,424	124
	Total area actually reporting.............	100.0%	216	2	11	29	174	2,973	233	2,592	148
	Rate per 100,000 inhabitants.............		268.9	2.5	13.7	36.1	216.6	3,700.9	290.0	3,226.6	184.2
Greeley, CO M.S.A.											
	Includes Weld County........................	233,271									
	City of Greeley..................................	89,252	467	2	53	50	362	4,324	841	3,163	320
	Total area actually reporting.............	99.3%	827	4	92	72	659	8,180	1,823	5,619	738
	Estimated total................................	100.0%	832	4	93	73	662	8,238	1,833	5,660	745
	Rate per 100,000 inhabitants.............		356.7	1.7	39.9	31.3	283.8	3,531.5	785.8	2,426.4	319.4
Green Bay, WI M.S.A.											
	Includes Brown, Kewaunee, and Oconto Counties...............................	298,584									
	City of Green Bay..............................	101,574	558	2	50	106	400	2,874	687	1,986	201
	Total area actually reporting.............	100.0%	678	2	78	114	484	6,856	1,390	5,074	392
	Rate per 100,000 inhabitants.............		227.1	0.7	26.1	38.2	162.1	2,296.2	465.5	1,699.4	131.3
Greensboro-High Point, NC M.S.A.											
	Includes Guilford, Randolph, and Rockingham Counties........................	687,959									
	City of Greensboro............................	236,591	2,062	27	86	901	1,048	14,336	4,129	9,000	1,207
	City of High Point..............................	95,482	688	8	40	265	375	5,567	1,672	3,397	498
	Total area actually reporting.............	99.8%	3,466	48	162	1,334	1,922	31,564	9,031	20,062	2,471
	Estimated total................................	100.0%	3,472	48	162	1,336	1,926	31,632	9,047	20,110	2,475
	Rate per 100,000 inhabitants.............		504.7	7.0	23.5	194.2	280.0	4,597.9	1,315.0	2,923.1	359.8
Greenville, NC M.S.A.											
	Includes Greene and Pitt Counties....	165,841									
	City of Greenville	70,904	640	6	22	240	372	4,537	1,323	2,932	282
	Total area actually reporting.............	100.0%	1,137	12	68	321	736	7,774	2,294	5,044	436
	Rate per 100,000 inhabitants.............		685.6	7.2	41.0	193.6	443.8	4,687.6	1,383.3	3,041.5	262.9
Greenville-Mauldin-Easley, SC M.S.A.											
	Includes Greenville, Laurens, and Pickens Counties.............................	600,445									
	City of Greenville	57,557	567	8	25	141	393	3,762	761	2,671	330
	City of Mauldin	19,644	125	0	6	6	113	485	75	343	67
	City of Easley	19,145	75	1	2	14	58	846	124	680	42
	Total area actually reporting.............	100.0%	4,024	40	214	717	3,053	23,304	6,096	14,916	2,292
	Rate per 100,000 inhabitants.............		670.2	6.7	35.6	119.4	508.5	3,881.1	1,015.2	2,484.2	381.7

[4] The data collection methodology for the offense of forcible rape used by the Minnesota state UCR Program does not comply with national UCR Program guidelines. Consequently, their figures for forcible rape and violent crime (of which forcible rape is a part) are not published in this table.

[6] The FBI determined that the agency's data were inflated. Consequently, affected data are not included in this table.

Table 6. Crime, by Metropolitan Statistical Area, 2006 (*Contd.*)

(Number, percent, rate per 100,000 population.)

Metropolitan statistical area	Counties/principal cities	Population	Violent crime	Murder and non-negligent man-slaughter	Forcible rape	Robbery	Aggra-vated assault	Property crime	Burglary	Larceny-theft	Motor vehicle theft
Hagerstown-Martinsburg, MD-WV M.S.A.											
	Includes Washington County, MD and Berkeley and Morgan Counties, WV	251,797									
	City of Hagerstown, MD	38,431	295	4	8	117	166	1,610	303	1,159	148
	City of Martinsburg, WV	16,010	117	0	4	40	73	893	116	728	49
	Total area actually reporting	99.5%	842	6	42	222	572	6,415	1,384	4,475	556
	Estimated total	100.0%	845	6	42	223	574	6,455	1,392	4,504	559
	Rate per 100,000 inhabitants		335.6	2.4	16.7	88.6	228.0	2,563.6	552.8	1,788.7	222.0
Hanford-Corcoran, CA M.S.A.											
	Includes Kings County	144,712									
	City of Hanford	47,913	191	1	0	51	139	1,718	244	1,222	252
	City of Corcoran	22,658	58	0	7	3	48	224	98	94	32
	Total area actually reporting	100.0%	535	4	31	83	417	3,623	682	2,253	688
	Rate per 100,000 inhabitants		369.7	2.8	21.4	57.4	288.2	2,503.6	471.3	1,556.9	475.4
Harrisburg-Carlisle, PA M.S.A.											
	Includes Cumberland, Dauphin, and Perry Counties	522,275									
	City of Harrisburg	47,514	803	10	51	461	281	2,443	629	1,655	159
	City of Carlisle	18,124	42	1	4	24	13	633	65	552	16
	Total area actually reporting	95.0%	1,704	15	144	686	859	11,065	2,022	8,528	515
	Estimated total	100.0%	1,768	16	148	704	900	11,623	2,105	8,966	552
	Rate per 100,000 inhabitants		338.5	3.1	28.3	134.8	172.3	2,225.5	403.0	1,716.7	105.7
Harrisonburg, VA M.S.A.											
	Includes Rockingham County and Harrisonburg City	112,802									
	City of Harrisonburg	40,841	130	4	16	28	82	1,261	254	925	82
	Total area actually reporting	100.0%	173	5	30	33	105	1,877	421	1,345	111
	Rate per 100,000 inhabitants		153.4	4.4	26.6	29.3	93.1	1,664.0	373.2	1,192.4	98.4
Hartford-West Hartford-East Hartford, CT M.S.A.											
	Includes Hartford, Middlesex, and Tolland Counties	1,001,896									
	City of Hartford	124,203	1,590	24	47	758	761	8,824	1,158	5,957	1,709
	City of West Hartford	61,077	110	0	1	59	50	1,538	279	1,157	102
	City of East Hartford	49,096	235	1	27	99	108	1,757	286	1,249	222
	City of Middletown	47,364	60	1	3	25	31	1,472	222	1,101	149
	Total area actually reporting	98.1%	3,133	38	177	1,430	1,488	31,118	5,048	22,341	3,729
	Estimated total	100.0%	3,160	38	180	1,442	1,500	31,551	5,119	22,665	3,767
	Rate per 100,000 inhabitants		315.4	3.8	18.0	143.9	149.7	3,149.1	510.9	2,262.2	376.0
Hattiesburg, MS M.S.A.[1]											
	Includes Forrest, Lamar,[1] and Perry Counties	131,395									
	City of Hattiesburg	47,006	226	10	18	125	73	2,777	816	1,694	267
	Total area actually reporting	75.2%	295	11	41	139	104	3,733	1,162	2,243	328
	Estimated total	100.0%	346	13	48	150	135	4,438	1,352	2,665	421
	Rate per 100,000 inhabitants		263.3	9.9	36.5	114.2	102.7	3,377.6	1,029.0	2,028.2	320.4
Holland-Grand Haven, MI M.S.A.											
	Includes Ottawa County	254,770									
	City of Holland	26,958	118	0	37	12	69	947	157	762	28
	City of Grand Haven	10,560	37	0	7	3	27	420	80	332	8
	Total area actually reporting	97.2%	499	0	157	44	298	4,863	993	3,675	195
	Estimated total	100.0%	521	0	160	49	312	5,080	1,031	3,828	221
	Rate per 100,000 inhabitants		204.5	0.0	62.8	19.2	122.5	1,994.0	404.7	1,502.5	86.7
Honolulu, HI M.S.A.											
	Includes Honolulu County	912,693									
	City of Honolulu	912,693	2,745	17	229	956	1,543	38,310	5,482	26,540	6,288
	Total area actually reporting	100.0%	2,745	17	229	956	1,543	38,310	5,482	26,540	6,288
	Rate per 100,000 inhabitants		300.8	1.9	25.1	104.7	169.1	4,197.5	600.6	2,907.9	689.0

[1] Because of changes in the state/local agency's reporting practices, figures are not comparable to previous years' data.

Table 6. Crime, by Metropolitan Statistical Area, 2006 (*Contd.*)

(Number, percent, rate per 100,000 population.)

Metropolitan statistical area	Counties/principal cities	Population	Violent crime	Murder and non-negligent man-slaughter	Forcible rape	Robbery	Aggra-vated assault	Property crime	Burglary	Larceny-theft	Motor vehicle theft
Hot Springs, AR M.S.A.											
	Includes Garland County....................	94,619									
	City of Hot Springs............................	38,279	511	4	23	133	351	4,614	1,162	3,215	237
	Total area actually reporting.............	100.0%	615	5	38	146	426	7,046	2,145	4,462	439
	Rate per 100,000 inhabitants..............		650.0	5.3	40.2	154.3	450.2	7,446.7	2,267.0	4,715.8	464.0
Houma-Bayou Cane-Thibodaux, LA M.S.A.											
	Includes Lafourche and Terrebonne Parishes......................................	189,259									
	City of Houma....................................	30,431	337	4	21	69	243	1,676	283	1311	82
	City of Thibodaux..............................	13,657	131	1	11	26	93	616	107	502	7
	Total area actually reporting.............	100.0%	1,035	9	78	155	793	7,202	1,412	5,266	524
	Rate per 100,000 inhabitants..............		546.9	4.8	41.2	81.9	419.0	3,805.4	746.1	2,782.4	276.9
Houston-Sugar Land-Baytown, TX M.S.A.											
	Includes Austin, Brazoria, Chambers, Fort Bend, Galveston, Harris, Liberty, Montgomery, San Jacinto, and Waller Counties	5,429,705									
	City of Houston.................................	2,073,729	24,250	377	854	11,371	11,648	121,053	26,869	73,091	21,093
	City of Sugar Land.............................	77,901	101	0	6	45	50	1,609	212	1,322	75
	City of Baytown	70,309	350	3	46	137	164	3,233	789	2,115	329
	City of Galveston	59,094	593	4	120	166	303	3,239	657	2,278	304
	Total area actually reporting.............	99.9%	38,397	519	1,881	15,181	20,816	223,826	52,388	139,572	31,866
	Estimated total..................................	100.0%	38,398	519	1,881	15,181	20,817	223,846	52,392	139,587	31,867
	Rate per 100,000 inhabitants..............		707.2	9.6	34.6	279.6	383.4	4,122.6	964.9	2,570.8	586.9
Huntington-Ashland, WV-KY-OH M.S.A.											
	Includes Boyd and Greenup Counties, KY; Lawrence County, OH; and Cabell and Wayne Counties, WV	286,889									
	City of Huntington, WV	49,242	349	0	45	180	124	3,834	1,208	2,321	305
	City of Ashland, KY...........................	21,678	69	1	16	20	32	1,185	243	885	57
	Total area actually reporting.............	93.7%	620	3	82	244	291	8,768	2,335	5,798	635
	Estimated total..................................	100.0%	657	3	87	258	309	9,332	2,442	6,221	669
	Rate per 100,000 inhabitants..............		229.0	1.0	30.3	89.9	107.7	3,252.8	851.2	2,168.4	233.2
Huntsville, AL M.S.A.											
	Includes Limestone and Madison Counties.................................	371,995									
	City of Huntsville..............................	167,817	1,439	16	100	617	706	11,495	2,493	7,643	1,359
	Total area actually reporting.............	83.9%	1,754	17	127	675	935	14,708	3,402	9,654	1,652
	Estimated total..................................	100.0%	2,005	20	146	769	1070	17,101	3,886	11,383	1,832
	Rate per 100,000 inhabitants..............		539.0	5.4	39.2	206.7	287.6	4,597.1	1,044.6	3,060.0	492.5
Idaho Falls, ID M.S.A.											
	Includes Bonneville and Jefferson Counties.............................	116,402									
	City of Idaho Falls	53,707	189	2	49	12	126	2,048	458	1,463	127
	Total area actually reporting.............	100.0%	295	2	69	20	204	3,258	693	2,327	238
	Rate per 100,000 inhabitants..............		253.4	1.7	59.3	17.2	175.3	2,798.9	595.4	1,999.1	204.5
Indianapolis-Carmel, IN M.S.A.											
	Includes Boone, Brown, Hamilton, Hancock, Hendricks, Johnson, Marion, Morgan, Putnam, and Shelby Counties	1,651,458									
	City of Indianapolis...........................	800,969	7,689	140	549	3,249	3,751	49,599	11,734	28,929	8,936
	City of Carmel	59,635	26	0	6	13	7	1,016	130	833	53
	Total area actually reporting.............	83.4%	8,642	151	641	3,552	4,298	63,451	13,941	39,530	9,980
	Estimated total..................................	100.0%	9,032	156	678	3,633	4,565	68,963	15,085	43,426	10,452
	Rate per 100,000 inhabitants..............		546.9	9.4	41.1	220.0	276.4	4,175.9	913.4	2,629.6	632.9

Table 6. Crime, by Metropolitan Statistical Area, 2006 (*Contd.*)

(Number, percent, rate per 100,000 population.)

Metropolitan statistical area	Counties/principal cities	Popula-tion	Violent crime	Murder and non-negligent man-slaughter	Forcible rape	Robbery	Aggra-vated assault	Property crime	Burglary	Larceny-theft	Motor vehicle theft
Iowa City, IA M.S.A.											
	Includes Johnson and Washington Counties	139,260									
	City of Iowa City................................	63,221	211	0	30	39	142	1,374	294	999	81
	Total area actually reporting	94.8%	379	0	64	56	259	2,746	529	2,072	145
	Estimated total....................................	100.0%	394	0	66	58	270	2,933	560	2,220	153
	Rate per 100,000 inhabitants..............		282.9	0.0	47.4	41.6	193.9	2,106.1	402.1	1,594.1	109.9
Ithaca, NY M.S.A.											
	Includes Tompkins County.................	100,286									
	City of Ithaca.....................................	29,846	62	0	4	28	30	1,167	147	995	25
	Total area actually reporting	98.4%	151	1	30	33	87	2,539	329	2,137	73
	Estimated total....................................	100.0%	154	1	30	34	89	2,570	334	2,162	74
	Rate per 100,000 inhabitants..............		153.6	1.0	29.9	33.9	88.7	2,562.7	333.0	2,155.8	73.8
Jackson, MI M.S.A.											
	Includes Jackson County	163,221									
	City of Jackson...................................	34,792	289	2	43	80	164	2,308	371	1,819	118
	Total area actually reporting	98.6%	647	4	111	108	424	5,020	995	3,729	296
	Estimated total....................................	100.0%	654	4	112	110	428	5,089	1,007	3,778	304
	Rate per 100,000 inhabitants..............		400.7	2.5	68.6	67.4	262.2	3,117.9	617.0	2,314.7	186.3
Jackson, MS M.S.A.											
	Includes Copiah, Hinds, Madison, Rankin, and Simpson Counties..........	520,697									
	City of Jackson...................................	177,334	1,736	40	160	1,022	514	13,208	3,817	7,534	1,857
	Total area actually reporting	86.4%	2,209	54	256	1,138	761	18,792	5,388	11,137	2,267
	Estimated total....................................	100.0%	2,375	58	282	1193	842	21,199	5,951	12,759	2,489
	Rate per 100,000 inhabitants..............		456.1	11.1	54.2	229.1	161.7	4,071.3	1,142.9	2,450.4	478.0
Jackson, TN M.S.A.											
	Includes Chester and Madison Counties	112,267									
	City of Jackson...................................	62,889	785	11	28	189	557	4,492	1,160	2,876	456
	Total area actually reporting	100.0%	987	14	40	204	729	5,796	1,527	3,719	550
	Rate per 100,000 inhabitants..............		879.2	12.5	35.6	181.7	649.3	5,162.7	1,360.2	3,312.6	489.9
Jacksonville, FL M.S.A.[6]											
	Includes Baker, Clay, Duval, Nas-sau,[6] and St. Johns Counties...............	1,269,424									
	City of Jacksonville............................	795,822	6,663	110	218	2,304	4,031	43,103	9,615	29,167	4,321
	Total area actually reporting	99.9%		134	340	2,624		57,396	12,806	39,305	5,285
	Estimated total....................................	100.0%		134	340	2,627		57,465	12,821	39,352	5,292
	Rate per 100,000 inhabitants..............			10.6	26.8	206.9		4,526.9	1,010.0	3,100.0	416.9
Jacksonville, NC M.S.A.[1]											
	Includes Onslow County.....................	155,482									
	City of Jacksonville[1]	73,696	208	2	26	48	132	2,002	408	1,476	118
	Total area actually reporting	100.0%	557	8	65	114	370	4,932	1,374	3,220	338
	Rate per 100,000 inhabitants..............		358.2	5.1	41.8	73.3	238.0	3,172.1	883.7	2,071.0	217.4
Janesville, WI M.S.A.											
	Includes Rock County.........................	158,116									
	City of Janesville................................	62,189	134	0	43	42	49	2,974	555	2,315	104
	Total area actually reporting	100.0%	372	4	67	132	169	5,891	1,167	4,473	251
	Rate per 100,000 inhabitants..............		235.3	2.5	42.4	83.5	106.9	3,725.7	738.1	2,828.9	158.7
Jefferson City, MO M.S.A.											
	Includes Callaway, Cole, Moniteau, and Osage Counties...........................	144,919									
	City of Jefferson City	39,348	324	2	19	40	263	1,567	250	1,241	76
	Total area actually reporting	100.0%	533	4	39	58	432	3,519	723	2,585	211
	Rate per 100,000 inhabitants..............		367.8	2.8	26.9	40.0	298.1	2,428.3	498.9	1,783.8	145.6

[1] Because of changes in the state/local agency's reporting practices, figures are not comparable to previous years' data.
[6] The FBI determined that the agency's data were inflated. Consequently, affected data are not included in this table.

Table 6. Crime, by Metropolitan Statistical Area, 2006 (*Contd.*)

(Number, percent, rate per 100,000 population.)

Metropolitan statistical area	Counties/principal cities	Population	Violent crime	Murder and non-negligent man-slaughter	Forcible rape	Robbery	Aggra-vated assault	Property crime	Burglary	Larceny-theft	Motor vehicle theft
Johnson City, TN M.S.A.											
	Includes Carter, Unicoi, and Washington Counties	191,348									
	City of Johnson City	59,465	329	6	19	63	241	3,397	701	2,493	203
	Total area actually reporting	100.0%	731	11	35	87	598	6,336	1,585	4,381	370
	Rate per 100,000 inhabitants		382.0	5.7	18.3	45.5	312.5	3,311.2	828.3	2,289.5	193.4
Johnstown, PA M.S.A.											
	Includes Cambria County	148,204									
	City of Johnstown	24,144	132	2	5	43	82	1,017	266	704	47
	Total area actually reporting	86.5%	315	6	21	65	223	2,828	609	2,079	140
	Estimated total	100.0%	363	6	24	79	254	3,256	673	2,415	168
	Rate per 100,000 inhabitants		244.9	4.0	16.2	53.3	171.4	2,197.0	454.1	1,629.5	113.4
Jonesboro, AR M.S.A.											
	Includes Craighead and Poinsett Counties	113,363									
	City of Jonesboro	60,035	467	3	39	88	337	3,807	1,579	2,080	148
	Total area actually reporting	100.0%	637	6	55	106	470	5,446	2,192	3,036	218
	Rate per 100,000 inhabitants		561.9	5.3	48.5	93.5	414.6	4,804.0	1,933.6	2,678.1	192.3
Joplin, MO M.S.A.											
	Includes Jasper and Newton Counties	167,393									
	City of Joplin	47,528	419	4	54	95	266	3,887	733	2,877	277
	Total area actually reporting	100.0%	702	6	79	122	495	7,194	1,495	5,158	541
	Rate per 100,000 inhabitants		419.4	3.6	47.2	72.9	295.7	4,297.7	893.1	3,081.4	323.2
Kalamazoo-Portage, MI M.S.A.											
	Includes Kalamazoo and Van Buren Counties	318,553									
	City of Kalamazoo	72,519	737	5	55	238	439	4,966	1,327	3,243	396
	City of Portage	45,164	122	0	27	24	71	2,072	337	1,664	71
	Total area actually reporting	99.1%	1,426	8	171	345	902	12,907	3,213	8,855	839
	Estimated total	100.0%	1,434	8	172	347	907	12,992	3,228	8,915	849
	Rate per 100,000 inhabitants		450.2	2.5	54.0	108.9	284.7	4,078.4	1,013.3	2,798.6	266.5
Kansas City, MO-KS M.S.A.[1]											
	Includes Franklin, Johnson, Leavenworth, Linn, Miami, and Wyandotte Counties, KS and Bates, Caldwell, Cass, Clay, Clinton, Jackson, Lafayette, Platte, and Ray Counties, MO	1,961,734									
	City of Kansas City, MO1	448,218	6,471	112	321	2,044	3,994	31,100	7,399	18,186	5,515
	City of Overland Park, KS	165,975	332	0	48	63	221	4,541	584	3,571	386
	City of Kansas City, KS	145,229	1,245	45	91	439	670	10,281	2,265	5,691	2,325
	Total area actually reporting	99.9%	11,689	174	858	3,119	7,538	81,913	16,680	53,763	11,470
	Estimated total	100.0%	11,690	174	858	3,119	7,539	81,922	16,681	53,770	11,471
	Rate per 100,000 inhabitants		595.9	8.9	43.7	159.0	384.3	4,176.0	850.3	2,740.9	584.7
Kennewick-Richland-Pasco, WA M.S.A.											
	Includes Benton and Franklin Counties	224,758									
	City of Kennewick	62,045	296	2	28	33	233	2,651	484	1,993	174
	City of Richland	45,078	100	0	10	14	76	1,438	282	1,069	87
	City of Pasco	47,293	159	3	19	34	103	1,781	388	1,199	194
	Total area actually reporting	100.0%	651	6	69	89	487	7,253	1,490	5,211	552
	Rate per 100,000 inhabitants		289.6	2.7	30.7	39.6	216.7	3,227.0	662.9	2,318.5	245.6
Killeen-Temple-Fort Hood, TX M.S.A.[7]											
	Includes Bell, Coryell, and Lampasas Counties	361,489									
	City of Killeen	103,073	787	8	81	246	452	5,471	2,121	3,108	242
	City of Temple[7]	57,018		2		62	90	2,878	668	2,045	165
	Total area actually reporting	99.1%		11		362	741	12,684	3,956	8,131	597
	Estimated total	100.0%		11		364	747	12,798	3,979	8,214	605
	Rate per 100,000 inhabitants			3.0		100.7	206.6	3,540.4	1,100.7	2,272.3	167.4

[1] Because of changes in the state/local agency's reporting practices, figures are not comparable to previous years' data.
[7] It was determined that the agency did not follow national UCR Program guidelines for reporting an offense. Consequently, this figure is not included in this table.

Table 6. Crime, by Metropolitan Statistical Area, 2006 (*Contd.*)

(Number, percent, rate per 100,000 population.)

Metropolitan statistical area	Counties/principal cities	Population	Violent crime	Murder and non-negligent man-slaughter	Forcible rape	Robbery	Aggra-vated assault	Property crime	Burglary	Larceny-theft	Motor vehicle theft
Kingsport-Bristol-Bristol, TN-VA M.S.A.											
	Includes Hawkins and Sullivan Counties, TN and Scott and Washington Counties and Bristol City, VA...........	304,872									
	City of Kingsport, TN...............	44,691	387	3	29	79	276	2,667	440	2,062	165
	City of Bristol, TN	25,312	159	0	10	17	132	1,432	229	1,094	109
	City of Bristol, VA	17,508	97	3	9	16	69	800	121	630	49
	Total area actually reporting	99.5%	1,371	12	104	156	1,099	10,652	2,365	7,552	735
	Estimated total...................	100.0%	1,378	12	105	158	1,103	10,710	2,374	7,597	739
	Rate per 100,000 inhabitants...............		452.0	3.9	34.4	51.8	361.8	3,512.9	778.7	2,491.9	242.4
Kingston, NY M.S.A.											
	Includes Ulster County	183,182									
	City of Kingston.....................	23,129	89	1	11	43	34	798	147	625	26
	Total area actually reporting	100.0%	513	5	50	77	381	3,405	698	2,553	154
	Rate per 100,000 inhabitants...............		280.0	2.7	27.3	42.0	208.0	1,858.8	381.0	1,393.7	84.1
Knoxville, TN M.S.A.											
	Includes Anderson, Blount, Knox, Loudon, and Union Counties...........	663,737									
	City of Knoxville.....................	182,421	1,894	18	89	538	1,249	11,063	2,281	7,684	1,098
	Total area actually reporting	100.0%	3,408	34	192	744	2,438	24,028	5,638	16,187	2,203
	Rate per 100,000 inhabitants...............		513.5	5.1	28.9	112.1	367.3	3,620.1	849.4	2,438.8	331.9
Kokomo, IN M.S.A.											
	Includes Howard and Tipton Counties............	102,034									
	City of Kokomo	46,484	217	5	23	65	124	3,042	642	2,260	140
	Total area actually reporting	89.0%	292	5	27	70	190	3,865	953	2,746	166
	Estimated total...................	100.0%	304	5	28	72	199	4,046	995	2,869	182
	Rate per 100,000 inhabitants...............		297.9	4.9	27.4	70.6	195.0	3,965.3	975.2	2,811.8	178.4
La Crosse, WI-MN M.S.A.[4]											
	Includes Houston County, MN[4] and La Crosse County, WI	129,432									
	City of La Crosse, WI......................	50,471	172	0	27	25	120	1,938	270	1,585	83
	Total area actually reporting	100.0%		0		29	179	3,234	428	2,671	135
	Rate per 100,000 inhabitants.............			0.0		22.4	138.3	2,498.6	330.7	2,063.6	104.3
Lafayette, IN M.S.A.											
	Includes Benton, Carroll, and Tippecanoe Counties..........	184,554									
	City of Lafayette	60,859	262	2	45	77	138	3,440	779	2,448	213
	Total area actually reporting	85.6%	394	2	72	90	230	5,325	1,154	3,875	296
	Estimated total...................	100.0%	425	2	75	95	253	5,804	1,259	4,208	337
	Rate per 100,000 inhabitants...............		230.3	1.1	40.6	51.5	137.1	3,144.9	682.2	2,280.1	182.6
Lake Charles, LA M.S.A.											
	Includes Calcasieu and Cameron Parishes................	184,811									
	City of Lake Charles	66,876	708	4	51	158	495	3,557	1,843	1,351	363
	Total area actually reporting	86.7%	1,181	10	138	258	775	7,765	2,805	4,276	684
	Estimated total...................	100.0%	1,373	12	147	291	923	9,170	3,056	5,338	776
	Rate per 100,000 inhabitants...............		742.9	6.5	79.5	157.5	499.4	4,961.8	1,653.6	2,888.4	419.9
Lake Havasu City-Kingman, AZ M.S.A.											
	Includes Mohave County...................	194,356									
	City of Lake Havasu City	57,453	101	3	10	11	77	1,715	321	1,243	151
	City of Kingman.....................	26,524	123	4	7	29	83	2,164	465	1,503	196
	Total area actually reporting	100.0%	589	17	27	102	443	9,045	2,426	5,656	963
	Rate per 100,000 inhabitants...............		303.1	8.7	13.9	52.5	227.9	4,653.8	1,248.2	2,910.1	495.5

[4] The data collection methodology for the offense of forcible rape used by the Minnesota state UCR Program does not comply with national UCR Program guidelines. Consequently, their figures for forcible rape and violent crime (of which forcible rape is a part) are not published in this table.

Table 6. Crime, by Metropolitan Statistical Area, 2006 (*Contd.*)

(Number, percent, rate per 100,000 population.)

Metropolitan statistical area	Counties/principal cities	Popula-tion	Violent crime	Murder and non-negligent man-slaughter	Forcible rape	Robbery	Aggra-vated assault	Property crime	Burglary	Larceny-theft	Motor vehicle theft
Lakeland, FL M.S.A.											
	Includes Polk County.........................	552,068									
	City of Lakeland...............................	90,209	593	3	57	202	331	5,158	1,140	3,666	352
	Total area actually reporting..............	99.5%	3,061	21	244	731	2,065	20,845	5,955	13,330	1,560
	Estimated total..................................	100.0%	3,078	21	245	736	2076	20,953	5,979	13,403	1,571
	Rate per 100,000 inhabitants..............		557.5	3.8	44.4	133.3	376.0	3,795.4	1,083.0	2,427.8	284.6
Lancaster, PA M.S.A.											
	Includes Lancaster County................	490,996									
	City of Lancaster...............................	54,805	532	7	44	244	237	3,164	535	2,312	317
	Total area actually reporting..............	93.6%	986	21	85	389	491	10,768	2,018	7,957	793
	Estimated total..................................	100.0%	1,062	22	90	410	540	11,440	2,118	8,485	837
	Rate per 100,000 inhabitants..............		216.3	4.5	18.3	83.5	110.0	2,330.0	431.4	1,728.1	170.5
Lansing-East Lansing, MI M.S.A.											
	Includes Clinton, Eaton, and Ingham Counties..	454,180									
	City of Lansing.................................	115,230	1,173	6	105	262	800	4,656	1,249	2,928	479
	City of East Lansing	46,303	172	0	14	28	130	1,093	248	785	60
	Total area actually reporting..............	98.6%	1,927	11	273	390	1,253	12,635	2,769	8,923	943
	Estimated total..................................	100.0%	1,947	11	275	395	1,266	12,831	2,804	9,061	966
	Rate per 100,000 inhabitants..............		428.7	2.4	60.5	87.0	278.7	2,825.1	617.4	1,995.0	212.7
Laredo, TX M.S.A.											
	Includes Webb County.......................	231,062									
	City of Laredo..................................	214,670	1,198	22	96	266	814	12,511	1,643	9,661	1,207
	Total area actually reporting..............	100.0%	1,261	24	96	270	871	12,981	1,778	9,956	1,247
	Rate per 100,000 inhabitants..............		545.7	10.4	41.5	116.9	377.0	5,618.0	769.5	4,308.8	539.7
Las Cruces, NM M.S.A.											
	Includes Dona Ana County................	192,019									
	City of Las Cruces	83,795	515	3	94	97	321	3,906	760	2,864	282
	Total area actually reporting..............	98.8%	879	5	132	113	629	5,943	1,326	4,122	495
	Estimated total..................................	100.0%	893	5	133	115	640	6,008	1,343	4,162	503
	Rate per 100,000 inhabitants..............		465.1	2.6	69.3	59.9	333.3	3,128.9	699.4	2,167.5	262.0
Las Vegas-Paradise, NV M.S.A.											
	Includes Clark County	1,767,730									
	City of Las Vegas Metropolitan Police Department............................	1,315,625	12,931	152	718	5,381	6,680	61,405	14,913	26,815	19,677
	Total area actually reporting..............	100.0%	15,506	181	845	6,293	8,187	79,277	19,476	35,849	23,952
	Rate per 100,000 inhabitants..............		877.2	10.2	47.8	356.0	463.1	4,484.7	1,101.8	2,028.0	1,355.0
Lawrence, KS M.S.A.											
	Includes Douglas County...................	103,641									
	City of Lawrence...............................	82,394	500	3	48	79	370	4,914	603	4,106	205
	Total area actually reporting..............	100.0%	556	5	57	79	415	5,751	794	4,718	239
	Rate per 100,000 inhabitants..............		536.5	4.8	55.0	76.2	400.4	5,549.0	766.1	4,552.3	230.6
Lawton, OK M.S.A.											
	Includes Comanche County	113,422									
	City of Lawton	91,031	929	8	82	169	670	4,727	1,550	2,886	291
	Total area actually reporting..............	100.0%	975	8	86	173	708	4,979	1,632	3,038	309
	Rate per 100,000 inhabitants..............		859.6	7.1	75.8	152.5	624.2	4,389.8	1,438.9	2,678.5	272.4
Lebanon, PA M.S.A.											
	Includes Lebanon County	125,689									
	City of Lebanon	24,007	152	2	9	61	80	892	175	659	58
	Total area actually reporting..............	90.6%	352	4	51	79	218	2,335	400	1,793	142
	Estimated total..................................	100.0%	380	4	53	87	236	2,587	437	1,991	159
	Rate per 100,000 inhabitants..............		302.3	3.2	42.2	69.2	187.8	2,058.3	347.7	1,584.1	126.5
Lewiston, ID-WA M.S.A.											
	Includes Nez Perce County, ID and Asotin County, WA	60,465									
	City of Lewiston, ID..........................	31,894	34	1	5	4	24	1,327	258	1,015	54
	Total area actually reporting..............	100.0%	72	1	9	4	58	1,977	368	1,510	99
	Rate per 100,000 inhabitants..............		119.1	1.7	14.9	6.6	95.9	3,269.7	608.6	2,497.3	163.7

Table 6. Crime, by Metropolitan Statistical Area, 2006 (*Contd.*)

(Number, percent, rate per 100,000 population.)

Metropolitan statistical area	Counties/principal cities	Popula-tion	Violent crime	Murder and non-negligent man-slaughter	Forcible rape	Robbery	Aggra-vated assault	Property crime	Burglary	Larceny-theft	Motor vehicle theft
Lewiston-Auburn, ME M.S.A.											
	Includes Androscoggin County..........	108,045									
	City of Lewiston..................................	36,052	91	1	21	42	27	1,191	213	938	40
	City of Auburn....................................	23,603	23	0	6	7	10	803	142	632	29
	Total area actually reporting.............	100.0%	146	1	38	54	53	2,792	545	2,140	107
	Rate per 100,000 inhabitants..............		135.1	0.9	35.2	50.0	49.1	2,584.1	504.4	1,980.7	99.0
Lexington-Fayette, KY M.S.A.[1]											
	Includes Bourbon, Clark, Fayette, Jessamine, Scott, and Woodford Counties.....................................	433,254									
	City of Lexington[1]	270,179	1,712	9	128	505	1,070	10,437	2,184	7,550	703
	Total area actually reporting.............	92.0%	1,930	10	161	562	1,197	15,090	3,191	10,947	952
	Estimated total....................................	100.0%	1,966	10	167	572	1,217	15,631	3,322	11,317	992
	Rate per 100,000 inhabitants..............		453.8	2.3	38.5	132.0	280.9	3,607.8	766.8	2,612.1	229.0
Lima, OH M.S.A.											
	Includes Allen County	106,363									
	City of Lima...	38,655	378	9	55	109	205	2,563	824	1,588	151
	Total area actually reporting.............	91.9%	440	10	72	134	224	4,025	1,169	2,658	198
	Estimated total....................................	100.0%	455	10	74	140	231	4,289	1,219	2,856	214
	Rate per 100,000 inhabitants..............		427.8	9.4	69.6	131.6	217.2	4,032.4	1,146.1	2,685.1	201.2
Lincoln, NE M.S.A.											
	Includes Lancaster and Seward Counties...................................	283,081									
	City of Lincoln	240,511	1,256	5	100	162	989	12,237	1,922	9,884	431
	Total area actually reporting.............	99.3%	1,279	5	107	163	1,004	13,278	2,093	10,716	469
	Estimated total....................................	100.0%	1,281	5	108	163	1,005	13,328	2,099	10,757	472
	Rate per 100,000 inhabitants..............		452.5	1.8	38.2	57.6	355.0	4,708.2	741.5	3,800.0	166.7
Little Rock-North Little Rock-Conway, AR M.S.A.											
	Includes Faulkner, Grant, Lonoke, Perry, Pulaski, and Saline Counties	650,613									
	City of Little Rock..............................	186,670	3,324	58	151	899	2,216	15,789	3,866	10,611	1,312
	City of North Little Rock	59,474	866	13	64	240	549	5,621	1,263	3,814	544
	City of Conway	52,592	187	3	35	61	88	2,420	393	1,843	184
	Total area actually reporting.............	97.7%	5,814	92	370	1,350	4,002	36,064	9,093	23,988	2,983
	Estimated total....................................	100.0%	5,891	93	377	1,362	4,059	36,705	9,280	24,409	3,016
	Rate per 100,000 inhabitants..............		905.5	14.3	57.9	209.3	623.9	5,641.6	1,426.3	3,751.7	463.6
Logan, UT-ID M.S.A.											
	Includes Franklin County, ID and Cache County, UT......................	113,944									
	City of Logan, UT................................	48,900	43	1	10	6	26	844	142	678	24
	Total area actually reporting.............	100.0%	86	2	23	7	54	1,879	298	1,527	54
	Rate per 100,000 inhabitants..............		75.5	1.8	20.2	6.1	47.4	1,649.1	261.5	1,340.1	47.4
Longview, TX M.S.A.											
	Includes Gregg, Rusk, and Upshur Counties..	207,210									
	City of Longview.................................	76,037	703	10	55	114	524	4,794	1,079	3,245	470
	Total area actually reporting.............	99.4%	1,158	16	109	167	866	9,576	2,219	6,475	882
	Estimated total....................................	100.0%	1,161	16	109	168	868	9,620	2,228	6,507	885
	Rate per 100,000 inhabitants..............		560.3	7.7	52.6	81.1	418.9	4,642.6	1,075.2	3,140.3	427.1
Longview, WA M.S.A.											
	Includes Cowlitz County....................	98,997									
	City of Longview.................................	36,758	146	3	40	39	64	2,906	593	2,045	268
	Total area actually reporting.............	100.0%	291	7	79	68	137	5,268	1,223	3,519	526
	Rate per 100,000 inhabitants..............		293.9	7.1	79.8	68.7	138.4	5,321.4	1,235.4	3,554.7	531.3

[1] Because of changes in the state/local agency's reporting practices, figures are not comparable to previous years' data.

Table 6. Crime, by Metropolitan Statistical Area, 2006 (*Contd.*)

(Number, percent, rate per 100,000 population.)

Metropolitan statistical area	Counties/principal cities	Popula-tion	Violent crime	Murder and non-negligent man-slaughter	Forcible rape	Robbery	Aggra-vated assault	Property crime	Burglary	Larceny-theft	Motor vehicle theft
Los Angeles-Long Beach-Santa Ana, CA M.S.A.											
	Includes Metropolitan Divisions of Los Angeles-Long Beach-Glendale and Santa Ana-Anaheim-Irvine	13,039,935									
	City of Los Angeles	3,879,455	30,526	480	1,059	14,353	14,634	105,459	20,359	59,711	25,389
	City of Long Beach	478,283	3,420	41	134	1,440	1,805	12,778	2,896	6,598	3,284
	City of Santa Ana	343,433	1,998	26	73	787	1,112	8,630	1,074	4,956	2,600
	City of Anaheim	334,792	1,524	10	107	584	823	8,817	1,886	5,277	1,654
	City of Glendale	201,867	368	2	14	167	185	3,935	672	2,685	578
	City of Irvine	188,535	126	4	17	50	55	3,034	634	2,147	253
	City of Pomona	155,172	1,255	19	17	464	755	5,227	1,027	2,781	1,419
	City of Torrance	143,666	354	1	18	203	132	3,171	666	1,998	507
	City of Pasadena	145,025	611	11	19	247	334	4,398	892	2,998	508
	City of Orange	136,165	298	1	13	147	137	3,291	549	2,309	433
	City of Fullerton	133,983	469	2	47	172	248	4,337	764	2,962	611
	City of Costa Mesa	110,819	306	6	30	123	147	3,380	524	2,449	407
	City of Burbank	105,046	252	1	10	75	166	2,721	567	1,683	471
	City of Compton	96,520	1,672	39	50	534	1,049	2,411	578	931	902
	City of Carson	94,801	738	15	16	268	439	2,823	619	1,502	702
	City of Santa Monica	88,591	590	2	26	256	306	3,314	733	2,187	394
	City of Newport Beach	80,553	130	1	4	32	93	2,431	575	1,682	174
	City of Tustin	69,718	155	1	11	45	98	1,780	396	1,148	236
	City of Montebello	63,860	278	3	14	122	139	2,007	330	1,011	666
	City of Monterey Park	62,624	164	1	7	108	48	1,374	313	744	317
	City of Gardena	60,430	506	8	13	290	195	1,515	407	616	492
	City of Paramount	57,049	383	5	12	155	211	1,777	346	739	692
	City of Fountain Valley	56,446	96	0	4	36	56	1,375	309	942	124
	City of Arcadia	56,659	157	1	5	73	78	1,783	409	1,208	166
	City of Cerritos	53,034	172	4	4	115	49	1,912	300	1,316	296
	Total area actually reporting	100.0%	73,407	1,092	2,817	30,798	38,700	336,940	68,227	193,468	75,245
	Rate per 100,000 inhabitants		562.9	8.4	21.6	236.2	296.8	2,583.9	523.2	1,483.7	577.0
Los Angeles-Long Beach-Glendale, CA M.D.											
	Includes Los Angeles County	10,024,953									
	Total area actually reporting	100.0%	65,044	1,012	2,342	27,731	33,959	269,334	55,499	149,138	64,697
	Rate per 100,000 inhabitants		648.8	10.1	23.4	276.6	338.7	2,686.6	553.6	1,487.7	645.4
Santa Ana-Anaheim-Irvine, CA M.D.											
	Includes Orange County	3,014,982									
	Total area actually reporting	100.0%	8,363	80	475	3,067	4,741	67,606	12,728	44,330	10,548
	Rate per 100,000 inhabitants		277.4	2.7	15.8	101.7	157.2	2,242.3	422.2	1,470.3	349.9
Louisville-Jefferson County, KY-IN M.S.A.											
	Includes Clark, Floyd, Harrison, and Washington Counties, IN and Bullitt, Henry, Jefferson, Meade, Nelson, Oldham, Shelby, Spencer, and Trimble Counties, KY	1,217,627									
	City of Louisville Metro, KY	626,018	3,836	50	175	1,738	1,873	29,136	7,587	17,855	3,694
	Total area actually reporting	94.7%	4,838	56	258	2,114	2,410	43,372	10,786	27,683	4,903
	Estimated total	100.0%	4,922	57	267	2,130	2,468	44,585	11,048	28,531	5,006
	Rate per 100,000 inhabitants		404.2	4.7	21.9	174.9	202.7	3,661.6	907.3	2,343.2	411.1
Lubbock, TX M.S.A.											
	Includes Crosby and Lubbock Counties	266,308									
	City of Lubbock	215,681	2,169	13	98	367	1,691	12,373	3,070	8,610	693
	Total area actually reporting	100.0%	2,316	14	115	378	1,809	13,779	3,447	9,508	824
	Rate per 100,000 inhabitants		869.7	5.3	43.2	141.9	679.3	5,174.1	1,294.4	3,570.3	309.4

Table 6. Crime, by Metropolitan Statistical Area, 2006 *(Contd.)*

(Number, percent, rate per 100,000 population.)

Metropolitan statistical area	Counties/principal cities	Population	Violent crime	Murder and non-negligent man-slaughter	Forcible rape	Robbery	Aggra-vated assault	Property crime	Burglary	Larceny-theft	Motor vehicle theft
Lynchburg, VA M.S.A.											
	Includes Amherst, Appomattox, Bedford, and Campbell Counties and Bedford and Lynchburg Cities	239,271									
	City of Lynchburg	67,640	340	2	34	91	213	2,402	442	1,796	164
	Total area actually reporting	99.5%	550	7	69	119	355	4,692	872	3,532	288
	Estimated total	100.0%	555	7	69	121	358	4,739	879	3,569	291
	Rate per 100,000 inhabitants		232.0	2.9	28.8	50.6	149.6	1,980.6	367.4	1,491.6	121.6
Macon, GA M.S.A.											
	Includes Bibb, Crawford, Jones, Monroe, and Twiggs Counties	236,057									
	City of Macon	97,345	853	12	53	358	430	9,486	2,355	5,891	1,240
	Total area actually reporting	99.2%	1,239	18	92	411	718	14,268	3,361	9,096	1,811
	Estimated total	100.0%	1,248	18	92	414	724	14,359	3,378	9,161	1,820
	Rate per 100,000 inhabitants		528.7	7.6	39.0	175.4	306.7	6,082.9	1,431.0	3,880.8	771.0
Madera, CA M.S.A.											
	Includes Madera County	144,074									
	City of Madera	52,617	435	0	29	97	309	1,225	318	649	258
	Total area actually reporting	100.0%	777	2	55	129	591	3,478	1,074	1,791	613
	Rate per 100,000 inhabitants		539.3	1.4	38.2	89.5	410.2	2,414.0	745.5	1,243.1	425.5
Madison, WI M.S.A.											
	Includes Columbia, Dane, and Iowa Counties	539,008									
	City of Madison	222,364	973	4	64	434	471	7,498	1,619	5,404	475
	Total area actually reporting	100.0%	1,411	4	139	542	726	15,283	2,753	11,717	813
	Rate per 100,000 inhabitants		261.8	0.7	25.8	100.6	134.7	2,835.4	510.8	2,173.8	150.8
Manchester-Nash-ua, NH M.S.A.											
	Includes Hillsborough County	402,810									
	City of Manchester	110,106	313	4	44	157	108	3,454	781	2,423	250
	City of Nashua	87,651	190	1	21	47	121	2,241	333	1,801	107
	Total area actually reporting	92.9%	614	5	90	227	292	8,007	1,472	6,029	506
	Estimated total	100.0%	634	5	94	231	304	8,276	1,516	6,236	524
	Rate per 100,000 inhabitants		157.4	1.2	23.3	57.3	75.5	2,054.6	376.4	1,548.1	130.1
Mansfield, OH M.S.A.											
	Includes Richland County	128,105									
	City of Mansfield	50,677	221	3	48	101	69	3,357	946	2,330	81
	Total area actually reporting	98.5%	303	3	72	125	103	6,197	1,515	4,527	155
	Estimated total	100.0%	307	3	73	126	105	6,256	1,526	4,571	159
	Rate per 100,000 inhabitants		239.6	2.3	57.0	98.4	82.0	4,883.5	1,191.2	3,568.2	124.1
McAllen-Edinburg-Mission, TX M.S.A.											
	Includes Hidalgo County	697,496									
	City of McAllen	127,125	383	4	28	123	228	6,926	637	5,820	469
	City of Edinburg	64,513	263	1	13	49	200	4,059	681	2,969	409
	City of Mission	61,850	64	2	2	24	36	2,769	275	2,206	288
	City of Pharr	60,658	190	4	26	62	98	3,339	597	2,525	217
	Total area actually reporting	99.8%	2,636	32	179	544	1,881	31,422	5,922	22,895	2,605
	Estimated total	100.0%	2,640	32	179	545	1,884	31,477	5,933	22,935	2,609
	Rate per 100,000 inhabitants		378.5	4.6	25.7	78.1	270.1	4,512.9	850.6	3,288.2	374.1
Medford, OR M.S.A.											
	Includes Jackson County	198,525									
	City of Medford	71,297	252	1	22	36	193	3,381	456	2,748	177
	Total area actually reporting	99.8%	490	3	55	66	366	6,095	958	4,799	338
	Estimated total	100.0%	491	3	55	66	367	6,109	960	4,810	339
	Rate per 100,000 inhabitants		247.3	1.5	27.7	33.2	184.9	3,077.2	483.6	2,422.9	170.8
Memphis, TN-MS-AR M.S.A.											
	Includes Crittenden County, AR; DeSoto, Marshall, Tate, and Tunica Counties, MS; and Fayette, Shelby, and Tipton Counties, TN	1,273,452									
	City of Memphis	680,828	13,544	147	425	5,311	7,661	56,905	16,450	33,736	6,719
	Total area actually reporting	95.6%	15,960	172	570	5,802	9,416	74,851	21,239	45,314	8,298
	Estimated total	100.0%	16,080	175	589	5,839	9,477	76,570	21,653	46,447	8,470
	Rate per 100,000 inhabitants		1,262.7	13.7	46.3	458.5	744.2	6,012.8	1,700.3	3,647.3	665.1

Table 6. Crime, by Metropolitan Statistical Area, 2006 (*Contd.*)

(Number, percent, rate per 100,000 population.)

Metropolitan statistical area	Counties/principal cities	Popula-tion	Violent crime	Murder and non-negligent man-slaughter	Forcible rape	Robbery	Aggra-vated assault	Property crime	Burglary	Larceny-theft	Motor vehicle theft
Merced, CA M.S.A.											
	Includes Merced County....................	243,883									
	City of Merced	74,431	603	9	22	165	407	3,876	819	2,611	446
	Total area actually reporting	100.0%	1,616	22	81	286	1,227	8,995	2,526	5,250	1,219
	Rate per 100,000 inhabitants		662.6	9.0	33.2	117.3	503.1	3,688.2	1,035.7	2,152.7	499.8
Miami-Fort Lauderdale-Miami Beach, FL M.S.A.											
	Includes Metropolitan Divisions of Fort Lauderdale-Pompano Beach-Deerfield Beach, Miami-Miami Beach-Kendall, and West Palm Beach-Boca Raton-Boynton Beach	5,513,643									
	City of Miami	392,934	5,931	77	101	2,111	3,642	20,288	4,442	11,967	3,879
	City of Fort Lauderdale	170,203	1,683	21	83	832	747	9,937	2,239	6,678	1,020
	City of Pompano Beach	105,936	1,367	10	54	441	862	4,985	1,049	3,398	538
	City of West Palm Beach	99,142	1,174	17	46	574	537	7,332	1,591	4,775	966
	City of Miami Beach	89,408	1,115	4	81	432	598	7,582	1,372	5,357	853
	City of Boca Raton.............................	88,093	238	3	13	72	150	2,951	551	2,232	168
	City of Deerfield Beach	77,636	561	7	23	141	390	2,591	478	1,835	278
	City of Boynton Beach........................	68,013	660	9	8	183	460	3,412	693	2,361	358
	City of Delray Beach..........................	65,849	678	5	22	150	501	3,332	587	2,430	315
	Total area actually reporting	100.0%	43,556	419	1,759	14,131	27,247	240,839	50,611	160,079	30,149
	Rate per 100,000 inhabitants		790.0	7.6	31.9	256.3	494.2	4,368.1	917.9	2,903.3	546.8
Fort Lauderdale-Pompano Beach-Deerfield Beach, FL M.D.											
	Includes Broward County...................	1,807,618									
	Total area actually reporting	100.0%	10,764	87	477	3,685	6,515	64,550	13,218	44,240	7,092
	Rate per 100,000 inhabitants		595.5	4.8	26.4	203.9	360.4	3,571.0	731.2	2,447.4	392.3
Miami-Miami Beach-Kendall, FL M.D.											
	Includes Miami-Dade County............	2,416,083									
	Total area actually reporting	100.0%	23,520	240	822	7,538	14,920	121,826	24,525	80,282	17,019
	Rate per 100,000 inhabitants		973.5	9.9	34.0	312.0	617.5	5,042.3	1,015.1	3,322.8	704.4
West Palm Beach-Boca Raton-Boynton Beach, FL M.D.											
	Includes Palm Beach County	1,289,942									
	Total area actually reporting	100.0%	9,272	92	460	2,908	5,812	54,463	12,868	35,557	6,038
	Rate per 100,000 inhabitants		718.8	7.1	35.7	225.4	450.6	4,222.1	997.6	2,756.5	468.1
Michigan City-La Porte, IN M.S.A.											
	Includes La Porte County...................	111,244									
	City of Michigan City	32,418	142	3	28	63	48	1,787	256	1,388	143
	City of La Porte	21,232	44	0	3	18	23	1,532	184	1,253	95
	Total area actually reporting	92.0%	223	3	37	88	95	4,388	711	3,336	341
	Estimated total....................................	100.0%	250	3	39	97	111	4,728	766	3,593	369
	Rate per 100,000 inhabitants		224.7	2.7	35.1	87.2	99.8	4,250.1	688.6	3,229.8	331.7
Midland, TX M.S.A.											
	Includes Midland County	124,810									
	City of Midland..................................	101,877	373	5	58	76	234	3,705	859	2,614	232
	Total area actually reporting	100.0%	443	5	68	81	289	4,256	1,005	2,997	254
	Rate per 100,000 inhabitants		354.9	4.0	54.5	64.9	231.6	3,410.0	805.2	2,401.2	203.5
Milwaukee-Waukesha-West Allis, WI M.S.A.											
	Includes Milwaukee, Ozaukee, Washington, and Waukesha Counties..	1,518,404									
	City of Milwaukee	581,005	7,698	103	112	3,608	3,875	38,233	5,651	24,343	8,239
	City of Waukesha...............................	67,906	112	1	23	28	60	1,417	309	1,029	79
	City of West Allis...............................	59,014	242	0	0	106	136	2,682	462	2,005	215
	Total area actually reporting	100.0%	8,800	112	216	4,052	4,420	59,620	8,856	41,360	9,404
	Rate per 100,000 inhabitants		579.6	7.4	14.2	266.9	291.1	3,926.5	583.2	2,723.9	619.3

Table 6. Crime, by Metropolitan Statistical Area, 2006 (*Contd.*)

(Number, percent, rate per 100,000 population.)

Metropolitan statistical area	Counties/principal cities	Popula-tion	Violent crime	Murder and non-negligent man-slaughter	Forcible rape	Robbery	Aggra-vated assault	Property crime	Burglary	Larceny-theft	Motor vehicle theft
Minneapolis-St. Paul-Bloomington, MN-WI M.S.A.[4]											
	Includes Anoka, Carver, Chisago, Dakota, Hennepin, Isanti, Ramsey, Scott, Sherburne, Washington, and Wright Counties, MN;[4] and Pierce and St. Croix Counties, WI	3,163,432									
	City of Minneapolis, MN[4]	375,302		57		3,028	2,836	22,561	5,826	13,110	3,625
	City of St. Paul, MN[4]	276,989		17		849	1,403	12,103	3,349	6,616	2,138
	City of Bloominton, MN[4]	81,706		5		59	77	2,892	331	2,398	163
	City of Plymouth, MN[4]	70,167		0		19	26	1,396	265	1,071	60
	City of Eagan, MN[4]	64,090		0		27	28	1,677	261	1,358	58
	City of Eden Prairie, MN[4]	61,054		0		20	37	1,239	146	1,058	35
	City of Minnetonka, MN[4]	50,379		0		8	14	952	148	769	35
	Total area actually reporting	98.0%		109		4,952	6,480	109,687	20,396	78,728	10,563
	Estimated total	100.0%		110		4,984	6,546	111,819	20,704	80,415	10,700
	Rate per 100,000 inhabitants			3.5		157.6	206.9	3,534.7	654.5	2,542.0	338.2
Missoula, MT M.S.A.											
	Includes Missoula County	101,045									
	City of Missoula	63,526	186	0	38	30	118	3,125	331	2,644	150
	Total area actually reporting	100.0%	269	0	50	32	187	3,792	466	3,126	200
	Rate per 100,000 inhabitants		266.2	0.0	49.5	31.7	185.1	3,752.8	461.2	3,093.7	197.9
Mobile, AL M.S.A.											
	Includes Mobile County	405,058									
	City of Mobile[8]	250,152	1,167	34	83	685	365	15,849	3,662	10,857	1,330
	Total area actually reporting	93.9%	1,491	46	112	794	539	19,608	4,760	13,052	1,796
	Estimated total	100.0%	1,594	47	120	833	594	20,591	4,959	13,762	1,870
	Rate per 100,000 inhabitants		393.5	11.6	29.6	205.6	146.6	5,083.5	1,224.3	3,397.5	461.7
Modesto, CA M.S.A.											
	Includes Stanislaus County	510,058									
	City of Modesto	208,875	1,418	11	73	462	872	11,804	1,762	8,018	2,024
	Total area actually reporting	100.0%	3,056	29	151	767	2,109	25,230	5,002	15,586	4,642
	Rate per 100,000 inhabitants		599.1	5.7	29.6	150.4	413.5	4,946.5	980.7	3,055.7	910.1
Monroe, LA M.S.A.											
	Includes Ouachita and Union Parishes	162,215									
	City of Monroe	49,207	425	12	27	71	315	4,592	1,170	3,270	152
	Total area actually reporting	98.8%	830	14	64	127	625	8,584	2,364	5,896	324
	Estimated total	100.0%	846	14	65	130	637	8,696	2,384	5,981	331
	Rate per 100,000 inhabitants		521.5	8.6	40.1	80.1	392.7	5,360.8	1,469.7	3,687.1	204.1
Monroe, MI M.S.A.											
	Includes Monroe County	153,551									
	City of Monroe	21,737	84	0	11	10	63	660	116	520	24
	Total area actually reporting	100.0%	347	1	56	47	243	3,744	867	2,582	295
	Rate per 100,000 inhabitants		226.0	0.7	36.5	30.6	158.3	2,438.3	564.6	1,681.5	192.1
Montgomery, AL M.S.A.											
	Includes Autauga, Elmore, Lowndes, and Montgomery Counties	360,475									
	City of Montgomery	201,937	1,184	27	74	686	397	13,086	3,380	8,579	1,127
	Total area actually reporting	93.7%	1,509	32	112	776	589	16,451	4,231	10,937	1,283
	Estimated total	100.0%	1,561	33	117	790	621	16,978	4,399	11,248	1,331
	Rate per 100,000 inhabitants		433.0	9.2	32.5	219.2	172.3	4,709.9	1,220.3	3,120.3	369.2
Morgantown, WV M.S.A.											
	Includes Monongalia and Preston Counties	114,603									
	City of Morgantown	28,317	113	1	26	29	57	1,013	233	739	41
	Total area actually reporting	96.8%	266	4	41	54	167	2,665	666	1,811	188
	Estimated total	100.0%	275	4	42	56	173	2,783	689	1,898	196
	Rate per 100,000 inhabitants		240.0	3.5	36.6	48.9	151.0	2,428.4	601.2	1,656.2	171.0

[4] The data collection methodology for the offense of forcible rape used by the Minnesota state UCR Program does not comply with national UCR Program guidelines. Consequently, their figures for forcible rape and violent crime (of which forcible rape is a part) are not published in this table.

[8] The population for the city of Mobile, Alabama, includes 56,876 inhabitants from the jurisdiction of the Mobile County Sheriff's Department.

Table 6. Crime, by Metropolitan Statistical Area, 2006 (*Contd.*)

(Number, percent, rate per 100,000 population.)

Metropolitan statistical area	Counties/principal cities	Population	Violent crime	Murder and non-negligent man-slaughter	Forcible rape	Robbery	Aggra-vated assault	Property crime	Burglary	Larceny-theft	Motor vehicle theft
Morristown, TN M.S.A.											
	Includes Grainger, Hamblen, and Jefferson Counties	132,236									
	City of Morristown	26,520	251	1	19	30	201	1,685	175	1,396	114
	Total area actually reporting	100.0%	571	2	33	58	478	4,461	834	3,277	350
	Rate per 100,000 inhabitants		431.8	1.5	25.0	43.9	361.5	3,373.5	630.7	2,478.1	264.7
Mount Vernon-Anacortes, WA M.S.A.											
	Includes Skagit County	115,116									
	City of Mount Vernon	29,774	76	0	19	24	33	2,154	265	1,709	180
	City of Anacortes	16,359	30	0	6	5	19	690	111	555	24
	Total area actually reporting	100.0%	259	2	71	60	126	6,689	1,150	5,010	529
	Rate per 100,000 inhabitants		225.0	1.7	61.7	52.1	109.5	5,810.7	999.0	4,352.1	459.5
Muncie, IN M.S.A.											
	Includes Delaware County	117,133									
	City of Muncie	66,602	340	3	45	95	197	3,111	633	2,315	163
	Total area actually reporting	100.0%	403	4	66	100	233	4,108	847	3,011	250
	Rate per 100,000 inhabitants		344.1	3.4	56.3	85.4	198.9	3,507.1	723.1	2,570.6	213.4
Muskegon-Norton Shores, MI M.S.A.											
	Includes Muskegon County	175,117									
	City of Muskegon	39,820	447	1	52	101	293	2,671	453	2,048	170
	City of Norton Shores	23,421	52	0	10	17	25	1,030	140	842	48
	Total area actually reporting	100.0%	961	4	145	194	618	8,520	1,378	6,671	471
	Rate per 100,000 inhabitants		548.8	2.3	82.8	110.8	352.9	4,865.3	786.9	3,809.5	269.0
Myrtle Beach-Conway-North Myrtle Beach, SC M.S.A.											
	Includes Horry County	230,522									
	City of Myrtle Beach	27,007	555	8	67	203	277	4,887	778	3,590	519
	City of Conway	13,651	204	3	6	41	154	1,102	210	838	54
	City of North Myrtle Beach	14,315	60	0	12	19	29	1,313	222	1,049	42
	Total area actually reporting	100.0%	1,958	25	164	444	1,325	15,298	3,130	10,541	1,627
	Rate per 100,000 inhabitants		849.4	10.8	71.1	192.6	574.8	6,636.2	1,357.8	4,572.7	705.8
Napa, CA M.S.A.		133,960									
	Includes Napa County										
	City of Napa	75,455	336	1	21	70	244	2,164	401	1,563	200
	Total area actually reporting	100.0%	463	2	36	84	341	3,233	708	2,169	356
	Rate per 100,000 inhabitants		345.6	1.5	26.9	62.7	254.6	2,413.4	528.5	1,619.1	265.8
Naples-Marco Island, FL M.S.A.											
	Includes Collier County	312,424									
	City of Naples	22,075	53	1	6	8	38	859	118	714	27
	City of Marco Island	16,381	15	0	1	2	12	207	36	168	3
	Total area actually reporting	100.0%	1,377	7	82	291	997	6,199	1,456	4,379	364
	Rate per 100,000 inhabitants		440.7	2.2	26.2	93.1	319.1	1,984.2	466.0	1,401.6	116.5
Nashville-Davidson Murfreesboro-Franklin, TN M.S.A.											
	Includes Cannon, Cheatham, Davidson, Dickson, Hickman, Macon, Robertson, Rutherford, Smith, Sumner, Trousdale, Williamson, and Wilson Counties	1,440,638									
	City of Nashville	560,813	8,565	80	320	2,425	5,740	32,625	6,370	23,234	3,021
	City of Murfreesboro	87,897	706	6	39	179	482	4,324	895	3,144	285
	City of Franklin	53,989	94	1	11	17	65	954	127	783	44
	Total area actually reporting	100.0%	12,357	104	593	2,947	8,713	55,350	11,413	39,143	4,794
	Rate per 100,000 inhabitants		857.7	7.2	41.2	204.6	604.8	3,842.0	792.2	2,717.1	332.8

Table 6. Crime, by Metropolitan Statistical Area, 2006 (*Contd.*)

(Number, percent, rate per 100,000 population.)

Metropolitan statistical area	Counties/principal cities	Popula-tion	Violent crime	Murder and non-negligent man-slaughter	Forcible rape	Robbery	Aggra-vated assault	Property crime	Burglary	Larceny-theft	Motor vehicle theft
New Orleans-Metairie-Kenner, LA M.S.A.											
	Includes Jefferson, Orleans, Plaquemines, St. Bernard, St. Charles, St. John the Baptist, and St. Tammany Parishes	1,250,582									
	City of New Orleans	431,153	2,255	162	87	761	1,245	12,178	4,087	5,228	2,863
	City of Kenner	66,266	370	9	17	114	230	2,698	555	1,701	442
	Total area actually reporting	94.9%	6,620	266	278	1,674	4,402	39,499	10,864	22,715	5,920
	Estimated total	100.0%	6,953	272	299	1,727	4,655	41,679	11,415	24,145	6,119
	Rate per 100,000 inhabitants		556.0	21.7	23.9	138.1	372.2	3,332.8	912.8	1,930.7	489.3
New York-Northern New Jersey-Long Island, NY-NJ-PA M.S.A.											
	Includes Metropolitan Divisions of Edison, NJ; Nassau-Suffolk County, NY; Newark-Union, NJ-PA; and New York-Wayne-White Plains, NY-NJ	18,785,139									
	City of New York, NY	8,165,001	52,086	596	1,071	23,511	26,908	153,436	22,137	115,363	15,936
	City of Newark, NJ	280,877	2,839	105	87	1,288	1,359	11,456	1,982	4,377	5,097
	City of Edison Township, NJ	100,575	295	1	15	86	193	2,320	368	1,684	268
	City of White Plains, NY	56,885	157	1	6	48	102	1,181	69	1,077	35
	City of Union Township, NJ	55,368	152	2	2	69	79	1,582	231	1,144	207
	City of Wayne Township, NJ	55,192	39	0	2	21	16	1,255	174	1,003	78
	Total area actually reporting	99.8%	82,273	978	2,101	37,098	42,096	356,978	58,098	257,798	41,082
	Estimated total	100.0%	82,359	978	2,106	37,129	42,146	357,850	58,230	258,495	41,125
	Rate per 100,000 inhabitants		438.4	5.2	11.2	197.7	224.4	1,905.0	310.0	1,376.1	218.9
Edison, NJ M.D.											
	Includes Middlesex, Monmouth, Ocean, and Somerset Counties	2,305,462									
	Total area actually reporting	100.0%	4,252	47	233	1,597	2,375	43,830	8,432	32,482	2,916
	Rate per 100,000 inhabitants		184.4	2.0	10.1	69.3	103.0	1,901.1	365.7	1,408.9	126.5
Nassau-Suffolk, NY M.D.											
	Includes Nassau and Suffolk Counties	2,815,582									
	Total area actually reporting	99.9%	5,679	59	200	2,408	3,012	48,132	6,978	37,087	4,067
	Estimated total	100.0%	5,682	59	200	2,409	3,014	48,162	6,983	37,111	4,068
	Rate per 100,000 inhabitants		201.8	2.1	7.1	85.6	107.0	1,710.6	248.0	1,318.1	144.5
Newark-Union, NJ-PA M.D.											
	Includes Essex, Hunterdon, Morris, Sussex, and Union Counties, NJ and Pike County, PA	2,154,623									
	Total area actually reporting	99.8%	8,936	188	296	4,268	4,184	50,400	9,512	29,736	11,152
	Estimated total	100.0%	8,948	188	297	4,271	4,192	50,507	9,528	29,820	11,159
	Rate per 100,000 inhabitants		415.3	8.7	13.8	198.2	194.6	2,344.1	442.2	1,384.0	517.9
New York-White Plains-Wayne, NY-NJ M.D.											
	Includes Bergen, Hudson, and Pas-saic Counties, NJ and Bronx, Kings, New York, Putnam, Queens, Rich-mond, Rockland, and Westchester Counties, NY	11,509,472									
	Total area actually reporting	99.7%	63,406	684	1,372	28,825	32,525	214,616	33,176	158,493	22,947
	Estimated total	100.0%	63,477	684	1,376	28,852	32,565	215,351	33,287	159,082	22,982
	Rate per 100,000 inhabitants		551.5	5.9	12.0	250.7	282.9	1,871.1	289.2	1,382.2	199.7
Niles-Benton Harbor, MI M.S.A.											
	Includes Berrien County	162,206									
	City of Niles	11,709	97	0	14	24	59	523	99	397	27
	City of Benton Harbor	10,722	174	2	9	10	153	384	136	209	39
	Total area actually reporting	97.3%	760	8	108	104	540	5,139	1,016	3,876	247
	Estimated total	100.0%	774	8	110	107	549	5,273	1,040	3,970	263
	Rate per 100,000 inhabitants		477.2	4.9	67.8	66.0	338.5	3,250.8	641.2	2,447.5	162.1

Table 6. Crime, by Metropolitan Statistical Area, 2006 *(Contd.)*

(Number, percent, rate per 100,000 population.)

Metropolitan statistical area	Counties/principal cities	Popula-tion	Violent crime	Murder and non-negligent man-slaughter	Forcible rape	Robbery	Aggra-vated assault	Property crime	Burglary	Larceny-theft	Motor vehicle theft
Ocala, FL M.S.A.											
	Includes Marion County	308,560									
	City of Ocala	50,584	718	3	43	179	493	3,283	647	2,455	181
	Total area actually reporting	100.0%	2,326	15	177	277	1,857	8,064	2,118	5,376	570
	Rate per 100,000 inhabitants		753.8	4.9	57.4	89.8	601.8	2,613.4	686.4	1,742.3	184.7
Ocean City, NJ M.S.A.											
	Includes Cape May County	99,362									
	City of Ocean City	15,342	23	0	0	4	19	1,042	182	852	8
	Total area actually reporting	100.0%	344	1	29	79	235	4,709	888	3,696	125
	Rate per 100,000 inhabitants		346.2	1.0	29.2	79.5	236.5	4,739.2	893.7	3,719.7	125.8
Odessa, TX M.S.A.											
	Includes Ector County	128,891									
	City of Odessa	96,197	614	2	12	88	512	3,654	774	2,624	256
	Total area actually reporting	100.0%	673	3	14	96	560	4,721	1,004	3,405	312
	Rate per 100,000 inhabitants		522.1	2.3	10.9	74.5	434.5	3,662.8	779.0	2,641.8	242.1
Ogden-Clearfield, UT M.S.A.											
	Includes Davis, Morgan, and Weber Counties	502,708									
	City of Ogden	80,861	415	2	37	123	253	5,029	820	3,773	436
	City of Clearfield	28,306	56	2	9	6	39	918	135	736	47
	Total area actually reporting	98.4%	848	9	146	181	512	14,631	2,399	11,345	887
	Estimated total	100.0%	861	9	148	183	521	14,851	2,442	11,501	908
	Rate per 100,000 inhabitants		171.3	1.8	29.4	36.4	103.6	2,954.2	485.8	2,287.8	180.6
Oklahoma City, OK M.S.A.											
	Includes Canadian, Cleveland, Grady, Lincoln, Logan, McClain, and Oklahoma Counties	1,167,026									
	City of Oklahoma City	536,016	4,301	55	327	1,179	2,740	34,292	9,304	20,169	4,819
	Total area actually reporting	100.0%	6,015	82	543	1,452	3,938	53,838	14,169	33,305	6,364
	Rate per 100,000 inhabitants		515.4	7.0	46.5	124.4	337.4	4,613.3	1,214.1	2,853.8	545.3
Olympia, WA M.S.A.											
	Includes Thurston County	232,799									
	City of Olympia	44,872	149	0	28	38	83	2,149	282	1,661	206
	Total area actually reporting	100.0%	596	4	75	112	405	7,796	1,686	5,426	684
	Rate per 100,000 inhabitants		256.0	1.7	32.2	48.1	174.0	3,348.8	724.2	2,330.8	293.8
Omaha-Council Bluffs, NE-IA M.S.A.											
	Includes Harrison, Mills, and Pot-tawattamie Counties, IA and Cass, Douglas, Sarpy, Saunders, and Washington Counties, NE	817,568									
	City of Omaha, NE	416,770	2,505	33	187	848	1,437	21,787	3,172	15,172	3,443
	City of Council Bluffs, IA	59,884	539	2	68	72	397	4,648	878	3,137	633
	Total area actually reporting	100.0%	3,403	39	307	965	2,092	33,351	5,256	23,550	4,545
	Rate per 100,000 inhabitants		416.2	4.8	37.6	118.0	255.9	4,079.3	642.9	2,880.5	555.9
Orlando-Kissim-mee, FL M.S.A.											
	Includes Lake, Orange, Osceola, and Seminole Counties	1,965,859									
	City of Orlando	216,819	4,300	49	163	1,528	2,560	18,318	3,662	12,320	2,336
	City of Kissimmee	60,365	476	7	14	134	321	2,349	665	1,458	226
	Total area actually reporting	99.9%	17,273	160	791	5,176	11,146	84,874	21,586	52,896	10,392
	Estimated total	100.0%	17,284	160	792	5,179	11,153	84,945	21,602	52,944	10,399
	Rate per 100,000 inhabitants		879.2	8.1	40.3	263.4	567.3	4,321.0	1,098.9	2,693.2	529.0
Oshkosh-Neenah, WI M.S.A.											
	Includes Winnebago County	160,067									
	City of Oshkosh	63,718	197	4	8	14	171	2,143	313	1,748	82
	City of Neenah	24,686	35	0	6	1	28	486	93	377	16
	Total area actually reporting	100.0%	329	4	23	20	282	3,698	627	2,922	149
	Rate per 100,000 inhabitants		205.5	2.5	14.4	12.5	176.2	2,310.3	391.7	1,825.5	93.1

Table 6. Crime, by Metropolitan Statistical Area, 2006 *(Contd.)*

(Number, percent, rate per 100,000 population.)

Metropolitan statistical area	Counties/principal cities	Popula-tion	Violent crime	Murder and non-negligent man-slaughter	Forcible rape	Robbery	Aggra-vated assault	Property crime	Burglary	Larceny-theft	Motor vehicle theft
Oxnard-Thousand Oaks-Ventura, CA M.S.A.											
	Includes Ventura County	803,276									
	City of Oxnard	185,282	841	13	34	418	376	4,376	946	2,816	614
	City of Thousand Oaks	125,479	182	0	13	41	128	1,794	367	1,296	131
	City of Ventura	104,954	335	1	24	130	180	3,686	730	2,604	352
	City of Camarillo	62,131	114	2	10	28	74	1,119	231	789	99
	Total area actually reporting	100.0%	2,223	29	128	802	1,264	16,590	3,516	11,314	1,760
	Rate per 100,000 inhabitants		276.7	3.6	15.9	99.8	157.4	2,065.3	437.7	1,408.5	219.1
Palm Bay-Melbourne-Titus-ville, FL M.S.A.											
	Includes Brevard County	540,209									
	City of Palm Bay	94,399	601	1	66	72	462	3,141	1,101	1,754	286
	City of Melbourne	77,939	884	2	30	211	641	4,010	928	2,840	242
	City of Titusville	44,505	356	7	26	99	224	1,622	386	1,064	172
	Total area actually reporting	100.0%	3,622	22	223	635	2,742	18,282	4,735	12,270	1,277
	Rate per 100,000 inhabitants		670.5	4.1	41.3	117.5	507.6	3,384.2	876.5	2,271.3	236.4
Palm Coast, FL M.S.A.											
	Includes Flagler County	77,699									
	Total area actually reporting	98.1%	182	4	8	26	144	1,883	446	1,289	148
	Estimated total	100.0%	191	4	8	29	150	1,946	460	1,332	154
	Rate per 100,000 inhabitants		245.8	5.1	10.3	37.3	193.1	2,504.5	592.0	1,714.3	198.2
Panama City-Lynn Haven, FL M.S.A.											
	Includes Bay County	164,283									
	City of Panama City	37,815	401	0	34	98	269	2,130	369	1,631	130
	City of Lynn Haven	15,941	267	0	1	5	261	361	98	241	22
	Total area actually reporting	100.0%	1,300	5	97	184	1,014	6,485	1,386	4,720	379
	Rate per 100,000 inhabitants		791.3	3.0	59.0	112.0	617.2	3,947.5	843.7	2,873.1	230.7
Pascagoula, MS M.S.A.											
	Includes George and Jackson Counties	156,631									
	City of Pascagoula	25,082	116	2	26	74	14	2,236	798	1,113	325
	Total area actually reporting	100.0%	388	9	55	155	169	6,611	2,040	3,570	1,001
	Rate per 100,000 inhabitants		247.7	5.7	35.1	99.0	107.9	4,220.7	1,302.4	2,279.2	639.1
Pensacola-Ferry Pass-Brent, FL M.S.A.											
	Includes Escambia and Santa Rosa Counties	447,295									
	City of Pensacola	54,967	506	1	30	118	357	2,913	599	2,153	161
	Total area actually reporting	100.0%	2,808	14	200	613	1,981	15,447	3,994	10,272	1,181
	Rate per 100,000 inhabitants		627.8	3.1	44.7	137.0	442.9	3,453.4	892.9	2,296.5	264.0
Philadelphia-Camden-Wilmington, PA-NJ-DE-MD M.S.A.											
	Includes Metropolitan Divisions of Camden, NJ; Philadelphia, PA; and Wilmington, DE-MD-NJ	5,834,113									
	City of Philadelphia, PA	1,464,576	22,883	406	960	10,971	10,546	62,612	11,542	39,413	11,657
	City of Camden, NJ	80,071	1,693	32	66	773	822	4,787	1,179	2,430	1,178
	City of Wilmington, DE	73,645	1,353	18	48	565	722	4,090	972	2,345	773
	Total area actually reporting	99.1%	38,328	553	1,882	16,203	19,690	168,226	30,485	116,796	20,945
	Estimated total	100.0%	38,459	554	1,890	16,240	19,775	169,390	30,658	117,710	21,022
	Rate per 100,000 inhabitants		659.2	9.5	32.4	278.4	339.0	2,903.4	525.5	2,017.6	360.3
Camden, NJ M.D.											
	Includes Burlington, Camden, and Gloucester Counties	1,246,850									
	Total area actually reporting	100.0%	4,387	58	305	1,674	2,350	33,126	6,618	23,515	2,993
	Rate per 100,000 inhabitants		351.8	4.7	24.5	134.3	188.5	2,656.8	530.8	1,886.0	240.0

Table 6. Crime, by Metropolitan Statistical Area, 2006 (*Contd.*)

(Number, percent, rate per 100,000 population.)

Metropolitan statistical area	Counties/principal cities	Popula-tion	Violent crime	Murder and non-negligent man-slaughter	Forcible rape	Robbery	Aggra-vated assault	Property crime	Burglary	Larceny-theft	Motor vehicle theft
Philadelphia, PA M.D.											
	Includes Bucks, Chester, Delaware, Montgomery, and Philadelphia Counties	3,893,625									
	Total area actually reporting	98.6%	29,329	457	1,356	12,922	14,594	111,402	18,778	77,280	15,344
	Estimated total	100.0%	29,460	458	1,364	12,959	14,679	112,566	18,951	78,194	15,421
	Rate per 100,000 inhabitants		756.6	11.8	35.0	332.8	377.0	2,891.0	486.7	2,008.3	396.1
Wilmington, DE-MD-NJ M.D.											
	Includes New Castle County, DE; Cecil County, MD; and Salem County, NJ	693,638									
	Total area actually reporting	100.0%	4,612	38	221	1,607	2,746	23,698	5,089	16,001	2,608
	Rate per 100,000 inhabitants		664.9	5.5	31.9	231.7	395.9	3,416.5	733.7	2,306.8	376.0
Phoenix-Mesa-Scottsdale, AZ M.S.A.											
	Includes Maricopa and Pinal Counties	4,012,817									
	City of Phoenix	1,517,443	11,194	234	550	4,363	6,047	90,050	16,150	49,811	24,089
	City of Mesa	459,705	2,003	26	203	508	1,266	21,304	3,283	14,367	3,654
	City of Scottsdale	234,652	505	5	65	153	282	8,315	1,721	5,476	1,118
	City of Tempe	167,303	1,094	5	71	426	592	12,589	1,795	8,374	2,420
	Total area actually reporting	98.3%	20,194	347	1,251	6,656	11,940	192,739	38,533	113,531	40,675
	Estimated total	100.0%	20,461	349	1,269	6,719	12,124	195,751	39,272	115,375	41,104
	Rate per 100,000 inhabitants		509.9	8.7	31.6	167.4	302.1	4,878.1	978.7	2,875.2	1,024.3
Pine Bluff, AR M.S.A.											
	Includes Cleveland, Jefferson, and Lincoln Counties	106,062									
	City of Pine Bluff	53,294	798	12	36	203	547	3,980	1,512	2,053	415
	Total area actually reporting	100.0%	919	15	49	212	643	5,122	2,039	2,576	507
	Rate per 100,000 inhabitants		866.5	14.1	46.2	199.9	606.2	4,829.3	1,922.5	2,428.8	478.0
Pittsburgh, PA M.S.A.											
	Includes Allegheny, Armstrong, Beaver, Butler, Fayette, Washington, and Westmoreland Counties	2,388,185									
	City of Pittsburgh	324,604	3,473	56	102	1,722	1,593	15,236	3,713	9,658	1,865
	Total area actually reporting	89.7%	7,997	101	414	2,946	4,536	50,473	10,456	35,502	4,515
	Estimated total	100.0%	8,594	106	452	3,114	4,922	55,754	11,241	39,650	4,863
	Rate per 100,000 inhabitants		359.9	4.4	18.9	130.4	206.1	2,334.6	470.7	1,660.3	203.6
Pittsfield, MA M.S.A.											
	Includes Berkshire County	132,660									
	City of Pittsfield	44,124	343	1	40	36	266	1,240	348	804	88
	Total area actually reporting	94.0%	573	2	68	40	463	2,781	832	1,782	167
	Estimated total	100.0%	595	2	70	45	478	2,939	871	1,886	182
	Rate per 100,000 inhabitants		448.5	1.5	52.8	33.9	360.3	2,215.4	656.6	1,421.7	137.2
Pocatello, ID M.S.A.											
	Includes Bannock and Power Counties	88,155									
	City of Pocatello	54,768	181	0	32	15	134	1,580	207	1,310	63
	Total area actually reporting	100.0%	283	1	42	16	224	2,441	325	2,012	104
	Rate per 100,000 inhabitants		321.0	1.1	47.6	18.1	254.1	2,769.0	368.7	2,282.3	118.0
Portland-South Portland-Bidd-eford, ME M.S.A.											
	Includes Cumberland, Sagadahoc, and York Counties	514,252									
	City of Portland	63,892	276	3	36	149	88	3,441	539	2,709	193
	City of South Portland	23,743	51	1	8	13	29	930	92	809	29
	City of Biddeford	22,073	53	0	19	14	20	877	152	696	29
	Total area actually reporting	100.0%	714	5	141	245	323	13,495	2,693	10,179	623
	Rate per 100,000 inhabitants		138.8	1.0	27.4	47.6	62.8	2,624.2	523.7	1,979.4	121.1

Table 6. Crime, by Metropolitan Statistical Area, 2006 (*Contd.*)

(Number, percent, rate per 100,000 population.)

Metropolitan statistical area	Counties/principal cities	Popula-tion	Violent crime	Murder and non-negligent man-slaughter	Forcible rape	Robbery	Aggra-vated assault	Property crime	Burglary	Larceny-theft	Motor vehicle theft
Portland-Vancou-ver-Beaverton, OR-WA M.S.A.											
	Includes Clackamas, Columbia, Multnomah, Washington, and Yamhill Counties, OR and Clark and Skamania Counties, WA	2,130,553									
	City of Portland, OR	542,174	3,872	20	293	1,297	2,262	31,996	5,485	22,033	4,478
	City of Vancouver, WA	160,199	598	4	103	139	352	6,527	1,001	4,584	942
	City of Beaverton, OR	87,181	208	1	18	30	159	2,205	311	1,634	260
	City of Hillsboro, OR	85,919	192	2	34	77	79	2,752	299	2,204	249
	Total area actually reporting	98.9%	6,864	48	840	2,092	3,884	77,124	13,076	54,499	9,549
	Estimated total	100.0%	6,898	48	845	2,099	3,906	77,650	13,190	54,858	9,602
	Rate per 100,000 inhabitants		323.8	2.3	39.7	98.5	183.3	3,644.6	619.1	2,574.8	450.7
Port St. Lucie, FL M.S.A.											
	Includes Martin and St. Lucie Counties	387,459									
	City of Port St. Lucie	133,913	340	7	36	34	263	3,563	1,065	2,355	143
	Total area actually reporting	100.0%	2,098	19	114	462	1,503	12,311	3,222	8,257	832
	Rate per 100,000 inhabitants		541.5	4.9	29.4	119.2	387.9	3,177.4	831.6	2,131.1	214.7
Poughkeepsie-Newburgh-Middle-town, NY M.S.A.											
	Includes Dutchess and Orange Counties	669,529									
	City of Poughkeepsie	30,436	417	4	13	173	227	1,122	242	792	88
	City of Newburgh	28,624	386	1	16	134	235	1,080	264	750	66
	City of Middletown	26,137	177	2	13	94	68	946	129	781	36
	Total area actually reporting	97.9%	1,821	16	100	604	1,101	12,515	2,107	9,853	555
	Estimated total	100.0%	1,847	16	101	614	1,116	12,791	2,149	10,074	568
	Rate per 100,000 inhabitants		275.9	2.4	15.1	91.7	166.7	1,910.4	321.0	1,504.6	84.8
Prescott, AZ M.S.A.											
	Includes Yavapai County	206,296									
	City of Prescott	41,903	181	3	12	32	134	1,541	318	1,133	90
	Total area actually reporting	99.8%	881	10	47	56	768	5,337	1,112	3,807	418
	Estimated total	100.0%	882	10	47	56	769	5,352	1,116	3,816	420
	Rate per 100,000 inhabitants		427.5	4.8	22.8	27.1	372.8	2,594.3	541.0	1,849.8	203.6
Provo-Orem, UT M.S.A.											
	Includes Juab and Utah Counties	467,608									
	City of Provo	117,156	169	2	38	24	105	2,859	541	2,121	197
	City of Orem	92,637	60	1	16	18	25	2,564	269	2,152	143
	Total area actually reporting	99.1%	430	3	108	62	257	11,567	2,153	8,787	627
	Estimated total	100.0%	437	3	109	63	262	11,680	2,175	8,867	638
	Rate per 100,000 inhabitants		93.5	0.6	23.3	13.5	56.0	2,497.8	465.1	1,896.2	136.4
Pueblo, CO M.S.A.											
	Includes Pueblo County	154,183									
	City of Pueblo	105,452	628	6	49	170	403	6,317	1,453	4,409	455
	Total area actually reporting	100.0%	674	6	50	178	440	7,888	1,791	5,580	517
	Rate per 100,000 inhabitants		437.1	3.9	32.4	115.4	285.4	5,116.0	1,161.6	3,619.1	335.3
Punta Gorda, FL M.S.A.											
	Includes Charlotte County	160,193									
	City of Punta Gorda	17,400	46	0	2	5	39	444	158	264	22
	Total area actually reporting	100.0%	739	2	15	95	627	5,454	1,343	3,754	357
	Rate per 100,000 inhabitants		461.3	1.2	9.4	59.3	391.4	3,404.6	838.4	2,343.4	222.9
Racine, WI M.S.A.											
	Includes Racine County	196,426									
	City of Racine	79,683	475	7	16	245	207	4,594	1,113	3,116	365
	Total area actually reporting	100.0%	533	8	21	265	239	6,809	1,399	4,945	465
	Rate per 100,000 inhabitants		271.3	4.1	10.7	134.9	121.7	3,466.4	712.2	2,517.5	236.7

Table 6. Crime, by Metropolitan Statistical Area, 2006 (*Contd.*)

(Number, percent, rate per 100,000 population.)

Metropolitan statistical area	Counties/principal cities	Popula-tion	Violent crime	Murder and non-negligent man-slaughter	Forcible rape	Robbery	Aggra-vated assault	Property crime	Burglary	Larceny-theft	Motor vehicle theft
Raleigh-Cary, NC M.S.A.											
	Includes Franklin, Johnston, and Wake Counties	968,631									
	City of Raleigh	348,345	2,223	19	97	782	1,325	12,650	2,978	8,666	1,006
	City of Cary	108,563	131	0	14	42	75	2,189	554	1,520	115
	Total area actually reporting	99.7%	3,471	37	202	1,075	2,157	28,281	7,490	18,752	2,039
	Estimated total	100.0%	3,485	37	203	1,079	2,166	28,434	7,527	18,860	2,047
	Rate per 100,000 inhabitants		359.8	3.8	21.0	111.4	223.6	2,935.5	777.1	1,947.1	211.3
Rapid City, SD M.S.A.											
	Includes Meade and Pennington Counties	119,115									
	City of Rapid City	62,647	232	0	56	38	138	2,190	407	1,679	104
	Total area actually reporting	100.0%	321	0	96	38	187	2,905	590	2,168	147
	Rate per 100,000 inhabitants		269.5	0.0	80.6	31.9	157.0	2,438.8	495.3	1,820.1	123.4
Reading, PA M.S.A.											
	Includes Berks County	396,665									
	City of Reading	80,927	1,001	10	44	465	482	4,637	1,128	2,288	1,221
	Total area actually reporting	95.3%	1,459	12	80	557	810	9,944	1,922	6,257	1,765
	Estimated total	100.0%	1,504	12	83	570	839	10,341	1,981	6,569	1,791
	Rate per 100,000 inhabitants		379.2	3.0	20.9	143.7	211.5	2,607.0	499.4	1,656.1	451.5
Redding, CA M.S.A.											
	Includes Shasta County	181,524									
	City of Redding	90,448	388	2	72	66	248	3,389	719	2,174	496
	Total area actually reporting	100.0%	648	8	94	85	461	4,986	1,202	2,964	820
	Rate per 100,000 inhabitants		357.0	4.4	51.8	46.8	254.0	2,746.7	662.2	1,632.8	451.7
Reno-Sparks, NV M.S.A.											
	Includes Storey and Washoe Counties	407,115									
	City of Reno	210,354	1,478	23	100	523	832	10,797	2,105	7,061	1,631
	City of Sparks	84,794	380	3	40	124	213	3,452	893	2,104	455
	Total area actually reporting	100.0%	2,075	30	141	671	1,233	16,337	3,621	10,395	2,321
	Rate per 100,000 inhabitants		509.7	7.4	34.6	164.8	302.9	4,012.9	889.4	2,553.3	570.1
Richmond, VA M.S.A.											
	Includes Amelia, Caroline, Charles City, Chesterfield, Cumberland, Dinwiddie, Goochland, Hanover, Henrico, King and Queen, King William, Louisa, New Kent, Powhatan, Prince George, and Sussex Counties and Colonial Heights, Hopewell, Petersburg, and Richmond Cities	1,187,370									
	City of Richmond	195,708	2,041	76	76	987	902	10,092	2,284	6,351	1,457
	Total area actually reporting	99.9%	4,482	117	279	1,957	2,129	35,209	6,773	25,265	3,171
	Estimated total	100.0%	4,489	117	280	1,959	2,133	35,264	6,781	25,308	3,175
	Rate per 100,000 inhabitants		378.1	9.9	23.6	165.0	179.6	2,969.9	571.1	2,131.4	267.4
Riverside-San Bernardino-Ontario, CA M.S.A.											
	Includes Riverside and San Bernardino Counties	3,945,166									
	City of Riverside	292,698	2,014	11	83	814	1,106	12,267	2,372	7,471	2,424
	City of San Bernardino	200,338	2,017	46	50	904	1,017	9,760	2,135	4,708	2,917
	City of Ontario	174,234	1,011	13	74	418	506	6,337	967	3,592	1,778
	City of Victorville	92,086	560	8	26	219	307	4,157	1,173	2,218	766
	City of Temecula	86,572	277	0	13	57	207	2,820	674	1,789	357
	City of Chino	78,277	228	0	8	108	112	2,390	530	1,426	434
	City of Redlands	70,625	379	3	22	114	240	2,537	501	1,610	426
	City of Hemet	68,676	520	6	26	170	318	3,207	947	1,835	425
	City of Colton	51,812	344	5	13	132	194	1,743	477	847	419
	Total area actually reporting	100.0%	19,301	271	1,054	6,601	11,375	135,378	33,166	73,633	28,579
	Rate per 100,000 inhabitants		489.2	6.9	26.7	167.3	288.3	3,431.5	840.7	1,866.4	724.4

Table 6. Crime, by Metropolitan Statistical Area, 2006 (*Contd.*)

(Number, percent, rate per 100,000 population.)

Metropolitan statistical area	Counties/principal cities	Population	Violent crime	Murder and non-negligent man-slaughter	Forcible rape	Robbery	Aggra-vated assault	Property crime	Burglary	Larceny-theft	Motor vehicle theft
Roanoke, VA M.S.A.											
	Includes Botetourt, Craig, Franklin, and Roanoke Counties and Roanoke and Salem Cities	295,903									
	City of Roanoke.................................	93,554	953	12	60	220	661	5,295	978	3,887	430
	Total area actually reporting	100.0%	1,243	14	96	263	870	8,450	1,515	6,319	616
	Rate per 100,000 inhabitants..............		420.1	4.7	32.4	88.9	294.0	2,855.7	512.0	2,135.5	208.2
Rochester, MN M.S.A.[4]											
	Includes Dodge, Olmsted, and Wabasha Counties	178,166									
	City of Rochester[4]	95,585		2		81	152	2,525	486	1,892	147
	Total area actually reporting	91.4%		2		85	175	3,542	757	2,564	221
	Estimated total................................	100.0%		2		88	187	3,879	820	2,814	245
	Rate per 100,000 inhabitants..............			1.1		49.4	105.0	2,177.2	460.2	1,579.4	137.5
Rochester, NY M.S.A.											
	Includes Livingston, Monroe, Ontario, Orleans, and Wayne Counties.....................	1,041,811									
	City of Rochester	211,656	2,666	49	92	1,332	1,193	12,999	2,673	7,913	2,413
	Total area actually reporting	98.4%	3,732	56	237	1,614	1,825	30,763	5,534	21,986	3,243
	Estimated total................................	100.0%	3,764	56	239	1,626	1,843	31,094	5,584	22,251	3,259
	Rate per 100,000 inhabitants..............		361.3	5.4	22.9	156.1	176.9	2,984.6	536.0	2,135.8	312.8
Rocky Mount, NC M.S.A.											
	Includes Edgecombe and Nash County..	148,410									
	City of Rocky Mount	57,756	577	12	22	225	318	5,617	1,696	3,535	386
	Total area actually reporting	100.0%	821	18	35	283	485	7,908	2,492	4,834	582
	Rate per 100,000 inhabitants..............		553.2	12.1	23.6	190.7	326.8	5,328.5	1,679.1	3,257.2	392.2
Rome, GA M.S.A.											
	Includes Floyd County.......................	97,223									
	City of Rome.....................................	36,966	309	1	19	53	236	2,354	433	1,798	123
	Total area actually reporting	100.0%	527	4	36	64	423	4,018	788	2,908	322
	Rate per 100,000 inhabitants..............		542.1	4.1	37.0	65.8	435.1	4,132.8	810.5	2,991.1	331.2
Sacramento–Arden-Arcade–Roseville, CA M.S.A.											
	Includes El Dorado, Placer, Sacramento, and Yolo Counties	2,060,675									
	City of Sacramento............................	460,552	5,556	57	196	2,188	3,115	26,112	6,175	12,762	7,175
	City of Roseville	106,894	378	3	24	134	217	3,884	588	2,722	574
	City of Folsom...................................	66,202	97	0	11	36	50	1,639	286	1,189	164
	City of Woodland..............................	51,479	128	0	15	44	69	1,793	382	1,164	247
	Total area actually reporting	100.0%	13,098	112	653	4,377	7,956	80,995	19,181	43,274	18,540
	Rate per 100,000 inhabitants..............		635.6	5.4	31.7	212.4	386.1	3,930.5	930.8	2,100.0	899.7
Saginaw-Saginaw Township North, MI M.S.A.											
	Includes Saginaw County....................	207,837									
	City of Saginaw	58,216	1,738	24	79	271	1,364	2,752	1,369	1,043	340
	Total area actually reporting	100.0%	2,265	28	158	351	1,728	7,075	2,348	4,099	628
	Rate per 100,000 inhabitants..............		1,089.8	13.5	76.0	168.9	831.4	3,404.1	1,129.7	1,972.2	302.2
Salem, OR M.S.A.											
	Includes Marion and Polk Counties...................................	381,718									
	City of Salem	151,190	691	9	74	129	479	8,267	1,073	6,363	831
	Total area actually reporting	100.0%	1,074	14	128	205	727	15,210	2,192	11,525	1,493
	Rate per 100,000 inhabitants..............		281.4	3.7	33.5	53.7	190.5	3,984.6	574.2	3,019.2	391.1
Salinas, CA M.S.A.											
	Includes Monterey County.................	415,815									
	City of Salinas	147,750	1,118	7	45	383	683	6,023	907	3,718	1,398
	Total area actually reporting	100.0%	2,014	15	116	599	1,284	13,118	2,712	8,204	2,202
	Rate per 100,000 inhabitants..............		484.4	3.6	27.9	144.1	308.8	3,154.8	652.2	1,973.0	529.6

[4] The data collection methodology for the offense of forcible rape used by the Minnesota state UCR Program does not comply with national UCR Program guidelines. Consequently, their figures for forcible rape and violent crime (of which forcible rape is a part) are not published in this table.

Table 6. Crime, by Metropolitan Statistical Area, 2006 (Contd.)

(Number, percent, rate per 100,000 population.)

Metropolitan statistical area	Counties/principal cities	Population	Violent crime	Murder and non-negligent man-slaughter	Forcible rape	Robbery	Aggra-vated assault	Property crime	Burglary	Larceny-theft	Motor vehicle theft
Salisbury, MD M.S.A.											
	Includes Somerset and Wicomico Counties	116,566									
	City of Salisbury	26,367	569	5	26	213	325	2,582	638	1,813	131
	Total area actually reporting	100.0%	1,058	10	49	284	715	5,298	1,400	3,603	295
	Rate per 100,000 inhabitants		907.6	8.6	42.0	243.6	613.4	4,545.1	1,201.0	3,091.0	253.1
Salt Lake City, UT M.S.A.											
	Includes Salt Lake, Summit, and Tooele Counties	1,068,196									
	City of Salt Lake City	183,901	1,494	8	95	507	884	15,420	2,244	11,136	2,040
	Total area actually reporting	99.8%	3,686	23	472	943	2,248	51,739	7,935	37,717	6,087
	Estimated total	100.0%	3,690	23	473	944	2,250	51,806	7,946	37,767	6,093
	Rate per 100,000 inhabitants		345.4	2.2	44.3	88.4	210.6	4,849.9	743.9	3,535.6	570.4
San Angelo, TX M.S.A.											
	Included Irion and Tom Green Counties	108,353									
	City of San Angelo	90,508	396	3	53	62	278	4,557	974	3,359	224
	Total area actually reporting	100.0%	423	3	56	62	302	4,928	1,075	3,617	236
	Rate per 100,000 inhabitants		390.4	2.8	51.7	57.2	278.7	4,548.1	992.1	3,338.2	217.8
San Antonio, TX M.S.A.											
	Includes Atascosa, Bandera, Bexar, Comal, Guadalupe, Kendall, Medina, and Wilson Counties	1,943,351									
	City of San Antonio	1,292,116	7,977	119	514	2,321	5,023	78,621	14,629	57,377	6,615
	Total area actually reporting	100.0%	9,659	137	714	2,559	6,249	99,173	19,367	72,134	7,672
	Rate per 100,000 inhabitants		497.0	7.0	36.7	131.7	321.6	5,103.2	996.6	3,711.8	394.8
San Diego-Carlsbad-San Marcos, CA M.S.A.											
	Includes San Diego County	2,959,880									
	City of San Diego	1,266,847	6,391	68	348	2,164	3,811	45,209	7,746	24,125	13,338
	City of Carlsbad	91,590	329	1	11	77	240	2,455	587	1,648	220
	City of San Marcos	74,149	286	3	19	75	189	1,735	484	918	333
	City of National City	61,972	524	2	9	211	302	2,463	453	1,125	885
	Total area actually reporting	100.0%	13,578	126	777	4,313	8,362	93,354	17,855	51,454	24,045
	Rate per 100,000 inhabitants		458.7	4.3	26.3	145.7	282.5	3,154.0	603.2	1,738.4	812.4
Sandusky, OH M.S.A.											
	Includes Erie County	78,761									
	City of Sandusky	26,698	231	0	12	46	173	1,796	359	1,345	92
	Total area actually reporting	99.5%	266	0	14	54	198	2,869	588	2,152	129
	Estimated total	100.0%	266	0	14	54	198	2,881	590	2,161	130
	Rate per 100,000 inhabitants		337.7	0.0	17.8	68.6	251.4	3,657.9	749.1	2,743.7	165.1
San Francisco-Oakland-Fremont, CA M.S.A.											
	Includes Metropolitan Divisions of Oakland-Fremont-Hayward and San Francisco-San Mateo-Redwood City	4,190,087									
	City of San Francisco	746,085	6,533	86	154	3,858	2,435	36,992	6,465	23,891	6,636
	City of Oakland	398,834	7,599	145	306	3,534	3,614	24,344	5,070	8,725	10,549
	City of Fremont	202,273	569	6	29	256	278	5,298	1,325	3,113	860
	City of Hayward	141,556	776	4	33	423	316	5,736	1,196	2,343	2,197
	City of Berkeley	101,651	646	4	22	414	206	7,323	1,152	5,096	1,075
	City of San Mateo	91,901	325	2	18	83	222	2,488	274	1,920	294
	City of San Leandro	78,882	650	4	28	309	309	4,196	773	2,176	1,247
	City of Redwood City	73,772	300	6	16	80	198	2,179	307	1,523	349
	City of Pleasanton	66,544	68	0	6	25	37	1,536	214	1,181	141
	City of Walnut Creek	64,774	113	0	3	41	69	2,469	438	1,773	258
	City of South San Francisco	61,282	230	0	15	78	137	1,403	444	695	264
	City of San Rafael	56,218	237	2	16	81	138	1,927	327	1,251	349
	Total area actually reporting	100.0%	26,646	375	1,079	12,942	12,250	164,668	30,914	95,040	38,714
	Rate per 100,000 inhabitants		635.9	8.9	25.8	308.9	292.4	3,929.9	737.8	2,268.2	923.9

Table 6. Crime, by Metropolitan Statistical Area, 2006 *(Contd.)*

(Number, percent, rate per 100,000 population.)

Metropolitan statistical area	Counties/principal cities	Popula-tion	Violent crime	Murder and non-negligent man-slaughter	Forcible rape	Robbery	Aggra-vated assault	Property crime	Burglary	Larceny-theft	Motor vehicle theft
Oakland-Fremont-Hayward, CA M.D.											
	Includes Alameda and Contra Costa Counties	2,488,907									
	Total area actually reporting	100.0%	17,208	265	723	8,123	8,097	102,843	19,988	54,401	28,454
	Rate per 100,000 inhabitants		691.4	10.6	29.0	326.4	325.3	4,132.1	803.1	2,185.7	1,143.2
San Francisco-San Mateo-Redwood City, CA M.D.											
	Includes Marin, San Francisco, and San Mateo Counties	1,701,180									
	Total area actually reporting	100.0%	9,438	110	356	4,819	4,153	61,825	10,926	40,639	10,260
	Rate per 100,000 inhabitants		554.8	6.5	20.9	283.3	244.1	3,634.2	642.3	2,388.9	603.1
San Jose-Sunnyvale-Santa Clara, CA M.S.A.											
	Includes San Benito and Santa Clara Counties	1,770,793									
	City of San Jose	920,548	3,561	29	217	1,030	2,285	24,240	4,423	12,678	7,139
	City of Sunnyvale	130,063	184	1	21	81	81	2,632	524	1,699	409
	City of Santa Clara	106,351	180	3	16	59	102	3,354	595	2,283	476
	City of Mountain View	69,900	300	0	10	71	219	2,244	271	1,648	325
	City of Milpitas	63,954	182	0	15	52	115	2,143	334	1,523	286
	City of Palo Alto	57,495	62	0	1	32	29	1,871	399	1,333	139
	City of Cupertino	52,641	109	0	0	23	86	1,094	338	710	46
	Total area actually reporting	100.0%	5,607	40	338	1,555	3,674	48,117	9,165	28,751	10,201
	Rate per 100,000 inhabitants		316.6	2.3	19.1	87.8	207.5	2,717.3	517.6	1,623.6	576.1
San Luis Obispo-Paso Robles, CA M.S.A.											
	Includes San Luis Obispo County	257,779									
	City of San Luis Obispo	43,901	160	0	22	25	113	1,727	358	1,273	96
	City of Paso Robles	27,724	89	1	15	12	61	989	230	666	93
	Total area actually reporting	100.0%	736	6	79	95	556	6,711	1,486	4,737	488
	Rate per 100,000 inhabitants		285.5	2.3	30.6	36.9	215.7	2,603.4	576.5	1,837.6	189.3
Santa Barbara-Santa Maria-Goleta, CA M.S.A.											
	Includes Santa Barbara County	404,371									
	City of Santa Barbara	86,673	458	1	33	103	321	2,483	544	1,781	158
	City of Santa Maria	85,106	742	2	43	113	584	2,410	372	1,550	488
	City of Goleta	29,631	40	7	1	11	21	400	118	259	23
	Total area actually reporting	100.0%	1,752	13	131	299	1,309	9,092	1,927	6,268	897
	Rate per 100,000 inhabitants		433.3	3.2	32.4	73.9	323.7	2,248.4	476.5	1,550.1	221.8
Santa Cruz-Watsonville, CA M.S.A.											
	Includes Santa Cruz County	251,914									
	City of Santa Cruz	55,253	399	3	38	107	251	3,198	537	2,412	249
	City of Watsonville	48,359	304	6	17	82	199	2,007	359	1,485	163
	Total area actually reporting	100.0%	1,083	16	96	227	744	9,936	1,961	7,118	857
	Rate per 100,000 inhabitants		429.9	6.4	38.1	90.1	295.3	3,944.2	778.4	2,825.6	340.2
Santa Fe, NM M.S.A.											
	Includes Santa Fe County	142,770									
	City of Santa Fe	71,591	419	9	42	104	264	4,249	2,209	1,824	216
	Total area actually reporting	98.0%	618	9	66	114	429	5,254	2,955	2,082	217
	Estimated total	100.0%	636	9	68	116	443	5,335	2,976	2,132	227
	Rate per 100,000 inhabitants		445.5	6.3	47.6	81.2	310.3	3,736.8	2,084.5	1,493.3	159.0
Santa Rosa-Petaluma, CA M.S.A.											
	Includes Sonoma County	470,678									
	City of Santa Rosa	154,537	891	6	75	175	635	4,212	833	2,887	492
	City of Petaluma	55,340	211	2	18	25	166	1,178	136	964	78
	Total area actually reporting	100.0%	2,163	11	173	300	1,679	10,083	2,209	6,903	971
	Rate per 100,000 inhabitants		459.5	2.3	36.8	63.7	356.7	2,142.2	469.3	1,466.6	206.3

Table 6. Crime, by Metropolitan Statistical Area, 2006 (*Contd.*)

(Number, percent, rate per 100,000 population.)

Metropolitan statistical area	Counties/principal cities	Popula-tion	Violent crime	Murder and non-negligent man-slaughter	Forcible rape	Robbery	Aggra-vated assault	Property crime	Burglary	Larceny-theft	Motor vehicle theft
Sarasota-Bradenton-Venice, FL M.S.A.											
	Includes Manatee and Sarasota Counties	684,386									
	City of Sarasota	54,617	565	4	23	196	342	3,583	847	2,484	252
	City of Bradenton	54,826	410	4	10	137	259	2,640	580	1,799	261
	City of Venice	21,328	53	0	3	7	43	599	127	449	23
	Total area actually reporting	100.0%	4,624	30	188	997	3,409	28,197	6,838	19,358	2,001
	Rate per 100,000 inhabitants		675.6	4.4	27.5	145.7	498.1	4,120.0	999.1	2,828.5	292.4
Savannah, GA M.S.A.[2]											
	Includes Bryan, Chatham, and Effingham[2] Counties	323,964									
	City of Savannah-Chatham Metropolitan	213,488	1,184	29	65	690	400	9,924	2,039	6,665	1,220
	Total area actually reporting	98.4%		32	89	779		13,160	2,688	8,967	1,505
	Estimated total	100.0%		32	90	789		13,421	2,736	9,155	1,530
	Rate per 100,000 inhabitants			9.9	27.8	243.5		4,142.7	844.5	2,825.9	472.3
Scranton–Wilkes-Barre, PA M.S.A.											
	Includes Lackawanna, Luzerne, and Wyoming Counties	551,034									
	City of Scranton	73,185	334	0	26	100	208	2,544	635	1,742	167
	City of Wilkes-Barre	41,374	209	6	31	110	62	1,686	298	1,256	132
	Total area actually reporting	83.5%	1,447	17	125	327	978	11,300	2,207	8,337	756
	Estimated total	100.0%	1,668	19	139	389	1,121	13,249	2,497	9,868	884
	Rate per 100,000 inhabitants		302.7	3.4	25.2	70.6	203.4	2,404.4	453.1	1,790.8	160.4
Seattle-Tacoma-Bellevue, WA M.S.A.											
	Includes Metropolitan Divisions of Seattle-Bellevue-Everett and Tacoma	3,258,355									
	City of Seattle	583,772	4,152	30	129	1,667	2,326	39,532	7,505	23,880	8,147
	City of Tacoma	199,264	2,076	21	142	680	1,233	16,540	3,276	9,663	3,601
	City of Bellevue	119,150	184	3	42	71	68	4,245	591	3,178	476
	City of Everett	98,264	602	3	43	240	316	9,063	1,352	5,468	2,243
	City of Kent	83,206	563	2	83	224	254	6,252	1,223	3,466	1,563
	City of Renton	56,776	259	2	26	128	103	4,412	690	2,739	983
	Total area actually reporting	99.9%	13,551	117	1,285	4,688	7,461	163,178	31,672	98,608	32,898
	Estimated total	100.0%	13,552	117	1,285	4,688	7,462	163,199	31,676	98,622	32,901
	Rate per 100,000 inhabitants		415.9	3.6	39.4	143.9	229.0	5,008.6	972.1	3,026.7	1,009.7
Seattle-Bellevue-Everett, WA M.D.											
	Includes King and Snohomish Counties	2,491,616									
	Total area actually reporting	100.0%	9,343	82	932	3,512	4,817	124,339	23,246	75,295	25,798
	Rate per 100,000 inhabitants		375.0	3.3	37.4	141.0	193.3	4,990.3	933.0	3,021.9	1,035.4
Tacoma, WA M.D.											
	Includes Pierce County	766,739									
	Total area actually reporting	99.9%	4,208	35	353	1,176	2,644	38,839	8,426	23,313	7,100
	Estimated total	100.0%	4,209	35	353	1,176	2,645	38,860	8,430	23,327	7,103
	Rate per 100,000 inhabitants		548.9	4.6	46.0	153.4	345.0	5,068.2	1,099.5	3,042.4	926.4
Sebastian-Vero Beach, FL M.S.A.											
	Includes Indian River County	130,763									
	City of Sebastian	19,974	51	0	3	8	40	512	141	348	23
	City of Vero Beach	17,366	76	0	7	23	46	642	121	498	23
	Total area actually reporting	100.0%	479	7	38	121	313	3,943	888	2,852	203
	Rate per 100,000 inhabitants		366.3	5.4	29.1	92.5	239.4	3,015.4	679.1	2,181.0	155.2
Sheboygan, WI M.S.A.											
	Includes Sheboygan County	115,030									
	City of Sheboygan	49,051	79	1	29	11	38	2,381	320	1,973	88
	Total area actually reporting	100.0%	134	1	46	13	74	3,334	454	2,775	105
	Rate per 100,000 inhabitants		116.5	0.9	40.0	11.3	64.3	2,898.4	394.7	2,412.4	91.3

[2] The FBI determined that the agency's data were underreported. Consequently, affected data are not included in this table.

Table 6. Crime, by Metropolitan Statistical Area, 2006 (*Contd.*)

(Number, percent, rate per 100,000 population.)

Metropolitan statistical area	Counties/principal cities	Popula-tion	Violent crime	Murder and non-negligent man-slaughter	Forcible rape	Robbery	Aggra-vated assault	Property crime	Burglary	Larceny-theft	Motor vehicle theft
Sherman-Denison, TX M.S.A.											
	Includes Grayson County	120,145									
	City of Sherman	37,833	153	0	12	25	116	1,611	349	1,208	54
	City of Denison	24,318	92	1	5	23	63	1,128	270	793	65
	Total area actually reporting	100.0%	300	1	25	53	221	3,954	1,006	2,726	222
	Rate per 100,000 inhabitants		249.7	0.8	20.8	44.1	183.9	3,291.0	837.3	2,268.9	184.8
Shreveport-Bossier City, LA M.S.A.											
	Includes Bossier, Caddo, and De Soto Parishes	363,251									
	City of Shreveport	188,505	2,249	28	140	586	1,495	12,693	2,922	8,508	1,263
	City of Bossier City	57,350	1,201	1	40	91	1,069	2,866	582	2,010	274
	Total area actually reporting	100.0%	4,315	41	207	706	3,361	18,432	4,091	12,576	1,765
	Rate per 100,000 inhabitants		1,187.9	11.3	57.0	194.4	925.3	5,074.2	1,126.2	3,462.1	485.9
Sioux City, IA-NE-SD M.S.A.											
	Includes Woodbury County, IA; Dakota and Dixon Counties, NE; and Union County, SD	143,363									
	City of Sioux City, IA	83,590	398	0	51	51	296	3,384	702	2,491	191
	Total area actually reporting	97.0%	469	1	59	58	351	3,996	847	2,922	227
	Estimated total....................................	100.0%	473	1	60	58	354	4,046	858	2,958	230
	Rate per 100,000 inhabitants		329.9	0.7	41.9	40.5	246.9	2,822.2	598.5	2,063.3	160.4
Sioux Falls, SD M.S.A.											
	Includes Lincoln, McCook, Min-nehaha, and Turner Counties............	209,523									
	City of Sioux Falls	140,593	426	7	115	34	270	3,596	768	2,616	212
	Total area actually reporting	97.2%	475	7	125	34	309	4,134	958	2,928	248
	Estimated total....................................	100.0%	481	7	126	34	314	4,200	972	2,976	252
	Rate per 100,000 inhabitants		229.6	3.3	60.1	16.2	149.9	2,004.6	463.9	1,420.4	120.3
South Bend-Mishawaka, IN-MI M.S.A.											
	Includes St. Joseph County, IN and Cass County, MI...............................	319,789									
	City of South Bend, IN	105,959	805	14	67	430	294	7,411	1,930	4,895	586
	City of Mishawaka, IN	48,818	176	0	12	62	102	3,452	389	2,885	178
	Total area actually reporting	96.7%	1,170	17	108	526	519	13,909	3,003	9,915	991
	Estimated total....................................	100.0%	1,203	17	112	535	539	14,257	3,063	10,166	1,028
	Rate per 100,000 inhabitants		376.2	5.3	35.0	167.3	168.5	4,458.3	957.8	3,179.0	321.5
Spartanburg, SC M.S.A.											
	Includes Spartanburg County	270,958									
	City of Spartanburg	38,976	715	5	19	194	497	3,628	870	2,494	264
	Total area actually reporting	99.8%	1,827	19	76	440	1,292	12,807	3,178	8,674	955
	Estimated total....................................	100.0%	1,830	19	76	441	1,294	12,829	3,182	8,691	956
	Rate per 100,000 inhabitants		675.4	7.0	28.0	162.8	477.6	4,734.7	1,174.4	3,207.5	352.8
Spokane, WA M.S.A.											
	Includes Spokane County	448,278									
	City of Spokane..................................	200,200	1,197	10	91	392	704	11,804	2,165	7,340	2,299
	Total area actually reporting	100.0%	1,799	17	129	468	1,185	18,427	3,547	11,590	3,290
	Rate per 100,000 inhabitants		401.3	3.8	28.8	104.4	264.3	4,110.6	791.3	2,585.4	733.9
Springfield, MA M.S.A.[3]											
	Includes Franklin, Hampden, and Hampshire Counties.........................	691,394									
	City of Springfield.............................	152,644	2,260	15	115	682	1,448	8,747	2,178	4,963	1,606
	Total area actually reporting	97.3%		21	287	957		20,746	5,262	12,638	2,846
	Estimated total....................................	100.0%		21	291	969		21,117	5,353	12,882	2,882
	Rate per 100,000 inhabitants			3.0	42.1	140.2		3,054.3	774.2	1,863.2	416.8
Springfield, MO M.S.A.											
	Includes Christian, Dallas, Greene, Polk, and Webster Counties	401,034									
	City of Springfield.............................	151,397	1,001	6	82	252	661	13,161	1,972	10,358	831
	Total area actually reporting	100.0%	1,947	7	115	275	1,550	18,027	3,135	13,744	1,148
	Rate per 100,000 inhabitants		485.5	1.7	28.7	68.6	386.5	4,495.1	781.7	3,427.1	286.3

[3] The data collection methodology for the offense of aggravated assault used by this agency does not comply with national Uniform Crime Reporting (UCR) Program guidelines. Consequently, the figures for aggravated assault and violent crime (of which aggravated assault is a part) are not included in this table.

Table 6. Crime, by Metropolitan Statistical Area, 2006 *(Contd.)*

(Number, percent, rate per 100,000 population.)

Metropolitan statistical area	Counties/principal cities	Population	Violent crime	Murder and non-negligent manslaughter	Forcible rape	Robbery	Aggravated assault	Property crime	Burglary	Larceny-theft	Motor vehicle theft
Springfield, OH M.S.A.											
	Includes Clark County	142,549									
	City of Springfield	63,379	535	4	56	309	166	6,331	1,978	3,856	497
	Total area actually reporting	92.7%	600	6	70	331	193	8,340	2,493	5,222	625
	Estimated total	100.0%	620	6	73	339	202	8,658	2,553	5,461	644
	Rate per 100,000 inhabitants		434.9	4.2	51.2	237.8	141.7	6,073.7	1,791.0	3,831.0	451.8
State College, PA M.S.A.											
	Includes Centre County	140,685									
	City of State College	52,225	39	2	7	12	18	997	122	856	19
	Total area actually reporting	97.9%	137	3	25	24	85	2,789	452	2,259	78
	Estimated total	100.0%	144	3	25	26	90	2,852	461	2,309	82
	Rate per 100,000 inhabitants		102.4	2.1	17.8	18.5	64.0	2,027.2	327.7	1,641.3	58.3
St. Cloud, MN M.S.A.[4]											
	Includes Benton and Stearns Counties	182,369									
	City of St. Cloud[4]	66,232		0		54	153	3,062	377	2,555	130
	Total area actually reporting	99.3%		1		60	226	5,115	671	4,223	221
	Estimated total	100.0%		1		61	227	5,158	677	4,257	224
	Rate per 100,000 inhabitants			0.5		33.4	124.5	2,828.3	371.2	2,334.3	122.8
St. Joseph, MO-KS M.S.A.[1]											
	Includes Doniphan County, KS and Andrew, Buchanan, and De Kalb Counties, MO	122,851									
	City of St. Joseph, MO[1]	73,192	213	0	11	67	135	3,863	761	2,782	320
	Total area actually reporting	98.4%	329	2	20	68	239	4,769	1,018	3,366	385
	Estimated total	100.0%	335	2	21	69	243	4,825	1,027	3,409	389
	Rate per 100,000 inhabitants		272.7	1.6	17.1	56.2	197.8	3,927.5	836.0	2,774.9	316.6
St. Louis, MO-IL M.S.A.											
	Includes Bond, Calhoun, Clinton, Jersey, Macoupin, Madison, Monroe, and St. Clair Counties, IL and Franklin, Jefferson, Lincoln, St. Charles, St. Louis, Warren, and Washington Counties and St. Louis City, MO	2,798,956									
	City of St. Louis, MO	346,879	8,605	129	337	3,147	4,992	40,751	8,510	23,596	8,645
	City of St. Charles, MO	62,759	158	1	14	44	99	1,981	280	1,568	133
	Total area actually reporting	75.3%	13,802	173	638	4,166	8,825	90,265	16,367	61,074	12,824
	Estimated total	100.0%	15,846	185	639	4,676	10,346	104,435	18,997	71,794	13,644
	Rate per 100,000 inhabitants		566.1	6.6	22.8	167.1	369.6	3,731.2	678.7	2,565.0	487.5
Stockton, CA M.S.A.											
	Includes San Joaquin County	670,097									
	City of Stockton	289,510	4,288	37	102	1,519	2,630	19,719	3,836	12,202	3,681
	Total area actually reporting	100.0%	6,079	57	165	1,916	3,941	36,202	7,234	22,705	6,263
	Rate per 100,000 inhabitants		907.2	8.5	24.6	285.9	588.1	5,402.5	1,079.5	3,388.3	934.6
Sumter, SC M.S.A.											
	Includes Sumter County	107,158									
	City of Sumter	40,296	532	4	14	87	427	2,087	495	1,478	114
	Total area actually reporting	100.0%	1,333	10	40	142	1,141	4,641	1,407	2,912	322
	Rate per 100,000 inhabitants		1,244.0	9.3	37.3	132.5	1,064.8	4,331.0	1,313.0	2,717.5	300.5
Syracuse, NY M.S.A.											
	Includes Madison, Onondaga, and Oswego Counties	653,507									
	City of Syracuse	142,062	1,515	12	66	534	903	6,677	1,904	4,037	736
	Total area actually reporting	99.3%	2,102	18	145	684	1,255	15,960	3,761	11,191	1,008
	Estimated total	100.0%	2,110	18	145	687	1,260	16,048	3,774	11,262	1,012
	Rate per 100,000 inhabitants		322.9	2.8	22.2	105.1	192.8	2,455.7	577.5	1,723.3	154.9

[1] Because of changes in the state/local agency's reporting practices, figures are not comparable to previous years' data.

[4] The data collection methodology for the offense of forcible rape used by the Minnesota state UCR Program does not comply with national UCR Program guidelines. Consequently, their figures for forcible rape and violent crime (of which forcible rape is a part) are not published in this table.

Table 6. Crime, by Metropolitan Statistical Area, 2006 (*Contd.*)

(Number, percent, rate per 100,000 population.)

Metropolitan statistical area	Counties/principal cities	Population	Violent crime	Murder and non-negligent man-slaughter	Forcible rape	Robbery	Aggra-vated assault	Property crime	Burglary	Larceny-theft	Motor vehicle theft
Tallahassee, FL M.S.A.											
	Includes Gadsden, Jefferson, Leon, and Wakulla Counties	340,534									
	City of Tallahassee..............................	161,173	1,615	10	155	452	998	7,709	2,168	4,935	606
	Total area actually reporting	99.5%	2,778	11	238	580	1,949	12,675	3,874	7,862	939
	Estimated total...................................	100.0%	2,789	11	239	583	1,956	12,749	3,891	7,912	946
	Rate per 100,000 inhabitants..............		819.0	3.2	70.2	171.2	574.4	3,743.8	1,142.6	2,323.4	277.8
Tampa-St. Peters-burg-Clearwater, FL M.S.A.											
	Includes Hernando, Hillsborough, Pasco, and Pinellas Counties..............	2,692,311									
	City of Tampa	331,487	3,839	25	133	1,211	2,470	18,789	4,451	11,251	3,087
	City of St. Petersburg	253,280	3,753	21	112	1,032	2,588	16,409	3,466	10,182	2,761
	City of Clearwater	110,520	862	4	44	200	614	4,837	882	3,527	428
	City of Largo	75,729	439	2	35	102	300	2,733	485	2,016	232
	Total area actually reporting	100.0%	19,095	133	1,025	4,511	13,426	113,752	26,017	74,405	13,330
	Rate per 100,000 inhabitants..............		709.2	4.9	38.1	167.6	498.7	4,225.1	966.3	2,763.6	495.1
Texarkana, TX-Texarkana, AR M.S.A.											
	Includes Miller County, AR and Bowie County, TX	136,867									
	Texarkana, TX	36,759	462	3	30	75	354	2,376	451	1,803	122
	Texarkana, AR	30,348	490	3	18	81	388	1,530	406	1,023	101
	Total area actually reporting	100.0%	1,179	14	67	167	931	5,230	1,247	3,639	344
	Rate per 100,000 inhabitants..............		861.4	10.2	49.0	122.0	680.2	3,821.2	911.1	2,658.8	251.3
Toledo, OH M.S.A.											
	Includes Fulton, Lucas, Ottawa, and Wood Counties....................................	657,496									
	City of Toledo.....................................	301,652	3,461	35	169	1,248	2,009	22,711	6,915	13,239	2,557
	Total area actually reporting	95.8%	3,713	37	226	1,307	2,143	31,741	8,435	20,328	2,978
	Estimated total...................................	100.0%	3,764	37	234	1,327	2,166	32,581	8,593	20,960	3,028
	Rate per 100,000 inhabitants..............		572.5	5.6	35.6	201.8	329.4	4,955.3	1,306.9	3,187.9	460.5
Topeka, KS M.S.A.											
	Includes Jackson, Jefferson, Osage, Shawnee, and Wabaunsee Counties.....................................	230,694									
	City of Topeka.....................................	122,807	669	9	57	310	293	8,748	1,478	6,645	625
	Total area actually reporting	98.3%	895	12	95	320	468	11,711	2,080	8,850	781
	Estimated total...................................	100.0%	905	12	96	321	476	11,821	2,097	8,935	789
	Rate per 100,000 inhabitants..............		392.3	5.2	41.6	139.1	206.3	5,124.1	909.0	3,873.1	342.0
Trenton-Ewing, NJ M.S.A.											
	Includes Mercer County	366,535									
	City of Trenton....................................	84,703	1,274	18	31	632	593	2,477	806	1,211	460
	City of Ewing Township......................	37,265	114	0	8	57	49	780	173	559	48
	Total area actually reporting	100.0%	1,781	21	66	867	827	8,086	1,860	5,403	823
	Rate per 100,000 inhabitants..............		485.9	5.7	18.0	236.5	225.6	2,206.1	507.5	1,474.1	224.5
Tucson, AZ M.S.A.[7]											
	Includes Pima County	960,135									
	City of Tucson[7]..................................	535,232	4,580	51	294	1,675	2,560		5,121		7,376
	Total area actually reporting	100.0%	5,682	72	400	1,975	3,235		8,365		9,592
	Rate per 100,000 inhabitants..............		591.8	7.5	41.7	205.7	336.9		871.2		999.0
Tulsa, OK M.S.A.											
	Includes Creek, Okmulgee, Osage, Pawnee, Rogers, Tulsa, and Wagoner Counties..	895,554									
	City of Tulsa..	385,834	4,816	53	289	997	3,477	24,011	6,315	14,523	3,173
	Total area actually reporting	100.0%	6,158	67	408	1,113	4,570	34,196	8,972	21,106	4,118
	Rate per 100,000 inhabitants..............		687.6	7.5	45.6	124.3	510.3	3,818.4	1,001.8	2,356.8	459.8
Tuscaloosa, AL M.S.A.											
	Includes Greene, Hale, and Tuscaloosa Counties........................	198,666									
	City of Tuscaloosa..............................	82,094	604	15	47	221	321	5,234	1,256	3,709	269
	Total area actually reporting	83.6%	953	22	84	260	587	8,167	2,096	5,518	553
	Estimated total...................................	100.0%	1,073	23	94	303	653	9,322	2,352	6,327	643
	Rate per 100,000 inhabitants..............		540.1	11.6	47.3	152.5	328.7	4,692.3	1,183.9	3,184.7	323.7

[7] It was determined that the agency did not follow national UCR Program guidelines for reporting an offense. Consequently, this figure is not included in this table.

Table 6. Crime, by Metropolitan Statistical Area, 2006 (*Contd.*)

(Number, percent, rate per 100,000 population.)

Metropolitan statistical area	Counties/principal cities	Population	Violent crime	Murder and non-negligent man-slaughter	Forcible rape	Robbery	Aggra-vated assault	Property crime	Burglary	Larceny-theft	Motor vehicle theft
Tyler, TX M.S.A.											
	Includes Smith County......................	195,995									
	City of Tyler....................................	94,541	563	5	41	110	407	4,313	842	3,280	191
	Total area actually reporting.............	98.9%	904	6	75	136	687	6,882	1,643	4,845	394
	Estimated total..................................	100.0%	910	6	76	137	691	6,959	1,658	4,901	400
	Rate per 100,000 inhabitants..............		464.3	3.1	38.8	69.9	352.6	3,550.6	845.9	2,500.6	204.1
Utica-Rome, NY M.S.A.											
	Includes Herkimer and Oneida Counties..	298,683									
	City of Utica	59,495	425	3	20	138	264	2,799	763	1,889	147
	City of Rome	34,436	45	1	3	10	31	566	154	381	31
	Total area actually reporting.............	96.8%	811	7	54	168	582	6,555	1,591	4,700	264
	Estimated total..................................	100.0%	829	7	55	175	592	6,746	1,620	4,853	273
	Rate per 100,000 inhabitants..............		277.6	2.3	18.4	58.6	198.2	2,258.6	542.4	1,624.8	91.4
Valdosta, GA M.S.A.											
	Includes Brooks, Echols, Lanier, and Lowndes Counties	127,788									
	City of Valdosta...............................	46,657	298	2	23	97	176	3,054	699	2,228	127
	Total area actually reporting.............	96.6%	527	3	37	126	361	5,251	1,178	3,835	238
	Estimated total..................................	100.0%	543	3	38	132	370	5,386	1,214	3,915	257
	Rate per 100,000 inhabitants..............		424.9	2.3	29.7	103.3	289.5	4,214.8	950.0	3,063.7	201.1
Vallejo-Fairfield, CA M.S.A.											
	Includes Solano County......................	415,300									
	City of Vallejo	118,541	1,206	6	31	430	739	5,971	1,155	3,300	1,516
	City of Fairfield	105,417	654	6	36	241	371	4,363	745	2,912	706
	Total area actually reporting.............	100.0%	2,531	14	129	849	1,539	15,129	2,884	9,329	2,916
	Rate per 100,000 inhabitants..............		609.4	3.4	31.1	204.4	370.6	3,642.9	694.4	2,246.3	702.1
Victoria, TX M.S.A.											
	Includes Calhoun, Goliad, and Victoria Counties................................	116,568									
	City of Victoria...............................	63,541	337	5	32	89	211	2,973	688	2,112	173
	Total area actually reporting.............	100.0%	454	7	58	92	297	4,005	958	2,797	250
	Rate per 100,000 inhabitants..............		389.5	6.0	49.8	78.9	254.8	3,435.8	821.8	2,399.5	214.5
Vineland-Millville-Bridgeton, NJ M.S.A.											
	Includes Cumberland County	153,369									
	City of Vineland	58,208	539	6	19	167	347	2,737	539	2,068	130
	City of Millville	27,907	240	8	8	98	126	1,534	398	1,083	53
	City of Bridgeton	23,977	359	0	21	156	182	1,040	288	666	86
	Total area actually reporting.............	100.0%	1,243	15	50	434	744	6,197	1,532	4,329	336
	Rate per 100,000 inhabitants..............		810.5	9.8	32.6	283.0	485.1	4,040.6	998.9	2,822.6	219.1
Virginia Beach-Norfolk-Newport News, VA-NC M.S.A.											
	Includes Currituck County, NC and Gloucester, Isle of Wight, James City, Mathews, Surry, and York Counties and Chesapeake, Hampton, Newport News, Norfolk, Poquoson, Portsmouth, Suffolk, Virginia Beach, and Williamsburg Cities, VA.............	1,663,994									
	City of Virginia Beach, VA................	442,784	1,256	19	115	678	444	12,855	2,048	10,212	595
	City of Norfolk, VA..........................	234,266	1,844	28	100	948	768	11,683	1,614	9,032	1,037
	City of Newport News, VA.................	181,692	1,422	19	109	473	821	7,578	1,661	5,160	757
	City of Hampton, VA.........................	147,030	571	11	53	269	238	4,861	767	3,594	500
	City of Portsmouth, VA	101,167	870	18	37	336	479	5,045	1,100	3,591	354
	Total area actually reporting.............	100.0%	7,693	121	547	3,180	3,845	56,616	9,877	42,653	4,086
	Rate per 100,000 inhabitants..............		462.3	7.3	32.9	191.1	231.1	3,402.4	593.6	2,563.3	245.6
Visalia-Porterville, CA M.S.A.											
	Includes Tulare County......................	414,574									
	City of Visalia	109,648	871	8	50	213	600	6,466	1,368	3,817	1,281
	City of Porterville	45,364	250	9	21	61	159	2,413	534	1,480	399
	Total area actually reporting.............	100.0%	2,442	49	130	466	1,797	19,326	4,611	10,858	3,857
	Rate per 100,000 inhabitants..............		589.0	11.8	31.4	112.4	433.5	4,661.7	1,112.2	2,619.1	930.4

Table 6. Crime, by Metropolitan Statistical Area, 2006 (*Contd.*)

(Number, percent, rate per 100,000 population.)

Metropolitan statistical area	Counties/principal cities	Popula-tion	Violent crime	Murder and non-negligent man-slaughter	Forcible rape	Robbery	Aggra-vated assault	Property crime	Burglary	Larceny-theft	Motor vehicle theft
Waco, TX M.S.A.											
	Includes McLennan County	231,035									
	City of Waco...	123,879	952	9	72	257	614	7,512	2,188	4,869	455
	Total area actually reporting	100.0%	1,283	10	122	292	859	10,819	2,960	7,222	637
	Rate per 100,000 inhabitants..............		555.3	4.3	52.8	126.4	371.8	4,682.8	1,281.2	3,125.9	275.7
Warner Robins, GA M.S.A.											
	Includes Houston County	130,215									
	City of Warner Robins	59,605	310	3	15	127	165	3,049	659	2,230	160
	Total area actually reporting	100.0%	505	3	31	148	323	4,316	916	3,149	251
	Rate per 100,000 inhabitants..............		387.8	2.3	23.8	113.7	248.1	3,314.5	703.5	2,418.3	192.8
Washington-Arlington-Alexan-dria, DC-VA-MD-WV M.S.A.[1]											
	Metropolitan Divisions of Bethesda-Frederick-Gaithersburg, MD and Washington-Arlington-Alexandria, DC-VA-MD-WV	5,275,654									
	City of Washington, D.C.	581,530	8,408	169	182	3,604	4,453	26,015	3,826	15,132	7,057
	City of Alexandria, VA	136,686	448	7	27	206	208	3,194	380	2,439	375
	City of Frederick, MD.......................	58,066	530	4	17	152	357	1,744	354	1,287	103
	Total area actually reporting	99.7%	25,161	389	998	11,058	12,716	151,800	21,670	102,445	27,685
	Estimated total....................................	100.0%	25,229	390	1,004	11,079	12,756	152,388	21,759	102,905	27,724
	Rate per 100,000 inhabitants..............		478.2	7.4	19.0	210.0	241.8	2,888.5	412.4	1,950.6	525.5
Bethesda-Gaith-ersburg-Frederick, MD M.D.											
	Includes Frederick and Montgomery Counties..	1,151,428									
	Total area actually reporting	100.0%	3,055	27	180	1,442	1,406	28,016	4,804	20,348	2,864
	Rate per 100,000 inhabitants..............		265.3	2.3	15.6	125.2	122.1	2,433.2	417.2	1,767.2	248.7
Washington-Arlington-Alexandria, DC-VA-MD-WV M.D.[1]											
	Includes District of Columbia; Cal-vert, Charles, and Prince George's[1] Counties, MD; Arlington, Clarke, Fairfax, Fauquier, Loudoun, Prince William, Spotsylvania, Stafford, and Warren Counties and Alexandria, Fairfax, Falls Church, Fredericks-burg, Manassas, and Manassas Park Cities, VA; and Jefferson County, WV	4,124,226									
	Total area actually reporting	99.6%	22,106	362	818	9,616	11,310	123,784	16,866	82,097	24,821
	Estimated total....................................	100.0%	22,174	363	824	9,637	11,350	124,372	16,955	82,557	24,860
	Rate per 100,000 inhabitants..............		537.7	8.8	20.0	233.7	275.2	3,015.6	411.1	2,001.8	602.8
Waterloo-Cedar Falls, IA M.S.A.											
	Includes Black Hawk, Bremer, and Grundy Counties	162,756									
	City of Waterloo	66,836	342	1	41	83	217	3,057	907	2,035	115
	City of Cedar Falls	36,665	86	0	13	5	68	881	140	703	38
	Total area actually reporting	100.0%	533	3	63	90	377	4,658	1,241	3,234	183
	Rate per 100,000 inhabitants..............		327.5	1.8	38.7	55.3	231.6	2,862.0	762.5	1,987.0	112.4
Wausau, WI M.S.A.											
	Includes Marathon County.................	129,414									
	City of Wausau	37,429	109	1	12	21	75	1,323	237	1,030	56
	Total area actually reporting	100.0%	205	4	18	25	158	2,482	480	1,898	104
	Rate per 100,000 inhabitants..............		158.4	3.1	13.9	19.3	122.1	1,917.9	370.9	1,466.6	80.4
Wenatchee, WA M.S.A.											
	Includes Chelan and Douglas Counties..	106,568									
	City of Wenatchee	29,879	95	0	14	22	59	1,550	224	1,255	71
	Total area actually reporting	100.0%	214	2	30	40	142	3,946	629	3,130	187
	Rate per 100,000 inhabitants..............		200.8	1.9	28.2	37.5	133.2	3,702.8	590.2	2,937.1	175.5

[1] Because of changes in the state/local agency's reporting practices, figures are not comparable to previous years' data.

Table 6. Crime, by Metropolitan Statistical Area, 2006 (*Contd.*)

(Number, percent, rate per 100,000 population.)

Metropolitan statistical area	Counties/principal cities	Popula-tion	Violent crime	Murder and non-negligent man-slaughter	Forcible rape	Robbery	Aggra-vated assault	Property crime	Burglary	Larceny-theft	Motor vehicle theft
Wheeling, WV-OH M.S.A.											
	Includes Belmont County, OH and Marshall and Ohio Counties, WV	148,832									
	City of Wheeling, WV	29,665	118	1	18	26	73	985	245	652	88
	Total area actually reporting	88.4%	217	1	33	40	143	2,046	521	1,355	170
	Estimated total....................................	100.0%	251	1	38	53	159	2,579	622	1,754	203
	Rate per 100,000 inhabitants		168.6	0.7	25.5	35.6	106.8	1,732.8	417.9	1,178.5	136.4
Wichita, KS M.S.A.											
	Includes Butler, Harvey, Sedgwick, and Sumner Counties........................	591,201									
	City of Wichita	357,372	3,319	26	240	520	2,533	19,562	3,800	13,786	1,976
	Total area actually reporting	99.9%	3,962	29	314	547	3,072	26,264	5,102	18,820	2,342
	Estimated total....................................	100.0%	3,964	29	314	547	3074	26,288	5,106	18,838	2,344
	Rate per 100,000 inhabitants		670.5	4.9	53.1	92.5	520.0	4,446.5	863.7	3,186.4	396.5
Wichita Falls, TX M.S.A.											
	Includes Archer, Clay, and Wichita Counties..	150,422									
	City of Wichita Falls..........................	102,675	491	9	27	169	286	6,285	1,291	4,574	420
	Total area actually reporting	100.0%	533	9	40	172	312	7,120	1,583	5,062	475
	Rate per 100,000 inhabitants		354.3	6.0	26.6	114.3	207.4	4,733.4	1,052.4	3,365.2	315.8
Williamsport, PA M.S.A.											
	Includes Lycoming County................	118,500									
	City of Williamsport	30,139	112	1	4	72	35	1,489	296	1,110	83
	Total area actually reporting	93.7%	180	1	18	79	82	2,715	632	1,949	134
	Estimated total....................................	100.0%	198	1	19	84	94	2,876	656	2,075	145
	Rate per 100,000 inhabitants		167.1	0.8	16.0	70.9	79.3	2,427.0	553.6	1,751.1	122.4
Wilmington, NC M.S.A.											
	Includes Brunswick, New Hanover, and Pender Counties.........................	321,432									
	City of Wilmington	97,381	857	7	62	409	379	6,207	1,694	3,865	648
	Total area actually reporting	98.5%	1,457	15	132	511	799	14,816	4,595	9,025	1,196
	Estimated total....................................	100.0%	1,480	15	134	517	814	15,078	4,658	9,210	1,210
	Rate per 100,000 inhabitants		460.4	4.7	41.7	160.8	253.2	4,690.9	1,449.1	2,865.3	376.4
Winchester, VA-WV M.S.A.											
	Includes Frederick County and Winchester City, VA and Hampshire County, WV	117,226									
	City of Winchester, VA	25,369	107	0	5	48	54	1,395	201	1,122	72
	Total area actually reporting	100.0%	267	6	39	71	151	3,164	650	2,270	244
	Rate per 100,000 inhabitants		227.8	5.1	33.3	60.6	128.8	2,699.1	554.5	1,936.4	208.1
Winston-Salem, NC M.S.A.											
	Includes Davie, Forsyth, Stokes, and Yadkin Counties	457,581									
	City of Winston-Salem	197,621	1,654	20	126	669	839	13,449	4,289	8,126	1,034
	Total area actually reporting	99.4%	2,457	24	170	777	1,486	20,812	6,320	13,017	1,475
	Estimated total....................................	100.0%	2,471	24	171	781	1,495	20,961	6,356	13,122	1,483
	Rate per 100,000 inhabitants		540.0	5.2	37.4	170.7	326.7	4,580.8	1,389.0	2,867.7	324.1
Worcester, MA M.S.A.[3]											
	Includes Worcester County	787,969									
	City of Worcester	176,956	1,496	6	124	388	978	5,671	1,231	3,452	988
	Total area actually reporting	99.1%		9	304	584		14,594	3,500	9,432	1,662
	Estimated total....................................	100.0%		9	305	589		14,737	3,535	9,526	1,676
	Rate per 100,000 inhabitants			1.1	38.7	74.7		1,870.3	448.6	1,208.9	212.7
Yakima, WA M.S.A.											
	Includes Yakima County....................	235,565									
	City of Yakima	82,609	449	3	62	158	226	7,159	1,469	4,687	1,003
	Total area actually reporting	100.0%	756	10	126	233	387	14,974	3,518	9,280	2,176
	Rate per 100,000 inhabitants		320.9	4.2	53.5	98.9	164.3	6,356.6	1,493.4	3,939.5	923.7

[3] The data collection methodology for the offense of aggravated assault used by this agency does not comply with national Uniform Crime Reporting (UCR) Program guidelines. Consequently, the figures for aggravated assault and violent crime (of which aggravated assault is a part) are not included in this table.

Table 6. Crime, by Metropolitan Statistical Area, 2006 *(Contd.)*

(Number, percent, rate per 100,000 population.)

Metropolitan statistical area	Counties/principal cities	Population	Violent crime	Murder and non-negligent man-slaughter	Forcible rape	Robbery	Aggra-vated assault	Property crime	Burglary	Larceny-theft	Motor vehicle theft
Yuba City, CA M.S.A.											
	Includes Sutter and Yuba Counties...	157,434									
	City of Yuba City	59,156	250	2	21	50	177	2,029	459	1,326	244
	Total area actually reporting	100.0%	748	7	62	134	545	5,253	1,637	2,840	776
	Rate per 100,000 inhabitants		475.1	4.4	39.4	85.1	346.2	3,336.6	1,039.8	1,803.9	492.9
Yuma, AZ M.S.A.											
	Includes Yuma County........................	188,206									
	City of Yuma	87,925	542	3	33	84	422	4,066	809	2,512	745
	Total area actually reporting	88.1%	786	6	40	118	622	5,912	1,186	3,714	1,012
	Estimated total........................	100.0%	873	7	46	138	682	6,889	1,426	4,312	1,151
	Rate per 100,000 inhabitants		463.9	3.7	24.4	73.3	362.4	3,660.4	757.7	2,291.1	611.6
Aguadilla-Isa-bela-San Sebastian, Puerto Rico M.S.A.											
	Includes Aguada, Aguadilla, Anasco, Isabela, Lares, Moca, Rincon, and San Sebastian Municipios	325,397									
	Total area actually reporting	100.0%	197	8	2	93	94	1,761	781	869	111
	Rate per 100,000 inhabitants		60.5	2.5	0.6	28.6	28.9	541.2	240.0	267.1	34.1
Fajardo, Puerto Rico M.S.A.											
	Includes Ceiba, Fajardo, and Luquillo Municipios	81,048									
	Total area actually reporting	100.0%	145	14	3	69	59	1,087	477	551	59
	Rate per 100,000 inhabitants		178.9	17.3	3.7	85.1	72.8	1,341.2	588.5	679.8	72.8
Guayama, Puerto Rico M.S.A.											
	Includes Arroyo, Guayama, and Patillas Municipios.............................	85,639									
	Total area actually reporting	100.0%	119	13	4	46	56	399	289	45	65
	Rate per 100,000 inhabitants		139.0	15.2	4.7	53.7	65.4	465.9	337.5	52.5	75.9
Mayaguez, Puerto Rico M.S.A.											
	Includes Hormigueros and Mayaguez Municipios	116,770									
	Total area actually reporting	100.0%	206	11	4	127	64	2,537	731	1,653	153
	Rate per 100,000 inhabitants		176.4	9.4	3.4	108.8	54.8	2,172.6	626.0	1,415.6	131.0
Ponce, Puerto Rico M.S.A.											
	Includes Juana Diaz, Ponce, and Villalba Municipios............................	270,985									
	Total area actually reporting	100.0%	651	75	19	265	292	3,863	1,179	2,355	329
	Rate per 100,000 inhabitants		240.2	27.7	7.0	97.8	107.8	1,425.5	435.1	869.1	121.4
San German-Cabo Rojo, Puerto Rico M.S.A.											
	Includes Cabo Rojo, Lajas, Sabana Grande, and San German Municipios	141,652									
	Total area actually reporting	100.0%	76	7	6	37	26	864	444	351	69
	Rate per 100,000 inhabitants		53.7	4.9	4.2	26.1	18.4	609.9	313.4	247.8	48.7
San Juan-Caguas-Guaynabo, Puerto Rico M.S.A.											
	Includes Aguas Buenas, Aibonito, Arecibo, Barceloneta, Barranquitas, Bayamon, Caguas, Camuy, Canova-nas, Carolina, Catano, Cayey, Ciales, Cidra, Comerio, Corozal, Dorado, Florida, Guaynabo, Gurabo, Hatillo, Humacao, Juncos, Las Piedras, Loiza, Manati, Maunabo, Morovis, Naguabo, Naranjito, Orocovis, Quebradillas, Rio Grande, San Juan, San Lorenzo, Toa Alta, Toa Baja, Trujillo Alto, Vega Alta, Vega Baja,and Yabucoa Municipios...........	2,586,865									
	Total area actually reporting	100.0%	7,032	564	66	4,403	1,999	39,787	11,500	20,794	7,493
	Rate per 100,000 inhabitants		271.8	21.8	2.6	170.2	77.3	1,538.0	444.6	803.8	289.7
Yauco, Puerto Rico M.S.A.											
	Includes Guanica, Guayanilla, Penu-elas, and Yauco Municipios	122,282									
	Total area actually reporting	100.0%	222	28	9	89	96	975	382	521	72
	Rate per 100,000 inhabitants		181.5	22.9	7.4	72.8	78.5	797.3	312.4	426.1	58.9

Table 7. Offense Analysis, 2002–2006

(Number.)

Classification		2002	2003	2004	2005[1]	2006
Murder		16,229	16,528	16,148	16,740	17,034
Forcible rape		95,235	93,883	95,089	94,347	92,455
Robbery:	Total[2]	420,806	414,235	401,470	417,438	447,403
Robbery by location:	Street/highway	180,058	179,657	171,812	184,188	199,241
	Commercial house	61,312	60,615	59,006	59,694	61,014
	Gas or service station	11,254	11,385	10,893	11,889	12,075
	Convenience store	27,183	25,826	24,653	23,822	24,921
	Residence	56,723	56,755	55,525	59,207	64,024
	Bank	9,693	9,523	9,775	8,766	9,591
	Miscellaneous	74,584	70,474	69,806	69,871	76,537
Burglary:	Total[2]	2,151,252	2,154,834	2,144,446	2,155,448	2,183,746
Burglary by location:	Residence (dwelling):	1,415,561	1,418,423	1,409,253	1,417,440	1,445,557
	Residence Night	418,094	409,188	405,556	402,881	411,558
	Residence Day	673,781	668,759	666,345	669,579	705,175
	Residence Unknown	323,687	340,477	337,351	344,980	328,824
	Nonresidence (store, office, etc.):	735,691	736,411	735,193	738,008	738,189
	Nonresidence Night	312,516	310,187	307,702	305,729	307,076
	Nonresidence Day	228,698	221,240	223,012	221,183	234,458
	Nonresidence Unknown	194,477	204,984	204,479	211,096	196,655
Larceny-theft (except motor vehicle theft):	Total[2]	7,057,379	7,026,802	6,937,089	6,783,447	6,607,013
Larceny-theft by type:	Pocket-picking	32,451	31,966	29,840	29,221	28,770
	Purse-snatching	38,896	42,181	42,345	42,040	39,997
	Shoplifting	986,296	1,013,265	1,009,214	940,411	872,635
	From motor vehicles (except accessories)	1,866,922	1,857,619	1,758,241	1,752,280	1,752,432
	Motor vehicle accessories	756,250	781,279	749,173	693,225	638,678
	Bicycles	277,003	271,801	249,813	248,792	231,238
	From buildings	883,847	868,621	861,197	852,462	829,756
	From coin-operated machines	52,374	52,373	45,927	40,885	35,264
	All others	2,163,340	2,107,696	2,191,338	2,184,131	2,178,243
Larceny-theft by value:	Over $200	2,796,465	2,761,752	2,711,560	2,715,997	2,805,338
	$50 to $200	1,592,830	1,586,672	1,562,672	1,522,810	1,474,693
	Under $50	2,668,084	2,678,377	2,662,857	2,544,640	2,326,982
Motor vehicle theft		1,246,646	1,261,226	1,237,851	1,235,859	1,192,809

[1] The 2005 crime figures have been adjusted.

[2] Because of rounding, the number of offenses may not add to the total.

Table 8. Offenses Known to Law Enforcement, by State and City, 2006

(Number.)

State	City	Popula-tion	Violent crime	Murder and non-negligent man-slaughter	Forcible rape	Robbery	Aggra-vated assault	Property crime	Burglary	Larceny-theft	Motor vehicle theft	Arson[1]
ALABAMA	Abbeville	2,990	11	0	1	0	10	92	23	66	3	
	Adamsville	4,889	44	0	2	13	29	289	38	228	23	
	Alabaster	27,766	27	0	0	8	19	650	39	561	50	
	Aliceville	2,487	33	1	1	2	29	89	23	62	4	
	Andalusia	8,770	49	0	8	8	33	532	120	389	23	
	Anniston	23,956	521	14	29	161	317	3,044	990	1,812	242	
	Ardmore	1,116	1	0	0	0	1	11	0	9	2	
	Ashford	1,949	3	0	0	0	3	26	7	15	4	
	Ashville	2,451	5	0	1	1	3	57	18	34	5	
	Atmore	7,598	69	0	2	11	56	531	98	407	26	
	Auburn	50,380	120	4	10	38	68	2,151	537	1,543	71	
	Autaugaville	873	0	0	0	0	0	29	13	15	1	
	Bayou La Batre	2,750	16	0	2	5	9	274	69	171	34	
	Bear Creek	1,030	2	0	0	0	2	15	2	12	1	
	Berry	1,237	0	0	0	0	0	3	0	2	1	
	Bessemer	28,900	493	5	37	200	251	3,400	875	2,218	307	
	Birmingham	233,577	3,175	104	220	1,429	1,422	19,007	4,813	12,113	2,081	228
	Blountsville	1,940	3	0	1	0	2	54	13	37	4	
	Boaz	7,964	20	1	2	3	14	544	91	437	16	
	Brantley	917	2	0	0	0	2	23	7	15	1	
	Brent	4,166	7	0	1	1	5	34	8	24	2	
	Brilliant	740	2	0	0	0	2	32	10	20	2	
	Butler	1,796	0	0	0	0	0	8	6	1	1	
	Camden	2,248	7	0	0	1	6	46	11	33	2	
	Centre	3,346	0	0	0	0	0	28	3	24	1	
	Centreville	2,530	4	0	0	1	3	25	7	18	0	
	Chatom	1,189	1	0	0	1	0	22	4	18	0	
	Cherokee	1,194	2	0	0	1	1	6	3	3	0	
	Clanton	8,411	59	2	1	9	47	240	45	178	17	
	Clayton	1,415	16	0	0	1	15	44	14	29	1	
	Cleveland	1,375	0	0	0	0	0	4	1	3	0	
	Coffeeville	357	1	0	0	0	1	7	1	4	2	
	Collinsville	1,682	8	0	0	3	5	53	8	42	3	
	Coosada	1,497	0	0	0	0	0	12	2	9	1	
	Cordova	2,357	6	0	1	1	4	110	30	73	7	
	Cottonwood	1,182	3	0	0	0	3	24	3	19	2	
	Courtland	772	1	0	0	0	1	14	6	7	1	
	Crossville	1,462	0	0	0	0	0	9	5	1	3	
	Cullman	14,868	24	0	6	9	9	864	122	687	55	
	Dadeville	3,173	21	0	1	1	19	209	28	176	5	
	Daleville	4,586	8	0	3	1	4	91	26	57	8	
	Daphne	18,749	20	0	4	9	7	576	95	453	28	
	Dauphin Island	1,547	3	0	1	0	2	24	7	17	0	
	Decatur	55,406	249	2	25	80	142	3,629	716	2,630	283	
	Dora	2,413	5	0	0	2	3	115	16	84	15	
	Dothan	63,280	381	7	58	189	127	3,350	881	2,266	203	
	Double Springs	992	4	0	0	2	2	26	3	20	3	
	East Brewton	2,446	6	0	1	0	5	83	14	64	5	
	Elba	4,219	19	0	0	2	17	126	36	85	5	
	Eutaw	1,816	29	0	1	4	24	120	28	79	13	
	Evergreen	3,473	18	1	1	2	14	116	21	92	3	
	Fairfield	11,802	98	1	3	46	48	792	170	528	94	
	Falkville	1,188	4	0	0	0	4	22	6	13	3	
	Fayette	4,804	18	0	3	3	12	181	26	145	10	
	Flomaton	1,574	2	1	0	0	1	44	10	27	7	
	Florala	1,910	19	1	2	0	16	93	14	77	2	
	Fultondale	6,915	24	0	3	8	13	433	75	327	31	
	Gadsden	37,743	326	2	41	195	88	3,251	829	2,174	248	
	Geraldine	823	2	0	0	0	2	7	0	6	1	
	Gordo	1,610	10	0	1	0	9	48	18	27	3	
	Grant	683	4	0	0	0	4	9	2	4	3	
	Guin	2,266	4	0	0	1	3	30	3	25	2	
	Gulf Shores	7,329	47	0	4	11	32	449	104	326	19	
	Hackleburg	1,488	7	0	0	1	6	20	4	15	1	

[1] The FBI does not publish arson data unless it receives data from either the agency or the state for all 12 months of the calendar year.

Table 8. Offenses Known to Law Enforcement, by State and City, 2006 (*Contd.*)

(Number.)

State	City	Population	Violent crime	Murder and non-negligent man-slaughter	Forcible rape	Robbery	Aggravated assault	Property crime	Burglary	Larceny-theft	Motor vehicle theft	Arson[1]
	Hamilton	6,555	8	0	4	1	3	238	52	161	25	0
	Hammondville	534	0	0	0	0	0	1	0	1	0	
	Hanceville	3,155	3	0	0	0	3	20	4	16	0	
	Harpersville	1,645	0	0	0	0	0	2	0	2	0	
	Hartselle	13,198	9	1	1	1	6	328	54	263	11	
	Hayneville	1,151	14	1	0	1	12	46	15	30	1	
	Heflin	3,338	27	0	2	3	22	112	21	85	6	
	Henagar	2,530	3	0	0	0	3	27	9	13	5	
	Hobson City	868	3	0	0	0	3	5	1	3	1	
	Hodges	260	0	0	0	0	0	1	1	0	0	
	Hokes Bluff	4,356	1	0	0	0	1	42	9	29	4	
	Hollywood	937	1	0	0	0	1	8	1	6	1	
	Homewood	24,180	134	0	8	98	28	1,141	243	812	86	
	Hoover	68,079	129	2	17	81	29	2,387	312	1,917	158	5
	Hueytown	15,329	10	1	1	5	3	87	29	52	6	
	Huntsville	167,817	1,439	16	100	617	706	11,495	2,493	7,643	1,359	
	Ider	694	0	0	0	0	0	5	2	1	2	
	Irondale	9,617	64	1	2	31	30	652	155	423	74	
	Jacksonville	8,942	60	3	3	19	35	549	173	347	29	
	Jemison	2,509	21	0	2	1	18	190	34	138	18	
	Lafayette	3,130	47	2	1	5	39	145	29	101	15	
	Lake View	1,662	3	0	0	1	2	60	15	42	3	
	Leeds	11,153	89	0	10	33	46	601	114	455	32	
	Leighton	843	1	0	0	0	1	8	3	4	1	
	Level Plains	1,543	18	0	0	0	18	84	11	73	0	0
	Lincoln	4,966	25	0	0	12	13	468	85	333	50	
	Lipscomb	2,339	1	0	0	1	0	1	0	1	0	
	Littleville	956	0	0	0	0	0	47	8	34	5	
	Livingston	3,076	12	0	0	7	5	152	44	98	10	
	Lockhart	547	0	0	0	0	0	1	0	1	0	
	Louisville	585	2	0	0	0	2	5	3	2	0	
	Loxley	1,448	4	0	1	1	2	143	35	88	20	
	Luverne	2,692	2	0	0	0	2	71	19	51	1	
	McIntosh	241	3	0	0	0	3	16	4	9	3	
	McKenzie	629	1	0	0	1	0	6	0	5	1	
	Midland City	1,814	26	0	2	2	22	39	11	27	1	
	Millbrook	14,939	4	0	1	2	1	106	17	88	1	
	Mobile[2]	250,152	1,167	34	83	685	365	15,849	3,662	10,857	1,330	112
	Montevallo	5,138	27	0	5	8	14	219	40	166	13	
	Montgomery	201,937	1,184	27	74	686	397	13,086	3,380	8,579	1,127	
	Moody	10,861	9	0	1	7	1	329	56	249	24	0
	Morris	1,885	1	0	0	1	0	24	3	21	0	
	Mosses	1,084	0	0	0	0	0	23	14	8	1	
	Moundville	2,208	21	0	0	1	20	54	14	34	6	2
	Mountain Brook	21,009	17	0	2	2	13	395	52	331	12	
	Mount Vernon	826	4	0	0	0	4	5	0	5	0	
	Napier Field	405	0	0	0	0	0	0	0	0	0	
	New Brockton	1,247	0	0	0	0	0	22	2	20	0	0
	New Hope	2,695	2	0	0	0	2	44	9	33	2	
	North Courtland	805	0	0	0	0	0	2	0	1	1	
	Notasulga	859	0	0	0	0	0	41	18	20	3	
	Odenville	1,214	15	0	1	0	14	34	15	15	4	
	Ohatchee	1,222	4	1	2	1	0	36	14	20	2	
	Oneonta	6,596	23	0	1	6	16	314	26	256	32	
	Opp	6,718	26	0	2	2	22	263	55	207	1	0
	Orange Beach	5,101	27	1	5	6	15	372	55	302	15	
	Ozark	14,967	146	0	12	32	102	777	200	517	60	
	Parrish	1,270	14	0	0	3	11	88	9	73	6	
	Pelham	19,626	47	1	2	31	13	558	52	472	34	0
	Pell City	11,110	93	0	10	15	68	606	103	465	38	
	Pennington	335	0	0	0	0	0	3	2	1	0	
	Phil Campbell	1,059	0	0	0	0	0	18	5	9	4	
	Pine Hill	931	13	0	0	0	13	19	4	15	0	
	Powell	968	0	0	0	0	0	3	2	1	0	

[1] The FBI does not publish arson data unless it receives data from either the agency or the state for all 12 months of the calendar year.
[2] The population for the city of Mobile, Alabama, includes 56,876 inhabitants from the jurisdiction of the Mobile County Sheriff's Department.

Table 8. Offenses Known to Law Enforcement, by State and City, 2006 (*Contd.*)

(Number.)

State	City	Popula-tion	Violent crime	Murder and non-negligent man-slaughter	Forcible rape	Robbery	Aggra-vated assault	Property crime	Burglary	Larceny-theft	Motor vehicle theft	Arson[1]
	Prattville	30,315	124	1	15	47	61	1,317	220	1,042	55	
	Priceville	2,253	0	0	0	0	0	58	17	40	1	0
	Prichard	28,216	94	7	4	35	48	650	131	388	131	
	Ragland	2,045	3	0	1	1	1	32	7	23	2	
	Ranburne	475	0	0	0	0	0	19	3	12	4	
	Red Level	555	0	0	0	0	0	1	1	0	0	
	Riverside	1,765	2	0	0	0	2	17	4	12	1	
	Roanoke	6,710	24	1	4	6	13	200	29	161	10	
	Rogersville	1,197	3	0	0	0	3	22	6	14	2	
	Russellville	8,873	32	0	5	12	15	103	20	73	10	
	Samson	2,043	3	0	0	0	3	47	15	31	1	
	Sardis City	1,935	3	0	0	0	3	35	11	21	3	
	Satsuma	6,005	10	0	2	5	3	93	19	60	14	0
	Scottsboro	14,974	28	2	4	5	17	631	29	585	17	
	Selma	19,576	315	3	29	96	187	2,497	711	1,623	163	
	Shorter	340	1	0	0	1	0	2	0	2	0	
	Silverhill	701	1	0	0	0	1	27	4	22	1	
	Sipsey	553	0	0	0	0	0	0	0	0	0	
	Skyline	847	0	0	0	0	0	12	2	9	1	
	Slocomb	2,051	2	0	0	0	2	25	10	11	4	
	Snead	824	1	0	0	0	1	26	2	22	2	
	Somerville	360	0	0	0	0	0	19	5	14	0	
	Southside	7,909	12	0	0	0	12	208	56	144	8	
	Steele	1,164	0	0	0	0	0	0	0	0	0	
	Stevenson	2,157	34	0	0	1	33	128	24	80	24	
	St. Florian	438	1	0	1	0	0	11	1	10	0	
	Sulligent	2,051	1	0	0	0	1	22	1	19	2	
	Sumiton	2,605	11	1	0	9	1	296	37	230	29	
	Summerdale	679	5	0	0	3	2	80	21	50	9	
	Sylacauga	13,073	56	0	7	23	26	874	163	693	18	
	Sylvania	1,249	0	0	0	0	0	8	6	0	2	
	Tallassee	5,078	51	0	0	4	47	345	38	289	18	
	Tarrant City	6,752	104	1	6	49	48	598	174	356	68	0
	Thorsby	1,999	0	0	0	0	0	7	1	6	0	
	Town Creek	1,220	0	0	0	0	0	7	2	5	0	
	Trinity	1,859	0	0	0	0	0	8	2	4	2	
	Troy	14,061	42	0	3	29	10	805	125	645	35	
	Trussville	16,912	46	0	6	25	15	875	84	757	34	
	Tuscaloosa	82,094	604	15	47	221	321	5,234	1,256	3,709	269	
	Tuscumbia	8,244	11	0	1	6	4	327	66	250	11	
	Vernon	2,002	0	0	0	0	0	13	3	9	1	
	Vestavia Hills	31,303	36	0	4	17	15	287	88	172	27	
	Wetumpka	6,967	27	0	2	13	12	410	96	304	10	
	Woodville	762	0	0	0	0	0	1	0	1	0	
ALASKA	Anchorage	277,692	2,592	17	248	465	1,862	11,721	1,733	8,543	1,445	106
	Bethel	6,322	61	2	6	4	49	99	44	28	27	1
	Bristol Bay Borough	1,123	12	0	0	0	12	23	8	11	4	0
	Cordova	2,349	11	0	0	0	11	41	3	26	12	1
	Craig	1,229	16	0	0	0	16	19	8	7	4	0
	Dillingham	2,492	49	1	19	1	28	69	6	60	3	0
	Fairbanks	31,626	268	1	67	47	153	1,617	297	1,163	157	14
	Haines	2,294	4	0	0	0	4	52	7	43	2	0
	Homer	5,416	39	0	0	1	38	216	26	173	17	2
	Houston	1,630	9	0	0	2	7	33	10	17	6	4
	Juneau	31,285	123	2	32	9	80	1,475	194	1,225	56	4
	Kenai	7,536	19	0	2	1	16	319	25	274	20	2
	Ketchikan	7,481	36	0	10	3	23	509	53	425	31	6
	Kodiak	6,333	25	0	0	2	23	196	24	147	25	1
	Kotzebue	3,268	13	0	1	0	12	33	9	13	11	0
	North Pole	1,795	4	0	1	1	2	110	21	78	11	2
	North Slope Borough	6,991	58	1	12	7	38	154	57	70	27	7
	Palmer	6,987	61	0	2	6	53	235	16	211	8	2
	Petersburg	3,039	0	0	0	0	0	123	8	102	13	0
	Seward	3,045	10	0	0	3	7	130	12	112	6	0
	Sitka	9,073	16	0	4	1	11	297	24	255	18	1

[1] The FBI does not publish arson data unless it receives data from either the agency or the state for all 12 months of the calendar year.

Table 8. Offenses Known to Law Enforcement, by State and City, 2006 (Contd.)

(Number.)

State	City	Population	Violent crime	Murder and non-negligent man-slaughter	Forcible rape	Robbery	Aggra-vated assault	Property crime	Burglary	Larceny-theft	Motor vehicle theft	Arson[1]
	Skagway	836	1	0	0	0	1	12	4	8	0	0
	Soldotna	4,126	22	0	3	0	19	279	33	232	14	1
	St. Paul	464	12	1	0	1	10	0	0	0	0	0
	Unalaska	4,389	11	0	1	1	9	80	10	65	5	0
	Wrangell	2,137	4	1	0	1	2	97	6	88	3	0
ARIZONA	Apache Junction[3]	33,532	163	0	13	19	131			1,280	225	14
	Benson	5,123	11	0	1	4	6	246	55	163	28	1
	Bisbee	6,413	15	0	0	0	15	272	46	212	14	0
	Bullhead City	40,596	160	1	6	39	114	2,049	472	1,349	228	19
	Camp Verde	10,543	50	0	4	0	46	274	37	204	33	4
	Casa Grande	34,111	248	1	4	49	194	3,093	1,042	1,678	373	17
	Chandler	243,919	959	9	56	236	658	8,724	1,401	6,152	1,171	70
	Chino Valley	10,081	15	0	1	1	13	189	52	126	11	2
	Clarkdale	3,896	13	0	0	0	13	55	20	28	7	0
	Clifton	2,352	3	0	0	0	3	24	7	14	3	1
	Colorado City	4,538	1	0	0	1	0	6	3	2	1	0
	Coolidge	8,466	81	1	4	24	52	790	213	476	101	13
	Cottonwood	11,310	44	0	0	2	42	438	54	357	27	5
	Eagar	4,284	16	0	0	0	16	93	26	57	10	1
	El Mirage	23,018	122	2	12	17	91	835	194	458	183	14
	Eloy	11,270	83	0	4	33	46	676	196	418	62	25
	Flagstaff	59,585	428	3	46	89	290	4,024	497	3,340	187	59
	Florence[4]	17,705	38	1	0	1	36			103	21	0
	Fredonia	1,091	2	0	0	0	2	5	3	2	0	0
	Gilbert	180,640	254	3	37	53	161	4,935	949	3,516	470	23
	Glendale	248,587	1,539	21	75	466	977	12,094	3,756	5,625	2,713	85
	Globe	7,462	72	0	0	2	70	394	90	284	20	1
	Goodyear	45,621	90	0	14	27	49	2,675	1,443	862	370	4
	Holbrook	5,322	91	0	8	3	80	432	116	298	18	7
	Huachuca City	1,962	2	0	0	0	2	44	14	21	9	0
	Kearny	2,871	18	0	0	0	18	54	16	38	0	0
	Kingman	26,524	123	4	7	29	83	2,164	465	1,503	196	15
	Lake Havasu City	57,453	101	3	10	11	77	1,715	321	1,243	151	11
	Mammoth	2,250	13	0	0	0	13	28	11	15	2	0
	Marana	27,096	78	1	4	14	59	1,167	235	796	136	7
	Mesa	459,705	2,003	26	203	508	1,266	21,304	3,283	14,367	3,654	38
	Miami	1,911	37	0	0	3	34	99	47	49	3	6
	Nogales	21,629	79	0	0	14	65	573	117	322	134	3
	Oro Valley	39,907	29	1	2	5	21	741	101	578	62	9
	Paradise Valley	15,114	14	0	0	3	11	341	202	124	15	2
	Payson	15,292	14	1	2	1	10	394	100	280	14	2
	Peoria	143,483	317	2	41	77	197	5,719	1,075	3,672	972	20
	Phoenix	1,517,443	11,194	234	550	4,363	6,047	90,050	16,150	49,811	24,089	525
	Pima	2,040	5	0	0	0	5	53	10	39	4	0
	Prescott	41,903	181	3	12	32	134	1,541	318	1,133	90	19
	Prescott Valley	34,332	207	2	15	9	181	910	187	687	36	4
	Quartzsite	3,527	17	0	2	0	15	123	3	108	12	1
	Sahuarita	9,351	30	0	6	2	22	445	54	348	43	1
	Scottsdale	234,652	505	5	65	153	282	8,315	1,721	5,476	1,118	50
	Sedona	11,649	23	0	3	2	18	241	43	185	13	0
	Show Low	10,382	98	0	7	2	89	478	159	294	25	1
	Sierra Vista	43,510	109	1	10	16	82	1,957	217	1,575	165	12
	Snowflake-Taylor	9,101	79	0	0	1	78	270	75	179	16	3
	Somerton	10,456	20	0	1	2	17	224	32	164	28	1
	South Tucson	5,775	156	1	3	55	97	960	134	733	93	3
	Springerville	2,031	20	0	3	0	17	95	28	63	4	0
	St. Johns	3,673	23	0	0	0	23	216	78	129	9	2
	Surprise	77,255	106	0	17	21	68	2,253	360	1,610	283	11
	Tempe	167,303	1,094	5	71	426	592	12,589	1,795	8,374	2,420	74
	Thatcher	4,279	4	1	0	0	3	141	27	110	4	2
	Tolleson[4]	6,202	69	0	3	26	40		386	518		5
	Tucson[5]	535,232	4,580	51	294	1,675	2,560		5,121		7,376	301

[1] The FBI does not publish arson data unless it receives data from either the agency or the state for all 12 months of the calendar year.
[3] The FBI determined that the agency's data were inflated. Consequently, affected data are not included in this table.
[4] The FBI determined that the agency's data were underreported. Consequently, affected data are not included in this table.
[5] It was determined that the agency did not follow national Uniform Crime Reporting (UCR) Program guidelines for reporting an offense. Consequently, this figure is not included in this table.

Table 8. Offenses Known to Law Enforcement, by State and City, 2006 (*Contd.*)

(Number.)

State	City	Popula-tion	Violent crime	Murder and non-negligent man-slaughter	Forcible rape	Robbery	Aggra-vated assault	Property crime	Burglary	Larceny-theft	Motor vehicle theft	Arson[1]
	Wellton	1,933	9	0	0	0	9	45	15	29	1	0
	Wickenburg	6,462	11	0	0	0	11	181	51	110	20	0
	Willcox	3,913	8	0	3	0	5	316	90	191	35	2
	Williams	3,212	34	0	0	3	31	137	13	121	3	3
	Winslow	10,311	52	1	2	8	41	506	105	372	29	8
	Youngtown	4,175	32	1	2	2	27	141	54	54	33	0
	Yuma	87,925	542	3	33	84	422	4,066	809	2,512	745	45
ARKANSAS	Altheimer	1,174	2	0	0	0	2	30	19	10	1	0
	Arkadelphia	10,668	41	0	3	10	28	381	162	208	11	0
	Arkansas City	555	3	0	0	0	3	12	9	3	0	0
	Ashdown	4,644	12	0	0	5	7	149	25	121	3	0
	Atkins	2,923	1	0	0	0	1	83	33	49	1	0
	Augusta	2,484	16	1	0	0	15	120	14	102	4	3
	Austin	695	6	0	0	0	6	14	4	10	0	0
	Bald Knob	3,354	8	0	0	1	7	62	21	36	5	0
	Barling	4,367	9	0	1	0	8	76	21	51	4	0
	Bay	1,975	2	0	1	0	1	44	26	17	1	0
	Bearden	1,059	0	0	0	0	0	35	17	18	0	0
	Beebe	5,687	30	0	2	3	25	407	114	271	22	1
	Benton	25,966	82	0	10	9	63	1,615	258	1,264	93	1
	Bentonville	29,875	72	0	19	9	44	802	118	642	42	3
	Berryville	4,991	17	0	15	1	1	226	74	139	13	2
	Blytheville	16,828	141	2	19	36	84	1,466	491	889	86	9
	Booneville	4,210	9	0	2	1	6	165	54	108	3	1
	Bradford	837	3	0	0	0	3	15	4	6	5	0
	Brinkley	3,560	1	0	0	1	0	39	34	5	0	0
	Bull Shoals	2,084	2	0	0	0	2	15	8	7	0	0
	Cabot	21,279	151	0	12	6	133	884	245	601	38	5
	Caddo Valley	611	1	0	0	0	1	18	8	9	1	0
	Camden	12,343	68	0	5	16	47	824	202	596	26	6
	Caraway	1,370	0	0	0	0	0	2	2	0	0	0
	Carlisle	2,447	3	0	0	0	3	59	29	29	1	0
	Cave Springs	1,440	1	0	0	0	1	7	1	6	0	0
	Centerton	5,540	21	0	6	1	14	119	44	72	3	0
	Charleston	3,060	3	0	0	0	3	36	10	24	2	0
	Cherokee Village	4,686	6	1	2	0	3	70	16	53	1	2
	Clinton	2,503	2	0	0	0	2	68	13	45	10	0
	Conway	52,592	187	3	35	61	88	2,420	393	1,843	184	6
	Corning	3,495	5	0	0	0	5	48	17	29	2	0
	Crossett	5,868	43	0	5	6	32	271	66	201	4	5
	Danville	2,470	6	0	1	0	5	14	7	7	0	0
	Dardanelle	4,386	23	0	2	2	19	70	62	7	1	0
	Decatur	1,367	6	0	1	0	5	29	17	11	1	0
	De Queen	6,021	29	3	3	1	22	269	90	156	23	1
	Des Arc	1,842	8	0	0	1	7	34	16	17	1	0
	De Witt	3,453	10	0	0	3	7	158	38	113	7	0
	Diaz	1,214	2	0	0	0	2	21	9	12	0	0
	Dierks	1,266	0	0	0	0	0	13	8	4	1	0
	Dover	1,375	3	0	0	0	3	23	10	11	2	0
	Dumas	4,917	50	0	7	20	23	187	54	124	9	1
	Earle	2,928	7	0	1	0	6	90	76	14	0	3
	El Dorado	20,701	182	2	1	34	145	1,277	518	714	45	6
	England	3,063	16	0	0	1	15	72	28	39	5	1
	Etowah	349	0	0	0	0	0	5	2	3	0	0
	Eureka Springs	2,377	18	0	0	1	17	89	20	69	0	0
	Fairfield Bay	2,531	3	0	0	0	3	44	14	29	1	0
	Farmington	4,426	7	0	2	0	5	60	19	36	5	0
	Fayetteville	67,416	357	0	41	35	281	3,229	602	2,455	172	11
	Flippin	1,412	6	0	0	1	5	44	12	32	0	0
	Fordyce	4,459	45	3	2	10	30	190	76	103	11	1
	Forrest City	14,239	132	0	8	42	82	1,071	207	806	58	5
	Fort Smith	83,422	876	11	83	131	651	5,491	1,089	4,039	363	28
	Gassville	1,953	1	1	0	0	0	33	11	22	0	0
	Gentry	2,643	9	0	1	0	8	44	22	22	0	0
	Gosnell	3,703	49	0	1	4	44	109	50	54	5	4

[1] The FBI does not publish arson data unless it receives data from either the agency or the state for all 12 months of the calendar year.

Table 8. Offenses Known to Law Enforcement, by State and City, 2006 (*Contd.*)

(Number.)

State	City	Popula-tion	Violent crime	Murder and non-negligent man-slaughter	Forcible rape	Robbery	Aggra-vated assault	Property crime	Burglary	Larceny-theft	Motor vehicle theft	Arson[1]
	Gravette	2,301	5	0	1	0	4	30	14	15	1	2
	Greenbrier	3,656	0	0	0	0	0	6	0	6	0	0
	Green Forest	2,892	7	0	2	0	5	41	10	31	0	0
	Greenland	1,073	5	0	0	0	5	29	13	14	2	0
	Greenwood	8,004	19	0	2	1	16	152	48	102	2	1
	Greers Ferry	977	6	0	0	0	6	12	7	5	0	1
	Gurdon	2,258	17	0	0	0	17	61	17	42	2	0
	Hamburg	2,876	11	0	3	3	5	49	15	34	0	1
	Hampton	1,529	3	0	0	1	2	16	5	11	0	0
	Harrisburg	2,190	3	0	0	0	3	146	67	68	11	1
	Harrison	12,910	54	0	9	1	44	567	163	375	29	4
	Hazen	1,580	7	0	0	0	7	31	4	26	1	1
	Heber Springs	7,096	14	0	7	1	6	330	83	244	3	1
	Helena-West Helena	13,718	236	3	5	26	202	1,147	475	621	51	11
	Hermitage	771	1	0	1	0	0	9	7	2	0	0
	Highland	1,035	3	0	0	0	3	28	10	18	0	1
	Hope	10,586	108	2	8	17	81	917	267	612	38	5
	Horseshoe Bend	2,313	1	0	0	0	1	68	26	39	3	1
	Hot Springs	38,279	511	4	23	133	351	4,614	1,162	3,215	237	2
	Hoxie	2,748	2	0	1	0	1	22	8	10	4	0
	Jacksonville	30,714	222	4	12	46	160	1,815	440	1,252	123	9
	Jonesboro	60,035	467	3	39	88	337	3,807	1,579	2,080	148	7
	Kensett	1,727	8	0	0	2	6	37	19	17	1	0
	Lake City	2,025	0	0	0	0	0	17	12	5	0	0
	Lakeview	815	2	0	0	0	2	9	2	7	0	0
	Lake Village	2,638	5	0	2	1	2	89	30	57	2	1
	Leachville	1,868	6	0	1	0	5	37	17	19	1	2
	Lepanto	2,103	16	0	1	2	13	89	30	53	6	0
	Lincoln	1,926	1	0	0	0	1	38	20	12	6	2
	Little Flock	2,813	2	0	2	0	0	19	14	5	0	0
	Little Rock	186,670	3,324	58	151	899	2,216	15,789	3,866	10,611	1,312	145
	Lonoke	4,604	12	0	0	4	8	219	69	140	10	0
	Lowell	7,122	18	1	1	3	13	204	67	125	12	0
	Luxora	1,257	5	0	1	1	3	7	4	3	0	0
	Magnolia	10,598	55	0	2	21	32	540	288	188	64	2
	Marianna	4,847	32	1	1	8	22	242	102	140	0	3
	Marion	9,904	37	0	4	2	31	309	82	219	8	1
	Marked Tree	2,751	4	0	0	2	2	94	21	73	0	0
	Marmaduke	1,176	4	0	1	0	3	40	6	33	1	1
	Marvell	1,264	2	0	2	0	0	40	10	29	1	0
	Maumelle	14,481	24	3	2	2	17	352	164	169	19	2
	McCrory	1,707	2	0	0	1	1	32	13	16	3	1
	McGehee	4,281	12	0	0	0	12	100	31	67	2	0
	McRae	689	5	0	0	0	5	50	13	35	2	0
	Mena	5,672	8	0	0	0	8	90	13	75	2	0
	Mineral Springs	1,308	2	0	0	0	2	15	9	6	0	0
	Monticello	9,433	48	0	4	6	38	554	184	357	13	2
	Morrilton	6,682	32	0	5	5	22	500	128	350	22	3
	Mountain Home	12,032	6	1	4	0	1	513	25	471	17	1
	Mountain View	3,032	5	0	1	0	4	54	16	35	3	1
	Nashville	4,985	20	1	2	6	11	421	252	166	3	1
	Newport	7,364	61	1	6	13	41	518	130	364	24	1
	North Little Rock	59,474	866	13	64	240	549	5,621	1,263	3,814	544	23
	Ola	1,220	3	0	0	0	3	11	8	3	0	1
	Osceola	8,221	116	1	8	10	97	443	121	304	18	3
	Ozark	3,627	9	2	2	0	5	55	20	33	2	0
	Pangburn	669	10	0	2	0	8	15	6	7	2	0
	Paragould	24,046	128	0	12	14	102	1,381	312	979	90	6
	Paris	3,749	15	0	1	0	14	92	36	50	6	0
	Pea Ridge	3,382	4	0	1	0	3	58	16	41	1	0
	Piggott	3,703	2	0	0	0	2	11	6	5	0	0
	Pine Bluff	53,294	798	12	36	203	547	3,980	1,512	2,053	415	77
	Plainview	765	0	0	0	0	0	2	1	0	1	0
	Plummerville	883	4	0	0	0	4	19	6	10	3	0
	Pocahontas	6,842	6	0	0	0	6	99	23	75	1	0

[1] The FBI does not publish arson data unless it receives data from either the agency or the state for all 12 months of the calendar year.

Table 8. Offenses Known to Law Enforcement, by State and City, 2006 (Contd.)

(Number.)

State	City	Population	Violent crime	Murder and non-negligent man-slaughter	Forcible rape	Robbery	Aggra-vated assault	Property crime	Burglary	Larceny-theft	Motor vehicle theft	Arson[1]
	Pottsville	1,534	10	0	0	0	10	35	15	16	4	0
	Prairie Grove	3,030	6	0	2	0	4	83	22	59	2	0
	Prescott	4,334	32	0	0	5	27	115	38	75	2	0
	Quitman	749	0	0	0	0	0	15	2	13	0	0
	Redfield	1,186	2	0	0	0	2	31	15	12	4	0
	Rogers	48,905	101	0	44	13	44	2,520	292	2,147	81	8
	Rose Bud	453	2	0	0	0	2	7	0	6	1	0
	Russellville	25,811	105	1	24	10	70	1,170	269	830	71	5
	Salem	1,605	3	0	1	0	2	25	8	16	1	1
	Searcy	20,899	99	1	4	8	86	854	66	741	47	0
	Sheridan	4,399	12	0	0	0	12	81	16	61	4	0
	Sherwood	23,413	105	1	9	9	86	965	142	744	79	2
	Siloam Springs	13,759	23	0	7	3	13	569	94	441	34	2
	Smackover	1,951	6	0	0	1	5	19	3	14	2	0
	Springdale	60,782	281	2	61	36	182	2,617	471	1,942	204	14
	Star City	2,347	8	1	1	1	5	53	14	39	0	1
	Stuttgart	9,483	50	1	3	10	36	514	186	324	4	2
	Sulphur Springs	697	2	0	1	0	1	22	20	2	0	0
	Swifton	820	0	0	0	0	0	3	2	1	0	0
	Texarkana	30,348	490	3	18	81	388	1,530	406	1,023	101	14
	Trumann	7,001	51	2	3	11	35	530	153	371	6	2
	Tuckerman	1,741	2	0	0	0	2	15	8	7	0	0
	Van Buren	21,492	73	1	19	0	53	901	241	622	38	2
	Vilonia	2,750	10	0	1	0	9	66	11	53	2	0
	Waldron	3,596	61	0	1	2	58	129	59	65	5	6
	Walnut Ridge	4,778	3	0	0	0	3	61	20	39	2	3
	Ward	3,308	17	0	2	0	15	98	39	51	8	0
	Warren	6,334	32	1	1	9	21	128	86	39	3	1
	Weiner	764	2	0	1	0	1	12	3	9	0	0
	West Fork	2,220	3	0	0	1	2	21	9	12	0	0
	West Memphis	28,503	530	10	35	124	361	1,899	832	959	108	18
	White Hall	5,172	4	0	0	1	3	123	17	96	10	0
	Wynne	8,667	34	0	1	8	25	379	183	190	6	1
CALIFORNIA	Adelanto	24,579	136	2	14	35	85	692	238	305	149	7
	Agoura Hills	22,970	41	0	3	7	31	338	86	229	23	3
	Alameda	71,212	221	2	7	81	131	1,912	323	1,297	292	9
	Albany	16,138	54	0	4	40	10	796	134	539	123	5
	Alhambra	88,197	297	1	19	158	119	2,472	443	1,572	457	14
	Aliso Viejo	41,915	38	0	4	2	32	436	72	324	40	13
	Alturas	2,928	16	0	4	2	10	93	27	56	10	3
	American Canyon	15,469	28	0	3	11	14	270	76	155	39	2
	Anaheim	334,792	1,524	10	107	584	823	8,817	1,886	5,277	1,654	65
	Anderson	10,623	35	0	3	6	26	441	110	298	33	2
	Antioch	101,537	657	10	35	285	327	2,844	840	1,124	880	56
	Apple Valley	65,743	247	2	17	74	154	2,103	652	1,077	374	25
	Arcadia	56,659	157	1	5	73	78	1,783	409	1,208	166	3
	Arcata	17,066	55	0	4	17	34	699	182	474	43	1
	Arroyo Grande	16,462	48	1	4	7	36	375	67	295	13	5
	Artesia	16,822	95	2	5	42	46	276	65	160	51	2
	Arvin	14,857	68	1	3	27	37	667	166	424	77	21
	Atascadero	27,374	72	0	2	13	57	661	130	496	35	6
	Atherton	7,242	15	0	2	2	11	168	32	131	5	7
	Atwater	27,351	96	1	4	25	66	1,022	305	607	110	14
	Auburn	13,028	65	1	5	3	56	433	105	267	61	6
	Avalon	3,364	27	0	2	2	23	193	44	85	64	2
	Avenal	16,781	53	0	2	2	49	138	50	76	12	3
	Azusa	47,544	185	1	10	43	131	1,468	292	923	253	2
	Bakersfield	298,198	1,575	24	43	549	959	15,915	3,729	9,623	2,563	193
	Baldwin Park	79,571	323	6	11	123	183	2,046	363	882	801	10
	Banning	29,572	203	4	9	39	151	876	305	443	128	0
	Barstow	23,951	290	2	18	80	190	1,022	374	418	230	13
	Bear Valley	4,555	2	0	0	0	2	13	7	6	0	0
	Beaumont	20,715	91	1	7	14	69	689	157	406	126	2
	Bell	37,859	162	3	10	64	85	439	126	117	196	0
	Bellflower	75,242	474	5	16	236	217	2,219	476	1,060	683	13

[1] The FBI does not publish arson data unless it receives data from either the agency or the state for all 12 months of the calendar year.

Table 8. Offenses Known to Law Enforcement, by State and City, 2006 (*Contd.*)

(Number.)

State	City	Population	Violent crime	Murder and non-negligent man-slaughter	Forcible rape	Robbery	Aggra-vated assault	Property crime	Burglary	Larceny-theft	Motor vehicle theft	Arson[1]
	Bell Gardens	45,541	281	6	15	77	183	804	182	243	379	3
	Belmont	24,743	7	0	2	5	0	563	87	432	44	1
	Belvedere	2,091	1	0	0	0	1	29	5	22	2	0
	Benicia	26,728	66	0	7	12	47	496	116	308	72	8
	Berkeley	101,651	646	4	22	414	206	7,323	1,152	5,096	1,075	36
	Beverly Hills	35,394	135	0	7	82	46	1,057	273	729	55	4
	Big Bear Lake	6,213	54	0	5	5	44	274	90	166	18	3
	Biggs	1,819	22	0	1	0	21	51	24	24	3	0
	Bishop	3,638	15	0	1	1	13	137	24	107	6	2
	Blue Lake	1,138	25	0	0	0	25	115	51	53	11	2
	Blythe	22,329	127	0	4	16	107	707	249	412	46	34
	Bradbury	1,023	0	0	0	0	0	12	4	5	3	0
	Brawley	22,635	61	0	4	25	32	1,244	386	680	178	13
	Brea	38,811	77	0	9	31	37	1,456	225	1,088	143	12
	Brentwood	44,188	123	3	8	33	79	1,191	208	868	115	32
	Brisbane	3,588	11	0	0	0	11	122	21	89	12	2
	Broadmoor	4,334	15	0	0	6	9	116	30	59	27	1
	Buellton	4,332	11	0	2	1	8	87	19	63	5	1
	Buena Park	79,887	274	1	19	114	140	1,960	410	1,091	459	44
	Burbank	105,046	252	1	10	75	166	2,721	567	1,683	471	14
	Burlingame	27,627	75	0	6	32	37	891	153	636	102	17
	Calabasas	22,105	24	0	1	3	20	322	80	215	27	4
	Calexico	36,329	117	1	1	42	73	1,350	364	566	420	31
	California City	11,896	43	2	1	6	34	302	120	160	22	0
	Calimesa	7,558	22	0	1	12	9	181	47	105	29	0
	Calipatria	7,795	1	0	0	1	0	36	14	18	4	0
	Calistoga	5,237	8	0	1	0	7	106	26	74	6	0
	Camarillo	62,131	114	2	10	28	74	1,119	231	789	99	7
	Campbell	37,376	77	0	7	24	46	1,238	243	829	166	17
	Canyon Lake	11,389	18	0	2	2	14	165	34	91	40	2
	Capitola	9,639	61	0	3	9	49	934	122	770	42	0
	Carlsbad	91,590	329	1	11	77	240	2,455	587	1,648	220	18
	Carmel	4,030	7	0	2	1	4	148	38	104	6	0
	Carpinteria	13,671	23	0	3	5	15	236	72	147	17	2
	Carson	94,801	738	15	16	268	439	2,823	619	1,502	702	37
	Cathedral City	52,179	233	4	15	62	152	1,709	501	871	337	0
	Ceres	40,936	180	2	12	57	109	2,094	333	1,300	461	19
	Cerritos	53,034	172	4	4	115	49	1,912	300	1,316	296	6
	Chico	72,070	337	1	66	92	178	2,658	741	1,559	358	78
	Chino	78,277	228	0	8	108	112	2,390	530	1,426	434	19
	Chino Hills	76,404	127	1	7	26	93	1,214	275	776	163	6
	Chowchilla	16,674	26	0	5	2	19	295	84	183	28	0
	Chula Vista	212,393	947	7	70	351	519	7,034	1,184	3,817	2,033	41
	City of Angels	3,795	11	0	1	2	8	76	30	41	5	3
	Claremont	35,499	88	1	6	29	52	989	293	620	76	5
	Clayton	11,242	12	0	0	3	9	184	36	137	11	5
	Clearlake	14,861	75	3	4	7	61	507	162	267	78	8
	Cloverdale	8,088	25	0	3	3	19	169	38	121	10	3
	Clovis	87,306	148	1	11	59	77	3,154	630	2,139	385	37
	Coachella	32,724	255	5	11	88	151	1,649	392	783	474	13
	Coalinga	17,506	42	0	5	5	32	455	126	282	47	6
	Colma	1,407	10	0	1	4	5	359	9	321	29	0
	Colton	51,812	344	5	13	132	194	1,743	477	847	419	9
	Colusa	5,878	18	0	1	2	15	208	56	131	21	0
	Commerce	13,576	117	6	5	56	50	1,159	153	606	400	12
	Compton	96,520	1,672	39	50	534	1,049	2,411	578	931	902	99
	Concord	124,362	520	2	20	248	250	5,386	941	3,258	1,187	4
	Corcoran	22,658	58	0	7	3	48	224	98	94	32	8
	Corning	7,204	60	0	3	6	51	339	82	228	29	19
	Corona	150,732	328	1	31	152	144	4,042	730	2,492	820	30
	Coronado	26,662	23	0	3	9	11	516	67	379	70	1
	Costa Mesa	110,819	306	6	30	123	147	3,380	524	2,449	407	11
	Cotati	7,202	56	0	1	4	51	148	50	83	15	3
	Covina	48,281	171	0	5	68	98	1,800	412	1,190	198	26
	Crescent City	7,895	40	0	6	11	23	359	86	232	41	1

[1] The FBI does not publish arson data unless it receives data from either the agency or the state for all 12 months of the calendar year.

Table 8. Offenses Known to Law Enforcement, by State and City, 2006 *(Contd.)*

(Number.)

State	City	Popula-tion	Violent crime	Murder and non-negligent man-slaughter	Forcible rape	Robbery	Aggra-vated assault	Property crime	Burglary	Larceny-theft	Motor vehicle theft	Arson[1]
	Cudahy	25,229	111	3	3	41	64	350	44	132	174	0
	Culver City	39,960	206	1	10	164	31	1,153	176	798	179	1
	Cupertino	52,641	109	0	0	23	86	1,094	338	710	46	14
	Cypress	47,810	67	2	1	32	32	919	183	596	140	20
	Daly City	101,243	289	3	18	134	134	2,344	243	1,587	514	23
	Dana Point	36,190	48	0	2	11	35	462	72	350	40	6
	Danville	42,229	33	1	5	12	15	595	105	458	32	2
	Davis	61,256	209	0	21	45	143	1,842	565	1,098	179	29
	Delano	45,941	337	5	11	72	249	2,577	950	832	795	77
	Del Mar	4,417	26	0	1	7	18	274	54	190	30	0
	Del Rey Oaks	1,598	0	0	0	0	0	24	11	8	5	0
	Desert Hot Springs	20,677	297	3	20	74	200	1,778	743	660	375	0
	Diamond Bar	58,497	108	1	4	49	54	1,023	311	591	121	4
	Dinuba	19,482	220	4	2	26	188	1,164	278	670	216	8
	Dixon	17,486	68	0	8	12	48	602	104	423	75	13
	Dorris	883	4	0	1	0	3	19	5	13	1	1
	Dos Palos	5,081	44	0	3	4	37	168	51	100	17	1
	Downey	110,706	451	4	21	249	177	3,616	575	1,897	1,144	4
	Duarte	22,394	123	1	5	44	73	508	95	320	93	2
	Dublin	39,682	85	0	4	27	54	723	167	428	128	4
	Dunsmuir	1,887	5	0	0	2	3	40	18	17	5	0
	East Palo Alto	32,532	293	6	22	121	144	1,076	342	400	334	0
	El Cajon	93,320	473	4	28	154	287	3,612	638	1,954	1,020	26
	El Centro	39,993	328	0	6	59	263	1,973	721	986	266	0
	El Cerrito	23,074	193	2	2	139	50	1,445	238	924	283	6
	El Monte	123,616	628	5	25	187	411	3,199	831	1,435	933	20
	El Segundo	16,666	28	1	2	16	9	644	156	420	68	5
	Emeryville	8,605	125	1	4	87	33	1,154	127	843	184	2
	Encinitas	60,061	163	3	8	48	104	1,198	324	704	170	3
	Escalon	7,236	34	0	3	0	31	244	45	177	22	2
	Escondido	135,293	713	3	33	235	442	4,407	758	2,687	962	17
	Etna	803	2	0	2	0	0	3	1	2	0	0
	Eureka	25,809	172	3	20	50	99	1,473	405	841	227	15
	Exeter	10,064	56	0	3	6	47	391	114	223	54	1
	Fairfax	7,170	9	0	1	2	6	143	27	104	12	0
	Fairfield	105,417	654	6	36	241	371	4,363	745	2,912	706	35
	Farmersville	10,007	52	1	0	12	39	242	37	146	59	0
	Ferndale	1,407	0	0	0	0	0	22	4	18	0	0
	Fillmore	15,029	61	0	2	6	53	330	56	235	39	6
	Firebaugh	7,064	9	0	1	0	8	240	23	185	32	0
	Folsom	66,202	97	0	11	36	50	1,639	286	1,189	164	22
	Fontana	165,336	863	5	40	254	564	3,309	779	1,375	1,155	12
	Fort Bragg	6,875	40	0	3	5	32	459	93	348	18	4
	Fort Jones	675	2	0	1	0	1	9	2	5	2	0
	Fortuna	11,255	23	0	7	6	10	447	74	340	33	7
	Foster City	29,015	30	1	4	8	17	437	68	332	37	2
	Fountain Valley	56,446	96	0	4	36	56	1,375	309	942	124	6
	Fowler	4,755	21	0	0	2	19	256	36	174	46	0
	Fremont	202,273	569	6	29	256	278	5,298	1,325	3,113	860	27
	Fresno	465,269	3,524	52	133	1,282	2,057	23,407	4,366	14,097	4,944	260
	Fullerton	133,983	469	2	47	172	248	4,337	764	2,962	611	25
	Galt	23,382	66	3	5	14	44	805	270	398	137	7
	Gardena	60,430	506	8	13	290	195	1,515	407	616	492	8
	Garden Grove	167,571	695	9	29	247	410	4,165	715	2,665	785	33
	Gilroy	46,130	233	1	12	67	153	2,061	273	1,485	303	37
	Glendale	201,867	368	2	14	167	185	3,935	672	2,685	578	14
	Glendora	50,995	73	3	2	22	46	1,438	205	1,110	123	19
	Goleta	29,631	40	7	1	11	21	400	118	259	23	2
	Gonzales	8,575	46	0	0	9	37	318	130	146	42	2
	Grand Terrace	12,453	22	0	1	5	16	241	67	101	73	3
	Grass Valley	12,561	82	0	4	6	72	391	78	275	38	4
	Greenfield	13,450	39	0	0	28	11	494	115	320	59	2
	Gridley	5,638	65	0	3	6	56	257	61	170	26	0
	Grover Beach	13,003	40	1	2	10	27	396	77	285	34	0
	Guadalupe	6,403	28	0	0	3	25	88	16	55	17	0

[1] The FBI does not publish arson data unless it receives data from either the agency or the state for all 12 months of the calendar year.

Table 8. Offenses Known to Law Enforcement, by State and City, 2006 (*Contd.*)

(Number.)

State	City	Popula-tion	Violent crime	Murder and non-negligent man-slaughter	Forcible rape	Robbery	Aggra-vated assault	Property crime	Burglary	Larceny-theft	Motor vehicle theft	Arson[1]
	Gustine	5,372	27	4	0	3	20	149	43	100	6	1
	Half Moon Bay	12,313	20	0	1	4	15	216	30	176	10	4
	Hanford	47,913	191	1	0	51	139	1,718	244	1,222	252	39
	Hawaiian Gardens	15,537	159	2	6	44	107	357	65	188	104	6
	Hawthorne	86,469	623	9	29	265	320	2,101	491	961	649	14
	Hayward	141,556	776	4	33	423	316	5,736	1,196	2,343	2,197	74
	Healdsburg	11,151	21	0	3	5	13	250	66	173	11	4
	Hemet	68,676	520	6	26	170	318	3,207	947	1,835	425	14
	Hercules	24,326	42	0	1	20	21	510	80	327	103	2
	Hermosa Beach	19,676	65	0	10	17	38	582	152	394	36	0
	Hesperia	78,686	241	7	17	56	161	2,040	562	930	548	13
	Hidden Hills	2,012	0	0	0	0	0	17	1	16	0	0
	Highland	51,350	230	2	13	100	115	1,395	380	631	384	14
	Hillsborough	10,711	2	0	0	0	2	97	12	80	5	0
	Hollister	36,265	126	2	6	28	90	980	316	530	134	14
	Holtville	5,519	1	0	0	1	0	93	28	49	16	1
	Hughson	5,756	4	0	0	1	3	138	33	86	19	0
	Huntington Beach	196,208	407	2	31	141	233	4,468	961	3,044	463	39
	Huntington Park	63,054	554	7	22	346	179	2,641	235	1,242	1,164	13
	Huron	7,252	59	3	1	18	37	307	75	211	21	1
	Imperial	9,794	8	0	2	3	3	216	28	153	35	3
	Imperial Beach	26,612	168	1	17	34	116	747	169	342	236	3
	Indian Wells	4,977	5	0	1	1	3	259	81	165	13	1
	Indio	71,177	385	4	22	154	205	3,108	908	1,486	714	0
	Industry	875	124	4	2	66	52	1,745	279	1,010	456	8
	Inglewood	115,498	1,051	36	36	486	493	2,926	675	1,194	1,057	16
	Ione	7,676	14	1	8	2	3	86	23	60	3	2
	Irvine	188,535	126	4	17	50	55	3,034	634	2,147	253	35
	Irwindale	1,493	16	0	1	4	11	232	86	76	70	4
	Isleton	827	7	0	0	3	4	28	11	10	7	0
	Jackson	4,342	44	0	3	3	38	163	65	76	22	1
	Kensington	5,313	5	0	0	2	3	121	21	80	20	0
	Kerman	11,324	30	0	0	3	27	410	100	230	80	4
	King City	11,103	53	1	7	5	40	446	155	229	62	5
	Kingsburg	11,248	23	0	1	6	16	428	81	240	107	2
	La Canada Flintridge	21,187	19	0	0	5	14	336	101	223	12	4
	Lafayette	24,990	22	0	0	15	7	493	119	317	57	2
	Laguna Beach	24,344	48	0	6	8	34	622	142	434	46	2
	Laguna Hills	32,488	47	0	1	19	27	630	113	466	51	5
	Laguna Niguel	65,246	54	0	3	13	38	645	118	486	41	10
	Laguna Woods	18,458	10	1	1	6	2	98	12	79	7	3
	La Habra	59,860	182	2	5	51	124	1,694	317	1,097	280	3
	La Habra Heights	6,024	2	0	0	1	1	101	38	50	13	2
	Lake Elsinore	39,612	201	4	13	55	129	1,573	299	955	319	2
	Lake Forest	77,100	97	1	6	25	65	1,104	205	793	106	18
	Lakeport	5,288	23	0	0	2	21	130	27	91	12	0
	Lake Shastina	2,358	0	0	0	0	0	27	4	23	0	0
	Lakewood	81,192	407	4	11	220	172	2,255	394	1,427	434	11
	La Mesa	53,559	235	3	8	111	113	2,497	447	1,459	591	16
	La Mirada	50,087	108	2	7	41	58	1,073	194	654	225	10
	Lancaster	135,239	1,274	19	56	432	767	5,027	1,539	2,440	1,048	46
	La Palma	15,947	22	0	0	11	11	308	89	200	19	1
	La Puente	42,138	255	8	7	76	164	853	194	378	281	2
	La Quinta	38,576	101	1	2	31	67	1,885	558	1,164	163	4
	La Verne	33,484	60	1	5	23	31	821	170	595	56	7
	Lawndale	32,483	202	1	7	76	118	535	152	237	146	11
	Lemon Grove	24,341	170	1	12	65	92	793	211	319	263	9
	Lemoore	22,903	91	2	9	13	67	643	110	448	85	15
	Lincoln	33,099	57	0	10	9	38	553	220	276	57	7
	Lindsay	10,864	69	0	0	10	59	546	162	250	134	3
	Livermore	79,115	147	1	16	57	73	1,703	395	1,083	225	23
	Livingston	12,698	79	2	9	7	61	291	118	116	57	1
	Lodi	62,693	245	2	10	54	179	2,881	555	1,854	472	2
	Loma Linda	21,089	21	1	5	6	9	575	122	276	177	4
	Lomita	20,700	93	0	4	49	40	351	105	178	68	6

[1] The FBI does not publish arson data unless it receives data from either the agency or the state for all 12 months of the calendar year.

Table 8. Offenses Known to Law Enforcement, by State and City, 2006 (*Contd.*)

(Number.)

State	City	Popula-tion	Violent crime	Murder and non-negligent man-slaughter	Forcible rape	Robbery	Aggra-vated assault	Property crime	Burglary	Larceny-theft	Motor vehicle theft	Arson[1]
	Lompoc	40,345	235	3	18	42	172	1,043	189	779	75	4
	Long Beach	478,283	3,420	41	134	1,440	1,805	12,778	2,896	6,598	3,284	103
	Los Altos	27,340	4	0	0	2	2	421	172	230	19	3
	Los Altos Hills	8,238	0	0	0	0	0	152	47	103	2	7
	Los Angeles	3,879,455	30,526	480	1,059	14,353	14,634	105,459	20,359	59,711	25,389	2,356
	Los Banos	33,808	265	0	7	42	216	1,046	290	615	141	7
	Los Gatos	28,281	35	0	3	12	20	557	145	379	33	14
	Lynwood	71,849	693	18	23	258	394	1,628	301	483	844	41
	Madera	52,617	435	0	29	97	309	1,225	318	649	258	0
	Malibu	13,327	20	0	2	7	11	270	74	167	29	2
	Mammoth Lakes	7,220	26	0	7	1	18	309	87	208	14	0
	Manhattan Beach	36,810	47	0	7	24	16	900	205	635	60	7
	Manteca	63,215	231	1	14	73	143	2,793	434	1,803	556	19
	Marina	19,177	65	0	3	14	48	514	145	323	46	6
	Martinez	36,239	98	0	12	23	63	1,273	222	830	221	0
	Marysville	12,240	134	0	14	32	88	574	171	285	118	1
	Maywood	28,858	144	4	7	44	89	328	56	120	152	7
	Menlo Park	29,928	75	0	7	27	41	728	150	498	80	3
	Merced	74,431	603	9	22	165	407	3,876	819	2,611	446	62
	Millbrae	20,525	42	2	4	14	22	384	143	199	42	11
	Mill Valley	13,406	13	0	1	6	6	265	71	177	17	1
	Milpitas	63,954	182	0	15	52	115	2,143	334	1,523	286	15
	Mission Viejo	95,837	70	0	1	29	40	1,399	260	1,016	123	29
	Modesto	208,875	1,418	11	73	462	872	11,804	1,762	8,018	2,024	110
	Monrovia	38,296	154	0	10	49	95	1,196	193	844	159	2
	Montague	1,518	3	0	0	0	3	23	11	10	2	0
	Montclair	35,793	255	4	10	114	127	2,451	278	1,729	444	4
	Montebello	63,860	278	3	14	122	139	2,007	330	1,011	666	53
	Monterey	29,480	181	0	19	31	131	1,139	230	819	90	4
	Monterey Park	62,624	164	1	7	108	48	1,374	313	744	317	2
	Monte Sereno	3,493	2	0	0	0	2	22	13	6	3	0
	Moorpark	36,167	45	0	1	10	34	391	86	283	22	6
	Moraga	17,021	15	0	2	4	9	215	43	153	19	13
	Moreno Valley	179,973	968	16	61	479	412	6,899	2,239	3,272	1,388	14
	Morgan Hill	35,166	60	0	5	10	45	988	170	704	114	31
	Morro Bay	10,300	23	0	4	4	15	167	47	109	11	2
	Mountain View	69,900	300	0	10	71	219	2,244	271	1,648	325	19
	Mount Shasta	3,656	9	0	1	1	7	115	16	84	15	0
	Murrieta	83,523	113	2	9	31	71	1,974	563	1,187	224	7
	Napa	75,455	336	1	21	70	244	2,164	401	1,563	200	19
	National City	61,972	524	2	9	211	302	2,463	453	1,125	885	12
	Needles	5,396	73	1	5	6	61	270	92	140	38	10
	Nevada City	3,059	16	0	0	2	14	74	18	47	9	0
	Newark	42,334	211	1	7	79	124	1,942	369	1,239	334	7
	Newman	9,710	19	0	2	1	16	242	63	144	35	3
	Newport Beach	80,553	130	1	4	32	93	2,431	575	1,682	174	19
	Norco	27,203	78	0	6	22	50	933	165	642	126	3
	Norwalk	106,787	567	7	21	240	299	2,602	504	1,301	797	25
	Novato	50,788	139	0	14	39	86	1,137	319	641	177	19
	Oakdale	18,728	40	1	8	11	20	956	261	611	84	1
	Oakland	398,834	7,599	145	306	3,534	3,614	24,344	5,070	8,725	10,549	307
	Oakley	27,422	95	2	5	22	66	763	199	430	134	4
	Oceanside	167,604	936	8	48	245	635	4,873	979	3,261	633	21
	Ojai	8,017	19	0	1	1	17	237	53	178	6	1
	Ontario	174,234	1,011	13	74	418	506	6,337	967	3,592	1,778	56
	Orange	136,165	298	1	13	147	137	3,291	549	2,309	433	51
	Orinda	18,423	11	0	1	7	3	330	77	230	23	0
	Orland	6,818	33	0	1	6	26	184	49	113	22	2
	Oroville	13,589	135	4	15	17	99	967	284	529	154	2
	Oxnard	185,282	841	13	34	418	376	4,376	946	2,816	614	54
	Pacifica	37,426	68	0	5	13	50	609	143	425	41	9
	Pacific Grove	15,227	18	0	2	6	10	403	83	311	9	4
	Palmdale	135,782	989	15	58	341	575	4,212	1,169	2,353	690	54
	Palm Desert	47,482	169	3	18	66	82	2,755	730	1,792	233	4
	Palm Springs	47,506	305	3	21	128	153	3,192	858	1,888	446	29

[1] The FBI does not publish arson data unless it receives data from either the agency or the state for all 12 months of the calendar year.

Table 8. Offenses Known to Law Enforcement, by State and City, 2006 (*Contd.*)

(Number.)

State	City	Popula-tion	Violent crime	Murder and non-negligent man-slaughter	Forcible rape	Robbery	Aggra-vated assault	Property crime	Burglary	Larceny-theft	Motor vehicle theft	Arson[1]
	Palo Alto	57,495	62	0	1	32	29	1,871	399	1,333	139	21
	Palos Verdes Estates	13,936	6	0	1	0	5	107	38	66	3	1
	Paradise	26,756	56	0	8	5	43	680	218	412	50	5
	Paramount	57,049	383	5	12	155	211	1,777	346	739	692	20
	Parlier	13,142	85	0	5	17	63	446	73	259	114	2
	Pasadena	145,025	611	11	19	247	334	4,398	892	2,998	508	27
	Paso Robles	27,724	89	1	15	12	61	989	230	666	93	12
	Patterson	15,640	32	0	4	8	20	680	217	356	107	10
	Perris	46,082	389	7	17	137	228	2,269	474	1,098	697	6
	Petaluma	55,340	211	2	18	25	166	1,178	136	964	78	12
	Pico Rivera	65,261	306	10	10	104	182	1,479	246	731	502	15
	Piedmont	10,654	19	0	0	16	3	303	71	157	75	4
	Pinole	19,233	129	2	8	50	69	830	126	489	215	11
	Pismo Beach	8,495	49	2	1	4	42	426	109	291	26	0
	Pittsburg	63,110	218	8	8	130	72	2,623	468	1,494	661	7
	Placentia	50,243	105	1	3	26	75	848	214	539	95	17
	Placerville	10,276	56	1	2	7	46	297	63	177	57	1
	Pleasant Hill	33,452	136	0	9	56	71	1,524	257	1,100	167	11
	Pleasanton	66,544	68	0	6	25	37	1,536	214	1,181	141	14
	Pomona	155,172	1,255	19	17	464	755	5,227	1,027	2,781	1,419	22
	Porterville	45,364	250	9	21	61	159	2,413	534	1,480	399	3
	Port Hueneme	22,230	114	3	3	42	66	469	109	290	70	3
	Poway	48,913	103	0	13	21	69	784	210	455	119	5
	Rancho Cucamonga	170,878	362	3	25	144	190	3,966	715	2,550	701	22
	Rancho Mirage	16,663	27	0	3	7	17	988	288	633	67	5
	Rancho Palos Verdes	42,327	40	0	4	10	26	464	133	295	36	10
	Rancho Santa Margarita	51,138	35	0	3	9	23	464	78	360	26	17
	Red Bluff	14,186	143	3	1	11	128	589	115	417	57	5
	Redding	90,448	388	2	72	66	248	3,389	719	2,174	496	29
	Redlands	70,625	379	3	22	114	240	2,537	501	1,610	426	31
	Redondo Beach	67,426	234	0	14	85	135	1,560	315	1,113	132	3
	Redwood City	73,772	300	6	16	80	198	2,179	307	1,523	349	19
	Reedley	22,569	117	3	5	13	96	662	156	367	139	14
	Rialto	100,409	708	12	30	299	367	2,708	607	1,141	960	19
	Richmond	103,106	1,224	42	41	504	637	5,495	1,031	2,211	2,253	30
	Ridgecrest	26,208	147	0	20	16	111	792	240	507	45	8
	Rio Dell	3,186	13	0	3	1	9	50	16	31	3	0
	Rio Vista	7,141	1	0	0	0	1	74	20	43	11	1
	Ripon	13,781	19	0	3	5	11	330	38	257	35	1
	Riverbank	19,905	40	0	4	15	21	818	195	505	118	1
	Riverside	292,698	2,014	11	83	814	1,106	12,267	2,372	7,471	2,424	131
	Rocklin	50,073	74	0	7	21	46	1,295	275	899	121	8
	Rohnert Park	41,471	207	1	17	18	171	790	128	595	67	16
	Rolling Hills	1,950	3	0	0	0	3	14	4	10	0	0
	Rolling Hills Estates	8,178	8	0	3	1	4	130	25	98	7	0
	Rosemead	55,615	270	6	12	112	140	1,421	385	670	366	10
	Roseville	106,894	378	3	24	134	217	3,884	588	2,722	574	13
	Ross	2,304	0	0	0	0	0	20	5	13	2	0
	Sacramento	460,552	5,556	57	196	2,188	3,115	26,112	6,175	12,762	7,175	294
	Salinas	147,750	1,118	7	45	383	683	6,023	907	3,718	1,398	29
	San Anselmo	12,126	21	0	0	2	19	312	73	215	24	4
	San Bernardino	200,338	2,017	46	50	904	1,017	9,760	2,135	4,708	2,917	85
	San Bruno	40,110	129	0	7	49	73	1,055	101	760	194	5
	San Carlos	27,063	21	0	3	7	11	599	150	401	48	6
	San Clemente	60,777	88	1	1	26	60	807	147	577	83	19
	Sand City	306	4	0	1	0	3	107	5	98	4	0
	San Diego	1,266,847	6,391	68	348	2,164	3,811	45,209	7,746	24,125	13,338	185
	San Dimas	36,173	94	0	6	33	55	844	171	593	80	3
	San Fernando	24,425	127	2	5	44	76	614	141	330	143	1
	San Francisco	746,085	6,533	86	154	3,858	2,435	36,992	6,465	23,891	6,636	226
	San Gabriel	41,426	223	3	5	95	120	979	234	618	127	7
	Sanger	22,239	116	3	4	24	85	697	161	394	142	3
	San Jacinto	30,525	127	1	10	44	72	1,333	361	745	227	8
	San Jose	920,548	3,561	29	217	1,030	2,285	24,240	4,423	12,678	7,139	437
	San Juan Capistrano	34,985	49	1	2	19	27	440	94	282	64	9

[1] The FBI does not publish arson data unless it receives data from either the agency or the state for all 12 months of the calendar year.

Table 8. Offenses Known to Law Enforcement, by State and City, 2006 *(Contd.)*

(Number.)

State	City	Population	Violent crime	Murder and non-negligent man-slaughter	Forcible rape	Robbery	Aggra-vated assault	Property crime	Burglary	Larceny-theft	Motor vehicle theft	Arson[1]
	San Leandro	78,882	650	4	28	309	309	4,196	773	2,176	1,247	12
	San Luis Obispo	43,901	160	0	22	25	113	1,727	358	1,273	96	41
	San Marcos	74,149	286	3	19	75	189	1,735	484	918	333	14
	San Marino	13,284	6	0	0	3	3	227	83	135	9	1
	San Mateo	91,901	325	2	18	83	222	2,488	274	1,920	294	20
	San Pablo	31,283	397	7	17	217	156	1,870	371	843	656	11
	San Rafael	56,218	237	2	16	81	138	1,927	327	1,251	349	11
	San Ramon	50,449	64	1	1	25	37	907	169	659	79	5
	Santa Ana	343,433	1,998	26	73	787	1,112	8,630	1,074	4,956	2,600	88
	Santa Barbara	86,673	458	1	33	103	321	2,483	544	1,781	158	31
	Santa Clara	106,351	180	3	16	59	102	3,354	595	2,283	476	14
	Santa Clarita	169,768	392	3	26	130	233	3,444	766	2,253	425	24
	Santa Cruz	55,253	399	3	38	107	251	3,198	537	2,412	249	32
	Santa Fe Springs	17,212	123	2	3	61	57	1,710	315	979	416	2
	Santa Maria	85,106	742	2	43	113	584	2,410	372	1,550	488	16
	Santa Monica	88,591	590	2	26	256	306	3,314	733	2,187	394	12
	Santa Paula	28,734	96	1	5	39	51	648	138	408	102	5
	Santa Rosa	154,537	891	6	75	175	635	4,212	833	2,887	492	27
	Santee	52,777	151	0	14	44	93	1,054	270	585	199	8
	Saratoga	29,930	26	0	2	2	22	525	161	345	19	3
	Sausalito	7,249	9	0	1	1	7	170	42	114	14	0
	Scotts Valley	11,254	13	0	2	2	9	334	60	262	12	2
	Seal Beach	24,514	35	0	1	11	23	521	107	359	55	2
	Seaside	34,522	189	0	12	41	136	742	114	556	72	6
	Sebastopol	7,666	17	0	0	8	9	156	32	111	13	0
	Selma	22,461	92	2	13	34	43	1,313	200	777	336	3
	Shafter	14,700	61	1	9	7	44	582	170	337	75	17
	Sierra Madre	11,087	12	1	1	3	7	186	51	125	10	0
	Signal Hill	10,949	76	1	3	33	39	512	108	341	63	0
	Simi Valley	119,756	199	3	21	58	117	2,060	425	1,475	160	22
	Solana Beach	12,831	26	1	0	12	13	277	77	160	40	1
	Soledad	27,455	49	1	6	21	21	527	179	306	42	0
	Solvang	5,187	9	0	0	1	8	91	24	64	3	2
	Sonoma	9,974	51	0	7	5	39	290	74	201	15	8
	Sonora	4,710	19	0	5	3	11	359	59	274	26	2
	South El Monte	21,861	132	4	5	46	77	745	184	285	276	9
	South Gate	99,788	506	16	14	271	205	2,764	416	1,102	1,246	26
	South Lake Tahoe	24,232	148	0	15	21	112	699	236	389	74	3
	South Pasadena	25,113	42	1	3	23	15	627	178	360	89	4
	South San Francisco	61,282	230	0	15	78	137	1,403	444	695	264	14
	Stallion Springs	1,639	3	0	0	0	3	30	5	23	2	0
	Stanton	38,000	149	5	3	63	78	750	147	442	161	8
	St. Helena	5,991	14	0	2	0	12	73	29	41	3	1
	Stockton	289,510	4,288	37	102	1,519	2,630	19,719	3,836	12,202	3,681	56
	Suisun City	27,003	110	1	14	30	65	691	180	375	136	12
	Sunnyvale	130,063	184	1	21	81	81	2,632	524	1,699	409	23
	Susanville	18,264	54	1	5	5	43	340	110	220	10	1
	Sutter Creek	2,773	10	0	4	0	6	78	17	56	5	1
	Taft	9,188	33	0	2	4	27	318	73	218	27	21
	Temecula	86,572	277	0	13	57	207	2,820	674	1,789	357	6
	Temple City	37,699	70	1	0	27	42	642	214	355	73	0
	Thousand Oaks	125,479	182	0	13	41	128	1,794	367	1,296	131	17
	Tiburon	8,749	4	0	0	1	3	93	22	65	6	0
	Torrance	143,666	354	1	18	203	132	3,171	666	1,998	507	46
	Tracy	80,684	134	0	3	66	65	2,825	366	2,018	441	32
	Trinidad	312	0	0	0	0	0	34	17	17	0	0
	Truckee	15,879	47	0	5	4	38	340	115	189	36	4
	Tulare	50,578	425	6	20	69	330	2,897	793	1,623	481	69
	Tulelake	1,019	1	0	0	0	1	12	2	10	0	0
	Turlock	68,278	429	5	18	114	292	3,104	604	1,778	722	21
	Tustin	69,718	155	1	11	45	98	1,780	396	1,148	236	26
	Twentynine Palms	28,665	83	2	7	13	61	495	186	243	66	17
	Twin Cities	21,032	22	0	3	12	7	677	173	409	95	2
	Ukiah	15,602	83	1	19	11	52	417	165	201	51	7
	Union City	69,799	444	1	12	215	216	2,266	508	1,219	539	21

[1] The FBI does not publish arson data unless it receives data from either the agency or the state for all 12 months of the calendar year.

Table 8. Offenses Known to Law Enforcement, by State and City, 2006 *(Contd.)*

(Number.)

State	City	Popula-tion	Violent crime	Murder and non-negligent man-slaughter	Forcible rape	Robbery	Aggra-vated assault	Property crime	Burglary	Larceny-theft	Motor vehicle theft	Arson[1]
	Upland	74,252	270	1	12	120	137	2,934	509	1,962	463	8
	Vacaville	93,822	280	1	25	112	142	2,384	320	1,733	331	33
	Vallejo	118,541	1,206	6	31	430	739	5,971	1,155	3,300	1,516	83
	Ventura	104,954	335	1	24	130	180	3,686	730	2,604	352	13
	Vernon	93	53	0	1	32	20	478	80	225	173	4
	Victorville	92,086	560	8	26	219	307	4,157	1,173	2,218	766	14
	Villa Park	6,080	4	0	0	3	1	112	20	88	4	0
	Visalia	109,648	871	8	50	213	600	6,466	1,368	3,817	1,281	30
	Vista	91,216	446	1	34	152	259	2,838	729	1,522	587	19
	Walnut	31,707	46	0	6	25	15	605	183	348	74	4
	Walnut Creek	64,774	113	0	3	41	69	2,469	438	1,773	258	14
	Waterford	8,234	43	0	0	0	43	350	64	242	44	3
	Watsonville	48,359	304	6	17	82	199	2,007	359	1,485	163	21
	Weed	3,142	13	0	1	1	11	89	22	59	8	0
	West Covina	109,159	419	2	13	200	204	4,030	679	2,439	912	2
	West Hollywood	37,063	309	1	21	129	158	1,433	286	945	202	8
	Westlake Village	8,662	33	0	2	0	31	149	47	96	6	3
	Westminster	90,329	314	1	20	117	176	2,594	509	1,664	421	23
	Westmorland	2,286	8	0	0	1	7	33	20	7	6	1
	West Sacramento	42,120	428	2	15	76	335	1,344	483	516	345	32
	Wheatland	3,671	7	0	0	1	6	68	18	33	17	2
	Whittier	85,234	313	4	12	118	179	2,760	421	1,865	474	8
	Williams	4,798	21	0	0	4	17	90	17	57	16	1
	Willits	5,112	32	0	1	5	26	90	40	43	7	3
	Willows	6,353	30	0	4	0	26	318	63	240	15	0
	Windsor	25,193	86	0	5	8	73	335	83	235	17	1
	Winters	6,825	7	0	1	0	6	155	49	91	15	5
	Woodlake	7,280	35	1	0	2	32	315	67	176	72	2
	Woodland	51,479	128	0	15	44	69	1,793	382	1,164	247	55
	Yorba Linda	65,057	51	0	4	16	31	990	212	699	79	9
	Yountville	3,337	2	0	0	0	2	40	6	32	2	0
	Yreka	7,361	53	0	0	3	50	235	32	189	14	3
	Yuba City	59,156	250	2	21	50	177	2,029	459	1,326	244	22
	Yucaipa	49,542	92	4	8	15	65	785	185	467	133	6
	Yucca Valley	19,873	106	1	12	20	73	537	155	294	88	16
COLORADO	Alamosa	8,846	62	0	6	6	50	538	73	447	18	0
	Arvada	105,932	193	0	31	42	120	3,202	539	2,303	360	13
	Aspen	5,914	19	0	2	2	15	408	43	351	14	2
	Ault	1,452	11	1	0	0	10	49	13	31	5	1
	Aurora	302,855	1,858	17	217	600	1,024	12,805	2,470	8,292	2,043	116
	Avon	6,469	14	0	3	2	9	250	44	192	14	1
	Basalt	3,064	14	0	1	0	13	38	4	26	8	0
	Bayfield	1,670	4	0	0	0	4	37	12	24	1	0
	Berthoud	5,151	4	0	0	2	2	101	26	73	2	3
	Black Hawk	109	8	0	0	4	4	169	1	164	4	0
	Boulder	93,418	229	1	35	29	164	3,016	487	2,372	157	72
	Bow Mar	823	1	0	0	1	0	5	0	5	0	0
	Brighton	28,543	115	0	15	14	86	1,188	206	855	127	10
	Broomfield	44,300	40	0	8	9	23	1,439	128	1,202	109	13
	Brush	5,284	22	0	1	2	19	184	38	142	4	0
	Buena Vista	2,215	0	0	0	0	0	6	3	3	0	0
	Burlington	3,559	8	0	2	0	6	108	20	85	3	0
	Campo	138	0	0	0	0	0	0	0	0	0	0
	Canon City	16,302	129	0	13	7	109	778	101	647	30	10
	Carbondale	5,935	10	0	1	1	8	174	13	144	17	0
	Castle Rock	36,421	42	2	0	3	37	525	107	367	51	14
	Cedaredge	2,189	0	0	0	0	0	26	5	20	1	0
	Centennial	100,100	180	0	25	36	119	1,618	340	1,122	156	37
	Center	2,544	2	0	0	0	2	22	3	17	2	0
	Central City	500	8	0	1	0	7	49	2	46	1	0
	Collbran	416	2	0	0	0	2	1	1	0	0	0
	Colorado Springs	376,807	2,145	15	251	612	1,267	18,076	3,347	12,940	1,789	115
	Columbine Valley	1,243	0	0	0	0	0	16	5	10	1	0
	Commerce City	34,835	177	2	14	27	134	1,664	401	1,005	258	5
	Cortez	8,400	24	0	0	2	22	312	32	269	11	0

[1] The FBI does not publish arson data unless it receives data from either the agency or the state for all 12 months of the calendar year.

Table 8. Offenses Known to Law Enforcement, by State and City, 2006 (*Contd.*)

(Number.)

State	City	Popula-tion	Violent crime	Murder and non-negligent man-slaughter	Forcible rape	Robbery	Aggra-vated assault	Property crime	Burglary	Larceny-theft	Motor vehicle theft	Arson[1]
	Craig	9,316	20	0	9	0	11	236	43	178	15	6
	Crested Butte	1,575	3	0	1	1	1	56	6	43	7	0
	Cripple Creek	1,085	27	0	4	1	22	101	22	75	4	0
	Dacono	3,596	17	0	1	1	15	76	16	39	21	2
	De Beque	481	0	0	0	0	0	16	9	7	0	0
	Delta	8,289	50	2	6	2	40	312	89	205	18	7
	Denver	568,465	4,325	51	342	1,280	2,652	26,266	6,543	13,376	6,347	198
	Dillon	789	7	0	1	0	6	77	3	74	0	0
	Durango	15,794	128	1	27	4	96	947	100	800	47	0
	Eagle	4,357	2	0	0	0	2	106	19	84	3	0
	Eaton	4,006	2	0	1	0	1	49	19	30	0	0
	Edgewater	5,310	26	1	1	10	14	330	27	256	47	2
	Empire	345	3	0	0	0	3	5	0	5	0	0
	Englewood	32,962	307	3	30	54	220	2,117	369	1,338	410	8
	Erie	12,585	8	0	3	0	5	187	60	109	18	5
	Estes Park	5,922	14	0	2	0	12	165	33	125	7	0
	Evans	17,800	36	0	4	6	26	646	164	404	78	10
	Federal Heights	11,927	32	0	10	11	11	663	84	500	79	7
	Firestone	6,531	18	0	3	1	14	269	66	187	16	1
	Florence	3,755	11	0	3	1	7	73	9	53	11	1
	Fort Collins	130,446	493	0	76	36	381	4,570	701	3,585	284	24
	Fort Lupton	7,256	22	0	4	5	13	232	51	158	23	8
	Fort Morgan	11,049	19	1	1	4	13	373	50	311	12	2
	Fountain	19,442	24	1	11	12	0	597	134	409	54	5
	Fraser/Winter Park	1,634	17	0	1	0	16	120	30	82	8	0
	Frederick	6,745	19	0	0	1	18	162	6	144	12	0
	Frisco	2,464	32	0	0	0	32	4	1	3	0	0
	Fruita	7,008	20	0	3	2	15	191	32	147	12	1
	Glenwood Springs	8,726	40	0	7	1	32	553	61	449	43	3
	Grand Junction	46,155	288	3	37	39	209	2,850	440	2,176	234	26
	Greeley	89,252	467	2	53	50	362	4,324	841	3,163	320	30
	Green Mountain Falls	799	12	0	0	0	12	36	13	22	1	0
	Greenwood Village	13,059	24	0	4	7	13	566	83	427	56	7
	Gunnison	5,398	17	0	5	0	12	317	40	262	15	4
	Hayden	1,568	6	0	0	0	6	30	3	24	3	0
	Hotchkiss	1,063	28	0	2	1	25	36	10	22	4	0
	Idaho Springs	1,841	21	0	2	0	19	80	6	66	8	0
	Ignacio	692	1	0	0	0	1	3	1	2	0	0
	Johnstown	7,387	17	1	1	1	14	175	39	128	8	3
	Kersey	1,427	5	0	0	0	5	45	8	32	5	0
	Kiowa	607	8	0	0	0	8	22	7	14	1	0
	Kremmling	1,583	6	0	0	1	5	18	1	13	4	0
	Lafayette	24,336	54	0	4	6	44	514	81	404	29	9
	La Junta	7,397	39	1	14	7	17	344	61	270	13	10
	Lakeside	20	8	0	0	3	5	73	2	65	6	0
	Lakewood	143,331	702	4	98	176	424	6,995	1,182	4,710	1,103	24
	Lamar	8,573	21	0	4	5	12	365	65	283	17	3
	Las Animas	2,591	11	0	0	0	11	75	22	53	0	0
	Leadville	2,739	11	0	0	0	11	47	5	40	2	0
	Limon	1,915	8	0	2	0	6	31	5	20	6	0
	Littleton	41,160	30	1	1	17	11	1,481	265	1,034	182	25
	Lone Tree	8,716	14	0	2	6	6	388	43	314	31	0
	Louisville	18,705	26	0	0	3	23	321	69	223	29	9
	Loveland	60,689	98	0	9	18	71	1,807	242	1,465	100	16
	Manitou Springs	5,134	9	0	0	3	6	168	36	124	8	1
	Milliken	5,699	9	0	2	1	6	90	21	63	6	1
	Monte Vista	4,292	17	0	2	0	15	164	39	119	6	1
	Montrose	15,772	33	1	6	3	23	631	89	510	32	2
	Monument	2,555	25	0	1	0	24	165	28	133	4	1
	Morrison	418	6	0	0	0	6	19	8	8	3	0
	Mountain View	539	3	0	0	1	2	26	17	8	1	1
	Mount Crested Butte	770	4	0	0	0	4	35	2	31	2	0
	Nederland	1,362	3	0	0	0	3	6	2	4	0	0
	New Castle	3,074	10	0	0	1	9	53	6	42	5	0
	Northglenn	33,528	94	1	8	16	69	1,349	196	936	217	13

[1] The FBI does not publish arson data unless it receives data from either the agency or the state for all 12 months of the calendar year.

Table 8. Offenses Known to Law Enforcement, by State and City, 2006 (*Contd.*)

(Number.)

State	City	Popula-tion	Violent crime	Murder and non-negligent man-slaughter	Forcible rape	Robbery	Aggra-vated assault	Property crime	Burglary	Larceny-theft	Motor vehicle theft	Arson[1]
	Oak Creek	812	7	0	0	0	7	7	2	0	5	0
	Olathe	1,711	2	0	2	0	0	27	9	13	5	0
	Pagosa Springs	1,659	5	0	1	0	4	95	11	79	5	0
	Palisade	2,734	0	0	0	0	0	16	3	13	0	0
	Parachute	1,115	2	0	1	0	1	46	9	28	9	0
	Parker	39,155	24	1	6	0	17	752	149	548	55	9
	Platteville	2,647	16	0	0	0	16	33	12	17	4	0
	Pueblo	105,452	628	6	49	170	403	6,317	1,453	4,409	455	55
	Rangely	2,077	3	0	0	1	2	20	4	14	2	1
	Rocky Ford	4,199	27	0	1	3	23	79	18	57	4	0
	Salida	5,580	24	0	4	1	19	174	16	151	7	0
	Sheridan	5,587	14	0	2	4	8	448	75	298	75	0
	Silt	2,303	5	0	0	1	4	50	5	41	4	0
	Silverthorne	3,678	9	0	1	1	7	128	10	116	2	2
	Snowmass Village	1,800	1	0	0	0	1	95	8	85	2	0
	South Fork	586	4	0	0	0	4	17	2	12	3	0
	Springfield	1,389	2	0	0	0	2	5	0	5	0	0
	Steamboat Springs	9,531	67	0	4	3	60	430	72	324	34	1
	Sterling	12,827	29	0	4	1	24	452	158	275	19	3
	Telluride	2,347	12	0	0	0	12	171	20	145	6	0
	Thornton	107,171	366	4	75	46	241	4,711	722	3,339	650	52
	Trinidad	9,249	25	0	4	5	16	212	75	131	6	2
	Vail	4,676	13	0	1	2	10	386	32	339	15	1
	Victor	427	3	0	0	0	3	12	1	11	0	0
	Walsh	695	0	0	0	0	0	2	0	0	2	0
	Westminster	107,071	285	5	37	53	190	4,366	653	3,121	592	16
	Wheat Ridge	31,833	128	0	33	33	62	1,769	334	1,200	235	7
	Windsor	15,155	7	0	2	1	4	320	84	217	19	1
	Woodland Park	6,786	12	0	0	0	12	177	22	144	11	3
	Wray	2,188	2	0	0	0	2	19	2	16	1	0
	Yuma	3,292	2	0	0	0	2	54	10	41	3	1
CONNECTICUT	Ansonia	18,715	22	0	3	6	13	383	52	297	34	2
	Avon	17,182	5	0	3	0	2	208	30	170	8	0
	Berlin	19,559	19	6	1	10	2	421	88	293	40	3
	Bethel	18,731	7	0	1	3	3	121	22	93	6	1
	Bridgeport	138,791	1,509	28	69	659	753	6,987	1,362	4,400	1,225	
	Bristol	61,257	173	1	13	58	101	1,692	466	1,098	128	8
	Cantonv	9,916	4	0	0	0	4	129	17	100	12	1
	Cheshire	29,052	8	0	3	3	2	247	41	191	15	3
	Danbury	78,613	132	4	11	62	55	1,601	257	1,191	153	1
	Darien	20,420	47	0	0	3	44	185	21	159	5	0
	East Hampton	12,175	1	0	0	0	1	110	20	80	10	1
	East Hartford	49,096	235	1	27	99	108	1,757	286	1,249	222	10
	East Haven	28,710	25	1	1	17	6	581	99	386	96	5
	Easton	7,476	4	0	1	0	3	42	14	22	6	0
	East Windsor	10,431	12	0	3	5	4	399	70	274	55	2
	Enfield	45,370	94	1	8	31	54	1,133	174	836	123	4
	Fairfield	57,723	36	1	3	11	21	1,110	167	871	72	1
	Farmington	24,902	14	0	3	10	1	662	58	560	44	0
	Glastonbury	33,037	16	0	1	7	8	399	77	315	7	3
	Granby	11,071	3	0	0	0	3	133	21	106	6	1
	Greenwich	62,139	25	2	1	10	12	514	58	428	28	3
	Groton	9,478	26	0	4	9	13	247	41	196	10	4
	Groton Long Point	679	1	0	0	0	1	4	0	4	0	0
	Groton Town	31,144	17	0	3	7	7	540	60	456	24	3
	Guilford	22,272	33	0	7	1	25	320	58	246	16	0
	Hamden	58,089	97	1	13	67	16	1,727	183	1,371	173	5
	Hartford	124,203	1,590	24	47	758	761	8,824	1,158	5,957	1,709	87
	Madison	18,783	8	0	0	0	8	173	34	137	2	1
	Manchester	55,485	151	0	9	58	84	2,193	276	1,738	179	18
	Meriden	59,560	222	3	11	135	73	2,111	433	1,463	215	28
	Middlebury	6,963	1	0	0	0	1	70	11	55	4	0
	Middletown	47,364	60	1	3	25	31	1,472	222	1,101	149	0
	Milford	54,716	80	1	12	19	48	1,775	218	1,421	136	5
	Monroe	19,619	8	0	1	1	6	154	32	108	14	0

[1] The FBI does not publish arson data unless it receives data from either the agency or the state for all 12 months of the calendar year.

Table 8. Offenses Known to Law Enforcement, by State and City, 2006 (Contd.)

(Number.)

State	City	Popula-tion	Violent crime	Murder and non-negligent man-slaughter	Forcible rape	Robbery	Aggra-vated assault	Property crime	Burglary	Larceny-theft	Motor vehicle theft	Arson[1]
	New Britain	71,143	333	4	10	194	125	3,270	761	2,119	390	1
	New Canaan	19,953	3	0	1	0	2	189	35	147	7	0
	Newington	29,630	24	0	11	13	0	934	217	643	74	2
	New Milford	28,622	21	1	4	3	13	237	45	175	17	2
	North Branford	14,375	18	0	1	2	15	202	31	161	10	1
	Norwich	36,541	181	1	23	68	89	1,019	178	754	87	5
	Old Saybrook	10,496	4	0	0	4	0	269	25	235	9	1
	Orange	13,948	6	0	1	3	2	396	51	326	19	0
	Plainfield	15,419	9	0	2	1	6	125	29	76	20	2
	Plainville	17,355	19	0	0	9	10	644	65	552	27	3
	Plymouth	12,164	18	0	2	4	12	233	51	168	14	4
	Putnam	9,273	23	0	2	4	17	230	47	174	9	3
	Redding	8,632	1	0	0	0	1	59	6	53	0	2
	Ridgefield	24,172	2	0	1	1	0	83	10	72	1	1
	Seymour	16,119	31	0	5	5	21	234	51	165	18	4
	Shelton	39,415	20	0	2	11	7	449	88	299	62	1
	Simsbury	23,619	5	0	0	4	1	143	16	123	4	2
	South Windsor	25,944	15	0	4	5	6	423	82	322	19	0
	Stonington	18,307	6	0	0	5	1	325	34	284	7	0
	Stratford	49,865	98	0	5	58	35	1,541	209	1,070	262	2
	Thomaston	7,926	1	0	0	0	1	139	28	99	12	2
	Trumbull	35,244	14	0	3	9	2	546	62	436	48	0
	Wallingford	44,666	37	0	7	18	12	902	115	732	55	4
	Waterbury	107,733	408	7	39	216	146	6,039	1,045	4,374	620	20
	Waterford	18,910	37	0	3	10	24	512	45	453	14	3
	Watertown	22,295	16	0	1	0	15	435	94	317	24	0
	West Hartford	61,077	110	0	1	59	50	1,538	279	1,157	102	0
	West Haven	52,840	175	1	1	58	115	1,781	233	1,284	264	13
	Weston	10,260	1	0	0	0	1	60	8	51	1	2
	Westport	26,573	12	0	1	3	8	319	59	249	11	1
	Wethersfield	26,179	34	0	5	17	12	601	68	468	65	2
	Wilton	17,932	1	0	0	1	0	144	17	123	4	0
	Winchester	10,840	21	0	6	1	14	248	71	161	16	5
	Windsor	28,733	20	0	2	5	13	508	49	424	35	1
	Windsor Locks	12,392	6	0	2	2	2	278	27	219	32	1
	Wolcott	16,203	6	0	2	2	2	210	52	138	20	1
	Woodbridge	9,250	4	0	0	4	0	86	10	72	4	1
DELAWARE	Bethany Beach	954	9	0	1	1	7	148	21	127	0	0
	Blades	1,011	4	0	1	0	3	23	5	18	0	0
	Bridgeville	1,597	12	0	0	0	12	63	15	47	1	0
	Camden	2,308	14	0	2	3	9	169	14	149	6	0
	Cheswold	349	4	0	0	1	3	26	2	23	1	0
	Clayton	1,417	6	0	1	1	4	20	6	14	0	0
	Dagsboro	562	0	0	0	0	0	6	2	4	0	0
	Delaware City	1,528	8	0	0	2	6	33	11	21	1	0
	Delmar	1,500	6	0	2	1	3	71	25	43	3	0
	Dewey Beach	315	21	0	1	1	19	92	22	69	1	1
	Dover	34,693	289	2	17	47	223	1,702	142	1,435	125	12
	Ellendale	348	2	0	0	0	2	6	1	5	0	0
	Elsmere	5,790	24	0	2	10	12	221	54	130	37	1
	Felton	848	2	0	1	0	1	17	1	16	0	0
	Fenwick Island	361	0	0	0	0	0	1	0	1	0	0
	Georgetown	4,969	84	0	6	28	50	226	52	164	10	1
	Greenwood	893	3	0	0	2	1	21	2	19	0	0
	Harrington	3,274	25	0	4	1	20	121	42	74	5	1
	Laurel	3,867	69	0	5	11	53	207	43	149	15	1
	Lewes	3,153	3	0	1	0	2	109	41	66	2	0
	Milford	7,286	63	0	3	16	44	489	65	398	26	0
	Millsboro	2,535	13	0	1	4	8	144	45	93	6	0
	Milton	1,812	15	0	2	3	10	105	45	59	1	1
	Newark	30,415	183	0	14	78	91	1,169	215	840	114	10
	New Castle	4,893	38	0	3	10	25	279	42	218	19	0
	Newport	1,119	16	1	0	1	14	41	10	28	3	0
	Ocean View	1,107	6	0	1	0	5	34	14	18	2	0
	Rehoboth Beach	1,574	13	0	4	1	8	235	25	206	4	0

[1] The FBI does not publish arson data unless it receives data from either the agency or the state for all 12 months of the calendar year.

Table 8. Offenses Known to Law Enforcement, by State and City, 2006 *(Contd.)*

(Number.)

State	City	Population	Violent crime	Murder and non-negligent manslaughter	Forcible rape	Robbery	Aggravated assault	Property crime	Burglary	Larceny-theft	Motor vehicle theft	Arson[1]
	Seaford	7,080	82	2	6	32	42	409	79	318	12	0
	Selbyville	1,763	7	0	0	1	6	51	11	39	1	0
	Smyrna	7,500	46	0	5	11	30	243	26	199	18	3
	South Bethany	520	0	0	0	0	0	8	1	7	0	0
	Wilmington	73,645	1,354	19	48	565	722	4,090	972	2,345	773	4
	Wyoming	1,257	8	0	2	1	5	36	11	23	2	0
DISTRICT OF COLUMBIA	Washington	581,530	8,408	169	182	3,604	4,453	26,015	3,826	15,132	7,057	34
FLORIDA	Alachua	7,684	81	0	1	11	69	407	89	285	33	5
	Altamonte Springs	41,749	212	0	14	69	129	1,678	255	1,236	187	8
	Altha	520	1	0	0	0	1	8	3	5	0	0
	Apalachicola	2,379	2	0	0	0	2	89	33	55	1	0
	Apopka	35,314	393	1	18	133	241	1,762	459	1,171	132	12
	Arcadia	7,272	70	0	3	11	56	247	60	175	12	0
	Atlantic Beach	13,663	61	1	4	13	43	482	123	335	24	0
	Atlantis	2,178	10	0	0	1	9	41	6	31	4	0
	Auburndale	12,590	87	0	1	39	47	765	187	545	33	0
	Aventura	29,887	60	0	1	46	13	1,737	126	1,542	69	0
	Avon Park	9,022	115	0	3	9	103	361	151	210	0	0
	Bal Harbour Village	3,327	7	0	1	2	4	74	6	67	1	1
	Bartow	16,553	203	1	14	47	141	1,061	299	688	74	0
	Bay Harbor Island	5,179	13	0	0	4	9	79	17	56	6	0
	Belleair	4,240	1	0	0	0	1	56	4	50	2	0
	Belleair Beach	1,655	1	0	0	0	1	16	3	12	1	0
	Belleair Bluffs	2,262	12	0	0	2	10	53	4	41	8	0
	Belle Glade	15,683	204	1	18	58	127	794	219	498	77	1
	Belleview	3,921	29	1	5	7	16	269	61	201	7	3
	Biscayne Park	3,181	5	0	0	1	4	82	51	24	7	0
	Blountstown	2,474	6	0	0	0	6	50	11	35	4	0
	Boca Raton	88,093	238	3	13	72	150	2,951	551	2,232	168	2
	Bonifay	2,757	2	0	0	0	2	48	30	12	6	0
	Bowling Green	2,977	16	0	0	1	15	68	18	42	8	0
	Boynton Beach	68,013	660	9	8	183	460	3,412	693	2,361	358	8
	Bradenton	54,826	410	4	10	137	259	2,640	580	1,799	261	1
	Bradenton Beach	1,587	8	1	0	2	5	79	11	63	5	0
	Brooksville	7,766	74	0	3	12	59	415	75	320	20	3
	Bushnell	2,155	19	0	0	5	14	120	18	95	7	0
	Cape Coral	142,371	406	6	52	83	265	4,908	1,462	3,115	331	21
	Carrabelle	1,312	4	0	0	0	4	46	19	22	5	0
	Casselberry	24,708	129	0	9	30	90	965	200	685	80	5
	Cedar Grove	5,314	10	0	3	1	6	107	30	70	7	0
	Cedar Key	974	1	0	0	0	1	15	5	10	0	1
	Center Hill	974	15	0	1	0	14	7	6	1	0	0
	Chattahoochee	3,783	58	0	3	2	53	81	25	52	4	0
	Chiefland	2,130	36	0	0	4	32	196	47	149	0	0
	Chipley	3,744	24	0	0	3	21	127	48	73	6	0
	Clearwater	110,520	862	4	44	200	614	4,837	882	3,527	428	31
	Clermont	11,813	128	0	14	18	96	659	177	455	27	2
	Clewiston	7,294	60	3	3	22	32	265	40	205	20	0
	Cocoa	17,183	398	5	21	76	296	1,159	356	716	87	5
	Cocoa Beach	12,645	124	0	9	19	96	1,056	115	871	70	3
	Coconut Creek	49,844	103	0	7	24	72	1,096	175	801	120	2
	Coleman	690	0	0	0	0	0	6	1	4	1	0
	Cooper City	30,528	88	0	2	18	68	572	113	426	33	6
	Coral Gables	43,594	118	0	4	35	79	2,133	366	1,653	114	1
	Coral Springs	130,976	292	2	2	86	202	2,949	487	2,209	253	7
	Crescent City	1,848	36	1	1	5	29	110	29	74	7	0
	Crestview	18,006	98	1	11	16	70	714	70	599	45	1
	Cross City	1,838	11	0	0	4	7	119	42	76	1	0
	Crystal River	3,661	38	0	3	6	29	321	68	238	15	1
	Dade City	6,938	90	0	3	22	65	354	121	203	30	1
	Dania	29,267	225	2	8	72	143	1,471	275	991	205	1
	Davenport	2,051	7	0	0	0	7	72	25	41	6	0
	Davie	85,624	295	2	20	80	193	2,865	450	2,102	313	7
	Daytona Beach	65,507	896	4	55	302	535	5,132	1,615	2,873	644	19

[1] The FBI does not publish arson data unless it receives data from either the agency or the state for all 12 months of the calendar year.

Table 8. Offenses Known to Law Enforcement, by State and City, 2006 (*Contd.*)

(Number.)

State	City	Population	Violent crime	Murder and non-negligent manslaughter	Forcible rape	Robbery	Aggravated assault	Property crime	Burglary	Larceny-theft	Motor vehicle theft	Arson[1]
	Daytona Beach Shores......	4,898	29	0	2	7	20	283	126	130	27	0
	Deerfield Beach	77,636	561	7	23	141	390	2,591	478	1,835	278	10
	Deland..............................	24,786	206	2	3	76	125	2,096	645	1,295	156	1
	Delray Beach....................	65,849	678	5	22	150	501	3,332	587	2,430	315	5
	Doral................................	22,264	126	2	10	29	85	2,654	349	2,033	272	0
	Dundee.............................	3,116	35	0	2	6	27	199	31	152	16	1
	Dunedin	37,309	131	3	20	15	93	907	172	673	62	4
	Dunnellon........................	2,004	16	0	3	4	9	51	16	35	0	0
	Eatonville........................	2,430	57	0	5	9	43	87	15	42	30	1
	Edgewater........................	21,488	73	2	4	8	59	631	163	441	27	4
	Edgewood........................	2,133	10	0	2	4	4	127	32	89	6	0
	El Portal	2,468	13	0	1	2	10	98	38	48	12	0
	Eustis...............................	17,981	64	3	2	10	49	375	91	258	26	1
	Fellsmere	4,881	13	1	0	4	8	61	23	30	8	0
	Fernandina Beach.............	11,454	49	1	2	8	38	510	113	369	28	2
	Flagler Beach	3,233	12	0	1	1	10	164	30	126	8	0
	Florida City......................	9,063	269	0	7	84	178	1,196	259	843	94	5
	Fort Lauderdale	170,203	1,683	21	83	832	747	9,937	2,239	6,678	1,020	49
	Fort Meade	5,839	31	0	1	5	25	220	63	146	11	0
	Fort Myers	59,413	937	15	38	327	557	2,910	561	1,691	658	22
	Fort Pierce	39,202	800	4	37	231	528	2,926	831	1,797	298	15
	Fort Walton Beach............	20,151	138	1	15	32	90	844	163	608	73	1
	Frostproof........................	3,000	5	0	0	0	5	102	28	64	10	0
	Fruitland Park	3,638	9	0	1	3	5	101	24	66	11	1
	Gainesville........................	110,009	1,090	7	96	250	737	5,763	1,420	3,877	466	11
	Golden Beach....................	921	3	0	0	0	3	15	2	12	1	0
	Graceville.........................	2,464	0	0	0	0	0	76	17	55	4	0
	Greenacres City	33,074	332	2	11	60	259	1,232	295	827	110	1
	Green Cove Springs	6,188	77	0	1	10	66	256	81	158	17	0
	Greensboro.......................	625	15	0	0	5	10	39	28	10	1	0
	Groveland.........................	5,293	12	0	0	2	10	160	48	102	10	0
	Gulf Breeze	6,564	5	0	0	5	0	179	32	140	7	3
	Gulfport...........................	12,875	57	0	1	19	37	626	188	379	59	0
	Gulf Stream	764	1	0	0	0	1	8	1	7	0	0
	Haines City.......................	16,647	99	0	3	46	50	932	276	618	38	0
	Hallandale	37,708	392	1	8	98	285	1,579	340	1,073	166	2
	Havana..............................	1,730	20	0	0	1	19	69	21	41	7	0
	Hialeah.............................	224,203	1,263	5	26	374	858	8,674	1,673	5,416	1,585	28
	Hialeah Gardens...............	20,266	63	1	1	23	38	788	198	465	125	0
	Highland Beach	4,193	5	0	0	1	4	39	7	27	5	0
	High Springs.....................	4,227	15	0	1	2	12	194	55	121	18	1
	Hillsboro Beach	2,368	3	0	0	0	3	18	3	14	1	0
	Holly Hill	12,843	118	2	7	35	74	866	219	520	127	2
	Hollywood	148,085	738	8	58	384	288	6,254	1,338	4,113	803	10
	Holmes Beach	5,186	12	0	0	2	10	164	30	125	9	0
	Homestead........................	45,244	1,039	5	7	437	590	3,115	958	1,833	324	8
	Howey-in-the-Hills...........	1,214	0	0	0	0	0	5	0	5	0	0
	Hypoluxo	2,656	5	0	1	0	4	34	14	14	6	0
	Indialantic........................	3,128	8	0	0	4	4	92	20	68	4	0
	Indian Creek Village	39	0	0	0	0	0	0	0	0	0	0
	Indian Harbour Beach	8,583	14	0	1	6	7	87	19	66	2	2
	Indian River Shores..........	3,610	0	0	0	0	0	35	11	23	1	0
	Indian Rocks Beach	5,354	17	0	3	1	13	138	21	107	10	0
	Indian Shores	3,917	7	0	2	0	5	74	15	47	12	0
	Inglis................................	1,638	8	0	0	0	8	41	4	32	5	0
	Jacksonville	795,822	6,663	110	218	2,304	4,031	43,103	9,615	29,167	4,321	172
	Jacksonville Beach............	22,137	200	3	9	57	131	1,461	219	1,124	118	12
	Juno Beach	3,452	4	0	0	1	3	103	20	81	2	0
	Jupiter	48,717	163	2	11	55	95	1,353	340	937	76	10
	Jupiter Inlet Colony	397	0	0	0	0	0	10	3	7	0	0
	Jupiter Island...................	672	2	2	0	0	0	17	9	8	0	0
	Kenneth City	4,494	31	0	2	9	20	186	33	137	16	0
	Key Biscayne....................	10,329	6	0	1	0	5	285	29	241	15	0
	Key Colony Beach............	809	1	0	0	0	1	16	0	16	0	0
	Key West..........................	24,339	207	1	30	71	105	1,627	366	1,021	240	0

[1] The FBI does not publish arson data unless it receives data from either the agency or the state for all 12 months of the calendar year.

Table 8. Offenses Known to Law Enforcement, by State and City, 2006 (*Contd.*)

(Number.)

State	City	Population	Violent crime	Murder and non-negligent man-slaughter	Forcible rape	Robbery	Aggra-vated assault	Property crime	Burglary	Larceny-theft	Motor vehicle theft	Arson[1]
	Kissimmee	60,365	476	7	14	134	321	2,349	665	1,458	226	13
	Lady Lake	13,467	32	0	3	5	24	332	81	217	34	0
	Lake Alfred	3,996	12	0	1	1	10	130	27	93	10	0
	Lake City	11,155	187	1	6	27	153	861	131	700	30	6
	Lake Clarke Shores	3,518	1	0	0	0	1	48	25	15	8	0
	Lake Hamilton	1,438	6	0	0	2	4	91	36	45	10	5
	Lake Helen	2,863	4	0	0	0	4	69	21	33	15	0
	Lakeland	90,209	593	3	57	202	331	5,158	1,140	3,666	352	12
	Lake Mary	14,885	31	0	1	12	18	297	110	174	13	0
	Lake Park	9,191	81	0	9	31	41	656	128	423	105	1
	Lake Placid	1,814	32	0	0	12	20	108	22	83	3	1
	Lake Wales	13,183	54	1	2	20	31	706	198	473	35	2
	Lake Worth	36,955	664	6	24	361	273	2,856	914	1,587	355	6
	Lantana	10,675	81	0	4	21	56	545	160	309	76	1
	Largo	75,729	439	2	35	102	300	2,733	485	2,016	232	6
	Lauderdale-by-the-Sea	6,091	22	0	1	8	13	180	63	108	9	0
	Lauderdale Lakes	32,363	406	4	12	126	264	1,423	362	834	227	8
	Lauderhill	60,627	631	5	21	157	448	2,346	674	1,340	332	10
	Lawtey	696	0	0	0	0	0	13	4	7	2	0
	Leesburg	19,408	295	2	23	83	187	1,272	370	821	81	4
	Lighthouse Point	11,452	14	1	0	7	6	234	29	187	18	2
	Live Oak	7,039	56	0	2	14	40	313	122	173	18	0
	Longboat Key	7,711	1	0	0	0	1	95	14	81	0	0
	Longwood	13,809	95	1	4	19	71	677	186	442	49	2
	Lynn Haven	15,941	267	0	1	5	261	361	98	241	22	0
	Madeira Beach	4,539	46	1	2	3	40	318	56	242	20	0
	Madison	3,244	32	1	3	6	22	187	44	139	4	0
	Maitland	14,363	41	2	4	14	21	389	110	234	45	1
	Manalapan	347	5	0	0	1	4	10	2	8	0	0
	Mangonia Park	1,305	97	1	2	40	54	367	76	238	53	0
	Marco Island	16,381	15	0	1	2	12	207	36	168	3	0
	Margate	56,946	196	0	6	43	147	966	247	632	87	4
	Marianna	6,381	60	0	1	8	51	236	47	178	11	2
	Mascotte	4,725	8	0	1	1	6	78	18	51	9	1
	Medley	1,077	18	0	0	4	14	378	112	207	59	0
	Melbourne	77,939	884	2	30	211	641	4,010	928	2,840	242	9
	Melbourne Beach	3,370	1	0	0	0	1	42	25	12	5	0
	Melbourne Village	714	1	0	0	0	1	7	2	5	0	0
	Mexico Beach	1,212	5	0	0	0	5	43	10	31	2	0
	Miami	392,934	5,931	77	101	2,111	3,642	20,288	4,442	11,967	3,879	110
	Miami Beach	89,408	1,115	4	81	432	598	7,582	1,372	5,357	853	6
	Miami Gardens	101,115	1,868	18	66	550	1,234	6,281	1,287	4,181	813	23
	Miami Lakes	22,697	81	0	7	26	48	918	128	658	132	0
	Miami Shores	10,209	63	1	4	32	26	637	178	408	51	0
	Miami Springs	13,392	43	1	2	16	24	445	111	282	52	0
	Milton	8,268	54	1	2	11	40	448	104	333	11	2
	Miramar	108,421	555	6	45	127	377	3,219	800	1,988	431	12
	Monticello	2,589	33	0	1	3	29	65	38	22	5	0
	Mount Dora	11,668	97	0	5	23	69	468	118	318	32	4
	Mulberry	3,288	25	0	4	4	17	265	83	152	30	3
	Naples	22,075	53	1	6	8	38	859	118	714	27	2
	Neptune Beach	7,136	21	0	1	8	12	284	53	206	25	0
	New Port Richey	17,213	218	0	20	42	156	1,000	326	601	73	1
	New Smyrna Beach	22,733	127	0	2	23	102	805	209	549	47	4
	Niceville	12,794	20	0	1	5	14	173	35	120	18	0
	North Bay Village	7,743	16	0	1	2	13	193	46	119	28	0
	North Lauderdale	42,975	320	2	14	78	226	938	239	593	106	2
	North Miami	58,626	652	7	28	292	325	3,653	862	2,312	479	8
	North Miami Beach	40,107	419	6	30	176	207	2,216	638	1,290	288	5
	North Palm Beach	12,846	51	0	0	21	30	346	101	213	32	1
	North Port	42,966	150	2	21	27	100	1,193	466	669	58	7
	North Redington Beach	1,543	0	0	0	0	0	30	6	23	1	0
	Oak Hill	1,509	14	0	3	1	10	56	32	19	5	0
	Oakland	1,111	3	0	0	1	2	39	19	14	6	0
	Oakland Park	32,248	504	1	17	180	306	2,451	566	1,623	262	7

[1] The FBI does not publish arson data unless it receives data from either the agency or the state for all 12 months of the calendar year.

Table 8. Offenses Known to Law Enforcement, by State and City, 2006 (*Contd.*)

(Number.)

State	City	Popula-tion	Violent crime	Murder and non-negligent man-slaughter	Forcible rape	Robbery	Aggra-vated assault	Property crime	Burglary	Larceny-theft	Motor vehicle theft	Arson[1]
	Ocala	50,584	718	3	43	179	493	3,283	647	2,455	181	12
	Ocean Ridge	1,728	1	0	0	0	1	53	10	40	3	0
	Ocoee	30,352	154	0	8	63	83	1,507	303	1,082	122	11
	Okeechobee	6,000	43	1	1	18	23	312	59	240	13	2
	Oldsmar	13,781	56	0	14	7	35	528	103	401	24	3
	Opa Locka	16,029	427	11	8	182	226	1,592	797	558	237	30
	Orange City	7,995	94	0	1	18	75	877	156	660	61	2
	Orange Park	9,360	58	0	5	8	45	301	60	219	22	0
	Orlando	216,819	4,300	49	163	1,528	2,560	18,318	3,662	12,320	2,336	63
	Ormond Beach	39,264	123	1	7	20	95	1,160	236	872	52	0
	Oviedo	30,351	70	0	1	7	62	457	82	358	17	1
	Pahokee	6,665	141	0	6	21	114	347	98	231	18	2
	Palatka	11,127	192	0	7	44	141	913	157	713	43	0
	Palm Bay	94,399	601	1	66	72	462	3,141	1,101	1,754	286	18
	Palm Beach	10,018	6	0	1	1	4	212	25	170	17	0
	Palm Beach Gardens	49,815	142	0	7	43	92	1,814	365	1,326	123	2
	Palm Beach Shores	1,541	3	0	0	1	2	84	26	49	9	0
	Palmetto	13,738	287	1	7	58	221	838	252	539	47	5
	Palmetto Bay	23,988	106	2	3	42	59	896	126	699	71	0
	Palm Springs	15,524	96	1	1	32	62	971	216	582	173	1
	Panama City	37,815	401	0	34	98	269	2,130	369	1,631	130	7
	Panama City Beach	11,671	93	1	9	16	67	822	187	627	8	2
	Parker	4,751	13	0	0	2	11	127	38	74	15	0
	Parkland	22,518	26	0	3	3	20	275	48	217	10	0
	Pembroke Park	5,580	72	0	4	19	49	439	175	232	32	0
	Pembroke Pines	152,916	363	1	15	134	213	4,886	831	3,581	474	15
	Pensacola	54,967	506	1	30	118	357	2,913	599	2,153	161	4
	Perry	6,848	123	1	4	9	109	166	76	80	10	1
	Pinellas Park	48,151	254	1	22	51	180	2,664	468	2,011	185	13
	Plantation	87,439	262	3	5	131	123	3,675	622	2,708	345	6
	Plant City	31,980	316	2	16	120	178	1,819	272	1,321	226	13
	Pompano Beach	105,936	1,367	10	54	441	862	4,985	1,049	3,398	538	19
	Ponce Inlet	3,256	5	0	0	1	4	44	7	34	3	0
	Port Orange	54,652	71	6	2	7	56	1,242	241	943	58	3
	Port Richey	3,389	34	1	1	12	20	315	58	241	16	1
	Port St. Joe	3,663	22	0	0	1	21	76	25	49	2	0
	Port St. Lucie	133,913	340	7	36	34	263	3,563	1,065	2,355	143	15
	Punta Gorda	17,400	46	0	2	5	39	444	158	264	22	1
	Quincy	7,111	82	0	5	10	67	458	158	287	13	1
	Redington Beaches	1,551	3	0	1	1	1	27	6	19	2	0
	Riviera Beach	34,342	903	10	13	254	626	3,149	1,073	1,590	486	20
	Rockledge	24,654	62	0	0	20	42	720	171	499	50	2
	Royal Palm Beach	31,407	87	0	4	16	67	848	190	585	73	3
	Safety Harbor	17,812	40	2	6	5	27	285	72	191	22	1
	Sanford	48,054	234	5	18	112	99	3,474	748	2,262	464	5
	Sanibel	6,174	2	1	0	0	1	99	36	60	3	0
	Sarasota	54,617	565	4	23	196	342	3,583	847	2,484	252	9
	Satellite Beach	9,976	31	0	3	3	25	252	93	153	6	0
	Sea Ranch Lakes	774	1	0	0	1	0	15	0	15	0	0
	Sebastian	19,974	51	0	3	8	40	512	141	348	23	0
	Sebring	10,607	86	0	5	15	66	564	184	351	29	4
	Seminole	18,817	70	0	6	9	55	679	92	555	32	4
	Sewall's Point	2,093	2	0	0	0	2	22	9	13	0	0
	Sneads	1,976	2	0	0	1	1	28	9	16	3	0
	South Bay	4,127	67	0	2	16	49	145	30	105	10	2
	South Daytona	13,965	60	0	5	18	37	548	112	388	48	1
	South Miami	11,335	98	1	1	50	46	769	141	584	44	2
	South Palm Beach	1,556	0	0	0	0	0	13	1	12	0	0
	South Pasadena	5,811	11	0	2	5	4	264	44	199	21	5
	Southwest Ranches	7,513	25	0	3	5	17	161	31	105	25	0
	Springfield	9,196	90	0	3	20	67	407	104	271	32	3
	Starke	5,943	59	0	3	6	50	166	3	152	11	0
	St. Augustine	12,470	120	1	5	17	97	825	112	662	51	5
	St. Augustine Beach	5,850	20	0	3	3	14	159	26	128	5	0
	St. Cloud	22,888	170	0	12	18	140	1,150	275	817	58	12

[1] The FBI does not publish arson data unless it receives data from either the agency or the state for all 12 months of the calendar year.

Table 8. Offenses Known to Law Enforcement, by State and City, 2006 (*Contd.*)

(Number.)

State	City	Population	Violent crime	Murder and non-negligent man-slaughter	Forcible rape	Robbery	Aggra-vated assault	Property crime	Burglary	Larceny-theft	Motor vehicle theft	Arson[1]
	St. Pete Beach	10,345	52	0	5	9	38	551	220	312	19	9
	St. Petersburg	253,280	3,753	21	112	1,032	2,588	16,409	3,466	10,182	2,761	75
	Stuart	16,030	96	2	6	31	57	827	114	679	34	2
	Sunny Isles Beach	15,684	35	0	2	11	22	521	175	275	71	1
	Sunrise	92,117	426	3	15	177	231	3,343	576	2,449	318	4
	Surfside	4,789	40	0	1	9	30	124	26	92	6	0
	Sweetwater	13,973	27	0	0	9	18	231	27	165	39	0
	Tallahassee	161,173	1,615	10	155	452	998	7,709	2,168	4,935	606	31
	Tamarac	60,934	167	1	12	69	85	1,221	292	796	133	5
	Tampa	331,487	3,839	25	133	1,211	2,470	18,789	4,451	11,251	3,087	45
	Tarpon Springs	23,033	213	0	3	25	185	780	212	516	52	5
	Tavares	11,817	51	0	2	7	42	261	49	189	23	0
	Temple Terrace	22,349	117	2	7	35	73	982	258	594	130	3
	Tequesta	6,090	15	0	1	2	12	105	14	84	7	3
	Titusville	44,505	356	7	26	99	224	1,622	386	1,064	172	11
	Treasure Island	7,669	15	0	4	3	8	282	54	218	10	2
	Trenton	1,823	6	1	0	0	5	64	21	39	4	0
	Umatilla	2,692	38	0	3	2	33	93	17	70	6	1
	Valparaiso	6,472	11	0	1	1	9	90	17	61	12	1
	Venice	21,328	53	0	3	7	43	599	127	449	23	5
	Vero Beach	17,366	76	0	7	23	46	642	121	498	23	6
	Village of Pinecrest	19,528	31	1	0	12	18	623	75	519	29	1
	Virginia Gardens	2,298	3	0	0	0	3	30	3	23	4	0
	Waldo	789	1	0	0	0	1	9	5	1	3	0
	Wauchula	4,525	35	0	2	3	30	204	42	152	10	0
	Webster	852	14	0	0	3	11	28	11	15	2	0
	Welaka	625	1	0	0	1	0	10	4	4	2	0
	Wellington	54,487	163	0	21	34	108	1,719	280	1,287	152	3
	West Melbourne	15,308	21	1	0	6	14	355	163	175	17	0
	West Miami	5,927	17	0	1	6	10	155	33	99	23	1
	Weston	66,787	96	0	6	16	74	967	157	749	61	11
	West Palm Beach	99,142	1,174	17	46	574	537	7,332	1,591	4,775	966	6
	White Springs	829	8	0	0	0	8	24	5	18	1	0
	Wildwood	3,486	71	0	10	10	51	199	73	116	10	1
	Williston	2,550	42	0	1	3	38	183	32	139	12	0
	Wilton Manors	13,075	76	0	2	33	41	661	177	420	64	0
	Windermere	2,037	1	0	0	0	1	26	6	18	2	0
	Winter Garden	25,930	278	3	12	59	204	1,121	308	693	120	2
	Winter Haven	29,999	226	1	30	80	115	2,040	496	1,395	149	9
	Winter Park	28,654	90	2	5	35	48	976	229	658	89	0
	Winter Springs	33,133	96	0	8	15	73	632	166	428	38	0
	Zephyrhills	12,465	64	1	3	21	39	816	164	596	56	10
	Zolfo Springs	1,694	1	0	0	1	0	15	9	6	0	0
GEORGIA	Adairsville	3,189	11	0	0	2	9	259	49	189	21	
	Albany	77,815	553	8	31	243	271	5,279	1,645	3,235	399	
	Alpharetta	41,417	119	0	13	40	66	1,560	162	1,317	81	
	Aragon	1,092	0	0	0	0	0	38	9	29	0	1
	Athens-Clarke County	106,700	373	5	53	125	190	5,634	1,116	4,154	364	21
	Atlanta	485,804	7,548	110	171	2,959	4,308	32,231	7,401	18,952	5,878	175
	Attapulgus	496	0	0	0	0	0	10	2	8	0	0
	Avondale Estates	2,707	2	0	0	2	0	78	14	55	9	
	Ball Ground	837	1	0	0	0	1	30	7	21	2	
	Blythe	813	0	0	0	0	0	21	4	16	1	0
	Bowdon	2,026	0	0	0	0	0	97	13	83	1	0
	Bremen	5,522	15	0	1	1	13	216	38	169	9	
	Brooklet	1,214	6	2	0	0	4	56	3	49	4	
	Broxton	1,515	12	0	0	0	12	77	14	61	2	
	Brunswick	16,468	449	2	8	89	350	1,343	345	930	68	
	Buchanan	1,051	1	0	0	0	1	57	13	42	2	
	Byron	3,355	14	0	1	3	10	114	19	80	15	
	Calhoun	14,006	47	2	2	23	20	743	90	619	34	
	Carrollton	22,538	167	4	6	60	97	1,729	278	1,390	61	
	Cartersville	18,220	121	1	11	42	67	1,218	281	819	118	
	Chamblee	10,077	88	1	1	72	14	719	85	540	94	
	Clarkesville	1,553	7	0	0	2	5	134	23	108	3	

[1] The FBI does not publish arson data unless it receives data from either the agency or the state for all 12 months of the calendar year.

Table 8. Offenses Known to Law Enforcement, by State and City, 2006 (Contd.)

(Number.)

State	City	Popula-tion	Violent crime	Murder and non-negligent man-slaughter	Forcible rape	Robbery	Aggra-vated assault	Property crime	Burglary	Larceny-theft	Motor vehicle theft	Arson[1]
	Clarkston[3]	7,305		0	3	20		275	141	86	48	
	College Park	20,829	327	3	17	137	170	1,979	392	1,247	340	
	Columbus	191,221	1,187	17	19	582	569	13,825	2,773	9,202	1,850	
	Commerce	6,044	37	0	3	2	32	355	49	290	16	
	Conyers	12,597	84	0	6	41	37	1,040	155	755	130	
	Coolidge	576	0	0	0	0	0	8	2	5	1	0
	Cordele	11,862	71	2	9	24	36	847	188	631	28	
	Cornelia	3,892	20	0	0	0	20	199	16	176	7	
	Covington	14,301	72	1	12	21	38	812	224	512	76	0
	Cumming	5,988	15	1	1	2	11	382	36	327	19	
	Dalton	33,172	148	1	10	32	105	1,390	209	1,065	116	
	Dillard	260	0	0	0	0	0	0	0	0	0	0
	Doraville	10,189	51	2	1	16	32	450	59	314	77	
	Douglasville	28,453	186	2	7	55	122	2,688	387	2,067	234	
	Duluth	25,268	91	0	1	15	75	536	103	391	42	
	East Point	41,986	413	7	14	203	189	2,803	816	1,533	454	
	Elberton	4,865	42	0	2	15	25	473	91	377	5	
	Emerson	1,344	17	0	0	1	16	61	9	47	5	
	Euharlee	3,983	7	0	0	0	7	59	18	40	1	
	Fairburn	8,839	54	1	1	27	25	586	185	327	74	
	Fayetteville	14,824	20	0	0	10	10	628	51	538	39	
	Forest Park	22,914	218	3	4	125	86	1,385	272	934	179	8
	Fort Gaines	1,093	2	0	0	0	2	6	2	4	0	
	Fort Oglethorpe	9,252	58	0	3	9	46	669	81	558	30	
	Fort Valley	8,460	143	0	0	24	119	517	131	373	13	
	Gainesville	33,486	217	2	17	77	121	1,959	228	1,584	147	
	Greensboro	3,409	25	0	0	4	21	249	39	188	22	
	Hahira	1,977	0	0	0	0	0	40	6	30	4	0
	Hampton	4,895	10	0	0	4	6	116	42	66	8	0
	Helen	690	9	0	0	0	9	71	6	60	5	0
	Jackson	4,498	2	0	0	2	0	145	14	127	4	0
	Jasper	2,928	6	0	0	1	5	154	16	132	6	
	Jonesboro	4,048	23	0	1	13	9	248	68	146	34	0
	LaGrange	28,241	174	1	26	70	77	1,878	369	1,394	115	
	Lake Park	578	0	0	0	0	0	17	4	11	2	0
	Lawrenceville	29,305	120	2	6	59	53	1,182	323	714	145	0
	Luthersville	871	1	0	0	1	0	40	19	21	0	0
	Macon	97,345	853	12	53	358	430	9,486	2,355	5,891	1,240	115
	Madison	3,956	11	0	2	1	8	192	38	149	5	0
	Manchester	3,838	21	0	0	4	17	254	84	150	20	0
	Marietta	63,228	400	1	19	235	145	2,622	548	1,626	448	0
	McDonough	16,022	188	0	4	23	161	859	161	621	77	0
	McIntyre	739	2	0	0	0	2	19	4	14	1	0
	McRae	4,421	42	2	1	2	37	141	38	100	3	0
	Milledgeville	20,020	70	2	8	21	39	871	139	683	49	3
	Molena	503	0	0	0	0	0	0	0	0	0	0
	Monroe	12,725	82	1	3	21	57	675	117	497	61	2
	Montezuma	4,125	20	0	0	2	18	175	39	127	9	1
	Morrow	5,453	64	1	0	39	24	1,075	60	896	119	0
	Newington	329	0	0	0	0	0	1	0	1	0	0
	Newnan	25,446	174	0	8	38	128	1,288	223	985	80	2
	Newton	895	0	0	0	0	0	2	2	0	0	0
	Norcross	10,205	159	0	4	80	75	558	140	296	122	1
	Norman Park	887	0	0	0	0	0	17	6	8	3	0
	Oglethorpe	1,194	15	0	0	1	14	17	9	6	2	0
	Omega	1,404	2	0	0	0	2	6	3	2	1	0
	Oxford	2,285	3	0	0	0	3	26	7	13	6	0
	Palmetto	4,826	17	0	0	7	10	149	40	98	11	0
	Peachtree City	35,633	16	1	2	5	8	384	37	285	62	1
	Pearson	1,962	16	0	2	1	13	142	35	100	7	0
	Pendergrass	493	0	0	0	0	0	5	0	2	3	0
	Perry	11,372	50	0	2	4	44	231	52	158	21	0
	Pine Mountain	1,271	7	0	0	4	3	92	13	73	6	0
	Powder Springs	14,973	55	0	5	10	40	374	99	248	27	0

[1] The FBI does not publish arson data unless it receives data from either the agency or the state for all 12 months of the calendar year.
[3] The FBI determined that the agency's data were inflated. Consequently, affected data are not included in this table.

Table 8. Offenses Known to Law Enforcement, by State and City, 2006 *(Contd.)*

(Number.)

State	City	Popula-tion	Violent crime	Murder and non-negligent man-slaughter	Forcible rape	Robbery	Aggra-vated assault	Property crime	Burglary	Larceny-theft	Motor vehicle theft	Arson[1]
	Reidsville	2,477	12	0	2	3	7	134	18	108	8	0
	Riverdale	15,972	115	0	2	75	38	1,045	224	636	185	0
	Rockmart	4,448	18	0	5	4	9	162	32	116	14	0
	Rome	36,966	309	1	19	53	236	2,354	433	1,798	123	17
	Rossville	3,526	10	0	1	5	4	276	53	203	20	0
	Roswell	88,679	178	0	12	93	73	2,218	445	1,586	187	1
	Sandersville	6,225	42	0	6	9	27	451	87	345	19	1
	Savannah-Chatham Metropolitan	213,488	1,184	29	65	690	400	9,924	2,039	6,665	1,220	76
	Senoia	2,806	2	0	0	1	1	60	18	40	2	0
	Shiloh	446	0	0	0	0	0	2	1	1	0	0
	Sky Valley	224	0	0	0	0	0	0	0	0	0	0
	Smyrna	49,173	223	1	7	126	89	1,949	454	1,208	287	2
	Snellville	19,856	51	0	0	20	31	858	118	672	68	0
	St. Marys	16,931	59	0	6	12	41	482	129	333	20	3
	Stone Mountain	7,307	17	0	4	6	7	206	114	35	57	0
	Suwanee	12,956	29	0	1	16	12	362	57	275	30	0
	Sylvania	2,674	18	0	2	2	14	104	17	85	2	0
	Tallulah Falls	164	0	0	0	0	0	3	1	0	2	0
	Tifton	16,851	174	0	6	50	118	1,395	199	1,149	47	0
	Trenton	2,224	5	0	0	0	5	35	5	26	4	0
	Trion	2,114	5	0	0	0	5	65	11	48	6	0
	Tunnel Hill	1,106	7	0	0	1	6	60	9	43	8	0
	Valdosta	46,657	298	2	23	97	176	3,054	699	2,228	127	0
	Vidalia	11,391	104	2	5	28	69	741	215	498	28	0
	Villa Rica	10,215	77	0	6	16	55	806	120	626	60	0
	Warm Springs	494	0	0	0	0	0	5	3	2	0	0
	Warner Robins	59,767	310	3	15	127	165	3,058	661	2,237	160	11
	Washington	4,283	25	0	2	1	22	116	22	88	6	0
	Waverly Hall	799	0	0	0	0	0	12	3	8	1	0
	Waycross	15,597	121	1	8	28	84	1,047	160	835	52	5
	Waynesboro	6,192	66	1	1	26	38	531	73	420	38	0
	Willacoochee	1,554	2	0	0	0	2	18	5	13	0	0
	Winterville	1,093	0	0	0	0	0	1	0	1	0	0
	Wrens	2,334	12	1	0	3	8	101	23	72	6	0
	Zebulon	1,232	1	0	0	0	1	23	5	16	2	0
HAWAII	Honolulu	912,693	2,745	17	229	956	1,543	38,310	5,482	26,540	6,288	588
IDAHO	Aberdeen	1,876	2	0	0	0	2	10	3	6	1	0
	American Falls	4,271	9	0	1	0	8	69	12	53	4	0
	Bellevue	2,261	1	0	0	0	1	8	3	5	0	0
	Blackfoot	11,111	35	0	4	2	29	431	49	367	15	1
	Boise	198,212	772	6	127	111	528	6,616	1,165	5,074	377	52
	Bonners Ferry	2,796	3	0	1	2	0	46	9	33	4	1
	Buhl	4,120	23	0	1	0	22	111	32	66	13	3
	Caldwell	35,333	179	1	23	18	137	1,688	489	1,012	187	12
	Cascade	1,031	1	0	0	0	1	8	2	5	1	0
	Chubbuck	10,987	67	0	5	1	61	516	43	455	18	4
	Coeur d'Alene	41,106	269	0	35	17	217	1,911	369	1,428	114	25
	Cottonwood	1,098	0	0	0	0	0	4	1	3	0	0
	Emmett	6,284	23	0	6	0	17	124	15	102	7	1
	Filer	1,814	4	0	0	1	3	8	5	2	1	0
	Fruitland	4,521	24	1	4	0	19	111	27	73	11	1
	Garden City	11,723	48	1	6	4	37	507	128	353	26	4
	Gooding	3,407	2	0	0	0	2	74	6	64	4	1
	Grangeville	3,233	16	0	3	0	13	117	11	94	12	0
	Hagerman	860	0	0	0	0	0	8	1	5	2	0
	Hailey	7,781	5	0	2	1	2	46	7	30	9	1
	Heyburn	2,827	0	0	0	0	0	17	7	10	0	0
	Idaho City	501	0	0	0	0	0	19	3	15	1	0
	Idaho Falls	53,707	189	2	49	12	126	2,048	458	1,463	127	20
	Jerome	8,725	23	0	4	1	18	255	56	187	12	3
	Kamiah	1,178	4	0	1	1	2	9	1	8	0	0
	Kellogg	2,358	8	0	1	0	7	53	12	37	4	0
	Ketchum	3,227	15	0	0	1	14	108	14	89	5	0
	Kimberly	2,756	4	0	0	0	4	19	4	13	2	1

[1] The FBI does not publish arson data unless it receives data from either the agency or the state for all 12 months of the calendar year.

Table 8. Offenses Known to Law Enforcement, by State and City, 2006 (*Contd.*)

(Number.)

State	City	Popula-tion	Violent crime	Murder and non-negligent man-slaughter	Forcible rape	Robbery	Aggra-vated assault	Property crime	Burglary	Larceny-theft	Motor vehicle theft	Arson[1]
	Lewiston	31,894	34	1	5	4	24	1,327	258	1,015	54	6
	McCall	2,478	15	0	4	3	8	169	36	123	10	0
	Meridian	53,606	109	1	14	9	85	1,283	270	934	79	16
	Montpelier	2,573	1	0	0	0	1	6	1	4	1	0
	Nampa	73,588	240	3	41	31	165	2,488	538	1,658	292	27
	Orofino	3,227	4	1	0	0	3	57	9	46	2	1
	Osburn	1,496	1	0	1	0	0	19	3	15	1	0
	Parma	1,846	6	0	0	2	4	52	9	38	5	0
	Payette	7,758	7	0	0	0	7	176	44	122	10	2
	Pinehurst	1,630	0	0	0	0	0	17	5	12	0	0
	Pocatello	54,768	181	0	32	15	134	1,580	207	1,310	63	9
	Ponderay	715	1	0	0	1	0	89	20	67	2	0
	Post Falls	23,768	62	0	15	6	41	659	116	490	53	6
	Preston	5,150	3	1	1	0	1	52	8	44	0	0
	Rathdrum	5,890	8	0	5	0	3	151	36	104	11	2
	Rexburg	26,952	7	0	2	0	5	296	76	210	10	1
	Rigby	3,330	3	0	1	0	2	88	13	72	3	0
	Rupert	5,362	0	0	0	0	0	69	11	55	3	0
	Salmon	3,152	8	1	0	0	7	38	3	35	0	1
	Sandpoint	8,317	17	0	0	1	16	321	87	223	11	1
	Shelley	4,239	3	0	1	0	2	55	11	42	2	0
	Soda Springs	3,341	1	0	0	0	1	27	8	19	0	0
	Spirit Lake	1,539	10	0	1	0	9	20	7	12	1	1
	St. Anthony	3,436	3	0	0	0	3	27	5	19	3	0
	St. Maries	2,703	8	0	0	0	8	27	4	21	2	0
	Sun Valley	1,482	2	0	0	0	2	35	7	26	2	0
	Twin Falls	39,640	131	0	22	20	89	1,820	351	1,367	102	13
	Weiser	5,562	13	1	0	1	11	98	22	71	5	0
	Wendell	2,459	6	0	1	0	5	77	7	63	7	2
	Wilder	1,489	5	0	0	0	5	35	7	24	4	0
ILLINOIS[6,7]	Aurora	169,085		4		178	531	4,936	917	3,734	285	24
	Chicago	2,857,796		468		15,863	17,445	129,718	24,153	83,737	21,828	712
	Joliet	136,940		14		191	387	4,049	882	3,016	151	51
	Naperville	142,340		0		25	75	2,231	185	1,972	74	6
	Peoria	113,291		17		386	554	6,547	1,590	4,395	562	50
	Rockford[8]	153,738	1,841	19	132	555	1,135	11,240	2,986	7,476	778	25
	Springfield	116,290		6		356	1,329	7,747	1,953	5,373	421	58
INDIANA	Albion	2,338	0	0	0	0	0	6	1	5	0	0
	Alexandria	5,907	4	0	0	3	1	323	43	265	15	1
	Anderson	57,881	287	6	42	75	164	2,794	607	1,961	226	17
	Angola	7,942	9	0	3	4	2	553	34	505	14	2
	Attica	3,407	6	0	1	1	4	107	29	72	6	2
	Auburn	12,771	28	0	3	16	9	493	83	389	21	0
	Bargersville	2,477	0	0	0	0	0	0	0	0	0	0
	Bedford	13,641	33	0	4	3	26	388	72	297	19	0
	Beech Grove	14,162	48	1	9	30	8	476	89	333	54	3
	Berne	4,185	5	0	2	1	2	82	18	62	2	0
	Bloomington	69,474	238	1	26	65	146	2,884	663	2,077	144	28
	Bluffton	9,523	4	0	0	2	2	191	29	159	3	0
	Boonville	6,827	2	0	0	1	1	164	1	160	3	0
	Brazil	8,268	3	0	0	1	2	214	36	161	17	0
	Bremen	4,599	4	0	2	0	2	80	17	61	2	2
	Brownsburg	18,411	6	0	1	3	2	388	47	326	15	1
	Burns Harbor	825	1	0	0	0	1	30	7	20	3	0
	Carmel	59,635	26	0	6	13	7	1,016	130	833	53	5
	Cedar Lake	9,967	13	0	1	1	11	404	79	312	13	1
	Charlestown[9]	8,105	4	0	1	0	3	321	64	245	12	0
	Chesterfield	2,816	2	0	0	1	1	83	16	65	2	0
	Chesterton	12,112	1	0	1	0	0	321	71	229	21	2
	Clarks Hill	664	1	0	0	0	1	21	10	10	1	1
	Clarksville	21,200	94	0	9	39	46	2,020	279	1,579	162	4

[1] The FBI does not publish arson data unless it receives data from either the agency or the state for all 12 months of the calendar year.
[6] Limited data for 2006 were available for Illinois.
[7] The data collection methodology for the offense of forcible rape used by the Illinois (with the exception of Rockford, Illinois) and the Minnesota state UCR Programs does not comply with national UCR Program guidelines. Consequently, their figures for forcible rape and violent crime (of which forcible rape is a part) are not published in this table.
[8] Because of changes in the state/local agency's reporting practices, figures are not comparable to previous years' data.
[9] Due to an annexation, population and figures may not be comparable to previous years' data.

Table 8. Offenses Known to Law Enforcement, by State and City, 2006 *(Contd.)*

(Number.)

State	City	Popula-tion	Violent crime	Murder and non-negligent man-slaughter	Forcible rape	Robbery	Aggra-vated assault	Property crime	Burglary	Larceny-theft	Motor vehicle theft	Arson[1]
	Clinton	4,938	4	0	0	0	4	59	3	44	12	3
	Columbia City	8,077	12	0	1	3	8	103	17	81	5	1
	Columbus	39,641	76	2	12	15	47	2,554	277	2,153	124	9
	Connersville	14,463	14	0	2	3	9	1,127	199	886	42	1
	Corydon	2,805	0	0	0	0	0	34	6	24	4	0
	Crawfordsville	15,255	25	0	7	8	10	807	159	628	20	1
	Crown Point	22,847	20	0	1	5	14	695	71	566	58	4
	Culver	1,536	7	0	0	0	7	18	4	13	1	0
	Danville	7,474	8	0	1	1	6	85	10	62	13	1
	Decatur	9,610	13	0	1	5	7	84	14	57	13	0
	Delphi	3,000	12	0	0	2	10	107	22	79	6	0
	Dyer	15,171	8	0	2	1	5	418	33	363	22	1
	East Chicago	31,151	304	15	7	137	145	2,119	441	1,357	321	13
	Elkhart	52,616	284	12	26	230	16	4,069	936	2,857	276	36
	Elwood	9,228	1	0	1	0	0	458	109	334	15	1
	Evansville	116,686	540	6	61	185	288	5,307	1,131	3,933	243	69
	Fairmount	2,833	9	0	0	0	9	96	16	80	0	0
	Fishers	57,599	27	0	5	14	8	643	78	530	35	4
	Fort Wayne[9]	224,820	708	18	80	404	206	10,767	2,128	7,934	705	126
	Frankfort	16,541	21	0	3	3	15	907	113	763	31	7
	Franklin	21,891	85	2	6	7	70	1,079	113	949	17	0
	Gary	99,369	707	48	61	336	262	5,564	1,818	2,680	1,066	
	Gas City	5,858	4	1	0	3	0	189	29	154	6	0
	Georgetown	2,700	6	0	0	0	6	13	3	7	3	0
	Goshen	31,476	77	2	18	22	35	1,301	199	1,047	55	10
	Greendale	4,386	32	0	2	1	29	101	6	90	5	1
	Greenfield	16,764	21	0	3	3	15	372	64	286	22	5
	Greensburg	10,606	9	0	1	5	3	357	69	274	14	4
	Greenwood	42,516	157	2	6	15	134	1,629	134	1,417	78	7
	Griffith	16,776	32	0	3	14	15	641	88	483	70	2
	Hagerstown	1,684	1	0	0	0	1	79	17	58	4	1
	Hammond	79,742	580	8	29	249	294	4,226	970	2,694	562	60
	Hartford City	6,728	9	0	0	3	6	251	49	191	11	0
	Hebron	3,594	1	0	0	0	1	27	2	20	5	2
	Highland	23,325	33	0	2	16	15	963	142	742	79	2
	Hobart	27,952	164	0	10	26	128	1,501	154	1,207	140	8
	Indianapolis	800,969	7,689	140	549	3,249	3,751	49,599	11,734	28,929	8,936	347
	Jasper	13,858	6	1	1	2	2	180	34	133	13	1
	Kendallville	10,084	14	0	3	3	8	337	57	262	18	0
	Knox	3,691	57	0	1	1	55	294	51	219	24	0
	Kokomo	46,484	217	5	23	65	124	3,042	642	2,260	140	0
	Lafayette	60,859	262	2	45	77	138	3,440	779	2,448	213	17
	La Porte	21,232	44	0	3	18	23	1,532	184	1,253	95	0
	Lawrence	41,230	140	3	3	114	20	1,063	222	674	167	0
	Ligonier	4,452	5	0	0	0	5	68	14	47	7	0
	Long Beach	1,564	2	0	0	0	2	20	3	17	0	0
	Lowell	8,092	16	0	0	3	13	178	28	143	7	1
	Madison	12,525	24	1	5	1	17	461	125	302	34	0
	Martinsville	11,734	42	0	4	2	36	961	103	828	30	3
	Merrillville	31,734	94	1	2	27	64	1,102	93	857	152	0
	Michigan City	32,418	142	3	28	63	48	1,787	256	1,388	143	19
	Mishawaka	48,818	176	0	12	62	102	3,452	389	2,885	178	28
	Monticello	5,498	2	0	0	0	2	135	18	114	3	1
	Mooresville	11,185	5	0	1	3	1	379	53	297	29	0
	Muncie	66,602	340	3	45	95	197	3,111	633	2,315	163	37
	Munster[8]	22,495	24	0	0	15	9	547	63	454	30	3
	Nappanee	7,001	2	0	2	0	0	238	21	208	9	1
	New Albany	37,016	173	1	5	73	94	2,333	409	1,725	199	46
	New Castle	18,842	18	0	7	9	2	1,936	464	1,402	70	1
	New Whiteland	4,460	8	0	0	0	8	99	13	82	4	2
	Noblesville	39,082	43	1	7	11	24	884	209	630	45	6
	North Liberty	1,371	17	0	0	0	17	8	1	6	1	0
	North Manchester	6,020	4	0	0	1	2	193	36	152	5	0

[1] The FBI does not publish arson data unless it receives data from either the agency or the state for all 12 months of the calendar year.
[8] Because of changes in the state/local agency's reporting practices, figures are not comparable to previous years' data.
[9] Due to an annexation, population and figures may not be comparable to previous years' data.

Table 8. Offenses Known to Law Enforcement, by State and City, 2006 (*Contd.*)

(Number.)

State	City	Population	Violent crime	Murder and non-negligent man-slaughter	Forcible rape	Robbery	Aggra-vated assault	Property crime	Burglary	Larceny-theft	Motor vehicle theft	Arson[1]
	North Vernon	6,476	6	0	2	1	3	352	50	291	11	1
	Plainfield	23,688	37	0	7	12	18	990	140	777	73	0
	Plymouth	10,948	15	0	1	6	8	385	51	314	20	0
	Portage	35,923	105	1	7	15	82	1,198	180	920	98	1
	Portland	6,232	1	0	0	1	0	273	19	250	4	0
	Rensselaer	6,275	37	0	0	0	37	278	60	206	12	5
	Richmond	37,809	170	1	14	58	97	1,559	330	1,054	175	66
	Rushville	5,717	13	0	0	0	13	143	24	119	0	2
	Salem	6,496	2	0	0	0	2	23	14	9	0	0
	Schererville	28,582	14	0	1	9	4	801	82	658	61	0
	Scottsburg	6,100	51	0	0	8	43	442	80	350	12	0
	Seymour	19,015	104	0	7	8	89	1,306	119	1,121	66	1
	South Bend	105,959	805	14	67	430	294	7,411	1,930	4,895	586	86
	South Whitley	1,859	3	0	0	0	3	31	10	19	2	1
	Speedway	12,490	77	2	6	52	17	547	71	373	103	0
	St. John	10,854	5	1	0	0	4	188	12	160	16	0
	Tell City	7,741	2	0	1	0	1	178	39	137	2	2
	Terre Haute	57,270	173	2	27	91	53	5,373	1,024	3,854	495	32
	Tipton	5,289	0	0	0	0	0	131	32	98	1	0
	Valparaiso	29,295	102	0	7	4	91	1,030	93	889	48	3
	Vincennes	18,197	25	0	5	7	13	1,188	268	860	60	3
	Wabash	11,283	7	1	1	3	2	203	70	125	8	0
	Warsaw	12,819	10	0	4	6	0	694	113	557	24	2
	Waterloo	2,213	12	0	1	0	11	81	21	51	9	0
	Westfield[9]	24,075	14	0	3	4	7	493	60	405	28	3
	West Lafayette	28,788	73	0	14	5	54	487	71	398	18	0
	Whiting	4,925	9	0	0	6	3	194	30	142	22	4
	Winchester	4,877	9	0	2	0	7	266	43	208	15	2
	Winona Lake	4,263	5	0	1	0	4	30	8	21	1	0
IOWA	Adel	4,067	3	0	0	0	3	114	13	93	8	0
	Albia	3,699	9	0	0	0	9	67	11	53	3	2
	Ames	52,541	147	0	24	17	106	1,465	363	1,061	41	5
	Anamosa	5,646	5	0	0	0	5	99	16	81	2	3
	Ankeny	36,876	36	0	6	6	24	806	140	626	40	4
	Belmond	2,464	0	0	0	0	0	18	10	4	4	0
	Bettendorf	32,059	75	1	9	13	52	832	156	644	32	6
	Bloomfield	2,611	2	0	1	0	1	23	7	15	1	0
	Boone	12,899	33	0	15	0	18	412	112	285	15	3
	Burlington	25,571	120	1	8	13	98	1,226	296	881	49	23
	Camanche	4,283	2	0	0	0	2	84	13	70	1	0
	Carlisle	3,563	3	0	0	0	3	10	2	7	1	1
	Carter Lake	3,422	15	1	0	2	12	304	46	239	19	0
	Cedar Falls	36,665	86	0	13	5	68	881	140	703	38	9
	Cedar Rapids	123,773	401	6	39	136	220	5,872	1,114	4,460	298	21
	Centerville	5,819	21	0	1	2	18	327	54	261	12	1
	Chariton	4,633	10	0	1	0	9	175	41	126	8	2
	Cherokee	5,054	7	0	0	0	7	91	14	71	6	1
	Clarinda	5,552	12	0	2	0	10	202	73	114	15	3
	Clarion	2,888	6	0	1	0	5	71	13	55	3	4
	Clinton	27,230	160	1	13	18	128	1,443	300	1,059	84	16
	Clive	13,925	40	0	3	5	32	469	70	379	20	6
	Coralville	17,906	49	0	11	14	24	744	65	658	21	6
	Council Bluffs	59,884	539	2	68	72	397	4,648	878	3,137	633	39
	Cresco	3,794	9	0	0	0	9	117	26	83	8	3
	Creston	7,398	18	0	1	2	15	221	53	145	23	3
	Decorah	8,127	14	0	1	0	13	127	21	97	9	1
	Denison	7,413	11	0	0	0	11	127	22	97	8	0
	Des Moines[8]	195,194	1,306	6	62	374	864	13,505	2,189	10,331	985	62
	De Witt	5,232	3	0	0	0	3	174	104	68	2	0
	Dubuque	58,105	354	0	21	16	317	1,694	436	1,179	79	43
	Dyersville	4,064	1	0	0	0	1	32	1	30	1	0
	Eagle Grove	3,534	4	0	0	0	4	31	9	19	3	0
	Eldridge	4,508	5	0	1	0	4	213	26	170	17	0

[1] The FBI does not publish arson data unless it receives data from either the agency or the state for all 12 months of the calendar year.

[8] Because of changes in the state/local agency's reporting practices, figures are not comparable to previous years' data.

[9] Due to an annexation, population and figures may not be comparable to previous years' data.

Table 8. Offenses Known to Law Enforcement, by State and City, 2006 (Contd.)

(Number.)

State	City	Popula-tion	Violent crime	Murder and non-negligent man-slaughter	Forcible rape	Robbery	Aggra-vated assault	Property crime	Burglary	Larceny-theft	Motor vehicle theft	Arson[1]
	Emmetsburg	3,726	3	0	1	0	2	35	8	26	1	1
	Estherville	6,381	18	0	3	0	15	128	49	72	7	0
	Evansdale	4,609	3	0	0	1	2	112	33	74	5	2
	Fort Dodge	25,628	138	0	11	28	99	1,913	469	1,333	111	14
	Fort Madison	11,107	15	0	0	4	11	374	88	270	16	6
	Glenwood	5,680	8	0	0	0	8	137	11	118	8	3
	Grinnell	9,382	17	0	6	1	10	286	59	214	13	8
	Hampton	4,246	10	0	0	0	10	26	10	12	4	0
	Hawarden	2,453	5	0	1	0	4	13	5	8	0	0
	Humboldt	4,389	1	0	0	0	1	36	8	23	5	0
	Independence	6,086	1	0	0	0	1	127	29	91	7	2
	Indianola	14,018	22	0	5	0	17	269	39	212	18	5
	Iowa City	63,221	211	0	30	39	142	1,374	294	999	81	7
	Iowa Falls	5,139	3	0	3	0	0	186	19	164	3	0
	Jefferson	4,430	0	0	0	0	0	42	0	39	3	0
	Le Mars	9,399	23	4	5	2	12	272	41	222	9	4
	Leon	1,934	4	0	1	0	3	27	2	21	4	0
	Manchester	5,101	13	0	0	0	13	72	16	54	2	1
	Maquoketa	6,086	17	0	2	0	15	203	76	113	14	2
	Marion	30,394	28	1	7	1	19	523	101	390	32	12
	Marshalltown	26,115	204	0	1	9	194	1,099	225	816	58	3
	Mason City	28,057	74	1	11	14	48	1,424	291	1,080	53	11
	Monticello	3,721	3	0	0	0	3	23	3	17	3	0
	Mount Pleasant	8,814	17	0	2	1	14	286	77	197	12	3
	Mount Vernon	4,073	5	0	2	0	3	72	9	61	2	0
	Muscatine	22,878	139	1	21	3	114	608	147	415	46	13
	Nevada	6,162	32	0	1	0	31	163	27	132	4	2
	New Hampton	3,547	4	0	1	0	3	41	14	24	3	0
	Newton	15,690	14	0	0	3	11	483	74	390	19	1
	North Liberty	8,855	28	0	6	1	21	57	23	23	11	1
	Norwalk	7,919	6	0	0	0	6	136	21	110	5	2
	Oelwein	6,405	20	0	7	1	12	182	102	74	6	0
	Ogden	2,030	5	0	1	0	4	16	5	9	2	1
	Orange City	5,806	1	0	0	0	1	54	11	39	4	0
	Osage	3,480	1	0	0	0	1	54	18	30	6	0
	Osceola	4,808	4	0	0	0	4	171	24	142	5	2
	Oskaloosa	11,085	34	0	6	4	24	322	56	250	16	3
	Ottumwa	24,930	180	0	18	4	158	1,386	320	1,007	59	7
	Perry	8,912	23	0	1	1	21	184	27	146	11	4
	Pleasant Hill	6,262	14	0	1	0	13	170	67	90	13	3
	Polk City	2,956	1	0	0	0	1	36	5	31	0	0
	Red Oak	5,950	7	1	2	0	4	230	65	158	7	3
	Sergeant Bluff	3,839	11	0	1	1	9	85	10	73	2	2
	Sheldon	4,833	3	0	0	0	3	68	19	43	6	0
	Shenandoah	5,267	1	0	0	0	1	111	11	95	5	0
	Sioux City	83,590	398	0	51	51	296	3,384	702	2,491	191	24
	Spencer	11,176	1	0	0	0	1	345	72	258	15	0
	Spirit Lake	4,614	2	0	1	0	1	105	15	88	2	1
	Story City	3,158	4	0	0	2	2	39	14	24	1	0
	Urbandale	34,880	65	0	14	15	36	825	145	659	21	13
	Vinton	5,247	6	0	0	1	5	96	30	61	5	3
	Waterloo	66,836	342	1	41	83	217	3,057	907	2,035	115	39
	Waukee	9,262	19	0	1	1	17	183	53	120	10	1
	Waverly	9,347	60	0	3	0	57	175	33	132	10	1
	Webster City	8,120	36	0	5	0	31	238	52	177	9	0
	West Burlington	3,248	11	0	1	0	10	257	30	222	5	0
	West Des Moines	53,048	98	0	20	9	69	1,847	241	1,538	68	13
	West Liberty	3,622	5	0	0	0	5	53	5	44	4	0
	West Union	2,498	3	0	0	0	3	7	2	4	1	0
	Williamsburg	2,766	4	0	0	0	4	17	6	10	1	0
	Wilton	2,881	8	0	0	0	8	45	17	26	2	0
	Winterset	4,903	7	0	0	1	6	94	15	75	4	0
KANSAS	Abilene	6,454	2	0	1	0	1	274	31	233	10	6
	Andover	9,178	8	0	2	0	6	289	48	224	17	0
	Anthony	2,318	10	0	3	0	7	25	3	21	1	0

[1] The FBI does not publish arson data unless it receives data from either the agency or the state for all 12 months of the calendar year.

Table 8. Offenses Known to Law Enforcement, by State and City, 2006 (*Contd.*)

(Number.)

State	City	Popula-tion	Violent crime	Murder and non-negligent man-slaughter	Forcible rape	Robbery	Aggra-vated assault	Property crime	Burglary	Larceny-theft	Motor vehicle theft	Arson[1]
	Arkansas City	11,663	75	0	9	1	65	480	60	395	25	5
	Atchison	10,241	41	1	4	5	31	333	60	260	13	2
	Atwood	1,147	1	0	1	0	0	24	1	22	1	0
	Auburn	1,139	0	0	0	0	0	0	0	0	0	0
	Augusta	8,669	21	0	3	2	16	466	49	402	15	1
	Baldwin City	3,772	4	1	2	0	1	122	16	104	2	0
	Basehor	3,310	3	0	0	0	3	78	9	63	6	1
	Baxter Springs	4,276	6	0	1	0	5	120	19	91	10	3
	Bel Aire	6,603	3	0	0	0	3	40	7	32	1	0
	Belle Plaine	1,629	1	0	0	0	1	41	9	26	6	0
	Beloit	3,729	5	0	0	0	5	69	16	48	5	2
	Bonner Springs	6,985	16	0	2	1	13	363	51	261	51	12
	Buhler	1,344	1	0	0	0	1	21	3	18	0	0
	Chanute	9,070	43	0	6	2	35	306	66	228	12	3
	Chapman	1,252	1	0	1	0	0	16	4	12	0	0
	Chetopa	1,240	5	0	0	0	5	32	7	21	4	0
	Claflin	693	1	0	0	0	1	5	2	3	0	0
	Clay Center	4,409	14	0	4	0	10	144	36	102	6	2
	Coffeyville	10,432	101	2	14	15	70	699	145	514	40	7
	Colby	5,066	20	0	6	0	14	192	41	139	12	1
	Colony	393	0	0	0	0	0	0	0	0	0	0
	Columbus	3,282	8	0	1	0	7	94	29	62	3	4
	Concordia	5,409	21	0	4	0	17	171	38	123	10	1
	Council Grove	2,291	11	0	0	0	11	55	11	42	2	0
	Derby	20,688	35	0	7	5	23	670	79	562	29	6
	Dodge City	26,288	136	1	23	23	89	1,356	254	1,056	46	2
	Edwardsville	4,535	14	0	1	4	9	146	30	92	24	0
	El Dorado	12,748	34	0	4	2	28	648	123	491	34	3
	Elkhart	2,050	6	0	0	0	6	56	16	38	2	2
	Ellinwood	2,134	1	0	0	0	1	45	8	35	2	0
	Ellis	1,825	4	0	1	0	3	23	0	21	2	0
	Ellsworth	2,907	3	0	2	0	1	49	8	40	1	0
	Elwood	1,161	12	0	0	0	12	89	40	44	5	1
	Emporia	26,643	117	3	29	14	71	1,683	254	1,389	40	8
	Eudora	5,321	13	0	2	0	11	133	23	99	11	1
	Fairway	3,867	4	0	1	0	3	56	17	36	3	1
	Florence	655	0	0	0	0	0	21	4	16	1	1
	Fort Scott	8,046	41	0	7	6	28	339	75	245	19	5
	Fredonia	2,472	5	0	0	1	4	106	28	73	5	0
	Frontenac	3,123	2	0	0	0	2	73	16	49	8	0
	Galena	3,185	10	0	0	1	9	93	15	74	4	0
	Garden City	27,289	132	1	18	8	105	1,327	232	1,025	70	6
	Gardner	14,418	70	0	12	1	57	453	66	366	21	6
	Garnett	3,362	10	0	1	1	8	136	27	99	10	1
	Girard	2,705	10	0	3	1	6	75	14	60	1	0
	Goddard	3,361	4	0	0	0	4	104	16	86	2	0
	Grandview Plaza	1,046	9	0	0	1	8	31	8	20	3	2
	Great Bend[5]	15,549		0	7	4		757	161	561	35	4
	Halstead	1,926	0	0	0	0	0	4	1	3	0	0
	Hays	19,771	72	0	12	6	54	624	87	508	29	2
	Haysville	9,886	42	1	9	0	32	406	54	334	18	4
	Herington	2,485	2	0	0	0	2	48	13	29	6	1
	Hesston	3,657	6	0	0	1	5	60	10	47	3	1
	Hiawatha	3,259	10	0	0	0	10	77	19	50	8	1
	Hill City	1,461	2	0	1	0	1	23	5	16	2	0
	Hillsboro	2,750	5	0	1	0	4	57	29	24	4	0
	Holcomb	1,901	1	0	0	0	1	27	5	22	0	0
	Holton	3,424	9	0	2	0	7	144	14	125	5	0
	Horton	1,856	12	0	1	0	11	31	9	20	2	1
	Hugoton	3,670	4	0	0	0	4	33	0	32	1	0
	Hutchinson	41,250	217	1	19	19	178	2,438	565	1,789	84	25
	Independence	9,350	51	1	2	5	43	453	100	331	22	5
	Inman	1,202	0	0	0	0	0	8	1	6	1	0
	Iola	6,050	38	0	3	3	31	264	41	217	6	7

[1] The FBI does not publish arson data unless it receives data from either the agency or the state for all 12 months of the calendar year.
[5] It was determined that the agency did not follow national Uniform Crime Reporting (UCR) Program guidelines for reporting an offense. Consequently, this figure is not included in this table.

Table 8. Offenses Known to Law Enforcement, by State and City, 2006 *(Contd.)*

(Number.)

State	City	Popula-tion	Violent crime	Murder and non-negligent man-slaughter	Forcible rape	Robbery	Aggra-vated assault	Property crime	Burglary	Larceny-theft	Motor vehicle theft	Arson[1]
	Junction City	16,518	167	1	11	13	142	893	172	685	36	8
	Kansas City	145,229	1,245	45	91	439	670	10,281	2,265	5,691	2,325	
	Kechi	1,251	4	0	0	0	4	16	3	12	1	0
	Kiowa	972	0	0	0	0	0	4	1	1	2	0
	La Cygne	1,154	2	0	0	1	1	36	8	24	4	0
	Lansing	10,286	29	1	1	2	25	197	21	151	25	2
	Larned	3,901	15	0	0	2	13	156	30	123	3	1
	Lawrence	82,394	500	3	48	79	370	4,914	603	4,106	205	13
	Leavenworth	35,462	317	2	12	74	229	1,639	310	1,218	111	18
	Leawood	30,358	47	0	4	4	39	404	70	326	8	1
	Lebo	957	0	0	0	0	0	20	7	13	0	0
	Lenexa	43,741	61	0	10	9	42	1,046	150	820	76	9
	Liberal	20,400	124	0	18	18	88	1,473	266	1,136	71	1
	Lindsborg	3,328	1	0	1	0	0	86	12	72	2	2
	Louisburg	3,336	4	0	1	0	3	76	15	58	3	0
	Lyons	3,579	22	1	3	0	18	67	13	47	7	1
	Maize	2,132	1	0	0	1	0	74	14	59	1	0
	Maple Hill	495	0	0	0	0	0	0	0	0	0	0
	Marysville	3,173	12	0	1	0	11	45	7	32	6	3
	McPherson	13,792	21	0	4	1	16	472	151	290	31	5
	Meade	1,641	0	0	0	0	0	7	2	5	0	0
	Meriden	713	0	0	0	0	0	2	0	2	0	0
	Minneapolis	2,029	4	0	2	0	2	29	12	13	4	0
	Mission	9,820	31	0	1	13	17	465	43	352	70	2
	Mission Hills	3,548	1	0	0	0	1	31	10	19	2	0
	Moran	545	0	0	0	0	0	0	0	0	0	0
	Moundridge	1,655	1	0	0	0	1	7	2	5	0	2
	Mulvane	5,668	5	0	2	1	2	147	11	133	3	0
	Neodesha	2,671	8	0	1	0	7	78	16	61	1	2
	Newton	18,358	116	0	21	9	86	790	119	634	37	8
	Nickerson	1,172	0	0	0	0	0	53	36	17	0	1
	North Newton	1,585	0	0	0	0	0	22	3	18	1	0
	Norton	2,826	3	0	2	0	1	18	6	12	0	0
	Oakley	1,998	1	0	0	0	1	26	2	24	0	0
	Oberlin	1,824	2	0	1	0	1	28	9	16	3	0
	Olathe	112,120	288	3	64	33	188	2,277	353	1,689	235	
	Osage City	3,008	12	0	3	0	9	95	22	63	10	2
	Osawatomie	4,649	11	0	1	0	10	210	45	159	6	2
	Oswego	2,010	3	0	1	0	2	32	17	13	2	0
	Ottawa	12,686	54	0	11	1	42	485	86	377	22	3
	Overland Park	165,975	332	0	48	63	221	4,541	584	3,571	386	23
	Oxford	1,125	1	0	0	0	1	23	6	17	0	0
	Paola	5,329	5	0	1	0	4	135	17	110	8	0
	Park City	7,224	28	0	1	1	26	249	38	197	14	2
	Parsons	11,291	70	0	4	8	58	536	113	398	25	6
	Peabody	1,311	1	0	0	0	1	36	7	27	2	0
	Pittsburg	19,350	118	3	23	11	81	1,268	278	930	60	11
	Prairie Village	21,606	20	0	2	5	13	249	29	201	19	2
	Pratt	6,493	15	0	0	0	15	114	34	76	4	1
	Roeland Park	7,024	22	0	1	4	17	285	27	222	36	1
	Rose Hill	3,924	7	0	2	0	5	92	10	78	4	0
	Russell	4,373	23	0	0	0	23	93	23	65	5	1
	Sabetha	2,541	6	0	0	0	6	28	10	16	2	0
	Salina	46,281	115	1	32	14	68	3,150	422	2,626	102	21
	Scott City	3,499	16	0	2	0	14	92	16	73	3	0
	Seneca	2,083	4	0	1	1	2	39	12	27	0	0
	Shawnee	58,035	102	0	15	17	70	1,333	196	977	160	13
	South Hutchinson	2,499	6	1	1	0	4	86	7	79	0	0
	Spring Hill	4,526	11	0	0	0	11	107	15	86	6	0
	Stafford	1,075	5	0	0	0	5	7	3	3	1	0
	Sterling	2,594	2	0	0	0	2	38	9	26	3	2
	St. Marys	2,269	4	0	0	0	4	29	5	21	3	2
	Tonganoxie	3,801	16	0	1	2	13	181	35	138	8	3
	Topeka	122,807	669	9	57	310	293	8,748	1,478	6,645	625	11
	Ulysses	5,690	13	0	0	0	13	82	16	59	7	0

[1] The FBI does not publish arson data unless it receives data from either the agency or the state for all 12 months of the calendar year.

Table 8. Offenses Known to Law Enforcement, by State and City, 2006 (*Contd.*)

(Number.)

State	City	Population	Violent crime	Murder and non-negligent manslaughter	Forcible rape	Robbery	Aggravated assault	Property crime	Burglary	Larceny-theft	Motor vehicle theft	Arson[1]
	Valley Center	5,547	9	0	0	0	9	102	13	86	3	0
	Wamego	4,273	5	0	2	0	3	101	14	83	4	0
	Wathena	1,299	7	0	1	0	6	30	3	25	2	0
	Wellington	8,155	19	0	5	0	14	468	96	350	22	3
	Wellsville	1,643	10	0	0	0	10	47	15	31	1	1
	Westwood	1,493	3	0	1	0	2	80	22	50	8	2
	Wichita	357,372	3,319	26	240	520	2,533	19,562	3,800	13,786	1,976	156
	Winfield	11,945	42	0	11	0	31	513	91	397	25	0
	Yates Center	1,504	8	0	0	0	8	5	0	4	1	0
KENTUCKY	Adairville	937	0	0	0	0	0	6	1	5	0	0
	Albany	2,306	0	0	0	0	0	5	4	1	0	0
	Alexandria	8,059	12	0	0	3	9	181	28	144	9	0
	Anchorage	2,549	1	0	0	0	1	63	12	50	1	0
	Ashland	21,678	69	1	16	20	32	1,185	243	885	57	11
	Auburn	1,501	1	0	0	0	1	13	8	5	0	0
	Audubon Park	1,547	6	0	0	2	4	40	8	25	7	0
	Barbourville	3,548	2	0	0	0	2	28	8	14	6	0
	Bardstown	11,070	18	0	6	5	7	255	61	179	15	0
	Beattyville	1,162	1	0	0	0	1	18	4	11	3	0
	Bellefonte	853	0	0	0	0	0	7	2	3	2	0
	Berea	13,334	15	0	1	6	8	373	85	265	23	0
	Bowling Green	52,681	369	5	59	103	202	2,735	559	2,033	143	1
	Brandenburg	2,231	1	0	1	0	0	36	11	24	1	0
	Brodhead	1,203	0	0	0	0	0	10	5	4	1	0
	Burnside	678	2	0	0	0	2	20	6	14	0	0
	Butler	639	0	0	0	0	0	3	0	3	0	0
	Cadiz	2,570	14	0	0	5	9	127	29	93	5	0
	Calhoun	819	0	0	0	0	0	12	7	5	0	0
	Campbellsville	10,991	48	0	4	15	29	398	80	307	11	1
	Caneyville	658	0	0	0	0	0	6	2	4	0	0
	Carlisle	2,046	2	0	0	0	2	17	6	8	3	0
	Carrollton	3,891	6	0	1	1	4	93	21	68	4	0
	Catlettsburg	1,942	2	0	1	1	0	63	20	37	6	0
	Cave City	2,070	4	0	1	0	3	41	13	25	3	0
	Central City	5,830	3	0	0	1	2	49	8	35	6	0
	Clinton	1,375	0	0	0	0	0	4	2	1	1	0
	Cold Spring	5,296	6	0	0	3	3	174	13	158	3	0
	Columbia	4,207	4	0	1	0	3	51	9	38	4	0
	Corbin	8,294	17	0	6	5	6	281	57	217	7	0
	Crescent Springs	4,006	12	0	2	7	3	148	21	117	10	0
	Crofton	831	1	0	1	0	0	9	3	4	2	0
	Cumberland	2,348	8	0	0	0	8	24	8	16	0	0
	Cynthiana	6,360	18	0	4	2	12	269	57	202	10	0
	Danville	15,530	43	0	1	17	25	553	120	394	39	0
	Dawson Springs	2,976	5	0	4	0	1	32	19	12	1	0
	Earlington	1,614	0	0	0	0	0	28	13	13	2	0
	Edmonton	1,613	1	0	0	0	1	16	6	10	0	0
	Elizabethtown	23,634	85	0	12	36	37	1,088	218	821	49	0
	Elkton	1,956	3	0	0	2	1	20	6	12	2	0
	Elsmere	8,010	21	1	5	11	4	199	45	133	21	0
	Eminence	2,275	2	0	1	0	1	12	3	8	1	0
	Erlanger	16,984	28	1	2	11	14	473	70	364	39	0
	Falmouth	2,112	5	0	1	2	2	74	20	48	6	0
	Flatwoods	7,681	3	0	1	1	1	74	24	41	9	0
	Flemingsburg	3,128	3	0	0	0	3	47	17	29	1	1
	Florence	26,555	159	0	11	47	101	1,427	168	1,177	82	2
	Fort Mitchell	7,665	6	1	2	1	2	163	24	132	7	1
	Fort Thomas	15,714	13	0	6	0	7	157	33	109	15	0
	Fort Wright	5,481	22	0	2	17	3	299	23	258	18	0
	Frankfort	27,423	125	1	20	55	49	1,390	300	977	113	2
	Franklin	8,142	12	0	0	6	6	252	55	185	12	0
	Fulton	2,584	6	0	0	3	3	72	21	46	5	1
	Georgetown	20,144	39	0	5	11	23	1,059	193	819	47	0
	Glasgow	14,172	23	0	5	3	15	260	89	152	19	1
	Glencoe	252	0	0	0	0	0	5	2	3	0	0

[1] The FBI does not publish arson data unless it receives data from either the agency or the state for all 12 months of the calendar year.

Table 8. Offenses Known to Law Enforcement, by State and City, 2006 (Contd.)

(Number.)

State	City	Population	Violent crime	Murder and non-negligent man-slaughter	Forcible rape	Robbery	Aggravated assault	Property crime	Burglary	Larceny-theft	Motor vehicle theft	Arson[1]
	Graymoor-Devondale	2,960	2	0	0	2	0	72	13	56	3	0
	Grayson	4,017	2	0	0	1	1	139	50	79	10	0
	Greenville	4,306	1	0	0	0	1	8	3	5	0	0
	Guthrie	1,445	5	0	1	1	3	5	2	3	0	0
	Hardinsburg	2,471	0	0	0	0	0	6	3	3	0	0
	Harlan	1,927	6	0	1	1	4	134	26	103	5	0
	Harrodsburg	8,190	26	1	6	3	16	116	49	54	13	2
	Hartford	2,673	3	0	0	2	1	45	12	32	1	0
	Hawesville	989	0	0	0	0	0	4	0	4	0	0
	Hazard	4,857	15	0	5	2	8	213	37	152	24	1
	Heritage Creek	1,538	0	0	0	0	0	21	7	9	5	1
	Hickman	2,390	7	0	0	3	4	37	9	24	4	0
	Hillview	7,407	9	0	0	3	6	119	34	78	7	0
	Hodgenville	2,810	8	0	0	3	5	25	10	14	1	0
	Hopkinsville	29,047	141	3	17	52	69	1,706	388	1,227	91	9
	Horse Cave	2,332	8	0	1	0	7	20	4	13	3	0
	Indian Hills	3,000	1	0	0	1	0	45	12	32	1	0
	Irvine	2,735	7	0	0	0	7	73	21	48	4	0
	Irvington	1,370	2	0	0	0	2	3	1	1	1	1
	Jackson	2,432	3	0	0	2	1	61	14	40	7	1
	Jamestown	1,724	2	0	0	0	2	50	17	32	1	0
	Jeffersontown	26,304	66	0	9	42	15	593	96	423	74	0
	Jenkins	2,315	0	0	0	0	0	13	5	8	0	0
	La Grange	6,093	9	0	3	6	0	171	39	123	9	0
	Lakeside Park-Crestview Hills	6,096	2	0	0	0	2	147	15	128	4	0
	Lawrenceburg	9,477	11	0	2	1	8	159	30	118	11	0
	Lebanon Junction	1,949	0	0	0	0	0	31	5	21	5	0
	Leitchfield	6,513	7	0	2	0	5	132	53	72	7	0
	Lewisburg	925	0	0	0	0	0	9	4	5	0	0
	Lexington[8]	270,179	1,712	9	128	505	1,070	10,437	2,184	7,550	703	36
	Liberty	1,907	1	0	0	0	1	10	2	7	1	1
	London	7,848	30	0	6	8	16	415	51	327	37	0
	Lone Oak	442	0	0	0	0	0	11	6	5	0	0
	Louisa	2,067	1	0	0	0	1	21	4	14	3	1
	Louisville Metro	626,018	3,836	50	175	1,738	1,873	29,136	7,587	17,855	3,694	295
	Lynch	851	0	0	0	0	0	6	4	2	0	0
	Lynnview	968	0	0	0	0	0	10	3	6	1	0
	Manchester	1,983	0	0	0	0	0	44	13	27	4	0
	Marion	3,057	3	0	1	0	2	60	16	42	2	0
	Maysville	9,208	42	0	3	8	31	481	95	368	18	0
	Morganfield	3,457	12	0	1	3	8	139	34	97	8	0
	Mortons Gap	963	1	0	1	0	0	14	2	12	0	0
	Mount Sterling	6,366	24	0	3	12	9	291	50	220	21	0
	Mount Vernon	2,619	7	0	2	2	3	57	9	39	9	1
	Mount Washington	8,692	7	0	1	3	3	137	42	78	17	0
	Muldraugh	1,357	0	0	0	0	0	12	5	6	1	0
	Munfordville	1,616	5	0	5	0	0	17	6	9	2	0
	New Castle	936	0	0	0	0	0	5	1	4	0	0
	New Haven	871	0	0	0	0	0	2	1	0	1	0
	Newport	16,036	129	1	25	72	31	1,393	257	1,009	127	6
	Nortonville	1,262	1	0	1	0	0	4	1	3	0	0
	Oak Grove	7,629	23	1	4	6	12	263	120	129	14	2
	Olive Hill	1,837	3	0	0	1	2	19	4	13	2	0
	Owenton	1,482	1	0	0	0	1	6	3	3	0	0
	Paducah	25,775	176	3	19	37	117	1,583	219	1,241	123	12
	Paintsville	4,173	3	0	0	0	3	98	13	77	8	1
	Paris	9,407	25	0	1	4	20	204	60	131	13	0
	Park Hills	2,825	1	0	0	0	1	14	2	10	2	0
	Pewee Valley	1,558	0	0	0	0	0	10	6	4	0	0
	Pikeville	6,361	18	0	3	3	12	487	44	403	40	0
	Pineville	2,030	2	0	0	0	2	56	10	45	1	0
	Pioneer Village	2,652	0	0	0	0	0	23	10	10	3	0
	Powderly	850	2	0	0	1	1	46	10	36	0	0

[1] The FBI does not publish arson data unless it receives data from either the agency or the state for all 12 months of the calendar year.
[8] Because of changes in the state/local agency's reporting practices, figures are not comparable to previous years' data.

Table 8. Offenses Known to Law Enforcement, by State and City, 2006 *(Contd.)*

(Number.)

State	City	Population	Violent crime	Murder and non-negligent manslaughter	Forcible rape	Robbery	Aggravated assault	Property crime	Burglary	Larceny-theft	Motor vehicle theft	Arson[1]
	Prestonsburg	3,735	4	0	0	0	4	118	31	82	5	0
	Princeton	6,497	21	1	2	4	14	221	70	145	6	0
	Prospect	4,915	0	0	0	0	0	4	3	1	0	0
	Providence	3,577	9	0	2	3	4	44	21	21	2	0
	Raceland	2,496	2	0	0	2	0	32	8	20	4	0
	Radcliff[3]	21,639		0	15	16		608	149	430	29	4
	Richmond	31,135	95	2	10	16	67	1,268	291	897	80	6
	Russell	3,625	12	0	2	6	4	140	20	114	6	0
	Russell Springs	2,557	8	0	4	2	2	97	29	66	2	0
	Russellville	7,328	18	1	1	3	13	295	70	219	6	1
	Sadieville	296	0	0	0	0	0	1	1	0	0	0
	Science Hill	658	0	0	0	0	0	5	3	2	0	0
	Scottsville	4,560	1	0	0	0	1	12	1	10	1	0
	Shelbyville	10,814	51	0	3	24	24	335	92	216	27	1
	Shepherdsville	8,943	13	0	4	1	8	451	65	362	24	3
	Shively	15,331	87	2	10	50	25	723	249	367	107	3
	Silver Grove	1,183	0	0	0	0	0	9	4	5	0	0
	Somerset	12,231	41	1	5	15	20	451	85	358	8	0
	Southgate	3,382	2	0	0	0	2	45	6	32	7	0
	Springfield	2,828	4	0	0	2	2	46	21	22	3	0
	Stanford	3,479	5	0	0	0	5	26	3	18	5	0
	Stanton	3,133	3	0	0	2	1	70	17	50	3	1
	St. Matthews	17,444	33	0	1	20	12	820	112	664	44	0
	Sturgis	2,024	2	0	0	0	2	24	8	15	1	0
	Taylor Mill	6,786	0	0	0	0	0	26	6	14	6	0
	Taylorsville	1,182	3	0	0	1	2	23	6	16	1	0
	Tompkinsville	2,654	0	0	0	0	0	12	2	6	4	0
	Uniontown	1,071	0	0	0	0	0	1	0	1	0	0
	Vanceburg	1,711	5	0	0	1	4	21	4	15	2	0
	Villa Hills	7,810	0	0	0	0	0	44	12	28	4	0
	Vine Grove	4,014	4	0	0	0	4	65	13	49	3	0
	West Buechel	1,333	8	0	0	8	0	172	5	151	16	0
	West Liberty	3,375	3	0	0	0	3	43	7	36	0	0
	West Point	1,040	0	0	0	0	0	16	5	7	4	0
	Wilder	3,004	1	0	0	0	1	42	4	36	2	0
	Williamsburg	5,202	5	0	3	0	2	65	21	39	5	1
	Williamstown	3,450	3	0	0	1	2	62	21	36	5	0
	Wilmore	5,872	1	0	1	0	0	47	14	30	3	0
	Winchester	16,623	61	0	7	13	41	901	221	633	47	1
	Worthington	1,692	0	0	0	0	0	2	0	2	0	0
LOUISIANA	Addis	2,303	11	0	0	0	11	2	0	2	0	0
	Alexandria	43,311	1,054	4	29	185	836	4,494	1,299	2,937	258	11
	Baker	12,559	57	1	6	10	40	750	146	545	59	5
	Basile	2,258	4	0	0	0	4	14	3	11	0	0
	Baton Rouge	210,486	2,954	57	93	1,049	1,755	14,684	4,021	9,209	1,454	223
	Blanchard	2,208	1	0	0	0	1	36	13	23	0	
	Bogalusa	12,288	168	4	19	37	108	896	271	548	77	5
	Bossier City	57,350	1,201	1	40	91	1,069	2,866	582	2,010	274	25
	Broussard	6,402	42	0	2	9	31	504	72	412	20	0
	Clinton	1,822	42	0	2	2	38	94	21	71	2	0
	Coushatta	2,090	29	0	2	2	25	76	22	50	4	0
	Covington	8,860	67	1	4	8	54	276	62	193	21	2
	Crowley	13,138	110	3	8	14	85	703	226	453	24	0
	Denham Springs	9,674	159	1	6	53	99	1,149	212	853	84	0
	De Ridder	9,456	28	0	5	6	17	158	43	115	0	0
	Eunice	10,926	26	3	0	9	14	716	177	500	39	1
	Farmerville	3,471	51	0	2	11	38	178	48	129	1	0
	Folsom	617	2	0	0	0	2	11	6	5	0	0
	Franklin	7,414	67	1	1	5	60	545	73	442	30	
	French Settlement	998	2	0	0	0	2	14	1	12	1	0
	Golden Meadow	2,033	4	0	0	0	4	14	1	11	2	0
	Gonzales	8,056	32	0	1	5	26	218	18	178	22	0
	Gramercy	6,422	27	0	0	2	25	109	8	96	5	0
	Gretna	16,266	169	1	7	49	112	811	182	517	112	

[1] The FBI does not publish arson data unless it receives data from either the agency or the state for all 12 months of the calendar year.
[3] The FBI determined that the agency's data were inflated. Consequently, affected data are not included in this table.

Table 8. Offenses Known to Law Enforcement, by State and City, 2006 *(Contd.)*

(Number.)

State	City	Population	Violent crime	Murder and non-negligent man-slaughter	Forcible rape	Robbery	Aggravated assault	Property crime	Burglary	Larceny-theft	Motor vehicle theft	Arson[1]
	Hammond......................	17,152	453	2	19	113	319	2,619	1,024	1,461	134	
	Harahan......................	9,209	24	0	0	3	21	131	28	95	8	3
	Haughton......................	2,645	30	0	0	2	28	16	1	15	0	
	Homer......................	3,367	35	0	0	5	30	170	68	101	1	0
	Houma	30,431	337	4	21	69	243	1,676	283	1,311	82	13
	Iowa......................	2,456	18	0	1	2	15	123	19	97	7	0
	Jackson......................	3,577	24	0	1	1	22	65	8	57	0	0
	Jeanerette	5,635	15	0	1	0	14	118	22	86	10	0
	Jennings	10,097	79	0	7	7	65	464	97	323	44	
	Kenner......................	66,266	370	9	17	114	230	2,698	555	1,701	442	17
	Kentwood	2,058	16	0	0	1	15	170	25	140	5	1
	Lafayette......................	106,189	1,142	10	73	231	828	6,393	1,296	4,566	531	17
	Lake Arthur	2,760	11	1	2	0	8	117	21	87	9	0
	Lake Charles	66,876	708	4	51	158	495	3,557	1,843	1,351	363	2
	Lake Providence	4,345	48	0	2	3	43	32	19	12	1	0
	Leesville	5,839	54	0	2	3	49	350	46	294	10	0
	Mamou	3,254	49	1	4	0	44	144	29	110	5	0
	Mandeville	11,026	43	1	2	5	35	481	57	407	17	1
	Minden	12,589	35	1	0	7	27	223	72	139	12	0
	Monroe......................	49,207	425	12	27	71	315	4,592	1,170	3,270	152	
	Morgan City	11,308	63	1	4	9	49	490	145	326	19	0
	New Orleans......................	431,153	2,255	162	87	761	1,245	12,178	4,087	5,228	2,863	
	Olla......................	1,288	3	0	0	0	3	58	11	45	2	0
	Pearl River......................	1,937	20	0	0	2	18	137	13	116	8	0
	Pineville	13,349	52	0	10	5	37	680	128	513	39	0
	Plaquemine......................	6,367	80	2	1	8	69	346	44	298	4	2
	Pollock	359	0	0	0	0	0	7	3	4	0	0
	Ponchatoula......................	5,482	74	1	5	6	62	581	188	363	30	0
	Ruston......................	19,589	125	0	2	29	94	723	159	544	20	0
	Shreveport	188,505	2,249	28	140	586	1,495	12,693	2,922	8,508	1,263	166
	Slidell......................	25,441	192	2	8	39	143	2,019	338	1,506	175	0
	Sterlington	1,181	3	0	0	1	2	7	2	5	0	0
	St. Gabriel......................	5,186	39	1	2	0	36	131	64	63	4	13
	Thibodaux......................	13,657	131	1	11	26	93	616	107	502	7	2
	Tickfaw......................	609	5	0	1	1	3	41	6	34	1	0
	Vidalia......................	3,990	25	0	0	1	24	172	47	125	0	0
	Westlake......................	4,327	22	0	0	0	22	183	25	141	17	3
	West Monroe......................	12,358	87	1	11	16	59	883	176	673	34	2
	Westwego......................	9,942	41	1	1	12	27	263	54	176	33	2
	Zachary......................	11,619	31	0	2	2	27	257	45	181	31	0
MAINE	Ashland......................	1,467	1	0	0	0	1	8	4	2	2	0
	Auburn......................	23,603	23	0	6	7	10	803	142	632	29	0
	Augusta......................	18,627	66	0	22	13	31	1,165	198	926	41	18
	Baileyville......................	1,618	6	0	0	0	6	67	18	48	1	0
	Bangor......................	31,076	52	2	1	24	25	1,897	216	1,633	48	9
	Bar Harbor	5,118	3	0	0	0	3	38	15	21	2	1
	Bath......................	9,257	8	0	1	3	4	309	36	265	8	4
	Belfast	6,872	12	0	2	1	9	232	38	185	9	0
	Berwick	7,348	6	0	1	1	4	103	17	79	7	4
	Bethel......................	2,583	1	0	0	0	1	14	5	5	4	0
	Biddeford......................	22,073	53	0	19	14	20	877	152	696	29	7
	Boothbay Harbor..............	2,345	2	0	1	0	1	68	13	54	1	0
	Brewer......................	9,138	4	0	2	1	1	340	26	307	7	0
	Bridgton......................	5,216	2	0	1	0	1	161	35	123	3	0
	Brownville	1,286	1	0	1	0	0	44	14	30	0	0
	Brunswick	21,821	13	0	10	1	2	535	88	426	21	9
	Bucksport......................	4,961	16	0	1	0	15	81	16	61	4	1
	Buxton......................	8,163	9	0	0	2	7	115	29	74	12	0
	Calais......................	3,308	35	0	4	0	31	175	15	159	1	0
	Camden......................	5,341	1	0	0	0	1	99	20	76	3	0
	Cape Elizabeth..................	8,922	3	0	0	0	3	139	17	117	5	2
	Caribou	8,308	8	0	0	4	4	281	54	218	9	0
	Carrabassett Valley...........	441	0	0	0	0	0	151	5	143	3	0
	Clinton	3,422	1	0	0	1	0	80	16	60	4	0
	Cumberland......................	7,656	2	0	0	1	1	66	18	44	4	0

[1] The FBI does not publish arson data unless it receives data from either the agency or the state for all 12 months of the calendar year.

Table 8. Offenses Known to Law Enforcement, by State and City, 2006 (*Contd.*)

(Number.)

State	City	Popula-tion	Violent crime	Murder and non-negligent man-slaughter	Forcible rape	Robbery	Aggra-vated assault	Property crime	Burglary	Larceny-theft	Motor vehicle theft	Arson[1]
	Damariscotta	2,006	0	0	0	0	0	63	6	55	2	0
	Dexter	3,789	17	0	2	0	15	153	45	106	2	0
	Dixfield	2,525	5	0	2	0	3	46	15	29	2	0
	Dover-Foxcroft	4,374	18	0	2	0	16	141	28	110	3	0
	East Millinocket	3,228	0	0	0	0	0	31	5	26	0	0
	Eastport	1,594	0	0	0	0	0	20	9	10	1	0
	Eliot	6,413	9	0	2	0	7	43	10	32	1	0
	Ellsworth	7,021	3	0	0	0	3	305	21	274	10	2
	Fairfield	6,702	9	0	5	0	4	351	52	289	10	0
	Falmouth	10,602	2	0	0	1	1	171	30	136	5	2
	Farmington	7,504	7	0	2	3	2	294	29	259	6	0
	Fort Fairfield	3,521	8	0	0	0	8	25	7	18	0	1
	Fort Kent	4,202	1	0	0	0	1	27	0	25	2	0
	Freeport	8,066	4	0	1	0	3	202	25	173	4	4
	Fryeburg	3,284	3	0	0	0	3	35	11	22	2	0
	Gardiner	6,237	6	0	1	1	4	88	19	67	2	1
	Gorham	15,301	18	0	5	5	8	223	90	115	18	2
	Gouldsboro	2,017	0	0	0	0	0	8	8	0	0	0
	Greenville	1,727	8	0	0	0	8	57	10	46	1	0
	Hallowell	2,535	1	0	0	0	1	70	9	56	5	0
	Hampden	6,773	2	0	0	0	2	105	11	89	5	0
	Holden	2,940	3	0	0	1	2	43	5	37	1	0
	Houlton	6,317	6	0	5	0	1	218	46	166	6	2
	Jay	4,857	6	0	3	0	3	114	37	74	3	0
	Kennebunk	11,511	2	0	2	0	0	211	20	183	8	2
	Kennebunkport	4,033	0	0	0	0	0	44	9	34	1	1
	Kittery	10,454	6	0	4	0	2	137	17	111	9	0
	Lewiston	36,052	91	1	21	42	27	1,191	213	938	40	8
	Lincoln	5,258	3	0	0	0	3	15	4	10	1	0
	Lisbon	9,444	3	0	0	3	0	135	14	115	6	3
	Livermore Falls	3,235	3	0	1	0	2	58	8	49	1	0
	Machias	2,277	3	0	1	0	2	59	15	41	3	2
	Madawaska	4,466	0	0	0	0	0	34	9	22	3	0
	Madison	4,589	2	0	1	0	1	127	24	100	3	1
	Mechanic Falls	3,238	3	0	0	1	2	40	11	28	1	0
	Mexico	2,939	3	0	1	1	1	111	24	84	3	1
	Milbridge	1,311	0	0	0	0	0	40	5	35	0	0
	Millinocket	5,034	0	0	0	0	0	124	17	101	6	0
	Milo	2,431	10	1	1	0	8	47	11	34	2	0
	Monmouth	3,788	0	0	0	0	0	44	8	34	2	0
	Mount Desert	2,197	0	0	0	0	0	32	4	27	1	0
	Newport	3,104	3	0	0	1	2	125	19	101	5	0
	North Berwick	4,802	0	0	0	0	0	3	3	0	0	0
	Norway	4,778	8	0	2	0	6	115	22	91	2	0
	Oakland	6,190	6	0	4	0	2	110	14	92	4	0
	Ogunquit	1,295	0	0	0	0	0	47	6	41	0	0
	Old Orchard Beach	9,350	21	0	9	3	9	404	119	271	14	2
	Old Town	7,792	2	0	0	1	1	164	31	130	3	0
	Orono	9,463	3	0	2	0	1	178	20	156	2	3
	Oxford	3,934	5	0	3	0	2	192	30	152	10	0
	Paris	4,998	3	0	2	0	1	107	19	86	2	0
	Phippsburg	2,212	0	0	0	0	0	14	1	13	0	0
	Pittsfield	4,249	8	0	0	0	8	167	21	141	5	0
	Portland	63,892	276	3	36	149	88	3,441	539	2,709	193	15
	Presque Isle	9,377	9	0	3	1	5	306	36	265	5	2
	Rangeley	1,122	3	0	0	0	3	35	9	26	0	0
	Richmond	3,425	1	0	0	0	1	36	4	29	3	1
	Rockland	7,658	20	0	10	2	8	463	44	408	11	0
	Rockport	3,504	1	0	0	0	1	42	3	38	1	0
	Rumford	6,429	8	0	6	0	2	266	53	210	3	3
	Sabattus	4,670	5	0	1	0	4	77	21	54	2	0
	Saco	18,231	13	0	4	2	7	662	170	461	31	2
	Sanford	21,735	38	0	16	6	16	807	134	648	25	7
	Scarborough	18,898	9	0	1	4	4	401	78	305	18	1
	Searsport	2,679	2	1	0	0	1	56	21	33	2	0

[1] The FBI does not publish arson data unless it receives data from either the agency or the state for all 12 months of the calendar year.

Table 8. Offenses Known to Law Enforcement, by State and City, 2006 (*Contd.*)

(Number.)

State	City	Popula-tion	Violent crime	Murder and non-negligent man-slaughter	Forcible rape	Robbery	Aggra-vated assault	Property crime	Burglary	Larceny-theft	Motor vehicle theft	Arson[1]
	Skowhegan	8,833	12	0	3	3	6	382	58	320	4	2
	South Berwick	7,304	5	0	3	0	2	74	19	54	1	0
	South Portland	23,743	51	1	8	13	29	930	92	809	29	2
	Southwest Harbor	1,983	4	1	0	0	3	68	7	61	0	0
	Swan's Island	316	0	0	0	0	0	0	0	0	0	0
	Thomaston	4,169	0	0	0	0	0	64	7	54	3	1
	Topsham	9,940	4	0	0	1	3	175	24	144	7	1
	Van Buren	2,502	1	0	0	0	1	24	13	8	3	0
	Veazie	1,865	1	0	0	0	1	33	5	25	3	0
	Waldoboro	5,114	3	0	0	0	3	109	32	77	0	0
	Washburn	1,617	0	0	0	0	0	34	17	17	0	0
	Waterville	15,622	34	0	10	5	19	557	84	455	18	0
	Wells	10,089	9	0	0	1	8	228	37	182	9	0
	Westbrook	16,109	38	1	5	22	10	552	137	380	35	6
	Wilton	4,166	9	0	1	2	6	105	22	80	3	1
	Windham	16,372	12	0	0	2	10	395	72	296	27	4
	Winslow	7,968	5	0	3	0	2	139	32	101	6	0
	Winter Harbor	976	0	0	0	0	0	11	0	11	0	0
	Winthrop	6,480	5	0	3	1	1	65	13	48	4	1
	Wiscasset	3,807	0	0	0	0	0	86	11	69	6	0
	Yarmouth	8,257	5	0	3	2	0	87	16	70	1	1
	York	13,491	4	0	1	0	3	260	53	203	4	0
MARYLAND	Aberdeen	14,344	102	1	2	41	58	792	95	635	62	7
	Annapolis	36,399	515	7	13	231	264	1,958	508	1,267	183	17
	Baltimore	637,556	10,816	276	138	4,229	6,173	32,321	7,608	18,451	6,262	428
	Baltimore City Sheriff		0	0	0	0	0	0	0	0	0	0
	Bel Air	10,041	74	1	0	19	54	474	60	384	30	4
	Berlin	3,721	5	0	0	1	4	160	22	135	3	0
	Berwyn Heights	3,076	11	0	0	6	5	103	19	60	24	1
	Bladensburg	7,940	110	3	2	60	45	606	96	312	198	0
	Boonsboro	2,990	1	0	0	0	1	24	7	13	4	0
	Brunswick	5,256	5	0	0	0	5	73	19	53	1	3
	Cambridge	11,119	123	0	3	24	96	759	157	571	31	6
	Capitol Heights	4,325	19	0	0	17	2	47	4	25	18	0
	Centreville	2,667	8	0	0	0	8	85	21	63	1	0
	Chestertown	4,686	45	0	2	15	28	198	41	148	9	0
	Cheverly	6,686	55	0	0	47	8	206	61	106	39	2
	Cottage City	1,179	15	0	0	9	6	48	9	24	15	0
	Crisfield	2,816	22	0	0	6	16	180	26	150	4	1
	Cumberland	20,972	188	1	20	25	142	1,284	311	936	37	21
	Delmar	2,296	13	0	1	6	6	111	25	81	5	1
	Denton	3,261	9	0	0	1	8	178	38	129	11	1
	District Heights	6,313	44	0	2	16	26	186	31	101	54	0
	Easton	13,484	81	0	4	24	53	577	91	476	10	0
	Edmonston	1,394	6	0	0	3	3	112	9	75	28	0
	Elkton	14,506	162	2	2	50	108	912	181	656	75	7
	Fairmount Heights	1,570	5	0	0	1	4	39	13	15	11	0
	Federalsburg	2,644	26	0	1	9	16	181	47	132	2	0
	Forest Heights	2,686	2	0	0	0	2	76	37	32	7	0
	Frederick	58,066	530	4	17	152	357	1,744	354	1,287	103	27
	Frostburg	7,980	26	0	2	4	20	211	61	140	10	0
	Fruitland	3,964	77	0	0	7	70	278	46	227	5	2
	Glenarden	6,397	7	0	1	3	3	41	7	26	8	0
	Greenbelt	22,303	219	2	6	158	53	1,074	102	715	257	1
	Greensboro	1,949	11	0	1	0	10	55	19	34	2	0
	Hagerstown	38,431	295	4	8	117	166	1,610	303	1,159	148	36
	Hampstead	5,466	6	0	0	1	5	85	10	67	8	1
	Hancock	1,741	9	0	0	5	4	41	13	27	1	0
	Havre de Grace	11,917	74	0	0	17	57	462	64	376	22	1
	Hurlock	2,008	8	0	0	3	5	150	49	89	12	1
	Hyattsville	16,723	145	0	6	111	28	1,061	119	766	176	0
	Landover Hills	1,593	4	0	0	0	4	23	5	13	5	0
	La Plata	8,465	31	0	0	10	21	211	32	163	16	3
	Laurel	22,186	141	0	1	75	65	1,226	191	821	214	3
	Lonaconing	1,167	1	0	0	1	0	3	0	3	0	0

[1] The FBI does not publish arson data unless it receives data from either the agency or the state for all 12 months of the calendar year.

Table 8. Offenses Known to Law Enforcement, by State and City, 2006 (*Contd.*)

(Number.)

State	City	Popula-tion	Violent crime	Murder and non-negligent man-slaughter	Forcible rape	Robbery	Aggra-vated assault	Property crime	Burglary	Larceny-theft	Motor vehicle theft	Arson[1]
	Luke	76	0	0	0	0	0	0	0	0	0	0
	Manchester	3,567	9	0	1	0	8	52	13	31	8	2
	Morningside	1,463	3	0	0	2	1	54	10	31	13	0
	Mount Rainier	8,775	139	2	3	109	25	435	67	204	164	2
	New Carrollton	12,853	41	0	2	9	30	227	45	130	52	0
	North East	2,825	9	0	1	3	5	138	18	104	16	0
	Oakland	1,901	1	0	0	0	1	58	9	48	1	0
	Ocean City	7,068	176	0	9	33	134	1,380	229	1,102	49	5
	Ocean Pines	11,129	9	0	2	0	7	126	26	91	9	0
	Oxford	748	0	0	0	0	0	3	2	1	0	0
	Perryville	3,780	6	0	0	0	6	89	25	62	2	3
	Pocomoke City	3,920	15	2	2	3	8	281	31	238	12	4
	Port Deposit	695	2	0	0	0	2	14	9	5	0	0
	Preston	584	1	0	0	0	1	11	4	5	2	0
	Princess Anne	2,808	26	0	0	7	19	184	67	108	9	0
	Ridgely	1,358	14	0	1	1	12	46	8	38	0	0
	Rising Sun	1,790	3	0	0	0	3	72	13	57	2	0
	Riverdale Park	6,648	86	0	0	49	37	385	37	260	88	0
	Rock Hall	2,573	2	0	0	0	2	44	16	27	1	0
	Salisbury	26,367	569	5	26	213	325	2,582	638	1,813	131	24
	Seat Pleasant	5,077	47	2	1	18	26	194	34	116	44	1
	Smithsburg	2,867	6	0	0	2	4	48	9	37	2	0
	Snow Hill	2,329	10	0	1	1	8	31	12	19	0	0
	St. Michaels	1,124	7	0	1	2	4	78	17	58	3	1
	Sykesville	4,452	3	0	0	1	2	30	9	21	0	2
	Takoma Park	18,591	124	4	2	89	29	670	115	424	131	15
	Taneytown	5,468	4	0	0	1	3	138	11	123	4	2
	Thurmont	6,053	10	0	0	2	8	71	19	47	5	2
	University Park	2,408	3	0	0	2	1	58	15	38	5	0
	Upper Marlboro	685	1	0	0	0	1	18	1	14	3	0
	Westernport	2,026	1	0	0	0	1	25	6	19	0	1
	Westminster	17,810	133	1	0	25	107	734	102	604	28	16
MASSACHU-SETTS	Abington	16,449	51	0	4	7	40	291	104	145	42	0
	Acton	20,686	11	0	6	3	2	372	58	300	14	5
	Acushnet	10,607	25	0	1	2	22	138	65	62	11	3
	Adams	8,506	25	0	5	0	20	180	53	119	8	0
	Agawam	28,771	43	0	4	4	35	441	172	225	44	6
	Amesbury	16,743	48	0	3	3	42	255	46	195	14	1
	Amherst	34,252	70	0	15	14	41	363	171	158	34	1
	Arlington	41,472	51	1	8	8	34	612	216	360	36	12
	Ashburnham	6,017	6	1	0	0	5	63	34	26	3	0
	Ashfield	1,836	0	0	0	0	0	9	6	2	1	0
	Ashland	15,644	26	0	7	0	19	76	26	43	7	1
	Attleboro	43,643	134	0	10	31	93	931	212	612	107	10
	Auburn[10]	16,499		0	7	4		463	89	349	25	5
	Avon	4,366	28	0	0	13	15	155	13	133	9	0
	Ayer	7,271	26	0	6	0	20	97	31	60	6	3
	Barnstable	48,113	330	1	33	32	264	1,320	508	725	87	7
	Barre	5,412	33	0	5	0	28	90	30	49	11	0
	Becket	1,797	2	0	0	0	2	33	16	16	1	
	Bedford	12,537	2	0	0	0	2	104	22	80	2	0
	Belchertown	14,042	23	0	3	1	19	201	72	113	16	3
	Bellingham	15,879	18	0	1	3	14	268	69	186	13	1
	Belmont	23,511	14	0	2	2	10	196	62	118	16	2
	Berkley	6,413	9	0	0	0	9	45	15	23	7	0
	Berlin	2,705	3	0	0	3	0	26	0	24	2	0
	Beverly	40,116	112	0	13	19	80	664	99	533	32	0
	Billerica	40,203	32	0	2	4	26	634	87	500	47	0
	Blackstone	9,111	26	0	3	2	21	134	31	96	7	0
	Bolton	4,462	5	0	1	0	4	40	12	27	1	1
	Boston	562,393	7,533	75	275	2,698	4,485	25,094	4,121	16,897	4,076	
	Bourne[10]	19,472		1	0	5		647	257	348	42	10

[1] The FBI does not publish arson data unless it receives data from either the agency or the state for all 12 months of the calendar year.
[10] The data collection methodology for the offense of aggravated assault used by this agency does not comply with national UCR Program guidelines. Consequently, the figures for aggravated assault and violent crime (of which aggravated assault is a part) are not included in this table.

Table 8. Offenses Known to Law Enforcement, by State and City, 2006 (*Contd.*)

(Number.)

State	City	Population	Violent crime	Murder and non-negligent man-slaughter	Forcible rape	Robbery	Aggra-vated assault	Property crime	Burglary	Larceny-theft	Motor vehicle theft	Arson[1]
	Boxborough	5,092	6	0	1	0	5	29	2	26	1	0
	Boylston	4,285	1	0	0	0	1	38	9	29	0	0
	Brewster	10,304	6	0	2	1	3	183	53	129	1	0
	Bridgewater	25,875	15	0	0	3	12	248	98	137	13	0
	Brimfield	3,661	4	0	0	0	4	11	4	6	1	0
	Brockton[10]	95,200		8	42	266		3,498	673	2,163	662	22
	Brookline[10]	55,924		1	7	47		1,050	218	778	54	
	Buckland	2,007	3	0	0	0	3	12	3	8	1	0
	Burlington	23,439	30	0	0	12	18	697	163	506	28	0
	Cambridge	100,737	458	2	11	208	237	3,283	684	2,376	223	
	Canton	21,701	37	0	2	5	30	218	45	164	9	0
	Carlisle	4,858	1	0	0	0	1	11	3	8	0	0
	Carver	11,631	28	1	3	2	22	103	42	53	8	4
	Charlton	12,550	27	0	1	1	25	144	34	90	20	1
	Chelmsford	33,962	40	0	2	5	33	615	81	497	37	0
	Chelsea[10]	32,713		0	27	179		1,318	345	665	308	8
	Cheshire	3,377	0	0	0	0	0	3	2	1	0	0
	Chicopee	55,009	368	1	22	58	287	1,723	425	1,072	226	11
	Clinton	14,079	15	0	0	1	14	60	15	45	0	1
	Cohasset	7,265	8	0	0	0	8	116	25	89	2	3
	Concord	16,934	16	0	1	0	15	187	35	150	2	4
	Cummington	994	0	0	0	0	0	12	8	3	1	0
	Dalton	6,740	18	0	2	1	15	100	27	70	3	2
	Danvers	26,202	57	1	3	8	45	929	74	799	56	3
	Dartmouth	31,578	111	1	4	16	90	1,004	213	727	64	7
	Dedham	23,879	16	0	0	9	7	435	48	354	33	0
	Deerfield	4,815	7	0	0	0	7	110	32	70	8	2
	Dennis	15,986	63	1	2	7	53	552	175	351	26	0
	Douglas	7,932	9	0	1	1	7	33	15	15	3	1
	Dracut	29,066	33	0	3	9	21	362	73	253	36	0
	Dudley	10,877	29	0	0	0	29	60	39	21	0	0
	East Bridgewater	13,942	22	0	0	1	21	150	39	98	13	0
	East Brookfield	2,124	5	0	0	0	5	16	5	9	2	0
	Easthampton[10]	16,100		0	0	1		181	53	112	16	6
	Easton	23,166	19	0	0	10	9	193	36	146	11	1
	Edgartown	3,959	7	0	0	0	7	129	14	115	0	0
	Egremont	1,364	1	0	0	0	1	45	11	32	2	0
	Erving	1,553	1	0	0	0	1	20	8	10	2	0
	Everett	37,058	128	0	6	55	67	1,110	262	664	184	2
	Fairhaven	16,319	75	2	3	11	59	531	208	298	25	0
	Falmouth	33,846	157	1	11	22	123	1,084	489	523	72	10
	Fitchburg[10]	40,286		1	26	47		1,089	306	693	90	4
	Foxborough	16,411	51	0	8	4	39	160	69	83	8	
	Framingham	65,451	163	2	8	33	120	1,571	223	1,160	188	
	Franklin	31,079	8	0	3	1	4	110	17	80	13	0
	Freetown	9,033	35	0	2	3	30	138	34	92	12	1
	Gardner	21,034	109	0	8	19	82	544	147	354	43	9
	Georgetown	8,089	2	0	0	0	2	56	10	46	0	
	Gill	1,401	2	0	0	0	2	33	7	24	2	0
	Gloucester	30,898	43	0	7	12	24	565	80	460	25	0
	Goshen	963	2	0	0	0	2	4	1	1	2	0
	Grafton	16,991	25	0	2	3	20	83	29	43	11	2
	Granby	6,382	7	0	1	0	6	78	22	46	10	0
	Great Barrington	7,486	27	0	2	2	23	124	23	94	7	0
	Greenfield[10]	17,941		0	15	12		511	227	244	40	5
	Groton	10,500	2	0	1	1	0	28	10	17	1	0
	Hadley	4,851	9	0	1	3	5	151	36	104	11	0
	Halifax	7,856	9	0	0	1	8	48	14	30	4	0
	Hamilton	8,399	5	0	1	0	4	64	30	30	4	0
	Hanover	14,186	1	0	0	1	0	266	41	220	5	0
	Hanson[10]	9,986		0	2	1		114	30	78	6	4
	Hardwick	2,671	16	0	2	0	14	27	10	15	2	0
	Harvard	6,110	7	0	1	0	6	28	8	18	2	3

[1] The FBI does not publish arson data unless it receives data from either the agency or the state for all 12 months of the calendar year.

[10] The data collection methodology for the offense of aggravated assault used by this agency does not comply with national UCR Program guidelines. Consequently, the figures for aggravated assault and violent crime (of which aggravated assault is a part) are not included in this table.

Table 8. Offenses Known to Law Enforcement, by State and City, 2006 (*Contd.*)

(Number.)

State	City	Population	Violent crime	Murder and non-negligent man-slaughter	Forcible rape	Robbery	Aggravated assault	Property crime	Burglary	Larceny-theft	Motor vehicle theft	Arson[1]
	Harwich	12,751	32	0	1	1	30	217	95	110	12	2
	Hatfield	3,302	1	0	0	1	0	18	14	4	0	0
	Haverhill	60,604	285	0	15	56	214	1,698	769	721	208	15
	Hingham	21,636	23	0	1	3	19	344	46	283	15	1
	Hinsdale	1,822	9	0	0	0	9	14	10	1	3	0
	Holbrook	10,840	12	0	3	2	7	216	76	131	9	
	Holden	16,692	21	0	2	0	19	87	6	76	5	2
	Holliston	13,930	7	0	1	0	6	72	18	48	6	2
	Holyoke[10]	40,198		2	38	81		2,154	374	1,472	308	12
	Hopedale	6,281	7	0	1	0	6	54	16	30	8	1
	Hopkinton	14,197	6	2	1	0	3	99	9	85	5	0
	Hubbardston	4,378	15	0	2	0	13	36	10	23	3	2
	Hudson	19,057	3	0	1	1	1	182	19	135	28	0
	Hull[10]	11,348		1	4	1		122	48	63	11	2
	Ipswich	13,382	5	0	1	0	4	199	97	96	6	0
	Kingston	12,532	22	0	0	3	19	274	25	228	21	3
	Lakeville	10,703	5	0	0	0	5	116	28	76	12	1
	Lancaster	6,886	17	0	5	3	9	51	14	32	5	1
	Lawrence	71,743	658	5	12	195	446	1,652	528	597	527	
	Lee	5,920	21	0	0	0	21	41	7	33	1	0
	Leicester	11,033	21	0	2	2	17	147	28	105	14	1
	Lenox	5,187	1	0	0	0	1	57	15	41	1	0
	Leominster[10]	42,055		0	15	46		1,144	217	833	94	6
	Lexington	30,448	16	0	1	0	15	245	52	186	7	1
	Lincoln	7,979	4	0	0	0	4	36	8	28	0	0
	Littleton	8,641	9	0	1	1	7	52	9	40	3	0
	Longmeadow	15,663	8	0	1	3	4	191	54	133	4	1
	Lowell	103,729	920	13	40	213	654	3,352	753	2,073	526	
	Ludlow	22,078	15	0	0	7	8	274	61	179	34	0
	Lunenburg	10,084	11	0	1	2	8	133	34	95	4	0
	Lynn	89,322	852	4	34	269	545	3,000	980	1,439	581	
	Lynnfield	11,615	17	0	0	5	12	173	62	96	15	2
	Malden	56,207	266	0	5	94	167	1,416	341	912	163	4
	Manchester-by-the-Sea	5,367	0	0	0	0	0	78	0	75	3	0
	Mansfield	23,115	37	0	2	5	30	371	140	219	12	2
	Marblehead	20,419	13	0	2	1	10	255	48	193	14	3
	Marion	5,351	13	0	0	2	11	116	26	86	4	2
	Marshfield	25,040	15	0	2	3	10	220	27	177	16	0
	Mashpee	14,366	57	0	1	4	52	335	97	216	22	8
	Mattapoisett	6,518	16	0	0	1	15	85	8	76	1	0
	Maynard	10,291	14	0	1	1	12	36	3	31	2	0
	Medfield	12,417	11	0	0	2	9	67	20	43	4	1
	Medford	53,845	69	1	7	45	16	1,421	261	1,035	125	
	Medway	12,889	5	0	0	1	4	80	10	68	2	0
	Melrose	26,523	44	0	1	12	31	326	78	226	22	0
	Mendon	5,789	12	0	1	0	11	36	10	22	4	0
	Merrimac	6,398	5	0	1	0	4	61	21	35	5	1
	Methuen	44,877	92	0	3	26	63	1,012	209	704	99	3
	Middleboro	21,325	59	0	4	5	50	430	144	235	51	1
	Middleton	9,329	12	0	0	0	12	71	0	69	2	0
	Millbury[10]	13,540		0	6	0		189	48	123	18	3
	Millville	2,961	3	0	0	0	3	14	6	6	2	0
	Milton	26,190	25	0	0	12	13	246	29	205	12	
	Monson	8,816	17	0	1	0	16	113	54	48	11	1
	Montague	8,459	38	0	1	2	35	161	58	90	13	1
	Nahant[10]	3,613		0	0	0		38	5	32	1	0
	Natick	32,135	49	0	4	4	41	686	94	552	40	2
	Needham	28,589	5	0	0	4	1	238	39	195	4	1
	New Bedford	93,661	1,143	7	58	283	795	3,140	842	1,866	432	38
	Newburyport	17,519	23	0	4	2	17	203	43	149	11	0
	Newton	83,658	143	1	8	23	111	1,055	189	829	37	10
	Norfolk	10,553	2	0	0	0	2	53	6	42	5	0
	North Adams	14,094	93	1	15	1	76	571	240	297	34	1

[1] The FBI does not publish arson data unless it receives data from either the agency or the state for all 12 months of the calendar year.
[10] The data collection methodology for the offense of aggravated assault used by this agency does not comply with national UCR Program guidelines. Consequently, the figures for aggravated assault and violent crime (of which aggravated assault is a part) are not included in this table.

Table 8. Offenses Known to Law Enforcement, by State and City, 2006 (*Contd.*)

(Number.)

State	City	Population	Violent crime	Murder and non-negligent manslaughter	Forcible rape	Robbery	Aggravated assault	Property crime	Burglary	Larceny-theft	Motor vehicle theft	Arson[1]
	Northampton	28,888	113	0	6	12	95	822	117	634	71	4
	North Attleboro	28,302	47	1	1	6	39	728	95	591	42	2
	Northborough	14,763	0	0	0	0	0	119	19	96	4	1
	Northbridge	14,301	23	0	6	0	17	197	58	124	15	3
	North Brookfield[10]	4,843		0	1	2		28	12	13	3	0
	Northfield	3,249	6	0	1	0	5	68	26	34	8	0
	North Reading	14,033	6	0	0	3	3	54	21	27	6	0
	Norwell	10,458	10	0	1	2	7	119	34	82	3	0
	Norwood	28,649	45	0	1	12	32	603	94	439	70	1
	Oak Bluffs	3,810	13	0	1	0	12	84	34	50	0	0
	Oakham	1,908	3	0	0	0	3	27	6	16	5	2
	Orange	7,713	35	0	2	1	32	198	82	100	16	2
	Orleans[10]	6,497		0	0	0		170	26	140	4	0
	Oxford	13,800	47	0	5	3	39	93	31	46	16	3
	Palmer	13,003	43	0	4	14	25	253	86	149	18	8
	Paxton	4,585	19	0	0	2	17	21	10	10	1	0
	Peabody	51,547	121	2	4	27	88	1,166	186	879	101	3
	Pembroke	18,204	28	0	0	3	25	209	58	140	11	0
	Pepperell	11,477	7	0	0	0	7	110	31	75	4	1
	Pittsfield	44,124	343	1	40	36	266	1,240	348	804	88	5
	Plainville	8,070	34	0	1	5	28	163	46	106	11	0
	Plymouth	55,253	105	0	5	22	78	681	145	506	30	2
	Princeton	3,544	2	0	0	0	2	18	8	10	0	0
	Provincetown[10]	3,447		0	1	1		192	13	175	4	0
	Quincy	90,792	305	3	23	92	187	1,684	473	1,058	153	16
	Randolph	30,651	156	1	19	31	105	721	95	544	82	1
	Raynham	13,579	31	0	4	5	22	429	61	320	48	1
	Reading	23,303	16	0	0	7	9	202	35	157	10	0
	Rehoboth	11,324	20	0	4	2	14	143	33	94	16	0
	Revere	46,082	255	0	12	68	175	1,539	297	949	293	12
	Rochester	5,342	4	0	0	0	4	59	33	24	2	0
	Rockland	17,946	20	0	1	8	11	341	61	222	58	
	Rowley	5,880	8	1	0	3	4	44	16	27	1	1
	Royalston	1,376	11	0	1	0	10	11	7	3	1	0
	Rutland	7,491	14	0	3	0	11	45	18	22	5	0
	Salem	42,007	122	0	10	26	86	877	191	627	59	0
	Salisbury[10]	8,334		0	8	2		186	75	91	20	2
	Sandwich	20,851	49	0	5	1	43	263	107	143	13	1
	Saugus[10]	27,077		0	10	40		1,011	333	601	77	2
	Savoy	729	2	0	1	0	1	3	3	0	0	0
	Scituate	18,229	18	0	0	0	18	151	41	103	7	0
	Seekonk	13,750	34	0	2	11	21	500	79	378	43	0
	Sharon	17,310	4	0	0	1	3	126	22	99	5	2
	Shelburne	2,066	0	0	0	0	0	11	2	8	1	0
	Sherborn	4,248	1	0	1	0	0	26	13	11	2	2
	Shirley	7,658	3	0	0	0	3	24	7	14	3	0
	Shrewsbury	33,373	26	0	9	2	15	344	30	297	17	1
	Somerset	18,682	55	0	1	1	53	351	67	260	24	4
	Somerville	75,413	322	2	19	129	172	1,954	434	1,204	316	6
	Southampton[10]	5,876		0	0	0		50	8	39	3	1
	Southborough	9,616	1	0	0	0	1	51	12	33	6	0
	Southbridge	17,338	76	0	7	16	53	355	154	177	24	4
	South Hadley	17,166	31	0	8	1	22	269	66	190	13	3
	Southwick	9,605	10	0	2	0	8	139	36	92	11	2
	Spencer	12,165	37	0	0	4	33	157	29	110	18	1
	Springfield	152,644	2,260	15	115	682	1,448	8,747	2,178	4,963	1,606	75
	Sterling	7,817	13	0	1	0	12	57	35	16	6	1
	Stockbridge	2,270	9	0	0	0	9	56	14	39	3	1
	Stoneham	21,712	24	0	0	6	18	382	82	276	24	
	Stow	6,216	4	0	0	1	3	42	25	16	1	1
	Sturbridge	8,913	21	0	3	0	18	143	37	101	5	0
	Sudbury	17,169	3	0	1	0	2	88	12	75	1	0
	Sunderland	3,826	11	0	0	1	10	33	16	17	0	1

[1] The FBI does not publish arson data unless it receives data from either the agency or the state for all 12 months of the calendar year.

[10] The data collection methodology for the offense of aggravated assault used by this agency does not comply with national UCR Program guidelines. Consequently, the figures for aggravated assault and violent crime (of which aggravated assault is a part) are not included in this table.

Table 8. Offenses Known to Law Enforcement, by State and City, 2006 (Contd.)

(Number.)

State	City	Population	Violent crime	Murder and non-negligent man-slaughter	Forcible rape	Robbery	Aggra-vated assault	Property crime	Burglary	Larceny-theft	Motor vehicle theft	Arson[1]
	Sutton	9,043	8	0	1	1	6	94	37	50	7	1
	Swansea	16,348	40	2	3	5	30	299	56	203	40	1
	Taunton	56,589	290	1	9	68	212	1,088	407	537	144	2
	Templeton	7,536	11	0	1	3	7	85	45	28	12	3
	Tewksbury	29,218	42	0	7	7	28	489	72	376	41	1
	Tisbury	3,835	13	0	1	0	12	141	31	100	10	0
	Topsfield	6,220	1	0	0	0	1	36	6	28	2	0
	Townsend	9,341	1	0	0	1	0	106	22	82	2	0
	Truro	2,177	0	0	0	0	0	19	1	18	0	0
	Tyngsboro	11,406	18	0	0	3	15	156	38	101	17	2
	Upton	6,435	3	0	0	0	3	55	11	36	8	1
	Uxbridge	12,484	21	0	3	0	18	123	49	64	10	2
	Wakefield	24,723	57	2	3	9	43	270	45	202	23	0
	Walpole	23,251	18	0	6	0	12	271	33	220	18	0
	Waltham	59,914	98	0	8	20	70	690	113	528	49	1
	Ware	10,065	32	0	7	3	22	154	42	97	15	8
	Wareham[10]	21,424		1	5	24		695	231	406	58	2
	Warren	5,075	35	0	6	0	29	40	20	15	5	2
	Watertown	32,497	37	0	2	9	26	549	77	452	20	0
	Wayland	13,080	5	0	2	2	1	93	12	76	5	0
	Webster	16,952	80	0	8	17	55	310	102	175	33	3
	Wellesley	27,140	19	0	2	0	17	250	73	174	3	1
	Wellfleet	2,839	8	0	0	0	8	83	11	71	1	0
	Wenham	4,678	1	0	0	1	0	50	26	23	1	0
	Westborough	18,845	28	0	2	2	24	267	53	189	25	3
	West Boylston	7,745	10	0	2	0	8	166	20	137	9	0
	West Brookfield	3,918	11	0	0	0	11	44	13	25	6	0
	Westfield[10]	40,769		1	11	9		643	260	331	52	9
	Westford	21,590	3	0	2	0	1	148	12	134	2	0
	Westhampton	1,577	1	0	0	0	1	7	2	5	0	0
	West Newbury	4,332	15	0	1	0	14	25	6	17	2	0
	Westport	15,162	34	0	1	1	32	216	109	93	14	0
	West Springfield	28,157	106	1	10	29	66	1,270	235	905	130	5
	West Tisbury	2,687	0	0	0	0	0	9	0	9	0	0
	Westwood	13,984	12	0	0	2	10	153	22	121	10	2
	Whately	1,594	5	0	0	1	4	33	7	25	1	0
	Wilbraham	14,087	26	0	4	0	22	189	32	143	14	1
	Williamstown	8,288	9	0	3	0	6	202	27	166	9	1
	Wilmington	21,601	30	0	4	4	22	393	68	307	18	
	Winchendon	10,165	49	0	2	0	47	184	58	109	17	3
	Winchester	21,308	11	0	0	3	8	307	49	241	17	0
	Winthrop	17,172	66	0	3	6	57	154	74	77	3	1
	Woburn	37,370	91	0	5	29	57	803	100	641	62	2
	Worcester	176,956	1,496	6	124	388	978	5,671	1,231	3,452	988	16
	Yarmouth[10]	24,769		0	4	11		736	318	387	31	3
MICHIGAN	Adrian	21,730	145	1	36	20	88	835	154	630	51	6
	Adrian Township	6,803	0	0	0	0	0	16	3	12	1	0
	Albion	9,325	101	0	7	19	75	365	96	263	6	1
	Algonac	4,587	19	0	5	0	14	54	9	44	1	1
	Allegan	4,951	72	0	1	1	70	110	15	89	6	0
	Allen Park	28,013	44	0	6	10	28	662	250	280	132	6
	Alma	9,237	6	0	3	0	3	20	14	6	0	0
	Almont	2,867	14	0	1	1	12	102	23	73	6	0
	Alpena	10,765	45	0	6	4	35	394	79	303	12	4
	Ann Arbor	112,989	344	0	32	85	227	2,923	631	2,119	173	22
	Argentine Township	7,163	9	0	5	0	4	140	28	104	8	1
	Armada	1,646	0	0	0	0	0	31	8	19	4	0
	Auburn Hills	20,959	78	0	8	36	34	1,147	111	950	86	5
	Bad Axe	3,238	9	0	1	0	8	144	11	131	2	2
	Bangor	1,877	8	0	1	2	5	89	8	78	3	0
	Baraga	1,249	2	0	1	0	1	16	1	13	2	0
	Bath Township	10,559	10	0	1	2	7	128	21	90	17	0
	Battle Creek	62,628	781	7	67	116	591	3,477	831	2,428	218	23

[1] The FBI does not publish arson data unless it receives data from either the agency or the state for all 12 months of the calendar year.
[10] The data collection methodology for the offense of aggravated assault used by this agency does not comply with national UCR Program guidelines. Consequently, the figures for aggravated assault and violent crime (of which aggravated assault is a part) are not included in this table.

Table 8. Offenses Known to Law Enforcement, by State and City, 2006 (*Contd.*)

(Number.)

State	City	Popula-tion	Violent crime	Murder and non-negligent man-slaughter	Forcible rape	Robbery	Aggra-vated assault	Property crime	Burglary	Larceny-theft	Motor vehicle theft	Arson[1]
	Bay City	34,792	145	0	29	32	84	1,340	340	880	120	9
	Beaverton	1,115	4	0	1	0	3	15	2	13	0	0
	Belding	5,880	16	0	2	1	13	313	40	266	7	2
	Benton Harbor	10,722	174	2	9	10	153	384	136	209	39	4
	Benton Township	15,894	177	1	7	42	127	1,471	195	1,197	79	10
	Berkley	15,051	16	0	2	4	10	207	41	149	17	1
	Berrien Springs-Oronoko Township	9,627	11	0	4	0	7	187	31	154	2	3
	Beverly Hills	10,061	12	0	1	7	4	172	25	146	1	1
	Big Rapids	10,677	32	0	7	6	19	308	65	232	11	3
	Birch Run	1,715	12	0	2	0	10	159	9	148	2	0
	Birmingham	19,033	48	0	3	8	37	527	81	417	29	2
	Blackman Township	24,785	51	0	8	9	34	578	96	455	27	4
	Blissfield	3,248	1	0	1	0	0	48	8	40	0	0
	Bloomfield Hills	3,841	3	0	1	0	2	76	9	63	4	0
	Bloomfield Township	41,547	28	1	4	13	10	727	137	551	39	4
	Bloomingdale	510	2	0	0	1	1	21	4	17	0	0
	Boyne City	3,284	10	0	5	1	4	120	11	104	5	0
	Breckenridge	1,315	1	0	0	0	1	5	2	3	0	0
	Bridgeport Township	11,301	38	0	1	3	34	342	109	200	33	1
	Bridgman	2,443	5	0	0	1	4	96	14	80	2	1
	Brighton	7,121	11	0	1	3	7	282	22	251	9	1
	Bronson	2,340	5	0	0	0	5	67	7	58	2	0
	Brownstown Township	29,074	76	1	13	9	53	643	130	413	100	6
	Buchanan	4,520	1	0	0	0	1	15	3	12	0	0
	Buena Vista Township	9,836	130	2	11	19	98	515	197	264	54	13
	Burr Oak	769	0	0	0	0	0	6	0	6	0	0
	Burton	30,839	126	1	11	33	81	1,447	343	921	183	6
	Cadillac	10,142	37	0	12	3	22	512	75	414	23	0
	Calumet	810	4	0	0	0	4	17	6	10	1	3
	Cambridge Township	5,878	0	0	0	0	0	5	0	5	0	0
	Canton Township	85,862	102	3	32	15	52	1,708	309	1,258	141	17
	Capac	2,227	4	0	1	0	3	56	3	52	1	0
	Carleton	2,867	5	0	0	0	5	37	4	33	0	0
	Caro	4,183	13	0	3	1	9	177	17	152	8	0
	Carrollton Township	6,261	15	0	3	2	10	226	57	155	14	2
	Carsonville	492	0	0	0	0	0	2	1	1	0	0
	Caseville	885	2	0	1	0	1	43	4	39	0	0
	Caspian	2,086	1	0	0	0	1	9	2	6	1	1
	Cass City	2,600	2	0	0	0	2	47	5	40	2	0
	Cedar Springs	3,226	13	0	2	1	10	89	18	69	2	0
	Center Line	8,287	23	0	4	6	13	335	49	168	118	1
	Charlevoix	2,769	7	0	3	1	3	75	11	63	1	0
	Charlotte	9,046	40	0	17	6	17	279	50	219	10	1
	Cheboygan	5,178	21	0	6	2	13	196	24	165	7	1
	Chelsea	4,789	3	0	0	0	3	142	17	120	5	2
	Chesterfield Township	43,729	180	1	11	18	150	1,152	157	910	85	7
	Chikaming Township	3,700	8	2	0	2	4	73	17	54	2	0
	Chocolay Township	6,000	1	0	0	0	1	56	5	48	3	0
	Clare	3,225	5	0	0	0	5	177	15	157	5	0
	Clawson	12,306	7	0	3	1	3	144	30	101	13	1
	Clayton Township	7,770	3	0	0	0	3	117	38	69	10	1
	Clay Township	9,842	8	0	3	0	5	140	39	95	6	1
	Clinton	2,348	2	0	0	0	2	50	5	42	3	0
	Clinton Township	96,587	328	1	21	77	229	2,461	522	1,623	316	16
	Clio	2,612	9	0	1	0	8	110	22	85	3	1
	Coldwater	10,756	35	0	9	2	24	568	74	474	20	0
	Coleman	1,263	3	0	0	1	2	37	10	27	0	0
	Coloma Township	6,720	13	0	4	0	9	215	74	138	3	0
	Colon	1,186	2	0	0	0	2	34	1	33	0	0
	Columbia Township	7,610	27	0	0	2	25	185	24	149	12	1
	Constantine	2,156	13	0	2	2	9	123	13	99	11	4
	Covert Township	3,130	26	0	0	4	22	99	30	61	8	1
	Croswell	2,542	5	0	0	0	5	72	11	57	4	2
	Davison	5,359	8	0	1	1	6	100	30	63	7	2

[1] The FBI does not publish arson data unless it receives data from either the agency or the state for all 12 months of the calendar year.

Table 8. Offenses Known to Law Enforcement, by State and City, 2006 (*Contd.*)

(Number.)

State	City	Popula-tion	Violent crime	Murder and non-negligent man-slaughter	Forcible rape	Robbery	Aggra-vated assault	Property crime	Burglary	Larceny-theft	Motor vehicle theft	Arson[1]
	Davison Township	18,604	30	0	6	6	18	388	115	232	41	1
	Dearborn	93,856	456	2	21	164	269	4,947	670	3,242	1,035	48
	Dearborn Heights	56,036	195	3	8	68	116	1,638	406	862	370	9
	Decatur	1,885	23	0	2	0	21	198	31	156	11	5
	Denton Township	5,690	10	0	2	0	8	114	39	70	5	0
	Detroit	884,462	21,394	418	593	7,240	13,143	62,338	18,134	21,287	22,917	859
	Dewitt	4,430	3	0	3	0	0	49	10	36	3	0
	Dewitt Township	13,052	23	0	3	2	18	164	46	96	22	1
	Douglas	2,230	8	0	1	0	7	81	14	61	6	1
	Dryden Township	4,746	3	0	1	0	2	56	6	42	8	0
	Durand	3,858	5	0	1	0	4	57	12	44	1	0
	East Grand Rapids	10,358	3	0	1	1	1	126	32	88	6	0
	East Jordan	2,332	2	0	1	0	1	92	11	78	3	0
	East Lansing	46,303	172	0	14	28	130	1,093	248	785	60	20
	Eastpointe	33,097	255	0	15	80	160	1,443	202	687	554	9
	East Tawas	2,845	9	0	2	0	7	144	34	102	8	5
	Eaton Rapids	5,253	15	0	6	2	7	182	12	166	4	1
	Eau Claire	641	5	0	1	0	4	21	1	20	0	0
	Elk Rapids	1,706	1	0	0	0	1	39	8	31	0	0
	Elkton	804	0	0	0	0	0	29	1	28	0	0
	Emmett Township	12,101	47	0	4	6	37	552	72	457	23	1
	Erie Township	4,776	5	0	0	0	5	107	36	65	6	2
	Essexville	3,581	5	0	2	2	1	95	13	79	3	2
	Evart	1,730	6	0	0	0	6	52	6	44	2	1
	Fairgrove	617	0	0	0	0	0	0	0	0	0	0
	Farmington	10,010	22	0	2	4	16	251	45	194	12	1
	Farmington Hills	80,023	134	0	14	32	88	1,553	325	1,060	168	11
	Fenton	11,916	39	0	7	3	29	278	56	206	16	2
	Ferndale	21,407	119	0	9	43	67	771	157	418	196	6
	Flat Rock	9,536	18	0	1	5	12	256	58	164	34	2
	Flint	118,256	3,070	54	143	627	2,246	8,117	3,058	3,538	1,521	186
	Flint Township	32,941	174	2	22	67	83	1,937	402	1,342	193	4
	Flushing	8,090	6	0	3	1	2	133	16	111	6	0
	Flushing Township	10,475	9	1	4	0	4	120	35	76	9	0
	Forsyth Township	4,845	4	0	2	0	2	67	21	41	5	1
	Fowlerville	3,124	8	0	2	0	6	89	14	66	9	0
	Frankenmuth	4,791	7	0	2	0	5	100	9	88	3	0
	Frankfort	1,489	1	0	1	0	0	39	9	27	3	1
	Franklin	2,951	2	0	0	0	2	43	3	39	1	0
	Fraser	15,057	34	0	9	8	17	476	69	359	48	0
	Fremont	4,245	5	0	1	0	4	87	9	74	4	0
	Fruitport	1,084	34	0	2	5	27	753	66	673	14	0
	Garden City	28,888	94	0	7	20	67	661	124	438	99	13
	Gaylord	3,721	12	0	4	0	8	235	63	157	15	1
	Genesee Township	24,185	111	4	17	31	59	789	249	426	114	8
	Gerrish Township	3,169	5	0	3	0	2	62	28	32	2	0
	Gladstone	5,242	4	0	1	0	3	152	22	129	1	2
	Gladwin	3,010	10	0	3	1	6	123	23	97	3	0
	Grand Beach	237	0	0	0	0	0	13	1	9	3	0
	Grand Blanc	7,878	23	0	3	2	18	189	30	143	16	0
	Grand Blanc Township	35,033	68	1	10	8	49	775	161	542	72	6
	Grand Haven	10,560	37	0	7	3	27	420	80	332	8	8
	Grand Ledge	7,749	8	0	0	2	6	281	19	253	9	2
	Grand Rapids	193,297	1,923	22	65	700	1,136	10,103	2,484	6,922	697	122
	Grayling	1,938	3	0	0	2	1	70	4	63	3	0
	Green Oak Township	17,654	15	0	3	2	10	286	73	196	17	0
	Greenville	8,285	31	1	10	2	18	414	68	333	13	1
	Grosse Ile Township	10,610	2	0	0	0	2	91	7	81	3	0
	Grosse Pointe	5,412	8	0	2	5	1	228	24	155	49	0
	Grosse Pointe Farms	9,302	5	0	0	2	3	185	24	132	29	0
	Grosse Pointe Park	11,875	23	0	0	12	11	345	41	206	98	1
	Grosse Pointe Shores	2,701	0	0	0	0	0	0	0	0	0	0
	Grosse Pointe Woods	16,276	21	0	1	4	16	309	36	219	54	1
	Hamburg Township	21,956	15	0	2	0	13	277	63	203	11	2
	Hampton Township	9,848	22	0	2	0	20	342	53	277	12	0

[1] The FBI does not publish arson data unless it receives data from either the agency or the state for all 12 months of the calendar year.

Table 8. Offenses Known to Law Enforcement, by State and City, 2006 (*Contd.*)

(Number.)

State	City	Population	Violent crime	Murder and non-negligent man-slaughter	Forcible rape	Robbery	Aggra-vated assault	Property crime	Burglary	Larceny-theft	Motor vehicle theft	Arson[1]
	Hamtramck	21,939	296	1	7	172	116	1,236	272	430	534	11
	Hancock	4,212	3	0	1	0	2	95	16	71	8	0
	Harbor Beach	1,715	1	0	1	0	0	46	4	41	1	0
	Harbor Springs	1,590	2	0	0	0	2	39	7	32	0	0
	Harper Woods	13,587	114	1	4	59	50	1,486	119	892	475	5
	Hart	1,991	6	0	0	0	6	112	23	82	7	1
	Hartford	2,427	19	0	2	2	15	112	25	78	9	0
	Hastings	7,148	19	0	6	1	12	206	15	188	3	3
	Hazel Park	18,345	105	0	16	31	58	775	134	384	257	5
	Hillsdale	7,884	14	0	6	1	7	158	26	127	5	0
	Holland	34,343	150	0	47	15	88	1,207	200	971	36	5
	Holly	6,359	16	0	6	5	5	139	30	103	6	1
	Homer	1,814	5	0	1	1	3	11	5	6	0	0
	Houghton	7,058	6	0	2	1	3	130	13	114	3	1
	Howard City	1,613	11	0	2	1	8	86	12	72	2	1
	Howell	9,733	38	0	5	0	33	338	46	271	21	4
	Hudson	2,409	8	0	3	1	4	77	9	68	0	1
	Huntington Woods	5,913	3	0	0	2	1	90	7	76	7	0
	Huron Township	15,787	30	0	4	4	22	351	66	211	74	0
	Imlay City	3,840	16	0	3	3	10	111	9	100	2	0
	Inkster	28,798	350	6	27	75	242	1,161	403	501	257	12
	Ionia	12,305	31	0	12	2	17	264	52	198	14	4
	Iron Mountain	8,153	9	0	3	0	6	187	25	159	3	2
	Iron River	3,104	10	0	6	0	4	101	18	64	19	1
	Ishpeming	6,491	17	0	8	1	8	180	21	143	16	0
	Jackson	34,792	289	2	43	80	164	2,308	371	1,819	118	20
	Jonesville	2,287	8	0	1	1	6	100	15	82	3	2
	Kalamazoo	72,519	737	5	55	238	439	4,966	1,327	3,243	396	44
	Kalamazoo Township	21,511	60	0	7	16	37	824	248	512	64	5
	Kalkaska	2,200	3	0	1	0	2	148	9	135	4	2
	Keego Harbor	2,784	11	0	0	0	11	55	3	48	4	0
	Kentwood	46,375	164	1	33	27	103	1,990	366	1,526	98	10
	Kingsford	5,551	4	0	1	1	2	84	3	80	1	0
	Kinross Township	8,062	3	0	1	0	2	53	18	32	3	0
	Laingsburg	1,267	6	0	0	0	6	31	7	23	1	0
	Lake Linden	1,041	2	0	0	0	2	21	8	12	1	0
	Lake Odessa	2,282	3	0	2	0	1	40	7	31	2	0
	Lake Orion	2,749	11	0	0	2	9	79	9	68	2	1
	Lakeview	1,119	1	0	0	0	1	76	22	53	1	0
	Lansing	115,230	1,173	6	105	262	800	4,656	1,249	2,928	479	43
	Lansing Township	7,993	40	0	3	16	21	374	83	269	22	0
	Lapeer	9,347	36	3	8	2	23	395	38	335	22	1
	Lapeer Township	5,193	0	0	0	0	0	27	3	23	1	0
	Lathrup Village	4,147	27	0	0	9	18	75	18	49	8	0
	Laurium	2,041	2	0	0	0	2	31	3	26	2	0
	Lawton	1,847	3	0	0	0	3	57	14	43	0	0
	Lennon	504	1	0	0	0	1	5	2	3	0	0
	Leoni Township	13,801	26	0	2	3	21	286	57	211	18	1
	Leslie	2,262	4	0	1	1	2	38	7	31	0	0
	Lincoln Park	38,142	140	2	13	51	74	1,876	299	1,200	377	4
	Lincoln Township	14,379	8	0	3	0	5	301	39	251	11	4
	Linden	3,443	0	0	0	0	0	26	2	24	0	0
	Litchfield	1,425	5	0	0	0	5	56	7	47	2	0
	Livonia	97,733	167	0	19	65	83	2,318	366	1,639	313	15
	Lowell	4,130	1	0	0	0	1	34	8	23	3	0
	Ludington	8,271	37	0	8	3	26	334	60	265	9	3
	Luna Pier	1,519	5	0	0	0	5	70	10	54	6	1
	Mackinac Island	490	4	0	2	0	2	343	2	340	1	0
	Mackinaw City	860	2	0	0	0	2	43	7	35	1	0
	Madison Heights	30,176	70	0	11	25	34	1,159	117	767	275	4
	Madison Township	7,889	2	0	1	0	1	53	9	39	5	0
	Mancelona	1,383	3	0	0	1	2	36	6	28	2	0
	Manistee	6,639	16	0	4	1	11	191	25	162	4	3
	Manton	1,216	0	0	0	0	0	16	7	9	0	0
	Marion	835	0	0	0	0	0	14	3	11	0	0

[1] The FBI does not publish arson data unless it receives data from either the agency or the state for all 12 months of the calendar year.

Table 8. Offenses Known to Law Enforcement, by State and City, 2006 (*Contd.*)

(Number.)

State	City	Popula-tion	Violent crime	Murder and non-negligent man-slaughter	Forcible rape	Robbery	Aggra-vated assault	Property crime	Burglary	Larceny-theft	Motor vehicle theft	Arson[1]
	Marlette	2,065	6	0	5	0	1	60	8	49	3	0
	Marquette	20,530	31	0	14	3	14	465	43	392	30	2
	Marshall	7,345	26	0	3	2	21	198	22	173	3	2
	Marysville	10,017	8	0	2	0	6	254	32	211	11	2
	Mason	7,965	20	0	3	1	16	244	25	214	5	1
	Mattawan	2,831	0	0	0	0	0	117	8	109	0	0
	Mayville	1,031	1	0	0	0	1	14	3	10	1	0
	Melvindale	10,586	42	0	2	15	25	306	48	169	89	0
	Memphis	1,120	1	0	1	0	0	42	0	40	2	0
	Mendon	931	0	0	0	0	0	12	1	11	0	0
	Menominee	8,731	22	0	5	4	13	312	71	233	8	2
	Meridian Township	38,245	50	1	12	14	23	970	171	752	47	6
	Metamora Township	4,648	8	0	1	2	5	66	27	35	4	0
	Midland	41,656	63	0	16	6	41	967	143	795	29	3
	Milan	5,363	17	0	2	1	14	186	15	161	10	0
	Milford	16,114	12	1	7	1	3	184	46	129	9	4
	Monroe	21,737	84	0	11	10	63	660	116	520	24	1
	Montague	2,333	2	0	0	0	2	73	5	68	0	1
	Montrose Township	7,949	11	0	1	2	8	162	38	112	12	0
	Morenci	2,346	3	0	2	0	1	78	7	70	1	1
	Morrice	886	0	0	0	0	0	1	0	1	0	0
	Mount Morris	3,313	40	0	3	8	29	139	27	97	15	0
	Mount Morris Township	23,244	185	2	31	48	104	1,220	475	566	179	15
	Mount Pleasant	26,188	45	0	10	9	26	651	96	524	31	4
	Mundy Township	14,007	41	1	3	13	24	589	87	475	27	4
	Munising	2,380	0	0	0	0	0	19	3	15	1	0
	Muskegon	39,820	447	1	52	101	293	2,671	453	2,048	170	31
	Muskegon Heights	11,792	247	2	27	53	165	879	198	579	102	22
	Muskegon Township	18,557	50	1	20	7	22	1,209	141	1,015	53	3
	Napoleon Township	7,087	5	0	2	0	3	96	29	65	2	0
	Nashville	1,701	12	0	2	0	10	36	3	30	3	0
	Negaunee	4,460	7	0	2	0	5	119	34	82	3	1
	Newaygo	1,681	9	0	3	0	6	96	11	83	2	1
	New Baltimore	11,137	25	4	5	2	14	249	26	210	13	4
	New Haven	4,696	4	0	1	1	2	1	0	1	0	0
	New Lothrop	597	1	0	0	1	0	15	5	10	0	0
	Niles	11,709	97	0	14	24	59	523	99	397	27	8
	North Branch	1,005	8	0	0	1	7	31	4	26	1	0
	Northfield Township	8,358	25	0	3	0	22	236	43	180	13	1
	North Muskegon	4,002	4	0	1	1	2	149	15	132	2	0
	Northville	6,295	1	0	1	0	0	85	23	58	4	2
	Northville Township	25,216	20	0	6	6	8	546	127	378	41	1
	Norton Shores	23,421	52	0	10	17	25	1,030	140	842	48	2
	Norway	2,966	8	0	2	0	6	80	7	70	3	0
	Novi	52,983	50	0	5	11	34	1,208	106	1,056	46	2
	Oak Park	31,116	159	0	12	70	77	1,102	227	618	257	1
	Ontwa Township-Edwardsburg	5,952	29	0	3	1	25	263	46	197	20	4
	Orchard Lake	2,219	5	0	0	0	5	60	5	53	2	0
	Oscoda Township	7,091	22	0	4	6	12	265	84	169	12	2
	Otsego	3,931	15	0	3	0	12	112	19	91	2	1
	Ovid	1,435	1	0	0	0	1	8	0	8	0	0
	Owosso	15,384	78	0	23	3	52	647	116	501	30	6
	Oxford	3,555	3	0	0	0	3	53	12	38	3	1
	Parchment	1,808	3	0	0	0	3	83	4	78	1	0
	Parma-Sandstone	6,817	7	0	0	1	6	62	14	43	5	3
	Paw Paw	3,320	8	0	2	1	5	139	10	129	0	1
	Pentwater	982	0	0	0	0	0	27	5	22	0	0
	Perry	2,047	5	0	2	0	3	28	4	24	0	0
	Petoskey	6,183	7	0	0	1	6	168	21	146	1	0
	Pigeon	1,127	1	0	0	0	1	24	0	24	0	0
	Pinckney	2,429	4	0	0	0	4	60	8	48	4	0
	Pinconning	1,346	1	0	0	0	1	51	8	41	2	2
	Pittsfield Township	33,539	64	0	12	20	32	965	163	698	104	2
	Plainwell	3,986	5	0	5	0	0	140	2	137	1	2

[1] The FBI does not publish arson data unless it receives data from either the agency or the state for all 12 months of the calendar year.

Table 8. Offenses Known to Law Enforcement, by State and City, 2006 (*Contd.*)

(Number.)

State	City	Popula-tion	Violent crime	Murder and non-negligent man-slaughter	Forcible rape	Robbery	Aggra-vated assault	Property crime	Burglary	Larceny-theft	Motor vehicle theft	Arson[1]
	Pleasant Ridge	2,495	3	0	0	3	0	32	7	23	2	0
	Plymouth	9,077	16	0	2	5	9	168	16	135	17	0
	Plymouth Township	27,153	14	0	0	6	8	434	72	326	36	2
	Pontiac	67,163	1,221	8	86	276	851	3,425	1,566	1,294	565	73
	Portage	45,164	122	0	27	24	71	2,072	337	1,664	71	12
	Port Austin	690	0	0	0	0	0	13	2	11	0	0
	Port Huron	31,423	285	1	41	80	163	1,596	337	1,154	105	8
	Portland	3,812	4	0	1	1	2	93	16	72	5	1
	Prairieville Township	3,450	1	0	0	1	0	30	23	7	0	0
	Raisin Township	7,157	4	0	0	0	4	27	4	20	3	1
	Redford Township	49,431	212	2	1	103	106	2,169	520	1,087	562	10
	Reed City	2,412	5	0	1	0	4	45	8	35	2	0
	Reese	1,362	0	0	0	0	0	4	1	2	1	0
	Richfield Township, Genesee County	8,740	5	0	1	0	4	133	50	64	19	0
	Richfield Township, Roscommon County	4,222	4	0	1	0	3	51	7	43	1	1
	Richland Township	4,371	1	0	1	0	0	37	18	19	0	0
	Richmond	5,593	39	0	5	0	34	122	28	88	6	0
	Riverview	12,712	9	2	0	4	3	234	22	182	30	0
	Rochester	11,181	28	0	3	2	23	137	19	113	5	0
	Rockford	5,049	5	0	2	0	3	158	15	141	2	1
	Rockwood	3,403	5	0	1	1	3	68	10	43	15	1
	Rogers City	3,193	10	0	2	0	8	71	7	64	0	0
	Romeo	3,805	5	0	2	0	3	82	13	67	2	0
	Romulus	23,794	181	1	19	30	131	1,026	233	627	166	13
	Roosevelt Park	3,801	7	0	3	2	2	177	14	157	6	0
	Roseville	47,589	229	1	17	72	139	2,552	307	1,695	550	9
	Rothbury	442	2	0	0	0	2	10	0	10	0	0
	Royal Oak	58,154	108	0	17	32	59	1,416	282	942	192	9
	Saginaw	58,216	1,738	24	79	271	1,364	2,752	1,369	1,043	340	163
	Saginaw Township	39,916	89	0	6	32	51	1,105	203	846	56	8
	Saline	8,804	3	0	0	1	2	184	26	155	3	1
	Sand Lake	511	0	0	0	0	0	8	3	5	0	0
	Sandusky	2,687	18	0	13	0	5	150	16	129	5	1
	Sault Ste. Marie	14,282	40	0	11	3	26	576	93	454	29	0
	Schoolcraft	1,500	5	0	1	0	4	71	17	49	5	1
	Scottville	1,270	3	0	1	0	2	52	13	39	0	0
	Shelby Township	69,735	148	1	26	11	110	1,164	206	843	115	7
	Southfield	76,627	1,041	1	36	164	840	3,604	894	2,003	707	3
	Southgate	29,498	120	0	7	31	82	1,205	124	919	162	14
	South Haven	5,144	25	0	5	7	13	179	30	143	6	2
	South Lyon	11,012	13	1	1	1	10	141	17	122	2	3
	South Rockwood	1,586	2	0	0	0	2	16	3	12	1	0
	Sparta	4,036	5	0	2	0	3	147	17	125	5	0
	Spaulding Township	2,295	1	0	0	0	1	0	0	0	0	0
	Spring Arbor Township	8,304	5	0	0	0	5	84	22	54	8	1
	Springfield	5,190	40	0	8	3	29	249	58	178	13	1
	Spring Lake-Ferrysburg	5,363	4	0	3	0	1	154	26	126	2	3
	St. Charles	2,145	8	0	2	0	6	74	8	63	3	1
	St. Clair	5,918	5	0	0	1	4	117	28	84	5	0
	St. Clair Shores	61,408	147	1	19	30	97	1,454	261	903	290	26
	Sterling Heights	127,715	256	2	17	30	207	3,415	356	2,716	343	22
	St. Ignace	2,440	3	0	0	0	3	62	10	51	1	0
	St. Johns	7,417	13	0	5	3	5	161	24	130	7	0
	St. Joseph	8,653	13	0	4	2	7	375	41	323	11	3
	St. Joseph Township	9,928	19	1	1	2	15	184	22	156	6	1
	St. Louis	6,497	7	0	6	0	1	79	9	70	0	0
	Stockbridge	1,276	1	0	1	0	0	42	7	30	5	0
	Sturgis	11,106	58	0	15	7	36	301	59	226	16	2
	Summit Township	22,003	39	0	3	3	33	270	59	197	14	1
	Sumpter Township	11,892	39	1	10	1	27	224	81	128	15	11
	Swartz Creek	5,328	10	1	4	1	4	181	28	143	10	1
	Sylvan Lake	1,672	1	0	0	0	1	41	6	33	2	1
	Taylor	64,800	234	4	33	78	119	2,736	382	1,983	371	37

[1] The FBI does not publish arson data unless it receives data from either the agency or the state for all 12 months of the calendar year.

Table 8. Offenses Known to Law Enforcement, by State and City, 2006 (*Contd.*)

(Number.)

State	City	Population	Violent crime	Murder and non-negligent manslaughter	Forcible rape	Robbery	Aggravated assault	Property crime	Burglary	Larceny-theft	Motor vehicle theft	Arson[1]
	Tecumseh	8,841	5	0	2	1	2	77	18	57	2	0
	Thomas Township	12,602	31	0	4	1	26	387	66	308	13	2
	Three Rivers	7,324	86	0	11	11	64	530	102	405	23	5
	Tittabawassee Township	8,820	6	0	1	1	4	165	26	133	6	2
	Traverse City	14,477	46	0	12	2	32	480	69	389	22	7
	Trenton	19,263	1	0	1	0	0	59	3	51	5	0
	Troy	80,966	93	2	10	26	55	2,018	321	1,550	147	7
	Tuscarora Township	3,158	5	0	2	0	3	91	11	79	1	0
	Unadilla Township	3,398	4	0	3	0	1	52	13	37	2	0
	Union City	1,772	9	0	1	0	8	86	16	69	1	0
	Utica	4,901	13	0	4	0	9	198	17	165	16	1
	Van Buren Township	27,073	32	1	3	4	24	198	21	131	46	4
	Vassar	2,769	5	0	0	0	5	25	3	22	0	0
	Vicksburg	2,184	3	0	0	0	3	15	2	12	1	1
	Walker	23,362	49	0	13	12	24	1,055	127	893	35	3
	Walled Lake	6,902	35	0	1	2	32	125	16	97	12	2
	Warren	134,974	842	5	75	241	521	4,883	790	2,288	1,805	41
	Waterford Township	71,491	177	1	44	46	86	1,922	385	1,381	156	12
	Wayland	3,938	0	0	0	0	0	44	2	40	2	0
	Wayne	18,543	149	1	16	30	102	702	156	419	127	9
	West Bloomfield Township	64,834	48	1	5	11	31	835	153	640	42	5
	West Branch	1,900	1	0	1	0	0	108	13	92	3	1
	Westland	85,410	367	2	64	85	216	2,758	523	1,789	446	41
	White Cloud	1,428	4	0	1	0	3	82	12	69	1	0
	Whitehall	2,832	13	0	2	1	10	160	19	138	3	1
	White Lake Township	29,846	20	0	4	1	15	545	74	448	23	4
	White Pigeon	1,595	1	0	0	0	1	38	9	28	1	0
	Williamston	3,781	1	0	0	0	1	70	12	53	5	0
	Wixom	13,351	36	0	3	9	24	432	46	350	36	0
	Wolverine Lake	4,258	3	0	0	0	3	47	7	37	3	0
	Woodhaven	13,321	36	0	3	4	29	366	28	307	31	2
	Wyandotte	26,873	57	0	8	12	37	717	91	587	39	8
	Wyoming	69,947	325	0	60	64	201	2,207	603	1,346	258	17
	Yale	1,988	4	0	0	0	4	21	9	12	0	1
	Ypsilanti	21,778	278	4	13	76	185	1,296	357	813	126	11
	Zeeland	5,518	12	0	3	0	9	74	8	66	0	1
	Zilwaukee	1,731	2	0	0	0	2	13	9	4	0	0
MINNESOTA[7]	Albany	2,020		0		0	0	9	0	9	0	0
	Albert Lea	18,035		0		2	25	473	46	402	25	1
	Alexandria	10,674		0		2	14	275	15	245	15	7
	Annandale	3,016		0		0	3	70	4	64	2	0
	Anoka	17,726		0		15	27	813	139	628	46	8
	Appleton	2,889		0		0	1	48	5	43	0	0
	Apple Valley	50,189		0		14	42	1,541	179	1,315	47	11
	Austin	23,626		0		17	49	1,076	146	870	60	1
	Avon	1,277		0		1	1	20	3	17	0	0
	Baxter	7,449		0		1	8	324	20	293	11	1
	Bayport	3,271		0		1	0	46	9	35	2	1
	Becker	3,894		0		0	1	9	2	7	0	0
	Belle Plaine	4,576		0		0	3	106	22	83	1	0
	Bemidji	13,385		0		6	42	1,095	125	916	54	5
	Benson	3,210		0		0	2	87	19	58	10	0
	Big Lake	8,863		0		0	9	380	39	334	7	1
	Blackduck	760		0		0	0	8	0	8	0	0
	Blaine	54,445		2		15	74	2,404	256	2,057	91	20
	Blooming Prairie	1,975		0		0	1	31	6	18	7	0
	Bloomington	81,706		5		59	77	2,892	331	2,398	163	8
	Blue Earth	3,475		0		0	4	103	15	87	1	0
	Brainerd	13,775		0		7	51	715	115	555	45	15
	Breckenridge	3,396		1		0	2	50	3	43	4	0
	Brooklyn Center	27,735		1		87	64	1,997	203	1,563	231	12
	Brooklyn Park	69,008		2		155	168	3,258	612	2,320	326	18
	Browns Valley	635		0		0	0	2	0	2	0	0

[1] The FBI does not publish arson data unless it receives data from either the agency or the state for all 12 months of the calendar year.

[7] The data collection methodology for the offense of forcible rape used by the Illinois (with the exception of Rockford, Illinois) and the Minnesota state UCR Programs does not comply with national UCR Program guidelines. Consequently, their figures for forcible rape and violent crime (of which forcible rape is a part) are not published in this table.

Table 8. Offenses Known to Law Enforcement, by State and City, 2006 (*Contd.*)

(Number.)

State	City	Population	Violent crime	Murder and non-negligent manslaughter	Forcible rape	Robbery	Aggravated assault	Property crime	Burglary	Larceny-theft	Motor vehicle theft	Arson[1]
	Brownton	797		0		0	0	4	1	3	0	0
	Buffalo	13,379		0		0	20	393	40	343	10	1
	Burnsville	59,554		1		35	62	2,164	297	1,742	125	16
	Caledonia	2,959		0		0	5	59	5	49	5	
	Cambridge	7,246		0		1	9	326	40	273	13	4
	Cannon Falls	3,940		0		0	3	234	39	181	14	0
	Centennial Lakes	11,275		0		0	8	199	37	154	8	0
	Champlin	23,458		0		5	10	589	83	495	11	3
	Chaska	22,973		1		1	12	428	45	375	8	3
	Chisholm	4,732		0		0	8	155	27	121	7	0
	Cloquet	11,553		1		2	18	408	51	339	18	4
	Cold Spring	3,670		0		0	4	80	16	64	0	0
	Columbia Heights	18,231		1		45	54	978	229	679	70	14
	Coon Rapids	62,834		1		26	76	3,152	306	2,706	140	22
	Corcoran	5,721		0		0	3	63	9	46	8	0
	Cottage Grove	32,771		0		8	25	766	135	588	43	7
	Crookston	7,982		0		1	8	27	9	8	10	2
	Crosby	2,237		0		0	6	130	13	113	4	0
	Crystal	21,790		0		21	32	674	106	515	53	5
	Dawson	1,458		0		0	1	23	12	11	0	0
	Dayton	4,653		0		0	5	49	4	14	31	0
	Deephaven-Woodland	4,211		0		0	1	41	12	27	2	2
	Detroit Lakes	7,967		0		3	15	385	22	344	19	3
	Dilworth	3,475		0		0	5	30	3	27	0	0
	Duluth	85,463		1		116	224	4,057	630	3,214	213	12
	Eagan	64,090		0		27	28	1,677	261	1,358	58	16
	Eagle Lake	2,042		0		0	0	27	6	20	1	0
	East Grand Forks	7,786		0		1	13	261	43	204	14	0
	Eden Prairie	61,054		0		20	37	1,239	146	1,058	35	12
	Edina	45,872		0		20	13	1,017	170	828	19	7
	Elk River	21,472		1		3	11	841	141	669	31	8
	Elmore	701		0		0	0	7	4	2	1	0
	Ely	3,657		0		0	1	63	8	53	2	0
	Eveleth	3,685		0		0	8	123	26	92	5	0
	Fairmont	10,575		0		1	10	387	77	303	7	1
	Falcon Heights	5,506		0		0	0	155	33	116	6	0
	Faribault	22,194		0		6	47	991	206	738	47	10
	Farmington	17,859		1		0	5	254	53	188	13	1
	Fergus Falls	13,814		0		3	27	407	84	303	20	3
	Floodwood	506		0		0	0	8	0	6	2	0
	Forest Lake	17,469		0		4	3	543	55	432	56	0
	Fridley	26,692		2		32	38	1,423	164	1,095	164	5
	Gilbert	1,784		0		0	1	40	6	27	7	0
	Glencoe	5,590		0		0	3	146	16	123	7	0
	Glenwood	2,581		0		0	2	20	2	16	2	1
	Golden Valley	20,137		0		22	22	601	99	459	43	1
	Goodview	3,361		0		0	2	106	14	88	4	0
	Grand Rapids	8,332		0		3	13	327	39	285	3	0
	Granite Falls	3,008		0		0	5	28	7	18	3	0
	Hastings	21,050		0		1	15	513	56	435	22	6
	Hermantown	8,920		0		1	3	302	27	266	9	1
	Hibbing	16,619		0		1	15	116	38	68	10	0
	Hilltop	765		0		8	8	91	14	67	10	2
	Hokah	599		0		0	0	6	2	3	1	0
	Hopkins	16,937		0		19	30	444	73	326	45	2
	Houston	1,008		0		0	2	14	2	10	2	0
	Hutchinson	13,814		0		2	22	438	74	347	17	7
	International Falls	6,374		0		1	8	262	38	200	24	2
	Inver Grove Heights	33,404		0		12	29	791	100	611	80	23
	Jackson	3,477		0		1	8	70	10	59	1	0
	Janesville	2,162		0		0	0	21	7	12	2	0
	Jordan	5,154		0		0	1	214	19	193	2	3
	Kimball	692		0		0	3	23	4	17	2	0
	La Crescent	5,129		0		0	3	82	2	76	4	0
	Lake City	5,317		0		0	1	121	5	110	6	0

[1] The FBI does not publish arson data unless it receives data from either the agency or the state for all 12 months of the calendar year.

Table 8. Offenses Known to Law Enforcement, by State and City, 2006 (*Contd.*)

(Number.)

State	City	Popula-tion	Violent crime	Murder and non-negligent man-slaughter[1]	Forcible rape	Robbery	Aggra-vated assault	Property crime	Burglary	Larceny-theft	Motor vehicle theft	Arson[1]
	Lake Crystal	2,533		0		0	0	41	14	27	0	0
	Lakefield	1,709		0		0	0	13	4	9	0	1
	Lakes Area	7,052		1		0	10	190	32	147	11	2
	Lakeville	51,828		0		8	29	1,104	225	847	32	7
	Lauderdale	2,230		0		2	1	67	10	52	5	0
	Lester Prairie	1,612		0		0	1	30	4	23	3	0
	Lino Lakes	19,554		0		1	5	282	35	227	20	1
	Litchfield	6,702		0		0	6	170	28	131	11	3
	Little Falls	8,193		0		0	6	293	26	253	14	0
	Long Prairie	2,964		0		0	0	82	8	74	0	0
	Mankato	35,210		0		28	63	1,874	332	1,467	75	2
	Maple Grove	60,155		0		20	22	1,507	312	1,151	44	11
	Maplewood	35,319		1		24	63	2,492	353	1,931	208	20
	Marshall	12,373		0		0	21	395	55	330	10	1
	Medina	4,775		0		1	5	102	23	74	5	0
	Melrose	3,166		0		0	0	33	2	31	0	0
	Minneapolis	375,302		57		3,028	2,836	22,561	5,826	13,110	3,625	232
	Minnetonka	50,379		0		8	14	952	148	769	35	14
	Minnetrista	7,874		0		0	4	85	19	64	2	0
	Montevideo	5,401		0		0	6	180	27	145	8	1
	Montgomery	3,097		0		0	4	135	25	107	3	1
	Moorhead	34,309		0		8	39	875	114	702	59	6
	Mora	3,472		0		1	8	222	33	178	11	2
	Morris	5,125		2		0	8	100	9	90	1	0
	Mound	9,479		0		0	5	219	40	174	5	0
	Mounds View	12,187		0		8	26	531	88	394	49	8
	New Brighton	20,877		0		12	18	552	91	412	49	3
	New Hope	20,432		0		20	29	848	110	687	51	4
	Newport	3,678		0		1	5	165	22	124	19	1
	New Prague	6,482		0		1	9	162	33	128	1	0
	New Ulm	13,710		0		0	4	329	60	261	8	1
	North Branch	10,302		0		2	10	380	36	332	12	0
	Northfield	18,796		0		2	10	632	133	482	17	1
	North Mankato	12,159		0		1	3	245	6	228	11	8
	North St. Paul	11,431		0		3	10	431	36	365	30	3
	Oakdale	27,572		0		16	37	1,148	114	953	81	13
	Oak Park Heights	4,092		0		2	4	294	20	258	16	0
	Olivia	2,521		0		1	2	70	16	50	4	
	Orono	11,896		0		0	2	191	35	153	3	0
	Owatonna	24,294		0		4	19	664	135	499	30	10
	Park Rapids	3,468		0		1	9	323	49	234	40	3
	Paynesville	2,258		0		0	4	97	26	70	1	1
	Plymouth	70,167		0		19	26	1,396	265	1,071	60	18
	Princeton	4,725		0		1	7	161	10	142	9	0
	Prior Lake	22,316		0		4	23	469	104	341	24	5
	Proctor	2,798		0		0	3	124	7	115	2	1
	Ramsey	22,222		0		2	13	778	69	672	37	6
	Red Wing	15,905		0		5	27	688	132	506	50	5
	Redwood Falls	5,307		0		1	12	242	43	195	4	1
	Richfield	33,721		1		61	61	1,210	234	886	90	10
	Robbinsdale	13,420		0		17	18	516	88	377	51	1
	Rochester	95,585		2		81	152	2,525	486	1,892	147	55
	Roseau	2,833		0		0	1	69	10	59	0	1
	Rosemount	19,440		0		1	7	447	79	351	17	5
	Roseville	32,293		0		21	28	1,520	201	1,216	103	6
	Sartell	12,753		0		0	4	188	29	156	3	0
	Sauk Centre	3,941		0		0	5	235	32	202	1	0
	Sauk Rapids	11,600		0		2	4	149	18	110	21	0
	Savage	26,759		0		2	25	752	136	592	24	7
	Shakopee	31,442		0		5	46	1,124	187	889	48	4
	Silver Lake	789		0		0	1	11	5	6	0	0
	Slayton	1,966		0		0	3	29	7	21	1	0
	South Lake Minnetonka	12,152		0		0	5	268	44	213	11	3
	South St. Paul	19,491		1		6	17	710	120	520	70	7
	Spring Grove	1,290		0		0	0	20	1	17	2	0

[1] The FBI does not publish arson data unless it receives data from either the agency or the state for all 12 months of the calendar year.

Table 8. Offenses Known to Law Enforcement, by State and City, 2006 (*Contd.*)

(Number.)

State	City	Population	Violent crime	Murder and non-negligent man-slaughter	Forcible rape	Robbery	Aggra-vated assault	Property crime	Burglary	Larceny-theft	Motor vehicle theft	Arson[1]
	Spring Lake Park	6,744		0		3	22	440	60	333	47	3
	St. Anthony	7,611		0		6	2	319	46	254	19	4
	Staples	3,142		0		0	3	92	12	76	4	0
	St. Charles	3,550		0		0	2	36	4	28	4	0
	St. Cloud	66,232		0		54	153	3,062	377	2,555	130	18
	Stewart	551		0		0	0	2	1	1	0	0
	St. Francis	7,148		0		0	6	170	21	139	10	0
	Stillwater	17,494		0		3	6	455	62	376	17	8
	St. James	4,467		0		1	4	147	13	132	2	2
	St. Louis Park	43,585		0		31	44	1,337	192	1,057	88	4
	St. Paul	276,989		17		849	1,403	12,103	3,349	6,616	2,138	182
	St. Paul Park	5,228		0		0	4	235	54	158	23	0
	St. Peter	10,599		0		1	12	336	59	268	9	3
	Thief River Falls	8,433		0		0	9	236	21	201	14	0
	Two Harbors	3,557		0		0	3	59	16	40	3	1
	Virginia	8,724		0		7	40	494	100	370	24	3
	Wabasha	2,570		0		0	4	78	4	74	0	0
	Waite Park	6,878		0		3	5	574	32	530	12	3
	Warroad	1,710		0		0	0	73	5	65	3	1
	Waseca	9,508		0		3	18	274	29	233	12	3
	Wayzata	3,967		0		1	0	185	28	147	10	0
	Wells	2,502		0		0	0	18	4	13	1	1
	West Hennepin	5,647		0		0	2	107	36	67	4	0
	West St. Paul	19,082		0		23	28	1,095	112	925	58	2
	Wheaton	1,498		0		0	1	36	7	29	0	0
	White Bear Lake	23,892		0		8	39	802	178	561	63	6
	Willmar	18,305		0		8	35	737	111	597	29	9
	Windom	4,446		0		0	12	115	28	82	5	0
	Winnebago	1,428		0		0	2	35	11	21	3	0
	Winona	26,765		1		4	16	582	100	462	20	6
	Winsted	2,383		0		0	5	41	8	27	6	1
	Woodbury	52,830		0		10	10	1,142	158	937	47	2
	Worthington	11,166		0		9	23	258	91	155	12	0
	Wyoming	3,846		0		0	4	107	16	88	3	0
	Zumbrota	2,986		0		1	1	80	6	70	4	0
MISSISSIPPI	Aberdeen	6,205	24	1	5	4	14	150	33	110	7	0
	Amory[8]	7,388	8	0	1	3	4	311	59	242	10	2
	Batesville	7,680	16	1	0	11	4	429	67	335	27	0
	Bay St. Louis	8,287	22	0	4	11	7	450	103	319	28	2
	Belzoni	2,532	0	0	0	0	0	0	0	0	0	0
	Booneville	8,554	9	0	0	4	5	193	60	132	1	0
	Brandon	19,320	5	0	2	1	2	200	38	146	16	4
	Brookhaven	9,871	18	2	0	7	9	270	29	231	10	0
	Bruce	2,025	1	0	0	0	1	0	0	0	0	0
	Byhalia	713	6	0	0	2	4	89	22	52	15	0
	Canton	12,462	59	1	11	15	32	417	226	183	8	0
	Charleston	2,047	23	0	1	3	19	93	31	60	2	2
	Cleveland	12,772	28	1	0	6	21	746	112	617	17	1
	Collins	2,751	12	1	0	9	2	149	37	101	11	0
	Columbia	6,385	8	1	5	2	0	1	0	0	1	0
	Columbus	24,337	61	4	4	30	23	1,061	179	841	41	2
	Corinth	14,205	64	1	11	23	29	1,011	246	740	25	1
	Edwards	1,300	6	0	0	0	6	10	2	8	0	0
	Fulton	4,087	2	0	1	0	1	79	15	61	3	1
	Gloster	1,056	10	0	0	2	8	8	7	1	0	0
	Greenville[8]	38,584	206	5	16	70	115	2,377	928	1,338	111	74
	Greenwood	17,281	118	5	5	43	65	1,038	339	611	88	0
	Grenada	14,516	90	3	5	29	53	634	165	426	43	0
	Gulfport	72,202	280	12	25	150	93	5,216	1,430	3,372	414	26
	Hattiesburg	47,006	226	10	18	125	73	2,777	816	1,694	267	20
	Heidelberg	807	1	1	0	0	0	25	3	15	7	0
	Holly Springs	7,985	68	1	3	17	47	252	47	166	39	1
	Horn Lake	22,071	34	0	1	21	12	1,175	169	905	101	1
	Indianola	11,280	86	0	16	14	56	618	188	409	21	6

[1] The FBI does not publish arson data unless it receives data from either the agency or the state for all 12 months of the calendar year.
[8] Because of changes in the state/local agency's reporting practices, figures are not comparable to previous years' data.

Table 8. Offenses Known to Law Enforcement, by State and City, 2006 (Contd.)

(Number.)

State	City	Population	Violent crime	Murder and non-negligent man-slaughter	Forcible rape	Robbery	Aggra-vated assault	Property crime	Burglary	Larceny-theft	Motor vehicle theft	Arson[1]
	Iuka	2,976	13	0	2	1	10	77	22	49	6	0
	Jackson	177,334	1,736	40	160	1,022	514	13,208	3,817	7,534	1,857	65
	Kosciusko	7,308	21	1	1	7	12	226	106	120	0	0
	Laurel[8]	18,232	183	4	19	121	39	1,532	508	962	62	3
	Leakesville	1,003	0	0	0	0	0	0	0	0	0	0
	Leland	5,138	23	1	0	3	19	203	72	129	2	1
	Lexington	1,934	9	1	0	1	7	17	10	7	0	0
	Long Beach	17,221	7	1	0	3	3	315	28	271	16	0
	Louisville	6,772	8	0	0	2	6	114	58	56	0	0
	Lucedale	2,880	7	2	0	1	4	91	19	72	0	0
	Madison	16,677	7	0	1	4	2	211	10	195	6	0
	Magee	4,278	5	1	1	2	1	115	27	76	12	0
	Magnolia	2,071	3	0	0	0	3	42	17	21	4	0
	McComb	13,196	50	0	2	28	20	844	178	611	55	0
	Meridian	38,466	201	2	34	70	95	1,910	776	1,017	117	12
	Morton	3,429	5	0	0	4	1	43	26	11	6	1
	Moss Point	15,070	105	5	12	48	40	1,350	491	624	235	3
	Natchez	16,905	47	2	8	12	25	938	173	755	10	0
	New Albany	7,980	34	0	1	5	28	59	24	28	7	3
	Newton	3,687	13	1	2	2	8	79	39	36	4	0
	Olive Branch	27,863	96	1	17	31	47	2,025	342	1,560	123	4
	Oxford	13,569	35	0	3	4	28	399	85	290	24	0
	Pascagoula	25,082	116	2	26	74	14	2,236	798	1,113	325	1
	Pass Christian	6,826	14	0	1	4	9	252	70	168	14	2
	Pearl	23,028	102	0	45	19	38	864	247	544	73	3
	Pelahatchie	1,485	0	0	0	0	0	0	0	0	0	0
	Petal	10,052	13	0	3	6	4	155	68	75	12	0
	Philadelphia	7,590	45	0	7	26	12	355	97	237	21	0
	Picayune	10,791	40	0	7	9	24	498	74	384	40	5
	Port Gibson	1,759	4	1	2	1	0	22	10	11	1	0
	Richland	7,026	21	0	12	1	8	328	103	213	12	0
	Ridgeland	21,159	55	1	0	21	33	761	65	655	41	1
	Ripley	5,613	11	0	0	0	11	92	32	51	9	0
	Roxie	562	0	0	0	0	0	0	0	0	0	0
	Southaven	38,700	93	1	10	39	43	1,682	239	1,288	155	1
	Starkville	22,051	72	0	9	26	37	620	182	420	18	0
	Summit	1,597	0	0	0	0	0	82	23	57	2	0
	Tupelo	35,544	102	1	21	41	39	1,692	332	1,247	113	2
	Vicksburg	25,659	234	2	32	37	163	1,895	445	1,344	106	20
	West Point	11,540	31	0	4	9	18	408	153	253	2	1
	Winona	4,916	7	0	1	4	2	22	9	11	2	0
MISSOURI	Adrian	1,852	2	0	1	1	0	12	3	7	2	1
	Advance	1,225	2	1	0	0	1	11	2	9	0	0
	Alma	381	0	0	0	0	0	0	0	0	0	0
	Alton	653	2	0	1	0	1	2	1	1	0	1
	Anderson	1,916	2	0	0	0	2	82	7	69	6	1
	Annapolis	300	0	0	0	0	0	0	0	0	0	0
	Appleton City	1,328	4	0	0	0	4	33	1	32	0	0
	Arbyrd	511	0	0	0	0	0	3	1	2	0	0
	Archie	965	0	0	0	0	0	26	4	19	3	0
	Arnold	20,562	37	0	3	6	28	1,391	82	1,277	32	1
	Ash Grove	1,502	2	0	0	0	2	13	3	10	0	1
	Ashland	2,191	6	0	0	0	6	45	11	30	4	0
	Aurora	7,360	37	1	1	1	34	647	132	476	39	1
	Auxvasse	1,003	5	0	0	1	4	23	6	15	2	0
	Ava	3,101	21	0	0	2	19	116	27	78	11	3
	Ballwin	30,704	14	0	3	4	7	288	46	232	10	0
	Bates City	242	0	0	0	0	0	24	4	19	1	0
	Battlefield	3,638	3	0	1	0	2	84	29	51	4	0
	Bella Villa	660	2	0	0	0	2	8	2	4	2	0
	Belle	1,358	0	0	0	0	0	6	0	4	2	1
	Bellefontaine Neighbors[5]	10,694		0	3		32	433	118	235	80	4

[1] The FBI does not publish arson data unless it receives data from either the agency or the state for all 12 months of the calendar year.

[5] It was determined that the agency did not follow national Uniform Crime Reporting (UCR) Program guidelines for reporting an offense. Consequently, this figure is not included in this table.

[8] Because of changes in the state/local agency's reporting practices, figures are not comparable to previous years' data.

Table 8. Offenses Known to Law Enforcement, by State and City, 2006 (*Contd.*)

(Number.)

State	City	Popula-tion	Violent crime	Murder and non-negligent man-slaughter	Forcible rape	Robbery	Aggra-vated assault	Property crime	Burglary	Larceny-theft	Motor vehicle theft	Arson[1]
	Bellerive	261	0	0	0	0	0	4	0	3	1	0
	Bellflower	417	0	0	0	0	0	2	2	0	0	0
	Bel-Nor	1,537	1	0	0	1	0	43	13	24	6	2
	Bel-Ridge	2,992	38	0	4	9	25	155	44	83	28	2
	Belton	24,316	57	0	8	8	41	651	69	535	47	4
	Berkeley	9,701	106	1	6	27	72	627	200	304	123	6
	Bernie	1,814	2	0	0	0	2	19	13	3	3	0
	Bethany	3,082	11	0	1	0	10	78	19	59	0	0
	Beverly Hills	579	0	0	0	0	0	4	4	0	0	0
	Billings	1,150	2	0	0	0	2	36	3	28	5	0
	Birch Tree	624	6	0	0	0	6	13	11	1	1	0
	Blackburn	280	0	0	0	0	0	0	0	0	0	0
	Bland	575	0	0	0	0	0	5	5	0	0	0
	Bloomfield	1,902	9	0	0	0	9	30	9	21	0	0
	Blue Springs	53,487	98	1	11	21	65	1,754	242	1,377	135	12
	Bolivar	10,253	66	0	8	4	54	422	74	332	16	5
	Bonne Terre	6,568	9	0	2	2	5	65	13	44	8	0
	Boonville	8,732	14	0	1	4	9	229	30	194	5	0
	Bourbon	1,418	14	0	1	0	13	34	2	30	2	0
	Bowling Green	5,223	6	0	0	0	6	118	27	88	3	1
	Branson	7,061	150	1	9	10	130	1,088	127	929	32	0
	Branson West	489	1	0	0	0	1	24	1	22	1	0
	Braymer	969	1	0	0	0	1	12	4	8	0	0
	Breckenridge Hills	4,642	20	1	2	4	13	246	44	166	36	3
	Brentwood	7,419	16	1	7	4	4	313	26	270	17	0
	Bridgeton	15,371	95	0	7	17	71	994	120	779	95	5
	Brookfield	4,539	5	0	1	1	3	116	23	85	8	0
	Bucklin	500	1	0	0	0	1	4	2	1	1	2
	Buckner	2,744	12	0	0	0	12	135	21	102	12	1
	Buffalo	3,028	11	0	0	1	10	173	31	138	4	2
	Bunker	440	0	0	0	0	0	0	0	0	0	0
	Butler	4,280	0	0	0	0	0	122	31	87	4	0
	Butterfield Village	419	0	0	0	0	0	0	0	0	0	0
	Byrnes Mill	2,766	1	0	0	0	1	10	4	5	1	0
	Cabool	2,156	6	1	1	1	3	41	12	25	4	1
	California	4,167	33	0	3	1	29	89	23	66	0	2
	Calverton Park	1,313	2	0	0	0	2	10	4	4	2	0
	Camden Point	551	0	0	0	0	0	0	0	0	0	0
	Camdenton	3,083	18	0	1	0	17	172	26	144	2	2
	Cameron	9,208	11	0	1	0	10	178	21	149	8	4
	Campbell	1,886	0	0	0	0	0	38	1	33	4	0
	Canton	2,520	21	0	0	0	21	49	14	34	1	2
	Cape Girardeau	36,469	229	1	9	33	186	1,983	279	1,649	55	10
	Cardwell	756	2	0	0	1	1	14	2	9	3	0
	Carl Junction	6,530	9	0	0	0	9	149	37	106	6	0
	Carterville	1,930	5	0	2	0	3	48	11	33	4	1
	Carthage	13,192	31	0	3	6	22	401	74	298	29	4
	Caruthersville	6,497	25	0	1	8	16	309	83	214	12	1
	Cassville	3,118	6	0	0	0	6	128	26	98	4	1
	Center	642	3	0	0	0	3	6	2	2	2	0
	Centralia[8]	3,684	23	0	2	0	21	99	13	80	6	1
	Chaffee	3,028	5	0	0	1	4	68	10	55	3	0
	Charlack	1,390	3	0	1	0	2	70	4	61	5	0
	Charleston	5,166	22	1	0	1	20	125	29	86	10	0
	Chesterfield	47,364	33	0	1	5	27	769	89	667	13	3
	Chillicothe	8,749	15	1	3	1	10	307	45	246	16	3
	Clarkson Valley	2,621	2	0	0	0	2	38	4	33	1	0
	Clarkton	1,289	5	0	2	0	3	28	10	17	1	0
	Claycomo	1,289	7	0	2	1	4	52	7	39	6	0
	Clayton	16,178	20	1	0	4	15	412	70	308	34	5
	Cleveland	679	1	0	0	0	1	19	4	12	3	0
	Clever	1,251	2	0	0	0	2	3	2	1	0	0

[1] The FBI does not publish arson data unless it receives data from either the agency or the state for all 12 months of the calendar year.
[8] Because of changes in the state/local agency's reporting practices, figures are not comparable to previous years' data.

Table 8. Offenses Known to Law Enforcement, by State and City, 2006 (*Contd.*)

(Number.)

State	City	Popula-tion	Violent crime	Murder and non-negligent man-slaughter	Forcible rape	Robbery	Aggra-vated assault	Property crime	Burglary	Larceny-theft	Motor vehicle theft	Arson[1]
	Clinton	9,483	16	0	2	3	11	451	70	353	28	3
	Cole Camp	1,168	1	0	0	0	1	18	11	6	1	0
	Columbia	92,485	460	2	23	113	322	3,105	544	2,335	226	12
	Concordia	2,431	5	0	0	1	4	39	10	27	2	0
	Cool Valley	1,041	10	0	0	2	8	85	15	55	15	0
	Cooter	440	0	0	0	0	0	2	1	1	0	0
	Corder	429	0	0	0	0	0	8	3	5	0	0
	Cottleville	2,350	3	0	0	0	3	36	1	35	0	0
	Country Club Hills	1,328	3	0	1	1	1	50	17	26	7	1
	Country Club Village	1,911	2	0	0	0	2	26	8	16	2	0
	Crane	1,453	1	0	0	0	1	21	4	16	1	1
	Crestwood	11,776	13	0	0	4	9	699	19	665	15	0
	Creve Coeur	17,099	14	0	1	2	11	275	41	217	17	0
	Crocker	1,017	5	0	0	3	2	17	7	10	0	1
	Crystal City	4,541	16	1	1	2	12	109	16	79	14	0
	Cuba	3,472	18	0	5	2	11	322	40	254	28	1
	Dellwood	5,064	29	0	3	8	18	176	82	67	27	0
	Delta	540	0	0	0	0	0	0	0	0	0	0
	Desloge	5,181	14	0	0	5	9	141	16	113	12	1
	De Soto	6,600	91	0	1	2	88	187	15	161	11	0
	Des Peres	8,682	14	0	2	7	5	405	19	375	11	0
	Dexter	7,652	13	0	1	0	12	206	51	143	12	2
	Diamond	852	0	0	0	0	0	2	2	0	0	1
	Dixon	1,559	0	0	0	0	0	65	16	47	2	6
	Doniphan	1,938	6	1	0	0	5	138	44	87	7	1
	Drexel	1,123	2	0	0	0	2	17	3	13	1	1
	Duenweg	1,076	6	0	1	0	5	51	19	30	2	2
	Duquesne	1,704	8	0	2	0	6	23	7	16	0	0
	East Prairie	3,140	20	0	0	1	19	43	4	35	4	0
	Edgerton	550	1	0	0	0	1	7	4	3	0	0
	Edina	1,170	0	0	0	0	0	0	0	0	0	0
	Edmundson	809	13	0	0	1	12	71	4	48	19	0
	Eldon	4,970	35	0	0	1	34	168	23	130	15	4
	El Dorado Springs	3,877	27	0	3	3	21	192	52	130	10	0
	Ellington	1,020	0	0	0	0	0	19	4	13	2	1
	Ellisville	9,421	10	0	0	1	9	128	21	95	12	0
	Eminence	554	1	0	0	0	1	3	1	2	0	0
	Emma	241	0	0	0	0	0	8	4	4	0	0
	Eureka	9,022	10	0	0	0	10	222	19	196	7	2
	Everton	324	0	0	0	0	0	2	2	0	0	0
	Excelsior Springs	11,556	65	0	3	7	55	432	97	314	21	2
	Exeter	742	0	0	0	0	0	3	0	3	0	0
	Fair Grove	1,292	0	0	0	0	0	23	6	17	0	0
	Fair Play	442	4	0	0	0	4	26	5	21	0	1
	Farmington	15,287	65	0	1	4	60	514	56	447	11	4
	Fayette	2,721	4	0	0	0	4	15	5	10	0	0
	Ferrelview	592	5	0	0	0	5	13	5	6	2	0
	Festus	10,985	127	0	2	4	121	240	39	190	11	3
	Flordell Hills	893	11	0	0	3	8	43	25	13	5	1
	Florissant	52,191	63	3	5	36	19	1,049	182	767	100	1
	Fordland	751	0	0	0	0	0	1	0	1	0	0
	Forsyth	1,718	2	0	0	0	2	64	7	54	3	2
	Fredericktown	4,064	17	0	0	0	17	140	24	110	6	4
	Freeman	607	0	0	0	0	0	0	0	0	0	0
	Frontenac	3,543	6	0	0	2	4	55	6	45	4	0
	Fulton	12,189	49	0	4	6	39	493	93	375	25	2
	Gallatin	1,789	8	0	0	0	8	55	6	47	2	0
	Garden City	1,679	1	0	0	0	1	25	2	20	3	0
	Gerald	1,247	4	0	0	0	4	8	6	2	0	2
	Gideon	1,026	0	0	0	0	0	10	5	5	0	0
	Gladstone	27,506	64	0	4	27	33	753	120	540	93	5
	Glasgow	1,214	2	0	0	0	2	12	5	7	0	1
	Glendale	5,636	4	0	0	0	4	31	1	28	2	0
	Goodman	1,242	2	0	0	0	2	24	12	9	3	1
	Gower	1,443	6	0	2	0	4	18	3	14	1	0

[1] The FBI does not publish arson data unless it receives data from either the agency or the state for all 12 months of the calendar year.

Table 8. Offenses Known to Law Enforcement, by State and City, 2006 (*Contd.*)

(Number.)

State	City	Popula-tion	Violent crime	Murder and non-negligent man-slaughter	Forcible rape	Robbery	Aggra-vated assault	Property crime	Burglary	Larceny-theft	Motor vehicle theft	Arson[1]
	Grain Valley	8,707	14	1	3	1	9	199	43	135	21	1
	Granby	2,246	7	0	0	0	7	58	13	41	4	0
	Grandin	238	0	0	0	0	0	0	0	0	0	0
	Grandview[8]	24,728	168	0	14	47	107	1,105	226	696	183	3
	Greendale	713	1	0	0	0	1	8	0	5	3	0
	Greenfield	1,308	10	0	0	1	9	28	11	17	0	0
	Greenwood	4,545	9	0	6	0	3	41	14	26	1	0
	Hallsville	962	1	0	0	0	1	9	1	8	0	0
	Hamilton	1,824	10	0	0	2	8	22	7	15	0	2
	Hannibal	17,778	98	0	12	15	71	1,312	155	1,123	34	7
	Harrisonville	9,862	28	0	2	2	24	730	58	653	19	0
	Hartville	607	0	0	0	0	0	7	4	3	0	0
	Hawk Point	528	0	0	0	0	0	2	1	0	1	0
	Hayti	3,088	11	0	2	1	8	183	31	147	5	1
	Hayti Heights	787	8	0	0	0	8	8	3	5	0	1
	Hazelwood	25,722	159	0	6	34	119	1,028	144	772	112	1
	Henrietta	454	0	0	0	0	0	2	0	2	0	0
	Herculaneum	3,195	1	1	0	0	0	281	10	267	4	0
	Hermann	2,755	21	0	0	0	21	78	9	69	0	0
	Higginsville	4,694	5	0	1	0	4	187	28	152	7	0
	High Hill	228	1	0	0	0	1	5	3	2	0	0
	Highlandville	928	2	0	0	0	2	8	3	3	2	0
	Hillsboro	1,797	5	0	0	1	4	183	7	174	2	1
	Hillsdale[4]	1,431		0	1	7			41		4	2
	Holcomb	702	0	0	0	0	0	1	0	1	0	0
	Holden	2,562	14	0	0	1	13	118	22	91	5	1
	Hollister	3,863	37	0	4	2	31	161	35	116	10	2
	Holt	439	0	0	0	0	0	17	2	15	0	0
	Holts Summit	3,409	13	0	0	3	10	75	20	53	2	2
	Houston	2,020	6	0	0	1	5	43	8	33	2	0
	Humansville	993	0	0	0	0	0	29	21	7	1	0
	Huntsville	1,637	3	0	0	0	3	16	2	14	0	0
	Iberia	678	1	0	0	0	1	6	1	5	0	1
	Independence	111,014	813	2	61	138	612	7,608	1,236	5,538	834	40
	Indian Point	618	0	0	0	0	0	1	0	1	0	0
	Iron Mountain Lake	711	1	0	1	0	0	20	13	7	0	0
	Ironton	1,372	5	0	0	0	5	45	9	35	1	1
	Jackson	13,077	25	0	1	2	22	263	40	207	16	0
	JASCO Metropolitan	2,460	15	0	0	1	14	47	14	30	3	0
	Jasper	1,045	1	0	0	0	1	4	0	1	3	2
	Jefferson City	39,348	324	2	19	40	263	1,567	250	1,241	76	7
	Jennings	15,035	159	0	9	42	108	1,018	325	500	193	4
	Jonesburg	712	3	0	0	0	3	17	3	13	1	0
	Joplin	47,528	419	4	54	95	266	3,887	733	2,877	277	37
	Kahoka	2,209	4	0	1	0	3	36	16	19	1	0
	Kansas City[8]	448,218	6,471	112	321	2,044	3,994	31,100	7,399	18,186	5,515	403
	Kearney	7,453	6	0	0	1	5	114	15	91	8	2
	Kennett	11,109	42	1	2	12	27	700	185	487	28	8
	Keytesville	520	0	0	0	0	0	0	0	0	0	0
	Kimberling City	2,538	6	0	0	1	5	39	4	34	1	0
	Kimmswick	94	5	0	0	0	5	5	4	0	1	0
	Kirksville	17,110	103	2	0	3	98	527	78	437	12	2
	Kirkwood[5]	27,236		0	7	10		726	104	589	33	9
	Knob Noster	2,754	8	0	0	0	8	142	22	114	6	1
	Ladue	8,329	13	0	0	3	10	122	15	101	6	0
	La Grange	956	5	0	0	0	5	4	3	1	0	0
	Lake Lafayette	377	1	0	0	0	1	7	1	5	1	0
	Lake Lotawana	1,935	3	0	1	0	2	31	10	20	1	0
	Lake Ozark	1,929	12	0	2	0	10	90	15	72	3	5
	Lakeshire	1,328	3	0	0	0	3	23	8	14	1	0
	Lake St. Louis	13,378	9	0	1	2	6	233	32	194	7	1

[1] The FBI does not publish arson data unless it receives data from either the agency or the state for all 12 months of the calendar year.
[4] The FBI determined that the agency's data were underreported. Consequently, affected data are not included in this table.
[5] It was determined that the agency did not follow national Uniform Crime Reporting (UCR) Program guidelines for reporting an offense. Consequently, this figure is not included in this table.
[8] Because of changes in the state/local agency's reporting practices, figures are not comparable to previous years' data.

Table 8. Offenses Known to Law Enforcement, by State and City, 2006 (*Contd.*)
(Number.)

State	City	Popula-tion	Violent crime	Murder and non-negligent man-slaughter	Forcible rape	Robbery	Aggra-vated assault	Property crime	Burglary	Larceny-theft	Motor vehicle theft	Arson[1]
	Lake Tapawingo	815	1	0	0	0	1	4	0	4	0	0
	Lake Waukomis	920	0	0	0	0	0	10	0	10	0	0
	Lake Winnebago	1,073	0	0	0	0	0	6	2	4	0	1
	Lamar	4,636	20	0	4	0	16	170	38	128	4	0
	La Monte	1,070	3	0	0	0	3	14	5	8	1	0
	Lanagan	438	1	0	0	0	1	8	3	5	0	0
	La Plata	1,453	1	0	1	0	0	9	1	8	0	0
	Lathrop	2,345	8	0	0	0	8	50	13	33	4	0
	Laurie	708	4	0	0	0	4	52	6	44	2	0
	Lawson	2,424	1	0	0	1	0	31	3	24	4	0
	Leadington	221	0	0	0	0	0	8	1	4	3	0
	Lebanon	13,433	72	0	5	1	66	694	121	542	31	3
	Lee's Summit	80,925	125	2	15	23	85	2,315	314	1,856	145	7
	Leeton	631	0	0	0	0	0	17	2	15	0	0
	Lexington	4,666	21	0	2	1	18	163	46	106	11	0
	Liberal	817	2	0	0	0	2	1	1	0	0	0
	Liberty	29,254	70	0	10	10	50	632	98	492	42	10
	Licking	2,755	4	0	1	1	2	52	7	42	3	0
	Lilbourn	1,246	0	0	0	0	0	0	0	0	0	1
	Lincoln	1,111	3	0	1	0	2	33	17	15	1	0
	Linn	1,434	3	0	1	0	2	12	2	8	2	1
	Linn Creek	297	4	0	0	0	4	9	3	5	1	0
	Lockwood	969	0	0	0	0	0	2	1	1	0	2
	Lone Jack	702	3	0	0	0	3	47	36	9	2	0
	Lowry City	743	11	0	3	0	8	15	10	5	0	0
	Macon	5,468	23	0	0	2	21	179	34	142	3	4
	Malden	4,669	7	0	0	1	6	109	29	78	2	6
	Manchester[5]	19,109	10	0	2	0	8			238		2
	Mansfield	1,362	1	0	0	0	1	23	5	18	0	1
	Maplewood	8,872	34	0	3	15	16	346	40	252	54	3
	Marble Hill	1,523	10	0	2	0	8	45	8	36	1	0
	Marceline	2,423	7	0	0	0	7	13	5	8	0	0
	Marionville	2,177	4	0	0	2	2	129	15	113	1	0
	Marquand	268	0	0	0	0	0	2	2	0	0	0
	Marshall	12,494	29	3	5	1	20	251	51	196	4	3
	Marshfield	6,812	12	0	0	0	12	158	30	122	6	1
	Marston	567	0	0	0	0	0	0	0	0	0	0
	Marthasville	870	0	0	0	0	0	4	3	1	0	0
	Martinsburg	330	0	0	0	0	0	0	0	0	0	0
	Maryland Heights	26,738	32	1	0	7	24	1,023	133	810	80	3
	Maryville	10,644	21	0	2	0	19	376	39	325	12	0
	Matthews	556	1	0	0	0	1	8	1	6	1	0
	Memphis	2,018	2	0	0	0	2	14	1	12	1	1
	Merriam Woods	1,141	0	0	0	0	0	10	6	4	0	1
	Mexico	11,099	12	0	2	6	4	251	50	195	6	3
	Milan	1,863	12	0	0	0	12	31	13	15	3	0
	Miller	798	0	0	0	0	0	17	2	15	0	0
	Miner	1,277	14	0	1	0	13	56	7	46	3	0
	Moberly	14,023	21	1	0	9	11	579	90	471	18	8
	Monett	8,410	19	0	2	6	11	456	90	336	30	5
	Monroe City[8]	2,575	8	0	0	0	8	82	26	54	2	1
	Montgomery City	2,531	16	1	0	0	15	33	2	26	5	2
	Morehouse	967	1	0	0	0	1	7	2	4	1	3
	Mosby	245	2	0	0	1	1	9	2	5	2	0
	Mound City	1,118	1	0	0	0	1	14	3	11	0	0
	Mountain Grove	4,628	12	0	0	3	9	122	26	92	4	0
	Mountain View	2,565	16	0	1	0	15	96	17	74	5	0
	Mount Vernon	4,434	21	0	0	0	21	242	40	190	12	1
	Napoleon	203	0	0	0	0	0	1	1	0	0	0
	Naylor	618	0	0	0	0	0	6	6	0	0	0
	Neosho	11,211	31	0	2	6	23	438	74	344	20	9
	Nevada	8,519	70	0	5	4	61	707	111	550	46	5

[1] The FBI does not publish arson data unless it receives data from either the agency or the state for all 12 months of the calendar year.
[5] It was determined that the agency did not follow national Uniform Crime Reporting (UCR) Program guidelines for reporting an offense. Consequently, this figure is not included in this table.
[8] Because of changes in the state/local agency's reporting practices, figures are not comparable to previous years' data.

Table 8. Offenses Known to Law Enforcement, by State and City, 2006 (*Contd.*)

(Number.)

State	City	Population	Violent crime	Murder and non-negligent man-slaughter	Forcible rape	Robbery	Aggra-vated assault	Property crime	Burglary	Larceny-theft	Motor vehicle theft	Arson[1]
	New Bloomfield	693	0	0	0	0	0	5	1	4	0	2
	Newburg	483	8	0	0	1	7	4	2	1	1	0
	New Florence	783	1	0	0	0	1	27	2	24	1	2
	New Franklin	1,121	6	0	0	0	6	4	0	3	1	0
	New Haven	1,964	16	0	1	0	15	57	11	40	6	0
	New London	999	4	0	0	0	4	10	4	6	0	4
	New Madrid	3,154	1	1	0	0	0	45	9	36	0	0
	New Melle	289	0	0	0	0	0	9	5	4	0	0
	Niangua	488	2	0	0	0	2	1	1	0	0	0
	Nixa	16,041	15	0	0	1	14	249	42	194	13	1
	Norborne	798	0	0	0	0	0	1	0	1	0	0
	North Kansas City	5,427	42	0	7	20	15	513	65	385	63	0
	Northmoor	410	2	0	0	1	1	13	4	5	4	2
	Northwoods[5]	4,467	11	0	1	6	4			48	30	1
	Oak Grove	6,812	8	0	5	0	3	212	33	161	18	0
	Oakland[5]	1,591	1	0	0	0	1		3		1	0
	Oakview Village	389	2	0	0	0	2	3	1	2	0	0
	Odessa	4,876	7	0	2	0	5	112	31	77	4	10
	O'Fallon	70,203	59	0	6	10	43	1,768	178	1,548	42	5
	Old Monroe	285	1	0	0	0	1	1	0	1	0	0
	Olivette	7,509	23	0	1	4	18	205	40	152	13	0
	Olympian Village	682	0	0	0	0	0	2	0	2	0	0
	Oran	1,268	3	0	0	0	3	6	1	5	0	2
	Orrick	873	3	0	0	0	3	18	4	12	2	2
	Osage Beach	4,290	39	0	2	0	37	381	32	334	15	0
	Osceola	824	2	0	0	0	2	5	1	2	2	1
	Overland	16,200	68	1	3	32	32	831	124	654	53	0
	Ozark	15,377	14	1	3	1	9	436	80	324	32	2
	Pacific	7,150	24	0	1	1	22	175	27	138	10	0
	Palmyra	3,468	6	0	1	0	5	40	4	35	1	4
	Park Hills	8,587	6	0	1	1	4	178	20	149	9	1
	Parkville	5,153	5	0	2	3	0	156	13	135	8	0
	Parma	811	2	0	0	1	1	19	6	12	1	2
	Peculiar	3,860	8	0	1	0	7	133	19	111	3	0
	Perry	662	0	0	0	0	0	1	0	1	0	0
	Perryville	7,993	11	1	0	0	10	180	44	132	4	4
	Pevely	4,239	12	0	1	2	9	178	30	137	11	1
	Piedmont	1,989	3	0	0	0	3	35	5	29	1	2
	Pilot Grove	744	5	0	0	0	5	17	2	14	1	0
	Pilot Knob	689	0	0	0	0	0	9	1	8	0	1
	Pineville	874	1	0	0	0	1	3	3	0	0	1
	Platte City	4,943	12	0	1	2	9	105	19	75	11	0
	Platte Woods	465	0	0	0	0	0	27	4	22	1	0
	Plattsburg	2,460	10	0	3	0	7	58	8	48	2	0
	Pleasant Hill	6,796	3	0	1	0	2	156	31	113	12	0
	Pleasant Hope	579	0	0	0	0	0	3	0	3	0	0
	Pleasant Valley	3,470	8	0	2	2	4	65	14	44	7	1
	Poplar Bluff	17,036	87	0	3	21	63	1,265	223	950	92	12
	Portageville	3,093	7	1	0	0	6	20	7	10	3	0
	Potosi	2,729	6	1	0	0	5	46	7	38	1	4
	Purdy	1,154	3	0	1	1	1	48	21	25	2	1
	Puxico	1,158	1	0	0	0	1	8	3	5	0	0
	Randolph	49	0	0	0	0	0	4	2	2	0	0
	Raymore	15,644	11	0	2	1	8	398	37	350	11	1
	Raytown	29,134	74	0	7	30	37	950	245	602	103	9
	Republic	10,715	44	0	1	2	41	307	72	221	14	1
	Rich Hill	1,511	7	0	0	0	7	52	26	23	3	0
	Richland	1,789	7	0	1	0	6	35	4	29	2	3
	Richmond	6,119	17	0	1	2	14	208	45	150	13	3
	Richmond Heights	9,377	28	0	2	6	20	585	43	501	41	0
	Risco	367	0	0	0	0	0	0	0	0	0	0
	Riverside	2,986	9	0	4	4	1	191	22	147	22	0
	Riverview	3,017	40	0	0	2	38	123	35	62	26	0

[1] The FBI does not publish arson data unless it receives data from either the agency or the state for all 12 months of the calendar year.
[5] It was determined that the agency did not follow national Uniform Crime Reporting (UCR) Program guidelines for reporting an offense. Consequently, this figure is not included in this table.

Table 8. Offenses Known to Law Enforcement, by State and City, 2006 (*Contd.*)

(Number.)

State	City	Population	Violent crime	Murder and non-negligent manslaughter	Forcible rape	Robbery	Aggravated assault	Property crime	Burglary	Larceny-theft	Motor vehicle theft	Arson[1]
	Rockaway Beach	592	5	0	0	0	5	8	5	2	1	0
	Rock Hill	4,734	10	0	0	4	6	94	17	65	12	0
	Rock Port	1,353	1	0	0	0	1	4	2	2	0	0
	Rogersville	2,255	14	0	0	0	14	66	12	51	3	1
	Rolla	17,847	79	0	7	14	58	944	158	740	46	4
	Salem	4,824	31	0	0	0	31	137	25	105	7	5
	Sarcoxie	1,350	1	0	0	0	1	29	8	18	3	0
	Savannah	4,961	10	0	0	0	10	61	18	41	2	1
	Scott City	4,618	2	0	0	0	2	8	4	3	1	0
	Sedalia	20,579	180	0	6	13	161	1,378	233	1,107	38	15
	Seligman	907	0	0	0	0	0	0	0	0	0	0
	Senath	1,653	0	0	0	0	0	2	0	2	0	1
	Seneca	2,253	0	0	0	0	0	79	16	55	8	1
	Seymour	1,974	1	0	1	0	0	49	11	37	1	0
	Shelbina	1,900	7	0	1	0	6	41	27	12	2	1
	Shrewsbury	6,440	6	0	0	3	3	99	8	82	9	2
	Sikeston	17,306	228	5	7	32	184	803	188	553	62	7
	Silex	234	3	0	0	0	3	0	0	0	0	1
	Slater	1,968	11	0	0	0	11	60	1	55	4	0
	Smithville	7,170	14	0	3	2	9	100	14	83	3	2
	Southwest City	926	10	0	4	0	6	41	15	25	1	1
	Sparta	1,235	2	0	1	0	1	4	1	3	0	0
	Springfield	151,397	1,001	6	82	252	661	13,161	1,972	10,358	831	72
	St. Ann	13,188	95	0	5	11	79	761	62	657	42	1
	St. Charles	62,759	158	1	14	44	99	1,981	280	1,568	133	12
	St. Clair	4,437	32	1	0	2	29	308	45	256	7	2
	Steele	2,185	4	0	1	1	2	55	16	38	1	1
	Steelville	1,465	15	0	0	1	14	51	14	32	5	0
	Ste. Genevieve	4,487	3	1	0	1	1	91	37	51	3	5
	St. George	1,251	3	0	0	0	3	29	2	19	8	0
	St. James	4,071	33	0	0	0	33	257	68	168	21	1
	St. John	6,606	24	1	4	8	11	274	30	217	27	3
	St. Joseph[8]	73,192	213	0	11	67	135	3,863	761	2,782	320	46
	St. Louis	346,879	8,605	129	337	3,147	4,992	40,751	8,510	23,596	8,645	431
	St. Marys	391	3	0	1	0	2	11	1	7	3	0
	Stover	1,029	17	0	0	0	17	37	14	22	1	0
	St. Peters	54,605	102	0	14	11	77	1,306	129	1,124	53	9
	Sturgeon	920	5	0	0	0	5	15	3	10	2	0
	Sugar Creek	3,624	20	0	1	4	15	159	40	98	21	3
	Sullivan	6,661	14	0	1	1	12	222	47	167	8	1
	Summersville	559	2	0	0	0	2	28	13	13	2	0
	Sunset Hills	8,435	23	0	1	4	18	275	28	218	29	0
	Sweet Springs	1,562	4	0	0	0	4	39	11	28	0	0
	Tarkio	1,880	2	0	0	1	1	7	0	6	1	0
	Thayer	2,187	1	0	0	1	0	0	0	0	0	0
	Theodosia	255	0	0	0	0	0	5	4	1	0	0
	Tipton	3,165	2	0	1	0	1	14	3	10	1	0
	Town and Country	10,886	14	0	1	4	9	130	16	112	2	3
	Tracy	213	0	0	0	0	0	20	1	19	0	0
	Trenton	6,166	22	1	2	2	17	204	44	149	11	8
	Trimble	489	0	0	0	0	0	3	0	2	1	0
	Troy	9,934	37	1	1	0	35	461	51	387	23	0
	Truesdale	493	0	0	0	0	0	11	2	6	3	0
	Union	8,962	21	0	0	0	21	424	46	372	6	0
	Unionville	1,995	1	0	0	0	1	6	4	2	0	1
	University City[5]	37,442		3	8		192	1,923	397	1,289	237	10
	Uplands Park	452	1	0	0	0	1	10	3	5	2	0
	Urbana	429	2	0	0	0	2	11	3	7	1	0
	Van Buren	823	3	0	0	0	3	39	11	25	3	0
	Vandalia	4,097	13	0	1	0	12	57	16	39	2	0
	Velda City	1,553	3	0	0	0	3	29	17	7	5	0
	Verona	725	0	0	0	0	0	5	4	1	0	0
	Versailles	2,681	3	0	0	0	3	121	11	105	5	0

[1] The FBI does not publish arson data unless it receives data from either the agency or the state for all 12 months of the calendar year.

[5] It was determined that the agency did not follow national Uniform Crime Reporting (UCR) Program guidelines for reporting an offense. Consequently, this figure is not included in this table.

[8] Because of changes in the state/local agency's reporting practices, figures are not comparable to previous years' data.

Table 8. Offenses Known to Law Enforcement, by State and City, 2006 (*Contd.*)

(Number.)

State	City	Popula-tion	Violent crime	Murder and non-negligent man-slaughter	Forcible rape	Robbery	Aggra-vated assault	Property crime	Burglary	Larceny-theft	Motor vehicle theft	Arson[1]
	Viburnum	817	1	0	0	0	1	8	3	5	0	0
	Vienna	640	2	0	0	0	2	18	8	10	0	0
	Vinita Park	1,850	10	0	0	3	7	63	8	45	10	0
	Walnut Grove	631	3	0	0	1	2	20	2	17	1	0
	Wardell	264	0	0	0	0	0	8	3	5	0	0
	Warrensburg	17,899	42	2	3	1	36	588	151	417	20	7
	Warrenton	6,660	18	0	0	0	18	318	33	279	6	2
	Warsaw	2,285	30	0	0	1	29	67	19	44	4	1
	Warson Woods	1,920	3	0	0	0	3	27	5	22	0	0
	Washburn	471	0	0	0	0	0	2	0	2	0	0
	Washington	14,239	31	0	0	3	28	298	37	245	16	2
	Waverly	813	2	0	0	0	2	17	10	5	2	1
	Waynesville	3,537	33	0	0	3	30	122	25	92	5	1
	Weatherby Lake	1,884	6	0	0	0	6	21	5	15	1	0
	Webb City	10,843	9	1	0	1	7	353	64	256	33	4
	Webster Groves	23,063	21	0	0	7	14	350	74	255	21	1
	Wellington	789	1	0	0	0	1	3	1	2	0	0
	Wellsville	1,408	3	0	0	0	3	13	6	7	0	0
	Wentzville	18,120	27	0	9	4	14	595	51	526	18	2
	Weston	1,656	4	0	1	0	3	29	10	14	5	0
	West Plains	11,431	57	1	2	7	47	822	138	645	39	9
	Westwood	298	0	0	0	0	0	1	0	1	0	0
	Willard	3,354	17	0	1	0	16	42	13	27	2	0
	Willow Springs	2,131	6	0	0	0	6	44	14	29	1	0
	Windsor	3,289	5	0	1	0	4	73	9	60	4	2
	Winfield	856	3	0	0	0	3	16	0	14	2	0
	Winona	1,327	5	0	0	0	5	14	11	1	2	1
	Wood Heights	782	0	0	0	0	0	4	2	2	0	0
	Woodson Terrace	4,141	17	2	2	3	10	147	23	86	38	1
	Wright City	2,458	9	0	1	2	6	86	10	70	6	0
MONTANA	Baker	1,644	4	0	0	0	4	18	4	12	2	0
	Belgrade	7,100	12	0	5	0	7	226	21	186	19	7
	Billings	99,667	209	2	28	44	135	4,304	465	3,518	321	33
	Boulder	1,450	5	0	4	0	1	15	2	13	0	1
	Bozeman	33,856	85	0	13	13	59	1,476	132	1,228	116	22
	Colstrip	2,353	5	0	0	0	5	54	8	45	1	2
	Columbia Falls	4,483	16	0	0	1	15	191	6	178	7	0
	Columbus	1,915	8	0	2	0	6	80	11	68	1	1
	Cut Bank	3,197	34	0	2	0	32	133	15	117	1	0
	Dillon	4,026	8	1	0	0	7	87	5	75	7	0
	East Helena	1,866	5	0	1	0	4	35	2	29	4	0
	Eureka	1,038	2	0	0	0	2	77	5	71	1	1
	Fort Benton	1,489	6	0	1	0	5	37	8	28	1	1
	Glasgow	3,047	5	0	4	0	1	57	7	45	5	0
	Glendive	4,715	7	0	1	0	6	150	10	137	3	0
	Great Falls	56,878	186	2	11	29	144	2,772	224	2,424	124	49
	Hamilton	4,486	24	0	3	0	21	243	35	201	7	2
	Havre	9,480	51	1	5	1	44	458	37	400	21	1
	Helena	27,645	83	2	12	9	60	1,071	127	892	52	14
	Kalispell	18,657	61	1	9	1	50	1,052	69	912	71	7
	Laurel	6,403	10	0	1	0	9	215	14	192	9	1
	Lewistown	6,157	7	0	1	0	6	93	13	74	6	0
	Libby	2,673	14	0	1	0	13	125	6	114	5	0
	Livingston	7,214	19	0	2	1	16	189	23	150	16	2
	Missoula	63,526	186	0	38	30	118	3,125	331	2,644	150	19
	Plains	1,259	5	0	0	0	5	30	5	23	2	0
	Polson	4,874	28	0	1	2	25	254	19	217	18	0
	Red Lodge	2,424	12	0	3	0	9	66	15	43	8	0
	Ronan City	1,987	15	0	1	1	13	63	12	44	7	0
	Stevensville	1,873	24	0	2	0	22	48	1	44	3	1
	Thompson Falls	1,405	7	0	0	0	7	46	5	38	3	0
	Whitefish	7,135	16	0	0	1	15	243	44	188	11	0
NEBRASKA	Alliance	8,376	18	0	1	5	12	167	28	133	6	8
	Ashland	2,507	0	0	0	0	0	13	1	12	0	0
	Auburn	3,093	4	0	3	0	1	89	10	74	5	0

[1] The FBI does not publish arson data unless it receives data from either the agency or the state for all 12 months of the calendar year.

Table 8. Offenses Known to Law Enforcement, by State and City, 2006 (*Contd.*)

(Number.)

State	City	Popula-tion	Violent crime	Murder and non-negligent man-slaughter	Forcible rape	Robbery	Aggra-vated assault	Property crime	Burglary	Larceny-theft	Motor vehicle theft	Arson[1]
	Aurora	4,305	6	0	0	0	6	67	6	60	1	0
	Bayard	1,161	1	0	1	0	0	30	10	20	0	0
	Beatrice	12,960	45	0	15	1	29	610	118	475	17	8
	Bellevue	47,591	67	0	10	20	37	1,236	139	989	108	11
	Blair	7,807	9	0	6	2	1	152	13	129	10	2
	Bridgeport	1,501	2	0	0	0	2	25	6	18	1	0
	Broken Bow	3,329	3	0	0	0	3	69	10	59	0	0
	Central City	2,907	2	0	0	0	2	82	5	72	5	1
	Chadron	5,349	4	0	0	1	3	55	16	34	5	0
	Columbusv	21,022	9	0	1	3	5	710	126	544	40	0
	Cozad	4,245	3	0	1	0	2	92	12	77	3	0
	Crete	6,342	9	0	2	0	7	173	22	146	5	0
	David City	2,572	2	0	0	0	2	57	9	47	1	0
	Elkhorn	8,236	0	0	0	0	0	88	17	68	3	0
	Emerson	820	0	0	0	0	0	5	1	2	2	0
	Falls City	4,241	2	0	0	1	1	96	18	74	4	1
	Fremont	25,451	37	2	14	1	20	714	91	592	31	3
	Gering	7,809	2	0	0	0	2	191	35	152	4	1
	Gothenburg	3,712	1	0	0	0	1	58	13	44	1	0
	Grand Island	44,788	99	1	4	15	79	2,459	411	1,939	109	5
	Hastings	25,575	48	0	13	6	29	972	183	775	14	10
	Holdrege	5,378	9	0	6	0	3	147	18	122	7	1
	Imperial	1,886	4	0	0	0	4	10	4	6	0	0
	Kearney	29,115	56	0	22	3	31	924	142	745	37	5
	La Vista	15,777	16	0	5	2	9	372	34	323	15	3
	Lexington	10,140	23	0	12	2	9	410	86	313	11	1
	Lincoln	240,511	1,256	5	100	162	989	12,237	1,922	9,884	431	4
	Lyons	917	4	0	0	0	4	18	1	17	0	0
	McCook	7,722	12	0	4	0	8	143	22	116	5	2
	Minden	2,929	0	0	0	0	0	72	6	66	0	2
	Mitchell	1,806	0	0	0	0	0	25	0	25	0	1
	Nebraska City	7,073	8	0	1	2	5	237	31	193	13	1
	Norfolk	24,076	23	0	15	2	6	785	98	655	32	0
	Ogallala	4,721	6	0	1	1	4	196	16	173	7	0
	Omaha	416,770	2,505	33	187	848	1,437	21,787	3,172	15,172	3,443	
	O'Neill	3,502	3	0	1	0	2	44	7	33	4	1
	Papillion	20,542	10	1	5	0	4	303	27	261	15	3
	Plainview	1,286	0	0	0	0	0	5	2	3	0	0
	Plattsmouth	7,061	7	0	3	0	4	169	19	139	11	0
	Ralston	6,227	10	0	0	4	6	187	17	156	14	3
	Scottsbluff	14,894	45	0	16	8	21	983	126	823	34	2
	Seward	6,813	2	0	2	0	0	105	9	90	6	1
	Sidney	6,477	14	0	4	1	9	214	22	185	7	0
	St. Paul	2,280	2	0	0	0	2	15	2	10	3	0
	Superior	1,913	1	0	1	0	0	7	1	6	0	0
	Syracuse	1,845	0	0	0	0	0	22	4	18	0	0
	Valley	1,839	3	0	1	0	2	64	6	57	1	1
	Wahoo	4,085	1	0	1	0	0	72	15	51	6	0
	Waterloo	509	0	0	0	0	0	0	0	0	0	0
	West Point	3,495	0	0	0	0	0	22	6	11	5	0
	Wymore	1,624	6	0	0	0	6	36	2	32	2	0
	York	7,931	1	0	1	0	0	199	27	169	3	0
NEVADA	Boulder City	15,684	19	1	2	5	11	254	106	126	22	3
	Carlin	2,153	31	0	0	0	31	32	18	9	5	0
	Elko	17,243	47	0	7	8	32	609	135	422	52	8
	Fallon	8,374	18	0	0	4	14	435	62	347	26	0
	Henderson	239,906	588	5	63	237	283	6,674	1,600	3,614	1,460	88
	Las Vegas Metropolitan Police Department	1,315,625	12,931	152	718	5,381	6,680	61,405	14,913	26,815	19,677	391
	Lovelock	1,941	8	0	0	0	8	40	17	20	3	0
	Mesquite	13,975	31	1	2	3	25	360	15	290	55	0
	North Las Vegas	182,540	1,695	22	57	584	1,032	8,617	2,523	3,456	2,638	58
	Reno	210,354	1,478	23	100	523	832	10,797	2,105	7,061	1,631	37
	Sparks	84,794	380	3	40	124	213	3,452	893	2,104	455	20
	West Wendover	5,132	17	1	2	4	10	200	49	133	18	3

[1] The FBI does not publish arson data unless it receives data from either the agency or the state for all 12 months of the calendar year.

Table 8. Offenses Known to Law Enforcement, by State and City, 2006 (*Contd.*)

(Number.)

State	City	Popula-tion	Violent crime	Murder and non-negligent man-slaughter	Forcible rape	Robbery	Aggra-vated assault	Property crime	Burglary	Larceny-theft	Motor vehicle theft	Arson[1]
	Winnemucca	7,984	18	1	2	3	12	110	32	63	15	8
	Yerington	3,603	0	0	0	0	0	49	35	14	0	0
NEW HAMPSHIRE	Alstead	2,034	3	0	0	0	3	21	8	12	1	0
	Alton	5,093	12	0	2	2	8	69	13	47	9	1
	Amherst	11,658	9	0	0	1	8	217	16	189	12	6
	Antrim	2,593	8	0	1	0	7	32	9	20	3	1
	Ashland	2,012	2	0	1	0	1	55	14	37	4	0
	Auburn	5,141	2	0	1	0	1	63	9	45	9	2
	Barnstead	4,578	3	0	1	1	1	63	19	37	7	0
	Barrington	8,193	6	0	0	0	6	129	37	87	5	0
	Bartlett	2,929	6	1	1	0	4	66	11	52	3	1
	Belmont	7,350	12	2	4	4	2	122	27	91	4	3
	Bennington	1,474	3	0	0	0	3	58	4	52	2	0
	Berlin	10,519	17	0	1	2	14	203	56	140	7	5
	Boscawen	3,875	4	0	1	0	3	58	16	36	6	0
	Bow	8,050	3	0	0	1	2	56	14	41	1	0
	Brentwood	3,791	1	0	0	0	1	37	9	14	14	0
	Bristol	3,130	6	0	0	0	6	85	20	62	3	1
	Campton	2,958	10	1	2	1	6	75	22	44	9	0
	Candia	4,181	1	0	0	0	1	48	6	36	6	2
	Charlestown	5,001	7	0	3	0	4	40	19	18	3	1
	Chester	4,654	4	0	1	0	3	60	12	44	4	0
	Claremont	13,439	23	0	5	2	16	331	35	285	11	8
	Colebrook	2,406	2	0	1	0	1	19	7	10	2	0
	Concord	42,496	62	0	13	18	31	1,016	171	802	43	18
	Conway	9,243	20	0	2	7	11	344	62	262	20	3
	Danville	4,411	1	0	1	0	0	53	11	41	1	0
	Deerfield	4,131	4	0	1	0	3	47	6	32	9	3
	Deering	2,036	1	0	1	0	0	19	7	9	3	1
	Derry	34,420	76	0	8	13	55	726	139	533	54	31
	Dover	28,594	29	1	8	10	10	536	48	479	9	5
	Dublin	1,562	1	0	1	0	0	23	4	19	0	0
	Enfield	4,848	4	0	1	0	3	34	8	25	1	1
	Epping	6,110	13	1	3	2	7	123	18	100	5	2
	Epsom	4,483	0	0	0	0	0	71	14	55	2	0
	Exeter	14,760	8	0	2	0	6	151	24	119	8	0
	Farmington	6,463	18	0	6	0	12	120	31	85	4	6
	Fitzwilliam	2,306	6	0	2	0	4	15	3	9	3	0
	Freedom	1,444	0	0	0	0	0	30	18	10	2	0
	Fremont	3,999	10	0	0	0	10	37	14	16	7	2
	Gilford	7,538	12	0	1	2	9	187	27	153	7	1
	Gilmanton	3,550	1	0	0	0	1	21	14	7	0	2
	Goffstown	17,754	6	0	1	0	5	336	47	287	2	2
	Gorham	2,944	4	0	0	0	4	42	4	32	6	2
	Grantham	2,512	0	0	0	0	0	13	1	12	0	0
	Greenland	3,395	2	0	1	0	1	33	5	27	1	1
	Hampstead	8,772	6	0	2	0	4	89	13	70	6	0
	Hampton	15,508	21	0	2	9	10	355	45	301	9	2
	Hancock	1,810	0	0	0	0	0	9	2	7	0	0
	Hanover	11,198	4	1	2	0	1	237	19	215	3	0
	Haverhill	4,570	14	0	2	1	11	74	22	45	7	1
	Henniker	4,885	4	0	2	0	2	115	18	94	3	0
	Hill	1,098	0	0	0	0	0	12	3	8	1	0
	Hinsdale	4,223	11	0	3	2	6	79	16	58	5	0
	Hooksett	13,329	8	0	2	2	4	281	48	227	6	3
	Hopkinton	5,641	6	0	3	0	3	35	8	26	1	0
	Hudson	24,661	26	0	9	7	10	401	66	292	43	6
	Jaffrey	5,733	5	0	0	0	5	64	18	41	5	3
	Keene	22,864	53	0	8	11	34	721	65	622	34	11
	Kingston	6,264	4	0	0	0	4	57	18	29	10	1
	Laconia	17,125	38	0	7	8	23	738	93	618	27	7
	Lancaster	3,371	3	0	2	0	1	78	18	56	4	1
	Lebanon	12,654	16	0	11	2	3	390	31	353	6	2
	Lee	4,422	5	0	2	0	3	39	2	33	4	0

[1] The FBI does not publish arson data unless it receives data from either the agency or the state for all 12 months of the calendar year.

SECTION II: OFFENSES REPORTED 153

Table 8. Offenses Known to Law Enforcement, by State and City, 2006 (*Contd.*)

(Number.)

State	City	Popula-tion	Violent crime	Murder and non-negligent man-slaughter	Forcible rape	Robbery	Aggra-vated assault	Property crime	Burglary	Larceny-theft	Motor vehicle theft	Arson[1]
	Lincoln	1,305	1	0	0	0	1	96	8	84	4	0
	Lisbon	1,648	4	0	0	0	4	24	4	19	1	0
	Litchfield	8,308	6	0	2	2	2	91	21	66	4	4
	Littleton	6,162	5	0	1	1	3	71	11	58	2	1
	Londonderry	24,931	28	0	3	7	18	327	47	242	38	4
	Loudon	5,081	3	0	0	0	3	51	9	38	4	0
	Madison	2,277	2	0	0	0	2	54	9	45	0	0
	Manchester	110,106	313	4	44	157	108	3,454	781	2,423	250	66
	Marlborough	2,102	3	0	3	0	0	33	8	25	0	0
	Merrimack	26,753	3	0	0	1	2	300	30	265	5	1
	Middleton	1,695	1	0	1	0	0	27	7	20	0	0
	Milford	14,918	20	0	4	3	13	205	32	162	11	5
	Milton	4,368	25	0	2	1	22	74	14	47	13	1
	Moultonborough	4,971	2	0	1	0	1	46	23	23	0	0
	Nashua	87,651	190	1	21	47	121	2,241	333	1,801	107	33
	New Boston	4,898	1	0	0	0	1	22	11	7	4	1
	New Durham	2,463	1	0	1	0	0	54	12	39	3	1
	Newfields	1,595	3	0	0	0	3	15	2	13	0	0
	New Hampton	2,243	2	0	0	0	2	35	8	25	2	0
	New Ipswich	5,037	0	0	0	0	0	62	9	48	5	1
	New London	4,480	0	0	0	0	0	30	6	22	2	0
	Newmarket	9,210	8	0	3	2	3	78	25	49	4	1
	Newport	6,586	12	0	1	3	8	265	37	215	13	2
	Newton	4,474	6	0	0	1	5	41	9	29	3	0
	Northfield	4,991	6	0	1	2	3	82	9	66	7	0
	Northumberland	2,426	3	0	0	0	3	24	7	14	3	0
	Northwood	3,994	2	0	0	1	1	34	21	6	7	1
	Nottingham	4,389	1	0	0	0	1	49	6	41	2	0
	Ossipee	4,655	5	0	1	0	4	125	23	94	8	1
	Pelham	12,521	5	0	1	2	2	170	31	107	32	3
	Pembroke	7,394	7	0	2	2	3	83	20	57	6	0
	Peterborough	6,096	9	0	2	1	6	114	19	94	1	1
	Plaistow	7,798	4	0	1	3	0	184	17	147	20	1
	Plymouth	6,227	5	0	0	0	5	232	29	194	9	1
	Portsmouth	20,752	45	0	9	16	20	670	86	554	30	11
	Raymond	10,160	18	0	7	1	10	156	25	121	10	2
	Rindge	6,326	7	0	2	1	4	58	14	37	7	2
	Rochester	30,117	73	0	19	8	46	689	114	537	38	5
	Rollinsford	2,635	1	0	0	0	1	22	5	16	1	1
	Rye	5,261	1	0	0	0	1	31	9	22	0	1
	Sandown	5,747	2	0	0	0	2	43	17	18	8	0
	Sandwich	1,353	0	0	0	0	0	40	9	31	0	0
	Seabrook	8,466	21	0	2	8	11	205	26	169	10	1
	Strafford	3,994	1	0	0	0	1	26	7	16	3	0
	Thornton	2,029	0	0	0	0	0	15	6	8	1	0
	Tilton	3,650	2	0	1	0	1	94	10	84	0	0
	Troy	2,069	0	0	0	0	0	30	4	21	5	0
	Warner	2,984	0	0	0	0	0	18	3	13	2	0
	Washington	1,047	1	0	0	0	1	11	6	5	0	0
	Weare	8,763	3	0	2	0	1	50	10	32	8	0
	Webster	1,830	1	0	0	0	1	16	6	8	2	3
	Wilton	3,899	4	0	2	0	2	77	28	47	2	1
	Windham	12,769	10	0	0	0	10	151	28	109	14	0
	Wolfeboro	6,685	3	0	0	1	2	93	22	53	18	2
	Woodstock	1,175	3	0	2	0	1	28	7	19	2	0
NEW JERSEY	Aberdeen Township	18,347	29	0	4	12	13	243	40	189	14	4
	Absecon	7,995	35	1	3	14	17	281	41	228	12	2
	Allendale	6,759	4	0	1	2	1	59	16	41	2	1
	Allenhurst	707	2	0	0	1	1	16	2	13	1	0
	Allentown	1,859	2	0	0	0	2	19	3	15	1	0
	Alpha	2,457	13	0	0	0	13	31	3	28	0	0
	Alpine	2,370	1	0	0	0	1	5	2	3	0	1
	Andover Township	6,527	3	0	0	0	3	53	9	41	3	0
	Asbury Park	16,637	386	8	7	193	178	916	284	539	93	11
	Atlantic City	40,399	842	18	46	355	423	3,859	507	3,148	204	7

[1] The FBI does not publish arson data unless it receives data from either the agency or the state for all 12 months of the calendar year.

Table 8. Offenses Known to Law Enforcement, by State and City, 2006 (*Contd.*)

(Number.)

State	City	Population	Violent crime	Murder and non-negligent manslaughter	Forcible rape	Robbery	Aggravated assault	Property crime	Burglary	Larceny-theft	Motor vehicle theft	Arson[1]
	Atlantic Highlands.............	4,629	5	0	0	2	3	57	3	54	0	0
	Audubon..........................	9,054	8	0	1	4	3	254	37	210	7	3
	Audubon Park...................	1,081	1	0	0	0	1	32	8	21	3	0
	Avalon.............................	2,135	6	0	1	0	5	303	45	254	4	1
	Avon-by-the-Sea	2,190	3	0	1	0	2	106	18	87	1	0
	Barnegat Light	823	0	0	0	0	0	36	1	35	0	0
	Barnegat Township...........	20,323	30	0	1	3	26	209	51	152	6	5
	Barrington	7,055	11	0	1	2	8	62	11	41	10	1
	Bay Head	1,260	1	0	0	0	1	50	10	39	1	0
	Bayonne...........................	60,033	193	1	4	86	102	860	188	573	99	9
	Beach Haven	1,353	4	0	1	0	3	128	11	113	4	0
	Beachwood	10,746	10	0	0	4	6	239	29	204	6	3
	Bedminster Township........	8,394	3	0	1	0	2	73	17	51	5	1
	Belleville	34,928	128	0	2	57	69	876	160	501	215	2
	Bellmawr..........................	11,167	13	0	1	4	8	253	46	182	25	0
	Belmar.............................	5,967	35	0	0	3	32	333	37	281	15	0
	Belvidere..........................	2,734	2	0	0	0	2	18	3	14	1	0
	Bergenfield	26,076	22	0	0	5	17	239	50	168	21	3
	Berkeley Heights Township..........................	13,581	5	0	0	1	4	86	8	76	2	0
	Berkeley Township...........	42,532	44	0	3	8	33	689	167	511	11	13
	Berlin...............................	7,850	8	0	0	5	3	215	35	170	10	2
	Berlin Township................	5,403	15	0	0	3	12	187	31	144	12	7
	Bernards Township...........	26,958	7	1	3	0	3	163	42	115	6	3
	Bernardsville	7,618	2	0	1	0	1	66	7	58	1	0
	Beverly.............................	2,672	15	0	5	0	10	66	18	38	10	1
	Blairstown Township........	5,980	6	0	1	0	5	55	12	43	0	0
	Bloomfield	46,181	128	1	4	82	41	1,329	192	881	256	5
	Bloomingdale	7,660	1	0	0	0	1	74	14	50	10	1
	Bogota..............................	8,156	5	0	0	2	3	86	14	69	3	0
	Boonton	8,562	9	0	0	0	9	58	4	46	8	1
	Boonton Township	4,379	3	0	0	0	3	25	6	17	2	0
	Bordentown......................	3,992	4	0	0	2	2	38	8	25	5	0
	Bordentown Township......	10,323	17	0	1	8	8	165	32	108	25	0
	Bound Brook....................	10,176	31	0	1	17	13	223	64	147	12	0
	Bradley Beach..................	4,786	6	0	0	3	3	188	44	140	4	0
	Branchburg Township.......	14,954	3	0	1	1	1	111	28	78	5	0
	Brick Township	78,214	83	0	3	19	61	1,463	303	1,100	60	0
	Bridgeton.........................	23,977	359	0	21	156	182	1,040	288	666	86	3
	Bridgewater Township	44,490	16	0	0	8	8	659	99	531	29	4
	Brielle..............................	4,882	5	0	1	0	4	46	25	20	1	0
	Brigantine	12,871	8	0	0	3	5	225	51	169	5	2
	Brooklawn	2,317	5	1	1	2	1	242	30	196	16	0
	Buena	3,851	22	0	1	1	20	114	45	66	3	1
	Burlington........................	9,798	55	2	5	23	25	178	46	115	17	1
	Burlington Township.........	21,932	34	1	7	14	12	443	60	356	27	3
	Butler	8,097	9	0	0	0	9	155	45	95	15	0
	Byram Township................	8,694	2	0	1	0	1	52	17	34	1	2
	Caldwell...........................	7,495	2	0	1	0	1	49	9	37	3	0
	Camden............................	80,071	1,693	32	66	773	822	4,787	1,179	2,430	1,178	131
	Cape May..........................	3,763	7	0	0	2	5	283	20	259	4	3
	Cape May Point	236	0	0	0	0	0	29	4	25	0	0
	Carlstadt..........................	6,023	7	0	1	2	4	135	8	105	22	0
	Carney's Point Township ..	7,952	25	1	0	9	15	172	55	105	12	2
	Carteret............................	21,476	63	3	4	21	35	359	61	274	24	0
	Cedar Grove Township.....	12,708	6	0	0	0	6	205	36	162	7	4
	Chatham...........................	8,445	5	0	1	3	1	93	22	66	5	0
	Chatham Township............	10,211	0	0	0	0	0	46	15	31	0	0
	Cherry Hill Township........	71,876	107	1	4	40	62	2,262	266	1,883	113	6
	Chesilhurst.......................	1,866	2	0	0	0	2	54	21	31	2	0
	Chester.............................	1,654	2	0	0	0	2	22	2	20	0	0
	Chesterfield Township.......	6,190	1	1	0	0	0	41	12	27	2	0
	Chester Township	7,846	1	0	0	0	1	51	3	47	1	0
	Cinnaminson Township.....	15,161	25	1	2	12	10	343	57	256	30	1
	Clark Township.................	14,646	11	0	0	1	10	203	15	168	20	1

[1] The FBI does not publish arson data unless it receives data from either the agency or the state for all 12 months of the calendar year.

Table 8. Offenses Known to Law Enforcement, by State and City, 2006 *(Contd.)*

(Number.)

State	City	Population	Violent crime	Murder and non-negligent manslaughter	Forcible rape	Robbery	Aggravated assault	Property crime	Burglary	Larceny-theft	Motor vehicle theft	Arson[1]
	Clayton	7,453	14	0	0	4	10	224	22	197	5	0
	Clementon	4,948	36	0	0	12	24	208	38	154	16	2
	Cliffside Park	23,053	15	0	0	5	10	215	55	138	22	0
	Clifton	79,983	179	1	2	78	98	1,911	361	1,259	291	1
	Clinton	2,623	2	0	0	1	1	18	1	17	0	0
	Clinton Township	13,999	3	0	0	0	3	77	12	62	3	0
	Closter	8,676	1	0	0	0	1	72	18	52	2	0
	Collingswood	14,094	23	0	1	7	15	410	66	315	29	0
	Colts Neck Township	11,637	2	0	0	1	1	93	15	76	2	4
	Cranbury Township	3,950	8	0	1	2	5	63	15	43	5	0
	Cranford Township	22,495	5	1	0	3	1	284	31	247	6	1
	Cresskill	8,455	1	0	0	0	1	35	8	26	1	0
	Deal	1,044	3	0	0	0	3	40	5	35	0	0
	Delanco Township	3,968	4	0	0	1	3	86	20	61	5	1
	Delaware Township	4,724	2	0	0	0	2	37	21	16	0	1
	Delran Township	17,427	20	0	0	8	12	239	43	183	13	2
	Demarest	5,009	0	0	0	0	0	46	3	43	0	0
	Denville Township	16,510	6	0	1	1	4	182	33	138	11	1
	Deptford Township	29,767	108	1	1	37	69	1,440	209	1,157	74	13
	Dover	18,455	64	0	2	30	32	353	85	238	30	1
	Dumont	17,487	10	0	2	0	8	171	17	147	7	1
	Dunellen	6,999	7	0	0	3	4	139	19	114	6	2
	Eastampton Township	6,734	13	0	1	4	8	66	11	46	9	0
	East Brunswick Township	48,293	36	0	0	9	27	889	137	712	40	2
	East Greenwich Township	6,373	5	0	2	1	2	104	31	69	4	1
	East Hanover Township	11,603	11	0	0	3	8	262	21	219	22	0
	East Newark	2,264	10	1	1	1	7	20	3	11	6	0
	East Orange	68,242	719	10	25	371	313	2,451	593	1,222	636	50
	East Rutherford	8,967	10	1	0	2	7	294	35	216	43	0
	East Windsor Township	26,893	41	1	3	8	29	356	73	257	26	7
	Eatontown	14,099	36	0	4	16	16	603	50	536	17	0
	Edgewater	9,653	22	0	0	5	17	178	30	135	13	0
	Edgewater Park Township	8,025	27	0	9	8	10	201	56	123	22	1
	Edison Township	100,575	295	1	15	86	193	2,320	368	1,684	268	12
	Egg Harbor City	4,500	13	0	0	6	7	93	28	63	2	0
	Egg Harbor Township	38,122	93	7	6	35	45	1,197	282	884	31	13
	Elizabeth	125,905	894	17	35	536	306	4,774	682	2,860	1,232	11
	Elk Township	3,795	11	0	3	3	5	121	29	86	6	2
	Elmer	1,380	0	0	0	0	0	28	4	23	1	0
	Elmwood Park	18,919	32	0	0	16	16	365	59	275	31	0
	Elsinboro Township	1,080	1	0	0	0	1	24	9	14	1	0
	Emerson	7,340	4	0	0	0	4	44	7	36	1	1
	Englewood	26,227	67	1	3	19	44	584	177	371	36	0
	Englewood Cliffs	5,742	2	0	0	0	2	98	22	73	3	0
	Englishtown	1,791	0	0	0	0	0	16	3	11	2	0
	Essex Fells	2,105	0	0	0	0	0	16	2	13	1	2
	Evesham Township	46,996	42	0	6	8	28	723	92	607	24	8
	Ewing Township	37,265	114	0	8	57	49	780	173	559	48	13
	Fairfield Township, Essex County	7,763	13	0	0	3	10	373	44	300	29	0
	Fair Haven	5,903	5	0	0	1	4	38	3	35	0	0
	Fair Lawn	31,432	38	0	3	11	24	453	60	373	20	5
	Fairview	13,575	57	0	6	25	26	253	113	119	21	1
	Fanwood	7,234	2	0	0	0	2	62	12	50	0	0
	Far Hills	920	1	0	0	0	1	11	2	9	0	0
	Flemington	4,174	13	0	0	6	7	83	12	69	2	3
	Florence Township	11,445	9	0	0	3	6	116	38	60	18	2
	Florham Park	12,636	6	0	1	1	4	104	10	88	6	0
	Fort Lee	37,203	19	1	0	5	13	339	65	256	18	7
	Franklin	5,237	2	0	0	1	1	94	18	74	2	2
	Franklin Lakes	11,311	1	0	1	0	0	115	17	97	1	0
	Franklin Township, Gloucester County	16,673	21	1	0	4	16	328	114	199	15	1

[1] The FBI does not publish arson data unless it receives data from either the agency or the state for all 12 months of the calendar year.

Table 8. Offenses Known to Law Enforcement, by State and City, 2006 (*Contd.*)

(Number.)

State	City	Popula-tion	Violent crime	Murder and non-negligent man-slaughter	Forcible rape	Robbery	Aggra-vated assault	Property crime	Burglary	Larceny-theft	Motor vehicle theft	Arson[1]
	Franklin Township, Hunterdon County	3,157	0	0	0	0	0	27	2	23	2	1
	Franklin Township, Somerset County	58,505	88	1	5	45	37	862	190	569	103	12
	Freehold.............................	11,448	49	0	1	26	22	260	35	211	14	3
	Freehold Township	33,889	36	0	8	11	17	921	76	831	14	4
	Frenchtown........................	1,504	1	0	0	0	1	23	2	21	0	0
	Galloway Township	35,860	90	0	6	27	57	759	200	524	35	4
	Garfield	29,795	62	0	1	28	33	464	122	275	67	0
	Garwood	4,148	3	0	0	1	2	49	11	37	1	0
	Gibbsboro..........................	2,470	5	0	0	2	3	49	17	31	1	5
	Glassboro..........................	19,305	77	0	14	26	37	738	133	579	26	6
	Glen Ridge	7,025	5	0	2	2	1	210	46	153	11	1
	Glen Rock..........................	11,466	1	0	0	1	0	73	15	53	5	0
	Gloucester City	11,591	33	1	3	16	13	299	55	219	25	0
	Gloucester Township........	66,590	174	0	24	46	104	1,778	340	1,321	117	21
	Green Brook Township.....	6,709	10	0	3	0	7	146	35	97	14	0
	Greenwich Township, Gloucester County.............	4,984	3	0	0	1	2	140	24	114	2	1
	Greenwich Township, Warren County..................	5,232	6	0	1	2	3	125	12	108	5	0
	Guttenberg	10,893	49	0	2	28	19	189	75	90	24	3
	Hackensack	43,771	147	0	5	61	81	1,090	83	885	122	1
	Hackettstown	9,382	8	0	0	0	8	239	26	204	9	1
	Haddonfield......................	11,600	12	0	2	6	4	268	40	223	5	11
	Haddon Heights................	7,433	6	0	1	3	2	137	19	116	2	3
	Haddon Township.............	14,586	29	0	1	19	9	398	51	332	15	2
	Haledon	8,404	13	0	0	7	6	98	27	60	11	1
	Hamburg............................	3,570	2	0	1	0	1	63	22	39	2	0
	Hamilton Township, Atlantic County	23,917	56	1	2	18	35	1,091	199	844	48	6
	Hamilton Township, Mercer County..................	90,062	208	1	9	109	89	1,871	440	1,246	185	10
	Hammonton	13,595	32	2	2	6	22	188	35	134	19	2
	Hanover Township	13,702	10	0	0	4	6	174	20	144	10	3
	Harding Township	3,316	0	0	0	0	0	16	8	7	1	0
	Hardyston Township	7,920	9	0	0	2	7	103	25	74	4	0
	Harrington Park................	4,910	0	0	0	0	0	11	1	10	0	0
	Harrison............................	14,071	46	1	3	27	15	359	60	188	111	0
	Harrison Township	11,310	5	0	1	3	1	171	39	126	6	4
	Harvey Cedars	386	0	0	0	0	0	19	0	19	0	0
	Hasbrouck Heights...........	11,652	0	0	0	0	0	177	31	128	18	0
	Haworth............................	3,417	0	0	0	0	0	8	4	4	0	0
	Hawthorne........................	18,282	10	1	0	3	6	246	42	189	15	0
	Hazlet Township	21,003	9	0	2	0	7	375	96	258	21	0
	Helmetta	2,052	3	0	0	0	3	5	0	5	0	0
	High Bridge	3,773	4	0	0	0	4	38	4	32	2	0
	Highland Park	14,279	16	0	1	5	10	227	32	180	15	0
	Highlands..........................	5,002	7	0	0	0	7	78	16	59	3	1
	Hightstown	5,297	17	0	3	6	8	107	25	76	6	1
	Hillsborough Township.....	37,837	22	0	6	5	11	347	80	251	16	2
	Hillsdale	10,097	3	0	0	0	3	89	7	81	1	0
	Hillside Township	21,760	102	1	10	53	38	654	129	374	151	2
	Hi-Nella	1,016	9	0	0	3	6	14	5	8	1	0
	Hoboken............................	39,930	115	2	0	46	67	1,064	281	667	116	0
	Ho-Ho-Kus........................	4,093	0	0	0	0	0	14	3	11	0	0
	Holland Township.............	5,317	1	0	0	0	1	19	5	14	0	0
	Holmdel Township	16,957	5	0	2	1	2	218	25	186	7	2
	Hopatcong	16,013	4	0	0	1	3	146	17	124	5	0
	Hopewell...........................	2,038	0	0	0	0	0	12	5	7	0	0
	Hopewell Township..........	17,756	6	0	0	2	4	116	28	84	4	1
	Howell Township	50,550	59	0	1	11	47	476	94	348	34	6
	Independence Township ...	5,775	2	0	0	0	2	69	8	60	1	0
	Interlaken	886	0	0	0	0	0	3	1	2	0	0
	Irvington	58,921	1,311	21	23	676	591	3,160	924	1,282	954	20
	Island Heights	1,862	0	0	0	0	0	15	4	10	1	0
	Jackson Township.............	51,909	30	0	1	8	21	580	105	438	37	18

[1] The FBI does not publish arson data unless it receives data from either the agency or the state for all 12 months of the calendar year.

Table 8. Offenses Known to Law Enforcement, by State and City, 2006 *(Contd.)*

(Number.)

State	City	Popula-tion	Violent crime	Murder and non-negligent man-slaughter	Forcible rape	Robbery	Aggra-vated assault	Property crime	Burglary	Larceny-theft	Motor vehicle theft	Arson[1]
	Jamesburg	6,526	12	0	3	3	6	60	20	33	7	0
	Jefferson Township	21,620	14	0	1	6	7	232	67	154	11	2
	Jersey City	239,794	2,890	22	60	1,553	1,255	7,590	1,670	4,425	1,495	96
	Keansburg	10,627	67	0	3	6	58	304	57	235	12	1
	Kearny	38,801	104	1	1	44	58	984	152	614	218	14
	Kenilworth	7,749	1	0	0	1	0	144	9	126	9	0
	Keyport	7,511	12	0	2	6	4	163	30	117	16	8
	Kinnelon	9,638	1	0	0	0	1	69	26	38	5	0
	Lacey Township	26,249	16	1	0	1	14	601	94	494	13	1
	Lake Como	1,760	6	0	0	3	3	51	7	41	3	0
	Lakehurst	2,685	8	0	2	3	3	28	5	22	1	0
	Lakewood Township	68,886	225	4	10	138	73	1,661	573	952	136	8
	Lambertville	3,843	10	0	0	2	8	58	16	41	1	0
	Laurel Springs	1,940	2	0	0	0	2	54	18	35	1	0
	Lavallette	2,749	1	0	0	0	1	31	7	24	0	0
	Lawnside	2,780	15	0	0	4	11	102	13	88	1	0
	Lawrence Township, Mercer County	31,425	50	0	2	27	21	1,023	127	849	47	7
	Lebanon Township	6,318	1	0	0	0	1	56	16	34	6	0
	Leonia	8,860	4	0	0	2	2	82	24	54	4	2
	Lincoln Park	10,907	8	0	2	1	5	79	13	62	4	0
	Linden	40,044	132	4	3	67	58	1,316	186	918	212	2
	Lindenwold	17,278	163	1	8	89	65	676	235	356	85	10
	Linwood	7,404	9	0	1	3	5	85	30	48	7	4
	Little Egg Harbor Township	19,849	31	0	2	5	24	458	83	360	15	4
	Little Falls Township	11,907	25	0	6	4	15	419	72	319	28	0
	Little Ferry	10,783	5	0	1	0	4	115	23	71	21	0
	Little Silver	6,142	0	0	0	0	0	63	12	49	2	0
	Livingston Township	27,764	30	1	1	8	20	513	43	439	31	1
	Loch Arbour	275	0	0	0	0	0	18	4	14	0	0
	Lodi	24,329	41	0	0	9	32	312	64	195	53	1
	Logan Township	6,211	9	1	1	0	7	108	21	76	11	0
	Long Beach Township	3,464	5	0	0	0	5	223	24	199	0	0
	Long Branch	32,115	172	4	2	76	90	803	230	538	35	0
	Long Hill Township	8,804	1	0	0	0	1	52	9	43	0	0
	Longport	1,091	0	0	0	0	0	33	15	17	1	0
	Lopatcong Township	8,252	11	1	0	4	6	88	19	67	2	0
	Lower Alloways Creek Township	1,927	1	0	0	0	1	15	3	10	2	0
	Lower Township	21,458	42	0	2	6	34	470	119	335	16	4
	Lumberton Township	12,433	29	0	1	10	18	330	69	250	11	14
	Lyndhurst Township	19,455	13	0	2	3	8	323	40	257	26	2
	Madison	15,930	18	0	1	1	16	166	24	139	3	0
	Magnolia	4,392	18	0	2	1	15	100	34	54	12	0
	Mahwah Township	24,652	8	0	1	0	7	146	15	116	15	1
	Manalapan Township	36,867	25	3	2	7	13	368	56	296	16	1
	Manasquan	6,206	4	0	0	1	3	163	13	150	0	1
	Manchester Township	41,934	19	0	2	6	11	316	72	233	11	13
	Mansfield Township, Burlington County	7,927	3	0	0	1	2	144	7	120	17	0
	Mansfield Township, Warren County	8,280	9	0	1	1	7	116	20	89	7	2
	Mantoloking	450	0	0	0	0	0	15	2	13	0	0
	Mantua Township	14,884	31	0	6	7	18	292	60	221	11	6
	Manville	10,412	11	0	0	2	9	207	17	164	26	1
	Maple Shade Township	19,517	47	0	12	10	25	461	84	327	50	2
	Maplewood Township	23,142	67	0	3	30	34	531	74	357	100	3
	Margate City	8,673	5	0	0	0	5	180	44	132	4	0
	Marlboro Township	39,695	16	0	1	8	7	399	73	313	13	8
	Matawan	8,826	11	0	1	6	4	94	24	62	8	0
	Maywood	9,449	4	0	0	1	3	98	17	78	3	1
	Medford Lakes	4,188	1	0	0	0	1	34	5	29	0	1
	Medford Township	23,534	20	0	5	1	14	240	43	192	5	6
	Mendham	5,176	2	0	0	0	2	38	2	36	0	0
	Mendham Township	5,615	1	0	0	0	1	49	5	44	0	0

[1] The FBI does not publish arson data unless it receives data from either the agency or the state for all 12 months of the calendar year.

Table 8. Offenses Known to Law Enforcement, by State and City, 2006 (*Contd.*)

(Number.)

State	City	Popula-tion	Violent crime	Murder and non-negligent man-slaughter	Forcible rape	Robbery	Aggra-vated assault	Property crime	Burglary	Larceny-theft	Motor vehicle theft	Arson[1]
	Merchantville	3,823	4	0	0	2	2	118	16	100	2	1
	Metuchen	13,393	11	0	0	2	9	254	40	201	13	1
	Middlesex	13,949	11	1	0	3	7	162	31	116	15	0
	Middle Township	16,632	108	1	12	21	74	732	154	549	29	9
	Middletown Township	67,877	57	0	6	11	40	806	120	651	35	3
	Midland Park	6,957	3	0	0	1	2	40	4	35	1	0
	Millburn Township	19,384	17	0	1	11	5	764	66	626	72	1
	Milltown	7,135	8	0	2	2	4	166	29	128	9	0
	Millville	27,907	240	8	8	98	126	1,534	398	1,083	53	14
	Mine Hill Township	3,680	2	0	1	0	1	33	8	22	3	0
	Monmouth Beach	3,596	4	0	0	0	4	31	1	27	3	1
	Monroe Township, Gloucester County	31,485	48	0	2	17	29	776	186	536	54	10
	Monroe Township, Middlesex County	34,033	19	0	1	1	17	281	52	217	12	0
	Montclair	37,827	90	1	1	27	61	994	251	663	80	1
	Montgomery Township	22,758	3	0	2	0	1	240	69	170	1	1
	Montvale	7,312	1	0	1	0	0	51	3	47	1	0
	Montville Township	21,428	8	1	0	0	7	230	41	172	17	2
	Moonachie	2,814	2	0	0	0	2	88	10	66	12	0
	Moorestown Township	20,026	21	0	4	6	11	441	53	379	9	1
	Morris Plains	5,633	5	0	0	2	3	78	11	60	7	2
	Morristown	18,865	106	0	3	37	66	727	111	580	36	3
	Morris Township	21,442	38	0	4	3	31	181	31	135	15	0
	Mountain Lakes	4,339	2	0	1	0	1	84	22	60	2	1
	Mountainside	6,640	3	0	0	0	3	70	14	49	7	0
	Mount Arlington	5,336	4	0	0	0	4	52	12	37	3	0
	Mount Ephraim	4,470	22	0	0	10	12	168	26	126	16	1
	Mount Holly Township	10,674	55	0	0	24	31	335	55	256	24	2
	Mount Laurel Township	40,666	37	2	9	15	11	760	107	632	21	2
	Mount Olive Township	25,956	4	0	0	2	2	245	54	169	22	1
	Mullica Township	6,114	12	0	1	0	11	93	16	72	5	1
	National Park	3,225	5	1	0	1	3	57	18	35	4	0
	Neptune City	5,180	17	0	2	3	12	160	30	122	8	1
	Neptune Township	28,257	161	1	8	78	74	1,377	251	1,032	94	14
	Netcong	3,297	5	0	1	2	2	108	23	74	11	0
	Newark	280,877	2,839	105	87	1,288	1,359	11,456	1,982	4,377	5,097	166
	New Brunswick	50,194	360	7	19	207	127	1,914	515	1,192	207	7
	Newfield	1,662	2	0	0	0	2	32	13	18	1	0
	New Hanover Township	9,644	1	0	0	0	1	19	10	7	2	0
	New Milford	16,330	3	0	0	1	2	130	18	110	2	2
	New Providence	11,914	5	0	0	0	5	140	19	120	1	0
	Newton	8,422	8	0	0	0	8	137	9	123	5	0
	North Arlington	15,191	15	0	3	4	8	251	35	187	29	1
	North Bergen Township	57,735	121	1	4	58	58	912	166	560	186	1
	North Brunswick Township	39,703	90	0	1	34	55	850	204	582	64	7
	North Caldwell	7,290	1	0	0	1	0	50	8	39	3	2
	Northfield	8,031	6	0	1	3	2	94	22	68	4	2
	North Haledon	9,080	6	0	0	1	5	60	24	34	2	0
	North Hanover Township	7,608	5	0	0	2	3	73	19	48	6	0
	North Plainfield	21,624	46	2	1	33	10	569	177	340	52	0
	Northvale	4,567	1	0	0	0	1	28	6	20	2	0
	North Wildwood	4,782	18	0	7	3	8	351	50	295	6	0
	Norwood	6,254	1	0	0	0	1	37	8	28	1	3
	Nutley Township	27,476	39	0	3	5	31	439	94	315	30	12
	Oakland	13,655	1	0	0	1	0	128	13	114	1	3
	Oaklyn	4,119	5	0	0	2	3	110	27	80	3	1
	Ocean City	15,342	23	0	0	4	19	1,042	182	852	8	0
	Ocean Gate	2,111	6	0	0	0	6	51	12	37	2	0
	Oceanport	5,784	1	0	1	0	0	39	9	26	4	3
	Ocean Township, Monmouth County	27,510	42	0	5	14	23	761	118	612	31	5
	Ocean Township, Ocean County	7,826	4	0	0	0	4	97	10	87	0	0

[1] The FBI does not publish arson data unless it receives data from either the agency or the state for all 12 months of the calendar year.

Table 8. Offenses Known to Law Enforcement, by State and City, 2006 (*Contd.*)

(Number.)

State	City	Population	Violent crime	Murder and non-negligent man-slaughter	Forcible rape	Robbery	Aggravated assault	Property crime	Burglary	Larceny-theft	Motor vehicle theft	Arson[1]
	Ogdensburg	2,633	0	0	0	0	0	7	2	5	0	0
	Old Bridge Township	64,903	54	0	5	18	31	942	239	621	82	8
	Old Tappan	5,907	4	0	0	0	4	30	3	27	0	0
	Oradell	8,011	4	0	0	0	4	70	16	54	0	1
	Orange	32,142	413	5	10	257	141	1,415	358	625	432	5
	Oxford Township	2,631	1	0	0	0	1	14	3	10	1	0
	Palisades Park	18,871	16	0	0	8	8	163	48	105	10	1
	Palmyra	7,647	21	0	0	9	12	175	26	131	18	1
	Paramus	26,565	77	0	0	34	43	1,669	87	1,478	104	7
	Park Ridge	8,966	3	0	0	1	2	48	3	42	3	1
	Parsippany-Troy Hills Township	51,655	35	0	2	9	24	897	246	575	76	2
	Passaic	68,390	646	5	3	273	365	1,677	394	919	364	8
	Paterson	149,957	1,672	15	37	808	812	4,360	1,361	1,994	1,005	17
	Paulsboro	6,101	52	0	1	21	30	231	54	163	14	2
	Peapack and Gladstone	2,467	1	0	0	0	1	13	4	9	0	0
	Pemberton	1,324	3	0	2	0	1	34	9	25	0	0
	Pemberton Township	28,917	74	2	4	26	42	699	250	402	47	11
	Pennington	2,698	1	0	1	0	0	22	3	19	0	1
	Pennsauken Township	35,555	141	1	16	49	75	1,366	323	909	134	9
	Penns Grove	4,828	46	0	0	21	25	234	59	157	18	1
	Pennsville Township	13,324	14	0	0	4	10	381	86	285	10	4
	Pequannock Township	15,598	0	0	0	0	0	154	31	110	13	0
	Perth Amboy	48,834	207	4	2	95	106	1,163	268	735	160	5
	Phillipsburg	14,931	38	1	2	21	14	364	102	227	35	1
	Pine Beach	2,027	0	0	0	0	0	27	4	22	1	0
	Pine Hill	11,314	40	0	1	13	26	285	82	183	20	11
	Pine Valley	22	0	0	0	0	0	0	0	0	0	0
	Piscataway Township	52,734	74	0	4	26	44	818	180	581	57	13
	Pitman	9,258	3	1	0	1	1	148	10	131	7	1
	Plainfield	47,678	571	10	12	260	289	1,615	494	947	174	21
	Plainsboro Township	21,380	13	0	3	1	9	212	35	163	14	10
	Pleasantville	19,046	183	1	7	78	97	602	196	355	51	9
	Plumsted Township	8,053	5	0	2	0	3	61	15	31	15	2
	Pohatcong Township	3,414	26	0	0	1	25	132	8	114	10	0
	Point Pleasant	19,876	16	0	0	2	14	330	51	269	10	0
	Point Pleasant Beach	5,401	13	0	3	1	9	199	23	172	4	0
	Pompton Lakes	11,322	6	0	0	1	5	102	24	66	12	0
	Princeton	13,505	21	0	1	11	9	339	68	262	9	0
	Princeton Township	17,260	16	0	4	5	7	167	35	126	6	0
	Prospect Park	5,764	10	1	0	2	7	97	14	72	11	0
	Rahway	27,584	76	1	3	46	26	632	117	433	82	5
	Ramsey	14,569	15	1	0	3	11	166	19	138	9	1
	Randolph Township	25,755	8	0	0	6	2	204	24	170	10	1
	Raritan	6,396	9	0	1	4	4	115	29	82	4	0
	Raritan Township	22,686	8	0	2	3	3	194	19	164	11	0
	Readington Township	16,369	14	0	3	1	10	153	35	116	2	4
	Red Bank	11,885	50	0	5	27	18	325	36	277	12	0
	Ridgefield	11,022	10	0	0	4	6	98	28	57	13	0
	Ridgefield Park	12,756	14	0	1	3	10	191	20	152	19	0
	Ridgewood	24,809	10	0	0	2	8	238	42	193	3	2
	Ringwood	12,819	7	0	2	1	4	62	14	47	1	1
	Riverdale	2,637	0	0	0	0	0	79	18	53	8	0
	River Edge	10,919	7	0	1	2	4	123	22	97	4	0
	Riverside Township	7,996	23	0	4	4	15	118	24	88	6	1
	Riverton	2,741	0	0	0	0	0	37	6	31	0	2
	River Vale Township	9,772	4	0	0	1	3	39	1	37	1	0
	Rochelle Park Township	5,863	6	0	0	0	6	107	18	83	6	0
	Rockaway	6,424	4	0	0	0	4	76	10	59	7	0
	Rockaway Township	25,559	15	0	3	6	6	482	38	424	20	2
	Rockleigh	395	2	0	0	0	2	9	2	7	0	0
	Roseland	5,406	1	0	0	0	1	39	6	29	4	0
	Roselle	21,281	87	1	4	54	28	414	109	242	63	0
	Roselle Park	13,199	8	0	0	1	7	223	35	169	19	0
	Roxbury Township	23,872	21	0	2	9	10	319	66	229	24	0

[1] The FBI does not publish arson data unless it receives data from either the agency or the state for all 12 months of the calendar year.

Table 8. Offenses Known to Law Enforcement, by State and City, 2006 *(Contd.)*

(Number.)

State	City	Popula-tion	Violent crime	Murder and non-negligent man-slaughter	Forcible rape	Robbery	Aggra-vated assault	Property crime	Burglary	Larceny-theft	Motor vehicle theft	Arson[1]
	Rumson	7,239	2	0	0	0	2	82	23	56	3	2
	Runnemede	8,526	29	0	1	6	22	315	47	250	18	1
	Rutherford	17,981	12	0	0	2	10	263	47	189	27	1
	Saddle Brook Township	13,357	7	0	1	3	3	310	45	238	27	1
	Saddle River	3,769	1	0	0	0	1	24	8	16	0	0
	Salem	5,816	86	1	0	28	57	275	80	184	11	10
	Sayreville	43,050	74	0	5	13	56	777	129	566	82	5
	Scotch Plains Township	23,230	24	0	2	10	12	295	47	230	18	1
	Sea Bright	1,791	1	0	0	0	1	16	0	16	0	0
	Sea Girt	2,071	6	0	0	0	6	34	5	28	1	0
	Sea Isle City	2,970	18	0	0	0	18	297	16	276	5	0
	Seaside Heights	3,222	93	0	3	16	74	254	54	182	18	0
	Seaside Park	2,303	1	0	1	0	0	85	10	73	2	0
	Secaucus	15,635	20	0	0	12	8	701	37	577	87	3
	Ship Bottom	1,419	7	0	0	0	7	86	25	61	0	1
	Shrewsbury	3,745	9	0	1	4	4	70	16	48	6	0
	Somerdale	5,159	23	0	3	11	9	148	32	104	12	1
	Somers Point	11,710	41	0	0	18	23	310	72	231	7	4
	Somerville	12,487	28	0	0	20	8	251	34	199	18	0
	South Amboy	7,981	13	2	0	1	10	132	32	84	16	1
	South Bound Brook	4,508	0	0	0	0	0	4	2	0	2	0
	South Brunswick Township	40,626	31	0	2	12	17	599	142	418	39	1
	South Hackensack Township	2,323	11	0	3	2	6	67	15	38	14	0
	South Harrison Township	2,889	3	0	0	0	3	27	6	20	1	1
	South Orange	16,625	43	1	1	23	18	428	74	260	94	0
	South Plainfield	23,082	27	0	0	13	14	491	84	365	42	6
	South River	16,072	20	0	1	4	15	211	43	159	9	0
	South Toms River	3,701	6	0	1	1	4	88	21	56	11	0
	Sparta Township	19,333	2	1	0	1	0	109	15	93	1	0
	Spotswood	8,243	5	0	0	0	5	110	19	85	6	1
	Springfield	14,749	17	0	0	9	8	182	25	134	23	7
	Springfield Township	3,561	3	0	0	1	2	70	31	23	16	1
	Spring Lake	3,509	0	0	0	0	0	80	5	68	7	0
	Spring Lake Heights	5,139	2	0	0	0	2	32	5	26	1	0
	Stafford Township	25,541	21	4	0	1	16	481	42	414	25	6
	Stanhope	3,704	4	0	1	1	2	66	18	47	1	0
	Stillwater Township	4,400	1	0	0	0	1	26	2	21	3	0
	Stone Harbor	1,063	5	0	1	0	4	43	7	35	1	0
	Stratford	7,189	15	0	1	7	7	208	29	169	10	1
	Summit	21,216	8	0	2	2	4	245	15	218	12	0
	Surf City	1,528	1	0	0	1	0	41	3	37	1	0
	Swedesboro	2,052	6	0	1	3	2	41	13	27	1	0
	Tavistock	24	0	0	0	0	0	0	0	0	0	0
	Teaneck Township	39,665	65	1	0	27	37	621	127	449	45	9
	Tenafly	14,373	1	0	0	1	0	106	22	78	6	2
	Teterboro	18	4	0	0	0	4	27	1	24	2	0
	Tewksbury Township	6,055	3	0	1	0	2	34	11	21	2	0
	Tinton Falls	17,287	17	0	3	7	7	315	49	250	16	0
	Toms River Township	94,732	112	0	12	44	56	1,958	312	1,548	98	17
	Totowa	10,600	9	0	0	6	3	327	53	234	40	0
	Trenton	84,703	1,274	18	31	632	593	2,477	806	1,211	460	23
	Tuckerton	3,783	4	0	0	0	4	67	15	48	4	0
	Union Beach	6,664	6	0	0	0	6	41	13	27	1	0
	Union City	65,178	407	1	4	214	188	1,576	405	931	240	6
	Union Township	55,368	152	2	2	69	79	1,582	231	1,144	207	0
	Upper Saddle River	8,515	5	0	0	0	5	37	10	23	4	2
	Ventnor City	12,747	18	0	2	8	8	315	103	199	13	0
	Vernon Township	25,559	10	1	0	2	7	491	44	445	2	3
	Verona	13,135	9	0	1	0	8	205	38	145	22	1
	Vineland	58,208	539	6	19	167	347	2,737	539	2,068	130	14
	Voorhees Township	28,980	59	0	6	16	37	827	124	687	16	7
	Waldwick	9,657	4	0	0	2	2	87	9	78	0	2
	Wallington	11,500	11	0	0	8	3	159	33	103	23	0

[1] The FBI does not publish arson data unless it receives data from either the agency or the state for all 12 months of the calendar year.

Table 8. Offenses Known to Law Enforcement, by State and City, 2006 (*Contd.*)

(Number.)

State	City	Popula-tion	Violent crime	Murder and non-negligent man-slaughter	Forcible rape	Robbery	Aggra-vated assault	Property crime	Burglary	Larceny-theft	Motor vehicle theft	Arson[1]
	Wall Township	26,034	27	0	0	7	20	480	120	341	19	2
	Wanaque	10,624	5	0	0	0	5	137	27	101	9	1
	Warren Township	15,648	3	0	0	2	1	103	13	88	2	1
	Washington	6,881	9	1	0	1	7	174	37	127	10	6
	Washington Township, Bergen County	9,672	5	2	0	1	2	32	1	29	2	0
	Washington Township, Gloucester County	50,928	80	1	10	27	42	1,021	221	732	68	12
	Washington Township, Mercer County	11,628	8	0	1	2	5	122	18	95	9	0
	Washington Township, Morris County	18,626	8	0	0	0	8	129	18	101	10	0
	Washington Township, arren County	6,950	4	0	0	0	4	61	10	51	0	0
	Watchung	6,175	6	0	0	6	0	311	13	284	14	0
	Waterford Township	10,721	15	0	1	5	9	174	29	134	11	3
	Wayne Township	55,192	39	0	2	21	16	1,255	174	1,003	78	3
	Weehawken Township	12,943	35	1	1	16	17	328	75	218	35	0
	Wenonah	2,334	2	0	0	0	2	17	6	11	0	0
	Westampton Township	8,668	24	0	3	3	18	230	24	182	24	0
	West Amwell Township	2,933	5	0	1	0	4	24	4	19	1	0
	West Caldwell Township	10,959	4	0	0	1	3	111	10	93	8	1
	West Cape May	1,039	0	0	0	0	0	38	6	31	1	0
	West Deptford Township	20,927	42	1	11	5	25	539	93	398	48	8
	Westfield	29,941	15	0	2	6	7	337	66	259	12	3
	West Long Branch	8,292	10	0	2	2	6	268	31	231	6	1
	West Milford Township	28,202	24	0	7	3	14	443	120	313	10	5
	West New York	46,703	186	3	5	85	93	835	215	464	156	1
	West Orange	44,264	81	0	0	51	30	1,061	196	684	181	0
	West Paterson	11,254	12	0	0	6	6	260	53	188	19	1
	Westville	4,469	10	0	0	2	8	116	30	71	15	2
	West Wildwood	413	0	0	0	0	0	19	6	13	0	0
	West Windsor Township	26,005	17	1	1	7	8	544	53	472	19	1
	Westwood	11,002	7	0	4	1	2	142	17	118	7	0
	Wharton	6,227	2	0	0	0	2	120	20	96	4	0
	Wildwood	5,295	78	0	4	35	39	449	110	314	25	2
	Wildwood Crest	3,875	5	0	0	1	4	199	56	137	6	0
	Willingboro Township	33,152	130	3	12	56	59	637	133	434	70	6
	Winfield Township	1,499	0	0	0	0	0	8	1	6	1	0
	Winslow Township	37,536	184	0	7	52	125	830	246	535	49	14
	Woodbine	2,571	2	0	0	1	1	8	0	8	0	0
	Woodbridge Township	100,655	260	0	17	80	163	2,804	415	2,113	276	15
	Woodbury	10,443	55	0	5	24	26	656	100	533	23	3
	Woodbury Heights	3,024	10	0	0	4	6	99	23	71	5	0
	Woodcliff Lake	5,891	1	0	0	0	1	31	0	30	1	0
	Woodlynne	2,747	18	0	0	4	14	109	20	69	20	0
	Wood-Ridge	7,640	7	0	0	2	5	54	7	42	5	0
	Woodstown	3,315	4	0	0	2	2	61	14	46	1	0
	Woolwich Township	7,569	4	0	0	1	3	79	8	69	2	0
	Wyckoff Township	17,219	4	0	0	1	3	111	18	92	1	0
NEW MEXICO	Alamogordo	36,738	118	1	19	9	89	915	145	742	28	4
	Albuquerque	500,955	4,550	34	286	1,171	3,059	31,757	6,352	19,890	5,515	61
	Artesia	10,623	41	0	4	8	29	589	298	267	24	0
	Aztec	7,180	63	1	6	4	52	257	50	184	23	3
	Bayard	2,430	7	0	0	0	7	48	11	37	0	0
	Belen	7,218	64	1	2	10	51	491	167	242	82	5
	Bloomfield	7,543	131	0	7	2	122	211	48	149	14	0
	Bosque Farms	4,023	2	0	0	0	2	50	7	27	16	1
	Clovis	33,810	221	3	22	46	150	2,075	540	1,434	101	30
	Corrales	7,742	9	0	1	0	8	67	33	33	1	0
	Deming	15,078	23	0	1	6	16	681	231	362	88	0
	Dexter	1,247	6	0	0	0	6	22	9	12	1	0
	Eunice	2,637	11	0	0	1	10	77	41	35	1	0
	Farmington	43,748	300	1	56	31	212	1,406	378	897	131	10
	Grants	9,166	59	0	0	10	49	367	201	134	32	1
	Hobbs	29,400	453	6	21	47	379	2,012	388	1,552	72	9

[1] The FBI does not publish arson data unless it receives data from either the agency or the state for all 12 months of the calendar year.

Table 8. Offenses Known to Law Enforcement, by State and City, 2006 *(Contd.)*

(Number.)

State	City	Population	Violent crime	Murder and non-negligent man-slaughter	Forcible rape	Robbery	Aggra-vated assault	Property crime	Burglary	Larceny-theft	Motor vehicle theft	Arson[1]
	Jal	2,048	0	0	0	0	0	15	4	11	0	0
	Las Cruces	83,795	515	3	94	97	321	3,906	760	2,864	282	14
	Las Vegas	14,211	164	0	20	14	130	671	210	401	60	10
	Los Alamos	19,078	45	0	9	2	34	307	62	239	6	1
	Los Lunas	11,492	58	0	7	14	37	495	121	285	89	1
	Lovington	9,734	48	0	2	4	42	292	103	176	13	0
	Milan	2,558	11	1	0	0	10	111	27	74	10	0
	Moriarty	1,833	10	0	0	2	8	84	36	41	7	0
	Raton	7,038	29	1	0	1	27	121	48	69	4	1
	Red River	502	9	0	4	2	3	17	1	15	1	0
	Rio Rancho	67,504	265	0	16	15	234	1,589	484	925	180	10
	Roswell	45,813	344	3	21	45	275	2,265	508	1,651	106	17
	Ruidoso	8,932	41	0	6	5	30	330	145	162	23	0
	Ruidoso Downs	1,999	5	0	0	0	5	121	42	71	8	0
	Santa Fe	71,591	419	9	42	104	264	4,249	2,209	1,824	216	17
	Silver City	10,135	91	2	7	7	75	717	198	467	52	3
	Taos	5,196	43	1	7	2	33	422	90	314	18	0
	Truth or Consequences	7,167	32	0	1	4	27	314	84	214	16	0
NEW YORK	Adams Village	1,667	0	0	0	0	0	7	0	7	0	0
	Addison Town and Village	2,595	7	0	0	0	7	27	7	19	1	1
	Akron Village	3,075	3	0	0	0	3	30	5	21	4	0
	Albany	93,773	1,217	5	50	388	774	4,820	1,058	3,521	241	
	Albion Village	5,781	30	0	2	7	21	373	50	315	8	1
	Alexandria Bay Village	1,103	5	0	0	0	5	16	4	12	0	0
	Alfred Village	5,022	8	0	1	0	7	49	9	38	2	0
	Allegany Village	1,836	2	0	0	0	2	17	0	17	0	0
	Altamont Village	1,725	2	0	0	2	0	1	0	1	0	0
	Amherst Town	112,284	122	2	11	31	78	1,882	277	1,571	34	6
	Amity Town and Belmont Village	2,197	0	0	0	0	0	1	1	0	0	0
	Amityville Village	9,502	10	0	0	5	5	231	60	159	12	1
	Amsterdam	17,797	89	0	0	2	87	163	36	126	1	2
	Angelica Village	879	0	0	0	0	0	1	1	0	0	0
	Angola Village	2,200	1	0	0	0	1	59	13	45	1	0
	Arcade Village	1,956	11	0	3	0	8	64	5	57	2	7
	Ardsley Village	4,828	1	0	0	0	1	41	11	30	0	0
	Asharoken Village	652	0	0	0	0	0	2	1	1	0	0
	Attica Village	2,503	3	0	1	0	2	29	3	26	0	0
	Baldwinsville Village	7,168	8	0	0	1	7	226	26	191	9	0
	Ballston Spa Village	5,589	2	0	1	0	1	127	18	107	2	1
	Batavia	15,703	37	1	5	8	23	655	88	560	7	0
	Bath Village	5,604	14	0	7	1	6	170	24	145	1	
	Beacon	14,876	83	0	2	37	44	282	72	180	30	6
	Bedford Town	18,546	7	0	0	2	5	149	17	125	7	1
	Bethlehem Town	32,991	24	0	1	5	18	568	87	464	17	2
	Binghamton	45,614	206	2	9	63	132	2,353	288	2,016	49	5
	Blooming Grove Town	12,241	11	0	0	0	11	157	38	110	9	0
	Bolivar Village	1,142	2	0	0	0	2	11	1	10	0	0
	Bolton Town	2,169	1	0	0	0	1	8	2	6	0	0
	Boonville Village	2,101	3	0	0	0	3	8	1	6	1	0
	Brant Town	1,876	0	0	0	0	0	9	0	9	0	0
	Briarcliff Manor Village	7,959	2	0	0	0	2	51	8	37	6	0
	Brighton Town	34,713	33	0	3	11	19	1,052	140	862	50	1
	Brockport Village	8,156	14	0	2	5	7	162	30	130	2	2
	Bronxville Village	6,472	1	0	0	1	0	38	3	24	11	0
	Buffalo	280,494	3,957	74	174	1,708	2,001	15,436	4,447	8,864	2,125	159
	Cairo Town	6,655	0	0	0	0	0	32	3	29	0	0
	Caledonia Village	2,229	2	0	0	0	2	74	14	60	0	0
	Cambridge Village	1,880	2	0	0	0	2	43	12	30	1	0
	Camden Village	2,294	5	0	0	0	5	39	9	28	2	0
	Camillus Town and Village	23,330	13	0	0	3	10	286	52	218	16	0
	Canisteo Village	2,287	11	0	2	0	9	50	16	34	0	0
	Cape Vincent Village	782	0	0	0	0	0	4	2	1	1	0
	Carmel Town	34,804	28	0	1	10	17	314	63	236	15	3

[1] The FBI does not publish arson data unless it receives data from either the agency or the state for all 12 months of the calendar year.

Table 8. Offenses Known to Law Enforcement, by State and City, 2006 (*Contd.*)

(Number.)

State	City	Popula-tion	Violent crime	Murder and non-negligent man-slaughter	Forcible rape	Robbery	Aggra-vated assault	Property crime	Burglary	Larceny-theft	Motor vehicle theft	Arson[1]
	Carroll Town	3,547	2	0	0	0	2	11	3	8	0	0
	Carthage Village	3,800	6	0	0	0	6	83	11	70	2	1
	Catskill Village	4,379	12	3	2	1	6	194	23	162	9	1
	Cattaraugus Village	1,032	2	0	0	0	2	4	4	0	0	0
	Cayuga Heights Village	3,709	0	0	0	0	0	45	0	45	0	0
	Cazenovia Village	2,705	0	0	0	0	0	10	0	9	1	0
	Central Square Village	1,662	1	0	0	0	1	19	2	17	0	0
	Chatham Village	1,766	16	0	1	2	13	67	18	47	2	0
	Cheektowaga Town	80,995	221	2	14	75	130	2,419	415	1,867	137	5
	Chester Town	9,710	1	0	0	0	1	36	12	22	2	3
	Chester Village	3,614	10	0	1	5	4	168	6	160	2	2
	Chittenango Village	4,914	6	0	0	0	6	102	20	78	4	1
	Cicero Town	28,045	25	0	0	11	14	449	70	367	12	0
	Clarkstown Town	78,642	66	1	5	15	45	1,602	103	1,436	63	1
	Clayton Village	1,871	2	0	0	0	2	13	8	4	1	0
	Clay Town	54,356	16	0	1	7	8	502	96	392	14	
	Clifton Springs Village	2,201	3	0	0	0	3	33	5	28	0	0
	Clyde Village	2,187	5	0	0	0	5	94	22	71	1	0
	Cobleskill Village	4,719	10	1	0	1	8	163	16	142	5	0
	Coeymans Town	8,057	20	0	0	2	18	63	11	50	2	0
	Cohoes	15,125	50	0	2	5	43	187	55	115	17	1
	Colchester Town	2,061	1	0	0	0	1	3	3	0	0	0
	Cold Spring Village	2,014	3	0	0	0	3	25	10	15	0	0
	Colonie Town	77,357	94	0	2	31	61	2,890	310	2,472	108	20
	Cooperstown Village	1,943	3	0	0	1	2	38	3	35	0	0
	Copake Town	3,357	2	0	0	0	2	26	9	15	2	0
	Corning	10,579	51	1	5	12	33	460	61	391	8	7
	Cornwall-on-Hudson Village	3,118	4	0	0	1	3	34	4	29	1	0
	Cornwall Town	9,742	12	0	1	2	9	16	6	10	0	0
	Cortland	18,572	77	0	18	8	51	393	86	290	17	5
	Coxsackie Village	2,861	6	0	0	0	6	21	3	15	3	0
	Crawford Town	9,276	10	0	1	3	6	180	33	138	9	0
	Croton-on-Hudson Village	7,824	2	0	0	2	0	91	15	69	7	0
	Cuba Town	3,382	16	0	0	0	16	38	11	25	2	0
	Dansville Village	4,652	6	0	0	0	6	264	12	249	3	0
	Deerpark Town	8,347	8	0	1	0	7	168	38	120	10	0
	Delhi Village	2,727	6	0	0	0	6	2	0	2	0	0
	Depew Village	15,840	24	0	3	6	15	321	53	260	8	1
	Deposit Village	1,640	12	0	2	0	10	13	7	5	1	1
	Dewitt Town	22,015	24	0	0	16	8	552	95	436	21	1
	Dexter Village	1,141	0	0	0	0	0	0	0	0	0	0
	Dobbs Ferry Village	11,100	11	0	0	5	6	136	22	109	5	1
	Dolgeville Village	2,101	4	0	0	0	4	46	6	38	2	0
	Dryden Village	1,838	4	0	1	1	2	93	8	83	2	0
	Dunkirk	12,526	62	0	6	17	39	323	59	260	4	2
	Durham Town	2,748	0	0	0	0	0	0	0	0	0	0
	East Aurora-Aurora Town	13,824	3	0	0	1	2	188	20	163	5	1
	Eastchester Town	18,675	11	0	0	7	4	199	20	170	9	0
	East Fishkill Town	28,835	101	1	1	1	98	380	38	324	18	
	East Greenbush Town	16,374	25	0	3	3	19	438	56	370	12	0
	East Hampton Town	18,989	30	0	4	3	23	382	97	271	14	1
	East Hampton Village	1,361	1	0	0	0	1	148	16	131	1	0
	East Rochester Village	6,383	21	0	0	5	16	133	28	102	3	4
	East Syracuse Village	3,084	14	0	1	7	6	146	12	129	5	2
	Eden Town	7,938	3	0	0	0	3	54	9	41	4	0
	Ellenville Village	3,965	11	2	2	5	2	158	24	130	4	1
	Ellicott Town	5,403	5	0	1	1	3	270	48	218	4	0
	Ellicottville	1,846	2	0	0	0	2	106	7	96	3	0
	Elmira	30,008	113	1	2	45	65	1,457	281	1,146	30	3
	Elmira Heights Village	4,022	5	0	1	0	4	123	12	107	4	0
	Elmira Town	6,023	1	0	0	0	1	11	7	3	1	0
	Elmsford Village	4,740	10	0	0	2	8	76	12	55	9	0
	Endicott Village	12,673	47	2	6	14	25	489	83	400	6	0

[1] The FBI does not publish arson data unless it receives data from either the agency or the state for all 12 months of the calendar year.

Table 8. Offenses Known to Law Enforcement, by State and City, 2006 *(Contd.)*

(Number.)

State	City	Popula-tion	Violent crime	Murder and non-negligent man-slaughter	Forcible rape	Robbery	Aggra-vated assault	Property crime	Burglary	Larceny-theft	Motor vehicle theft	Arson[1]
	Evans Town	15,080	15	0	2	1	12	312	73	226	13	4
	Fairport Village	5,591	0	0	0	0	0	66	13	47	6	4
	Fallsburg Town	11,772	24	0	2	3	19	213	87	116	10	0
	Fishkill Town	18,691	11	1	2	3	5	250	39	194	17	0
	Fishkill Village	1,754	9	0	0	0	9	64	12	52	0	0
	Floral Park Village	15,779	6	0	0	6	0	132	19	106	7	3
	Florida Village	2,788	0	0	0	0	0	22	6	16	0	0
	Fort Edward Village	3,128	10	0	1	0	9	72	13	58	1	4
	Fort Plain Village	2,217	2	0	0	0	2	14	3	11	0	0
	Frankfort Town	4,967	8	0	0	0	8	25	8	14	3	0
	Frankfort Village	2,459	0	0	0	0	0	33	5	27	1	0
	Franklinville Village	1,783	9	0	0	0	9	10	3	7	0	0
	Fredonia Village	10,764	14	0	0	0	14	228	17	207	4	0
	Freeport Village	43,636	234	1	2	123	108	879	114	642	123	5
	Freeville Village	508	0	0	0	0	0	9	3	6	0	0
	Friendship Town	1,888	5	0	0	1	4	14	5	8	1	0
	Fulton City	11,556	22	0	2	6	14	513	42	464	7	3
	Garden City Village	21,755	8	0	1	2	5	328	37	279	12	1
	Gates Town	28,754	61	0	3	30	28	1,047	106	867	74	1
	Geddes Town	10,747	5	0	0	1	4	195	30	160	5	3
	Geneseo Village	7,830	8	0	5	0	3	241	22	217	2	0
	Geneva	13,545	36	0	7	11	18	362	89	271	2	0
	Germantown Town	2,040	0	0	0	0	0	1	0	1	0	0
	Glen Cove	26,704	30	1	1	13	15	273	54	203	16	2
	Glen Park Village	499	0	0	0	0	0	0	0	0	0	0
	Glens Falls	14,146	26	0	2	8	16	616	79	529	8	0
	Glenville Town	20,988	11	0	1	2	8	317	55	251	11	0
	Gloversville	15,324	55	0	6	6	43	585	94	459	32	
	Goshen Town	8,325	2	0	0	1	1	81	14	59	8	1
	Goshen Village	5,452	6	0	0	1	5	113	12	98	3	0
	Gouverneur Village	4,138	9	1	0	0	8	189	36	148	5	0
	Gowanda Village	2,723	6	0	2	0	4	74	16	56	2	0
	Granville Village	2,630	3	1	0	0	2	44	14	29	1	0
	Great Neck Estates Village	2,745	1	0	0	1	0	5	2	2	1	0
	Greece Town	94,233	97	2	12	40	43	2,321	255	1,954	112	3
	Greenburgh Town	43,354	36	0	0	19	17	780	80	652	48	0
	Greene Village	1,695	0	0	0	0	0	4	0	4	0	0
	Green Island Village	2,579	4	0	0	2	2	58	13	40	5	1
	Greenport Town	4,147	5	0	0	0	5	71	6	65	0	0
	Greenwich Village	1,891	1	0	0	0	1	34	12	19	3	0
	Greenwood Lake Village	3,470	4	0	0	1	3	38	2	34	2	0
	Groton Village	2,439	0	0	0	0	0	55	5	49	1	0
	Guilderland Town	33,078	9	0	0	4	5	791	52	730	9	4
	Hamburg Town	44,390	5	0	0	0	5	259	40	206	13	0
	Hamburg Village	9,663	17	0	2	4	11	224	42	178	4	0
	Hamilton Village	3,560	0	0	0	0	0	23	1	22	0	0
	Hancock Village	1,142	0	0	0	0	0	10	4	6	0	0
	Harriman Village	2,290	2	0	1	0	1	47	9	35	3	1
	Harrison Town	25,896	28	0	2	3	23	305	45	250	10	2
	Hastings-on-Hudson Village	7,723	22	0	0	2	20	120	14	103	3	2
	Haverstraw Town	24,463	93	0	5	35	53	562	118	428	16	4
	Hempstead Village	52,970	326	4	10	181	131	950	220	551	179	3
	Herkimer Village	7,283	88	0	14	5	69	427	65	362	0	0
	Highland Falls Village	3,771	0	0	0	0	0	7	3	4	0	0
	Homer Village	3,312	0	0	0	0	0	62	8	54	0	0
	Hoosick Falls Village	3,359	21	0	1	0	20	65	12	52	1	0
	Hornell	8,785	51	0	7	0	44	230	34	196	0	1
	Horseheads Village	6,383	6	0	2	2	2	151	12	137	2	0
	Hudson Falls Village	6,882	6	0	0	0	6	106	17	82	7	0
	Huntington Bay Village	1,497	0	0	0	0	0	4	0	4	0	0
	Hyde Park Town	20,922	1	0	0	1	0	93	17	66	10	
	Ilion Village	8,352	20	0	2	1	17	126	32	88	6	1
	Irondequoit Town	51,209	93	1	8	42	42	1,618	205	1,291	122	6

[1] The FBI does not publish arson data unless it receives data from either the agency or the state for all 12 months of the calendar year.

Table 8. Offenses Known to Law Enforcement, by State and City, 2006 (*Contd.*)

(Number.)

State	City	Popula-tion	Violent crime	Murder and non-negligent man-slaughter	Forcible rape	Robbery	Aggra-vated assault	Property crime	Burglary	Larceny-theft	Motor vehicle theft	Arson[1]
	Irvington Village	6,633	1	0	0	0	1	40	8	30	2	1
	Ithaca	29,846	62	0	4	28	30	1,167	147	995	25	0
	Jamestown	30,462	170	0	21	35	114	1,206	365	795	46	10
	Johnson City Village	14,995	88	0	11	21	56	801	106	678	17	3
	Johnstown	8,595	12	0	2	0	10	301	32	258	11	0
	Jordan Village	1,350	0	0	0	0	0	13	3	10	0	0
	Kenmore Village	15,597	32	0	3	21	8	297	46	240	11	2
	Kensington Village	1,198	0	0	0	0	0	0	0	0	0	0
	Kent Town	14,438	5	0	0	0	5	121	34	83	4	1
	Kings Point Village	5,271	1	0	0	0	1	12	0	10	2	0
	Kingston	23,129	89	1	11	43	34	798	147	625	26	4
	Kirkland Town	8,293	7	0	0	1	6	112	17	91	4	0
	Lackawanna	18,224	87	0	5	14	68	453	124	298	31	5
	Lake Placid Village	2,764	4	0	0	0	4	63	8	54	1	2
	Lake Success Village	2,832	1	0	0	1	0	75	5	62	8	0
	Lakewood-Busti	7,598	6	0	1	3	2	175	29	146	0	0
	Lancaster Town	23,212	16	1	1	5	9	475	70	396	9	1
	Larchmont Village	6,504	3	0	0	0	3	99	13	82	4	0
	Le Roy Village	4,301	5	0	1	1	3	207	7	198	2	1
	Lewisboro Town	12,516	0	0	0	0	0	60	1	57	2	0
	Lewiston Town and Village	16,677	9	0	2	1	6	166	29	128	9	0
	Liberty Village	3,934	33	0	2	7	24	188	39	142	7	2
	Liverpool Village	2,421	2	0	0	0	2	35	6	29	0	0
	Lloyd Harbor Village	3,712	1	0	0	0	1	27	4	22	1	0
	Lloyd Town	10,527	10	0	1	0	9	125	24	90	11	1
	Lockport	21,328	53	1	5	21	26	780	198	545	37	7
	Long Beach	35,431	51	0	0	23	28	273	19	248	6	0
	Lowville Village	3,259	7	0	1	0	6	78	14	62	2	0
	Lynbrook Village	19,693	33	0	1	22	10	181	26	141	14	1
	Lyons Village	3,563	28	0	2	7	19	267	47	202	18	0
	Macedon Town and Village	8,985	1	0	0	1	0	49	8	38	3	0
	Malone Village	5,945	23	1	6	0	16	147	22	125	0	0
	Malverne Village	8,856	0	0	0	0	0	11	0	8	3	0
	Mamaroneck Town	11,382	3	0	0	1	2	191	18	165	8	0
	Manchester Village	1,461	0	0	0	0	0	0	0	0	0	0
	Manlius Town	25,072	27	1	0	7	19	317	45	264	8	1
	Marcellus Village	1,798	1	0	0	0	1	13	3	10	0	0
	Marlborough Town	8,394	18	0	1	1	16	142	33	100	9	1
	Massena Village	10,888	23	1	6	1	15	241	33	206	2	2
	Maybrook Village	4,079	1	0	0	0	1	52	7	44	1	0
	McGraw Village	976	0	0	0	0	0	1	1	0	0	0
	Mechanicville	5,010	35	0	0	1	34	64	19	43	2	1
	Medina Village	6,252	22	0	1	1	20	96	26	69	1	1
	Menands Village	3,835	5	0	0	1	4	147	20	120	7	1
	Middleport Village	1,831	0	0	0	0	0	52	5	46	1	0
	Middletown	26,137	177	2	13	94	68	946	129	781	36	
	Millbrook Village	1,563	0	0	0	0	0	9	1	8	0	0
	Mohawk Village	2,576	2	0	0	0	2	59	10	49	0	2
	Monroe Village	8,149	22	0	0	4	18	240	25	211	4	0
	Montgomery Town	8,805	6	0	0	2	4	131	13	110	8	1
	Monticello Village	6,667	75	0	3	23	49	351	97	243	11	3
	Moravia Village	1,330	1	0	0	0	1	11	0	10	1	0
	Moriah Town	3,629	1	0	0	0	1	11	2	8	1	0
	Mount Hope Town	7,393	2	0	0	0	2	43	14	26	3	0
	Mount Kisco Village	10,359	14	1	0	5	8	155	13	140	2	
	Mount Morris Village	2,986	4	0	1	0	3	113	15	97	1	0
	Mount Pleasant Town	26,438	9	0	0	4	5	178	29	140	9	0
	Mount Vernon	68,106	719	2	14	398	305	1,717	383	1,124	210	12
	Newark Village	9,436	33	0	9	6	18	405	49	344	12	1
	New Berlin Town	1,695	0	0	0	0	0	30	9	21	0	0
	Newburgh	28,624	386	1	16	134	235	1,080	264	750	66	14
	Newburgh Town	30,590	34	0	1	18	15	920	120	783	17	4
	New Castle Town	17,679	5	1	0	3	1	77	21	53	3	0

[1] The FBI does not publish arson data unless it receives data from either the agency or the state for all 12 months of the calendar year.

Table 8. Offenses Known to Law Enforcement, by State and City, 2006 (*Contd.*)

(Number.)

State	City	Popula-tion	Violent crime	Murder and non-negligent man-slaughter	Forcible rape	Robbery	Aggra-vated assault	Property crime	Burglary	Larceny-theft	Motor vehicle theft	Arson[1]
	New Hartford Town and Village	19,662	5	0	0	2	3	654	45	602	7	0
	New Paltz Town and Village	14,046	63	0	5	4	54	269	39	223	7	0
	New Rochelle	73,162	242	4	4	168	66	1,628	215	1,314	99	2
	New Windsor Town	25,033	29	1	1	7	20	579	90	470	19	4
	New York	8,165,001	52,086	596	1,071	23,511	26,908	153,436	22,137	115,363	15,936	
	New York Mills Village	3,154	1	0	0	0	1	56	15	36	5	0
	Niagara Falls	53,008	643	4	35	201	403	2,788	791	1,802	195	37
	Niagara Town	8,672	12	0	0	6	6	307	60	226	21	4
	Niskayuna Town	21,511	11	1	0	5	5	434	62	357	15	1
	Nissequogue Village	1,575	0	0	0	0	0	16	0	16	0	0
	North Castle Town	12,027	7	0	1	1	5	110	10	97	3	0
	North Greenbush Town	11,699	30	0	1	1	28	151	16	135	0	1
	Northport Village	7,607	2	0	0	1	1	70	8	60	2	4
	North Syracuse Village	6,744	12	0	0	6	6	53	7	46	0	0
	North Tonawanda	32,158	68	0	8	18	42	540	107	403	30	2
	Northville Village	1,162	2	0	0	0	2	9	3	6	0	0
	Norwich	7,252	19	0	7	2	10	359	75	280	4	1
	Nunda Town And Village	2,995	3	0	3	0	0	81	5	76	0	0
	Ocean Beach Village	146	3	0	0	0	3	161	12	149	0	0
	Ogdensburg	11,453	9	0	5	0	4	542	91	436	15	1
	Ogden Town	19,224	19	0	2	5	12	347	69	258	20	0
	Old Brookville Village	2,250	2	0	0	1	1	124	27	95	2	0
	Old Westbury Village	5,048	3	0	0	0	3	57	17	39	1	1
	Olean	14,839	12	0	2	10	0	676	96	574	6	1
	Olive Town	4,714	0	0	0	0	0	17	8	9	0	0
	Oneida	10,952	20	0	4	5	11	339	74	261	4	1
	Oneonta City	13,241	51	0	8	10	33	356	82	263	11	1
	Orangetown Town	35,966	27	0	4	13	10	565	71	487	7	1
	Orchard Park Town	28,345	32	0	4	7	21	548	113	414	21	1
	Oriskany Village	1,427	0	0	0	0	0	15	3	11	1	0
	Ossining Town	5,697	3	0	0	1	2	56	11	45	0	0
	Ossining Village	23,610	67	1	2	42	22	290	58	218	14	3
	Oswego City	17,752	39	0	7	6	26	607	81	515	11	4
	Owego Village	3,804	8	0	2	0	6	23	3	20	0	0
	Oxford Village	1,575	1	0	0	0	1	49	8	41	0	0
	Oyster Bay Cove Village	2,273	0	0	0	0	0	10	5	5	0	0
	Painted Post Village	1,810	2	0	0	0	2	30	1	29	0	0
	Palmyra Village	3,438	2	0	0	1	1	53	11	41	1	0
	Peekskill	24,108	67	0	2	23	42	193	39	143	11	0
	Pelham Manor Village	5,409	5	0	1	4	0	103	10	82	11	1
	Pelham Village	6,381	18	0	0	7	11	146	12	118	16	0
	Penn Yan Village	5,184	4	0	2	2	0	127	16	109	2	0
	Perry Village	3,802	8	1	2	1	4	124	42	78	4	1
	Phelps Village	1,955	3	0	0	0	3	7	2	5	0	0
	Piermont Village	2,605	0	0	0	0	0	49	2	45	2	0
	Pine Plains Town	2,718	0	0	0	0	0	20	0	20	0	0
	Plattekill Town	10,839	0	0	0	0	0	32	7	21	4	0
	Plattsburgh City	19,232	24	1	5	4	14	608	136	458	14	7
	Pleasantville Village	7,149	1	0	0	0	1	0	0	0	0	0
	Port Byron Village	1,271	0	0	0	0	0	3	1	2	0	0
	Port Chester Village	27,961	85	0	2	61	22	777	107	648	22	1
	Port Dickinson Village	1,630	2	0	0	0	2	26	4	20	2	0
	Port Jervis	9,227	29	0	1	10	18	233	48	171	14	
	Portville Village	997	0	0	0	0	0	35	7	28	0	0
	Port Washington	18,427	13	0	0	0	13	135	33	94	8	4
	Potsdam Village	9,731	4	0	0	1	3	217	24	184	9	0
	Poughkeepsie	30,436	417	4	13	173	227	1,122	242	792	88	4
	Poughkeepsie Town	43,809	36	0	1	20	15	1,271	111	1,142	18	1
	Pulaski Village	2,351	8	0	0	1	7	61	11	50	0	0
	Quogue Village	1,119	0	0	0	0	0	36	18	17	1	0
	Ramapo Town	74,747	85	1	4	20	60	717	114	560	43	1
	Rensselaer City	7,880	18	1	1	6	10	245	60	179	6	0

[1] The FBI does not publish arson data unless it receives data from either the agency or the state for all 12 months of the calendar year.

Table 8. Offenses Known to Law Enforcement, by State and City, 2006 (*Contd.*)

(Number.)

State	City	Popula-tion	Violent crime	Murder and non-negligent man-slaughter	Forcible rape	Robbery	Aggra-vated assault	Property crime	Burglary	Larceny-theft	Motor vehicle theft	Arson[1]
	Rhinebeck Village	3,134	0	0	0	0	0	26	3	23	0	0
	Riverhead Town	34,332	146	0	8	66	72	1,003	166	815	22	0
	Rochester	211,656	2,666	49	92	1,332	1,193	12,999	2,673	7,913	2,413	239
	Rockville Centre Village	24,302	21	0	1	17	3	304	42	240	22	0
	Rome	34,436	45	1	3	10	31	566	154	381	31	5
	Rosendale Town	6,381	2	0	0	0	2	46	11	34	1	0
	Rotterdam Town	29,160	38	0	2	18	18	833	143	671	19	1
	Rouses Point Village	2,406	0	0	0	0	0	3	2	1	0	0
	Rye	15,032	9	0	0	2	7	229	16	202	11	0
	Sackets Harbor Village	1,422	0	0	0	0	0	13	2	11	0	2
	Sag Harbor Village	2,374	8	0	1	1	6	44	13	26	5	0
	Salamanca	5,867	25	0	2	2	21	288	58	222	8	2
	Sands Point Village	2,846	3	0	0	0	3	11	4	7	0	0
	Saranac Lake Village	4,936	11	0	0	1	10	110	26	83	1	0
	Saratoga Springs	28,111	50	0	4	7	39	676	139	513	24	4
	Saugerties Town	15,490	10	0	5	3	2	259	52	199	8	4
	Saugerties Village	3,941	16	0	0	0	16	76	7	68	1	0
	Scarsdale Village	17,811	5	0	0	4	1	163	21	135	7	1
	Schenectady	61,444	712	6	52	309	345	3,449	1,119	1,994	336	42
	Schodack Town	11,277	6	0	2	0	4	169	44	120	5	0
	Schoharie Village	991	3	0	0	0	3	7	1	6	0	0
	Scotia Village	7,979	15	0	1	6	8	207	22	181	4	0
	Seneca Falls Village	6,855	11	0	0	1	10	31	8	22	1	0
	Shandaken Town	3,168	4	0	0	0	4	68	16	49	3	1
	Shawangunk Town	12,741	11	0	0	1	10	116	20	90	6	0
	Shelter Island Town	2,450	0	0	0	0	0	58	11	47	0	0
	Sherburne Village	1,450	1	0	0	0	1	45	6	38	1	0
	Sherrill	3,172	2	0	0	1	1	17	5	12	0	0
	Shortsville Village	1,301	0	0	0	0	0	1	0	1	0	0
	Sidney Village	3,915	11	0	1	0	10	209	25	179	5	2
	Silver Creek Village	2,871	9	0	0	0	9	46	7	37	2	0
	Skaneateles Village	2,596	0	0	0	0	0	14	4	10	0	0
	Sleepy Hollow Village	10,004	0	0	0	0	0	0	0	0	0	0
	Sodus Village	1,677	2	0	0	1	1	43	5	38	0	0
	Solvay Village	6,624	13	0	2	4	7	155	24	122	9	0
	Southampton Town	50,311	79	0	7	21	51	990	241	691	58	2
	Southampton Village	4,120	6	0	0	1	5	142	11	127	4	0
	South Glens Falls Village	3,454	10	0	1	1	8	109	20	87	2	0
	South Nyack Village	3,502	7	0	1	2	4	55	9	46	0	0
	Spring Valley Village	25,423	181	1	6	69	105	413	93	284	36	1
	Stillwater Town	6,324	4	0	0	0	4	28	7	19	2	1
	Stony Point Town	14,950	5	0	0	3	2	103	9	88	6	0
	Suffern Village	10,926	4	0	0	1	3	82	16	61	5	
	Syracuse	142,062	1,515	12	66	534	903	6,677	1,904	4,037	736	57
	Tarrytown Village	11,376	4	0	0	2	2	100	13	82	5	0
	Tonawanda	15,376	49	0	5	12	32	425	42	367	16	5
	Tonawanda Town	58,720	165	0	11	55	99	1,145	229	841	75	2
	Troy	48,439	373	1	18	120	234	2,279	614	1,482	183	
	Tuckahoe Village	6,273	6	0	1	1	4	33	1	31	1	0
	Tupper Lake Village	3,866	13	0	3	0	10	97	15	76	6	0
	Tuxedo Park Village	734	0	0	0	0	0	0	0	0	0	0
	Tuxedo Town	2,978	3	0	0	0	3	5	1	3	1	0
	Ulster Town	12,915	9	2	1	4	2	263	37	206	20	0
	Utica	59,495	425	3	20	138	264	2,799	763	1,889	147	6
	Vernon Village	1,174	1	0	1	0	0	17	2	14	1	0
	Vestal Town	27,496	22	0	0	4	18	560	39	515	6	3
	Walden Village	6,773	11	0	0	3	8	87	15	65	7	1
	Wallkill Town	27,071	45	1	2	26	16	687	81	565	41	2
	Walton Village	2,959	13	0	0	0	13	84	27	56	1	1
	Wappingers Falls Village	5,099	10	0	0	4	6	146	19	125	2	3
	Warsaw Village	3,711	7	0	0	0	7	111	14	95	2	0
	Warwick Town	19,829	0	0	0	0	0	180	30	146	4	0
	Washingtonville Village	6,253	1	0	0	1	0	91	7	80	4	0
	Waterford Town & Village	8,746	8	0	1	0	7	90	18	68	4	1

[1] The FBI does not publish arson data unless it receives data from either the agency or the state for all 12 months of the calendar year.

Table 8. Offenses Known to Law Enforcement, by State and City, 2006 (*Contd.*)

(Number.)

State	City	Popula-tion	Violent crime	Murder and non-negligent man-slaughter	Forcible rape	Robbery	Aggra-vated assault	Property crime	Burglary	Larceny-theft	Motor vehicle theft	Arson[1]
	Waterloo Village	5,148	12	0	0	1	11	255	22	227	6	0
	Watertown	27,293	178	1	10	42	125	1,509	292	1,101	116	8
	Watervliet	9,915	31	0	0	11	20	241	54	170	17	0
	Watkins Glen Village	2,105	2	0	0	1	1	75	7	66	2	0
	Waverly Village	4,505	2	0	0	0	2	143	26	112	5	1
	Wayland Village	1,847	1	0	0	0	1	9	6	3	0	0
	Webster Town & Village	41,120	24	0	1	12	11	623	76	514	33	1
	Weedsport Village	1,975	0	0	0	0	0	54	0	54	0	1
	Wellsville Village	4,786	29	1	0	1	27	177	24	149	4	2
	West Carthage Village	2,164	2	0	0	0	2	17	1	16	0	0
	Westfield Village	3,473	2	0	0	0	2	54	7	44	3	0
	Westhampton Beach Village	1,962	1	0	1	0	0	95	10	85	0	0
	West Seneca Town	44,829	66	0	4	23	39	932	178	711	43	
	Whitehall Village	2,655	1	0	0	0	1	51	18	30	3	0
	White Plains	56,885	157	1	6	48	102	1,181	69	1,077	35	1
	Whitesboro Village	3,864	14	0	0	2	12	41	6	34	1	0
	Whitestown Town	9,230	1	0	0	0	1	40	6	33	1	1
	Windham Town	1,868	0	0	0	0	0	47	11	36	0	0
	Woodbury Town	10,266	3	0	0	0	3	153	8	139	6	0
	Woodridge Village	1,050	0	0	0	0	0	3	2	1	0	2
	Woodstock Town	6,268	6	0	0	1	5	84	28	56	0	1
	Yonkers	196,951	978	8	31	498	441	3,502	651	2,400	451	33
NORTH CAROLINA	Aberdeen	4,890	25	1	1	12	11	293	54	216	23	6
	Ahoskie	4,410	37	1	0	7	29	228	54	166	8	3
	Albemarle	15,631	118	3	6	31	78	1,040	209	786	45	9
	Andrews	1,737	5	1	0	0	4	47	7	34	6	0
	Angier	4,189	25	0	3	5	17	182	46	128	8	3
	Archdale	9,616	23	0	0	9	14	404	103	249	52	4
	Asheboro	24,111	50	1	8	18	23	1,599	418	1,070	111	3
	Asheville	73,672	473	4	49	206	214	4,099	793	2,834	472	25
	Atlantic Beach	1,839	14	0	1	0	13	189	57	132	0	0
	Aulander	911	1	0	0	1	0	30	17	11	2	0
	Ayden	4,894	11	1	1	3	6	266	71	191	4	1
	Badin	1,275	2	0	0	1	1	3	0	3	0	0
	Bailey	688	2	0	0	0	2	44	11	22	11	0
	Banner Elk	977	0	0	0	0	0	39	8	27	4	0
	Beaufort	4,201	30	0	1	1	28	158	38	112	8	1
	Beech Mountain	312	0	0	0	0	0	24	8	15	1	0
	Belhaven	2,004	14	0	2	1	11	68	18	50	0	1
	Belmont	8,954	41	0	0	15	26	434	111	299	24	1
	Benson	3,347	85	0	1	12	72	306	81	209	16	0
	Bethel	1,723	13	0	1	3	9	55	7	45	3	1
	Beulaville	1,120	5	0	0	4	1	61	15	45	1	1
	Biltmore Forest	1,527	1	0	0	0	1	24	3	20	1	0
	Biscoe	1,749	2	0	0	1	1	204	22	174	8	0
	Black Mountain	7,803	14	0	1	6	7	166	60	96	10	1
	Bladenboro	1,747	29	0	1	4	24	135	35	91	9	0
	Blowing Rock	1,452	2	0	0	0	2	71	13	56	2	0
	Boiling Spring Lakes	4,189	2	0	1	0	1	75	21	47	7	0
	Boone	13,455	28	0	5	4	19	405	58	330	17	0
	Brevard	6,776	33	0	3	3	27	242	58	177	7	2
	Bryson City	1,388	26	1	1	1	23	126	1	116	9	0
	Burgaw	3,831	14	0	0	4	10	106	18	80	8	0
	Burlington	48,542	445	4	17	110	314	3,118	692	2,251	175	16
	Burnsville	1,660	2	0	1	1	0	61	14	44	3	0
	Butner	6,373	18	0	0	9	9	310	67	232	11	2
	Cameron	160	1	0	0	1	0	17	4	10	3	0
	Canton	4,082	13	0	0	0	13	238	75	150	13	1
	Cape Carteret	1,428	0	0	0	0	0	33	1	32	0	0
	Carolina Beach	5,496	13	0	2	4	7	428	103	314	11	9
	Carrboro	16,753	74	0	5	28	41	931	209	692	30	1
	Carthage	1,974	15	0	0	5	10	79	18	59	2	5
	Cary	108,563	131	0	14	42	75	2,189	554	1,520	115	11
	Caswell Beach	475	1	0	0	0	1	5	2	2	1	0

[1] The FBI does not publish arson data unless it receives data from either the agency or the state for all 12 months of the calendar year.

Table 8. Offenses Known to Law Enforcement, by State and City, 2006 *(Contd.)*

(Number.)

State	City	Popula-tion	Violent crime	Murder and non-negligent man-slaughter	Forcible rape	Robbery	Aggra-vated assault	Property crime	Burglary	Larceny-theft	Motor vehicle theft	Arson[1]
	Catawba	754	1	0	0	0	1	17	5	11	1	0
	Chadbourn	2,147	28	0	3	7	18	189	51	125	13	1
	Chapel Hill	50,532	252	2	24	81	145	2,211	528	1,609	74	12
	Charlotte-Mecklenburg	699,398	7,532	83	346	3,207	3,896	48,886	13,582	28,154	7,150	346
	Cherryville	5,564	17	0	1	5	11	232	95	129	8	1
	China Grove	3,788	14	0	0	5	9	134	22	102	10	1
	Chocowinity	746	5	0	1	0	4	20	5	13	2	0
	Claremont	1,126	0	0	0	0	0	88	15	64	9	0
	Clayton	13,201	40	1	5	16	18	453	106	330	17	2
	Cleveland	839	3	0	1	0	2	59	17	42	0	0
	Clinton	8,943	73	1	4	21	47	536	139	361	36	4
	Clyde	1,384	2	0	0	0	2	25	12	13	0	0
	Concord	62,311	280	3	14	98	165	2,924	459	2,149	316	12
	Creedmoor	3,218	17	0	3	2	12	104	13	85	6	3
	Dobson	1,538	1	0	0	0	1	40	7	32	1	0
	Drexel	1,932	2	1	0	0	1	32	8	22	2	0
	Dunn	10,086	113	0	8	29	76	732	261	403	68	5
	Durham[8]	208,932	1,957	13	98	977	869	11,866	3,098	7,617	1,151	48
	Edenton	5,101	19	0	1	4	14	227	46	167	14	0
	Elizabethtown	3,921	23	1	0	8	14	285	53	221	11	0
	Elkin	4,401	22	0	2	3	17	225	32	183	10	0
	Elon	7,242	11	0	2	3	6	115	32	82	1	0
	Emerald Isle	3,760	1	0	0	1	0	220	107	108	5	0
	Enfield	2,348	14	0	1	3	10	142	61	77	4	0
	Erwin	4,888	7	0	0	1	6	211	73	120	18	0
	Fairmont	2,670	56	0	1	7	48	289	120	149	20	1
	Farmville	4,637	47	0	1	15	31	266	71	189	6	1
	Fayetteville	132,521	1,299	15	61	510	713	13,091	3,519	8,549	1,023	49
	Fletcher	4,612	12	0	0	6	6	194	37	134	23	0
	Four Oaks	1,800	6	0	0	1	5	47	15	24	8	0
	Franklin	3,683	10	0	1	0	9	188	70	107	11	1
	Franklinton	1,937	4	0	1	1	2	131	31	96	4	0
	Fuquay-Varina	12,443	71	0	3	14	54	492	106	360	26	2
	Garner	22,810	73	0	9	26	38	1,169	220	906	43	2
	Garysburg	1,226	9	0	0	0	9	56	34	21	1	0
	Gastonia	70,340	710	4	30	220	456	5,816	1,271	4,056	489	62
	Goldsboro	39,442	328	4	3	95	226	2,435	633	1,650	152	3
	Graham	14,230	106	0	3	16	87	772	166	538	68	7
	Granite Falls	4,664	11	0	0	2	9	232	95	132	5	0
	Granite Quarry	2,277	3	0	0	2	1	78	25	50	3	1
	Greensboro	236,591	2,062	27	86	901	1,048	14,336	4,129	9,000	1,207	109
	Greenville	70,904	640	6	22	240	372	4,537	1,323	2,932	282	16
	Grifton	2,107	3	0	0	3	0	82	18	62	2	2
	Hamlet	5,940	44	2	1	12	29	385	107	245	33	3
	Havelock	22,097	65	0	8	16	41	568	125	415	28	5
	Henderson	16,537	182	5	4	79	94	1,491	366	1,049	76	7
	Hendersonville	11,623	104	2	6	21	75	993	154	765	74	1
	Hertford	2,146	8	0	1	3	4	123	48	68	7	1
	Hickory	41,035	320	1	26	115	178	3,063	736	2,082	245	10
	Highlands	960	0	0	0	0	0	69	26	40	3	0
	High Point	96,983	699	8	41	269	381	5,652	1,697	3,449	506	28
	Hillsborough	5,489	48	0	1	11	36	300	69	208	23	1
	Holden Beach	864	2	0	0	0	2	87	57	28	2	0
	Holly Ridge	776	1	0	0	0	1	58	15	40	3	0
	Holly Springs	15,532	22	1	0	3	18	215	66	142	7	0
	Hope Mills	13,037	63	0	4	28	31	866	178	646	42	1
	Hudson	3,122	5	0	0	0	5	120	26	91	3	1
	Huntersville	37,103	101	0	11	30	60	1,180	268	858	54	15
	Jacksonville[8]	73,696	208	2	26	48	132	2,002	408	1,476	118	7
	Jefferson	1,393	0	0	0	0	0	13	4	9	0	0
	Jonesville	2,321	10	0	0	3	7	170	54	108	8	0
	Kannapolis	39,820	155	4	12	54	85	1,037	292	636	109	13
	Kenansville	899	0	0	0	0	0	49	6	42	1	1
	Kenly	1,867	19	0	0	7	12	176	68	98	10	0

[1] The FBI does not publish arson data unless it receives data from either the agency or the state for all 12 months of the calendar year.
[8] Because of changes in the state/local agency's reporting practices, figures are not comparable to previous years' data.

Table 8. Offenses Known to Law Enforcement, by State and City, 2006 (*Contd.*)

(Number.)

State	City	Popula-tion	Violent crime	Murder and non-negligent man-slaughter	Forcible rape	Robbery	Aggra-vated assault	Property crime	Burglary	Larceny-theft	Motor vehicle theft	Arson[1]
	Kernersville	21,787	127	0	5	25	97	1,050	202	801	47	6
	Kill Devil Hills	6,681	40	0	7	8	25	432	105	305	22	1
	King	6,480	23	1	4	4	14	261	35	219	7	3
	Kings Mountain	11,079	38	2	1	20	15	520	114	387	19	2
	Kinston	23,307	237	5	9	44	179	1,887	396	1,397	94	14
	Kitty Hawk	3,425	6	0	2	0	4	135	33	96	6	0
	Knightdale	6,445	27	0	1	8	18	292	62	219	11	2
	La Grange	2,860	30	0	1	1	28	120	34	83	3	0
	Landis	3,125	7	2	1	2	2	158	24	115	19	1
	Laurel Park	2,125	0	0	0	0	0	23	1	19	3	0
	Laurinburg	16,125	121	0	10	32	79	835	284	496	55	15
	Leland	4,529	19	0	4	3	12	365	166	188	11	0
	Lenoir	18,269	58	2	0	26	30	808	226	529	53	1
	Lexington	20,805	181	1	10	37	133	1,151	319	771	61	7
	Liberty	2,766	2	0	1	1	0	58	11	43	4	0
	Lillington	3,225	15	1	0	4	10	99	41	49	9	0
	Lincolnton	10,600	64	3	1	18	42	766	162	563	41	2
	Longview	4,937	24	0	9	4	11	399	166	185	48	5
	Louisburg	3,423	8	0	3	2	3	199	54	137	8	0
	Lumberton	22,022	267	5	12	120	130	2,444	638	1,597	209	9
	Madison	2,284	36	0	0	0	36	160	43	117	0	0
	Maiden	3,329	12	0	0	2	10	145	26	114	5	0
	Manteo	1,327	1	0	0	0	1	73	22	49	2	0
	Marion	5,113	30	0	1	5	24	459	154	289	16	3
	Mars Hill	1,871	3	0	0	0	3	34	16	17	1	0
	Marshville	2,876	17	0	0	5	12	105	24	75	6	1
	Matthews	25,811	60	1	6	21	32	1,164	192	897	75	15
	Mayodan	2,547	3	0	0	0	3	100	23	77	0	0
	Maysville	1,010	3	0	0	0	3	11	3	7	1	0
	Mebane	9,123	57	0	0	6	51	389	87	277	25	4
	Middlesex	868	4	0	0	0	4	49	20	25	4	0
	Mint Hill	18,228	66	0	3	30	33	395	219	141	35	4
	Mocksville	4,553	16	0	1	5	10	299	42	250	7	0
	Monroe	30,585	230	2	7	65	156	1,963	505	1,277	181	9
	Mooresville	20,897	73	0	5	27	41	1,058	117	881	60	10
	Morehead City	9,024	71	1	6	10	54	506	113	373	20	2
	Morrisville	12,435	10	0	2	2	6	360	81	256	23	0
	Mount Airy	8,623	39	0	6	16	17	669	147	482	40	9
	Mount Gilead	1,415	6	0	0	2	4	67	44	23	0	0
	Mount Holly	9,869	61	1	2	12	46	289	86	178	25	2
	Mount Olive	4,531	67	0	1	8	58	332	56	258	18	0
	Murfreesboro	2,265	21	0	1	7	13	149	32	116	1	1
	Murphy	1,596	12	0	1	1	10	100	13	83	4	1
	Nags Head	3,137	23	0	6	3	14	298	74	216	8	1
	Nashville	4,566	23	0	2	6	15	111	43	60	8	0
	New Bern	24,587	150	0	18	49	83	1,434	307	1,056	71	2
	Newland	700	0	0	0	0	0	21	5	15	1	0
	Newport	3,917	7	0	1	1	5	97	27	67	3	0
	Newton	13,276	40	2	0	21	17	806	202	547	57	0
	North Topsail Beach	877	3	0	0	1	2	63	25	33	5	0
	North Wilkesboro	4,288	21	0	2	7	12	323	70	240	13	0
	Norwood	2,203	13	0	0	4	9	91	40	49	2	3
	Oak Island	7,832	30	2	4	4	20	306	138	154	14	0
	Ocean Isle Beach	514	4	0	0	0	4	131	49	76	6	0
	Old Fort	987	2	0	0	2	0	19	9	10	0	1
	Oxford	8,700	125	0	5	36	84	634	224	374	36	4
	Pembroke	2,747	23	3	1	8	11	286	147	124	15	4
	Pine Level	1,479	3	0	2	0	1	54	4	43	7	0
	Pinebluff	1,244	3	0	0	3	0	28	12	16	0	0
	Pinehurst	11,665	8	0	0	0	8	119	3	111	5	1
	Pine Knoll Shores	1,601	3	0	0	0	3	48	16	30	2	0
	Pineville	3,723	82	1	4	45	32	1,061	110	870	81	5
	Pittsboro	2,501	8	0	4	3	1	97	26	69	2	1
	Plymouth	4,043	50	0	2	1	47	208	84	122	2	0
	Raeford	3,666	27	0	3	12	12	256	99	144	13	0

[1] The FBI does not publish arson data unless it receives data from either the agency or the state for all 12 months of the calendar year.

Table 8. Offenses Known to Law Enforcement, by State and City, 2006 (*Contd.*)

(Number.)

State	City	Popula-tion	Violent crime	Murder and non-negligent man-slaughter	Forcible rape	Robbery	Aggra-vated assault	Property crime	Burglary	Larceny-theft	Motor vehicle theft	Arson[1]
	Raleigh	348,345	2,223	19	97	782	1,325	12,650	2,978	8,666	1,006	71
	Ramseur	1,738	3	0	0	2	1	117	33	82	2	0
	Randleman	3,726	11	0	0	0	11	310	77	226	7	2
	Red Springs	3,554	39	0	0	18	21	378	208	140	30	2
	Reidsville	15,073	65	2	0	22	41	1,277	314	902	61	6
	Richlands	844	1	0	0	0	1	49	7	39	3	0
	River Bend	2,810	0	0	0	0	0	10	4	6	0	0
	Roanoke Rapids	16,786	110	2	2	37	69	1,008	278	661	69	7
	Robersonville	1,670	14	0	0	6	8	104	34	64	6	1
	Rockingham	9,404	76	0	5	18	53	1,075	265	772	38	2
	Rockwell	2,022	3	0	0	1	2	43	10	31	2	0
	Rocky Mount	57,756	577	12	22	225	318	5,617	1,696	3,535	386	11
	Rose Hill	1,404	3	0	0	1	2	42	18	23	1	0
	Rowland	1,171	10	0	1	4	5	69	37	23	9	0
	Roxboro	8,930	87	0	7	11	69	567	191	348	28	0
	Rutherfordton	4,181	1	0	0	1	0	134	18	107	9	0
	Salisbury	28,113	281	3	17	131	130	2,132	461	1,521	150	15
	Sanford	27,243	127	2	9	67	49	1,702	411	1,208	83	5
	Scotland Neck	2,285	51	0	1	8	42	250	82	164	4	2
	Selma	6,779	75	1	6	28	40	479	233	219	27	3
	Shallotte	1,620	10	0	1	5	4	265	43	209	13	1
	Sharpsburg	2,509	9	0	0	2	7	29	12	15	2	2
	Shelby	21,687	180	5	14	67	94	1,319	373	855	91	5
	Siler City	8,240	48	0	5	7	36	326	68	232	26	1
	Smithfield	12,209	112	1	5	30	76	915	183	670	62	4
	Southern Pines	12,118	71	3	3	24	41	614	181	402	31	3
	Southern Shores	2,695	3	0	0	1	2	75	29	44	2	0
	Southport	2,779	19	0	1	2	16	133	31	93	9	1
	Sparta	1,833	1	0	1	0	0	41	10	29	2	1
	Spencer	3,412	16	0	0	9	7	234	79	154	1	3
	Spindale	3,999	20	0	0	9	11	218	73	135	10	1
	Spring Hope	1,297	4	0	0	1	3	50	18	30	2	0
	Spring Lake	8,361	78	1	5	31	41	727	283	386	58	3
	Stallings	3,931	57	3	2	14	38	236	80	127	29	0
	Stanley	3,156	10	0	1	5	4	146	58	84	4	1
	Statesville	25,371	243	2	6	100	135	2,174	777	1,273	124	7
	St. Pauls	2,309	7	0	0	4	3	117	47	62	8	3
	Sugar Mountain	224	0	0	0	0	0	10	5	5	0	0
	Sunset Beach	2,219	0	0	0	0	0	99	50	47	2	0
	Surf City	1,750	8	0	0	0	8	157	54	97	6	0
	Swansboro	1,365	8	0	0	3	5	73	15	48	10	2
	Sylva	2,446	34	1	1	2	30	205	35	163	7	1
	Tabor City	2,681	17	0	1	3	13	154	59	85	10	0
	Tarboro	10,812	50	0	1	17	32	485	126	350	9	2
	Taylorsville	1,892	10	1	3	2	4	111	37	67	7	0
	Thomasville	26,388	189	2	3	47	137	1,608	442	1,071	95	6
	Trent Woods	4,040	5	0	0	0	5	46	2	44	0	0
	Troutman	1,740	3	0	1	0	2	120	33	81	6	0
	Troy	3,334	26	0	0	3	23	256	51	201	4	3
	Tryon	1,787	5	0	1	1	3	45	10	33	2	0
	Valdese	4,620	13	0	0	1	12	100	27	70	3	2
	Vanceboro	863	3	0	0	3	0	27	19	7	1	0
	Vass	785	6	0	0	2	4	55	6	48	1	0
	Wadesboro	5,368	46	0	7	14	25	407	145	248	14	2
	Wake Forest	20,528	40	0	3	7	30	689	171	504	14	1
	Wallace	3,601	18	2	0	5	11	165	58	101	6	1
	Warsaw	3,154	24	0	2	5	17	187	31	148	8	3
	Washington	10,037	64	0	9	23	32	473	117	326	30	2
	Waxhaw	3,271	14	0	0	4	10	142	44	85	13	2
	Waynesville	9,573	28	0	3	4	21	405	135	241	29	2
	Weaverville	2,558	8	0	1	2	5	80	13	64	3	0
	Wendell	4,606	22	1	0	3	18	130	30	94	6	0
	Whispering Pines	2,180	1	0	0	0	1	17	7	10	0	0
	Whitakers	788	7	0	1	1	5	35	13	21	1	0
	White Lake	543	9	0	1	2	6	85	27	53	5	0

[1] The FBI does not publish arson data unless it receives data from either the agency or the state for all 12 months of the calendar year.

Table 8. Offenses Known to Law Enforcement, by State and City, 2006 *(Contd.)*

(Number.)

State	City	Popula-tion	Violent crime	Murder and non-negligent man-slaughter	Forcible rape	Robbery	Aggra-vated assault	Property crime	Burglary	Larceny-theft	Motor vehicle theft	Arson[1]
	Whiteville	5,316	86	0	1	24	61	735	137	554	44	2
	Wilkesboro	3,268	13	0	1	5	7	333	61	261	11	1
	Williamston	5,763	64	0	3	8	53	365	102	250	13	0
	Wilmington	97,381	857	7	62	409	379	6,207	1,694	3,865	648	22
	Wilson	47,904	310	1	13	91	205	2,204	494	1,602	108	17
	Windsor	2,276	2	0	0	1	1	116	29	82	5	0
	Wingate	2,923	11	0	0	3	8	114	49	52	13	1
	Winston-Salem	197,621	1,654	20	126	669	839	13,449	4,289	8,126	1,034	10
	Winterville	4,782	23	0	1	3	19	238	45	181	12	2
	Winton	938	4	0	1	0	3	11	6	4	1	1
	Woodfin	3,342	11	0	0	5	6	133	41	84	8	0
	Woodland	813	8	0	0	1	7	34	10	21	3	0
	Wrightsville Beach	2,618	3	0	1	0	2	190	45	143	2	0
	Yadkinville	2,924	16	0	3	3	10	165	22	138	5	2
	Yanceyville	2,190	10	0	0	2	8	89	26	57	6	0
	Youngsville	726	1	0	0	0	1	39	17	22	0	1
	Zebulon	4,302	47	0	2	19	26	340	61	267	12	0
NORTH DAKOTA	Beulah	3,032	2	0	1	0	1	25	4	18	3	0
	Bismarck	57,304	138	1	15	10	112	1,590	256	1,242	92	11
	Cavalier	1,441	1	0	0	0	1	18	4	14	0	0
	Devils Lake	6,807	19	0	1	2	16	335	40	278	17	1
	Dickinson	15,646	7	0	1	2	4	571	97	436	38	2
	Emerado	482	4	0	0	0	4	21	7	12	2	0
	Fargo	90,818	231	2	69	19	141	2,679	525	1,930	224	17
	Fessenden	546	0	0	0	0	0	3	2	1	0	0
	Grafton	4,243	6	0	2	0	4	122	18	96	8	0
	Grand Forks	50,239	91	1	19	12	59	1,800	281	1,370	149	8
	Harvey	1,757	1	0	0	0	1	31	5	26	0	3
	Hillsboro	1,527	0	0	0	0	0	30	8	19	3	0
	Jamestown	14,807	27	0	11	2	14	321	84	225	12	3
	Lincoln	2,294	1	0	1	0	0	11	2	9	0	0
	Mandan	17,203	34	1	8	1	24	408	90	298	20	4
	Mayville	1,929	1	0	1	0	0	19	4	14	1	0
	Minot	34,939	57	0	16	9	32	915	140	690	85	8
	Northwood	883	0	0	0	0	0	13	2	10	1	0
	Portland	577	0	0	0	0	0	1	0	0	1	0
	Rolla	1,440	1	0	0	0	1	110	11	92	7	1
	Rugby	2,685	0	0	0	0	0	30	2	26	2	1
	Steele	693	0	0	0	0	0	12	3	9	0	0
	Thompson	961	0	0	0	0	0	3	2	1	0	0
	Valley City	6,431	6	1	0	1	4	88	10	73	5	2
	Wahpeton	8,210	11	0	1	1	9	176	19	142	15	0
	Watford City	1,355	1	0	0	0	1	9	1	5	3	0
	West Fargo	19,462	16	0	3	1	12	373	73	274	26	3
	Williston	12,177	13	0	5	1	7	170	25	120	25	5
OHIO	Ada	5,854	2	0	1	0	1	72	15	55	2	0
	Alliance	22,829	89	0	23	24	42	1,054	244	768	42	7
	Amberley Village	3,280	1	0	1	0	0	39	9	28	2	0
	Amherst	11,886	8	0	1	6	1	195	31	163	1	2
	Arcanum	2,034	0	0	0	0	0	30	10	17	3	0
	Archbold	4,510	1	0	0	1	0	77	6	69	2	0
	Ashland	21,576	21	1	11	6	3	612	82	519	11	1
	Ashville	3,256	2	0	1	0	1	134	23	104	7	1
	Athens	20,943	26	0	7	7	12	569	102	457	10	2
	Aurora	14,370	10	0	4	2	4	154	26	124	4	3
	Austintown	36,659	53	1	0	38	14	1,766	272	1,372	122	0
	Bainbridge Township	11,265	7	0	0	3	4	347	45	299	3	0
	Barberton	27,225	44	0	12	15	17	1,240	236	919	85	6
	Beavercreek	39,703	43	0	6	15	22	1,205	121	1,020	64	8
	Beaver Township	6,210	3	0	2	1	0	178	38	132	8	1
	Bedford Heights	10,868	29	0	1	10	18	292	53	176	63	2
	Bellaire	4,744	10	0	2	4	4	45	5	35	5	0
	Bellbrook	6,968	3	0	1	1	1	104	11	92	1	1
	Bellefontaine	13,025	60	0	5	6	49	696	94	575	27	0

[1] The FBI does not publish arson data unless it receives data from either the agency or the state for all 12 months of the calendar year.

Table 8. Offenses Known to Law Enforcement, by State and City, 2006 (*Contd.*)

(Number.)

State	City	Popula-tion	Violent crime	Murder and non-negligent man-slaughter	Forcible rape	Robbery	Aggra-vated assault	Property crime	Burglary	Larceny-theft	Motor vehicle theft	Arson[1]
	Bellville	1,756	2	0	0	2	0	99	2	96	1	0
	Belpre	6,568	7	0	3	0	4	136	32	96	8	0
	Berea	18,264	14	0	1	5	8	400	48	332	20	3
	Bethel	2,593	5	0	0	2	3	247	23	217	7	1
	Bethesda	1,381	1	0	0	0	1	8	4	4	0	0
	Bexley	12,337	33	0	2	23	8	421	128	277	16	0
	Blendon Township	7,621	8	0	2	5	1	249	45	187	17	1
	Blue Ash	11,761	8	0	1	6	1	338	41	280	17	0
	Bluffton	4,018	2	0	0	0	2	88	23	60	5	0
	Boardman	40,954	85	0	9	51	25	1,900	240	1,541	119	4
	Bowling Green	29,829	32	0	1	10	21	1,056	99	909	48	0
	Bradford	1,893	0	0	0	0	0	8	2	6	0	0
	Brecksville	13,266	4	0	0	0	4	67	15	50	2	0
	Brimfield Township	7,930	11	0	3	3	5	220	49	161	10	2
	Broadview Heights	17,526	24	1	1	5	17	107	18	71	18	0
	Brooklyn	10,914	52	0	5	25	22	627	73	480	74	0
	Brooklyn Heights	1,512	0	0	0	0	0	37	7	26	4	0
	Brook Park	20,083	24	0	7	7	10	389	44	309	36	0
	Brookville	5,323	7	0	3	2	2	88	20	65	3	0
	Bryan	8,370	18	0	8	1	9	313	55	239	19	2
	Buckeye Lake	3,064	7	0	4	2	1	89	34	36	19	0
	Byesville	2,600	0	0	0	0	0	5	0	5	0	0
	Cambridge	11,576	34	0	9	8	17	1,088	163	872	53	
	Canal Fulton	5,060	9	0	2	3	4	142	28	110	4	0
	Canfield	7,162	0	0	0	0	0	99	8	91	0	1
	Canton	79,575	813	9	67	459	278	6,222	1,812	3,871	539	28
	Celina	10,361	19	0	5	1	13	403	71	308	24	3
	Centerville	23,190	13	0	4	3	6	647	72	554	21	6
	Champion Township	9,546	18	2	2	2	12	194	36	133	25	0
	Chardon	5,286	9	0	0	2	7	87	7	77	3	2
	Cheviot	8,245	17	0	4	7	6	269	49	207	13	2
	Chillicothe	22,108	58	0	12	35	11	2,390	340	1,963	87	13
	Cincinnati	309,104	3,766	89	291	2,339	1,047	22,107	6,009	13,523	2,575	270
	Circleville	13,576	21	0	4	8	9	976	228	703	45	3
	Cleveland	452,759	7,004	75	445	4,288	2,196	28,220	9,650	12,036	6,534	502
	Cleveland Heights	48,088	19	1	0	17	1	605	80	438	87	0
	Cleves	2,577	4	0	0	1	3	101	17	78	6	0
	Clinton Township	4,025	28	0	1	25	2	537	80	412	45	3
	Clyde	6,150	6	0	0	3	3	209	41	161	7	2
	Coldwater	4,443	2	0	2	0	0	104	24	70	10	0
	Columbus	731,547	5,948	104	586	3,646	1,612	52,098	14,816	30,882	6,400	559
	Conneaut	12,663	37	0	2	3	32	509	118	368	23	1
	Cortland	6,648	3	0	1	0	2	64	9	54	1	0
	Covington	2,578	2	0	2	0	0	45	7	38	0	1
	Crestline	4,970	12	0	2	2	8	41	13	26	2	0
	Creston	2,143	1	1	0	0	0	78	13	64	1	1
	Cridersville	1,798	3	0	0	1	2	39	9	28	2	1
	Cross Creek Township	5,711	2	0	0	1	1	55	8	44	3	2
	Cuyahoga Falls	50,556	72	1	24	20	27	1,870	212	1,543	115	2
	Dayton	159,067	1,721	37	120	810	754	11,759	3,525	6,037	2,197	168
	Deer Park	5,622	10	0	0	6	4	117	14	98	5	1
	Defiance	16,170	33	1	21	3	8	663	86	565	12	7
	Delaware	31,360	64	2	29	17	16	1,030	249	751	30	15
	Delhi Township	30,358	32	0	10	5	17	431	65	353	13	1
	Delphos	6,828	7	0	4	0	3	197	56	137	4	0
	Delta	2,931	3	0	1	0	2	82	26	52	4	0
	Dover	12,531	12	0	6	2	4	137	22	107	8	1
	Dublin	35,007	18	0	6	11	1	700	141	539	20	6
	Eastlake	19,819	25	1	3	14	7	387	27	333	27	5
	Eaton	8,252	17	0	3	6	8	404	65	327	12	1
	Edgerton	2,017	1	0	1	0	0	77	16	61	0	1
	Elyria	56,129	232	4	24	89	115	2,718	745	1,807	166	17
	Englewood	12,743	24	0	4	6	14	424	25	378	21	2
	Euclid	49,679	203	0	18	95	90	1,788	479	1,098	211	12
	Fairborn[8]	31,689	118	0	30	32	56	1,239	216	940	83	6

[1] The FBI does not publish arson data unless it receives data from either the agency or the state for all 12 months of the calendar year.
[8] Because of changes in the state/local agency's reporting practices, figures are not comparable to previous years' data.

Table 8. Offenses Known to Law Enforcement, by State and City, 2006 (*Contd.*)

(Number.)

State	City	Popula-tion	Violent crime	Murder and non-negligent man-slaughter	Forcible rape	Robbery	Aggra-vated assault	Property crime	Burglary	Larceny-theft	Motor vehicle theft	Arson[1]
	Fairfield	42,346	203	3	19	27	154	1,570	282	1,200	88	10
	Fairfield Township	16,673	186	0	2	5	179	576	102	443	31	0
	Fairlawn	7,211	9	0	0	5	4	400	16	364	20	0
	Fairport Harbor	3,227	14	0	3	1	10	186	50	132	4	3
	Findlay	39,166	98	0	23	24	51	1,904	317	1,529	58	11
	Forest	1,457	0	0	0	0	0	21	7	14	0	1
	Fredericktown	2,529	1	0	0	1	0	90	20	70	0	1
	Fremont	17,070	49	1	0	17	31	1,250	167	1,053	30	5
	Gahanna	33,117	66	1	5	21	39	872	177	670	25	9
	Galion	11,463	34	0	12	4	18	515	90	411	14	3
	Gallipolis	4,217	17	0	5	7	5	555	103	439	13	2
	Garfield Heights	29,077	125	0	12	58	55	1,013	243	696	74	5
	Gates Mills	2,373	0	0	0	0	0	8	0	8	0	0
	Georgetown	3,725	5	1	0	2	2	179	41	130	8	4
	German Township, Montgomery County	3,188	3	0	1	0	2	63	31	30	2	0
	Gibsonburg	2,463	2	0	1	0	1	97	7	89	1	0
	Glendale	2,142	0	0	0	0	0	34	8	24	2	0
	Grandview Heights	6,281	8	0	2	5	1	212	58	138	16	0
	Granville	5,287	2	0	2	0	0	54	9	44	1	1
	Greenfield	5,152	24	0	2	14	8	378	71	287	20	2
	Greenhills	3,763	0	0	0	0	0	64	12	50	2	1
	Greenville	13,182	36	0	9	6	21	491	103	349	39	11
	Grove City	30,930	57	0	13	36	8	818	153	614	51	12
	Groveport	4,759	9	0	1	0	8	212	37	169	6	6
	Hamilton	62,018	494	1	69	189	235	4,410	1,052	2,895	463	36
	Harrison	7,831	4	0	0	2	2	373	25	334	14	1
	Hartville	2,392	0	0	0	0	0	42	7	34	1	1
	Heath	8,899	21	0	4	5	12	536	68	458	10	1
	Hebron	2,152	1	0	0	1	0	93	10	82	1	0
	Highland Heights	8,632	6	0	1	4	1	122	9	110	3	0
	Highland Hills	1,423	0	0	0	0	0	1	0	0	1	0
	Hilliard	26,688	30	0	3	19	8	904	153	724	27	10
	Hillsboro	6,685	7	0	1	1	5	214	24	187	3	2
	Holland	1,328	0	0	0	0	0	118	10	107	1	1
	Howland Township	17,041	25	0	0	4	21	671	137	501	33	0
	Hubbard Township	5,907	8	0	0	5	3	241	39	188	14	0
	Huber Heights	38,135	70	0	13	30	27	1,339	235	985	119	32
	Hunting Valley	712	0	0	0	0	0	2	2	0	0	0
	Huron	7,590	3	0	2	1	0	164	19	136	9	0
	Independence	6,877	8	0	1	5	2	162	19	126	17	0
	Indian Hill	5,668	0	0	0	0	0	67	6	59	2	3
	Jackson Township, Mahoning County	2,276	4	0	3	0	1	73	19	48	6	1
	Johnstown	3,888	2	0	1	1	0	73	23	45	5	0
	Junction City	859	0	0	0	0	0	32	10	20	2	1
	Kent	28,169	60	0	7	24	29	805	179	596	30	47
	Kenton	8,179	17	0	4	7	6	571	127	431	13	1
	Kettering	55,549	66	0	23	21	22	1,695	296	1,278	121	26
	Kirtland	7,260	2	0	0	1	1	59	9	46	4	0
	Kirtland Hills	745	1	0	0	0	1	15	3	12	0	0
	Lakemore	2,652	1	0	1	0	0	131	36	94	1	0
	Lakewood	53,309	108	1	4	61	42	1,278	261	862	155	9
	Lawrence Township	8,458	10	0	0	2	8	89	23	64	2	0
	Lebanon	20,002	32	0	14	7	11	479	98	367	14	4
	Lexington	4,229	3	0	3	0	0	91	35	53	3	0
	Liberty Township	12,319	33	0	6	19	8	505	109	353	43	2
	Lima	38,655	378	9	55	109	205	2,563	824	1,588	151	19
	Lockland	3,397	36	0	0	13	23	158	59	73	26	1
	Logan	7,099	10	0	5	4	1	454	62	376	16	2
	London	9,407	15	0	4	8	3	396	83	293	20	4
	Lorain	67,903	294	5	5	135	149	2,455	862	1,447	146	28
	Lordstown	3,640	3	0	0	0	3	46	16	28	2	0
	Loudonville	2,986	2	0	0	0	2	69	6	62	1	0
	Lyndhurst	14,468	4	0	1	0	3	0	0	0	0	0
	Madeira	8,340	2	0	0	0	2	71	11	57	3	0

[1] The FBI does not publish arson data unless it receives data from either the agency or the state for all 12 months of the calendar year.

Table 8. Offenses Known to Law Enforcement, by State and City, 2006 (*Contd.*)

(Number.)

State	City	Popula-tion	Violent crime	Murder and non-negligent man-slaughter	Forcible rape	Robbery	Aggra-vated assault	Property crime	Burglary	Larceny-theft	Motor vehicle theft	Arson[1]
	Magnolia	936	2	0	1	1	0	84	27	55	2	0
	Manchester	2,085	7	0	0	0	7	18	8	9	1	1
	Mansfield	50,677	221	3	48	101	69	3,357	946	2,330	81	14
	Mariemont	3,131	0	0	0	0	0	49	3	46	0	0
	Marietta	14,287	25	0	12	7	6	548	113	411	24	1
	Marion	36,538	90	0	33	29	28	1,842	479	1,316	47	10
	Maumee	14,302	11	0	1	7	3	674	70	561	43	3
	Mayfield Heights	18,402	8	0	1	3	4	377	13	347	17	0
	Mayfield Village	3,246	3	2	0	0	1	63	7	56	0	1
	McComb	1,690	6	0	0	1	5	37	6	31	0	1
	Mentor	51,548	42	0	5	15	22	1,167	154	948	65	11
	Mentor-on-the-Lake	8,303	4	0	2	2	0	66	16	48	2	1
	Miamisburg	19,820	54	0	10	20	24	826	129	620	77	9
	Miami Township	39,327	25	0	6	7	12	823	140	655	28	3
	Middlefield	2,414	2	0	1	0	1	55	7	46	2	0
	Middletown	51,535	213	1	37	80	95	4,021	860	3,009	152	17
	Milford[8]	6,333	12	0	4	6	2	316	25	271	20	0
	Millersburg	3,586	5	0	2	0	3	81	16	65	0	0
	Milton Township	2,908	2	0	1	0	1	68	14	44	10	0
	Minerva	3,981	24	0	0	4	20	189	37	149	3	0
	Mingo Junction	3,430	26	0	0	1	25	69	21	43	5	0
	Mogadore	3,971	1	0	0	0	1	52	16	35	1	1
	Monroe	12,892	54	0	2	9	43	716	118	574	24	2
	Montgomery	10,027	6	0	2	2	2	254	31	215	8	2
	Montpelier	4,140	14	0	4	2	8	249	43	199	7	1
	Montville Township	7,032	3	0	0	2	1	72	17	52	3	0
	Mount Gilead	3,551	1	0	0	1	0	127	25	99	3	1
	Mount Healthy	6,608	10	0	2	4	4	115	12	94	9	1
	Mount Sterling	1,842	9	0	0	0	9	109	15	91	3	0
	Napoleon	9,180	9	0	3	0	6	478	71	397	10	2
	Navarre	1,433	2	0	1	1	0	46	21	22	3	0
	New Albany	5,834	0	0	0	0	0	77	7	63	7	0
	New Bremen	2,997	0	0	0	0	0	58	4	54	0	0
	Newcomerstown	3,957	9	0	0	0	9	131	18	103	10	1
	New Franklin	14,978	8	0	4	2	2	159	45	104	10	1
	New Lebanon	4,213	8	0	3	3	2	134	39	87	8	0
	New London	2,671	1	0	1	0	0	47	17	26	4	0
	New Middletown	1,622	0	0	0	0	0	26	11	14	1	2
	New Richmond	2,466	9	0	4	3	2	150	27	119	4	0
	Newtown	3,696	0	0	0	0	0	57	3	50	4	0
	North Canton	16,800	13	0	1	7	5	342	66	267	9	2
	North College Hill	9,370	62	0	6	36	20	514	107	385	22	4
	North Olmsted	32,693	31	0	2	16	13	530	93	386	51	5
	North Ridgeville	26,140	37	0	8	7	22	396	108	276	12	2
	Northwood	5,506	10	0	1	3	6	313	44	258	11	6
	Oakwood	8,760	10	0	2	1	7	172	25	133	14	0
	Oberlin	8,290	17	0	4	9	4	166	35	130	1	2
	Olmsted Falls	8,447	9	0	1	3	5	112	18	78	16	1
	Ontario	5,357	8	0	0	6	2	630	21	598	11	0
	Oregon	19,198	30	0	3	9	18	926	116	772	38	1
	Orrville	8,495	15	0	8	2	5	194	26	158	10	5
	Ottawa Hills	4,614	2	0	0	0	2	49	12	36	1	1
	Oxford	22,150	114	0	14	11	89	595	122	460	13	7
	Parma	81,568	113	0	14	47	52	1,699	496	1,049	154	18
	Parma Heights	20,682	25	0	4	7	14	441	108	304	29	9
	Perrysburg	17,001	19	0	3	2	14	435	50	367	18	1
	Perry Township, Franklin County	3,617	1	0	1	0	0	90	15	74	1	0
	Perry Township, Montgomery County	3,767	3	0	1	0	2	48	21	20	7	0
	Perry Township, Stark County	28,592	59	1	3	14	41	742	174	510	58	4
	Pickerington	15,897	20	0	1	10	9	390	50	327	13	2
	Pierce Township	10,809	11	0	7	2	2	428	120	296	12	5
	Piqua	20,908	45	1	18	19	7	1,302	242	1,024	36	8
	Plain City	3,466	1	0	1	0	0	31	6	24	1	1

[1] The FBI does not publish arson data unless it receives data from either the agency or the state for all 12 months of the calendar year.

Table 8. Offenses Known to Law Enforcement, by State and City, 2006 *(Contd.)*

(Number.)

State	City	Population	Violent crime	Murder and non-negligent man-slaughter	Forcible rape	Robbery	Aggravated assault	Property crime	Burglary	Larceny-theft	Motor vehicle theft	Arson[1]
	Poland Village	2,753	1	0	0	0	1	24	7	17	0	0
	Port Clinton	6,344	6	0	4	2	0	233	51	177	5	0
	Powhatan Point	1,705	1	0	0	0	1	5	3	2	0	0
	Ravenna	11,524	10	0	1	4	5	444	72	359	13	1
	Reading	10,333	35	0	7	17	11	416	48	309	59	2
	Reminderville	2,515	2	0	0	0	2	15	3	10	2	0
	Reynoldsburg	33,099	107	1	17	60	29	1,233	290	868	75	5
	Rittman	6,319	5	0	0	1	4	114	19	82	13	2
	Riverside	22,761	87	0	7	32	48	1,112	257	693	162	6
	Rocky Ridge	394	1	0	0	0	1	10	3	7	0	0
	Salem	12,020	6	0	0	5	1	100	12	70	18	0
	Sandusky	26,698	231	0	12	46	173	1,796	359	1,345	92	6
	Seven Hills	12,056	5	0	0	4	1	31	24	6	1	0
	Seville	2,465	0	0	0	0	0	43	10	31	2	0
	Sharon Township	2,326	1	0	0	1	0	35	14	17	4	0
	Sheffield Lake	9,168	7	0	0	5	2	227	40	182	5	0
	Shelby	9,483	7	0	0	6	1	480	70	405	5	1
	Silverton	4,740	21	0	3	11	7	182	36	123	23	0
	Smith Township	4,992	19	0	3	1	15	129	24	97	8	0
	Smithville	1,314	7	0	1	0	6	42	6	36	0	0
	Solon	22,362	14	0	4	4	6	270	49	219	2	2
	Somerset	1,579	0	0	0	0	0	47	9	37	1	1
	South Bloomfield	1,542	3	0	0	0	3	59	10	47	2	0
	South Russell	3,997	0	0	0	0	0	8	1	7	0	0
	South Solon	391	0	0	0	0	0	1	0	1	0	0
	Spencer	810	0	0	0	0	0	15	2	13	0	0
	Spencerville	2,212	1	0	1	0	0	9	4	5	0	0
	Springdale	9,821	44	0	8	26	10	940	72	821	47	1
	Springfield	63,379	535	4	56	309	166	6,331	1,978	3,856	497	19
	Springfield Township, Hamilton County	35,959	133	2	15	55	61	832	195	559	78	4
	Springfield Township, Mahoning County	6,159	3	0	0	0	3	103	42	55	6	0
	Springfield Township, Summit County	15,445	38	0	10	12	16	765	153	570	42	9
	St. Bernard	4,534	15	0	1	9	5	180	26	140	14	1
	Steubenville	19,338	77	3	7	32	35	976	185	752	39	6
	Stow	34,446	26	0	9	12	5	906	112	780	14	6
	St. Paris	1,985	1	0	1	0	0	59	3	54	2	0
	Sugarcreek Township	6,821	4	0	3	1	0	168	17	144	7	0
	Swanton	3,561	3	0	1	2	0	118	27	82	9	0
	Sycamore	895	1	0	0	0	1	10	3	6	1	0
	Sylvania Township	26,123	4	0	0	3	1	756	106	603	47	1
	Tallmadge	17,429	16	0	4	7	5	404	92	291	21	6
	Tiffin	17,459	21	0	6	11	4	785	158	599	28	2
	Tipp City	9,368	11	0	4	3	4	225	21	195	9	0
	Toledo	301,652	3,461	35	169	1,248	2,009	22,711	6,915	13,239	2,557	362
	Twinsburg	17,401	18	1	3	6	8	170	35	129	6	0
	Uniontown	2,833	4	0	0	1	3	109	34	74	1	3
	University Heights	13,258	20	0	3	10	7	247	66	166	15	1
	Upper Arlington	31,588	24	0	6	8	10	442	96	333	13	2
	Vandalia	14,315	18	0	4	7	7	438	77	335	26	6
	Van Wert	10,448	38	0	6	10	22	511	83	416	12	5
	Vermilion	11,013	7	0	1	0	6	337	68	254	15	2
	Wadsworth	19,975	14	0	9	3	2	397	54	325	18	0
	Waite Hill	526	0	0	0	0	0	3	2	1	0	0
	Walbridge	3,100	3	0	2	0	1	54	12	37	5	0
	Walton Hills	2,350	2	0	0	0	2	30	2	26	2	0
	Wapakoneta	9,614	10	0	0	2	8	202	47	155	0	1
	Warrensville Heights	14,240	52	0	10	37	5	404	136	176	92	0
	Warren Township	6,274	25	0	1	4	20	126	31	85	10	0
	Washington Court House	13,482	20	2	2	5	11	496	109	363	24	2
	Wauseon	7,320	4	0	2	2	0	189	30	159	0	0
	West Carrollton	13,214	44	2	12	14	16	512	120	321	71	3
	West Chester Township	54,267	102	2	24	37	39	1,730	247	1,431	52	15

[1] The FBI does not publish arson data unless it receives data from either the agency or the state for all 12 months of the calendar year.

Table 8. Offenses Known to Law Enforcement, by State and City, 2006 (Contd.)

(Number.)

State	City	Popula-tion	Violent crime	Murder and non-negligent man-slaughter	Forcible rape	Robbery	Aggra-vated assault	Property crime	Burglary	Larceny-theft	Motor vehicle theft	Arson[1]
	Westerville	34,764	33	0	6	22	5	887	124	738	25	18
	West Jefferson	4,292	7	0	1	0	6	164	29	128	7	1
	Whitehall	18,074	160	2	20	105	33	1,370	352	897	121	2
	Willard	6,826	3	0	0	1	2	217	29	173	15	0
	Williamsburg	2,335	2	0	1	0	1	88	20	67	1	1
	Willoughby	22,363	20	2	5	7	6	426	78	319	29	1
	Willoughby Hills	8,469	5	0	0	1	4	209	38	148	23	1
	Willowick	14,021	9	1	1	6	1	165	21	130	14	0
	Wilmington	12,489	26	0	6	9	11	711	59	648	4	1
	Windham	2,752	7	1	3	0	3	170	41	120	9	1
	Wintersville	3,894	3	0	1	1	1	81	2	75	4	0
	Woodlawn	2,587	15	0	1	7	7	194	32	157	5	0
	Wooster	25,699	72	1	15	30	26	1,051	206	828	17	18
	Wyoming	7,728	2	0	0	0	2	180	18	152	10	0
	Xenia	23,629	38	1	13	21	3	1,211	207	949	55	8
	Youngstown	82,938	993	32	48	358	555	4,854	2,017	2,136	701	321
	Zanesville	25,284	68	0	14	34	20	1,633	340	1,221	72	9
OKLAHOMA	Achille	525	6	0	0	0	6	10	3	7	0	0
	Ada	16,140	144	1	16	10	117	882	227	613	42	4
	Agra	361	0	0	0	0	0	0	0	0	0	0
	Altus	20,075	54	0	3	15	36	778	231	516	31	6
	Alva	4,943	4	0	3	0	1	139	18	116	5	0
	Anadarko	6,642	43	0	2	3	38	369	98	240	31	20
	Antlers	2,530	33	0	0	0	33	94	18	58	18	0
	Apache	1,611	5	0	2	0	3	28	11	11	6	2
	Ardmore	24,494	273	1	14	19	239	1,351	313	959	79	4
	Arkoma	2,210	3	0	0	2	1	24	9	14	1	0
	Atoka	3,071	14	0	2	1	11	120	34	81	5	1
	Bartlesville	35,041	118	0	11	12	95	1,284	270	942	72	10
	Beaver	1,426	3	0	0	1	2	28	11	17	0	0
	Beggs	1,387	4	0	0	0	4	35	10	24	1	0
	Bethany	19,961	60	0	6	14	40	759	184	484	91	11
	Bixby	18,764	21	1	4	3	13	317	76	204	37	2
	Blackwell	7,361	19	0	2	0	17	158	45	99	14	4
	Blanchard	3,710	2	0	0	0	2	114	34	68	12	0
	Boise City	1,334	0	0	0	0	0	18	6	10	2	0
	Boley	1,112	1	0	1	0	0	27	3	1	23	0
	Bristow	4,436	7	0	0	2	5	186	41	139	6	0
	Broken Arrow	86,989	178	1	13	23	141	1,673	420	1,118	135	20
	Broken Bow	4,207	19	0	0	3	16	300	74	204	22	4
	Caddo	974	8	0	0	1	7	20	15	5	0	0
	Calera	1,800	10	0	1	0	9	40	17	23	0	0
	Carnegie	1,617	10	0	1	0	9	30	13	12	5	0
	Catoosa	6,497	22	0	1	1	20	146	34	93	19	0
	Chandler	2,884	4	0	0	1	3	80	19	59	2	0
	Checotah	3,564	9	0	1	1	7	170	36	124	10	0
	Chelsea	2,282	8	0	4	0	4	29	5	24	0	0
	Cherokee	1,498	4	0	0	0	4	7	2	5	0	0
	Chickasha	16,998	147	1	9	6	131	884	229	581	74	5
	Choctaw[3]	10,622		2	1	2		216	75	126	15	2
	Chouteau	2,010	6	0	0	1	5	79	22	54	3	6
	Claremore	17,313	53	0	11	9	33	476	89	357	30	2
	Clayton	730	3	0	0	0	3	13	2	8	3	0
	Cleveland	3,276	8	0	0	0	8	76	20	54	2	0
	Clinton	8,437	21	1	1	3	16	218	42	161	15	1
	Coalgate	1,906	2	0	0	0	2	21	5	14	2	0
	Colbert	1,104	4	0	0	1	3	34	13	19	2	0
	Collinsville	4,363	7	0	0	1	6	87	28	50	9	0
	Comanche	1,529	7	0	0	0	7	79	20	58	1	0
	Cordell	2,910	19	0	1	0	18	31	3	28	0	0
	Coweta	8,426	19	0	3	0	16	199	49	135	15	3
	Crescent	1,348	3	0	0	0	3	17	4	12	1	3
	Cushing	8,340	38	0	2	2	34	289	53	216	20	3
	Davenport	894	2	0	1	0	1	9	4	4	1	0

[1] The FBI does not publish arson data unless it receives data from either the agency or the state for all 12 months of the calendar year.
[3] The FBI determined that the agency's data were inflated. Consequently, affected data are not included in this table.

Table 8. Offenses Known to Law Enforcement, by State and City, 2006 (Contd.)

(Number.)

State	City	Popula-tion	Violent crime	Murder and non-negligent man-slaughter	Forcible rape	Robbery	Aggra-vated assault	Property crime	Burglary	Larceny-theft	Motor vehicle theft	Arson[1]
	Davis	2,671	6	0	2	0	4	54	17	33	4	1
	Del City	22,139	105	2	10	29	64	1,220	400	699	121	18
	Dewey	3,317	15	0	1	0	14	130	31	95	4	4
	Drumright	2,902	5	0	2	0	3	78	11	64	3	0
	Duncan	22,503	56	0	8	12	36	846	173	627	46	3
	Durant	14,926	56	0	10	11	35	719	193	474	52	1
	Edmond	75,542	91	1	30	14	46	1,961	370	1,499	92	8
	Elk City	10,838	5	0	2	0	3	185	12	166	7	0
	El Reno	16,239	79	1	7	14	57	546	176	339	31	10
	Enid	46,826	180	1	25	30	124	2,037	481	1,429	127	5
	Eufaula	2,814	7	0	0	2	5	124	30	82	12	2
	Fairfax	1,518	9	0	1	0	8	51	12	36	3	4
	Fairview	2,652	2	0	0	0	2	76	12	60	4	1
	Fort Gibson	4,290	8	0	1	0	7	34	5	28	1	0
	Frederick	4,232	11	0	0	4	7	122	38	80	4	1
	Geary	1,301	12	0	0	0	12	29	5	22	2	0
	Glenpool	9,039	9	0	1	1	7	145	29	101	15	0
	Goodwell	1,139	0	0	0	0	0	18	9	9	0	0
	Grove	5,803	18	0	0	0	18	199	38	152	9	1
	Guthrie	10,895	35	1	7	6	21	256	81	160	15	1
	Guymon	10,737	25	1	6	3	15	277	42	221	14	3
	Harrah	4,983	17	0	1	1	15	111	35	72	4	1
	Hartshorne	2,091	5	0	0	1	4	35	5	27	3	0
	Haskell	1,792	0	0	0	0	0	9	4	4	1	0
	Healdton	2,802	3	0	0	0	3	46	16	24	6	0
	Heavener[3]	3,275		0	8	2		84	23	55	6	0
	Henryetta	6,164	11	0	2	1	8	136	30	90	16	0
	Hinton	2,202	1	0	1	0	0	24	4	17	3	0
	Hobart	3,839	43	0	3	1	39	51	16	32	3	1
	Holdenville	5,587	19	0	2	1	16	90	18	59	13	2
	Hollis	2,105	6	0	1	0	5	54	20	33	1	0
	Hominy	3,766	37	0	1	0	36	68	39	28	1	2
	Hooker	1,736	1	0	0	0	1	24	8	10	6	0
	Hugo	5,570	13	1	0	1	11	136	58	73	5	1
	Hulbert	538	3	0	0	2	1	1	0	0	1	0
	Hydro	1,054	1	0	0	0	1	15	5	9	1	0
	Idabel	6,977	30	1	3	5	21	253	57	179	17	0
	Jay	2,865	9	0	0	0	9	67	18	44	5	2
	Jenks	13,211	16	0	1	1	14	244	57	176	11	0
	Jones	2,634	2	0	0	0	2	23	5	17	1	0
	Kingfisher	4,541	7	0	2	0	5	75	9	63	3	0
	Kingston	1,539	5	0	2	0	3	15	6	5	4	2
	Konawa	1,447	3	0	0	0	3	19	4	14	1	1
	Krebs	2,139	9	0	0	0	9	24	6	17	1	1
	Lawton	91,031	929	8	82	169	670	4,727	1,550	2,886	291	65
	Lexington	2,097	4	0	0	0	4	67	18	47	2	1
	Lindsay	2,916	5	0	1	0	4	64	24	34	6	0
	Locust Grove	1,590	5	0	0	0	5	68	13	46	9	0
	Lone Grove	5,120	11	0	0	1	10	122	19	95	8	1
	Luther	1,093	8	0	0	1	7	17	7	8	2	0
	Madill	3,721	19	0	2	2	15	172	41	118	13	1
	Mangum	2,769	13	0	0	0	13	53	7	45	1	1
	Mannford	2,782	13	0	1	0	12	45	14	29	2	0
	Marietta	2,548	11	0	1	2	8	119	26	82	11	1
	Marlow	4,571	57	0	8	1	48	85	18	58	9	0
	Maysville	1,307	3	0	0	0	3	19	9	7	3	1
	McAlester	18,265	50	0	4	17	29	887	126	725	36	2
	McLoud	4,086	9	0	0	2	7	53	23	24	6	0
	Meeker	998	4	0	0	0	4	45	23	22	0	1
	Miami	13,685	99	1	11	8	79	773	207	545	21	9
	Midwest City	55,375	266	3	25	50	188	2,186	484	1,522	180	16
	Minco	1,783	0	0	0	0	0	4	1	3	0	1
	Moore	48,118	115	0	14	22	79	1,907	396	1,344	167	14
	Mooreland	1,232	0	0	0	0	0	25	10	14	1	0

[1] The FBI does not publish arson data unless it receives data from either the agency or the state for all 12 months of the calendar year.
[3] The FBI determined that the agency's data were inflated. Consequently, affected data are not included in this table.

Table 8. Offenses Known to Law Enforcement, by State and City, 2006 (*Contd.*)

(Number.)

State	City	Popula-tion	Violent crime	Murder and non-negligent man-slaughter	Forcible rape	Robbery	Aggra-vated assault	Property crime	Burglary	Larceny-theft	Motor vehicle theft	Arson[1]
	Morris	1,338	0	0	0	0	0	22	7	11	4	0
	Mountain View	837	2	0	0	0	2	10	2	8	0	0
	Muldrow	3,196	12	0	5	2	5	111	42	66	3	2
	Muskogee	40,117	297	1	27	64	205	1,631	550	944	137	17
	Mustang	16,027	53	1	7	1	44	490	91	354	45	2
	Newcastle	6,359	12	3	1	3	5	186	53	120	13	2
	Newkirk	2,181	19	0	2	1	16	100	21	75	4	0
	Nichols Hills	4,032	2	0	0	1	1	71	10	57	4	0
	Nicoma Park	2,409	22	0	1	6	15	77	23	49	5	2
	Noble	5,567	4	0	2	0	2	126	33	81	12	1
	Norman	102,617	211	5	38	50	118	3,582	881	2,415	286	5
	Nowata	4,070	22	0	3	3	16	69	19	44	6	3
	Oilton	1,153	4	0	0	0	4	27	8	17	2	0
	Okemah	2,996	16	0	1	0	15	137	31	101	5	1
	Oklahoma City	536,016	4,301	55	327	1,179	2,740	34,292	9,304	20,169	4,819	201
	Okmulgee	12,968	78	1	5	12	60	390	100	263	27	0
	Oologah	1,131	1	0	0	0	1	24	10	12	2	0
	Owasso	23,981	81	0	12	6	63	550	85	410	55	10
	Pauls Valley	6,233	38	0	4	3	31	493	105	368	20	1
	Pawhuska	3,564	51	0	0	1	50	90	24	54	12	0
	Pawnee	2,223	4	0	0	0	4	35	11	23	1	0
	Perkins	2,205	7	0	0	1	6	81	19	60	2	0
	Perry	5,150	12	0	0	2	10	119	21	88	10	2
	Piedmont	4,708	10	0	0	1	9	56	17	37	2	0
	Pocola	4,412	20	0	2	0	18	56	32	16	8	0
	Ponca City	25,291	168	0	11	15	142	1,291	261	961	69	19
	Porum	739	0	0	0	0	0	14	3	10	1	0
	Poteau	8,224	47	0	5	0	42	314	45	249	20	5
	Prague	2,143	3	0	0	0	3	11	3	7	1	0
	Pryor	9,308	78	0	5	1	72	336	96	202	38	0
	Purcell	5,910	14	1	2	2	9	254	94	148	12	1
	Ringling	1,092	1	0	1	0	0	21	4	14	3	0
	Roland	3,137	7	0	0	1	6	27	8	18	1	0
	Rush Springs	1,336	5	0	1	0	4	24	8	15	1	0
	Sallisaw	8,697	84	0	4	5	75	316	66	233	17	3
	Sand Springs	17,823	30	0	3	10	17	511	114	322	75	2
	Sapulpa	20,801	62	0	3	11	48	676	145	478	53	12
	Sayre	2,861	7	0	3	1	3	64	9	47	8	1
	Seiling	828	10	0	0	0	10	11	2	8	1	0
	Seminole	6,974	20	1	2	5	12	366	100	241	25	0
	Shawnee	30,087	151	0	13	15	123	1,642	391	1,093	158	7
	Skiatook	6,346	15	0	2	1	12	279	81	167	31	2
	Snyder	1,465	9	0	1	1	7	38	15	20	3	0
	Spencer	3,874	11	0	5	0	6	70	22	34	14	0
	Spiro	2,307	11	1	0	1	9	44	13	29	2	0
	Stigler	2,846	12	0	0	0	12	59	14	44	1	0
	Stillwater	41,267	126	2	18	14	92	1,347	318	975	54	13
	Stilwell	3,503	6	0	0	1	5	123	8	108	7	0
	Stratford	1,497	3	0	0	0	3	17	5	11	1	0
	Stringtown	416	0	0	0	0	0	5	2	3	0	0
	Stroud	2,779	8	0	1	1	6	98	19	70	9	0
	Sulphur	4,920	17	0	3	2	12	139	45	91	3	0
	Tahlequah	16,217	42	0	11	5	26	619	153	409	57	1
	Talihina	1,245	10	0	1	3	6	33	10	20	3	1
	Tecumseh	6,574	53	0	2	2	49	193	62	119	12	3
	Texhoma	936	2	0	0	0	2	15	3	12	0	0
	The Village	9,914	51	1	1	13	36	354	100	225	29	1
	Tishomingo	3,164	10	0	2	0	8	82	16	59	7	3
	Tonkawa	3,160	7	0	0	0	7	103	33	65	5	7
	Tulsa	385,834	4,816	53	289	997	3,477	24,011	6,315	14,523	3,173	271
	Tushka	365	1	0	0	0	1	1	0	0	1	0
	Tuttle	5,412	8	0	2	0	6	137	44	86	7	0
	Valliant	766	9	0	1	4	4	25	4	20	1	0
	Vian	1,473	17	0	0	1	16	20	10	9	1	0
	Vinita	6,070	15	1	1	1	12	201	47	147	7	2

[1] The FBI does not publish arson data unless it receives data from either the agency or the state for all 12 months of the calendar year.

Table 8. Offenses Known to Law Enforcement, by State and City, 2006 (*Contd.*)

(Number.)

State	City	Popula-tion	Violent crime	Murder and non-negligent man-slaughter	Forcible rape	Robbery	Aggra-vated assault	Property crime	Burglary	Larceny-theft	Motor vehicle theft	Arson[1]
	Wagoner............................	7,947	68	1	0	7	60	362	104	241	17	0
	Walters..............................	2,633	11	1	2	0	8	53	20	31	2	0
	Warner..............................	1,456	3	0	0	0	3	10	3	6	1	0
	Warr Acres.........................	9,559	65	1	3	12	49	428	111	270	47	2
	Watonga............................	5,637	11	0	0	0	11	75	13	54	8	0
	Waukomis	1,212	0	0	0	0	0	19	5	13	1	0
	Waurika	1,873	0	0	0	0	0	15	7	7	1	0
	Waynoka	938	4	0	0	1	3	44	24	18	2	0
	Weatherford	9,824	34	0	2	3	29	352	85	247	20	0
	Weleetka	962	2	0	0	1	1	27	11	14	2	0
	Westville............................	1,667	17	0	2	0	15	109	14	88	7	0
	Wetumka	1,433	2	0	0	0	2	49	31	17	1	2
	Wewoka.............................	3,467	16	0	0	2	14	162	58	93	11	0
	Wilburton..........................	2,960	5	0	1	1	3	32	9	20	3	0
	Wilson	1,637	9	0	0	0	9	36	9	25	2	0
	Woodward..........................	12,036	23	1	6	4	12	685	173	490	22	0
	Wright City	821	4	0	0	0	4	22	6	15	1	2
	Wynnewood........................	2,334	6	0	0	0	6	47	16	30	1	0
	Yale...................................	1,265	5	0	0	0	5	7	3	4	0	0
	Yukon................................	22,227	33	0	5	7	21	615	122	461	32	1
OREGON	Albany................................	45,532	40	1	1	25	13	2,705	297	2,192	216	20
	Amity	1,487	0	0	0	0	0	49	5	41	3	0
	Astoria	9,944	27	0	2	4	21	464	93	335	36	1
	Athena	1,238	0	0	0	0	0	21	4	14	3	0
	Aumsville...........................	3,255	3	0	1	1	1	37	5	29	3	0
	Aurora...............................	893	0	0	0	0	0	14	6	7	1	0
	Baker City..........................	9,862	24	1	1	1	21	201	26	159	16	4
	Bandon..............................	2,956	1	0	0	1	0	67	16	50	1	1
	Banks................................	1,588	0	0	0	0	0	17	4	13	0	0
	Beaverton	87,181	208	1	18	30	159	2,205	311	1,634	260	28
	Bend..................................	68,253	149	1	22	32	94	2,912	489	2,193	230	27
	Boardman..........................	3,101	14	0	3	1	10	95	21	58	16	0
	Brookings..........................	6,400	6	1	0	3	2	211	22	180	9	1
	Burns................................	2,800	3	0	0	0	3	117	34	78	5	0
	Canby	15,235	23	0	6	4	13	388	60	304	24	1
	Cannon Beach....................	1,728	0	0	0	0	0	57	11	46	0	0
	Carlton..............................	1,526	0	0	0	0	0	15	6	9	0	0
	Central Point	15,929	3	0	3	0	0	315	46	256	13	1
	Clatskanie	1,658	9	0	2	1	6	51	7	41	3	0
	Coburg	1,015	1	0	0	0	1	31	5	23	3	0
	Columbia City....................	1,826	0	0	0	0	0	14	3	11	0	0
	Coos Bay............................	16,082	28	0	12	7	9	570	121	399	50	6
	Coquille.............................	4,324	0	0	0	0	0	61	15	46	0	3
	Cornelius...........................	10,997	11	0	1	5	5	274	69	177	28	4
	Cottage Grove....................	8,867	12	0	1	6	5	496	90	370	36	8
	Creswell	4,708	27	0	2	2	23	217	79	118	20	1
	Dallas	14,231	23	0	6	3	14	334	51	259	24	6
	Eagle Point	7,619	1	0	1	0	0	152	22	126	4	0
	Elgin.................................	1,669	2	0	0	0	2	31	9	19	3	0
	Enterprise	1,830	5	0	0	0	5	28	3	24	1	0
	Estacada............................	2,475	7	0	2	2	3	136	25	91	20	0
	Eugene	146,885	370	3	44	155	168	8,113	1,561	5,386	1,166	54
	Fairview	9,480	14	0	2	2	10	372	62	247	63	2
	Florence	7,970	9	0	2	2	5	308	37	249	22	1
	Forest Grove	20,012	10	0	3	1	6	656	83	539	34	2
	Gaston...............................	778	0	0	0	0	0	20	5	15	0	0
	Gearhart............................	1,095	1	0	0	1	0	10	2	7	1	0
	Gervais..............................	2,330	8	0	1	1	6	105	24	67	14	2
	Gladstone..........................	12,316	32	2	8	10	12	465	61	364	40	2
	Gold Beach........................	1,962	7	0	0	1	6	39	10	22	7	0
	Grants Pass	29,356	49	0	16	13	20	1,859	177	1,557	125	1
	Gresham............................	97,647	562	6	72	170	314	4,026	645	2,525	856	46
	Hermiston..........................	14,897	34	0	3	7	24	834	148	619	67	2
	Hillsboro	85,919	192	2	34	77	79	2,752	299	2,204	249	16
	Hines.................................	1,517	2	0	0	0	2	16	1	14	1	0

[1] The FBI does not publish arson data unless it receives data from either the agency or the state for all 12 months of the calendar year.

Table 8. Offenses Known to Law Enforcement, by State and City, 2006 (*Contd.*)

(Number.)

State	City	Population	Violent crime	Murder and non-negligent man-slaughter	Forcible rape	Robbery	Aggra-vated assault	Property crime	Burglary	Larceny-theft	Motor vehicle theft	Arson[1]
	Hood River	6,586	8	0	1	1	6	199	24	155	20	2
	Hubbard	2,587	2	0	0	1	1	52	10	37	5	1
	Independence	8,327	20	1	3	1	15	189	25	155	9	2
	Jacksonville	2,267	0	0	0	0	0	47	5	40	2	0
	John Day	1,631	10	0	0	0	10	46	13	29	4	0
	Junction City	5,457	3	0	1	1	1	64	21	37	6	3
	King City	2,092	0	0	0	0	0	58	4	51	3	0
	Klamath Falls	20,208	87	2	15	26	44	584	118	393	73	3
	La Grande	12,644	26	0	10	1	15	339	60	264	15	6
	Lake Oswego	37,101	25	0	3	6	16	567	127	412	28	19
	Lakeview	2,417	22	0	0	0	22	102	19	79	4	1
	Lincoln City	7,978	41	0	2	8	31	392	82	290	20	4
	Madras	5,387	33	1	1	0	31	320	51	223	46	2
	Malin	648	0	0	0	0	0	3	1	1	1	0
	Manzanita	625	1	0	0	0	1	35	6	28	1	0
	McMinnville	30,132	41	0	7	6	28	733	108	573	52	6
	Milton-Freewater	6,551	9	0	1	1	7	327	80	229	18	0
	Milwaukie	21,151	33	0	13	8	12	623	110	445	68	4
	Molalla	6,847	10	0	3	1	6	214	25	170	19	2
	Monmouth	9,134	15	0	3	0	12	212	24	180	8	0
	Mount Angel	3,410	10	0	1	0	9	127	22	96	9	4
	Myrtle Creek	3,586	7	0	6	0	1	127	36	82	9	0
	Newberg-Dundee	24,046	26	0	8	5	13	507	38	419	50	11
	North Bend	10,004	10	0	0	7	3	314	72	210	32	7
	North Plains	1,804	0	0	0	0	0	20	4	16	0	0
	Oakridge	3,199	3	0	0	1	2	114	20	88	6	0
	Ontario	11,307	85	0	6	7	72	718	122	564	32	1
	Oregon City	30,717	41	0	6	17	18	979	123	759	97	10
	Philomath	4,282	13	0	0	1	12	145	46	96	3	3
	Phoenix	4,447	7	0	4	2	1	130	12	112	6	0
	Portland	542,174	3,872	20	293	1,297	2,262	31,996	5,485	22,033	4,478	408
	Prineville	9,054	80	0	6	0	74	299	45	247	7	4
	Rainier	1,846	3	0	0	1	2	42	20	19	3	1
	Reedsport	4,433	2	0	1	1	0	117	16	93	8	0
	Rockaway Beach	1,329	1	0	0	0	1	64	25	37	2	0
	Rogue River	1,973	1	0	1	0	0	64	11	49	4	1
	Roseburg	21,067	53	0	11	19	23	1,102	177	875	50	10
	Salem	151,190	691	9	74	129	479	8,267	1,073	6,363	831	54
	Sandy	8,000	15	0	6	0	9	282	45	220	17	2
	Scappoose	6,010	8	0	1	0	7	164	20	132	12	1
	Seaside	6,216	21	1	1	8	11	518	81	424	13	7
	Shady Cove	2,339	0	0	0	0	0	65	15	44	6	0
	Sherwood	15,650	11	0	3	5	3	276	36	231	9	4
	Springfield	56,553	182	2	11	29	140	3,969	651	2,785	533	37
	St. Helens	12,069	30	1	5	4	20	316	53	239	24	10
	Sutherlin	7,400	12	0	3	2	7	204	48	138	18	1
	Sweet Home	8,527	28	0	2	4	22	560	139	399	22	3
	Talent	6,117	6	0	1	3	2	43	6	33	4	0
	The Dalles	12,089	21	0	5	2	14	574	108	429	37	9
	Tigard	48,755	93	0	7	37	49	2,022	268	1,650	104	18
	Toledo	3,490	3	0	1	1	1	109	23	80	6	1
	Troutdale	15,142	21	0	3	7	11	496	72	364	60	3
	Tualatin	26,305	33	0	2	13	18	827	122	630	75	0
	Turner	1,597	7	0	1	0	6	53	17	34	2	1
	Umatilla	6,409	5	0	1	1	3	119	22	82	15	1
	Veneta	3,534	50	0	12	2	36	282	115	138	29	2
	Vernonia	2,324	0	0	0	0	0	46	9	36	1	1
	Warrenton	4,381	2	0	2	0	0	133	19	107	7	0
	West Linn	25,505	25	0	5	5	15	299	61	226	12	2
	Weston	726	0	0	0	0	0	44	23	18	3	3
	Wilsonville	16,339	15	2	2	9	2	599	81	470	48	4
	Winston	4,842	8	0	3	1	4	171	38	119	14	2
	Yamhill	836	0	0	0	0	0	10	2	7	1	0
PENNSYL-VANIA	Abington Township	55,314	61	0	3	46	12	1,141	131	958	52	5

[1] The FBI does not publish arson data unless it receives data from either the agency or the state for all 12 months of the calendar year.

Table 8. Offenses Known to Law Enforcement, by State and City, 2006 (*Contd.*)

(Number.)

State	City	Popula-tion	Violent crime	Murder and non-negligent man-slaughter	Forcible rape	Robbery	Aggra-vated assault	Property crime	Burglary	Larceny-theft	Motor vehicle theft	Arson[1]
	Adamstown	1,302	0	0	0	0	0	17	1	14	2	0
	Adams Township, Butler County	8,160	9	0	2	0	7	76	6	66	4	0
	Akron	4,013	1	0	0	0	1	44	8	31	5	2
	Albion	1,559	1	0	0	0	1	20	9	10	1	1
	Alburtis	2,205	3	0	0	0	3	20	0	20	0	1
	Aldan	4,298	6	0	1	3	2	105	12	87	6	0
	Aliquippa	11,115	67	5	1	19	42	299	87	180	32	0
	Allegheny Township, Blair County	6,933	29	0	3	4	22	220	41	175	4	0
	Allegheny Township, Westmoreland County	8,170	3	0	0	0	3	65	8	51	6	0
	Allentown	107,087	1,081	16	42	684	339	6,059	1,433	4,131	495	35
	Altoona	47,218	245	0	32	84	129	1,502	439	976	87	23
	Ambler	6,355	5	0	0	4	1	157	12	125	20	0
	Amity Township	11,077	3	0	0	1	2	104	21	74	9	4
	Annville Township	4,679	10	0	3	0	7	51	14	35	2	0
	Arnold	5,406	21	0	2	8	11	95	29	44	22	0
	Ashland	3,162	3	0	0	0	3	55	9	46	0	0
	Ashley	2,728	0	0	0	0	0	16	0	10	6	0
	Ashville	267	0	0	0	0	0	0	0	0	0	0
	Aspinwall	2,791	5	0	1	3	1	28	9	17	2	0
	Aston Township	16,829	32	0	6	10	16	296	35	236	25	2
	Athens	3,304	4	0	1	0	3	73	14	59	0	0
	Auburn	814	0	0	0	0	0	2	0	2	0	0
	Avalon	4,966	7	0	0	5	2	93	18	64	11	0
	Baldwin Borough	18,859	23	0	0	1	22	168	26	119	23	0
	Baldwin Township	2,103	8	0	0	0	8	25	6	17	2	0
	Bally	1,103	0	0	0	0	0	2	1	1	0	0
	Bangor	5,310	30	0	5	2	23	164	19	131	14	0
	Barrett Township	4,283	4	0	0	0	4	59	16	42	1	1
	Beaver	4,554	4	0	0	1	3	136	14	117	5	0
	Beaver Falls	9,410	96	0	4	19	73	411	40	347	24	6
	Bedford	3,054	3	0	0	1	2	33	6	23	4	0
	Bedminster Township	4,944	6	1	0	0	5	81	9	70	2	0
	Bell Acres	1,385	0	0	0	0	0	3	3	0	0	0
	Bellefonte	6,166	1	0	1	0	0	148	12	135	1	0
	Bellwood	1,918	2	0	0	0	2	15	4	11	0	0
	Bensalem Township	58,797	122	2	10	50	60	2,272	321	1,706	245	8
	Berks-Lehigh Regional	26,655	10	0	4	3	3	350	53	276	21	3
	Berlin	2,132	0	0	0	0	0	0	0	0	0	0
	Bern Township	7,064	17	1	1	0	15	76	12	55	9	0
	Berwick	10,361	34	0	21	3	10	369	63	278	28	2
	Bessemer	1,127	0	0	0	0	0	3	1	1	1	0
	Bethel Park	32,342	18	0	1	5	12	339	48	279	12	1
	Bethel Township, Berks County	4,421	0	0	0	0	0	48	7	39	2	0
	Bethel Township, Delaware County	9,317	7	0	1	1	5	91	9	77	5	0
	Bethlehem Township	23,583	65	0	2	10	53	425	29	369	27	1
	Biglerville	1,153	1	0	0	0	1	19	0	16	3	0
	Birdsboro	5,196	9	0	2	1	6	83	10	67	6	1
	Birmingham Township	4,269	6	0	0	0	6	28	1	26	1	0
	Blairsville	3,463	10	1	0	3	6	103	12	82	9	0
	Blakely	6,823	5	0	0	4	1	51	9	39	3	0
	Blawnox	1,481	2	0	0	0	2	4	1	2	1	0
	Bloomsburg Town	12,926	18	0	2	2	14	201	25	172	4	2
	Boyertown	3,949	7	0	1	3	3	95	13	76	6	2
	Brackenridge	3,325	3	0	0	3	0	108	20	81	7	0
	Bradford	8,659	35	0	3	0	32	308	38	259	11	2
	Bradford Township	4,800	17	0	0	2	15	59	3	52	4	0
	Brandywine Regional	9,862	19	0	0	0	19	95	6	85	4	1
	Brecknock Township, Berks County	4,827	3	0	0	0	3	22	6	13	3	0
	Brentwood	9,820	22	0	2	10	10	187	26	137	24	0
	Bridgeport	4,406	15	0	0	1	14	151	19	119	13	0
	Bridgeville	5,026	8	0	2	2	4	68	16	43	9	0

[1] The FBI does not publish arson data unless it receives data from either the agency or the state for all 12 months of the calendar year.

Table 8. Offenses Known to Law Enforcement, by State and City, 2006 (*Contd.*)

(Number.)

State	City	Popula-tion	Violent crime	Murder and non-negligent man-slaughter	Forcible rape	Robbery	Aggra-vated assault	Property crime	Burglary	Larceny-theft	Motor vehicle theft	Arson[1]
	Brighton Township	7,975	6	0	0	1	5	50	4	44	2	0
	Bristol	9,819	30	0	3	16	11	438	54	347	37	2
	Brockway	2,103	0	0	0	0	0	6	1	5	0	0
	Brookhaven	7,856	22	0	0	3	19	227	19	193	15	0
	Brookville	4,081	8	0	2	0	6	72	3	67	2	0
	Brownsville	2,692	12	0	0	2	10	68	18	39	11	0
	Bryn Athyn	1,355	0	0	0	0	0	12	1	10	1	0
	Buckingham Township	18,486	8	0	0	0	8	173	22	146	5	0
	Buffalo Township	7,176	26	0	0	4	22	122	36	82	4	0
	Butler	14,534	92	3	5	18	66	639	112	527	0	3
	Butler Township, Butler County	17,045	40	1	1	6	32	478	31	435	12	2
	California	5,076	16	0	3	4	9	123	30	87	6	3
	Cambria Township	6,210	13	0	0	4	9	116	7	99	10	0
	Cambridge Springs	2,284	5	0	1	0	4	35	3	31	1	0
	Camp Hill	7,431	9	0	0	4	5	125	18	104	3	2
	Carbondale	9,356	12	0	5	1	6	178	31	138	9	0
	Carlisle	18,124	42	1	4	24	13	633	65	552	16	5
	Carnegie	8,156	29	1	3	8	17	216	42	152	22	1
	Carrolltown	997	1	0	0	0	1	30	1	29	0	0
	Carroll Township, Washington County	5,596	15	0	0	1	14	53	5	44	4	1
	Carroll Township, York County	5,168	9	1	2	1	5	157	21	129	7	0
	Castle Shannon	8,276	19	0	0	7	12	174	35	130	9	2
	Catawissa	1,558	3	0	0	0	3	60	10	49	1	0
	Center Township	11,756	21	0	2	7	12	365	47	300	18	1
	Centerville	3,297	0	0	0	0	0	25	10	13	2	0
	Central Berks Regional	7,474	19	1	3	10	5	164	25	112	27	0
	Chalfont	4,202	0	0	0	0	0	22	0	22	0	0
	Chambersburg	17,977	120	1	7	39	73	725	152	538	35	0
	Chartiers Township	7,220	3	0	0	2	1	69	9	56	4	0
	Cheltenham Township	36,812	110	1	6	74	29	955	159	693	103	1
	Chester	37,091	984	18	21	241	704	1,468	444	740	284	25
	Chester Township	4,509	63	0	3	9	51	38	10	16	12	0
	Cheswick	1,792	0	0	0	0	0	5	1	4	0	0
	Chippewa Township	9,877	4	0	0	2	2	234	19	212	3	0
	Christiana	1,092	1	0	0	0	1	4	1	3	0	0
	Churchill	3,353	18	0	0	1	17	40	8	30	2	0
	Clairton	8,088	56	0	5	29	22	288	93	171	24	0
	Clarion	5,512	6	0	0	3	3	113	12	99	2	0
	Claysville	696	0	0	0	0	0	13	0	13	0	0
	Clearfield	6,345	17	0	2	7	8	127	19	102	6	0
	Coaldale	2,172	4	0	0	0	4	3	1	2	0	0
	Coal Township	10,430	38	0	3	0	35	182	23	144	15	7
	Coatesville	11,505	151	4	3	81	63	486	101	325	60	3
	Colebrookdale District	6,413	9	0	1	1	7	165	23	135	7	1
	Collegeville	5,059	4	0	0	0	4	87	8	76	3	1
	Collier Township	5,961	8	0	1	4	3	209	20	184	5	5
	Collingdale	8,509	102	0	3	16	83	265	33	203	29	1
	Colonial Regional	18,691	22	0	2	9	11	515	53	453	9	2
	Columbia	10,101	33	1	2	8	22	264	65	176	23	1
	Colwyn	2,396	32	0	0	3	29	88	18	54	16	0
	Conemaugh Township, Cambria County	2,546	1	0	0	0	1	12	8	3	1	0
	Conewago Township, Adams County	6,074	6	0	4	0	2	64	6	57	1	3
	Conewango Township	3,711	7	0	1	0	6	97	17	77	3	2
	Conneaut Lake Regional	3,570	5	0	1	0	4	70	16	48	6	0
	Connellsville	8,652	18	0	3	5	10	368	55	306	7	1
	Conshohocken	7,718	24	0	3	2	19	200	0	175	25	0
	Coopersburg	2,572	3	0	0	0	3	44	6	36	2	0
	Coplay	3,374	9	0	0	2	7	61	5	55	1	0
	Coraopolis	5,759	66	0	1	9	56	209	43	151	15	0
	Cornwall	3,450	0	0	0	0	0	23	8	13	2	0
	Corry	6,554	33	0	1	1	31	60	24	34	2	2

[1] The FBI does not publish arson data unless it receives data from either the agency or the state for all 12 months of the calendar year.

Table 8. Offenses Known to Law Enforcement, by State and City, 2006 (*Contd.*)

(Number.)

State	City	Popula-tion	Violent crime	Murder and non-negligent man-slaughter	Forcible rape	Robbery	Aggra-vated assault	Property crime	Burglary	Larceny-theft	Motor vehicle theft	Arson[1]
	Covington Township..........	2,100	2	0	0	0	2	76	27	46	3	3
	Crafton................................	6,295	14	0	0	8	6	131	16	109	6	1
	Cranberry Township..........	27,057	45	0	0	14	31	362	23	330	9	2
	Cresson...............................	1,539	3	0	0	0	3	58	9	46	3	0
	Cresson Township..............	4,253	1	0	1	0	0	16	3	13	0	0
	Croyle Township................	2,249	1	0	0	0	1	21	0	21	0	0
	Cumru Township................	17,284	20	0	2	13	5	413	44	328	41	1
	Curwensville......................	2,542	6	0	0	0	6	59	17	42	0	1
	Dallas.................................	2,510	4	0	0	1	3	27	5	19	3	0
	Dallas Township.................	8,385	10	0	2	1	7	60	27	30	3	0
	Danville..............................	4,644	36	0	1	0	35	132	22	108	2	0
	Darby	10,055	354	0	15	52	287	483	112	280	91	3
	Decatur Township..............	3,088	2	0	1	0	1	28	3	25	0	0
	Delmont..............................	2,500	1	0	0	1	0	70	11	57	2	0
	Denver	3,649	1	0	1	0	0	125	31	91	3	2
	Derry Township, Dauphin County..............................	21,833	51	0	6	5	40	633	69	549	15	0
	Dickson City......................	5,972	17	0	2	7	8	383	17	356	10	0
	Donegal Township.............	2,586	2	0	0	0	2	17	2	13	2	0
	Dormont	8,704	51	0	2	5	44	140	27	103	10	4
	Douglass Township, Montgomery......................	10,226	22	0	3	4	15	194	18	160	16	2
	Downingtown.....................	7,865	34	1	2	7	24	353	33	307	13	0
	Doylestown........................	8,232	19	0	1	2	16	253	30	213	10	0
	Doylestown Township.......	18,812	18	0	2	4	12	238	44	187	7	2
	Dublin Borough................	2,185	2	0	0	0	2	3	0	3	0	0
	Du Bois..............................	7,845	34	0	8	1	25	400	47	339	14	0
	Duboistown........................	1,234	0	0	0	0	0	0	0	0	0	0
	Duncannon.........................	1,497	2	0	0	0	2	42	10	29	3	0
	Duncansville......................	1,195	0	0	0	0	0	34	6	27	1	0
	Duquesne...........................	6,881	100	5	9	26	60	368	127	202	39	9
	Earl Township	6,797	4	0	0	1	3	51	20	25	6	0
	East Bangor.......................	996	0	0	0	0	0	15	1	14	0	0
	East Berlin	1,431	2	0	0	1	1	4	0	4	0	0
	East Buffalo Township......	5,901	3	0	3	0	0	27	3	24	0	0
	East Cocalico Township	10,268	3	0	1	1	1	183	42	124	17	0
	East Conemaugh................	1,215	2	0	0	0	2	3	0	3	0	0
	East Coventry Township.....	5,703	6	0	0	0	6	65	7	57	1	0
	Eastern Adams Regional....	8,928	3	0	1	2	0	59	33	23	3	
	East Fallowfield Township..........................	6,717	11	0	0	1	10	73	8	63	2	0
	East Franklin Township	3,979	6	0	1	0	5	63	12	46	5	0
	East Hempfield Township..........................	22,647	11	0	1	5	5	588	84	478	26	5
	East Lampeter Township..........................	14,646	30	6	3	11	10	746	76	642	28	3
	East McKeesport	2,891	1	0	0	0	1	27	12	15	0	0
	East Norriton Township......	13,525	8	1	2	3	2	299	35	248	16	2
	Easton	26,290	166	4	16	54	92	1,424	188	1,037	199	23
	East Pennsboro Township..........................	19,627	20	0	3	10	7	392	51	325	16	2
	East Petersburg................	4,350	6	0	0	3	3	77	10	64	3	0
	East Pikeland Township......	6,824	3	0	1	0	2	91	19	68	4	1
	East Rochester..................	589	2	0	0	1	1	52	1	47	4	0
	East Taylor Township........	2,620	0	0	0	0	0	0	0	0	0	0
	Easttown Township............	10,409	11	0	1	2	8	103	21	79	3	0
	East Vincent Township	6,452	9	0	1	1	7	64	8	49	7	0
	East Washington	1,914	5	0	0	2	3	27	5	16	6	2
	East Whiteland Township..........................	10,314	6	0	2	1	3	151	6	131	14	1
	Ebensburg.........................	2,941	9	0	0	1	8	102	6	95	1	0
	Economy............................	9,299	0	0	0	0	0	5	3	2	0	0
	Eddystone.........................	2,383	35	0	0	8	27	274	20	239	15	0
	Edgewood..........................	3,101	17	0	1	11	5	295	26	264	5	1
	Edgeworth	1,624	0	0	0	0	0	0	0	0	0	0
	Edinboro............................	6,743	7	0	2	2	3	107	18	87	2	0
	Edwardsville......................	4,745	49	1	4	1	43	211	32	157	22	1

[1] The FBI does not publish arson data unless it receives data from either the agency or the state for all 12 months of the calendar year.

Table 8. Offenses Known to Law Enforcement, by State and City, 2006 (*Contd.*)

(Number.)

State	City	Popula-tion	Violent crime	Murder and non-negligent man-slaughter	Forcible rape	Robbery	Aggra-vated assault	Property crime	Burglary	Larceny-theft	Motor vehicle theft	Arson[1]
	Elizabethtown	11,903	19	1	2	5	11	226	43	172	11	10
	Elizabeth Township	13,097	25	0	0	0	25	101	25	66	10	0
	Elk Lick Township	2,205	2	0	0	0	2	4	1	2	1	0
	Ellwood City	8,269	40	0	0	18	22	203	39	155	9	5
	Emmaus	11,361	19	0	4	5	10	400	42	351	7	2
	Emporium	2,364	3	0	1	0	2	50	9	41	0	0
	Ephrata	13,104	12	0	2	7	3	270	52	196	22	4
	Ephrata Township	9,185	10	0	1	1	8	148	36	103	9	1
	Erie	102,703	554	2	69	275	208	2,987	740	2,106	141	38
	Etna	3,674	28	0	0	3	25	50	15	24	11	0
	Evans City	1,959	4	0	0	2	2	34	5	27	2	0
	Everett	1,890	4	0	0	0	4	56	14	40	2	0
	Exeter	6,012	15	0	0	2	13	147	16	124	7	0
	Exeter Township, Berks County	26,119	22	0	1	7	14	420	63	314	43	2
	Fairview Township, York County	15,946	32	0	3	8	21	348	50	283	15	3
	Falls Township, Bucks County	34,276	74	0	8	32	34	1,017	122	778	117	2
	Fawn Township	2,382	1	0	0	1	0	24	4	16	4	0
	Ferguson Township	15,766	15	0	4	1	10	182	30	142	10	1
	Findlay Township	5,126	10	0	0	0	10	91	9	75	7	0
	Fleetwood	4,010	2	0	0	0	2	62	12	47	3	1
	Folcroft	6,912	51	0	7	11	33	188	32	126	30	1
	Forest City	1,797	3	0	1	0	2	18	2	16	0	0
	Forest Hills	6,430	8	0	1	4	3	72	18	50	4	0
	Forks Township	12,864	13	0	1	0	12	199	8	181	10	2
	Forty Fort	4,335	2	0	0	0	2	104	16	81	7	0
	Foster Township	4,371	3	1	0	0	2	29	8	20	1	0
	Fountain Hill	4,599	23	0	4	3	16	182	24	151	7	1
	Fox Chapel	5,243	0	0	0	0	0	21	5	16	0	0
	Frackville	5,042	10	0	0	2	8	8	7	0	1	0
	Franklin	6,885	18	1	3	1	13	197	28	167	2	1
	Franklin Park	11,775	6	0	0	1	5	84	16	67	1	1
	Franklin Township, Carbon County	4,733	10	0	0	0	10	51	6	37	8	0
	Freedom	1,666	7	0	1	0	6	59	13	34	12	0
	Freeland	3,458	12	0	1	1	10	70	11	57	2	0
	Freemansburg	1,975	3	0	0	0	3	55	10	43	2	0
	Gallitzin	2,058	1	0	0	1	0	31	12	18	1	0
	Gettysburg	8,021	32	0	2	13	17	200	41	150	9	2
	Gilpin Township	2,542	2	0	0	0	2	11	7	2	2	0
	Girard	3,020	10	0	1	1	8	38	3	34	1	0
	Glenolden	7,315	34	0	3	8	23	173	18	145	10	2
	Granville Township	4,926	9	0	1	0	8	92	18	71	3	3
	Greencastle	3,841	6	0	0	3	3	98	15	80	3	0
	Greenfield Township, Blair County	3,812	15	0	0	2	13	202	27	173	2	0
	Greensburg	15,583	39	1	4	8	26	448	63	372	13	2
	Green Tree	4,457	2	0	1	0	1	106	15	83	8	1
	Greenwood Township	2,008	0	0	0	0	0	0	0	0	0	0
	Grove City	7,771	9	1	2	1	5	131	17	109	5	0
	Halifax Regional	4,199	0	0	0	0	0	10	1	9	0	0
	Hamburg	4,187	10	0	1	1	8	88	16	61	11	0
	Hamiltonban Township	2,606	8	0	0	0	8	7	2	4	1	1
	Hampton Township	17,203	20	0	3	3	14	176	34	138	4	0
	Hanover	15,003	40	0	3	19	18	626	76	525	25	3
	Harmar Township	3,077	6	0	0	3	3	134	15	109	10	1
	Harmony Township	3,189	1	0	0	1	0	92	13	74	5	0
	Harrisburg	47,514	803	10	51	461	281	2,443	629	1,655	159	32
	Harrison Township	10,281	29	0	0	11	18	416	76	321	19	0
	Hatboro	7,294	18	0	1	8	9	118	32	80	6	2
	Heidelberg Township, Berks County	1,742	1	0	0	0	1	9	0	9	0	0
	Hellam Township	8,581	32	0	3	4	25	132	33	87	12	0
	Hellertown	5,620	27	0	1	2	24	140	24	112	4	0
	Hemlock Township	2,137	2	0	0	1	1	158	3	153	2	0

[1] The FBI does not publish arson data unless it receives data from either the agency or the state for all 12 months of the calendar year.

Table 8. Offenses Known to Law Enforcement, by State and City, 2006 (*Contd.*)

(Number.)

State	City	Population	Violent crime	Murder and non-negligent man-slaughter	Forcible rape	Robbery	Aggra-vated assault	Property crime	Burglary	Larceny-theft	Motor vehicle theft	Arson[1]
	Hermitage	16,586	16	0	1	4	11	551	63	477	11	1
	Highspire	2,627	34	0	2	5	27	103	15	80	8	1
	Hilltown Township	12,751	39	0	2	3	34	225	38	179	8	0
	Hollidaysburg	5,524	9	0	0	4	5	130	13	113	4	0
	Homestead	3,538	54	2	2	27	23	387	64	269	54	0
	Honesdale	4,853	5	0	2	1	2	170	23	142	5	0
	Hooversville	733	1	0	0	0	1	4	3	1	0	0
	Horsham Township	25,093	15	0	0	6	9	281	24	238	19	1
	Hughesville	2,116	0	0	0	0	0	19	1	18	0	
	Huntingdon	6,882	14	0	0	0	14	117	10	106	1	0
	Independence Township, Beaver County	2,768	1	0	0	0	1	51	11	31	9	0
	Indiana	15,029	56	0	6	6	44	281	44	235	2	2
	Indiana Township	6,913	2	0	1	1	0	64	14	48	2	1
	Industry	1,847	0	0	0	0	0	31	7	23	1	0
	Ingram	3,481	18	0	0	4	14	34	5	27	2	0
	Irwin	4,191	15	0	0	3	12	112	14	95	3	0
	Jackson Township, Butler County	3,833	15	0	0	1	14	95	24	70	1	0
	Jackson Township, Cambria County	4,845	10	0	4	2	4	147	11	128	8	0
	Jackson Township, Luzerne County	4,633	9	0	0	0	9	13	3	10	0	0
	Jenkins Township	4,841	6	0	2	0	4	110	22	76	12	1
	Jersey Shore	4,430	8	0	2	0	6	153	29	119	5	0
	Jim Thorpe	4,896	15	0	0	1	14	116	16	92	8	4
	Johnsonburg	2,819	4	0	0	3	1	70	18	50	2	2
	Johnstown	24,144	132	2	5	43	82	1,017	266	704	47	7
	Juniata Valley Regional	434	1	0	0	0	1	7	0	7	0	0
	Kane	3,896	4	0	0	0	4	17	4	12	1	0
	Kennedy Township	8,618	21	0	0	5	16	194	16	169	9	0
	Kidder Township	1,333	14	0	2	0	12	129	23	105	1	4
	Kingston	13,188	55	0	4	11	40	335	48	272	15	7
	Kingston Township	7,066	12	0	1	2	9	84	10	67	7	2
	Kiskiminetas Township	4,859	5	0	0	0	5	56	14	38	4	0
	Kline Township	1,509	1	0	1	0	0	26	3	21	2	0
	Koppel	809	3	0	0	0	3	82	11	71	0	1
	Kutztown	4,930	10	0	0	2	8	207	35	149	23	0
	Laflin Borough	1,508	2	0	0	0	2	27	3	24	0	0
	Lake City	2,984	7	0	0	1	6	29	8	21	0	0
	Lancaster	54,805	532	7	44	244	237	3,164	535	2,312	317	36
	Lancaster Township, Butler County	2,579	0	0	0	0	0	8	0	7	1	0
	Lancaster Township, Lancaster County	14,241	38	0	1	26	11	463	90	342	31	4
	Lansdale	15,927	29	0	5	9	15	418	44	343	31	13
	Lansdowne	10,799	54	0	1	16	37	323	59	239	25	0
	Larksville	4,523	5	0	1	1	3	79	7	67	5	1
	Latimore-York Springs Regional	3,419	3	0	1	0	2	23	1	17	5	0
	Latrobe	8,662	39	0	2	4	33	186	20	163	3	2
	Lawrence Park Township	3,845	9	0	1	0	8	50	8	40	2	0
	Lawrence Township	7,672	52	0	2	2	48	244	36	204	4	3
	Lebanon	24,007	152	2	9	61	80	892	175	659	58	9
	Leet Township	1,540	0	0	0	0	0	0	0	0	0	0
	Lehighton	5,528	19	1	2	5	11	191	30	147	14	4
	Lehigh Township, Northampton County	10,588	10	0	1	1	8	108	13	88	7	1
	Lehman Township	3,272	6	0	0	0	6	33	9	23	1	0
	Lewisburg	5,567	6	0	1	0	5	69	8	58	3	0
	Liberty Township, Bedford County	1,461	0	0	0	0	0	0	0	0	0	0
	Lilly	896	0	0	0	0	0	1	0	0	1	0
	Limerick Township	16,423	7	0	0	1	6	283	38	234	11	1
	Lincoln	1,152	2	0	0	0	2	12	5	6	1	0
	Linesville	1,123	0	0	0	0	0	0	0	0	0	0
	Lititz	9,016	5	0	0	1	4	129	16	103	10	8

[1] The FBI does not publish arson data unless it receives data from either the agency or the state for all 12 months of the calendar year.

Table 8. Offenses Known to Law Enforcement, by State and City, 2006 (*Contd.*)

(Number.)

State	City	Popula-tion	Violent crime	Murder and non-negligent man-slaughter	Forcible rape	Robbery	Aggra-vated assault	Property crime	Burglary	Larceny-theft	Motor vehicle theft	Arson[1]
	Littlestown	4,135	24	0	2	3	19	155	27	122	6	0
	Lock Haven	8,792	19	0	6	3	10	339	63	265	11	4
	Locust Township	2,508	1	0	0	0	1	22	3	19	0	0
	Logan Township	11,882	30	0	0	9	21	305	67	227	11	2
	Lower Burrell	12,455	13	0	1	2	10	173	33	133	7	0
	Lower Gwynedd Township	11,185	22	0	0	3	19	195	26	160	9	0
	Lower Heidelberg Township	4,962	2	0	0	1	1	31	2	28	1	0
	Lower Makefield Township	32,732	6	0	1	0	5	399	69	318	12	0
	Lower Merion Township	58,271	62	1	0	48	13	1,043	172	809	62	1
	Lower Moreland Township	11,722	22	0	4	0	18	193	53	133	7	2
	Lower Paxton Township	44,949	104	0	13	32	59	1,212	164	1,023	25	14
	Lower Pottsgrove Township	12,058	28	0	1	3	24	263	43	204	16	0
	Lower Providence Township	24,959	11	1	2	4	4	296	52	231	13	0
	Lower Salford Township	14,123	7	0	0	0	7	98	8	87	3	0
	Lower Saucon Township	11,053	18	0	1	2	15	104	10	93	1	3
	Lower Southampton Township	19,264	63	0	0	8	55	520	83	393	44	5
	Lower Swatara Township	8,350	10	0	3	1	6	130	27	101	2	1
	Lower Windsor Township	7,743	11	0	0	0	11	91	27	55	9	1
	Luzerne Township	6,029	0	0	0	0	0	30	5	23	2	1
	Madison Township	1,611	0	0	0	0	0	0	0	0	0	0
	Mahanoy City	4,466	0	0	0	0	0	23	0	22	1	0
	Mahoning Township, Montour County	4,260	51	0	0	0	51	35	5	26	4	0
	Malvern	3,103	1	0	0	0	1	43	4	36	3	0
	Manheim	4,663	8	0	1	1	6	112	18	90	4	0
	Manheim Township	35,608	56	0	3	23	30	936	146	735	55	8
	Manor Township, Armstrong County	4,047	1	0	0	0	1	5	1	3	1	0
	Mansfield	3,357	1	0	0	1	0	9	1	7	1	0
	Marion Township, Beaver County	909	1	0	0	0	1	5	0	5	0	0
	Marlborough Township	3,274	5	0	1	0	4	40	7	32	1	1
	Marple Township	23,591	17	0	6	2	9	340	25	306	9	2
	Martinsburg	2,159	3	1	1	1	0	56	7	46	3	1
	Masontown	3,472	3	0	0	0	3	82	22	49	11	1
	McCandless	27,782	23	0	3	3	17	412	36	367	9	0
	McDonald Borough	2,183	24	0	1	0	23	49	5	40	4	2
	McSherrystown	2,806	7	0	1	1	5	53	2	50	1	0
	Meadville	13,380	29	1	7	7	14	314	41	263	10	2
	Mechanicsburg	8,826	39	1	2	5	31	200	15	176	9	0
	Media	5,456	18	0	2	3	13	28	8	18	2	1
	Mercer	2,299	0	0	0	0	0	27	3	23	1	0
	Mercersburg	1,550	6	0	0	0	6	41	4	37	0	0
	Middlesex Township, Cumberland County	6,801	17	0	3	6	8	218	17	188	13	0
	Middletown	8,952	21	0	4	4	13	194	32	156	6	4
	Middletown Township	47,490	59	0	2	18	39	1,627	171	1,358	98	3
	Midland	2,972	16	0	1	4	11	124	40	73	11	0
	Mifflinburg	3,581	4	0	0	0	4	11	1	10	0	0
	Mifflin County Regional	22,502	80	1	11	4	64	687	135	532	20	3
	Mifflin Township	2,274	1	0	1	0	0	17	1	15	1	0
	Milford	2,832	6	0	0	0	6	25	6	18	1	0
	Millcreek Township	52,713	47	2	8	9	28	918	191	685	42	0
	Millersburg	2,493	16	0	0	1	15	61	12	47	2	1
	Millersville	7,590	11	0	1	3	7	96	21	66	9	0
	Millvale	3,775	13	0	2	0	11	14	14	0	0	0
	Millville	958	1	0	0	0	1	1	0	1	0	0
	Milton	6,490	31	1	3	1	26	106	10	93	3	2
	Mohnton	3,074	5	0	0	0	5	23	7	15	1	0

[1] The FBI does not publish arson data unless it receives data from either the agency or the state for all 12 months of the calendar year.

Table 8. Offenses Known to Law Enforcement, by State and City, 2006 (*Contd.*)

(Number.)

State	City	Population	Violent crime	Murder and non-negligent manslaughter	Forcible rape	Robbery	Aggravated assault	Property crime	Burglary	Larceny-theft	Motor vehicle theft	Arson[1]
	Monaca	5,978	16	0	1	2	13	126	24	94	8	4
	Monessen	8,314	62	0	2	5	55	270	55	203	12	6
	Monroeville	28,200	84	0	3	29	52	767	110	561	96	3
	Montgomery Township	24,234	11	0	0	6	5	555	27	520	8	2
	Montoursville	4,632	2	0	0	1	1	102	13	85	4	
	Montrose	1,597	4	0	0	0	4	6	1	5	0	0
	Moon Township	22,664	27	1	2	9	15	334	55	249	30	1
	Moore Township	9,336	2	0	0	0	2	62	12	45	5	0
	Moosic	5,743	42	0	3	3	36	253	26	204	23	6
	Morrisville	9,819	40	0	0	14	26	291	64	196	31	0
	Morton	2,667	12	0	1	2	9	84	8	70	6	1
	Moscow	1,918	7	0	1	0	6	22	3	19	0	0
	Mount Carmel	6,058	46	0	0	2	44	93	15	75	3	2
	Mount Gretna Borough	234	0	0	0	0	0	0	0	0	0	0
	Mount Jewett	1,027	1	0	0	0	1	0	0	0	0	0
	Mount Joy	6,950	5	0	2	2	1	134	35	92	7	0
	Mount Lebanon	31,286	72	1	2	9	60	269	36	222	11	3
	Mount Oliver	3,775	52	0	5	27	20	205	43	114	48	3
	Muhlenberg Township	17,763	28	0	0	19	9	665	59	510	96	0
	Munhall	11,523	11	0	0	3	8	241	47	162	32	0
	Nanticoke	10,391	37	0	5	6	26	442	119	307	16	2
	Narberth	4,158	3	0	0	1	2	56	6	48	2	0
	Nazareth Area	6,028	8	0	1	4	3	149	9	137	3	0
	Neshannock Township	9,418	9	0	0	6	3	174	23	143	8	0
	Newberry Township	15,268	17	0	6	4	7	271	38	219	14	5
	New Bethlehem	1,008	0	0	0	0	0	5	1	4	0	1
	New Britain	2,315	10	0	0	1	9	43	5	37	1	1
	New Britain Township	10,745	4	0	0	0	4	76	10	66	0	1
	New Cumberland	7,133	16	0	2	10	4	136	24	111	1	0
	New Hanover Township	8,861	10	0	0	0	10	83	13	62	8	1
	New Holland	5,145	2	0	0	1	1	121	21	93	7	0
	New Hope	2,278	16	0	0	0	16	67	7	58	2	0
	New Kensington	14,097	60	2	8	20	30	493	103	356	34	5
	Newport	1,468	18	0	1	1	16	67	13	53	1	1
	New Sewickley Township	7,738	2	0	0	1	1	120	26	87	7	1
	Newtown	2,258	4	0	0	0	4	26	1	24	1	0
	Newtown Township, Bucks County	19,161	29	0	1	6	22	196	18	171	7	2
	Newtown Township, Delaware County	11,861	15	0	1	4	10	131	24	104	3	0
	Newville	1,324	7	0	0	0	7	46	4	41	1	0
	Norristown	30,716	523	5	20	239	259	1,665	358	1,113	194	8
	Northampton	9,708	8	0	0	0	8	155	22	127	6	1
	Northampton Township	41,054	16	0	2	7	7	390	79	296	15	10
	North Apollo	1,356	1	0	1	0	0	8	1	5	2	1
	North Catasauqua	2,866	3	0	0	0	3	79	15	58	6	0
	North Cornwall Township	6,497	22	0	1	3	18	111	6	96	9	0
	North Coventry Township	7,623	12	0	3	2	7	320	34	262	24	3
	North East	4,335	10	0	0	1	9	91	15	75	1	2
	Northeastern Regional	10,387	20	1	6	3	10	173	24	144	5	0
	Northern Berks Regional	11,545	10	0	0	1	9	113	19	86	8	6
	Northern Cambria Borough	4,026	13	0	2	1	10	120	27	84	9	0
	Northern Regional	26,802	3	0	0	1	2	353	27	313	13	1
	Northern York Regional	60,162	65	1	2	19	43	1,161	124	977	60	3
	North Fayette Township	12,900	13	0	0	5	8	258	24	221	13	0
	North Franklin Township	4,747	8	0	1	6	1	133	21	105	7	0
	North Huntingdon Township	29,368	15	0	1	3	11	412	79	304	29	0
	North Lebanon Township	10,844	52	0	3	4	45	324	33	275	16	0
	North Londonderry Township	6,903	2	0	0	1	1	95	11	81	3	0

[1] The FBI does not publish arson data unless it receives data from either the agency or the state for all 12 months of the calendar year.

Table 8. Offenses Known to Law Enforcement, by State and City, 2006 *(Contd.)*

(Number.)

State	City	Popula-tion	Violent crime	Murder and non-negligent man-slaughter	Forcible rape	Robbery	Aggra-vated assault	Property crime	Burglary	Larceny-theft	Motor vehicle theft	Arson[1]
	North Middleton Township	10,611	3	1	1	1	0	75	7	61	7	1
	North Strabane Township	11,691	16	0	0	3	13	241	24	209	8	0
	Northumberland	3,589	1	0	0	0	1	106	25	79	2	1
	North Versailles Township	12,564	38	0	3	7	28	341	39	289	13	2
	North Wales	3,302	4	0	0	1	3	80	11	65	4	0
	Northwest Lancaster County Regional	17,424	4	1	0	1	2	164	3	158	3	0
	Northwest Lawrence County Regional	6,891	11	0	1	1	9	89	21	60	8	2
	Norwood	5,857	12	0	1	2	9	106	13	92	1	0
	O'Hara Township	9,488	10	0	0	3	7	104	15	85	4	0
	Oil City	10,952	9	1	2	0	6	156	17	129	10	0
	Old Forge	8,566	24	0	0	1	23	72	14	47	11	0
	Old Lycoming Township	5,380	0	0	0	0	0	12	3	8	1	0
	Orwigsburg	2,998	2	1	0	0	1	47	6	40	1	0
	Paint Township	3,241	9	0	0	0	9	13	2	7	4	0
	Palmerton	5,284	17	0	0	0	17	138	20	115	3	0
	Palmyra	6,963	25	0	2	4	19	142	27	106	9	0
	Parkesburg	3,448	13	0	7	2	4	28	7	19	2	0
	Patterson Area	3,698	8	1	3	1	3	77	17	58	2	0
	Patton Township	12,556	9	1	5	2	1	176	21	154	1	1
	Paxtang	1,506	3	0	0	0	3	30	4	23	3	2
	Pen Argyl	3,673	5	0	1	0	4	72	16	48	8	1
	Penn Hills	44,839	177	1	10	81	85	1,102	274	672	156	7
	Pennridge Regional	10,310	17	0	2	0	15	121	16	101	4	0
	Penn Township, Butler County	5,262	5	0	0	2	3	50	4	45	1	0
	Penn Township, Lancaster County	7,830	11	0	0	1	10	149	31	86	32	1
	Penn Township, Westmoreland County	20,243	12	0	0	0	12	41	14	27	0	1
	Penn Township, York County	15,607	28	0	1	5	22	256	40	204	12	1
	Pequea Township	4,444	2	0	0	0	2	55	21	30	4	2
	Perkasie	8,744	14	0	3	3	8	185	18	163	4	1
	Perry Township, Lawrence County	1,926	0	0	0	0	0	3	3	0	0	0
	Peters Township	19,632	15	0	4	2	9	209	48	150	11	4
	Philadelphia	1,464,576	22,883	406	960	10,971	10,546	62,612	11,542	39,413	11,657	
	Phoenixville	15,434	52	0	4	4	44	413	24	372	17	1
	Pittsburgh	324,604	3,473	56	102	1,722	1,593	15,236	3,713	9,658	1,865	70
	Pittston	7,696	9	0	1	0	8	158	31	119	8	4
	Plains Township	10,568	49	1	3	8	37	339	56	256	27	1
	Pleasant Hills	7,947	5	0	0	3	2	125	12	103	10	1
	Plum	26,475	2	0	2	0	0	170	55	113	2	4
	Plumstead Township	11,904	5	0	0	2	3	116	27	84	5	4
	Plymouth Township, Montgomery County	16,257	32	1	1	23	7	722	94	602	26	5
	Pocono Mountain Regional	34,104	94	1	22	26	45	875	375	439	61	8
	Pocono Township	11,055	36	0	1	15	20	348	62	272	14	5
	Point Township	3,817	6	0	1	0	5	34	8	25	1	0
	Portage	2,688	3	0	0	0	3	28	1	27	0	0
	Port Allegany	2,262	0	0	0	0	0	0	0	0	0	0
	Pottstown	21,570	206	2	19	70	115	1,217	220	910	87	26
	Pottsville	14,777	41	0	3	1	37	261	19	222	20	5
	Prospect Park	6,455	23	0	0	4	19	129	10	107	12	0
	Punxsutawney	6,041	28	0	5	0	23	134	10	120	4	1
	Pymatuning Township	3,710	10	0	0	1	9	142	40	85	17	0
	Radnor Township	31,028	37	0	0	6	31	377	44	322	11	2
	Rankin	2,170	20	0	2	7	11	52	22	18	12	0
	Reading	80,927	1,001	10	44	465	482	4,637	1,128	2,288	1,221	49
	Reynoldsville	2,611	2	0	0	0	2	21	6	13	2	0
	Rice Township	2,689	2	0	0	0	2	11	4	7	0	0

[1] The FBI does not publish arson data unless it receives data from either the agency or the state for all 12 months of the calendar year.

Table 8. Offenses Known to Law Enforcement, by State and City, 2006 (Contd.)

(Number.)

State	City	Popula-tion	Violent crime	Murder and non-negligent man-slaughter	Forcible rape	Robbery	Aggra-vated assault	Property crime	Burglary	Larceny-theft	Motor vehicle theft	Arson[1]
	Richland Township, Bucks County	12,427	17	1	2	0	14	264	32	219	13	1
	Richland Township, Cambria County	12,654	14	0	0	3	11	409	29	375	5	0
	Ridgway	4,306	39	0	0	0	39	124	20	98	6	1
	Ridley Park	7,068	2	0	0	0	2	113	9	95	9	0
	Ridley Township	30,256	60	1	2	12	45	494	64	377	53	0
	Riverside	1,822	0	0	0	0	0	5	1	4	0	0
	Roaring Spring	2,311	0	0	0	0	0	42	5	36	1	0
	Robesonia	2,061	3	0	0	0	3	29	0	27	2	0
	Robeson Township	7,481	5	0	2	1	2	70	20	43	7	0
	Robinson Township, Allegheny County	13,537	33	0	5	9	19	428	31	377	20	2
	Robinson Township, Washington County	2,194	7	0	0	0	7	14	1	10	3	0
	Rochester	3,807	19	0	2	5	12	232	34	176	22	0
	Rochester Township	2,983	2	0	0	0	2	53	10	39	4	0
	Rockledge	2,539	10	0	0	2	8	55	5	45	5	0
	Rosslyn Farms	437	0	0	0	0	0	0	0	0	0	0
	Ross Township	31,197	44	1	0	12	31	820	119	678	23	1
	Rostraver Township	11,730	26	0	1	6	19	452	35	408	9	1
	Royersford	4,334	13	0	2	0	11	106	18	86	2	1
	Rush Township	3,652	0	0	0	0	0	38	4	26	8	2
	Rye Township	2,453	0	0	0	0	0	8	1	7	0	0
	Sadsbury Township, Chester County	3,240	0	0	0	0	0	4	1	1	2	0
	Sandy Lake	719	0	0	0	0	0	0	0	0	0	0
	Sandy Township	11,584	17	0	1	1	15	214	27	178	9	0
	Sankertown	646	0	0	0	0	0	1	0	1	0	0
	Saxton	773	0	0	0	0	0	0	0	0	0	0
	Sayre	5,611	15	0	4	0	11	232	45	181	6	2
	Schuylkill Haven	5,288	22	0	1	0	21	153	25	120	8	3
	Schuylkill Township, Chester County	7,646	2	0	1	0	1	95	7	83	5	0
	Scott Township, Columbia County	4,892	1	0	0	0	1	25	5	20	0	0
	Scott Township, Lackawanna County	4,927	3	0	0	1	2	11	1	6	4	0
	Scranton	73,185	334	0	26	100	208	2,544	635	1,742	167	20
	Selinsgrove	5,422	79	0	6	2	71	250	52	182	16	2
	Seven Springs	121	3	0	0	0	3	26	1	25	0	0
	Seward	466	0	0	0	0	0	0	0	0	0	0
	Sewickley	3,677	11	0	0	4	7	107	19	82	6	0
	Sewickley Heights	941	0	0	0	0	0	0	0	0	0	0
	Shaler Township	28,615	30	0	1	7	22	327	71	227	29	0
	Shamokin	7,588	43	1	0	1	41	105	11	85	9	6
	Shamokin Dam	1,467	0	0	0	0	0	44	3	41	0	0
	Sharon	15,518	114	1	6	23	84	623	114	470	39	2
	Sharon Hill	5,362	37	0	0	22	15	154	20	122	12	0
	Sharpsburg	3,369	9	0	0	1	8	45	19	13	13	0
	Sharpsville	4,285	18	0	1	1	16	104	13	86	5	0
	Shenandoah	5,301	13	0	2	2	9	219	49	148	22	5
	Shenango Township, Lawrence County	7,702	10	0	0	3	7	157	30	120	7	0
	Shillington	5,035	7	0	0	3	4	125	21	83	21	0
	Shippingport	228	0	0	0	0	0	2	0	2	0	0
	Silver Lake Township	1,775	0	0	0	0	0	11	3	7	1	4
	Silver Spring Township	12,473	0	0	0	0	0	20	0	20	0	0
	Sinking Spring	3,446	5	0	1	1	3	92	19	67	6	0
	Slippery Rock	3,213	4	0	1	0	3	70	7	63	0	0
	Smethport	1,618	1	0	0	0	1	17	3	13	1	0
	Solebury Township	8,866	10	0	1	1	8	76	10	63	3	2
	South Abington Township	9,430	25	0	3	1	21	140	26	108	6	0
	South Buffalo Township	2,821	2	0	0	1	1	20	5	13	2	0
	South Centre Township	1,923	1	0	0	0	1	15	1	13	1	0
	Southern Regional, Lancaster County	3,800	4	0	2	0	2	34	11	21	2	0

[1] The FBI does not publish arson data unless it receives data from either the agency or the state for all 12 months of the calendar year.

Table 8. Offenses Known to Law Enforcement, by State and City, 2006 *(Contd.)*

(Number.)

State	City	Popula-tion	Violent crime	Murder and non-negligent man-slaughter	Forcible rape	Robbery	Aggra-vated assault	Property crime	Burglary	Larceny-theft	Motor vehicle theft	Arson[1]
	Southern Regional, York County	9,579	17	0	4	4	9	256	24	218	14	3
	South Fayette Township	13,053	45	0	2	2	41	82	12	60	10	1
	South Fork	1,071	0	0	0	0	0	20	5	14	1	0
	South Heidelberg Township	6,684	4	0	0	1	3	47	9	36	2	0
	South Lebanon Township	8,602	5	0	0	0	5	163	24	134	5	1
	South Londonderry Township	6,694	3	0	2	0	1	54	9	43	2	0
	South Park Township	14,190	11	0	2	2	7	32	11	18	3	1
	South Pymatuning Township	2,857	2	0	0	0	2	36	4	29	3	0
	South Strabane Township	8,572	26	0	9	7	10	361	24	322	15	1
	Southwestern Regional	17,113	13	0	3	2	8	218	31	184	3	2
	Southwest Greensburg	2,286	9	0	1	1	7	61	6	52	3	0
	Southwest Regional	2,213	9	0	0	0	9	20	6	10	4	0
	South Whitehall Township	18,954	59	0	3	17	39	756	53	682	21	2
	South Williamsport	6,194	9	0	1	3	5	137	20	115	2	0
	Spring City	3,287	5	0	1	0	4	91	25	61	5	0
	Springdale	3,600	9	0	0	1	8	51	6	43	2	0
	Springettsbury Township	24,348	41	0	2	25	14	985	59	898	28	2
	Springfield Township, Bucks County	5,077	9	0	2	1	6	61	15	44	2	2
	Springfield Township, Delaware County	23,112	28	0	1	15	12	677	35	614	28	0
	Springfield Township, Montgomery County	19,313	20	0	0	10	10	214	34	166	14	1
	Spring Garden Township	11,756	35	0	3	24	8	417	74	318	25	1
	Spring Township, Berks County	24,384	10	0	0	3	7	399	56	295	48	0
	Spring Township, Centre County	6,563	2	0	0	0	2	96	10	85	1	0
	State College	52,225	39	2	7	12	18	997	122	856	19	6
	Steelton	5,672	36	1	1	20	14	226	33	170	23	1
	Stewartstown	2,011	2	0	0	1	1	26	3	19	4	0
	St. Marys City	13,885	10	0	0	4	6	223	57	161	5	4
	Stoneboro	1,062	0	0	0	0	0	9	3	6	0	0
	Stonycreek Township	3,027	13	0	0	0	13	39	7	32	0	0
	Strasburg	2,747	3	0	0	0	3	30	5	24	1	0
	Stroud Area Regional	34,334	102	2	18	52	30	988	150	789	49	7
	Sugarcreek	5,120	13	0	0	0	13	142	5	137	0	1
	Summerhill Township	2,657	1	0	0	0	1	44	9	34	1	1
	Sunbury	10,095	79	0	13	7	59	305	50	238	17	4
	Susquehanna Township, Dauphin County	22,775	38	0	2	22	14	456	64	372	20	6
	Swarthmore	6,151	15	0	0	4	11	96	11	80	5	0
	Swatara Township	22,434	126	0	3	36	87	816	109	683	24	8
	Swissvale	9,051	58	2	0	16	40	210	68	123	19	1
	Swoyersville	7,741	15	0	0	0	15	174	27	137	10	0
	Tamaqua	6,760	15	0	3	1	11	223	10	212	1	0
	Tatamy	1,045	0	0	0	0	0	11	0	10	1	0
	Tidioute	747	0	0	0	0	0	9	0	9	0	0
	Tinicum Township, Bucks County	4,261	5	1	0	1	3	66	6	60	0	0
	Tinicum Township, Delaware County	4,258	32	0	4	4	24	259	20	213	26	0
	Titusville	5,867	10	0	2	2	6	172	11	159	2	0
	Towamencin Township	17,995	21	0	1	4	16	212	23	184	5	4
	Towanda	2,918	5	0	0	0	5	77	16	59	2	0
	Trainer	1,863	19	0	1	2	16	94	13	68	13	1
	Tredyffrin Township	29,010	22	0	2	5	15	310	46	258	6	1
	Troy	1,486	2	0	0	0	2	32	4	27	1	0
	Tullytown	2,002	7	0	0	0	7	69	12	48	9	0
	Tunkhannock	1,827	10	0	0	1	9	19	8	10	1	0

[1] The FBI does not publish arson data unless it receives data from either the agency or the state for all 12 months of the calendar year.

Table 8. Offenses Known to Law Enforcement, by State and City, 2006 *(Contd.)*

(Number.)

State	City	Population	Violent crime	Murder and non-negligent man-slaughter	Forcible rape	Robbery	Aggra-vated assault	Property crime	Burglary	Larceny-theft	Motor vehicle theft	Arson[1]
	Tunkhannock Township, Wyoming County	4,324	5	0	0	0	5	78	21	52	5	1
	Union City	3,367	2	0	0	0	2	21	5	14	2	0
	Union Township, Lawrence County	5,175	7	0	1	2	4	132	20	104	8	1
	Upper Chichester Township	17,393	72	0	3	26	43	466	68	356	42	4
	Upper Darby Township	79,690	310	2	12	231	65	2,158	287	1,635	236	4
	Upper Dublin Township	26,412	53	0	3	3	47	345	56	265	24	1
	Upper Gwynedd Township	14,607	20	0	3	1	16	142	7	131	4	3
	Upper Leacock Township	8,408	15	0	1	3	11	156	30	118	8	0
	Upper Makefield Township	8,426	5	0	0	0	5	60	18	41	1	0
	Upper Merion Township	26,993	20	1	1	6	12	1,387	79	1,249	59	0
	Upper Moreland Township	24,783	28	0	4	5	19	439	62	352	25	6
	Upper Nazareth Township	5,318	11	0	0	0	11	102	3	97	2	0
	Upper Perkiomen	6,462	22	0	3	3	16	150	25	106	19	2
	Upper Pottsgrove Township	4,930	8	0	1	1	6	58	9	47	2	1
	Upper Providence Township, Delaware County	11,161	6	0	0	4	2	46	11	33	2	0
	Upper Providence Township, Montgomery County	18,297	6	0	0	0	6	222	28	182	12	2
	Upper Saucon Township	13,947	10	0	2	1	7	127	17	106	4	1
	Upper Southampton Township	15,547	7	0	1	2	4	185	47	128	10	3
	Upper St. Clair Township	19,295	2	0	1	1	0	88	13	72	3	0
	Upper Uwchlan Township	8,059	4	0	1	0	3	127	19	101	7	1
	Uwchlan Township	18,333	21	0	4	3	14	240	41	192	7	21
	Vandergrift	5,195	28	0	2	4	22	29	6	20	3	0
	Vandling	708	0	0	0	0	0	4	0	4	0	0
	Vernon Township	5,397	4	0	1	0	3	49	5	42	2	0
	Verona	2,934	10	0	0	5	5	112	16	85	11	0
	Walnutport	2,138	1	0	0	0	1	56	6	49	1	0
	Warminster Township	33,009	46	0	10	20	16	655	79	539	37	4
	Warren	9,657	131	0	3	0	128	226	39	183	4	0
	Warrington Township	22,039	52	0	7	4	41	254	47	194	13	3
	Warwick Township, Bucks County	14,551	5	0	2	2	1	146	35	106	5	2
	Warwick Township, Lancaster County	17,024	6	0	0	1	5	101	7	85	9	0
	Washington, Washington County	15,149	119	0	12	46	61	821	106	604	111	8
	Washington Township, Fayette County	4,250	8	0	0	0	8	43	15	25	3	0
	Washington Township, Franklin County	11,895	11	0	3	3	5	315	56	238	21	1
	Washington Township, Northampton County	4,706	3	0	1	0	2	78	18	57	3	1
	Washington Township, Westmoreland County	7,499	10	0	1	3	6	43	10	30	3	0
	Watsontown	2,150	13	0	0	1	12	53	5	47	1	0
	Waynesburg	4,146	5	0	0	3	2	98	18	78	2	0
	Wellsboro	3,345	1	0	1	0	0	48	16	31	1	0
	Wernersville	2,395	4	0	1	2	1	70	9	59	2	0
	West Alexander	310	1	0	0	0	1	3	1	2	0	0
	West Brandywine Township	7,645	2	0	0	0	2	81	13	59	9	2
	West Brownsville	1,046	0	0	0	0	0	4	0	3	1	0
	West Chester	18,063	98	1	7	39	51	569	98	424	47	0
	West Cocalico Township	7,095	4	0	0	0	4	55	10	40	5	5

[1] The FBI does not publish arson data unless it receives data from either the agency or the state for all 12 months of the calendar year.

Table 8. Offenses Known to Law Enforcement, by State and City, 2006 *(Contd.)*

(Number.)

State	City	Popula-tion	Violent crime	Murder and non-negligent man-slaughter	Forcible rape	Robbery	Aggra-vated assault	Property crime	Burglary	Larceny-theft	Motor vehicle theft	Arson[1]
	West Cornwall Township	1,968	4	0	0	0	4	28	2	25	1	1
	West Earl Township	7,267	0	0	0	0	0	152	19	122	11	1
	Westfall Township	2,829	4	0	0	0	4	121	10	110	1	1
	West Goshen Township	21,195	58	1	2	5	50	495	50	422	23	3
	West Hempfield Township	15,813	16	0	0	8	8	256	27	209	20	1
	West Hills Regional	11,101	8	0	0	2	6	129	29	99	1	0
	West Homestead	2,062	0	0	0	0	0	0	0	0	0	0
	West Lampeter Township	14,974	15	0	1	10	4	200	33	159	8	0
	West Lebanon Township	840	2	0	0	0	2	54	3	51	0	0
	West Manchester Township	17,834	58	0	3	32	23	737	81	624	32	6
	West Manheim Township	6,599	1	0	0	1	0	46	12	31	3	0
	West Norriton Township	14,855	40	0	6	14	20	332	33	275	24	2
	West Pikeland Township	3,993	0	0	0	0	0	36	11	24	1	0
	West Pike Run	1,879	0	0	0	0	0	2	1	1	0	0
	West Pittston	4,874	1	0	0	1	0	74	15	56	3	0
	West Pottsgrove Township	3,836	33	0	0	3	30	113	29	79	5	0
	West Reading	4,009	27	0	1	7	19	231	29	169	33	0
	West Sadsbury Township	2,502	4	0	0	1	3	83	0	80	3	0
	West Shore Regional	6,608	36	0	1	6	29	43	23	14	6	0
	Westtown-East Goshen Regional	31,417	33	0	6	1	26	292	35	243	14	3
	West Whiteland Township	18,261	28	0	1	17	10	593	30	544	19	1
	West Wyoming	2,724	2	0	1	0	1	44	9	30	5	0
	West York	4,234	14	0	1	7	6	104	26	74	4	0
	Whitehall	13,756	13	0	2	2	9	78	13	56	9	2
	Whitehall Township	25,977	63	0	1	37	25	1,460	114	1,309	37	7
	White Haven Borough	1,154	2	0	0	1	1	12	2	10	0	1
	Whitemarsh Township	17,171	14	0	1	4	9	223	33	181	9	0
	Whitpain Township	18,922	26	0	3	0	23	213	39	162	12	2
	Wilkes-Barre	41,374	209	6	31	110	62	1,686	298	1,256	132	10
	Wilkes-Barre Township	3,091	14	0	0	14	0	385	13	362	10	1
	Wilkinsburg	18,024	165	10	8	48	99	698	274	285	139	4
	Wilkins Township	6,626	7	0	0	1	6	143	15	122	6	0
	Williamsport	30,139	112	1	4	72	35	1,489	296	1,110	83	20
	Willistown Township	10,752	5	0	0	0	5	82	20	57	5	0
	Windber	4,123	5	0	0	1	4	32	6	21	5	0
	Wind Gap	2,830	13	0	3	1	9	65	3	61	1	0
	Wyoming	3,056	5	0	0	1	4	110	7	102	1	0
	Wyomissing	10,443	10	0	0	5	5	417	27	348	42	0
	Yardley	2,544	4	0	0	1	3	19	5	14	0	0
	Yeadon	11,516	106	1	5	39	61	346	60	225	61	6
	York Area Regional	57,864	129	1	5	35	88	736	148	539	49	2
	Youngsville	1,725	6	0	0	0	6	31	0	31	0	0
RHODE ISLAND	Barrington	16,623	4	0	3	0	1	238	34	197	7	3
	Bristol	24,462	18	0	2	2	14	379	49	313	17	2
	Burrillville	16,431	9	0	3	0	6	142	32	101	9	2
	Central Falls	19,006	109	3	13	26	67	552	141	259	152	10
	Charlestown	8,203	5	0	2	0	3	123	28	91	4	2
	Coventry	34,800	31	0	7	5	19	397	112	247	38	13
	Cranston	80,963	128	1	16	45	66	1,876	299	1,309	268	25
	Cumberland	34,086	24	0	3	8	13	545	97	414	34	5
	East Greenwich	13,507	12	0	1	1	10	246	30	206	10	2
	East Providence	49,120	63	2	10	14	37	847	145	600	102	11
	Foster	4,469	3	0	0	0	3	40	12	21	7	0
	Glocester	10,518	5	0	0	0	5	69	22	44	3	1
	Hopkinton	8,056	6	0	1	0	5	121	34	82	5	4

[1] The FBI does not publish arson data unless it receives data from either the agency or the state for all 12 months of the calendar year.

Table 8. Offenses Known to Law Enforcement, by State and City, 2006 (*Contd.*)

(Number.)

State	City	Popula-tion	Violent crime	Murder and non-negligent man-slaughter	Forcible rape	Robbery	Aggra-vated assault	Property crime	Burglary	Larceny-theft	Motor vehicle theft	Arson[1]
	Jamestown	5,566	2	0	1	0	1	105	20	82	3	1
	Johnston	28,931	34	0	4	8	22	617	94	448	75	6
	Lincoln	21,930	27	1	2	6	18	424	56	340	28	3
	Little Compton	3,558	0	0	0	0	0	39	8	31	0	1
	Middletown	16,604	7	0	1	2	4	337	49	284	4	0
	Narragansett	16,771	12	0	3	1	8	281	70	200	11	1
	Newport	25,138	123	0	16	19	88	1,090	289	749	52	9
	New Shoreham	1,037	0	0	0	0	0	93	14	74	5	1
	North Kingstown	26,877	27	0	4	6	17	498	98	369	31	4
	North Providence	32,901	40	1	5	11	23	601	139	371	91	10
	North Smithfield	11,102	8	0	2	0	6	176	40	127	9	1
	Pawtucket	73,154	240	4	20	86	130	2,407	541	1,543	323	24
	Portsmouth	16,992	13	0	5	1	7	214	58	143	13	2
	Providence	175,452	972	11	52	379	530	8,585	1,746	5,106	1,733	3
	Richmond	7,707	4	0	0	2	2	86	13	67	6	0
	Scituate	10,884	2	0	0	0	2	106	24	75	7	1
	Smithfield	21,632	18	0	3	2	13	255	32	206	17	4
	South Kingstown	29,093	20	0	5	3	12	328	55	262	11	3
	Tiverton	15,214	7	0	0	1	6	263	79	154	30	1
	Warren	11,238	19	0	2	3	14	201	35	157	9	3
	Warwick	86,538	114	2	27	36	49	2,120	316	1,639	165	15
	Westerly	23,447	26	0	8	2	16	479	63	387	29	2
	West Greenwich	5,632	3	0	0	1	2	101	7	91	3	1
	West Warwick	29,745	68	2	18	18	30	573	107	404	62	8
	Woonsocket	43,975	175	0	31	45	99	1,363	307	943	113	11
SOUTH CAROLINA	Abbeville	5,821	139	3	4	6	126	282	63	200	19	0
	Aiken	27,917	148	1	8	31	108	1,239	205	958	76	2
	Allendale	3,958	58	1	3	9	45	199	94	99	6	0
	Anderson	26,302	256	4	22	39	191	1,601	324	1,144	133	7
	Andrews	3,158	21	1	1	3	16	158	26	121	11	1
	Atlantic Beach	379	15	0	1	3	11	33	11	17	5	1
	Aynor	596	37	0	0	2	35	58	6	50	2	0
	Bamberg	3,607	21	0	1	1	19	122	32	83	7	0
	Barnwell	4,950	41	0	1	7	33	357	77	274	6	0
	Batesburg-Leesville	5,662	28	0	1	1	26	243	64	163	16	1
	Beaufort[3]	12,246	151	0	9	34	108		186	591		8
	Belton	4,639	18	1	3	1	13	226	61	152	13	1
	Bennettsville	9,496	188	1	10	19	158	576	106	459	11	2
	Bishopville	3,891	39	2	0	2	35	268	58	200	10	2
	Blacksburg	1,928	41	0	0	5	36	169	37	124	8	1
	Blackville	2,964	18	0	0	4	14	42	18	22	2	2
	Bluffton	2,377	46	0	2	7	37	323	80	222	21	6
	Brunson	585	1	0	0	1	0	6	1	5	0	0
	Calhoun Falls	2,299	9	0	1	0	8	67	12	54	1	1
	Camden	7,109	120	0	1	12	107	447	73	351	23	0
	Cayce[3]	12,625	118	0	7	14	97		131	660		1
	Central	4,102	17	1	7	2	7	107	11	88	8	0
	Chapin	687	8	0	0	0	8	65	12	53	0	0
	Charleston	108,371	960	23	45	245	647	4,358	707	3,108	543	17
	Cheraw	5,559	66	0	2	15	49	318	41	267	10	3
	Chesnee	1,038	14	0	0	2	12	57	9	45	3	0
	Chester	6,295	164	1	2	10	151	370	106	243	21	1
	Chesterfield	1,359	9	0	0	0	9	62	7	52	3	0
	Clemson	12,556	25	0	3	8	14	281	61	192	28	0
	Clinton	9,212	96	3	2	17	74	555	103	427	25	2
	Clio	764	8	0	0	1	7	35	6	28	1	0
	Clover	4,317	147	0	2	0	145	186	35	136	15	0
	Columbia	118,909	1,290	7	56	375	852	6,994	1,254	5,086	654	27
	Conway	13,651	204	3	6	41	154	1,102	210	838	54	4
	Cowpens	2,366	8	0	0	1	7	153	43	104	6	0
	Darlington	6,626	164	2	11	27	124	661	111	520	30	4
	Denmark	3,179	31	0	1	7	23	159	86	64	9	2
	Due West	1,307	0	0	0	0	0	17	3	14	0	0
	Duncan	3,023	10	0	1	3	6	102	13	77	12	0

[1] The FBI does not publish arson data unless it receives data from either the agency or the state for all 12 months of the calendar year.
[3] The FBI determined that the agency's data were inflated. Consequently, affected data are not included in this table.

Table 8. Offenses Known to Law Enforcement, by State and City, 2006 (*Contd.*)

(Number.)

State	City	Popula-tion	Violent crime	Murder and non-negligent man-slaughter	Forcible rape	Robbery	Aggra-vated assault	Property crime	Burglary	Larceny-theft	Motor vehicle theft	Arson[1]
	Easley	19,145	75	1	2	14	58	846	124	680	42	2
	Edgefield	4,590	10	0	2	0	8	65	14	51	0	1
	Edisto Beach	716	2	0	0	0	2	29	9	19	1	0
	Ehrhardt	584	0	0	0	0	0	17	5	11	1	0
	Elgin	969	14	0	0	3	11	81	10	68	3	0
	Estill	2,431	47	0	1	2	44	102	39	58	5	1
	Eutawville	339	2	0	0	1	1	43	24	17	2	0
	Fairfax	3,227	22	0	0	2	20	33	20	10	3	0
	Florence	31,755	523	4	17	155	347	3,226	461	2,542	223	24
	Folly Beach	2,298	15	0	2	0	13	238	20	204	14	0
	Forest Acres	10,146	85	0	2	24	59	653	110	523	20	4
	Fort Lawn	846	12	0	0	2	10	54	12	39	3	1
	Fort Mill	8,385	64	2	2	10	50	254	37	193	24	0
	Fountain Inn	6,834	34	1	1	1	31	207	36	162	9	1
	Gaffney	13,135	137	0	11	35	91	994	174	756	64	3
	Georgetown	9,080	147	3	4	12	128	656	110	520	26	3
	Goose Creek	33,022	112	0	9	32	71	925	210	621	94	7
	Great Falls	2,128	26	0	2	2	22	105	25	74	6	3
	Greeleyville	426	1	0	0	0	1	3	1	2	0	0
	Greenville	57,557	567	8	25	141	393	3,762	761	2,671	330	11
	Greenwood	22,726	380	2	14	64	300	1,644	393	1,196	55	7
	Greer	21,754	81	0	8	29	44	717	127	522	68	3
	Hampton	2,843	30	0	0	6	24	294	97	186	11	0
	Hanahan	14,033	94	2	12	27	53	651	157	412	82	2
	Hardeeville	1,872	31	1	4	17	9	336	64	249	23	0
	Hartsville	7,529	179	0	7	31	141	1,112	173	906	33	3
	Hemingway	532	3	0	0	2	1	34	11	15	8	0
	Holly Hill	1,385	9	0	0	4	5	41	7	32	2	0
	Honea Path	3,653	33	0	1	1	31	209	34	165	10	0
	Inman	1,948	10	0	2	1	7	95	15	74	6	0
	Irmo	11,398	51	0	4	10	37	367	56	299	12	4
	Isle of Palms	4,650	2	0	0	0	2	144	18	116	10	0
	Iva	1,198	1	0	0	0	1	15	7	7	1	0
	Jackson	1,670	10	0	1	0	9	41	20	21	0	1
	Jamestown	97	0	0	0	0	0	5	1	4	0	0
	Johnsonville	1,483	4	0	0	3	1	70	14	54	2	0
	Johnston	2,389	25	1	0	1	23	81	24	52	5	1
	Kingstree	3,415	28	0	0	10	18	264	57	190	17	2
	Lake City	6,794	133	1	3	18	111	739	113	589	37	4
	Lake View	804	7	0	0	1	6	25	3	20	2	0
	Lamar	1,019	13	0	0	1	12	35	9	24	2	0
	Lancaster	8,501	170	1	9	20	140	632	151	458	23	9
	Landrum	2,557	4	0	0	0	4	77	10	65	2	0
	Latta	1,485	10	0	1	4	5	20	6	13	1	0
	Laurens	9,977	182	2	6	23	151	599	109	468	22	2
	Lexington[3]	13,797	16	0	3	1	12		29	439		1
	Liberty	3,051	4	0	0	0	4	107	25	76	6	1
	Lincolnville	890	0	0	0	0	0	0	0	0	0	0
	Lyman	2,808	7	0	1	1	5	96	19	75	2	2
	Manning	4,088	55	0	2	18	35	251	51	191	9	1
	Marion	7,106	136	0	4	22	110	471	96	358	17	0
	Mauldin	19,644	125	0	6	6	113	485	75	343	67	16
	McColl	2,446	25	2	0	3	20	182	46	125	11	7
	McCormick	2,698	20	0	0	1	19	46	1	42	3	0
	Moncks Corner	6,626	41	0	3	9	29	310	33	247	30	4
	Mount Pleasant	58,833	200	0	11	22	167	1,247	191	996	60	4
	Mullins	4,930	76	0	2	20	54	532	107	409	16	4
	Myrtle Beach	27,007	555	8	67	203	277	4,887	778	3,590	519	15
	Newberry	10,825	66	0	4	13	49	549	72	473	4	2
	New Ellenton	2,294	12	0	0	3	9	70	12	56	2	0
	Ninety Six	1,952	22	0	1	1	20	50	5	45	0	0
	North	800	6	0	0	3	3	53	12	38	3	1
	North Augusta	19,770	49	2	4	24	19	887	122	672	93	3
	North Charleston	87,655	1,481	28	81	544	828	7,470	1,331	5,040	1,099	21

[1] The FBI does not publish arson data unless it receives data from either the agency or the state for all 12 months of the calendar year.
[3] The FBI determined that the agency's data were inflated. Consequently, affected data are not included in this table.

Table 8. Offenses Known to Law Enforcement, by State and City, 2006 *(Contd.)*

(Number.)

State	City	Popula-tion	Violent crime	Murder and non-negligent man-slaughter	Forcible rape	Robbery	Aggra-vated assault	Property crime	Burglary	Larceny-theft	Motor vehicle theft	Arson[1]
	North Myrtle Beach	14,315	60	0	12	19	29	1,313	222	1,049	42	0
	Norway	375	2	0	1	0	1	4	0	4	0	0
	Orangeburg	14,685	71	1	3	24	43	803	232	523	48	3
	Pacolet	2,769	10	0	0	1	9	92	24	63	5	1
	Pageland	2,584	54	1	1	2	50	172	37	129	6	0
	Pamplico	1,176	8	0	0	2	6	51	21	28	2	1
	Pelion	596	2	0	0	1	1	24	5	19	0	0
	Pickens	3,020	8	0	0	0	8	139	33	101	5	0
	Pine Ridge	1,735	4	0	0	0	4	42	9	30	3	0
	Port Royal	9,492	28	0	1	10	17	266	44	214	8	3
	Prosperity	1,115	3	0	2	0	1	31	3	27	1	0
	Ridgeland	2,659	26	0	1	12	13	145	45	92	8	1
	Ridge Spring	809	0	0	0	0	0	0	0	0	0	0
	Ridgeville	1,990	0	0	0	0	0	0	0	0	0	0
	Rock Hill	60,480	747	6	32	113	596	2,716	484	2,015	217	24
	Saluda	3,015	39	0	4	9	26	82	7	73	2	1
	Scranton	1,015	2	0	0	2	0	13	2	11	0	0
	Seneca	8,086	96	0	6	13	77	462	110	325	27	1
	Simpsonville	15,370	94	0	6	7	81	707	126	541	40	4
	Society Hill	708	3	0	0	1	2	20	4	14	2	0
	South Congaree	2,370	7	0	1	0	6	53	14	37	2	0
	Spartanburg	38,976	715	5	19	194	497	3,628	870	2,494	264	37
	Springdale	2,963	9	0	0	1	8	99	8	82	9	1
	Springfield	498	4	0	1	2	1	3	1	2	0	0
	St. George	2,152	16	0	1	3	12	133	22	97	14	0
	St. Stephen	1,767	12	1	3	2	6	78	17	54	7	0
	Sullivans Island	1,926	6	1	1	0	4	42	6	33	3	0
	Summerton	1,069	21	0	1	5	15	119	26	90	3	0
	Summerville	38,300	137	0	16	44	77	1,444	168	1,159	117	8
	Sumter	40,296	532	4	14	87	427	2,087	495	1,478	114	11
	Surfside Beach	4,846	18	0	1	5	12	359	114	208	37	0
	Swansea	697	10	0	2	2	6	100	15	84	1	1
	Tega Cay	4,440	4	0	0	0	4	70	7	62	1	0
	Timmonsville	2,422	42	1	3	5	33	136	40	85	11	4
	Travelers Rest	4,303	10	0	1	5	4	194	10	166	18	1
	Turbeville	735	10	0	0	3	7	32	11	20	1	0
	Union	8,450	126	0	1	8	117	447	92	341	14	6
	Vance	205	1	0	0	0	1	3	2	1	0	0
	Wagener	886	3	0	0	0	3	34	14	17	3	1
	Walterboro	5,634	92	0	4	17	71	660	92	523	45	4
	Ware Shoals	2,414	12	0	1	0	11	86	13	68	5	2
	Wellford	2,317	12	0	1	5	6	59	11	40	8	2
	West Columbia	13,622	226	2	5	38	181	922	165	689	68	7
	Westminster	2,711	10	0	0	2	8	48	8	39	1	2
	West Pelzer	913	7	0	1	3	3	20	3	15	2	0
	West Union	306	0	0	0	0	0	4	1	3	0	0
	Whitmire	1,550	2	0	0	0	2	38	6	31	1	1
	Williamston	3,938	19	0	0	3	16	111	13	89	9	2
	Williston	3,311	18	0	1	3	14	130	24	102	4	1
	Winnsboro	3,668	51	0	2	4	45	215	21	190	4	0
	Woodruff	4,169	42	0	4	11	27	234	36	185	13	1
	Yemassee	852	5	0	0	0	5	23	7	15	1	0
	York	7,345	123	0	5	25	93	325	62	251	12	1
SOUTH DAKOTA	Aberdeen	24,284	64	0	17	2	45	469	84	355	30	6
	Avon	547	0	0	0	0	0	0	0	0	0	0
	Belle Fourche	4,711	3	0	2	0	1	6	1	5	0	0
	Bonesteel	272	0	0	0	0	0	0	0	0	0	0
	Box Elder	3,015	4	0	1	0	3	54	22	32	0	0
	Brandon	7,231	6	0	0	0	6	49	9	40	0	0
	Bridgewater	597	0	0	0	0	0	0	0	0	0	0
	Burke	611	0	0	0	0	0	0	0	0	0	0
	Canton	3,189	3	0	1	0	2	27	4	22	1	0
	Corsica	630	0	0	0	0	0	0	0	0	0	0
	Deadwood	1,306	2	0	0	0	2	43	3	39	1	0

[1] The FBI does not publish arson data unless it receives data from either the agency or the state for all 12 months of the calendar year.

Table 8. Offenses Known to Law Enforcement, by State and City, 2006 (*Contd.*)

(Number.)

State	City	Popula-tion	Violent crime	Murder and non-negligent man-slaughter	Forcible rape	Robbery	Aggra-vated assault	Property crime	Burglary	Larceny-theft	Motor vehicle theft	Arson[1]
	Delmont	246	0	0	0	0	0	0	0	0	0	0
	Estelline	692	0	0	0	0	0	8	0	8	0	0
	Eureka	996	0	0	0	0	0	0	0	0	0	0
	Faith	478	0	0	0	0	0	0	0	0	0	0
	Freeman	1,232	0	0	0	0	0	0	0	0	0	0
	Gettysburg	1,178	0	0	0	0	0	13	2	10	1	0
	Glenham	128	0	0	0	0	0	0	0	0	0	0
	Hermosa	338	0	0	0	0	0	0	0	0	0	0
	Hot Springs	4,134	1	1	0	0	0	43	24	19	0	1
	Jefferson	595	0	0	0	0	0	0	0	0	0	0
	Kadoka	673	1	0	0	0	1	9	8	1	0	0
	Kimball	698	0	0	0	0	0	0	0	0	0	0
	Lennox	2,108	0	0	0	0	0	4	1	3	0	0
	Leola	414	0	0	0	0	0	0	0	0	0	0
	Madison	6,271	3	0	2	0	1	138	29	104	5	2
	Martin	1,056	8	0	1	0	7	30	13	17	0	1
	McIntosh	219	0	0	0	0	0	0	0	0	0	0
	Menno	702	0	0	0	0	0	0	0	0	0	0
	Miller	1,375	0	0	0	0	0	8	0	8	0	0
	Mitchell	14,809	20	0	1	2	17	370	42	310	18	2
	New Effington	228	0	0	0	0	0	0	0	0	0	0
	North Sioux City	2,513	2	0	0	0	2	3	1	2	0	0
	Rapid City	62,647	232	0	56	38	138	2,190	407	1,679	104	12
	Rosholt	442	0	0	0	0	0	0	0	0	0	0
	Scotland	836	0	0	0	0	0	0	0	0	0	0
	Sioux Falls	140,593	426	7	115	34	270	3,596	768	2,616	212	27
	Springfield	1,534	0	0	0	0	0	0	0	0	0	0
	Sturgis	6,308	11	0	3	0	8	162	23	121	18	0
	Tyndall	1,164	0	0	0	0	0	0	0	0	0	0
	Vermillion	10,041	16	0	7	0	9	314	23	285	6	1
	Wagner	1,613	2	0	0	0	2	36	3	29	4	0
	Winner	2,940	3	0	2	0	1	44	3	37	4	0
	Yankton	13,822	28	0	10	3	15	293	35	249	9	1
TENNESSEE	Adamsville	2,088	3	0	0	0	3	17	0	15	2	0
	Alamo	2,410	2	0	0	0	2	40	17	21	2	0
	Alcoa	8,495	120	1	7	21	91	552	98	413	41	4
	Alexandria	871	1	0	0	0	1	17	6	9	2	0
	Algood	3,229	2	0	0	0	2	79	3	73	3	0
	Ardmore	1,130	10	0	1	0	9	48	13	29	6	0
	Ashland City	4,608	23	0	4	3	16	214	53	150	11	0
	Athens	14,055	184	0	6	20	158	1,250	262	891	97	1
	Atoka	5,748	22	0	2	0	20	160	27	127	6	1
	Baileyton	510	2	0	0	0	2	12	0	12	0	0
	Bartlett	43,813	116	0	4	32	80	1,041	211	770	60	0
	Baxter	1,350	3	0	1	0	2	44	7	30	7	0
	Bean Station	2,808	22	0	0	1	21	173	52	106	15	1
	Belle Meade	3,139	0	0	0	0	0	14	2	12	0	0
	Bells	2,336	4	0	0	0	4	57	18	34	5	2
	Benton	1,117	2	0	0	0	2	40	9	28	3	0
	Berry Hill	693	17	0	0	9	8	110	17	83	10	0
	Bethel Springs	781	0	0	0	0	0	0	0	0	0	0
	Big Sandy	525	3	0	1	0	2	7	1	5	1	0
	Blaine	1,739	4	0	0	0	4	26	5	19	2	0
	Bluff City	1,622	12	0	0	1	11	64	12	48	4	0
	Bolivar	5,724	53	1	2	11	39	339	90	223	26	3
	Bradford	1,087	0	0	0	0	0	13	7	3	3	0
	Brentwood	32,838	28	0	3	5	20	561	88	461	12	1
	Brighton	2,472	11	0	1	1	9	60	19	39	2	0
	Bristol	25,312	159	0	10	17	132	1,432	229	1,094	109	8
	Brownsville	10,856	197	2	5	18	172	634	199	399	36	5
	Bruceton	1,505	6	0	0	0	6	30	8	20	2	0
	Burns	1,420	6	0	0	0	6	5	0	5	0	0
	Calhoun	520	7	0	0	0	7	18	2	14	2	0
	Camden	3,784	9	0	1	0	8	157	38	106	13	0
	Carthage	2,297	5	0	0	1	4	50	11	36	3	0

[1] The FBI does not publish arson data unless it receives data from either the agency or the state for all 12 months of the calendar year.

Table 8. Offenses Known to Law Enforcement, by State and City, 2006 (*Contd.*)

(Number.)

State	City	Population	Violent crime	Murder and non-negligent man-slaughter	Forcible rape	Robbery	Aggra-vated assault	Property crime	Burglary	Larceny-theft	Motor vehicle theft	Arson[1]
	Caryville	2,410	9	0	2	3	4	86	18	63	5	0
	Celina	1,386	1	0	0	0	1	25	9	16	0	1
	Centerville	4,053	8	0	1	0	7	104	31	70	3	0
	Chapel Hill	1,032	4	0	0	2	2	30	13	16	1	0
	Charleston	652	4	0	0	1	3	24	6	18	0	0
	Chattanooga	156,730	1,935	17	118	532	1,268	12,275	2,273	8,876	1,126	10
	Church Hill	6,451	20	1	0	0	19	141	32	101	8	0
	Clarksburg	380	0	0	0	0	0	4	1	3	0	0
	Clarksville	114,314	1,023	6	50	195	772	4,242	1,348	2,611	283	21
	Cleveland	38,672	361	1	26	34	300	2,122	456	1,523	143	10
	Clifton	2,713	4	0	0	0	4	22	10	10	2	0
	Clinton	9,500	45	0	0	9	36	384	79	285	20	7
	Collegedale	7,307	8	0	3	2	3	222	42	175	5	0
	Collierville	38,042	60	0	4	22	34	798	111	627	60	4
	Collinwood	1,058	0	0	0	0	0	11	5	5	1	0
	Columbia	34,207	380	2	18	39	321	1,700	400	1,191	109	6
	Cookeville	28,096	133	0	18	30	85	1,339	280	981	78	1
	Coopertown	3,262	6	0	0	0	6	71	24	40	7	0
	Copperhill	488	1	0	0	0	1	23	3	15	5	0
	Cornersville	949	1	0	0	0	1	2	0	2	0	0
	Covington	9,133	101	0	3	21	77	536	140	371	25	2
	Cowan	1,778	6	0	0	0	6	31	5	20	6	0
	Cross Plains	1,536	3	0	0	0	3	26	5	19	2	0
	Crossville	10,557	91	0	5	6	80	840	220	554	66	1
	Crump	1,560	8	0	0	0	8	88	42	37	9	0
	Cumberland City	325	2	0	0	0	2	3	0	3	0	0
	Cumberland Gap	205	2	2	0	0	0	8	3	4	1	0
	Dandridge	2,377	5	0	0	2	3	236	19	210	7	0
	Dayton	6,525	21	1	2	0	18	283	44	229	10	0
	Decatur	1,468	3	0	0	0	3	73	14	52	7	0
	Decaturville	857	3	1	0	0	2	6	1	3	2	0
	Decherd	2,218	11	0	1	0	10	105	30	71	4	0
	Dickson	13,037	114	1	12	19	82	774	104	596	74	5
	Dover	1,514	5	0	0	0	5	20	3	16	1	0
	Dresden	2,737	13	0	1	0	12	69	18	51	0	0
	Dunlap	4,741	15	0	0	1	14	99	18	68	13	1
	Dyer	2,449	4	0	0	0	4	35	13	20	2	1
	Dyersburg	17,688	174	1	16	24	133	1,453	332	1,052	69	4
	Eagleville	464	0	0	0	0	0	6	4	2	0	0
	East Ridge	20,073	154	0	13	33	108	1,111	254	772	85	7
	Elizabethton	14,121	94	0	5	14	75	764	173	563	28	9
	Elkton	512	1	0	0	0	1	9	4	3	2	0
	Englewood	1,687	12	0	0	0	12	68	10	49	9	0
	Erin	1,460	6	0	0	0	6	58	9	44	5	0
	Erwin	5,860	18	0	0	1	17	235	40	185	10	1
	Estill Springs	2,207	6	0	0	2	4	34	6	26	2	0
	Ethridge	562	1	0	0	0	1	27	16	11	0	2
	Fairview	7,281	19	1	4	2	12	161	44	109	8	1
	Fayetteville	7,123	60	1	1	6	52	354	91	251	12	1
	Franklin	53,989	94	1	11	17	65	954	127	783	44	2
	Friendship	620	2	0	0	0	2	6	2	3	1	0
	Gadsden	567	2	0	0	1	1	10	5	4	1	0
	Gainesboro	870	3	0	0	0	3	27	4	23	0	0
	Gallatin	27,060	149	0	13	18	118	671	97	519	55	8
	Gallaway	721	9	0	1	0	8	14	5	8	1	0
	Gates	874	0	0	0	0	0	23	8	11	4	0
	Gatlinburg	4,482	41	0	5	4	32	447	138	287	22	4
	Germantown	37,957	39	0	5	10	24	720	170	512	38	2
	Gibson	412	2	0	0	0	2	16	1	13	2	0
	Gleason	1,444	6	0	0	0	6	29	11	15	3	0
	Goodlettsville	15,515	82	1	3	33	45	814	130	624	60	2
	Gordonsville	1,144	3	0	0	1	2	41	8	29	4	0
	Grand Junction	320	5	0	0	5	0	6	2	3	1	0
	Graysville	1,444	9	0	0	0	9	41	8	32	1	0
	Greenbrier	6,131	37	1	3	2	31	185	45	122	18	1

[1] The FBI does not publish arson data unless it receives data from either the agency or the state for all 12 months of the calendar year.

Table 8. Offenses Known to Law Enforcement, by State and City, 2006 (*Contd.*)

(Number.)

State	City	Population	Violent crime	Murder and non-negligent man-slaughter	Forcible rape	Robbery	Aggravated assault	Property crime	Burglary	Larceny-theft	Motor vehicle theft	Arson[1]
	Greeneville	15,579	88	0	4	29	55	1,262	272	935	55	1
	Greenfield	2,111	4	0	0	1	3	28	4	22	2	0
	Halls	2,264	19	0	2	1	16	41	19	18	4	0
	Henderson	6,138	23	2	2	4	15	234	40	189	5	1
	Hendersonville	45,447	206	2	11	21	172	1,002	204	744	54	6
	Henning	1,298	8	0	0	0	8	35	14	19	2	0
	Henry	536	2	0	0	0	2	8	2	5	1	0
	Hohenwald	3,839	16	0	0	1	15	103	27	68	8	0
	Hollow Rock	958	2	0	0	2	0	16	2	13	1	0
	Hornbeak	429	0	0	0	0	0	1	0	0	1	0
	Humboldt	9,387	140	0	4	16	120	617	195	383	39	9
	Huntingdon	4,239	14	0	0	1	13	106	29	70	7	0
	Huntland	897	2	0	0	0	2	18	7	8	3	0
	Jacksboro	2,017	11	0	0	1	10	194	10	175	9	1
	Jackson	62,889	785	11	28	189	557	4,492	1,160	2,876	456	18
	Jamestown	1,889	13	0	2	1	10	91	18	69	4	1
	Jasper	3,121	0	0	0	0	0	107	29	66	12	1
	Jefferson City	8,032	14	0	0	4	10	518	87	407	24	0
	Jellico	2,546	10	0	0	0	10	121	12	99	10	1
	Johnson City	59,465	329	6	19	63	241	3,397	701	2,493	203	14
	Jonesborough	4,608	13	0	0	0	13	123	24	95	4	0
	Kenton	1,318	5	0	0	0	5	9	5	4	0	0
	Kimball	1,370	10	0	1	2	7	85	4	75	6	0
	Kingsport	44,691	387	3	29	79	276	2,667	440	2,062	165	9
	Kingston	5,542	13	0	0	3	10	104	28	69	7	0
	Kingston Springs	2,907	2	0	0	0	2	34	6	26	2	0
	Knoxville	182,421	1,894	18	89	538	1,249	11,063	2,281	7,684	1,098	114
	Lafayette	4,230	6	0	2	1	3	88	30	54	4	0
	La Follette	8,270	68	0	3	5	60	473	170	265	38	0
	La Grange	148	0	0	0	0	0	2	0	1	1	0
	Lake City	1,867	3	0	0	1	2	120	23	85	12	3
	Lakewood	2,418	4	0	0	3	1	32	9	18	5	0
	La Vergne	26,214	166	0	7	10	149	670	170	432	68	5
	Lawrenceburg	11,050	107	0	7	11	89	713	169	497	47	3
	Lebanon	23,336	288	1	14	64	209	1,342	233	997	112	7
	Lenoir City	7,773	65	0	3	4	58	535	129	375	31	0
	Lewisburg	10,927	68	0	2	5	61	319	88	218	13	1
	Lexington	7,765	66	0	8	4	54	592	117	441	34	3
	Livingston	3,533	17	0	0	3	14	147	58	82	7	2
	Lookout Mountain	1,922	0	0	0	0	0	10	1	9	0	0
	Loretto	1,732	7	0	0	0	7	41	9	26	6	1
	Loudon	4,805	9	0	0	0	9	178	25	147	6	0
	Lynnville	343	0	0	0	0	0	0	0	0	0	0
	Madisonville	4,407	18	0	0	1	17	382	44	313	25	1
	Manchester	9,618	86	0	2	4	80	570	81	453	36	2
	Martin	10,280	37	0	4	3	30	310	57	250	3	0
	Maryville	26,180	66	1	8	18	39	682	135	497	50	3
	Mason	1,160	10	1	1	0	8	32	7	24	1	0
	Maury City	726	2	0	1	0	1	9	5	3	1	0
	Maynardville	1,939	1	0	0	0	1	59	20	36	3	0
	McEwen	1,689	1	0	0	0	1	11	1	9	1	0
	McKenzie	5,503	18	0	0	4	14	235	52	178	5	0
	McMinnville	13,410	78	1	9	3	65	574	137	397	40	3
	Medina	1,306	8	0	0	0	8	30	11	17	2	0
	Memphis	680,828	13,544	147	425	5,311	7,661	56,905	16,450	33,736	6,719	246
	Middleton	630	8	0	0	0	8	31	7	23	1	0
	Milan	7,923	61	0	3	2	56	386	70	300	16	3
	Millersville	6,192	37	0	2	2	33	98	24	56	18	0
	Millington	10,437	79	0	3	19	57	519	115	343	61	3
	Minor Hill	433	3	0	0	0	3	7	1	6	0	1
	Monteagle	1,236	6	0	0	0	6	34	11	19	4	1
	Monterey	2,826	4	0	0	3	1	72	23	45	4	0
	Morristown	26,520	251	1	19	30	201	1,685	175	1,396	114	12
	Moscow	548	3	0	0	0	3	17	6	10	1	0
	Mountain City	2,450	3	1	0	0	2	13	7	3	3	0

[1] The FBI does not publish arson data unless it receives data from either the agency or the state for all 12 months of the calendar year.

Table 8. Offenses Known to Law Enforcement, by State and City, 2006 (*Contd.*)

(Number.)

State	City	Popula-tion	Violent crime	Murder and non-negligent man-slaughter	Forcible rape	Robbery	Aggra-vated assault	Property crime	Burglary	Larceny-theft	Motor vehicle theft	Arson[1]
	Mount Carmel	5,337	9	0	0	1	8	77	16	55	6	1
	Mount Juliet	18,329	77	0	4	12	61	445	82	335	28	2
	Mount Pleasant	4,509	34	1	2	3	28	250	63	174	13	0
	Munford	5,724	23	0	1	0	22	159	32	112	15	3
	Murfreesboro	87,897	706	6	39	179	482	4,324	895	3,144	285	17
	Nashville	560,813	8,565	80	320	2,425	5,740	32,625	6,370	23,234	3,021	125
	Newbern	3,128	21	0	1	3	17	80	19	60	1	0
	New Hope	1,038	1	0	0	0	1	5	1	3	1	0
	New Johnsonville	1,989	3	0	1	0	2	14	3	11	0	0
	New Market	1,335	0	0	0	0	0	3	0	3	0	0
	Newport	7,392	97	0	6	14	77	754	75	627	52	2
	New Tazewell	2,919	17	0	3	2	12	203	34	158	11	0
	Niota	806	2	0	0	0	2	19	9	7	3	0
	Nolensville	2,604	4	0	0	1	3	48	17	30	1	0
	Norris	1,457	0	0	0	0	0	14	4	10	0	0
	Oakland	2,500	10	0	0	0	10	74	11	55	8	0
	Oak Ridge	27,644	148	1	17	35	95	1,615	347	1,159	109	6
	Obion	1,123	12	0	0	0	12	22	9	13	0	0
	Oliver Springs	3,317	10	0	0	3	7	148	26	107	15	1
	Oneida	3,724	17	0	2	1	14	201	32	165	4	1
	Paris	10,000	50	0	5	6	39	510	143	348	19	1
	Parsons	2,476	8	0	0	1	7	66	26	35	5	0
	Petersburg	604	1	0	0	0	1	8	1	5	2	0
	Pigeon Forge	5,858	48	0	6	6	36	730	168	510	52	1
	Piperton	962	2	0	0	0	2	20	2	17	1	0
	Pittman Center	566	0	0	0	0	0	9	1	6	2	0
	Pleasant View	3,497	5	0	0	0	5	64	11	49	4	0
	Portland	10,474	73	0	8	1	64	348	123	205	20	3
	Powells Crossroads	1,237	1	0	0	0	1	7	2	3	2	0
	Pulaski	8,018	74	0	11	10	53	424	116	292	16	3
	Puryear	679	1	0	0	1	0	28	2	26	0	0
	Red Bank	11,875	84	0	7	16	61	517	114	374	29	0
	Red Boiling Springs	1,072	2	0	1	0	1	26	11	14	1	0
	Ridgely	1,613	4	0	0	1	3	34	11	21	2	1
	Ridgetop	1,701	2	0	0	0	2	16	2	12	2	0
	Ripley	7,871	124	1	5	9	109	676	224	422	30	0
	Rockwood	5,495	20	0	0	4	16	329	55	258	16	0
	Rogersville	4,337	46	0	3	2	41	341	37	292	12	2
	Rossville	485	1	0	0	0	1	20	5	15	0	0
	Rutherford	1,261	9	0	1	1	7	22	5	15	2	1
	Rutledge	1,277	6	0	0	0	6	52	9	38	5	1
	Savannah	7,292	46	0	4	14	28	576	135	401	40	0
	Scotts Hill	926	0	0	0	0	0	13	7	6	0	0
	Selmer	4,677	42	0	0	4	38	280	58	201	21	1
	Sevierville	14,976	58	1	11	7	39	1,015	162	784	69	1
	Sewanee	2,506	1	0	1	0	0	65	34	30	1	0
	Sharon	947	5	0	0	0	5	15	8	6	1	0
	Shelbyville	18,885	90	0	6	21	63	662	161	450	51	1
	Signal Mountain	7,237	5	0	0	0	5	92	16	76	0	0
	Smithville	4,213	33	0	0	1	32	279	47	219	13	3
	Sneedville	1,334	3	0	0	1	2	69	19	48	2	0
	Soddy-Daisy	12,137	68	0	2	3	63	376	97	257	22	1
	Somerville	2,944	11	0	1	3	7	54	3	47	4	0
	South Carthage	1,338	3	0	0	0	3	62	24	36	2	0
	South Fulton	2,483	17	1	0	2	14	80	14	58	8	0
	South Pittsburg	3,163	14	0	0	1	13	165	39	112	14	0
	Sparta	4,827	19	0	3	2	14	367	80	271	16	5
	Spencer	1,716	2	0	0	0	2	7	4	3	0	0
	Spring City	2,035	1	0	0	0	1	36	6	30	0	0
	Springfield	16,118	217	2	15	30	170	945	132	748	65	4
	Spring Hill	17,366	29	0	3	1	25	179	46	128	5	1
	St. Joseph	869	2	0	0	0	2	12	4	8	0	0
	Surgoinsville	1,766	4	0	0	1	3	27	4	21	2	0
	Sweetwater	6,195	51	0	2	3	46	342	58	263	21	2
	Tazewell	2,177	15	0	0	2	13	167	32	126	9	1

[1] The FBI does not publish arson data unless it receives data from either the agency or the state for all 12 months of the calendar year.

Table 8. Offenses Known to Law Enforcement, by State and City, 2006 (*Contd.*)

(Number.)

State	City	Population	Violent crime	Murder and non-negligent man-slaughter	Forcible rape	Robbery	Aggra-vated assault	Property crime	Burglary	Larceny-theft	Motor vehicle theft	Arson[1]
	Tellico Plains	942	8	0	0	0	8	56	17	36	3	0
	Tiptonville	4,151	16	0	0	1	15	49	12	36	1	8
	Toone	363	0	0	0	0	0	3	1	2	0	0
	Townsend	261	0	0	0	0	0	14	4	10	0	0
	Trenton	4,635	27	0	1	3	23	238	64	172	2	1
	Trezevant	904	2	0	0	0	2	28	11	16	1	2
	Trimble	735	4	0	0	0	4	17	2	12	3	0
	Troy	1,265	3	0	0	0	3	60	16	41	3	1
	Tullahoma	19,150	68	2	6	18	42	924	257	623	44	3
	Tusculum	2,239	4	0	2	0	2	43	7	34	2	0
	Union City	10,925	61	0	0	7	54	712	136	552	24	3
	Vonore	1,401	10	0	0	1	9	84	11	70	3	2
	Wartburg	925	1	0	1	0	0	13	5	6	2	0
	Wartrace	571	1	0	0	0	1	6	2	4	0	0
	Watertown	1,410	4	0	0	1	3	56	12	41	3	1
	Waverly	4,187	11	0	0	0	11	68	18	48	2	1
	Waynesboro	2,203	10	0	0	0	10	51	16	32	3	1
	Westmoreland	2,193	9	0	0	1	8	68	11	55	2	1
	White Bluff	2,402	2	0	0	1	1	23	11	11	1	0
	White House	8,834	15	0	1	0	14	113	21	84	8	0
	White Pine	2,081	1	0	1	0	0	107	13	88	6	1
	Whiteville	4,546	12	0	0	1	11	70	22	42	6	1
	Whitwell	1,624	10	0	0	1	9	77	19	50	8	0
	Winchester	7,851	78	0	1	12	65	356	91	241	24	3
	Winfield	991	16	0	0	1	15	52	12	32	8	2
	Woodbury	2,556	4	0	0	0	4	45	7	33	5	1
TEXAS	Abernathy	2,840	2	0	1	0	1	36	9	26	1	0
	Abilene	118,009	554	5	67	107	375	5,045	1,282	3,460	303	33
	Addison	14,054	104	3	5	36	60	1,280	190	955	135	4
	Alamo	16,429	67	0	0	17	50	1,098	113	887	98	6
	Alamo Heights	7,315	13	0	0	9	4	258	42	208	8	0
	Alice	20,072	152	0	8	5	139	1,657	292	1,310	55	15
	Allen	71,184	59	0	7	16	36	1,872	333	1,468	71	4
	Alpine	6,237	13	0	1	0	12	81	32	45	4	0
	Alto	1,189	2	0	0	2	0	55	35	17	3	0
	Alton	7,257	7	0	0	3	4	355	84	229	42	0
	Alvarado	4,090	12	0	5	0	7	114	20	88	6	1
	Alvin	22,799	75	0	6	14	55	664	182	435	47	5
	Amarillo	188,208	1,623	5	98	401	1,119	11,080	2,412	7,617	1,051	93
	Andrews	9,657	31	0	8	3	20	263	59	193	11	2
	Angleton	19,293	100	0	15	14	71	570	144	390	36	1
	Anna	1,800	4	0	2	1	1	121	32	84	5	1
	Anthony	4,187	11	0	0	6	5	112	10	96	6	0
	Anton	1,205	0	0	0	0	0	5	0	2	3	0
	Aransas Pass	9,129	52	1	6	20	25	843	192	626	25	0
	Arcola	1,251	10	0	0	1	9	18	7	9	2	0
	Argyle	3,053	0	0	0	0	0	29	7	19	3	0
	Arlington	373,086	2,728	14	192	890	1,632	19,666	4,042	13,905	1,719	42
	Arp	958	1	0	0	0	1	13	5	7	1	1
	Athens	12,915	63	0	17	14	32	522	158	334	30	3
	Atlanta	5,838	36	0	5	10	21	219	55	154	10	0
	Austin	709,813	3,658	20	319	1,358	1,961	41,573	7,467	31,562	2,544	88
	Azle	10,643	37	0	2	9	26	521	108	388	25	4
	Baird	1,728	1	0	0	0	1	10	6	4	0	0
	Balch Springs	20,027	123	1	22	35	65	1,221	194	889	138	3
	Balcones Heights	3,076	56	0	4	18	34	661	102	519	40	0
	Ballinger	4,133	2	0	0	0	2	96	20	73	3	0
	Bangs	1,669	3	0	0	0	3	25	10	15	0	0
	Bastrop	7,504	17	0	2	4	11	434	43	373	18	0
	Bay City	18,842	166	1	3	58	104	894	210	651	33	2
	Bayou Vista	1,741	0	0	0	0	0	4	1	3	0	0
	Baytown	70,309	350	3	46	137	164	3,233	789	2,115	329	23
	Beaumont	114,967	1,155	10	75	344	726	6,962	1,887	4,525	550	33
	Bedford	49,761	254	0	19	38	197	1,615	314	1,180	121	5
	Beeville	13,944	35	0	0	2	33	454	154	292	8	2

[1] The FBI does not publish arson data unless it receives data from either the agency or the state for all 12 months of the calendar year.

Table 8. Offenses Known to Law Enforcement, by State and City, 2006 (*Contd.*)

(Number.)

State	City	Population	Violent crime	Murder and non-negligent man-slaughter	Forcible rape	Robbery	Aggra-vated assault	Property crime	Burglary	Larceny-theft	Motor vehicle theft	Arson[1]
	Bellaire	17,694	24	0	1	19	4	390	74	302	14	1
	Bellmead	9,826	117	0	6	14	97	727	93	589	45	7
	Bellville	4,425	4	0	1	0	3	118	25	88	5	0
	Belton	15,970	33	0	0	7	26	531	150	363	18	2
	Benbrook	22,543	28	2	1	11	14	522	108	379	35	4
	Beverly Hills	2,130	11	0	0	0	11	98	22	66	10	0
	Big Sandy	1,387	2	0	0	0	2	22	3	19	0	0
	Big Spring	24,940	138	1	17	15	105	1,159	348	751	60	6
	Bishop	3,295	7	0	0	0	7	214	14	199	1	0
	Blue Mound	2,425	1	0	0	0	1	70	8	54	8	0
	Boerne	8,282	13	1	1	1	10	218	33	176	9	0
	Bogata	1,351	2	0	1	0	1	19	7	11	1	1
	Bonham	10,855	50	0	4	0	46	379	117	248	14	1
	Borger	13,682	79	0	14	9	56	878	178	639	61	12
	Bovina	1,855	3	0	0	2	1	5	3	1	1	0
	Bowie	5,700	19	0	5	2	12	358	47	290	21	1
	Brady	5,496	26	0	2	0	24	122	76	45	1	1
	Brazoria	2,979	13	0	2	2	9	104	14	75	15	0
	Breckenridge	5,809	4	0	0	1	3	107	36	66	5	0
	Bremond	921	4	0	0	0	4	5	3	2	0	0
	Brenham[5]	14,562		0		12	52	419	112	264	43	1
	Bridge City	9,049	16	0	0	0	16	213	43	149	21	2
	Bridgeport	5,819	14	0	3	1	10	191	35	147	9	0
	Brookshire	3,703	18	1	1	7	9	112	50	44	18	0
	Brookside Village	2,053	9	0	0	0	9	25	13	10	2	0
	Brownsville	172,239	867	5	46	168	648	8,385	1,377	6,483	525	9
	Brownwood	20,120	128	0	18	14	96	1,123	284	800	39	1
	Bruceville-Eddy	1,577	4	0	0	1	3	21	5	15	1	0
	Bryan	68,185	589	6	31	100	452	3,760	1,004	2,570	186	35
	Bullard	1,606	2	0	0	0	2	78	7	68	3	0
	Bulverde	4,572	4	0	0	0	4	78	11	66	1	0
	Burkburnett	10,672	1	0	0	0	1	145	63	81	1	0
	Burleson	30,452	57	0	10	11	36	1,182	145	962	75	5
	Burnet	5,720	14	0	2	0	12	107	31	72	4	0
	Caddo Mills	1,245	6	0	1	0	5	25	6	19	0	0
	Caldwell	3,971	5	0	0	0	5	29	3	22	4	0
	Calvert	1,443	7	0	0	0	7	40	17	22	1	0
	Cameron	6,067	15	0	4	4	7	224	47	171	6	2
	Canton	3,693	0	0	0	0	0	99	25	70	4	0
	Canyon	13,731	10	0	0	1	9	151	16	128	7	0
	Carrollton	122,239	229	5	6	87	131	3,782	815	2,489	478	26
	Carthage	6,798	38	0	0	2	36	198	32	142	24	0
	Castle Hills	4,290	8	0	0	4	4	395	46	340	9	0
	Castroville	3,019	7	0	0	0	7	89	10	78	1	0
	Cedar Hill	42,760	117	2	6	30	79	1,436	375	941	120	6
	Cedar Park	49,503	94	1	18	7	68	798	154	608	36	6
	Celina	3,821	9	0	0	0	9	71	11	58	2	0
	Center	5,945	27	2	2	2	21	301	70	214	17	0
	Childress	6,793	24	0	0	1	23	118	33	75	10	3
	Cibolo	8,025	12	0	4	0	8	164	26	131	7	2
	Cisco	3,942	7	0	1	0	6	123	30	81	12	0
	Clarksville	3,713	5	0	0	1	4	57	23	34	0	1
	Cleburne	30,011	158	1	34	25	98	1,329	259	1,003	67	4
	Cleveland	8,260	56	1	15	8	32	572	95	435	42	2
	Clifton	3,745	9	0	0	0	9	59	21	34	4	0
	Clint	1,013	0	0	0	0	0	0	0	0	0	0
	Clute	11,035	56	0	9	8	39	515	118	364	33	3
	Clyde	3,777	10	0	1	0	9	69	14	45	10	0
	Cockrell Hill	4,411	11	0	0	3	8	117	34	43	40	1
	Coffee City	212	1	0	0	0	1	5	1	4	0	0
	Coleman	4,966	2	0	0	0	2	209	94	99	16	2
	College Station	74,439	210	0	39	33	138	2,860	549	2,192	119	0
	Colleyville	23,029	9	0	0	2	7	302	52	231	19	0
	Collinsville	1,513	2	0	0	0	2	20	9	6	5	0

[1] The FBI does not publish arson data unless it receives data from either the agency or the state for all 12 months of the calendar year.
[5] It was determined that the agency did not follow national Uniform Crime Reporting (UCR) Program guidelines for reporting an offense. Consequently, this figure is not included in this table.

Table 8. Offenses Known to Law Enforcement, by State and City, 2006 (*Contd.*)

(Number.)

State	City	Popula-tion	Violent crime	Murder and non-negligent man-slaughter	Forcible rape	Robbery	Aggra-vated assault	Property crime	Burglary	Larceny-theft	Motor vehicle theft	Arson[1]
	Colorado City	4,132	32	0	3	1	28	158	39	113	6	0
	Columbus	4,045	20	0	2	0	18	138	42	91	5	4
	Comanche	4,424	10	2	2	0	6	104	31	71	2	1
	Combes	2,920	16	0	3	2	11	79	38	33	8	0
	Commerce	9,225	36	0	7	13	16	335	68	256	11	0
	Conroe	48,375	238	5	20	58	155	2,414	450	1,780	184	8
	Converse	13,008	7	0	0	2	5	264	98	158	8	0
	Coppell	39,801	29	0	2	11	16	829	145	624	60	3
	Copperas Cove	31,511	109	1	16	24	68	1,058	238	795	25	5
	Corinth	18,490	16	0	4	3	9	238	54	166	18	0
	Corpus Christi	291,507	2,070	21	167	468	1,414	19,138	3,005	15,261	872	128
	Corrigan	1,986	4	0	0	2	2	22	12	10	0	4
	Corsicana	26,790	62	1	13	17	31	1,270	310	866	94	6
	Crane	3,130	3	0	0	0	3	24	6	18	0	0
	Crockett	7,238	52	0	2	4	46	359	81	265	13	0
	Crowell	1,092	1	0	0	0	1	3	2	1	0	0
	Crowley	9,966	29	0	6	4	19	229	52	162	15	1
	Crystal City	7,429	6	0	0	2	4	200	52	143	5	2
	Cuero	6,962	27	0	6	3	18	160	39	117	4	1
	Daingerfield	2,540	7	0	0	0	7	59	26	31	2	2
	Dalhart	7,349	37	0	3	5	29	214	60	145	9	0
	Dallas	1,248,223	15,058	187	665	6,914	7,292	85,592	21,653	50,009	13,930	1,058
	Dalworthington Gardens	2,426	3	0	1	0	2	45	11	32	2	0
	Danbury	1,714	1	0	0	0	1	13	5	8	0	0
	Dayton	6,810	13	0	2	3	8	212	46	142	24	1
	Decatur	6,202	13	0	2	2	9	275	42	216	17	0
	Deer Park	29,815	71	0	8	6	57	590	134	415	41	5
	De Kalb	1,841	8	0	0	1	7	54	25	29	0	0
	De Leon	2,454	3	0	0	0	3	29	4	24	1	1
	Del Rio	37,041	40	0	0	11	29	1,042	199	742	101	9
	Denison	24,318	92	1	5	23	63	1,128	270	793	65	0
	Denton	107,105	329	0	60	65	204	3,168	664	2,295	209	19
	Denver City	4,107	2	0	0	0	2	30	4	26	0	0
	DeSoto	45,918	103	2	6	34	61	1,415	446	835	134	9
	Devine	4,534	4	0	1	0	3	143	20	119	4	0
	Diboll	5,595	18	0	4	1	13	131	55	68	8	2
	Dickinson	18,405	56	3	8	19	26	526	145	335	46	1
	Dilley	4,285	17	0	0	1	16	80	34	40	6	1
	Dimmitt	4,094	9	0	0	1	8	162	57	102	3	2
	Donna	16,295	90	2	5	16	67	1,045	176	793	76	6
	Double Oak	2,945	1	0	0	0	1	13	5	7	1	0
	Driscoll	845	1	0	0	0	1	92	1	91	0	0
	Dublin	3,766	15	0	3	1	11	90	21	63	6	2
	Dumas	14,281	28	0	2	3	23	356	54	293	9	1
	Duncanville	36,146	110	1	12	60	37	1,451	366	914	171	0
	Eagle Lake	3,798	21	0	1	3	17	81	23	58	0	1
	Eagle Pass	26,296	102	2	0	15	85	1,064	151	867	46	0
	Early	2,853	1	0	0	0	1	86	20	59	7	0
	Eastland	3,921	4	0	0	2	2	134	15	113	6	1
	East Mountain	641	2	0	0	0	2	11	3	5	3	0
	Edcouch	4,551	11	0	0	4	7	106	43	52	11	3
	Eden	2,516	1	0	0	1	0	21	9	12	0	0
	Edgewood	1,492	10	0	1	1	8	36	13	22	1	0
	Edinburg	64,513	263	1	13	49	200	4,059	681	2,969	409	10
	Edna	6,036	15	0	5	0	10	133	29	101	3	1
	El Campo	11,192	39	0	4	15	20	387	62	309	16	4
	Electra	3,021	3	0	1	0	2	82	30	43	9	1
	Elgin	8,935	25	0	10	3	12	299	63	222	14	0
	El Paso[8]	615,553	2,413	13	291	503	1,606	20,576	2,212	14,845	3,519	93
	Elsa	6,641	100	0	0	7	93	477	108	327	42	0
	Ennis	19,266	69	3	6	29	31	838	152	637	49	0
	Euless	52,678	103	0	3	36	64	1,607	298	1,153	156	9
	Everman	5,895	32	0	6	7	19	167	46	102	19	3

[1] The FBI does not publish arson data unless it receives data from either the agency or the state for all 12 months of the calendar year.
[8] Because of changes in the state/local agency's reporting practices, figures are not comparable to previous years' data.

Table 8. Offenses Known to Law Enforcement, by State and City, 2006 (*Contd.*)

(Number.)

State	City	Popula-tion	Violent crime	Murder and non-negligent man-slaughter	Forcible rape	Robbery	Aggra-vated assault	Property crime	Burglary	Larceny-theft	Motor vehicle theft	Arson[1]
	Fairfield	3,607	25	0	0	2	23	47	6	36	5	0
	Fair Oaks Ranch	5,877	16	0	4	0	12	42	22	20	0	0
	Falfurrias	5,193	28	0	2	3	23	212	74	133	5	5
	Farmers Branch	27,238	65	1	3	29	32	1,192	238	755	199	1
	Farmersville	3,452	5	0	0	3	2	51	13	35	3	1
	Ferris	2,363	5	1	1	1	2	82	28	50	4	1
	Flatonia	1,461	3	0	1	0	2	11	0	9	2	0
	Florence	1,140	4	0	0	0	4	28	8	20	0	1
	Floresville	7,223	18	0	3	0	15	251	43	204	4	2
	Flower Mound	65,326	38	2	8	4	24	784	135	616	33	1
	Floydada	3,387	7	0	0	2	5	42	21	19	2	0
	Forest Hill	13,602	95	0	11	40	44	437	120	279	38	0
	Forney	10,879	17	0	4	2	11	307	60	220	27	0
	Fort Stockton	7,474	18	0	3	1	14	268	94	163	11	1
	Fort Worth	641,752	4,209	49	247	1,417	2,496	36,473	8,998	24,128	3,347	233
	Frankston	1,268	4	0	0	0	4	37	10	26	1	0
	Fredericksburg	10,728	9	0	0	0	9	210	18	190	2	0
	Freeport	12,962	47	1	9	9	28	405	135	244	26	0
	Freer	3,168	7	0	0	0	7	56	12	43	1	0
	Friendswood	34,032	42	0	8	5	29	491	101	365	25	2
	Friona	3,841	7	0	0	0	7	34	12	21	1	0
	Frisco	72,799	98	1	11	14	72	3,184	733	2,379	72	8
	Gainesville	17,039	130	2	7	19	102	896	235	608	53	3
	Galena Park	10,511	32	0	5	7	20	263	75	167	21	0
	Galveston	59,094	593	4	120	166	303	3,239	657	2,278	304	7
	Ganado	1,924	0	0	0	0	0	15	4	11	0	0
	Garland	222,477	576	3	50	223	300	7,884	1,889	5,278	717	41
	Gatesville	16,095	26	0	1	3	22	284	70	198	16	3
	Georgetown	40,121	50	0	9	9	32	600	87	470	43	1
	Giddings	5,596	27	0	4	0	23	181	44	133	4	0
	Gilmer	5,287	20	0	1	7	12	394	69	309	16	1
	Gladewater	6,473	14	0	0	3	11	288	57	205	26	0
	Glenn Heights	9,588	31	0	1	4	26	318	141	153	24	3
	Godley	1,020	5	0	0	1	4	7	3	3	1	1
	Gonzales	7,727	105	0	8	11	86	457	186	270	1	5
	Gorman	1,294	1	0	0	0	1	29	13	16	0	0
	Graham	8,962	15	0	3	2	10	298	44	242	12	3
	Granbury	7,569	15	0	0	4	11	416	9	396	11	0
	Grand Prairie	148,427	490	3	69	156	262	7,479	1,591	4,844	1,044	25
	Grand Saline	3,319	3	0	0	0	3	68	9	59	0	0
	Granger	1,369	8	0	0	0	8	18	8	10	0	0
	Granite Shoals	2,402	4	0	1	0	3	52	12	33	7	0
	Grapeland	1,461	4	0	0	1	3	39	13	20	6	0
	Grapevine	48,805	92	0	8	30	54	1,526	203	1,178	145	3
	Greenville	26,364	230	2	6	45	177	1,425	357	954	114	0
	Gregory	2,328	1	0	0	0	1	232	11	220	1	5
	Groesbeck	4,476	6	0	0	0	6	64	26	34	4	0
	Groves	15,431	38	1	0	20	17	500	135	330	35	0
	Gruver	1,154	0	0	0	0	0	2	1	1	0	0
	Gun Barrel City	6,131	44	1	10	2	31	290	72	210	8	0
	Hale Center	2,242	5	0	3	0	2	12	4	7	1	0
	Hallettsville	2,568	13	0	5	0	8	58	6	50	2	1
	Hallsville	2,979	1	0	0	0	1	44	11	27	6	0
	Haltom City	41,005	190	2	18	44	126	2,320	507	1,542	271	14
	Hamlin	2,075	6	0	1	1	4	9	5	2	2	0
	Harker Heights	21,942	27	0	5	13	9	790	217	527	46	1
	Harlingen	64,084	353	3	22	67	261	4,570	1,043	3,255	272	21
	Hart	1,132	0	0	0	0	0	23	11	11	1	0
	Haskell	2,861	12	0	0	0	12	65	18	42	5	0
	Hawk Cove	510	3	0	0	0	3	10	3	5	2	1
	Hawkins	1,513	2	0	0	0	2	22	3	16	3	1
	Hawley	620	0	0	0	0	0	9	9	0	0	0
	Hearne	4,843	28	0	2	1	25	179	35	138	6	3
	Heath	6,600	13	0	4	0	9	107	22	82	3	0
	Hedwig Village	2,360	12	0	2	6	4	252	33	201	18	0

[1] The FBI does not publish arson data unless it receives data from either the agency or the state for all 12 months of the calendar year.

Table 8. Offenses Known to Law Enforcement, by State and City, 2006 *(Contd.)*

(Number.)

State	City	Population	Violent crime	Murder and non-negligent man-slaughter	Forcible rape	Robbery	Aggra-vated assault	Property crime	Burglary	Larceny-theft	Motor vehicle theft	Arson[1]
	Helotes	6,362	5	0	0	1	4	96	29	65	2	0
	Hemphill	1,099	1	0	0	0	1	30	7	23	0	0
	Hempstead	6,732	37	1	3	6	27	241	61	159	21	2
	Henderson	11,822	125	0	11	14	100	871	161	663	47	3
	Hereford	14,882	60	0	1	4	55	589	113	447	29	4
	Hewitt	13,355	17	0	4	2	11	204	46	152	6	2
	Hickory Creek	3,130	6	0	2	2	2	71	1	67	3	0
	Hidalgo	11,198	27	1	2	5	19	294	66	182	46	1
	Highland Park[5]	9,042	6	0	0	1	5				7	0
	Highland Village	15,533	13	0	3	2	8	85	17	67	1	0
	Hill Country Village	1,103	1	0	0	0	1	46	9	34	3	1
	Hillsboro	9,255	33	0	9	10	14	261	57	186	18	0
	Hitchcock	7,397	29	0	11	2	16	232	68	130	34	1
	Holliday	1,729	0	0	0	0	0	13	5	6	2	0
	Hollywood Park	3,301	3	0	0	1	2	79	15	57	7	0
	Hondo	9,028	53	0	14	5	34	345	88	247	10	8
	Hooks	3,007	5	1	2	0	2	15	6	8	1	0
	Horizon City	8,941	20	0	1	0	19	201	32	141	28	9
	Horseshoe Bay	3,759	1	0	1	0	0	59	14	40	5	0
	Houston	2,073,729	24,250	377	854	11,371	11,648	121,053	26,869	73,091	21,093	1,121
	Howe	2,786	4	0	0	0	4	20	2	16	2	0
	Hubbard	1,728	1	0	0	0	1	19	5	12	2	0
	Hudson	4,169	3	0	0	0	3	47	43	4	0	0
	Hudson Oaks	1,885	3	0	0	1	2	105	16	85	4	0
	Humble	15,222	106	3	10	58	35	1,560	144	1,192	224	4
	Huntington	2,132	6	1	2	0	3	37	12	23	2	0
	Huntsville	37,739	142	2	8	39	93	1,057	176	823	58	0
	Hurst	39,043	203	1	18	46	138	2,239	293	1,815	131	5
	Hutchins	3,024	17	0	2	5	10	91	17	56	18	0
	Hutto	7,611	6	0	0	0	6	78	17	59	2	0
	Idalou	2,104	5	0	0	0	5	45	8	33	4	0
	Ingleside	9,801	16	0	7	1	8	204	52	138	14	6
	Ingram	1,890	2	0	0	1	1	63	16	47	0	0
	Iowa Park	6,350	5	0	2	0	3	115	30	76	9	0
	Irving	199,137	850	3	48	264	535	9,644	1,674	6,728	1,242	36
	Italy	2,150	18	0	0	0	18	53	15	36	2	1
	Itasca	1,664	3	1	0	1	1	29	8	19	2	0
	Jacinto City	10,227	79	1	1	12	65	363	93	228	42	1
	Jacksboro	4,741	3	0	2	0	1	37	10	25	2	1
	Jacksonville	14,803	85	1	12	14	58	657	188	437	32	1
	Jamaica Beach	1,147	2	0	0	0	2	29	11	17	1	0
	Jasper	7,744	69	0	7	13	49	477	101	354	22	5
	Jefferson	2,048	16	0	2	4	10	74	17	51	6	0
	Jersey Village	7,288	24	0	0	11	13	282	71	171	40	0
	Johnson City	1,511	1	0	0	0	1	41	5	35	1	0
	Jones Creek	2,190	1	0	0	0	1	12	2	9	1	0
	Jonestown	1,922	5	0	0	0	5	52	23	29	0	0
	Joshua	5,656	13	0	2	5	6	83	20	62	1	0
	Jourdanton	4,355	7	0	0	0	7	49	24	22	3	0
	Junction	2,729	24	0	1	0	23	71	14	56	1	2
	Karnes City	3,527	7	0	1	0	6	51	9	41	1	1
	Katy[5]	13,631		0	0	12		519	56	423	40	3
	Kaufman	8,095	20	1	4	3	12	354	77	247	30	1
	Keene	6,121	1	0	0	0	1	128	26	84	18	0
	Keller	36,718	25	2	7	4	12	550	99	431	20	0
	Kemah	2,454	10	0	3	1	6	96	9	81	6	0
	Kemp	1,294	6	0	0	1	5	62	11	49	2	0
	Kenedy	3,505	4	0	0	0	4	61	31	30	0	0
	Kennedale	6,733	42	0	4	5	33	342	120	198	24	3
	Kermit	5,431	10	0	1	0	9	62	18	42	2	1
	Kerrville	22,634	44	0	14	8	22	733	144	559	30	7
	Kilgore	12,194	41	0	11	8	22	915	153	713	49	2
	Killeen	103,073	787	8	81	246	452	5,471	2,121	3,108	242	44

[1] The FBI does not publish arson data unless it receives data from either the agency or the state for all 12 months of the calendar year.
[5] It was determined that the agency did not follow national Uniform Crime Reporting (UCR) Program guidelines for reporting an offense. Consequently, this figure is not included in this table.

Table 8. Offenses Known to Law Enforcement, by State and City, 2006 (*Contd.*)

(Number.)

State	City	Popula-tion	Violent crime	Murder and non-negligent man-slaughter	Forcible rape	Robbery	Aggra-vated assault	Property crime	Burglary	Larceny-theft	Motor vehicle theft	Arson[1]
	Kingsville	25,441	245	0	3	19	223	1,275	372	858	45	0
	Kirby	8,856	23	0	0	6	17	180	52	119	9	0
	Kirbyville	2,086	8	0	0	0	8	49	7	35	7	1
	Knox City	1,114	4	0	0	0	4	19	5	13	1	0
	Kountze	2,214	9	0	1	2	6	83	21	54	8	0
	Kress	801	0	0	0	0	0	5	2	2	1	0
	Kyle	18,274	4	0	0	0	4	134	21	113	0	1
	Lacy-Lakeview	5,968	25	0	6	3	16	260	51	181	28	1
	La Feria	7,008	21	0	4	0	17	514	85	427	2	0
	Lago Vista	5,731	5	0	0	2	3	101	27	68	6	1
	La Grange	4,751	5	0	1	2	2	91	45	45	1	0
	Laguna Vista	2,674	2	0	0	0	2	49	14	33	2	6
	La Joya	4,613	5	0	0	1	4	63	23	39	1	0
	Lake Dallas	7,198	15	0	3	2	10	145	32	102	11	0
	Lake Jackson	28,162	33	0	2	9	22	701	110	568	23	2
	Lakeside	1,197	0	0	0	0	0	26	7	18	1	0
	Lakeview	6,695	8	0	1	1	6	76	17	53	6	2
	Lakeway	9,103	7	0	1	0	6	156	31	120	5	0
	Lake Worth	4,814	54	0	0	9	45	647	57	558	32	0
	La Marque	14,253	92	1	16	29	46	585	225	298	62	1
	Lamesa	9,585	53	0	2	5	46	217	74	131	12	0
	Lampasas	7,677	31	0	18	0	13	204	28	164	12	5
	Lancaster	33,146	175	3	10	17	145	1,635	570	838	227	1
	La Porte	34,075	90	0	4	8	78	497	113	304	80	27
	Laredo	214,670	1,198	22	96	266	814	12,511	1,643	9,661	1,207	115
	La Vernia	1,118	4	0	0	0	4	44	8	36	0	0
	Lavon	433	0	0	0	0	0	22	9	13	0	0
	League City	63,233	83	0	18	24	41	1,678	342	1,249	87	6
	Leander	18,357	18	0	0	2	16	305	54	242	9	2
	Leon Valley	9,923	33	0	4	12	17	705	81	579	45	0
	Levelland	13,139	64	0	16	5	43	432	141	277	14	1
	Lewisville	92,908	214	2	37	70	105	3,045	508	2,150	387	15
	Lexington	1,280	6	0	0	0	6	59	14	45	0	1
	Liberty	8,672	5	0	0	2	3	221	49	148	24	1
	Lindale	4,144	3	0	0	1	2	157	8	147	2	0
	Linden	2,263	8	0	0	0	8	76	25	47	4	0
	Little Elm	18,522	20	0	4	1	15	140	22	104	14	0
	Littlefield[5]	6,508	19	0	7	2	10		51	104		3
	Live Oak	11,252	27	0	3	6	18	576	54	474	48	1
	Livingston	6,582	43	0	13	8	22	338	74	243	21	4
	Llano	3,443	4	0	1	0	3	69	16	50	3	0
	Lockhart	13,951	77	0	4	6	67	406	92	301	13	3
	Lockney	1,931	5	0	1	0	4	20	7	13	0	0
	Lone Star	1,634	7	0	0	0	7	75	18	55	2	0
	Longview	77,752	719	10	56	117	536	4,902	1,103	3,318	481	49
	Lorena	1,640	1	0	1	0	0	42	15	26	1	0
	Lorenzo	1,324	6	0	0	0	6	4	2	2	0	0
	Los Fresnos	5,339	5	0	1	1	3	98	31	63	4	2
	Lubbock	215,681	2,169	13	98	367	1,691	12,373	3,070	8,610	693	52
	Lufkin	34,472	221	1	33	38	149	1,403	332	975	96	2
	Luling	5,539	25	0	3	9	13	282	63	204	15	2
	Lumberton	9,910	19	0	2	3	14	382	76	294	12	0
	Lytle	2,721	3	0	0	2	1	99	17	78	4	3
	Madisonville	4,370	21	0	0	8	13	176	41	119	16	1
	Magnolia	1,221	7	0	1	4	2	25	7	15	3	0
	Malakoff	2,437	14	0	5	1	8	89	19	59	11	0
	Manor	1,930	14	0	0	2	12	143	18	115	10	0
	Mansfield	39,052	91	2	13	21	55	896	249	594	53	2
	Manvel	3,380	20	0	0	2	18	105	26	73	6	0
	Marble Falls	6,936	18	0	1	2	15	306	42	250	14	1
	Marfa	2,034	4	0	2	0	2	48	6	40	2	1
	Marion	1,150	1	0	0	0	1	25	5	19	1	0
	Marlin	6,382	24	0	4	6	14	117	31	75	11	0

[1] The FBI does not publish arson data unless it receives data from either the agency or the state for all 12 months of the calendar year.
[5] It was determined that the agency did not follow national Uniform Crime Reporting (UCR) Program guidelines for reporting an offense. Consequently, this figure is not included in this table.

Table 8. Offenses Known to Law Enforcement, by State and City, 2006 (*Contd.*)

(Number.)

State	City	Popula-tion	Violent crime	Murder and non-negligent man-slaughter	Forcible rape	Robbery	Aggra-vated assault	Property crime	Burglary	Larceny-theft	Motor vehicle theft	Arson[1]
	Marshall	24,686	141	4	16	20	101	1,092	322	704	66	6
	Mart	2,603	4	0	1	0	3	86	26	55	5	0
	Martindale	1,090	0	0	0	0	0	2	1	0	1	0
	Mathis	5,617	10	0	0	1	9	169	47	120	2	3
	McAllen	127,125	383	4	28	123	228	6,926	637	5,820	469	23
	McGregor	4,984	21	0	2	2	17	125	43	80	2	1
	McKinney	99,318	264	2	41	37	184	2,217	490	1,616	111	23
	Meadows Place	6,625	3	0	0	3	0	123	21	91	11	2
	Melissa	2,504	9	0	0	1	8	99	24	74	1	0
	Memorial Villages	11,904	10	0	2	6	2	165	63	98	4	0
	Memphis	2,471	7	0	1	0	6	60	32	24	4	0
	Mercedes	14,587	69	0	5	8	56	670	170	429	71	10
	Meridian	1,570	1	0	0	0	1	4	1	3	0	0
	Merkel	2,665	8	0	0	0	8	47	17	30	0	0
	Mesquite	133,583	496	5	10	171	310	5,374	926	3,743	705	46
	Mexia	6,933	41	0	5	13	23	486	86	385	15	2
	Midland	102,039	373	5	58	76	234	3,712	861	2,619	232	12
	Midlothian	13,562	18	0	3	2	13	262	63	177	22	0
	Milford	747	4	0	0	0	4	5	2	3	0	0
	Mineral Wells	17,398	55	1	10	8	36	889	194	653	42	2
	Mission	61,850	64	2	2	24	36	2,769	275	2,206	288	2
	Missouri City	71,923	145	1	9	55	80	1,110	282	710	118	29
	Monahans	6,504	16	2	0	0	14	153	48	103	2	0
	Mont Belvieu	2,597	6	0	3	2	1	175	13	149	13	1
	Montgomery	553	2	0	1	0	1	30	7	23	0	0
	Morgans Point Resort	4,176	2	0	0	0	2	35	9	23	3	0
	Mount Pleasant	15,178	41	0	1	10	30	476	96	344	36	1
	Muleshoe	4,709	18	0	3	0	15	140	44	90	6	0
	Munday	1,387	8	0	0	0	8	25	11	14	0	0
	Mustang Ridge	934	4	0	1	0	3	18	6	10	2	0
	Nacogdoches	31,679	92	2	17	25	48	970	202	718	50	0
	Nash	2,419	6	2	1	0	3	63	16	41	6	0
	Nassau Bay	4,171	11	0	1	4	6	114	21	86	7	0
	Navasota	7,459	36	0	5	8	23	420	107	292	21	1
	Nederland	17,226	66	0	14	22	30	686	160	491	35	1
	Needville	3,381	6	1	0	0	5	11	3	4	4	0
	New Boston	4,755	10	0	0	1	9	207	36	162	9	2
	New Braunfels	48,505	132	0	11	27	94	2,152	401	1,672	79	3
	New Deal	716	1	0	0	0	1	7	5	1	1	0
	Nocona	3,342	4	0	2	0	2	62	17	40	5	0
	Nolanville	2,321	7	0	1	1	5	110	43	56	11	0
	Northlake	1,048	1	0	1	0	0	9	1	8	0	0
	North Richland Hills	62,847	188	0	19	41	128	2,362	499	1,677	186	2
	Oak Ridge	261	1	0	0	0	1	3	1	2	0	2
	Oak Ridge North	3,400	5	0	0	1	4	126	17	96	13	3
	Odessa	96,197	614	2	12	88	512	3,654	774	2,624	256	33
	O'Donnell	1,002	0	0	0	0	0	3	0	3	0	0
	Olmos Park	2,380	2	0	1	1	0	39	6	26	7	1
	Olney	3,435	2	0	0	0	2	77	30	40	7	1
	Olton	2,339	7	0	0	2	5	68	26	41	1	0
	Onalaska	1,393	1	0	1	0	0	12	2	8	2	0
	Orange	18,564	195	0	17	48	130	1,252	332	826	94	14
	Orange Grove	1,442	6	0	0	1	5	17	13	2	2	0
	Overton	2,387	5	0	0	0	5	33	5	27	1	0
	Ovilla	3,887	2	0	1	1	0	46	14	28	4	1
	Oyster Creek	1,262	16	0	0	0	16	58	26	28	4	0
	Paducah	1,402	2	0	0	0	2	8	7	1	0	0
	Palacios	5,312	35	0	0	2	33	127	51	71	5	0
	Palestine	18,420	115	1	0	13	101	726	159	521	46	13
	Palmer	2,133	5	0	1	0	4	31	3	25	3	0
	Pampa	17,218	165	0	31	8	126	890	244	597	49	8
	Panhandle	2,683	3	0	0	0	3	11	4	7	0	0
	Pantego	2,396	5	0	0	2	3	160	43	112	5	0
	Paris[8]	27,291	220	2	15	27	176	1,781	414	1,334	33	13

[1] The FBI does not publish arson data unless it receives data from either the agency or the state for all 12 months of the calendar year.
[8] Because of changes in the state/local agency's reporting practices, figures are not comparable to previous years' data.

Table 8. Offenses Known to Law Enforcement, by State and City, 2006 (*Contd.*)

(Number.)

State	City	Population	Violent crime	Murder and nonnegligent manslaughter	Forcible rape	Robbery	Aggravated assault	Property crime	Burglary	Larceny-theft	Motor vehicle theft	Arson[1]
	Parker	2,584	4	0	0	0	4	15	2	11	2	0
	Pasadena	147,929	620	7	49	171	393	4,848	1,017	3,395	436	33
	Pearland	58,399	115	0	25	24	66	1,553	402	1,033	118	7
	Pearsall	7,992	32	2	0	1	29	258	88	164	6	0
	Pecos	8,485	31	0	0	3	28	136	28	103	5	0
	Pelican Bay	1,632	13	0	3	0	10	18	7	10	1	1
	Penitas	1,215	7	0	2	1	4	27	12	13	2	0
	Perryton	8,325	4	0	0	1	3	111	20	87	4	0
	Pflugerville	28,311	42	0	14	9	19	640	136	483	21	4
	Pharr	60,658	190	4	26	62	98	3,339	597	2,525	217	5
	Pilot Point	4,157	10	0	2	0	8	85	28	52	5	0
	Pinehurst	2,293	21	0	0	3	18	101	22	71	8	0
	Pittsburg	4,682	26	1	2	6	17	162	55	99	8	0
	Plainview	22,614	105	0	14	13	78	1,309	256	1,005	48	6
	Plano	257,183	743	4	42	154	543	8,618	1,394	6,642	582	69
	Pleasanton	9,641	36	0	10	2	24	287	57	220	10	2
	Point Comfort	757	1	0	0	0	1	2	2	0	0	0
	Ponder	870	2	0	0	0	2	27	6	19	2	0
	Port Aransas	3,771	25	0	0	4	21	289	43	230	16	1
	Port Arthur	58,290	394	2	12	140	240	2,075	814	1,014	247	42
	Port Isabel	5,525	36	0	12	1	23	327	58	259	10	0
	Portland	16,679	20	0	9	0	11	345	32	302	11	0
	Port Lavaca	12,027	31	0	10	2	19	317	67	224	26	1
	Port Neches	13,503	12	0	2	1	9	506	173	300	33	11
	Poteet	3,729	17	0	4	2	11	69	18	48	3	0
	Pottsboro	2,048	6	0	0	0	6	52	13	33	6	0
	Premont	2,916	6	0	1	0	5	71	18	47	6	0
	Presidio	4,910	4	0	0	0	4	29	9	14	6	1
	Primera	3,291	1	0	0	0	1	98	28	66	4	0
	Princeton	4,232	16	0	3	3	10	162	37	112	13	3
	Progreso	5,226	14	0	0	2	12	83	21	59	3	0
	Prosper	4,326	2	0	0	1	1	149	24	122	3	0
	Queen City	1,636	11	0	1	1	9	52	12	38	2	0
	Quinlan	1,498	4	0	0	0	4	40	9	20	11	0
	Quitman	2,260	8	0	2	1	5	39	10	26	3	1
	Ranger	2,607	3	0	0	0	3	63	34	27	2	0
	Ransom Canyon	1,091	1	0	0	0	1	10	0	9	1	0
	Raymondville	9,752	170	0	13	5	152	783	187	579	17	0
	Red Oak	7,374	11	0	0	0	11	219	65	136	18	0
	Refugio	2,876	1	0	0	0	1	43	15	26	2	0
	Reno	3,038	1	0	0	0	1	47	11	35	1	0
	Richardson	101,998	234	3	11	98	122	3,118	685	2,121	312	12
	Richland Hills	8,275	24	0	4	6	14	326	69	216	41	0
	Richmond	13,638	60	0	6	12	42	328	102	203	23	6
	Richwood	3,360	3	1	0	0	2	82	12	67	3	0
	Riesel	1,032	2	0	1	0	1	11	1	9	1	0
	Rio Grande City	14,038	25	0	3	7	15	430	100	263	67	0
	Rising Star	866	2	0	0	0	2	6	6	0	0	0
	River Oaks	7,106	13	0	5	0	8	200	60	125	15	0
	Roanoke	3,618	11	0	0	2	9	131	22	101	8	0
	Robinson	9,319	12	0	1	5	6	230	42	184	4	0
	Robstown[3]	12,838		0		6	20	647	262	369	16	3
	Rockdale	6,219	19	0	2	3	14	119	32	79	8	0
	Rockport	9,297	31	0	20	2	9	634	108	506	20	0
	Rockwall	30,186	64	0	8	10	46	812	142	615	55	0
	Rollingwood	1,398	0	0	0	0	0	31	10	17	4	0
	Roma	11,209	23	0	3	5	15	228	55	115	58	1
	Roman Forest	3,034	3	0	0	0	3	18	6	8	4	0
	Ropesville	539	0	0	0	0	0	5	2	3	0	0
	Roscoe	1,309	0	0	0	0	0	4	1	3	0	1
	Rosebud	1,434	0	0	0	0	0	25	12	13	0	0
	Rosenberg	31,181	78	0	17	10	51	829	188	570	71	5
	Round Rock	88,762	104	0	23	31	50	1,968	277	1,642	49	6

[1] The FBI does not publish arson data unless it receives data from either the agency or the state for all 12 months of the calendar year.
[3] The FBI determined that the agency's data were inflated. Consequently, affected data are not included in this table.

Table 8. Offenses Known to Law Enforcement, by State and City, 2006 (*Contd.*)

(Number.)

State	City	Population	Violent crime	Murder and non-negligent man-slaughter	Forcible rape	Robbery	Aggra-vated assault	Property crime	Burglary	Larceny-theft	Motor vehicle theft	Arson[1]
	Rowlett[5]	55,185		3		13	40		229	798		3
	Royse City	5,747	8	0	2	2	4	79	11	64	4	1
	Runaway Bay	1,367	0	0	0	0	0	41	9	32	0	0
	Rusk	5,382	15	0	0	1	14	59	22	34	3	0
	Sabinal	1,703	7	0	0	0	7	51	8	43	0	0
	Sachse	17,491	11	0	3	0	8	190	33	147	10	0
	Saginaw	18,203	32	1	2	9	20	490	84	364	42	2
	Salado	2,026	1	0	0	1	0	26	4	19	3	0
	San Angelo	90,508	396	3	53	62	278	4,557	974	3,359	224	20
	San Antonio	1,292,116	7,977	119	514	2,321	5,023	78,621	14,629	57,377	6,615	484
	San Augustine	2,535	20	0	1	0	19	57	20	34	3	0
	San Benito	25,399	76	1	10	14	51	1,558	331	1,172	55	8
	Sanger	6,534	14	1	6	1	6	214	48	156	10	0
	San Juan	31,645	104	1	0	14	89	1,602	276	1,204	122	0
	San Marcos	47,418	166	1	25	33	107	1,359	262	975	122	7
	San Saba	2,689	4	0	0	0	4	26	7	15	4	0
	Sansom Park Village	4,238	18	1	2	2	13	92	15	65	12	1
	Santa Anna	1,055	2	0	0	1	1	3	0	3	0	0
	Santa Fe	10,795	26	0	8	1	17	333	97	214	22	2
	Santa Rosa	3,029	15	0	0	2	13	64	19	42	3	3
	Schertz[3]	27,424		0	17	8		622	133	458	31	0
	Seabrook	11,216	33	0	5	3	25	189	49	124	16	0
	Seadrift	1,429	2	0	0	0	2	16	7	8	1	0
	Seagoville	11,427	38	0	2	12	24	616	152	387	77	0
	Seagraves	2,387	6	0	1	0	5	29	14	14	1	0
	Sealy	6,209	18	0	1	5	12	232	23	193	16	0
	Seguin	24,917	59	0	8	12	39	1,230	160	1,027	43	1
	Selma	2,351	14	0	1	4	9	221	20	192	9	0
	Seminole	6,123	7	1	2	3	1	86	18	67	1	0
	Seven Points	1,287	14	0	1	1	12	97	18	74	5	0
	Seymour[3]	2,781		0	1	1		70	11	55	4	0
	Shallowater	2,231	1	0	0	0	1	64	6	56	2	1
	Shamrock	1,893	3	1	1	1	0	21	3	16	2	0
	Shavano Park	2,355	2	0	0	0	2	90	28	62	0	0
	Shenandoah	1,764	4	0	0	4	0	245	8	231	6	
	Sherman	37,833	153	0	12	25	116	1,611	349	1,208	54	0
	Silsbee	6,912	12	0	0	3	9	131	34	92	5	0
	Sinton	5,665	13	1	1	2	9	193	43	147	3	3
	Slaton	5,889	16	0	0	2	14	133	28	98	7	1
	Smithville	4,494	24	0	3	3	18	146	29	115	2	2
	Snyder[3]	10,880		0	10	1		198	74	113	11	1
	Socorro[8]	30,526	107	1	4	14	88	564	131	357	76	8
	Somerset	1,829	1	0	0	0	1	36	6	27	3	0
	Somerville	1,803	5	0	0	2	3	39	13	21	5	0
	Sonora	3,093	11	0	0	0	11	49	10	38	1	1
	Sour Lake	1,765	3	0	1	0	2	42	6	32	4	0
	South Houston	16,679	124	1	7	67	49	763	171	440	152	1
	Southlake	25,608	13	0	0	3	10	582	106	455	21	3
	South Padre Island	2,661	80	0	12	5	63	659	105	521	33	0
	Southside Place	1,645	3	0	0	3	0	13	0	12	1	0
	Spearman	3,007	11	0	2	0	9	28	3	25	0	0
	Springtown	2,714	19	0	2	1	16	79	29	50	0	0
	Spring Valley	3,701	1	0	0	0	1	102	9	89	4	0
	Spur	1,056	2	2	0	0	0	7	7	0	0	0
	Stafford	19,772	84	2	4	33	45	876	147	634	95	0
	Stamford	3,345	13	0	1	0	12	89	33	48	8	0
	Stanton	2,326	3	0	1	1	1	27	6	20	1	0
	Stephenville	16,400	35	0	7	2	26	602	90	488	24	2
	Sugar Land	77,901	101	0	6	45	50	1,609	212	1,322	75	5
	Sullivan City	4,469	12	1	2	1	8	122	89	26	7	1
	Sulphur Springs	15,660	29	0	1	2	26	343	85	239	19	6
	Sunset Valley	492	1	0	0	1	0	145	2	142	1	0

[1] The FBI does not publish arson data unless it receives data from either the agency or the state for all 12 months of the calendar year.
[3] The FBI determined that the agency's data were inflated. Consequently, affected data are not included in this table.
[5] It was determined that the agency did not follow national Uniform Crime Reporting (UCR) Program guidelines for reporting an offense. Consequently, this figure is not included in this table.
[8] Because of changes in the state/local agency's reporting practices, figures are not comparable to previous years' data.

Table 8. Offenses Known to Law Enforcement, by State and City, 2006 (*Contd.*)

(Number.)

State	City	Popula-tion	Violent crime	Murder and non-negligent man-slaughter	Forcible rape	Robbery	Aggra-vated assault	Property crime	Burglary	Larceny-theft	Motor vehicle theft	Arson[1]
	Surfside Beach	850	0	0	0	0	0	31	15	12	4	0
	Sweeny	3,725	9	1	1	0	7	86	22	58	6	1
	Sweetwater	10,997	36	1	2	11	22	393	147	235	11	0
	Taft.....................................	3,526	0	0	0	0	0	148	20	127	1	0
	Tahoka................................	2,807	5	0	1	1	3	68	21	44	3	1
	Tatum	1,222	2	0	1	0	1	30	9	20	1	0
	Taylor	15,439	33	0	2	3	28	403	68	317	18	3
	Teague	4,761	8	0	0	3	5	23	5	11	7	0
	Temple[5]	57,018		2		62	90	2,878	668	2,045	165	3
	Terrell.................................	18,166	187	2	17	40	128	968	241	637	90	18
	Terrell Hills........................	5,253	2	0	0	1	1	114	50	59	5	0
	Texarkana	36,759	462	3	30	75	354	2,376	451	1,803	122	18
	Texas City	45,529	195	2	13	91	89	2,552	765	1,614	173	5
	The Colony	39,048	33	0	0	12	21	730	143	544	43	11
	Thorndale	1,368	3	0	0	1	2	12	5	6	1	0
	Thrall..................................	871	1	0	0	0	1	18	3	14	1	0
	Three Rivers.......................	1,814	3	1	0	0	2	57	17	38	2	0
	Tioga	903	1	0	0	0	1	18	9	8	1	0
	Tolar	661	0	0	0	0	0	3	0	3	0	0
	Tomball	10,220	43	1	7	9	26	397	61	307	29	0
	Tool.....................................	2,521	7	0	0	0	7	61	25	30	6	0
	Trinity.................................	2,859	18	1	0	3	14	82	17	61	4	1
	Trophy Club........................	7,542	3	0	0	2	1	77	14	59	4	1
	Tulia...................................	4,848	39	0	0	2	37	162	34	123	5	1
	Tye	1,173	2	0	1	0	1	42	14	24	4	1
	Tyler....................................	94,541	563	5	41	110	407	4,313	842	3,280	191	10
	Universal City	17,125	30	0	2	6	22	371	79	257	35	4
	University Park	24,481	20	0	2	9	9	483	70	394	19	0
	Uvalde	16,907	85	1	5	12	67	1,177	268	886	23	10
	Van......................................	2,647	2	0	0	2	0	72	24	44	4	1
	Van Alstyne	2,838	6	0	2	0	4	68	12	53	3	1
	Vernon................................	11,391	74	0	5	11	58	605	90	497	18	12
	Victoria	63,541	337	5	32	89	211	2,973	688	2,112	173	1
	Vidor	11,610	37	0	5	8	24	469	125	286	58	1
	Waco	123,879	952	9	72	257	614	7,512	2,188	4,869	455	28
	Wake Village	5,374	3	1	0	2	0	64	21	40	3	0
	Waller.................................	2,055	20	1	0	8	11	121	32	80	9	2
	Wallis..................................	1,307	1	0	0	0	1	71	16	54	1	0
	Watauga	24,215	53	0	2	22	29	665	127	491	47	5
	Waxahachie........................	26,175	104	0	14	8	82	1,014	219	742	53	5
	Weatherford	23,976	58	0	12	7	39	789	111	629	49	0
	Webster	9,103	65	1	16	25	23	1,024	103	803	118	3
	Weimar...............................	2,073	1	0	0	0	1	18	5	12	1	0
	Wells	814	5	0	0	0	5	7	6	0	1	3
	Weslaco	32,333	153	1	6	40	106	2,147	421	1,499	227	0
	West....................................	2,788	6	0	0	0	6	33	5	25	3	1
	West Columbia..................	4,360	5	0	1	0	4	107	19	83	5	0
	West Lake Hills..................	3,107	4	0	0	0	4	75	19	53	3	0
	West Orange......................	4,106	10	0	2	3	5	314	66	230	18	1
	Westover Hills...................	699	0	0	0	0	0	24	3	18	3	0
	West Tawakoni	1,702	8	0	2	0	6	54	17	33	4	0
	West University Place	15,308	5	0	0	5	0	275	65	204	6	0
	Westworth..........................	2,951	3	0	0	0	3	133	18	110	5	1
	Wharton..............................	9,640	50	0	1	4	45	375	69	297	9	2
	Whitehouse........................	7,324	11	0	3	0	8	83	14	61	8	3
	White Oak	6,304	5	0	1	1	3	138	31	96	11	0
	Whitesboro	4,114	3	0	0	0	3	87	3	78	6	0
	White Settlement	16,182	35	0	0	15	20	874	213	614	47	9
	Whitney..............................	2,107	2	0	0	0	2	72	12	60	0	1
	Wichita Falls.....................	102,675	491	9	27	169	286	6,285	1,291	4,574	420	64
	Willis..................................	4,290	27	0	1	8	18	222	54	143	25	0
	Willow Park	3,561	1	0	1	0	0	36	10	24	2	0
	Wills Point	3,964	4	0	0	3	1	32	16	14	2	0
	Wilmer................................	3,672	13	0	0	2	11	129	46	66	17	0

[1] The FBI does not publish arson data unless it receives data from either the agency or the state for all 12 months of the calendar year.
[5] It was determined that the agency did not follow national Uniform Crime Reporting (UCR) Program guidelines for reporting an offense. Consequently, this figure is not included in this table.

Table 8. Offenses Known to Law Enforcement, by State and City, 2006 (*Contd.*)

(Number.)

State	City	Popula-tion	Violent crime	Murder and non-negligent man-slaughter	Forcible rape	Robbery	Aggra-vated assault	Property crime	Burglary	Larceny-theft	Motor vehicle theft	Arson[1]
	Windcrest	5,234	17	0	1	4	12	363	49	298	16	1
	Wink	908	0	0	0	0	0	6	0	6	0	0
	Winnsboro	3,902	10	0	0	0	10	54	20	34	0	0
	Winters	2,805	3	0	0	1	2	30	10	15	5	1
	Wolfforth	3,025	5	0	2	1	2	60	10	44	6	1
	Woodville	2,379	5	0	0	1	4	15	5	10	0	0
	Woodway	8,935	9	0	2	0	7	166	39	121	6	1
	Wortham	1,120	2	0	0	0	2	10	4	6	0	0
	Wylie	29,885	28	0	5	3	20	562	121	413	28	1
	Yoakum	5,882	2	0	0	0	2	163	41	112	10	0
	Yorktown	2,329	22	0	6	1	15	47	20	27	0	1
UTAH	Alpine/Highland	23,143	6	0	1	0	5	263	101	155	7	0
	American Fork	22,068	29	0	7	6	16	1,050	246	744	60	0
	Blanding	3,237	6	0	2	0	4	34	13	21	0	1
	Bountiful	42,424	27	2	9	3	13	975	156	764	55	11
	Brian Head	120	0	0	0	0	0	31	6	25	0	0
	Brigham City	18,953	29	1	3	3	22	514	79	413	22	2
	Cedar City	24,765	36	1	11	5	19	750	107	603	40	3
	Clearfield	28,306	56	2	9	6	39	918	135	736	47	9
	Clinton	18,313	6	0	1	1	4	205	35	156	14	0
	Draper	36,263	26	0	6	7	13	1,083	211	797	75	2
	Ephraim	5,139	8	0	3	0	5	111	12	95	4	1
	Grantsville	7,738	8	0	4	1	3	156	19	120	17	4
	Gunnison	2,788	12	0	0	0	12	130	20	98	12	1
	Harrisville	5,184	7	0	2	2	3	178	18	151	9	0
	Heber	9,445	6	0	3	0	3	34	22	7	5	0
	Helper	1,939	5	0	0	0	5	29	7	18	4	0
	Hildale	2,037	0	0	0	0	0	1	1	0	0	0
	Hurricane	11,347	10	0	4	0	6	281	68	200	13	0
	Kaysville	23,244	12	0	7	1	4	441	66	357	18	2
	La Verkin	4,239	10	0	4	0	6	63	22	36	5	1
	Layton	63,795	100	1	30	12	57	1,953	271	1,612	70	12
	Lehi	32,764	26	0	6	2	18	665	214	411	40	0
	Logan	48,900	43	1	10	6	26	844	142	678	24	1
	Mapleton	6,167	2	0	1	1	0	81	23	57	1	0
	Midvale	28,055	90	1	20	25	44	1,618	207	1,177	234	3
	Moab	4,964	17	0	4	1	12	196	34	144	18	3
	Monticello	1,975	2	0	1	0	1	11	0	11	0	0
	Naples	1,507	2	1	0	0	1	121	20	86	15	0
	Nephi	5,209	7	0	1	0	6	95	25	65	5	0
	North Ogden	17,081	5	0	2	0	3	305	43	258	4	2
	North Park	9,900	3	0	0	0	3	171	28	138	5	0
	Ogden	80,861	415	2	37	123	253	5,029	820	3,773	436	0
	Orem	92,637	60	1	16	18	25	2,564	269	2,152	143	1
	Park City	8,329	26	0	9	3	14	534	77	427	30	0
	Parowan	2,615	1	0	0	0	1	11	2	8	1	0
	Payson	16,978	16	0	5	3	8	491	113	353	25	0
	Perry	3,181	1	0	0	0	1	64	15	45	4	1
	Pleasant Grove/Lindon	40,327	20	0	4	4	12	992	143	804	45	0
	Pleasant View	6,351	2	0	2	0	0	144	28	116	0	0
	Price	8,344	18	0	3	6	9	396	42	339	15	3
	Provo	117,156	169	2	38	24	105	2,859	541	2,121	197	19
	Richfield	7,274	7	0	3	0	4	291	45	243	3	1
	Riverdale	8,193	10	0	3	3	4	439	53	374	12	0
	Roosevelt	4,701	6	1	1	0	4	225	28	185	12	0
	Roy	36,377	46	0	14	8	24	685	91	564	30	11
	Salem	4,879	0	0	0	0	0	113	29	77	7	0
	Salina	2,460	7	0	2	2	3	111	14	94	3	0
	Salt Lake City	183,901	1,494	8	95	507	884	15,420	2,244	11,136	2,040	58
	Sandy	92,586	151	0	23	29	99	3,161	522	2,404	235	18
	Santaquin/Genola	8,330	4	0	2	0	2	150	22	123	5	0
	Smithfield	7,836	6	0	4	0	2	125	17	104	4	0
	South Jordan	41,519	35	0	7	6	22	876	131	673	72	1
	South Ogden	15,690	16	0	5	3	8	397	82	300	15	3
	South Salt Lake	22,109	187	2	40	48	97	2,276	367	1,501	408	5

[1] The FBI does not publish arson data unless it receives data from either the agency or the state for all 12 months of the calendar year.

Table 8. Offenses Known to Law Enforcement, by State and City, 2006 (*Contd.*)

(Number.)

State	City	Popula-tion	Violent crime	Murder and non-negligent man-slaughter	Forcible rape	Robbery	Aggra-vated assault	Property crime	Burglary	Larceny-theft	Motor vehicle theft	Arson[1]
	Spanish Fork	27,473	20	0	8	1	11	669	126	522	21	5
	Springville	26,134	32	0	9	3	20	654	104	522	28	2
	Stockton	592	0	0	0	0	0	4	0	4	0	0
	Sunset	5,108	5	0	0	0	5	140	37	99	4	1
	Syracuse	18,523	7	1	1	1	4	229	71	148	10	1
	Taylorsville City	59,899	141	1	22	34	84	2,576	344	1,908	324	7
	Tooele	29,293	59	0	18	5	36	865	147	649	69	9
	Tremonton	6,491	6	0	0	0	6	255	48	198	9	0
	Washington	14,114	18	0	3	2	13	315	61	228	26	0
	Wendover	1,673	12	0	2	0	10	55	11	40	4	0
	West Bountiful	5,056	20	0	1	2	17	112	7	101	4	0
	West Jordan	94,424	173	1	27	36	109	3,329	466	2,560	303	10
	West Valley	116,992	473	3	69	113	288	5,783	877	4,047	859	31
	Woods Cross	8,280	10	0	3	3	4	220	43	157	20	1
VERMONT	Barre	9,141	17	0	3	1	13	282	40	229	13	6
	Barre Town	8,013	1	0	1	0	0	144	31	105	8	0
	Bellows Falls	3,023	3	0	0	0	3	47	9	35	3	1
	Bennington	15,396	24	0	8	1	15	403	93	278	32	2
	Berlin	2,892	0	0	0	0	0	23	1	22	0	0
	Bradford	823	0	0	0	0	0	0	0	0	0	0
	Brandon	3,952	2	0	0	0	2	130	33	93	4	0
	Brattleboro	11,865	29	0	1	8	20	408	68	330	10	4
	Bristol	3,800	0	0	0	0	0	0	0	0	0	0
	Burlington	38,584	155	1	23	16	115	1,564	260	1,260	44	3
	Castleton	4,374	1	0	0	0	1	50	21	28	1	0
	Chester	3,116	6	0	0	0	6	60	21	36	3	0
	Colchester	17,189	24	0	1	4	19	569	90	462	17	3
	Dover	1,447	2	0	1	0	1	145	14	128	3	0
	Essex	19,172	17	2	3	2	10	453	72	369	12	0
	Fair Haven	2,973	1	0	0	0	1	28	6	20	2	0
	Hardwick	3,234	15	0	2	0	13	111	38	70	3	0
	Hinesburg	4,431	2	0	1	1	0	99	25	71	3	0
	Ludlow	2,698	1	0	0	0	1	38	5	33	0	0
	Lyndonville	1,224	0	0	0	0	0	0	0	0	0	0
	Manchester	4,365	7	0	2	1	4	103	23	75	5	0
	Milton	10,183	19	0	0	7	12	248	72	169	7	0
	Morristown	5,530	7	0	1	0	6	147	32	111	4	0
	Newport	5,214	3	0	1	1	1	121	13	106	2	0
	Northfield	5,824	12	0	1	1	10	61	8	49	4	0
	Norwich	3,572	1	0	0	0	1	47	13	33	1	0
	Randolph	5,061	4	0	1	0	3	41	9	31	1	1
	Richmond	4,116	0	0	0	0	0	36	12	22	2	0
	Rutland	17,069	49	0	5	8	36	872	121	719	32	30
	Shelburne	7,005	3	0	0	0	3	96	21	72	3	1
	Springfield	8,903	20	0	2	3	15	319	71	231	17	1
	St. Albans	7,486	56	0	3	9	44	391	55	325	11	0
	St. Johnsbury	7,505	12	0	2	2	8	103	18	83	2	0
	Stowe	4,739	4	0	0	0	4	208	34	173	1	0
	Swanton	6,463	2	0	0	0	2	68	30	36	2	0
	Thetford	2,788	0	0	0	0	0	13	3	7	3	0
	Vergennes	2,767	1	0	1	0	0	38	7	30	1	0
	Waterbury	5,218	3	0	0	0	3	39	6	33	0	0
	Weathersfield	2,857	3	0	0	0	3	24	10	13	1	0
	Williston	8,254	4	0	0	2	2	254	35	215	4	0
	Wilmington	2,334	1	0	0	0	1	72	11	57	4	0
	Windsor	3,740	11	0	1	4	6	60	34	23	3	2
	Winhall	763	0	0	0	0	0	103	18	85	0	1
	Winooski	6,362	29	0	7	9	13	288	66	214	8	1
	Woodstock	3,228	1	0	0	1	0	20	0	19	1	0
VIRGINIA	Abingdon	8,004	25	0	6	2	17	460	40	396	24	1
	Alexandria	136,686	448	7	27	206	208	3,194	380	2,439	375	7
	Altavista	3,419	10	0	1	3	6	101	8	83	10	3
	Amherst	2,247	3	0	0	0	3	23	5	18	0	0
	Appalachia	1,789	11	1	1	1	8	69	7	56	6	2
	Ashland	7,066	14	0	2	6	6	281	33	234	14	2

[1] The FBI does not publish arson data unless it receives data from either the agency or the state for all 12 months of the calendar year.

Table 8. Offenses Known to Law Enforcement, by State and City, 2006 (*Contd.*)

(Number.)

State	City	Popula-tion	Violent crime	Murder and non-negligent man-slaughter	Forcible rape	Robbery	Aggra-vated assault	Property crime	Burglary	Larceny-theft	Motor vehicle theft	Arson[1]
	Bedford	6,273	22	0	3	4	15	195	23	163	9	1
	Berryville	3,188	3	0	1	0	2	87	13	69	5	1
	Big Stone Gap	5,912	10	0	1	3	6	203	22	174	7	1
	Blacksburg	39,520	76	1	17	10	48	634	117	477	40	6
	Blackstone	3,593	13	1	1	4	7	134	18	105	11	2
	Bluefield	5,039	6	0	1	0	5	175	12	152	11	2
	Boykins	613	3	0	0	0	3	8	0	8	0	0
	Bridgewater	5,467	5	0	1	0	4	25	7	17	1	0
	Bristol	17,508	97	3	9	16	69	800	121	630	49	6
	Cape Charles	1,437	0	0	0	0	0	15	3	10	2	0
	Cedar Bluff	1,084	1	0	0	0	1	28	6	16	6	0
	Charlottesville	40,840	322	3	30	77	212	2,174	316	1,675	183	12
	Chase City	2,406	4	0	0	2	2	77	9	63	5	0
	Chesapeake	221,150	963	7	60	278	618	6,888	1,345	5,082	461	30
	Chilhowie	1,805	0	0	0	0	0	29	4	24	1	1
	Chincoteague	4,460	7	0	3	0	4	116	31	75	10	0
	Christiansburg	18,105	29	0	7	9	13	631	98	509	24	9
	Clarksville	1,302	2	0	0	1	1	44	2	39	3	0
	Clifton Forge	4,118	5	0	0	0	5	86	19	66	1	2
	Clinchco	417	0	0	0	0	0	1	1	0	0	0
	Clintwood	1,533	0	0	0	0	0	54	18	31	5	1
	Colonial Beach	3,550	14	1	1	3	9	73	14	53	6	1
	Colonial Heights	17,742	30	0	1	20	9	730	73	625	32	10
	Courtland	1,263	0	0	0	0	0	0	0	0	0	0
	Covington	6,267	13	0	3	3	7	165	27	128	10	5
	Crewe	2,314	4	0	0	2	2	85	14	68	3	2
	Culpeper	12,167	68	1	8	17	42	455	47	389	19	2
	Damascus	1,094	2	0	0	0	2	34	4	22	8	0
	Danville	46,603	193	4	5	75	109	2,105	426	1,569	110	11
	Dayton	1,358	1	0	0	0	1	9	0	8	1	0
	Dublin	2,230	2	0	0	0	2	61	8	50	3	0
	Dumfries	4,864	25	0	1	8	16	134	30	90	14	1
	Elkton	2,632	3	0	1	0	2	57	35	19	3	0
	Emporia	5,643	52	1	1	19	31	331	53	260	18	2
	Exmore	1,407	7	1	1	2	3	38	8	29	1	0
	Farmville	6,945	1	0	0	1	0	71	22	46	3	0
	Franklin	8,680	53	0	6	17	30	280	36	225	19	0
	Fredericksburg	20,939	106	1	15	29	61	937	71	791	75	6
	Fries	579	0	0	0	0	0	2	0	1	1	0
	Front Royal	14,644	31	0	6	12	13	441	34	371	36	8
	Galax	6,743	22	1	2	3	16	272	17	247	8	5
	Gate City	2,093	4	0	0	0	4	49	9	38	2	0
	Glasgow	1,029	1	0	0	0	1	5	2	3	0	0
	Glen Lyn	165	0	0	0	0	0	10	1	9	0	0
	Gordonsville	1,633	1	0	1	0	0	27	2	24	1	0
	Grottoes	2,190	3	0	2	0	1	20	7	11	2	1
	Halifax	1,306	0	0	0	0	0	12	4	8	0	0
	Hampton	147,030	571	11	53	269	238	4,861	767	3,594	500	37
	Harrisonburg	40,841	130	4	16	28	82	1,261	254	925	82	9
	Haymarket	1,094	1	0	1	0	0	15	1	13	1	0
	Herndon	22,184	86	1	7	24	54	489	44	421	24	3
	Hillsville	2,743	13	0	2	0	11	61	5	47	9	1
	Honaker	930	3	0	0	0	3	15	7	8	0	0
	Hopewell	22,916	148	1	13	50	84	1,008	177	710	121	13
	Independence	930	1	0	1	0	0	9	2	5	2	0
	Jonesville	990	0	0	0	0	0	14	6	8	0	0
	Kenbridge	1,332	7	0	1	0	6	9	0	8	1	0
	Lawrenceville	1,169	5	0	1	0	4	29	8	20	1	0
	Lebanon	3,257	8	0	3	2	3	146	22	119	5	1
	Leesburg	36,630	73	0	12	19	42	783	67	668	48	4
	Lexington	6,844	3	0	0	2	1	107	16	89	2	0
	Louisa	1,525	1	0	0	1	0	34	8	22	4	0
	Luray	4,913	5	0	1	0	4	131	11	117	3	0
	Lynchburg	67,640	340	2	34	91	213	2,402	442	1,796	164	23
	Manassas	37,943	195	2	15	72	106	1,206	160	927	119	12

[1] The FBI does not publish arson data unless it receives data from either the agency or the state for all 12 months of the calendar year.

Table 8. Offenses Known to Law Enforcement, by State and City, 2006 (*Contd.*)

(Number.)

State	City	Popula-tion	Violent crime	Murder and non-negligent man-slaughter	Forcible rape	Robbery	Aggra-vated assault	Property crime	Burglary	Larceny-theft	Motor vehicle theft	Arson[1]
	Manassas Park	11,738	38	0	6	8	24	334	34	254	46	1
	Marion	6,225	46	0	1	3	42	221	39	172	10	4
	Martinsville	15,074	45	0	3	12	30	536	72	426	38	3
	Middleburg	889	0	0	0	0	0	27	6	18	3	0
	Mount Jackson	1,784	2	0	0	1	1	36	9	26	1	0
	Narrows	2,171	1	0	0	1	0	17	3	14	0	0
	Newport News	181,692	1,422	19	109	473	821	7,578	1,661	5,160	757	87
	Norfolk	234,266	1,844	28	100	948	768	11,683	1,614	9,032	1,037	76
	Norton	3,714	17	0	3	1	13	200	20	172	8	1
	Occoquan	765	0	0	0	0	0	2	1	1	0	0
	Onancock	1,492	4	0	0	0	4	22	5	16	1	0
	Onley	501	1	0	0	1	0	36	0	36	0	0
	Orange	4,473	16	1	1	5	9	132	11	114	7	0
	Poquoson	11,929	15	0	0	1	14	132	24	104	4	1
	Portsmouth	101,167	870	18	37	336	479	5,045	1,100	3,591	354	12
	Pound	1,098	4	0	0	0	4	38	9	29	0	0
	Pulaski	9,179	32	0	5	10	17	368	92	256	20	4
	Purcellville	4,727	3	0	0	1	2	86	6	78	2	2
	Quantico	628	1	0	0	1	0	31	4	27	0	0
	Radford	14,720	55	1	8	7	39	540	111	401	28	5
	Richlands	4,157	22	3	2	3	14	252	61	184	7	3
	Richmond	195,708	2,041	76	76	987	902	10,092	2,284	6,351	1,457	70
	Roanoke	93,554	953	12	60	220	661	5,295	978	3,887	430	36
	Rocky Mount	4,614	14	0	3	5	6	115	9	98	8	2
	Rural Retreat	1,367	0	0	0	0	0	0	0	0	0	0
	Salem	24,900	31	0	3	16	12	660	89	542	29	1
	Saltville	2,290	6	0	2	0	4	58	10	44	4	2
	Shenandoah	1,889	4	0	0	0	4	39	5	31	3	0
	South Boston	8,196	46	0	5	15	26	397	78	304	15	5
	South Hill	4,653	29	0	1	6	22	235	24	191	20	0
	Stanley	1,344	3	0	0	0	3	23	0	22	1	0
	Staunton	23,570	52	0	5	12	35	790	115	637	38	11
	Stephens City	1,259	1	0	0	0	1	49	7	42	0	0
	St. Paul	974	0	0	0	0	0	2	0	1	1	0
	Strasburg	4,312	5	0	0	1	4	97	12	82	3	0
	Suffolk	79,781	395	8	25	106	256	2,515	427	1,943	145	27
	Tappahannock	2,176	13	0	2	1	10	132	8	118	6	0
	Tazewell	4,448	9	0	2	1	6	116	15	90	11	0
	Victoria	1,807	8	0	4	0	4	23	2	19	2	0
	Vinton	7,811	16	0	3	3	10	291	34	238	19	0
	Virginia Beach	442,784	1,256	19	115	678	444	12,855	2,048	10,212	595	165
	Warrenton	8,721	34	0	4	2	28	241	22	213	6	0
	Warsaw	1,380	1	0	0	1	0	9	0	9	0	0
	Waverly	2,198	6	1	0	0	5	27	5	19	3	0
	Waynesboro	21,481	104	0	4	13	87	646	106	495	45	11
	Weber City	1,296	5	0	0	1	4	53	13	38	2	0
	West Point	3,043	5	0	1	3	1	50	9	38	3	0
	Williamsburg	11,868	27	3	5	8	11	235	21	200	14	0
	Winchester	25,369	107	0	5	48	54	1,395	201	1,122	72	5
	Wise	3,315	6	0	2	1	3	103	14	85	4	0
	Woodstock	4,271	8	0	0	2	6	32	5	21	6	1
WASHINGTON	Aberdeen	16,639	41	0	5	11	25	1,021	160	759	102	3
	Airway Heights	4,727	24	0	3	1	20	166	33	112	21	2
	Algona	2,689	18	0	2	2	14	24	8	10	6	2
	Anacortes	16,359	30	0	6	5	19	690	111	555	24	8
	Arlington	15,539	28	0	3	4	21	1,204	139	863	202	1
	Asotin	1,143	4	0	1	0	3	34	12	18	4	1
	Auburn	47,895	305	0	24	122	159	3,544	686	2,216	642	37
	Bainbridge Island	22,328	30	0	6	4	20	508	125	367	16	8
	Battle Ground	13,464	30	0	12	3	15	505	85	391	29	5
	Bellevue	119,150	184	3	42	71	68	4,245	591	3,178	476	33
	Bellingham	75,828	196	0	33	76	87	5,334	791	4,267	276	20
	Bingen	701	1	0	0	1	0	27	8	16	3	0
	Black Diamond	3,997	4	0	4	0	0	50	10	37	3	0
	Blaine	4,404	11	0	1	3	7	191	41	144	6	2

[1] The FBI does not publish arson data unless it receives data from either the agency or the state for all 12 months of the calendar year.

Table 8. Offenses Known to Law Enforcement, by State and City, 2006 (*Contd.*)

(Number.)

State	City	Popula-tion	Violent crime	Murder and non-negligent man-slaughter	Forcible rape	Robbery	Aggra-vated assault	Property crime	Burglary	Larceny-theft	Motor vehicle theft	Arson[1]
	Bonney Lake	14,862	43	0	5	5	33	581	96	428	57	9
	Bothell	31,447	40	0	9	18	13	972	222	561	189	6
	Bremerton	38,478	346	1	70	76	199	1,687	407	1,102	178	17
	Brewster	2,177	28	0	2	1	25	148	42	101	5	1
	Brier	6,453	2	1	0	0	1	104	25	62	17	1
	Buckley	4,550	4	0	2	0	2	137	27	92	18	0
	Burien	31,265	179	2	14	59	104	1,899	383	1,009	507	21
	Burlington	8,389	31	0	7	16	8	1,169	109	958	102	2
	Camas	16,957	23	0	4	7	12	490	80	394	16	8
	Carnation	1,859	1	0	0	0	1	10	2	8	0	0
	Castle Rock	2,140	12	1	5	3	3	115	32	64	19	0
	Centralia	15,669	78	0	9	13	56	979	168	707	104	10
	Chehalis	7,329	33	0	9	4	20	549	59	463	27	3
	Cheney	10,534	18	0	3	4	11	289	54	225	10	1
	Chewelah	2,324	14	0	1	0	13	113	15	95	3	0
	Clarkston	7,430	12	0	1	0	11	362	33	304	25	0
	Cle Elum	1,827	2	0	0	0	2	195	37	135	23	0
	Clyde Hill	2,994	3	0	0	0	3	47	12	33	2	0
	Colfax	2,828	7	0	0	0	7	30	5	21	4	1
	College Place	9,099	4	0	3	0	1	135	8	124	3	0
	Colton	372	0	0	0	0	0	0	0	0	0	0
	Colville	5,115	6	0	2	3	1	171	24	142	5	0
	Connell	3,031	4	0	1	1	2	49	12	34	3	0
	Cosmopolis	1,674	6	0	0	0	6	37	6	30	1	0
	Coulee City	648	0	0	0	0	0	16	4	11	1	1
	Coulee Dam	1,099	4	0	0	0	4	19	1	16	2	0
	Coupeville	1,844	0	0	0	0	0	87	20	60	7	0
	Covington	16,895	35	0	9	15	11	525	136	315	74	8
	Des Moines	29,261	97	0	11	42	44	1,211	234	607	370	4
	Dupont	5,466	6	0	1	0	5	75	11	59	5	2
	Duvall	5,808	0	0	0	0	0	38	11	22	5	0
	East Wenatchee	8,971	36	0	4	10	22	751	111	617	23	3
	Eatonville	2,368	6	0	1	0	5	65	21	35	9	0
	Edgewood	9,885	6	0	1	1	4	239	94	124	21	1
	Edmonds	40,623	58	0	4	24	30	1,339	226	864	249	16
	Ellensburg	17,205	29	0	11	8	10	1,032	198	791	43	0
	Elma	3,218	5	0	2	1	2	275	55	192	28	0
	Enumclaw	11,083	5	0	4	0	1	326	50	219	57	14
	Ephrata	7,301	18	0	7	3	8	504	119	367	18	3
	Everett	98,264	602	3	43	240	316	9,063	1,352	5,468	2,243	12
	Everson	2,103	4	0	3	0	1	93	22	63	8	0
	Federal Way	84,516	331	1	64	146	120	5,182	753	3,230	1,199	26
	Ferndale	10,148	21	0	1	5	15	569	111	426	32	6
	Fife	5,663	34	0	4	13	17	745	117	478	150	0
	Fircrest	6,191	11	0	0	3	8	183	40	124	19	1
	Forks	3,247	13	0	6	1	6	200	49	148	3	0
	Gig Harbor	6,734	17	0	1	4	12	484	70	378	36	1
	Goldendale	3,777	5	0	0	0	5	179	34	130	15	1
	Grand Coulee	941	8	0	4	1	3	106	56	48	2	0
	Grandview	9,061	15	0	4	3	8	584	117	393	74	1
	Granger	2,885	10	0	3	0	7	163	53	96	14	1
	Granite Falls	2,912	6	0	0	0	6	145	32	88	25	3
	Hoquiam	9,185	14	2	5	2	5	502	111	346	45	0
	Ilwaco	998	2	0	1	0	1	40	17	20	3	0
	Issaquah	17,352	8	0	0	3	5	907	137	652	118	4
	Kalama	1,971	1	0	0	0	1	95	30	62	3	6
	Kelso	12,058	63	1	13	20	29	1,123	213	795	115	8
	Kenmore	19,900	33	0	6	14	13	580	176	334	70	12
	Kennewick	62,045	296	2	28	33	233	2,651	484	1,993	174	30
	Kent	83,206	563	2	83	224	254	6,252	1,223	3,466	1,563	39
	Kettle Falls	1,615	2	0	0	2	0	59	10	47	2	0
	Kirkland	46,601	91	6	18	33	34	1,846	316	1,288	242	29
	La Center	1,905	4	0	1	0	3	20	3	14	3	0
	Lacey	33,941	90	1	8	27	54	1,609	240	1,230	139	3
	Lake Forest Park	12,690	8	0	0	6	2	330	73	218	39	1

[1] The FBI does not publish arson data unless it receives data from either the agency or the state for all 12 months of the calendar year.

Table 8. Offenses Known to Law Enforcement, by State and City, 2006 (*Contd.*)

(Number.)

State	City	Popula-tion	Violent crime	Murder and non-negligent man-slaughter	Forcible rape	Robbery	Aggra-vated assault	Property crime	Burglary	Larceny-theft	Motor vehicle theft	Arson[1]
	Lake Stevens	7,688	18	0	4	3	11	381	80	259	42	1
	Lakewood	58,662	512	7	54	147	304	3,730	785	2,409	536	15
	Langley	1,035	1	0	1	0	0	49	14	34	1	0
	Liberty Lake	5,709	5	0	0	1	4	101	27	59	15	0
	Long Beach	1,410	5	1	0	1	3	91	21	66	4	0
	Longview	36,758	146	3	40	39	64	2,906	593	2,045	268	22
	Lynden	10,881	11	0	0	0	11	229	27	196	6	0
	Lynnwood	34,080	99	0	5	60	34	3,040	302	2,116	622	12
	Mabton	2,073	0	0	0	0	0	46	21	11	14	1
	Malden	204	3	0	1	0	2	7	5	1	1	0
	Maple Valley	15,413	25	1	4	2	18	334	85	200	49	8
	Marysville	30,403	75	1	13	20	41	1,328	238	752	338	13
	McCleary	1,500	3	0	0	0	3	34	14	17	3	0
	Medical Lake	4,262	3	0	1	0	2	79	25	54	0	0
	Medina	3,084	1	0	0	0	1	85	9	71	5	0
	Mercer Island	23,255	21	0	5	2	14	452	75	345	32	14
	Mill Creek	13,733	26	0	5	3	18	853	167	556	130	2
	Milton	6,579	31	0	7	9	15	308	61	203	44	1
	Monroe	15,922	51	1	13	7	30	605	83	432	90	9
	Montesano	3,457	2	0	0	0	2	124	23	92	9	1
	Morton	1,102	1	0	1	0	0	68	4	61	3	0
	Moses Lake	17,082	69	2	12	21	34	1,713	297	1,290	126	7
	Mountlake Terrace	20,599	40	0	5	18	17	922	157	542	223	13
	Mount Vernon	29,774	76	0	19	24	33	2,154	265	1,709	180	23
	Moxee	1,435	1	0	1	0	0	31	8	19	4	0
	Mukilteo	20,198	22	0	2	13	7	845	191	493	161	10
	Newcastle	9,447	6	0	2	1	3	302	56	190	56	2
	Normandy Park	6,284	1	0	0	0	1	131	28	87	16	0
	North Bend	4,668	15	0	2	2	11	186	45	118	23	3
	North Bonneville	728	4	0	1	0	3	23	3	19	1	0
	Oakesdale	402	1	0	0	0	1	5	2	3	0	1
	Oak Harbor	22,711	35	0	15	2	18	594	144	426	24	7
	Ocean Shores	4,544	6	0	1	2	3	216	61	146	9	0
	Odessa	958	2	0	2	0	0	23	5	18	0	0
	Olympia	44,872	149	0	28	38	83	2,149	282	1,661	206	9
	Omak	4,837	16	0	0	2	14	248	34	205	9	0
	Oroville	1,626	4	0	1	0	3	80	8	68	4	1
	Orting	4,871	4	0	1	2	1	62	7	49	6	0
	Othello	6,328	16	1	4	0	11	467	78	362	27	2
	Pacific	5,820	12	0	1	2	9	189	52	107	30	4
	Pasco	47,293	159	3	19	34	103	1,781	388	1,199	194	15
	Pe Ell	692	1	0	0	0	1	5	3	2	0	0
	Port Angeles	19,252	80	1	20	11	48	1,059	174	804	81	16
	Port Orchard	8,123	70	0	17	3	50	393	81	260	52	9
	Port Townsend	9,156	19	0	1	5	13	512	125	375	12	1
	Poulsbo	7,723	27	0	14	1	12	310	45	243	22	0
	Prosser	5,228	5	0	1	0	4	205	37	151	17	0
	Pullman	25,696	32	0	9	3	20	495	96	384	15	3
	Puyallup	36,477	102	1	14	41	46	2,938	389	2,053	496	15
	Quincy	5,664	28	0	1	10	17	427	126	265	36	0
	Rainier	1,677	1	0	0	0	1	43	13	29	1	0
	Raymond	3,046	10	0	0	1	9	60	30	28	2	1
	Reardan	620	0	0	0	0	0	26	5	19	2	0
	Redmond	48,397	64	0	12	20	32	1,738	208	1,332	198	6
	Renton	56,776	259	2	26	128	103	4,412	690	2,739	983	18
	Republic	1,005	1	0	0	0	1	12	1	10	1	0
	Richland	45,078	100	0	10	14	76	1,438	282	1,069	87	5
	Ridgefield	2,918	1	0	1	0	0	127	37	73	17	0
	Ritzville	1,751	1	0	0	0	1	68	10	58	0	0
	Rosalia	610	0	0	0	0	0	5	4	1	0	0
	Roy	695	1	0	0	0	1	4	4	0	0	1
	Ruston	759	2	0	0	2	0	16	4	9	3	0
	Sammamish	34,954	11	0	5	1	5	457	99	329	29	15
	SeaTac	25,512	139	4	23	57	55	2,032	384	1,084	564	8
	Seattle	583,772	4,152	30	129	1,667	2,326	39,532	7,505	23,880	8,147	235

[1] The FBI does not publish arson data unless it receives data from either the agency or the state for all 12 months of the calendar year.

Table 8. Offenses Known to Law Enforcement, by State and City, 2006 *(Contd.)*

(Number.)

State	City	Popula-tion	Violent crime	Murder and non-negligent man-slaughter	Forcible rape	Robbery	Aggra-vated assault	Property crime	Burglary	Larceny-theft	Motor vehicle theft	Arson[1]
	Sedro Woolley	10,218	28	0	9	9	10	718	125	533	60	3
	Selah	6,993	2	0	0	2	0	366	53	265	48	0
	Sequim	5,251	11	0	0	2	9	277	29	238	10	4
	Shelton	9,221	56	0	15	16	25	979	175	694	110	3
	Shoreline	52,918	135	0	21	60	54	2,048	381	1,226	441	27
	Snohomish	8,870	17	0	2	8	7	484	81	349	54	5
	Snoqualmie	6,187	7	0	1	1	5	143	26	97	20	1
	Soap Lake	1,876	1	0	0	0	1	92	28	59	5	0
	South Bend	1,862	0	0	0	0	0	31	11	15	5	0
	Spokane	200,200	1,197	10	91	392	704	11,804	2,165	7,340	2,299	66
	Spokane Valley	82,778	296	1	18	56	221	3,527	581	2,268	678	41
	Stanwood	5,155	7	0	1	3	3	269	30	216	23	2
	Steilacoom	6,246	10	0	0	4	6	122	22	87	13	3
	Sultan	4,011	7	0	2	1	4	185	49	121	15	4
	Sumas	1,087	2	0	0	0	2	50	14	33	3	0
	Sumner	9,458	38	1	2	8	27	504	116	329	59	5
	Sunnyside	14,674	35	1	4	6	24	1,077	204	713	160	5
	Tacoma	199,264	2,076	21	142	680	1,233	16,540	3,276	9,663	3,601	123
	Tenino	1,611	1	0	1	0	0	82	20	58	4	0
	Tieton	1,191	0	0	0	0	0	9	1	6	2	0
	Toledo	688	1	0	0	0	1	27	16	7	4	0
	Tonasket	987	1	0	0	0	1	117	10	106	1	0
	Toppenish	9,365	60	3	5	19	33	831	206	515	110	6
	Tukwila	17,261	178	1	18	91	68	3,212	312	2,270	630	10
	Tumwater	13,560	36	0	4	7	25	511	119	328	64	0
	Union Gap	5,805	20	0	8	6	6	872	117	681	74	0
	University Place	30,948	104	0	16	27	61	1,174	277	737	160	9
	Vader	623	0	0	0	0	0	16	2	13	1	0
	Vancouver	160,199	598	4	103	139	352	6,527	1,001	4,584	942	54
	Walla Walla	31,521	132	1	35	13	83	1,405	201	1,149	55	7
	Wapato	4,698	42	0	9	11	22	443	118	230	95	4
	Warden	2,680	4	0	2	0	2	139	25	104	10	0
	Washougal	10,916	15	0	0	2	13	348	80	247	21	1
	Wenatchee	29,879	95	0	14	22	59	1,550	224	1,255	71	4
	Westport	2,443	7	0	2	1	4	89	14	72	3	0
	West Richland	10,077	9	0	2	2	5	177	39	132	6	3
	White Salmon	2,319	4	0	1	1	2	55	8	41	6	0
	Wilbur	916	0	0	0	0	0	9	2	6	1	0
	Winthrop	365	0	0	0	0	0	12	1	11	0	0
	Woodinville	10,059	23	0	4	6	13	633	125	423	85	9
	Woodland	4,411	21	0	3	2	16	197	48	133	16	2
	Woodway	1,279	0	0	0	0	0	24	10	13	1	0
	Yakima	82,609	449	3	62	158	226	7,159	1,469	4,687	1,003	51
	Yarrow Point	1,040	0	0	0	0	0	16	4	10	2	0
	Yelm	4,621	22	0	2	6	14	283	76	188	19	0
	Zillah	2,644	9	0	4	0	5	203	56	137	10	2
WEST VIRGINIA	Anawalt	247	0	0	0	0	0	0	0	0	0	0
	Barboursville	3,188	9	0	0	1	8	378	20	353	5	1
	Beckley	16,951	167	0	4	40	123	1,186	167	947	72	7
	Bluefield	11,129	45	0	4	11	30	369	111	223	35	11
	Bramwell	412	0	0	0	0	0	0	0	0	0	0
	Bridgeport	7,493	7	1	2	0	4	239	28	202	9	1
	Buckhannon	5,692	15	0	1	1	13	106	29	70	7	1
	Cameron	1,143	1	0	0	0	1	9	3	6	0	0
	Ceredo	1,632	5	0	2	0	3	58	10	47	1	0
	Charleston	51,221	508	2	19	112	375	3,559	729	2,603	227	14
	Charles Town	3,707	6	0	1	0	5	92	13	74	5	0
	Clarksburg	16,454	67	2	8	14	43	727	159	518	50	11
	Clearview	564	0	0	0	0	0	0	0	0	0	0
	Dunbar	7,747	29	3	4	6	16	293	168	99	26	4
	Elkins	7,115	29	0	1	2	26	221	52	159	10	1
	Fairmont	19,066	51	1	6	10	34	400	111	255	34	8
	Follansbee	2,974	1	0	0	0	1	28	10	17	1	2
	Fort Gay	819	8	0	0	0	8	3	2	1	0	0

[1] The FBI does not publish arson data unless it receives data from either the agency or the state for all 12 months of the calendar year.

Table 8. Offenses Known to Law Enforcement, by State and City, 2006 *(Contd.)*

(Number.)

State	City	Popula-tion	Violent crime	Murder and non-negligent man-slaughter	Forcible rape	Robbery	Aggra-vated assault	Property crime	Burglary	Larceny-theft	Motor vehicle theft	Arson[1]
	Gauley Bridge	707	0	0	0	0	0	13	5	8	0	0
	Glen Dale	1,476	4	0	0	2	2	50	15	34	1	1
	Glenville	1,483	1	0	0	0	1	11	4	6	1	0
	Henderson	315	0	0	0	0	0	0	0	0	0	0
	Hinton	2,698	12	1	0	1	10	53	19	34	0	0
	Hundred	335	0	0	0	0	0	0	0	0	0	0
	Huntington	49,242	349	0	45	180	124	3,834	1,208	2,321	305	9
	Hurricane	5,973	4	0	0	2	2	189	18	151	20	0
	Kenova	3,394	5	0	0	0	5	164	34	117	13	0
	Kermit	227	0	0	0	0	0	0	0	0	0	0
	Keyser	5,415	15	0	5	6	4	193	43	144	6	0
	Lewisburg	3,598	1	0	1	0	0	42	2	37	3	0
	Logan	1,548	28	0	0	10	18	271	64	201	6	2
	Man	717	0	0	0	0	0	1	0	1	0	0
	Marlinton	1,248	0	0	0	0	0	9	4	5	0	0
	Martinsburg	16,010	117	0	4	40	73	893	116	728	49	4
	Matoaka	306	0	0	0	0	0	0	0	0	0	0
	McMechen	1,833	0	0	0	0	0	22	6	13	3	0
	Milton	2,264	8	2	0	3	3	71	19	48	4	0
	Montgomery	2,032	2	0	0	1	1	49	17	31	1	0
	Moorefield	2,410	4	0	0	0	4	52	14	35	3	0
	Morgantown	28,317	113	1	26	29	57	1,013	233	739	41	3
	Moundsville	9,575	19	0	5	2	12	207	51	140	16	4
	New Martinsville	5,796	3	0	0	0	3	81	16	60	5	0
	Nitro	6,756	13	0	0	2	11	262	72	172	18	3
	Paden City	2,739	0	0	0	0	0	7	0	5	2	0
	Parkersburg	32,048	93	2	16	27	48	1,719	392	1,203	124	28
	Philippi	2,829	10	0	1	0	9	51	11	34	6	2
	Piedmont	944	0	0	0	0	0	0	0	0	0	0
	Point Pleasant	4,485	21	0	0	4	17	196	40	149	7	0
	Princeton	6,228	95	2	2	7	84	488	88	372	28	5
	Ranson	3,796	11	0	0	4	7	64	8	42	14	0
	Ravenswood	3,995	4	0	0	0	4	17	1	14	2	0
	Ripley	3,269	4	0	0	0	4	79	10	63	6	1
	Rivesville	914	0	0	0	0	0	12	2	9	1	0
	Romney	1,977	3	0	0	0	3	18	3	15	0	1
	Ronceverte	1,545	3	0	0	2	1	32	4	26	2	1
	Shinnston	2,242	4	0	0	1	3	58	3	54	1	0
	Sophia	1,261	1	0	0	0	1	41	10	27	4	1
	South Charleston	12,711	69	0	3	12	54	609	97	475	37	4
	Spencer	2,260	3	0	0	0	3	86	8	75	3	0
	St. Albans	11,115	21	0	0	5	16	367	83	234	50	4
	Star City	1,370	4	0	0	0	4	27	6	20	1	0
	Summersville	3,372	2	0	0	0	2	58	5	49	4	0
	Triadelphia	797	0	0	0	0	0	0	0	0	0	0
	Welch	2,373	12	0	0	2	10	137	29	107	1	1
	West Milford	647	0	0	0	0	0	0	0	0	0	0
	Weston	4,245	3	1	0	1	1	9	1	7	1	0
	Westover	3,929	16	0	0	5	11	77	21	51	5	1
	Wheeling	29,665	118	1	18	26	73	985	245	652	88	8
	White Sulphur Springs	2,354	2	0	0	0	2	5	0	4	1	0
	Williamson	3,184	11	0	0	0	11	40	8	27	5	1
	Williamstown	2,958	1	0	0	1	0	55	2	48	5	0
WISCONSIN	Albany	1,137	2	0	1	0	1	17	2	14	1	0
	Altoona	6,472	5	0	2	1	2	150	23	123	4	0
	Amery	2,879	9	0	0	0	9	83	11	69	3	0
	Antigo	8,312	6	0	0	0	6	576	76	470	30	0
	Appleton	70,475	188	1	26	26	135	2,135	381	1,690	64	16
	Arcadia	2,357	3	0	0	1	2	73	10	58	5	0
	Ashland	8,336	33	0	6	2	25	432	58	358	16	0
	Ashwaubenon	16,973	13	0	5	4	4	927	81	819	27	0
	Baraboo	10,967	34	0	0	3	31	508	44	454	10	0
	Barron	3,163	7	0	1	2	4	45	9	33	3	0
	Bayfield	604	5	0	0	0	5	19	1	16	2	0
	Bayside	4,230	2	0	0	2	0	29	11	17	1	0

[1] The FBI does not publish arson data unless it receives data from either the agency or the state for all 12 months of the calendar year.

Table 8. Offenses Known to Law Enforcement, by State and City, 2006 *(Contd.)*

(Number.)

State	City	Popula-tion	Violent crime	Murder and non-negligent man-slaughter	Forcible rape	Robbery	Aggra-vated assault	Property crime	Burglary	Larceny-theft	Motor vehicle theft	Arson[1]
	Beaver Dam	15,209	5	0	1	0	4	543	74	464	5	0
	Belleville	2,122	1	0	0	0	1	45	4	39	2	0
	Beloit	35,752	185	2	17	79	87	1,898	344	1,442	112	0
	Beloit Town	7,429	4	0	0	3	1	156	47	105	4	2
	Berlin	5,232	5	0	1	0	4	152	16	134	2	0
	Black River Falls	3,498	7	0	3	0	4	169	14	152	3	0
	Blair	1,266	4	0	2	0	2	40	12	27	1	0
	Bloomer	3,292	0	0	0	0	0	82	11	66	5	0
	Boscobel	3,385	3	0	0	0	3	84	8	76	0	0
	Brillion	2,921	3	0	1	1	1	20	0	19	1	0
	Brodhead	3,079	6	0	3	0	3	45	6	37	2	0
	Brookfield	39,801	8	0	0	6	2	1,134	126	983	25	7
	Brookfield Township	6,315	2	0	0	2	0	166	14	147	5	1
	Brown Deer	11,654	18	0	0	12	6	465	55	369	41	0
	Burlington	11,189	7	0	2	2	3	273	15	240	18	1
	Burlington Town	6,720	8	0	0	1	7	67	6	58	3	1
	Butler	1,829	2	0	0	2	0	61	6	42	13	0
	Caledonia	24,516	5	1	1	2	1	314	56	231	27	0
	Campbellsport	1,937	0	0	0	0	0	30	1	29	0	0
	Cedarburg	11,339	5	0	0	3	2	126	13	112	1	1
	Chenequa	596	0	0	0	0	0	2	0	2	0	0
	Chetek	2,158	5	0	0	0	5	38	8	28	2	0
	Chilton	3,630	1	0	0	0	1	55	8	44	3	0
	Chippewa Falls	13,423	29	0	3	4	22	265	30	222	13	0
	Cleveland	1,406	0	0	0	0	0	5	1	3	1	0
	Clinton	3,135	0	0	0	0	0	60	6	53	1	0
	Clintonville	4,415	5	0	1	2	2	229	16	203	10	0
	Colby-Abbotsford	3,578	4	0	0	0	4	38	7	27	4	0
	Columbus	5,120	2	0	0	0	2	101	14	86	1	0
	Combined Locks	3,011	1	0	0	0	1	10	0	10	0	0
	Cornell	1,397	3	0	0	0	3	35	5	30	0	0
	Cottage Grove	5,290	12	0	2	5	5	129	25	98	6	0
	Crandon	1,874	3	0	0	0	3	68	12	54	2	1
	Cross Plains	3,431	2	0	0	0	2	38	6	31	1	0
	Cuba City	2,112	1	0	0	0	1	39	7	29	3	1
	Cudahy	18,383	38	0	5	13	20	642	123	487	32	13
	Cumberland	2,250	0	0	0	0	0	43	5	35	3	0
	Dane	899	0	0	0	0	0	2	1	1	0	0
	Darien	1,641	1	0	1	0	0	50	13	35	2	0
	Darlington	2,350	5	0	0	0	5	34	4	29	1	0
	Deerfield	2,210	0	0	0	0	0	21	6	12	3	0
	Deforest	8,469	10	0	0	1	9	205	25	173	7	0
	Delafield	6,792	1	0	0	0	1	147	10	132	5	0
	Delavan	8,401	16	0	1	3	12	259	32	210	17	0
	Delavan Town	4,587	5	0	4	0	1	171	68	92	11	0
	Denmark	1,997	0	0	0	0	0	15	4	9	2	0
	De Pere	23,461	6	0	1	0	5	370	62	301	7	2
	Dodgeville	4,858	3	0	1	0	2	108	6	98	4	0
	Durand	1,905	3	0	2	0	1	10	3	5	2	0
	Eagle River	1,614	2	0	1	0	1	87	2	81	4	1
	East Troy	4,239	4	0	0	1	3	225	17	204	4	2
	Eau Claire	62,799	100	0	8	13	79	2,191	390	1,707	94	7
	Edgar	1,332	0	0	0	0	0	34	15	19	0	0
	Edgerton	5,121	1	0	0	0	1	88	7	78	3	0
	Eleva	657	0	0	0	0	0	9	2	7	0	0
	Elkhart Lake	1,072	0	0	0	0	0	33	2	30	1	0
	Elkhorn	9,054	3	0	0	0	3	283	31	246	6	1
	Elk Mound	818	7	0	4	0	3	5	0	5	0	0
	Ellsworth	3,071	5	0	0	0	5	56	10	40	6	0
	Elm Grove	6,205	5	0	1	3	1	138	32	100	6	0
	Elroy	1,533	1	0	0	0	1	41	12	26	3	0
	Evansville	4,675	1	0	0	0	1	104	14	87	3	0
	Everest	15,136	18	1	0	1	16	318	59	244	15	0
	Fennimore	2,366	1	0	1	0	0	39	8	29	2	1
	Fitchburg	22,121	59	0	13	19	27	689	61	590	38	2

[1] The FBI does not publish arson data unless it receives data from either the agency or the state for all 12 months of the calendar year.

Table 8. Offenses Known to Law Enforcement, by State and City, 2006 *(Contd.)*

(Number.)

State	City	Population	Violent crime	Murder and non-negligent man-slaughter	Forcible rape	Robbery	Aggra-vated assault	Property crime	Burglary	Larceny-theft	Motor vehicle theft	Arson[1]
	Fond du Lac	42,591	124	0	23	16	85	1,182	162	986	34	2
	Fontana	1,958	2	0	0	0	2	33	3	30	0	0
	Fort Atkinson	11,993	9	0	0	2	7	313	18	293	2	0
	Fox Lake	1,463	0	0	0	0	0	21	4	17	0	0
	Fox Point	6,766	3	0	1	1	1	70	13	57	0	1
	Fox Valley	17,163	4	0	3	0	1	500	54	436	10	2
	Franklin	33,385	43	0	5	9	29	558	121	410	27	0
	Frederic	1,238	0	0	0	0	0	22	8	12	2	0
	Geneva Town	4,196	2	0	0	0	2	119	23	95	1	0
	Genoa City	2,752	2	0	0	0	2	77	22	53	2	0
	Germantown	19,316	8	0	2	4	2	382	29	346	7	1
	Glendale	12,927	31	0	0	23	8	625	58	515	52	0
	Grafton	11,668	3	0	0	1	2	176	15	158	3	1
	Grand Chute	20,350	23	1	8	6	8	919	80	811	28	0
	Grand Rapids	7,608	0	0	0	0	0	57	24	30	3	0
	Grantsburg	1,402	4	0	0	0	4	21	13	7	1	0
	Green Bay	101,574	558	2	50	106	400	2,874	687	1,986	201	31
	Greendale	13,911	11	0	1	3	7	559	20	535	4	1
	Greenfield	35,884	63	0	3	31	29	1,167	151	931	85	5
	Green Lake	1,129	1	0	0	0	1	23	2	21	0	0
	Hales Corners	7,563	11	0	3	2	6	128	21	100	7	0
	Hartford	13,065	13	0	0	4	9	352	79	253	20	9
	Hartland	8,704	2	0	0	0	2	124	21	103	0	0
	Hazel Green	1,209	2	0	0	0	2	2	2	0	0	0
	Hobart-Lawrence	7,872	0	0	0	0	0	65	19	41	5	0
	Horicon	3,617	1	0	0	0	1	80	6	70	4	0
	Hortonville	2,640	3	0	0	0	3	93	11	79	3	0
	Hudson	11,409	12	3	3	1	5	561	55	484	22	0
	Hurley	1,684	11	0	0	1	10	73	5	52	16	0
	Independence	1,251	1	0	0	0	1	16	2	10	4	0
	Iron Ridge	991	0	0	0	0	0	14	1	12	1	0
	Jackson	6,058	8	0	3	1	4	60	9	47	4	0
	Janesville	62,189	134	0	43	42	49	2,974	555	2,315	104	13
	Jefferson	7,620	26	0	0	2	24	212	10	183	19	0
	Juneau	2,596	1	0	0	0	1	59	10	48	1	0
	Kaukauna	14,710	7	0	1	0	6	318	21	288	9	1
	Kenosha	95,589	347	4	52	152	139	2,909	626	2,084	199	11
	Kewaskum	3,620	5	1	0	0	4	40	8	31	1	1
	Kiel	3,520	6	0	1	2	3	117	14	101	2	0
	Kohler	1,998	0	0	0	0	0	55	1	54	0	0
	La Crosse	50,471	172	0	27	25	120	1,938	270	1,585	83	6
	Ladysmith	3,803	2	0	0	0	2	143	13	129	1	0
	Lake Delton	3,064	16	0	3	2	11	480	35	439	6	0
	Lake Geneva	8,253	18	0	5	2	11	365	24	330	11	0
	Lake Hallie	4,495	5	0	2	0	3	189	28	156	5	1
	Lake Mills	5,260	3	0	2	0	1	76	10	63	3	0
	Lancaster	3,992	1	0	0	0	1	65	7	57	1	0
	Lodi	3,041	0	0	0	0	0	122	17	101	4	0
	Madison	222,364	973	4	64	434	471	7,498	1,619	5,404	475	109
	Manitowoc	34,041	178	1	4	7	166	1,156	221	893	42	3
	Maple Bluff	1,302	0	0	0	0	0	27	7	20	0	1
	Marathon City	1,535	8	0	0	0	8	47	3	44	0	0
	Marinette	11,316	8	0	2	3	3	423	55	362	6	2
	Marion	1,246	1	0	1	0	0	10	1	7	2	0
	Markesan	1,354	1	0	0	0	1	42	9	32	1	0
	Marshall Village	3,574	5	0	5	0	0	63	10	51	2	0
	Marshfield	18,865	8	0	3	1	4	508	79	422	7	3
	Mauston	4,307	43	0	4	1	38	152	16	131	5	1
	Mayville	5,074	1	0	0	0	1	17	3	13	1	0
	McFarland	7,410	11	0	2	0	9	181	22	152	7	0
	Medford	4,204	4	0	2	0	2	145	14	129	2	0
	Menasha	16,366	39	0	4	2	33	421	70	333	18	1
	Menomonee Falls	34,250	24	0	3	10	11	698	85	560	53	0
	Menomonie	15,300	20	0	6	2	12	449	100	330	19	3
	Mequon	23,907	5	1	0	1	3	228	58	167	3	0

[1] The FBI does not publish arson data unless it receives data from either the agency or the state for all 12 months of the calendar year.

Table 8. Offenses Known to Law Enforcement, by State and City, 2006 *(Contd.)*

(Number.)

State	City	Popula-tion	Violent crime	Murder and non-negligent man-slaughter	Forcible rape	Robbery	Aggra-vated assault	Property crime	Burglary	Larceny-theft	Motor vehicle theft	Arson[1]
	Merrill	10,182	10	0	5	1	4	411	45	354	12	0
	Middleton	15,874	24	0	3	11	10	451	63	370	18	0
	Milton	5,484	3	2	0	0	1	76	16	56	4	0
	Milwaukee	581,005	7,698	103	112	3,608	3,875	38,233	5,651	24,343	8,239	320
	Mineral Point	2,504	1	0	0	0	1	33	5	28	0	0
	Minocqua	4,891	9	0	2	1	6	185	18	160	7	0
	Mishicot	1,418	0	0	0	0	0	11	1	10	0	0
	Mondovi	2,628	0	0	0	0	0	27	8	18	1	0
	Monona	7,744	23	0	0	17	6	302	32	258	12	0
	Monroe	10,602	5	0	1	0	4	237	32	196	9	6
	Mosinee	4,011	2	0	0	1	1	113	30	83	0	0
	Mount Horeb	6,211	3	0	1	0	2	153	33	116	4	2
	Mount Pleasant	26,094	22	0	2	9	11	808	104	678	26	2
	Mukwonago	6,882	4	1	1	1	1	133	16	114	3	0
	Muskego	22,956	2	0	0	1	1	211	42	159	10	5
	Neenah	24,686	35	0	6	1	28	486	93	377	16	6
	Neillsville	2,704	0	0	0	0	0	79	11	68	0	0
	New Glarus	2,066	0	0	0	0	0	64	9	54	1	0
	New Holstein	3,212	5	0	1	1	3	57	4	50	3	0
	New Lisbon	2,473	2	0	0	0	2	21	2	19	0	0
	New London	6,951	4	0	1	0	3	165	24	135	6	0
	New Richmond	7,754	2	0	0	0	2	205	20	178	7	1
	Niagara	1,812	3	0	0	0	3	23	5	18	0	0
	North Hudson	3,761	0	0	0	0	0	23	1	21	1	0
	Oak Creek	32,431	28	2	8	11	7	999	108	855	36	6
	Oconomowoc	13,761	17	1	7	2	7	181	33	147	1	1
	Oconomowoc Town	8,038	4	0	1	1	2	62	22	39	1	0
	Oconto	4,581	39	0	3	1	35	216	25	185	6	0
	Oconto Falls	2,739	0	0	0	0	0	96	7	83	6	1
	Omro	3,294	6	0	0	0	6	9	6	0	3	0
	Onalaska	15,759	17	0	1	2	14	450	53	394	3	1
	Oregon	8,524	8	0	1	1	6	220	34	183	3	0
	Osceola	2,695	13	0	0	0	13	69	9	60	0	0
	Oshkosh	63,718	197	4	8	14	171	2,143	313	1,748	82	21
	Osseo	1,667	1	0	0	0	1	55	4	46	5	0
	Palmyra	1,769	4	0	3	0	1	64	6	54	4	0
	Park Falls	2,473	0	0	0	0	0	42	3	38	1	0
	Pepin	928	1	0	0	0	1	13	3	9	1	0
	Peshtigo	3,358	2	0	0	0	2	69	18	47	4	0
	Pewaukee	12,816	14	0	1	4	9	164	24	132	8	1
	Pewaukee Village	8,951	5	0	2	1	2	187	21	158	8	2
	Platteville	9,890	7	0	0	0	7	118	14	103	1	0
	Pleasant Prairie	18,619	12	0	2	4	6	275	33	231	11	1
	Plover	11,297	14	0	3	1	10	301	57	235	9	2
	Plymouth	8,247	6	0	3	1	2	222	15	205	2	0
	Portage	10,072	16	0	1	1	14	390	30	355	5	0
	Port Washington	10,932	3	0	2	0	1	220	25	189	6	0
	Poynette	2,572	1	0	0	0	1	42	6	35	1	0
	Prescott	4,024	3	0	2	0	1	152	16	135	1	0
	Princeton	1,468	0	0	0	0	0	29	3	18	8	0
	Pulaski	3,553	5	0	0	0	5	42	9	32	1	0
	Racine	79,683	475	7	16	245	207	4,594	1,113	3,116	365	19
	Reedsburg	8,528	8	0	4	1	3	208	9	194	5	1
	Rice Lake	8,392	20	3	2	0	15	311	39	266	6	2
	Richland Center	5,196	5	0	2	2	1	86	14	71	1	0
	Ripon	7,295	13	1	4	0	8	200	34	160	6	0
	River Falls	13,303	18	0	3	2	13	428	73	337	18	1
	River Hills	1,636	0	0	0	0	0	14	3	11	0	0
	Rome Town	2,866	1	0	0	0	1	73	12	60	1	0
	Rothschild	5,115	1	0	0	0	1	131	1	127	3	0
	Sauk Prairie	4,138	1	0	1	0	0	339	19	313	7	1
	Saukville	4,199	7	0	0	2	5	145	18	125	2	0
	Shawano	8,472	28	0	8	1	19	514	47	446	21	0
	Sheboygan	49,051	79	1	29	11	38	2,381	320	1,973	88	18
	Sheboygan Falls	7,555	4	0	4	0	0	85	10	73	2	4

[1] The FBI does not publish arson data unless it receives data from either the agency or the state for all 12 months of the calendar year.

Table 8. Offenses Known to Law Enforcement, by State and City, 2006 *(Contd.)*

(Number.)

State	City	Popula-tion	Violent crime	Murder and non-negligent man-slaughter	Forcible rape	Robbery	Aggra-vated assault	Property crime	Burglary	Larceny-theft	Motor vehicle theft	Arson[1]
	Shorewood	13,240	20	0	1	17	2	365	48	300	17	1
	Shorewood Hills	1,677	1	0	0	1	0	44	2	41	1	0
	Silver Lake	2,522	5	0	0	0	5	31	8	22	1	0
	Siren	1,019	7	0	0	1	6	39	6	30	3	0
	Slinger	4,374	1	0	0	0	1	113	17	92	4	0
	South Milwaukee	20,925	51	0	5	11	35	582	98	447	37	2
	Sparta	8,859	17	0	7	3	7	348	42	295	11	0
	Spencer	1,840	1	1	0	0	0	22	1	21	0	0
	Spooner	2,680	2	0	0	1	1	93	12	80	1	0
	Spring Green	1,441	0	0	0	0	0	35	5	30	0	0
	Stanley	3,316	8	0	1	0	7	73	17	55	1	0
	St. Croix Falls	2,140	0	0	0	0	0	57	1	56	0	0
	Stevens Point	24,387	75	0	9	5	61	830	149	656	25	1
	St. Francis	9,416	7	0	1	6	0	271	44	206	21	0
	Stoughton	12,692	13	0	0	6	7	299	39	258	2	0
	Strum	975	0	0	0	0	0	10	3	6	1	0
	Sturgeon Bay	9,214	9	0	1	0	8	177	18	156	3	1
	Sturtevant	6,213	3	0	0	3	0	122	26	91	5	0
	Summit	5,126	2	0	1	0	1	28	1	23	4	0
	Sun Prairie	25,485	31	0	6	5	20	434	39	374	21	0
	Superior	26,877	71	1	7	22	41	1,438	237	1,125	76	4
	Theresa	1,270	2	0	0	0	2	26	2	24	0	0
	Thiensville	3,134	4	0	0	0	4	23	3	20	0	0
	Tomah	8,652	17	0	1	3	13	506	41	445	20	0
	Tomahawk	3,843	13	0	0	0	13	122	32	83	7	0
	Town of East Troy	3,918	4	0	0	0	4	37	4	33	0	0
	Town of Madison	6,259	55	0	8	18	29	354	49	268	37	1
	Town of Menasha	15,659	18	0	4	3	11	220	51	154	15	0
	Trempealeau	1,464	0	0	0	0	0	2	1	0	1	0
	Twin Lakes	5,533	5	0	2	0	3	122	19	96	7	0
	Two Rivers	12,189	7	0	2	2	3	291	52	228	11	0
	Valders	999	0	0	0	0	0	1	1	0	0	0
	Verona	10,203	11	0	1	1	9	228	31	193	4	0
	Viroqua	4,440	4	0	1	0	3	80	5	75	0	0
	Walworth	2,692	6	0	1	0	5	48	7	41	0	0
	Washburn	2,289	0	0	0	0	0	67	4	62	1	0
	Waterloo	3,294	2	0	0	0	2	43	8	35	0	0
	Watertown	22,900	73	0	11	5	57	681	124	539	18	11
	Waukesha	67,906	112	1	23	28	60	1,417	309	1,029	79	8
	Waunakee	10,398	4	0	1	1	2	134	30	100	4	0
	Waupaca	5,899	12	0	2	1	9	275	26	247	2	0
	Wausau	37,429	109	1	12	21	75	1,323	237	1,030	56	12
	Wautoma	2,111	1	0	0	0	1	94	12	81	1	0
	Wauwatosa	45,179	131	1	6	87	37	1,906	266	1,486	154	0
	West Allis	59,014	242	0	0	106	136	2,682	462	2,005	215	26
	West Bend	29,657	31	0	0	7	24	793	47	733	13	0
	Westby	2,150	1	0	0	0	1	21	13	7	1	0
	West Milwaukee	4,027	20	0	0	10	10	304	45	218	41	0
	West Salem	4,726	5	0	0	0	5	73	4	69	0	3
	Whitefish Bay	13,558	6	0	0	2	4	149	15	131	3	0
	Whitehall	1,634	0	0	0	0	0	41	3	38	0	0
	Whitewater	14,363	25	0	11	0	14	281	46	229	6	1
	Williams Bay	2,678	5	0	2	0	3	49	8	40	1	0
	Winneconne	2,454	4	0	0	0	4	11	6	5	0	0
	Wisconsin Dells	2,568	22	0	4	1	17	304	16	277	11	0
	Wisconsin Rapids	17,686	18	0	5	2	11	868	130	713	25	3
	Woodruff	1,965	2	0	0	0	2	56	7	48	1	0
WYOMING	Afton	1,852	3	0	0	0	3	28	11	17	0	0
	Baggs	358	0	0	0	0	0	11	5	4	2	0
	Basin	1,238	2	0	0	0	2	26	4	21	1	0
	Buffalo	4,338	16	0	0	0	16	103	15	83	5	0
	Casper	52,318	130	0	20	12	98	2,581	441	2,023	117	14
	Cheyenne	56,356	117	2	29	23	63	2,364	266	1,975	123	14
	Cody	9,202	38	0	5	0	33	240	23	209	8	1
	Diamondville	703	1	0	0	0	1	21	11	10	0	0

[1] The FBI does not publish arson data unless it receives data from either the agency or the state for all 12 months of the calendar year.

Table 8. Offenses Known to Law Enforcement, by State and City, 2006 *(Contd.)*

(Number.)

State	City	Popula-tion	Violent crime	Murder and non-negligent man-slaughter	Forcible rape	Robbery	Aggra-vated assault	Property crime	Burglary	Larceny-theft	Motor vehicle theft	Arson[1]
	Douglas	5,644	14	0	0	0	14	159	22	133	4	0
	Evanston	11,587	12	0	4	1	7	414	36	365	13	0
	Evansville	2,354	6	0	1	1	4	108	9	92	7	0
	Gillette	22,939	27	0	4	2	21	1,004	64	893	47	12
	Glenrock	2,377	5	0	1	0	4	36	7	28	1	0
	Green River	11,919	75	0	2	0	73	386	64	301	21	1
	Guernsey	1,131	0	0	0	0	0	7	2	5	0	0
	Hanna	873	6	0	0	0	6	2	2	0	0	0
	Jackson	9,139	70	0	18	4	48	336	42	268	26	0
	Kemmerer	2,589	3	0	0	0	3	34	5	29	0	0
	Lander	6,975	16	0	0	0	16	231	27	196	8	3
	Laramie	26,342	30	2	1	1	26	844	126	662	56	2
	Lovell	2,303	4	0	0	0	4	41	2	39	0	0
	Lusk	1,363	1	0	0	0	1	21	1	19	1	0
	Mills	2,930	18	1	0	0	17	81	5	68	8	0
	Moorcroft	854	1	0	0	0	1	3	0	3	0	0
	Newcastle	3,257	5	0	2	0	3	109	31	77	1	1
	Pine Bluffs	1,175	1	0	0	0	1	34	15	18	1	0
	Powell	5,347	12	0	3	0	9	213	24	185	4	3
	Rawlins	8,755	40	0	2	4	34	399	47	332	20	2
	Riverton	9,536	38	0	5	3	30	380	55	303	22	9
	Rock Springs	18,982	136	1	10	5	120	800	146	601	53	12
	Saratoga	1,733	9	0	0	0	9	41	2	38	1	0
	Sheridan	16,516	16	0	1	1	14	482	68	398	16	1
	Sundance	1,197	2	0	0	0	2	40	3	37	0	0
	Thermopolis	2,938	3	0	0	0	3	121	0	119	2	0
	Torrington	5,595	25	0	2	0	23	187	30	150	7	0
	Wheatland	3,503	8	0	2	0	6	122	10	108	4	0
	Worland	5,023	11	0	0	0	11	40	9	30	1	0

[1] The FBI does not publish arson data unless it receives data from either the agency or the state for all 12 months of the calendar year.

Table 9. Offenses Known to Law Enforcement, by State and University and College, 2006

(Number.)

State	University/College	Campus	Student enroll-ment[1]	Violent crime	Murder and non-negligent man-slaughter	Forcible rape	Robbery	Aggra-vated assault
ALABAMA	Auburn University	Montgomery	5,128	0	0	0	0	0
	Jacksonville State University		9,110	0	0	0	0	0
	Troy University		26,880	1	0	0	0	1
	University of Alabama:	Huntsville	7,084	2	0	2	0	0
		Tuscaloosa	21,793	10	0	2	5	3
	University of Montevallo		2,999	1	0	1	0	0
	University of South Alabama		13,122	7	0	3	1	3
ALASKA	University of Alaska:	Anchorage	16,412	13	0	2	5	6
		Fairbanks	8,228	1	0	0	0	1
ARIZONA	Arizona State University	Main Campus	51,612	36	0	6	4	26
	Central Arizona College		6,388	1	0	1	0	0
	Northern Arizona University		18,773	17	0	5	3	9
	Pima Community College		30,884	2	0	1	1	0
	University of Arizona		37,036	24	0	2	9	13
	Yavapai College		7,422	1	0	0	1	0
ARKANSAS	Arkansas State University:	Beebe	3,976	0	0	0	0	0
		Jonesboro	10,414	5	0	1	2	2
	Arkansas Tech University		6,842	0	0	0	0	0
	Northwest Arkansas Community College		5,467	0	0	0	0	0
	Southern Arkansas University		3,109	1	0	0	0	1
	University of Arkansas:	Little Rock	11,896	13	0	0	7	6
		Monticello	2,959	1	0	0	0	1
	University of Central Arkansas		11,375	4	0	1	1	2
CALIFORNIA	Allan Hancock College		12,252	0	0	0	0	0
	California State Polytechnic University:	Pomona	19,885	1	0	0	0	1
		San Luis Obispo	18,475	3	0	2	1	0
	California State University:	Bakersfield	7,549	2	0	2	0	0
		Channel Islands	2,575	2	0	1	0	1
		Chico	15,919	9	0	2	2	5
		Dominguez Hills	12,357	10	0	1	3	6
		East Bay	12,535	2	0	2	0	0
		Fresno	20,371	6	0	0	0	6
		Fullerton	35,040	3	0	2	1	0
		Long Beach	34,547	5	0	1	1	3
		Los Angeles	20,034	6	0	0	5	1
		Monterey Bay	3,773	5	0	0	0	5
		Northridge	33,243	16	0	0	8	8
		Sacramento	27,932	3	0	1	1	1
		San Bernardino	16,431	7	0	0	1	6
		San Jose[3]		9	0	3	4	2
		San Marcos	7,502	2	0	1	0	1
		Stanislaus	8,137	0	0	0	0	0
	College of the Sequoias		10,317	1	0	0	0	1
	Contra Costa Community College		6,670	21	0	1	13	7
	Cuesta College		10,307	0	0	0	0	0
	El Camino College		23,895	5	0	0	3	2
	Foothill-De Anza College		39,817	1	0	0	1	0
	Fresno Community College		21,917	8	0	0	6	2
	Humboldt State University		7,462	3	0	3	0	0
	Kings River Community College[3]			0	0	0	0	0
	Marin Community College		6,447	2	0	1	0	1
	Pasadena Community College		27,199	9	0	1	6	2
	RiversideCommunity College		29,160	8	0	1	4	3
	San Bernardino Community College		12,390	0	0	0	0	0
	San Diego State University		31,802	25	0	7	13	5
	San Francisco State University		28,950	21	0	0	16	5
	San Jose/Evergreen Community College		18,772	4	0	0	2	2
	Santa Rosa Junior College		24,293	3	0	0	0	3
	Solano Community College		11,520	0	0	0	0	0
	Sonoma State University		7,749	1	0	1	0	0
	University of California:	Berkeley	33,547	44	0	6	24	14
		Davis	28,815	8	0	1	5	2

Note: Caution should be exercised in making any intercampus comparisons or ranking schools because university/college crime statistics are affected by a variety of factors. These include demographic characteristics of the surrounding community, ratio of male to female students, number of on-campus residents, accessibility of the campus to outside visitors, size of enrollment, etc.

[1] The student enrollment figures provided by the United States Department of Education are for the 2005 school year, the most recent available. The enrollment figures include full-time and part-time students.

[3] Student enrollment figures were not available.

Table 9. Offenses Known to Law Enforcement, by State and University and College, 2006

(Number.)

State	University/College	Campus	Property crime	Burglary	Larceny-theft	Motor vehicle theft	Arson[2]
ALABAMA	Auburn University	Montgomery	8	0	8	0	
	Jacksonville State University		98	28	70	0	
	Troy University		145	31	113	1	
	University of Alabama:..	Huntsville	106	11	95	0	
		Tuscaloosa	374	87	283	4	
	University of Montevallo...................................		23	0	23	0	
	University of South Alabama............................		176	29	141	6	
ALASKA	University of Alaska:...	Anchorage	109	11	94	4	0
		Fairbanks	182	18	162	2	3
ARIZONA	Arizona State University	Main Campus	1,183	141	966	76	4
	Central Arizona College....................................		32	8	23	1	0
	Northern Arizona University.............................		429	56	364	9	10
	Pima Community College....................................		203	7	177	19	0
	University of Arizona..		1,001	70	862	69	4
	Yavapai College		44	3	41	0	0
ARKANSAS	Arkansas State University:................................	Beebe	5	0	5	0	0
		Jonesboro	182	50	130	2	0
	Arkansas Tech University		82	10	72	0	0
	Northwest Arkansas Community College........		0	0	0	0	0
	Southern Arkansas University...........................		36	16	20	0	0
	University of Arkansas:	Little Rock	200	97	91	12	0
		Monticello	21	1	20	0	0
	University of Central Arkansas		242	104	134	4	1
CALIFORNIA	Allan Hancock College.......................................		30	11	19	0	0
	California State Polytechnic University:...........	Pomona	244	31	166	47	1
		San Luis Obispo	183	8	163	12	1
	California State University:................................	Bakersfield	86	20	62	4	1
		Channel Islands	6	0	6	0	0
		Chico	307	26	278	3	3
		Dominguez Hills	105	20	57	28	0
		East Bay	145	3	131	11	0
		Fresno	353	89	234	30	1
		Fullerton	194	37	129	28	0
		Long Beach	277	16	203	58	0
		Los Angeles	220	11	175	34	0
		Monterey Bay	84	29	48	7	5
		Northridge	312	62	225	25	0
		Sacramento	263	21	218	24	0
		San Bernardino	137	22	100	15	1
		San Jose[3]	352	20	325	7	10
		San Marcos	46	6	39	1	0
		Stanislaus	41	3	35	3	0
	College of the Sequoias......................................		120	60	47	13	0
	Contra Costa Community College		6,670	19	186	22	0
	Cuesta College		10,307	4	27	0	0
	El Camino College		23,895	14	115	15	2
	Foothill-De Anza College		39,817	31	60	2	0
	Fresno Community College................................		21,917	12	182	23	0
	Humboldt State University		7,462	10	128	3	0
	Kings River Community College[3]			1	43	3	0
	Marin Community College.................................		6,447	3	35	2	0
	Pasadena Community College		27,199	6	214	30	0
	RiversideCommunity College............................		29,160	14	104	9	0
	San Bernardino Community College		12,390	8	58	7	0
	San Diego State University		31,802	35	410	118	2
	San Francisco State University		28,950	84	333	27	2
	San Jose/Evergreen Community College		18,772	16	60	0	0
	Santa Rosa Junior College		24,293	10	75	2	1
	Solano Community College...............................		11,520	0	34	2	0
	Sonoma State University		7,749	14	133	4	3
	University of California:	Berkeley	33,547	89	814	22	1
		Davis	28,815	66	644	21	2

Note: Caution should be exercised in making any intercampus comparisons or ranking schools because university/college crime statistics are affected by a variety of factors. These include demographic characteristics of the surrounding community, ratio of male to female students, number of on-campus residents, accessibility of the campus to outside visitors, size of enrollment, etc.

[2] The FBI does not publish arson data unless it receives data from either the agency or the state for all 12 months of the calendar year.

[3] Student enrollment figures were not available.

Table 9. Offenses Known to Law Enforcement, by State and University and College, 2006 (*Contd.*)

(Number.)

State	University/College	Campus	Student enroll-ment[1]	Violent crime	Murder and non-negligent man-slaughter	Forcible rape	Robbery	Aggra-vated assault
		Hastings College of Law	1,286	7	0	0	3	4
		Irvine	24,400	3	0	0	0	3
		Lawrence-Livermore Laboratory[3]		0	0	0	0	0
		Los Angeles	35,625	41	0	4	18	19
		Medical Center, Sacramento[3]		2	0	0	0	2
		Riverside	16,622	12	0	1	5	6
		San Diego	25,320	3	0	0	1	2
		San Francisco	2,863	9	0	0	4	5
		Santa Barbara	21,016	11	0	6	2	3
		Santa Cruz	15,012	6	0	2	2	2
	West Valley-Mission College		17,986	2	0	0	0	2
COLORADO	Adams State College		9,157	2	0	1	0	1
	Arapahoe Community College		7,132	0	0	0	0	0
	Auraria Higher Education Center[3]			5	0	0	1	4
	Colorado School of Mines		4,318	2	0	0	0	2
	Colorado State University:	Fort Collins	27,780	4	0	2	0	2
		Pueblo	5,870	0	0	0	0	0
	Fort Lewis College		3,946	1	0	1	0	0
	Pikes Peak Community College		10,619	2	0	0	0	2
	Red Rocks Community College		6,600	0	0	0	0	0
	University of Colorado:	Boulder	31,589	22	0	4	3	15
		Colorado Springs	9,333	2	0	1	0	1
		Health Sciences Center[3]		0	0	0	0	0
		Health Sciences Center, Fitzsimons Campus[3]		0	0	0	0	0
	University of Northern Colorado		13,622	9	0	6	1	2
CONNECTICUT	Central Connecticut State University		12,315	5	0	0	1	4
	Eastern Connecticut State University		5,113	1	0	0	1	0
	University of Connecticut:	Health Center[3]		3	0	0	0	3
		Storrs, Avery Point, and Hartford[3]		7	0	2	2	3
	Western Connecticut State University		5,907	6	0	1	0	5
	Yale University		11,483	6	0	2	3	1
DELAWARE	Delaware State University		3,722	10	0	0	3	7
	University of Delaware		20,982	14	0	4	5	5
FLORIDA	Florida A&M University		12,154	8	0	0	6	2
	Florida Atlantic University		25,645	13	0	3	1	9
	Florida Gulf Coast University		7,249	2	0	0	1	1
	Florida International University		36,904	9	0	3	0	6
	Florida State University:	Panama City[3]		0	0	0	0	0
		Tallahassee	39,146	33	0	3	12	18
	New College of Florida		762	1	0	1	0	0
	Pensacola Junior College		9,858	0	0	0	0	0
	Santa Fe Community College		13,688	1	0	0	1	0
	Tallahassee Community College		13,029	1	0	0	0	1
	University of Central Florida		44,856	27	0	2	11	14
	University of Florida		49,693	21	0	2	2	17
	University of North Florida		15,234	4	0	0	1	3
	University of South Florida:	St. Petersburg[3]		1	0	1	0	0
		Tampa	42,660	12	1	2	3	6
	University of West Florida		9,632	3	0	2	0	1
GEORGIA	Abraham Baldwin Agricultural College		3,423	3	0	0	0	3
	Albany State University		3,649	0	0	0	0	0
	Armstrong Atlantic State University		6,688	3	0	0	1	2
	Augusta State University		6,312	1	0	0	0	1
	Clark Atlanta University		4,469	18	0	2	9	7
	Dalton State College		4,265	0	0	0	0	0
	Georgia Institute of Technology		17,135	11	0	1	5	5
	Georgia Perimeter College		20,461	4	0	0	0	4

Note: Caution should be exercised in making any intercampus comparisons or ranking schools because university/college crime statistics are affected by a variety of factors. These include demographic characteristics of the surrounding community, ratio of male to female students, number of on-campus residents, accessibility of the campus to outside visitors, size of enrollment, etc.

[1] The student enrollment figures provided by the United States Department of Education are for the 2005 school year, the most recent available. The enrollment figures include full-time and part-time students.

[3] Student enrollment figures were not available.

Table 9. Offenses Known to Law Enforcement, by State and University and College, 2006

(Number.)

State	University/College	Campus	Property crime	Burglary	Larceny-theft	Motor vehicle theft	Arson[2]
		Hastings College of Law	1,286	9	8	1	0
		Irvine	24,400	66	360	13	2
		Lawrence-Livermore Laboratory[3]		0	8	0	0
		Los Angeles	35,625	216	798	45	0
		Medical Center, Sacramento[3]		13	132	14	0
		Riverside	16,622	44	257	8	3
		San Diego	25,320	91	513	75	5
		San Francisco	2,863	43	398	16	0
		Santa Barbara	21,016	47	395	5	1
		Santa Cruz	15,012	53	249	3	2
	West Valley-Mission College		17,986	12	52	2	0
COLORADO	Adams State College		9,157	9	41	0	0
	Arapahoe Community College		7,132	0	16	0	0
	Auraria Higher Education Center[3]			17	234	11	0
	Colorado School of Mines		4,318	9	37	0	0
	Colorado State University:	Fort Collins	27,780	15	393	2	2
		Pueblo	5,870	0	46	2	1
	Fort Lewis College		3,946	22	49	2	2
	Pikes Peak Community College		10,619	2	24	0	0
	Red Rocks Community College		6,600	1	11	0	0
	University of Colorado:	Boulder	31,589	99	381	15	13
		Colorado Springs	9,333	14	57	4	1
		Health Sciences Center[3]		9	61	2	0
		Health Sciences Center, Fitzsimons Campus[3]		2	30	0	0
	University of Northern Colorado		13,622	48	254	8	2
CONNECTICUT	Central Connecticut State University		12,315	6	73	1	2
	Eastern Connecticut State University		5,113	3	84	6	0
	University of Connecticut:	Health Center[3]		0	51	0	0
		Storrs, Avery Point, and Hartford[3]		29	170	3	4
	Western Connecticut State University		5,907	14	33	1	1
	Yale University		11,483	112	305	2	0
DELAWARE	Delaware State University		3,722	15	52	1	0
	University of Delaware		20,982	59	280	2	10
FLORIDA	Florida A&M University		12,154	29	254	7	0
	Florida Atlantic University		25,645	51	195	20	1
	Florida Gulf Coast University		7,249	5	38	18	0
	Florida International University		36,904	92	386	63	1
	Florida State University:	Panama City[3]		0	12	0	0
		Tallahassee	39,146	53	438	16	3
	New College of Florida		762	4	76	2	1
	Pensacola Junior College		104	9	94	1	0
	Santa Fe Community College		98	2	95	1	0
	Tallahassee Community College		88	0	84	4	0
	University of Central Florida		460	105	328	27	6
	University of Florida		762	45	692	25	2
	University of North Florida		162	10	147	5	1
	University of South Florida:	St. Petersburg[3]	67	1	53	13	1
		Tampa	490	112	335	43	3
	University of West Florida		102	7	92	3	0
GEORGIA	Abraham Baldwin Agricultural College		49	10	39	0	0
	Albany State University		68	6	61	1	
	Armstrong Atlantic State University		57	9	43	5	
	Augusta State University		20	0	18	2	
	Clark Atlanta University		184	47	106	31	0
	Dalton State College		9	3	6	0	
	Georgia Institute of Technology		671	101	517	53	
	Georgia Perimeter College		152	5	135	12	

Note: Caution should be exercised in making any intercampus comparisons or ranking schools because university/college crime statistics are affected by a variety of factors. These include demographic characteristics of the surrounding community, ratio of male to female students, number of on-campus residents, accessibility of the campus to outside visitors, size of enrollment, etc.

[2] The FBI does not publish arson data unless it receives data from either the agency or the state for all 12 months of the calendar year.

[3] Student enrollment figures were not available.

Table 9. Offenses Known to Law Enforcement, by State and University and College, 2006 *(Contd.)*

(Number.)

State	University/College	Campus	Student enroll-ment[1]	Violent crime	Murder and non-negligent man-slaughter	Forcible rape	Robbery	Aggra-vated assault
	Georgia Southern University		16,646	2	0	0	2	0
	Georgia Southwestern State University		2,427	4	0	0	1	3
	Georgia State University		25,967	15	0	0	11	4
	Kennesaw State University		18,551	5	0	1	0	4
	Medical College of Georgia		2,131	1	0	0	1	0
	Mercer University		7,154	3	0	1	1	1
	Morehouse College		3,029	9	0	0	7	2
	Morris-Brown College[3]			0	0	0	0	0
	North Georgia College		4,767	0	0	0	0	0
	South Georgia College		1,504	0	0	0	0	0
	University of Georgia		33,660	6	0	1	3	2
	University of West Georgia		10,153	2	0	0	0	2
	Valdosta State University		10,503	9	0	2	3	4
	Wesleyan College		640	0	0	0	0	0
	Young Harris College		532	0	0	0	0	0
INDIANA	Ball State University		20,351	31	0	13	1	17
	Indiana State University		10,679	2	0	0	0	2
	Indiana University:	Bloomington	37,958	21	0	6	1	14
		Gary	4,987	1	0	0	1	0
		Indianapolis[3]		3	0	1	1	1
		New Albany	6,164	0	0	0	0	0
	Marian College		1,678	0	0	0	0	0
	Purdue University		40,151	10	0	1	2	7
IOWA	Iowa State University		25,741	11	0	6	0	5
	University of Iowa		28,426	8	0	3	1	4
	University of Northern Iowa		12,622	1	0	0	0	1
KANSAS	Emporia State University		6,288	4	0	2	0	2
	Kansas State University		23,182	7	0	3	0	4
	Pittsburg State University		6,628	2	0	0	0	2
	University of Kansas:	Main Campus	26,934	5	0	3	0	2
		Medical Center	2,015	6	0	0	3	3
	Washburn University		7,261	0	0	0	0	0
	Wichita State University		13,812	3	0	1	2	0
KENTUCKY	Eastern Kentucky University		16,219	3	0	1	1	1
	Kentucky State University		2,386	1	0	0	1	0
	Morehead State University		9,003	1	0	0	0	1
	Murray State University		10,266	6	0	3	1	2
	Northern Kentucky University		14,004	1	0	1	0	0
	University of Kentucky		25,672	8	0	2	1	5
	University of Louisville		20,726	5	0	0	4	1
	Western Kentucky University		18,634	4	0	1	3	0
LOUISIANA	Delgado Community College[3]			3	0	0	0	3
	Louisiana State University:	Baton Rouge[3]		24	0	0	11	13
		Health Sciences Center, New Orleans	2,207	0	0	0	0	0
		Health Sciences Center, Shrevport	713	15	0	0	1	14
		Shreveport	4,370	2	0	1	0	1
	Louisiana Tech University		11,593	4	0	1	0	3
	McNeese State University		8,980	5	0	1	2	2
	Nicholls State University		7,525	11	0	0	1	10
	Northwestern State University		9,847	2	0	0	1	1
	Southeastern Louisiana University		16,054	6	0	0	2	4
	Southern University and A&M College:	Baton Rouge	10,364	8	0	0	4	4
		New Orleans[3]		2	0	0	0	2
	Tulane University[3]			12	0	3	2	7
	University of Louisiana	Lafayette	9,278	10	0	1	5	4
	University of New Orleans		6,684	7	1	0	1	5
MAINE	University of Maine:	Farmington	2,452	1	0	0	1	0
		Orono	11,435	3	0	3	0	0
	University of Southern Maine		10,974	2	0	0	0	2

Note: Caution should be exercised in making any intercampus comparisons or ranking schools because university/college crime statistics are affected by a variety of
factors. These include demographic characteristics of the surrounding community, ratio of male to female students, number of on-campus residents, accessibility
of the campus to outside visitors, size of enrollment, etc.
[1] The student enrollment figures provided by the United States Department of Education are for the 2005 school year, the most recent available.
The enrollment figures include full-time and part-time students.
[3] Student enrollment figures were not available.

Table 9. Offenses Known to Law Enforcement, by State and University and College, 2006

(Number.)

State	University/College	Campus	Property crime	Burglary	Larceny-theft	Motor vehicle theft	Arson[2]
	Georgia Southern University		211	5	203	3	
	Georgia Southwestern State University		68	1	66	1	
	Georgia State University		359	13	335	11	
	Kennesaw State University		138	20	113	5	0
	Medical College of Georgia		170	3	160	7	0
	Mercer University		65	4	60	1	0
	Morehouse College		170	8	158	4	
	Morris-Brown College[3]		7	1	6	0	0
	North Georgia College		28	9	19	0	0
	South Georgia College		12	3	9	0	0
	University of Georgia		516	43	453	20	0
	University of West Georgia		240	83	156	1	1
	Valdosta State University		178	6	168	4	0
	Wesleyan College		13	3	10	0	0
	Young Harris College		0	0	0	0	0
INDIANA	Ball State University		329	88	238	3	1
	Indiana State University		272	10	259	3	0
	Indiana University:	Bloomington	567	73	480	14	1
		Gary	41	5	36	0	0
		Indianapolis[3]	380	82	275	23	0
		New Albany	43	4	39	0	0
	Marian College		25	1	24	0	0
	Purdue University		448	44	402	2	0
IOWA	Iowa State University		307	37	259	11	14
	University of Iowa		264	36	223	5	4
	University of Northern Iowa		99	10	88	1	0
KANSAS	Emporia State University		40	6	34	0	0
	Kansas State University		184	39	144	1	2
	Pittsburg State University		86	14	70	2	1
	University of Kansas:	Main Campus	288	78	208	2	1
		Medical Center	208	6	191	11	1
	Washburn University		65	7	58	0	0
	Wichita State University		154	13	139	2	1
KENTUCKY	Eastern Kentucky University		201	51	148	2	0
	Kentucky State University		6	2	4	0	0
	Morehead State University		42	8	34	0	0
	Murray State University		141	27	113	1	6
	Northern Kentucky University		138	9	128	1	0
	University of Kentucky		601	60	529	12	0
	University of Louisville		230	11	208	11	0
	Western Kentucky University		294	54	234	6	1
LOUISIANA	Delgado Community College[3]		14	1	12	1	0
	Louisiana State University:	Baton Rouge[3]	457	58	380	19	1
		Health Sciences Center, New Orleans	5	0	5	0	0
		Health Sciences Center, Shreveport	133	1	119	13	0
		Shreveport	20	10	10	0	1
	Louisiana Tech University		150	26	113	11	
	McNeese State University		78	16	62	0	1
	Nicholls State University		43	8	35	0	0
	Northwestern State University		98	54	41	3	0
	Southeastern Louisiana University		182	46	133	3	1
	Southern University and A&M College:	Baton Rouge	176	28	145	3	2
		New Orleans[3]	7	1	6	0	0
	Tulane University[3]		188	61	119	8	1
	University of Louisiana	Lafayette	141	26	113	2	
	University of New Orleans		93	12	77	4	0
MAINE	University of Maine:	Farmington	46	4	41	1	0
		Orono	237	11	222	4	17
	University of Southern Maine		99	10	89	0	5

Note: Caution should be exercised in making any intercampus comparisons or ranking schools because university/college crime statistics are affected by a variety of factors. These include demographic characteristics of the surrounding community, ratio of male to female students, number of on-campus residents, accessibility of the campus to outside visitors, size of enrollment, etc.

[2] The FBI does not publish arson data unless it receives data from either the agency or the state for all 12 months of the calendar year.

[3] Student enrollment figures were not available.

Table 9. Offenses Known to Law Enforcement, by State and University and College, 2006 (*Contd.*)

(Number.)

State	University/College	Campus	Student enroll-ment[1]	Violent crime	Murder and non-negligent man-slaughter	Forcible rape	Robbery	Aggra-vated assault
MARYLAND	Bowie State University		5,319	8	0	1	1	6
	Coppin State University		4,306	12	0	1	7	4
	Frostburg State University		5,041	6	0	0	1	5
	Morgan State University		6,438	24	0	0	15	9
	Salisbury University		7,009	2	0	0	1	1
	St. Mary's College		1,964	10	0	0	1	9
	Towson University		18,011	7	0	0	3	4
	University of Baltimore		4,895	4	0	0	3	1
	University of Maryland:	Baltimore City	5,526	12	0	0	5	7
		Baltimor County	11,650	2	0	0	2	0
		College Park	35,369	32	0	0	16	16
		Eastern Shore	3,870	4	0	1	1	2
MASSACHUSETTS	Assumption College		2,766	4	0	1	0	3
	Bentley College		5,619	10	0	2	2	6
	Boston College		14,829	13	0	1	0	12
	Brandeis University		5,189	4	0	0	0	4
	Bristol Community College		6,873	0	0	0	0	0
	Clark University		3,118	5	0	1	1	3
	Dean College		1,249	5	0	2	1	2
	Emerson College		4,326	4	0	1	1	2
	Fitchburg State College		5,340	7	0	4	1	2
	Framingham State College		5,874	2	0	1	0	1
	Harvard University		25,017	11	0	2	3	6
	Lasell College		1,253	2	0	1	0	1
	Massachusetts College of Art		2,127	0	0	0	0	0
	Massachusetts College of Liberal Arts		1,849	3	0	0	0	3
	Massachusetts Institute of Technology		10,206	12	0	5	1	6
	Massasoit Community College		6,706	1	0	0	0	1
	Merrimack College		2,231	8	0	2	0	6
	Mount Holyoke College		2,127	10	0	7	0	3
	Northeastern University		22,604	14	0	3	7	4
	North Shore Community College		6,604	1	0	0	0	1
	Quinsigamond Community College		5,970	1	0	0	0	1
	Salem State College		9,863	5	0	1	0	4
	Springfield College		5,025	13	0	1	5	7
	Tufts University:	Medford	9,776	13	0	3	3	7
		Suffolk[3]		0	0	0	0	0
		Worcester[3]		0	0	0	0	0
	University of Massachusetts:	Amherst	25,093	21	0	0	2	19
		Dartmouth	8,549	13	0	2	1	10
		Harbor Campus, Boston	11,862	0	0	0	0	0
		Medical Center, Worcester	1,008	12	0	0	0	12
	Wellesley College		2,331	0	0	0	0	0
	Western New England College		3,729	4	0	1	3	0
	Westfield State College		5,345	1	0	0	0	1
MICHIGAN	Central Michigan University		27,221	7	0	3	2	2
	Delta College		10,274	1	0	0	0	1
	Eastern Michigan University		23,486	5	1	4	0	0
	Ferris State University		12,547	9	0	5	1	3
	Grand Rapids Community College		14,798	0	0	0	0	0
	Grand Valley State University		22,565	0	0	0	0	0
	Lansing Community College		20,057	1	0	0	0	1
	Macomb Community College		20,596	1	0	0	1	0
	Michigan State University		45,166	29	0	7	6	16
	Michigan Technological University		6,506	0	0	0	0	0
	Mott Community College		10,299	2	0	0	0	2
	Northern Michigan University		9,500	5	0	3	0	2
	Oakland Community College		24,287	2	0	0	0	2
	Oakland University		17,339	3	0	1	0	2
	Saginaw Valley State University		9,569	2	0	1	0	1

Note: Caution should be exercised in making any intercampus comparisons or ranking schools because university/college crime statistics are affected by a variety of factors. These include demographic characteristics of the surrounding community, ratio of male to female students, number of on-campus residents, accessibility of the campus to outside visitors, size of enrollment, etc.

[1] The student enrollment figures provided by the United States Department of Education are for the 2005 school year, the most recent available. The enrollment figures include full-time and part-time students.

[3] Student enrollment figures were not available.

Table 9. Offenses Known to Law Enforcement, by State and University and College, 2006

(Number.)

State	University/College	Campus	Property crime	Burglary	Larceny-theft	Motor vehicle theft	Arson[2]
MARYLAND	Bowie State University		100	44	54	2	0
	Coppin State University		60	12	45	3	0
	Frostburg State University		125	36	89	0	0
	Morgan State University		143	34	104	5	0
	Salisbury University		103	4	97	2	0
	St. Mary's College		82	7	75	0	0
	Towson University		205	46	156	3	3
	University of Baltimore		79	5	70	4	0
	University of Maryland:	Baltimore City	137	5	130	2	0
		Baltimor County	150	14	133	3	2
		College Park	830	191	582	57	4
		Eastern Shore	202	56	143	3	1
MASSACHUSETTS	Assumption College		55	4	51	0	0
	Bentley College		75	17	56	2	0
	Boston College		214	53	159	2	
	Brandeis University		63	12	50	1	0
	Bristol Community College		12	0	11	1	0
	Clark University		63	27	36	0	0
	Dean College		44	29	15	0	0
	Emerson College		59	9	49	1	0
	Fitchburg State College		79	0	79	0	0
	Framingham State College		23	6	16	1	0
	Harvard University		525	315	203	7	0
	Lasell College		23	7	16	0	0
	Massachusetts College of Art		50	2	48	0	0
	Massachusetts College of Liberal Arts		24	8	16	0	0
	Massachusetts Institute of Technology		450	64	384	2	0
	Massasoit Community College		18	0	18	0	0
	Merrimack College		60	19	41	0	0
	Mount Holyoke College		99	4	95	0	0
	Northeastern University		384	41	341	2	0
	North Shore Community College		9	1	7	1	0
	Quinsigamond Community College		29	0	25	4	0
	Salem State College		133	61	71	1	0
	Springfield College		80	11	62	7	0
	Tufts University:	Medford	149	28	121	0	0
		Suffolk[3]	28	1	27	0	0
		Worcester[3]	3	0	3	0	0
	University of Massachusetts:	Amherst	306	102	198	6	1
		Dartmouth	212	57	149	6	0
		Harbor Campus, Boston	137	35	102	0	0
		Medical Center, Worcester	83	2	81	0	0
	Wellesley College		49	17	32	0	0
	Western New England College		45	5	38	2	0
	Westfield State College		53	13	40	0	0
MICHIGAN	Central Michigan University		175	7	168	0	1
	Delta College		49	1	48	0	0
	Eastern Michigan University		355	15	325	15	8
	Ferris State University		103	6	96	1	0
	Grand Rapids Community College		163	2	161	0	0
	Grand Valley State University		126	8	117	1	0
	Lansing Community College		117	0	116	1	0
	Macomb Community College		120	6	111	3	0
	Michigan State University		818	150	658	10	3
	Michigan Technological University		78	0	77	1	0
	Mott Community College		159	1	149	9	0
	Northern Michigan University		130	3	125	2	1
	Oakland Community College		86	1	82	3	0
	Oakland University		125	6	112	7	0
	Saginaw Valley State University		93	22	70	1	0

Note: Caution should be exercised in making any intercampus comparisons or ranking schools because university/college crime statistics are affected by a variety of factors. These include demographic characteristics of the surrounding community, ratio of male to female students, number of on-campus residents, accessibility of the campus to outside visitors, size of enrollment, etc.

[2] The FBI does not publish arson data unless it receives data from either the agency or the state for all 12 months of the calendar year.

[3] Student enrollment figures were not available.

Table 9. Offenses Known to Law Enforcement, by State and University and College, 2006 *(Contd.)*

(Number.)

State	University/College	Campus	Student enroll-ment[1]	Violent crime	Murder and non-negligent man-slaughter	Forcible rape	Robbery	Aggra-vated assault
	University of Michigan:...............................	Ann Arbor	39,993	16	0	2	4	10
		Dearborn	8,369	0	0	0	0	0
		Flint	6,422	1	0	0	1	0
MINNESOTA[4]	University of Minnesota:	Duluth	10,496		0		1	0
		Morris	1,684		0		0	0
		Twin Cities	51,175		0		14	9
MISSISSIPPI	Coahoma Community College....................		1,946	0	0	0	0	0
	Itawamba Community College		4,979	0	0	0	0	0
	Jackson State University..............................		8,416	8	0	1	5	2
	Mississippi State University..........................		16,101	0	0	0	0	0
	University of Mississippi:	Medical Center	2,027	2	0	0	2	0
		Oxford	14,901	1	1	0	0	0
MISSOURI	Central Missouri State University		10,604	13	0	0	0	13
	Lincoln University...		3,180	2	0	0	0	2
	Mineral Area College...................................		2,930	0	0	0	0	0
	Missouri Western State University.................		5,248	3	0	0	1	2
	Northwest Missouri State University...............		6,328	3	0	3	0	0
	Southeast Missouri State University		10,288	6	0	2	1	3
	St. Louis Community College	Meramec	11,611	3	0	1	0	2
	Truman State University................................		5,881	0	0	0	0	0
	University of Missouri:..................................	Columbia	27,930	13	0	0	2	11
		Kansas City	14,310	2	0	0	1	1
		Rolla	5,600	2	0	0	0	2
		St. Louis	15,548	3	0	0	1	2
	Washington University...................................		13,383	0	0	0	0	0
NEBRASKA	University of Nebraska:	Kearney	6,445	0	0	0	0	0
		Lincoln	21,675	4	0	1	1	2
NEVADA	Truckee Meadows Community College............		11,431	0	0	0	0	0
	University of Nevada:	Las Vegas	28,134	6	0	0	2	4
		Reno	16,336	6	0	1	0	5
NEW JERSEY	Brookdale Community College		13,279	1	0	0	0	1
	Essex County College		10,435	0	0	0	0	0
	Kean University of New Jersey........................		12,958	6	0	1	2	3
	Middlesex County College		11,898	1	0	0	1	0
	Monmouth University....................................		6,351	3	0	2	1	0
	Montclair State University		16,063	12	0	6	1	5
	New Jersey Institute of Technology		8,058	13	1	0	7	5
	Richard Stockton College...............................		7,035	1	0	0	0	1
	Rowan University...		9,762	5	0	2	3	0
	Rutgers University:..	Camden	5,321	4	0	0	4	0
		Newark	10,246	12	0	0	6	6
		New Brunswick	34,449	14	0	4	5	5
	Stevens Institute of Technology........................		4,690	0	0	0	0	0
	The College of New Jersey...............................		6,768	2	0	1	0	1
	University of Medicine and Dentistry:.............	Camden[3]		2	0	0	2	0
		Newark	5,574	48	0	0	22	26
		New Brunswick[3]		3	0	0	0	3
		Piscataway[3]		0	0	0	0	0
	William Paterson University		10,970	3	0	1	1	1
NEW MEXICO	Eastern New Mexico University........................		4,033	1	0	1	0	0
	New Mexico State University...........................		16,072	24	0	1	0	23
NEW YORK	Cornell University		19,642	4	0	1	0	3
	State University of New York:	Albany	17,040	10	0	6	1	3
		Buffalo	27,220	5	0	0	2	3
		Downstate Medical Center[3]		5	0	0	2	3
		Maritime Colege	1,294	0	0	0	0	0
		Stony Brook[3]		8	0	2	0	6
		Upstate Medical Center[3]		4	0	0	0	4

Note: Caution should be exercised in making any intercampus comparisons or ranking schools because university/college crime statistics are affected by a variety of factors. These include demographic characteristics of the surrounding community, ratio of male to female students, number of on-campus residents, accessibility of the campus to outside visitors, size of enrollment, etc.

[1] The student enrollment figures provided by the United States Department of Education are for the 2005 school year, the most recent available. The enrollment figures include full-time and part-time students.

[3] Student enrollment figures were not available.

[4] The data collection methodology for the offense of forcible rape used by the Minnesota state Uniform Crime Reporting (UCR) program does not comply with national UCR guidelines. Consequently, their figures for forcible rape and violent crime (of which forcible rape is a part) are not published in this table.

Table 9. Offenses Known to Law Enforcement, by State and University and College, 2006

(Number.)

State	University/College	Campus	Property crime	Burglary	Larceny-theft	Motor vehicle theft	Arson[2]
	University of Michigan:	Ann Arbor	884	45	827	12	8
		Dearborn	55	0	50	5	0
		Flint	69	3	64	2	0
MINNESOTA[4]	University of Minnesota:	Duluth	88	10	75	3	1
		Morris	21	1	20	0	0
		Twin Cities	797	59	718	20	1
MISSISSIPPI	Coahoma Community College		12	10	2	0	0
	Itawamba Community College		31	2	29	0	0
	Jackson State University		216	18	194	4	0
	Mississippi State University		150	8	139	3	1
	University of Mississippi:	Medical Center	171	2	163	6	0
		Oxford	182	3	177	2	0
MISSOURI	Central Missouri State University		142	40	99	3	2
	Lincoln University		59	27	32	0	0
	Mineral Area College		4	1	3	0	0
	Missouri Western State University		105	28	72	5	0
	Northwest Missouri State University		57	8	48	1	0
	Southeast Missouri State University		86	26	58	2	0
	St. Louis Community College	Meramec	32	0	31	1	0
	Truman State University		80	8	72	0	0
	University of Missouri:	Columbia	365	21	341	3	5
		Kansas City	220	39	170	11	1
		Rolla	66	16	49	1	0
		St. Louis	123	19	96	8	0
	Washington University		208	29	172	7	0
NEBRASKA	University of Nebraska:	Kearney	60	22	38	0	0
		Lincoln	393	49	337	7	0
NEVADA	Truckee Meadows Community College		16	3	13	0	1
	University of Nevada:	Las Vegas	354	64	246	44	1
		Reno	192	14	166	12	0
NEW JERSEY	Brookdale Community College		51	0	51	0	0
	Essex County College		69	1	67	1	0
	Kean University of New Jersey		142	16	122	4	0
	Middlesex County College		61	0	60	1	0
	Monmouth University		59	7	50	2	0
	Montclair State University		301	38	253	10	0
	New Jersey Institute of Technology		143	5	109	29	0
	Richard Stockton College		70	3	67	0	1
	Rowan University		176	23	148	5	0
	Rutgers University:	Camden	111	23	85	3	0
		Newark	164	26	123	15	2
		New Brunswick	591	138	442	11	6
	Stevens Institute of Technology		42	2	39	1	0
	The College of New Jersey		94	16	77	1	1
	University of Medicine and Dentistry:	Camden[3]	7	0	7	0	0
		Newark	282	10	236	36	0
		New Brunswick[3]	39	2	34	3	0
		Piscataway[3]	25	1	24	0	0
	William Paterson University		109	24	80	5	0
NEW MEXICO	Eastern New Mexico University		81	9	71	1	0
	New Mexico State University		448	29	401	18	3
NEW YORK	Cornell University		366	23	334	9	2
	State University of New York:	Albany	239	20	219	0	3
		Buffalo	416	106	308	2	11
		Downstate Medical Center[3]	71	2	68	1	1
		Maritime Colege	83	19	63	1	1
		Stony Brook[3]	591	28	551	12	3
		Upstate Medical Center[3]	180	0	180	0	0

Note: Caution should be exercised in making any intercampus comparisons or ranking schools because university/college crime statistics are affected by a variety of factors. These include demographic characteristics of the surrounding community, ratio of male to female students, number of on-campus residents, accessibility of the campus to outside visitors, size of enrollment, etc.

[2] The FBI does not publish arson data unless it receives data from either the agency or the state for all 12 months of the calendar year.

[3] Student enrollment figures were not available.

[4] The data collection methodology for the offense of forcible rape used by the Minnesota state Uniform Crime Reporting (UCR) program does not comply with national UCR guidelines. Consequently, their figures for forcible rape and violent crime (of which forcible rape is a part) are not published in this table.

Table 9. Offenses Known to Law Enforcement, by State and University and College, 2006 *(Contd.)*

(Number.)

State	University/College	Campus	Student enroll-ment[1]	Violent crime	Murder and non-negligent man-slaughter	Forcible rape	Robbery	Aggra-vated assault
	State University of New York Agricultural and Technical College:	Alfred	3,304	1	0	0	1	0
		Canton	2,481	2	0	0	0	2
		Cobleskill	2,478	0	0	0	0	0
		Farmingdale[3]		0	0	0	0	1
		Morrisville[3]		2	0	1	0	1
	State University of New York College:.............	Buffalo	11,006	12	0	1	2	9
		Cortland	7,224	1	0	0	0	1
		Fredonia	5,432	0	0	0	0	0
		Geneseo	5,484	0	0	0	0	0
		New Paltz	7,822	3	0	0	1	2
		Old Westbury	3,398	0	0	0	0	0
		Oneonta	5,859	0	0	0	0	0
		Oswego	8,282	3	0	2	0	1
		Plattsburgh	6,044	4	0	2	0	2
		Potsdam	4,329	4	0	2	0	2
		Purchase	3,811	7	0	1	1	5
	United States Merchant Marine Academy		927	1	0	0	0	1
NORTH CAROLINA	Appalachian State University		14,653	2	0	0	0	2
	Duke University..		14,075	8	0	1	1	6
	East Carolina University		23,164	14	0	5	3	6
	Elizabeth City State University		2,664	2	0	1	1	0
	Elon University..		4,956	0	0	0	0	0
	Fayetteville State University		6,072	3	0	1	0	2
	North Carolina Agricultural and Technical State University		11,103	22	0	0	8	14
	North Carolina Central University....................		8,219	20	0	2	9	9
	North Carolina State University	Raleigh	30,148	11	0	1	2	8
	University of North Carolina:	Asheville	3,499	1	0	0	0	1
		Chapel Hill	27,276	14	0	1	3	10
		Charlotte	20,772	6	0	0	2	4
		Greensboro	16,147	14	0	3	7	4
		Pembroke	5,632	0	0	0	0	0
		Wilmington	11,839	5	0	2	1	2
	Wake Forest University		6,716	6	0	1	0	5
	Western Carolina University.............................		8,665	7	0	5	0	2
NORTH DAKOTA	North Dakota State College of Science		2,457	2	0	0	0	2
	North Dakota State University........................		12,099	1	0	1	0	0
	University of North Dakota		12,954	3	0	1	1	1
OHIO	Bowling Green State University.......................		19,016	5	0	2	1	2
	Cleveland State University...............................		15,482	4	0	0	3	1
	Cuyahoga Community College		24,788	2	0	0	1	1
	Kent State University..		23,622	0	0	0	0	0
	Lakeland Community College		8,310	0	0	0	0	0
	Miami University...		16,722	2	0	0	0	2
	Ohio State University..		50,504	20	0	5	6	9
	Ohio University		20,461	6	0	1	2	3
	University of Akron		21,049	16	0	5	9	2
	University of Cincinnati....................................		27,932	15	0	4	8	3
	University of Toledo..		19,201	5	0	0	1	4
	Wright State University		16,207	5	0	3	1	1
	Youngstown State University		12,912	3	0	0	1	2
OKLAHOMA	Cameron University...		5,880	0	0	0	0	0
	East Central University		4,627	1	0	0	0	1
	Murray State College		2,242	1	0	0	0	1
	Northeastern Oklahoma A&M College		2,019	2	0	0	0	2
	Northeastern State University		9,575	3	0	0	1	2
	Oklahoma State University:..............................	Main Campus	23,692	6	0	2	0	4
		Okmulgee	2,705	1	0	0	1	0
		Tulsa[3]		0	0	0	0	0
	Rogers State University		3,880	0	0	0	0	0
	Seminole State College		2,107	0	0	0	0	0

Note: Caution should be exercised in making any intercampus comparisons or ranking schools because university/college crime statistics are affected by a variety of factors. These include demographic characteristics of the surrounding community, ratio of male to female students, number of on-campus residents, accessibility of the campus to outside visitors, size of enrollment, etc.

[1] The student enrollment figures provided by the United States Department of Education are for the 2005 school year, the most recent available. The enrollment figures include full-time and part-time students.

[3] Student enrollment figures were not available.

Table 9. Offenses Known to Law Enforcement, by State and University and College, 2006

(Number.)

State	University/College	Campus	Property crime	Burglary	Larceny-theft	Motor vehicle theft	Arson[2]
	State University of New York Agricultural and Technical College:..	Alfred	97	10	86	1	0
		Canton	62	1	61	0	0
		Cobleskill	80	19	61	0	0
		Farmingdale[3]	43	2	38	3	0
		Morrisville[3]	87	11	76	0	0
	State University of New York College:............	Buffalo	255	53	197	5	0
		Cortland	87	18	69	0	0
		Fredonia	109	13	96	0	0
		Geneseo	127	13	112	2	0
		New Paltz	106	13	93	0	0
		Old Westbury	74	3	65	6	0
		Oneonta	74	6	68	0	0
		Oswego	140	24	115	1	0
		Plattsburgh	104	20	84	0	0
		Potsdam	105	18	84	3	0
		Purchase	176	35	141	0	0
	United States Merchant Marine Academy........		5	2	3	0	0
NORTH CAROLINA	Appalachian State University		161	24	130	7	10
	Duke University..		730	48	675	7	0
	East Carolina University		242	11	229	2	2
	Elizabeth City State University		100	42	56	2	0
	Elon University...		68	21	46	1	0
	Fayetteville State University		133	5	118	10	0
	North Carolina Agricultural and Technical State University		297	17	270	10	1
	North Carolina Central University..................		360	82	271	7	0
	North Carolina State University	Raleigh	442	85	348	9	1
	University of North Carolina:...........................	Asheville	51	13	38	0	0
		Chapel Hill	438	19	417	2	0
		Charlotte	261	36	215	10	3
		Greensboro	264	3	249	12	1
		Pembroke	92	14	78	0	0
		Wilmington	273	35	231	7	3
	Wake Forest University		145	22	122	1	1
	Western Carolina University............................		170	6	162	2	1
NORTH DAKOTA	North Dakota State College of Science		34	3	30	1	0
	North Dakota State University.........................		117	18	98	1	3
	University of North Dakota		163	16	143	4	1
OHIO	Bowling Green State University.......................		286	27	257	2	0
	Cleveland State University...............................		225	10	201	14	0
	Cuyahoga Community College		106	2	103	1	0
	Kent State University.......................................		189	25	163	1	0
	Lakeland Community College		25	1	24	0	0
	Miami University...		192	27	163	2	5
	Ohio State University.......................................		926	328	584	14	4
	Ohio University		257	37	220	0	0
	University of Akron		328	24	289	15	2
	University of Cincinnati..................................		666	45	618	3	2
	University of Toledo..		406	90	309	7	3
	Wright State University		197	7	182	8	0
	Youngstown State University...........................		154	14	137	3	0
OKLAHOMA	Cameron University		32	0	32	0	0
	East Central University		29	7	20	2	0
	Murray State College		4	2	1	1	0
	Northeastern Oklahoma A&M College		22	12	10	0	0
	Northeastern State University		78	19	57	2	0
	Oklahoma State University:..............................	Main Campus	220	48	166	6	1
		Okmulgee	26	2	24	0	0
		Tulsa[3]	10	1	7	2	0
	Rogers State University...................................		21	3	18	0	0
	Seminole State College		18	0	18	0	0

Note: Caution should be exercised in making any intercampus comparisons or ranking schools because university/college crime statistics are affected by a variety of factors. These include demographic characteristics of the surrounding community, ratio of male to female students, number of on-campus residents, accessibility of the campus to outside visitors, size of enrollment, etc.

[2] The FBI does not publish arson data unless it receives data from either the agency or the state for all 12 months of the calendar year.

[3] Student enrollment figures were not available.

Table 9. Offenses Known to Law Enforcement, by State and University and College, 2006 (*Contd.*)

(Number.)

State	University/College	Campus	Student enroll-ment[1]	Violent crime	Murder and non-negligent man-slaughter	Forcible rape	Robbery	Aggra-vated assault
	Southeastern Oklahoma State University		3,951	0	0	0	0	0
	Southwestern Oklahoma State University		5,057	1	0	1	0	0
	Tulsa Community College		16,770	0	0	0	0	0
	University of Central Oklahoma		15,859	8	0	0	2	6
	University of Oklahoma:	Health Sciences Center	3,638	9	0	1	1	7
		Norman	26,506	4	0	2	2	0
PENNSYLVANIA	Bloomsburg University.....................................		8,570	0	0	0	0	0
	California University.......................................		7,184	2	0	0	0	2
	Cheyney University..		1,560	9	0	0	1	8
	Clarion University..		6,338	5	0	1	0	4
	Dickenson College...		2,352	2	0	1	0	1
	East Stroudsburg University		6,793	6	0	0	0	6
	Edinboro University..		7,691	2	0	0	0	2
	Elizabethtown College		2,206	0	0	0	0	0
	Indiana University		14,081	16	0	3	0	13
	Kutztown University		9,864	8	0	6	1	1
	Lehigh University...		6,748	0	0	0	0	0
	Lock Haven University......................................		5,283	1	0	0	1	0
	Mansfield University		3,390	0	0	0	0	0
	Millersville University......................................		7,919	6	0	1	0	5
	Moravian College		2,007	3	0	0	2	1
	Pennsylvania State University:..........................	Altoona	3,647	1	0	1	0	0
		Beaver	641	0	0	0	0	0
		Behrend	3,542	3	0	1	0	2
		Berks	2,488	1	0	0	1	0
		Harrisburg	3,736	0	0	0	0	0
		McKeesport	682	1	0	0	0	1
		Mont Alto	932	3	0	1	0	2
		University Park	40,709	13	0	1	4	8
	Shippensburg University....................................		7,485	0	0	0	0	0
	Slippery Rock University...................................		8,105	1	0	0	0	1
	University of Pittsburgh:	Bradford	1,318	1	0	0	0	1
		Pittsburgh	26,559	22	0	2	11	9
	West Chester University		12,988	13	0	0	2	11
RHODE ISLAND	Brown University..		8,261	3	0	0	1	2
	University of Rhode Island		15,095	6	0	2	0	4
SOUTH CAROLINA	Aiken Technical College....................................		2,506	0	0	0	0	0
	Benedict College...		2,552	18	0	1	1	16
	Bob Jones University[3].....................................			0	0	0	0	0
	Clemson University..		17,165	9	0	1	2	6
	Coastal Carolina University		7,613	0	0	0	0	0
	College of Charleston.......................................		11,332	5	0	1	2	2
	Columbia College		1,493	0	0	0	0	0
	Denmark Technical College..............................		1,408	8	0	0	0	8
	Erskine College		890	0	0	0	0	0
	Francis Marion University.................................		4,008	4	0	1	1	2
	Lander University...		2,703	2	0	0	1	1
	Medical University of South Carolina		2,499	6	0	2	0	4
	Midlands Technical College		10,779	0	0	0	0	0
	South Carolina State University		4,446	25	0	1	11	13
	Trident Technical College.................................		11,407	1	0	0	1	0
	University of South Carolina:	Aiken	3,303	0	0	0	0	0
		Columbia	27,065	18	0	3	6	9
		Upstate	4,484	1	0	0	0	1
	Winthrop University..		6,480	7	0	2	2	3
TENNESSEE	Austin Peay State University		8,813	6	0	0	2	4
	Christian Brothers University		1,783	3	0	2	1	0
	East Tennessee State University.......................		11,894	6	0	3	0	3
	Middle Tennessee State University		22,554	13	0	3	5	5
	Northeast State Technical Community College		4,860	0	0	0	0	0
	Southwest Tennessee Community College.......		11,556	1	0	0	1	0

Note: Caution should be exercised in making any intercampus comparisons or ranking schools because university/college crime statistics are affected by a variety of factors. These include demographic characteristics of the surrounding community, ratio of male to female students, number of on-campus residents, accessibility of the campus to outside visitors, size of enrollment, etc.

[1] The student enrollment figures provided by the United States Department of Education are for the 2005 school year, the most recent available. The enrollment figures include full-time and part-time students.
[3] Student enrollment figures were not available.

Table 9. Offenses Known to Law Enforcement, by State and University and College, 2006

(Number.)

State	University/College	Campus	Property crime	Burglary	Larceny-theft	Motor vehicle theft	Arson[2]
	Southeastern Oklahoma State University		45	8	36	1	0
	Southwestern Oklahoma State University		42	12	29	1	0
	Tulsa Community College		48	3	41	4	0
	University of Central Oklahoma		119	12	105	2	0
	University of Oklahoma:	Health Sciences Center	227	9	217	1	0
		Norman	287	56	215	16	0
PENNSYLVANIA	Bloomsburg University		72	7	65	0	2
	California University		81	4	77	0	1
	Cheyney University		71	26	45	0	3
	Clarion University		36	14	22	0	0
	Dickenson College		39	1	38	0	0
	East Stroudsburg University		66	41	24	1	0
	Edinboro University		81	6	74	1	0
	Elizabethtown College		11	1	10	0	1
	Indiana University		93	21	72	0	2
	Kutztown University		151	19	129	3	0
	Lehigh University		75	4	70	1	0
	Lock Haven University		28	2	25	1	1
	Mansfield University		30	6	23	1	0
	Millersville University		75	29	44	2	1
	Moravian College		44	3	41	0	0
	Pennsylvania State University:	Altoona	40	1	37	2	0
		Beaver	9	0	9	0	0
		Behrend	44	7	36	1	1
		Berks	51	6	37	8	0
		Harrisburg	14	0	14	0	0
		McKeesport	0	0	0	0	0
		Mont Alto	23	5	17	1	0
		University Park	516	46	467	3	2
	Shippensburg University		56	23	33	0	0
	Slippery Rock University		106	2	103	1	0
	University of Pittsburgh:	Bradford	11	0	11	0	0
		Pittsburgh	616	35	578	3	0
	West Chester University		133	46	81	6	0
RHODE ISLAND	Brown University		178	57	121	0	0
	University of Rhode Island		210	34	168	8	1
SOUTH CAROLINA	Aiken Technical College		14	0	14	0	0
	Benedict College		273	124	145	4	3
	Bob Jones University[3]		0	0	0	0	0
	Clemson University		257	32	211	14	0
	Coastal Carolina University		117	23	94	0	0
	College of Charleston		159	32	125	2	1
	Columbia College		19	0	19	0	0
	Denmark Technical College		4	2	2	0	0
	Erskine College		1	0	1	0	0
	Francis Marion University		52	11	40	1	0
	Lander University		49	12	36	1	0
	Medical University of South Carolina		179	5	169	5	0
	Midlands Technical College		49	0	47	2	0
	South Carolina State University		195	55	135	5	1
	Trident Technical College		32	1	31	0	0
	University of South Carolina:	Aiken	16	2	14	0	0
		Columbia	461	49	400	12	0
		Upstate	36	3	33	0	0
	Winthrop University		87	15	72	0	0
TENNESSEE	Austin Peay State University		77	1	73	3	0
	Christian Brothers University		33	7	24	2	1
	East Tennessee State University		147	27	114	6	4
	Middle Tennessee State University		222	42	175	5	5
	Northeast State Technical Community College		13	5	8	0	0
	Southwest Tennessee Community College		84	4	77	3	0

Note: Caution should be exercised in making any intercampus comparisons or ranking schools because university/college crime statistics are affected by a variety of factors. These include demographic characteristics of the surrounding community, ratio of male to female students, number of on-campus residents, accessibility of the campus to outside visitors, size of enrollment, etc.

[2] The FBI does not publish arson data unless it receives data from either the agency or the state for all 12 months of the calendar year.

[3] Student enrollment figures were not available.

Table 9. Offenses Known to Law Enforcement, by State and University and College, 2006 (*Contd.*)

(Number.)

State	University/College	Campus	Student enroll-ment[1]	Violent crime	Murder and non-negligent man-slaughter	Forcible rape	Robbery	Aggra-vated assault
	Tennessee State University....................................		8,880	9	0	0	1	8
	Tennessee Technological University		9,313	4	0	4	0	0
	University of Memphis.....................................		20,465	15	0	1	8	6
	University of Tennessee:..................................	Chattanooga	8,656	10	0	1	4	5
		Knoxville	28,512	8	0	1	3	4
		Martin	6,478	2	0	1	0	1
		Memphis[3]		2	0	0	1	1
	Vanderbilt University..		11,479	22	0	3	5	14
	Volunteer State Community College		7,150	1	0	0	1	0
	Walters State Community College		5,891	0	0	0	0	0
TEXAS	Abilene Christian University		4,685	5	0	0	1	4
	Alvin Community College.................................		3,935	0	0	0	0	0
	Amarillo College...		10,573	3	0	0	0	3
	Angelo State University...................................		6,156	2	0	1	0	1
	Austin College...		1,327	0	0	0	0	0
	Baylor Health Care System[3]			4	0	0	1	3
	Baylor University	Waco	13,975	7	0	0	0	7
	Central Texas College		17,792	0	0	0	0	0
	College of the Mainland		3,992	0	0	0	0	0
	Eastfield College..		11,915	1	0	0	1	0
	El Paso Community College		26,667	2	0	0	2	0
	Grayson County College		3,768	1	0	0	0	1
	Hardin-Simmons University.............................		2,427	0	0	0	0	0
	Houston Baptist University.............................		2,294	0	0	0	0	0
	Lamar University	Beaumont	10,595	11	0	0	2	9
	Laredo Community College...............................		8,298	1	0	0	0	1
	McLennan Community College.........................		7,663	1	0	0	0	1
	Midwestern State University............................		6,279	1	0	1	0	0
	Mountain View College		6,494	1	0	0	0	1
	North Lake College...		9,268	0	0	0	0	0
	Paris Junior College		4,272	0	0	0	0	0
	Prairie View A&M University		7,912	10	0	4	0	6
	Rice University		5,095	5	0	3	1	1
	Richland College..		14,399	5	0	0	5	0
	Southern Methodist University.........................		11,152	6	0	6	0	0
	South Plains College...		9,273	4	0	1	0	3
	Southwestern University...................................		1,309	3	0	2	0	1
	Stephen F. Austin State University		11,435	5	0	2	0	3
	St. Mary's University		3,925	1	0	0	1	0
	Sul Ross State University		2,927	0	0	0	0	0
	Tarleton State University..................................		9,141	0	0	0	0	0
	Texas A&M International University..............		4,298	1	0	0	0	1
	Texas A&M University:....................................	College Station	44,910	11	0	9	1	1
		Commerce	8,777	3	0	2	0	1
		Corpus Christi	8,365	2	0	0	0	2
		Galveston	1,677	3	0	0	0	3
		Kingsville	6,662	3	0	1	1	1
	Texas Christian University		8,749	4	0	3	0	1
	Texas Southern University		11,903	17	0	3	8	6
	Texas State Technical College:........................	Harlingen	4,209	0	0	0	0	0
		Marshall	565	0	0	0	0	0
		Waco	4,452	4	0	1	1	2
	Texas State University:	San Marcos	27,129	2	0	2	0	0
	Texas Technological University	Lubbock	28,001	5	0	3	0	2
	Texas Woman's University................................		11,344	0	0	0	0	0
	Trinity University		2,685	0	0	0	0	0
	Tyler Junior College		9,310	0	0	0	0	0
	University of Houston:......................................	Central Campus	35,344	11	0	2	5	4
		Clearlake	7,853	0	0	0	0	0
		DowntownCampus	11,484	4	0	0	1	3
	University of Mary Hardin-Baylor..................		2,724	0	0	0	0	0

Note: Caution should be exercised in making any intercampus comparisons or ranking schools because university/college crime statistics are affected by a variety of factors. These include demographic characteristics of the surrounding community, ratio of male to female students, number of on-campus residents, accessibility of the campus to outside visitors, size of enrollment, etc.

[1] The student enrollment figures provided by the United States Department of Education are for the 2005 school year, the most recent available. The enrollment figures include full-time and part-time students.

[3] Student enrollment figures were not available.

Table 9. Offenses Known to Law Enforcement, by State and University and College, 2006

(Number.)

State	University/College	Campus	Property crime	Burglary	Larceny-theft	Motor vehicle theft	Arson[2]
	Tennessee State University..................................		145	25	112	8	1
	Tennessee Technological University		75	7	68	0	3
	University of Memphis.......................................		257	47	198	12	1
	University of Tennessee:...................................	Chattanooga	267	77	187	3	1
		Knoxville	382	6	364	12	4
		Martin	53	5	48	0	0
		Memphis[3]	126	7	115	4	0
	Vanderbilt University...		612	91	513	8	1
	Volunteer State Community College		23	0	23	0	0
	Walters State Community College		9	1	8	0	0
TEXAS	Abilene Christian University		115	27	81	7	1
	Alvin Community College..................................		8	0	8	0	0
	Amarillo College		39	3	35	1	0
	Angelo State University....................................		78	6	70	2	1
	Austin College		29	4	23	2	1
	Baylor Health Care System[3]		510	25	463	22	0
	Baylor University	Waco	279	25	250	4	0
	Central Texas College		31	0	30	1	0
	College of the Mainland		28	7	19	2	0
	Eastfield College...		56	1	50	5	1
	El Paso Community College		111	0	105	6	0
	Grayson County College		23	8	15	0	0
	Hardin-Simmons University.............................		50	24	26	0	0
	Houston Baptist University...............................		17	7	9	1	0
	Lamar University	Beaumont	128	9	114	5	0
	Laredo Community College...............................		26	1	23	2	0
	McLennan Community College.........................		26	0	26	0	0
	Midwestern State University.............................		71	9	62	0	0
	Mountain View College		58	0	52	6	0
	North Lake College		63	1	59	3	0
	Paris Junior College		21	2	19	0	0
	Prairie View A&M University		243	86	143	14	1
	Rice University		236	47	183	6	1
	Richland College		79	2	65	12	0
	Southern Methodist University.........................		292	33	251	8	6
	South Plains College		19	0	18	1	0
	Southwestern University....................................		34	5	28	1	0
	Stephen F. Austin State University		213	37	176	0	2
	St. Mary's University		85	16	68	1	0
	Sul Ross State University		52	23	27	2	0
	Tarleton State University..................................		38	6	32	0	0
	Texas A&M International University..............		52	13	38	1	0
	Texas A&M University:....................................	College Station	578	27	541	10	0
		Commerce	72	16	53	3	0
		Corpus Christi	102	13	86	3	0
		Galveston	49	6	43	0	0
		Kingsville	81	12	68	1	0
	Texas Christian University		171	21	139	11	1
	Texas Southern University		285	82	196	7	0
	Texas State Technical College:.........................	Harlingen	31	6	25	0	2
		Marshall	4	1	3	0	0
		Waco	141	58	81	2	0
	Texas State University:	San Marcos	282	43	237	2	1
	Texas Technological University	Lubbock	290	16	270	4	1
	Texas Woman's University................................		53	6	47	0	0
	Trinity University..		142	51	83	8	0
	Tyler Junior College		130	9	121	0	0
	University of Houston:......................................	Central Campus	529	28	469	32	0
		Clearlake	16	0	16	0	0
		DowntownCampus	79	3	71	5	0
	University of Mary Hardin-Baylor....................		33	5	28	0	0

Note: Caution should be exercised in making any intercampus comparisons or ranking schools because university/college crime statistics are affected by a variety of factors. These include demographic characteristics of the surrounding community, ratio of male to female students, number of on-campus residents, accessibility of the campus to outside visitors, size of enrollment, etc.

[2] The FBI does not publish arson data unless it receives data from either the agency or the state for all 12 months of the calendar year.

[3] Student enrollment figures were not available.

Table 9. Offenses Known to Law Enforcement, by State and University and College, 2006 (*Contd.*)

(Number.)

State	University/College	Campus	Student enroll-ment[1]	Violent crime	Murder and non-negligent man-slaughter	Forcible rape	Robbery	Aggra-vated assault
	University of North Texas:	Denton	31,958	11	0	2	1	8
		Health Science Center	1,049	1	0	0	0	1
	University of Texas:...	Arlington	25,432	11	0	0	9	2
		Austin	49,696	12	0	0	3	9
		Brownsville	13,316	5	0	0	0	5
		Dallas	14,480	6	0	0	1	5
		El Paso	19,268	5	0	1	1	3
		Health Science Center, San Antonio	2,781	0	0	0	0	0
		Health Science Center, Tyler[3]		1	0	0	1	0
		Houston[3]		5	0	0	2	3
		Medical Branch	2,172	1	0	0	0	1
		Pan American	17,048	3	0	0	0	3
		Permian Basin	3,406	1	0	0	0	1
		San Antonio	27,337	5	0	0	1	4
		Southwestern Medical School	2,393	2	0	1	0	1
		Tyler	5,777	1	0	0	0	1
	West Texas A&M University		7,302	1	0	1	0	0
UTAH	Brigham Young University		34,067	3	0	0	0	3
	College of Eastern Utah		2,178	0	0	0	0	0
	Southern Utah University		6,859	0	0	0	0	0
	University of Utah..		30,558	5	0	2	0	3
	Utah State University..		14,458	2	0	2	0	0
	Utah Valley State College................................		24,180	4	0	1	0	3
	Weber State University.....................................		18,142	3	0	0	1	2
VERMONT	University of Vermont		11,597	5	0	1	0	4
VIRGINIA	Christopher Newport University		4,699	2	0	2	0	0
	College of William and Mary		7,544	1	0	0	1	0
	Emory and Henry College................................		1,101	0	0	0	0	0
	Ferrum College		993	4	0	1	1	2
	George Mason University		29,728	10	0	1	2	7
	Hampton University..		6,309	2	0	0	1	1
	James Madison University................................		16,938	3	0	2	0	1
	Longwood College..		4,374	5	0	3	1	1
	Norfolk State University..................................		6,096	6	0	0	5	1
	Northern Virginia Community College		37,740	1	0	0	1	0
	Old Dominion University..................................		21,274	9	0	4	3	2
	Radford University..		9,552	11	0	1	0	10
	University of Richmond....................................		4,542	2	0	1	0	1
	University of Virginia..		23,765	6	0	2	3	1
	University of Virginia..	College at Wise	1,953	0	0	0	0	0
	Virginia Commonwealth University		29,168	23	0	0	13	10
	Virginia Military Institute................................		1,369	1	0	1	0	0
	Virginia Polytechnic Institute and State University		27,979	3	0	3	0	0
	Virginia State University		5,055	5	0	0	2	3
WASHINGTON	Central Washington University.........................		10,190	2	0	2	0	0
	Eastern Washington University........................		10,908	1	0	1	0	0
	Evergreen State College		4,470	6	0	6	0	0
	University of Washington		39,251	8	0	1	2	5
	Washington State University:	Pullman	23,544	6	0	4	0	2
		Vancouver[3]		0	0	0	0	0
	Western Washington University		14,247	0	0	0	0	0
WEST VIRGINIA	Fairmont State University		7,759	1	0	0	0	1
	Marshall University..		13,988	7	0	0	1	6
	Potomac State College		1,279	2	0	0	1	1
	Shepherd University..		3,901	3	2	0	0	1
	West Virginia State University.........................		3,491	1	0	1	0	0
	West Virginia University...................................		26,051	3	0	0	3	0
WISCONSIN	University of Wisconsin:..................................	Eau Claire	10,688	0	0	0	0	0
		Green Bay	5,628	1	0	1	0	0
		La Crosse	9,397	1	0	0	0	1

Note: Caution should be exercised in making any intercampus comparisons or ranking schools because university/college crime statistics are affected by a variety of factors. These include demographic characteristics of the surrounding community, ratio of male to female students, number of on-campus residents, accessibility of the campus to outside visitors, size of enrollment, etc.

[1] The student enrollment figures provided by the United States Department of Education are for the 2005 school year, the most recent available. The enrollment figures include full-time and part-time students.

[3] Student enrollment figures were not available.

Table 9. Offenses Known to Law Enforcement, by State and University and College, 2006

(Number.)

State	University/College	Campus	Property crime	Burglary	Larceny-theft	Motor vehicle theft	Arson[2]
	University of North Texas:	Denton	225	39	179	7	1
		Health Science Center	19	1	18	0	0
	University of Texas:..	Arlington	357	51	297	9	0
		Austin	649	47	598	4	2
		Brownsville	70	0	56	14	0
		Dallas	163	10	146	7	2
		El Paso	163	7	145	11	2
		Health Science Center, San Antonio	53	2	50	1	0
		Health Science Center, Tyler[3]	16	0	16	0	0
		Houston[3]	399	12	385	2	0
		Medical Branch	195	11	184	0	0
		Pan American	147	6	131	10	0
		Permian Basin	25	3	21	1	0
		San Antonio	244	25	197	22	0
		Southwestern Medical School	202	15	168	19	0
		Tyler	26	6	20	0	1
	West Texas A&M University		40	9	31	0	1
UTAH	Brigham Young University.................................		298	34	262	2	2
	College of Eastern Utah		9	4	5	0	0
	Southern Utah University		46	8	38	0	0
	University of Utah		582	16	527	39	0
	Utah State University..		140	10	130	0	0
	Utah Valley State College.................................		66	10	55	1	0
	Weber State University.....................................		81	9	71	1	0
VERMONT	University of Vermont		186	24	161	1	0
VIRGINIA	Christopher Newport University		153	7	140	6	0
	College of William and Mary		176	17	159	0	2
	Emory and Henry College.................................		0	0	0	0	0
	Ferrum College		26	7	19	0	3
	George Mason University		314	8	304	2	0
	Hampton University...		166	23	142	1	0
	James Madison University.................................		169	4	165	0	0
	Longwood College..		104	6	97	1	0
	Norfolk State University....................................		140	41	94	5	2
	Northern Virginia Community College		179	4	173	2	1
	Old Dominion University...................................		197	16	180	1	0
	Radford University..		117	5	112	0	6
	University of Richmond....................................		129	21	108	0	1
	University of Virginia..		396	64	328	4	2
	University of Virginia..	College at Wise	0	0	0	0	0
	Virginia Commonwealth University		620	11	599	10	6
	Virginia Military Institute.................................		18	2	16	0	0
	Virginia Polytechnic Institute and State University		254	27	225	2	2
	Virginia State University		175	5	162	8	1
WASHINGTON	Central Washington University.........................		176	14	159	3	0
	Eastern Washington University........................		111	17	93	1	0
	Evergreen State College		99	11	86	2	0
	University of Washington		747	87	629	31	5
	Washington State University:	Pullman	200	30	167	3	3
		Vancouver[3]	9	0	8	1	0
	Western Washington University		236	37	196	3	0
WEST VIRGINIA	Fairmont State University		62	15	47	0	0
	Marshall University...		138	17	120	1	1
	Potomac State College		17	0	16	1	0
	Shepherd University...		33	1	30	2	2
	West Virginia State University		39	13	25	1	0
	West Virginia University...................................		217	8	206	3	1
WISCONSIN	University of Wisconsin:	Eau Claire	65	0	65	0	0
		Green Bay	40	0	40	0	0
		La Crosse	88	7	80	1	0

Note: Caution should be exercised in making any intercampus comparisons or ranking schools because university/college crime statistics are affected by a variety of factors. These include demographic characteristics of the surrounding community, ratio of male to female students, number of on-campus residents, accessibility of the campus to outside visitors, size of enrollment, etc.

[2] The FBI does not publish arson data unless it receives data from either the agency or the state for all 12 months of the calendar year.

[3] Student enrollment figures were not available.

Table 9. Offenses Known to Law Enforcement, by State and University and College, 2006 (Contd.)

(Number.)

State	University/College	Campus	Student enroll-ment[1]	Violent crime	Murder and non-negligent man-slaughter	Forcible rape	Robbery	Aggra-vated assault
		Madison	40,793	18	0	4	5	9
		Milwaukee	27,502	5	0	1	3	1
		Oshkosh	11,433	1	0	0	0	1
		Parkside	4,923	0	0	0	0	0
		Platteville	6,493	2	0	0	0	2
		Stevens Point	8,747	0	0	0	0	0
		Stout	8,227	4	0	1	0	3
		Superior	2,872	0	0	0	0	0
		Whitewater	10,750	1	0	0	0	1
WYOMING	Sheridan College..		2,849	0	0	0	0	0
	University of Wyoming..		13,126	0	0	0	0	0

Note: Caution should be exercised in making any intercampus comparisons or ranking schools because university/college crime statistics are affected by a variety of factors. These include demographic characteristics of the surrounding community, ratio of male to female students, number of on-campus residents, accessibility of the campus to outside visitors, size of enrollment, etc.

[1] The student enrollment figures provided by the United States Department of Education are for the 2005 school year, the most recent available. The enrollment figures include full-time and part-time students.

Table 9. Offenses Known to Law Enforcement, by State and University and College, 2006

(Number.)

State	University/College	Campus	Property crime	Burglary	Larceny-theft	Motor vehicle theft	Arson[2]
		Madison	642	43	590	9	10
		Milwaukee	327	33	294	0	1
		Oshkosh	90	9	80	1	0
		Parkside	88	0	88	0	0
		Platteville	104	26	77	1	0
		Stevens Point	111	7	104	0	0
		Stout	145	21	124	0	0
		Superior	56	23	33	0	0
		Whitewater	141	52	86	3	0
WYOMING	Sheridan College..		4	1	3	0	0
	University of Wyoming.....................................		161	12	147	2	0

Note: Caution should be exercised in making any intercampus comparisons or ranking schools because university/college crime statistics are affected by a variety of factors. These include demographic characteristics of the surrounding community, ratio of male to female students, number of on-campus residents, accessibility of the campus to outside visitors, size of enrollment, etc.

[2] The FBI does not publish arson data unless it receives data from either the agency or the state for all 12 months of the calendar year.

Table 10. Offenses Known to Law Enforcement, by State Metropolitan and Nonmetropolitan Counties, 2006

(Number.)

State	County	Violent crime	Murder and non-negligent man-slaughter	Forcible rape	Robbery	Aggra-vated assault	Property crime	Burglary	Larceny-theft	Motor vehicle theft	Arson[1]
ALABAMA- **Metropolitan Counties**	Autauga	33	0	2	4	27	375	120	215	40	
	Bibb	15	0	1	1	13	78	26	46	6	
	Colbert	0	0	0	0	0	2	0	1	1	
	Elmore	44	2	13	9	20	659	209	422	28	
	Geneva	22	0	0	3	19	214	70	104	40	
	Henry	14	0	0	1	13	164	53	100	11	
	Houston	9	0	0	4	5	373	114	229	30	
	Jefferson	642	9	57	227	349	5,260	1,779	2,949	532	23
	Lawrence	44	2	9	6	27	524	139	360	25	
	Lee	49	2	11	19	17	1,349	476	801	72	
	Limestone	26	0	0	6	20	362	90	243	29	
	Lowndes	44	1	5	11	27	145	119	20	6	
	Madison	284	1	25	52	206	2,679	797	1,623	259	
	Mobile	190	5	17	63	105	2,537	843	1,413	281	
	Shelby	79	2	19	16	42	996	397	498	101	
	St. Clair	40	1	9	1	29	321	102	191	28	
	Tuscaloosa	255	5	31	21	198	2,013	593	1,191	229	
	Walker	21	0	4	1	16	532	196	319	17	
ALABAMA- **Nonmetropolitan Counties**	Baldwin	93	0	9	7	77	861	296	542	23	
	Butler	6	0	0	0	6	58	18	36	4	
	Chambers	31	1	4	7	19	195	57	138	0	
	Cleburne	27	0	1	2	24	222	78	121	23	
	Coosa	36	3	4	5	24	208	63	130	15	
	Crenshaw	16	0	3	1	12	185	55	116	14	
	Cullman	118	2	18	8	90	1,482	415	923	144	
	Dale	4	0	0	1	3	23	15	8	0	
	De Kalb	195	1	23	2	169	674	358	210	106	
	Fayette	15	0	2	1	12	176	77	82	17	
	Franklin	4	1	1	0	2	18	10	5	3	
	Jackson	65	3	9	6	47	602	214	305	83	
	Lamar	0	0	0	0	0	5	2	3	0	
	Macon	21	0	2	0	19	232	108	94	30	
	Marengo	18	0	0	3	15	130	57	65	8	
	Marion	23	0	1	0	22	226	83	133	10	
	Marshall	36	0	5	0	31	475	144	307	24	
	Perry	10	2	0	2	6	62	26	30	6	
	Pickens	15	0	4	0	11	58	16	41	1	
	Pike	5	0	0	1	4	86	32	49	5	
	Wilcox	3	1	1	0	1	44	9	26	9	
ARIZONA- **Metropolitan Counties**	Maricopa	850	25	30	94	701	6,698	1,734	3,936	1,028	69
	Mohave	204	9	4	22	169	3,111	1,165	1,559	387	26
	Pima	783	18	88	214	463	13,674	2,643	9,237	1,794	121
	Pinal	298	11	39	42	206	5,079	1,067	3,176	836	24
	Yavapai	354	5	13	10	326	1,703	408	1,092	203	7
	Yuma	215	3	6	32	174	1,577	330	1,009	238	9
ARIZONA- **Nonmetropolitan Counties**	Cochise[2]		0	17	22		1,531	580	755	196	15
	Gila	100	1	7	6	86	559	229	264	66	7
	Graham	243	0	2	1	240	203	58	134	11	8
	La Paz	84	0	0	6	78	417	82	290	45	1
	Navajo	61	1	7	2	51	661	386	189	86	8
	Santa Cruz	8	0	1	2	5	368	136	164	68	0
ARKANSAS- **Metropolitan Counties**	Benton	126	1	29	4	92	919	404	473	42	22
	Cleveland	4	0	0	1	3	156	79	61	16	3
	Craighead	34	1	6	0	27	376	144	198	34	2
	Crittenden	93	0	4	5	84	510	229	235	46	8
	Faulkner	43	0	6	0	37	729	206	440	83	9
	Garland	104	1	15	13	75	2,432	983	1,247	202	17
	Grant	26	0	1	0	25	150	69	76	5	0
	Jefferson	87	2	11	5	69	591	286	248	57	8

Note: The data shown in this table do not reflect county totals but are the number of offenses reported by the sheriff's office or county police department.
[1] The FBI does not publish arson data unless it receives data from either the agency or the state for all 12 months of the calendar year.
[2] It was determined that the agency did not follow national Uniform Crime Reporting (UCR) Program guidelines for reporting an offense. Consequently, this figure is not included in this table.

Table 10. Offenses Known to Law Enforcement, by State Metropolitan and Nonmetropolitan Counties, 2006 *(Contd.)*

(Number.)

State	County	Violent crime	Murder and non-negligent man-slaughter	Forcible rape	Robbery	Aggra-vated assault	Property crime	Burglary	Larceny-theft	Motor vehicle theft	Arson[1]
	Lincoln	6	0	1	1	4	106	57	45	4	0
	Lonoke	114	3	15	7	89	747	290	409	48	6
	Madison	26	2	4	0	20	93	40	45	8	1
	Miller	77	1	5	2	69	319	98	195	26	3
	Perry	30	0	2	0	28	73	38	31	4	1
	Poinsett	51	0	3	1	47	119	94	15	10	4
	Pulaski	443	6	20	56	361	2,449	949	1,175	325	12
	Sebastian	41	0	3	0	38	337	157	166	14	8
	Washington	130	3	19	2	106	748	255	412	81	6
ARKANSAS- **Nonmetropolitan Counties**	Arkansas	3	0	0	0	3	106	37	51	18	0
	Ashley	15	0	3	2	10	182	53	113	16	4
	Baxter	51	1	8	0	42	511	105	369	37	0
	Boone	73	2	5	0	66	391	239	109	43	2
	Bradley	3	0	0	0	3	14	9	5	0	0
	Calhoun	1	0	0	0	1	28	15	11	2	0
	Carroll	8	0	3	0	5	125	27	79	19	2
	Chicot	0	0	0	0	0	99	11	73	15	0
	Clark	24	1	1	2	20	144	65	75	4	4
	Clay	18	0	3	0	15	82	31	51	0	1
	Cleburne	22	0	4	2	16	362	175	151	36	4
	Columbia	52	0	0	4	48	248	80	158	10	2
	Cross	37	0	5	0	32	133	38	84	11	1
	Dallas	12	0	1	2	9	21	9	11	1	0
	Drew	36	0	1	0	35	112	30	75	7	2
	Fulton	1	0	0	0	1	90	42	42	6	0
	Greene	14	0	3	1	10	173	73	95	5	9
	Howard	10	0	0	3	7	98	28	69	1	0
	Independence........	17	1	0	4	12	1,012	50	878	84	1
	Izard	4	0	1	0	3	112	57	42	13	4
	Jackson..................	14	0	6	1	7	148	39	92	17	3
	Lawrence	2	0	0	0	2	120	46	74	0	3
	Lee........................	14	0	1	0	13	18	14	4	0	0
	Logan	8	0	2	0	6	189	61	113	15	2
	Marion...................	9	0	1	0	8	91	42	47	2	1
	Mississippi.............	41	0	4	4	33	351	104	218	29	4
	Monroe..................	0	0	0	0	0	51	18	22	11	0
	Ouachita................	29	2	4	3	20	221	95	118	8	2
	Pike.......................	11	1	2	0	8	54	23	28	3	0
	Polk.......................	18	1	2	0	15	154	77	72	5	0
	Pope......................	38	1	8	0	29	368	168	176	24	2
	Prairie	1	0	0	0	1	50	21	21	8	1
	Randolph	0	0	0	0	0	80	27	52	1	0
	Scott.....................	16	0	3	1	12	94	42	45	7	2
	Searcy...................	8	0	0	0	8	15	9	3	3	2
	Sevier....................	29	1	7	1	20	258	82	157	19	2
	Sharp	20	2	3	1	14	149	82	66	1	4
	St. Francis	46	1	4	8	33	336	101	234	1	3
	Union	31	3	2	8	18	419	99	283	37	0
	Van Buren..............	20	0	0	1	19	124	52	58	14	0
	White	52	1	5	2	44	845	323	419	103	2
	Yell.......................	67	0	11	2	54	91	54	30	7	3
CALIFORNIA- **Metropolitan Counties**	Alameda.................	545	3	25	280	237	3,152	635	1,510	1,007	40
	Butte.....................	154	6	18	22	108	1,699	727	950	22	75
	Contra Costa	587	13	26	195	353	3,486	1,115	2,342	29	17
	El Dorado..............	410	3	23	23	361	2,127	694	1,411	22	10
	Fresno...................	612	10	35	152	415	6,659	1,631	3,873	1,155	304
	Imperial.................	136	2	5	7	122	1,092	471	580	41	32
	Kern......................	1,915	32	110	378	1,395	11,715	3,226	6,743	1,746	253
	Kings.....................	131	1	13	14	103	596	180	409	7	5
	Los Angeles...........	7,290	135	222	2,008	4,925	20,127	4,890	9,042	6,195	374
	Madera...................	315	2	21	30	262	1,581	672	888	21	1
	Marin.....................	179	1	10	52	116	999	284	714	1	12

Note: The data shown in this table do not reflect county totals but are the number of offenses reported by the sheriff's office or county police department.

[1] The FBI does not publish arson data unless it receives data from either the agency or the state for all 12 months of the calendar year.

Table 10. Offenses Known to Law Enforcement, by State Metropolitan and Nonmetropolitan Counties, 2006 (*Contd.*)

(Number.)

State	County	Violent crime	Murder and non-negligent man-slaughter	Forcible rape	Robbery	Aggra-vated assault	Property crime	Burglary	Larceny-theft	Motor vehicle theft	Arson[1]
	Merced	500	6	36	40	418	1,905	896	992	17	12
	Monterey	239	6	19	60	154	1,737	568	1,144	25	18
	Napa	50	1	9	3	37	451	169	276	6	2
	Orange	244	2	12	46	184	1,542	361	974	207	19
	Placer	234	2	28	24	180	2,040	684	1,321	35	12
	Riverside	2,101	34	119	409	1,539	15,952	3,835	8,395	3,722	71
	Sacramento	4,857	37	251	1,640	2,929	25,051	7,368	15,486	2,197	238
	San Benito	41	0	2	4	35	282	143	129	10	1
	San Bernardino	1,076	36	89	181	770	6,400	1,950	2,896	1,554	108
	San Diego	1,403	20	93	279	1,011	8,548	2,297	4,215	2,036	61
	San Joaquin	995	17	29	188	761	5,409	1,564	3,649	196	14
	San Luis Obispo	201	1	26	17	157	1,413	433	975	5	15
	San Mateo	224	1	24	38	161	1,688	230	1,206	252	5
	Santa Barbara	192	0	25	18	149	1,636	515	1,118	3	18
	Santa Clara	372	4	18	32	318	2,455	517	1,516	422	7
	Santa Cruz	298	7	33	25	233	2,596	830	1,750	16	25
	Shasta	221	6	19	12	184	920	373	449	98	14
	Solano	144	0	8	12	124	457	243	200	14	23
	Sonoma	591	2	43	48	498	1,931	739	1,172	20	24
	Stanislaus	847	10	30	98	709	4,416	1,463	2,436	517	231
	Sutter	164	2	9	14	139	973	376	520	77	9
	Tulare[3]	460	20	34	67	339		1,196	2,067		613
	Ventura	209	6	13	29	161	1,303	370	814	119	29
	Yolo	39	2	3	5	29	355	130	212	13	13
	Yuba	193	3	18	37	135	1,252	610	628	14	16
CALIFORNIA- **Nonmetropolitan Counties**	Alpine	13	0	2	0	11	83	22	61	0	0
	Amador	63	1	14	5	43	472	223	246	3	2
	Calaveras	45	1	10	10	24	740	334	400	6	4
	Colusa	41	0	9	1	31	297	91	193	13	6
	Del Norte	54	0	15	2	37	244	130	111	3	4
	Glenn	13	1	2	1	9	149	73	70	6	2
	Humboldt	117	3	16	20	78	1,007	322	664	21	10
	Inyo	59	0	2	0	57	151	11	139	1	2
	Lake	231	4	12	17	198	790	385	400	5	12
	Lassen	35	0	5	0	30	142	55	84	3	4
	Mariposa	49	1	6	1	41	318	100	218	0	3
	Mendocino	324	5	18	23	278	662	275	381	6	14
	Modoc	33	0	4	1	28	96	40	54	2	0
	Mono	14	0	1	0	13	90	27	62	1	0
	Nevada	152	2	9	8	133	630	208	406	16	3
	Plumas	36	0	3	1	32	487	196	289	2	3
	Sierra	10	0	2	1	7	53	15	37	1	0
	Siskiyou	59	0	11	2	46	264	95	164	5	11
	Tehama	247	2	3	6	236	439	245	194	0	18
	Trinity	23	0	4	4	15	108	77	30	1	2
	Tuolumne	123	0	10	12	101	811	377	422	12	6
COLORADO- **Metropolitan Counties**	Adams	437	6	41	74	316	3,383	796	1,907	680	45
	Arapahoe	246	1	32	37	176	1,740	404	1,063	273	40
	Boulder	87	1	14	4	68	753	246	446	61	21
	Clear Creek	18	0	1	0	17	92	16	71	5	3
	Douglas	184	2	60	25	97	2,746	526	2,100	120	29
	El Paso	1,016	2	57	35	922	2,745	784	1,607	354	35
	Gilpin	6	0	0	0	6	2	1	1	0	0
	Jefferson	250	2	55	27	166	3,793	983	2,445	365	30
	Larimer	104	5	24	5	70	1,347	361	868	118	21
	Mesa	58	3	3	7	45	1,580	367	1,036	177	33
	Park	23	3	0	0	20	57	28	24	5	1
	Pueblo	45	0	1	8	36	1,519	338	1,121	60	5
	Teller	18	0	1	1	16	103	52	42	9	4
	Weld	137	0	13	4	120	1,186	383	621	182	13

Note: The data shown in this table do not reflect county totals but are the number of offenses reported by the sheriff's office or county police department.
[1] The FBI does not publish arson data unless it receives data from either the agency or the state for all 12 months of the calendar year.
[3] The motor vehicle thefts for this county are collected by the Tulare County Highway Patrol. These data can be found in Table 11.

Table 10. Offenses Known to Law Enforcement, by State Metropolitan and Nonmetropolitan Counties, 2006 (*Contd.*)

(Number.)

State	County	Violent crime	Murder and non-negligent man-slaughter	Forcible rape	Robbery	Aggra-vated assault	Property crime	Burglary	Larceny-theft	Motor vehicle theft	Arson[1]
COLORADO- **Nonmetropolitan Counties**	Alamosa................	8	0	1	0	7	64	14	50	0	2
	Archuleta..............	29	0	6	0	23	116	30	75	11	1
	Baca......................	2	0	0	0	2	2	0	2	0	0
	Bent......................	3	0	0	0	3	28	6	20	2	2
	Chaffee.................	9	1	3	0	5	90	16	73	1	2
	Cheyenne..............	0	0	0	0	0	11	3	8	0	0
	Crowley.................	1	0	0	0	1	1	1	0	0	0
	Custer...................	11	0	0	0	11	42	10	30	2	1
	Delta.....................	15	0	4	0	11	150	38	95	17	4
	Dolores.................	0	0	0	0	0	31	5	21	5	0
	Eagle....................	38	0	9	2	27	487	62	416	9	2
	Fremont................	17	0	2	0	15	216	51	147	18	1
	Garfield................	62	1	2	2	57	311	80	204	27	7
	Grand...................	16	0	0	0	16	201	57	136	8	0
	Gunnison..............	14	0	0	0	14	33	4	24	5	0
	Hinsdale...............	0	0	0	0	0	3	0	3	0	0
	Huerfano..............	9	0	1	1	7	110	2	106	2	1
	Jackson.................	1	0	0	0	1	6	4	1	1	0
	Lake......................	21	0	2	0	19	22	9	9	4	0
	La Plata................	25	0	5	1	19	285	80	186	19	0
	Logan	12	0	0	2	10	56	17	31	8	1
	Moffat...................	10	0	1	0	9	31	12	17	2	0
	Montezuma...........	28	0	1	2	25	189	54	121	14	0
	Montrose...............	20	1	4	0	15	189	56	109	24	2
	Morgan.................	0	0	0	0	0	78	21	46	11	1
	Otero....................	27	0	1	0	26	87	19	56	12	1
	Pitkin...................	11	0	3	0	8	147	19	116	12	1
	Prowers................	9	0	0	0	9	38	10	25	3	0
	Rio Grande...........	4	0	0	0	4	30	19	9	2	1
	Routt	26	0	0	0	26	78	12	63	3	0
	Saguache..............	3	0	0	0	3	23	7	16	0	1
	San Juan...............	4	0	0	0	4	22	3	18	1	0
	San Miguel...........	2	0	0	0	2	42	7	31	4	0
	Sedgwick...............	3	0	0	0	3	24	14	7	3	1
	Summit..................	14	0	3	0	11	552	28	516	8	2
	Washington...........	7	0	0	0	7	37	6	27	4	0
	Yuma	2	0	0	0	2	18	1	16	1	0
DELAWARE- **Metropolitan Counties**	New Castle County Police Department	1,438	9	122	357	950	6,917	1,771	4,333	813	10
FLORIDA- **Metropolitan Counties**	Alachua.................	1,048	5	81	116	846	3,868	1,163	2,457	248	19
	Baker....................	93	2	4	7	80	402	30	339	33	0
	Bay.......................	420	4	47	42	327	2,476	550	1,763	163	5
	Brevard	1,120	6	67	119	928	5,735	1,356	4,043	336	35
	Broward	554	4	19	125	406	1,266	208	945	113	7
	Charlotte...............	691	2	13	90	586	5,006	1,185	3,486	335	8
	Clay......................	693	7	59	83	544	4,031	877	2,895	259	21
	Collier...................	1,308	6	75	281	946	5,132	1,302	3,496	334	33
	Escambia...............	1,927	10	137	443	1,337	9,804	2,595	6,335	874	31
	Flagler..................	169	4	7	25	133	1,723	417	1,166	140	9
	Gadsden................	248	1	12	17	218	800	305	412	83	0
	Gilchrist	16	0	0	0	16	191	80	86	25	2
	Hernando..............	613	5	67	48	493	5,116	1,498	3,345	273	14
	Hillsborough..........	4,947	30	207	1,095	3,615	30,549	6,507	20,494	3,548	126
	Indian River	339	6	28	86	219	2,685	592	1,945	148	4
	Jefferson................	92	0	7	8	77	123	56	61	6	1
	Lake......................	929	4	53	55	817	3,746	1,249	2,164	333	27
	Lee........................	1,808	26	106	454	1,222	11,835	3,670	6,870	1,295	93
	Leon	457	0	42	59	356	1,799	826	828	145	20
	Manatee	2,394	14	91	443	1,846	11,347	2,634	7,874	839	18
	Marion..................	1,562	11	126	87	1,338	4,460	1,394	2,684	382	5
	Martin...................	524	3	11	130	380	3,006	647	2,185	174	3
	Miami-Dade	9,047	98	413	2,356	6,180	49,794	9,194	33,552	7,048	147

Note: The data shown in this table do not reflect county totals but are the number of offenses reported by the sheriff's office or county police department.
[1] The FBI does not publish arson data unless it receives data from either the agency or the state for all 12 months of the calendar year.

Table 10. Offenses Known to Law Enforcement, by State Metropolitan and Nonmetropolitan Counties, 2006 (Contd.)

(Number.)

State	County	Violent crime	Murder and non-negligent man-slaughter	Forcible rape	Robbery	Aggra-vated assault	Property crime	Burglary	Larceny-theft	Motor vehicle theft	Arson[1]
	Nassau[4]		3	9	17		1,355	458	784	113	5
	Okaloosa	438	3	29	52	354	3,511	752	2,474	285	28
	Orange	7,341	64	297	2,423	4,557	30,988	8,134	18,032	4,822	1
	Osceola	789	6	44	172	567	5,891	2,347	3,085	459	5
	Palm Beach	3,057	35	228	831	1,963	18,578	4,604	11,767	2,207	131
	Pasco	1,402	26	110	238	1,028	12,784	3,761	7,918	1,105	47
	Pinellas	1,259	6	168	154	931	7,545	1,800	5,082	663	54
	Polk	1,671	15	129	279	1,248	9,103	3,066	5,251	786	0
	Santa Rosa	306	2	29	36	239	1,895	648	1,123	124	6
	Sarasota	737	4	32	125	576	7,571	1,872	5,195	504	25
	Seminole	592	11	43	99	439	3,937	928	2,539	470	2
	St. Johns	533	5	18	52	458	3,160	882	2,073	205	14
	St. Lucie	328	1	24	36	267	1,939	547	1,210	182	8
	Volusia	872	4	71	110	687	5,129	1,624	2,925	580	22
	Wakulla	113	0	10	5	98	570	167	361	42	11
FLORIDA-Nonmetropolitan Counties	Bradford	61	0	5	7	49	323	107	188	28	1
	Calhoun	13	0	0	1	12	50	23	18	9	0
	Citrus	387	1	37	30	319	2,521	575	1,787	159	29
	Columbia	236	1	17	16	202	1,114	368	640	106	19
	DeSoto	167	1	8	27	131	663	263	377	23	4
	Dixie	66	1	4	8	53	344	116	216	12	7
	Franklin	22	1	0	3	18	140	53	77	10	3
	Glades	61	1	3	8	49	288	87	171	30	9
	Gulf	77	0	3	1	73	176	48	116	12	0
	Hamilton	51	0	1	9	41	226	66	149	11	0
	Hardee	92	0	6	12	74	455	97	320	38	0
	Hendry	239	1	9	36	193	967	356	517	94	4
	Highlands	174	2	13	41	118	1,922	800	1,015	107	15
	Holmes	47	0	9	1	37	165	48	93	24	0
	Jackson	206	1	4	9	192	574	217	309	48	0
	Lafayette	18	0	0	0	18	52	14	35	3	1
	Levy	140	0	19	10	111	847	307	493	47	8
	Liberty	6	0	2	0	4	42	20	14	8	2
	Madison	104	2	7	5	90	413	154	230	29	1
	Monroe	247	0	15	32	200	1,998	422	1,454	122	4
	Okeechobee	259	5	14	20	220	915	408	433	74	8
	Putnam	594	5	21	26	542	2,227	926	1,106	195	10
	Sumter	147	2	26	21	98	713	248	420	45	11
	Suwannee	140	0	7	6	127	463	141	278	44	2
	Taylor	63	0	5	0	58	142	78	56	8	0
	Union	56	1	2	9	44	211	71	118	22	1
	Walton	118	2	6	2	108	919	180	659	80	0
	Washington	22	1	0	2	19	177	50	100	27	1
GEORGIA-Metropolitan Counties	Augusta-Richmond	1,035	17	139	619	260	13,755	2,844	9,075	1,836	
	Baker	1	0	0	0	1	0	0	0	0	0
	Barrow[5]	305	1	4	5	295			613	138	
	Brantley	32	0	1	3	28	363	118	210	35	2
	Brooks	75	1	0	1	73	296	84	186	26	3
	Catoosa	70	3	9	6	52	909	203	578	128	
	Clayton County Police Department	1,126	34	42	544	506	8,203	2,979	3,574	1,650	42
	Cobb County Police Department	1,393	22	94	560	717	12,859	3,075	8,175	1,609	49
	Coweta	70	5	2	19	44	1,352	404	805	143	
	Dawson	12	0	1	2	9	547	105	382	60	
	Dekalb County Police Department	4,454	85	167	2,179	2,023	28,719	8,062	14,116	6,541	175
	Dougherty County Police Department	34	0	4	10	20	500	166	298	36	
	Effingham[5]		1	4	0		434	189	180	65	
	Fayette	27	0	4	6	17	631	139	428	64	3

Note: The data shown in this table do not reflect county totals but are the number of offenses reported by the sheriff's office or county police department.
[1] The FBI does not publish arson data unless it receives data from either the agency or the state for all 12 months of the calendar year.
[4] The FBI determined that the agency's data were inflated. Consequently, affected data are not included in this table.
[5] The FBI determined that the agency's data were underreported. Consequently, affected data are not included in this table.

Table 10. Offenses Known to Law Enforcement, by State Metropolitan and Nonmetropolitan Counties, 2006 (*Contd.*)

(Number.)

State	County	Violent crime	Murder and non-negligent man-slaughter	Forcible rape	Robbery	Aggra-vated assault	Property crime	Burglary	Larceny-theft	Motor vehicle theft	Arson[1]
	Floyd County Police Department	195	2	14	10	169	1,606	342	1,065	199	
	Forsyth	89	5	13	14	57	2,447	443	1,871	133	6
	Fulton	2	0	0	2	0	16	0	14	2	
	Fulton County Police Department	984	17	62	497	408	8,574	2,654	4,633	1,287	
	Glynn	0	0	0	0	0	0	0	0	0	0
	Glynn County Police Department	279	2	19	68	190	2,382	516	1,732	134	
	Gwinnett County Police Department	1,890	35	97	1,050	708	19,228	5,466	11,245	2,517	152
	Hall	210	1	19	15	175	2,907	674	1,747	486	13
	Haralson	13	0	0	3	10	489	78	360	51	0
	Henry	0	0	0	0	0	0	0	0	0	0
	Lamar	20	0	0	1	19	167	49	100	18	0
	Liberty	61	3	6	13	39	616	133	462	21	4
	Long	27	0	1	7	19	182	73	96	13	0
	Lowndes	63	0	8	14	41	1,152	269	820	63	1
	Madison	66	0	7	4	55	424	44	340	40	5
	Meriwether	39	0	5	4	30	435	127	233	75	0
	Newton	337	2	14	25	296	1,580	560	786	234	2
	Paulding	168	1	19	12	136	2,547	621	1,623	303	6
	Rockdale	289	1	14	58	216	2,161	617	1,234	310	8
	Walker	333	0	5	6	322	1,156	296	770	90	2
	Walton	16	1	2	4	9	962	289	598	75	0
	Whitfield	219	1	16	9	193	2,011	542	1,284	185	7
GEORGIA- **Nonmetropolitan Counties**	Chattooga	39	0	2	2	35	214	65	139	10	
	Clay	3	0	0	0	3	6	1	2	3	0
	Clinch	4	0	0	0	4	60	19	39	2	0
	Decatur	33	1	0	7	25	330	96	222	12	
	Dooly	10	0	0	4	6	63	17	45	1	
	Early	47	1	4	3	39	231	72	147	12	
	Fannin	2	0	0	0	2	130	66	63	1	
	Gordon	70	0	5	1	64	516	134	345	37	
	Habersham	51	0	5	4	42	490	151	302	37	
	Jackson	60	0	3	3	54	863	225	568	70	3
	Laurens	71	3	6	6	56	574	172	337	65	2
	Lumpkin	34	0	9	0	25	433	97	296	40	0
	Peach	28	0	4	3	21	332	108	177	47	0
	Polk	0	0	0	0	0	0	0	0	0	0
	Polk County Police Department	116	1	3	10	102	760	263	392	105	0
	Putnam	63	0	1	2	60	305	105	185	15	0
	Seminole	14	3	1	0	10	63	35	26	2	0
	Stephens	28	2	4	1	21	464	109	291	64	0
	Treutlen	13	0	1	1	11	150	50	94	6	1
	Troup	47	0	1	6	40	1,132	157	926	49	0
	Turner	4	0	1	1	2	105	31	60	14	0
	Upson	94	1	3	1	89	371	105	236	30	0
	White	14	0	2	2	10	327	81	203	43	1
	Wilkes	7	0	0	0	7	12	3	7	2	0
HAWAII- **Nonmetropolitan Counties** **IDAHO-** **Metropolitan Counties**	Hawaii Police Department	432	3	65	88	276	6,327	1,426	4,293	608	50
	Bannock	19	1	2	0	16	222	55	156	11	1
	Boise	4	1	1	0	2	114	21	84	9	0
	Canyon	74	2	8	3	61	773	265	399	109	8
	Franklin	3	0	0	0	3	38	2	35	1	0
	Gem	9	0	1	0	8	32	17	9	6	1
	Jefferson	19	0	7	1	11	177	35	122	20	0
	Kootenai	102	1	21	4	76	1,060	346	639	75	7
	Nez Perce	8	0	2	0	6	83	26	55	2	0
	Owyhee	25	0	10	0	15	129	33	85	11	0
	Power	7	0	2	0	5	54	8	38	8	0

Note: The data shown in this table do not reflect county totals but are the number of offenses reported by the sheriff's office or county police department.

[1] The FBI does not publish arson data unless it receives data from either the agency or the state for all 12 months of the calendar year.

Table 10. Offenses Known to Law Enforcement, by State Metropolitan and Nonmetropolitan Counties, 2006 (*Contd.*)

(Number.)

State	County	Violent crime	Murder and non-negligent man-slaughter	Forcible rape	Robbery	Aggra-vated assault	Property crime	Burglary	Larceny-theft	Motor vehicle theft	Arson[1]
IDAHO- Nonmetropolitan Counties	Adams	3	0	0	0	3	40	6	30	4	0
	Bear Lake	1	0	0	0	1	31	9	20	2	0
	Benewah	9	1	0	0	8	19	5	14	0	0
	Blaine	12	0	0	0	12	51	23	25	3	1
	Bonner	61	0	13	1	47	575	144	385	46	1
	Boundary	5	0	1	0	4	72	27	42	3	0
	Butte	2	0	0	0	2	9	0	9	0	0
	Camas	0	0	0	0	0	5	3	2	0	0
	Caribou	2	0	0	0	2	50	28	21	1	0
	Cassia	48	1	2	2	43	532	105	401	26	2
	Clark	2	0	0	0	2	18	3	15	0	0
	Clearwater	10	0	0	0	10	93	16	70	7	1
	Elmore	9	0	3	0	6	93	29	52	12	0
	Fremont	10	0	1	0	9	92	15	70	7	0
	Gooding	23	6	2	0	15	56	17	24	15	1
	Idaho	26	1	3	0	22	75	11	60	4	0
	Jerome	16	0	4	0	12	117	53	56	8	0
	Latah	20	0	4	1	15	185	70	101	14	0
	Lemhi	5	0	0	0	5	23	7	15	1	1
	Lewis	4	0	2	0	2	24	9	11	4	0
	Lincoln	5	0	2	0	3	11	5	1	5	2
	Madison	10	0	3	0	7	93	11	78	4	0
	Minidoka	19	1	2	1	15	126	30	86	10	2
	Oneida	3	0	0	0	3	31	8	21	2	0
	Payette	16	0	3	1	12	51	22	17	12	1
	Shoshone	29	0	2	0	27	141	24	104	13	0
	Teton	8	0	1	0	7	54	25	25	4	0
	Twin Falls	28	1	2	0	25	226	97	110	19	5
	Valley	28	0	7	2	19	133	47	72	14	0
	Washington	8	0	2	0	6	33	12	20	1	1
INDIANA- Metropolitan Counties	Allen[6]	67	0	13	15	39	1,143	293	724	126	4
	Bartholomew	69	0	4	1	64	500	103	393	4	1
	Brown	2	0	0	0	2	68	23	39	6	1
	Delaware	29	1	8	4	16	642	125	436	81	3
	Elkhart	52	1	12	29	10	1,526	379	1,019	128	11
	Floyd	4	0	0	0	4	734	124	566	44	0
	Greene	15	0	1	3	11	218	73	129	16	0
	Howard	68	0	4	5	59	676	276	375	25	4
	Johnson	11	0	7	4	0	802	151	628	23	0
	Lake	35	2	0	12	21	1,161	157	781	223	0
	La Porte	28	0	5	4	19	943	268	593	82	1
	Monroe	47	1	5	7	34	564	202	316	46	2
	Newton	7	0	1	2	4	163	55	90	18	1
	Owen	60	0	1	3	56	659	248	396	15	0
	Porter	57	0	0	6	51	1,152	166	906	80	0
	Putnam	112	0	1	2	109	446	213	197	36	0
	Shelby	29	0	0	2	27	360	90	223	47	1
	St. Joseph	88	2	14	26	46	1,871	381	1,357	133	12
	Tippecanoe	25	0	10	3	12	769	223	494	52	10
	Vanderburgh	49	0	5	8	36	1,324	167	1,084	73	1
	Warrick	122	0	7	3	112	661	84	547	30	12
	Wells	5	0	1	0	4	147	55	71	21	2
INDIANA- Nonmetropolitan Counties	Blackford	0	0	0	0	0	52	10	33	9	0
	Cass	20	0	4	1	15	224	55	155	14	0
	Daviess	3	0	0	0	3	108	20	76	12	1
	Fayette	3	0	0	0	3	231	59	160	12	3
	Grant	15	0	5	3	7	343	82	240	21	0
	Henry	9	0	4	4	1	755	246	451	58	1
	Huntington	7	0	1	1	5	149	35	102	12	0
	Kosciusko	16	1	7	2	6	547	108	398	41	5
	LaGrange	1	0	1	0	0	248	51	183	14	0

Note: The data shown in this table do not reflect county totals but are the number of offenses reported by the sheriff's office or county police department.
[1] The FBI does not publish arson data unless it receives data from either the agency or the state for all 12 months of the calendar year.
[6] Due to an annexation, figures may not be comparable to previous years' data.

Table 10. Offenses Known to Law Enforcement, by State Metropolitan and Nonmetropolitan Counties, 2006 *(Contd.)*
(Number.)

State	County	Violent crime	Murder and non-negligent man-slaughter	Forcible rape	Robbery	Aggra-vated assault	Property crime	Burglary	Larceny-theft	Motor vehicle theft	Arson[1]
	Lawrence	6	1	1	2	2	229	81	140	8	1
	Martin...................	2	0	1	1	0	28	10	14	4	0
	Noble....................	16	1	1	2	12	220	84	131	5	7
	Randolph	7	0	7	0	0	142	55	86	1	0
	Ripley...................	0	0	0	0	0	247	52	180	15	1
	Starke	21	0	3	1	17	397	104	222	71	3
	Steuben	19	0	8	3	8	632	115	479	38	0
	Union	3	0	0	0	3	17	9	7	1	0
	Wabash.................	1	0	0	1	0	156	29	123	4	0
	Wayne	0	0	0	0	0	128	58	65	5	0
IOWA- **Metropolitan Counties**	Benton..................	4	0	0	0	4	62	2	58	2	0
	Black Hawk	30	0	6	1	23	212	82	121	9	4
	Bremer	7	1	0	0	6	50	14	32	4	0
	Dallas	1	0	0	0	1	144	40	98	6	3
	Dubuque...............	48	0	2	0	46	220	96	97	27	5
	Grundy.................	3	0	0	0	3	54	20	33	1	0
	Guthrie.................	0	0	0	0	0	64	29	33	2	0
	Harrison	21	0	3	1	17	154	39	96	19	1
	Jones....................	4	0	0	0	4	53	10	38	5	0
	Linn.....................	57	0	9	1	47	393	158	209	26	5
	Mills....................	16	0	2	0	14	198	70	105	23	0
	Polk.....................	91	1	2	14	74	1,032	242	693	97	6
	Pottawattamie	27	1	5	1	20	578	207	324	47	3
	Scott....................	32	2	5	1	24	259	66	178	15	2
	Story	11	0	4	0	7	166	71	83	12	1
	Warren..................	43	1	6	2	34	268	73	170	25	3
	Washington	22	0	4	0	18	54	26	26	2	0
	Woodbury	33	1	3	2	27	115	47	63	5	3
IOWA- **Nonmetropolitan Counties**	Adair	8	0	0	0	8	34	10	19	5	0
	Adams	3	0	1	0	2	41	8	28	5	0
	Audubon...............	0	0	0	0	0	24	0	21	3	1
	Boone	11	0	2	0	9	43	22	17	4	3
	Buchanan	6	0	0	2	4	138	57	79	2	1
	Buena Vista	7	0	1	1	5	103	37	58	8	0
	Butler	3	1	1	0	1	32	15	15	2	0
	Calhoun.................	5	1	1	0	3	103	38	61	4	2
	Cass......................	2	0	0	1	1	36	12	16	8	0
	Cedar....................	16	0	4	1	11	104	24	66	14	2
	Cerro Gordo..........	12	0	1	0	11	108	38	57	13	0
	Chickasaw.............	4	1	1	0	2	34	16	15	3	0
	Clarke...................	4	0	2	0	2	84	40	37	7	0
	Clay......................	8	0	0	0	8	60	16	41	3	0
	Clayton.................	6	1	2	0	3	77	21	47	9	1
	Davis....................	8	0	0	0	8	11	3	8	0	0
	Delaware...............	8	0	0	0	8	32	12	19	1	1
	Des Moines............	17	0	0	0	17	193	57	125	11	4
	Emmet...................	4	2	0	0	2	23	14	9	0	0
	Fayette	9	0	1	0	8	51	6	37	8	0
	Hamilton...............	18	0	0	0	18	107	66	37	4	1
	Hancock	8	0	0	0	8	41	17	21	3	1
	Hardin	11	0	5	0	6	134	52	78	4	0
	Henry	13	0	0	0	13	74	20	52	2	1
	Howard	2	0	0	1	1	113	17	87	9	0
	Humboldt..............	1	0	0	0	1	42	21	19	2	1
	Ida.......................	7	0	0	0	7	43	6	33	4	0
	Iowa.....................	8	0	0	0	8	80	16	55	9	1
	Jasper	8	0	1	1	6	138	49	81	8	4
	Jefferson...............	6	0	1	1	4	78	19	53	6	0
	Keokuk.................	0	0	0	0	0	9	3	6	0	0
	Kossuth	9	0	0	0	9	49	16	30	3	0
	Lee.......................	11	0	0	0	11	122	73	44	5	2
	Louisa...................	14	1	4	0	9	116	42	60	14	0
	Lucas	6	0	0	1	5	86	31	47	8	1

Note: The data shown in this table do not reflect county totals but are the number of offenses reported by the sheriff's office or county police department.
[1] The FBI does not publish arson data unless it receives data from either the agency or the state for all 12 months of the calendar year.

Table 10. Offenses Known to Law Enforcement, by State Metropolitan and Nonmetropolitan Counties, 2006 (*Contd.*)

(Number.)

State	County	Violent crime	Murder and non-negligent man-slaughter	Forcible rape	Robbery	Aggra-vated assault	Property crime	Burglary	Larceny-theft	Motor vehicle theft	Arson[1]
	Lyon......................	8	0	3	0	5	71	17	52	2	1
	Mahaska................	36	0	2	0	34	103	45	54	4	4
	Marion..................	3	0	0	0	3	115	39	64	12	1
	Marshall	33	0	4	0	29	88	47	34	7	3
	Monona................	0	0	0	0	0	1	0	0	1	0
	Monroe..................	4	0	1	0	3	40	9	25	6	2
	Muscatine..............	19	0	5	0	14	137	64	61	12	4
	O'Brien	10	0	2	0	8	117	55	54	8	0
	Osceola.................	2	0	1	0	1	84	29	52	3	0
	Page	4	0	0	0	4	90	26	52	12	0
	Palo Alto...............	7	0	0	0	7	45	21	21	3	0
	Plymouth...............	18	0	3	1	14	67	28	37	2	1
	Pocahontas............	2	0	0	0	2	40	19	12	9	0
	Poweshiek..............	3	0	1	1	1	177	44	113	20	3
	Sac........................	1	0	0	0	1	39	18	21	0	1
	Sioux.....................	2	0	0	0	2	83	26	53	4	0
	Tama.....................	36	1	1	2	32	155	70	80	5	8
	Taylor	3	0	0	0	3	49	27	22	0	0
	Union	4	0	2	0	2	39	14	23	2	7
	Van Buren..............	14	5	2	0	7	86	39	45	2	0
	Wapello	8	0	2	0	6	189	102	75	12	5
	Wayne....................	4	0	0	0	4	26	6	17	3	0
	Webster..................	30	0	2	0	28	262	91	137	34	1
	Winneshiek............	1	0	0	0	1	38	11	25	2	0
	Worth....................	2	0	1	0	1	123	45	66	12	0
	Wright...................	1	0	0	0	1	62	31	25	6	0
KANSAS- **Metropolitan Counties**	Butler	61	1	9	0	51	534	171	330	33	3
	Doniphan..............	4	0	0	0	4	73	24	46	3	0
	Douglas	34	1	2	0	31	294	74	201	19	2
	Franklin................	59	1	4	1	53	236	93	128	15	3
	Harvey...................	12	0	2	0	10	88	23	54	11	2
	Jackson..................	20	0	3	0	17	172	42	118	12	3
	Jefferson................	29	0	3	1	25	413	103	281	29	6
	Johnson.................	102	0	24	3	75	391	107	274	10	9
	Leavenworth	50	0	1	1	48	258	95	123	40	8
	Linn	7	0	0	0	7	122	61	50	11	1
	Miami	25	1	3	0	21	209	87	101	21	11
	Osage....................	23	1	3	1	18	144	64	69	11	2
	Shawnee................	97	0	19	7	71	1,556	278	1,210	68	25
	Wabaunsee............	10	0	3	0	7	89	14	69	6	2
KANSAS- **Nonmetropolitan Counties**	Allen......................	13	0	2	0	11	55	16	31	8	8
	Anderson	9	0	2	0	7	66	22	38	6	1
	Atchison................	18	0	1	1	16	59	16	39	4	9
	Barber	2	0	0	0	2	33	16	16	1	0
	Barton	21	0	1	0	20	93	18	75	0	
	Bourbon................	6	0	0	1	5	112	33	64	15	7
	Brown....................	7	0	0	0	7	63	24	30	9	0
	Chase....................	2	0	0	0	2	19	8	8	3	2
	Chautauqua	7	0	0	0	7	39	11	26	2	1
	Cherokee	32	1	2	2	27	282	130	132	20	12
	Cheyenne..............	2	0	2	0	0	31	10	17	4	0
	Clay.......................	9	1	0	0	8	64	26	34	4	2
	Cloud....................	4	0	0	0	4	43	13	29	1	0
	Coffey...................	10	0	2	0	8	71	25	40	6	2
	Cowley	40	0	3	0	37	221	84	123	14	3
	Crawford...............	35	0	5	2	28	364	144	198	22	20
	Dickinson..............	6	0	0	0	6	112	27	75	10	4
	Elk	10	0	1	0	9	96	45	45	6	1
	Ellis.......................	8	0	1	0	7	74	22	49	3	4
	Ellsworth...............	4	0	1	0	3	32	7	22	3	2
	Finney...................	34	0	5	2	27	280	65	202	13	6
	Ford......................	18	0	1	1	16	46	19	20	7	1
	Geary.....................	2	0	1	0	1	48	14	32	2	0
	Gove......................	3	0	2	0	1	33	0	32	1	0

Note: The data shown in this table do not reflect county totals but are the number of offenses reported by the sheriff's office or county police department.
[1] The FBI does not publish arson data unless it receives data from either the agency or the state for all 12 months of the calendar year.

Table 10. Offenses Known to Law Enforcement, by State Metropolitan and Nonmetropolitan Counties, 2006 (*Contd.*)

(Number.)

State	County	Violent crime	Murder and non-negligent man-slaughter	Forcible rape	Robbery	Aggra-vated assault	Property crime	Burglary	Larceny-theft	Motor vehicle theft	Arson[1]
	Graham	0	0	0	0	0	18	8	9	1	0
	Grant	6	0	0	0	6	21	2	17	2	1
	Gray	1	0	0	0	1	10	1	8	1	1
	Greenwood	9	0	0	0	9	102	17	79	6	1
	Harper	2	0	1	0	1	37	13	21	3	0
	Haskell	2	0	1	0	1	54	17	35	2	0
	Hodgeman	2	0	0	0	2	50	11	35	4	0
	Kearny	9	0	3	0	6	110	27	79	4	2
	Kingman	9	0	1	0	8	76	23	50	3	1
	Kiowa	6	1	0	0	5	26	6	18	2	0
	Labette	14	0	0	0	14	81	30	47	4	9
	Lane	3	0	0	0	3	44	8	33	3	0
	Lincoln	1	0	0	0	1	36	7	28	1	0
	Logan	1	0	0	0	1	17	1	15	1	0
	Lyon	12	0	3	0	9	93	15	76	2	1
	Marion	2	0	0	1	1	46	17	25	4	0
	Marshall	5	0	0	0	5	35	9	22	4	1
	McPherson	7	0	1	2	4	69	25	39	5	0
	Meade	1	0	1	0	0	28	9	18	1	2
	Montgomery	7	0	0	0	7	140	48	79	13	8
	Morris	4	0	0	0	4	43	9	29	5	6
	Morton	3	0	1	0	2	38	15	20	3	0
	Nemaha	12	1	1	0	10	50	17	29	4	0
	Neosho	9	0	3	0	6	87	39	37	11	4
	Norton	1	0	1	0	0	4	1	3	0	0
	Ottawa	10	0	2	1	7	71	13	54	4	0
	Pawnee	14	0	0	0	14	63	40	20	3	0
	Phillips	4	0	0	0	4	10	6	3	1	0
	Pottawatomie	45	1	4	0	40	402	76	300	26	2
	Pratt	1	0	0	0	1	56	24	30	2	3
	Rawlins	2	0	0	0	2	26	11	14	1	1
	Reno	33	0	3	0	30	340	128	188	24	6
	Republic	2	0	1	0	1	36	12	23	1	7
	Rice	13	0	1	0	12	54	18	34	2	0
	Riley County Police Department	260	0	38	24	198	1,732	254	1,410	68	26
	Rooks	4	0	1	0	3	5	3	2	0	0
	Rush	5	0	0	1	4	32	16	11	5	0
	Russell	7	0	0	0	7	41	8	27	6	1
	Saline	18	1	3	2	12	227	55	155	17	5
	Scott	1	0	0	0	1	29	6	22	1	0
	Seward	5	0	1	1	3	99	12	80	7	3
	Sherman	6	0	0	0	6	31	14	16	1	0
	Smith	5	1	2	0	2	43	15	26	2	1
	Stafford	0	0	0	0	0	41	7	32	2	0
	Stanton	1	1	0	0	0	18	4	11	3	0
	Stevens	14	0	3	2	9	114	61	48	5	0
	Thomas	12	0	1	0	11	52	14	35	3	0
	Trego	3	0	2	0	1	14	10	4	0	0
	Washington	1	0	0	0	1	11	3	5	3	0
	Wichita	0	0	0	0	0	32	8	18	6	0
	Wilson	6	0	0	0	6	16	5	9	2	1
	Woodson	3	0	1	0	2	40	8	28	4	0
KENTUCKY-Metropolitan Counties	Boone	131	0	11	17	103	1,217	259	878	80	4
	Boyd	12	0	2	4	6	207	74	103	30	0
	Boyd County Police Department	0	0	0	0	0	85	22	59	4	0
	Bullitt	22	0	5	4	13	476	154	267	55	1
	Campbell County Police Department	32	1	23	0	8	277	89	165	23	1
	Christian	13	1	1	2	9	285	106	148	31	3
	Christian County Police Department	6	0	0	0	6	1	0	1	0	0

Note: The data shown in this table do not reflect county totals but are the number of offenses reported by the sheriff's office or county police department.

[1] The FBI does not publish arson data unless it receives data from either the agency or the state for all 12 months of the calendar year.

Table 10. Offenses Known to Law Enforcement, by State Metropolitan and Nonmetropolitan Counties, 2006 (*Contd.*)

(Number.)

State	County	Violent crime	Murder and non-negligent man-slaughter	Forcible rape	Robbery	Aggra-vated assault	Property crime	Burglary	Larceny-theft	Motor vehicle theft	Arson[1]
	Clark......................	6	0	4	1	1	244	83	152	9	1
	Daviess.................	28	0	4	1	23	501	120	356	25	3
	Edmonson.............	1	0	0	0	1	32	8	16	8	0
	Gallatin	2	0	0	1	1	24	7	10	7	0
	Grant	5	0	0	3	2	96	28	49	19	0
	Greenup................	3	0	0	0	3	42	14	24	4	0
	Hancock................	0	0	0	0	0	15	4	6	5	0
	Hardin	4	0	0	1	3	66	23	38	5	1
	Henderson	19	1	2	1	15	152	70	73	9	0
	Jefferson...............	0	0	0	0	0	12	0	3	9	0
	Jessamine	15	0	3	3	9	278	106	146	26	0
	Kenton	1	0	0	1	0	5	0	5	0	0
	Larue	0	0	0	0	0	44	16	24	4	0
	McLean	0	0	0	0	0	18	6	10	2	0
	Meade...................	5	0	0	2	3	141	60	70	11	0
	Nelson	16	0	4	1	11	225	83	125	17	0
	Oldham	1	0	0	0	1	7	2	4	1	0
	Oldham County Police Department	20	2	5	7	6	468	136	312	20	0
	Pendleton..............	0	0	0	0	0	86	22	54	10	0
	Scott.....................	14	0	3	4	7	243	86	139	18	0
	Shelby...................	25	0	1	6	18	427	103	287	37	0
	Spencer.................	4	0	1	1	2	39	20	17	2	0
	Trigg.....................	2	0	1	0	1	96	36	51	9	0
	Trimble.................	0	0	0	0	0	7	1	5	1	0
	Warren..................	17	0	0	2	15	584	161	390	33	0
KENTUCKY- **Nonmetropolitan Counties**	Allen......................	3	0	0	0	3	93	23	55	15	0
	Anderson	0	0	0	0	0	99	35	60	4	0
	Ballard..................	2	0	1	0	1	83	24	45	14	1
	Barren	1	0	1	0	0	130	41	73	16	0
	Bell	9	0	0	2	7	128	37	83	8	0
	Boyle	3	0	1	0	2	77	27	45	5	0
	Caldwell................	5	0	1	1	3	41	17	22	2	0
	Calloway	21	0	2	1	18	341	149	166	26	0
	Carlisle	0	0	0	0	0	7	4	3	0	0
	Carter	10	0	1	0	9	161	60	87	14	0
	Casey	0	0	0	0	0	17	5	7	5	0
	Clay......................	4	0	0	0	4	99	22	62	15	0
	Clinton	1	0	0	0	1	4	3	1	0	0
	Crittenden.............	0	0	0	0	0	54	24	25	5	0
	Estill	0	0	0	0	0	25	7	17	1	0
	Fleming	2	0	0	0	2	28	10	15	3	0
	Floyd....................	4	0	0	1	3	126	45	64	17	0
	Franklin................	9	0	0	2	7	187	59	108	20	0
	Fulton...................	3	1	0	0	2	38	11	24	3	0
	Garrard	2	0	0	0	2	106	18	81	7	0
	Graves...................	13	0	2	0	11	84	35	35	14	1
	Grayson.................	3	0	0	0	3	125	72	36	17	0
	Harlan	13	0	0	4	9	65	23	41	1	0
	Harrison................	3	0	1	0	2	96	46	43	7	0
	Hart	0	0	0	0	0	60	36	22	2	0
	Hopkins.................	13	0	3	0	10	198	81	108	9	0
	Jackson.................	0	0	0	0	0	17	4	11	2	0
	Johnson	2	0	0	0	2	29	5	16	8	0
	Knott	0	0	0	0	0	64	9	49	6	0
	Knox.....................	1	0	0	1	0	134	67	54	13	0
	Laurel...................	9	0	1	1	7	590	184	357	49	0
	Letcher.................	3	1	0	1	1	58	24	30	4	0
	Lewis	0	0	0	0	0	82	37	32	13	0
	Lincoln..................	4	0	1	0	3	173	59	102	12	0
	Livingston	3	0	0	0	3	132	67	57	8	0
	Logan	12	0	1	0	11	175	68	99	8	0
	Lyon......................	1	0	0	0	1	26	12	14	0	0

Note: The data shown in this table do not reflect county totals but are the number of offenses reported by the sheriff's office or county police department.
[1] The FBI does not publish arson data unless it receives data from either the agency or the state for all 12 months of the calendar year.

Table 10. Offenses Known to Law Enforcement, by State Metropolitan and Nonmetropolitan Counties, 2006 (*Contd.*)

(Number.)

State	County	Violent crime	Murder and non-negligent man-slaughter	Forcible rape	Robbery	Aggra-vated assault	Property crime	Burglary	Larceny-theft	Motor vehicle theft	Arson[1]
	Madison	12	0	1	0	11	322	103	204	15	0
	Marion	2	0	0	0	2	47	15	27	5	0
	Marshall	22	1	3	2	16	364	144	202	18	3
	Martin	7	0	0	3	4	71	29	26	16	0
	Mason	10	0	0	0	10	103	39	60	4	0
	McCreary	3	0	0	0	3	40	7	25	8	0
	Metcalfe	4	0	0	0	4	36	9	24	3	0
	Montgomery	15	0	0	5	10	345	126	189	30	0
	Morgan	0	0	0	0	0	1	1	0	0	0
	Muhlenberg	6	0	0	0	6	17	4	10	3	0
	Ohio	2	0	0	0	2	87	33	47	7	0
	Owen	1	0	0	0	1	64	30	33	1	0
	Owsley	0	0	0	0	0	8	1	7	0	0
	Pike	0	0	0	0	0	35	8	23	4	0
	Pulaski	15	0	4	4	7	358	108	227	23	3
	Rockcastle	3	0	0	1	2	31	17	10	4	1
	Simpson	6	1	0	1	4	84	24	56	4	0
	Taylor	4	0	0	1	3	116	50	60	6	3
	Todd	0	0	0	0	0	2	1	0	1	0
	Union	5	0	0	0	5	103	49	49	5	0
	Washington	3	0	1	1	1	45	26	18	1	0
	Wayne	3	0	0	1	2	58	20	31	7	0
	Whitley	1	0	0	0	1	94	35	46	13	1
	Wolfe	1	0	0	0	1	32	12	19	1	0
LOUISIANA- **Metropolitan Counties**	Ascension	424	6	29	26	363	2,896	666	1,908	322	9
	Bossier	273	1	11	3	258	596	72	468	56	1
	Caddo	175	10	9	18	138	981	206	670	105	17
	Cameron	30	0	1	0	29	212	43	152	17	1
	East Baton Rouge	961	16	31	248	666	8,872	1,837	6,450	585	52
	Jefferson	2,580	66	84	547	1,883	13,834	3,731	8,444	1,659	173
	Lafayette	271	1	24	29	217	1,586	477	986	123	13
	Lafourche	179	2	8	20	149	1,886	317	1,446	123	0
	Livingston	260	5	28	12	215	1,162	603	426	133	1
	Ouachita	216	1	24	25	166	2,719	943	1,643	133	9
	Plaquemines	57	3	3	2	49	477	106	353	18	3
	St. Charles	121	4	10	40	67	1,460	450	889	121	
	St. John the Baptist	202	4	17	58	123	1,533	366	1,006	161	
	St. Tammany	453	11	35	31	376	2,883	754	1,860	269	28
	Terrebonne	373	2	38	39	294	2,967	696	1,961	310	15
	West Baton Rouge	133	3	7	19	104	577	53	467	57	1
	West Feliciana	63	2	6	3	52	127	22	98	7	0
LOUISIANA- **Nonmetropolitan Counties**	Acadia	36	1	6	2	27	697	117	529	51	0
	Assumption	153	1	0	2	150	349	40	294	15	0
	Bienville	37	1	2	3	31	121	34	83	4	0
	Caldwell	18	0	3	0	15	142	70	65	7	0
	East Carroll	20	0	1	4	15	57	19	34	4	1
	Evangeline	44	0	6	0	38	479	131	289	59	
	Franklin	41	0	3	2	36	199	77	112	10	1
	Lincoln	33	1	1	7	24	313	100	195	18	0
	Madison	38	2	1	5	30	155	50	93	12	3
	Morehouse	33	2	3	3	25	325	58	256	11	4
	Natchitoches	91	0	7	5	79	463	179	248	36	0
	Red River	43	1	2	4	36	107	47	53	7	0
	Richland	10	1	2	1	6	132	42	80	10	0
	Sabine	50	0	0	0	50	308	109	190	9	
	St. James	127	1	5	13	108	628	174	419	35	4
	Tangipahoa	610	4	36	46	524	2,662	1,085	1,474	103	2
	Washington	106	1	8	4	93	672	165	437	70	0
	Webster	63	1	4	3	55	258	114	125	19	1
	West Carroll	33	0	0	0	33	309	103	178	28	0

Note: The data shown in this table do not reflect county totals but are the number of offenses reported by the sheriff's office or county police department.

[1] The FBI does not publish arson data unless it receives data from either the agency or the state for all 12 months of the calendar year.

Table 10. Offenses Known to Law Enforcement, by State Metropolitan and Nonmetropolitan Counties, 2006 (*Contd.*)

(Number.)

State	County	Violent crime	Murder and non-negligent man-slaughter	Forcible rape	Robbery	Aggra-vated assault	Property crime	Burglary	Larceny-theft	Motor vehicle theft	Arson[1]
MAINE- Metropolitan Counties	Androscoggin	10	0	8	1	1	339	80	241	18	1
	Cumberland	26	0	1	6	19	615	280	295	40	6
	Penobscot	8	0	0	4	4	826	250	540	36	1
	Sagadahoc	7	0	0	1	6	196	50	141	5	1
	York	46	0	6	2	38	353	158	173	22	1
MAINE- Nonmetropolitan Counties	Aroostook	7	0	0	0	7	91	22	67	2	1
	Franklin	8	0	0	0	8	110	40	68	2	0
	Hancock	3	0	0	0	3	210	49	146	15	0
	Kennebec	13	1	8	0	4	288	111	162	15	2
	Knox	9	0	1	0	8	194	53	127	14	2
	Lincoln	11	0	5	3	3	204	67	124	13	2
	Oxford	13	0	6	2	5	231	76	146	9	0
	Piscataquis	1	0	1	0	0	99	21	74	4	0
	Somerset	15	0	5	5	5	362	155	185	22	1
	Waldo	9	0	4	0	5	200	58	125	17	0
	Washington	5	0	0	1	4	108	53	52	3	0
MARYLAND- Metropolitan Counties	Allegany	12	0	1	1	10	112	31	74	7	0
	Anne Arundel	1	0	0	0	1	0	0	0	0	0
	Anne Arundel County Police Department	2,634	16	97	709	1,812	15,245	2,906	10,892	1,447	132
	Baltimore County	0	0	0	0	0	0	0	0	0	0
	Baltimore County Police Department	5,664	34	141	2,084	3,405	26,203	4,752	18,022	3,429	361
	Calvert	184	0	4	9	171	1,245	233	935	77	1
	Carroll	56	0	18	0	38	295	78	206	11	1
	Cecil	81	0	2	19	60	891	321	449	121	0
	Charles	695	4	24	192	475	4,019	673	2,933	413	0
	Frederick	134	2	13	18	101	1,552	354	1,106	92	7
	Harford	439	4	31	91	313	2,503	638	1,617	248	24
	Howard	0	0	0	0	0	0	0	0	0	0
	Howard County Police Department	615	4	42	277	292	7,124	1,323	5,170	631	86
	Montgomery	0	0	0	0	0	0	0	0	0	0
	Montgomery County Police Department	2,155	15	141	1,166	833	23,157	3,804	16,860	2,493	324
	Prince George's[7]	353	0	2	3	348	9	0	9	0	0
	Prince George's County Police Department	6,892	117	255	3,341	3,179	38,398	5,729	21,354	11,315	354
	Queen Anne's	87	0	3	7	77	625	175	426	24	2
	Somerset	4	0	0	0	4	30	10	18	2	0
	Washington	199	0	19	29	151	1,392	377	900	115	3
	Wicomico	168	1	11	27	129	961	298	600	63	2
MARYLAND- Nonmetropolitan Counties	Caroline	55	0	0	5	50	339	130	199	10	0
	Dorchester	28	0	3	4	21	339	99	202	38	2
	Garrett	28	1	3	1	23	280	77	193	10	0
	Kent	25	0	0	0	25	108	52	53	3	0
	St. Mary's	233	4	13	53	163	2,058	484	1,438	136	7
	Talbot	15	0	4	3	8	166	52	105	9	0
	Worcester	88	0	4	1	83	109	28	66	15	0
MICHIGAN- Metropolitan Counties	Barry	52	0	11	0	41	352	63	261	28	2
	Bay	56	1	13	10	32	521	123	361	37	3
	Berrien	137	1	27	13	96	823	207	576	40	9
	Calhoun	69	3	6	3	57	541	177	322	42	1
	Cass	29	1	6	4	18	750	207	491	52	6
	Clinton	23	2	4	2	15	253	80	143	30	1
	Eaton	121	0	25	26	70	1,341	250	968	123	3
	Genesee	60	1	11	5	43	641	143	453	45	2
	Ingham	129	2	37	16	74	1,136	255	810	71	20
	Ionia	47	0	16	0	31	394	113	250	31	3

Note: The data shown in this table do not reflect county totals but are the number of offenses reported by the sheriff's office or county police department.

[1] The FBI does not publish arson data unless it receives data from either the agency or the state for all 12 months of the calendar year.

[7] Because of changes in the state/local agency's reporting practices, figures are not comparable to previous years' data.

Table 10. Offenses Known to Law Enforcement, by State Metropolitan and Nonmetropolitan Counties, 2006 (*Contd.*)

(Number.)

State	County	Violent crime	Murder and non-negligent man-slaughter	Forcible rape	Robbery	Aggra-vated assault	Property crime	Burglary	Larceny-theft	Motor vehicle theft	Arson[1]
	Jackson	106	1	25	5	75	651	174	427	50	7
	Kalamazoo	223	0	34	48	141	2,515	664	1,719	132	18
	Kent	296	0	37	29	230	4,242	1,134	2,922	186	36
	Lapeer	68	2	10	5	51	541	132	369	40	5
	Livingston	83	0	9	2	72	1,091	266	742	83	8
	Macomb	604	0	47	61	496	2,831	532	1,993	306	24
	Monroe	181	1	33	27	120	2,594	632	1,730	232	48
	Muskegon	64	0	12	5	47	1,019	214	758	47	12
	Newaygo	64	1	34	2	27	392	130	238	24	6
	Oakland	457	5	72	60	320	4,552	898	3,409	245	50
	Ottawa	320	0	102	29	189	3,062	696	2,210	156	20
	Saginaw	115	2	15	13	85	819	177	569	73	3
	St. Clair	205	2	35	11	157	1,886	465	1,254	167	26
	Van Buren	62	1	15	2	44	710	190	452	68	3
	Washtenaw	267	3	39	78	147	2,131	638	1,189	304	21
	Wayne	235	4	7	79	145	581	146	226	209	6
MICHIGAN- **Nonmetropolitan Counties**	Alcona	22	1	1	0	20	190	69	115	6	2
	Alger	0	0	0	0	0	6	1	4	1	0
	Allegan	71	0	35	5	31	933	215	659	59	7
	Alpena	3	0	1	0	2	41	11	26	4	0
	Antrim	20	1	5	1	13	266	96	158	12	3
	Arenac	31	0	8	2	21	225	79	126	20	2
	Baraga	3	0	0	1	2	15	5	10	0	1
	Benzie	18	2	3	0	13	199	79	116	4	0
	Branch	20	0	11	0	9	280	64	196	20	1
	Charlevoix	20	1	11	0	8	203	60	136	7	1
	Cheboygan	7	0	1	0	6	117	40	73	4	2
	Chippewa	9	0	1	0	8	71	24	44	3	0
	Clare	73	0	14	3	56	990	451	495	44	8
	Crawford	33	0	9	1	23	203	78	107	18	3
	Delta	6	0	2	0	4	81	27	47	7	1
	Dickinson	4	0	1	0	3	74	16	51	7	0
	Emmet	24	0	11	0	13	201	38	157	6	0
	Gladwin	18	0	5	0	13	161	68	88	5	2
	Grand Traverse	99	0	28	2	69	1,061	275	750	36	12
	Gratiot	15	1	8	0	6	200	74	110	16	0
	Hillsdale	30	2	7	3	18	239	89	135	15	0
	Houghton	14	0	1	1	12	96	21	73	2	0
	Huron	13	1	5	1	6	227	59	156	12	1
	Iosco	1	0	0	0	1	10	3	6	1	0
	Iron	5	0	2	0	3	43	11	29	3	0
	Isabella	46	0	11	2	33	534	150	361	23	6
	Kalkaska	31	0	4	1	26	217	75	135	7	3
	Keweenaw	1	0	0	0	1	56	25	29	2	1
	Lake	20	2	3	0	15	263	124	129	10	3
	Leelanau	18	0	5	0	13	156	52	103	1	1
	Lenawee	38	0	14	0	24	290	100	168	22	1
	Mackinac	5	0	0	0	5	74	32	36	6	2
	Manistee	11	0	3	0	8	89	26	59	4	4
	Marquette	12	0	2	1	9	136	41	88	7	0
	Mason	34	1	10	1	22	542	147	375	20	0
	Mecosta	26	0	1	1	24	614	214	350	50	2
	Menominee	8	0	1	0	7	72	38	32	2	0
	Midland	50	0	26	1	23	460	99	347	14	3
	Missaukee	11	0	4	0	7	186	61	121	4	4
	Montcalmv	61	2	33	0	26	636	233	351	52	9
	Montmorency	11	0	1	0	10	58	29	27	2	0
	Oceana	42	0	3	0	39	286	80	196	10	4
	Ogemaw	17	0	6	2	9	215	96	110	9	1
	Ontonagon	5	0	1	0	4	22	8	12	2	0
	Osceola	23	1	6	1	15	165	53	103	9	0
	Oscoda	7	0	2	0	5	185	48	131	6	3
	Otsego	8	0	1	0	7	91	32	56	3	0
	Roscommon	28	1	5	1	21	321	83	207	31	0
	Sanilac	16	0	1	0	15	213	81	116	16	0

Note: The data shown in this table do not reflect county totals but are the number of offenses reported by the sheriff's office or county police department.
[1] The FBI does not publish arson data unless it receives data from either the agency or the state for all 12 months of the calendar year.

Table 10. Offenses Known to Law Enforcement, by State Metropolitan and Nonmetropolitan Counties, 2006 (*Contd.*)

(Number.)

State	County	Violent crime	Murder and non-negligent man-slaughter	Forcible rape	Robbery	Aggra-vated assault	Property crime	Burglary	Larceny-theft	Motor vehicle theft	Arson[1]
	Shiawassee	57	1	12	8	36	473	120	316	37	1
	St. Joseph	20	0	7	0	13	274	80	177	17	3
	Tuscola	25	0	9	0	16	318	97	190	31	3
	Wexford	28	0	6	0	22	371	147	212	12	4
MINNESOTA- **Metropolitan Counties[8]**	Anoka		0		3	25	1,012	227	712	73	6
	Benton		0		2	6	352	65	254	33	6
	Carlton		0		0	9	134	35	85	14	0
	Carver		0		4	41	1,152	159	928	65	4
	Chisago		2		1	18	689	132	506	51	2
	Clay		0		0	5	116	41	64	11	0
	Dakota		0		1	10	236	75	139	22	1
	Dodge		0		2	2	311	72	212	27	1
	Hennepin		0		2	14	198	33	158	7	2
	Houston		0		0	3	58	11	42	5	1
	Isanti		1		0	12	332	100	185	47	2
	Olmsted		0		2	13	498	185	271	42	6
	Polk		0		0	22	228	81	137	10	4
	Ramsey		0		11	42	1,227	158	943	126	24
	Scott		0		1	14	183	49	114	20	1
	Sherburne		2		2	42	685	142	486	57	2
	Stearns		0		3	49	512	100	388	24	0
	St. Louis		1		2	48	913	350	488	75	4
	Washington		2		4	38	1,054	210	780	64	9
	Wright		2		9	53	2,139	257	1,733	149	9
MINNESOTA **Nonmetropolitan Counties[8]**	Aitkin		1		0	7	394	137	223	34	1
	Becker		0		1	25	252	88	127	37	5
	Beltrami		0		3	32	507	122	343	42	3
	Big Stone		0		0	2	55	20	33	2	2
	Blue Earth		0		0	6	244	67	164	13	9
	Brown		0		1	1	19	4	12	3	3
	Cass		0		8	55	661	218	386	57	1
	Clearwater		0		0	13	134	30	97	7	2
	Cook		0		1	7	127	10	106	11	0
	Cottonwood		0		0	2	51	18	33	0	3
	Crow Wing		0		1	34	587	185	374	28	3
	Douglas		0		0	13	297	64	220	13	1
	Faribault		0		0	4	82	52	25	5	0
	Fillmore		0		0	10	111	44	55	12	1
	Freeborn		0		0	7	173	48	112	13	0
	Goodhue		0		2	15	425	135	243	47	1
	Grant		0		2	7	71	23	45	3	0
	Hubbard		0		1	13	319	121	179	19	1
	Itasca		1		2	32	422	151	239	32	5
	Jackson		0		0	2	33	12	21	0	0
	Kanabec		0		0	14	277	113	142	22	2
	Kandiyohi		0		1	16	302	81	200	21	4
	Kittson		0		0	2	60	5	51	4	0
	Koochiching		0		0	5	134	35	83	16	1
	Lac Qui Parle		0		0	2	52	19	30	3	0
	Lake		0		0	0	91	31	58	2	0
	Lake of the Woods		0		0	2	75	11	58	6	0
	Le Sueur		0		0	9	120	5	109	6	0
	Lincoln		0		0	7	26	3	23	0	0
	Lyon		0		0	1	67	16	45	6	0
	McLeod		0		0	14	117	36	68	13	1
	Meeker		1		0	6	298	81	195	22	0
	Mille Lacs		0		2	32	581	126	403	52	4
	Morrison		0		0	13	411	50	331	30	8
	Mower		0		0	21	272	85	152	35	3
	Murray		0		0	1	59	12	40	7	0
	Nicollet		0		0	7	101	20	70	11	1

Note: The data shown in this table do not reflect county totals but are the number of offenses reported by the sheriff's office or county police department.

[1] The FBI does not publish arson data unless it receives data from either the agency or the state for all 12 months of the calendar year.

[8] The data collection methodology for the offense of forcible rape used by the Minnesota state UCR Program does not comply with national UCR Program guidelines. Consequently, its figures for forcible rape and violent crime (of which forcible rape is a part) are not published in this table.

Table 10. Offenses Known to Law Enforcement, by State Metropolitan and Nonmetropolitan Counties, 2006 (*Contd.*)
(Number.)

State	County	Violent crime	Murder and non-negligent man-slaughter	Forcible rape	Robbery	Aggra-vated assault	Property crime	Burglary	Larceny-theft	Motor vehicle theft	Arson[1]
	Nobles		0		0	5	49	20	27	2	0
	Otter Tail		2		1	25	490	192	262	36	9
	Pennington		0		0	3	56	20	32	4	0
	Pine		0		4	23	1,068	313	683	72	3
	Pipestone		0		0	3	92	18	69	5	1
	Pope		0		0	3	36	10	23	3	1
	Redwood		1		0	10	119	37	74	8	1
	Renville		1		0	9	169	58	99	12	1
	Rice		0		1	11	289	130	124	35	11
	Rock		0		0	26	68	19	42	7	0
	Roseau		0		0	0	126	17	105	4	0
	Steele		0		0	8	193	97	84	12	1
	Stevens		0		0	2	34	15	16	3	1
	Todd		1		0	7	260	108	137	15	5
	Wadena		1		0	8	82	31	46	5	0
	Waseca		0		0	3	78	39	36	3	1
	Watonwan		0		0	4	93	38	50	5	0
	Winona		0		0	9	111	24	76	11	0
	Yellow Medicine		0		0	3	57	15	39	3	0
MISSISSIPPI- **Metropolitan Counties**	Desoto	46	2	8	13	23	704	126	456	122	0
	Harrison	77	6	20	14	37	2,155	508	1,365	282	5
	Jackson	111	0	11	19	81	2,024	463	1,221	340	0
	Lamar[7]	52	1	20	8	23	778	259	471	48	6
	Madison	67	3	5	16	43	453	126	291	36	0
	Rankin	54	2	3	2	47	749	302	407	40	10
	Simpson	18	3	4	2	9	199	98	76	25	1
	Stone	30	0	3	0	27	75	13	55	7	2
	Tate	14	2	0	3	9	227	83	85	59	1
	Tunica	104	5	2	38	59	772	128	546	98	0
MISSISSIPPI- **Nonmetropolitan Counties**	Adams	35	2	5	3	25	489	149	305	35	1
	Chickasaw	16	0	0	3	13	50	29	19	2	0
	Claiborne	24	2	2	6	14	146	97	47	2	1
	Coahoma	12	3	0	4	5	121	54	48	19	0
	Grenada	6	0	0	1	5	151	52	81	18	0
	Issaquena	0	0	0	0	0	0	0	0	0	0
	Itawamba	5	0	2	1	2	144	62	73	9	0
	Jefferson	33	1	4	3	25	39	23	16	0	0
	Lauderdale	41	0	8	8	25	497	247	213	37	0
	Leflore	185	4	5	17	159	513	195	281	37	5
	Lincoln[4]		1	1	0		298	50	211	37	11
	Lowndes	101	1	15	18	67	506	172	306	28	2
	Marion	45	3	6	14	22	340	159	139	42	0
	Oktibbeha	6	0	0	0	6	32	13	18	1	1
	Panola	53	0	7	11	35	560	268	243	49	0
	Pearl River	21	1	12	7	1	691	254	367	70	2
	Pike	30	0	5	4	21	426	164	230	32	
	Sharkey	9	0	0	0	9	27	18	7	2	0
	Tippah	26	1	1	1	23	23	4	18	1	1
	Tishomingo	24	0	0	23	1	97	89	3	5	0
	Union	9	1	0	6	2	224	122	78	24	9
	Warren	14	1	2	1	10	361	131	190	40	0
	Washington	19	2	9	1	7	315	111	172	32	5
MISSOURI- **Metropolitan Counties**	Andrew	2	2	0	0	0	151	37	96	18	0
	Bates	27	0	0	0	27	148	58	74	16	1
	Boone	150	0	6	19	125	907	211	607	89	8
	Buchanan	35	0	0	0	35	221	73	136	12	3
	Caldwell	18	0	0	4	14	95	34	46	15	1
	Callaway	42	2	4	5	31	576	137	399	40	4
	Cass	80	0	12	2	66	421	129	257	35	1
	Christian	157	0	2	0	155	294	91	168	35	0
	Clay	32	2	3	0	27	225	70	120	35	3

Note: The data shown in this table do not reflect county totals but are the number of offenses reported by the sheriff's office or county police department.
[1] The FBI does not publish arson data unless it receives data from either the agency or the state for all 12 months of the calendar year.
[4] The FBI determined that the agency's data were inflated. Consequently, affected data are not included in this table.
[7] Because of changes in the state/local agency's reporting practices, figures are not comparable to previous years' data.

Table 10. Offenses Known to Law Enforcement, by State Metropolitan and Nonmetropolitan Counties, 2006 (*Contd.*)

(Number.)

State	County	Violent crime	Murder and non-negligent man-slaughter	Forcible rape	Robbery	Aggra-vated assault	Property crime	Burglary	Larceny-theft	Motor vehicle theft	Arson[1]
	Clinton	16	0	6	1	9	156	50	88	18	2
	Cole	40	0	6	2	32	495	130	321	44	5
	Dallas	55	0	5	0	50	221	95	107	19	5
	De Kalb	31	0	7	0	24	57	14	31	12	1
	Franklin	58	0	2	1	55	848	188	615	45	5
	Greene	442	0	6	11	425	1,488	303	1,078	107	1
	Howard	9	1	2	0	6	56	33	16	7	0
	Jackson	55	1	4	11	39	644	187	392	65	7
	Jasper	73	0	10	10	53	703	202	423	78	1
	Jefferson	398	3	36	17	342	3,599	421	2,944	234	40
	Lafayette	21	0	1	0	20	183	74	90	19	0
	Lincoln	87	0	4	1	82	266	70	170	26	1
	McDonald	68	0	12	4	52	419	106	243	70	2
	Moniteau	7	0	1	0	6	38	13	15	10	0
	Newton	87	1	5	3	78	922	221	630	71	21
	Osage	13	0	0	0	13	73	18	46	9	1
	Platte	26	0	0	3	23	295	67	220	8	5
	Polk	31	0	2	1	28	258	107	142	9	1
	Ray	33	0	4	0	29	164	69	73	22	1
	St. Charles	218	0	6	16	196	1,808	292	1,433	83	36
	St. Louis County Police Department	1,240	14	60	312	854	10,547	1,961	7,433	1,153	105
	Warren	63	1	4	3	55	252	60	152	40	3
	Washington	73	0	4	1	68	218	57	129	32	7
	Webster	39	0	2	1	36	315	112	177	26	4
MISSOURI- Nonmetropolitan Counties	Adair	17	1	0	1	15	20	6	8	6	3
	Atchison	3	0	2	1	0	8	3	2	3	1
	Audrain	12	0	1	1	10	158	44	105	9	1
	Barry	46	2	8	1	35	521	183	306	32	6
	Barton	23	0	3	1	19	127	27	99	1	4
	Benton	36	0	1	0	35	268	82	168	18	2
	Bollinger	10	0	0	0	10	86	35	48	3	3
	Butler	37	1	0	3	33	505	152	295	58	4
	Camden	61	1	0	1	59	578	179	370	29	4
	Cape Girardeau	87	0	2	1	84	228	58	161	9	0
	Carroll	3	0	1	0	2	68	14	49	5	0
	Carter	1	0	0	0	1	56	16	27	13	0
	Cedar	10	0	0	2	8	102	39	61	2	3
	Clark	4	0	2	0	2	58	28	26	4	0
	Cooper	34	1	1	0	32	164	35	117	12	0
	Crawford	44	0	0	1	43	289	98	170	21	3
	Dade	7	0	2	0	5	35	21	10	4	2
	Daviess	7	2	0	0	5	68	37	26	5	0
	Dent	17	0	0	0	17	131	47	63	21	0
	Douglas	36	0	0	2	34	122	47	58	17	6
	Dunklin	16	0	3	1	12	168	53	113	2	0
	Gasconade	34	0	3	1	30	90	41	41	8	1
	Gentry	6	0	0	0	6	72	45	16	11	0
	Grundy	5	0	0	0	5	42	21	19	2	2
	Harrison	6	0	1	0	5	54	16	36	2	1
	Henry	18	1	2	1	14	224	86	123	15	19
	Hickory	1	0	1	0	0	146	52	79	15	0
	Holt	3	0	0	2	1	96	35	42	19	1
	Howell	126	0	0	0	126	445	132	259	54	7
	Iron	13	0	0	1	12	114	55	43	16	5
	Johnson	37	0	1	0	36	370	142	211	17	0
	Knox	5	0	0	0	5	110	15	94	1	0
	Laclede	24	0	1	4	19	361	125	218	18	1
	Lawrence	12	0	0	0	12	249	106	120	23	4
	Lewis	8	0	1	0	7	86	31	52	3	2
	Linn	23	0	0	0	23	37	14	16	7	3
	Livingston	1	0	0	0	1	51	16	34	1	1
	Macon	19	0	2	0	17	58	23	30	5	8
	Madison	15	0	3	0	12	85	36	42	7	1

Note: The data shown in this table do not reflect county totals but are the number of offenses reported by the sheriff's office or county police department.
[1] The FBI does not publish arson data unless it receives data from either the agency or the state for all 12 months of the calendar year.

Table 10. Offenses Known to Law Enforcement, by State Metropolitan and Nonmetropolitan Counties, 2006 (*Contd.*)

(Number.)

State	County	Violent crime	Murder and non-negligent man-slaughter	Forcible rape	Robbery	Aggra-vated assault	Property crime	Burglary	Larceny-theft	Motor vehicle theft	Arson[1]
	Maries	12	0	0	0	12	72	35	33	4	1
	Marion	8	0	0	0	8	99	24	74	1	0
	Mercer	6	0	0	0	6	30	23	5	2	0
	Miller	51	0	4	0	47	190	78	93	19	6
	Mississippi	25	2	2	0	21	64	23	35	6	0
	Monroe	4	0	1	0	3	63	23	36	4	1
	Montgomery	6	0	0	0	6	131	50	69	12	3
	Morgan	117	0	0	0	117	231	110	107	14	4
	New Madrid	39	1	3	1	34	71	26	34	11	0
	Nodaway	8	0	1	0	7	139	43	90	6	1
	Oregon	12	0	0	0	12	28	13	13	2	3
	Ozark	16	0	2	2	12	77	25	43	9	2
	Pemiscot	15	1	1	3	10	90	36	50	4	1
	Perry	11	0	0	0	11	67	27	38	2	0
	Pettis	29	0	1	2	26	232	73	147	12	1
	Phelps	143	2	8	3	130	451	141	271	39	2
	Pike	6	1	1	0	4	56	33	22	1	3
	Pulaski	106	1	16	6	83	263	113	124	26	3
	Putnam	0	0	0	0	0	10	4	6	0	0
	Ralls	34	0	0	1	33	111	43	58	10	3
	Randolph	13	0	1	2	10	159	54	99	6	1
	Reynolds	6	0	3	0	3	14	10	1	3	0
	Ripley	21	0	2	0	19	269	88	151	30	5
	Saline	6	0	0	0	6	128	33	86	9	0
	Schuyler	8	1	0	1	6	22	10	7	5	3
	Scotland	1	0	0	0	1	39	8	31	0	0
	Scott	19	0	3	1	15	195	53	124	18	1
	Shannon	12	0	0	0	12	62	24	24	14	1
	Shelby	4	0	0	0	4	52	24	28	0	0
	St. Clair	14	0	0	0	14	130	38	92	0	0
	Ste. Genevieve	32	0	5	1	26	173	53	114	6	4
	St. Francois	63	0	8	1	54	493	149	284	60	10
	Stoddard	24	1	1	0	22	131	45	75	11	1
	Stone	252	1	11	0	240	742	260	409	73	7
	Sullivan	13	0	1	0	12	49	23	20	6	1
	Taney	97	0	9	2	86	506	150	330	26	2
	Texas	50	3	2	0	45	179	61	89	29	8
	Vernon	31	0	1	0	30	270	87	167	16	8
	Wayne	2	0	0	0	2	107	36	58	13	3
	Worth	0	0	0	0	0	18	9	7	2	0
	Wright	15	0	1	1	13	75	13	54	8	1
MONTANA-**Metropolitan Counties**	Carbon	1	0	0	0	1	33	3	28	2	0
	Yellowstone	36	1	5	4	26	666	108	507	51	9
MONTANA-**Nonmetropolitan Counties**	Beaverhead	8	0	0	0	8	42	8	29	5	0
	Big Horn	56	0	2	1	53	232	11	191	30	3
	Blaine	16	0	0	0	16	35	5	25	5	1
	Broadwater	12	0	1	0	11	181	4	166	11	0
	Chouteau	3	0	0	0	3	19	5	13	1	0
	Dawson	8	0	0	0	8	74	13	57	4	2
	Deer Lodge	34	1	5	0	28	102	12	78	12	0
	Fergus	6	0	0	0	6	36	5	21	10	0
	Flathead[5]	149	0	18	4	127		174	723		0
	Gallatin	51	1	9	2	39	401	68	281	52	2
	Glacier	24	0	2	1	21	43	10	28	5	1
	Granite	3	0	0	0	3	33	7	23	3	0
	Hill	23	0	1	1	21	179	13	157	9	1
	Jefferson	20	0	5	0	15	46	9	28	9	1
	Lake	75	1	8	3	63	340	56	250	34	4
	Lewis and Clark	45	0	6	0	39	374	69	271	34	6
	Lincoln	29	0	2	1	26	238	41	180	17	1
	Madison	6	0	0	0	6	57	9	40	8	4
	Mineral	27	0	0	2	25	25	13	8	4	1
	Park	20	0	1	0	19	77	19	53	5	2

Note: The data shown in this table do not reflect county totals but are the number of offenses reported by the sheriff's office or county police department.
[1] The FBI does not publish arson data unless it receives data from either the agency or the state for all 12 months of the calendar year.
[5] The FBI determined that the agency's data were underreported. Consequently, affected data are not included in this table.

Table 10. Offenses Known to Law Enforcement, by State Metropolitan and Nonmetropolitan Counties, 2006 (Contd.)

(Number.)

State	County	Violent crime	Murder and non-negligent manslaughter	Forcible rape	Robbery	Aggra-vated assault	Property crime	Burglary	Larceny-theft	Motor vehicle theft	Arson[1]
	Phillips	8	0	0	0	8	69	20	44	5	0
	Powell	15	0	0	0	15	155	14	128	13	1
	Roosevelt	7	1	0	0	6	30	6	24	0	1
	Rosebud	19	0	2	0	17	44	20	18	6	1
	Sanders	20	0	2	0	18	151	23	115	13	4
	Sheridan	1	0	0	0	1	17	4	12	1	0
	Silver Bow	149	2	4	4	139	992	129	769	94	6
	Stillwater	3	0	1	0	2	24	9	13	2	0
	Sweet Grass	8	1	1	0	6	30	2	24	4	0
	Teton	9	0	1	0	8	52	5	35	12	0
	Toole	18	0	2	0	16	64	12	43	9	1
NEBRASKA- **Metropolitan Counties**	Dixon	5	0	3	0	2	82	29	49	4	1
	Douglas	122	1	6	12	103	1,528	343	1,090	95	0
	Lancaster	15	0	3	0	12	452	98	341	13	3
	Sarpy	13	0	1	0	12	843	84	712	47	4
	Saunders	1	0	0	0	1	88	19	61	8	0
	Washington	2	0	0	1	1	98	28	68	2	0
NEBRASKA- **Nonmetropolitan Counties**	Adams	0	0	0	0	0	125	41	77	7	1
	Antelope	0	0	0	0	0	30	7	22	1	1
	Arthur	0	0	0	0	0	2	1	0	1	0
	Box Butte	0	0	0	0	0	2	0	2	0	1
	Brown	2	0	0	2	0	60	9	50	1	0
	Buffalo	11	0	3	0	8	219	65	144	10	4
	Burt	1	0	0	0	1	78	33	44	1	0
	Butler	2	0	0	0	2	52	5	47	0	1
	Chase	1	0	0	0	1	17	3	12	2	0
	Cherry	3	0	0	0	3	8	2	4	2	0
	Colfax	7	0	0	0	7	53	5	47	1	0
	Cuming	1	0	1	0	0	20	8	8	4	0
	Custer	2	0	0	1	1	79	12	66	1	0
	Deuel	0	0	0	0	0	31	10	18	3	0
	Dodge	10	2	1	1	6	138	18	111	9	1
	Franklin	2	0	0	0	2	19	2	16	1	0
	Frontier	1	0	0	0	1	28	5	23	0	1
	Furnas	2	0	0	0	2	21	5	16	0	0
	Gage	3	0	0	0	3	168	26	136	6	1
	Garden	1	0	0	0	1	9	2	7	0	0
	Hall	11	0	5	1	5	259	63	184	12	0
	Hamilton	1	0	0	0	1	56	16	28	12	0
	Hitchcock	0	0	0	0	0	4	1	3	0	2
	Hooker	0	0	0	0	0	0	0	0	0	0
	Howard	7	0	2	0	5	24	5	19	0	0
	Jefferson	5	1	1	0	3	64	23	39	2	1
	Kearney	6	0	2	0	4	42	12	30	0	0
	Keith	0	0	0	0	0	67	23	39	5	1
	Keya Paha	0	0	0	0	0	1	0	1	0	0
	Kimball	1	0	0	0	1	17	6	11	0	0
	Knox	1	0	0	0	1	30	1	26	3	0
	Lincoln	6	0	0	0	6	122	25	93	4	0
	Madison	4	0	2	0	2	86	21	60	5	1
	Merrick	1	0	0	0	1	90	22	60	8	0
	Nance	1	0	1	0	0	24	8	8	8	0
	Nemaha	3	1	1	1	0	32	9	19	4	1
	Pawnee	3	1	0	1	1	52	11	39	2	1
	Platte	7	0	1	0	6	227	65	146	16	1
	Polk	0	0	0	0	0	48	8	35	5	0
	Red Willow	3	0	0	0	3	58	6	49	3	0
	Richardson	0	0	0	0	0	30	11	17	2	0
	Rock	1	0	0	0	1	21	12	8	1	0
	Saline	7	0	1	0	6	82	19	58	5	0
	Scotts Bluff	7	0	0	0	7	126	24	88	14	0
	Sheridan	5	0	2	0	3	46	13	29	4	0
	Sioux	0	0	0	0	0	0	0	0	0	0
	Stanton	5	0	0	0	5	81	31	48	2	0

Note: The data shown in this table do not reflect county totals but are the number of offenses reported by the sheriff's office or county police department.
[1] The FBI does not publish arson data unless it receives data from either the agency or the state for all 12 months of the calendar year.

Table 10. Offenses Known to Law Enforcement, by State Metropolitan and Nonmetropolitan Counties, 2006 (*Contd.*)

(Number.)

State	County	Violent crime	Murder and non-negligent man-slaughter	Forcible rape	Robbery	Aggra-vated assault	Property crime	Burglary	Larceny-theft	Motor vehicle theft	Arson[1]
	Thayer	1	0	0	0	1	89	24	62	3	0
	Wayne	0	0	0	0	0	11	3	8	0	0
	Webster	3	0	1	1	1	17	2	12	3	0
	Wheeler	0	0	0	0	0	4	0	4	0	0
	York	2	0	2	0	0	66	13	49	4	0
NEVADA- **Metropolitan Counties**	Carson City	195	2	2	22	169	1,247	291	819	137	11
	Storey	0	0	0	0	0	65	17	45	3	0
	Washoe	199	4	0	22	173	1,631	566	846	219	10
NEVADA- **Nonmetropolitan Counties**	Churchill	52	1	9	0	42	295	118	155	22	3
	Douglas	87	2	24	2	59	1,008	207	740	61	8
	Elko	19	1	6	0	12	192	87	87	18	3
	Esmeralda	3	0	0	0	3	6	1	4	1	0
	Eureka	6	0	1	0	5	24	9	11	4	0
	Humboldt	51	0	0	2	49	49	13	30	6	1
	Lander	43	0	11	2	30	104	43	54	7	0
	Lincoln	4	0	0	0	4	46	8	29	9	2
	Lyon	85	1	5	5	74	728	207	444	77	17
	Mineral	7	0	1	0	6	46	23	18	5	1
	Nye	124	2	9	10	103	936	271	475	190	29
	Pershing	73	1	10	0	62	64	36	26	2	0
	White Pine	39	1	4	1	33	202	61	111	30	1
NEW HAMPSHIRE- **Metropolitan Counties**	Rockingham	17	0	0	0	17	19	0	17	2	0
NEW HAMPSHIRE- **Nonmetropolitan Counties**	Carroll	6	0	2	1	3	33	16	16	1	0
	Cheshire	0	0	0	0	0	7	0	6	1	0
	Merrimack	7	0	5	0	2	9	1	8	0	1
NEW JERSEY- **Metropolitan Counties**	Essex County Police Department	119	2	2	73	42	124	20	85	19	3
NEW MEXICO- **Metropolitan Counties**	Bernalillo	821	13	46	115	647	2,556	878	1,258	420	65
	Sandoval	29	1	1	0	27	164	91	69	4	2
	San Juan	269	2	31	9	227	1,074	233	771	70	9
	Santa Fe	199	0	24	10	165	1,005	746	258	1	16
	Valencia	145	4	13	17	111	1,329	642	360	327	26
NEW MEXICO- **Nonmetropolitan Counties**	Chaves	35	1	5	0	29	425	202	192	31	2
	Cibola	50	0	3	1	46	130	66	45	19	0
	Eddy	63	0	11	4	48	382	149	215	18	0
	Grant	7	0	1	0	6	96	58	38	0	0
	Harding	0	0	0	0	0	2	2	0	0	0
	Lea	58	0	23	1	34	416	162	230	24	2
	McKinley	117	0	0	12	105	299	113	146	40	9
	Mora	6	1	0	2	3	16	13	1	2	0
	Otero[4]		0	5	2		218	91	114	13	1
	Rio Arriba	44	0	2	0	42	85	68	9	8	2
	Sierra	7	0	2	0	5	63	28	30	5	0
	Socorro	25	0	0	1	24	68	18	37	13	2
NEW YORK- **Metropolitan Counties**	Albany	32	0	1	2	29	113	25	86	2	0
	Broome	51	1	4	8	38	1,045	183	827	35	1
	Chemung	12	0	1	5	6	378	58	296	24	3
	Dutchess	68	0	7	11	50	762	159	573	30	2
	Erie	113	2	8	7	96	858	229	613	16	11
	Herkimer	0	0	0	0	0	8	0	8	0	0
	Livingston	34	1	7	3	23	816	91	708	17	1
	Madison	7	0	3	0	4	227	82	137	8	0
	Monroe	219	1	19	68	131	3,948	675	3,080	193	18
	Nassau	1,813	14	74	866	859	14,713	2,170	11,372	1,171	
	Niagara	94	0	13	22	59	1,322	373	874	75	10
	Oneida	58	1	3	3	51	571	147	398	26	7
	Onondaga	166	2	22	51	91	1,876	399	1,397	80	24
	Ontario	53	1	9	7	36	967	228	669	70	

Note: The data shown in this table do not reflect county totals but are the number of offenses reported by the sheriff's office or county police department.
[1] The FBI does not publish arson data unless it receives data from either the agency or the state for all 12 months of the calendar year.
[4] The FBI determined that the agency's data were inflated. Consequently, affected data are not included in this table.

Table 10. Offenses Known to Law Enforcement, by State Metropolitan and Nonmetropolitan Counties, 2006 (*Contd.*)

(Number.)

State	County	Violent crime	Murder and non-negligent man-slaughter	Forcible rape	Robbery	Aggra-vated assault	Property crime	Burglary	Larceny-theft	Motor vehicle theft	Arson[1]
	Orange	4	0	0	0	4	7	0	7	0	0
	Orleans	26	0	3	4	19	286	107	169	10	3
	Oswego	34	0	7	3	24	487	155	309	23	0
	Rensselaer	42	0	5	8	29	222	61	148	13	0
	Rockland	7	0	0	1	6	37	3	34	0	0
	Saratoga	40	1	4	6	29	1,094	204	846	44	6
	Schenectady	6	0	0	4	2	11	0	8	3	0
	Schoharie	2	1	0	0	1	75	16	54	5	0
	Suffolk	264	0	0	1	263	13	0	13	0	0
	Suffolk County Police Department	2,481	37	86	1,027	1,331	24,811	3,373	19,110	2,328	268
	Tioga	12	0	2	1	9	227	75	138	14	0
	Tompkins	30	0	18	2	10	475	93	360	22	0
	Ulster	52	0	3	5	44	340	69	247	24	1
	Warren	43	0	11	5	27	842	174	643	25	6
	Washington	31	1	6	0	24	397	126	260	11	4
	Wayne	49	0	7	9	33	676	200	440	36	1
	Westchester Public Safety	75	0	4	12	59	305	18	281	6	1
NEW YORK- **Nonmetropolitan Counties**	Allegany	2	0	0	0	2	4	0	4	0	1
	Cattaraugus	52	0	11	0	41	589	146	414	29	4
	Cayuga	15	0	3	1	11	331	93	226	12	4
	Chautauqua	46	0	15	4	27	742	180	531	31	4
	Chenango	28	0	1	0	27	335	80	248	7	4
	Clinton	3	0	0	0	3	12	0	11	1	1
	Columbia	21	3	2	6	10	432	93	334	5	3
	Cortland	16	0	8	0	8	311	54	250	7	3
	Delaware	16	1	1	0	14	132	37	89	6	0
	Franklin	0	0	0	0	0	0	0	0	0	0
	Fulton	14	0	2	1	11	427	112	281	34	0
	Genesee	41	0	6	7	28	700	139	536	25	4
	Greene	2	0	0	0	2	40	10	25	5	1
	Hamilton	1	0	0	0	1	10	2	8	0	0
	Jefferson	39	0	8	5	26	534	114	405	15	2
	Lewis	5	0	0	0	5	159	105	44	10	
	Montgomery	13	0	0	1	12	398	51	335	12	0
	Otsego	15	1	4	0	10	156	48	103	5	3
	Schuyler	7	0	1	0	6	92	27	60	5	1
	Seneca	8	0	1	1	6	158	17	133	8	3
	Steuben	18	0	2	0	16	123	33	89	1	0
	St. Lawrence	25	0	3	1	21	369	116	231	22	5
	Sullivan	40	1	4	5	30	508	107	372	29	1
	Wyoming	41	0	2	2	37	294	79	197	18	0
	Yates	12	0	1	1	10	197	51	139	7	0
NORTH CAROLINA- **Metropolitan Counties**	Alamance	130	2	7	10	111	1,281	452	737	92	7
	Alexander	60	2	6	6	46	716	328	336	52	4
	Anson	56	5	2	11	38	566	249	275	42	2
	Brunswick	148	6	20	27	95	2,339	1,038	1,078	223	12
	Buncombe	220	1	17	48	154	2,717	1,069	1,389	259	11
	Cabarrus	34	2	2	13	17	1,277	595	626	56	4
	Caldwell	64	1	6	9	48	1,379	528	771	80	22
	Catawba	135	4	11	30	90	1,635	622	862	151	16
	Chatham	117	2	4	17	94	898	384	428	86	6
	Cumberland	554	11	20	95	428	4,896	1,624	2,931	341	40
	Currituck	63	1	6	9	47	502	194	287	21	2
	Davie	67	1	4	4	58	682	254	383	45	4
	Durham	64	3	0	15	46	904	222	600	82	5
	Edgecombe	78	1	4	18	55	662	273	325	64	7
	Forsyth	331	2	17	49	263	2,867	799	1,884	184	56
	Franklin	14	0	2	5	7	727	330	348	49	2
	Greene	72	1	18	19	34	523	197	299	27	2
	Guilford	217	3	12	37	165	1,984	750	1,074	160	32
	Haywood	101	1	8	2	90	980	417	473	90	7
	Henderson	105	3	16	12	74	1,409	551	696	162	2

Note: The data shown in this table do not reflect county totals but are the number of offenses reported by the sheriff's office or county police department.
[1] The FBI does not publish arson data unless it receives data from either the agency or the state for all 12 months of the calendar year.

Table 10. Offenses Known to Law Enforcement, by State Metropolitan and Nonmetropolitan Counties, 2006 (Contd.)

(Number.)

State	County	Violent crime	Murder and non-negligent man-slaughter	Forcible rape	Robbery	Aggra-vated assault	Property crime	Burglary	Larceny-theft	Motor vehicle theft	Arson[1]
	Hoke	115	3	11	20	81	1,229	654	507	68	32
	Johnston	141	9	8	23	101	2,315	789	1,275	251	7
	Madison	19	0	2	0	17	192	80	94	18	2
	Nash	57	5	5	11	36	777	282	407	88	7
	New Hanover	258	0	30	39	189	2,738	735	1,881	122	8
	Onslow	335	6	39	62	228	2,660	895	1,567	198	27
	Orange	23	1	2	14	6	769	330	371	68	2
	Pender	65	0	4	13	48	905	320	483	102	6
	Person	93	1	3	5	84	577	277	276	24	2
	Pitt	314	4	19	32	259	1,572	553	921	98	11
	Rockingham	67	4	3	8	52	1,490	504	873	113	2
	Stokes	116	0	4	8	104	924	329	510	85	11
	Union[5]		4	7	25		2,662	1,009	1,550	103	12
	Wake	208	4	22	35	147	2,828	1,062	1,487	279	18
	Wayne	194	3	4	38	149	2,047	834	1,096	117	4
	Yadkin	86	0	4	5	77	648	263	335	50	1
NORTH CAROLINA-Nonmetropolitan Counties	Ashe	45	0	5	3	37	369	190	155	24	3
	Avery	11	0	2	0	9	128	30	86	12	0
	Beaufort	121	0	5	25	91	776	253	475	48	7
	Bertie	19	0	2	4	13	326	125	148	53	3
	Bladen	135	7	2	12	114	932	332	540	60	3
	Camden	10	2	2	1	5	68	34	29	5	6
	Carteret	67	0	20	6	41	641	220	382	39	2
	Caswell	89	0	9	12	68	419	154	231	34	2
	Clay	22	0	4	2	16	136	66	62	8	0
	Cleveland	66	1	17	33	15	1,580	556	845	179	2
	Columbus	149	2	6	34	107	1,718	729	820	169	24
	Craven	132	0	3	22	107	1,270	398	770	102	2
	Dare	31	0	0	0	31	624	172	441	11	0
	Davidson	179	2	2	25	150	2,053	157	1,683	213	16
	Duplin	126	3	3	16	104	851	424	356	71	5
	Granville	83	3	5	8	67	823	349	444	30	1
	Halifax	92	1	4	26	61	1,123	602	439	82	12
	Harnett	267	1	19	28	219	2,269	924	1,116	229	36
	Hertford	51	2	10	7	32	343	150	176	17	2
	Jackson	89	0	5	6	78	695	299	342	54	4
	Jones	32	1	1	2	28	242	48	168	26	1
	Lee	28	1	7	8	12	645	282	265	98	24
	Lenoir	109	3	8	7	91	972	281	635	56	9
	Macon	15	1	4	1	9	457	168	259	30	3
	McDowell	52	2	5	15	30	631	268	316	47	8
	Montgomery	32	0	2	2	28	487	162	283	42	0
	Moore	83	5	9	12	57	948	404	468	76	12
	Northampton	35	2	1	6	26	332	174	133	25	1
	Pasquotank	45	1	6	7	31	437	158	249	30	4
	Perquimans	5	1	1	3	0	176	107	47	22	2
	Polk	18	1	2	1	14	312	96	202	14	2
	Richmond	140	0	8	35	97	1,329	534	712	83	17
	Robeson	503	22	20	96	365	3,767	1,882	1,469	416	29
	Rutherford	150	3	19	17	111	874	383	401	90	17
	Sampson	148	4	20	34	90	1,339	683	520	136	14
	Scotland	57	1	11	14	31	488	227	213	48	17
	Stanly	37	0	17	2	18	349	150	183	16	2
	Surry	126	1	9	16	100	1,495	560	744	191	23
	Swain	23	0	0	1	22	330	87	220	23	5
	Transylvania	35	0	0	2	33	281	136	123	22	6
	Tyrrell	15	0	3	3	9	53	14	34	5	1
	Vance	73	2	8	16	47	1,314	625	598	91	10
	Warren	39	7	6	9	17	565	246	279	40	5
	Watauga	19	0	4	1	14	537	205	301	31	5
	Wilkes	90	3	3	7	77	1,038	424	531	83	4
	Wilson	82	3	2	4	73	852	220	575	57	8
	Yancey	12	0	0	0	12	70	32	34	4	5

Note: The data shown in this table do not reflect county totals but are the number of offenses reported by the sheriff's office or county police department.
[1] The FBI does not publish arson data unless it receives data from either the agency or the state for all 12 months of the calendar year.
[5] The FBI determined that the agency's data were underreported. Consequently, affected data are not included in this table.

Table 10. Offenses Known to Law Enforcement, by State Metropolitan and Nonmetropolitan Counties, 2006 (*Contd.*)

(Number.)

State	County	Violent crime	Murder and non-negligent man-slaughter	Forcible rape	Robbery	Aggra-vated assault	Property crime	Burglary	Larceny-theft	Motor vehicle theft	Arson[1]
NORTH DAKOTA- **Metropolitan Counties**	Burleigh	11	0	2	0	9	148	47	86	15	1
	Cass	21	0	6	2	13	179	44	111	24	0
	Grand Forks[4]	8	1	2	0	5			64	19	0
	Morton	7	0	3	0	4	67	17	43	7	0
NORTH DAKOTA- **Nonmetropolitan Counties**	Adams	2	0	0	0	2	11	0	10	1	0
	Barnes	2	0	0	0	2	27	11	15	1	0
	Bottineau	2	0	2	0	0	81	29	47	5	2
	Burke	0	0	0	0	0	29	11	16	2	0
	Cavalier	4	0	0	0	4	46	4	37	5	0
	Dickey	0	0	0	0	0	35	4	31	0	0
	Dunn	0	0	0	0	0	0	0	0	0	0
	Eddy	5	0	1	4	0	30	4	19	7	0
	Emmons	1	0	0	0	1	32	11	21	0	1
	Foster	0	0	0	0	0	2	1	1	0	0
	Grant	0	0	0	0	0	5	0	5	0	1
	Hettinger	1	0	0	0	1	7	2	3	2	0
	Lamoure	0	0	0	0	0	11	0	9	2	0
	Logan	0	0	0	0	0	4	0	3	1	0
	McHenry	1	0	0	0	1	43	16	23	4	0
	McKenzie	1	0	0	0	1	35	6	25	4	0
	McLean	0	0	0	0	0	76	13	54	9	0
	Mercer	3	0	3	0	0	17	6	9	2	1
	Mountrail	0	0	0	0	0	42	8	26	8	4
	Nelson	1	0	0	0	1	39	10	25	4	1
	Pembina	1	0	0	0	1	22	9	13	0	1
	Pierce	0	0	0	0	0	6	0	6	0	0
	Ramsey	1	0	0	0	1	36	12	20	4	0
	Ransom	2	0	0	0	2	17	6	5	6	1
	Renville	0	0	0	0	0	12	1	11	0	0
	Richland	1	0	0	0	1	110	39	63	8	0
	Rolette	4	0	1	0	3	25	15	10	0	2
	Sargent	1	0	1	0	0	21	4	15	2	0
	Sheridan	2	0	0	0	2	28	5	22	1	1
	Stark	2	0	0	0	2	40	3	32	5	0
	Stutsman	3	0	1	0	2	62	35	19	8	1
	Towner	0	0	0	0	0	16	7	9	0	0
	Traill	2	0	2	0	0	26	10	10	6	0
	Walsh	3	0	1	0	2	143	29	89	25	4
	Ward	13	0	2	1	10	165	49	103	13	0
	Wells	0	0	0	0	0	28	13	14	1	2
	Williams	4	1	1	0	2	86	13	57	16	1
OHIO- **Metropolitan Counties**	Allen	53	1	14	25	13	1,215	267	909	39	0
	Clark	65	2	14	22	27	2,009	515	1,366	128	12
	Clermont	73	0	39	10	24	1,811	398	1,299	114	15
	Delaware	46	0	18	12	16	1,212	408	747	57	15
	Erie	20	0	0	4	16	453	160	273	20	11
	Geauga	5	0	5	0	0	305	101	191	13	3
	Greene	21	0	10	4	7	486	129	319	38	0
	Hamilton	300	6	61	170	63	7,772	1,111	6,297	364	56
	Jefferson	48	1	5	6	36	418	132	253	33	1
	Lawrence	23	0	0	1	22	134	51	67	16	2
	Licking	10	0	2	6	2	613	176	363	74	11
	Lorain	47	0	10	25	12	1,204	692	482	30	38
	Lucas	38	0	12	7	19	1,128	277	778	73	3
	Miami	23	1	9	4	9	563	205	304	54	9
	Morrow	16	0	9	2	5	415	160	218	37	2
	Pickaway	45	0	5	8	32	1,115	418	646	51	12
	Portage	27	0	14	7	6	1,632	452	1,097	83	2
	Preble	25	1	9	1	14	439	158	251	30	5
	Richland	63	0	22	10	31	1,540	441	1,045	54	12
	Stark	144	0	29	59	56	2,885	807	1,925	153	20
	Summit	53	1	16	23	13	1,553	319	1,168	66	4

Note: The data shown in this table do not reflect county totals but are the number of offenses reported by the sheriff's office or county police department.
[1] The FBI does not publish arson data unless it receives data from either the agency or the state for all 12 months of the calendar year.
[4] The FBI determined that the agency's data were inflated. Consequently, affected data are not included in this table.

Table 10. Offenses Known to Law Enforcement, by State Metropolitan and Nonmetropolitan Counties, 2006 (*Contd.*)

(Number.)

State	County	Violent crime	Murder and non-negligent man-slaughter	Forcible rape	Robbery	Aggra-vated assault	Property crime	Burglary	Larceny-theft	Motor vehicle theft	Arson[1]
	Trumbull	31	0	4	5	22	480	168	230	82	3
	Union	25	0	8	0	17	303	87	199	17	3
	Washington	20	0	11	1	8	411	127	248	36	4
	Wood	12	0	5	2	5	620	156	436	28	4
OHIO- **Nonmetropolitan Counties**	Ashland	20	0	5	2	13	277	107	160	10	2
	Auglaize	3	0	2	1	0	118	59	52	7	0
	Clinton	10	1	4	1	4	286	77	194	15	0
	Crawford	8	0	4	0	4	194	36	156	2	0
	Darke	37	0	23	0	14	354	133	202	19	13
	Defiance[4]	8	0	6	0	2			198	8	3
	Fayette	17	2	6	6	3	709	205	488	16	4
	Gallia	17	0	8	7	2	789	303	437	49	11
	Hancock	16	0	3	0	13	298	86	187	25	5
	Hardin	3	1	0	0	2	232	92	126	14	1
	Harrison	10	1	2	1	6	187	58	110	19	2
	Highland	18	0	4	1	13	459	211	233	15	4
	Hocking	13	0	2	2	9	379	113	225	41	5
	Holmes	18	0	4	0	14	336	101	218	17	2
	Huron	6	0	2	4	0	496	182	274	40	1
	Logan	9	0	1	2	6	269	136	117	16	1
	Marion	51	1	9	14	27	954	195	737	22	4
	Meigs	14	0	5	4	5	235	92	118	25	4
	Mercer	8	0	5	1	2	264	74	175	15	1
	Morgan	1	0	0	1	0	143	46	81	16	7
	Muskingum	56	1	32	14	9	1,247	380	771	96	
	Paulding	14	0	2	1	11	182	54	128	0	1
	Perry	4	0	2	2	0	60	17	41	2	0
	Pike	16	3	2	6	5	511	193	267	51	8
	Ross	46	1	11	13	21	1,727	403	1,188	136	15
	Scioto	49	0	10	14	25	2,137	670	1,395	72	0
	Seneca	5	0	0	3	2	184	65	110	9	1
	Van Wert	4	0	1	0	3	219	77	135	7	2
	Wayne	20	0	4	5	11	573	208	335	30	10
	Williams	12	0	8	2	2	309	64	230	15	1
OKLAHOMA- **Metropolitan Counties**	Canadian	21	0	4	1	16	73	43	17	13	0
	Cleveland	44	0	8	3	33	377	163	177	37	2
	Creek	57	3	10	0	44	603	187	366	50	7
	Grady	24	1	5	0	18	314	98	194	22	7
	Le Flore	37	0	7	0	30	221	90	122	9	3
	Lincoln	38	1	5	1	31	287	77	167	43	3
	Logan	36	0	2	3	31	265	95	158	12	2
	McClain	24	1	5	2	16	107	40	54	13	2
	Oklahoma	17	1	4	1	11	278	72	159	47	1
	Okmulgee	20	0	4	6	10	245	91	126	28	2
	Osage	50	1	6	3	40	461	154	260	47	17
	Pawnee	67	0	9	0	58	142	47	78	17	3
	Rogers	4	2	0	0	2	219	78	93	48	0
	Sequoyah	70	0	4	1	65	287	79	170	38	8
	Tulsa	292	4	15	14	259	1,119	313	683	123	15
	Wagoner	28	0	5	2	21	309	125	143	41	2
OKLAHOMA- **Nonmetropolitan Counties**	Adair	31	0	8	0	23	183	51	97	35	4
	Alfalfa	4	0	1	0	3	51	10	39	2	1
	Atoka	16	0	3	0	13	118	36	75	7	4
	Beaver	7	0	0	0	7	57	16	35	6	0
	Beckham	7	0	0	0	7	81	29	41	11	0
	Blaine	11	0	0	1	10	65	27	38	0	1
	Bryan	61	1	12	3	45	328	135	142	51	9
	Caddo	71	0	4	3	64	247	76	132	39	5
	Carter	54	3	2	8	41	150	37	95	18	2
	Choctaw	48	1	0	2	45	127	56	58	13	2
	Cimarron	1	0	0	0	1	4	0	4	0	0
	Coal	6	1	0	0	5	92	22	63	7	1

Note: The data shown in this table do not reflect county totals but are the number of offenses reported by the sheriff's office or county police department.
[1] The FBI does not publish arson data unless it receives data from either the agency or the state for all 12 months of the calendar year.
[4] The FBI determined that the agency's data were inflated. Consequently, affected data are not included in this table.

Table 10. Offenses Known to Law Enforcement, by State Metropolitan and Nonmetropolitan Counties, 2006 (Contd.)

(Number.)

State	County	Violent crime	Murder and non-negligent man-slaughter	Forcible rape	Robbery	Aggra-vated assault	Property crime	Burglary	Larceny-theft	Motor vehicle theft	Arson[1]
	Cotton	1	0	0	0	1	10	2	7	1	0
	Craig	12	0	1	0	11	102	41	53	8	1
	Custer	5	0	1	0	4	58	19	36	3	2
	Delaware	83	4	12	2	65	464	213	185	66	27
	Dewey	2	0	0	0	2	17	7	5	5	0
	Ellis	2	0	0	1	1	21	7	10	4	0
	Garfield	10	0	2	0	8	101	21	68	12	3
	Garvin	19	3	2	2	12	187	54	114	19	5
	Grant	2	0	0	0	2	43	12	27	4	0
	Greer	0	0	0	0	0	16	4	11	1	0
	Harmon	1	1	0	0	0	16	9	6	1	0
	Harper	0	0	0	0	0	18	10	8	0	0
	Haskell	63	1	4	0	58	50	15	25	10	1
	Hughes	3	0	0	0	3	127	41	59	27	2
	Jackson	3	0	0	0	3	92	22	45	25	1
	Jefferson	7	0	0	0	7	54	13	36	5	0
	Johnston	13	0	1	1	11	47	25	14	8	0
	Kay	30	0	4	3	23	200	68	123	9	6
	Kingfisher	9	0	0	1	8	73	11	60	2	2
	Kiowa	3	0	0	0	3	31	8	21	2	0
	Latimer	23	0	2	1	20	61	19	35	7	0
	Love	7	2	2	1	2	96	24	64	8	1
	Major	9	0	3	0	6	60	18	39	3	1
	Marshall	30	0	4	0	26	155	49	85	21	2
	Mayes	36	3	3	2	28	226	63	139	24	1
	McCurtain	37	2	8	0	27	477	178	263	36	25
	McIntosh	9	0	0	0	9	112	44	60	8	1
	Murray	6	0	2	0	4	64	27	31	6	1
	Muskogee	66	1	6	5	54	217	78	88	51	9
	Noble	13	0	2	0	11	97	41	49	7	0
	Nowata	7	1	1	0	5	91	38	49	4	2
	Okfuskee	4	0	0	1	3	76	35	24	17	0
	Ottawa	7	2	0	0	5	144	67	63	14	2
	Payne	31	0	2	0	29	229	58	151	20	3
	Pittsburg	15	2	2	0	11	378	145	228	5	11
	Pontotoc	19	0	2	1	16	166	54	98	14	6
	Pottawatomie	56	1	12	3	40	616	206	358	52	7
	Pushmataha	12	2	2	0	8	90	40	41	9	3
	Roger Mills	1	0	0	0	1	65	18	45	2	0
	Seminole	39	0	1	0	38	270	81	171	18	7
	Stephens	19	0	1	0	18	147	46	95	6	1
	Texas	3	0	0	0	3	22	3	19	0	0
	Tillman	2	0	0	0	2	53	12	36	5	1
	Washington	17	0	3	1	13	132	41	88	3	3
	Washita	8	1	2	0	5	37	16	18	3	0
	Woods	2	0	0	0	2	21	5	15	1	0
	Woodward	6	0	1	0	5	92	41	49	2	3
OREGON-Metropolitan Counties	Benton	18	0	2	1	15	345	95	223	27	3
	Clackamas	256	4	44	101	107	6,191	1,061	4,455	675	35
	Jackson	178	2	11	14	151	980	234	668	78	11
	Lane	253	3	22	21	207	1,693	701	758	234	16
	Marion	92	2	20	31	39	2,896	470	2,112	314	13
	Multnomah	30	0	3	5	22	837	144	615	78	8
	Washington	223	3	46	63	111	3,635	833	2,497	305	44
OREGON-Nonmetropolitan Counties	Baker	3	0	0	0	3	47	23	18	6	1
	Clatsop	5	0	0	0	5	201	61	107	33	3
	Crook	36	0	3	0	33	128	50	66	12	5
	Curry	19	1	0	2	16	201	66	128	7	2
	Gilliam	0	0	0	0	0	33	2	26	5	0
	Grant	0	0	0	0	0	45	13	30	2	0
	Harney	0	0	0	0	0	9	3	3	3	1
	Hood River	22	0	2	1	19	292	57	222	13	1
	Jefferson	31	0	3	2	26	210	48	120	42	3
	Josephine	29	1	3	1	24	903	189	601	113	0

Note: The data shown in this table do not reflect county totals but are the number of offenses reported by the sheriff's office or county police department.

[1] The FBI does not publish arson data unless it receives data from either the agency or the state for all 12 months of the calendar year.

Table 10. Offenses Known to Law Enforcement, by State Metropolitan and Nonmetropolitan Counties, 2006 *(Contd.)*

(Number.)

State	County	Violent crime	Murder and non-negligent man-slaughter	Forcible rape	Robbery	Aggra-vated assault	Property crime	Burglary	Larceny-theft	Motor vehicle theft	Arson[1]
	Lake	1	0	0	0	1	42	10	27	5	0
	Linn	16	1	3	9	3	1,433	396	916	121	11
	Malheur	7	1	4	2	0	152	58	82	12	2
	Morrow	17	0	6	0	11	296	75	187	34	3
	Sherman	0	0	0	0	0	38	5	30	3	1
	Union	6	0	1	0	5	104	29	67	8	5
	Wallowa	1	0	0	0	1	63	17	41	5	0
	Wasco	1	0	0	1	0	250	59	164	27	0
	Wheeler	1	0	0	0	1	21	6	12	3	2
PENNSYLVANIA- **Metropolitan Counties**	Allegheny	14	0	0	1	13	2	1	0	1	0
	Allegheny County Police Department	39	0	4	3	32	268	7	240	21	96
	Beaver	8	0	0	1	7	6	1	5	0	0
	Cumberland	0	0	0	0	0	0	0	0	0	0
	Pike	0	0	0	0	0	0	0	0	0	0
	Washington	0	0	0	0	0	0	0	0	0	0
	York	3	0	0	0	3	2	0	0	2	0
PENNSYLVANIA- **Nonmetropolitan Counties**	Adams	0	0	0	0	0	0	0	0	0	0
	Bradford	0	0	0	0	0	0	0	0	0	0
	Clarion	0	0	0	0	0	1	0	1	0	0
	Elk	0	0	0	0	0	0	0	0	0	0
	Greene	0	0	0	0	0	0	0	0	0	0
	Snyder	0	0	0	0	0	2	0	2	0	0
	Tioga	0	0	0	0	0	0	0	0	0	0
SOUTH CAROLINA- **Metropolitan Counties**	Aiken	364	7	46	72	239	3,096	909	1,832	355	2
	Anderson	799	13	63	109	614	5,888	1,484	3,809	595	45
	Berkeley	659	14	39	131	475	3,258	1,008	1,822	428	19
	Calhoun	25	0	1	2	22	249	58	157	34	1
	Charleston	838	5	38	110	685	2,951	832	1,729	390	11
	Darlington	688	0	22	48	618	2,228	768	1,244	216	30
	Dorchester	429	2	26	54	347	2,551	618	1,686	247	6
	Edgefield	46	1	3	5	37	355	90	233	32	0
	Fairfield	238	7	10	12	209	583	188	342	53	5
	Florence	575	4	15	101	455	3,164	713	2,139	312	10
	Greenville	2,262	17	101	444	1,700	11,223	3,447	6,595	1,181	37
	Horry	0	0	0	0	0	50	0	49	1	0
	Horry County Police Department	1,063	14	77	171	801	7,321	1,754	4,612	955	40
	Laurens	246	3	25	22	196	1,619	573	800	246	12
	Lexington	547	9	35	88	415	4,024	943	2,652	429	7
	Pickens	216	4	23	7	182	1,737	489	1,044	204	13
	Richland	1,882	31	92	316	1,443	8,115	1,791	5,490	834	26
	Saluda	33	0	3	5	25	142	26	105	11	1
	Spartanburg	959	14	45	206	694	7,892	2,078	5,210	604	34
	Sumter	801	6	26	55	714	2,554	912	1,434	208	36
	York	674	3	40	65	566	2,995	724	2,001	270	18
SOUTH CAROLINA- **Nonmetropolitan Counties**	Abbeville	42	0	1	2	39	307	91	195	21	0
	Allendale	17	1	0	1	15	75	25	47	3	1
	Bamberg	46	4	3	2	37	203	80	92	31	2
	Barnwell	101	1	1	4	95	333	106	216	11	1
	Beaufort	750	6	37	128	579	4,062	1,078	2,716	268	19
	Cherokee	186	1	15	29	141	1,533	376	1,009	148	7
	Chester	245	4	8	16	217	826	200	582	44	8
	Chesterfield	144	0	3	3	138	764	226	476	62	8
	Clarendon	232	1	13	38	180	876	218	541	117	2
	Colleton	247	2	11	19	215	1,057	255	678	124	13
	Dillon	169	2	16	42	109	798	279	424	95	9
	Georgetown	201	1	11	21	168	1,371	346	915	110	6
	Greenwood	353	3	21	10	319	1,646	359	1,184	103	3
	Hampton	76	0	3	1	72	315	107	191	17	5
	Jasper	152	7	10	26	109	711	245	385	81	2

Note: The data shown in this table do not reflect county totals but are the number of offenses reported by the sheriff's office or county police department.
[1] The FBI does not publish arson data unless it receives data from either the agency or the state for all 12 months of the calendar year.

Table 10. Offenses Known to Law Enforcement, by State Metropolitan and Nonmetropolitan Counties, 2006 (Contd.)

(Number.)

State	County	Violent crime	Murder and non-negligent man-slaughter	Forcible rape	Robbery	Aggra-vated assault	Property crime	Burglary	Larceny-theft	Motor vehicle theft	Arson[1]
	Lancaster	228	2	28	40	158	1,695	433	1,179	83	9
	Lee	79	3	4	7	65	380	99	242	39	6
	Marion	145	1	4	12	128	696	202	432	62	4
	Marlboro	202	2	11	10	179	515	166	312	37	3
	McCormick	22	0	1	0	21	91	26	51	14	1
	Newberry	65	0	6	10	49	468	70	382	16	2
	Oconee	210	3	17	9	181	1,114	308	725	81	7
	Orangeburg[4]	273	7	41	61	164		1,362	1,703		16
	Union	146	0	12	12	122	484	144	304	36	6
	Williamsburg	136	4	6	15	111	855	293	439	123	23
SOUTH DAKOTA- **Metropolitan Counties**	Lincoln	3	0	1	0	2	72	34	31	7	0
	McCook	8	0	0	0	8	37	2	30	5	0
	Meade	27	0	5	0	22	114	27	77	10	0
	Minnehaha	29	0	8	0	21	301	110	170	21	1
	Pennington	47	0	31	0	16	385	111	259	15	0
	Turner	0	0	0	0	0	39	24	13	2	0
	Union	0	0	0	0	0	8	5	3	0	0
SOUTH DAKOTA- **Nonmetropolitan Counties**	Aurora	1	0	0	0	1	3	2	1	0	0
	Bennett	18	0	0	0	18	10	6	2	2	0
	Butte	7	0	1	0	6	30	9	11	10	1
	Clay	2	0	0	0	2	10	0	10	0	0
	Corson	1	0	1	0	0	13	1	12	0	1
	Davison	1	0	0	0	1	7	1	4	2	0
	Deuel	0	0	0	0	0	27	5	22	0	0
	Edmunds	0	0	0	0	0	1	1	0	0	0
	Hamlin	2	0	0	0	2	12	5	6	1	1
	Hanson	0	0	0	0	0	10	3	7	0	1
	Hughes	5	0	3	1	1	15	9	6	0	0
	Hutchinson	0	0	0	0	0	0	0	0	0	0
	Lawrence	2	0	0	0	2	72	28	39	5	0
	Marshall	4	0	1	0	3	56	15	39	2	0
	McPherson	0	0	0	0	0	0	0	0	0	0
	Miner	0	0	0	0	0	23	11	11	1	1
	Moody	0	0	0	0	0	0	0	0	0	0
	Perkins	0	0	0	0	0	9	4	4	1	0
	Potter	0	0	0	0	0	2	0	1	1	0
	Stanley	2	0	0	0	2	55	1	53	1	0
	Tripp	0	0	0	0	0	4	1	2	1	0
	Walworth	0	0	0	0	0	3	1	2	0	0
	Yankton	3	0	0	0	3	39	16	21	2	0
TENNESSEE- **Metropolitan Counties**	Anderson	84	0	8	10	66	868	294	468	106	7
	Blount	366	3	39	14	310	1,586	477	929	180	3
	Bradley	316	0	11	3	302	1,139	335	698	106	10
	Cannon	29	1	0	1	27	127	48	51	28	0
	Carter	48	1	1	1	45	633	262	316	55	6
	Cheatham	101	1	10	3	87	465	120	274	71	3
	Chester	20	1	0	0	19	135	39	86	10	1
	Dickson	131	1	15	8	107	673	208	396	69	4
	Fayette	142	0	12	4	126	494	178	237	79	4
	Grainger	27	0	2	0	25	293	55	218	20	0
	Hamblen	140	1	1	12	126	603	179	374	50	4
	Hamilton	300	5	16	14	265	1,640	460	1,055	125	14
	Hartsville-Trousdale	24	0	0	0	24	115	26	84	5	0
	Hawkins	71	1	6	6	58	952	345	541	66	3
	Hickman	76	1	5	5	65	474	145	297	32	3
	Jefferson	100	0	10	9	81	747	239	404	104	4
	Knox	499	9	22	84	384	5,089	1,434	3,224	431	39
	Loudon	72	1	0	6	65	656	187	395	74	7
	Macon	39	0	2	1	36	187	62	104	21	5
	Madison	159	0	10	11	138	930	287	564	79	2
	Montgomery	122	1	16	3	102	653	169	412	72	4

Note: The data shown in this table do not reflect county totals but are the number of offenses reported by the sheriff's office or county police department.
[1] The FBI does not publish arson data unless it receives data from either the agency or the state for all 12 months of the calendar year.
[4] The FBI determined that the agency's data were inflated. Consequently, affected data are not included in this table.

Table 10. Offenses Known to Law Enforcement, by State Metropolitan and Nonmetropolitan Counties, 2006 *(Contd.)*

(Number.)

State	County	Violent crime	Murder and non-negligent man-slaughter	Forcible rape	Robbery	Aggra-vated assault	Property crime	Burglary	Larceny-theft	Motor vehicle theft	Arson[1]
	Robertson	81	1	5	6	69	419	127	253	39	0
	Rutherford.............	241	1	28	7	205	1,239	319	792	128	5
	Sequatchie	13	1	2	0	10	122	25	76	21	1
	Shelby...................	523	3	19	71	430	3,628	1,294	2,015	319	10
	Smith	28	0	1	1	26	85	26	46	13	1
	Stewart	32	0	5	1	26	142	45	70	27	3
	Sullivan..................	434	1	27	17	389	1,914	689	1,037	188	38
	Sumner...................	132	1	17	7	107	652	179	414	59	10
	Tipton....................	161	0	14	9	138	699	222	389	88	8
	Unicoi....................	31	0	0	0	31	107	25	73	9	2
	Union	35	0	0	3	32	286	114	144	28	2
	Washington............	192	4	7	8	173	947	337	554	56	18
	Williamson.............	82	1	5	0	76	550	165	344	41	2
	Wilson	177	0	10	12	155	936	296	516	124	7
TENNESSEE **Nonmetropolitan Counties**	Bedford..................	60	1	1	2	56	378	147	153	78	7
	Benton....................	30	0	1	1	28	311	122	161	28	1
	Campbell................	66	2	3	4	57	635	233	342	60	7
	Carroll	39	0	2	1	36	200	87	81	32	1
	Claiborne	82	0	11	1	70	581	215	318	48	2
	Clay.......................	8	0	0	0	8	87	38	46	3	0
	Cocke	91	2	5	10	74	785	282	412	91	18
	Coffee....................	52	0	0	2	50	430	81	307	42	0
	Crockett	19	0	1	3	15	132	38	72	22	1
	Cumberland...........	86	1	2	6	77	720	251	410	59	15
	Decatur	18	0	1	0	17	163	56	88	19	1
	DeKalb...................	40	1	2	1	36	425	165	212	48	6
	Dyer.......................	46	0	3	0	43	311	87	193	31	1
	Fentress.................	64	1	2	0	61	376	179	177	20	7
	Franklin.................	56	1	9	·2	44	282	90	157	35	6
	Gibson...................	56	0	1	2	53	244	84	121	39	5
	Giles......................	80	0	2	3	75	347	144	171	32	1
	Greene	217	3	12	9	193	1,319	528	700	91	21
	Grundy...................	87	1	0	0	86	97	39	23	35	6
	Hancock.................	3	0	0	1	2	106	41	60	5	0
	Hardeman..............	116	0	9	9	98	415	159	183	73	2
	Hardin....................	117	3	1	4	109	574	232	295	47	8
	Haywood................	35	0	3	6	26	206	63	105	38	0
	Henderson	55	1	6	3	45	438	173	222	43	4
	Henry	63	0	9	4	50	536	211	280	45	0
	Houston	15	1	0	0	14	102	42	51	9	3
	Humphreys.............	27	1	0	0	26	139	40	78	21	1
	Jackson..................	23	0	1	1	21	252	73	171	8	2
	Johnson.................	62	1	0	2	59	175	74	80	21	2
	Lake.......................	19	0	0	1	18	20	2	14	4	1
	Lawrence	136	1	1	2	132	729	308	356	65	6
	Lewis	10	0	1	0	9	172	74	88	10	2
	Lincoln	99	3	0	8	88	482	217	214	51	7
	Marshall	30	0	0	4	26	228	70	131	27	1
	Maury....................	145	2	8	6	129	742	171	478	93	13
	McMinn..................	152	1	7	8	136	1,025	394	544	87	7
	Meigs.....................	35	0	1	1	33	311	95	173	43	2
	Monroe...................	117	0	9	2	106	785	280	419	86	11
	Moore.....................	11	0	0	0	11	91	25	60	6	1
	Morgan...................	9	0	0	0	9	221	85	105	31	2
	Obion	38	1	5	1	31	250	51	176	23	6
	Overton..................	24	0	0	0	24	310	144	152	14	3
	Perry......................	15	0	0	1	14	212	66	116	30	3
	Putnam...................	61	1	1	3	56	682	121	507	54	3
	Rhea	59	0	5	0	54	365	69	264	32	7
	Roane	108	3	7	5	93	932	373	476	83	7
	Scott......................	104	1	3	1	99	544	146	350	48	1
	Sevier....................	138	1	18	6	113	1,850	774	952	124	4
	Van Buren..............	11	1	1	0	9	41	4	34	3	2
	Warren...................	54	1	2	2	49	370	102	228	40	4

Note: The data shown in this table do not reflect county totals but are the number of offenses reported by the sheriff's office or county police department.
[1] The FBI does not publish arson data unless it receives data from either the agency or the state for all 12 months of the calendar year.

Table 10. Offenses Known to Law Enforcement, by State Metropolitan and Nonmetropolitan Counties, 2006 (*Contd.*)

(Number.)

State	County	Violent crime	Murder and non-negligent man-slaughter	Forcible rape	Robbery	Aggra-vated assault	Property crime	Burglary	Larceny-theft	Motor vehicle theft	Arson[1]
	Wayne	30	1	1	1	27	135	69	55	11	2
	Weakley	52	0	6	2	44	213	70	113	30	2
	White	48	0	0	4	44	290	109	152	29	10
TEXAS- **Metropolitan Counties**	Aransas	28	1	10	1	16	672	242	404	26	1
	Archer	6	0	1	0	5	78	26	43	9	2
	Armstrong	3	0	0	0	3	13	3	9	1	0
	Atascosa	39	1	0	2	36	251	83	143	25	0
	Austin	20	0	3	1	16	174	66	97	11	0
	Bandera	24	1	1	1	21	231	87	130	14	1
	Bastrop	92	2	2	9	79	1,007	448	487	72	1
	Bell	75	0	32	3	40	938	317	575	46	3
	Bexar	493	11	57	79	346	5,927	1,817	3,723	387	104
	Bowie	118	3	11	5	99	602	188	338	76	0
	Brazoria	107	0	5	29	73	1,441	518	802	121	1
	Brazos	53	1	5	3	44	514	183	287	44	4
	Burleson	30	0	4	3	23	127	56	65	6	4
	Caldwell	63	0	9	10	44	253	93	141	19	1
	Calhoun	27	0	3	0	24	161	49	104	8	2
	Callahan[7]	12	0	3	0	9	58	20	35	3	3
	Cameron	193	2	15	16	160	1,725	740	827	158	11
	Chambers	92	1	0	6	85	487	229	229	29	3
	Clay	16	0	3	2	11	178	56	106	16	0
	Collin	96	1	24	1	70	681	237	373	71	1
	Comal	159	1	21	10	127	906	300	567	39	4
	Coryell	9	0	1	0	8	107	56	46	5	0
	Crosby	0	0	0	0	0	4	2	2	0	0
	Dallas	42	3	0	4	35	343	74	230	39	17
	Delta	4	0	0	2	2	107	52	53	2	8
	Denton	78	0	3	6	69	934	285	616	33	8
	Ector	54	1	2	8	43	910	230	622	58	0
	Ellis	157	2	3	9	143	1,071	396	558	117	3
	El Paso	218	8	25	19	166	1,216	310	763	143	18
	Fort Bend	703	14	42	127	520	3,458	1,138	2,049	271	23
	Galveston	140	1	11	17	111	812	353	394	65	18
	Goliad	1	0	0	0	1	33	14	18	1	0
	Grayson	32	0	6	5	21	898	327	493	78	7
	Gregg	77	2	23	11	41	885	209	571	105	6
	Guadalupe	103	1	8	2	92	799	287	458	54	4
	Hardin	46	1	10	2	33	406	128	204	74	2
	Harris	7,539	67	338	2,214	4,920	43,004	11,543	25,710	5,751	463
	Hays	72	0	4	2	66	585	217	342	26	0
	Hidalgo	1,067	15	88	167	797	6,093	2,124	3,505	464	
	Hunt	36	3	0	9	24	1,006	374	537	95	9
	Irion	0	0	0	0	0	30	15	14	1	0
	Jefferson	42	4	2	8	28	471	141	269	61	1
	Johnson	137	3	0	6	128	1,429	443	836	150	15
	Jonesv	8	0	0	0	8	37	12	18	7	0
	Kaufman	200	1	10	10	179	1,550	609	754	187	15
	Kendall	37	1	9	1	26	192	44	139	9	3
	Lampasas	2	0	0	0	2	56	23	30	3	1
	Liberty	139	5	11	11	112	767	283	350	134	17
	McLennan	90	1	25	7	57	858	301	493	64	34
	Medina	51	1	7	3	40	288	126	151	11	0
	Midland	62	0	10	4	48	443	131	293	19	1
	Montgomery	791	10	49	112	620	6,600	1,874	4,094	632	62
	Nueces	62	0	23	3	36	311	101	177	33	0
	Orange	142	0	19	9	114	957	359	469	129	6
	Parker	86	1	16	4	65	1,064	337	638	89	1
	Potter	25	2	0	1	22	211	47	142	22	4
	Randall	52	0	4	3	45	327	95	208	24	10
	Robertson	8	1	0	1	6	153	54	81	18	0
	Rockwall	49	0	0	0	49	242	105	122	15	1
	Rusk	75	4	3	5	63	612	221	302	89	6

Note: The data shown in this table do not reflect county totals but are the number of offenses reported by the sheriff's office or county police department.

[1] The FBI does not publish arson data unless it receives data from either the agency or the state for all 12 months of the calendar year.

[7] Because of changes in the state/local agency's reporting practices, figures are not comparable to previous years' data.

Table 10. Offenses Known to Law Enforcement, by State Metropolitan and Nonmetropolitan Counties, 2006 (*Contd.*)

(Number.)

State	County	Violent crime	Murder and non-negligent man-slaughter	Forcible rape	Robbery	Aggra-vated assault	Property crime	Burglary	Larceny-theft	Motor vehicle theft	Arson[1]
	San Jacinto	60	0	0	4	56	540	218	255	67	32
	San Patricio	40	1	0	0	39	329	99	203	27	0
	Smith	315	1	31	24	259	1,809	714	906	189	28
	Tarrant	90	0	17	11	62	1,289	405	752	132	0
	Taylor	14	1	1	0	12	148	59	76	13	4
	Tom Green	25	0	2	0	23	263	80	174	9	5
	Travis	281	4	37	31	209	3,454	1,096	2,155	203	10
	Upshur	87	0	3	4	80	591	221	306	64	0
	Victoria	55	2	13	1	39	503	131	331	41	1
	Waller	20	1	7	0	12	284	128	118	38	0
	Webb	58	2	0	4	52	319	114	168	37	2
	Wichita	10	0	5	1	4	153	73	71	9	15
	Williamson	201	1	32	14	154	1,745	447	1,200	98	13
	Wilson	23	0	4	1	18	159	37	109	13	2
	Wise	152	1	7	2	142	640	206	425	9	0
TEXAS- **Nonmetropolitan Counties**	Anderson	77	1	21	1	54	382	190	163	29	8
	Andrews	1	0	0	0	1	67	24	40	3	1
	Angelina	217	0	11	11	195	542	212	280	50	0
	Bailey	1	1	0	0	0	33	15	17	1	0
	Baylor	0	0	0	0	0	15	7	7	1	0
	Bee	28	1	5	0	22	154	52	89	13	0
	Blanco	5	0	1	0	4	36	19	14	3	0
	Borden	1	0	0	0	1	4	1	3	0	0
	Bosque	18	0	3	4	11	143	39	93	11	0
	Brewster	8	0	0	0	8	31	15	13	3	0
	Briscoe	1	0	0	0	1	6	5	1	0	0
	Brooks	0	0	0	0	0	13	4	9	0	0
	Brown	27	0	2	1	24	213	62	136	15	4
	Burnet	34	0	8	1	25	276	104	149	23	4
	Camp	17	0	0	1	16	127	58	63	6	2
	Cass	21	1	8	2	10	269	101	129	39	3
	Castro	6	0	2	0	4	27	8	17	2	0
	Cherokee	97	0	16	3	78	497	206	229	62	3
	Childress	1	0	0	0	1	24	9	12	3	0
	Cochran	3	0	0	1	2	68	32	34	2	0
	Coke	0	0	0	0	0	9	5	4	0	0
	Coleman	2	0	1	0	1	37	10	27	0	0
	Collingsworth	0	0	0	0	0	0	0	0	0	0
	Colorado	16	1	3	3	9	179	46	115	18	2
	Comanche	6	0	2	0	4	116	41	67	8	1
	Concho	1	0	0	0	1	12	7	5	0	2
	Cooke	58	1	3	4	50	263	88	139	36	5
	Cottle	0	0	0	0	0	1	0	1	0	0
	Crane	2	0	0	0	2	41	10	26	5	0
	Crockett	20	0	4	0	16	38	12	24	2	1
	Culberson	0	0	0	0	0	4	1	3	0	0
	Dallam	3	0	0	0	3	18	5	13	0	1
	Dawson	3	0	0	1	2	33	16	13	4	2
	Deaf Smith	6	0	0	1	5	52	10	29	13	3
	Dewitt	12	0	1	0	11	61	18	38	5	1
	Dickens	1	0	0	0	1	2	2	0	0	0
	Dimmit	45	1	2	1	41	315	136	147	32	2
	Donley	5	0	0	1	4	30	16	12	2	0
	Duval	14	0	2	0	12	109	41	59	9	1
	Eastland	1	0	0	0	1	83	36	40	7	0
	Edwards	3	0	0	1	2	29	8	19	2	0
	Erath	17	0	2	0	15	186	64	101	21	0
	Falls	23	1	2	0	20	84	31	47	6	6
	Fannin	23	0	3	3	17	306	138	156	12	1
	Fayette	2	1	0	0	1	139	51	85	3	0
	Fisher	8	0	4	0	4	60	27	31	2	2
	Floyd	2	0	0	0	2	12	3	7	2	0
	Foard	2	0	1	0	1	0	0	0	0	0
	Franklin	4	1	1	0	2	130	42	77	11	0

Note: The data shown in this table do not reflect county totals but are the number of offenses reported by the sheriff's office or county police department.
[1] The FBI does not publish arson data unless it receives data from either the agency or the state for all 12 months of the calendar year.

Table 10. Offenses Known to Law Enforcement, by State Metropolitan and Nonmetropolitan Counties, 2006 (*Contd.*)

(Number.)

State	County	Violent crime	Murder and non-negligent man-slaughter	Forcible rape	Robbery	Aggra-vated assault	Property crime	Burglary	Larceny-theft	Motor vehicle theft	Arson[1]
	Freestone	14	0	2	2	10	109	35	63	11	0
	Frio	0	0	0	0	0	51	24	24	3	0
	Gaines	4	0	0	0	4	60	13	43	4	0
	Garza	3	0	1	0	2	94	31	57	6	1
	Gillespie	3	0	0	0	3	100	21	77	2	0
	Glasscock	0	0	0	0	0	0	0	0	0	0
	Gonzales	31	0	4	0	27	125	45	74	6	2
	Gray	11	0	0	2	9	85	26	45	14	1
	Grimes	31	0	5	2	24	295	121	149	25	1
	Hale	9	0	2	0	7	128	63	61	4	0
	Hall	0	0	0	0	0	19	4	10	5	0
	Hamilton	10	0	0	1	9	127	43	74	10	2
	Hansford	3	0	1	0	2	13	5	7	1	1
	Hardeman	10	0	4	3	3	122	57	58	7	1
	Harrison	142	2	4	0	136	933	313	573	47	5
	Hartley	0	0	0	0	0	18	7	8	3	0
	Haskell	1	0	0	0	1	23	11	12	0	0
	Hemphill	15	0	1	1	13	44	11	29	4	0
	Henderson	246	2	1	11	232	1,137	483	591	63	0
	Hill	14	1	2	3	8	345	120	196	29	1
	Hockley	12	0	1	0	11	69	19	43	7	0
	Hood	48	1	0	8	39	714	204	451	59	6
	Hopkins	35	0	13	0	22	239	100	124	15	1
	Houston	16	0	3	1	12	127	63	56	8	0
	Howard	12	0	2	1	9	61	30	27	4	0
	Hudspeth	9	0	0	0	9	32	16	15	1	0
	Hutchinson	12	0	0	0	12	73	27	43	3	1
	Jack	6	0	2	0	4	23	11	9	3	0
	Jackson	13	0	0	0	13	86	27	56	3	1
	Jasper	85	2	2	4	77	312	113	180	19	0
	Jeff Davis	7	0	0	1	6	12	7	5	0	0
	Jim Hogg	10	0	0	0	10	71	25	43	3	0
	Jim Wells	202	2	11	3	186	383	183	172	28	5
	Karnes	16	0	2	1	13	77	25	51	1	0
	Kenedy	2	0	0	0	2	5	3	2	0	0
	Kent	3	1	0	0	2	22	9	13	0	0
	Kerr	27	2	5	4	16	348	108	222	18	3
	Kimble	1	0	0	0	1	7	2	4	1	1
	King	0	0	0	0	0	2	2	0	0	0
	Kinney	0	0	0	0	0	5	1	1	3	1
	Kleberg	29	0	3	1	25	935	50	881	4	0
	Knox	2	0	0	0	2	19	5	12	2	0
	Lamar	41	0	1	2	38	315	130	168	17	1
	Lamb	6	0	1	0	5	86	31	49	6	0
	La Salle	6	0	0	0	6	83	27	56	0	0
	Lavaca	15	4	1	0	10	34	13	19	2	0
	Lee	16	1	2	0	13	140	55	77	8	0
	Leon	40	1	4	1	34	182	83	84	15	0
	Limestone	10	0	1	0	9	227	65	150	12	1
	Lipscomb	3	0	0	0	3	11	5	6	0	0
	Live Oak	1	0	0	0	1	57	24	27	6	1
	Llano	11	0	3	0	8	209	62	140	7	2
	Loving	0	0	0	0	0	3	1	1	1	0
	Lynn	0	0	0	0	0	16	9	5	2	1
	Madison	17	1	0	1	15	96	33	53	10	1
	Marion	42	0	6	5	31	195	92	84	19	2
	Martin	0	0	0	0	0	7	2	4	1	0
	Mason	9	0	1	1	7	60	16	43	1	0
	Matagorda	42	2	2	2	36	282	97	169	16	5
	Maverick	88	0	7	0	81	672	153	479	40	0
	McCulloch	1	0	0	0	1	28	12	15	1	0
	McMullen	1	0	0	0	1	12	2	10	0	0
	Menard	2	0	0	0	2	11	2	8	1	2
	Milam	18	0	3	1	14	168	84	73	11	2
	Mills	2	0	0	0	2	24	15	8	1	0

Note: The data shown in this table do not reflect county totals but are the number of offenses reported by the sheriff's office or county police department.
[1] The FBI does not publish arson data unless it receives data from either the agency or the state for all 12 months of the calendar year.

Table 10. Offenses Known to Law Enforcement, by State Metropolitan and Nonmetropolitan Counties, 2006 (*Contd.*)

(Number.)

State	County	Violent crime	Murder and non-negligent man-slaughter	Forcible rape	Robbery	Aggra-vated assault	Property crime	Burglary	Larceny-theft	Motor vehicle theft	Arson[1]
	Mitchell	0	0	0	0	0	19	2	16	1	0
	Montague	17	1	6	0	10	105	29	69	7	0
	Moore	0	0	0	0	0	63	23	34	6	5
	Morris	20	0	0	1	19	84	33	42	9	0
	Motley	0	0	0	0	0	3	2	1	0	0
	Nacogdoches	85	2	11	5	67	339	141	160	38	2
	Navarro	30	2	5	1	22	549	199	328	22	7
	Newton	22	0	3	0	19	215	62	147	6	1
	Nolan	5	0	1	2	2	34	11	20	3	0
	Ochiltree	8	0	0	0	8	36	6	27	3	0
	Oldham	6	0	1	0	5	13	3	9	1	0
	Palo Pinto	10	1	0	1	8	135	61	67	7	0
	Panola	71	2	2	3	64	310	89	176	45	4
	Parmer	3	0	0	1	2	60	28	30	2	0
	Pecos	5	0	0	0	5	25	7	17	1	0
	Polk	77	2	26	6	43	724	302	359	63	3
	Presidio	1	0	0	0	1	0	0	0	0	0
	Rains	18	0	1	0	17	181	67	94	20	1
	Reagan	1	0	0	0	1	34	7	22	5	0
	Real	0	0	0	0	0	13	8	5	0	0
	Red River	20	1	0	1	18	136	61	67	8	0
	Reeves	9	0	0	0	9	80	14	60	6	0
	Refugio	23	0	0	0	23	57	16	38	3	0
	Roberts	2	0	0	0	2	33	8	22	3	1
	Runnels	8	0	0	1	7	21	12	9	0	0
	Sabine	30	1	0	1	28	118	49	64	5	3
	San Augustine	7	2	0	0	5	74	38	34	2	0
	San Saba	3	0	3	0	0	36	22	11	3	0
	Schleicher	3	0	0	0	3	14	3	9	2	0
	Scurry	19	2	2	0	15	68	25	40	3	0
	Shackelford	7	0	2	0	5	18	4	11	3	1
	Shelby	29	2	3	4	20	204	66	110	28	3
	Sherman	0	0	0	0	0	3	0	2	1	0
	Somervell	10	2	0	0	8	114	30	81	3	0
	Starr	45	5	0	4	36	357	170	133	54	1
	Stephens	5	1	2	0	2	29	6	22	1	0
	Sterling	0	0	0	0	0	8	4	4	0	0
	Stonewall	2	0	0	0	2	5	0	5	0	2
	Sutton	3	1	0	1	1	13	2	9	2	1
	Swisher	3	0	0	0	3	27	13	12	2	0
	Terrell	3	0	0	0	3	11	7	4	0	1
	Terry	1	0	1	0	0	27	6	16	5	0
	Throckmorton	1	0	0	0	1	5	1	4	0	0
	Titus	69	2	17	2	48	311	125	159	27	7
	Trinity	53	1	7	4	41	120	48	56	16	4
	Tyler	51	1	6	2	42	199	121	70	8	1
	Upton	6	2	2	0	2	17	4	13	0	0
	Uvalde	28	0	3	1	24	137	61	69	7	0
	Val Verde	0	0	0	0	0	134	50	68	16	0
	Van Zandt	83	0	0	7	76	923	316	505	102	12
	Walker	73	1	15	6	51	377	152	191	34	3
	Ward	4	0	0	1	3	13	5	6	2	0
	Washington	26	1	3	3	19	145	81	55	9	1
	Wharton	71	3	3	4	61	463	222	203	38	2
	Wheeler	4	0	0	1	3	24	9	15	0	0
	Wilbarger	3	0	0	0	3	25	11	12	2	7
	Willacy	24	0	0	2	22	171	72	92	7	1
	Winkler	3	0	0	0	3	41	11	28	2	0
	Wood	143	2	1	0	140	537	254	264	19	2
	Yoakum	2	0	0	0	2	41	5	33	3	0
	Young	15	0	2	0	13	80	24	54	2	1
	Zapata	34	0	1	5	28	214	84	105	25	0
	Zavala	15	0	0	1	14	48	20	28	0	0

Note: The data shown in this table do not reflect county totals but are the number of offenses reported by the sheriff's office or county police department.
[1] The FBI does not publish arson data unless it receives data from either the agency or the state for all 12 months of the calendar year.

Table 10. Offenses Known to Law Enforcement, by State Metropolitan and Nonmetropolitan Counties, 2006 (*Contd.*)

(Number.)

State	County	Violent crime	Murder and non-negligent man-slaughter	Forcible rape	Robbery	Aggra-vated assault	Property crime	Burglary	Larceny-theft	Motor vehicle theft	Arson[1]
UTAH- **Metropolitan Counties**	Cache	26	0	6	1	19	509	91	398	20	0
	Salt Lake	578	3	86	88	401	9,038	1,697	6,371	970	56
	Summit	18	0	6	2	10	642	98	510	34	0
	Tooele	14	2	3	1	8	184	53	121	10	2
	Utah	32	0	9	0	23	524	147	339	38	8
	Washington	9	1	2	1	5	201	49	130	22	0
	Weber	48	1	10	7	30	1,056	219	784	53	7
UTAH- **Nonmetropolitan Counties**	Beaver	11	0	0	2	9	76	17	56	3	0
	Box Elder	6	0	5	0	1	221	42	173	6	1
	Carbon	7	0	3	1	3	166	50	100	16	5
	Daggett	0	0	0	0	0	13	7	5	1	0
	Duchesne	6	0	0	0	6	141	22	104	15	1
	Emery	8	1	2	1	4	107	22	83	2	0
	Grand	8	0	0	0	8	100	26	67	7	1
	Iron	17	0	2	1	14	158	40	86	32	1
	Kane	4	0	1	0	3	40	27	13	0	0
	Millard	20	2	5	1	12	304	63	230	11	0
	Rich	1	0	0	0	1	50	14	35	1	0
	San Juan	3	0	0	0	3	32	7	23	2	1
	Sevier	9	0	1	0	8	159	33	120	6	0
	Uintah	57	0	15	2	40	259	62	163	34	9
	Wasatch	12	0	1	0	11	191	30	153	8	0
	Wayne	11	0	0	0	11	148	14	134	0	1
VERMONT- **Metropolitan Counties**	Franklin	20	0	3	3	14	210	64	130	16	0
	Grand Isle	1	0	0	0	1	109	44	62	3	0
VERMONT- **Nonmetropolitan Counties**	Addison	0	0	0	0	0	0	0	0	0	0
	Bennington	1	0	0	0	1	3	0	2	1	0
	Lamoille	7	0	1	0	6	102	35	59	8	1
	Orange	0	0	0	0	0	48	16	28	4	0
	Orleans	0	0	0	0	0	1	0	1	0	0
	Rutland	0	0	0	0	0	148	5	139	4	0
	Washington	0	0	0	0	0	0	0	0	0	0
	Windham	1	0	0	0	1	15	1	14	0	0
	Windsor	0	0	0	0	0	0	0	0	0	0
VIRGINIA- **Metropolitan Counties**	Albemarle County Police Department	142	1	25	42	74	2,200	353	1,735	112	14
	Amelia	14	1	1	0	12	101	34	61	6	2
	Amherst	39	0	10	8	21	392	60	312	20	6
	Appomattox	4	0	1	1	2	117	18	97	2	0
	Arlington County Police Department	405	4	44	167	190	3,985	356	3,289	340	12
	Bedford	56	1	10	1	44	671	136	497	38	7
	Botetourt	16	0	0	0	16	376	58	297	21	3
	Campbell	74	4	10	11	49	782	180	558	44	6
	Caroline	76	3	6	9	58	460	72	382	6	4
	Charles City	4	0	0	0	4	41	17	19	5	0
	Chesterfield County Police Department	702	6	66	324	306	7,092	1,396	5,266	430	101
	Cumberland	14	0	4	0	10	80	35	36	9	0
	Dinwiddie	49	3	1	14	31	369	75	246	48	2
	Fairfax County Police Department	745	10	58	410	267	15,218	1,450	12,323	1,445	123
	Fauquier	81	2	3	9	67	700	103	556	41	9
	Fluvanna	27	0	3	4	20	171	33	121	17	3
	Franklin	35	2	8	2	23	532	79	401	52	0
	Frederick	105	6	28	21	50	1,418	330	947	141	7
	Giles	14	1	7	3	3	189	25	147	17	6
	Gloucester	15	0	4	2	9	464	49	389	26	8
	Goochland	58	3	0	3	52	191	34	149	8	0
	Greene	27	0	1	3	23	276	31	154	91	3

Note: The data shown in this table do not reflect county totals but are the number of offenses reported by the sheriff's office or county police department.
[1] The FBI does not publish arson data unless it receives data from either the agency or the state for all 12 months of the calendar year.

Table 10. Offenses Known to Law Enforcement, by State Metropolitan and Nonmetropolitan Counties, 2006 (*Contd.*)

(Number.)

State	County	Violent crime	Murder and non-negligent man-slaughter	Forcible rape	Robbery	Aggra-vated assault	Property crime	Burglary	Larceny-theft	Motor vehicle theft	Arson[1]
	Hanover	58	3	0	22	33	1,013	85	888	40	5
	Henrico County Police Department	570	9	43	290	228	8,575	1,432	6,572	571	91
	Isle of Wight	29	1	4	7	17	457	105	313	39	2
	James City County Police Department	64	1	10	19	34	892	147	687	58	28
	King and Queen	7	1	0	0	6	52	22	28	2	1
	King William	12	0	0	1	11	59	12	41	6	0
	Loudoun	172	2	27	42	101	2,946	299	2,432	215	86
	Louisa	24	1	9	4	10	436	80	335	21	1
	Mathews	5	0	0	0	5	130	33	89	8	9
	Montgomery	55	1	6	5	43	574	163	361	50	5
	Nelson	8	0	0	0	8	281	55	205	21	0
	New Kent	22	0	3	5	14	256	52	189	15	1
	Powhatan	7	0	1	3	3	234	65	151	18	6
	Prince George County Police Department	51	0	10	11	30	423	98	281	44	2
	Prince William County Police Department	809	14	32	366	397	7,462	1,420	5,376	666	85
	Pulaski	39	3	9	4	23	493	75	391	27	8
	Roanoke County Police Department	162	0	17	15	130	1,100	251	796	53	8
	Rockingham	26	1	8	5	12	302	101	183	18	0
	Scott	33	3	4	2	24	439	149	250	40	0
	Spotsylvania	201	4	18	19	160	1,658	9	1,585	64	15
	Surry	32	0	3	4	25	83	42	39	2	0
	Sussex	34	1	6	3	24	212	62	130	20	2
	Warren	11	0	2	1	8	259	60	173	26	5
	Washington	56	0	10	11	35	1,135	212	878	45	3
	York	61	4	8	21	28	1,043	162	850	31	12
VIRGINIA-Nonmetropolitan Counties	Accomack	83	5	5	39	34	511	119	336	56	2
	Alleghany	4	0	0	0	4	89	23	62	4	1
	Bland	4	0	1	0	3	97	41	55	1	0
	Brunswick	20	2	0	1	17	155	40	94	21	5
	Buchanan	40	1	9	5	25	596	113	445	38	9
	Buckingham	19	0	1	3	15	170	64	97	9	0
	Carroll	44	1	3	3	37	384	117	219	48	1
	Charlotte	26	1	1	2	22	150	39	91	20	0
	Culpeper	25	0	1	2	22	202	33	157	12	1
	Dickenson	21	0	2	0	19	264	67	182	15	8
	Essex	11	0	2	2	7	85	13	59	13	1
	Floyd	15	0	1	0	14	152	28	103	21	2
	Grayson	22	0	3	1	18	183	90	75	18	2
	Greensville	36	3	8	4	21	261	69	174	18	0
	Halifax	18	1	1	4	12	257	66	162	29	0
	Henry	157	8	12	32	105	1,193	308	811	74	14
	King George	21	0	5	1	15	447	109	313	25	1
	Lancaster	15	2	2	1	10	93	20	72	1	2
	Lee	34	0	2	4	28	446	170	270	6	0
	Lunenburg	1	0	1	0	0	83	27	49	7	2
	Madison	7	0	1	0	6	184	26	147	11	0
	Mecklenburg	48	0	11	11	26	402	87	266	49	9
	Middlesex	16	1	4	1	10	121	39	72	10	2
	Northampton	14	1	0	8	5	216	75	137	4	2
	Northumberland	12	0	5	1	6	124	40	79	5	0
	Nottoway	16	0	1	3	12	95	17	66	12	0
	Orange	25	2	6	2	15	233	50	170	13	2
	Page	25	1	5	1	18	295	106	173	16	6
	Patrick	36	0	7	2	27	378	71	261	46	5
	Prince Edward	9	0	1	1	7	24	10	14	0	0
	Rappahannock	7	1	1	2	3	51	24	24	3	0
	Richmond	8	0	2	1	5	100	4	80	16	0

Note: The data shown in this table do not reflect county totals but are the number of offenses reported by the sheriff's office or county police department.
[1] The FBI does not publish arson data unless it receives data from either the agency or the state for all 12 months of the calendar year.

Table 10. Offenses Known to Law Enforcement, by State Metropolitan and Nonmetropolitan Counties, 2006 (*Contd.*)

(Number.)

State	County	Violent crime	Murder and non-negligent man-slaughter	Forcible rape	Robbery	Aggra-vated assault	Property crime	Burglary	Larceny-theft	Motor vehicle theft	Arson[1]
	Rockbridge	15	0	6	2	7	279	55	210	14	1
	Russell	29	2	5	2	20	294	89	168	37	7
	Shenandoah	27	0	0	3	24	247	54	179	14	0
	Smyth	43	1	9	0	33	374	108	235	31	10
	Southampton	34	1	4	5	24	258	71	167	20	3
	Tazewell	27	0	4	3	20	571	165	368	38	1
	Westmoreland	27	2	0	5	20	179	27	142	10	2
	Wise	50	1	13	2	34	467	155	276	36	35
	Wythe	23	1	2	2	18	220	37	155	28	2
WASHINGTON- **Metropolitan Counties**	Asotin	14	0	0	0	14	171	39	118	14	0
	Benton	61	1	6	4	50	735	184	495	56	6
	Chelan	32	1	6	5	20	1,014	142	816	56	4
	Clark	253	1	94	45	113	4,536	1,080	2,873	583	50
	Cowlitz	48	2	18	4	24	836	308	423	105	5
	Douglas	50	1	6	3	40	628	152	439	37	4
	Franklin	17	0	2	1	14	217	64	138	15	1
	King	657	15	101	185	356	8,769	2,594	4,483	1,692	233
	Kitsap	541	2	124	41	374	3,623	1,084	2,206	333	38
	Pierce	1,197	5	102	228	862	10,870	2,997	6,019	1,854	82
	Skagit	85	2	27	5	51	1,873	529	1,188	156	32
	Skamania	8	0	4	0	4	319	75	216	28	1
	Spokane	255	6	12	14	223	2,350	645	1,439	266	6
	Thurston	289	3	26	33	227	3,008	921	1,839	248	23
	Whatcom	125	0	36	6	83	1,728	632	934	162	11
	Yakima	113	3	26	28	56	3,190	1,095	1,527	568	46
WASHINGTON- **Nonmetropolitan Counties**	Adams	16	0	3	1	12	277	84	171	22	3
	Clallam	69	1	22	4	42	843	239	543	61	7
	Columbia	1	0	0	0	1	162	31	122	9	0
	Ferry	5	0	2	0	3	32	9	20	3	0
	Garfield	8	0	2	0	6	70	13	48	9	0
	Grant	71	0	7	20	44	1,868	555	1,107	206	5
	Grays Harbor	40	2	2	8	28	558	202	304	52	5
	Island	29	0	10	2	17	1,295	414	782	99	3
	Jefferson	49	0	5	8	36	537	204	311	22	1
	Kittitas	18	0	4	2	12	665	159	477	29	0
	Klickitat	11	0	0	2	9	125	84	13	28	0
	Lewis	41	0	6	2	33	885	292	502	91	9
	Lincoln	6	0	2	0	4	204	37	157	10	0
	Mason	103	1	23	15	64	1,857	620	1,012	225	10
	Okanogan	59	1	18	5	35	608	162	399	47	0
	Pacific	22	0	6	1	15	603	228	337	38	1
	Pend Oreille	7	1	2	0	4	493	145	319	29	2
	San Juan	9	0	3	2	4	248	64	161	23	0
	Stevens	35	1	12	3	19	741	346	293	102	1
	Wahkiakum	8	0	1	0	7	38	16	17	5	0
	Walla Walla	28	0	7	1	20	403	114	261	28	0
	Whitman	13	0	5	0	8	64	14	44	6	3
WEST VIRGINIA- **Metropolitan Counties**	Berkeley	58	1	0	17	40	931	216	634	81	6
	Boone	29	0	2	0	27	112	38	62	12	2
	Brooke	30	0	2	1	27	89	36	44	9	0
	Cabell	46	0	10	21	15	844	248	517	79	1
	Hampshire	12	0	0	0	12	82	39	34	9	0
	Jefferson	45	0	2	2	41	415	103	270	42	2
	Kanawha	184	11	16	36	121	1,495	521	776	198	40
	Marshall	6	0	1	0	5	170	50	109	11	0
	Mineral	19	0	0	0	19	55	15	38	2	0
	Monongalia	58	1	5	8	44	463	139	290	34	1
	Morgan	7	0	0	0	7	70	19	42	9	2
	Ohio	15	0	0	2	13	37	5	28	4	0
	Preston	18	1	1	0	16	66	26	27	13	0
	Putnam	89	2	16	13	58	936	195	623	118	6
	Wayne	3	0	0	0	3	115	67	43	5	0
	Wirt	5	0	1	1	3	17	5	11	1	2

Note: The data shown in this table do not reflect county totals but are the number of offenses reported by the sheriff's office or county police department.

[1] The FBI does not publish arson data unless it receives data from either the agency or the state for all 12 months of the calendar year.

Table 10. Offenses Known to Law Enforcement, by State Metropolitan and Nonmetropolitan Counties, 2006 (*Contd.*)

(Number.)

State	County	Violent crime	Murder and non-negligent man-slaughter	Forcible rape	Robbery	Aggra-vated assault	Property crime	Burglary	Larceny-theft	Motor vehicle theft	Arson[1]
WEST VIRGINIA-Nonmetropolitan Counties	Braxton	25	0	0	0	25	53	14	34	5	0
	Fayette	54	0	13	7	34	414	153	218	43	4
	Gilmer	0	0	0	0	0	12	3	7	2	0
	Grant	8	0	0	0	8	50	33	16	1	0
	Greenbrier	9	0	0	0	9	90	35	46	9	0
	Hardy	4	0	0	0	4	20	9	9	2	0
	Harrison	74	5	2	10	57	397	140	229	28	9
	Jackson	14	0	1	1	12	78	18	43	17	1
	Lewis	9	0	0	0	9	34	6	26	2	0
	Logan	14	3	1	0	10	40	11	28	1	0
	Marion	18	0	2	1	15	250	58	176	16	1
	Mason	10	0	0	0	10	128	16	79	33	3
	McDowell	9	0	0	1	8	100	39	46	15	0
	Mercer	102	3	5	10	84	569	218	297	54	10
	Monroe	3	0	0	0	3	42	18	20	4	1
	Nicholas	31	0	2	1	28	493	105	337	51	3
	Pocahontas	1	0	0	0	1	37	16	17	4	0
	Raleigh	63	1	0	12	50	1,140	180	847	113	11
	Randolph	7	0	0	0	7	43	17	18	8	0
	Ritchie	6	0	1	0	5	69	36	28	5	1
	Roane	8	0	1	0	7	112	5	89	18	0
	Summers	14	0	1	0	13	68	29	33	6	1
	Upshur	15	0	1	0	14	49	18	25	6	1
	Wyoming	7	0	0	3	4	197	103	80	14	0
WISCONSIN-Metropolitan Counties	Brown	43	0	14	0	29	1,451	323	1,059	69	7
	Calumet	6	0	0	1	5	211	36	171	4	1
	Chippewa	2	0	2	0	0	399	75	290	34	0
	Columbia	23	0	5	0	18	488	124	326	38	4
	Dane	59	0	14	10	35	1,208	314	820	74	9
	Douglas	9	0	1	1	7	303	126	153	24	0
	Eau Claire	49	0	0	3	46	405	129	261	15	1
	Fond du Lac	40	0	9	1	30	301	84	200	17	2
	Iowa	18	0	3	2	13	172	37	115	20	19
	Kenosha	37	0	7	7	23	732	172	518	42	0
	Kewaunee	4	0	2	0	2	60	16	40	4	1
	La Crosse	24	0	3	2	19	245	45	184	16	1
	Marathon	65	1	6	2	56	469	130	310	29	4
	Milwaukee	1	0	0	1	0	8	0	8	0	0
	Oconto	5	0	0	3	2	498	141	307	50	1
	Outagamie	29	0	13	4	12	498	90	375	33	3
	Ozaukee	14	0	1	2	11	203	42	151	10	2
	Pierce	21	0	0	1	20	254	94	145	15	0
	Racine	13	0	0	3	10	631	79	531	21	1
	Rock	44	0	7	8	29	536	178	338	20	5
	Sheboygan	45	0	10	1	34	558	106	440	12	1
	St. Croix	50	1	7	1	41	490	138	321	31	1
	Washington	31	1	10	2	18	684	192	444	48	4
	Waukesha	22	0	4	5	13	566	88	452	26	3
	Winnebago	29	0	1	0	28	314	78	222	14	4
WISCONSIN-Nonmetropolitan Counties	Adams	8	0	0	0	8	37	21	14	2	0
	Ashland	31	0	2	0	29	83	18	57	8	1
	Barron	1	0	0	1	0	258	102	149	7	1
	Bayfield	26	0	1	0	25	221	72	136	13	15
	Buffalo	1	0	0	0	1	90	21	57	12	0
	Burnett	28	0	4	0	24	243	87	139	17	0
	Clark	19	0	3	1	15	245	66	155	24	0
	Crawford	2	1	1	0	0	134	1	128	5	0
	Dodge	37	1	7	6	23	286	117	154	15	2
	Door	4	0	0	0	4	203	32	169	2	1
	Dunn	28	0	2	0	26	309	91	193	25	0
	Florence	4	0	0	0	4	143	50	90	3	0
	Forest	40	0	1	1	38	140	36	88	16	1
	Grant	36	0	2	0	34	160	54	88	18	0

Note: The data shown in this table do not reflect county totals but are the number of offenses reported by the sheriff's office or county police department.

[1] The FBI does not publish arson data unless it receives data from either the agency or the state for all 12 months of the calendar year.

Table 10. Offenses Known to Law Enforcement, by State Metropolitan and Nonmetropolitan Counties, 2006 (Contd.)

(Number.)

State	County	Violent crime	Murder and non-negligent man-slaughter	Forcible rape	Robbery	Aggra-vated assault	Property crime	Burglary	Larceny-theft	Motor vehicle theft	Arson[1]
	Green	9	1	4	1	3	161	33	116	12	0
	Green Lake	5	0	1	0	4	100	26	69	5	0
	Iron	8	0	0	0	8	55	16	38	1	0
	Jackson	11	0	3	2	6	279	85	170	24	0
	Jefferson	49	0	4	3	42	456	111	325	20	2
	Juneau	19	0	2	1	16	274	96	164	14	0
	Lafayette	3	1	1	0	1	118	21	91	6	2
	Langlade	10	0	1	0	9	261	87	160	14	1
	Lincoln	12	0	3	1	8	251	139	98	14	6
	Manitowoc	43	0	7	0	36	257	85	159	13	3
	Marquette	5	0	3	1	1	147	25	97	25	0
	Menominee	2	0	1	0	1	50	18	28	4	0
	Monroe	16	0	0	1	15	205	43	148	14	0
	Oneida	18	0	10	0	8	273	90	174	9	1
	Pepin	4	0	1	0	3	31	28	1	2	1
	Polk	20	1	12	1	6	344	158	162	24	0
	Portage	9	2	3	1	3	387	138	237	12	1
	Price	11	0	1	0	10	77	24	52	1	2
	Richland	1	0	0	0	1	141	43	93	5	0
	Rusk	21	0	1	0	20	149	43	93	13	0
	Sauk	36	1	5	6	24	589	98	455	36	0
	Shawano	8	0	4	0	4	439	123	287	29	3
	Taylor	11	0	5	0	6	144	47	87	10	0
	Trempealeau	8	1	3	0	4	111	37	67	7	0
	Vernon	11	0	0	0	11	146	51	92	3	0
	Vilas	9	0	0	0	9	187	42	131	14	2
	Walworth	5	0	2	2	1	357	83	251	23	1
	Washburn	21	0	4	1	16	206	74	124	8	1
	Waupaca	23	0	6	1	16	483	129	296	58	1
	Waushara	16	0	2	1	13	354	93	246	15	1
	Wood	10	0	4	1	5	288	103	172	13	2
WYOMING- **Metropolitan Counties**	Laramie	50	0	9	6	35	516	120	363	33	0
	Natrona	15	1	0	3	11	416	137	268	11	1
WYOMING- **Nonmetropolitan Counties**	Albany	6	0	0	0	6	60	12	43	5	0
	Campbell	46	0	1	0	45	290	68	194	28	3
	Carbon	1	0	0	0	1	41	6	33	2	0
	Converse	1	0	0	0	1	43	8	32	3	1
	Crook	5	0	0	0	5	45	14	27	4	0
	Fremont	9	0	2	0	7	183	49	115	19	0
	Goshen	37	0	2	0	35	83	15	61	7	0
	Hot Springs	0	0	0	0	0	29	3	26	0	1
	Johnson	3	0	0	0	3	30	10	19	1	0
	Lincoln	9	0	0	2	7	133	27	102	4	0
	Niobrara	1	0	0	0	1	10	2	5	3	0
	Park	28	0	3	0	25	71	18	50	3	0
	Platte	2	0	0	0	2	25	9	14	2	2
	Sheridan	12	0	1	0	11	101	14	78	9	0
	Sublette	31	1	2	1	27	234	27	196	11	3
	Sweetwater	22	1	2	2	17	238	56	165	17	1
	Teton	7	0	1	0	6	125	27	95	3	1
	Uinta	7	0	2	0	5	172	7	154	11	0
	Washakie	8	0	0	0	8	7	0	4	3	0
	Weston	1	0	0	0	1	8	5	3	0	0

Note: The data shown in this table do not reflect county totals but are the number of offenses reported by the sheriff's office or county police department.
[1] The FBI does not publish arson data unless it receives data from either the agency or the state for all 12 months of the calendar year.

Table 11. Offenses Known to Law Enforcement, by State and Other Agencies, 2006

(Number.)

State	State/Other Agency	Unit/Office	Violent crime	Murder and non-negligent man-slaughter	Forcible rape	Robbery	Aggra-vated assault	Property crime	Burglary	Larceny-theft	Motor vehicle theft	Arson[1]
ALABAMA-State Agencies	Alabama Alcoholic Beverage Control Board......		0	0	0	0	0	0	0	0	0	
ALABAMA-Other Agencies	2nd Judicial Circuit Drug Task Force		0	0	0	0	0	0	0	0	0	
	22nd Judicial Circuit Drug Task Force		0	0	0	0	0	0	0	0	0	
	24th Judicial Circuit Drug and Violent Crime Task Force		0	0	0	0	0	1	1	0	0	
	Marshall County Drug Enforcement Unit................		0	0	0	0	0	0	0	0	0	
ALASKA-State Agencies	Alaska State Troopers..........		981	9	85	28	859	4,635	1,338	2,790	507	58
	Alcohol Beverage Control Board......................................		1	0	0	0	1	1	0	1	0	0
ALASKA-Other Agencies	Anchorage International Airport		0	0	0	0	0	116	1	101	14	1
	Fairbanks International Airport		1	0	0	0	1	20	1	16	3	0
ARIZONA-State Agencies	Arizona Department of Public Safety........................		3	0	0	0	3	0	0	0	0	0
ARKANSAS-State Agencies	Camp Robinson		2	0	1	0	1	12	2	8	2	0
	State Capitol Police		0	0	0	0	0	18	3	13	2	0
CALIFORNIA-State Agencies	Atascadero State Hospital..................................		27	0	0	0	27	0	0	0	0	0
	California State Fair		9	0	0	1	8	68	3	62	3	0
	Department of Parks and Recreation:	Angeles	0	0	0	0	0	12	0	12	0	0
		Bay Area	0	0	0	0	0	5	0	5	0	0
		Calaveras County	0	0	0	0	0	11	5	6	0	0
		Capital	1	0	0	0	1	17	9	8	0	0
		Channel Coast	5	0	0	0	5	40	3	37	0	3
		Colorado	0	0	0	0	0	1	1	0	0	0
		Four Rivers District	0	0	0	0	0	13	3	10	0	1
		Gold Fields District	5	0	1	2	2	117	12	98	7	4
		Hollister Hills	0	0	0	0	0	0	0	0	0	1
		Hungry Valley	0	0	0	0	0	4	0	0	4	0
		Inland Empire	0	0	0	0	0	2	0	2	0	0
		Marin County	1	0	0	0	1	6	3	3	0	1
		Mendocino Headquarters	0	0	0	0	0	25	0	25	0	0
		Monterey County	0	0	0	0	0	62	2	60	0	0
		North Coast Redwoods	0	0	0	0	0	70	46	24	0	0
		Northern Buttes	0	0	0	0	0	16	2	13	1	0
		Oceano Dunes	20	0	1	2	17	130	22	87	21	1
		Ocotillo Wells	2	0	0	0	2	2	0	0	2	1
		Orange Coast	3	0	0	1	2	41	13	25	3	0
		Russian River	2	0	0	1	1	55	2	53	0	1
		San Diego Coast	1	0	0	0	1	60	2	52	6	0
		San Joaquin	0	0	0	0	0	3	0	3	0	0
		San Luis Obispo Coast	0	0	0	0	0	32	1	31	0	0
		Santa Cruz Mountains	2	0	1	0	1	99	0	98	1	3
		Sierra	2	0	0	0	2	14	9	5	0	0
		Silverado	0	0	0	0	0	21	3	18	0	0
		Twin Cities	1	0	0	0	1	0	0	0	0	1
	Fairview Developmental Center......................................		13	0	0	0	13	8	3	5	0	0
	Highway Patrol:	Alameda County	2	0	0	0	2	250	0	30	220	0
		Alpine County	0	0	0	0	0	5	0	0	5	0

[1] The FBI does not publish arson data unless it receives data from either the agency or the state for all 12 months of the calendar year.

Table 11. Offenses Known to Law Enforcement, by State and Other Agencies, 2006 *(Contd.)*

(Number.)

State	State/Other Agency	Unit/Office	Violent crime	Murder and non-negligent man-slaughter	Forcible rape	Robbery	Aggra-vated assault	Property crime	Burglary	Larceny-theft	Motor vehicle theft	Arson[1]
		Amador County	0	0	0	0	0	45	0	0	45	0
		Butte County	2	0	0	0	2	465	2	70	393	0
		Calaveras County	0	0	0	0	0	117	0	16	101	0
		Colusa County	0	0	0	0	0	29	0	1	28	0
		Contra Costa County	0	0	0	0	0	1,246	1	46	1,199	0
		Del Norte County	0	0	0	0	0	64	0	0	64	0
		El Dorado County	0	0	0	0	0	365	0	50	315	0
		Fresno County	3	0	0	0	3	381	0	37	344	1
		Glenn County	1	0	0	0	1	19	0	7	12	0
		Humboldt County	0	0	0	0	0	196	1	8	187	0
		Imperial County	2	0	0	0	2	189	0	13	176	0
		Inyo County	0	0	0	0	0	35	0	10	25	0
		Kern County	3	0	0	0	3	457	0	52	405	0
		Kings County	0	0	0	0	0	300	0	0	300	0
		Lake County	0	0	0	0	0	128	0	18	110	0
		Lassen County	0	0	0	0	0	24	0	10	14	0
		Los Angeles County	35	0	0	4	31	423	6	25	392	0
		Madera County	1	0	0	0	1	377	0	71	306	0
		Marin County	2	0	0	0	2	132	0	11	121	0
		Mariposa County	0	0	0	0	0	30	0	6	24	0
		Mendocino County	0	0	0	0	0	115	2	30	83	0
		Merced County	2	0	0	0	2	513	0	88	425	0
		Modoc County	0	0	0	0	0	5	0	1	4	0
		Mono County	0	0	0	0	0	5	0	3	2	0
		Monterey County	1	0	0	0	1	338	1	7	330	0
		Napa County	0	0	0	0	0	127	1	26	100	0
		Nevada County	1	0	0	1	0	92	0	40	52	0
		Orange County	4	0	0	0	4	52	6	12	34	0
		Placer County	2	0	0	0	2	367	0	92	275	0
		Plumas County	0	0	0	0	0	49	0	9	40	0
		Riverside County	11	0	0	0	11	109	8	11	90	0
		Sacramento County	3	0	0	0	3	6,432	11	345	6,076	0
		San Benito County	1	0	0	0	1	35	0	1	34	0
		San Bernardino County	8	0	0	0	8	49	5	10	34	0
		San Diego County	16	0	0	0	16	110	12	22	76	0
		San Francisco County	0	0	0	0	0	6	0	0	6	0
		San Joaquin County	0	0	0	0	0	1,175	0	322	853	0
		San Luis Obispo County	4	0	0	0	4	181	0	39	142	0
		San Mateo County	0	0	0	0	0	33	0	2	31	0
		Santa Barbara County	3	0	0	0	3	140	0	37	103	0
		Santa Clara County	2	0	0	0	2	107	0	17	90	0
		Santa Cruz County	0	0	0	0	0	462	0	91	371	0
		Shasta County	1	0	0	1	0	226	0	33	193	0
		Sierra County	0	0	0	0	0	10	0	0	10	0
		Siskiyou County	2	0	0	0	2	32	0	10	22	0
		Solano County	1	0	0	0	1	55	1	1	53	0
		Sonoma County	0	0	0	0	0	302	0	75	227	0
		Stanislaus County	0	0	0	0	0	534	0	26	508	0
		Sutter County	0	0	0	0	0	70	0	8	62	0
		Tehama County	0	0	0	0	0	87	0	7	80	0
		Trinity County	0	0	0	0	0	77	0	0	77	0
		Tulare County	3	0	0	0	3	1,493	1	344	1,148	0
		Tuolumne County	0	0	0	0	0	188	0	15	173	0
		Ventura County	0	0	0	0	0	50	1	13	36	2

[1] The FBI does not publish arson data unless it receives data from either the agency or the state for all 12 months of the calendar year.

Table 11. Offenses Known to Law Enforcement, by State and Other Agencies, 2006 (*Contd.*)

(Number.)

State	State/Other Agency	Unit/Office	Violent crime	Murder and non-negligent man-slaughter	Forcible rape	Robbery	Aggra-vated assault	Property crime	Burglary	Larceny-theft	Motor vehicle theft	Arson[1]
CALIFORNIA-Other Agencies		Yolo County	0	0	0	0	0	37	2	0	35	0
		Yuba County	0	0	0	0	0	265	0	21	244	0
	Lanterman State Hospital.....		2	0	0	0	2	4	2	2	0	0
	Napa State Hospital		25	0	0	0	25	2	0	2	0	2
	Porterville Developmental Center........................		11	0	0	0	11	3	0	3	0	0
	Sonoma Developmental Center........................		1	0	0	0	1	8	1	7	0	0
	East Bay Municipal Utility..		0	0	0	0	0	28	2	25	1	0
	East Bay Regional Parks:	Alameda County	7	0	4	1	2	138	9	118	11	9
		Contra Costa County	21	0	1	16	4	171	7	159	5	6
	Fontana Unified School District		14	0	0	7	7	339	60	270	9	18
	Grant Joint Union High School..................................		37	0	2	10	25	82	35	43	4	4
	Los Angeles County Metro-politan Transportation Authority		10	0	0	3	7	26	5	21	0	0
	Los Angeles Transportation Services Bureau		539	0	7	341	191	651	24	477	150	4
	Monterey Peninsula Airport		0	0	0	0	0	11	0	6	5	0
	Port of San Diego Harbor.................................		16	0	0	5	11	579	24	553	2	0
	San Bernardino Unified School District......................		88	0	0	72	16	340	206	105	29	14
	San Francisco Bay Area Rapid Transit:.......................	Alameda County	193	0	2	152	39	1,665	5	1,280	380	1
		Contra Costa County	53	0	1	43	9	770	5	561	204	0
		San Francisco County	35	0	0	26	9	166	2	161	3	0
		San Mateo County	13	0	0	11	2	232	0	197	35	0
	Santa Clara Transit District ...		34	0	0	19	15	125	2	102	21	0
	Stockton Unified School District		124	0	1	11	112	522	139	376	7	19
	Union Pacific Railroad:........	Alameda County	5	0	0	0	5	323	278	45	0	0
		Amador County	0	0	0	0	0	0	0	0	0	0
		Butte County	7	0	0	0	7	7	0	7	0	0
		Calaveras County	0	0	0	0	0	0	0	0	0	0
		Colusa County	0	0	0	0	0	0	0	0	0	0
		Contra Costa County	8	0	0	0	8	9	7	2	0	0
		El Dorado County	0	0	0	0	0	0	0	0	0	0
		Fresno County	0	0	0	0	0	2	1	1	0	0
		Glenn County	0	0	0	0	0	0	0	0	0	0
		Humboldt County	0	0	0	0	0	0	0	0	0	0
		Imperial County	1	0	0	0	1	162	160	2	0	1
		Inyo County	0	0	0	0	0	0	0	0	0	0
		Kern County	0	0	0	0	0	10	6	4	0	0
		Kings County	0	0	0	0	0	1	0	1	0	0
		Lassen County	0	0	0	0	0	0	0	0	0	0
		Los Angeles County	12	0	0	0	12	349	321	28	0	0
		Madera County	0	0	0	0	0	0	0	0	0	0
		Marin County	0	0	0	0	0	0	0	0	0	0
		Mendocino County	0	0	0	0	0	0	0	0	0	0
		Merced County	0	0	0	0	0	8	1	7	0	0
		Modoc County	0	0	0	0	0	0	0	0	0	0
		Monterey County	0	0	0	0	0	1	0	1	0	0
		Napa County	0	0	0	0	0	0	0	0	0	0
		Nevada County	0	0	0	0	0	0	0	0	0	0
		Orange County	0	0	0	0	0	0	0	0	0	0
		Placer County	3	0	0	0	3	29	7	22	0	0
		Plumas County	0	0	0	0	0	2	0	2	0	0
		Riverside County	4	0	0	0	4	207	180	27	0	0

[1] The FBI does not publish arson data unless it receives data from either the agency or the state for all 12 months of the calendar year.

Table 11. Offenses Known to Law Enforcement, by State and Other Agencies, 2006 (*Contd.*)

(Number.)

State	State/Other Agency	Unit/Office	Violent crime	Murder and non-negligent man-slaughter	Forcible rape	Robbery	Aggra-vated assault	Property crime	Burglary	Larceny-theft	Motor vehicle theft	Arson[1]
		Sacramento County	7	0	0	0	7	34	11	23	0	0
		San Benito County	0	0	0	0	0	0	0	0	0	0
		San Bernardino County	0	0	0	0	0	141	110	31	0	0
		San Francisco County	0	0	0	0	0	0	0	0	0	0
		San Joaquin County	9	0	0	0	9	304	257	47	0	2
		San Luis Obispo County	0	0	0	0	0	0	0	0	0	0
		San Mateo County	0	0	0	0	0	0	0	0	0	0
		Santa Barbara County	0	0	0	0	0	1	0	1	0	0
		Santa Clara County	0	0	0	0	0	4	0	4	0	0
		Santa Cruz County	0	0	0	0	0	1	0	1	0	0
		Shasta County	3	0	0	0	3	10	0	10	0	0
		Sierra County	0	0	0	0	0	0	0	0	0	0
		Siskiyou County	0	0	0	0	0	0	0	0	0	0
		Solano County	1	0	0	0	1	0	0	0	0	0
		Sonoma County	0	0	0	0	0	0	0	0	0	0
		Stanislaus County	4	0	0	0	4	53	4	49	0	1
		Sutter County	0	0	0	0	0	14	1	13	0	0
		Tehama County	3	0	0	0	3	2	0	2	0	0
		Trinity County	0	0	0	0	0	0	0	0	0	0
		Tulare County	0	0	0	0	0	16	1	15	0	0
		Ventura County	0	0	0	0	0	1	1	0	0	0
		Yolo County	2	0	0	0	2	2	0	2	0	0
		Yuba County	0	0	0	0	0	8	2	6	0	0
COLORADO- **State Agencies**	Colorado Mental Health Institute		1	0	0	0	1	4	0	4	0	0
	Colorado State Patrol		27	0	0	0	27	40	0	6	34	0
CONNECTICUT- **State Agencies**	Connecticut State Police		338	3	68	67	200	3,880	1,020	2,471	389	80
	State Capitol Police		0	0	0	0	0	12	1	11	0	0
DELAWARE- **State Agencies**	Attorney General:	Kent County	0	0	0	0	0	0	0	0	0	0
		New Castle County	0	0	0	0	0	0	0	0	0	0
		Sussex County	0	0	0	0	0	0	0	0	0	0
	Division of Alcohol and Tobacco Enforcement		0	0	0	0	0	0	0	0	0	0
	Environmental Control		0	0	0	0	0	0	0	0	0	0
	Fish and Wildlife		2	0	0	1	1	20	0	20	0	0
	Park Rangers		1	0	1	0	0	40	2	37	1	0
	River and Bay Authority		4	0	0	1	3	9	0	9	0	0
	State Capitol Police		1	0	0	1	0	18	2	16	0	0
	State Fire Marshal		29	0	0	0	29	18	18	0	0	301
	State Police:	Kent County	417	6	58	63	290	1,799	592	1,044	163	1
		New Castle County	835	3	20	408	404	5,890	608	4,842	440	3
		Sussex County	637	0	62	64	511	3,420	1,060	2,152	208	5
DELAWARE- **Other Agencies**	Amtrak Police		0	0	0	0	0	0	0	0	0	0
	Drug Enforcement Administration, Wilmington Resident Office		0	0	0	0	0	0	0	0	0	0
	Wilmington Fire Department		0	0	0	0	0	0	0	0	0	0
DISTRICT OF COLUMBIA- **Other Agencies**	Metro Transit Police		362	0	2	225	135	1,025	7	755	263	1
	National Zoological Park		2	0	1	0	1	23	2	20	1	0
FLORIDA- **State Agencies**	Capitol Police		0	0	0	0	0	27	0	27	0	0

[1] The FBI does not publish arson data unless it receives data from either the agency or the state for all 12 months of the calendar year.

Table 11. Offenses Known to Law Enforcement, by State and Other Agencies, 2006 (*Contd.*)

(Number.)

State	State/Other Agency	Unit/Office	Violent crime	Murder and non-negligent manslaughter	Forcible rape	Robbery	Aggravated assault	Property crime	Burglary	Larceny-theft	Motor vehicle theft	Arson[1]
	Department of Agriculture .		153	2	5	47	99	506	111	317	78	2
	Department of Environmental Protection, Division of Law Enforcement:....................	Alachua County	0	0	0	0	0	2	0	2	0	0
		Baker County	0	0	0	0	0	1	0	1	0	0
		Bay County	0	0	0	0	0	0	0	0	0	0
		Brevard County	0	0	0	0	0	3	0	3	0	0
		Broward County	0	0	0	0	0	2	0	2	0	0
		Charlotte County	0	0	0	0	0	4	0	4	0	0
		Citrus County	0	0	0	0	0	0	0	0	0	0
		Clay County	0	0	0	0	0	0	0	0	0	0
		Collier County	0	0	0	0	0	1	0	1	0	0
		Columbia County	0	0	0	0	0	0	0	0	0	0
		Duval County	0	0	0	0	0	2	0	2	0	0
		Escambia County	0	0	0	0	0	0	0	0	0	0
		Flagler County	0	0	0	0	0	0	0	0	0	0
		Franklin County	0	0	0	0	0	0	0	0	0	0
		Gilchrist County	0	0	0	0	0	0	0	0	0	0
		Hamilton County	0	0	0	0	0	0	0	0	0	0
		Hernando County	0	0	0	0	0	0	0	0	0	0
		Highlands County	0	0	0	0	0	0	0	0	0	0
		Hillsborough County	0	0	0	0	0	1	0	1	0	0
		Holmes County	0	0	0	0	0	0	0	0	0	0
		Indian River County	0	0	0	0	0	8	0	8	0	0
		Lake County	0	0	0	0	0	0	0	0	0	0
		Lee County	0	0	0	0	0	7	0	7	0	0
		Leon County	0	0	0	0	0	0	0	0	0	0
		Levy County	0	0	0	0	0	1	0	0	1	0
		Manatee County	0	0	0	0	0	0	0	0	0	0
		Marion County	0	0	0	0	0	0	0	0	0	0
		Martin County	0	0	0	0	0	0	0	0	0	0
		Miami-Dade County	0	0	0	0	0	3	0	3	0	0
		Monroe County	0	0	0	0	0	4	0	4	0	0
		Nassau County	1	0	0	0	1	1	0	1	0	0
		Okaloosa County	0	0	0	0	0	1	0	1	0	0
		Okeechobee County	0	0	0	0	0	0	0	0	0	0
		Orange County	0	0	0	0	0	3	0	3	0	0
		Palm Beach County	0	0	0	0	0	0	0	0	0	0
		Pasco County	0	0	0	0	0	0	0	0	0	0
		Pinellas County	0	0	0	0	0	6	0	6	0	0
		Polk County	0	0	0	0	0	0	0	0	0	0
		Putnam County	0	0	0	0	0	0	0	0	0	0
		Santa Rosa County	0	0	0	0	0	2	0	2	0	0
		Sarasota County	0	0	0	0	0	1	0	1	0	0
		Seminole County	0	0	0	0	0	2	0	2	0	0
		St. Johns County	0	0	0	0	0	1	0	1	0	0
		St. Lucie County	0	0	0	0	0	4	0	4	0	0
		Volusia County	0	0	0	0	0	11	0	11	0	0
		Wakulla County	0	0	0	0	0	0	0	0	0	0
		Walton County	0	0	0	0	0	0	0	0	0	0
		Washington County	0	0	0	0	0	0	0	0	0	0
	Department of Insurance:....	Broward County	0	0	0	0	0	0	0	0	0	0
		Duval County	0	0	0	0	0	0	0	0	0	0
		Escambia County	0	0	0	0	0	0	0	0	0	0
		Hillsboro County	0	0	0	0	0	0	0	0	0	0
		Lee County	0	0	0	0	0	0	0	0	0	0
		Miami-Dade County	0	0	0	0	0	0	0	0	0	0
		Orange County	0	0	0	0	0	0	0	0	0	0

[1] The FBI does not publish arson data unless it receives data from either the agency or the state for all 12 months of the calendar year.

Table 11. Offenses Known to Law Enforcement, by State and Other Agencies, 2006 (*Contd.*)

(Number.)

State	State/Other Agency	Unit/Office	Violent crime	Murder and non-negligent man-slaughter	Forcible rape	Robbery	Aggra-vated assault	Property crime	Burglary	Larceny-theft	Motor vehicle theft	Arson[1]
	Department of Law Enforcement:........................	Palm Beach County	0	0	0	0	0	0	0	0	0	0
		Duval County, Jacksonville	1	1	0	0	0	0	0	0	0	0
		Escambia County, Pensacola	1	0	0	0	1	0	0	0	0	0
		Hillsborough County, Tampa	0	0	0	0	0	0	0	0	0	0
		Leon County, Tallahassee	2	0	0	0	2	50	0	50	0	0
		Miami-Dade County, Miami	1	0	1	0	0	1	0	1	0	0
		Orange County, Orlando	0	0	0	0	0	0	0	0	0	0
	Florida Game Commission:...	Alachua County	0	0	0	0	0	0	0	0	0	0
		Baker County	0	0	0	0	0	0	0	0	0	0
		Bay County	0	0	0	0	0	0	0	0	0	0
		Bradford County	0	0	0	0	0	0	0	0	0	0
		Brevard County	0	0	0	0	0	0	0	0	0	0
		Broward County	0	0	0	0	0	0	0	0	0	0
		Calhoun County	0	0	0	0	0	0	0	0	0	0
		Charlotte County	0	0	0	0	0	0	0	0	0	0
		Citrus County	0	0	0	0	0	0	0	0	0	0
		Clay County	0	0	0	0	0	0	0	0	0	0
		Collier County	0	0	0	0	0	0	0	0	0	0
		Columbia County	0	0	0	0	0	0	0	0	0	0
		DeSoto County	0	0	0	0	0	0	0	0	0	0
		Dixie County	0	0	0	0	0	0	0	0	0	0
		Duval County	0	0	0	0	0	0	0	0	0	0
		Escambia County	0	0	0	0	0	0	0	0	0	0
		Flagler County	0	0	0	0	0	0	0	0	0	0
		Franklin County	0	0	0	0	0	0	0	0	0	0
		Gadsden County	0	0	0	0	0	0	0	0	0	0
		Gilchrist County	0	0	0	0	0	0	0	0	0	0
		Glades County	0	0	0	0	0	0	0	0	0	0
		Gulf County	0	0	0	0	0	0	0	0	0	0
		Hamilton County	0	0	0	0	0	0	0	0	0	0
		Hardee County	0	0	0	0	0	0	0	0	0	0
		Hendry County	0	0	0	0	0	0	0	0	0	0
		Hernando County	0	0	0	0	0	0	0	0	0	0
		Highlands County	0	0	0	0	0	0	0	0	0	0
		Hillsborough County	0	0	0	0	0	0	0	0	0	0
		Holmes County	0	0	0	0	0	0	0	0	0	0
		Indian River County	0	0	0	0	0	0	0	0	0	0
		Jackson County	0	0	0	0	0	0	0	0	0	0
		Jefferson County	0	0	0	0	0	0	0	0	0	0
		Lafayette County	0	0	0	0	0	0	0	0	0	0
		Lake County	0	0	0	0	0	0	0	0	0	0
		Lee County	0	0	0	0	0	0	0	0	0	0
		Leon County	0	0	0	0	0	0	0	0	0	0
		Levy County	0	0	0	0	0	0	0	0	0	0
		Liberty County	0	0	0	0	0	0	0	0	0	0
		Madison County	0	0	0	0	0	0	0	0	0	0
		Manatee County	0	0	0	0	0	0	0	0	0	0
		Marion County	0	0	0	0	0	0	0	0	0	0
		Martin County	0	0	0	0	0	50	0	50	0	0
		Miami-Dade County	0	0	0	0	0	0	0	0	0	0
		Monroe County	0	0	0	0	0	0	0	0	0	0
		Nassau County	0	0	0	0	0	0	0	0	0	0
		Okaloosa County	0	0	0	0	0	0	0	0	0	0
		Okeechobee County	0	0	0	0	0	0	0	0	0	0
		Orange County	0	0	0	0	0	0	0	0	0	0

[1] The FBI does not publish arson data unless it receives data from either the agency or the state for all 12 months of the calendar year.

Table 11. Offenses Known to Law Enforcement, by State and Other Agencies, 2006 (*Contd.*)

(Number.)

State	State/Other Agency	Unit/Office	Violent crime	Murder and non-negligent man-slaughter	Forcible rape	Robbery	Aggra-vated assault	Property crime	Burglary	Larceny-theft	Motor vehicle theft	Arson[1]
		Osceola County	0	0	0	0	0	0	0	0	0	0
		Palm Beach County	0	0	0	0	0	0	0	0	0	0
		Pasco County	0	0	0	0	0	0	0	0	0	0
		Pinellas County	0	0	0	0	0	0	0	0	0	0
		Polk County	4	0	0	0	4	0	0	0	0	0
		Putnam County	0	0	0	0	0	0	0	0	0	0
		Santa Rosa County	0	0	0	0	0	0	0	0	0	0
		Sarasota County	0	0	0	0	0	0	0	0	0	0
		Seminole County	0	0	0	0	0	0	0	0	0	0
		St. Johns County	0	0	0	0	0	0	0	0	0	0
		St. Lucie County	0	0	0	0	0	0	0	0	0	0
		Sumter County	0	0	0	0	0	0	0	0	0	0
		Suwannee County	0	0	0	0	0	0	0	0	0	0
		Taylor County	0	0	0	0	0	0	0	0	0	0
		Union County	0	0	0	0	0	0	0	0	0	0
		Volusia County	0	0	0	0	0	0	0	0	0	0
		Wakulla County	0	0	0	0	0	0	0	0	0	0
		Walton County	0	0	0	0	0	0	0	0	0	0
		Washington County	0	0	0	0	0	0	0	0	0	0
	Highway Patrol:	Alachua County	3	1	0	0	2	0	0	0	0	0
		Baker County	0	0	0	0	0	0	0	0	0	0
		Bay County	1	0	0	0	1	0	0	0	0	0
		Bradford County	0	0	0	0	0	0	0	0	0	0
		Brevard County	1	0	0	0	1	0	0	0	0	0
		Broward County	62	0	0	1	61	148	0	41	107	0
		Calhoun County	0	0	0	0	0	0	0	0	0	0
		Charlotte County	2	0	0	0	2	0	0	0	0	0
		Citrus County	0	0	0	0	0	0	0	0	0	0
		Clay County	0	0	0	0	0	0	0	0	0	0
		Collier County	1	0	0	0	1	0	0	0	0	0
		Columbia County	0	0	0	0	0	0	0	0	0	0
		DeSoto County	0	0	0	0	0	0	0	0	0	0
		Dixie County	0	0	0	0	0	0	0	0	0	0
		Duval County	4	0	0	0	4	2	0	1	1	0
		Escambia County	5	0	0	0	5	0	0	0	0	0
		Flagler County	1	0	0	0	1	0	0	0	0	0
		Franklin County	0	0	0	0	0	0	0	0	0	0
		Gadsden County	0	0	0	0	0	0	0	0	0	0
		Gilchrist County	0	0	0	0	0	1	0	0	1	0
		Glades County	0	0	0	0	0	0	0	0	0	0
		Gulf County	0	0	0	0	0	0	0	0	0	0
		Hamilton County	1	0	0	0	1	0	0	0	0	0
		Hardee County	0	0	0	0	0	0	0	0	0	0
		Hendry County	0	0	0	0	0	0	0	0	0	0
		Hernando County	0	0	0	0	0	0	0	0	0	0
		Highlands County	0	0	0	0	0	0	0	0	0	0
		Hillsborough County	21	0	0	0	21	6	0	4	2	0
		Holmes County	1	0	0	0	1	0	0	0	0	0
		Indian River County	0	0	0	0	0	0	0	0	0	0
		Jackson County	0	0	0	0	0	0	0	0	0	0
		Jefferson County	0	0	0	0	0	0	0	0	0	0
		Lafayette County	0	0	0	0	0	0	0	0	0	0
		Lake County	1	0	0	0	1	0	0	0	0	0
		Lee County	1	0	0	0	1	0	0	0	0	0
		Leon County	0	0	0	0	0	0	0	0	0	0
		Levy County	0	0	0	0	0	0	0	0	0	0
		Liberty County	0	0	0	0	0	0	0	0	0	0
		Madison County	0	0	0	0	0	0	0	0	0	0
		Manatee County	1	0	0	0	1	0	0	0	0	0

[1] The FBI does not publish arson data unless it receives data from either the agency or the state for all 12 months of the calendar year.

Table 11. Offenses Known to Law Enforcement, by State and Other Agencies, 2006 (*Contd.*)

(Number.)

State	State/Other Agency	Unit/Office	Violent crime	Murder and non-negligent man-slaughter	Forcible rape	Robbery	Aggra-vated assault	Property crime	Burglary	Larceny-theft	Motor vehicle theft	Arson[1]
		Marion County	1	0	0	0	1	1	0	1	0	0
		Martin County	1	0	0	0	1	0	0	0	0	0
		Miami-Dade County	33	0	0	0	33	71	0	10	61	0
		Monroe County	3	0	0	0	3	0	0	0	0	0
		Nassau County	1	0	0	0	1	0	0	0	0	0
		Okaloosa County	1	0	0	0	1	0	0	0	0	0
		Okeechobee County	0	0	0	0	0	1	0	1	0	0
		Orange County	14	0	0	0	14	8	0	7	1	0
		Osceola County	4	0	0	0	4	3	0	2	1	0
		Palm Beach County Turnpike Station	29	0	0	1	28	34	0	14	20	0
		Pasco County	9	0	0	0	9	0	0	0	0	0
		Pinellas County	2	0	0	0	2	2	0	1	1	0
		Polk County	3	0	0	0	3	1	0	1	0	0
		Putnam County	0	0	0	0	0	0	0	0	0	0
		Santa Rosa County	1	0	0	0	1	0	0	0	0	0
		Sarasota County	5	0	0	0	5	3	0	2	1	0
		Seminole County	2	0	0	0	2	1	0	1	0	0
		St. Johns County	3	0	0	0	3	0	0	0	0	0
		St. Lucie County	5	0	0	0	5	7	0	6	1	0
		Sumter County	3	0	0	0	3	0	0	0	0	0
		Suwannee County	1	0	0	0	1	0	0	0	0	0
		Taylor County	0	0	0	0	0	0	0	0	0	0
		Union County	0	0	0	0	0	0	0	0	0	0
		Volusia County	5	0	0	0	5	3	0	1	2	0
		Wakulla County	1	0	0	0	1	0	0	0	0	0
		Walton County	1	0	0	0	1	0	0	0	0	0
		Washington County	1	0	0	0	1	0	0	0	0	0
FLORIDA– **Other Agencies**		State Treasurer's Office, Division of Insurance Fraud	0	0	0	0	0	0	0	0	0	0
		Duval County Schools	123	0	2	36	85	801	139	632	30	6
		Florida School for the Deaf and Blind	2	0	0	0	2	0	0	0	0	2
		Fort Lauderdale Airport	1	0	0	0	1	316	4	264	48	0
		Jacksonville Airport Authority	1	0	0	0	1	97	8	61	28	0
		Lee County Port Authority	1	0	0	1	0	223	2	217	4	0
		Melbourne International Airport	0	0	0	0	0	1	0	1	0	0
		Miami-Dade County Public Schools	430	0	7	182	241	2,859	562	2,244	53	28
		Miccosukee Tribal	25	0	3	1	21	95	26	58	11	1
		Palm Beach County School District	95	0	4	25	66	656	152	500	4	3
		Port Everglades	4	0	0	0	4	35	4	30	1	0
		Sarasota-Bradenton International Airport	0	0	0	0	0	2	1	1	0	0
		Seminole Tribal	81	1	7	22	51	560	55	424	81	0
		St. Petersburg-Clearwater International Airport	0	0	0	0	0	5	0	2	3	0
		Tampa International Airport	6	0	0	0	6	248	7	179	62	0
		Volusia County Beach Management	19	0	0	10	9	183	0	180	3	0
GEORGIA– **State Agencies**		Georgia World Congress	10	0	0	6	4	422	19	397	6	0
		Ports Authority, Savannah	0	0	0	0	0	16	1	15	0	0
GEORGIA– **Other Agencies**		Augusta Board of Education	0	0	0	0	0	121	1	120	0	0
		Cherokee County Marshal	0	0	0	0	0	0	0	0	0	0
		Fulton County Marshal	79	0	1	8	70	162	7	132	23	

[1] The FBI does not publish arson data unless it receives data from either the agency or the state for all 12 months of the calendar year.

Table 11. Offenses Known to Law Enforcement, by State and Other Agencies, 2006 (*Contd.*)

(Number.)

State	State/Other Agency	Unit/Office	Violent crime	Murder and non-negligent man-slaughter	Forcible rape	Robbery	Aggra-vated assault	Property crime	Burglary	Larceny-theft	Motor vehicle theft	Arson[1]
	Gwinnett County Public Schools....................................		12	0	0	8	4	406	76	327	3	
	Hartsfield-Jackson Atlanta International Airport		16	0	0	4	12	323	1	277	45	
	Metropolitan Atlanta Rapid Transit Authority.................		163	1	0	71	91	340	5	273	62	2
	Muscogee City Marshal		0	0	0	0	0	0	0	0	0	0
	Stone Mountain Park		2	0	0	0	2	40	0	39	1	0
	Twiggs County Board of Education..............................		2	0	1	0	1	3	0	3	0	0
	Washington County Board of Education		0	0	0	0	0	1	0	1	0	0
IDAHO- **State Agencies**	Idaho State Police		7	0	3	0	4	5	0	5	0	0
INDIANA- **State Agencies**	Northern Indiana Commuter Transportation District		2	0	0	2	0	85	0	70	15	0
	State Police:[2]........................	Adams County	0	0	0			4	2	2	0	0
		Allen County	0	1	1			43	3	38	2	0
		Bartholomew County	1	0	1			2	0	1	1	0
		Benton County	0	0	0			2	2	0	0	1
		Blackford County	0	0	1			1	0	1	0	0
		Boone County	0	0	0			9	0	6	3	0
		Brown County	0	0	0			0	0	0	0	0
		Carroll County	0	0	1			6	0	5	1	0
		Cass County	0	1	0			17	9	7	1	1
		Clark County	0	2	4			72	8	49	15	0
		Clay County	0	2	0			25	3	17	5	0
		Clinton County	0	1	0			11	1	9	1	0
		Crawford County	0	2	0			33	5	26	2	0
		Daviess County	0	1	0			20	5	13	2	0
		Dearborn County	0	1	0			38	5	29	4	0
		Decatur County	1	0	0			26	3	22	1	0
		De Kalb County	0	0	1			5	0	3	2	1
		Delaware County	0	0	0			26	1	22	3	0
		Dubois County	0	1	0			44	8	33	3	0
		Elkhart County	0	0	0			21	4	15	2	0
		Fayette County	0	1	0			13	3	7	3	0
		Floyd County	0	2	1			36	4	24	8	0
		Fountain County	0	0	0			9	2	6	1	0
		Franklin County	1	1	0			29	12	13	4	0
		Fulton County	0	0	0			5	1	2	2	0
		Gibson County	0	0	0			26	1	24	1	0
		Grant County	0	0	0			10	0	8	2	0
		Greene County	2	1	0			25	13	11	1	0
		Hamilton County	0	2	1			12	1	7	4	0
		Hancock County	0	0	0			12	0	8	4	0
		Harrison County	0	1	1			49	16	27	6	0
		Hendricks County	0	0	1			19	3	12	4	0
		Henry County	1	0	0			25	7	17	1	0
		Howard County	0	0	0			11	0	11	0	0
		Huntington County	0	0	0			10	2	7	1	0
		Jackson County	2	2	4			64	15	45	4	0
		Jasper County	0	0	0			5	0	3	2	0
		Jay County	0	0	0			12	3	6	3	0
		Jefferson County	1	1	0			35	12	20	3	0
		Jennings County	1	0	0			10	4	5	1	0
		Johnson County	0	1	0			4	0	2	2	0
		Knox County	0	0	0			24	9	12	3	0
		Kosciusko County	1	0	0			8	2	6	0	0
		LaGrange County	0	0	1			46	10	35	1	1
		Lake County	0	1	1			82	1	41	40	0
		La Porte County	0	1	1			21	0	15	6	0
		Lawrence County	0	0	0			12	3	9	0	1

[1] The FBI does not publish arson data unless it receives data from either the agency or the state for all 12 months of the calendar year.

[2] It was determined that the agency did not follow national Uniform Crime Reporting (UCR) Program guidelines for reporting this offense. Consequently, this figure is not included in this table.

Table 11. Offenses Known to Law Enforcement, by State and Other Agencies, 2006 *(Contd.)*

(Number.)

State	State/Other Agency	Unit/Office	Violent crime	Murder and non-negligent man-slaughter	Forcible rape	Robbery	Aggra-vated assault	Property crime	Burglary	Larceny-theft	Motor vehicle theft	Arson[1]
		Madison County		0	0	0		16	1	11	4	0
		Marion County		0	3	4		272	3	174	95	0
		Marshall County		0	0	0		17	1	13	3	0
		Martin County		0	1	0		17	11	5	1	0
		Miami County		0	0	0		64	22	39	3	2
		Monroe County		0	5	0		49	8	39	2	0
		Montgomery County		0	1	0		11	3	7	1	2
		Morgan County		0	1	0		18	2	8	8	0
		Newton County		0	1	0		4	1	3	0	0
		Noble County		0	0	0		17	3	10	4	0
		Ohio County		0	0	0		4	1	3	0	0
		Orange County		1	5	1		32	16	13	3	1
		Owen County		0	0	0		6	2	4	0	0
		Parke County		0	1	0		11	1	8	2	0
		Perry County		1	3	0		26	5	18	3	0
		Pike County		3	0	1		10	1	7	2	0
		Porter County		0	0	1		19	0	15	4	1
		Posey County		1	0	0		23	7	16	0	0
		Pulaski County		1	0	0		2	0	2	0	1
		Putnam County		0	0	0		24	8	12	4	0
		Randolph County		0	0	0		5	3	1	1	0
		Ripley County		0	1	0		112	35	72	5	1
		Rush County		0	0	0		5	2	3	0	0
		Scott County		1	1	2		26	5	13	8	1
		Shelby County		0	0	1		3	0	2	1	0
		Spencer County		0	2	0		45	7	35	3	0
		Starke County		0	0	0		5	1	2	2	0
		Steuben County		0	0	0		21	7	12	2	1
		St. Joseph County		0	1	0		18	1	13	4	0
		Sullivan County		0	2	0		14	2	11	1	0
		Switzerland County		0	0	0		15	3	11	1	0
		Tippecanoe County		0	2	0		45	3	39	3	0
		Tipton County		0	0	0		5	3	2	0	0
		Union County		0	0	0		7	2	3	2	0
		Vanderburgh County		0	0	0		29	1	26	2	0
		Vermillion County		0	1	0		11	2	8	1	0
		Vigo County		0	2	1		83	16	59	8	1
		Wabash County		0	0	0		14	7	7	0	0
		Warren County		0	0	1		1	0	1	0	0
		Warrick County		0	0	0		18	1	14	3	0
		Washington County		1	0	0		19	5	8	6	0
		Wayne County		0	0	2		57	8	43	6	0
		Wells County		0	0	0		5	0	4	1	0
		White County		1	2	0		10	2	7	1	0
		Whitley County		0	0	0		17	3	13	1	0
INDIANA-Other Agencies	St. Joseph County Airport Authority		0	0	0	0	0	17	0	11	6	0
KANSAS-State Agencies	Kansas Alcoholic Beverage Control		0	0	0	0	0	0	0	0	0	0
	Kansas Bureau of Investigation		5	2	0	0	3	3	0	3	0	0
	Kansas Department of Wildlife and Parks		1	0	0	1	0	35	4	31	0	0
	Kansas Highway Patrol		40	1	1	1	37	118	6	88	24	0
	Kansas Racing Commission Security Division		0	0	0	0	0	0	0	0	0	0
KANSAS-Other Agencies	Johnson County Park		1	0	0	0	1	31	2	29	0	2
	Potawatomi Tribal		3	0	0	0	3	68	6	60	2	0
	Unified School District:........	Goddard	0	0	0	0	0	21	1	20	0	2

[1] The FBI does not publish arson data unless it receives data from either the agency or the state for all 12 months of the calendar year.

Table 11. Offenses Known to Law Enforcement, by State and Other Agencies, 2006 *(Contd.)*

(Number.)

State	State/Other Agency	Unit/Office	Violent crime	Murder and non-negligent manslaughter	Forcible rape	Robbery	Aggravated assault	Property crime	Burglary	Larceny-theft	Motor vehicle theft	Arson[1]
		Topeka	7	0	1	1	5	47	8	36	3	1
	Wyandotte County Parks and Recreation		6	0	0	1	5	9	1	7	1	8
KENTUCKY-State Agencies	Alcohol Beverage Control		0	0	0	0	0	0	0	0	0	0
	Fish and Wildlife Enforcement		0	0	0	0	0	0	0	0	0	0
	Kentucky Fairgrounds Security		0	0	0	0	0	17	0	14	3	0
	Kentucky Horse Park		0	0	0	0	0	55	4	51	0	0
	Motor Vehicle Enforcement		4	0	0	0	4	8	0	6	2	0
	South Central Kentucky Drug Task Force		2	0	0	1	1	2	1	1	0	0
	State Police		1,085	55	361	129	540	7,224	2,899	3,560	765	
	Unlawful Narcotics Investigation, Treatment and Education		0	0	0	0	0	5	0	5	0	0
KENTUCKY-Other Agencies	Buffalo Trace-Gateway Narcotics Task Force		0	0	0	0	0	0	0	0	0	0
	Cincinnati-Northern Kentucky International Airport		0	0	0	0	0	118	6	89	23	0
	FIVCO Area Drug Task Force		0	0	0	0	0	1	0	1	0	0
	Greater Hardin County Narcotics Task Force		0	0	0	0	0	1	0	0	1	0
	Jefferson County Board of Education		39	0	0	2	37	244	119	122	3	0
	Lake Cumberland Area Drug Enforcement Task Force		0	0	0	0	0	1	0	1	0	0
	Louisville Regional Airport Authority		0	0	0	0	0	24	0	5	19	0
	McCracken County Public Schools		1	0	0	0	1	1	0	1	0	1
	Northern Kentucky Narcotics Enforcement Unit		0	0	0	0	0	0	0	0	0	0
	Pennyrile Narcotics Task Force		0	0	0	0	0	2	1	1	0	0
LOUISIANA-State Agencies	Department of Public Safety, State Capitol Detail		8	0	1	3	4	24	2	20	2	0
	Tensas Basin Levee District		0	0	0	0	0	11	0	10	1	12
MAINE-State Agencies	Drug Enforcement Agency:	Androscoggin County	0	0	0	0	0	0	0	0	0	0
		Aroostook County	0	0	0	0	0	0	0	0	0	0
		Cumberland County	0	0	0	0	0	0	0	0	0	0
		Franklin County	0	0	0	0	0	0	0	0	0	0
		Hancock County	0	0	0	0	0	0	0	0	0	0
		Kennebec County	0	0	0	0	0	0	0	0	0	0
		Knox County	0	0	0	0	0	0	0	0	0	0
		Lincoln County	0	0	0	0	0	0	0	0	0	0
		Oxford County	0	0	0	0	0	0	0	0	0	0
		Penobscot County	0	0	0	0	0	0	0	0	0	0
		Piscataquis County	0	0	0	0	0	0	0	0	0	0
		Sagadahoc County	0	0	0	0	0	0	0	0	0	0
		Somerset County	0	0	0	0	0	0	0	0	0	0
		Waldo County	0	0	0	0	0	0	0	0	0	0
		Washington County	0	0	0	0	0	0	0	0	0	0
		York County	0	0	0	0	0	0	0	0	0	0
	State Police:	Androscoggin County	8	0	1	0	7	149	56	83	10	1
		Aroostook County	8	0	3	0	5	277	80	186	11	0
		Cumberland County	5	0	0	1	4	171	51	109	11	0
		Franklin County	7	0	0	0	7	87	35	50	2	1
		Hancock County	1	0	0	0	1	217	46	154	17	0
		Kennebec County	14	0	3	2	9	410	132	254	24	3

[1] The FBI does not publish arson data unless it receives data from either the agency or the state for all 12 months of the calendar year.

Table 11. Offenses Known to Law Enforcement, by State and Other Agencies, 2006 (*Contd.*)

(Number.)

State	State/Other Agency	Unit/Office	Violent crime	Murder and non-negligent man-slaughter	Forcible rape	Robbery	Aggra-vated assault	Property crime	Burglary	Larceny-theft	Motor vehicle theft	Arson[1]
		Knox County	2	0	0	0	2	82	33	45	4	0
		Lincoln County	1	0	0	0	1	15	5	7	3	0
		Oxford County	12	4	1	0	7	182	91	86	5	2
		Penobscot County	10	1	4	1	4	355	119	216	20	0
		Piscataquis County	1	0	0	0	1	10	6	3	1	0
		Sagadahoc County	2	0	1	1	0	4	1	2	1	0
		Somerset County	12	6	2	0	4	190	80	93	17	2
		Waldo County	1	0	0	0	1	159	47	106	6	5
		Washington County	2	0	1	0	1	229	78	140	11	0
		York County	3	0	1	1	1	205	46	147	12	0
MARYLAND-State Agencies	Comptroller of the Treasury, Field Enforcement Division..................................		0	0	0	0	0	0	0	0	0	0
	Department of Public Safety and Correctional Services, Internal Investigations Unit		208	6	0	0	202	0	0	0	0	0
	General Services:	Annapolis, Anne Arundel County	1	0	0	0	1	20	0	19	1	0
		Baltimore City	1	0	0	1	0	43	0	43	0	0
	Maryland State Police Statewide		7	0	1	0	6	0	0	0	0	0
	Natural Resources Police.....		0	0	0	0	0	208	10	196	2	178
	Rosewood		13	0	1	0	12	22	0	22	0	0
	Springfield Hospital..............		0	0	0	0	0	13	0	13	0	0
	State Fire Marshal		0	0	0	0	0	0	0	0	0	1
	State Police:	Allegany County	48	0	6	5	37	451	97	325	29	13
		Anne Arundel County	16	0	0	3	13	68	6	39	23	0
		Baltimore City	2	0	0	0	2	3	0	3	0	0
		Baltimore County	27	1	1	1	24	52	0	24	28	0
		Calvert County	73	1	2	3	67	333	62	246	25	39
		Caroline County	33	0	4	2	27	135	45	73	17	7
		Carroll County	163	0	5	28	130	1,358	339	951	68	17
		Cecil County	227	2	2	30	193	926	317	515	94	50
		Charles County	3	0	0	0	3	36	9	21	6	36
		Dorchester County	22	1	1	1	19	80	33	39	8	6
		Frederick County	72	2	5	9	56	538	126	389	23	15
		Garrett County	34	1	4	2	27	186	70	105	11	5
		Harford County	137	3	3	34	97	528	133	320	75	35
		Howard County	9	1	0	2	6	36	1	10	25	0
		Kent County	4	0	0	0	4	41	16	21	4	2
		Montgomery County	4	0	0	0	4	19	0	8	11	9
		Prince George's County	11	0	0	0	11	195	0	77	118	0
		Queen Anne's County	33	0	1	4	28	278	72	185	21	18
		Somerset County	71	2	3	4	62	288	111	158	19	12
		St. Mary's County	77	1	2	7	67	256	66	149	41	23
		Talbot County	13	0	0	2	11	114	24	77	13	3
		Washington County	58	0	1	5	52	338	77	231	30	36
		Wicomico County	102	2	7	12	81	379	119	208	52	13
		Worcester County	45	0	2	3	40	237	76	143	18	6
	Transit Administration.........		0	0	0	0	0	0	0	0	0	0
	Transportation Authority		19	0	2	1	16	219	2	179	38	0
MARYLAND-Other Agencies	Maryland-National Capital Park Police:	Montgomery County	21	0	2	6	13	192	13	174	5	6
		Prince George's County	81	4	5	37	35	259	25	206	28	3
MASSACHUSETTS-State Agencies	Massachusetts Bay Transportation Authority:	Bristol County	0	0	0	0	0	4	0	3	1	
		Essex County	4	0	0	1	3	15	1	13	1	
		Middlesex County	39	0	0	19	20	140	8	130	2	
		Norfolk County	13	0	0	5	8	90	0	71	19	

[1] The FBI does not publish arson data unless it receives data from either the agency or the state for all 12 months of the calendar year.

Table 11. Offenses Known to Law Enforcement, by State and Other Agencies, 2006 (*Contd.*)

(Number.)

State	State/Other Agency	Unit/Office	Violent crime	Murder and non-negligent man-slaughter	Forcible rape	Robbery	Aggra-vated assault	Property crime	Burglary	Larceny-theft	Motor vehicle theft	Arson[1]
		Plymouth County	0	0	0	0	0	32	0	27	5	
		Suffolk County	307	0	3	191	113	504	11	481	12	
		Worcester County	0	0	0	0	0	5	0	1	4	
	State Police:..........................	Barnstable County	9	0	0	0	9	4	0	3	1	0
		Berkshire County	8	0	0	0	8	78	23	48	7	0
		Dukes County	0	0	0	0	0	0	0	0	0	0
		Hampden County	20	0	0	0	20	81	4	9	68	0
		Hampshire County	4	0	0	1	3	9	4	5	0	0
		Norfolk County	11	0	0	0	11	6	2	1	3	0
		Plymouth County	13	0	0	0	13	9	0	3	6	0
MICHIGAN-State Agencies	State Police:..........................	Alcona County	3	0	2	0	1	32	17	15	0	1
		Alger County	7	0	5	0	2	74	30	44	0	2
		Allegan County	55	0	20	2	33	481	140	301	40	3
		Alpena County	22	0	7	0	15	219	67	140	12	0
		Antrim County	12	0	6	0	6	50	31	18	1	0
		Arenac County	8	0	4	0	4	65	29	31	5	5
		Baraga County	7	0	3	1	3	37	18	17	2	1
		Barry County	65	0	28	2	35	475	181	265	29	5
		Bay County	50	1	18	6	25	404	122	239	43	0
		Benzie County	8	0	4	0	4	39	12	25	2	0
		Berrien County	90	1	34	8	47	404	133	249	22	4
		Branch County	50	1	16	2	31	209	64	127	18	1
		Calhoun County	35	1	7	3	24	311	104	182	25	5
		Cass County	21	0	5	3	13	119	48	60	11	3
		Charlevoix County	8	0	7	0	1	22	5	14	3	0
		Cheboygan County	27	0	8	0	19	119	45	66	8	2
		Chippewa County	22	1	3	1	17	221	100	101	20	2
		Clare County	14	0	11	0	3	41	16	23	2	2
		Clinton County	5	0	4	0	1	41	14	25	2	0
		Crawford County	4	0	1	0	3	8	3	4	1	0
		Delta County	15	0	6	0	9	111	40	69	2	4
		Dickinson County	14	0	6	0	8	28	10	17	1	0
		Eaton County	20	0	10	0	10	106	30	70	6	1
		Emmet County	28	0	13	0	15	167	51	109	7	0
		Genesee County	75	0	23	7	45	358	132	182	44	0
		Gladwin County	23	0	8	1	14	92	33	53	6	2
		Gogebic County	12	0	3	0	9	29	6	22	1	2
		Grand Traverse County	24	0	14	1	9	261	57	192	12	1
		Gratiot County	31	0	8	0	23	144	38	101	5	0
		Hillsdale County	42	0	15	2	25	202	83	103	16	3
		Houghton County	23	0	5	0	18	144	52	88	4	2
		Huron County	8	0	2	0	6	86	30	54	2	0
		Ingham County	25	0	12	1	12	84	6	73	5	0
		Ionia County	59	1	20	1	37	324	106	195	23	3
		Iosco County	21	0	8	0	13	321	150	152	19	8
		Iron County	9	0	3	1	5	44	16	28	0	1
		Isabella County	52	0	34	3	15	242	69	160	13	2
		Jackson County	81	1	21	5	54	425	127	262	36	3
		Kalamazoo County	9	1	2	0	6	36	11	23	2	3
		Kalkaska County	14	0	7	0	7	106	51	54	1	1
		Kent County	20	0	7	0	13	39	0	35	4	4
		Lake County	5	0	0	0	5	8	3	4	1	2
		Lapeer County	26	0	12	0	14	163	67	80	16	4
		Leelanau County	1	0	1	0	0	11	2	9	0	0
		Lenawee County	35	0	11	1	23	117	45	58	14	2
		Livingston County	48	0	13	2	33	502	116	349	37	3
		Luce County	16	0	11	0	5	70	20	44	6	0
		Mackinac County	24	0	9	0	15	109	46	53	10	0

[1] The FBI does not publish arson data unless it receives data from either the agency or the state for all 12 months of the calendar year.

Table 11. Offenses Known to Law Enforcement, by State and Other Agencies, 2006 *(Contd.)*

(Number.)

State	State/Other Agency	Unit/Office	Violent crime	Murder and non-negligent man-slaughter	Forcible rape	Robbery	Aggra-vated assault	Property crime	Burglary	Larceny-theft	Motor vehicle theft	Arson[1]
		Macomb County	20	2	8	0	10	71	14	48	9	2
		Manistee County	30	1	11	0	18	241	104	128	9	2
		Marquette County	33	1	14	2	16	320	104	188	28	3
		Mason County	16	0	9	0	7	100	33	63	4	3
		Mecosta County	27	0	17	0	10	87	35	47	5	0
		Menominee County	13	0	2	0	11	129	58	68	3	1
		Midland County	5	0	3	0	2	52	19	31	2	1
		Missaukee County	8	0	7	0	1	44	18	23	3	0
		Monroe County	59	0	11	10	38	191	60	109	22	3
		Montcalm County	42	1	25	1	15	338	138	175	25	7
		Montmorency County	4	0	3	0	1	40	22	17	1	0
		Muskegon County	41	0	16	2	23	400	113	261	26	8
		Newaygo County	55	1	22	2	30	366	124	216	26	1
		Oakland County	63	0	10	6	47	356	98	213	45	4
		Oceana County	25	0	8	1	16	148	50	88	10	4
		Ogemaw County	34	0	20	0	14	186	96	84	6	3
		Ontonagon County	7	0	2	0	5	28	7	18	3	0
		Osceola County	24	0	9	0	15	182	77	85	20	1
		Oscoda County	7	0	3	1	3	39	18	17	4	0
		Otsego County	24	0	9	0	15	228	63	151	14	3
		Ottawa County	8	0	5	0	3	80	18	62	0	0
		Presque Isle County	0	0	0	0	0	19	9	7	3	0
		Roscommon County	33	0	11	4	18	230	85	129	16	0
		Saginaw County	68	0	30	7	31	288	69	189	30	3
		Sanilac County	33	0	15	0	18	189	87	83	19	4
		Schoolcraft County	10	0	3	0	7	108	47	53	8	3
		Shiawassee County	18	0	9	0	9	188	56	117	15	1
		St. Clair County	43	1	12	1	29	264	93	151	20	10
		St. Joseph County	55	0	21	1	33	306	83	196	27	6
		Tuscola County	25	0	13	1	11	253	105	123	25	1
		Van Buren County	88	1	18	0	69	586	253	271	62	9
		Washtenaw County	44	1	8	3	32	302	117	156	29	11
		Wayne County	62	2	13	4	43	145	6	93	46	1
		Wexford County	14	1	4	1	8	180	46	125	9	0
MICHIGAN- Other Agencies	Bishop International Airport		0	0	0	0	0	28	1	8	19	0
	Huron-Clinton Metropolitan Authority	Kensington Metropark	0	0	0	0	0	23	1	22	0	0
	Wayne County Airport		3	0	0	0	3	297	2	264	31	0
MINNESOTA- State Agencies[3]	Capitol Security, St. Paul			0		0	0	32	0	31	1	0
MINNESOTA- Other Agencies[3]	Minneapolis-St. Paul Inter-national Airport			0		1	4	88	0	12	76	0
	Three Rivers Park District			0		0	1	109	4	105	0	0
MISSOURI- Other Agencies	Clay County Park Authority		2	0	0	1	1	24	2	20	2	2
	Jackson County Park Rangers		0	0	0	0	0	0	0	0	0	0
	Lambert-St. Louis Interna-tional Airport		19	0	1	1	17	233	1	224	8	0
	St. Charles County Park Rangers		0	0	0	0	0	0	0	0	0	0
NEBRASKA- State Agencies	Nebraska State Patrol		7	0	0	0	7	2	1	1	0	0
	State Patrol:	Adams County	1	0	0	0	1	1	0	1	0	0
		Antelope County	0	0	0	0	0	2	2	0	0	0
		Arthur County	0	0	0	0	0	0	0	0	0	0
		Banner County	0	0	0	0	0	0	0	0	0	0

[1] The FBI does not publish arson data unless it receives data from either the agency or the state for all 12 months of the calendar year.
[3] The data collection methodology for the offense of forcible rape used by the Minnesota state UCR Program does not comply with national UCR Program guidelines. Consequently, their figures for forcible rape and violent crime (of which forcible rape is a part) are not published in this table.

Table 11. Offenses Known to Law Enforcement, by State and Other Agencies, 2006 *(Contd.)*

(Number.)

State	State/Other Agency	Unit/Office	Violent crime	Murder and non-negligent man-slaughter	Forcible rape	Robbery	Aggra-vated assault	Property crime	Burglary	Larceny-theft	Motor vehicle theft	Arson[1]
		Blaine County	0	0	0	0	0	0	0	0	0	0
		Boone County	0	0	0	0	0	0	0	0	0	0
		Box Butte County	0	0	0	0	0	1	1	0	0	0
		Boyd County	0	0	0	0	0	0	0	0	0	0
		Brown County	0	0	0	0	0	0	0	0	0	0
		Buffalo County	0	0	0	0	0	1	0	1	0	0
		Burt County	0	0	0	0	0	0	0	0	0	0
		Butler County	2	0	2	0	0	0	0	0	0	0
		Cass County	1	0	1	0	0	0	0	0	0	0
		Cedar County	0	0	0	0	0	0	0	0	0	0
		Chase County	0	0	0	0	0	0	0	0	0	0
		Cherry County	0	0	0	0	0	0	0	0	0	0
		Cheyenne County	0	0	0	0	0	1	0	1	0	0
		Clay County	0	0	0	0	0	1	0	0	1	0
		Colfax County	0	0	0	0	0	0	0	0	0	0
		Cuming County	0	0	0	0	0	0	0	0	0	0
		Custer County	1	0	0	0	1	1	0	1	0	0
		Dakota County	0	0	0	0	0	1	0	0	1	0
		Dawes County	0	0	0	0	0	2	1	1	0	0
		Dawson County	0	0	0	0	0	0	0	0	0	0
		Deuel County	0	0	0	0	0	0	0	0	0	0
		Dixon County	0	0	0	0	0	0	0	0	0	0
		Dodge County	0	0	0	0	0	0	0	0	0	0
		Douglas County	0	0	0	0	0	2	0	2	0	0
		Dundy County	0	0	0	0	0	0	0	0	0	0
		Fillmore County	1	0	0	0	1	0	0	0	0	0
		Franklin County	0	0	0	0	0	0	0	0	0	0
		Frontier County	0	0	0	0	0	0	0	0	0	0
		Furnas County	0	0	0	0	0	0	0	0	0	0
		Gage County	0	0	0	0	0	1	0	1	0	0
		Garden County	0	0	0	0	0	0	0	0	0	0
		Garfield County	0	0	0	0	0	0	0	0	0	0
		Gosper County	0	0	0	0	0	0	0	0	0	0
		Grant County	0	0	0	0	0	0	0	0	0	0
		Greeley County	0	0	0	0	0	0	0	0	0	0
		Hall County	0	0	0	0	0	3	0	2	1	0
		Hamilton County	0	0	0	0	0	0	0	0	0	0
		Harlan County	0	0	0	0	0	0	0	0	0	0
		Hayes County	0	0	0	0	0	0	0	0	0	0
		Hitchcock County	0	0	0	0	0	0	0	0	0	0
		Holt County	0	0	0	0	0	0	0	0	0	0
		Hooker County	0	0	0	0	0	0	0	0	0	0
		Howard County	0	0	0	0	0	0	0	0	0	0
		Jefferson County	0	0	0	0	0	0	0	0	0	0
		Johnson County	0	0	0	0	0	0	0	0	0	0
		Kearney County	0	0	0	0	0	0	0	0	0	0
		Keith County	0	0	0	0	0	0	0	0	0	0
		Keya Paha County	0	0	0	0	0	0	0	0	0	0
		Kimball County	0	0	0	0	0	0	0	0	0	0
		Knox County	0	0	0	0	0	0	0	0	0	0
		Lancaster County	1	0	1	0	0	4	1	2	1	0
		Lincoln County	0	0	0	0	0	0	0	0	0	0
		Logan County	0	0	0	0	0	0	0	0	0	0
		Loup County	0	0	0	0	0	0	0	0	0	0
		Madison County	0	0	0	0	0	1	0	1	0	0
		McPherson County	0	0	0	0	0	0	0	0	0	0
		Merrick County	0	0	0	0	0	0	0	0	0	0
		Morrill County	0	0	0	0	0	0	0	0	0	0
		Nance County	0	0	0	0	0	0	0	0	0	0
		Nemaha County	0	0	0	0	0	0	0	0	0	0
		Nuckolls County	0	0	0	0	0	0	0	0	0	0
		Otoe County	0	0	0	0	0	0	0	0	0	0

[1] The FBI does not publish arson data unless it receives data from either the agency or the state for all 12 months of the calendar year.

Table 11. Offenses Known to Law Enforcement, by State and Other Agencies, 2006 (*Contd.*)

(Number.)

State	State/Other Agency	Unit/Office	Violent crime	Murder and non-negligent man-slaughter	Forcible rape	Robbery	Aggra-vated assault	Property crime	Burglary	Larceny-theft	Motor vehicle theft	Arson[1]
		Pawnee County	0	0	0	0	0	0	0	0	0	0
		Perkins County	0	0	0	0	0	0	0	0	0	0
		Phelps County	1	0	1	0	0	0	0	0	0	0
		Pierce County	1	0	0	0	1	4	3	1	0	0
		Platte County	0	0	0	0	0	0	0	0	0	0
		Polk County	0	0	0	0	0	0	0	0	0	0
		Red Willow County	0	0	0	0	0	3	2	1	0	0
		Richardson County	1	1	0	0	0	0	0	0	0	0
		Rock County	0	0	0	0	0	0	0	0	0	0
		Saline County	0	0	0	0	0	0	0	0	0	0
		Sarpy County	0	0	0	0	0	1	0	1	0	0
		Saunders County	0	0	0	0	0	0	0	0	0	0
		Scotts Bluff County	0	0	0	0	0	0	0	0	0	0
		Seward County	0	0	0	0	0	0	0	0	0	0
		Sheridan County	0	0	0	0	0	0	0	0	0	0
		Sherman County	0	0	0	0	0	1	1	0	0	0
		Sioux County	0	0	0	0	0	0	0	0	0	0
		Stanton County	0	0	0	0	0	1	0	1	0	0
		Thayer County	0	0	0	0	0	0	0	0	0	0
		Thomas County	0	0	0	0	0	0	0	0	0	0
		Thurston County	0	0	0	0	0	1	1	0	0	0
		Valley County	1	0	0	0	1	0	0	0	0	0
		Washington County	0	0	0	0	0	0	0	0	0	0
		Wayne County	0	0	0	0	0	0	0	0	0	0
		Webster County	0	0	0	0	0	0	0	0	0	0
		Wheeler County	0	0	0	0	0	0	0	0	0	0
		York County	0	0	0	0	0	0	0	0	0	0
NEVADA-State Agencies	Taxicab Authority		126	0	0	34	92	425	0	414	11	0
NEVADA-Other Agencies	Clark County School District....................		110	0	3	47	60	1,188	255	888	45	76
	Washoe County School District.....................		12	0	0	2	10	184	23	160	1	18
NEW HAMPSHIRE-State Agencies	Liquor Commission..............		0	0	0	0	0	0	0	0	0	0
NEW JERSEY-State Agencies	Human Services, Woodland Township..............................		16	0	0	0	16	13	5	8	0	0
	Hunterdon Developmental Center...........................		0	0	0	0	0	13	0	13	0	0
	New Jersey Transit Police		82	0	0	36	46	260	4	240	16	0
	Palisades Interstate Parkway		6	0	0	0	6	1	1	0	0	0
	Port Authority of New York and New Jersey[4]..................		55	0	0	15	40	658	10	593	55	0
	State Police:.........................	Atlantic County	54	0	1	24	29	1,015	99	890	26	1
		Bergen County	9	0	0	2	7	141	4	113	24	0
		Burlington County	45	1	2	5	37	526	106	365	55	7
		Camden County	10	1	1	0	8	29	0	25	4	0
		Cape May County	32	0	2	6	24	446	113	313	20	1
		Cumberland County	105	1	2	13	89	886	307	512	67	11
		Essex County	13	0	0	4	9	30	1	27	2	0
		Gloucester County	4	0	0	0	4	12	0	11	1	0
		Hudson County	4	0	0	3	1	10	1	9	0	1
		Hunterdon County	15	0	0	1	14	193	56	117	20	3
		Mercer County	8	0	2	1	5	150	6	140	4	2
		Middlesex County	10	0	0	0	10	103	1	87	15	0
		Monmouth County	17	0	0	5	12	249	44	180	25	5
		Morris County	12	0	2	3	7	27	6	15	6	0
		Ocean County	10	0	0	0	10	75	4	63	8	0

[1] The FBI does not publish arson data unless it receives data from either the agency or the state for all 12 months of the calendar year.
[4] Figures reported are the number of crimes occurring in New Jersey.

Table 11. Offenses Known to Law Enforcement, by State and Other Agencies, 2006 (*Contd.*)

(Number.)

State	State/Other Agency	Unit/Office	Violent crime	Murder and non-negligent man-slaughter	Forcible rape	Robbery	Aggra-vated assault	Property crime	Burglary	Larceny-theft	Motor vehicle theft	Arson[1]
		Passaic County	1	0	0	0	1	32	1	30	1	0
		Salem County	31	0	1	4	26	476	153	283	40	5
		Somerset County	3	0	0	0	3	7	1	5	1	0
		Sussex County	51	0	4	6	41	454	97	320	37	8
		Union County	6	0	0	1	5	14	2	7	5	0
		Warren County	21	0	0	2	19	256	73	158	25	5
NEW MEXICO-State Agencies	New Mexico State Police		219	10	57	27	125	1,322	616	486	220	6
NEW MEXICO-Other Agencies	Acoma Tribal		25	0	0	1	24	21	5	15	1	0
	Laguna Tribal........................		125	0	16	3	106	63	12	47	4	0
	Taos Pueblo Tribal		45	0	3	2	40	32	8	18	6	2
NEW YORK-State Agencies	State Park:.............................	Albany County	1	0	0	0	1	5	0	5	0	0
		Allegany County	0	0	0	0	0	0	0	0	0	0
		Bronx County	1	0	0	1	0	11	3	8	0	0
		Cattaraugus County	0	0	0	0	0	7	2	5	0	0
		Cayuga County	1	0	0	0	1	7	2	5	0	0
		Chautauqua County	0	0	0	0	0	1	0	1	0	0
		Chemung County	0	0	0	0	0	0	0	0	0	0
		Chenango County	0	0	0	0	0	0	0	0	0	0
		Clinton County	0	0	0	0	0	4	0	4	0	0
		Cortland County	0	0	0	0	0	0	0	0	0	0
		Delaware County	0	0	0	0	0	0	0	0	0	0
		Erie County	0	0	0	0	0	6	0	6	0	0
		Fulton County	0	0	0	0	0	0	0	0	0	0
		Genesee County	0	0	0	0	0	0	0	0	0	0
		Greene County	0	0	0	0	0	0	0	0	0	0
		Herkimer County	0	0	0	0	0	0	0	0	0	0
		Jefferson County	0	0	0	0	0	15	1	14	0	0
		Kings County	0	0	0	0	0	1	0	1	0	0
		Lewis County	0	0	0	0	0	0	0	0	0	0
		Livingston County	0	0	0	0	0	2	0	2	0	0
		Madison County	0	0	0	0	0	3	0	3	0	0
		Monroe County	0	0	0	0	0	5	0	5	0	0
		Montgomery County	0	0	0	0	0	0	0	0	0	0
		Nassau County	5	0	0	0	5	37	0	37	0	0
		New York County	3	0	0	3	0	76	0	76	0	0
		Niagara County	3	0	0	0	3	14	1	13	0	0
		Oneida County	0	0	0	0	0	3	1	2	0	0
		Onondaga County	0	0	0	0	0	9	0	9	0	0
		Ontario County	0	0	0	0	0	1	0	1	0	0
		Orange County	0	0	0	0	0	5	1	4	0	0
		Orleans County	0	0	0	0	0	0	0	0	0	0
		Oswego County	1	0	0	0	1	4	2	2	0	0
		Otsego County	0	0	0	0	0	3	0	3	0	0
		Queens County	0	0	0	0	0	0	0	0	0	0
		Rennselaer County	0	0	0	0	0	2	1	1	0	0
		Richmond County	0	0	0	0	0	1	0	1	0	0
		Rockland County	2	0	0	0	2	19	2	15	2	0
		Saratoga County	6	0	0	1	5	19	0	19	0	0
		Schenectady County	0	0	0	0	0	0	0	0	0	0
		Schoharie County	0	0	0	0	0	0	0	0	0	0
		Schuyler County	0	0	0	0	0	3	0	3	0	0
		Seneca County	0	0	0	0	0	4	2	2	0	0
		Steuben County	0	0	0	0	0	2	0	2	0	0
		St. Lawrence County	0	0	0	0	0	11	0	11	0	2
		Suffolk County	5	0	0	1	4	43	5	36	2	1
		Sullivan County	0	0	0	0	0	0	0	0	0	0

[1] The FBI does not publish arson data unless it receives data from either the agency or the state for all 12 months of the calendar year.

Table 11. Offenses Known to Law Enforcement, by State and Other Agencies, 2006 (*Contd.*)

(Number.)

State	State/Other Agency	Unit/Office	Violent crime	Murder and non-negligent man-slaughter	Forcible rape	Robbery	Aggra-vated assault	Property crime	Burglary	Larceny-theft	Motor vehicle theft	Arson[1]
		Taconic Region	0	0	0	0	0	39	7	31	1	0
		Tioga County	0	0	0	0	0	0	0	0	0	0
		Tompkins County	0	0	0	0	0	8	0	8	0	0
		Ulster County	0	0	0	0	0	1	0	1	0	0
		Washington County	0	0	0	0	0	0	0	0	0	0
		Wayne County	0	0	0	0	0	4	0	4	0	0
		Wyoming County	0	0	0	0	0	1	0	1	0	0
		Yates County	0	0	0	0	0	0	0	0	0	0
	State Police:	Albany County	31	0	7	0	24	231	31	182	18	
		Allegany County	56	1	12	0	43	326	87	233	6	5
		Broome County	70	1	30	6	33	602	139	452	11	1
		Cattaraugus County	59	0	5	4	50	325	116	206	3	0
		Cayuga County	55	0	5	2	48	326	77	244	5	6
		Chautauqua County	15	2	1	0	12	148	29	109	10	1
		Chemung County	56	1	14	4	37	267	52	213	2	
		Chenango County	47	0	6	0	41	151	57	90	4	0
		Clinton County	97	1	19	2	75	945	304	622	19	
		Columbia County	33	0	11	3	19	294	94	189	11	4
		Cortland County	18	0	0	2	16	203	27	174	2	
		Delaware County	30	0	4	1	25	280	102	169	9	
		Dutchess County	116	2	13	14	87	654	185	451	18	5
		Erie County	50	0	14	2	34	443	74	356	13	2
		Essex County	46	0	3	2	41	310	113	186	11	
		Franklin County	110	0	9	1	100	453	233	197	23	
		Fulton County	17	0	2	0	15	95	23	68	4	0
		Genesee County	23	0	5	0	18	84	12	69	3	0
		Greene County	162	1	6	4	151	445	166	265	14	
		Hamilton County	5	0	2	0	3	43	14	29	0	
		Herkimer County	39	1	2	4	32	220	91	124	5	
		Jefferson County	67	0	16	5	46	575	165	395	15	
		Lewis County	14	0	6	0	8	85	44	39	2	0
		Livingston County	29	0	13	1	15	84	11	72	1	
		Madison County	25	0	10	0	15	271	88	177	6	0
		Monroe County	24	1	2	1	20	75	3	70	2	1
		Montgomery County	23	0	5	1	17	96	23	70	3	0
		Nassau County	8	0	0	1	7	25	0	21	4	0
		New York County	0	0	0	0	0	55	2	53	0	
		Niagara County	17	0	5	4	8	231	34	183	14	
		Oneida County	83	1	9	1	72	640	197	423	20	3
		Onondaga County	38	2	6	10	20	556	128	413	15	
		Ontario County	22	0	11	1	10	231	38	189	4	0
		Orange County	146	3	22	27	94	837	165	632	40	
		Orleans County	9	0	1	0	8	64	13	46	5	0
		Oswego County	42	1	11	3	27	714	244	457	13	
		Otsego County	77	1	19	4	53	419	93	321	5	0
		Putnam County	19	1	1	4	13	150	23	124	3	3
		Rensselaer County	38	0	11	2	25	445	135	295	15	
		Rockland County	26	0	4	0	22	21	1	16	4	
		Saratoga County	85	1	20	8	56	810	166	625	19	
		Schenectady County	6	0	3	0	3	142	14	121	7	
		Schoharie County	13	0	5	0	8	127	26	98	3	
		Schuyler County	3	0	1	0	2	28	7	20	1	0
		Seneca County	15	0	3	1	11	96	32	63	1	
		Steuben County	104	0	67	1	36	410	113	277	20	
		St. Lawrence County	62	0	13	2	47	622	283	327	12	
		Suffolk County	26	0	0	6	20	34	9	23	2	
		Sullivan County	118	1	17	9	91	444	156	252	36	
		Tioga County	14	0	3	0	11	159	34	122	3	1

[1] The FBI does not publish arson data unless it receives data from either the agency or the state for all 12 months of the calendar year.

Table 11. Offenses Known to Law Enforcement, by State and Other Agencies, 2006 (*Contd.*)

(Number.)

State	State/Other Agency	Unit/Office	Violent crime	Murder and non-negligent man-slaughter	Forcible rape	Robbery	Aggra-vated assault	Property crime	Burglary	Larceny-theft	Motor vehicle theft	Arson[1]
NEW YORK- **Other Agencies**		Tompkins County	49	1	4	2	42	208	31	163	14	1
		Ulster County	207	0	21	7	179	503	161	312	30	
		Warren County	41	0	10	1	30	226	41	184	1	2
		Washington County	40	0	8	0	32	227	68	148	11	
		Wayne County	45	0	12	3	30	491	170	307	14	6
		Westchester County	85	2	9	10	64	438	89	331	18	6
		Wyoming County	30	0	4	0	26	30	14	14	2	0
		Yates County	7	0	1	0	6	26	3	23	0	0
	Board of Water:	Delaware County	0	0	0	0	0	2	2	0	0	0
		Sullivan County	1	0	0	0	1	4	1	3	0	0
		Westchester County	0	0	0	0	0	23	0	23	0	0
	Broome County Special Investigations Task Force		1	0	0	0	1	2	0	2	0	0
	CSX Transportation:	Albany County	0	0	0	0	0	6	0	6	0	0
		Bronx County	0	0	0	0	0	61	0	61	0	0
		Cattaraugus County	0	0	0	0	0	0	0	0	0	0
		Cayuga County	0	0	0	0	0	1	0	1	0	0
		Chautauqua County	0	0	0	0	0	2	0	2	0	0
		Columbia County	0	0	0	0	0	0	0	0	0	0
		Dutchess County	0	0	0	0	0	0	0	0	0	0
		Erie County	0	0	0	0	0	25	0	25	0	0
		Genesee County	0	0	0	0	0	1	0	1	0	0
		Greene County	0	0	0	0	0	1	0	1	0	0
		Herkimer County	0	0	0	0	0	3	0	3	0	0
		Jefferson County	0	0	0	0	0	0	0	0	0	0
		Madison County	0	0	0	0	0	0	0	0	0	0
		Monroe County	0	0	0	0	0	7	2	4	1	0
		Montgomery County	0	0	0	0	0	3	0	3	0	0
		Niagara County	0	0	0	0	0	2	0	2	0	0
		Oneida County	0	0	0	0	0	1	0	1	0	0
		Onondaga County	0	0	0	0	0	4	2	2	0	0
		Ontario County	0	0	0	0	0	0	0	0	0	0
		Orange County	0	0	0	0	0	1	0	1	0	0
		Orleans County	0	0	0	0	0	0	0	0	0	0
		Oswego County	0	0	0	0	0	1	0	1	0	0
		Queens County	0	0	0	0	0	0	0	0	0	0
		Rensselaer County	0	0	0	0	0	0	0	0	0	0
		Rockland County	0	0	0	0	0	3	0	3	0	
		Schenectady County	0	0	0	0	0	2	0	2	0	0
		Seneca County	0	0	0	0	0	0	0	0	0	0
		St. Lawrence County	0	0	0	0	0	0	0	0	0	0
		Ulster County	0	0	0	0	0	0	0	0	0	0
		Wayne County	0	0	0	0	0	1	0	1	0	0
		Westchester County	0	0	0	0	0	0	0	0	0	0
	New York City Metropolitan Transportation Authority:	Bronx County	9	0	0	6	3	22	0	20	2	0
		Dutchess County	0	0	0	0	0	25	0	22	3	0
		Kings County	9	0	0	9	0	11	0	10	1	0
		Nassau County	17	1	0	9	7	34	1	33	0	1
		New York County	19	0	0	8	11	237	8	229	0	0
		Orange County	0	0	0	0	0	9	1	8	0	0
		Putnam County	0	0	0	0	0	15	0	13	2	0
		Queens County	6	0	0	3	3	44	0	43	1	0
		Richmond County	14	0	1	9	4	10	0	10	0	0
		Rockland County	0	0	0	0	0	3	0	3	0	0
		Suffolk County	8	1	0	7	0	52	1	49	2	1

[1] The FBI does not publish arson data unless it receives data from either the agency or the state for all 12 months of the calendar year.

Table 11. Offenses Known to Law Enforcement, by State and Other Agencies, 2006 (*Contd.*)

(Number.)

State	State/Other Agency	Unit/Office	Violent crime	Murder and non-negligent manslaughter	Forcible rape	Robbery	Aggravated assault	Property crime	Burglary	Larceny-theft	Motor vehicle theft	Arson[1]
		Westchester County	20	0	0	14	6	88	1	84	3	0
	Onondaga County Parks......		0	0	0	0	0	41	6	35	0	0
	Suffolk County Parks............		4	0	0	1	3	67	10	57	0	0
NORTH CAROLINA- **State Agencies**	Department of Human Resources...............................		11	0	0	0	11	18	5	12	1	0
	Department of Wildlife		5	0	0	0	5	0	0	0	0	0
	Division of Alcohol Law Enforcement...........................		0	0	0	0	0	0	0	0	0	0
	North Carolina Highway Patrol		0	0	0	0	0	0	0	0	0	0
	State Capitol Police..............		0	0	0	0	0	47	7	39	1	0
	State Park Rangers:...............	Crowders Mountain	0	0	0	0	0	9	0	9	0	0
		Dismal Swamp	0	0	0	0	0	0	0	0	0	0
		Elk Knob	0	0	0	0	0	0	0	0	0	0
		Eno River	0	0	0	0	0	1	0	0	1	0
		Goose Creek	0	0	0	0	0	0	0	0	0	0
		Hanging Rock	0	0	0	0	0	4	0	4	0	0
		Jordan Lake Recreation Area	1	0	0	1	0	14	0	13	1	0
		Lake James	0	0	0	0	0	7	0	7	0	0
		Medoc Mountain	0	0	0	0	0	0	0	0	0	0
		Merchants Millpond	0	0	0	0	0	0	0	0	0	0
		Morrow Mountain	0	0	0	0	0	0	0	0	0	0
		Mt. Mitchell	0	0	0	0	0	0	0	0	0	0
		New River-Mount Jefferson	0	0	0	0	0	0	0	0	0	0
		Pettigrew	0	0	0	0	0	2	0	2	0	0
		Pilot Mountain	0	0	0	0	0	0	0	0	0	0
		Raven Rock	0	0	0	0	0	0	0	0	0	0
		Stone Mountain	0	0	0	0	0	1	0	1	0	0
		Weymouth Woods Sandhills Preserve	0	0	0	0	0	0	0	0	0	0
NORTH CAROLINA- **Other Agencies**	Raleigh-Durham International Airport............		3	0	0	1	2	78	2	72	4	0
	Wilmington International Airport..................................		0	0	0	0	0	12	2	7	3	0
OHIO- **State Agencies**	Ohio State Highway Patrol		294	2	8	14	270	532	18	385	129	10
OHIO- **Other Agencies**	Cleveland Metropolitan Park District		6	0	0	2	4	222	5	211	6	0
	Hamilton County Park District.................................		1	0	1	0	0	47	5	42	0	0
	Lake Metroparks..................		1	0	0	0	1	12	2	10	0	2
	Port Columbus International Airport..................................		0	0	0	0	0	139	4	107	28	0
OKLAHOMA- **State Agencies**	Capitol Park Police		1	0	0	0	1	25	0	23	2	0
OKLAHOMA- **Other Agencies**	Jenks Public Schools.............		2	0	0	0	2	26	0	25	1	0
	Madill Public Schools		0	0	0	0	0	1	0	1	0	1
	McAlester Public Schools....		3	0	0	0	3	2	1	1	0	1
	Norman Public Schools		1	0	0	0	1	70	8	57	5	0
	Putnam City Campus............		3	0	0	0	3	112	15	95	2	0
OREGON- **Other Agencies**	Port of Portland		0	0	0	0	2	412	3	353	56	0
PENNSYLVANIA- **State Agencies**	Bureau of Narcotics:	Allegheny County	0	0	0	0	0	0	0	0	0	0
		Bedford County	0	0	0	0	0	0	0	0	0	0
		Berks County	0	0	0	0	0	0	0	0	0	0
		Blair County	0	0	0	0	0	0	0	0	0	0
		Bradford County	0	0	0	0	0	0	0	0	0	0
		Bucks County	0	0	0	0	0	0	0	0	0	0
		Cambria County	0	0	0	0	0	0	0	0	0	0
		Cameron County	0	0	0	0	0	0	0	0	0	0
		Carbon County	0	0	0	0	0	0	0	0	0	0
		Centre County	0	0	0	0	0	0	0	0	0	0
		Chester County	0	0	0	0	0	0	0	0	0	0

[1] The FBI does not publish arson data unless it receives data from either the agency or the state for all 12 months of the calendar year.

Table 11. Offenses Known to Law Enforcement, by State and Other Agencies, 2006 (*Contd.*)

(Number.)

State	State/Other Agency	Unit/Office	Violent crime	Murder and non-negligent man-slaughter	Forcible rape	Robbery	Aggra-vated assault	Property crime	Burglary	Larceny-theft	Motor vehicle theft	Arson[1]
		Clearfield County	0	0	0	0	0	0	0	0	0	0
		Clinton County	0	0	0	0	0	0	0	0	0	0
		Columbia County	0	0	0	0	0	0	0	0	0	0
		Crawford County	0	0	0	0	0	0	0	0	0	0
		Delaware County	0	0	0	0	0	0	0	0	0	0
		Elk County	0	0	0	0	0	0	0	0	0	0
		Erie County	0	0	0	0	0	0	0	0	0	0
		Fayette County	0	0	0	0	0	0	0	0	0	0
		Forest County	0	0	0	0	0	0	0	0	0	0
		Greene County	0	0	0	0	0	0	0	0	0	0
		Huntingdon County	0	0	0	0	0	0	0	0	0	0
		Juniata County	0	0	0	0	0	0	0	0	0	0
		Lackawanna County	0	0	0	0	0	0	0	0	0	0
		Lehigh County	0	0	0	0	0	0	0	0	0	0
		Luzerne County	0	0	0	0	0	0	0	0	0	0
		Lycoming County	0	0	0	0	0	0	0	0	0	0
		McKean County	0	0	0	0	0	0	0	0	0	0
		Mifflin County	0	0	0	0	0	0	0	0	0	0
		Monroe County	0	0	0	0	0	0	0	0	0	0
		Montgomery County	0	0	0	0	0	0	0	0	0	0
		Montour County	0	0	0	0	0	0	0	0	0	0
		Northampton County	0	0	0	0	0	1	0	1	0	0
		Northumberland County	0	0	0	0	0	0	0	0	0	0
		Philadelphia County	0	0	0	0	0	0	0	0	0	0
		Pike County	0	0	0	0	0	0	0	0	0	0
		Potter County	0	0	0	0	0	0	0	0	0	0
		Schuylkill County	0	0	0	0	0	0	0	0	0	0
		Snyder County	0	0	0	0	0	0	0	0	0	0
		Somerset County	0	0	0	0	0	0	0	0	0	0
		Sullivan County	0	0	0	0	0	0	0	0	0	0
		Susquehanna County	0	0	0	0	0	0	0	0	0	0
		Tioga County	0	0	0	0	0	0	0	0	0	0
		Union County	0	0	0	0	0	0	0	0	0	0
		Venango County	0	0	0	0	0	0	0	0	0	0
		Warren County	0	0	0	0	0	0	0	0	0	0
		Washington County	0	0	0	0	0	0	0	0	0	0
		Wayne County	0	0	0	0	0	0	0	0	0	0
		Westmoreland County	0	0	0	0	0	0	0	0	0	0
		Wyoming County	0	0	0	0	0	0	0	0	0	0
	Department of Environmental Resources...........................		0	0	0	0	0	12	0	12	0	0
	State Capitol Police..............		6	0	0	1	5	49	1	45	3	0
	State Park Police, Pymatuning............................		0	0	0	0	0	40	1	39	0	0
	State Police:...........................	Adams County	41	2	11	7	21	521	167	313	41	8
		Allegheny County	42	0	0	2	40	36	4	25	7	0
		Armstrong County	55	1	9	14	31	561	159	364	38	14
		Beaver County	30	0	5	7	18	222	69	126	27	13
		Bedford County	66	0	10	9	47	695	214	444	37	26
		Berks County	191	0	10	6	175	698	184	448	66	10
		Blair County	37	0	11	4	22	441	134	263	44	5
		Bradford County	27	2	8	2	15	487	162	283	42	11
		Bucks County	36	0	4	3	29	353	84	231	38	4
		Butler County	76	0	3	10	63	860	241	560	59	8
		Cambria County	57	4	8	6	39	402	162	191	49	8
		Cameron County	2	0	2	0	0	72	33	38	1	0

[1] The FBI does not publish arson data unless it receives data from either the agency or the state for all 12 months of the calendar year.

Table 11. Offenses Known to Law Enforcement, by State and Other Agencies, 2006 (*Contd.*)

(Number.)

State	State/Other Agency	Unit/Office	Violent crime	Murder and non-negligent man-slaughter	Forcible rape	Robbery	Aggra-vated assault	Property crime	Burglary	Larceny-theft	Motor vehicle theft	Arson[1]
		Carbon County	99	0	2	3	94	349	122	209	18	12
		Centre County	46	0	7	5	34	674	211	420	43	10
		Chester County	151	1	22	27	101	1,254	440	710	104	26
		Clarion County	53	0	20	2	31	473	140	307	26	15
		Clearfield County	48	1	16	3	28	722	219	440	63	29
		Clinton County	20	0	7	3	10	517	148	330	39	5
		Columbia County	17	2	4	2	9	206	92	99	15	1
		Crawford County	32	0	13	4	15	673	300	315	58	4
		Cumberland County	65	0	6	4	55	636	161	412	63	10
		Delaware County	71	2	7	24	38	1,030	138	825	67	6
		Elizabethville	79	0	17	14	48	640	135	464	41	4
		Elk County	10	0	2	2	6	181	55	118	8	5
		Erie County	126	0	26	19	81	1,213	359	748	106	7
		Fayette County	198	1	36	67	94	1,838	533	1,070	235	85
		Franklin County	130	3	15	15	97	1,099	247	784	68	27
		Fulton County	22	0	6	4	12	182	62	102	18	2
		Greene County	28	1	10	11	6	442	123	285	34	2
		Huntingdon County	70	2	12	4	52	470	157	292	21	13
		Indiana County	75	0	17	16	42	1,076	277	721	78	36
		Jefferson County	32	3	5	1	23	364	117	218	29	6
		Juniata County	12	0	3	1	8	227	72	141	14	1
		Lackawanna County	28	0	7	2	19	199	67	112	20	33
		Lancaster County	100	5	15	14	66	1,047	381	587	79	44
		Lawrence County	53	0	7	13	33	557	145	352	60	51
		Lebanon County	47	1	8	5	33	380	80	265	35	3
		Lehigh County	91	1	6	27	57	942	196	693	53	19
		Luzerne County	277	8	8	27	234	980	262	613	105	32
		Lycoming County	49	0	11	3	35	803	270	494	39	4
		McKean County	14	0	4	1	9	157	64	85	8	2
		Mercer County	46	1	9	7	29	527	181	321	25	7
		Mifflin County	9	0	0	2	7	139	44	85	10	2
		Monroe County	247	1	21	26	199	1,290	501	699	90	8
		Montour County	1	0	0	0	1	84	24	57	3	0
		Northampton County	29	1	6	3	19	355	99	217	39	8
		Northumberland County	102	0	5	3	94	323	85	212	26	0
		Perry County	66	1	11	6	48	577	220	333	24	6
		Philadelphia County	0	0	0	0	0	5	0	5	0	0
		Pike County	91	1	12	20	58	797	290	447	60	33
		Potter County	19	0	7	0	12	250	106	133	11	2
		Schuylkill County	111	0	7	9	95	687	126	487	74	17
		Skippack	93	1	1	5	86	439	103	310	26	15
		Snyder County	16	0	1	5	10	389	78	281	30	2
		Somerset County	49	0	14	5	30	560	188	330	42	15
		Sullivan County	2	0	1	0	1	94	26	64	4	2
		Susquehanna County	30	0	7	5	18	516	133	342	41	6
		Tioga County	18	0	5	3	10	264	91	154	19	5
		Tionesta	27	0	8	0	19	121	63	47	11	2
		Union County	11	0	7	1	3	154	52	89	13	4
		Venango County	37	0	4	5	28	409	140	238	31	4
		Warren County	34	0	10	0	24	270	104	145	21	10
		Washington County	86	2	15	15	54	802	286	424	92	30
		Wayne County	53	3	21	4	25	555	190	321	44	21
		Westmoreland County	210	1	28	70	111	1,946	507	1,294	145	33
		Wyoming County	23	0	6	4	13	296	97	181	18	4
		York County	277	2	20	10	245	579	151	361	67	18

[1] The FBI does not publish arson data unless it receives data from either the agency or the state for all 12 months of the calendar year.

Table 11. Offenses Known to Law Enforcement, by State and Other Agencies, 2006 (*Contd.*)

(Number.)

State	State/Other Agency	Unit/Office	Violent crime	Murder and non-negligent man-slaughter	Forcible rape	Robbery	Aggra-vated assault	Property crime	Burglary	Larceny-theft	Motor vehicle theft	Arson[1]
PENNSYLVANIA-Other Agencies	Allegheny County Port Authority		59	0	1	33	25	139	2	120	17	1
	County Detective:	Berks County	2	0	1	0	1	5	0	5	0	0
		Butler County	2	0	0	0	2	0	0	0	0	0
		Dauphin County	9	0	3	0	6	31	0	31	0	0
		Lebanon County	26	1	23	0	2	0	0	0	0	0
		Lehigh County	0	0	0	0	0	0	0	0	0	0
		Westmoreland County	4	0	0	0	4	87	0	87	0	0
		York County	3	0	0	0	3	29	1	28	0	0
	Delaware County District Attorney, Criminal Investigation Division		25	0	11	0	14	1	0	1	0	0
	Harrisburg International Airport		0	0	0	0	0	13	0	11	2	1
	Westmoreland County Park		1	0	0	0	1	5	0	5	0	0
RHODE ISLAND-State Agencies	Department of Environmental Management		0	0	0	0	0	50	2	46	2	3
	Rhode Island State Police Headquarters		15	1	2	0	12	46	1	17	28	1
	State Police:	Chepachet	4	0	3	0	1	25	0	17	8	0
		Hope Valley	9	0	4	0	5	90	20	62	8	2
		Lincoln	10	0	3	1	6	73	3	34	36	0
		Portsmouth	1	0	0	0	1	7	2	5	0	0
		Wickford	3	0	1	0	2	22	1	15	6	0
SOUTH CAROLINA-State Agencies	Department of Mental Health		12	0	1	0	11	38	0	38	0	0
	Department of Natural Resources:	Abbeville County	0	0	0	0	0	0	0	0	0	0
		Aiken County	0	0	0	0	0	0	0	0	0	0
		Allendale County	0	0	0	0	0	0	0	0	0	0
		Anderson County	0	0	0	0	0	0	0	0	0	0
		Bamberg County	0	0	0	0	0	0	0	0	0	0
		Beaufort County	0	0	0	0	0	0	0	0	0	0
		Berkeley County	0	0	0	0	0	0	0	0	0	0
		Calhoun County	0	0	0	0	0	0	0	0	0	0
		Charleston County	0	0	0	0	0	0	0	0	0	0
		Cherokee County	0	0	0	0	0	0	0	0	0	0
		Chester County	0	0	0	0	0	0	0	0	0	0
		Chesterfield County	0	0	0	0	0	0	0	0	0	0
		Clarendon County	0	0	0	0	0	0	0	0	0	0
		Colleton County	0	0	0	0	0	0	0	0	0	0
		Dorchester County	0	0	0	0	0	0	0	0	0	0
		Edgefield County	0	0	0	0	0	0	0	0	0	0
		Fairfield County	0	0	0	0	0	0	0	0	0	0
		Florence County	0	0	0	0	0	0	0	0	0	0
		Georgetown County	0	0	0	0	0	0	0	0	0	0
		Greenville County	0	0	0	0	0	0	0	0	0	0
		Greenwood County	0	0	0	0	0	0	0	0	0	0
		Hampton County	0	0	0	0	0	0	0	0	0	0
		Horry County	0	0	0	0	0	0	0	0	0	0
		Jasper County	0	0	0	0	0	0	0	0	0	0
		Kershaw County	0	0	0	0	0	0	0	0	0	0
		Lancaster County	0	0	0	0	0	0	0	0	0	0
		Laurens County	0	0	0	0	0	0	0	0	0	0
		Lee County	0	0	0	0	0	0	0	0	0	0
		Lexington County	0	0	0	0	0	0	0	0	0	0
		Marion County	0	0	0	0	0	0	0	0	0	0
		Marlboro County	0	0	0	0	0	0	0	0	0	0
		McCormick County	0	0	0	0	0	0	0	0	0	0
		Newberry County	0	0	0	0	0	0	0	0	0	0

[1] The FBI does not publish arson data unless it receives data from either the agency or the state for all 12 months of the calendar year.

Table 11. Offenses Known to Law Enforcement, by State and Other Agencies, 2006 (*Contd.*)

(Number.)

State	State/Other Agency	Unit/Office	Violent crime	Murder and non-negligent man-slaughter	Forcible rape	Robbery	Aggra-vated assault	Property crime	Burglary	Larceny-theft	Motor vehicle theft	Arson[1]
		Oconee County	0	0	0	0	0	0	0	0	0	0
		Orangeburg County	0	0	0	0	0	0	0	0	0	0
		Pickens County	0	0	0	0	0	0	0	0	0	0
		Saluda County	0	0	0	0	0	0	0	0	0	0
		Spartanburg County	0	0	0	0	0	0	0	0	0	0
		Union County	0	0	0	0	0	0	0	0	0	0
		Williamsburg County	0	0	0	0	0	0	0	0	0	0
		York County	0	0	0	0	0	0	0	0	0	0
	Forestry Commission:...........	Abbeville County	0	0	0	0	0	0	0	0	0	1
		Aiken County	0	0	0	0	0	1	0	1	0	15
		Allendale County	0	0	0	0	0	0	0	0	0	3
		Anderson County	0	0	0	0	0	0	0	0	0	0
		Bamberg County	0	0	0	0	0	0	0	0	0	2
		Barnwell County	0	0	0	0	0	2	0	2	0	1
		Beaufort County	0	0	0	0	0	0	0	0	0	17
		Calhoun County	0	0	0	0	0	1	0	1	0	1
		Charleston County	0	0	0	0	0	0	0	0	0	6
		Cherokee County	0	0	0	0	0	0	0	0	0	0
		Chester County	0	0	0	0	0	0	0	0	0	0
		Chesterfield County	0	0	0	0	0	0	0	0	0	5
		Clarendon County	0	0	0	0	0	0	0	0	0	13
		Colleton County	0	0	0	0	0	0	0	0	0	4
		Darlington County	0	0	0	0	0	0	0	0	0	7
		Dillon County	0	0	0	0	0	0	0	0	0	1
		Dorchester County	0	0	0	0	0	0	0	0	0	8
		Fairfield County	0	0	0	0	0	1	0	1	0	2
		Florence County	0	0	0	0	0	0	0	0	0	3
		Georgetown County	0	0	0	0	0	1	0	1	0	4
		Greenville County	0	0	0	0	0	0	0	0	0	4
		Greenwood County	0	0	0	0	0	0	0	0	0	0
		Hampton County	0	0	0	0	0	0	0	0	0	15
		Horry County	0	0	0	0	0	0	0	0	0	12
		Jasper County	0	0	0	0	0	0	0	0	0	17
		Kershaw County	0	0	0	0	0	0	0	0	0	1
		Lancaster County	0	0	0	0	0	0	0	0	0	2
		Laurens County	0	0	0	0	0	0	0	0	0	0
		Lexington County	0	0	0	0	0	0	0	0	0	0
		Marion County	0	0	0	0	0	0	0	0	0	5
		Marlboro County	0	0	0	0	0	0	0	0	0	2
		McCormick County	0	0	0	0	0	0	0	0	0	0
		Newberry County	0	0	0	0	0	0	0	0	0	0
		Oconee County	0	0	0	0	0	0	0	0	0	2
		Orangeburg County	0	0	0	0	0	0	0	0	0	10
		Pickens County	0	0	0	0	0	0	0	0	0	1
		Richland County	0	0	0	0	0	2	0	2	0	2
		Saluda County	0	0	0	0	0	0	0	0	0	0
		Spartanburg County	0	0	0	0	0	0	0	0	0	0
		Sumter County	0	0	0	0	0	0	0	0	0	13
		Union County	0	0	0	0	0	0	0	0	0	0
		Williamsburg County	0	0	0	0	0	0	0	0	0	3
		York County	0	0	0	0	0	0	0	0	0	0
	Highway Patrol:	Abbeville County	0	0	0	0	0	0	0	0	0	0
		Aiken County	0	0	0	0	0	0	0	0	0	0

[1] The FBI does not publish arson data unless it receives data from either the agency or the state for all 12 months of the calendar year.

Table 11. Offenses Known to Law Enforcement, by State and Other Agencies, 2006 *(Contd.)*

(Number.)

State	State/Other Agency	Unit/Office	Violent crime	Murder and non-negligent man-slaughter	Forcible rape	Robbery	Aggra-vated assault	Property crime	Burglary	Larceny-theft	Motor vehicle theft	Arson[1]
		Anderson County	1	0	0	0	1	0	0	0	0	0
		Barnwell County	0	0	0	0	0	0	0	0	0	0
		Beaufort County	0	0	0	0	0	0	0	0	0	0
		Berkeley County	1	0	0	0	1	2	0	0	2	0
		Charleston County	0	0	0	0	0	0	0	0	0	0
		Cherokee County	0	0	0	0	0	0	0	0	0	0
		Chester County	0	0	0	0	0	0	0	0	0	0
		Chesterfield County	0	0	0	0	0	0	0	0	0	0
		Clarendon County	1	0	0	0	1	0	0	0	0	0
		Colleton County	0	0	0	0	0	0	0	0	0	0
		Darlington County	0	0	0	0	0	0	0	0	0	0
		Dillon County	0	0	0	0	0	0	0	0	0	0
		Dorchester County	0	0	0	0	0	0	0	0	0	0
		Edgefield County	0	0	0	0	0	1	0	0	1	0
		Fairfield County	0	0	0	0	0	0	0	0	0	0
		Florence County	0	0	0	0	0	0	0	0	0	0
		Greenville County	0	0	0	0	0	2	0	0	2	0
		Greenwood County	0	0	0	0	0	0	0	0	0	0
		Hampton County	0	0	0	0	0	0	0	0	0	0
		Horry County	1	0	0	0	1	5	0	0	5	0
		Jasper County	0	0	0	0	0	1	0	0	1	0
		Kershaw County	1	0	0	0	1	2	0	1	1	0
		Lancaster County	0	0	0	0	0	0	0	0	0	0
		Laurens County	0	0	0	0	0	0	0	0	0	0
		Lee County	0	0	0	0	0	0	0	0	0	0
		Lexington County	0	0	0	0	0	0	0	0	0	0
		Marion	0	0	0	0	0	0	0	0	0	0
		Marlboro County	0	0	0	0	0	0	0	0	0	0
		McCormick County	0	0	0	0	0	0	0	0	0	0
		Newberry County	0	0	0	0	0	1	0	0	1	0
		Oconee County	0	0	0	0	0	0	0	0	0	0
		Orangeburg County	0	0	0	0	0	2	0	0	2	0
		Pickens County	0	0	0	0	0	0	0	0	0	0
		Richland County	1	0	0	0	1	0	0	0	0	0
		Saluda County	0	0	0	0	0	0	0	0	0	0
		Spartanburg County	0	0	0	0	0	1	0	1	0	0
		Sumter County	0	0	0	0	0	0	0	0	0	0
		Union County	0	0	0	0	0	0	0	0	0	0
		Williamsburg County	0	0	0	0	0	0	0	0	0	0
		York County	0	0	0	0	0	0	0	0	0	0
	South Carolina Law Enforcement Division Vice:	Abbeville County	0	0	0	0	0	0	0	0	0	0
		Aiken County	0	0	0	0	0	0	0	0	0	0
		Allendale County	0	0	0	0	0	0	0	0	0	0
		Anderson County	0	0	0	0	0	0	0	0	0	0
		Bamberg County	0	0	0	0	0	0	0	0	0	0
		Barnwell County	0	0	0	0	0	0	0	0	0	0
		Beaufort County	0	0	0	0	0	0	0	0	0	0
		Berkeley County	0	0	0	0	0	0	0	0	0	0
		Calhoun County	0	0	0	0	0	0	0	0	0	0
		Charleston County	0	0	0	0	0	0	0	0	0	0
		Cherokee County	0	0	0	0	0	0	0	0	0	0
		Chester County	0	0	0	0	0	0	0	0	0	0
		Chesterfield County	0	0	0	0	0	0	0	0	0	0
		Colleton County	0	0	0	0	0	0	0	0	0	0

[1] The FBI does not publish arson data unless it receives data from either the agency or the state for all 12 months of the calendar year.

Table 11. Offenses Known to Law Enforcement, by State and Other Agencies, 2006 (*Contd.*)

(Number.)

State	State/Other Agency	Unit/Office	Violent crime	Murder and non-negligent man-slaughter	Forcible rape	Robbery	Aggra-vated assault	Property crime	Burglary	Larceny-theft	Motor vehicle theft	Arson[1]
		Dorchester County	0	0	0	0	0	0	0	0	0	0
		Edgefield County	0	0	0	0	0	0	0	0	0	0
		Fairfield County	0	0	0	0	0	0	0	0	0	0
		Florence County	0	0	0	0	0	0	0	0	0	0
		Georgetown County	0	0	0	0	0	0	0	0	0	0
		Greenville County	0	0	0	0	0	0	0	0	0	0
		Greenwood County	0	0	0	0	0	0	0	0	0	0
		Hampton County	0	0	0	0	0	0	0	0	0	0
		Horry County	0	0	0	0	0	0	0	0	0	0
		Lancaster County	0	0	0	0	0	0	0	0	0	0
		Laurens County	0	0	0	0	0	0	0	0	0	0
		Lee County	0	0	0	0	0	0	0	0	0	0
		Lexington County	0	0	0	0	0	0	0	0	0	0
		Marion County	0	0	0	0	0	0	0	0	0	0
		Marlboro County	0	0	0	0	0	0	0	0	0	0
		McCormick County	0	0	0	0	0	0	0	0	0	0
		Newberry County	0	0	0	0	0	0	0	0	0	0
		Oconee County	0	0	0	0	0	0	0	0	0	0
		Pickens County	0	0	0	0	0	0	0	0	0	0
		Saluda County	0	0	0	0	0	0	0	0	0	0
		Spartanburg County	0	0	0	0	0	0	0	0	0	0
		Union County	0	0	0	0	0	0	0	0	0	0
		Williamsburg County	0	0	0	0	0	0	0	0	0	0
		York County	0	0	0	0	0	0	0	0	0	0
	State Ports Authority............		0	0	0	0	0	9	3	6	0	0
	State Transport Police:	Abbeville County	0	0	0	0	0	0	0	0	0	0
		Aiken County	0	0	0	0	0	0	0	0	0	0
		Allendale County	0	0	0	0	0	0	0	0	0	0
		Anderson County	0	0	0	0	0	0	0	0	0	0
		Bamberg County	0	0	0	0	0	0	0	0	0	0
		Barnwell County	0	0	0	0	0	0	0	0	0	0
		Beaufort County	0	0	0	0	0	0	0	0	0	0
		Berkeley County	0	0	0	0	0	0	0	0	0	0
		Calhoun County	0	0	0	0	0	0	0	0	0	0
		Charleston County	0	0	0	0	0	0	0	0	0	0
		Cherokee County	0	0	0	0	0	0	0	0	0	0
		Chester County	0	0	0	0	0	0	0	0	0	0
		Chesterfield County	0	0	0	0	0	0	0	0	0	0
		Clarendon County	0	0	0	0	0	0	0	0	0	0
		Darlington County	0	0	0	0	0	0	0	0	0	0
		Dillon County	0	0	0	0	0	0	0	0	0	0
		Dorchester County	0	0	0	0	0	0	0	0	0	0
		Edgefield County	0	0	0	0	0	0	0	0	0	0
		Fairfield County	0	0	0	0	0	0	0	0	0	0
		Florence County	0	0	0	0	0	0	0	0	0	0
		Georgetown County	0	0	0	0	0	0	0	0	0	0
		Greenville County	0	0	0	0	0	1	0	0	1	0
		Greenwood County	0	0	0	0	0	0	0	0	0	0
		Hampton County	0	0	0	0	0	0	0	0	0	0
		Horry County	0	0	0	0	0	0	0	0	0	0
		Jasper County	0	0	0	0	0	0	0	0	0	0
		Lancaster County	0	0	0	0	0	0	0	0	0	0
		Laurens County	0	0	0	0	0	0	0	0	0	0
		Lee County	0	0	0	0	0	0	0	0	0	0
		Lexington County	0	0	0	0	0	0	0	0	0	0
		Marion County	0	0	0	0	0	0	0	0	0	0
		Marlboro County	0	0	0	0	0	0	0	0	0	0

[1] The FBI does not publish arson data unless it receives data from either the agency or the state for all 12 months of the calendar year.

Table 11. Offenses Known to Law Enforcement, by State and Other Agencies, 2006 (*Contd.*)

(Number.)

State	State/Other Agency	Unit/Office	Violent crime	Murder and non-negligent man-slaughter	Forcible rape	Robbery	Aggra-vated assault	Property crime	Burglary	Larceny-theft	Motor vehicle theft	Arson[1]
		McCormick County	0	0	0	0	0	0	0	0	0	0
		Newberry County	0	0	0	0	0	0	0	0	0	0
		Oconee County	0	0	0	0	0	0	0	0	0	0
		Orangeburg County	0	0	0	0	0	0	0	0	0	0
		Pickens County	0	0	0	0	0	0	0	0	0	0
		Saluda County	0	0	0	0	0	0	0	0	0	0
		Spartanburg County	0	0	0	0	0	0	0	0	0	0
		Union County	0	0	0	0	0	0	0	0	0	0
		Williamsburg County	0	0	0	0	0	0	0	0	0	0
		York County	0	0	0	0	0	0	0	0	0	0
SOUTH CAROLINA-Other Agencies	United States Department of Energy, Savannah River Plant		0	0	0	0	0	35	0	35	0	0
	Charleston County Aviation Authority		0	0	0	0	0	27	2	15	10	0
	Columbia Metropolitan Airport		1	0	0	0	1	18	0	15	3	0
	Greenville-Spartanburg International Airport		0	0	0	0	0	12	0	7	5	0
	Whitten Center		3	0	0	0	3	9	1	7	1	0
SOUTH DAKOTA-State Agencies	Division of Criminal Investigation		18	0	8	1	9	1	1	0	0	0
TENNESSEE-State Agencies	Alcoholic Beverage Commission		0	0	0	0	0	0	0	0	0	0
	Department of Correction Internal Affairs		0	0	0	0	0	0	0	0	0	0
	Department of Safety		23	0	0	0	23	50	0	3	47	0
	State Fire Marshal		0	0	0	0	0	0	0	0	0	34
	State Park Rangers:	Bicentennial Capitol Mall	0	0	0	0	0	0	0	0	0	0
		Big Hill Pond	0	0	0	0	0	0	0	0	0	0
		Big Ridge	0	0	0	0	0	0	0	0	0	0
		Bledsoe Creek	0	0	0	0	0	0	0	0	0	0
		Booker T. Washington	0	0	0	0	0	1	0	1	0	0
		Burgess Falls Natural Area	0	0	0	0	0	0	0	0	0	0
		Cedars of Lebanon	0	0	0	0	0	0	0	0	0	0
		Chickasaw	0	0	0	0	0	3	0	3	0	1
		Cove Lake	0	0	0	0	0	0	0	0	0	0
		Cumberland Mountain	0	0	0	0	0	0	0	0	0	0
		Cumberland Trail	0	0	0	0	0	0	0	0	0	0
		David Crockett	0	0	0	0	0	0	0	0	0	0
		David Crockett Birthplace	0	0	0	0	0	0	0	0	0	0
		Dunbar Cave Natural Area	0	0	0	0	0	0	0	0	0	0
		Edgar Evins	0	0	0	0	0	5	0	5	0	0
		Fall Creek Falls	0	0	0	0	0	0	0	0	0	0
		Fort Loudon State Historic Park	0	0	0	0	0	0	0	0	0	0
		Fort Pillow State Historic Park	0	0	0	0	0	0	0	0	0	0
		Frozen Head Natural Area	0	0	0	0	0	0	0	0	0	0
		Harpeth Scenic Rivers	0	0	0	0	0	1	0	0	1	1
		Harrison Bay	1	0	1	0	0	0	0	0	0	0
		Henry Horton	0	0	0	0	0	3	0	3	0	1
		Hiwassee/Ocoee State Scenic Rivers	0	0	0	0	0	0	0	0	0	0
		Indian Mountain	0	0	0	0	0	3	1	2	0	0

[1] The FBI does not publish arson data unless it receives data from either the agency or the state for all 12 months of the calendar year.

Table 11. Offenses Known to Law Enforcement, by State and Other Agencies, 2006 (*Contd.*)

(Number.)

State	State/Other Agency	Unit/Office	Violent crime	Murder and non-negligent man-slaughter	Forcible rape	Robbery	Aggra-vated assault	Property crime	Burglary	Larceny-theft	Motor vehicle theft	Arson[1]
		Johnsonville State Historic Park	0	0	0	0	0	0	0	0	0	0
		Long Hunter	0	0	0	0	0	0	0	0	0	0
		Meeman-Shelby Forest	0	0	0	0	0	5	0	5	0	0
		Montgomery Bell	0	0	0	0	0	3	1	2	0	0
		Mousetail Landing	0	0	0	0	0	2	0	2	0	0
		Natchez Trace	1	0	0	0	1	4	0	2	2	0
		Nathan Bedford Forrest	0	0	0	0	0	0	0	0	0	0
		Norris Dam	0	0	0	0	0	1	0	1	0	0
		Old Stone Fort State Archaeo-logical Area	0	0	0	0	0	0	0	0	0	0
		Panther Creek	0	0	0	0	0	4	0	4	0	0
		Paris Landing	0	0	0	0	0	0	0	0	0	0
		Pickett	0	0	0	0	0	0	0	0	0	0
		Pickwick Landing	0	0	0	0	0	0	0	0	0	0
		Pinson Mounds State Archaeo-logical Park	0	0	0	0	0	0	0	0	0	0
		Radnor Lake Natural Area	0	0	0	0	0	0	0	0	0	0
		Red Clay State Historic Park	0	0	0	0	0	0	0	0	0	0
		Reelfoot Lake	0	0	0	0	0	0	0	0	0	0
		Roan Mountain	0	0	0	0	0	0	0	0	0	0
		Rock Island	0	0	0	0	0	1	0	1	0	0
		Sgt. Alvin C. York	0	0	0	0	0	0	0	0	0	0
		South Cumberland Recreation Area	0	0	0	0	0	1	0	1	0	0
		Standing Stone	0	0	0	0	0	0	0	0	0	0
		Sycamore Shoals State Historic Park	0	0	0	0	0	0	0	0	0	0
		Tim's Ford	0	0	0	0	0	1	0	1	0	0
		T.O. Fuller	0	0	0	0	0	2	0	2	0	0
		Warrior's Path	0	0	0	0	0	6	0	6	0	0
	Tennessee Bureau of Investigation............................		0	0	0	0	0	0	0	0	0	1
	TennCare Office of Inspector General.................		0	0	0	0	0	0	0	0	0	0
	Tennessee Department of Revenue, Special Investigations Unit...............		1	0	0	0	1	0	0	0	0	0
	Wildlife Resources Agency:....................................	Region 1	0	0	0	0	0	0	0	0	0	0
		Region 2	0	0	0	0	0	0	0	0	0	0
		Region 3	1	0	0	0	1	0	0	0	0	0
		Region 4	1	0	0	0	1	5	0	2	3	0
TENNESSEE-Other Agencies	Chattanooga Metropolitan Airport....................................		0	0	0	0	0	1	1	0	0	0
	Drug Task Force:..................	1st Judicial District	1	0	0	0	1	0	0	0	0	0
		2nd Judicial District	0	0	0	0	0	0	0	0	0	0
		3rd Judicial District	0	0	0	0	0	0	0	0	0	0
		4th Judicial District	0	0	0	0	0	1	0	1	0	0
		5th Judicial District	2	0	0	0	2	2	0	1	1	0
		8th Judicial District	0	0	0	0	0	0	0	0	0	0
		9th Judicial District	0	0	0	0	0	0	0	0	0	0
		10th Judicial District	0	0	0	0	0	1	0	0	1	0
		12th Judicial District	0	0	0	0	0	0	0	0	0	0
		13th Judicial District	0	0	0	0	0	0	0	0	0	0
		14th Judicial District	0	0	0	0	0	0	0	0	0	0
		15th Judicial District	0	0	0	0	0	0	0	0	0	0
		17th Judicial District	0	0	0	0	0	0	0	0	0	0

[1] The FBI does not publish arson data unless it receives data from either the agency or the state for all 12 months of the calendar year.

Table 11. Offenses Known to Law Enforcement, by State and Other Agencies, 2006 (*Contd.*)

(Number.)

State	State/Other Agency	Unit/Office	Violent crime	Murder and non-negligent man-slaughter	Forcible rape	Robbery	Aggra-vated assault	Property crime	Burglary	Larceny-theft	Motor vehicle theft	Arson[1]
		18th Judicial District	0	0	0	0	0	0	0	0	0	0
		19th Judicial District	0	0	0	0	0	0	0	0	0	0
		21st Judicial District	0	0	0	0	0	0	0	0	0	0
		22nd Judicial District	0	0	0	0	0	0	0	0	0	0
		23rd Judicial District	0	0	0	0	0	1	0	1	0	0
		24th Judicial District	0	0	0	0	0	0	0	0	0	0
		27th Judicial District	2	0	0	0	2	0	0	0	0	0
		31st Judicial District	0	0	0	0	0	0	0	0	0	0
	Knoxville Metropolitan Airport..................................		0	0	0	0	0	14	0	12	2	0
	Memphis International Airport..................................		3	0	0	1	2	192	10	172	10	0
	Metropolitan Board of Parks and Recreation, Nashville-Davidson		6	0	0	3	3	84	16	65	3	3
	Nashville International Airport..................................		0	0	0	0	0	69	0	61	8	1
	Tri-Cities Regional Airport..................................		0	0	0	0	0	1	0	1	0	0
	West Tennessee Violent Crime Task Force		2	0	0	0	2	0	0	0	0	0
TEXAS- **Other Agencies**	Amarillo International Airport..................................		0	0	0	0	0	4	0	4	0	0
	Cameron County Park Rangers..................................		8	1	0	1	6	65	7	54	4	0
	Dallas-Fort Worth International Airport............		5	0	0	0	5	455	16	400	39	0
	Hospital District:	Dallas County	5	0	1	1	3	443	11	422	10	0
		Tarrant County	6	0	0	0	6	173	3	168	2	0
	Houston Metropolitan Transit Authority..................		0	0	0	0	0	27	0	19	8	0
	Independent School District:..................................	Aldine	3	0	0	2	1	171	27	131	13	0
		Alvin	8	0	1	0	7	112	3	108	1	1
		Angleton	1	0	0	0	1	3	0	3	0	0
		Austin	32	0	1	14	17	636	37	592	7	21
		Bay City	0	0	0	0	0	69	3	66	0	0
		Cedar Hill	4	0	0	1	3	80	4	76	0	1
		Conroe	8	0	1	0	7	281	12	267	2	2
		Corpus Christi	38	0	0	0	38	358	66	291	1	6
		East Central	0	0	0	0	0	4	2	2	0	0
		Ector County	12	0	0	1	11	179	7	172	0	2
		El Paso	20	0	0	1	19	553	45	508	0	2
		Fort Bend	38	0	1	2	35	430	32	392	6	5
		Humble	16	0	0	0	16	104	9	92	3	8
		Katy	12	0	9	2	1	435	5	428	2	5
		Kaufman	2	0	0	0	2	9	0	8	1	0
		Killeen	6	0	0	2	4	132	7	124	1	3
		Klein	6	0	1	0	5	223	10	209	4	9
		Mexia	4	0	0	0	4	16	8	8	0	0
		Midland	0	0	0	0	0	61	5	56	0	0
		North East	5	0	0	1	4	518	11	507	0	0
		Pasadena	7	0	3	1	3	215	20	185	10	1
		Raymondville	1	0	0	0	1	23	4	19	0	0
		Socorro	8	0	0	0	8	160	24	136	0	10
		Spring	41	0	1	0	40	159	6	152	1	8
		Spring Branch	8	0	1	0	7	192	11	170	11	0
		Taft	3	0	0	0	3	12	1	11	0	0
		United	3	0	0	0	3	73	7	66	0	0
UTAH-State Agencies	Parks and Recreation		7	0	0	0	7	51	4	47	0	0

[1] The FBI does not publish arson data unless it receives data from either the agency or the state for all 12 months of the calendar year.

Table 11. Offenses Known to Law Enforcement, by State and Other Agencies, 2006 *(Contd.)*

(Number.)

State	State/Other Agency	Unit/Office	Violent crime	Murder and non-negligent man-slaughter	Forcible rape	Robbery	Aggra-vated assault	Property crime	Burglary	Larceny-theft	Motor vehicle theft	Arson[1]
UTAH- **Other Agencies**	Cache-Rich Drug Task Force		0	0	0	0	0	5	3	2	0	0
	Davis Metropolitan Narcotics Strike Force		0	0	0	0	0	0	0	0	0	0
	Granite School District		28	0	1	0	27	93	17	75	1	6
	Utah County Attorney Investigations Division		0	0	0	0	0	0	0	0	0	0
	Utah County Major Crime Task Force		0	0	0	0	0	3	0	3	0	0
VERMONT- **State Agencies**	Attorney General		0	0	0	0	0	13	1	12	0	0
	Department of Liquor Control, Division of Enforce-ment and Licensing		0	0	0	0	0	0	0	0	0	0
	Department of Motor Vehicles		0	0	0	0	0	0	0	0	0	0
	Fish and Wildlife Department, Law Enforcement Division		0	0	0	0	0	1	1	0	0	0
	State Police:	Bethel	20	0	5	2	13	224	100	108	16	1
		Bradford	18	0	2	0	16	191	69	103	19	1
		Brattleboro	19	1	3	2	13	182	94	80	8	2
		Derby	12	0	3	1	8	314	110	188	16	0
		Middlebury	10	1	4	1	4	265	115	133	17	1
		Middlesex	4	1	1	1	1	244	117	127	0	0
		Rockingham	17	1	1	0	15	190	68	105	17	1
		Rutland	15	1	1	2	11	499	200	272	27	0
		Shaftsbury	16	1	5	2	8	142	58	67	17	0
		St. Albans	44	0	24	5	15	702	229	407	66	19
		St. Johnsbury	25	2	4	3	16	413	115	275	23	7
		Williston	25	1	5	2	17	338	94	226	18	8
	Vermont State Police		0	0	0	0	0	0	0	0	0	0
	Vermont State Police Head-quarters, Bureau of Criminal Investigations		0	0	0	0	0	0	0	0	0	0
VIRGINIA- **State Agencies**	Alcoholic Beverage Control Commission		0	0	0	0	0	34	0	34	0	0
	Department of Conservation and Recreation		2	0	0	0	2	16	2	13	1	0
	Southside Virginia Training Center		8	0	1	0	7	31	0	31	0	0
	State Police:	Accomack County	1	0	1	0	0	13	1	10	2	0
		Albemarle County	3	0	0	0	3	8	0	6	2	0
		Alleghany County	2	0	0	0	2	8	0	5	3	0
		Amelia County	0	0	0	0	0	2	0	2	0	0
		Augusta County	0	0	0	0	0	2	0	2	0	2
		Bedford County	2	0	0	0	2	6	0	5	1	0
		Bland County	3	0	0	1	2	18	0	18	0	2
		Botetourt County	1	0	0	0	1	4	0	3	1	0
		Brunswick County	0	0	0	0	0	1	0	1	0	0
		Buchanan County	0	0	0	0	0	2	2	0	0	2
		Campbell County	0	0	0	0	0	0	0	0	0	0
		Caroline County	1	0	0	0	1	24	0	13	11	0
		Carroll County	2	0	0	0	2	11	0	11	0	0
		Chesapeake	0	0	0	0	0	1	0	1	0	0
		Chesterfield County	0	0	0	0	0	13	0	10	3	0
		Craig County	0	0	0	0	0	5	0	3	2	1
		Culpeper County	7	0	0	0	7	3	0	3	0	1
		Dickenson County	0	0	0	0	0	0	0	0	0	1
		Dinwiddie County	0	0	0	0	0	3	2	0	1	0
		Fairfax County	19	0	0	1	18	28	1	11	16	0
		Fauquier County	1	0	1	0	0	14	3	10	1	0
		Floyd County	1	0	0	0	1	0	0	0	0	0
		Franklin County	0	0	0	0	0	2	0	2	0	2
		Frederick County	1	0	0	0	1	6	1	2	3	0
		Fredericksburg	0	0	0	0	0	0	0	0	0	0

[1] The FBI does not publish arson data unless it receives data from either the agency or the state for all 12 months of the calendar year.

Table 11. Offenses Known to Law Enforcement, by State and Other Agencies, 2006 *(Contd.)*

(Number.)

State	State/Other Agency	Unit/Office	Violent crime	Murder and non-negligent man-slaughter	Forcible rape	Robbery	Aggra-vated assault	Property crime	Burglary	Larceny-theft	Motor vehicle theft	Arson[1]
		Gloucester County	0	0	0	0	0	1	0	1	0	0
		Greensville County	0	0	0	0	0	2	0	2	0	0
		Halifax County	2	0	0	0	2	5	0	3	2	0
		Hampton	1	0	0	0	1	3	0	2	1	0
		Hanover County	1	0	0	0	1	5	0	2	3	0
		Harrisonburg	0	0	0	0	0	0	0	0	0	0
		Henrico County	2	0	1	0	1	11	0	10	1	0
		Henry County	3	0	0	0	3	4	0	1	3	0
		Hopewell	0	0	0	0	0	4	0	3	1	0
		Isle of Wight County	2	0	0	0	2	1	0	0	1	0
		James City County	0	0	0	0	0	0	0	0	0	0
		King George County	0	0	0	0	0	2	0	2	0	0
		Lee County	0	0	0	0	0	11	0	5	6	8
		Loudoun County	5	0	0	0	5	19	0	8	11	1
		Louisa County	0	0	0	0	0	2	0	2	0	0
		Lunenburg County	0	0	0	0	0	0	0	0	0	0
		Madison County	0	0	0	0	0	2	0	2	0	0
		Mecklenburg County	0	0	0	0	0	3	1	0	2	1
		Middlesex County	0	0	0	0	0	1	0	1	0	1
		Montgomery County	2	1	0	0	1	9	1	6	2	0
		Nelson County	4	0	0	0	4	5	1	3	1	1
		New Kent County	1	0	0	0	1	8	0	6	2	0
		Newport News	2	0	0	0	2	1	0	1	0	0
		Norfolk	7	1	0	0	6	2	0	1	1	0
		Northampton County	0	0	0	0	0	2	0	2	0	0
		Nottoway County	1	0	0	0	1	1	0	1	0	1
		Orange County	2	1	1	0	0	1	0	1	0	1
		Page County	0	0	0	0	0	7	0	5	2	0
		Pittsylvania County	0	0	0	0	0	28	2	7	19	0
		Powhatan County	4	0	0	0	4	2	0	2	0	0
		Prince William County	4	0	0	0	4	20	0	9	11	0
		Pulaski County	0	0	0	0	0	12	1	9	2	0
		Richmond	2	0	0	1	1	3	0	3	0	0
		Roanoke	1	0	0	0	1	1	0	0	1	0
		Roanoke County	1	0	1	0	0	2	0	2	0	0
		Rockbridge County	0	0	0	0	0	15	0	15	0	0
		Rockingham County	0	0	0	0	0	0	0	0	0	0
		Russell County	0	0	0	0	0	1	0	0	1	2
		Scott County	0	0	0	0	0	6	2	3	1	1
		Shenandoah County	3	0	0	0	3	5	0	3	2	0
		Smyth County	1	0	0	0	1	13	1	11	1	2
		Spotsylvania County	0	0	0	0	0	2	0	2	0	0
		Stafford County	0	0	0	0	0	1	0	1	0	0
		Sussex County	2	0	0	0	2	4	1	2	1	0
		Tazewell County	2	0	0	0	2	2	0	2	0	0
		Virginia Beach	2	0	0	0	2	2	0	0	2	0
		Warren County	1	1	0	0	0	1	0	1	0	0
		Washington County	5	0	0	0	5	13	0	11	2	1
		Waynesboro	0	0	0	0	0	0	0	0	0	0
		Winchester	0	0	0	0	0	1	0	1	0	0
		Wise County	2	0	0	0	2	13	1	10	2	1
		Wythe County	4	0	0	1	3	69	4	60	5	1

[1] The FBI does not publish arson data unless it receives data from either the agency or the state for all 12 months of the calendar year.

Table 11. Offenses Known to Law Enforcement, by State and Other Agencies, 2006 (*Contd.*)

(Number.)

State	State/Other Agency	Unit/Office	Violent crime	Murder and non-negligent man-slaughter	Forcible rape	Robbery	Aggra-vated assault	Property crime	Burglary	Larceny-theft	Motor vehicle theft	Arson[1]
		York County	0	0	0	0	0	0	0	0	0	0
VIRGINIA- **Other Agencies**	Virginia State Capitol		1	0	0	0	1	62	0	61	1	0
	Norfolk Airport Authority		0	0	0	0	0	50	1	49	0	0
	Reagan National Airport.....		16	1	1	3	11	393	1	324	68	0
	Richmond International Airport....................		1	0	0	0	1	35	0	31	4	0
WASHINGTON- **Other Agencies**	Lummi Tribal.....................		54	1	1	8	44	354	126	209	19	2
	Nisqually Tribal....................		2	0	0	1	1	12	4	7	1	0
	Nooksack Tribal...................		8	0	1	0	7	56	17	36	3	0
	Port of Seattle		18	1	1	4	12	1,318	34	1,073	211	0
	Swinomish Tribal..................		9	0	3	1	5	85	11	67	7	0
WEST VIRGINIA- **State Agencies**	Capitol Protective Services....................		0	0	0	0	0	0	0	0	0	0
	Department of Natural Resources:...........................	Boone County	0	0	0	0	0	0	0	0	0	0
		Cabell County	0	0	0	0	0	0	0	0	0	0
		Calhoun County	0	0	0	0	0	0	0	0	0	0
		Fayette County	0	0	0	0	0	0	0	0	0	0
		Greenbrier County	0	0	0	0	0	0	0	0	0	0
		Logan County	0	0	0	0	0	0	0	0	0	0
		Mason County	0	0	0	0	0	0	0	0	0	0
		McDowell County	0	0	0	0	0	0	0	0	0	0
		Mercer County	0	0	0	0	0	0	0	0	0	0
		Mingo County	0	0	0	0	0	0	0	0	0	0
		Nicholas County	0	0	0	0	0	0	0	0	0	0
		Raleigh County	0	0	0	0	0	0	0	0	0	0
		Ritchie County	0	0	0	0	0	0	0	0	0	0
		Roane County	0	0	0	0	0	0	0	0	0	0
		Summers County	0	0	0	0	0	0	0	0	0	0
		Webster County	0	0	0	0	0	0	0	0	0	0
		Wirt County	0	0	0	0	0	0	0	0	0	0
		Wood County	0	0	0	0	0	0	0	0	0	0
		Wyoming County	0	0	0	0	0	0	0	0	0	0
	State Police:...........................	Beckley	51	1	2	5	43	500	154	308	38	5
		Berkeley Springs	7	0	1	0	6	100	33	60	7	1
		Bridgeport	17	0	2	0	15	205	35	140	30	1
		Buckeye	28	0	0	0	28	66	16	47	3	1
		Buckhannon	6	0	1	0	5	131	29	95	7	0
		Clay	13	0	0	0	13	87	28	45	14	1
		Danville	23	1	4	3	15	305	55	218	32	1
		Elizabeth	7	0	2	0	5	82	32	43	7	3
		Elkins	34	0	4	3	27	244	80	151	13	1
		Fairmont	15	0	1	0	14	122	24	85	13	0
		Franklin	7	0	1	0	6	20	4	16	0	1
		Gauley Bridge	5	0	0	0	5	63	17	41	5	1
		Gilbert	20	0	1	2	17	92	30	55	7	1
		Glenville	5	1	1	0	3	35	10	24	1	1
		Grafton	4	0	3	0	1	18	8	10	0	0
		Grantsville	19	0	2	0	17	67	28	29	10	0
		Hamlin	49	0	5	4	40	439	103	277	59	6
		Harrisville	12	2	1	0	9	91	25	55	11	1
		Hinton	6	0	0	0	6	48	20	24	4	0
		Hundred	4	0	0	0	4	26	4	21	1	3
		Huntington	14	0	3	1	10	878	134	692	52	1
		Kearneysville	28	2	2	1	23	330	82	206	42	4
		Keyser	54	0	4	2	48	229	90	114	25	3
		Kingwood	19	0	2	2	15	134	49	63	22	3
		Lewisburg	17	1	2	1	13	98	18	70	10	2
		Logan	97	2	8	6	81	908	223	596	89	16
		Martinsburg	85	1	9	7	68	968	214	644	110	1
		Moorefield	10	1	1	0	8	69	36	29	4	3
		Morgantown	33	1	7	7	18	626	172	388	66	1

[1] The FBI does not publish arson data unless it receives data from either the agency or the state for all 12 months of the calendar year.

Table 11. Offenses Known to Law Enforcement, by State and Other Agencies, 2006 (*Contd.*)

(Number.)

State	State/Other Agency	Unit/Office	Violent crime	Murder and non-negligent man-slaughter	Forcible rape	Robbery	Aggra-vated assault	Property crime	Burglary	Larceny-theft	Motor vehicle theft	Arson[1]
		Moundsville	8	0	0	0	8	34	10	20	4	0
		New Cumberland	3	0	2	0	1	17	3	12	2	1
		Oak Hill	4	0	0	1	3	198	49	138	11	0
		Paden City	7	0	0	0	7	47	7	34	6	0
		Parkersburg	9	0	0	1	8	326	65	247	14	6
		Parsons	6	0	0	0	6	37	15	20	2	2
		Petersburg	5	0	0	0	5	33	9	17	7	1
		Philippi	14	1	0	0	13	62	16	36	10	2
		Point Pleasant	9	0	3	0	6	116	38	65	13	3
		Princeton	56	3	2	4	47	463	104	307	52	3
		Quincy	14	2	0	2	10	231	48	135	48	4
		Rainelle	3	0	0	0	3	61	19	35	7	3
		Ripley	7	0	2	0	5	52	12	35	5	2
		Romney	33	0	2	1	30	153	56	80	17	2
		South Charleston	47	0	2	6	39	963	160	730	73	2
		Spencer	21	0	0	1	20	44	14	23	7	2
		Summersville	6	0	1	1	4	88	11	67	10	1
		Sutton	18	0	3	0	15	137	22	95	20	2
		Union	9	1	0	2	6	57	17	35	5	1
		Upperglade	23	0	0	0	23	111	42	60	9	0
		Wayne	40	0	0	2	38	313	98	183	32	0
		Welch	10	0	0	0	10	55	30	24	1	1
		Wellsburg	1	0	0	0	1	14	0	14	0	0
		Weston	7	0	3	0	4	108	17	78	13	0
		West Union	9	0	0	0	9	31	15	9	7	0
		Wheeling	7	0	2	0	5	83	17	62	4	1
		Whitesville	5	0	0	0	5	115	31	74	10	2
		Williamson	33	0	5	1	27	202	43	132	27	5
		Winfield	16	1	3	0	12	208	23	172	13	4
	State Police, Bureau of Criminal Investigation:	Beckley	0	0	0	0	0	0	0	0	0	0
		Buckhannon	0	0	0	0	0	0	0	0	0	0
		Fairmont	0	0	0	0	0	0	0	0	0	0
	State Police, Parkway Authority:	Kanawha County	0	0	0	0	0	7	1	5	1	0
		Mercer County	0	0	0	0	0	4	0	4	0	0
		Raleigh County	2	0	0	2	0	8	0	8	0	0
WEST VIRGINIA-Other Agencies	Central West Virginia Drug Task Force		0	0	0	0	0	0	0	0	0	0
	Harrison County Drug and Violent Crime Task Force		0	0	0	0	0	0	0	0	0	0
	Metropolitan Drug Enforcement Network Team		0	0	0	0	0	1	0	1	0	0
	Ohio Valley Drug and Violent Crime Task Force		0	0	0	0	0	0	0	0	0	0
	Parkersburg Narcotics and Violent Crime Task Force		0	0	0	0	0	0	0	0	0	0
	Southern Regional Drug and Violent Crime Task Force		4	0	0	2	2	0	0	0	0	0
WISCONSIN-State Agencies	Capitol Police		3	0	0	3	0	181	4	177	0	0
	Department of Natural Resources		0	0	0	0	0	0	0	0	0	0
	Wisconsin State Patrol		2	0	0	0	2	0	0	0	0	0
WISCONSIN-Other Agencies	Lac du Flambeau Tribal		16	0	2	2	12	306	41	239	26	4
	Menominee Tribal		30	0	2	1	27	134	25	80	29	2
	Oneida Tribal		4	0	2	0	2	151	13	125	13	0
PUERTO RICO AND OTHER OUTLYING AREAS	Puerto Rico		8,929	739	118	5,245	2,827	53,197	16,668	27,936	8,593	
FEDERAL AGENCIES	National Institutes of Health		3	0	0	0	3	150	5	145	0	0
	United States Department of the Interior:	Bureau of Indian Affairs	7,193	121	757	416	5,899	37,767	4,565	11,874	21,328	1,046
		Bureau of Land Management	10	2	2	0	6	556	23	493	40	109

[1] The FBI does not publish arson data unless it receives data from either the agency or the state for all 12 months of the calendar year.

Table 11. Offenses Known to Law Enforcement, by State and Other Agencies, 2006 *(Contd.)*

(Number.)

State	State/Other Agency	Unit/Office	Violent crime	Murder and non-negligent man-slaughter	Forcible rape	Robbery	Aggra-vated assault	Property crime	Burglary	Larceny-theft	Motor vehicle theft	Arson[1]
		Bureau of Reclamation	3	0	0	0	3	6	2	2	2	1
		Fish and Wildlife Service	113	4	6	31	72	361	123	163	75	134
		National Park Service	367	10	35	61	261	4,022	411	3,465	146	79

[1] The FBI does not publish arson data unless it receives data from either the agency or the state for all 12 months of the calendar year.

Table 12. Crime Trends, by Population Group, 2005–2006

(Number, percent change.)

Population group		Violent crime	Murder and non-negligent man-slaughter	Forcible rape	Robbery	Aggra-vated assault	Property crime	Burglary	Larceny-theft	Motor vehicle theft	Arson	Number of agencies	2006 estimated population
TOTAL ALL AGENCIES:	2005	1,284,185	15,568	81,674	395,510	791,433	9,288,388	1,973,124	6,150,982	1,164,282	64,733		
	2006	1,308,436	15,854	80,414	422,375	789,793	9,080,788	1,990,468	5,971,647	1,118,673	66,065	13,048	269,116,153
	Percent change	+1.9	+1.8	-1.5	+6.8	-0.2	-2.2	+0.9	-2.9	-3.9	+2.1		
TOTAL CITIES	2005	1,024,110	12,250	60,197	346,251	605,412	7,301,826	1,455,331	4,910,707	935,788	47,520		
	2006	1,044,375	12,483	59,501	368,886	603,505	7,109,568	1,467,168	4,745,380	897,020	48,580	9,342	180,561,790
	Percent change	+2.0	+1.9	-1.2	+6.5	-0.3	-2.6	+0.8	-3.4	-4.1	+2.2		
GROUP I (250,000 and over)	2005	492,570	6,587	20,327	195,365	270,291	2,522,159	517,553	1,548,399	456,207	19,469		
	2006	497,476	6,875	19,677	204,495	266,429	2,450,869	520,809	1,490,873	439,187	19,291	70	53,487,428
	Percent change	+1.0	+4.4	-3.2	+4.7	-1.4	-2.8	+0.6	-3.7	-3.7	-0.9		
1,000,000 and over (Group I subset)	2005	216,601	2,891	7,093	94,309	112,308	963,317	184,430	598,587	180,300	6,727		
	2006	217,072	3,087	6,739	97,212	110,034	933,155	180,151	579,452	173,552	6,832	10	25,080,811
	Percent change	+0.2	+6.8	-5.0	+3.1	-2.0	-3.1	-2.3	-3.2	-3.7	+1.6		
500,000 to 999,999 (Group I subset)	2005	150,566	2,088	7,128	54,614	86,736	850,158	182,862	516,025	151,271	6,313		
	2006	150,827	2,107	6,935	57,042	84,743	832,624	189,200	496,716	146,708	6,387	23	15,374,394
	Percent change	+0.2	+0.9	-2.7	+4.4	-2.3	-2.1	+3.5	-3.7	-3.0	+1.2		
250,000 to 499,999 (Group I subset)	2005	125,403	1,608	6,106	46,442	71,247	708,684	150,261	433,787	124,636	6,429		
	2006	129,577	1,681	6,003	50,241	71,652	685,090	151,458	414,705	118,927	6,072	37	13,032,223
	Percent change	+3.3	+4.5	-1.7	+8.2	+0.6	-3.3	+0.8	-4.4	-4.6	-5.6		
GROUP II (100,000 to 249,999)	2005	170,215	2,192	10,429	57,147	100,447	1,278,174	259,441	846,656	172,077	7,909		
	2006	174,186	2,157	10,342	62,416	99,271	1,235,046	261,270	811,664	162,112	7,874	186	27,908,022
	Percent change	+2.3	-1.6	-0.8	+9.2	-1.2	-3.4	+0.7	-4.1	-5.8	-0.4		
GROUP III (50,000 to 99,999)	2005	130,009	1,409	9,205	40,197	79,198	1,085,500	222,861	739,162	123,477	6,464		
	2006	134,619	1,335	9,318	43,378	80,588	1,060,259	224,139	716,467	119,653	7,152	417	28,595,956
	Percent change	+3.5	-5.3	+1.2	+7.9	+1.8	-2.3	+0.6	-3.1	-3.1	+10.6		
GROUP IV (25,000 to 49,999)	2005	92,546	904	7,821	25,586	58,235	894,445	172,036	641,104	81,305	5,270		
	2006	96,065	903	7,629	28,251	59,282	874,003	174,604	621,757	77,642	5,420	725	25,030,551
	Percent change	+3.8	-0.1	-2.5	+10.4	+1.8	-2.3	+1.5	-3.0	-4.5	+2.8		
GROUP V (10,000 to 24,999)	2005	75,143	664	6,790	17,857	49,832	816,256	154,388	600,628	61,240	4,384		
	2006	77,279	716	6,865	19,403	50,295	798,600	156,728	582,994	58,878	4,651	1,594	25,246,097
	Percent change	+2.8	+7.8	+1.1	+8.7	+0.9	-2.2	+1.5	-2.9	-3.9	+6.1		
GROUP VI (under 10,000)	2005	63,627	494	5,625	10,099	47,409	705,292	129,052	534,758	41,482	4,024		
	2006	64,750	497	5,670	10,943	47,640	690,791	129,618	521,625	39,548	4,192	6,350	20,293,736
	Percent change	+1.8	+0.6	+0.8	+8.4	+0.5	-2.1	+0.4	-2.5	-4.7	+4.2		
METROPOLITAN COUNTIES	2005	207,758	2,426	15,444	45,372	144,516	1,561,909	381,613	986,909	193,387	13,217		
	2006	213,839	2,575	15,201	49,490	146,573	1,556,482	390,885	977,608	187,989	13,573	1,549	63,500,951
	Percent change	+2.9	+6.1	-1.6	+9.1	+1.4	-0.3	+2.4	-0.9	-2.8	+2.7		
NONMETROPOL-ITAN COUNTIES[1]	2005	52,317	892	6,033	3,887	41,505	424,653	136,180	253,366	35,107	3,996		
	2006	50,222	796	5,712	3,999	39,715	414,738	132,415	248,659	33,664	3,912	2,157	25,053,412
	Percent change	-4.0	-10.8	-5.3	+2.9	-4.3	-2.3	-2.8	-1.9	-4.1	-2.1		
SUBURBAN AREA[2]	2005	348,523	3,635	26,915	81,744	236,229	3,082,730	660,245	2,093,579	328,906	21,744		
	2006	359,075	3,852	26,682	89,646	238,895	3,058,006	675,520	2,065,196	317,290	22,621	6,908	112,961,096
	Percent change	+3.0	+6.0	-0.9	+9.7	+1.1	-0.8	+2.3	-1.4	-3.5	+4.0		

[1] Includes state police agencies that report aggregately for the entire state.

[2] Suburban area includes law enforcement agencies in cities with less than 50,000 inhabitants and county law enforcement agencies that are within a Metropolitan Statistical Area. Suburban area excludes all metropolitan agencies associated with a principal city. The agencies associated with suburban areas also appear in other groups within this table.

Table 13. Crime Trends, by Suburban and Nonsuburban Cities[1] by Population Group, 2005–2006

(Number, percent change.)

Population group		Violent crime	Murder and non-negligent man-slaughter	Forcible rape	Robbery	Aggra-vated assault	Property crime	Burglary	Larceny-theft	Motor vehicle theft	Arson	Number of agencies	2006 estimated popula-tion
TOTAL SUBUR-BAN CITIES:	2005	140,669	1,209	11,375	36,372	91,713	1,520,821	278,632	1,106,670	135,519	8,527		
	2006	145,236	1,277	11,481	40,156	92,322	1,501,524	284,635	1,087,588	129,301	9,048	5,359	49,460,145
	Percent change	+3.2	+5.6	+0.9	+10.4	+0.7	-1.3	+2.2	-1.7	-4.6	+6.1		
GROUP IV (25,000 to 49,999)	2005	55,340	521	4,116	16,497	34,206	555,187	105,849	389,387	59,951	3,246		
	2006	57,846	535	4,054	18,379	34,878	545,714	107,579	381,250	56,885	3,323	536	18,292,185
	Percent change	+4.5	+2.7	-1.5	+11.4	+2.0	-1.7	+1.6	-2.1	-5.1	+2.4		
GROUP V (10,000 to 24,999)	2005	48,797	435	4,204	12,811	31,347	529,995	98,691	384,322	46,982	2,819		
	2006	50,065	470	4,176	14,076	31,343	523,293	100,741	377,493	45,059	3,125	1,183	18,866,148
	Percent change	+2.6	+8.0	-0.7	+9.9	*	-1.3	+2.1	-1.8	-4.1	+10.9		
GROUP VI (under 10,000)	2005	36,532	253	3,055	7,064	26,160	435,639	74,092	332,961	28,586	2,462		
	2006	37,325	272	3,251	7,701	26,101	432,517	76,315	328,845	27,357	2,600	3,640	12,301,812
	Percent change	+2.2	+7.5	+6.4	+9.0	-0.2	-0.7	+3.0	-1.2	-4.3	+5.6		
TOTAL NON-SUBURBAN CITIES:	2005	90,647	853	8,861	17,170	63,763	895,172	176,844	669,820	48,508	5,151		
	2006	92,858	839	8,683	18,441	64,895	861,870	176,315	638,788	46,767	5,215	3,310	21,110,239
	Percent change	+2.4	-1.6	-2.0	+7.4	+1.8	-3.7	-0.3	-4.6	-3.6	+1.2		
GROUP IV (25,000 to 49,999)	2005	37,206	383	3,705	9,089	24,029	339,258	66,187	251,717	21,354	2,024		
	2006	38,219	368	3,575	9,872	24,404	328,289	67,025	240,507	20,757	2,097	189	6,738,366
	Percent change	+2.7	-3.9	-3.5	+8.6	+1.6	-3.2	+1.3	-4.5	-2.8	+3.6		
GROUP V (10,000 to 24,999)	2005	26,346	229	2,586	5,046	18,485	286,261	55,697	216,306	14,258	1,565		
	2006	27,214	246	2,689	5,327	18,952	275,307	55,987	205,501	13,819	1,526	411	6,379,949
	Percent change	+3.3	+7.4	+4.0	+5.6	+2.5	-3.8	+0.5	-5.0	-3.1	-2.5		
GROUP VI (under 10,000)	2005	27,095	241	2,570	3,035	21,249	269,653	54,960	201,797	12,896	1,562		
	2006	27,425	225	2,419	3,242	21,539	258,274	53,303	192,780	12,191	1,592	2,710	7,991,924
	Percent change	+1.2	-6.6	-5.9	+6.8	+1.4	-4.2	-3.0	-4.5	-5.5	+1.9		

[1] Suburban cities include law enforcement agencies in cities with less than 50,000 inhabitants that are within a Metropolitan Statistical Area. Suburban cities exclude all metropolitan agencies associated with a principal city. Nonsuburban cities include law enforcement agencies in cities with less than 50,000 inhabitants that are not associated with a Metropolitan Statistical Area.
* Less than one-tenth of 1 percent.

Table 14. Crime Trends, by Metropolitan and Nonmetropolitan Counties[1] by Population Group, 2005–2006

(Number, percent change.)

Population group	Population range		Violent crime	Murder and non-negligent man-slaughter	Forcible rape	Robbery	Aggra-vated assault	Property crime	Burglary	Larceny-theft	Motor vehicle theft	Arson	Number of agen-cies	2006 estimated popula-tion
METROPOLITAN-COUNTIES	100,000 and over	2005	148,660	1,710	9,401	38,405	99,144	1,041,525	240,278	668,493	132,754	8,582		
		2006	153,120	1,815	9,233	41,845	100,227	1,037,502	248,386	660,031	129,085	8,948	144	38,414,528
		Percent change	+3.0	+6.1	-1.8	+9.0	+1.1	-0.4	+3.4	-1.3	-2.8	+4.3		
	25,000 to 99,999	2005	43,386	563	4,482	4,745	33,596	392,693	112,974	245,631	34,088	2,985		
		2006	45,016	569	4,375	5,145	34,927	394,833	114,260	246,345	34,228	2,999	406	20,997,448
		Percent change	+3.8	+1.1	-2.4	+8.4	+4.0	+0.5	+1.1	+0.3	+0.4	+0.5		
	Under 25,000	2005	15,667	153	1,552	2,219	11,743	127,273	28,286	72,477	26,510	1,642		
		2006	15,601	191	1,569	2,497	11,344	123,756	28,132	70,958	24,666	1,617	998	4,066,252
		Percent change	-0.4	+24.8	+1.1	+12.5	-3.4	-2.8	-0.5	-2.1	-7.0	-1.5		
NONMETRO-POLITAN COUNTIES	25,000 and over	2005	21,689	313	2,276	1,911	17,189	186,920	61,546	111,014	14,360	1,473		
		2006	20,850	301	2,099	2,014	16,436	183,229	60,432	108,523	14,274	1,538	271	10,674,001
		Percent change	-3.9	-3.8	-7.8	+5.4	-4.4	-2.0	-1.8	-2.2	-0.6	+4.4		
	10,000 to 24,999	2005	15,830	274	1,522	960	13,074	123,740	40,899	73,094	9,747	1,084		
		2006	14,983	236	1,464	955	12,328	120,670	39,357	72,047	9,266	1,149	549	8,845,670
		Percent change	-5.4	-13.9	-3.8	-0.5	-5.7	-2.5	-3.8	-1.4	-4.9	+6.0		
	Under 10,000	2005	8,505	151	1,220	319	6,815	63,876	19,783	38,215	5,878	818		
		2006	8,402	148	1,270	353	6,631	63,196	19,479	38,083	5,634	851	1,183	3,786,660
		Percent change	-1.2	-2.0	+4.1	+10.7	-2.7	-1.1	-1.5	-0.3	-4.2	+4.0		

[1] Metropolitan counties include sheriffs and county law enforcement agencies associated with a Metropolitan Statistical Area. Nonmetropolitan counties include sheriffs and county law enforcement agencies that are not associated with a Metropolitan Statistical Area. The offenses from state police agencies are not included in this table.

Table 15. Crime Trends, by Population Group, 2005–2006

(Number, Percent change.)

Population group		Forcible rape		Robbery				Aggravated assault			
		Rape by force	Assault to rape-attempts	Firearm	Knife or cutting instrument	Other weapon	Strong-arm	Firearm	Knife or cutting in-strument	Other weapon	Hands, fists, feet, etc.
TOTAL ALL AGENCIES:	2005.........................	71,544	6,469	141,307	30,010	31,695	135,088	151,527	136,537	251,806	180,245
	2006.........................	70,812	6,237	153,285	31,694	33,759	146,698	155,770	136,005	249,739	180,680
	Percent change	-1.0	-3.6	+8.5	+5.6	+6.5	+8.6	+2.8	-0.4	-0.8	+0.2
TOTAL CITIES	2005.........................	51,890	5,077	119,583	26,040	26,630	118,390	118,433	106,355	184,593	126,587
	2006.........................	51,625	4,899	129,959	27,287	28,508	128,171	122,188	105,776	183,066	125,877
	Percent change	-0.5	-3.5	+8.7	+4.8	+7.1	+8.3	+3.2	-0.5	-0.8	-0.6
GROUP I (250,000 and over)	2005.........................	16,138	2,014	65,538	12,317	12,149	56,116	62,378	42,202	74,075	32,917
	2006.........................	15,786	2,050	70,019	12,946	13,137	60,007	63,434	41,722	73,579	31,649
	Percent change	-2.2	+1.8	+6.8	+5.1	+8.1	+6.9	+1.7	-1.1	-0.7	-3.9
1,000,000 and over (Group I subset)	2005.........................	4,856	825	25,025	5,256	4,241	19,101	21,424	13,833	21,653	9,505
	2006.........................	4,796	872	26,598	5,530	4,620	21,090	21,050	13,460	21,401	9,770
	Percent change	-1.2	+5.7	+6.3	+5.2	+8.9	+10.4	-1.7	-2.7	-1.2	+2.8
500,000 to 999,999 (Group I subset)	2005.........................	5,827	612	22,463	3,836	4,128	17,003	22,879	15,396	26,461	11,054
	2006.........................	5,579	669	22,717	4,027	4,676	18,144	22,683	15,343	26,853	9,940
	Percent change	-4.3	+9.3	+1.1	+5.0	+13.3	+6.7	-0.9	-0.3	+1.5	-10.1
250,000 to 499,999 (Group I subset)	2005.........................	5,455	577	18,050	3,225	3,780	20,012	18,075	12,973	25,961	12,358
	2006.........................	5,411	509	20,704	3,389	3,841	20,773	19,701	12,919	25,325	11,939
	Percent change	-0.8	-11.8	+14.7	+5.1	+1.6	+3.8	+9.0	-0.4	-2.4	-3.4
GROUP II (100,000 to 249,999)	2005.........................	8,686	811	21,239	4,762	5,072	20,192	19,802	19,139	34,750	17,264
	2006.........................	8,616	709	23,535	4,951	5,195	22,726	20,678	18,729	33,911	16,573
	Percent change	-0.8	-12.6	+10.8	+4.0	+2.4	+12.5	+4.4	-2.1	-2.4	-4.0
GROUP III (50,000 to 99,999)	2005.........................	8,479	637	14,079	3,869	3,812	18,025	14,754	15,836	27,298	20,291
	2006.........................	8,600	632	15,252	3,961	4,190	19,477	15,459	16,319	27,309	20,551
	Percent change	+1.4	-0.8	+8.3	+2.4	+9.9	+8.1	+4.8	+3.1	*	+1.3
GROUP IV (25,000 to 49,999)	2005.........................	7,235	567	8,739	2,490	2,874	11,435	9,103	11,538	19,786	17,738
	2006.........................	7,068	544	10,158	2,663	2,965	12,434	9,890	11,596	19,871	17,825
	Percent change	-2.3	-4.1	+16.2	+6.9	+3.2	+8.7	+8.6	+0.5	+0.4	+0.5
GROUP V (10,000 to 24,999)	2005.........................	6,264	523	6,438	1,657	1,777	7,974	6,943	9,461	15,825	17,541
	2006.........................	6,396	467	7,119	1,813	1,992	8,460	7,214	9,528	15,622	17,875
	Percent change	+2.1	-10.7	+10.6	+9.4	+12.1	+6.1	+3.9	+0.7	-1.3	+1.9
GROUP VI (under 10,000)	2005.........................	5,088	525	3,550	945	946	4,648	5,453	8,179	12,859	20,836
	2006.........................	5,159	497	3,876	953	1,029	5,067	5,513	7,882	12,774	21,404
	Percent change	+1.4	-5.3	+9.2	+0.8	+8.8	+9.0	+1.1	-3.6	-0.7	+2.7
METROPOLITAN COUNTIES	2005.........................	14,025	993	20,314	3,555	4,529	15,178	26,065	24,035	54,871	37,685
	2006.........................	13,829	985	21,810	4,009	4,694	17,002	26,739	24,316	54,975	39,565
	Percent change	-1.4	-0.8	+7.4	+12.8	+3.6	+12.0	+2.6	+1.2	+0.2	+5.0
NONMETROPOLI-TAN COUNTIES	2005.........................	5,629	399	1,410	415	536	1,520	7,029	6,147	12,342	15,973
	2006.........................	5,358	353	1,516	398	557	1,525	6,843	5,913	11,698	15,238
	Percent change	-4.8	-11.5	+7.5	-4.1	+3.9	+0.3	-2.6	-3.8	-5.2	-4.6
SUBURBAN AREA[1]	2005.........................	24,522	1,937	33,514	6,818	8,204	31,358	38,246	40,343	84,602	71,050
	2006.........................	24,442	1,826	36,629	7,580	8,750	34,641	39,649	40,569	84,503	72,070
	Percent change	-0.3	-5.7	+9.3	+11.2	+6.7	+10.5	+3.7	+0.6	-0.1	+1.4

[1] Suburban area includes law enforcement agencies in cities with less than 50,000 inhabitants and county law enforcement agencies that are within a Metropolitan Statistical Area. Suburban area excludes all metropolitan agencies associated with a principal city. The agencies associated with suburban areas also appear in other groups within this table.
* Less than one-tenth of 1 percent.

Table 15. Crime Trends, by Population Group, 2005–2006 (*Contd.*)

(Number, Percent change.)

Population group		Burglary			Motor vehicle theft			Arson			Number of agencies	2006 estimated population
		Forcible entry	Unlawful entry	Attempted forcible entry	Autos	Trucks and buses	Other vehicles	Structure	Mobile	Other		
TOTAL ALL AGENCIES:	2005	1,121,947	607,756	116,814	779,905	192,635	95,234	26,318	17,695	16,821		
	2006	1,135,984	607,694	123,283	753,081	184,255	91,316	26,229	17,820	18,240	13,009	252,262,599
	Percent change	+1.3	*	+5.5	-3.4	-4.4	-4.1	-0.3	+0.7	+8.4		
TOTAL CITIES	2005	815,000	438,333	89,494	633,820	149,268	63,167	19,693	12,347	12,119		
	2006	826,859	435,006	93,568	609,144	143,586	60,591	19,501	12,678	13,248	9,309	165,022,332
	Percent change	+1.5	-0.8	+4.6	-3.9	-3.8	-4.1	-1.0	+2.7	+9.3		
GROUP I (250,000 and over)	2005	289,418	120,360	26,288	276,374	83,258	25,171	7,195	6,345	3,752		
	2006	297,844	114,366	28,451	268,846	80,293	23,878	6,901	6,403	3,987	64	40,498,965
	Percent change	+2.9	-5.0	+8.2	-2.7	-3.6	-5.1	-4.1	+0.9	+6.3		
1,000,000 and over (Group I subset)	2005	92,544	36,896	6,466	93,184	37,905	8,334	2,217	2,545	1,283		
	2006	91,080	35,901	6,880	89,034	38,542	8,212	2,059	2,580	1,481	8	14,058,014
	Percent change	-1.6	-2.7	+6.4	-4.5	+1.7	-1.5	-7.1	+1.4	+15.4		
500,000 to 999,999 (Group I subset)	2005	105,134	40,706	11,375	90,666	22,518	11,129	2,199	1,797	1,305		
	2006	112,445	37,371	12,537	91,340	19,898	10,532	2,274	1,781	1,365	21	13,935,869
	Percent change	+7.0	-8.2	+10.2	+0.7	-11.6	-5.4	+3.4	-0.9	+4.6		
250,000 to 499,999 (Group I subset)	2005	91,740	42,758	8,447	92,524	22,835	5,708	2,779	2,003	1,164		
	2006	94,319	41,094	9,034	88,472	21,853	5,134	2,568	2,042	1,141	35	12,505,082
	Percent change	+2.8	-3.9	+6.9	-4.4	-4.3	-10.1	-7.6	+1.9	-2.0		
GROUP II (100,000 to 249,999)	2005	142,441	73,559	16,147	120,148	25,048	10,210	3,256	1,926	1,990		
	2006	143,246	73,014	16,977	112,470	24,030	9,588	3,163	1,945	2,034	172	25,727,612
	Percent change	+0.6	-0.7	+5.1	-6.4	-4.1	-6.1	-2.9	+1.0	+2.2		
GROUP III (50,000 to 99,999)	2005	129,096	75,682	15,567	95,789	17,784	8,878	2,822	1,607	1,920		
	2006	129,346	76,669	15,385	92,608	16,987	8,910	2,994	1,726	2,311	414	28,415,901
	Percent change	+0.2	+1.3	-1.2	-3.3	-4.5	+0.4	+6.1	+7.4	+20.4		
GROUP IV (25,000 to 49,999)	2005	98,517	60,312	12,438	64,387	9,475	7,223	2,205	1,031	1,922		
	2006	100,303	61,209	12,736	61,081	9,180	7,197	2,153	1,092	2,059	721	24,881,889
	Percent change	+1.8	+1.5	+2.4	-5.1	-3.1	-0.4	-2.4	+5.9	+7.1		
GROUP V (10,000 to 24,999)	2005	86,527	57,282	10,341	46,506	8,391	6,174	2,090	837	1,352		
	2006	87,020	58,398	11,004	44,795	8,042	5,920	2,157	862	1,534	1,593	25,224,468
	Percent change	+0.6	+1.9	+6.4	-3.7	-4.2	-4.1	+3.2	+3.0	+13.5		
GROUP VI (under 10,000)	2005	69,001	51,138	8,713	30,616	5,312	5,511	2,125	601	1,183		
	2006	69,100	51,350	9,015	29,344	5,054	5,098	2,133	650	1,323	6,345	20,273,497
	Percent change	+0.1	+0.4	+3.5	-4.2	-4.9	-7.5	+0.4	+8.2	+11.8		
METROPOLITAN COUNTIES	2005	220,909	125,573	21,155	124,976	37,173	24,280	4,576	4,495	3,681		
	2006	224,906	130,686	23,646	123,062	35,089	23,546	4,755	4,303	3,998	1,544	62,193,418
	Percent change	+1.8	+4.1	+11.8	-1.5	-5.6	-3.0	+3.9	-4.3	+8.6		
NONMETROPOLITAN COUNTIES	2005	86,038	43,850	6,165	21,109	6,194	7,787	2,049	853	1,021		
	2006	84,219	42,002	6,069	20,875	5,580	7,179	1,973	839	994	2,156	25,046,849
	Percent change	-2.1	-4.2	-1.6	-1.1	-9.9	-7.8	-3.7	-1.6	-2.6		
SUBURBAN AREA[1]	2005	372,783	231,089	41,523	230,569	53,883	37,246	8,400	6,062	6,629		
	2006	378,436	239,174	42,790	223,842	51,053	35,608	8,661	5,974	7,254	6,897	111,495,563
	Percent change	+1.5	+3.5	+3.1	-2.9	-5.3	-4.4	+3.1	-1.5	+9.4		

[1] Suburban area includes law enforcement agencies in cities with less than 50,000 inhabitants and county law enforcement agencies that are within a Metropolitan Statistical Area. Suburban area excludes all metropolitan agencies associated with a principal city. The agencies associated with suburban areas also appear in other groups within this table.
* Less than one-tenth of 1 percent.

Table 16. Crime Per 100,000 Population, by Population Group, 2006

(Number, rate.)

Population group	Number of agencies	2006 estimated population	Violent crime		Murder and nonnegligent manslaughter		Forcible rape		Robbery		Aggravated assault	
			Number of offenses known	Rate	Number of offenses known	Rate	Number of offenses known	Rate	Number of offenses known	Rate	Number of offenses known	Rate
TOTAL ALL AGENCIES:	12,610	265,518,902	1,319,961	497.1	16,065	6.1	83,161	31.3	425,940	160.4	794,795	299.3
TOTAL CITIES	9,015	179,611,076	1,057,857	589.0	12,720	7.1	62,256	34.7	372,752	207.5	610,129	339.7
GROUP I (250,000 and over)	72	54,499,586	510,505	936.7	7,151	13.1	21,133	38.8	209,006	383.5	273,215	501.3
1,000,000 and over (Group I subset)	10	25,080,811	217,939	868.9	3,087	12.3	7,606	30.3	97,212	387.6	110,034	438.7
500,000 to 999,999 (Group I subset).........	24	15,955,399	158,525	993.6	2,210	13.9	7,047	44.2	60,650	380.1	88,618	555.4
250,000 to 499,999 (Group I subset).........	38	13,463,376	134,041	995.6	1,854	13.8	6,480	48.1	51,144	379.9	74,563	553.8
GROUP II (100,000 to 249,999)	185	27,695,654	175,503	633.7	2,144	7.7	10,749	38.8	62,210	224.6	100,400	362.5
GROUP III (50,000 to 99,999)....................	415	28,528,285	135,723	475.7	1,356	4.8	9,779	34.3	43,732	153.3	80,856	283.4
GROUP IV (25,000 to 49,999)....................	712	24,636,615	95,276	386.7	887	3.6	7,696	31.2	27,695	112.4	58,998	239.5
GROUP V (10,000 to 24,999)	1,540	24,421,216	76,123	311.7	694	2.8	7,045	28.8	19,047	78.0	49,337	202.0
GROUP VI (under 10,000)	6,091	19,829,720	64,727	326.4	488	2.5	5,854	29.5	11,062	55.8	47,323	238.6
METROPOLITAN COUNTIES.............	1,501	62,005,421	212,823	343.2	2,582	4.2	15,080	24.3	49,379	79.6	145,782	235.1
NONMETROPOLITAN COUNTIES[1]	2,094	23,902,405	49,281	206.2	763	3.2	5,825	24.4	3,809	15.9	38,884	162.7
SUBURBAN AREA[2]	6,678	110,390,760	357,295	323.7	3,839	3.5	26,782	24.3	89,277	80.9	237,397	215.1

Population group	Number of agencies	2006 estimated population	Property crime		Burglary		Larceny-theft		Motor vehicle theft	
			Number of offenses known	Rate	Number of offenses known	Rate	Number of offenses known	Rate	Number of offenses known	Rate
TOTAL ALL AGENCIES:	12,610	265,518,902	9,103,824	3,428.7	1,987,997	748.7	5,988,929	2,255.6	1,126,898	424.4
TOTAL CITIES	9,015	179,611,076	7,168,602	3,991.2	1,473,500	820.4	4,785,935	2,664.6	909,167	506.2
GROUP I (250,000 and over)	72	54,499,586	2,524,142	4,631.5	531,486	975.2	1,541,809	2,829.0	450,847	827.2
1,000,000 and over (Group I subset)	10	25,080,811	933,155	3,720.6	180,151	718.3	579,452	2,310.3	173,552	692.0
500,000 to 999,999 (Group I subset)........	24	15,955,399	888,943	5,571.4	194,851	1,221.2	539,145	3,379.1	154,947	971.1
250,000 to 499,999 (Group I subset)........	38	13,463,376	702,044	5,214.5	156,484	1,162.3	423,212	3,143.4	122,348	908.7
GROUP II (100,000 to 249,999)	185	27,695,654	1,231,537	4,446.7	259,991	938.7	808,998	2,921.0	162,548	586.9
GROUP III (50,000 to 99,999)....................	415	28,528,285	1,066,164	3,737.2	225,017	788.8	720,452	2,525.4	120,695	423.1
GROUP IV (25,000 to 49,999)....................	712	24,636,615	869,917	3,531.0	172,795	701.4	619,878	2,516.1	77,244	313.5
GROUP V (10,000 to 24,999)	1,540	24,421,216	782,273	3,203.3	154,176	631.3	570,300	2,335.3	57,797	236.7
GROUP VI (under 10,000)	6,091	19,829,720	694,569	3,502.7	130,035	655.8	524,498	2,645.0	40,036	201.9
METROPOLITAN COUNTIES.............	1,501	62,005,421	1,536,614	2,478.2	385,915	622.4	965,114	1,556.5	185,585	299.3
NONMETROPOLITAN COUNTIES[1]	2,094	23,902,405	398,608	1,667.6	128,582	537.9	237,880	995.2	32,146	134.5
SUBURBAN AREA[2]	6,678	110,390,760	3,031,023	2,745.7	668,688	605.7	2,047,728	1,855.0	314,607	285.0

[1] Includes state police agencies that report aggregately for the entire state.
[2] Suburban area includes law enforcement agencies in cities with less than 50,000 inhabitants and county law enforcement agencies that are within a Metropolitan Statistical Area. Suburban area excludes all metropolitan agencies associated with a principal city. The agencies associated with suburban areas also appear in other groups within this table.

Table 17. Crime Per 100,000 Population, by Suburban and Nonsuburban Cities and Population Groups, 2006

(Number, rate.)

Population group	Violent crime		Murder and nonnegligent manslaughter		Forcible rape		Robbery		Aggravated assault	
	Number of offenses known	Rate	Number of offenses known	Rate	Number of offenses known	Rate	Number of offenses known	Rate	Number of offenses known	Rate
TOTAL SUBURBAN CITIES:...............	144,470	298.6	1,257	2.6	11,700	24.2	39,898	82.5	91,615	189.3
GROUP IV (25,000 to 49,999)....................	57,601	319.4	531	2.9	4,096	22.7	18,195	100.9	34,779	192.9
GROUP V (10,000 to 24,999)	49,426	270.0	462	2.5	4,270	23.3	13,857	75.7	30,837	168.5
GROUP VI (under 10,000).........................	37,443	310.8	264	2.2	3,334	27.7	7,846	65.1	25,999	215.8
TOTAL NONSUBURBAN CITIES:........	91,651	447.0	812	4.0	8,890	43.4	17,906	87.3	64,043	312.4
GROUP IV (25,000 to 49,999)....................	37,653	570.1	356	5.4	3,578	54.2	9,500	143.8	24,219	366.7
GROUP V (10,000 to 24,999)	26,712	436.8	232	3.8	2,790	45.6	5,190	84.9	18,500	302.5
GROUP VI (under 10,000).........................	27,286	350.7	224	2.9	2,522	32.4	3,216	41.3	21,324	274.0

Population group	Property crime		Burglary		Larceny-theft		Motor vehicle theft		Number of agencies	2006 estimated population
	Number of offenses known	Rate	Number of offenses known	Rate	Number of offenses known	Rate	Number of offenses known	Rate		
TOTAL SUBURBAN CITIES:...............	1,494,431	3,088.6	282,773	584.4	1,082,614	2,237.5	129,044	266.7	5,177	48,385,339
GROUP IV (25,000 to 49,999)....................	544,966	3,022.3	107,143	594.2	380,937	2,112.6	56,886	315.5	527	18,031,521
GROUP V (10,000 to 24,999)	513,459	2,804.9	98,976	540.7	370,132	2,022.0	44,351	242.3	1,146	18,305,530
GROUP VI (under 10,000).........................	436,006	3,618.8	76,654	636.2	331,545	2,751.8	27,807	230.8	3,504	12,048,288
TOTAL NONSUBURBAN CITIES:........	852,328	4,157.2	174,233	849.8	632,062	3,082.9	46,033	224.5	3,166	20,502,212
GROUP IV (25,000 to 49,999)....................	324,951	4,919.7	65,652	994.0	238,941	3,617.5	20,358	308.2	185	6,605,094
GROUP V (10,000 to 24,999)	268,814	4,395.5	55,200	902.6	200,168	3,273.0	13,446	219.9	394	6,115,686
GROUP VI (under 10,000).........................	258,563	3,322.8	53,381	686.0	192,953	2,479.7	12,229	157.2	2,587	7,781,432

[1] Suburban cities include law enforcement agencies in cities with less than 50,000 inhabitants that are within a Metropolitan Statistical Area. Suburban cities exclude all metropolitan agencies associated with a principal city. Nonsuburban cities include law enforcement agencies in cities with less than 50,000 inhabitants that are not associated with a Metropolitan Statistical Area.

Table 18. Crime Per 100,000 Population, by Metropolitan and Nonmetropolitan Counties[1] by Population Group, 2006

(Number, rate.)

Population group	Population range	Violent crime		Murder and nonnegligent manslaughter		Forcible rape		Robbery		Aggravated assault	
		Number of offenses known	Rate	Number of offenses known	Rate	Number of offenses known	Rate	Number of offenses known	Rate	Number of offenses known	Rate
METROPOLITAN COUNTIES	100,000 and over	154,268	404.2	1,854	4.9	9,139	23.9	42,012	110.1	101,263	265.3
	25,000 to 99,999	42,938	215.3	534	2.7	4,305	21.6	4,894	24.5	33,205	166.5
	Under 25,000	15,631	401.3	194	5.0	1,650	42.4	2,473	63.5	11,314	290.5
NONMETROPOLITAN COUNTIES	25,000 and over	20,201	197.1	282	2.8	2,120	20.7	1,934	18.9	15,865	154.8
	10,000 to 24,999	15,105	176.4	230	2.7	1,522	17.8	919	10.7	12,434	145.2
	Under 10,000	8,218	236.1	142	4.1	1,321	38.0	332	9.5	6,423	184.5

Population group	Population range	Property crime		Burglary		Larceny-theft		Motor vehicle theft		Number of agencies	2006 estimated population
		Number of offenses known	Rate	Number of offenses known	Rate	Number of offenses known	Rate	Number of offenses known	Rate		
METROPOLITAN COUNTIES	100,000 and over	1,039,674	2,724.0	248,708	651.6	661,713	1,733.7	129,253	338.6	142	38,167,764
	25,000 to 99,999	375,195	1,881.4	109,382	548.5	233,720	1,172.0	32,093	160.9	390	19,942,456
	Under 25,000	121,804	3,127.0	27,825	714.3	69,681	1,788.9	24,298	623.8	969	3,895,201
NONMETROPOLITAN COUNTIES	25,000 and over	176,780	1,724.5	58,473	570.4	104,674	1,021.1	13,633	133.0	262	10,251,334
	10,000 to 24,999	118,512	1,383.7	39,004	455.4	70,379	821.7	9,129	106.6	528	8,564,553
	Under 10,000	61,038	1,753.7	18,783	539.7	36,811	1,057.7	5,444	156.4	1,155	3,480,451

[1] Metropolitan counties include sheriffs and county law enforcement agencies associated with a Metropolitan Statistical Area. Nonmetropolitan counties include sheriffs and county law enforcement agencies that are not associated with a Metropolitan Statistical Area. The offenses from state police agencies are not included in this table.

Table 19. Crime Per 100,000 Population, Selected Known Offenses, by Population Group, 2006

(Number, rate.)

Population group		Forcible rape		Robbery				Aggravated assault	
		Rape by force	Assault to rape attempts	Firearm	Knife or cutting instrument	Other weapon	Strong-arm	Firearm	Knife or cutting instrument
TOTAL ALL AGENCIES:	Number of offenses known ...	72,830	6,398	157,275	32,072	34,395	148,593	160,319	137,270
	Rate	29.2	2.6	63.0	12.8	13.8	59.5	64.2	55.0
TOTAL CITIES	Number of offenses known ...	53,551	5,056	133,672	27,680	29,193	129,939	127,162	107,607
	Rate	32.4	3.1	81.0	16.8	17.7	78.7	77.0	65.2
GROUP I (250,000 and over)	Number of offenses known ...	16,343	2,084	72,998	13,264	13,690	61,517	66,678	42,983
	Rate	39.1	5.0	174.7	31.7	32.8	147.2	159.6	102.9
1,000,000 and over (Group I subset)	Number of offenses known ...	4,796	872	26,598	5,530	4,620	21,090	21,050	13,460
	Rate	34.1	6.2	189.2	39.3	32.9	150.0	149.7	95.7
500,000 to 999,999 (Group I subset)	Number of offenses known ...	5,690	670	24,885	4,212	5,128	18,947	24,472	15,734
	Rate	39.2	4.6	171.4	29.0	35.3	130.5	168.6	108.4
250,000 to 499,999 (Group I subset)	Number of offenses known ...	5,857	542	21,515	3,522	3,942	21,480	21,156	13,789
	Rate	44.3	4.1	162.8	26.7	29.8	162.6	160.1	104.4
GROUP II (100,000 to 249,999)	Number of offenses known....	9,133	753	24,147	5,055	5,286	23,141	22,204	19,271
	Rate..	35.0	2.9	92.5	19.4	20.3	88.7	85.1	73.8
GROUP III (50,000 to 99,999)	Number of offenses known....	9,083	671	15,725	4,046	4,253	19,688	15,807	16,598
	Rate..	31.9	2.4	55.2	14.2	14.9	69.1	55.5	58.3
GROUP IV (25,000 to 49,999)	Number of offenses known....	7,107	550	9,872	2,596	2,964	12,177	9,843	11,643
	Rate..	28.9	2.2	40.2	10.6	12.1	49.6	40.1	47.4
GROUP V (10,000 to 24,999)	Number of offenses known....	6,566	480	7,088	1,758	1,994	8,193	7,169	9,318
	Rate..	26.9	2.0	29.0	7.2	8.2	33.6	29.4	38.2
GROUP VI (under 10,000)	Number of offenses known....	5,319	518	3,842	961	1,006	5,223	5,461	7,794
	Rate..	26.9	2.6	19.4	4.9	5.1	26.4	27.6	39.4
METROPOLITAN COUNTIES	Number of offenses known....	13,857	984	22,169	4,011	4,678	17,204	26,540	24,007
	Rate..	22.8	1.6	36.4	6.6	7.7	28.3	43.6	39.5
NONMETROPOLITAN COUNTIES	Number of offenses known....	5,422	358	1,434	381	524	1,450	6,617	5,656
	Rate..	22.9	1.5	6.1	1.6	2.2	6.1	28.0	23.9
SUBURBAN AREA[1]	Number of offenses known....	24,674	1,838	36,825	7,575	8,687	34,814	39,485	40,331
	Rate..	22.6	1.7	33.7	6.9	8.0	31.9	36.2	37.0

[1] Suburban area includes law enforcement agencies in cities with less than 50,000 inhabitants and county law enforcement agencies that are within a Metropolitan Statistical Area. Suburban area excludes all metropolitan agencies associated with a principal city. The agencies associated with suburban areas also appear in other groups within this table.

Table 19. Crime Per 100,000 Population, Selected Known Offenses, by Population Group, 2006 *(Contd.)*

(Number, rate.)

Population group		Aggravated assault		Burglary			Motor vehicle theft			Number of agencies	2006 estimated population
		Other weapon	Hands, fists, feet, etc.	Forcible entry	Unlawful entry	Attempted forcible entry	Autos	Trucks and buses	Other vehicles		
TOTAL ALL AGENCIES:	Number of offenses known ...	252,109	181,531	1,149,577	613,260	124,275	777,634	188,450	91,311	12,565	249,598,585
	Rate	101.0	72.7	460.6	245.7	49.8	311.6	75.5	36.6		
TOTAL CITIES	Number of offenses known ...	186,164	127,458	843,170	444,773	95,176	635,367	147,893	61,178	8,986	165,111,407
	Rate	112.8	77.2	510.7	269.4	57.6	384.8	89.6	37.1		
GROUP I (250,000 and over)	Number of offenses known ...	75,528	33,384	311,546	121,047	29,599	287,845	84,428	24,282	67	41,788,112
	Rate	180.7	79.9	745.5	289.7	70.8	688.8	202.0	58.1		
1,000,000 and over (Group I subset)	Number of offenses known ...	21,401	9,770	91,080	35,901	6,880	89,034	38,542	8,212	8	14,058,014
	Rate	152.2	69.5	647.9	255.4	48.9	633.3	274.2	58.4		
500,000 to 999,999 (Group I subset)	Number of offenses known ...	27,607	10,881	120,239	41,995	13,275	105,700	23,292	10,757	22	14,516,874
	Rate	190.2	75.0	828.3	289.3	91.4	728.1	160.4	74.1		
250,000 to 499,999 (Group I subset)	Number of offenses known ...	26,520	12,733	100,227	43,151	9,444	93,111	22,594	5,313	37	13,213,224
	Rate	200.7	96.4	758.5	326.6	71.5	704.7	171.0	40.2		
GROUP II (100,000 to 249,999)	Number of offenses known....	34,796	17,307	147,553	75,205	17,391	118,590	24,282	9,780	175	26,102,993
	Rate......................................	133.3	66.3	565.3	288.1	66.6	454.3	93.0	37.5		
GROUP III (50,000 to 99,999)	Number of offenses known....	27,630	20,794	131,483	77,565	15,757	94,394	17,084	9,102	414	28,477,729
	Rate......................................	97.0	73.0	461.7	272.4	55.3	331.5	60.0	32.0		
GROUP IV (25,000 to 49,999)	Number of offenses known....	19,990	17,411	98,571	60,976	12,551	60,770	9,104	7,132	709	24,554,854
	Rate......................................	81.4	70.9	401.4	248.3	51.1	247.5	37.1	29.0		
GROUP V (10,000 to 24,999)	Number of offenses known....	15,556	17,238	85,145	58,152	10,762	43,956	7,922	5,823	1,539	24,399,587
	Rate......................................	63.8	70.6	349.0	238.3	44.1	180.2	32.5	23.9		
GROUP VI (under 10,000)	Number of offenses known....	12,664	21,324	68,872	51,828	9,116	29,812	5,073	5,059	6,082	19,788,132
	Rate......................................	64.0	107.8	348.0	261.9	46.1	150.7	25.6	25.6		
METROPOLITAN COUNTIES	Number of offenses known....	54,554	38,932	224,939	127,762	23,551	122,333	35,341	23,380	1,496	60,839,013
	Rate......................................	89.7	64.0	369.7	210.0	38.7	201.1	58.1	38.4		
NONMETROPOLITAN COUNTIES	Number of offenses known....	11,391	15,141	81,468	40,725	5,548	19,934	5,216	6,753	2,083	23,648,165
	Rate......................................	48.2	64.0	344.5	172.2	23.5	84.3	22.1	28.6		
SUBURBAN AREA[1]	Number of offenses known....	84,148	71,888	377,432	236,718	44,285	223,264	51,225	35,381	6,665	109,136,000
	Rate......................................	77.1	65.9	345.8	216.9	40.6	204.6	46.9	32.4		

[1] Suburban area includes law enforcement agencies in cities with less than 50,000 inhabitants and county law enforcement agencies that are within a Metropolitan Statistical Area. Suburban area excludes all metropolitan agencies associated with a principal city. The agencies associated with suburban areas also appear in other groups within this table.

Table 20. Murder, by State and Type of Weapon, 2006

(Number.)

State	Total murders[1]	Total firearms	Handguns	Rifles	Shotguns	Firearms (type unknown)	Knives or cutting instruments	Other weapons	Hands, fists, feet, etc.[2]
Alabama	349	247	226	0	21	0	35	51	16
Alaska	35	22	15	5	1	1	8	2	3
Arizona	462	343	269	33	14	27	53	46	20
Arkansas	201	134	82	15	10	27	22	34	11
California	2,485	1,822	1,623	74	69	56	315	218	130
Colorado	156	85	38	0	8	39	35	16	20
Connecticut	100	65	57	0	2	6	18	12	5
Delaware	41	27	14	0	3	10	7	6	1
Georgia	548	403	351	13	19	20	64	67	14
Hawaii	21	7	5	0	0	2	3	6	5
Idaho	36	22	9	2	2	9	6	5	3
Illinois[3]	487	392	380	4	6	2	46	35	14
Indiana	339	239	171	20	10	38	36	45	19
Iowa	54	23	8	1	5	9	13	11	7
Kansas	126	70	33	6	4	27	14	33	9
Kentucky	150	98	78	6	8	6	22	16	14
Louisiana	488	396	335	29	7	25	35	37	20
Maine	23	12	7	2	1	2	1	8	2
Maryland	546	403	372	5	17	9	72	46	25
Massachusetts	185	111	66	2	3	40	42	28	4
Michigan	711	498	208	29	25	236	50	134	29
Minnesota	117	75	67	1	7	0	20	9	13
Mississippi	173	121	93	5	7	16	18	24	10
Missouri	334	246	96	13	14	123	36	41	11
Montana	17	4	4	0	0	0	3	7	3
Nebraska	16	5	2	1	0	2	2	7	2
Nevada	224	133	88	4	9	32	34	45	12
New Hampshire	12	3	2	0	1	0	6	1	2
New Jersey	428	289	270	0	7	12	69	47	23
New Mexico	99	57	48	3	3	3	21	7	14
New York	921	400	308	14	8	70	141	351	29
North Carolina	530	338	227	23	28	60	59	75	58
North Dakota	8	1	1	0	0	0	4	3	0
Ohio	487	334	233	3	8	90	40	84	29
Oklahoma	207	133	85	12	12	24	18	35	21
Oregon	85	44	16	4	2	22	22	12	7
Pennsylvania	719	554	474	14	11	55	51	87	27
Rhode Island	28	7	3	0	0	4	8	11	2
South Carolina	359	253	163	10	14	66	44	42	20
South Dakota	8	2	0	0	0	2	2	4	0
Tennessee	409	271	211	11	12	37	43	71	24
Texas	1,381	949	711	53	71	114	162	183	87
Utah	46	21	9	1	2	9	6	9	10
Vermont	12	7	7	0	0	0	1	2	2
Virginia	398	264	142	6	13	103	49	70	15
Washington	186	107	90	3	12	2	31	28	20
West Virginia	71	40	24	4	1	11	9	18	4
Wisconsin	163	95	72	3	3	17	23	29	16
Wyoming	9	5	2	2	1	0	3	0	1

[1] Total number of murders for which supplemental homicide data were received.
[2] Pushed is included in hands, fists, feet, etc.
[3] Limited supplemental homicide data were received.

Table 21. Robbery by State, Type of Weapon, 2006

(Number.)

State	Total robberies[1]	Firearms	Knives or cutting instruments	Other weapons	Strong-arm	Agency count	Population
Alabama	2,562	1,519	164	180	699	220	2,453,070
Alaska	589	181	66	66	276	32	648,530
Arizona	9,002	4,437	1,113	770	2,682	78	5,763,933
Arkansas	2,599	1,247	168	291	893	218	2,440,466
California	70,890	24,384	6,828	6,679	32,999	723	36,332,437
Colorado	3,774	1,508	401	394	1,471	195	4,562,929
Connecticut	2,930	975	335	295	1,325	78	2,754,178
Delaware	1,735	729	154	149	703	53	853,476
District of Columbia	3,829	1,546	171	201	1,911	3	581,530
Florida	34,093	14,352	2,353	3,267	14,121	591	18,015,015
Georgia	12,490	7,540	605	1,066	3,279	211	5,788,935
Hawaii	1,044	149	80	78	737	2	1,081,338
Idaho	294	104	38	35	117	104	1,458,022
Illinois[2]	555	208	40	54	253	1	153,738
Indiana	3,485	1,598	285	281	1,321	164	3,900,622
Iowa	1,013	248	91	113	561	178	2,501,202
Kansas	1,781	758	195	222	606	238	2,305,606
Kentucky	3,260	1,281	253	566	1,160	263	3,274,856
Louisiana	5,103	2,642	328	400	1,733	116	3,296,886
Maine	384	78	80	36	190	163	1,319,259
Maryland	10,142	4,913	962	529	3,738	150	4,977,683
Massachusetts	6,748	1,765	1,267	764	2,952	284	5,170,140
Michigan	14,136	7,000	751	1,294	5,091	558	9,879,608
Minnesota	5,368	1,657	371	725	2,615	271	4,769,467
Mississippi	2,513	1,380	137	312	684	107	1,776,401
Missouri	7,495	3,557	491	552	2,895	557	5,759,961
Montana	152	44	18	27	63	64	721,431
Nebraska	1,092	497	94	97	404	208	1,502,765
Nevada	7,027	3,476	612	483	2,456	36	2,495,529
New Hampshire	380	75	72	52	181	122	1,039,150
New Jersey	13,356	4,313	1,323	958	6,762	515	8,720,592
New Mexico	1,855	819	262	125	649	53	1,493,052
New York	10,841	3,400	1,170	1,019	5,252	652	10,824,535
North Carolina	12,971	6,851	1,091	1,172	3,857	376	7,818,693
North Dakota	69	10	10	11	38	72	591,890
Ohio	16,866	6,545	893	1,790	7,638	357	7,961,904
Oklahoma	3,123	1,268	326	326	1,203	289	3,479,339
Oregon	2,512	614	271	251	1,376	137	3,134,046
Pennsylvania	19,660	8,558	1,414	1,240	8,448	837	10,869,846
Rhode Island	691	155	85	120	331	43	906,054
South Carolina	5,681	3,104	456	497	1,624	426	4,061,426
South Dakota	81	8	11	11	51	80	569,130
Tennessee	11,085	6,519	786	1,247	2,533	446	5,909,564
Texas	37,117	16,917	3,774	3,465	12,961	965	23,227,354
Utah	1,226	363	145	120	598	110	2,484,578
Vermont	105	42	19	14	30	75	571,164
Virginia	7,429	3,736	629	829	2,235	315	7,250,178
Washington	5,363	1,262	489	558	3,054	237	5,481,639
West Virginia	204	58	18	37	91	180	772,766
Wisconsin	5,564	2,867	368	620	1,709	351	5,389,771
Wyoming	71	18	9	7	37	61	502,901

[1] The number of robberies for which breakdowns by type of weapon were received from agencies that submitted 12 months of data in 2006.
[2] Limited data were received.

Table 22. Aggravated Assault by State, Type of Weapon, 2006

(Number.)

State	Total aggravated assaults[1]	Firearms	Knives or cutting instruments	Other weapons	Personal weapons	Agency count	Population
Alabama	4,903	1,523	775	1,015	1,590	220	2,453,070
Alaska	3,354	590	730	929	1,105	32	648,530
Arizona	18,155	5,353	3,026	5,633	4,143	78	5,763,933
Arkansas	10,094	2,577	1,578	2,736	3,203	218	2,440,466
California	111,327	23,494	18,185	40,426	29,222	723	36,332,437
Colorado	12,148	2,547	2,668	3,156	3,777	195	4,562,929
Connecticut	3,264	467	802	1,182	813	78	2,754,178
Delaware	3,640	804	799	1,644	393	53	853,476
District of Columbia	4,589	975	1,237	1,888	489	3	581,530
Florida	86,822	15,882	15,370	38,188	17,382	591	18,015,015
Georgia	17,300	4,831	3,446	5,685	3,338	211	5,788,935
Hawaii	1,819	188	440	671	520	2	1,081,338
Idaho	2,641	480	531	787	843	104	1,458,022
Illinois[2]	1,135	539	125	278	193	1	153,738
Indiana	5,091	701	649	1,130	2,611	164	3,900,622
Iowa	5,159	447	846	1,169	2,697	178	2,501,202
Kansas	7,520	2,234	1,523	2,217	1,546	238	2,305,606
Kentucky	5,292	1,070	780	2,079	1,363	263	3,274,856
Louisiana	17,373	4,797	3,127	4,654	4,795	116	3,296,886
Maine	780	46	160	215	359	163	1,319,259
Maryland	15,490	2,438	3,618	5,660	3,774	150	4,977,683
Massachusetts	16,347	1,787	3,640	8,371	2,549	284	5,170,140
Michigan	36,306	9,181	6,739	12,737	7,649	558	9,879,608
Minnesota	8,446	1,452	1,754	2,379	2,861	271	4,769,467
Mississippi	2,871	910	555	691	715	107	1,776,401
Missouri	21,827	5,517	3,120	6,544	6,646	557	5,759,961
Montana	1,539	215	263	468	593	64	721,431
Nebraska	3,018	455	520	1,528	515	208	1,502,765
Nevada	10,178	2,089	1,864	4,557	1,668	36	2,495,529
New Hampshire	884	140	309	244	191	122	1,039,150
New Jersey	15,647	2,609	3,430	4,705	4,903	515	8,720,592
New Mexico	7,382	1,604	1,314	2,452	2,012	53	1,493,052
New York	18,117	2,521	4,700	5,250	5,646	652	10,824,535
North Carolina	23,737	6,804	4,714	6,673	5,546	376	7,818,693
North Dakota	522	13	57	137	315	72	591,890
Ohio	13,311	3,557	2,605	4,124	3,025	357	7,961,904
Oklahoma	12,682	2,477	1,997	4,811	3,397	289	3,479,339
Oregon	5,502	736	1,055	1,837	1,874	137	3,134,046
Pennsylvania	26,825	5,762	3,919	6,616	10,528	837	10,869,846
Rhode Island	1,289	179	287	579	244	43	906,054
South Carolina	23,853	6,071	4,224	6,610	6,948	426	4,061,426
South Dakota	654	112	204	198	140	80	569,130
Tennessee	31,906	9,754	6,589	12,217	3,346	446	5,909,564
Texas	73,846	17,513	16,352	26,131	13,850	965	23,227,354
Utah	3,435	628	904	1,243	660	110	2,484,578
Vermont	561	70	116	131	244	75	571,164
Virginia	11,060	2,080	2,403	3,538	3,039	315	7,250,178
Washington	10,306	1,544	1,879	3,359	3,524	237	5,481,639
West Virginia	1,455	407	218	286	544	180	772,766
Wisconsin	8,842	2,056	954	2,058	3,774	351	5,389,771
Wyoming	985	93	170	293	429	61	502,901

[1] The number of aggravated assaults for which breakdowns by type of weapon were received from agencies that submitted 12 months of data in 2006.

[2] Limited data were received.

Table 23. Offense Analysis, by Classification and Value, 2005–2006

(Number, percent, dollars.)

Classification		Number of offenses 2006	Percent change from 2005	Percent distribution[1]	Average value
Murder		13,299	+1.3	-	-
Forcible rape		72,266	-3.4	-	-
Robbery:	Total..	343,282	+8.7	100.0	$1,268
Robbery by location:	Street/highway..................................	152,873	+10.5	44.5	980
	Commercial house	46,815	+3.5	13.6	1,589
	Gas or service station	9,265	+3.5	2.7	1,169
	Convenience store	19,121	+6.1	5.6	761
	Residence..	49,124	+8.0	14.3	1,469
	Bank..	7,359	+10.5	2.1	4,330
	Miscellaneous.....................................	58,725	+10.7	17.1	1,389
Burglary:	Total..	1,734,074	+1.3	100.0	1,834
Burglary by location:	Residence (dwelling):.........................	1,147,891	+1.6	66.2	1,823
	Residence Night	326,811	+0.3	18.8	1,464
	Residence Day	559,967	+3.4	32.3	1,917
	Residence Unknown.........................	261,113	-0.3	15.1	2,070
	Nonresidence (store, office, etc.):......	586,183	+0.7	33.8	1,855
	Nonresidence Night.........................	243,844	+0.2	14.1	1,602
	Nonresidence Day............................	186,179	+3.5	10.7	1,804
	Nonresidence Unknown....................	156,160	-1.7	9.0	2,311
Larceny-theft (except motor vehicle theft):	Total..	5,265,007	-2.7	100.0	855
Larceny-theft by type:	Pocket-picking....................................	22,926	+1.4	0.4	443
	Purse-snatching	31,873	-3.0	0.6	440
	Shoplifting	695,387	-7.2	13.2	194
	From motor vehicles (except accessories).............	1,396,481	-0.4	26.5	734
	Motor vehicle accessories...................	508,951	-8.5	9.7	522
	Bicycles	184,269	-4.8	3.5	263
	From buildings	661,217	-2.7	12.6	1,170
	From coin-operated machines..............	28,101	-15.3	0.5	317
	All others	1,735,802	-0.2	33.0	1,280
Larceny-theft by value:	Over $200..	2,235,522	+2.5	42.5	1,938
	$50 to $200	1,175,156	-3.1	22.3	111
	Under $50	1,854,329	-8.0	35.2	21
Motor vehicle theft		990,261	-3.2	-	6,649

[1] Because of rounding, the percentages may not add to 100.0.

Table 24. Property Stolen and Recovered, by Type and Value, 2006

(Dollars, percent.)

Type of property	Value of property		Percent recovered
	Stolen	Recovered	
Total..	$14,940,285,373	$4,625,247,564	31.0
Currency, notes, etc.	1,108,666,932	44,773,028	4.0
Jewelry and precious metals............................	1,215,235,529	59,464,987	4.9
Clothing and furs	250,515,900	31,344,315	12.5
Locally stolen motor vehicles..........................	6,891,284,744	4,068,866,634	59.0
Office equipment	601,742,665	27,177,888	4.5
Televisions, radios, stereos, etc.	867,735,960	39,290,382	4.5
Firearms..	103,559,485	9,475,233	9.1
Household goods	280,613,770	11,253,776	4.0
Consumable goods...	125,561,212	14,368,025	11.4
Livestock...	19,787,860	2,701,302	13.7
Miscellaneous...	3,475,581,316	316,531,994	9.1

SECTION III:
OFFENSES CLEARED

OFFENSES CLEARED

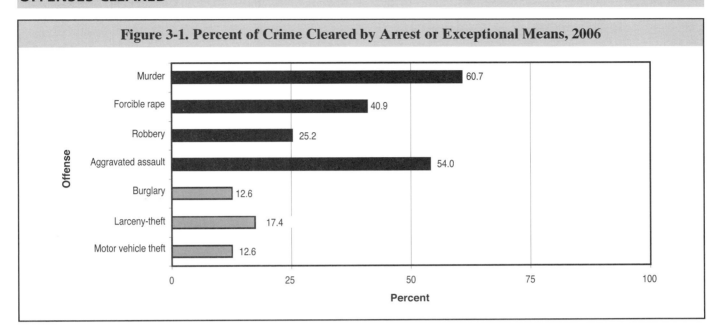

Figure 3-1. Percent of Crime Cleared by Arrest or Exceptional Means, 2006

Law enforcement agencies that report crime to the Federal Bureau of Investigation (FBI) can clear, or "close," offenses in one of two ways: by arrest or by exceptional means. However, the administrative closing of a case by a local law enforcement agency does not necessarily mean that the agency can clear an offense for UCR purposes. To clear an offense within the program's guidelines, the reporting agency must adhere to certain criteria, which are outlined in this section. (*Note:* The UCR Program does not distinguish between offenses cleared by arrest and those cleared by exceptional means in its data presentations. The distinction is made solely for the purpose of a definition and not for data collection and publication.) See Appendix I for information on the UCR Program's statistical methodology.

Cleared by Arrest

In the UCR Program, a law enforcement agency reports that an offense is cleared by arrest, or solved for crime reporting purposes, when at least one person is arrested, charged with the commission of the offense, and turned over to the court for prosecution (whether following arrest, court summons, or police notice). To qualify as a clearance, *all* of these conditions must be met.

In its calculations, the UCR Program counts the number of offenses that are cleared, not the number of arrestees. Therefore, the arrest of one person may clear several crimes, and the arrest of many persons may clear only one offense. In addition, some clearances recorded by an agency during a particular calendar year, such as 2006, may pertain to offenses that occurred in previous years.

Cleared by Exceptional Means

In certain situations, elements beyond law enforcement's control prevent the agency from arresting and formally charging the offender. When this occurs, the agency can clear the offense *exceptionally*. There are four UCR Program requirements that law enforcement must meet in order to clear an offense by exceptional means. The agency must have:

- Identified the offender

- Gathered enough evidence to support an arrest, make a charge, and turn over the offender to the court for prosecution

- Identified the offender's exact location so that the suspect could be taken into custody immediately

- Encountered a circumstance outside the control of law enforcement that prohibits the agency from arresting, charging, and prosecuting the offender

Examples of exceptional clearances include, but are not limited to, the death of the offender (e.g., suicide or justifiably killed by a law enforcement officer or a citizen), the victim's refusal to cooperate with the prosecution after the offender has been identified, or the denial of extradition because the offender committed a crime in another jurisdiction and is being prosecuted for that offense. In the UCR Program, the recovery of property does not clear an offense.

National Clearances

A review of the data for 2006 revealed law enforcement agencies in the United States cleared 44.3 percent of violent crimes (murder, forcible rape, robbery, and aggravated assault) and 15.8 percent of property crimes (burglary, larceny-theft, and motor vehicle theft) brought to their attention. In addition, law enforcement cleared 18.0 percent of arson offenses, which are reported in a slightly different manner than the other property crimes. (More details concerning this offense are furnished in the arson text in this section.)

As in most years, law enforcement agencies cleared a higher percentage of violent crimes than property crimes in 2006. As a rule, this long-term trend is attributed to the more vigorous investigative efforts put forth for violent crimes. In addition, violent crimes more often involve victims and/or witnesses who are able to identify the perpetrators.

A breakdown of the clearances for violent crimes for 2006 revealed that the nation's law enforcement agencies cleared 60.7 percent of murder offenses, 54.0 percent of aggravated assault offenses, 40.9 percent of forcible rape offenses, and 25.2 percent of robbery offenses. The data for property crimes showed that agencies cleared 17.4 percent of larceny-theft offenses, 12.6 percent of motor vehicle theft offenses, and 12.6 percent of burglary offenses. (Table 25)

Regional Clearances

The UCR Program divides the nation into four regions: the Northeast, the Midwest, the South, and the West. (See Appendix III for further details.) A review of clearance data for 2006 by region showed that agencies in the Northeast cleared the greatest proportion of their violent crime offenses (48.4 percent). Law enforcement agencies in the South cleared 46.4 percent of their violent crimes, while agencies in the West and Midwest cleared 42.2 percent and 38.4 percent, respectively.

Clearance data for 2006 showed that, among the regions, law enforcement agencies in the Northeast cleared the highest percentage of their property crimes (19.0 percent). Agencies in the South and Midwest cleared 16.4 percent and 15.2 percent, respectively. Agencies in the West cleared 13.7 percent of their property crimes. (Table 26)

Clearances by Population Groups

The UCR Program uses the following population group designations in its data presentations: cities (grouped according to population size) and counties (classified as either metropolitan or nonmetropolitan counties). (A breakdown of these classifications is furnished in Appendix III.)

Cities

In 2006, the clearance data collected showed that law enforcement agencies in the nation's cities cleared 42.0 percent of their violent crime offenses. Among the city population groups, agencies in the smallest cities, those with populations under 10,000 inhabitants, cleared the greatest proportion of their violent crime offenses (57.7 percent), and law enforcement in cities with 1,000,000 or more inhabitants cleared the smallest proportion of their violent crime offenses (32.6 percent). The clearance data for murder showed that among the city population groups, agencies in cities with populations of 10,000 to 24,999 inhabitants cleared the greatest percentage of their murders (73.6 percent). Law enforcement agencies in cities with 250,000 to 499,999 inhabitants cleared the lowest percentage of their murders (49.5 percent).

A further review of the clearance data for 2006 showed that agencies in the nation's cities collectively cleared 15.7

percent of their property crime offenses. Law enforcement in cities with 10,000 to 24,999 inhabitants cleared the highest proportion of the property crimes (19.5 percent) brought to their attention; as with the clearances for violent crime, agencies in cities with 500,000 to 999,999 inhabitants cleared the smallest proportion of their property crimes (11.0 percent).

Metropolitan Counties

An examination of clearance data submitted by law enforcement agencies in metropolitan counties in 2006 showed that these agencies cleared 50.7 percent of their violent crime offenses. Of the violent crimes made known to law enforcement agencies, murder offenses had the highest proportion of clearance (62.9 percent). Clearance data also showed that law enforcement agencies in metropolitan counties cleared 15.6 percent of their total property crimes. (Table 25)

Nonmetropolitan Counties

Clearance figures for nonmetropolitan counties showed that these agencies, like their counterparts in metropolitan counties, collectively cleared a greater proportion of their violent crimes than did the nation as a whole in 2006. A further breakdown of the clearance data revealed that agencies in nonmetropolitan counties cleared 59.3 percent of their violent crime offenses. Of the violent crimes known to them, law enforcement in nonmetropolitan counties had the highest number of clearances for murder (73.0 percent). The clearance data collected also showed that law enforcement agencies in nonmetropolitan counties cleared 16.8 percent of their property crime offenses. Among the property crimes known to these agencies, the highest percentage of offenses cleared was for arson at 24.6 percent. (Table 25)

Clearances and Juveniles

When an offender under 18 years of age is cited to appear in juvenile court or before other juvenile authorities, the UCR Program considers the incident for which the juvenile is being held responsible to be cleared by arrest, although a physical arrest may not have occurred. In addition, according to program definitions, clearances that include both adult and juvenile offenders are classified as clearances for crimes committed by adults. Therefore, because the clearance percentages for crimes committed by juveniles include only those clearances in which no adults were involved, the figures in this publication should not be used to present a definitive picture of juvenile involvement in crime.

Of the clearances for violent crimes that were reported in the nation in 2006, 12.6 percent involved only juveniles, up from 12.4 percent in 2005. In addition, 19.1 percent of clearances for property crime in 2006 involved only juveniles, down from 17.9 percent in 2005. In 2006, 16.6 percent of all reported robbery clearances involved only juveniles. Arson offenses had the highest percentage of clearances involving only juveniles—40.2 percent— nationally in 2006.

VIOLENT CRIME

National Clearances

In 2006, 44.3 percent of violent crime offenses in the nation was cleared by arrest or exceptional means. Murder had the highest percentage of offenses cleared (60.7 percent). Law enforcement agencies also cleared 54.0 percent of aggravated assaults, 40.9 percent of forcible rapes, and 25.2 percent of robberies. (Table 25)

Regional Clearances

A comparison of clearance data by region showed that law enforcement agencies in the Northeast cleared 48.4 percent of the violent crime reported to them, followed by the South (46.4 percent), the West (42.2 percent), and the Midwest (38.4 percent). For murder, the South cleared 65.9 percent of offenses, followed by the Northeast (61.4 percent), the West (56.4 percent) and the Midwest (51.9 percent each). Forcible rape offenses were cleared 45.5 percent of the time in the South, 45.0 percent of the time in the Northeast, 38.7 percent of the time in the West, and 31.8 percent of the time in the Midwest. For robbery, the Northeast cleared 28.4 percent of offenses, followed by the South (26.4 percent), the West (24.2 percent), and the Midwest (21.0 percent). The Northeast also had the highest proportion of clearances for aggravated assault (61.3 percent), followed by the South (55.1 percent), the West (52.1 percent), and the Midwest (48.1 percent). (Table 26)

Clearances by Population Group

Cities

In the nation's cities, law enforcement agencies collectively cleared 42.0 percent of violent crimes reported to them. Of the population groups with the *city* designation, the nation's smallest cities—those with under 10,000 inhabitants—had the highest percentage of violent crimes cleared (57.7 percent). Cities with 1,000,000 or more inhabitants had the lowest percentage of violent offenses cleared, 32.6 percent. Cities with 10,000 to 24,999 inhabitants cleared the highest percentage of their murder offenses (73.6 percent), while cities with 250,000 to 459,999 inhabitants cleared the lowest percentage of murder offenses (49.5 percent). For forcible rape, cities with under 10,000 inhabitants cleared the largest percentage of offenses at 41.7 percent; cities with 500,000 to 999,999 inhabitants cleared the lowest percentage of offenses at 36.1 percent. Cities with under 10,000 inhabitants also cleared the greatest percentage of their robbery offenses at 35.3 percent, and cities with 500,000 to 999,999 inhabitants cleared the lowest percentage of their robbery offenses at 20.4 percent. For aggravated assault, cities with under 10,000 inhabitants cleared the highest proportion of offenses (64.6 percent); cities with 1,000,000 or more inhabitants cleared the lowest percentage of offenses (40.6 percent). (Table 25)

Metropolitan and Nonmetropolitan Counties

Law enforcement agencies in the nation's metropolitan counties cleared 50.7 percent of their violent crimes, with 62.9 percent of murders, 45.7 percent of forcible rapes, 26.9 percent of robberies, and 58.8 percent of aggravated assaults being cleared. Agencies in nonmetropolitan counties cleared 59.3 percent of their violent crime offenses, with 73.0 percent of murders, 44.9 percent of forcible rapes, 39.6 percent of robberies, and 62.9 percent of aggravated assaults being cleared. (Table 25)

Clearances by Classification Group and Type

For forcible rape, by classification group and type, law enforcement agencies cleared 42.0 percent of assault to rape attempts and 39.5 percent of rapes by force in 2006. Cleared robbery offenses included 29.0 percent of offenses involving strong-arm tactics, 28.0 percent of offenses involving knives or other cutting instruments, 19.7 percent of offenses involving firearms, and 26.9 percent of offenses involving other weapons. For aggravated assault, agencies cleared 61.1 percent of offenses involving hands, feet, fists, etc.; 60.7 percent of offenses involving knives or other cutting instruments; 37.9 percent of offenses involving firearms; and 54.3 percent of offenses involving other weapons. (Table 27)

Clearances and Juveniles

When an individual under 18 years of age (a juvenile) is cited to appear before juvenile authorities, the incident is cleared by arrest despite the lack of a physical arrest. In addition, the UCR Program considers any clearance that involves both adults (those age 18 years or over) and juveniles as an adult clearance. Therefore, the juvenile clearance data are limited to those clearances involving juveniles only, and the figures in this publication should not be used to present a definitive picture of juvenile involvement in crime.

In 2006, 12.6 percent of violent crime clearances in the United States exclusively involved juveniles. In the nation's cities, collectively, 12.9 percent of violent crime clearances involved only juveniles, with juveniles in cities exclusively involved in 5.9 percent of murder clearances, 11.0 percent of forcible rape clearances, 16.8 percent of robbery clearances, and 12.1 percent of aggravated assault clearances. Of the nation's city population groups, cities with 25,000 to 49,999 inhabitants had the highest percentage of overall clearances for violent crime only involving juveniles (14.9 percent); cities with 250,000 or more inhabitants had the lowest percentage (11.4 percent). Law enforcement agencies in metropolitan counties reported that 12.4 percent of their violent crime clearances—including 5.1 percent of their murder clearances, 13.8 percent of their forcible rape clearances, 16.5 percent of their robbery clearances, and 11.9 percent of their aggravated assault clearances—involved only juveniles. Agencies in nonmetropolitan counties reported that 9.2 percent of their clearances for violent crime involved only juveniles, including 3.3 percent of their murder clearances, 12.9 percent of their forcible rape clearances, 7.5 percent of their robbery clearances, and 9.0 percent of their aggravated assault clearances. (Table 28)

PROPERTY CRIME

National Clearances

Law enforcement agencies throughout the nation collectively cleared 15.8 percent of property crime offenses in 2006, including 12.6 percent of burglary offenses, 17.4 percent of larceny-theft offenses, 12.6 percent of motor vehicle theft offenses, and 18.0 percent of arson offenses. (Table 25)

Regional Clearances

By region in 2006, agencies in the Northeast cleared the highest percentage of property crimes at 19.0 percent, followed by the South at 16.4 percent, the Midwest at 15.2 percent, and the West at 13.7 percent. Agencies in the Northeast also cleared the highest percentage of burglary offenses at 15.4 percent, followed by the South at 13.4 percent, the West at 11.1 percent, and the Midwest at 10.8 percent. For larceny-theft, the Northeast (20.6 percent) was followed by the South (17.6 percent), the Midwest (17.1 percent), and the West (15.7 percent). The South, at 15.6 percent, cleared the greatest percentage of their motor vehicle theft offenses, followed by the Northeast at 14.5 percent, the Midwest at 12.0 percent, and the West at 9.7 percent. The Northeast cleared the greatest percentage of their arson offenses (22.5 percent), followed by the South (20.6 percent), the Midwest (16.0 percent), and the West (14.8 percent). (Table 26)

Clearances by Population Group

Cities

Law enforcement agencies in cities cleared 15.7 percent of property crimes, 12.1 percent of burglaries, 17.7 percent of larceny-thefts, 11.6 percent of motor vehicle thefts, and 17.3 percent of arsons in 2006. (Table 25)

Agencies in cities with populations of 10,000 to 24,999 cleared the largest percentage of their property crimes (19.5 percent), while agencies in cities with populations of 500,000 to 999,999 cleared the smallest percentage of their property crimes (11.0 percent). For burglaries, cities with under 10,000 inhabitants cleared the largest percentage of their offenses, at 16.5 percent, while cities with 1,000,000 or more inhabitants cleared the smallest percentage of their offenses, at 8.5 percent. Cities with 10,000 to 24,999 inhabitants cleared the greatest percentage of their larceny-theft offenses (20.8 percent), and cities with 500,000 to 999,999 inhabitants cleared the lowest percentage of their larceny-theft offenses (12.3 percent). For motor vehicle theft and arson, cities with under 10,000 inhabitants cleared the highest percentages of their offenses, at 24.0 percent and 26.2 percent, respectively; cities with 1,000,000 or more inhabitants cleared the lowest percentages of their offenses, at 7.9 percent and 10.9 percent, respectively. (Table 25)

Metropolitan Counties and Nonmetropolitan Counties

Metropolitan county law enforcement agencies reported that 15.6 percent of their property crimes, 13.3 percent of their burglaries, 16.5 percent of their larceny-thefts, 15.3 percent of their motor vehicle thefts, and 18.3 percent of their arsons were cleared by arrest or exceptional means. Agencies in nonmetropolitan counties reported clearing 16.8 percent of their property crimes, 15.4 percent of their burglaries, 16.5 percent of their larceny-thefts, 24.5 percent of their motor vehicle thefts, and 24.6 percent of their arsons. (Table 25)

Clearances by Classification and Type

For property crime clearances grouped by classification and type, data showed that the highest percentage of burglary clearances in the nation in 2006 (13.9 percent) were of offenses that involved unlawful entry of structures. Law enforcement agencies cleared 11.8 percent of burglaries in which force was used to enter structures and 10.3 percent of attempted burglary offenses. For motor vehicle theft, agencies cleared 12.8 percent of motor vehicle theft offenses involving automobiles and 10.7 percent of motor vehicle theft offenses involving trucks and buses. (Table 27)

In 2006, 22.5 percent of structural arson offenses were cleared by arrest or exceptional means, while 8.2 percent of mobile arson offenses and 19.4 percent of other arson crimes were cleared. (Table 27)

Clearances and Juveniles

When an offender under 18 years of age is cited to appear in juvenile court or before other juvenile authorities, the UCR Program considers the incident for which the juvenile is being held responsible to be cleared by arrest, although a physical arrest may not have occurred. In addition, clearances that include both adult and juvenile offenders are classified as clearances for crimes committed by adults. Thus, juvenile clearance data may not reflect the total involvement of youthful offenders in crime.

In 2006, 19.1 percent of property crime clearances, 18.1 percent of burglary clearances, 19.8 percent of larceny-theft clearances, 16.1 percent of motor vehicle theft clearances, and 40.2 percent of arson clearances nationwide exclusively involved juveniles. (Table 28) Clearances of juveniles for arson were proportionally higher than those for any other crime.

In cities collectively, 20.6 percent of the clearances for property crime, 18.8 percent of clearances for burglary, 20.7 percent of clearances for larceny-theft, 16.6 percent of clearances for motor vehicle theft, and 43.0 percent of clearances for arson involved juveniles only. Among the population groups labeled *city*, the percentages of clearances involving only juveniles for overall property crime ranged from a low of 14.4 percent in cities with populations of 1,000,000 and over to a high of 26.1 percent in cities with populations of 100,000 to 249,999. Law enforcement in metropolitan counties reported 16.3 percent of property crime clearances, 17.3 percent of burglary clearances, 16.3 percent of larceny-theft clearances, 14.5 percent of motor vehicle theft clearances, and 37.3 percent of arson clearances involved persons under 18 years of age. In nonmetropolitan counties, 13.8 percent of property crime clearances, 14.3 percent of burglary clearances, 13.5 percent of larceny-theft clearances, 14.2 percent of motor vehicle theft clearances, and 24.4 percent of arson clearances involved juveniles exclusively. (Table 28)

Of clearances for structural arsons, 39.5 percent involved only juveniles. Approximately 20.8 percent of clearances for mobile arsons and 53.0 percent of other property type arsons involved only juveniles. (Unpublished Expanded Arson Table 2; see Appendix I for more information.)

Table 25. Percent of Offenses Cleared by Arrest or Exceptional Means, by Population Group, 2006

(Number, percent.)

Population group		Violent crime	Murder and nonnegligent manslaughter	Forcible rape	Robbery	Aggravated assault	Property crime
TOTAL ALL AGENCIES:	Offenses known	1,240,985	14,948	80,440	384,844	760,753	8,851,465
	Percent cleared by arrest	44.3	60.7	40.9	25.2	54.0	15.8
TOTAL CITIES	Offenses known	970,010	11,462	59,113	331,106	568,329	6,851,214
	Percent cleared by arrest	42.0	59.3	39.3	24.8	52.0	15.7
GROUP I (250,000 and over)	Offenses known	420,698	6,051	18,652	168,676	227,319	2,184,592
	Percent cleared by arrest	35.5	53.7	39.8	21.5	45.2	12.0
1,000,000 and over (Group I subset)	Offenses known	131,210	2,023	5,668	57,838	65,681	650,001
	Percent cleared by arrest	32.6	59.2	41.4	21.8	40.6	11.2
500,000 to 999,999 (Group I subset)	Offenses known	155,761	2,174	6,818	59,694	87,075	832,547
	Percent cleared by arrest	35.6	52.3	36.1	20.4	45.7	11.0
250,000 to 499,999 (Group I subset)	Offenses known	133,727	1,854	6,166	51,144	74,563	702,044
	Percent cleared by arrest	38.3	49.5	42.4	22.4	48.6	14.0
GROUP II (100,000 to 249,999)	Offenses known	168,765	1,981	10,269	60,056	96,459	1,183,719
	Percent cleared by arrest	40.8	60.9	40.4	24.5	50.6	14.9
GROUP III (50,000 to 99,999)	Offenses known	136,613	1,318	9,500	43,501	82,294	1,073,801
	Percent cleared by arrest	45.0	63.8	37.0	27.8	54.7	17.3
GROUP IV (25,000 to 49,999)	Offenses known	96,807	857	7,678	27,703	60,569	877,422
	Percent cleared by arrest	49.0	68.8	37.4	31.1	58.4	18.1
GROUP V (10,000 to 24,999)	Offenses known	78,824	720	7,072	19,564	51,468	812,047
	Percent cleared by arrest	52.1	73.6	39.5	32.6	60.9	19.5
GROUP VI (under 10,000)	Offenses known	68,303	535	5,942	11,606	50,220	719,633
	Percent cleared by arrest	57.7	71.0	41.7	35.3	64.6	19.0
METROPOLITAN COUNTIES	Offenses known	217,660	2,654	15,382	49,587	150,037	1,572,480
	Percent cleared by arrest	50.7	62.9	45.7	26.9	58.8	15.6
NONMETROPOLITAN COUNTIES	Offenses known	53,315	832	5,945	4,151	42,387	427,771
	Percent cleared by arrest	59.3	73.0	44.9	39.6	62.9	16.8
SUBURBAN AREA[2]	Offenses known	367,678	3,934	27,284	90,147	246,313	3,108,417
	Percent cleared by arrest	50.9	64.7	43.1	28.7	59.7	16.8

Population group		Burglary	Larceny-theft	Motor vehicle theft	Arson[1]	Number of agencies	2006 estimated population
TOTAL ALL AGENCIES:	Offenses known	1,956,175	5,810,638	1,084,652	65,939	13,760	260,278,125
	Percent cleared by arrest	12.6	17.4	12.6	18.0		
TOTAL CITIES	Offenses known	1,423,646	4,565,971	861,597	48,166	9,748	170,276,178
	Percent cleared by arrest	12.1	17.7	11.6	17.3		
GROUP I (250,000 and over)	Offenses known	479,714	1,298,083	406,795	18,436	69	42,564,096
	Percent cleared by arrest	9.5	13.8	9.1	13.2		
1,000,000 and over (Group I subset)	Offenses known	133,861	380,352	135,788	6,120	8	14,058,014
	Percent cleared by arrest	8.5	13.3	7.9	10.9		
500,000 to 999,999 (Group I subset)	Offenses known	189,369	494,519	148,659	6,212	23	15,042,706
	Percent cleared by arrest	8.7	12.3	9.4	15.3		
250,000 to 499,999 (Group I subset)	Offenses known	156,484	423,212	122,348	6,104	38	13,463,376
	Percent cleared by arrest	11.4	16.1	10.1	13.4		
GROUP II (100,000 to 249,999)	Offenses known	250,789	775,383	157,547	7,575	179	26,835,997
	Percent cleared by arrest	11.3	16.9	10.5	15.0		
GROUP III (50,000 to 99,999)	Offenses known	224,212	729,912	119,677	7,624	419	28,813,634
	Percent cleared by arrest	12.8	19.6	11.8	18.4		
GROUP IV (25,000 to 49,999)	Offenses known	173,592	627,093	76,737	5,472	733	25,344,757
	Percent cleared by arrest	13.0	19.9	14.5	19.1		
GROUP V (10,000 to 24,999)	Offenses known	159,979	592,748	59,320	4,752	1,615	25,598,860
	Percent cleared by arrest	15.1	20.8	18.2	25.2		
GROUP VI (under 10,000)	Offenses known	135,360	542,752	41,521	4,307	6,733	21,118,834
	Percent cleared by arrest	16.5	19.3	24.0	26.2		
METROPOLITAN COUNTIES	Offenses known	394,870	988,811	188,799	13,654	1,676	64,185,500
	Percent cleared by arrest	13.3	16.5	15.3	18.3		
NONMETROPOLITAN COUNTIES	Offenses known	137,659	255,856	34,256	4,119	2,336	25,816,447
	Percent cleared by arrest	15.4	16.5	24.5	24.6		
SUBURBAN AREA[2]	Offenses known	685,507	2,103,341	319,569	22,895	7,243	114,780,554
	Percent cleared by arrest	13.7	18.1	15.4	19.8		

[1] Not all agencies submit reports for arson to the FBI. As a result, the number of reports the FBI uses to compute the percent of offenses cleared for arson is less than the number it uses to compute the percent of offenses cleared for all other offenses.

[2] Suburban area includes law enforcement agencies in cities with less than 50,000 inhabitants and county law enforcement agencies that are within a Metropolitan Statistical Area. Suburban area excludes all metropolitan agencies associated with a principal city. The agencies associated with suburban areas also appear in other groups within this table.

Table 26. Percent of Offenses Cleared by Arrest or Exceptional Means, by Region and Geographic Division, 2006

(Number, percent.)

Geographic region/division		Violent crime	Murder and nonnegligent manslaughter	Forcible rape	Robbery	Aggravated assault
TOTAL ALL AGENCIES:	Offenses known	1,240,985	14,948	80,440	384,844	760,753
	Percent cleared by arrest	44.3	60.7	40.9	25.2	54.0
NORTHEAST	Offenses known	155,536	1,810	9,626	56,044	88,056
	Percent cleared by arrest	48.4	61.4	45.0	28.4	61.3
NEW ENGLAND	Offenses known	43,505	351	3,235	12,120	27,799
	Percent cleared by arrest	46.2	56.1	33.6	24.8	56.9
MIDDLE ATLANTIC	Offenses known	112,031	1,459	6,391	43,924	60,257
	Percent cleared by arrest	49.3	62.6	50.7	29.4	63.3
MIDWEST	Offenses known	196,174	2,336	16,199	60,678	116,961
	Percent cleared by arrest	38.4	51.9	31.8	21.0	48.1
EAST NORTH CENTRAL	Offenses known	127,263	1,658	11,762	44,247	69,596
	Percent cleared by arrest	33.8	46.1	30.1	19.8	43.0
WEST NORTH CENTRAL	Offenses known	68,911	678	4,437	16,431	47,365
	Percent cleared by arrest	46.9	66.1	36.3	24.2	55.5
SOUTH	Offenses known	571,133	6,987	33,681	164,820	365,645
	Percent cleared by arrest	46.4	65.9	45.5	26.4	55.1
SOUTH ATLANTIC	Offenses known	318,720	3,779	16,293	95,288	203,360
	Percent cleared by arrest	47.9	64.2	49.7	26.9	57.3
EAST SOUTH CENTRAL	Offenses known	73,040	917	4,947	21,223	45,953
	Percent cleared by arrest	45.1	68.3	36.2	24.7	55.0
WEST SOUTH CENTRAL	Offenses known	179,373	2,291	12,441	48,309	116,332
	Percent cleared by arrest	44.1	67.5	43.7	25.9	51.3
WEST	Offenses known	318,142	3,815	20,934	103,302	190,091
	Percent cleared by arrest	42.2	56.4	38.7	24.2	52.1
MOUNTAIN	Offenses known	90,580	1,073	7,723	23,557	58,227
	Percent cleared by arrest	42.7	59.8	32.6	21.2	52.4
PACIFIC	Offenses known	227,562	2,742	13,211	79,745	131,864
	Percent cleared by arrest	42.0	55.0	42.3	25.0	51.9

Geographic region/division		Property crime	Burglary	Larceny-theft	Motor vehicle theft	Arson[1]	Number of agencies	2006 estimated population
TOTAL ALL AGENCIES:	Offenses known	8,851,465	1,956,175	5,810,638	1,084,652	65,939	13,760	260,278,125
	Percent cleared by arrest	15.8	12.6	17.4	12.6	18.0		
NORTHEAST	Offenses known	1,016,894	200,501	716,830	99,563	7,104	2,882	43,895,527
	Percent cleared by arrest	19.0	15.4	20.6	14.5	22.5		
NEW ENGLAND	Offenses known	315,431	64,187	219,714	31,530	1,889	834	13,478,777
	Percent cleared by arrest	14.2	12.0	15.3	10.4	19.1		
MIDDLE ATLANTIC	Offenses known	701,463	136,314	497,116	68,033	5,215	2,048	30,416,750
	Percent cleared by arrest	21.1	16.9	22.9	16.4	23.7		
MIDWEST	Offenses known	1,617,882	347,773	1,100,943	169,166	13,896	3,433	47,475,585
	Percent cleared by arrest	15.2	10.8	17.1	12.0	16.0		
EAST NORTH CENTRAL	Offenses known	1,014,429	229,868	669,257	115,304	8,884	1,633	29,043,228
	Percent cleared by arrest	14.2	9.9	16.3	10.6	14.5		
WEST NORTH CENTRAL	Offenses known	603,453	117,905	431,686	53,862	5,012	1,800	18,432,357
	Percent cleared by arrest	16.9	12.5	18.4	14.9	18.6		
SOUTH	Offenses known	3,903,094	930,054	2,577,729	395,311	23,718	5,544	102,628,486
	Percent cleared by arrest	16.4	13.4	17.6	15.6	20.6		
SOUTH ATLANTIC	Offenses known	2,039,482	477,258	1,343,453	218,771	12,057	2,796	55,059,190
	Percent cleared by arrest	17.5	15.1	18.6	16.2	21.9		
EAST SOUTH CENTRAL	Offenses known	523,261	133,398	343,291	46,572	2,339	1,071	14,246,982
	Percent cleared by arrest	15.9	11.4	17.5	16.7	20.9		
WEST SOUTH CENTRAL	Offenses known	1,340,351	319,398	890,985	129,968	9,322	1,677	33,322,314
	Percent cleared by arrest	14.8	11.6	16.1	14.2	18.9		
WEST	Offenses known	2,313,595	477,847	1,415,136	420,612	21,221	1,901	66,278,527
	Percent cleared by arrest	13.7	11.1	15.7	9.7	14.8		
MOUNTAIN	Offenses known	745,583	154,462	469,147	121,974	5,362	765	19,991,251
	Percent cleared by arrest	14.1	9.3	16.6	10.6	19.7		
PACIFIC	Offenses known	1,568,012	323,385	945,989	298,638	15,859	1,136	46,287,276
	Percent cleared by arrest	13.5	12.0	15.3	9.3	13.2		

[1] Not all agencies submit reports for arson to the FBI. As a result, the number of reports the FBI uses to compute the percent of offenses cleared for arson is less than the number it uses to compute the percent of offenses cleared for all other offenses.

Table 27. Percent of Offenses Cleared by Arrest or Exceptional Means, by Population Group, 2006

(Number, percent.)

Population group		Forcible rape		Robbery				Aggravated assault			
		Rape by force	Assault to rape-attempts	Firearm	Knife or cutting instrument	Other weapon	Strong-arm	Firearm	Knife or cutting instrument	Other weapon	Hands, fists, feet, etc.
TOTAL ALL AGENCIES:	Offenses known	66,717	5,951	143,148	29,946	31,303	134,886	146,364	123,792	217,803	170,819
	Percent cleared by arrest	39.5	42.0	19.7	28.0	26.9	29.0	37.9	60.7	54.3	61.1
TOTAL CITIES	Offenses known	49,975	4,740	124,200	26,398	27,232	120,437	118,439	99,803	168,938	121,946
	Percent cleared by arrest	38.3	39.9	19.5	27.4	26.3	28.5	35.0	59.6	52.7	60.2
GROUP I (250,000 and over)	Offenses known	15,321	1,997	69,850	12,769	13,117	58,119	63,291	40,184	70,170	30,654
	Percent cleared by arrest	38.9	36.8	17.0	23.2	22.4	24.5	30.0	55.3	47.4	49.2
1,000,000 and over (Group I subset)	Offenses known	4,796	872	26,598	5,530	4,620	21,090	21,050	13,460	21,401	9,770
	Percent cleared by arrest	41.9	39.1	17.2	21.8	23.5	27.2	27.7	50.2	44.3	47.2
500,000 to 999,999 (Group I subset)	Offenses known	5,264	649	23,479	4,019	4,875	17,539	22,626	14,503	25,856	10,135
	Percent cleared by arrest	33.5	33.3	14.6	23.3	21.3	20.2	29.8	54.9	45.0	44.4
250,000 to 499,999 (Group I subset)	Offenses known	5,261	476	19,773	3,220	3,622	19,490	19,615	12,221	22,913	10,749
	Percent cleared by arrest	41.7	37.4	19.6	25.3	22.5	25.5	32.7	61.3	53.1	55.4
GROUP II (100,000 to 249,999)	Offenses known	8,375	683	21,672	4,765	4,885	21,276	20,146	17,386	30,330	16,043
	Percent cleared by arrest	39.1	40.4	20.3	27.4	25.9	27.9	35.0	59.7	52.3	58.4
GROUP III (50,000 to 99,999)	Offenses known	8,139	607	13,836	3,728	3,755	17,624	14,054	15,100	24,335	19,754
	Percent cleared by arrest	36.2	41.0	21.3	29.7	30.5	32.0	37.2	60.8	56.7	61.2
GROUP IV (25,000 to 49,999)	Offenses known	6,700	500	8,556	2,489	2,638	10,706	8,703	10,638	17,618	17,221
	Percent cleared by arrest	36.2	41.2	25.3	34.7	30.0	34.4	45.8	64.1	57.1	63.7
GROUP V (10,000 to 24,999)	Offenses known	6,202	447	6,493	1,691	1,839	7,621	6,714	8,779	14,151	16,525
	Percent cleared by arrest	39.0	41.8	27.3	38.1	34.7	36.8	47.5	65.3	59.7	67.0
GROUP VI (under 10,000)	Offenses known	5,238	506	3,793	956	998	5,091	5,531	7,716	12,334	21,749
	Percent cleared by arrest	40.6	47.2	28.7	38.2	37.6	39.5	54.6	67.3	61.6	68.0
METROPOLITAN COUNTIES	Offenses known	11,398	853	17,474	3,179	3,519	13,035	21,121	18,497	37,765	33,095
	Percent cleared by arrest	42.5	50.2	20.0	30.7	29.9	31.7	46.6	64.6	59.3	63.9
NONMETROPOLITAN COUNTIES	Offenses known	5,344	358	1,474	369	552	1,414	6,804	5,492	11,100	15,778
	Percent cleared by arrest	43.8	49.7	34.4	49.1	35.9	43.3	61.2	67.8	61.4	62.3
SUBURBAN AREA[2]	Offenses known	21,609	1,644	30,276	6,523	7,122	28,493	32,610	33,333	63,713	65,067
	Percent cleared by arrest	40.6	47.9	21.8	33.0	31.3	33.5	46.8	65.1	59.5	65.3

[2] Suburban area includes law enforcement agencies in cities with less than 50,000 inhabitants and county law enforcement agencies that are within a Metropolitan Statistical Area. Suburban area excludes all metropolitan agencies associated with a principal city. The agencies associated with suburban areas also appear in other groups within this table.

Table 27. Percent of Offenses Cleared by Arrest or Exceptional Means, by Population Group, 2006 *(Contd.)*

(Number, percent.)

Population group		Burglary			Motor vehicle theft			Arson[1]			Number of agencies	2006 estimated population
		Forcible entry	Unlaw-ful entry	At-tempted forcible entry	Autos	Trucks and buses	Other vehicles	Struc-ture	Mobile	Other		
TOTAL ALL AGENCIES:	Offenses known	1,061,741	569,166	113,712	728,191	170,385	82,549	25,595	17,361	17,925	13,159	238,918,460
	Percent cleared by arrest	11.8	13.9	10.3	12.8	10.7	10.3	22.5	8.2	19.4		
TOTAL CITIES	Offenses known	790,086	419,714	87,936	600,932	137,098	55,914	19,274	12,408	13,139	9,419	159,266,331
	Percent cleared by arrest	11.3	13.6	10.2	12.0	9.8	9.3	21.7	7.7	19.2		
GROUP I (250,000 and over)	Offenses known	293,246	114,345	27,145	272,993	80,426	22,800	6,864	6,147	3,834	62	39,101,896
	Percent cleared by arrest	8.5	10.8	8.7	9.6	7.4	6.6	18.0	4.6	16.7		
1,000,000 and over (Group I subset)	Offenses known	91,080	35,901	6,880	89,034	38,542	8,212	2,059	2,580	1,481	8	14,058,014
	Percent cleared by arrest	7.9	9.6	10.7	9.4	5.1	5.3	18.8	3.9	12.1		
500,000 to 999,999 (Group I subset)	Offenses known	109,522	38,578	12,312	98,535	20,895	9,710	2,193	1,603	1,197	20	12,808,359
	Percent cleared by arrest	7.4	8.8	7.2	9.4	9.6	5.0	18.5	6.1	18.0		
250,000 to 499,999 (Group I subset)	Offenses known	92,644	39,866	7,953	85,424	20,989	4,878	2,612	1,964	1,156	34	12,235,523
	Percent cleared by arrest	10.4	13.8	9.3	9.9	9.5	12.0	17.0	4.4	21.1		
GROUP II (100,000 to 249,999)	Offenses known	136,465	69,487	15,325	110,430	22,293	8,510	3,037	1,948	1,975	162	24,250,319
	Percent cleared by arrest	10.7	13.1	9.4	10.5	9.9	8.0	17.8	7.1	16.8		
GROUP III (50,000 to 99,999)	Offenses known	118,718	71,947	14,494	87,970	14,865	8,016	3,145	1,751	2,383	391	26,858,143
	Percent cleared by arrest	11.9	14.5	10.7	11.8	12.0	8.6	21.6	8.1	21.4		
GROUP IV (25,000 to 49,999)	Offenses known	91,392	57,048	11,570	56,887	7,805	6,396	2,021	1,069	2,065	699	24,071,954
	Percent cleared by arrest	12.5	13.5	10.8	14.4	14.9	11.6	25.4	9.7	16.9		
GROUP V (10,000 to 24,999)	Offenses known	80,971	55,789	10,370	42,974	6,834	5,232	2,088	844	1,529	1,541	24,397,493
	Percent cleared by arrest	14.9	16.3	11.5	19.0	17.2	13.7	28.8	17.3	24.0		
GROUP VI (under 10,000)	Offenses known	69,294	51,098	9,032	29,678	4,875	4,960	2,119	649	1,353	6,564	20,586,526
	Percent cleared by arrest	16.9	16.6	12.7	25.1	22.3	17.7	28.6	21.0	24.4		
METROPOLITAN COUNTIES	Offenses known	187,830	107,998	19,688	106,615	28,024	19,717	4,374	4,112	3,705	1,500	54,711,611
	Percent cleared by arrest	12.5	14.4	10.4	15.2	12.8	10.8	24.3	8.0	18.8		
NONMETROPOLITAN COUNTIES	Offenses known	83,825	41,454	6,088	20,644	5,263	6,918	1,947	841	1,081	2,240	24,940,518
	Percent cleared by arrest	15.5	15.2	11.9	26.4	23.8	16.7	27.1	16.6	22.8		
SUBURBAN AREA[2]	Offenses known	329,065	209,716	39,114	202,078	41,655	30,646	8,082	5,763	6,970	6,844	102,764,718
	Percent cleared by arrest	13.0	14.7	10.8	15.4	13.5	11.5	25.4	9.6	19.4		

[1] Not all agencies submit reports for arson to the FBI. As a result, the number of reports the FBI uses to compute the percent of offenses cleared for arson is less than the number it uses to compute the percent of offenses cleared for all other offenses. Agencies must report arson clearances by detailed property classification as specified on the Monthly Return of Arson Offenses Known to Law Enforcement to be included in this table; therefore, clearances in this table may differ from other clearance tables.

[2] Suburban area includes law enforcement agencies in cities with less than 50,000 inhabitants and county law enforcement agencies that are within a Metropolitan Statistical Area. Suburban area excludes all metropolitan agencies associated with a principal city. The agencies associated with suburban areas also appear in other groups within this table.

Table 28. Number of Offenses Cleared by Arrest or Exceptional Means Involving Persons Under 18 Years of Age, by Population Group, 2006

(Number, percent.)

Population group		Violent crime	Murder and non-negligent man-slaughter	Forcible rape	Robbery	Aggra-vated assault	Property crime	Burglary	Larceny-theft	Motor vehicle theft	Arson[1]	Number of agencies	2006 estimated population
TOTAL ALL AGENCIES:	Total clearances	463,182	7,798	28,080	82,188	345,116	1,223,700	212,768	892,686	118,246	10,816	12,797	233,121,330
	Percent under 18	12.6	5.6	11.7	16.6	11.9	19.1	18.1	19.8	16.1	40.2		
TOTAL CITIES	Total clearances	353,981	5,881	20,442	71,207	256,451	970,796	153,162	728,468	89,166	7,737	9,214	155,374,941
	Percent under 18	12.9	5.9	11.0	16.8	12.1	20.0	18.8	20.7	16.6	43.0		
GROUP I (250,000 and over)	Total clearances	127,963	2,744	6,564	31,440	87,215	231,117	38,949	158,780	33,388	2,206	61	38,520,366
	Percent under 18	11.4	6.3	8.3	15.8	10.2	16.6	15.7	17.1	15.3	38.1		
1,000,000 and over (Group I subset)	Total clearances	42,821	1,197	2,349	12,604	26,671	72,675	11,392	50,505	10,778	668	8	14,058,014
	Percent under 18	11.2	5.6	8.0	15.3	9.7	14.4	13.4	14.9	13.1	29.6		
500,000 to 999,999 (Group I subset)	Total clearances	39,409	706	1,844	8,363	28,496	71,563	11,696	48,307	11,560	758	19	12,226,829
	Percent under 18	12.2	5.9	8.3	17.2	11.2	17.8	18.0	18.0	16.5	45.0		
250,000 to 499,999 (Group I subset)	Total clearances	45,733	841	2,371	10,473	32,048	86,879	15,861	59,968	11,050	780	34	12,235,523
	Percent under 18	10.9	7.5	8.7	15.4	9.7	17.4	15.5	18.2	16.2	38.6		
GROUP II (100,000 to 249,999)	Total clearances	58,726	1,028	3,455	12,626	41,617	162,937	27,019	121,027	14,891	1,044	160	23,895,543
	Percent under 18	13.2	5.8	10.1	18.5	12.1	26.1	27.3	26.3	22.3	44.8		
GROUP III (50,000 to 99,999)	Total clearances	53,891	766	3,107	10,523	39,495	166,109	25,446	128,188	12,475	1,332	378	26,075,063
	Percent under 18	13.9	5.6	13.0	17.6	13.1	21.1	15.9	22.7	16.3	42.9		
GROUP IV (25,000 to 49,999)	Total clearances	41,775	540	2,590	7,373	31,272	143,594	19,941	113,804	9,849	969	681	23,498,333
	Percent under 18	14.5	7.2	13.9	18.5	13.7	21.3	18.3	22.2	17.2	49.1		
GROUP V (10,000 to 24,999)	Total clearances	35,410	451	2,448	5,543	26,968	139,823	21,097	109,293	9,433	1,114	1,470	23,256,780
	Percent under 18	13.9	5.5	13.0	16.2	13.7	18.7	18.1	19.1	14.5	48.0		
GROUP VI (under 10,000)	Total clearances	36,216	352	2,278	3,702	29,884	127,216	20,710	97,376	9,130	1,072	6,464	20,128,856
	Percent under 18	13.5	2.6	12.2	15.3	13.5	16.9	18.4	16.9	14.3	40.5		
METROPOLITAN COUNTIES	Total clearances	80,732	1,368	5,173	9,537	64,654	187,470	40,258	125,786	21,426	2,135	1,426	53,651,935
	Percent under 18	12.4	5.1	13.8	16.5	11.9	16.3	17.3	16.3	14.5	37.3		
NONMETROPOL-ITAN COUNTIES	Total clearances	28,469	549	2,465	1,444	24,011	65,434	19,348	38,432	7,654	944	2,157	24,094,454
	Percent under 18	9.2	3.3	12.9	7.5	9.0	13.8	14.3	13.5	14.2	24.4		
SUBURBAN AREA[2]	Total clearances	146,311	2,128	9,297	20,002	114,884	432,853	75,704	318,095	39,054	4,002	6,641	100,042,470
	Percent under 18	13.7	5.6	13.5	17.6	13.2	18.1	18.0	18.5	14.7	43.0		

[1] Not all agencies submit reports for arson to the FBI. As a result, the number of reports the FBI uses to compute the percent of offenses cleared for arson is less than the number it uses to compute the percent of offenses cleared for all other offenses.

[2] Suburban area includes law enforcement agencies in cities with less than 50,000 inhabitants and county law enforcement agencies that are within a Metropolitan Statistical Area. Suburban area excludes all metropolitan agencies associated with a principal city. The agencies associated with suburban areas also appear in other groups within this table.

SECTION IV:
PERSONS ARRESTED

PERSONS ARRESTED

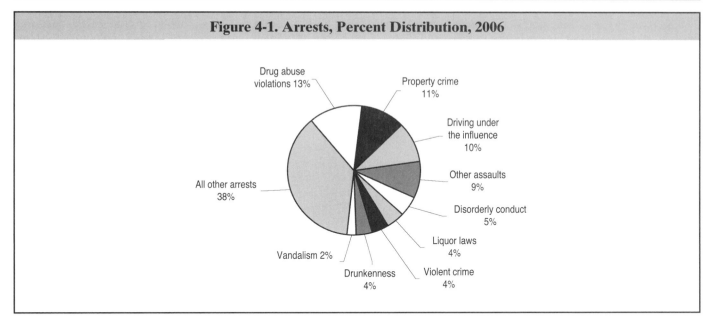

Figure 4-1. Arrests, Percent Distribution, 2006

In the Uniform Crime Reporting (UCR) Program, one arrest is counted for each separate instance in which an individual is arrested, cited, or summoned for criminal acts in Part I and Part II crimes. (See Appendix II for additional information concerning Part I and Part II crimes.) One person may be arrested multiple times during the year; as a result, the arrest figures in this section should not be taken as the total number of individuals arrested. Instead, it provides the number of arrest occurrences reported by law enforcement. Information regarding the UCR Program's statistical methodology and table construction can be found in Appendix I.

National Volume, Trends, and Rates

In 2006, the UCR Program estimated that there were over 14.3 million (14,380,370) arrests in the United States for all criminal offenses (except traffic violations). Law enforcement made an estimated 1.5 million arrests (10.7 percent of all arrests) for property crimes and 611,523 arrests (4.3 percent of all arrests) for violent crimes. More arrests were made for drug abuse violations (an estimated 1.9 million arrests and 13.1 percent of all arrests) than for any other offense. (Table 29)

The estimated overall arrest rate of in the nation in 2006 was 4,832.5 arrests per 100,000 inhabitants. Arrests for violent crimes were measured at a rate of 207.0 arrests per 100,000 inhabitants; for property crimes, the arrest rate was 524.5. (Table 30)

A comparison of arrest figures from 2005 to 2006 revealed a 0.9 percent increase. Arrests for violent crimes rose 0.3 percent, while arrests for property crimes fell 5.4 percent during the 2-year period. An examination of the 5-year and 10-year arrest trends showed that the total number of arrests in 2006 rose 3.7 percent from the 2002 total. Arrests for violent crimes showed a 1.0 percent increase

from 2002 to 2006, while property crimes showed a 5.8 percent decrease. In the 10-year trend data (1997 to 2006), the number of arrests showed a steeper decline (4.7 percent). For property crimes, the number of arrests fell 24.5 percent, while arrests for violent crimes fell 12.2 percent. (Tables 32, 34, and 36)

By Age, Sex, and Race

Law enforcement agencies that contributed arrest data to the UCR Program reported information on the age, sex, and race of the persons they arrested. According to the 2006 data, adults accounted for 84.5 percent of arrestees nationally. (Table 38)

A review of arrest data by age from 2005 to 2006 showed that arrests of adults increased 0.9 percent during this period. Arrests of adults for property crimes fell 5.4 percent, and arrests of adults for violent crimes decreased 0.3 percent over the same time span. The arrest total for juveniles (those under 18 years of age) in 2006 increased 0.8 percent from the 2005 figure. Over the 2-year period, arrests of juveniles for violent crimes rose 3.6 percent; juvenile arrests property crimes dropped 5.5 percent. (Table 36)

By gender, 76.3 percent of arrests in 2006 were of males. Males accounted for 82.2 percent of the total number of arrestees for violent crimes and 68.8 percent of the total number of arrestees for property crimes. Females accounted for 23.7 percent of all arrestees, 17.8 percent of violent crime arrestees, and 31.2 percent of property crime arrestees. (Table 42)

A review of the 2006 arrest data by race indicated that 69.7 percent of arrestees were White, 28.0 percent were Black, and 2.4 percent were of other races (American Indian or Alaskan Native and Asian or Pacific Islander). Of all arrestees for violent crimes, 58.5 percent were White, 39.3 percent were Black, and 2.2 percent were of other races. Of all arrestees for property crimes, 68.2 percent were White, 29.4 percent were Black, and 2.3 percent were of other races. White adults were most commonly arrested for driving under the influence (914,226 arrests) and drug abuse violations (875,101 arrests). Black adults were most frequently arrested for drug abuse violations (483,886 arrests) and other assaults (simple) (306,078 arrests). (Table 43)

Regional Arrest Rates

The UCR Program divides the United States into four regions: the Northeast, the Midwest, the South, and the West. (Appendix III provides a more information about the regions.)

Law enforcement agencies in the Northeast had an overall arrest rate of 3,901.2 arrests per 100,000 inhabitants, well below the national rate (4,832.5 arrests per 100,000 inhabitants). In this region, the arrest rate for violent crimes was 183.7 arrests per 100,000 inhabitants, and for property crime, the arrest rate was 432.7 arrests per 100,000 inhabitants. In the Midwest, law enforcement agencies reported an arrest rate of 5,025.4 arrests per 100,000 inhabitants. The arrest rate for violent crimes was 165.5 and the arrest rate for property crime was 549.8. Law enforcement agencies in the South, the nation's most populous region, reported an arrest rate of 5,406.8 per 100,000 inhabitants. Arrests for violent crime occurred at a rate of 200.3 arrests per 100,000 residents, and for property crime, the arrest rate was 568.1 arrests per 100,000 inhabitants. In the Western states, law enforcement agencies reported an overall arrest rate of 4,676.4 arrests per 100,000 inhabitants. The region's violent crime arrest rate was 257.4, while its property crime arrest rate was 518.7. (Table 30)

Population Groups: Trends and Rates

The national UCR Program aggregates data by various population groups, which include cities, metropolitan counties, and nonmetropolitan counties. Definitions of these groups can be found in Appendix III. The total number of arrests in U.S. cities rose 1.1 percent from 2005 to 2006. The number of arrests for property crimes fell 5.9 percent during the 2-year time frame; however, arrests for violent crimes in cities increased 0.4 percent. (Table 44)

In 2006, law enforcement agencies in cities collectively recorded an arrest rate of 5,229.1 arrests per 100,000 inhab-

itants. The nation's smallest cities, those with under 10,000 inhabitants, had the highest arrest rate among the city population groups with 6,342.7 arrests per 100,000 inhabitants. Law enforcement agencies in cities with 25,000 to 49,999 inhabitants recorded the lowest rate, 4,685.9. In the nation's metropolitan counties, law enforcement agencies reported an arrest rate of 3,859.2 per 100,000 inhabitants. Agencies in nonmetropolitan counties reported an arrest rate of 4,034.5. (Table 31)

By Age, Sex, and Race

In 2006, law enforcement agencies in the nation's cities reported that 83.1 percent of arrests in their jurisdictions were of adults and 16.9 percent of arrests were of juveniles. Adults accounted for 82.3 percent of arrestees for violent crimes, while juveniles accounted for 17.7 percent. Adults made up 73.0 percent of the arrestees for property crimes, and juveniles accounted for 27.0 percent. Of all arrests in the nation's cities in 2006, 46.1 percent were of individuals under 25 years of age. In metropolitan counties, 87.8 percent of arrests were of adults and 12.2 percent of arrests were of juveniles. In nonmetropolitan counties, 91.1 percent of persons arrested were adults and 8.9 percent were juveniles. (Tables 46, 47, 53, and 59)

A breakdown of arrests by gender showed that males accounted for 76.0 percent and females accounted for 24.0 percent of arrestees in the nation's cities in 2006. In metropolitan counties, males composed 77.1 percent of arrestees, and in nonmetropolitan counties, males represented 77.3 percent of all arrestees. (Tables 48, 54, and 60)

By race, 67.0 percent of arrestees in the nation's cities in 2006 were White, 30.5 percent were Black, and 2.5 percent were of other races (American Indian or Alaska Native and Asian or Pacific Islander). Whites accounted for 75.8 percent of arrestees in metropolitan counties in 2005, Blacks made up 23.0 percent of arrestees, and persons of other races made up 1.2 percent of the total. In nonmetropolitan counties, Whites made up 82.7 percent of arrestees, Blacks accounted for 13.7 percent of arrestees, and other races made up 3.6 percent of the total. (Tables 49, 55, and 61)

Of the estimated 611,523 arrests for violent crime in 2006, 447,948 (73.3 percent) were for aggravated assault, 125,605 (20.5 percent) were for robbery, 24,535 (4.0 percent) were for forcible rape, and 13435 (2.2 percent) were for murder.

VIOLENT CRIME

Arrest Trends

A look at 2-year, 5-year, and 10-year trend data showed that the number of arrests for violent crime increased 0.3 percent from 2005 to 2006, increased 1.0 percent from 2002 to 2006, and declined 12.2 percent from 1997 to 2006. The number of adults arrested for violent crime (arrestees age 18 years and over) decreased 0.3 percent from 2005 to 2006, decreased 0.2 percent from 2002 to 2006, and decreased 10.5 percent from 1997 to 2006. The number of juveniles arrested for violent crime (arrestees under 18 years of age) increased 3.6 percent from 2005 to 2006, increased 7.6 percent from 2002 to 2006, and decreased 20.1 percent from 1997 to 2006. (Tables 32, 34, and 36)

The trend data for murder showed that the number of arrests for this offense decreased 3.1 percent from 2005 to 2006, increased 4.5 percent from 2002 to 2006, and decreased 16.5 percent from 1997 to 2006. The number of adults arrested for murder fell 3.7 percent from 2005 to 2006, rose 3.2 percent from 2002 to 2006, and fell 12.5 percent from 1997 to 2006. The number of juveniles arrested for murder rose 3.4 percent from 2005 to 2006, rose 17.8 percent from 2002 to 2006, and fell 42.0 percent from 1997 to 2006. (Tables 32, 34, and 36)

For forcible rape, the 2-year trend data showed that arrests declined 3.8 percent from 2005 to 2006, with adult arrests dropping 2.7 percent and juvenile arrests dropping 9.9 percent. The 5-year trend data showed that arrests declined 11.3 percent from 2002 to 2006; adult arrests dropped 9.7 percent and juvenile arrests declined 19.7 percent during this period. The 10-year trend data showed that forcible rape arrests dropped 20.5 percent from 1997 to 2006, with adult arrests falling 18.4 percent and juvenile arrests falling 30.9 percent. (Tables 32, 34, and 36)

For robbery, the 2-year trend data showed that arrests increased 8.6 percent from 2005 to 2006, with adult arrests rising 5.4 percent and juvenile arrests increasing 18.9 percent. The 5-year trend data showed that total robbery arrests rose 14.9 percent from 2002 to 2006; adult arrests rose 9.0 percent and juvenile arrests rose 34.4 percent during this period. The 10-year trend data showed that arrests dropped 6.8 percent from 1997 to 2006, with adult arrests dropping 2.9 percent and juvenile arrests decreasing 15.9 percent. (Tables 32, 34, and 36)

The aggravated assault trend data showed that the number of arrests for this offense fell 1.3 percent from 2005 to 2006, dropped 1.6 percent from 2002 to 2006, and fell 12.9 percent from 1997 to 2006. The number of adults arrested for aggravated assault percent decreased 1.2 percent from 2005 to 2006, declined 1.6 percent from 2002 to 2006, and declined 11.6 percent from 1997 to 2006. The number of juveniles arrested for aggravated assault dropped 2.0 percent from 2005 to 2006, fell 1.3 percent from 2002 to 2006, and dropped 20.9 percent from 1997 to 2006. (Tables 32, 34, and 36)

Arrest Rates

Law enforcement agencies throughout the nation reported 207.0 violent crime arrests, 4.5 murder arrests, 8.2 forcible rape arrests, 43.2 robbery arrests, and 151.1 aggravated assault arrests per 100,000 inhabitants in 2006. By region, agencies reported violent crime arrest rates of 183.7 in the Northeast, 165.5 in the Midwest, 200.3 in the South, and 257.4 in the West. The regional murder arrest rates were 3.2 in the Northeast, 3.6 in the Midwest, 5.8 in the South, and 4.6 in the West. For forcible rape, the regional arrest rates were 7.5 in the Northeast, 9.1 in the Midwest, 9.0 in the South, and 7.2 in the West. Regional arrest rates for robbery were 48.4 in the Northeast, 35.0 in the Midwest, 43.9 in the South, and 44.7 in the West. For aggravated assault, the regional arrest rates were 124.6 in the Northeast, 117.7 in the Midwest, 141.6 in the South, and 200.8 in the West. (Table 30)

By population group, law enforcement agencies in the nation's cities collectively reported 229.8 violent crime arrests per 100,000 inhabitants in 2006. In the city population groups, cities with 250,000 or more inhabitants reported the highest violent crime arrest rate (312.3) and cities with 10,000 to 24,999 inhabitants reported the lowest violent crime arrest rate (159.4). Cities reported an overall murder arrest rate of 4.8 per 100,000 inhabitants; cities with 250,000 or more inhabitants had the highest murder arrest rate (8.0) and cities with under 10,000 inhabitants and cities with 10,000 to 24,999 inhabitants both had the lowest murder arrest rate (2.5). The collective city forcible rape arrest rate was 8.4 per 100,000 inhabitants, with the highest rate in cities with 250,000 or more inhabitants (10.0) and the lowest rate in cities with 25,000 to 49,999 inhabitants (7.1). The overall robbery arrest rate for cities was 53.0 per 100,000 inhabitants; cities with 250,000 or more inhabitants had the highest robbery arrest rate (86.9) and cities with under 10,000 inhabitants had the lowest robbery arrest rate (22.8). For aggravated assault, the collective city arrest rate was 163.6 per 100,000 inhabitants, with the greatest arrest rate in cities with 250,000 or more inhabitants (207.5) and the lowest arrest rate in cities with 10,000 to 24,999 inhabitants (120.2). (Table 31)

Agencies in metropolitan counties reported a violent crime arrest rate of 165.9 per 100,000 inhabitants, with arrest rates of 4.3 for murder, 7.4 for forcible rape, 24.7 for robbery, and 124.5 for aggravated assault. Agencies in nonmetropolitan counties reported arrest rates of 126.5 for violent crime, 3.2 for murder, 8.3 for forcible rape, 10.2 for robbery, and 104.8 for aggravated assault. (Table 31)

By Age, Sex, and Race

In 2006, most arrestees for violent crime (84.5 percent) were over 18 years of age. By sex, males accounted for 82.2 percent of arrestees for violent crime, 89.1 percent of arrestees for murder, 98.7 percent of arrestees for forcible rape, 88.7 percent of arrestees for robbery, and 79.3 percent of arrestees for aggravated assault. Females accounted for 17.8 percent of violent crime arrestees, 10.9 percent of murder arrestees, 1.3 percent of forcible rape arrestees, 11.3 percent of robbery arrestees, and 20.7 percent of aggravated assault arrestees. (Tables 38 and 42)

By race, 58.5 percent of arrestees for violent crime were White, 39.3 percent were Black, and 2.2 percent were of other races (American Indian or Alaska Native and Asian or Pacific Islander). For murder, 46.9 percent of arrestees were White, 50.9 percent were Black, and 2.2 percent were of other races. For forcible rape, 65.3 percent of arrestees were White, 32.5 percent were Black, and 2.2 percent were

of other races. For robbery, 42.2 percent of arrestees were White, 56.3 percent of arrestees were Black, and 1.6 percent were of other races. For aggravated assault, 63.2 percent of arrestees were White, 34.5 percent of arrestees were Black, and 2.3 percent were of other races. (Table 43)

Of the estimated 1,540,297 arrests for property crimes in 2006, 1,081,157 (70.2 percent) were for larceny-theft, 304,801 (19.8 percent) were for burglary, 137,757 (8.9 percent) were for motor vehicle theft, and 16,582 (1.1 percent) were for arson. (Table 29)

PROPERTY CRIME

Arrest Trends

The 2-year, 5-year, and 10-year trend data showed that the number of arrests for property crime dropped 5.4 percent from 2005 to 2006, decreased 5.8 percent from 2002 to 2006, and declined 24.5 percent from 1997 to 2006. The number of adults arrested for property crime offenses (arrestees age 18 years and over) decreased 5.4 percent from 2005 to 2006, increased 0.8 percent from 2002 to 2006, and decreased 13.7 percent from 1997 to 2006. The number of juveniles arrested for property crime (arrestees under 18 years of age) dropped 5.5 percent from 2005 to 2006, decreased 17.4 percent from 2002 to 2006, and decreased 44.0 percent from 1997 to 2006. (Tables 32, 34, and 36)

The trend data for burglary showed that the number of arrests for this offense increased 1.7 percent from 2005 to 2006, increased 4.4 percent from 2002 to 2006, and decreased 13.7 percent from 1997 to 2006. The number of adults arrested for burglary rose 0.4 percent from 2005 to 2006, rose 8.8 percent from 2002 to 2006, and rose 0.2 percent from 1997 to 2006. The number of juveniles arrested for burglary rose 5.1 percent from 2005 to 2006, decreased 5.8 percent from 2002 to 2006, and fell 37.0 percent from 1997 to 2006. (Tables 32, 34, and 36)

For larceny-theft, the 2-year trend data showed that arrests dropped 7.2 percent from 2005 to 2006, with adult arrests decreasing 6.9 percent and juvenile arrests dropping 8.0 percent. The 5-year trend data showed that total larceny-theft arrests declined 7.9 percent from 2002 to 2006; adult arrests decreased 3.1 percent and juvenile arrests declined 19.3 percent during this period. The 10-year trend data showed that larceny-theft arrests dropped 27.5 percent from 1997 to 2006, with adult arrests falling 18.1 percent and juvenile arrests falling 45.2 percent. (Tables 32, 34, and 36)

For motor vehicle theft, the 2-year trend data showed that arrests declined 6.4 percent from 2005 to 2006, with adult arrests decreasing 5.8 percent and juvenile arrests decreasing 8.3 percent. The 5-year trend data showed that total motor vehicle theft arrests fell 9.1 percent from 2002 to 2006; adult arrests declined 1.0 percent and juvenile arrests fell 27.7 percent during this period. The 10-year trend data showed that arrests dropped 22.7 percent from 1997 to 2006, with adult arrests falling 2.3 percent and juvenile arrests dropping 21.6 percent. (Tables 32, 34, and 36)

The arson trend data showed that the number of arrests for this offense decreased 0.7 percent from 2005 to 2006, fell 4.4 percent from 2002 to 2006, and fell 13.8 percent from 1997 to 2006. The number of adults arrested for arson fell 1.5 percent from 2005 to 2006, declined 3.8 percent from 2002 to 2006, and declined 4.1 percent from 1997 to 2006. The number of juveniles arrested for arson declined by less than one-tenth of one percent from 2005 to 2006, dropped 5.0 percent from 2002 to 2006, and dropped 21.6 percent from 1997 to 2006. (Tables 32, 34, and 36)

Arrest Rates

Law enforcement agencies throughout the nation reported 524.5 property crime arrests, 102.5 burglary arrests, 370.0 larceny-theft arrests, 46.5 motor vehicle theft arrests, and 5.5 arson arrests per 100,000 inhabitants in 2006. By region, agencies reported property crime arrest rates of 432.7 in the Northeast, 549.8 in the Midwest, 568.1 in the South, and 518.7 in the West. The regional burglary arrest rates were 80.4 in the Northeast, 83.8 in the Midwest, 113.7 in the South, and 117.5 in the West. For larceny-theft, the regional arrest rates were 320.2 in the Northeast, 409.5 in the Midwest, 412.9 in the South, and 328.5 in the West. Regional arrest rates for motor vehicle theft were 26.7 in the Northeast, 51.0 in the Midwest, 35.7 in the South, and 67.3 in the West. For arson, the regional arrest rates were 5.5 in the Northeast, 5.5 in the Midwest, 5.8 in the South, and 5.3 in the West. (Table 30)

By population group, law enforcement agencies in the nation's cities collectively reported 609.0 property crime arrests per 100,000 inhabitants in 2006. In the city population groups, cities with 100,000 to 249,999 inhabitants reported the highest property crime arrest rate (661.7) and cities with 10,000 to 24,9999 inhabitants reported the lowest property crime arrest rate (562.1). Cities reported an overall burglary arrest rate of 108.4 per 100,000 inhabitants; cities with 100,000 to 249,999 inhabitants had the highest burglary arrest rate (131.2) and cities with 25,000 to 49,999 inhabitants had the lowest burglary arrest rate (92.4). The collective city larceny-theft arrest rate was 443.1 per 100,000 inhabitants, with the highest rate in cities with 50,000 to 99,999 inhabitants (472.3) and the lowest rate in cities with 250,000 or more inhabitants (416.4). The overall motor vehicle theft arrest rate for cities was 46.5 per 100,000 inhabitants; cities with 250,000 or more inhabitants had the highest motor vehicle theft arrest rate (92.3), and cities with 10,000 to 24,999 inhabitants had the lowest motor vehicle theft arrest rate (28.7). For arson, the collective city arrest rate was 5.7 per 100,000 inhabitants, with the greatest arrest rate in cities with under 10,000 inhabitants (7.3) and the lowest arrest rate in cities with 250,000 or more inhabitants (4.8). (Table 31)

Agencies in metropolitan counties reported a property crime arrest rate of 350.1 per 100,000 inhabitants, with arrest rates of 86.6 for burglary, 220.6 for larceny-theft, 37.8 for motor vehicle theft, and 5.1 for arson. Agencies in nonmetropolitan counties reported arrest rates of 277.2 for property crime, 94.1 for burglary, 152.0 for larceny-theft, 26.2 for motor vehicle theft, and 5.0 for arson. (Table 31)

By Age, Sex, and Race

In 2006, most arrestees for property crime (73.7 percent) were over 18 years of age. By sex, males accounted for 68.8 percent of arrestees for property crime, 85.5 percent of arrestees for burglary, 62.3 percent of arrestees for larceny-theft, 82.3 percent of arrestees for motor vehicle theft, and 83.0 percent of arrestees for arson. Females accounted for 31.2 percent of property crime arrestees, 14.5 percent of burglary arrestees, 37.7 percent of larceny-theft arrestees, 17.7 percent of motor vehicle theft arrestees, and 17.0 percent of arson arrestees. (Tables 38 and 42)

By race, 68.2 percent of arrestees for property crime were White, 29.4 percent were Black, and 2.4 percent were of other races (American Indian or Alaska Native and Asian or Pacific Islander). For burglary, 69.0 percent of arrestees were White, 29.2 percent were Black, and 1.9 percent were of other races. For larceny-theft, 68.6 percent of arrestees were White, 28.9 percent were Black, and 2.5 percent were of other races. For motor vehicle theft, 62.7 percent of arrestees were White, 34.9 percent of arrestees were Black, and 2.4 percent were of other races. For arson, 76.0 percent of arrestees were White, 21.6 percent of arrestees were Black, and 2.4 percent were of other races. (Table 43)

Table 29. Estimated Number of Arrests, 2006

(Number.)

Offense	Arrests
TOTAL[1]	14,380,370
Murder and nonnegligent manslaughter	13,435
Forcible rape	24,535
Robbery	125,605
Aggravated assault	447,948
Burglary	304,801
Larceny-theft	1,081,157
Motor vehicle theft	137,757
Arson	16,582
Violent crime[2]	611,523
Property crime[2]	1,540,297
Other assaults	1,305,757
Forgery and counterfeiting	108,823
Fraud	280,693
Embezzlement	20,012
Stolen property; buying, receiving, possessing	122,722
Vandalism	300,679
Weapons; carrying, possessing, etc.	200,782
Prostitution and commercialized vice	79,673
Sex offenses (except forcible rape and prostitution)	87,252
Drug abuse violations	1,889,810
Gambling	12,307
Offenses against the family and children	131,491
Driving under the influence	1,460,498
Liquor laws	645,734
Drunkenness	553,188
Disorderly conduct	703,504
Vagrancy	36,471
All other offenses	4,022,068
Suspicion	2,482
Curfew and loitering law violations	152,907
Runaways	114,179

[1] Does not include suspicion.
[2] Violent crimes are offenses of murder, forcible rape, robbery, and aggravated assault. Property crimes are offenses of burglary, larceny-theft, motor vehicle theft, and arson.

Table 30. Number and Rate of Arrests, by Geographic Region, 2006

(Number, rate per 100,000.)

Offense charged	United States total (11,250 agencies; population 216,686,722)		Northeast (2,785 agencies; population 40,267,285)		Midwest (2,894 agencies; population 44,274,352)		South (3,904 agencies; population 67,897,508)		West (1,667 agencies; population 64,247,577)	
	Total	Rate	Total	Rate	Total	Rate	Total	Rate	Total	Rate
TOTAL[1]	10,471,387	4,832.5	1,570,891	3,901.2	2,224,956	5,025.4	3,671,094	5,406.8	3,004,446	4,676.4
Murder and nonnegligent manslaughter	9,815	4.5	1,280	3.2	1,599	3.6	3,967	5.8	2,969	4.6
Forcible rape	17,792	8.2	3,028	7.5	4,030	9.1	6,107	9.0	4,627	7.2
Robbery	93,527	43.2	19,509	48.4	15,510	35.0	29,794	43.9	28,714	44.7
Aggravated assault	327,478	151.1	50,174	124.6	52,119	117.7	96,145	141.6	129,040	200.8
Burglary	222,192	102.5	32,364	80.4	37,112	83.8	77,205	113.7	75,511	117.5
Larceny-theft	801,633	370.0	128,929	320.2	181,302	409.5	280,373	412.9	211,029	328.5
Motor vehicle theft	100,775	46.5	10,735	26.7	22,562	51.0	24,213	35.7	43,265	67.3
Arson	12,002	5.5	2,203	5.5	2,427	5.5	3,948	5.8	3,424	5.3
Violent crime[2]	448,612	207.0	73,991	183.7	73,258	165.5	136,013	200.3	165,350	257.4
Property crime[2]	1,136,602	524.5	174,231	432.7	243,403	549.8	385,739	568.1	333,229	518.7
Other assaults	952,741	439.7	151,954	377.4	200,061	451.9	377,020	555.3	223,706	348.2
Forgery and counterfeiting	79,477	36.7	12,159	30.2	13,483	30.5	32,381	47.7	21,454	33.4
Fraud	197,722	91.2	30,527	75.8	35,390	79.9	108,959	160.5	22,846	35.6
Embezzlement	14,769	6.8	1,273	3.2	2,110	4.8	7,591	11.2	3,795	5.9
Stolen property; buying, receiving, possessing	90,084	41.6	17,270	42.9	15,641	35.3	24,015	35.4	33,158	51.6
Vandalism	220,422	101.7	44,399	110.3	49,683	112.2	52,964	78.0	73,376	114.2
Weapons; carrying, possessing, etc.	147,623	68.1	19,251	47.8	27,824	62.8	50,018	73.7	50,530	78.6
Prostitution and commercialized vice	59,724	27.6	7,813	19.4	10,240	23.1	18,671	27.5	23,000	35.8
Sex offenses (except forcible rape and prostitution)	63,243	29.2	10,503	26.1	12,852	29.0	15,914	23.4	23,974	37.3
Drug abuse violations	1,379,887	636.8	214,395	532.4	258,438	583.7	464,263	683.8	442,791	689.2
Gambling	9,018	4.2	851	2.1	4,582	10.3	2,781	4.1	804	1.3
Offenses against the family and children	92,065	42.5	22,324	55.4	25,016	56.5	30,944	45.6	13,781	21.4
Driving under the influence	1,038,633	479.3	131,583	326.8	243,411	549.8	297,672	438.4	365,967	569.6
Liquor laws	469,186	216.5	58,652	145.7	171,294	386.9	115,020	169.4	124,220	193.3
Drunkenness	409,490	189.0	33,079	82.1	28,313	63.9	233,935	344.5	114,163	177.7
Disorderly conduct	519,046	239.5	122,835	305.0	164,607	371.8	158,496	233.4	73,108	113.8
Vagrancy	27,053	12.5	4,375	10.9	5,069	11.4	8,966	13.2	8,643	13.5
All other offenses (except traffic)	2,917,803	1,346.6	395,103	981.2	598,755	1,352.4	1,099,346	1,619.1	824,599	1,283.5
Suspicion	1,725	0.8	179	0.4	151	0.3	1,091	1.6	304	0.5
Curfew and loitering law violations	114,313	52.8	36,340	90.2	20,157	45.5	22,817	33.6	34,999	54.5
Runaways	83,874	38.7	7,983	19.8	21,369	48.3	27,569	40.6	26,953	42.0

[1] Does not include suspicion.

[2] Violent crimes are offenses of murder and nonnegligent manslaughter, forcible rape, robbery, and aggravated assault. Property crimes are offenses of burglary, larceny-theft, motor vehicle theft, and arson.

Table 31. Number and Rate of Arrests, by Population Group, 2006

(Number, rate per 100,000 population.)

Offense charged	Total (11,250 agencies; population 216,686,722)		Cities							
			Total cities (8,199 cities; population 151,460,208)		Group I (59 cities, 250,000 and over; population 40,435,530)		Group II (150 cities, 100,000 to 249,999; population 22,519,131)		Group III (368 cities, 50,000 to 99,999; population 25,265,390)	
	Total	Rate	Total	Rate	Total	Rate	Total	Rate	Total	Rate
TOTAL[3]	10,471,361	4,832.5	7,920,056	5,229.1	2,216,009	5,480.4	1,146,794	5,092.5	1,230,221	4,869.2
Murder and nonnegligent manslaughter	9,815	4.5	7,220	4.8	3,235	8.0	1,442	6.4	952	3.8
Forcible rape	17,766	8.2	12,768	8.4	4,029	10.0	2,008	8.9	1,861	7.4
Robbery	93,527	43.2	80,214	53.0	35,122	86.9	14,255	63.3	11,779	46.6
Aggravated assault	327,478	151.1	247,831	163.6	83,904	207.5	42,538	188.9	39,442	156.1
Burglary	222,192	102.5	164,247	108.4	44,404	109.8	29,543	131.2	28,322	112.1
Larceny-theft	801,633	370.0	671,068	443.1	168,391	416.4	105,792	469.8	119,329	472.3
Motor vehicle theft	100,775	46.5	78,390	51.8	37,337	92.3	12,494	55.5	9,481	37.5
Arson	12,002	5.5	8,702	5.7	1,947	4.8	1,187	5.3	1,480	5.9
Violent crime[4]	448,586	207.0	348,033	229.8	126,290	312.3	60,243	267.5	54,034	213.9
Property crime[4]	1,136,602	524.5	922,407	609.0	252,079	623.4	149,016	661.7	158,612	627.8
Other assaults	952,741	439.7	725,941	479.3	202,496	500.8	113,491	504.0	112,472	445.2
Forgery and counterfeiting	79,477	36.7	60,686	40.1	14,485	35.8	8,431	37.4	10,202	40.4
Fraud	197,722	91.2	110,740	73.1	16,567	41.0	13,163	58.5	18,340	72.6
Embezzlement	14,769	6.8	11,370	7.5	2,032	5.0	2,088	9.3	2,283	9.0
Stolen property; buying, receiving, possessing	90,084	41.6	68,677	45.3	16,949	41.9	11,421	50.7	13,585	53.8
Vandalism	220,422	101.7	175,466	115.8	44,508	110.1	25,223	112.0	28,142	111.4
Weapons; carrying, possessing, etc.	147,623	68.1	118,846	78.5	45,137	111.6	19,068	84.7	17,783	70.4
Prostitution and commercialized vice	59,724	27.6	56,792	37.5	40,315	99.7	7,968	35.4	4,514	17.9
Sex offenses (except forcible rape and prostitution)	63,243	29.2	45,733	30.2	16,658	41.2	6,246	27.7	7,010	27.7
Drug abuse violations	1,379,887	636.8	1,061,310	700.7	391,826	969.0	157,235	698.2	154,573	611.8
Gambling	9,018	4.2	7,806	5.2	5,894	14.6	427	1.9	330	1.3
Offenses against the family and children	92,065	42.5	43,328	28.6	5,647	14.0	8,403	37.3	7,855	31.1
Driving under the influence	1,038,633	479.3	650,167	429.3	124,322	307.5	84,072	373.3	96,859	383.4
Liquor laws	469,186	216.5	377,374	249.2	60,084	148.6	45,682	202.9	54,364	215.2
Drunkenness	409,490	189.0	350,973	231.7	81,300	201.1	55,584	246.8	56,862	225.1
Disorderly conduct	519,046	239.5	451,199	297.9	110,527	273.3	56,591	251.3	67,469	267.0
Vagrancy	27,053	12.5	24,095	15.9	14,565	36.0	2,443	10.8	3,050	12.1
All other offenses (except traffic)	2,917,803	1,346.6	2,136,472	1,410.6	564,915	1,397.1	298,622	1,326.1	336,971	1,333.7
Suspicion	1,725	0.8	1,000	0.7	0	0.0	221	1.0	142	0.6
Curfew and loitering law violations	114,313	52.8	109,350	72.2	62,528	154.6	8,872	39.4	13,111	51.9
Runaways	83,874	38.7	63,291	41.8	16,885	41.8	12,505	55.5	11,800	46.7

[3] Does not include suspicion.
[4] Violent crimes are offenses of murder and nonnegligent manslaughter, forcible rape, robbery, and aggravated assault. Property crimes are offenses of burglary, larceny-theft, motor vehicle theft, and arson.

Table 31. Number and Rate of Arrests, by Population Group, 2006 (Contd.)

(Number, rate per 100,000 population.)

Offense charged	Group IV (654 cities, 25,000 to 49,999; population 22,552,890)		Group V (1,419 cities, 10,000 to 24,999; population 22,395,901)		Group VI (5,549 cities, under 10,000; population 18,291,366)		Counties Metropolitan counties[1] (1,252 agencies; population 45,787,064)		Nonmetropolitan counties (1,799 agencies; population 19,439,450)		Suburban area[2] (6,122 agencies; population 94,714,217)	
	Total	Rate	Total	Rate	Total	Rate	Total	Rate	Total	Rate	Total	Rate
TOTAL[3]	1,056,810	4,685.9	1,110,055	4,956.5	1,160,167	6,342.7	1,767,021	3,859.2	784,284	4,034.5	4,119,107	4,349.0
Murder and nonnegligent manslaughter	636	2.8	570	2.5	385	2.1	1,969	4.3	626	3.2	3,074	3.2
Forcible rape	1,602	7.1	1,709	7.6	1,559	8.5	3,391	7.4	1,607	8.3	6,693	7.1
Robbery	8,384	37.2	6,502	29.0	4,172	22.8	11,323	24.7	1,990	10.2	26,620	28.1
Aggravated assault	29,910	132.6	26,924	120.2	25,113	137.3	59,274	129.5	20,373	104.8	117,886	124.5
Burglary	20,834	92.4	21,475	95.9	19,669	107.5	39,651	86.6	18,294	94.1	83,110	87.7
Larceny-theft	105,583	468.2	96,092	429.1	75,881	414.8	101,022	220.6	29,543	152.0	303,538	320.5
Motor vehicle theft	6,723	29.8	6,421	28.7	5,934	32.4	17,298	37.8	5,087	26.2	31,306	33.1
Arson	1,368	6.1	1,387	6.2	1,333	7.3	2,330	5.1	970	5.0	5,271	5.6
Violent crime[4]	40,532	179.7	35,705	159.4	31,229	170.7	75,957	165.9	24,596	126.5	154,273	162.9
Property crime[4]	134,508	596.4	125,375	559.8	102,817	562.1	160,301	350.1	53,894	277.2	423,225	446.8
Other assaults	99,680	442.0	97,154	433.8	100,648	550.2	159,136	347.6	67,664	348.1	362,365	382.6
Forgery and counterfeiting	9,138	40.5	9,672	43.2	8,758	47.9	13,652	29.8	5,139	26.4	32,418	34.2
Fraud	16,717	74.1	20,596	92.0	25,357	138.6	57,507	125.6	29,475	151.6	97,223	102.6
Embezzlement	2,009	8.9	1,758	7.8	1,200	6.6	2,625	5.7	774	4.0	5,931	6.3
Stolen property; buying, receiving, possessing	10,376	46.0	9,083	40.6	7,263	39.7	16,344	35.7	5,063	26.0	37,696	39.8
Vandalism	25,060	111.1	26,355	117.7	26,178	143.1	32,155	70.2	12,801	65.9	86,831	91.7
Weapons; carrying, possessing, etc.	13,127	58.2	11,413	51.0	12,318	67.3	21,591	47.2	7,186	37.0	49,206	52.0
Prostitution and commercialized vice	2,490	11.0	930	4.2	575	3.1	2,705	5.9	227	1.2	6,275	6.6
Sex offenses (except forcible rape and prostitution)	5,315	23.6	5,477	24.5	5,027	27.5	12,440	27.2	5,070	26.1	23,807	25.1
Drug abuse violations	121,673	539.5	116,436	519.9	119,567	653.7	226,189	494.0	92,388	475.3	493,312	520.8
Gambling	257	1.1	255	1.1	643	3.5	706	1.5	506	2.6	1,564	1.7
Offenses against the family and children	6,921	30.7	7,863	35.1	6,639	36.3	36,059	78.8	12,678	65.2	50,271	53.1
Driving under the influence	97,987	434.5	115,408	515.3	131,519	719.0	237,867	519.5	150,599	774.7	484,907	512.0
Liquor laws	48,928	216.9	66,031	294.8	102,285	559.2	55,614	121.5	36,198	186.2	197,822	208.9
Drunkenness	48,923	216.9	53,657	239.6	54,647	298.8	40,392	88.2	18,125	93.2	143,163	151.2
Disorderly conduct	57,429	254.6	74,621	333.2	84,562	462.3	45,960	100.4	21,887	112.6	196,035	207.0
Vagrancy	1,526	6.8	822	3.7	1,689	9.2	2,789	6.1	169	0.9	6,063	6.4
All other offenses (except traffic)	296,761	1,315.8	315,053	1,406.7	324,150	1,772.1	546,850	1,194.3	234,481	1,206.2	1,213,199	1,280.9
Suspicion	267	1.2	148	0.7	222	1.2	538	1.2	187	1.0	987	1.0
Curfew and loitering law violations	8,097	35.9	8,670	38.7	8,072	44.1	4,428	9.7	535	2.8	23,400	24.7
Runaways	9,356	41.5	7,721	34.5	5,024	27.5	15,754	34.4	4,829	24.8	30,121	31.8

[1] Includes only metropolitan county law enforcement agencies.
[2] Suburban area includes law enforcement agencies in cities with less than 50,000 inhabitants and county law enforcement agencies that are within a Metropolitan Statistical Area. Suburban area excludes all metropolitan agencies associated with a principal city. The agencies associated with suburban areas also appear in other groups within this table.
[3] Does not include suspicion.
[4] Violent crimes are offenses of murder and nonnegligent manslaughter, forcible rape, robbery, and aggravated assault. Property crimes are offenses of burglary, larceny-theft, motor vehicle theft, and arson.

Table 32. Ten-Year Arrest Trends, 1997 and 2006

(Number, percent change; 7,769 agencies; 2006 estimated population 172,264,090; 1997 estimated population 153,673,448.)

Offense charged	Number of persons arrested								
	Total all ages			Under 18 years of age			18 years of age and over		
	1997	2006	Percent change	1997	2006	Percent change	1997	2006	Percent change
TOTAL[1]	8,644,918	8,241,244	-4.7	1,670,353	1,268,950	-24.0	6,974,565	6,972,294	*
Murder and nonnegligent manslaughter	9,000	7,515	-16.5	1,224	710	-42.0	7,776	6,805	-12.5
Forcible rape	17,777	14,127	-20.5	3,047	2,104	-30.9	14,730	12,023	-18.4
Robbery	75,806	70,661	-6.8	22,845	19,219	-15.9	52,961	51,442	-2.9
Aggravated assault	299,789	261,040	-12.9	43,517	34,434	-20.9	256,272	226,606	-11.6
Burglary	209,972	181,287	-13.7	78,484	49,482	-37.0	131,488	131,805	+0.2
Larceny-theft	874,874	634,416	-27.5	302,506	165,840	-45.2	572,368	468,576	-18.1
Motor vehicle theft	91,797	70,934	-22.7	36,940	17,342	-53.1	54,857	53,592	-2.3
Arson	11,031	9,509	-13.8	6,112	4,794	-21.6	4,919	4,715	-4.1
Violent crime[2]	402,372	353,343	-12.2	70,633	56,467	-20.1	331,739	296,876	-10.5
Property crime[2]	1,187,674	896,146	-24.5	424,042	237,458	-44.0	763,632	658,688	-13.7
Other assaults	777,350	742,328	-4.5	138,719	141,986	+2.4	638,631	600,342	-6.0
Forgery and counterfeiting	71,042	62,098	-12.6	5,052	2,054	-59.3	65,990	60,044	-9.0
Fraud	234,057	170,200	-27.3	6,402	4,447	-30.5	227,655	165,753	-27.2
Embezzlement	11,346	13,074	+15.2	888	912	+2.7	10,458	12,162	+16.3
Stolen property; buying, receiving, possessing	86,621	73,173	-15.5	23,029	12,680	-44.9	63,592	60,493	-4.9
Vandalism	177,554	173,012	-2.6	79,986	68,868	-13.9	97,568	104,144	+6.7
Weapons; carrying, possessing, etc.	122,773	115,266	-6.1	30,140	27,198	-9.8	92,633	88,068	-4.9
Prostitution and commercialized vice	48,141	37,719	-21.6	688	788	+14.5	47,453	36,931	-22.2
Sex offenses (except forcible rape and prostitution)	55,900	48,441	-13.3	11,065	9,293	-16.0	44,835	39,148	-12.7
Drug abuse violations	884,598	1,045,377	+18.2	122,020	108,087	-11.4	762,578	937,290	+22.9
Gambling	6,172	3,164	-48.7	715	405	-43.4	5,457	2,759	-49.4
Offenses against the family and children	85,786	72,826	-15.1	5,775	2,978	-48.4	80,011	69,848	-12.7
Driving under the influence	814,757	809,753	-0.6	10,945	11,074	+1.2	803,812	798,679	-0.6
Liquor laws	356,230	352,636	-1.0	92,366	78,530	-15.0	263,864	274,106	+3.9
Drunkenness	462,690	363,221	-21.5	14,755	10,338	-29.9	447,935	352,883	-21.2
Disorderly conduct	412,053	387,696	-5.9	109,956	118,160	+7.5	302,097	269,536	-10.8
Vagrancy	16,490	15,918	-3.5	1,999	1,284	-35.8	14,491	14,634	+1.0
All other offenses (except traffic)	2,190,350	2,357,286	+7.6	280,216	227,376	-18.9	1,910,134	2,129,910	+11.5
Suspicion	3,924	1,575	-59.9	1,070	278	-74.0	2,854	1,297	-54.6
Curfew and loitering law violations	116,347	80,440	-30.9	116,347	80,440	-30.9	-	-	-
Runaways	124,615	68,127	-45.3	124,615	68,127	-45.3	-	-	-

[1] Does not include suspicion.
[2] Violent crimes are offenses of murder and nonnegligent manslaughter, forcible rape, robbery, and aggravated assault. Property crimes are offenses of burglary, larceny-theft, motor vehicle theft, and arson.
* Less than one-tenth of 1 percent.

Table 33. Ten-Year Arrest Trends, by Sex, 1997 and 2006

(Number, percent change; 7,769 agencies; 2006 estimated population 172,264,090; 1997 estimated population 153,673,448.)

Offense charged	Male						Female					
	Total			Under 18			Total			Under 18		
	1997	2006	Percent change	1997	2006	Percent change	1997	2006	Percent change	1997	2006	Percent change
TOTAL[1]	6,752,792	6,273,496	-7.1	1,222,353	899,669	-26.4	1,892,126	1,967,748	+4.0	448,000	369,281	-17.6
Murder and nonnegligent manslaughter	8,066	6,677	-17.2	1,148	675	-41.2	934	838	-10.3	76	35	-53.9
Forcible rape	17,574	13,945	-20.6	2,992	2,058	-31.2	203	182	-10.3	55	46	-16.4
Robbery	68,273	62,687	-8.2	20,680	17,425	-15.7	7,533	7,974	+5.9	2,165	1,794	-17.1
Aggravated assault	243,712	207,009	-15.1	34,632	26,440	-23.7	56,077	54,031	-3.6	8,885	7,994	-10.0
Burglary	184,181	153,960	-16.4	70,073	43,638	-37.7	25,791	27,327	+6.0	8,411	5,844	-30.5
Larceny-theft	570,438	394,104	-30.9	199,483	98,168	-50.8	304,436	240,312	-21.1	103,023	67,672	-34.3
Motor vehicle theft	78,241	58,098	-25.7	30,829	14,230	-53.8	13,556	12,836	-5.3	6,111	3,112	-49.1
Arson	9,536	7,926	-16.9	5,477	4,131	-24.6	1,495	1,583	+5.9	635	663	+4.4
Violent crime[2]	337,625	290,318	-14.0	59,452	46,598	-21.6	64,747	63,025	-2.7	11,181	9,869	-11.7
Property crime[2]	842,396	614,088	-27.1	305,862	160,167	-47.6	345,278	282,058	-18.3	118,180	77,291	-34.6
Other assaults	607,669	554,660	-8.7	98,601	94,367	-4.3	169,681	187,668	+10.6	40,118	47,619	+18.7
Forgery and counterfeiting	43,678	37,827	-13.4	3,073	1,360	-55.7	27,364	24,271	-11.3	1,979	694	-64.9
Fraud	125,476	91,852	-26.8	4,131	2,882	-30.2	108,581	78,348	-27.8	2,271	1,565	-31.1
Embezzlement	5,930	6,143	+3.6	493	502	+1.8	5,416	6,931	+28.0	395	410	+3.8
Stolen property; buying, receiving, possessing	73,033	59,214	-18.9	20,058	10,793	-46.2	13,588	13,959	+2.7	2,971	1,887	-36.5
Vandalism	151,227	144,165	-4.7	70,532	59,827	-15.2	26,327	28,847	+9.6	9,454	9,041	-4.4
Weapons; carrying, possessing, etc.	112,793	106,050	-6.0	27,537	24,471	-11.1	9,980	9,216	-7.7	2,603	2,727	+4.8
Prostitution and commercialized vice	19,761	13,534	-31.5	292	201	-31.2	28,380	24,185	-14.8	396	587	+48.2
Sex offenses (except forcible rape and prostitution)	51,499	45,054	-12.5	10,145	8,418	-17.0	4,401	3,387	-23.0	920	875	-4.9
Drug abuse violations	729,215	843,512	+15.7	104,616	90,326	-13.7	155,383	201,865	+29.9	17,404	17,761	+2.1
Gambling	5,397	2,713	-49.7	682	382	-44.0	775	451	-41.8	33	23	-30.3
Offenses against the family and children	68,052	55,112	-19.0	3,645	1,820	-50.1	17,734	17,714	-0.1	2,130	1,158	-45.6
Driving under the influence	689,380	647,914	-6.0	9,130	8,546	-6.4	125,377	161,839	+29.1	1,815	2,528	+39.3
Liquor laws	278,223	257,331	-7.5	64,393	50,162	-22.1	78,007	95,305	+22.2	27,973	28,368	+1.4
Drunkenness	405,996	308,242	-24.1	12,324	7,877	-36.1	56,694	54,979	-3.0	2,431	2,461	+1.2
Disorderly conduct	315,437	282,947	-10.3	80,312	78,637	-2.1	96,616	104,749	+8.4	29,644	39,523	+33.3
Vagrancy	12,697	12,619	-0.6	1,709	939	-45.1	3,793	3,299	-13.0	290	345	+19.0
All other offenses (except traffic)	1,743,500	1,814,493	+4.1	211,558	165,686	-21.7	446,850	542,793	+21.5	68,658	61,690	-10.1
Suspicion	3,101	1,220	-60.7	826	218	-73.6	823	355	-56.9	244	60	-75.4
Curfew and loitering law violations	81,890	56,042	-31.6	81,890	56,042	-31.6	34,457	24,398	-29.2	34,457	24,398	-29.2
Runaways	51,918	29,666	-42.9	51,918	29,666	-42.9	72,697	38,461	-47.1	72,697	38,461	-47.1

[1] Does not include suspicion.
[2] Violent crimes are offenses of murder and nonnegligent manslaughter, forcible rape, robbery, and aggravated assault. Property crimes are offenses of burglary, larceny-theft, motor vehicle theft, and arson.

Table 34. Five-Year Arrest Trends, by Age, 2002 and 2006

(Number, percent change; 9,187 agencies; 2006 estimated population 187,723,263; 2002 estimated population 180,980,321.)

Offense charged	Number of persons arrested								
	Total all ages			Under 18 years of age			18 years of age and over		
	2002	2006	Percent change	2002	2006	Percent change	2002	2006	Percent change
TOTAL[1]	8,646,175	8,970,388	+3.7	1,413,478	1,370,310	-3.1	7,232,697	7,600,078	+5.1
Murder and nonnegligent manslaughter	7,561	7,899	+4.5	634	747	+17.8	6,927	7,152	+3.2
Forcible rape	17,138	15,194	-11.3	2,857	2,294	-19.7	14,281	12,900	-9.7
Robbery	64,469	74,065	+14.9	14,927	20,055	+34.4	49,542	54,010	+9.0
Aggravated assault	280,559	276,133	-1.6	37,055	36,589	-1.3	243,504	239,544	-1.6
Burglary	183,256	191,271	+4.4	55,252	52,026	-5.8	128,004	139,245	+8.8
Larceny-theft	743,473	684,656	-7.9	221,194	178,464	-19.3	522,279	506,192	-3.1
Motor vehicle theft	85,837	77,998	-9.1	26,122	18,884	-27.7	59,715	59,114	-1.0
Arson	10,670	10,197	-4.4	5,462	5,187	-5.0	5,208	5,010	-3.8
Violent crime[2]	369,727	373,291	+1.0	55,473	59,685	+7.6	314,254	313,606	-0.2
Property crime[2]	1,023,236	964,122	-5.8	308,030	254,561	-17.4	715,206	709,561	-0.8
Other assaults	804,954	813,863	+1.1	147,075	154,433	+5.0	657,879	659,430	+0.2
Forgery and counterfeiting	73,966	67,351	-8.9	3,290	2,160	-34.3	70,676	65,191	-7.8
Fraud	215,764	184,405	-14.5	5,630	4,833	-14.2	210,134	179,572	-14.5
Embezzlement	13,009	13,629	+4.8	980	952	-2.9	12,029	12,677	+5.4
Stolen property; buying, receiving, possessing	74,118	76,492	+3.2	15,244	13,347	-12.4	58,874	63,145	+7.3
Vandalism	175,407	189,816	+8.2	67,873	74,899	+10.4	107,534	114,917	+6.9
Weapons; carrying, possessing, etc.	98,074	117,875	+20.2	21,438	28,060	+30.9	76,636	89,815	+17.2
Prostitution and commercialized vice	41,093	42,910	+4.4	724	838	+15.7	40,369	42,072	+4.2
Sex offenses (except forcible rape and prostitution)	55,551	50,597	-8.9	11,975	9,769	-18.4	43,576	40,828	-6.3
Drug abuse violations	958,031	1,117,815	+16.7	115,793	117,172	+1.2	842,238	1,000,643	+18.8
Gambling	3,734	3,990	+6.9	366	438	+19.7	3,368	3,552	+5.5
Offenses against the family and children	85,657	76,206	-11.0	5,996	3,607	-39.8	79,661	72,599	-8.9
Driving under the influence	918,647	910,477	-0.9	13,550	12,447	-8.1	905,097	898,030	-0.8
Liquor laws	409,154	397,966	-2.7	94,860	89,694	-5.4	314,294	308,272	-1.9
Drunkenness	386,036	389,083	+0.8	12,174	11,379	-6.5	373,862	377,704	+1.0
Disorderly conduct	400,506	418,791	+4.6	118,832	128,887	+8.5	281,674	289,904	+2.9
Vagrancy	14,628	18,147	+24.1	1,351	1,409	+4.3	13,277	16,738	+26.1
All other offenses (except traffic)	2,361,593	2,583,492	+9.4	249,534	241,670	-3.2	2,112,059	2,341,822	+10.9
Suspicion	2,710	1,575	-41.9	1,035	292	-71.8	1,675	1,283	-23.4
Curfew and loitering law violations	82,297	87,598	+6.4	82,297	87,598	+6.4	-	-	-
Runaways	80,993	72,472	-10.5	80,993	72,472	-10.5	-	-	-

[1] Does not include suspicion.
[2] Violent crimes are offenses of murder and nonnegligent manslaughter, forcible rape, robbery, and aggravated assault. Property crimes are offenses of burglary, larceny-theft, motor vehicle theft, and arson.

Table 35. Five-Year Arrest Trends, by Age and Sex, 2002 and 2006

(Number, percent change; 9,187 agencies; 2006 estimated population 187,723,263; 2002 estimated population 180,980,321.)

| Offense charged | Male | | | | | | Female | | | | | |
| | Total | | | Under 18 | | | Total | | | Under 18 | | |
	2002	2006	Percent change	2002	2006	Percent change	2002	2006	Percent change	2002	2006	Percent change
TOTAL[1]	6,642,688	6,812,478	+2.6	1,001,487	969,942	-3.1	2,003,487	2,157,910	+7.7	411,991	400,368	-2.8
Murder and nonnegligent manslaughter	6,702	7,004	+4.5	563	708	+25.8	859	895	+4.2	71	39	-45.1
Forcible rape	16,898	15,004	-11.2	2,755	2,251	-18.3	240	190	-20.8	102	43	-57.8
Robbery	57,747	65,656	+13.7	13,564	18,167	+33.9	6,722	8,409	+25.1	1,363	1,888	+38.5
Aggravated assault	224,373	219,256	-2.3	28,454	28,148	-1.1	56,186	56,877	+1.2	8,601	8,441	-1.9
Burglary	158,132	162,540	+2.8	48,868	45,926	-6.0	25,124	28,731	+14.4	6,384	6,100	-4.4
Larceny-theft	466,573	424,654	-9.0	133,987	105,524	-21.2	276,900	260,002	-6.1	87,207	72,940	-16.4
Motor vehicle theft	71,562	63,885	-10.7	21,488	15,512	-27.8	14,275	14,113	-1.1	4,634	3,372	-27.2
Arson	9,079	8,524	-6.1	4,846	4,487	-7.4	1,591	1,673	+5.2	616	700	+13.6
Violent crime[2]	305,720	306,920	+0.4	45,336	49,274	+8.7	64,007	66,371	+3.7	10,137	10,411	+2.7
Property crime[2]	705,346	659,603	-6.5	209,189	171,449	-18.0	317,890	304,519	-4.2	98,841	83,112	-15.9
Other assaults	610,669	606,984	-0.6	99,843	102,112	+2.3	194,285	206,879	+6.5	47,232	52,321	+10.8
Forgery and counterfeiting	44,264	40,603	-8.3	2,136	1,437	-32.7	29,702	26,748	-9.9	1,154	723	-37.3
Fraud	116,600	100,491	-13.8	3,716	3,134	-15.7	99,164	83,914	-15.4	1,914	1,699	-11.2
Embezzlement	6,511	6,424	-1.3	578	526	-9.0	6,498	7,205	+10.9	402	426	+6.0
Stolen property; buying, receiving, possessing	61,009	61,863	+1.4	12,971	11,359	-12.4	13,109	14,629	+11.6	2,273	1,988	-12.5
Vandalism	146,209	158,084	+8.1	58,501	65,005	+11.1	29,198	31,732	+8.7	9,372	9,894	+5.6
Weapons; carrying, possessing, etc.	90,018	108,422	+20.4	19,088	25,230	+32.2	8,056	9,453	+17.3	2,350	2,830	+20.4
Prostitution and commercialized vice	14,596	14,513	-0.6	271	216	-20.3	26,497	28,397	+7.2	453	622	+37.3
Sex offenses (except forcible rape and prostitution)	51,907	47,239	-9.0	10,923	8,864	-18.9	3,644	3,358	-7.8	1,052	905	-14.0
Drug abuse violations	780,707	899,996	+15.3	96,455	97,505	+1.1	177,324	217,819	+22.8	19,338	19,667	+1.7
Gambling	3,204	3,235	+1.0	347	399	+15.0	530	755	+42.5	19	39	+105.3
Offenses against the family and children	64,762	56,403	-12.9	3,634	2,196	-39.6	20,895	19,803	-5.2	2,362	1,411	-40.3
Driving under the influence	757,835	727,781	-4.0	10,944	9,597	-12.3	160,812	182,696	+13.6	2,606	2,850	+9.4
Liquor laws	308,572	288,786	-6.4	62,907	57,247	-9.0	100,582	109,180	+8.5	31,953	32,447	+1.5
Drunkenness	332,058	329,388	-0.8	9,535	8,557	-10.3	53,978	59,695	+10.6	2,639	2,822	+6.9
Disorderly conduct	299,480	306,485	+2.3	82,692	86,332	+4.4	101,026	112,306	+11.2	36,140	42,555	+17.8
Vagrancy	11,521	14,512	+26.0	1,032	1,045	+1.3	3,107	3,635	+17.0	319	364	+14.1
All other offenses (except traffic)	1,841,953	1,982,435	+7.6	181,642	176,147	-3.0	519,640	601,057	+15.7	67,892	65,523	-3.5
Suspicion	2,045	1,229	-39.9	699	232	-66.8	665	346	-48.0	336	60	-82.1
Curfew and loitering law violations	57,216	60,735	+6.2	57,216	60,735	+6.2	25,081	26,863	+7.1	25,081	26,863	+7.1
Runaways	32,531	31,576	-2.9	32,531	31,576	-2.9	48,462	40,896	-15.6	48,462	40,896	-15.6

[1] Does not include suspicion.
[2] Violent crimes are offenses of murder and nonnegligent manslaughter, forcible rape, robbery, and aggravated assault. Property crimes are offenses of burglary, larceny-theft, motor vehicle theft, and arson.

Table 36. Current Year Over Previous Year Arrest Trends, 2005–2006

(Number, percent change; 10,119 agencies; 2006 estimated population 194,654,690; 2005 estimated population 192,732,617.)

Offense charged	Number of persons arrested											
	Total all ages			Under 15 years of age			Under 18 years of age			18 years of age and over		
	2005	2006	Percent change	2005	2006	Percent change	2005	2006	Percent change	2005	2006	Percent change
TOTAL[1]	9,062,755	9,141,735	+0.9	420,884	406,717	-3.4	1,371,279	1,382,848	+0.8	7,691,476	7,758,887	+0.9
Murder and nonnegligent manslaughter	8,322	8,068	-3.1	77	68	-11.7	739	764	+3.4	7,583	7,304	-3.7
Forcible rape	15,970	15,357	-3.8	923	827	-10.4	2,527	2,278	-9.9	13,443	13,079	-2.7
Robbery	66,930	72,701	+8.6	3,600	4,211	+17.0	16,142	19,193	+18.9	50,788	53,508	+5.4
Aggravated assault	287,485	283,742	-1.3	12,907	11,992	-7.1	37,895	37,135	-2.0	249,590	246,607	-1.2
Burglary	194,344	197,570	+1.7	17,044	17,144	+0.6	51,549	54,158	+5.1	142,795	143,412	+0.4
Larceny-theft	761,646	707,018	-7.2	70,768	62,308	-12.0	200,825	184,723	-8.0	560,821	522,295	-6.9
Motor vehicle theft	85,622	80,125	-6.4	4,888	4,546	-7.0	21,089	19,347	-8.3	64,533	60,778	-5.8
Arson	10,757	10,678	-0.7	3,321	3,155	-5.0	5,449	5,447	*	5,308	5,231	-1.5
Violent crime[2]	378,707	379,868	+0.3	17,507	17,098	-2.3	57,303	59,370	+3.6	321,404	320,498	-0.3
Property crime[2]	1,052,369	995,391	-5.4	96,021	87,153	-9.2	278,912	263,675	-5.5	773,457	731,716	-5.4
Other assaults	845,753	842,877	-0.3	66,208	63,332	-4.3	162,056	161,107	-0.6	683,697	681,770	-0.3
Forgery and counterfeiting	76,379	70,103	-8.2	355	258	-27.3	2,821	2,268	-19.6	73,558	67,835	-7.8
Fraud	215,797	194,275	-10.0	914	784	-14.2	5,323	5,041	-5.3	210,474	189,234	-10.1
Embezzlement	13,364	14,264	+6.7	48	34	-29.2	831	998	+20.1	12,533	13,266	+5.8
Stolen property; buying, receiving, possessing	84,646	81,929	-3.2	3,550	3,495	-1.5	14,098	14,219	+0.9	70,548	67,710	-4.0
Vandalism	185,238	197,154	+6.4	29,148	31,660	+8.6	69,273	77,175	+11.4	115,965	119,979	+3.5
Weapons; carrying, possessing, etc.	121,098	123,305	+1.8	9,799	9,805	+0.1	28,181	28,844	+2.4	92,917	94,461	+1.7
Prostitution and commercialized vice	38,295	37,525	-2.0	107	127	+18.7	715	781	+9.2	37,580	36,744	-2.2
Sex offenses (except forcible rape and prostitution)	54,617	52,785	-3.4	5,467	4,707	-13.9	10,896	9,918	-9.0	43,721	42,867	-2.0
Drug abuse violations	1,103,178	1,125,895	+2.1	19,033	18,348	-3.6	115,273	117,286	+1.7	987,905	1,008,609	+2.1
Gambling	3,675	3,696	+0.6	91	78	-14.3	443	380	-14.2	3,232	3,316	+2.6
Offenses against the family and children	87,014	87,401	+0.4	1,261	1,114	-11.7	3,874	3,635	-6.2	83,140	83,766	+0.8
Driving under the influence	892,415	919,742	+3.1	209	390	+86.6	11,697	12,735	+8.9	880,718	907,007	+3.0
Liquor laws	395,333	417,317	+5.6	7,847	8,384	+6.8	84,485	92,076	+9.0	310,848	325,241	+4.6
Drunkenness	365,708	388,857	+6.3	1,232	1,317	+6.9	10,249	11,469	+11.9	355,459	377,388	+6.2
Disorderly conduct	432,401	440,561	+1.9	52,350	50,999	-2.6	129,830	130,268	+0.3	302,571	310,293	+2.6
Vagrancy	17,989	17,813	-1.0	1,040	1,186	+14.0	3,219	3,538	+9.9	14,770	14,275	-3.4
All other offenses (except traffic)	2,561,222	2,612,450	+2.0	64,793	63,909	-1.4	244,243	249,538	+2.2	2,316,979	2,362,912	+2.0
Suspicion	1,665	1,595	-4.2	76	59	-22.4	348	296	-14.9	1,317	1,299	-1.4
Curfew and loitering law violations	58,695	60,938	+3.8	16,851	16,786	-0.4	58,695	60,938	+3.8	-	-	-
Runaways	78,862	77,589	-1.6	27,053	25,753	-4.8	78,862	77,589	-1.6	-	-	-

[1] Does not include suspicion.
[2] Violent crimes are offenses of murder and nonnegligent manslaughter, forcible rape, robbery, and aggravated assault. Property crimes are offenses of burglary, larceny-theft, motor vehicle theft, and arson.
* Less than one-tenth of 1 percent.

Table 37. Current Year Over Previous Year Arrest Trends, by Age and Sex, 2005–2006

(Number, percent change; 10,119 agencies; 2006 estimated population 194,654,690; 2005 estimated population 192,732,617.)

Offense charged	Male						Female					
	Total			Under 18			Total			Under 18		
	2005	2006	Percent change	2005	2006	Percent change	2005	2006	Percent change	2005	2006	Percent change
TOTAL[1]	6,866,831	6,937,710	+1.0	957,856	976,304	+1.9	2,195,924	2,204,025	+0.4	413,423	406,544	-1.7
Murder and nonnegligent manslaughter	7,371	7,145	-3.1	660	724	+9.7	951	923	-2.9	79	40	-49.4
Forcible rape	15,779	15,155	-4.0	2,472	2,235	-9.6	191	202	+5.8	55	43	-21.8
Robbery	59,358	64,426	+8.5	14,641	17,366	+18.6	7,572	8,275	+9.3	1,501	1,827	+21.7
Aggravated assault	228,067	225,512	-1.1	28,968	28,623	-1.2	59,418	58,230	-2.0	8,927	8,512	-4.6
Burglary	165,767	168,433	+1.6	45,532	47,920	+5.2	28,577	29,137	+2.0	6,017	6,238	+3.7
Larceny-theft	464,283	438,207	-5.6	115,929	109,106	-5.9	297,363	268,811	-9.6	84,896	75,617	-10.9
Motor vehicle theft	70,280	65,540	-6.7	17,236	15,878	-7.9	15,342	14,585	-4.9	3,853	3,469	-10.0
Arson	9,058	8,922	-1.5	4,756	4,713	-0.9	1,699	1,756	+3.4	693	734	+5.9
Violent crime[2]	310,575	312,238	+0.5	46,741	48,948	+4.7	68,132	67,630	-0.7	10,562	10,422	-1.3
Property crime[2]	709,388	681,102	-4.0	183,453	177,617	-3.2	342,981	314,289	-8.4	95,459	86,058	-9.8
Other assaults	634,155	628,917	-0.8	108,148	106,896	-1.2	211,598	213,960	+1.1	53,908	54,211	+0.6
Forgery and counterfeiting	45,838	42,328	-7.7	1,904	1,509	-20.7	30,541	27,775	-9.1	917	759	-17.2
Fraud	116,384	105,481	-9.4	3,439	3,293	-4.2	99,413	88,794	-10.7	1,884	1,748	-7.2
Embezzlement	6,588	6,720	+2.0	466	554	+18.9	6,776	7,544	+11.3	365	444	+21.6
Stolen property; buying, receiving, possessing	68,415	66,416	-2.9	11,916	12,118	+1.7	16,231	15,513	-4.4	2,182	2,101	-3.7
Vandalism	153,053	163,956	+7.1	59,613	66,967	+12.3	32,185	33,198	+3.1	9,660	10,208	+5.7
Weapons; carrying, possessing, etc.	111,216	113,466	+2.0	25,266	26,030	+3.0	9,882	9,839	-0.4	2,915	2,814	-3.5
Prostitution and commercialized vice	13,611	13,606	*	177	212	+19.8	24,684	23,919	-3.1	538	569	+5.8
Sex offenses (except forcible rape and prostitution)	51,037	49,248	-3.5	9,930	9,023	-9.1	3,580	3,537	-1.2	966	895	-7.3
Drug abuse violations	886,704	905,139	+2.1	94,143	97,089	+3.1	216,474	220,756	+2.0	21,130	20,197	-4.4
Gambling	3,098	2,983	-3.7	425	344	-19.1	577	713	+23.6	18	36	+100.0
Offenses against the family and children	66,023	66,170	+0.2	2,366	2,227	-5.9	20,991	21,231	+1.1	1,508	1,408	-6.6
Driving under the influence	719,502	734,151	+2.0	9,126	9,776	+7.1	172,913	185,591	+7.3	2,571	2,959	+15.1
Liquor laws	291,467	304,090	+4.3	54,381	58,811	+8.1	103,866	113,227	+9.0	30,104	33,265	+10.5
Drunkenness	309,662	328,126	+6.0	7,779	8,563	+10.1	56,046	60,731	+8.4	2,470	2,906	+17.7
Disorderly conduct	316,811	322,446	+1.8	87,069	87,059	*	115,590	118,115	+2.2	42,761	43,209	+1.0
Vagrancy	14,112	13,782	-2.3	2,339	2,445	+4.5	3,877	4,031	+4.0	880	1,093	+24.2
All other offenses (except traffic)	1,966,674	2,002,670	+1.8	176,657	182,148	+3.1	594,548	609,780	+2.6	67,586	67,390	-0.3
Suspicion	1,317	1,240	-5.8	250	233	-6.8	348	355	+2.0	98	63	-35.7
Curfew and loitering law violations	39,762	41,056	+3.3	39,762	41,056	+3.3	18,933	19,882	+5.0	18,933	19,882	+5.0
Runaways	32,756	33,619	+2.6	32,756	33,619	+2.6	46,106	43,970	-4.6	46,106	43,970	-4.6

[1] Does not include suspicion.
[2] Violent crimes are offenses of murder and nonnegligent manslaughter, forcible rape, robbery, and aggravated assault. Property crimes are offenses of burglary, larceny-theft, motor vehicle theft, and arson.
* Less than one-tenth of 1 percent.

Table 38. Arrests, Distribution by Age, 2006

(Number, percent; 11,250 agencies; 2006 estimated population 216,686,722.)

Offense charged	Total all ages	Ages under 15	Ages under 18	Ages 18 and over	Under 10	10-12	13-14	15	16	17	18	19
TOTAL	10,472,432	474,555	1,626,523	8,845,909	13,420	98,167	362,968	324,351	395,741	431,876	488,119	501,989
Total percent distribution[1]	100.0	4.5	15.5	84.5	0.1	0.9	3.5	3.1	3.8	4.1	4.7	4.8
Murder and nonnegligent manslaughter	9,815	81	956	8,859	0	9	72	146	287	442	667	649
Forcible rape	17,112	916	2,519	14,593	13	203	700	433	560	610	858	881
Robbery	93,527	6,023	26,092	67,435	73	878	5,072	5,518	6,988	7,563	7,925	6,665
Aggravated assault	327,478	14,405	44,424	283,054	429	3,512	10,464	8,487	10,380	11,152	12,233	12,412
Burglary	222,192	19,514	61,155	161,037	716	3,994	14,804	12,555	14,375	14,711	16,348	13,320
Larceny-theft	801,633	69,542	206,187	595,446	1,831	15,686	52,025	41,364	46,741	48,540	47,111	38,575
Motor vehicle theft	100,775	5,913	25,338	75,437	45	620	5,248	6,003	6,791	6,631	6,692	5,594
Arson	12,002	3,416	5,888	6,114	346	1,097	1,973	1,019	862	591	555	462
Violent crime[2]	447,932	21,425	73,991	373,941	515	4,602	16,308	14,584	18,215	19,767	21,683	20,607
Violent crime percent distribution[1]	100.0	4.8	16.5	83.5	0.1	1.0	3.6	3.3	4.1	4.4	4.8	4.6
Property crime[2]	1,136,602	98,385	298,568	838,034	2,938	21,397	74,050	60,941	68,769	70,473	70,706	57,951
Property crime percent distribution[1]	100.0	8.7	26.3	73.7	0.3	1.9	6.5	5.4	6.1	6.2	6.2	5.1
Other assaults	952,741	71,704	181,965	770,776	2,252	18,233	51,219	36,029	38,597	35,635	31,191	30,981
Forgery and counterfeiting	79,477	283	2,583	76,894	17	50	216	342	696	1,262	2,640	3,404
Fraud	197,722	879	5,681	192,041	35	123	721	850	1,542	2,410	4,581	6,136
Embezzlement	14,769	41	1,037	13,732	2	10	29	41	312	643	1,135	1,134
Stolen property; buying, receiving, possessing	90,084	3,891	15,649	74,435	67	623	3,201	3,191	3,966	4,601	5,500	4,934
Vandalism	220,422	35,214	86,170	134,252	1,762	9,226	24,226	16,529	17,877	16,550	14,198	11,139
Weapons; carrying, possessing, etc.	147,623	11,605	34,700	112,923	376	2,868	8,361	6,521	7,819	8,755	9,750	9,041
Prostitution and commercialized vice	59,724	164	1,208	58,516	13	14	137	172	348	524	1,939	2,155
Sex offenses (except forcible rape and prostitution)	63,243	5,467	11,516	51,727	285	1,472	3,710	2,068	2,024	1,957	2,421	2,375
Drug abuse violations	1,379,887	21,846	143,639	1,236,248	271	2,298	19,277	24,801	40,044	56,948	80,952	82,514
Gambling	9,018	242	1,620	7,398	3	16	223	322	402	654	795	616
Offenses against the family and children	92,065	1,110	3,633	88,432	105	230	775	745	881	897	1,724	1,890
Driving under the influence	1,038,633	409	14,292	1,024,341	238	11	160	575	3,567	9,741	24,599	33,666
Liquor laws	469,186	9,386	102,755	366,431	112	643	8,631	15,736	29,943	47,690	77,637	82,030
Drunkenness	409,490	1,351	12,057	397,433	55	67	1,229	1,951	2,869	5,886	11,772	12,974
Disorderly conduct	519,046	59,389	153,231	365,815	1,214	14,079	44,096	32,289	32,464	29,089	23,715	21,137
Vagrancy	27,053	1,221	3,734	23,319	16	212	993	952	1,067	494	995	758
All other offenses (except traffic)	2,917,803	71,340	279,991	2,637,812	2,102	12,602	56,636	57,411	70,509	80,731	100,077	116,438
Suspicion	1,725	70	316	1,409	1	10	59	68	89	89	109	109
Curfew and loitering law violations	114,313	31,315	114,313	-	446	5,079	25,790	26,706	31,555	24,737	-	-
Runaways	83,874	27,818	83,874	-	595	4,302	22,921	21,527	22,186	12,343	-	-

[1] Because of rounding, the percentages may not add to 100.0.
[2] Violent crimes are offenses of murder and nonnegligent manslaughter, forcible rape, robbery, and aggravated assault. Property crimes are offenses of burglary, larceny-theft, motor vehicle theft, and arson.

Table 38. Arrests, Distribution by Age, 2006 *(Contd.)*

(Number, percent; 11,250 agencies; 2006 estimated population 216,686,722.)

Offense charged	20	21	22	23	24	25-29	30-34	35-39	40-44	45-49	50-54	55-59	60-64	65 and over
TOTAL	476,844	433,919	398,346	378,820	358,162	1,449,813	1,033,257	980,213	924,668	705,892	388,162	185,697	78,114	63,894
Total percent distribution[1]	4.6	4.1	3.8	3.6	3.4	13.8	9.9	9.4	8.8	6.7	3.7	1.8	0.7	0.6
Murder and nonnegligent manslaughter	636	538	505	461	454	1,689	986	703	569	423	247	167	72	93
Forcible rape	757	733	635	636	546	2,375	1,828	1,807	1,389	1,017	553	291	137	150
Robbery	5,344	4,498	3,639	3,267	2,914	10,533	6,689	6,060	4,945	2,944	1,306	467	152	87
Aggravated assault	12,317	12,768	12,361	12,161	11,864	50,029	36,275	33,187	31,031	22,578	12,556	5,890	2,756	2,636
Burglary	10,346	8,833	7,715	6,828	6,245	25,381	17,258	16,673	15,079	9,934	4,620	1,614	501	342
Larceny-theft	32,301	27,466	23,756	22,078	20,744	85,902	65,936	68,838	64,570	48,596	26,755	12,593	5,280	4,945
Motor vehicle theft	4,770	4,241	3,862	3,537	3,322	13,314	9,396	8,226	6,305	3,701	1,540	606	186	145
Arson	332	288	242	213	194	800	659	642	606	523	310	160	76	52
Violent crime[2]	19,054	18,537	17,140	16,525	15,778	64,626	45,778	41,757	37,934	26,962	14,662	6,815	3,117	2,966
Violent crime percent distribution[1]	4.3	4.1	3.8	3.7	3.5	14.4	10.2	9.3	8.5	6.0	3.3	1.5	0.7	0.7
Property crime[2]	47,749	40,828	35,575	32,656	30,505	125,397	93,249	94,379	86,560	62,754	33,225	14,973	6,043	5,484
Property crime percent distribution[1]	4.2	3.6	3.1	2.9	2.7	11.0	8.2	8.3	7.6	5.5	2.9	1.3	0.5	0.5
Other assaults	31,310	33,946	32,626	32,292	31,524	135,686	102,789	96,346	87,803	63,107	32,571	15,486	6,751	6,367
Forgery and counterfeiting	3,614	3,380	3,264	3,363	3,310	15,104	11,455	10,075	7,998	5,356	2,295	978	372	286
Fraud	7,039	6,970	6,658	7,181	7,139	34,097	29,642	28,079	22,843	15,403	8,526	4,355	1,869	1,523
Embezzlement	957	863	723	655	507	2,064	1,563	1,439	1,170	759	393	235	88	47
Stolen property; buying, receiving, possessing	4,502	4,034	3,537	3,488	3,228	13,011	9,047	8,429	6,970	4,398	2,081	786	312	178
Vandalism	9,311	8,988	7,467	6,563	5,985	21,345	13,407	11,844	10,330	7,209	3,488	1,660	686	632
Weapons; carrying, possessing, etc.	7,840	7,637	6,725	6,118	5,657	20,328	11,421	8,525	7,345	5,767	3,375	1,765	863	766
Prostitution and commercialized vice	2,285	2,182	2,206	2,097	2,000	8,844	7,942	9,060	8,118	5,200	2,486	1,050	494	458
Sex offenses (except forcible rape and prostitution)	2,206	2,123	1,869	1,778	1,660	6,922	5,764	6,238	5,976	4,632	3,233	1,959	1,144	1,427
Drug abuse violations	75,968	68,268	61,994	58,445	54,873	212,899	137,677	125,980	118,371	87,881	44,164	17,922	5,497	2,843
Gambling	562	495	386	303	300	1,074	603	522	434	401	300	252	158	197
Offenses against the family and children	2,137	2,484	2,691	2,787	3,016	15,998	15,032	14,501	12,366	7,827	3,573	1,429	574	403
Driving under the influence	38,067	52,762	51,517	50,138	47,107	183,447	123,455	110,350	106,752	88,898	55,957	31,234	14,567	11,825
Liquor laws	68,715	12,231	8,207	6,719	5,556	19,913	14,344	15,260	18,092	16,752	11,003	5,761	2,507	1,704
Drunkenness	13,308	19,712	17,614	16,538	14,814	56,905	41,867	43,466	50,456	46,459	28,239	13,882	5,682	3,745
Disorderly conduct	19,783	23,710	20,171	18,051	16,010	57,999	37,382	35,418	35,431	28,189	15,509	7,336	3,249	2,725
Vagrancy	724	621	571	575	571	2,566	2,200	3,050	3,410	3,494	2,228	987	382	187
All other offenses (except traffic)	121,649	124,073	117,328	112,479	108,554	451,375	328,503	315,336	296,172	224,341	120,809	56,808	23,753	20,117
Suspicion	64	75	77	69	68	213	137	159	137	103	45	24	6	14
Curfew and loitering law violations	-	-	-	-	-	-	-	-	-	-	-	-	-	-
Runaways	-	-	-	-	-	-	-	-	-	-	-	-	-	-

[1] Because of rounding, the percentages may not add to 100.0.
[2] Violent crimes are offenses of murder and nonnegligent manslaughter, forcible rape, robbery, and aggravated assault. Property crimes are offenses of burglary, larceny-theft, motor vehicle theft, and arson.

Table 39. Male Arrests, Distribution by Age, 2006

(Number, percent; 11,250 agencies; 2006 estimated population 216,686,722.)

Offense charged	Total all ages	Ages under 15	Ages under 18	Ages 18 and over	Under 10	10-12	13-14	15	16	17	18	19	20
TOTAL	7,985,505	328,637	1,156,871	6,828,634	11,000	72,395	245,242	222,654	282,570	323,010	378,523	390,316	369,913
Total percent distribution[1]	100.0	4.1	14.5	85.5	0.1	0.9	3.1	2.8	3.5	4.0	4.7	4.9	4.6
Murder and nonnegligent manslaughter	8,744	76	905	7,839	0	8	68	138	273	418	633	599	576
Forcible rape	16,888	894	2,469	14,419	12	197	685	427	545	603	850	874	748
Robbery	82,983	5,354	23,614	59,369	65	803	4,486	4,951	6,390	6,919	7,227	6,047	4,801
Aggravated assault	259,544	10,911	34,065	225,479	400	2,819	7,692	6,299	7,997	8,858	9,908	9,857	9,885
Burglary	190,065	17,083	54,250	135,815	624	3,450	13,009	11,173	12,856	13,138	14,480	11,734	8,911
Larceny-theft	499,270	42,339	121,934	377,336	1,349	10,223	30,767	23,834	27,139	28,622	29,264	23,861	19,890
Motor vehicle theft	82,939	4,771	21,107	61,832	43	522	4,206	4,898	5,753	5,685	5,731	4,772	3,992
Arson	9,967	2,962	5,072	4,895	311	992	1,659	858	747	505	483	396	287
Violent crime[2]	368,159	17,235	61,053	307,106	477	3,827	12,931	11,815	15,205	16,798	18,618	17,377	16,010
Violent crime percent distribution[1]	100.0	4.7	16.6	83.4	0.1	1.0	3.5	3.2	4.1	4.6	5.1	4.7	4.3
Property crime[2]	782,241	67,155	202,363	579,878	2,327	15,187	49,641	40,763	46,495	47,950	49,958	40,763	33,080
Property crime percent distribution[1]	100.0	8.6	25.9	74.1	0.3	1.9	6.3	5.2	5.9	6.1	6.4	5.2	4.2
Other assaults	714,100	48,040	120,800	593,300	1,886	13,349	32,805	22,868	25,405	24,487	22,398	22,501	22,862
Forgery and counterfeiting	48,419	194	1,733	46,686	4	31	159	244	465	830	1,735	2,139	2,268
Fraud	109,745	588	3,737	106,008	22	89	477	569	1,019	1,561	2,857	3,632	3,974
Embezzlement	6,981	25	575	6,406	2	7	16	30	175	345	564	527	435
Stolen property; buying, receiving, possessing	73,078	3,248	13,357	59,721	62	507	2,679	2,693	3,410	4,006	4,682	4,104	3,703
Vandalism	183,413	30,494	74,799	108,614	1,591	8,016	20,887	14,423	15,555	14,327	12,312	9,469	7,714
Weapons; carrying, possessing, etc.	135,835	10,180	31,197	104,638	349	2,536	7,295	5,748	7,162	8,107	9,200	8,537	7,396
Prostitution and commercialized vice	21,358	41	317	21,041	4	10	27	35	84	157	357	463	610
Sex offenses (except forcible rape and prostitution)	57,735	4,972	10,383	47,352	248	1,349	3,375	1,824	1,814	1,773	2,109	2,094	1,938
Drug abuse violations	1,118,697	17,244	120,899	997,798	227	1,826	15,191	20,528	34,068	49,059	69,097	70,138	63,889
Gambling	8,112	224	1,565	6,547	3	16	205	317	391	633	749	580	506
Offenses against the family and children	69,542	650	2,272	67,270	67	159	424	446	573	603	1,241	1,294	1,454
Driving under the influence	830,517	300	10,976	819,541	181	6	113	446	2,690	7,540	19,367	26,706	30,467
Liquor laws	342,063	4,807	65,580	276,483	77	335	4,395	9,130	19,127	32,516	54,322	59,160	50,441
Drunkenness	346,087	850	9,058	337,029	47	48	755	1,386	2,124	4,698	9,740	10,943	11,332
Disorderly conduct	383,341	38,659	102,693	280,648	1,001	9,857	27,801	20,886	22,147	21,001	18,039	16,177	15,044
Vagrancy	21,043	785	2,604	18,439	14	134	637	655	786	378	837	637	597
All other offenses (except traffic)	2,248,556	50,246	205,525	2,043,031	1,690	9,342	39,214	40,661	51,959	62,659	80,256	92,990	96,147
Suspicion	1,346	47	248	1,098	1	7	39	53	70	78	85	85	46
Curfew and loitering law violations	78,735	20,603	78,735	-	329	3,430	16,844	18,004	22,194	17,934	-	-	-
Runaways	36,402	12,050	36,402	-	391	2,327	9,332	9,130	9,652	5,570	-	-	-

[1] Because of rounding, the percentages may not add to 100.0.
[2] Violent crimes are offenses of murder and nonnegligent manslaughter, forcible rape, robbery, and aggravated assault. Property crimes are offenses of burglary, larceny-theft, motor vehicle theft, and arson.

Table 39. Male Arrests, Distribution by Age, 2006 *(Contd.)*

(Number, percent; 11,250 agencies; 2006 estimated population 216,686,722.)

Offense charged	21	22	23	24	25-29	30-34	35-39	40-44	45-49	50-54	55-59	60-64	65 and over
TOTAL	340,309	312,209	296,385	279,048	1,124,066	785,418	728,724	692,258	546,378	312,516	154,315	65,377	52,879
Total percent distribution[1]	4.3	3.9	3.7	3.5	14.1	9.8	9.1	8.7	6.8	3.9	1.9	0.8	0.7
Murder and nonnegligent manslaughter	481	451	395	419	1,514	870	584	471	350	212	144	64	76
Forcible rape	728	630	625	538	2,340	1,790	1,780	1,375	1,014	551	290	137	149
Robbery	4,053	3,252	2,893	2,565	9,097	5,740	5,170	4,206	2,553	1,143	426	122	74
Aggravated assault	10,245	9,993	9,678	9,420	39,982	28,686	25,764	24,110	17,927	10,336	4,974	2,384	2,330
Burglary	7,564	6,443	5,726	5,213	21,070	14,186	13,586	12,544	8,362	3,958	1,366	406	266
Larceny-theft	16,977	14,613	13,685	12,861	53,027	40,677	44,304	43,045	32,749	17,912	8,211	3,262	2,998
Motor vehicle theft	3,499	3,214	2,892	2,680	10,662	7,506	6,562	5,052	3,113	1,341	523	167	126
Arson	252	210	170	160	644	514	496	431	388	239	122	62	41
Violent crime[2]	15,507	14,326	13,591	12,942	52,933	37,086	33,298	30,162	21,844	12,242	5,834	2,707	2,629
Violent crime percent distribution[1]	4.2	3.9	3.7	3.5	14.4	10.1	9.0	8.2	5.9	3.3	1.6	0.7	0.7
Property crime[2]	28,292	24,480	22,473	20,914	85,403	62,883	64,948	61,072	44,612	23,450	10,222	3,897	3,431
Property crime percent distribution[1]	3.6	3.1	2.9	2.7	10.9	8.0	8.3	7.8	5.7	3.0	1.3	0.5	0.4
Other assaults	25,378	24,649	24,746	24,129	105,854	79,862	73,963	67,404	49,832	26,095	12,734	5,560	5,333
Forgery and counterfeiting	2,073	2,017	2,053	2,033	8,977	6,622	5,937	4,713	3,371	1,567	679	280	222
Fraud	3,910	3,691	3,888	3,806	17,964	15,374	14,996	12,849	9,169	5,073	2,724	1,193	908
Embezzlement	422	348	319	225	934	691	676	550	369	172	102	38	34
Stolen property; buying, receiving, possessing	3,249	2,830	2,761	2,558	10,129	7,053	6,570	5,563	3,617	1,785	677	272	168
Vandalism	7,439	6,122	5,396	4,857	17,047	10,556	9,060	7,854	5,562	2,779	1,351	564	532
Weapons; carrying, possessing, etc.	7,188	6,324	5,694	5,286	18,864	10,479	7,647	6,527	5,211	3,104	1,651	815	715
Prostitution and commercialized vice	600	688	722	706	3,496	2,969	2,944	2,533	2,002	1,329	780	417	425
Sex offenses (except forcible rape and prostitution)	1,869	1,657	1,602	1,490	6,263	5,267	5,703	5,490	4,330	3,101	1,896	1,128	1,415
Drug abuse violations	57,125	51,680	48,489	45,222	174,094	108,986	94,873	87,974	67,463	35,936	15,415	4,839	2,578
Gambling	454	371	291	281	987	532	432	339	291	229	197	136	172
Offenses against the family and children	1,683	1,815	1,895	2,067	11,658	11,417	11,234	9,961	6,536	3,006	1,211	476	322
Driving under the influence	41,368	41,012	40,253	37,960	150,348	101,216	86,882	81,176	68,561	45,173	26,321	12,454	10,277
Liquor laws	9,790	6,618	5,484	4,582	16,095	11,487	12,018	14,259	13,893	9,500	5,093	2,249	1,492
Drunkenness	16,952	15,180	14,319	12,786	49,097	35,707	35,443	40,763	38,746	24,715	12,531	5,247	3,528
Disorderly conduct	18,729	15,900	14,197	12,547	44,909	27,799	25,786	26,288	21,686	12,513	6,092	2,701	2,241
Vagrancy	527	475	425	445	1,977	1,610	2,198	2,626	2,846	1,860	871	340	168
All other offenses (except traffic)	97,695	91,961	87,735	84,159	346,876	247,713	233,994	224,051	176,354	98,852	47,913	20,058	16,277
Suspicion	59	65	52	53	161	109	122	104	83	35	21	6	12
Curfew and loitering law violations	-	-	-	-	-	-	-	-	-	-	-	-	-
Runaways	-	-	-	-	-	-	-	-	-	-	-	-	-

[1] Because of rounding, the percentages may not add to 100.0.
[2] Violent crimes are offenses of murder and nonnegligent manslaughter, forcible rape, robbery, and aggravated assault. Property crimes are offenses of burglary, larceny-theft, motor vehicle theft, and arson.

Table 40. Female Arrests, Distribution by Age, 2006

(Number, percent; 11,250 agencies; 2006 estimated population 216,686,722.)

Offense charged	Total all ages	Ages under 15	Ages under 18	Ages 18 and over	Under 10	10-12	13-14	15	16	17	18	19	20
TOTAL	2,486,927	145,918	469,652	2,017,275	2,420	25,772	117,726	101,697	113,171	108,866	109,596	111,673	106,931
Total percent distribution[1]	100.0	5.9	18.9	81.1	0.1	1.0	4.7	4.1	4.6	4.4	4.4	4.5	4.3
Murder and nonnegligent manslaughter	1,071	5	51	1,020	0	1	4	8	14	24	34	50	60
Forcible rape	224	22	50	174	1	6	15	6	15	7	8	7	9
Robbery	10,544	669	2,478	8,066	8	75	586	567	598	644	698	618	543
Aggravated assault	67,934	3,494	10,359	57,575	29	693	2,772	2,188	2,383	2,294	2,325	2,555	2,432
Burglary	32,127	2,431	6,905	25,222	92	544	1,795	1,382	1,519	1,573	1,868	1,586	1,435
Larceny-theft	302,363	27,203	84,253	218,110	482	5,463	21,258	17,530	19,602	19,918	17,847	14,714	12,411
Motor vehicle theft	17,836	1,142	4,231	13,605	2	98	1,042	1,105	1,038	946	961	822	778
Arson	2,035	454	816	1,219	35	105	314	161	115	86	72	66	45
Violent crime[2]	79,773	4,190	12,938	66,835	38	775	3,377	2,769	3,010	2,969	3,065	3,230	3,044
Violent crime percent distribution[1]	100.0	5.3	16.2	83.8	*	1.0	4.2	3.5	3.8	3.7	3.8	4.0	3.8
Property crime[2]	354,361	31,230	96,205	258,156	611	6,210	24,409	20,178	22,274	22,523	20,748	17,188	14,669
Property crime percent distribution[1]	100.0	8.8	27.1	72.9	0.2	1.8	6.9	5.7	6.3	6.4	5.9	4.9	4.1
Other assaults	238,641	23,664	61,165	177,476	366	4,884	18,414	13,161	13,192	11,148	8,793	8,480	8,448
Forgery and counterfeiting	31,058	89	850	30,208	13	19	57	98	231	432	905	1,265	1,346
Fraud	87,977	291	1,944	86,033	13	34	244	281	523	849	1,724	2,504	3,065
Embezzlement	7,788	16	462	7,326	0	3	13	11	137	298	571	607	522
Stolen property; buying, receiving, possessing	17,006	643	2,292	14,714	5	116	522	498	556	595	818	830	799
Vandalism	37,009	4,720	11,371	25,638	171	1,210	3,339	2,106	2,322	2,223	1,886	1,670	1,597
Weapons; carrying, possessing, etc.	11,788	1,425	3,503	8,285	27	332	1,066	773	657	648	550	504	444
Prostitution and commercialized vice	38,366	123	891	37,475	9	4	110	137	264	367	1,582	1,692	1,675
Sex offenses (except forcible rape and prostitution)	5,508	495	1,133	4,375	37	123	335	244	210	184	312	281	268
Drug abuse violations	261,190	4,602	22,740	238,450	44	472	4,086	4,273	5,976	7,889	11,855	12,376	12,079
Gambling	906	18	55	851	0	0	18	5	11	21	46	36	56
Offenses against the family and children	22,523	460	1,361	21,162	38	71	351	299	308	294	483	596	683
Driving under the influence	208,116	109	3,316	204,800	57	5	47	129	877	2,201	5,232	6,960	7,600
Liquor laws	127,123	4,579	37,175	89,948	35	308	4,236	6,606	10,816	15,174	23,315	22,870	18,274
Drunkenness	63,403	501	2,999	60,404	8	19	474	565	745	1,188	2,032	2,031	1,976
Disorderly conduct	135,705	20,730	50,538	85,167	213	4,222	16,295	11,403	10,317	8,088	5,676	4,960	4,739
Vagrancy	6,010	436	1,130	4,880	2	78	356	297	281	116	158	121	127
All other offenses (except traffic)	669,247	21,094	74,466	594,781	412	3,260	17,422	16,750	18,550	18,072	19,821	23,448	25,502
Suspicion	379	23	68	311	0	3	20	15	19	11	24	24	18
Curfew and loitering law violations	35,578	10,712	35,578	-	117	1,649	8,946	8,702	9,361	6,803	-	-	-
Runaways	47,472	15,768	47,472	-	204	1,975	13,589	12,397	12,534	6,773	-	-	-

[1] Because of rounding, the percentages may not add to 100.0.
[2] Violent crimes are offenses of murder and nonnegligent manslaughter, forcible rape, robbery, and aggravated assault. Property crimes are offenses of burglary, larceny-theft, motor vehicle theft, and arson.
* Less than one-tenth of 1 percent.

Table 40. Female Arrests, Distribution by Age, 2006 *(Contd.)*

(Number, percent; 11,250 agencies; 2006 estimated population 216,686,722.)

Offense charged	21	22	23	24	25-29	30-34	35-39	40-44	45-49	50-54	55-59	60-64	65 and over
TOTAL	93,610	86,137	82,435	79,114	325,747	247,839	251,489	232,410	159,514	75,646	31,382	12,737	11,015
Total percent distribution[1]	3.8	3.5	3.3	3.2	13.1	10.0	10.1	9.3	6.4	3.0	1.3	0.5	0.4
Murder and nonnegligent manslaughter	57	54	66	35	175	116	119	98	73	35	23	8	17
Forcible rape	5	5	11	8	35	38	27	14	3	2	1	0	1
Robbery	445	387	374	349	1,436	949	890	739	391	163	41	30	13
Aggravated assault	2,523	2,368	2,483	2,444	10,047	7,589	7,423	6,921	4,651	2,220	916	372	306
Burglary	1,269	1,272	1,102	1,032	4,311	3,072	3,087	2,535	1,572	662	248	95	76
Larceny-theft	10,489	9,143	8,393	7,883	32,875	25,259	24,534	21,525	15,847	8,843	4,382	2,018	1,947
Motor vehicle theft	742	648	645	642	2,652	1,890	1,664	1,253	588	199	83	19	19
Arson	36	32	43	34	156	145	146	175	135	71	38	14	11
Violent crime[2]	3,030	2,814	2,934	2,836	11,693	8,692	8,459	7,772	5,118	2,420	981	410	337
Violent crime percent distribution[1]	3.8	3.5	3.7	3.6	14.7	10.9	10.6	9.7	6.4	3.0	1.2	0.5	0.4
Property crime[2]	12,536	11,095	10,183	9,591	39,994	30,366	29,431	25,488	18,142	9,775	4,751	2,146	2,053
Property crime percent distribution[1]	3.5	3.1	2.9	2.7	11.3	8.6	8.3	7.2	5.1	2.8	1.3	0.6	0.6
Other assaults	8,568	7,977	7,546	7,395	29,832	22,927	22,383	20,399	13,275	6,476	2,752	1,191	1,034
Forgery and counterfeiting	1,307	1,247	1,310	1,277	6,127	4,833	4,138	3,285	1,985	728	299	92	64
Fraud	3,060	2,967	3,293	3,333	16,133	14,268	13,083	9,994	6,234	3,453	1,631	676	615
Embezzlement	441	375	336	282	1,130	872	763	620	390	221	133	50	13
Stolen property; buying, receiving, possessing	785	707	727	670	2,882	1,994	1,859	1,407	781	296	109	40	10
Vandalism	1,549	1,345	1,167	1,128	4,298	2,851	2,784	2,476	1,647	709	309	122	100
Weapons; carrying, possessing, etc.	449	401	424	371	1,464	942	878	818	556	271	114	48	51
Prostitution and commercialized vice	1,582	1,518	1,375	1,294	5,348	4,973	6,116	5,585	3,198	1,157	270	77	33
Sex offenses (except forcible rape and prostitution)	254	212	176	170	659	497	535	486	302	132	63	16	12
Drug abuse violations	11,143	10,314	9,956	9,651	38,805	28,691	31,107	30,397	20,418	8,228	2,507	658	265
Gambling	41	15	12	19	87	71	90	95	110	71	55	22	25
Offenses against the family and children	801	876	892	949	4,340	3,615	3,267	2,405	1,291	567	218	98	81
Driving under the influence	11,394	10,505	9,885	9,147	33,099	22,239	23,468	25,576	20,337	10,784	4,913	2,113	1,548
Liquor laws	2,441	1,589	1,235	974	3,818	2,857	3,242	3,833	2,859	1,503	668	258	212
Drunkenness	2,760	2,434	2,219	2,028	7,808	6,160	8,023	9,693	7,713	3,524	1,351	435	217
Disorderly conduct	4,981	4,271	3,854	3,463	13,090	9,583	9,632	9,143	6,503	2,996	1,244	548	484
Vagrancy	94	96	150	126	589	590	852	784	648	368	116	42	19
All other offenses (except traffic)	26,378	25,367	24,744	24,395	104,499	80,790	81,342	72,121	47,987	21,957	8,895	3,695	3,840
Suspicion	16	12	17	15	52	28	37	33	20	10	3	0	2
Curfew and loitering law violations	-	-	-	-	-	-	-	-	-	-	-	-	-
Runaways	-	-	-	-	-	-	-	-	-	-	-	-	-

[1] Because of rounding, the percentages may not add to 100.0.
[2] Violent crimes are offenses of murder and nonnegligent manslaughter, forcible rape, robbery, and aggravated assault. Property crimes are offenses of burglary, larceny-theft, motor vehicle theft, and arson.

Table 41. Arrests of Persons Under 15, 18, 21, and 25 Years of Age, 2006

(Number, percent; 11,250 agencies; 2006 estimated population 216,686,722.)

Offense charged	Total all ages	Number of persons arrested				Percent of total all ages			
		Under 15	Under 18	Under 21	Under 25	Under 15	Under 18	Under 21	Under 25
TOTAL..	10,472,432	474,555	1,626,523	3,093,475	4,662,722	4.5	15.5	29.5	44.5
Murder and nonnegligent manslaughter........................	9,815	81	956	2,908	4,866	0.8	9.7	29.6	49.6
Forcible rape..	17,112	916	2,519	5,015	7,565	5.4	14.7	29.3	44.2
Robbery...	93,527	6,023	26,092	46,026	60,344	6.4	27.9	49.2	64.5
Aggravated assault	327,478	14,405	44,424	81,386	130,540	4.4	13.6	24.9	39.9
Burglary..	222,192	19,514	61,155	101,169	130,790	8.8	27.5	45.5	58.9
Larceny-theft...	801,633	69,542	206,187	324,174	418,218	8.7	25.7	40.4	52.2
Motor vehicle theft	100,775	5,913	25,338	42,394	57,356	5.9	25.1	42.1	56.9
Arson..	12,002	3,416	5,888	7,237	8,174	28.5	49.1	60.3	68.1
Violent crime[1]...	447,932	21,425	73,991	135,335	203,315	4.8	16.5	30.2	45.4
Property crime[1]..	1,136,602	98,385	298,568	474,974	614,538	8.7	26.3	41.8	54.1
Other assaults..	952,741	71,704	181,965	275,447	405,835	7.5	19.1	28.9	42.6
Forgery and counterfeiting.......................................	79,477	283	2,583	12,241	25,558	0.4	3.2	15.4	32.2
Fraud..	197,722	879	5,681	23,437	51,385	0.4	2.9	11.9	26.0
Embezzlement..	14,769	41	1,037	4,263	7,011	0.3	7.0	28.9	47.5
Stolen property; buying, receiving, possessing.............	90,084	3,891	15,649	30,585	44,872	4.3	17.4	34.0	49.8
Vandalism...	220,422	35,214	86,170	120,818	149,821	16.0	39.1	54.8	68.0
Weapons; carrying, possessing, etc.	147,623	11,605	34,700	61,331	87,468	7.9	23.5	41.5	59.3
Prostitution and commercialized vice	59,724	164	1,208	7,587	16,072	0.3	2.0	12.7	26.9
Sex offenses (except forcible rape and prostitution)	63,243	5,467	11,516	18,518	25,948	8.6	18.2	29.3	41.0
Drug abuse violations..	1,379,887	21,846	143,639	383,073	626,653	1.6	10.4	27.8	45.4
Gambling..	9,018	242	1,620	3,593	5,077	2.7	18.0	39.8	56.3
Offenses against the family and children......................	92,065	1,110	3,633	9,384	20,362	1.2	3.9	10.2	22.1
Driving under the influence.......................................	1,038,633	409	14,292	110,624	312,148	*	1.4	10.7	30.1
Liquor laws...	469,186	9,386	102,755	331,137	363,850	2.0	21.9	70.6	77.5
Drunkenness..	409,490	1,351	12,057	50,111	118,789	0.3	2.9	12.2	29.0
Disorderly conduct	519,046	59,389	153,231	217,866	295,808	11.4	29.5	42.0	57.0
Vagrancy...	27,053	1,221	3,734	6,211	8,549	4.5	13.8	23.0	31.6
All other offenses (except traffic)...............................	2,917,803	71,340	279,991	618,155	1,080,589	2.4	9.6	21.2	37.0
Suspicion..	1,725	70	316	598	887	4.1	18.3	34.7	51.4
Curfew and loitering law violations............................	114,313	31,315	114,313	114,313	114,313	27.4	100.0	100.0	100.0
Runaways..	83,874	27,818	83,874	83,874	83,874	33.2	100.0	100.0	100.0

[1] Violent crimes are offenses of murder and nonnegligent manslaughter, forcible rape, robbery, and aggravated assault. Property crimes are offenses of burglary, larceny-theft, motor vehicle theft, and arson.
* Less than one-tenth of 1 percent.

Table 42. Arrests, Distribution by Sex, 2006

(Number, percent; 11,250 agencies; 2006 estimated population 216,686,722.)

Offense charged	Number of persons arrested			Percent male	Percent female	Percent distribution[1]		
	Total	Male	Female			Total	Male	Female
TOTAL	10,472,432	7,985,505	2,486,927	76.3	23.7	100.0	100.0	100.0
Murder and nonnegligent manslaughter	9,815	8,744	1,071	89.1	10.9	0.1	0.1	*
Forcible rape	17,112	16,888	224	98.7	1.3	0.2	0.2	*
Robbery	93,527	82,983	10,544	88.7	11.3	0.9	1.0	0.4
Aggravated assault	327,478	259,544	67,934	79.3	20.7	3.1	3.3	2.7
Burglary	222,192	190,065	32,127	85.5	14.5	2.1	2.4	1.3
Larceny-theft	801,633	499,270	302,363	62.3	37.7	7.7	6.3	12.2
Motor vehicle theft	100,775	82,939	17,836	82.3	17.7	1.0	1.0	0.7
Arson	12,002	9,967	2,035	83.0	17.0	0.1	0.1	0.1
Violent crime[2]	447,932	368,159	79,773	82.2	17.8	4.3	4.6	3.2
Property crime[2]	1,136,602	782,241	354,361	68.8	31.2	10.9	9.8	14.2
Other assaults	952,741	714,100	238,641	75.0	25.0	9.1	8.9	9.6
Forgery and counterfeiting	79,477	48,419	31,058	60.9	39.1	0.8	0.6	1.2
Fraud	197,722	109,745	87,977	55.5	44.5	1.9	1.4	3.5
Embezzlement	14,769	6,981	7,788	47.3	52.7	0.1	0.1	0.3
Stolen property; buying, receiving, possessing	90,084	73,078	17,006	81.1	18.9	0.9	0.9	0.7
Vandalism	220,422	183,413	37,009	83.2	16.8	2.1	2.3	1.5
Weapons; carrying, possessing, etc.	147,623	135,835	11,788	92.0	8.0	1.4	1.7	0.5
Prostitution and commercialized vice	59,724	21,358	38,366	35.8	64.2	0.6	0.3	1.5
Sex offenses (except forcible rape and prostitution)	63,243	57,735	5,508	91.3	8.7	0.6	0.7	0.2
Drug abuse violations	1,379,887	1,118,697	261,190	81.1	18.9	13.2	14.0	10.5
Gambling	9,018	8,112	906	90.0	10.0	0.1	0.1	*
Offenses against the family and children	92,065	69,542	22,523	75.5	24.5	0.9	0.9	0.9
Driving under the influence	1,038,633	830,517	208,116	80.0	20.0	9.9	10.4	8.4
Liquor laws	469,186	342,063	127,123	72.9	27.1	4.5	4.3	5.1
Drunkenness	409,490	346,087	63,403	84.5	15.5	3.9	4.3	2.5
Disorderly conduct	519,046	383,341	135,705	73.9	26.1	5.0	4.8	5.5
Vagrancy	27,053	21,043	6,010	77.8	22.2	0.3	0.3	0.2
All other offenses (except traffic)	2,917,803	2,248,556	669,247	77.1	22.9	27.9	28.2	26.9
Suspicion	1,725	1,346	379	78.0	22.0	*	*	*
Curfew and loitering law violations	114,313	78,735	35,578	68.9	31.1	1.1	1.0	1.4
Runaways	83,874	36,402	47,472	43.4	56.6	0.8	0.5	1.9

[1] Because of rounding, the percentages may not add to 100.0.
[2] Violent crimes are offenses of murder and nonnegligent manslaughter, forcible rape, robbery, and aggravated assault. Property crimes are offenses of burglary, larceny-theft, motor vehicle theft, and arson.
* Less than one-tenth of 1 percent.

Table 43. Arrests, Distribution by Race, 2006

(Number, percent; 11,249 agencies; 2006 estimated population 216,685,152.)

Offense charged	Total arrests					Percent distribution[1]					Arrests under 18			
	Total	White	Black	American Indian or Alaskan Native	Asian or Pacific Islander	Total	White	Black	American Indian or Alaskan Native	Asian or Pacific Islander	Total	White	Black	American Indian or Alaskan Native
TOTAL	10,437,620	7,270,214	2,924,724	130,589	112,093	100.0	69.7	28.0	1.3	1.1	1,621,167	1,088,376	490,838	18,592
Murder and nonnegligent manslaughter....................	9,801	4,595	4,990	110	106	100.0	46.9	50.9	1.1	1.1	956	374	566	6
Forcible rape	17,042	11,122	5,536	195	189	100.0	65.3	32.5	1.1	1.1	2,507	1,592	863	30
Robbery	93,393	39,419	52,541	611	822	100.0	42.2	56.3	0.7	0.9	26,060	8,074	17,569	116
Aggravated assault	326,721	206,417	112,645	3,949	3,710	100.0	63.2	34.5	1.2	1.1	44,314	24,697	18,652	439
Burglary	221,732	152,965	64,655	2,123	1,989	100.0	69.0	29.2	1.0	0.9	60,987	40,426	19,221	657
Larceny-theft...................	798,983	548,057	230,980	9,377	10,569	100.0	68.6	28.9	1.2	1.3	205,201	138,577	60,545	2,275
Motor vehicle theft..........	100,612	63,090	35,116	978	1,428	100.0	62.7	34.9	1.0	1.4	25,285	13,576	10,965	265
Arson.................................	11,972	9,101	2,591	116	164	100.0	76.0	21.6	1.0	1.4	5,868	4,646	1,075	49
Violent crime[2]	446,957	261,553	175,712	4,865	4,827	100.0	58.5	39.3	1.1	1.1	73,837	34,737	37,650	591
Property crime[2]...............	1,133,299	773,213	333,342	12,594	14,150	100.0	68.2	29.4	1.1	1.2	297,341	197,225	91,806	3,246
Other assaults..................	949,940	619,825	306,078	13,097	10,940	100.0	65.2	32.2	1.4	1.2	181,288	106,785	70,639	1,899
Forgery and counterfeiting...................	79,258	55,562	22,337	433	926	100.0	70.1	28.2	0.5	1.2	2,568	1,892	617	21
Fraud................................	196,930	135,329	59,087	1,213	1,301	100.0	68.7	30.0	0.6	0.7	5,656	3,623	1,938	34
Embezzlement.................	14,705	9,668	4,741	82	214	100.0	65.7	32.2	0.6	1.5	1,036	624	391	6
Stolen property; buying, receiving, possessing........	89,850	58,066	30,267	670	847	100.0	64.6	33.7	0.7	0.9	15,574	8,750	6,522	123
Vandalism........................	219,652	165,518	48,781	2,987	2,366	100.0	75.4	22.2	1.4	1.1	85,850	67,487	16,417	854
Weapons; carrying, possessing, etc.	147,312	84,929	59,863	1,134	1,386	100.0	57.7	40.6	0.8	0.9	34,611	21,142	12,745	285
Prostitution and commercialized vice	59,616	33,827	23,612	569	1,608	100.0	56.7	39.6	1.0	2.7	1,207	533	651	10
Sex offenses (except forcible rape and prostitution)	63,048	46,194	15,465	640	749	100.0	73.3	24.5	1.0	1.2	11,465	8,185	3,086	80
Drug abuse violations......	1,376,792	875,101	483,886	8,198	9,607	100.0	63.6	35.1	0.6	0.7	143,267	97,800	43,080	1,126
Gambling	9,001	2,358	6,467	12	164	100.0	26.2	71.8	0.1	1.8	1,620	140	1,471	1
Offenses against the family and children.........	91,618	61,278	28,086	1,678	576	100.0	66.9	30.7	1.8	0.6	3,621	2,737	823	26
Driving under the influence..........................	1,034,651	914,226	95,260	13,484	11,681	100.0	88.4	9.2	1.3	1.1	14,225	13,328	506	232
Liquor laws......................	466,323	398,068	50,035	12,831	5,389	100.0	85.4	10.7	2.8	1.2	102,230	93,368	4,987	2,635
Drunkenness	08,439	344,155	54,113	7,884	2,287	100.0	84.3	13.2	1.9	0.6	12,035	10,764	977	200
Disorderly conduct..........	517,264	325,991	179,733	7,606	3,934	100.0	63.0	34.7	1.5	0.8	152,869	88,420	61,438	1,799
Vagrancy	27,016	15,308	11,238	333	137	100.0	56.7	41.6	1.2	0.5	3,734	2,872	823	17
All other offenses (except traffic)..................	2,906,311	1,962,017	872,571	37,935	33,788	100.0	67.5	30.0	1.3	1.2	278,902	200,742	70,771	3,104
Suspicion..........................	1,723	1,011	658	41	13	100.0	58.7	38.2	2.4	0.8	316	205	108	0
Curfew and loitering law violations...................	114,166	69,624	42,496	814	1,232	100.0	61.0	37.2	0.7	1.1	114,166	69,624	42,496	814
Runaways.........................	83,749	57,393	20,896	1,489	3,971	100.0	68.5	25.0	1.8	4.7	83,749	57,393	20,896	1,489

[1] Because of rounding, the percentages may not add to 100.0.

[2] Violent crimes are offenses of murder and nonnegligent manslaughter, forcible rape, robbery, and aggravated assault. Property crimes are offenses of burglary, larceny-theft, motor vehicle theft, and arson.

Table 43. Arrests, Distribution by Race, 2006 *(Contd.)*

(Number, percent; 11,249 agencies; 2006 estimated population 216,685,152.)

Offense charged	Asian or Pacific Islander	Percent distribution[1]					Arrests 18 and over					Percent distribution[1]				
		Total	White	Black	American Indian or Alaskan Native	Asian or Pacific Islander	Total	White	Black	American Indian or Alaskan Native	Asian or Pacific Islander	Total	White	Black	American Indian or Alaskan Native	Asian or Pacific Islander
TOTAL	23,361	100.0	67.1	30.3	1.1	1.4	8,816,453	6,181,838	2,433,886	111,997	88,732	100.0	70.1	27.6	1.3	1.0
Murder and nonnegligent manslaughter	10	100.0	39.1	59.2	0.6	1.0	8,845	4,221	4,424	104	96	100.0	47.7	50.0	1.2	1.1
Forcible rape	22	100.0	63.5	34.4	1.2	0.9	14,535	9,530	4,673	165	167	100.0	65.6	32.1	1.1	1.1
Robbery	301	100.0	31.0	67.4	0.4	1.2	67,333	31,345	34,972	495	521	100.0	46.6	51.9	0.7	0.8
Aggravated assault	526	100.0	55.7	42.1	1.0	1.2	282,407	181,720	93,993	3,510	3,184	100.0	64.3	33.3	1.2	1.1
Burglary	683	100.0	66.3	31.5	1.1	1.1	160,745	112,539	45,434	1,466	1,306	100.0	70.0	28.3	0.9	0.8
Larceny-theft	3,804	100.0	67.5	29.5	1.1	1.9	593,782	409,480	170,435	7,102	6,765	100.0	69.0	28.7	1.2	1.1
Motor vehicle theft	479	100.0	53.7	43.4	1.0	1.9	75,327	49,514	24,151	713	949	100.0	65.7	32.1	0.9	1.3
Arson	98	100.0	79.2	18.3	0.8	1.7	6,104	4,455	1,516	67	66	100.0	73.0	24.8	1.1	1.1
Violent crime[2]	859	100.0	47.0	51.0	0.8	1.2	373,120	226,816	138,062	4,274	3,968	100.0	60.8	37.0	1.1	1.1
Property crime[2]	5,064	100.0	66.3	30.9	1.1	1.7	835,958	575,988	241,536	9,348	9,086	100.0	68.9	28.9	1.1	1.1
Other assaults	1,965	100.0	58.9	39.0	1.0	1.1	768,652	513,040	235,439	11,198	8,975	100.0	66.7	30.6	1.5	1.2
Forgery and counterfeiting	38	100.0	73.7	24.0	0.8	1.5	76,690	53,670	21,720	412	888	100.0	70.0	28.3	0.5	1.2
Fraud	61	100.0	64.1	34.3	0.6	1.1	191,274	131,706	57,149	1,179	1,240	100.0	68.9	29.9	0.6	0.6
Embezzlement	15	100.0	60.2	37.7	0.6	1.4	13,669	9,044	4,350	76	199	100.0	66.2	31.8	0.6	1.5
Stolen property; buying, receiving, possessing	179	100.0	56.2	41.9	0.8	1.1	74,276	49,316	23,745	547	668	100.0	66.4	32.0	0.7	0.9
Vandalism	1,092	100.0	78.6	19.1	1.0	1.3	133,802	98,031	32,364	2,133	1,274	100.0	73.3	24.2	1.6	1.0
Weapons; carrying, possessing, etc.	439	100.0	61.1	36.8	0.8	1.3	112,701	63,787	47,118	849	947	100.0	56.6	41.8	0.8	0.8
Prostitution and commercialized vice	13	100.0	44.2	53.9	0.8	1.1	58,409	33,294	22,961	559	1,595	100.0	57.0	39.3	1.0	2.7
Sex offenses (except forcible rape and prostitution)	114	100.0	71.4	26.9	0.7	1.0	51,583	38,009	12,379	560	635	100.0	73.7	24.0	1.1	1.2
Drug abuse violations	1,261	100.0	68.3	30.1	0.8	0.9	1,233,525	777,301	440,806	7,072	8,346	100.0	63.0	35.7	0.6	0.7
Gambling	8	100.0	8.6	90.8	0.1	0.5	7,381	2,218	4,996	11	156	100.0	30.1	67.7	0.1	2.1
Offenses against the family and children	35	100.0	75.6	22.7	0.7	1.0	87,997	58,541	27,263	1,652	541	100.0	66.5	31.0	1.9	0.6
Driving under the influence	159	100.0	93.7	3.6	1.6	1.1	1,020,426	900,898	94,754	13,252	11,522	100.0	88.3	9.3	1.3	1.1
Liquor laws	1,240	100.0	91.3	4.9	2.6	1.2	364,093	304,700	45,048	10,196	4,149	100.0	83.7	12.4	2.8	1.1
Drunkenness	94	100.0	89.4	8.1	1.7	0.8	396,404	333,391	53,136	7,684	2,193	100.0	84.1	13.4	1.9	0.6
Disorderly conduct	1,212	100.0	57.8	40.2	1.2	0.8	364,395	237,571	118,295	5,807	2,722	100.0	65.2	32.5	1.6	0.7
Vagrancy	22	100.0	76.9	22.0	0.5	0.6	23,282	12,436	10,415	316	115	100.0	53.4	44.7	1.4	0.5
All other offenses (except traffic)	4,285	100.0	72.0	25.4	1.1	1.5	2,627,409	1,761,275	801,800	34,831	29,503	100.0	67.0	30.5	1.3	1.1
Suspicion	3	100.0	64.9	34.2	0.0	0.9	1,407	806	550	41	10	100.0	57.3	39.1	2.9	0.7
Curfew and loitering law violations	1,232	100.0	61.0	37.2	0.7	1.1	-	-	-	-	-	-	-	-	-	-
Runaways	3,971	100.0	68.5	25.0	1.8	4.7	-	-	-	-	-	-	-	-	-	-

[1] Because of rounding, the percentages may not add to 100.0.
[2] Violent crimes are offenses of murder and nonnegligent manslaughter, forcible rape, robbery, and aggravated assault. Property crimes are offenses of burglary, larceny-theft, motor vehicle theft, and arson.

Table 44. City Arrest Trends, 2005–2006

(Number, percent change; 7,407 agencies; 2006 estimated population 130,339,315; 2005 estimated population 128,885,807.)

Offense charged	Number of persons arrested								
	Total all ages			Under 18 years of age			18 years of age and over		
	2005	2006	Percent change	2005	2006	Percent change	2005	2006	Percent change
TOTAL[1]	6,618,163	6,687,715	+1.1	1,104,310	1,112,347	+0.7	5,513,853	5,575,368	+1.1
Murder and nonnegligent manslaughter	5,762	5,553	-3.6	572	596	+4.2	5,190	4,957	-4.5
Forcible rape	10,945	10,577	-3.4	1,762	1,596	-9.4	9,183	8,981	-2.2
Robbery	55,400	60,320	+8.9	13,793	16,540	+19.9	41,607	43,780	+5.2
Aggravated assault	209,160	206,004	-1.5	29,228	28,595	-2.2	179,932	177,409	-1.4
Burglary	138,093	141,905	+2.8	38,448	40,024	+4.1	99,645	101,881	+2.2
Larceny-theft	632,568	583,049	-7.8	173,162	157,789	-8.9	459,406	425,260	-7.4
Motor vehicle theft	62,612	58,273	-6.9	16,183	14,883	-8.0	46,429	43,390	-6.5
Arson	7,631	7,644	+0.2	4,077	4,170	+2.3	3,554	3,474	-2.3
Violent crime[2]	281,267	282,454	+0.4	45,355	47,327	+4.3	235,912	235,127	-0.3
Property crime[2]	840,904	790,871	-5.9	231,870	216,866	-6.5	609,034	574,005	-5.8
Other assaults	613,774	618,864	+0.8	122,062	121,713	-0.3	491,712	497,151	+1.1
Forgery and counterfeiting	58,215	53,087	-8.8	2,124	1,779	-16.2	56,091	51,308	-8.5
Fraud	116,188	105,563	-9.1	4,183	3,976	-4.9	112,005	101,587	-9.3
Embezzlement	9,889	10,796	+9.2	649	785	+21.0	9,240	10,011	+8.3
Stolen property; buying, receiving, possessing	64,769	62,411	-3.6	11,944	11,856	-0.7	52,825	50,555	-4.3
Vandalism	142,797	153,237	+7.3	55,017	62,152	+13.0	87,780	91,085	+3.8
Weapons; carrying, possessing, etc.	93,558	95,649	+2.2	22,934	23,322	+1.7	70,624	72,327	+2.4
Prostitution and commercialized vice	35,401	34,726	-1.9	672	702	+4.5	34,729	34,024	-2.0
Sex offenses (except forcible rape and prostitution)	37,922	36,583	-3.5	7,674	7,039	-8.3	30,248	29,544	-2.3
Drug abuse violations	805,106	824,821	+2.4	90,222	91,898	+1.9	714,884	732,923	+2.5
Gambling	2,715	2,591	-4.6	411	335	-18.5	2,304	2,256	-2.1
Offenses against the family and children	40,024	40,283	+0.6	2,751	2,621	-4.7	37,273	37,662	+1.0
Driving under the influence	558,304	573,024	+2.6	7,996	8,577	+7.3	550,308	564,447	+2.6
Liquor laws	315,789	335,107	+6.1	64,475	70,602	+9.5	251,314	264,505	+5.2
Drunkenness	305,675	327,738	+7.2	8,801	9,872	+12.2	296,874	317,866	+7.1
Disorderly conduct	370,725	378,199	+2.0	112,624	112,571	*	258,101	265,628	+2.9
Vagrancy	15,723	15,810	+0.6	2,894	3,293	+13.8	12,829	12,517	-2.4
All other offenses (except traffic)	1,795,770	1,831,892	+2.0	196,004	201,052	+2.6	1,599,766	1,630,840	+1.9
Suspicion	1,105	928	-16.0	277	184	-33.6	828	744	-10.1
Curfew and loitering law violations	54,264	56,014	+3.2	54,264	56,014	+3.2	-	-	-
Runaways	59,384	57,995	-2.3	59,384	57,995	-2.3	-	-	-

[1] Does not include suspicion.
[2] Violent crimes are offenses of murder and nonnegligent manslaughter, forcible rape, robbery, and aggravated assault. Property crimes are offenses of burglary, larceny-theft, motor vehicle theft, and arson.
* Less than one-tenth of 1 percent.

Table 45. City Arrest Trends, by Age and Sex, 2005–2006

(Number, percent change; 7,407 agencies; 2006 estimated population 130,339,315; 2005 estimated population 128,885,807.)

Offense charged	Male						Female					
	Total			Under 18			Total			Under 18		
	2005	2006	Percent change	2005	2006	Percent change	2005	2006	Percent change	2005	2006	Percent change
TOTAL[1]	4,983,887	5,048,214	+1.3	766,967	781,549	+1.9	1,634,276	1,639,501	+0.3	337,343	330,798	-1.9
Murder and nonnegligent manslaughter	5,159	4,964	-3.8	522	570	+9.2	603	589	-2.3	50	26	-48.0
Forcible rape	10,833	10,457	-3.5	1,725	1,569	-9.0	112	120	+7.1	37	27	-27.0
Robbery	49,060	53,401	+8.8	12,523	14,941	+19.3	6,340	6,919	+9.1	1,270	1,599	+25.9
Aggravated assault	164,485	162,495	-1.2	22,212	21,943	-1.2	44,675	43,509	-2.6	7,016	6,652	-5.2
Burglary	117,193	120,262	+2.6	33,702	35,105	+4.2	20,900	21,643	+3.6	4,746	4,919	+3.6
Larceny-theft	378,810	355,147	-6.2	98,205	91,419	-6.9	253,758	227,902	-10.2	74,957	66,370	-11.5
Motor vehicle theft	51,320	47,652	-7.1	13,243	12,200	-7.9	11,292	10,621	-5.9	2,940	2,683	-8.7
Arson	6,359	6,351	-0.1	3,509	3,590	+2.3	1,272	1,293	+1.7	568	580	+2.1
Violent crime[2]	229,537	231,317	+0.8	36,982	39,023	+5.5	51,730	51,137	-1.1	8,373	8,304	-0.8
Property crime[2]	553,682	529,412	-4.4	148,659	142,314	-4.3	287,222	261,459	-9.0	83,211	74,552	-10.4
Other assaults	458,627	460,655	+0.4	81,124	80,365	-0.9	155,147	158,209	+2.0	40,938	41,348	+1.0
Forgery and counterfeiting	34,980	32,233	-7.9	1,396	1,173	-16.0	23,235	20,854	-10.2	728	606	-16.8
Fraud	65,704	60,020	-8.7	2,728	2,584	-5.3	50,484	45,543	-9.8	1,455	1,392	-4.3
Embezzlement	4,827	5,035	+4.3	361	421	+16.6	5,062	5,761	+13.8	288	364	+26.4
Stolen property; buying, receiving, possessing	52,161	50,474	-3.2	10,098	10,125	+0.3	12,608	11,937	-5.3	1,846	1,731	-6.2
Vandalism	117,638	127,325	+8.2	47,267	54,006	+14.3	25,159	25,912	+3.0	7,750	8,146	+5.1
Weapons; carrying, possessing, etc.	85,884	88,048	+2.5	20,626	21,166	+2.6	7,674	7,601	-1.0	2,308	2,156	-6.6
Prostitution and commercialized vice	12,120	12,339	+1.8	161	183	+13.7	23,281	22,387	-3.8	511	519	+1.6
Sex offenses (except forcible rape and prostitution)	35,120	33,922	-3.4	6,927	6,381	-7.9	2,802	2,661	-5.0	747	658	-11.9
Drug abuse violations	649,109	665,361	+2.5	73,861	76,442	+3.5	155,997	159,460	+2.2	16,361	15,456	-5.5
Gambling	2,364	2,116	-10.5	397	303	-23.7	351	475	+35.3	14	32	+128.6
Offenses against the family and children	27,028	26,953	-0.3	1,670	1,547	-7.4	12,996	13,330	+2.6	1,081	1,074	-0.6
Driving under the influence	445,468	452,488	+1.6	6,203	6,545	+5.5	112,836	120,536	+6.8	1,793	2,032	+13.3
Liquor laws	233,295	244,246	+4.7	41,569	45,177	+8.7	82,494	90,861	+10.1	22,906	25,425	+11.0
Drunkenness	259,469	277,274	+6.9	6,690	7,355	+9.9	46,206	50,464	+9.2	2,111	2,517	+19.2
Disorderly conduct	271,307	276,346	+1.9	75,290	74,842	-0.6	99,418	101,853	+2.4	37,334	37,729	+1.1
Vagrancy	12,482	12,367	-0.9	2,114	2,255	+6.7	3,241	3,443	+6.2	780	1,038	+33.1
All other offenses (except traffic)	1,371,644	1,397,662	+1.9	141,403	146,721	+3.8	424,126	434,230	+2.4	54,601	54,331	-0.5
Suspicion	869	708	-18.5	197	146	-25.9	236	220	-6.8	80	38	-52.5
Curfew and loitering law violations	36,901	37,758	+2.3	36,901	37,758	+2.3	17,363	18,256	+5.1	17,363	18,256	+5.1
Runaways	24,540	24,863	+1.3	24,540	24,863	+1.3	34,844	33,132	-4.9	34,844	33,132	-4.9

[1] Does not include suspicion.
[2] Violent crimes are offenses of murder and nonnegligent manslaughter, forcible rape, robbery, and aggravated assault. Property crimes are offenses of burglary, larceny-theft, motor vehicle theft, and arson.

Table 46. City Arrests, Distribution by Age, 2006

(Number, percent; 8,199 agencies; 2006 estimated population 151,460,208.)

Offense charged	Total all ages	Ages under 15	Ages under 18	Ages 18 and over	Under 10	10-12	13-14	15	16	17	18	19	20
TOTAL	7,920,504	399,936	1,341,825	6,578,679	10,697	82,790	306,449	271,380	324,457	346,052	379,958	387,757	365,142
Total percent distribution[1]	100.0	5.0	16.9	83.1	0.1	1.0	3.9	3.4	4.1	4.4	4.8	4.9	4.6
Murder and nonnegligent manslaughter	7,220	71	783	6,437	0	7	64	124	235	353	516	497	499
Forcible rape	12,216	671	1,845	10,371	6	151	514	318	406	450	572	616	546
Robbery	80,214	5,458	23,221	56,993	70	806	4,582	4,979	6,212	6,572	6,659	5,516	4,495
Aggravated assault	247,831	11,668	35,543	212,288	321	2,836	8,511	6,842	8,312	8,721	9,370	9,673	9,547
Burglary	164,247	15,345	46,214	118,033	570	3,164	11,611	9,657	10,734	10,478	11,393	9,372	7,248
Larceny-theft	671,068	61,264	178,034	493,034	1,616	13,918	45,730	35,839	39,990	40,941	39,501	32,166	26,746
Motor vehicle theft	78,390	4,899	20,686	57,704	35	522	4,342	4,949	5,561	5,277	5,260	4,311	3,714
Arson	8,702	2,764	4,568	4,134	294	921	1,549	781	632	391	361	287	220
Violent crime[2]	347,481	17,868	61,392	286,089	397	3,800	13,671	12,263	15,165	16,096	17,117	16,302	15,087
Violent crime percent distribution[1]	100.0	5.1	17.7	82.3	0.1	1.1	3.9	3.5	4.4	4.6	4.9	4.7	4.3
Property crime[2]	922,407	84,272	249,502	672,905	2,515	18,525	63,232	51,226	56,917	57,087	56,515	46,136	37,928
Property crime percent distribution[1]	100.0	9.1	27.0	73.0	0.3	2.0	6.9	5.6	6.2	6.2	6.1	5.0	4.1
Other assaults	725,941	56,680	141,334	584,607	1,672	14,354	40,654	28,037	29,494	27,123	24,038	24,146	24,600
Forgery and counterfeiting	60,686	221	2,045	58,641	14	37	170	278	570	976	2,069	2,703	2,873
Fraud	110,740	708	4,531	106,209	25	100	583	702	1,233	1,888	3,331	4,177	4,577
Embezzlement	11,370	35	824	10,546	2	7	26	29	229	531	894	933	795
Stolen property; buying, receiving, possessing	68,677	3,358	13,045	55,632	53	551	2,754	2,716	3,268	3,703	4,247	3,833	3,431
Vandalism	175,466	29,405	70,322	105,144	1,418	7,651	20,336	13,619	14,288	13,010	11,088	8,817	7,316
Weapons; carrying, possessing, etc.	118,846	9,595	28,992	89,854	299	2,344	6,952	5,464	6,574	7,359	8,137	7,563	6,439
Prostitution and commercialized vice	56,792	149	1,126	55,666	13	11	125	150	332	495	1,851	2,081	2,187
Sex offenses (except forcible rape and prostitution)	45,733	4,033	8,376	37,357	191	1,076	2,766	1,517	1,447	1,379	1,715	1,682	1,569
Drug abuse violations	1,061,310	18,115	116,857	944,453	200	1,890	16,025	20,782	32,707	45,253	62,780	63,368	57,857
Gambling	7,806	229	1,566	6,240	3	14	212	315	391	631	753	574	508
Offenses against the family and children	43,328	791	2,547	40,781	82	161	548	518	617	621	1,113	1,256	1,375
Driving under the influence	650,167	198	9,502	640,665	64	8	126	411	2,411	6,482	16,082	21,901	24,700
Liquor laws	377,374	7,459	78,986	298,388	82	522	6,855	12,391	23,014	36,122	61,364	65,703	55,338
Drunkenness	350,973	1,170	10,430	340,543	50	58	1,062	1,678	2,465	5,117	9,825	10,891	11,190
Disorderly conduct	451,199	52,660	134,224	316,975	1,001	12,582	39,077	28,292	28,062	25,210	20,638	18,649	17,531
Vagrancy	24,095	1,167	3,440	20,655	15	206	946	901	983	389	890	660	632
All other offenses (except traffic)	2,136,472	60,049	229,948	1,906,524	1,676	10,533	47,840	48,284	57,992	63,623	75,444	86,325	89,167
Suspicion	1,000	37	195	805	1	4	32	45	61	52	67	57	42
Curfew and loitering law violations	109,350	30,130	109,350	-	430	4,924	24,776	25,570	30,032	23,618	-	-	-
Runaways	63,291	21,607	63,291	-	494	3,432	17,681	16,192	16,205	9,287	-	-	-

[1] Because of rounding, the percentages may not add to 100.0.
[2] Violent crimes are offenses of murder and nonnegligent manslaughter, forcible rape, robbery, and aggravated assault. Property crimes are offenses of burglary, larceny-theft, motor vehicle theft, and arson.

Table 46. City Arrests, Distribution by Age, 2006 *(Contd.)*

(Number, percent; 8,199 agencies; 2006 estimated population 151,460,208.)

Offense charged	21	22	23	24	25-29	30-34	35-39	40-44	45-49	50-54	55-59	60-64	65 and over
TOTAL	329,372	300,203	283,833	267,017	1,067,358	749,959	712,451	678,567	525,459	290,914	137,669	57,073	45,947
Total percent distribution[1]	4.2	3.8	3.6	3.4	13.5	9.5	9.0	8.6	6.6	3.7	1.7	0.7	0.6
Murder and nonnegligent manslaughter	381	382	345	352	1,261	708	495	394	277	146	96	40	48
Forcible rape	503	454	472	396	1,742	1,327	1,256	980	730	398	192	86	101
Robbery	3,800	3,045	2,752	2,456	8,814	5,709	5,212	4,222	2,553	1,159	396	135	70
Aggravated assault	9,930	9,541	9,434	9,113	38,046	27,123	24,358	22,622	16,392	9,139	4,214	1,953	1,833
Burglary	6,266	5,530	4,846	4,561	18,438	12,655	12,503	11,701	7,922	3,678	1,271	400	249
Larceny-theft	22,661	19,454	18,078	16,971	69,994	53,996	56,837	53,758	40,971	22,636	10,679	4,422	4,164
Motor vehicle theft	3,242	2,960	2,688	2,548	10,109	7,134	6,298	4,762	2,837	1,166	465	119	91
Arson	199	165	156	133	535	445	442	420	363	214	111	51	32
Violent crime[2]	14,614	13,422	13,003	12,317	49,863	34,867	31,321	28,218	19,952	10,842	4,898	2,214	2,052
Violent crime percent distribution[1]	4.2	3.9	3.7	3.5	14.3	10.0	9.0	8.1	5.7	3.1	1.4	0.6	0.6
Property crime[2]	32,368	28,109	25,768	24,213	99,076	74,230	76,080	70,641	52,093	27,694	12,526	4,992	4,536
Property crime percent distribution[1]	3.5	3.0	2.8	2.6	10.7	8.0	8.2	7.7	5.6	3.0	1.4	0.5	0.5
Other assaults	26,875	25,845	25,483	24,831	105,106	77,594	71,108	64,451	46,491	23,963	11,063	4,698	4,315
Forgery and counterfeiting	2,578	2,554	2,551	2,534	11,435	8,743	7,594	6,036	4,045	1,721	724	270	211
Fraud	4,246	3,976	4,245	4,046	18,886	15,515	14,615	12,144	8,229	4,444	2,152	909	717
Embezzlement	686	577	533	400	1,591	1,170	1,055	816	559	278	167	59	33
Stolen property; buying, receiving, possessing	3,063	2,678	2,609	2,420	9,741	6,596	6,206	5,143	3,224	1,526	581	214	120
Vandalism	7,156	5,896	5,250	4,807	16,867	10,421	9,009	8,002	5,611	2,714	1,252	508	430
Weapons; carrying, possessing, etc.	6,236	5,469	4,979	4,540	16,360	8,954	6,494	5,469	4,270	2,501	1,265	639	539
Prostitution and commercialized vice	2,069	2,113	1,991	1,911	8,391	7,551	8,651	7,719	4,932	2,353	989	455	422
Sex offenses (except forcible rape and prostitution)	1,570	1,380	1,289	1,204	5,046	4,129	4,497	4,353	3,416	2,376	1,433	749	949
Drug abuse violations	51,572	46,940	44,377	41,369	160,990	104,511	96,543	90,997	68,081	34,541	14,062	4,300	2,165
Gambling	458	349	271	264	934	458	377	320	293	210	195	118	158
Offenses against the family and children	1,536	1,636	1,596	1,631	7,861	6,292	5,881	4,793	3,091	1,542	652	304	222
Driving under the influence	34,183	33,391	32,141	30,293	116,323	77,287	67,899	64,417	53,823	33,707	18,686	8,683	7,149
Liquor laws	10,105	6,695	5,468	4,507	16,039	11,733	12,782	15,508	14,685	9,724	5,115	2,168	1,454
Drunkenness	17,042	15,218	14,188	12,734	48,727	35,630	37,032	43,200	40,090	24,555	11,978	4,966	3,277
Disorderly conduct	21,156	17,917	15,984	14,089	50,684	32,090	29,888	30,185	23,917	13,195	6,188	2,690	2,174
Vagrancy	548	499	498	479	2,213	1,921	2,650	3,012	3,184	2,040	907	355	167
All other offenses (except traffic)	91,269	85,491	81,572	78,384	321,096	230,187	222,685	213,068	165,419	90,966	42,825	17,777	14,849
Suspicion	42	48	37	44	129	80	84	75	54	22	11	5	8
Curfew and loitering law violations	-	-	-	-	-	-	-	-	-	-	-	-	-
Runaways	-	-	-	-	-	-	-	-	-	-	-	-	-

[1] Because of rounding, the percentages may not add to 100.0.
[2] Violent crimes are offenses of murder and nonnegligent manslaughter, forcible rape, robbery, and aggravated assault. Property crimes are offenses of burglary, larceny-theft, motor vehicle theft, and arson.

Table 47. City Arrests of Persons Under 15, 18, 21, and 25 Years of Age, 2006

(Number, percent; 8,199 agencies; 2006 estimated population 151,460,208.)

Offense charged	Total all ages	Number of persons arrested				Percent of total all ages			
		Under 15	Under 18	Under 21	Under 25	Under 15	Under 18	Under 21	Under 25
TOTAL	7,920,504	399,936	1,341,825	2,474,682	3,655,107	5.0	16.9	31.2	46.1
Murder and nonnegligent manslaughter	7,220	71	783	2,295	3,755	1.0	10.8	31.8	52.0
Forcible rape	12,216	671	1,845	3,579	5,404	5.5	15.1	29.3	44.2
Robbery	80,214	5,458	23,221	39,891	51,944	6.8	28.9	49.7	64.8
Aggravated assault	247,831	11,668	35,543	64,133	102,151	4.7	14.3	25.9	41.2
Burglary	164,247	15,345	46,214	74,227	95,430	9.3	28.1	45.2	58.1
Larceny-theft	671,068	61,264	178,034	276,447	353,611	9.1	26.5	41.2	52.7
Motor vehicle theft	78,390	4,899	20,686	33,971	45,409	6.2	26.4	43.3	57.9
Arson	8,702	2,764	4,568	5,436	6,089	31.8	52.5	62.5	70.0
Violent crime[1]	347,481	17,868	61,392	109,898	163,254	5.1	17.7	31.6	47.0
Property crime[1]	922,407	84,272	249,502	390,081	500,539	9.1	27.0	42.3	54.3
Other assaults	725,941	56,680	141,334	214,118	317,152	7.8	19.5	29.5	43.7
Forgery and counterfeiting	60,686	221	2,045	9,690	19,907	0.4	3.4	16.0	32.8
Fraud	110,740	708	4,531	16,616	33,129	0.6	4.1	15.0	29.9
Embezzlement	11,370	35	824	3,446	5,642	0.3	7.2	30.3	49.6
Stolen property; buying, receiving, possessing	68,677	3,358	13,045	24,556	35,326	4.9	19.0	35.8	51.4
Vandalism	175,466	29,405	70,322	97,543	120,652	16.8	40.1	55.6	68.8
Weapons; carrying, possessing, etc.	118,846	9,595	28,992	51,131	72,355	8.1	24.4	43.0	60.9
Prostitution and commercialized vice	56,792	149	1,126	7,245	15,329	0.3	2.0	12.8	27.0
Sex offenses (except forcible rape and prostitution)	45,733	4,033	8,376	13,342	18,785	8.8	18.3	29.2	41.1
Drug abuse violations	1,061,310	18,115	116,857	300,862	485,120	1.7	11.0	28.3	45.7
Gambling	7,806	229	1,566	3,401	4,743	2.9	20.1	43.6	60.8
Offenses against the family and children	43,328	791	2,547	6,291	12,690	1.8	5.9	14.5	29.3
Driving under the influence	650,167	198	9,502	72,185	202,193	*	1.5	11.1	31.1
Liquor laws	377,374	7,459	78,986	261,391	288,166	2.0	20.9	69.3	76.4
Drunkenness	350,973	1,170	10,430	42,336	101,518	0.3	3.0	12.1	28.9
Disorderly conduct	451,199	52,660	134,224	191,042	260,188	11.7	29.7	42.3	57.7
Vagrancy	24,095	1,167	3,440	5,622	7,646	4.8	14.3	23.3	31.7
All other offenses (except traffic)	2,136,472	60,049	229,948	480,884	817,600	2.8	10.8	22.5	38.3
Suspicion	1,000	37	195	361	532	3.7	19.5	36.1	53.2
Curfew and loitering law violations	109,350	30,130	109,350	109,350	109,350	27.6	100.0	100.0	100.0
Runaways	63,291	21,607	63,291	63,291	63,291	34.1	100.0	100.0	100.0

[1] Violent crimes are offenses of murder and nonnegligent manslaughter, forcible rape, robbery, and aggravated assault. Property crimes are offenses of burglary, larceny-theft, motor vehicle theft, and arson.
* Less than one-tenth of 1 percent.

Table 48. City Arrests, Distribution by Sex, 2006

(Number, percent; 8,199 agencies; 2006 estimated population 151,460,208.)

Offense charged	Number of persons arrested			Percent male	Percent female	Percent distribution[1]		
	Total	Male	Female			Total	Male	Female
TOTAL	7,920,504	6,016,393	1,904,111	76.0	24.0	100.0	100.0	100.0
Murder and nonnegligent manslaughter	7,220	6,487	733	89.8	10.2	0.1	0.1	*
Forcible rape	12,216	12,072	144	98.8	1.2	0.2	0.2	*
Robbery	80,214	71,085	9,129	88.6	11.4	1.0	1.2	0.5
Aggravated assault	247,831	195,001	52,830	78.7	21.3	3.1	3.2	2.8
Burglary	164,247	139,851	24,396	85.1	14.9	2.1	2.3	1.3
Larceny-theft	671,068	411,930	259,138	61.4	38.6	8.5	6.8	13.6
Motor vehicle theft	78,390	64,588	13,802	82.4	17.6	1.0	1.1	0.7
Arson	8,702	7,195	1,507	82.7	17.3	0.1	0.1	0.1
Violent crime[2]	347,481	284,645	62,836	81.9	18.1	4.4	4.7	3.3
Property crime[2]	922,407	623,564	298,843	67.6	32.4	11.6	10.4	15.7
Other assaults	725,941	543,731	182,210	74.9	25.1	9.2	9.0	9.6
Forgery and counterfeiting	60,686	37,151	23,535	61.2	38.8	0.8	0.6	1.2
Fraud	110,740	64,622	46,118	58.4	41.6	1.4	1.1	2.4
Embezzlement	11,370	5,331	6,039	46.9	53.1	0.1	0.1	0.3
Stolen property; buying, receiving, possessing	68,677	55,550	13,127	80.9	19.1	0.9	0.9	0.7
Vandalism	175,466	145,845	29,621	83.1	16.9	2.2	2.4	1.6
Weapons; carrying, possessing, etc.	118,846	109,351	9,495	92.0	8.0	1.5	1.8	0.5
Prostitution and commercialized vice	56,792	20,215	36,577	35.6	64.4	0.7	0.3	1.9
Sex offenses (except forcible rape and prostitution)	45,733	41,193	4,540	90.1	9.9	0.6	0.7	0.2
Drug abuse violations	1,061,310	864,114	197,196	81.4	18.6	13.4	14.4	10.4
Gambling	7,806	7,146	660	91.5	8.5	0.1	0.1	*
Offenses against the family and children	43,328	29,005	14,323	66.9	33.1	0.5	0.5	0.8
Driving under the influence	650,167	514,739	135,428	79.2	20.8	8.2	8.6	7.1
Liquor laws	377,374	275,850	101,524	73.1	26.9	4.8	4.6	5.3
Drunkenness	350,973	297,303	53,670	84.7	15.3	4.4	4.9	2.8
Disorderly conduct	451,199	333,073	118,126	73.8	26.2	5.7	5.5	6.2
Vagrancy	24,095	18,943	5,152	78.6	21.4	0.3	0.3	0.3
All other offenses (except traffic)	2,136,472	1,641,718	494,754	76.8	23.2	27.0	27.3	26.0
Suspicion	1,000	770	230	77.0	23.0	*	*	*
Curfew and loitering law violations	109,350	75,416	33,934	69.0	31.0	1.4	1.3	1.8
Runaways	63,291	27,118	36,173	42.8	57.2	0.8	0.5	1.9

[1] Because of rounding, the percentages may not add to 100.0.
[2] Violent crimes are offenses of murder and nonnegligent manslaughter, forcible rape, robbery, and aggravated assault. Property crimes are offenses of burglary,
   larceny-theft, motor vehicle theft, and arson.
* Less than one-tenth of 1 percent.

Table 49. City Arrests, Distribution by Race, 2006

(Number, percent; 8,198 agencies; 2006 estimated population 151,458,638.)

Offense charged	Total arrests					Percent distribution[1]					Arrests under 18			
	Total	White	Black	American Indian or Alaskan Native	Asian or Pacific Islander	Total	White	Black	American Indian or Alaskan Native	Asian or Pacific Islander	Total	White	Black	American Indian or Alaskan Native
TOTAL	7,894,606	5,289,134	2,411,609	98,763	95,100	100.0	67.0	30.5	1.3	1.2	1,337,365	879,533	421,975	15,084
Murder and nonnegligent manslaughter	7,210	2,999	4,054	65	92	100.0	41.6	56.2	0.9	1.3	783	293	477	3
Forcible rape	12,162	7,346	4,524	120	172	100.0	60.4	37.2	1.0	1.4	1,837	1,080	723	14
Robbery	80,094	32,818	46,051	500	725	100.0	41.0	57.5	0.6	0.9	23,191	7,106	15,709	102
Aggravated assault	247,200	148,322	93,092	2,608	3,178	100.0	60.0	37.7	1.1	1.3	35,446	18,966	15,719	299
Burglary	163,865	107,527	53,360	1,327	1,651	100.0	65.6	32.6	0.8	1.0	46,074	29,347	15,759	419
Larceny-theft	668,651	453,091	197,904	8,124	9,532	100.0	67.8	29.6	1.2	1.4	177,117	119,646	51,922	2,050
Motor vehicle theft	78,263	45,711	30,588	717	1,247	100.0	58.4	39.1	0.9	1.6	20,643	10,262	9,752	200
Arson	8,677	6,385	2,074	77	141	100.0	73.6	23.9	0.9	1.6	4,551	3,551	871	43
Violent crime[2]	346,666	191,485	147,721	3,293	4,167	100.0	55.2	42.6	0.9	1.2	61,257	27,445	32,628	418
Property crime[2]	919,456	612,714	283,926	10,245	12,571	100.0	66.6	30.9	1.1	1.4	248,385	162,806	78,304	2,712
Other assaults	723,628	450,556	253,587	9,980	9,505	100.0	62.3	35.0	1.4	1.3	140,762	81,886	55,660	1,465
Forgery and counterfeiting	60,502	41,431	17,948	335	788	100.0	68.5	29.7	0.6	1.3	2,031	1,475	512	10
Fraud	110,207	72,475	36,007	731	994	100.0	65.8	32.7	0.7	0.9	4,514	2,748	1,688	25
Embezzlement	11,321	7,414	3,662	63	182	100.0	65.5	32.3	0.6	1.6	823	527	279	5
Stolen property; buying, receiving, possessing	68,481	41,854	25,416	465	746	100.0	61.1	37.1	0.7	1.1	12,979	6,916	5,806	95
Vandalism	174,816	128,541	41,837	2,327	2,111	100.0	73.5	23.9	1.3	1.2	70,048	54,446	13,903	686
Weapons; carrying, possessing, etc.	118,595	65,368	51,263	765	1,199	100.0	55.1	43.2	0.6	1.0	28,917	17,561	10,771	204
Prostitution and commercialized vice	56,689	31,990	22,759	558	1,382	100.0	56.4	40.1	1.0	2.4	1,125	492	612	10
Sex offenses (except forcible rape and prostitution)	45,587	31,771	12,709	460	647	100.0	69.7	27.9	1.0	1.4	8,341	5,688	2,488	57
Drug abuse violations	1,059,063	635,190	410,240	5,730	7,903	100.0	60.0	38.7	0.5	0.7	116,540	76,589	38,041	878
Gambling	7,796	1,587	6,084	5	120	100.0	20.4	78.0	0.1	1.5	1,566	125	1,433	1
Offenses against the family and children	43,084	29,951	11,912	788	433	100.0	69.5	27.6	1.8	1.0	2,535	1,791	688	23
Driving under the influence	647,719	567,649	62,806	8,620	8,644	100.0	87.6	9.7	1.3	1.3	9,465	8,831	365	143
Liquor laws	375,270	314,553	44,621	11,368	4,728	100.0	83.8	11.9	3.0	1.3	78,623	71,003	4,344	2,193
Drunkenness	350,099	291,715	49,436	6,871	2,077	100.0	83.3	14.1	2.0	0.6	10,414	9,287	869	175
Disorderly conduct	449,678	276,664	162,956	6,424	3,634	100.0	61.5	36.2	1.4	0.8	133,896	77,221	54,077	1,471
Vagrancy	24,059	13,317	10,302	317	123	100.0	55.4	42.8	1.3	0.5	3,440	2,624	785	13
All other offenses (except traffic)	2,128,477	1,375,362	697,101	27,392	28,622	100.0	64.6	32.8	1.3	1.3	229,096	162,990	59,733	2,477
Suspicion	1,000	607	378	3	12	100.0	60.7	37.8	0.3	1.2	195	142	51	0
Curfew and loitering law violations	109,221	65,596	41,677	774	1,174	100.0	60.1	38.2	0.7	1.1	109,221	65,596	41,677	774
Runaways	63,192	41,344	17,261	1,249	3,338	100.0	65.4	27.3	2.0	5.3	63,192	41,344	17,261	1,249

[1] Because of rounding, the percentages may not add to 100.0.
[2] Violent crimes are offenses of murder and nonnegligent manslaughter, forcible rape, robbery, and aggravated assault. Property crimes are offenses of burglary, larceny-theft, motor vehicle theft, and arson.

Table 49. City Arrests, Distribution by Race, 2006 *(Contd.)*

(Number, percent; 8,198 agencies; 2006 estimated population 151,458,638.)

Offense charged	Asian or Pacific Islander	Percent distribution[1]					Arrests 18 and over					Percent distribution[1]				
		Total	White	Black	American Indian or Alaskan Native	Asian or Pacific Islander	Total	White	Black	American Indian or Alaskan Native	Asian or Pacific Islander	Total	White	Black	American Indian or Alaskan Native	Asian or Pacific Islander
TOTAL	20,773	100.0	65.8	31.6	1.1	1.6	6,557,241	4,409,601	1,989,634	83,679	74,327	100.0	67.2	30.3	1.3	1.1
Murder and nonnegligent manslaughter	10	100.0	37.4	60.9	0.4	1.3	6,427	2,706	3,577	62	82	100.0	42.1	55.7	1.0	1.3
Forcible rape	20	100.0	58.8	39.4	0.8	1.1	10,325	6,266	3,801	106	152	100.0	60.7	36.8	1.0	1.5
Robbery	274	100.0	30.6	67.7	0.4	1.2	56,903	25,712	30,342	398	451	100.0	45.2	53.3	0.7	0.8
Aggravated assault	462	100.0	53.5	44.3	0.8	1.3	211,754	129,356	77,373	2,309	2,716	100.0	61.1	36.5	1.1	1.3
Burglary	549	100.0	63.7	34.2	0.9	1.2	117,791	78,180	37,601	908	1,102	100.0	66.4	31.9	0.8	0.9
Larceny-theft	3,499	100.0	67.6	29.3	1.2	2.0	491,534	333,445	145,982	6,074	6,033	100.0	67.8	29.7	1.2	1.2
Motor vehicle theft	429	100.0	49.7	47.2	1.0	2.1	57,620	35,449	20,836	517	818	100.0	61.5	36.2	0.9	1.4
Arson	86	100.0	78.0	19.1	0.9	1.9	4,126	2,834	1,203	34	55	100.0	68.7	29.2	0.8	1.3
Violent crime[2]	766	100.0	44.8	53.3	0.7	1.3	285,409	164,040	115,093	2,875	3,401	100.0	57.5	40.3	1.0	1.2
Property crime[2]	4,563	100.0	65.5	31.5	1.1	1.8	671,071	449,908	205,622	7,533	8,008	100.0	67.0	30.6	1.1	1.2
Other assaults	1,751	100.0	58.2	39.5	1.0	1.2	582,866	368,670	197,927	8,515	7,754	100.0	63.3	34.0	1.5	1.3
Forgery and counterfeiting	34	100.0	72.6	25.2	0.5	1.7	58,471	39,956	17,436	325	754	100.0	68.3	29.8	0.6	1.3
Fraud	53	100.0	60.9	37.4	0.6	1.2	105,693	69,727	34,319	706	941	100.0	66.0	32.5	0.7	0.9
Embezzlement	12	100.0	64.0	33.9	0.6	1.5	10,498	6,887	3,383	58	170	100.0	65.6	32.2	0.6	1.6
Stolen property; buying, receiving, possessing	162	100.0	53.3	44.7	0.7	1.2	55,502	34,938	19,610	370	584	100.0	62.9	35.3	0.7	1.1
Vandalism	1,013	100.0	77.7	19.8	1.0	1.4	104,768	74,095	27,934	1,641	1,098	100.0	70.7	26.7	1.6	1.0
Weapons; carrying, possessing, etc.	381	100.0	60.7	37.2	0.7	1.3	89,678	47,807	40,492	561	818	100.0	53.3	45.2	0.6	0.9
Prostitution and commercialized vice	11	100.0	43.7	54.4	0.9	1.0	55,564	31,498	22,147	548	1,371	100.0	56.7	39.9	1.0	2.5
Sex offenses (except forcible rape and prostitution)	108	100.0	68.2	29.8	0.7	1.3	37,246	26,083	10,221	403	539	100.0	70.0	27.4	1.1	1.4
Drug abuse violations	1,032	100.0	65.7	32.6	0.8	0.9	942,523	558,601	372,199	4,852	6,871	100.0	59.3	39.5	0.5	0.7
Gambling	7	100.0	8.0	91.5	0.1	0.4	6,230	1,462	4,651	4	113	100.0	23.5	74.7	0.1	1.8
Offenses against the family and children	33	100.0	70.7	27.1	0.9	1.3	40,549	28,160	11,224	765	400	100.0	69.4	27.7	1.9	1.0
Driving under the influence	126	100.0	93.3	3.9	1.5	1.3	638,254	558,818	62,441	8,477	8,518	100.0	87.6	9.8	1.3	1.3
Liquor laws	1,083	100.0	90.3	5.5	2.8	1.4	296,647	243,550	40,277	9,175	3,645	100.0	82.1	13.6	3.1	1.2
Drunkenness	83	100.0	89.2	8.3	1.7	0.8	339,685	282,428	48,567	6,696	1,994	100.0	83.1	14.3	2.0	0.6
Disorderly conduct	1,127	100.0	57.7	40.4	1.1	0.8	315,782	199,443	108,879	4,953	2,507	100.0	63.2	34.5	1.6	0.8
Vagrancy	18	100.0	76.3	22.8	0.4	0.5	20,619	10,693	9,517	304	105	100.0	51.9	46.2	1.5	0.5
All other offenses (except traffic)	3,896	100.0	71.1	26.1	1.1	1.7	1,899,381	1,212,372	637,368	24,915	24,726	100.0	63.8	33.6	1.3	1.3
Suspicion	2	100.0	72.8	26.2	0.0	1.0	805	465	327	3	10	100.0	57.8	40.6	0.4	1.2
Curfew and loitering law violations	1,174	100.0	60.1	38.2	0.7	1.1	-	-	-	-	-	-	-	-	-	-
Runaways	3,338	100.0	65.4	27.3	2.0	5.3	-	-	-	-	-	-	-	-	-	-

[1] Because of rounding, the percentages may not add to 100.0.

[2] Violent crimes are offenses of murder and nonnegligent manslaughter, forcible rape, robbery, and aggravated assault. Property crimes are offenses of burglary, larceny-theft, motor vehicle theft, and arson.

Table 50. Arrest Trends for Metropolitan Counties, 2005–2006

(Number, percent change; 1,095 agencies; 2006 estimated population 44,677,438; 2005 estimated population 44,305,110.)

Offense charged	Number of persons arrested								
	Total all ages			Under 18 years of age			18 years of age and over		
	2005	2006	Percent change	2005	2006	Percent change	2005	2006	Percent change
TOTAL[1]	1,690,997	1,703,478	+0.7	200,034	204,765	+2.4	1,490,963	1,498,713	+0.5
Murder and nonnegligent manslaughter	1,853	1,888	+1.9	130	146	+12.3	1,723	1,742	+1.1
Forcible rape	3,302	3,217	-2.6	483	464	-3.9	2,819	2,753	-2.3
Robbery	9,602	10,429	+8.6	2,111	2,459	+16.5	7,491	7,970	+6.4
Aggravated assault	57,500	57,239	-0.5	6,770	6,706	-0.9	50,730	50,533	-0.4
Burglary	37,585	37,748	+0.4	9,150	10,047	+9.8	28,435	27,701	-2.6
Larceny-theft	97,944	93,854	-4.2	22,341	22,083	-1.2	75,603	71,771	-5.1
Motor vehicle theft	17,440	16,679	-4.4	3,652	3,352	-8.2	13,788	13,327	-3.3
Arson	2,095	2,050	-2.1	1,037	984	-5.1	1,058	1,066	+0.8
Violent crime[2]	72,257	72,773	+0.7	9,494	9,775	+3.0	62,763	62,998	+0.4
Property crime[2]	155,064	150,331	-3.1	36,180	36,466	+0.8	118,884	113,865	-4.2
Other assaults	159,732	154,303	-3.4	31,056	30,721	-1.1	128,676	123,582	-4.0
Forgery and counterfeiting	12,847	12,057	-6.1	507	377	-25.6	12,340	11,680	-5.3
Fraud	63,556	55,401	-12.8	804	761	-5.3	62,752	54,640	-12.9
Embezzlement	2,633	2,670	+1.4	160	190	+18.8	2,473	2,480	+0.3
Stolen property; buying, receiving, possessing	14,684	14,702	+0.1	1,572	1,793	+14.1	13,112	12,909	-1.5
Vandalism	29,492	31,018	+5.2	10,348	11,284	+9.0	19,144	19,734	+3.1
Weapons; carrying, possessing, etc.	20,460	20,679	+1.1	4,445	4,659	+4.8	16,015	16,020	*
Prostitution and commercialized vice	2,733	2,557	-6.4	40	74	+85.0	2,693	2,483	-7.8
Sex offenses (except forcible rape and prostitution)	11,431	11,356	-0.7	2,228	2,050	-8.0	9,203	9,306	+1.1
Drug abuse violations	208,713	212,585	+1.9	18,945	19,321	+2.0	189,768	193,264	+1.8
Gambling	560	655	+17.0	26	32	+23.1	534	623	+16.7
Offenses against the family and children	34,156	34,637	+1.4	760	734	-3.4	33,396	33,903	+1.5
Driving under the influence	218,418	229,417	+5.0	2,220	2,345	+5.6	216,198	227,072	+5.0
Liquor laws	48,431	49,521	+2.3	12,390	13,421	+8.3	36,041	36,100	+0.2
Drunkenness	41,013	42,038	+2.5	1,020	1,136	+11.4	39,993	40,902	+2.3
Disorderly conduct	40,573	42,090	+3.7	12,357	13,224	+7.0	28,216	28,866	+2.3
Vagrancy	2,053	1,824	-11.2	312	227	-27.2	1,741	1,597	-8.3
All other offenses (except traffic)	533,515	543,592	+1.9	36,494	36,903	+1.1	497,021	506,689	+1.9
Suspicion	435	491	+12.9	48	90	+87.5	387	401	+3.6
Curfew and loitering law violations	3,852	4,325	+12.3	3,852	4,325	+12.3	-	-	-
Runaways	14,824	14,947	+0.8	14,824	14,947	+0.8	-	-	-

[1] Does not include suspicion.
[2] Violent crimes are offenses of murder and nonnegligent manslaughter, forcible rape, robbery, and aggravated assault. Property crimes are offenses of burglary, larceny-theft, motor vehicle theft, and arson.
* Less than one-tenth of 1 percent

Table 51. Arrest Trends for Metropolitan Counties, by Age and Sex, 2005–2006

(Number, percent change; 1,095 agencies; 2006 estimated population 44,677,438; 2005 estimated population 44,305,110.)

Offense charged	Male						Female					
	Total			Under 18			Total			Under 18		
	2005	2006	Percent change	2005	2006	Percent change	2005	2006	Percent change	2005	2006	Percent change
TOTAL[1]	1,303,107	1,312,978	+0.8	142,473	147,254	+3.4	387,890	390,500	+0.7	57,561	57,511	-0.1
Murder and nonnegligent manslaughter	1,605	1,636	+1.9	107	136	+27.1	248	252	+1.6	23	10	-56.5
Forcible rape	3,253	3,159	-2.9	475	452	-4.8	49	58	+18.4	8	12	+50.0
Robbery	8,603	9,319	+8.3	1,905	2,247	+18.0	999	1,110	+11.1	206	212	+2.9
Aggravated assault	46,517	46,315	-0.4	5,281	5,266	-0.3	10,983	10,924	-0.5	1,489	1,440	-3.3
Burglary	32,410	32,618	+0.6	8,241	9,133	+10.8	5,175	5,130	-0.9	909	914	+0.6
Larceny-theft	63,576	61,755	-2.9	13,932	14,194	+1.9	34,368	32,099	-6.6	8,409	7,889	-6.2
Motor vehicle theft	14,446	13,675	-5.3	3,024	2,807	-7.2	2,994	3,004	+0.3	628	545	-13.2
Arson	1,816	1,738	-4.3	934	868	-7.1	279	312	+11.8	103	116	+12.6
Violent crime[2]	59,978	60,429	+0.8	7,768	8,101	+4.3	12,279	12,344	+0.5	1,726	1,674	-3.0
Property crime[2]	112,248	109,786	-2.2	26,131	27,002	+3.3	42,816	40,545	-5.3	10,049	9,464	-5.8
Other assaults	120,731	115,724	-4.1	20,875	20,609	-1.3	39,001	38,579	-1.1	10,181	10,112	-0.7
Forgery and counterfeiting	7,801	7,306	-6.3	369	267	-27.6	5,046	4,751	-5.8	138	110	-20.3
Fraud	32,853	28,631	-12.9	505	509	+0.8	30,703	26,770	-12.8	299	252	-15.7
Embezzlement	1,341	1,297	-3.3	93	119	+28.0	1,292	1,373	+6.3	67	71	+6.0
Stolen property; buying, receiving, possessing	11,945	11,983	+0.3	1,316	1,492	+13.4	2,739	2,719	-0.7	256	301	+17.6
Vandalism	24,641	26,026	+5.6	8,921	9,771	+9.5	4,851	4,992	+2.9	1,427	1,513	+6.0
Weapons; carrying, possessing, etc.	18,832	19,014	+1.0	3,925	4,091	+4.2	1,628	1,665	+2.3	520	568	+9.2
Prostitution and commercialized vice	1,398	1,126	-19.5	13	25	+92.3	1,335	1,431	+7.2	27	49	81.5
Sex offenses (except forcible rape and prostitution)	10,934	10,752	-1.7	2,087	1,894	-9.2	497	604	+21.5	141	156	+10.6
Drug abuse violations	167,121	170,038	+1.7	15,496	15,820	+2.1	41,592	42,547	+2.3	3,449	3,501	+1.5
Gambling	421	497	+18.1	25	30	+20.0	139	158	+13.7	1	2	+100.0
Offenses against the family and children	28,602	29,146	+1.9	468	469	+0.2	5,554	5,491	-1.1	292	265	-9.2
Driving under the influence	179,172	186,261	+4.0	1,749	1,824	+4.3	39,246	43,156	+10.0	471	521	+10.6
Liquor laws	35,165	35,638	+1.3	7,912	8,462	+7.0	13,266	13,883	+4.7	4,478	4,959	+10.7
Drunkenness	34,350	35,083	+2.1	765	863	+12.8	6,663	6,955	+4.4	255	273	+7.1
Disorderly conduct	29,989	31,121	+3.8	8,492	9,106	+7.2	10,584	10,969	+3.6	3,865	4,118	+6.5
Vagrancy	1,470	1,269	-13.7	220	175	-20.5	583	555	-4.8	92	52	-43.5
All other offenses (except traffic)	415,372	422,208	+1.6	26,600	26,982	+1.4	118,143	121,384	+2.7	9,894	9,921	+0.3
Suspicion	348	385	+10.6	36	69	+91.7	87	106	+21.8	12	21	+75.0
Curfew and loitering law violations	2,510	2,870	+14.3	2,510	2,870	+14.3	1,342	1,455	+8.4	1,342	1,455	+8.4
Runaways	6,233	6,773	+8.7	6,233	6,773	+8.7	8,591	8,174	-4.9	8,591	8,174	-4.9

[1] Does not include suspicion.
[2] Violent crimes are offenses of murder and nonnegligent manslaughter, forcible rape, robbery, and aggravated assault. Property crimes are offenses of burglary, larceny-theft, motor vehicle theft, and arson.

Table 52. Arrests in Metropolitan Counties, Distribution by Age, 2006

(Number, percent; 1,252 agencies; 2006 estimated population 45,787,064.)

Offense charged	Total all ages	Ages under 15	Ages under 18	Ages 18 and over	Under 10	10-12	13-14	15	16	17	18	19	20
TOTAL	1,767,517	58,160	215,230	1,552,287	1,712	12,108	44,340	41,360	53,802	61,908	73,938	77,865	75,642
Total percent distribution[1]	100.0	3.3	12.2	87.8	0.1	0.7	2.5	2.3	3.0	3.5	4.2	4.4	4.3
Murder and nonnegligent manslaughter	1,969	7	150	1,819	0	2	5	16	43	84	127	125	100
Forcible rape	3,349	182	462	2,887	6	41	135	84	98	98	202	176	137
Robbery	11,323	542	2,672	8,651	2	71	469	519	715	896	1,114	997	713
Aggravated assault	59,274	2,234	7,007	52,267	88	562	1,584	1,340	1,600	1,833	2,160	2,045	2,066
Burglary	39,651	3,057	10,632	29,019	90	616	2,351	2,102	2,620	2,853	3,367	2,608	2,014
Larceny-theft	101,022	6,908	23,290	77,732	156	1,431	5,321	4,686	5,559	6,137	5,853	4,950	4,168
Motor vehicle theft	17,298	756	3,543	13,755	5	69	682	806	960	1,021	1,112	989	798
Arson	2,330	519	1,041	1,289	43	135	341	200	168	154	132	113	71
Violent crime[2]	75,915	2,965	10,291	65,624	96	676	2,193	1,959	2,456	2,911	3,603	3,343	3,016
Violent crime percent distribution[1]	100.0	3.9	13.6	86.4	0.1	0.9	2.9	2.6	3.2	3.8	4.7	4.4	4.0
Property crime[2]	160,301	11,240	38,506	121,795	294	2,251	8,695	7,794	9,307	10,165	10,464	8,660	7,051
Property crime percent distribution[1]	100.0	7.0	24.0	76.0	0.2	1.4	5.4	4.9	5.8	6.3	6.5	5.4	4.4
Other assaults	159,136	12,090	31,788	127,348	437	3,152	8,501	6,344	7,009	6,345	5,072	4,788	4,610
Forgery and counterfeiting	13,652	50	414	13,238	3	11	36	50	100	214	402	511	541
Fraud	57,507	121	838	56,669	5	15	101	111	228	378	778	1,243	1,622
Embezzlement	2,625	5	189	2,436	0	2	3	10	74	100	217	182	137
Stolen property; buying, receiving, possessing	16,344	413	2,004	14,340	8	55	350	370	526	695	940	837	831
Vandalism	32,155	4,404	12,017	20,138	208	1,207	2,989	2,273	2,694	2,646	2,113	1,630	1,408
Weapons; carrying, possessing, etc.	21,591	1,724	4,809	16,782	47	450	1,227	899	1,049	1,137	1,263	1,192	1,124
Prostitution and commercialized vice	2,705	15	77	2,628	0	3	12	22	13	27	81	74	86
Sex offenses (except forcible rape and prostitution)	12,440	1,073	2,263	10,177	67	314	692	401	398	391	486	465	437
Drug abuse violations	226,189	2,921	20,466	205,723	28	320	2,573	3,173	5,709	8,663	12,790	13,524	12,728
Gambling	706	10	40	666	0	1	9	7	8	15	24	20	34
Offenses against the family and children	36,059	219	757	35,302	6	45	168	172	186	180	381	403	520
Driving under the influence	237,867	23	2,530	235,337	4	2	17	82	604	1,821	5,020	7,058	8,174
Liquor laws	55,614	1,177	14,863	40,751	19	85	1,073	2,046	4,356	7,284	10,003	9,838	8,023
Drunkenness	40,392	142	1,168	39,224	4	8	130	204	290	532	1,365	1,444	1,472
Disorderly conduct	45,960	5,026	13,986	31,974	136	1,138	3,752	3,043	3,219	2,698	2,079	1,685	1,418
Vagrancy	2,789	49	271	2,518	1	4	44	47	81	94	100	95	88
All other offenses (except traffic)	546,850	8,704	37,677	509,173	265	1,583	6,856	7,197	9,480	12,296	16,716	20,828	22,302
Suspicion	538	25	94	444	0	2	23	15	22	32	41	45	20
Curfew and loitering law violations	4,428	1,026	4,428	-	10	125	891	1,026	1,368	1,008	-	-	-
Runaways	15,754	4,738	15,754	-	74	659	4,005	4,115	4,625	2,276	-	-	-

[1] Because of rounding, the percentages may not add to 100.0.
[2] Violent crimes are offenses of murder and nonnegligent manslaughter, forcible rape, robbery, and aggravated assault. Property crimes are offenses of burglary, larceny-theft, motor vehicle theft, and arson.

Table 52. Arrests in Metropolitan Counties, Distribution by Age, 2006 *(Contd.)*

(Number, percent; 1,252 agencies; 2006 estimated population 45,787,064.)

Offense charged	21	22	23	24	25-29	30-34	35-39	40-44	45-49	50-54	55-59	60-64	65 and over
TOTAL	71,784	67,248	65,609	62,960	264,487	195,649	185,656	169,435	122,552	64,835	31,120	12,923	10,584
Total percent distribution[1]	4.1	3.8	3.7	3.6	15.0	11.1	10.5	9.6	6.9	3.7	1.8	0.7	0.6
Murder and nonnegligent manslaughter	125	101	81	82	330	205	164	120	104	62	48	19	26
Forcible rape	161	126	113	105	436	347	385	272	197	107	64	32	27
Robbery	568	467	417	378	1,389	797	709	578	322	122	57	12	11
Aggravated assault	2,119	2,073	1,995	2,054	8,896	6,795	6,649	6,145	4,514	2,464	1,199	549	544
Burglary	1,684	1,448	1,310	1,117	4,642	3,120	2,916	2,386	1,394	680	221	53	59
Larceny-theft	3,641	3,216	2,985	2,868	11,943	8,913	9,076	8,407	5,903	3,178	1,430	647	554
Motor vehicle theft	792	729	663	613	2,524	1,756	1,467	1,192	654	282	101	49	34
Arson	52	43	25	40	168	139	141	129	113	67	28	17	11
Violent crime[2]	2,973	2,767	2,606	2,619	11,051	8,144	7,907	7,115	5,137	2,755	1,368	612	608
Violent crime percent distribution[1]	3.9	3.6	3.4	3.4	14.6	10.7	10.4	9.4	6.8	3.6	1.8	0.8	0.8
Property crime[2]	6,169	5,436	4,983	4,638	19,277	13,928	13,600	12,114	8,064	4,207	1,780	766	658
Property crime percent distribution[1]	3.8	3.4	3.1	2.9	12.0	8.7	8.5	7.6	5.0	2.6	1.1	0.5	0.4
Other assaults	4,924	4,613	4,679	4,648	20,955	17,174	17,231	15,885	11,359	5,856	3,004	1,292	1,258
Forgery and counterfeiting	566	512	599	554	2,619	1,959	1,843	1,417	967	427	187	78	56
Fraud	1,786	1,759	1,921	1,946	10,021	9,327	9,072	7,158	4,756	2,758	1,427	593	502
Embezzlement	149	121	109	86	368	285	268	229	129	85	43	20	8
Stolen property; buying, receiving, possessing	725	690	675	618	2,456	1,870	1,719	1,408	896	428	155	61	31
Vandalism	1,236	1,051	937	825	3,058	2,082	2,019	1,633	1,135	513	269	115	114
Weapons; carrying, possessing, etc.	1,069	955	856	843	2,971	1,802	1,402	1,275	942	541	284	132	131
Prostitution and commercialized vice	110	90	99	82	417	364	375	372	242	122	56	34	24
Sex offenses (except forcible rape and prostitution)	380	334	357	310	1,303	1,171	1,267	1,188	892	634	386	257	310
Drug abuse violations	11,722	10,508	9,857	9,423	36,610	23,556	21,037	19,521	13,920	6,662	2,636	820	409
Gambling	15	11	18	18	72	87	79	60	71	54	40	32	31
Offenses against the family and children	673	726	847	1,009	5,909	6,468	6,486	5,764	3,667	1,574	559	203	113
Driving under the influence	11,803	11,551	11,659	10,897	43,583	29,220	26,006	25,046	20,130	12,634	7,076	3,054	2,426
Liquor laws	1,214	860	723	598	2,264	1,523	1,488	1,520	1,225	807	352	178	135
Drunkenness	1,859	1,683	1,652	1,487	5,629	4,298	4,456	4,985	4,338	2,491	1,315	480	270
Disorderly conduct	1,650	1,527	1,356	1,245	4,786	3,437	3,636	3,432	2,842	1,501	716	362	302
Vagrancy	66	68	69	88	337	259	377	379	296	180	73	24	19
All other offenses (except traffic)	22,666	21,966	21,579	21,010	90,738	68,660	65,342	58,890	41,513	20,593	9,385	3,809	3,176
Suspicion	29	20	28	16	63	35	46	44	31	13	9	1	3
Curfew and loitering law violations	-	-	-	-	-	-	-	-	-	-	-	-	-
Runaways	-	-	-	-	-	-	-	-	-	-	-	-	-

[1] Because of rounding, the percentages may not add to 100.0.
[2] Violent crimes are offenses of murder and nonnegligent manslaughter, forcible rape, robbery, and aggravated assault. Property crimes are offenses of burglary, larceny-theft, motor vehicle theft, and arson.

Table 53. Arrests in Metropolitan Counties of Persons Under 15, 18, 21, and 25 Years of Age, 2006

(Number, percent; 1,252 agencies; 2006 estimated population 45,787,064.)

Offense charged	Total all ages	Number of persons arrested				Percent of total all ages			
		Under 15	Under 18	Under 21	Under 25	Under 15	Under 18	Under 21	Under 25
TOTAL	1,767,517	58,160	215,230	442,675	710,276	3.3	12.2	25.0	40.2
Murder and nonnegligent manslaughter	1,969	7	150	502	891	0.4	7.6	25.5	45.3
Forcible rape	3,349	182	462	977	1,482	5.4	13.8	29.2	44.3
Robbery	11,323	542	2,672	5,496	7,326	4.8	23.6	48.5	64.7
Aggravated assault	59,274	2,234	7,007	13,278	21,519	3.8	11.8	22.4	36.3
Burglary	39,651	3,057	10,632	18,621	24,180	7.7	26.8	47.0	61.0
Larceny-theft	101,022	6,908	23,290	38,261	50,971	6.8	23.1	37.9	50.5
Motor vehicle theft	17,298	756	3,543	6,442	9,239	4.4	20.5	37.2	53.4
Arson	2,330	519	1,041	1,357	1,517	22.3	44.7	58.2	65.1
Violent crime[1]	75,915	2,965	10,291	20,253	31,218	3.9	13.6	26.7	41.1
Property crime[1]	160,301	11,240	38,506	64,681	85,907	7.0	24.0	40.3	53.6
Other assaults	159,136	12,090	31,788	46,258	65,122	7.6	20.0	29.1	40.9
Forgery and counterfeiting	13,652	50	414	1,868	4,099	0.4	3.0	13.7	30.0
Fraud	57,507	121	838	4,481	11,893	0.2	1.5	7.8	20.7
Embezzlement	2,625	5	189	725	1,190	0.2	7.2	27.6	45.3
Stolen property; buying, receiving, possessing	16,344	413	2,004	4,612	7,320	2.5	12.3	28.2	44.8
Vandalism	32,155	4,404	12,017	17,168	21,217	13.7	37.4	53.4	66.0
Weapons; carrying, possessing, etc.	21,591	1,724	4,809	8,388	12,111	8.0	22.3	38.8	56.1
Prostitution and commercialized vice	2,705	15	77	318	699	0.6	2.8	11.8	25.8
Sex offenses (except forcible rape and prostitution)	12,440	1,073	2,263	3,651	5,032	8.6	18.2	29.3	40.5
Drug abuse violations	226,189	2,921	20,466	59,508	101,018	1.3	9.0	26.3	44.7
Gambling	706	10	40	118	180	1.4	5.7	16.7	25.5
Offenses against the family and children	36,059	219	757	2,061	5,316	0.6	2.1	5.7	14.7
Driving under the influence	237,867	23	2,530	22,782	68,692	*	1.1	9.6	28.9
Liquor laws	55,614	1,177	14,863	42,727	46,122	2.1	26.7	76.8	82.9
Drunkenness	40,392	142	1,168	5,449	12,130	0.4	2.9	13.5	30.0
Disorderly conduct	45,960	5,026	13,986	19,168	24,946	10.9	30.4	41.7	54.3
Vagrancy	2,789	49	271	554	845	1.8	9.7	19.9	30.3
All other offenses (except traffic)	546,850	8,704	37,677	97,523	184,744	1.6	6.9	17.8	33.8
Suspicion	538	25	94	200	293	4.6	17.5	37.2	54.5
Curfew and loitering law violations	4,428	1,026	4,428	4,428	4,428	23.2	100.0	100.0	100.0
Runaways	15,754	4,738	15,754	15,754	15,754	30.1	100.0	100.0	100.0

[1] Violent crimes are offenses of murder and nonnegligent manslaughter, forcible rape, robbery, and aggravated assault. Property crimes are offenses of burglary, larceny-theft, motor vehicle theft, and arson.
* Less than one-tenth of 1 percent.

Table 54. Arrests in Metropolitan Counties, Distribution by Sex, 2006

(Number, percent; 1,252 agencies; 2006 estimated population 45,787,064.)

Offense charged	Number of persons arrested			Percent male	Percent female	Percent distribution[1]		
	Total	Male	Female			Total	Male	Female
TOTAL	1,767,517	1,362,533	404,984	77.1	22.9	100.0	100.0	100.0
Murder and nonnegligent manslaughter	1,969	1,708	261	86.7	13.3	0.1	0.1	0.1
Forcible rape	3,349	3,294	55	98.4	1.6	0.2	0.2	*
Robbery	11,323	10,160	1,163	89.7	10.3	0.6	0.7	0.3
Aggravated assault	59,274	47,959	11,315	80.9	19.1	3.4	3.5	2.8
Burglary	39,651	34,290	5,361	86.5	13.5	2.2	2.5	1.3
Larceny-theft	101,022	66,317	34,705	65.6	34.4	5.7	4.9	8.6
Motor vehicle theft	17,298	14,216	3,082	82.2	17.8	1.0	1.0	0.8
Arson	2,330	1,962	368	84.2	15.8	0.1	0.1	0.1
Violent crime[2]	75,915	63,121	12,794	83.1	16.9	4.3	4.6	3.2
Property crime[2]	160,301	116,785	43,516	72.9	27.1	9.1	8.6	10.7
Other assaults	159,136	119,380	39,756	75.0	25.0	9.0	8.8	9.8
Forgery and counterfeiting	13,652	8,349	5,303	61.2	38.8	0.8	0.6	1.3
Fraud	57,507	29,969	27,538	52.1	47.9	3.3	2.2	6.8
Embezzlement	2,625	1,274	1,351	48.5	51.5	0.1	0.1	0.3
Stolen property; buying, receiving, possessing	16,344	13,356	2,988	81.7	18.3	0.9	1.0	0.7
Vandalism	32,155	27,003	5,152	84.0	16.0	1.8	2.0	1.3
Weapons; carrying, possessing, etc.	21,591	19,875	1,716	92.1	7.9	1.2	1.5	0.4
Prostitution and commercialized vice	2,705	1,005	1,700	37.2	62.8	0.2	0.1	0.4
Sex offenses (except forcible rape and prostitution)	12,440	11,763	677	94.6	5.4	0.7	0.9	0.2
Drug abuse violations	226,189	181,455	44,734	80.2	19.8	12.8	13.3	11.0
Gambling	706	545	161	77.2	22.8	*	*	*
Offenses against the family and children	36,059	30,340	5,719	84.1	15.9	2.0	2.2	1.4
Driving under the influence	237,867	193,082	44,785	81.2	18.8	13.5	14.2	11.1
Liquor laws	55,614	39,691	15,923	71.4	28.6	3.1	2.9	3.9
Drunkenness	40,392	33,755	6,637	83.6	16.4	2.3	2.5	1.6
Disorderly conduct	45,960	34,096	11,864	74.2	25.8	2.6	2.5	2.9
Vagrancy	2,789	1,962	827	70.3	29.7	0.2	0.1	0.2
All other offenses (except traffic)	546,850	425,163	121,687	77.7	22.3	30.9	31.2	30.0
Suspicion	538	419	119	77.9	22.1	*	*	*
Curfew and loitering law violations	4,428	2,933	1,495	66.2	33.8	0.3	0.2	0.4
Runaways	15,754	7,212	8,542	45.8	54.2	0.9	0.5	2.1

[1] Because of rounding, the percentages may not add to 100.0.
[2] Violent crimes are offenses of murder and nonnegligent manslaughter, forcible rape, robbery, and aggravated assault. Property crimes are offenses of burglary, larceny-theft, motor vehicle theft, and arson.
* Less than one-tenth of 1 percent.

Table 55. Arrests in Metropolitan Counties, Distribution by Race, 2006

(Number, percent; 1,252 agencies; 2006 estimated population 45,787,064.)

Offense charged	Total arrests					Percent distribution[1]				
	Total	White	Black	American Indian or Alaskan Native	Asian or Pacific Islander	Total	White	Black	American Indian or Alaskan Native	Asian or Pacific Islander
TOTAL	1,763,142	1,336,437	405,986	10,770	9,949	100.0	75.8	23.0	0.6	0.6
Murder and nonnegligent manslaughter	1,969	1,195	747	16	11	100.0	60.7	37.9	0.8	0.6
Forcible rape	3,344	2,550	754	29	11	100.0	76.3	22.5	0.9	0.3
Robbery	11,311	5,491	5,689	52	79	100.0	48.5	50.3	0.5	0.7
Aggravated assault	59,209	42,796	15,566	437	410	100.0	72.3	26.3	0.7	0.7
Burglary	39,614	30,332	8,854	204	224	100.0	76.6	22.4	0.5	0.6
Larceny-theft	100,903	70,724	28,939	512	728	100.0	70.1	28.7	0.5	0.7
Motor vehicle theft	17,281	13,132	3,961	83	105	100.0	76.0	22.9	0.5	0.6
Arson	2,327	1,888	413	11	15	100.0	81.1	17.7	0.5	0.6
Violent crime[2]	75,833	52,032	22,756	534	511	100.0	68.6	30.0	0.7	0.7
Property crime[2]	160,125	116,076	42,167	810	1,072	100.0	72.5	26.3	0.5	0.7
Other assaults	158,872	115,660	41,338	938	936	100.0	72.8	26.0	0.6	0.6
Forgery and counterfeiting	13,639	9,895	3,594	46	104	100.0	72.5	26.4	0.3	0.8
Fraud	57,359	39,741	17,242	147	229	100.0	69.3	30.1	0.3	0.4
Embezzlement	2,619	1,621	968	7	23	100.0	61.9	37.0	0.3	0.9
Stolen property; buying, receiving, possessing	16,322	12,109	4,034	97	82	100.0	74.2	24.7	0.6	0.5
Vandalism	32,086	26,072	5,615	225	174	100.0	81.3	17.5	0.7	0.5
Weapons; carrying, possessing, etc.	21,546	14,131	7,156	123	136	100.0	65.6	33.2	0.6	0.6
Prostitution and commercialized vice	2,700	1,671	816	9	204	100.0	61.9	30.2	0.3	7.6
Sex offenses (except forcible rape and prostitution)	12,413	9,933	2,329	74	77	100.0	80.0	18.8	0.6	0.6
Drug abuse violations	225,715	165,571	58,224	969	951	100.0	73.4	25.8	0.4	0.4
Gambling	699	446	217	1	35	100.0	63.8	31.0	0.1	5.0
Offenses against the family and children	35,958	22,449	13,261	125	123	100.0	62.4	36.9	0.3	0.3
Driving under the influence	237,226	212,813	21,689	1,371	1,353	100.0	89.7	9.1	0.6	0.6
Liquor laws	55,317	50,340	4,070	474	433	100.0	91.0	7.4	0.9	0.8
Drunkenness	40,311	36,458	3,341	351	161	100.0	90.4	8.3	0.9	0.4
Disorderly conduct	45,872	32,370	12,991	304	207	100.0	70.6	28.3	0.7	0.5
Vagrancy	2,789	1,867	900	8	14	100.0	66.9	32.3	0.3	0.5
All other offenses (except traffic)	545,050	399,118	138,962	4,007	2,963	100.0	73.2	25.5	0.7	0.5
Suspicion	538	279	258	0	1	100.0	51.9	48.0	0.0	0.2
Curfew and loitering law violations	4,412	3,545	801	23	43	100.0	80.3	18.2	0.5	1.0
Runaways	15,741	12,240	3,257	127	117	100.0	77.8	20.7	0.8	0.7

[1] Because of rounding, the percentages may not add to 100.0.
[2] Violent crimes are offenses of murder and nonnegligent manslaughter, forcible rape, robbery, and aggravated assault. Property crimes are offenses of burglary, larceny-theft, motor vehicle theft, and arson.

Table 55. Arrests in Metropolitan Counties, Distribution by Race, 2006 (*Contd.*)

(Number, percent; 1,252 agencies; 2006 estimated population 45,787,064.)

Offense charged	Arrests under 18					Percent distribution[1]				
	Total	White	Black	American Indian or Alaskan Native	Asian or Pacific Islander	Total	White	Black	American Indian or Alaskan Native	Asian or Pacific Islander
TOTAL	214,812	152,065	60,024	1,310	1,413	100.0	70.8	27.9	0.6	0.7
Murder and nonnegligent manslaughter	150	62	85	3	0	100.0	41.3	56.7	2.0	0.0
Forcible rape	461	335	120	4	2	100.0	72.7	26.0	0.9	0.4
Robbery	2,671	873	1,765	7	26	100.0	32.7	66.1	0.3	1.0
Aggravated assault	7,002	4,377	2,519	55	51	100.0	62.5	36.0	0.8	0.7
Burglary	10,621	7,566	2,930	47	78	100.0	71.2	27.6	0.4	0.7
Larceny-theft	23,261	14,852	8,072	108	229	100.0	63.8	34.7	0.5	1.0
Motor vehicle theft	3,540	2,392	1,095	21	32	100.0	67.6	30.9	0.6	0.9
Arson	1,038	844	184	2	8	100.0	81.3	17.7	0.2	0.8
Violent crime[2]	10,284	5,647	4,489	69	79	100.0	54.9	43.7	0.7	0.8
Property crime[2]	38,460	25,654	12,281	178	347	100.0	66.7	31.9	0.5	0.9
Other assaults	31,737	18,475	12,933	170	159	100.0	58.2	40.8	0.5	0.5
Forgery and counterfeiting	414	318	84	9	3	100.0	76.8	20.3	2.2	0.7
Fraud	834	609	214	3	8	100.0	73.0	25.7	0.4	1.0
Embezzlement	189	78	108	0	3	100.0	41.3	57.1	0.0	1.6
Stolen property; buying, receiving, possessing	2,000	1,342	630	12	16	100.0	67.1	31.5	0.6	0.8
Vandalism	11,988	9,632	2,227	70	59	100.0	80.3	18.6	0.6	0.5
Weapons; carrying, possessing, etc.	4,797	2,976	1,736	34	51	100.0	62.0	36.2	0.7	1.1
Prostitution and commercialized vice	77	36	39	0	2	100.0	46.8	50.6	0.0	2.6
Sex offenses (except forcible rape and prostitution)	2,255	1,714	533	6	2	100.0	76.0	23.6	0.3	0.1
Drug abuse violations	20,433	15,856	4,361	108	108	100.0	77.6	21.3	0.5	0.5
Gambling	40	5	34	0	1	100.0	12.5	85.0	0.0	2.5
Offenses against the family and children	757	655	97	3	2	100.0	86.5	12.8	0.4	0.3
Driving under the influence	2,519	2,412	75	27	5	100.0	95.8	3.0	1.1	0.2
Liquor laws	14,795	14,074	491	129	101	100.0	95.1	3.3	0.9	0.7
Drunkenness	1,164	1,046	101	8	9	100.0	89.9	8.7	0.7	0.8
Disorderly conduct	13,971	7,963	5,851	92	65	100.0	57.0	41.9	0.7	0.5
Vagrancy	271	230	34	3	4	100.0	84.9	12.5	1.1	1.5
All other offenses (except traffic)	37,580	27,519	9,594	239	228	100.0	73.2	25.5	0.6	0.6
Suspicion	94	39	54	0	1	100.0	41.5	57.4	0.0	1.1
Curfew and loitering law violations	4,412	3,545	801	23	43	100.0	80.3	18.2	0.5	1.0
Runaways	15,741	12,240	3,257	127	117	100.0	77.8	20.7	0.8	0.7

[1] Because of rounding, the percentages may not add to 100.0.
[2] Violent crimes are offenses of murder and nonnegligent manslaughter, forcible rape, robbery, and aggravated assault. Property crimes are offenses of burglary, larceny-theft, motor vehicle theft, and arson.

Table 55. Arrests in Metropolitan Counties, Distribution by Race, 2006 (*Contd.*)

(Number, percent; 1,252 agencies; 2006 estimated population 45,787,064.)

Offense charged	Arrests 18 and over					Percent distribution[1]				
	Total	White	Black	American Indian or Alaskan Native	Asian or Pacific Islander	Total	White	Black	American Indian or Alaskan Native	Asian or Pacific Islander
TOTAL	1,548,330	1,184,372	345,962	9,460	8,536	100.0	76.5	22.3	0.6	0.6
Murder and nonnegligent manslaughter..	1,819	1,133	662	13	11	100.0	62.3	36.4	0.7	0.6
Forcible rape	2,883	2,215	634	25	9	100.0	76.8	22.0	0.9	0.3
Robbery...	8,640	4,618	3,924	45	53	100.0	53.4	45.4	0.5	0.6
Aggravated assault	52,207	38,419	13,047	382	359	100.0	73.6	25.0	0.7	0.7
Burglary	28,993	22,766	5,924	157	146	100.0	78.5	20.4	0.5	0.5
Larceny-theft.......................................	77,642	55,872	20,867	404	499	100.0	72.0	26.9	0.5	0.6
Motor vehicle theft	13,741	10,740	2,866	62	73	100.0	78.2	20.9	0.5	0.5
Arson...	1,289	1,044	229	9	7	100.0	81.0	17.8	0.7	0.5
Violent crime[2]	65,549	46,385	18,267	465	432	100.0	70.8	27.9	0.7	0.7
Property crime[2]....................................	121,665	90,422	29,886	632	725	100.0	74.3	24.6	0.5	0.6
Other assaults......................................	127,135	97,185	28,405	768	777	100.0	76.4	22.3	0.6	0.6
Forgery and counterfeiting...................	13,225	9,577	3,510	37	101	100.0	72.4	26.5	0.3	0.8
Fraud...	56,525	39,132	17,028	144	221	100.0	69.2	30.1	0.3	0.4
Embezzlement......................................	2,430	1,543	860	7	20	100.0	63.5	35.4	0.3	0.8
Stolen property; buying, receiving, possessing..	14,322	10,767	3,404	85	66	100.0	75.2	23.8	0.6	0.5
Vandalism	20,098	16,440	3,388	155	115	100.0	81.8	16.9	0.8	0.6
Weapons; carrying, possessing, etc.	16,749	11,155	5,420	89	85	100.0	66.6	32.4	0.5	0.5
Prostitution and commercialized vice...	2,623	1,635	777	9	202	100.0	62.3	29.6	0.3	7.7
Sex offenses (except forcible rape and prostitution)...................................	10,158	8,219	1,796	68	75	100.0	80.9	17.7	0.7	0.7
Drug abuse violations...........................	205,282	149,715	53,863	861	843	100.0	72.9	26.2	0.4	0.4
Gambling..	659	441	183	1	34	100.0	66.9	27.8	0.2	5.2
Offenses against the family and children	35,201	21,794	13,164	122	121	100.0	61.9	37.4	0.3	0.3
Driving under the influence.................	234,707	210,401	21,614	1,344	1,348	100.0	89.6	9.2	0.6	0.6
Liquor laws..	40,522	36,266	3,579	345	332	100.0	89.5	8.8	0.9	0.8
Drunkenness	39,147	35,412	3,240	343	152	100.0	90.5	8.3	0.9	0.4
Disorderly conduct..............................	31,901	24,407	7,140	212	142	100.0	76.5	22.4	0.7	0.4
Vagrancy..	2,518	1,637	866	5	10	100.0	65.0	34.4	0.2	0.4
All other offenses (except traffic)........	507,470	371,599	129,368	3,768	2,735	100.0	73.2	25.5	0.7	0.5
Suspicion..	444	240	204	0	0	100.0	54.1	45.9	0.0	0.0
Curfew and loitering law violations.....	-	-	-	-	-	-	-	-	-	-
Runaways...	-	-	-	-	-	-	-	-	-	-

[1] Because of rounding, the percentages may not add to 100.0.
[2] Violent crimes are offenses of murder and nonnegligent manslaughter, forcible rape, robbery, and aggravated assault. Property crimes are offenses of burglary, larceny-theft, motor vehicle theft, and arson.

Table 56. Arrest Trends for Nonmetropolitan Counties, 2005–2006

(Number, percent change; 1,617 agencies; 2006 estimated population 19,637,937; 2005 estimated population 19,541,700.)

Offense charged	Number of persons arrested								
	Total all ages			Under 18 years of age			18 years of age and over		
	2005	2006	Percent change	2005	2006	Percent change	2005	2006	Percent change
TOTAL[1]	753,595	750,542	-0.4	66,935	65,736	-1.8	686,660	684,806	-0.3
Murder and nonnegligent manslaughter	707	627	-11.3	37	22	-40.5	670	605	-9.7
Forcible rape	1,723	1,563	-9.3	282	218	-22.7	1,441	1,345	-6.7
Robbery	1,928	1,952	+1.2	238	194	-18.5	1,690	1,758	+4.0
Aggravated assault	20,825	20,499	-1.6	1,897	1,834	-3.3	18,928	18,665	-1.4
Burglary	18,666	17,917	-4.0	3,951	4,087	+3.4	14,715	13,830	-6.0
Larceny-theft	31,134	30,115	-3.3	5,322	4,851	-8.9	25,812	25,264	-2.1
Motor vehicle theft	5,570	5,173	-7.1	1,254	1,112	-11.3	4,316	4,061	-5.9
Arson	1,031	984	-4.6	335	293	-12.5	696	691	-0.7
Violent crime[2]	25,183	24,641	-2.2	2,454	2,268	-7.6	22,729	22,373	-1.6
Property crime[2]	56,401	54,189	-3.9	10,862	10,343	-4.8	45,539	43,846	-3.7
Other assaults	72,247	69,710	-3.5	8,938	8,673	-3.0	63,309	61,037	-3.6
Forgery and counterfeiting	5,317	4,959	-6.7	190	112	-41.1	5,127	4,847	-5.5
Fraud	36,053	33,311	-7.6	336	304	-9.5	35,717	33,007	-7.6
Embezzlement	842	798	-5.2	22	23	+4.5	820	775	-5.5
Stolen property; buying, receiving, possessing	5,193	4,816	-7.3	582	570	-2.1	4,611	4,246	-7.9
Vandalism	12,949	12,899	-0.4	3,908	3,739	-4.3	9,041	9,160	+1.3
Weapons; carrying, possessing, etc.	7,080	6,977	-1.5	802	863	+7.6	6,278	6,114	-2.6
Prostitution and commercialized vice	161	242	+50.3	3	5	+66.7	158	237	+50.0
Sex offenses (except forcible rape and prostitution)	5,264	4,846	-7.9	994	829	-16.6	4,270	4,017	-5.9
Drug abuse violations	89,359	88,489	-1.0	6,106	6,067	-0.6	83,253	82,422	-1.0
Gambling	400	450	+12.5	6	13	+116.7	394	437	+10.9
Offenses against the family and children	12,834	12,481	-2.8	363	280	-22.9	12,471	12,201	-2.2
Driving under the influence	115,693	117,301	+1.4	1,481	1,813	+22.4	114,212	115,488	+1.1
Liquor laws	31,113	32,689	+5.1	7,620	8,053	+5.7	23,493	24,636	+4.9
Drunkenness	19,020	19,081	+0.3	428	461	+7.7	18,592	18,620	+0.2
Disorderly conduct	21,103	20,272	-3.9	4,849	4,473	-7.8	16,254	15,799	-2.8
Vagrancy	213	179	-16.0	13	18	+38.5	200	161	-19.5
All other offenses (except traffic)	231,937	236,966	+2.2	11,745	11,583	-1.4	220,192	225,383	+2.4
Suspicion	125	176	+40.8	23	22	-4.3	102	154	+51.0
Curfew and loitering law violations	579	599	+3.5	579	599	+3.5	-	-	-
Runaways	4,654	4,647	-0.2	4,654	4,647	-0.2	-	-	-

[1] Does not include suspicion.
[2] Violent crimes are offenses of murder and nonnegligent manslaughter, forcible rape, robbery, and aggravated assault. Property crimes are offenses of burglary, larceny-theft, motor vehicle theft, and arson.

Table 57. Arrest Trends for Nonmetropolitan Counties, by Age and Sex, 2005–2006

(Number, percent; 1,617 agencies; 2006 estimated population 19,637,937; 2005 estimated population 19,541,700.)

Offense charged	Male						Female					
	Total			Under 18			Total			Under 18		
	2005	2006	Percent change	2005	2006	Percent change	2005	2006	Percent change	2005	2006	Percent change
TOTAL[1]	579,837	576,518	-0.6	48,416	47,501	-1.9	173,758	174,024	+0.2	18,519	18,235	-1.5
Murder and nonnegligent manslaughter	607	545	-10.2	31	18	-41.9	100	82	-18.0	6	4	-33.3
Forcible rape	1,693	1,539	-9.1	272	214	-21.3	30	24	-20.0	10	4	-60.0
Robbery	1,695	1,706	+0.6	213	178	-16.4	233	246	+5.6	25	16	-36.0
Aggravated assault	17,065	16,702	-2.1	1,475	1,414	-4.1	3,760	3,797	+1.0	422	420	-0.5
Burglary	16,164	15,553	-3.8	3,589	3,682	+2.6	2,502	2,364	-5.5	362	405	+11.9
Larceny-theft	21,897	21,305	-2.7	3,792	3,493	-7.9	9,237	8,810	-4.6	1,530	1,358	-11.2
Motor vehicle theft	4,514	4,213	-6.7	969	871	-10.1	1,056	960	-9.1	285	241	-15.4
Arson	883	833	-5.7	313	255	-18.5	148	151	+2.0	22	38	+72.7
Violent crime[2]	21,060	20,492	-2.7	1,991	1,824	-8.4	4,123	4,149	+0.6	463	444	-4.1
Property crime[2]	43,458	41,904	-3.6	8,663	8,301	-4.2	12,943	12,285	-5.1	2,199	2,042	-7.1
Other assaults	54,797	52,538	-4.1	6,149	5,922	-3.7	17,450	17,172	-1.6	2,789	2,751	-1.4
Forgery and counterfeiting	3,057	2,789	-8.8	139	69	-50.4	2,260	2,170	-4.0	51	43	-15.7
Fraud	17,827	16,830	-5.6	206	200	-2.9	18,226	16,481	-9.6	130	104	-20.0
Embezzlement	420	388	-7.6	12	14	+16.7	422	410	-2.8	10	9	-10.0
Stolen property; buying, receiving, possessing	4,309	3,959	-8.1	502	501	-0.2	884	857	-3.1	80	69	-13.8
Vandalism	10,774	10,605	-1.6	3,425	3,190	-6.9	2,175	2,294	+5.5	483	549	+13.7
Weapons; carrying, possessing, etc.	6,500	6,404	-1.5	715	773	+8.1	580	573	-1.2	87	90	+3.4
Prostitution and commercialized vice	93	141	+51.6	3	4	+33.3	68	101	+48.5	0	1	-
Sex offenses (except forcible rape and prostitution)	4,983	4,574	-8.2	916	748	-18.3	281	272	-3.2	78	81	+3.8
Drug abuse violations	70,474	69,740	-1.0	4,786	4,827	+0.9	18,885	18,749	-0.7	1,320	1,240	-6.1
Gambling	313	370	+18.2	3	11	+266.7	87	80	-8.0	3	2	-33.3
Offenses against the family and children	10,393	10,071	-3.1	228	211	-7.5	2,441	2,410	-1.3	135	69	-48.9
Driving under the influence	94,862	95,402	+0.6	1,174	1,407	+19.8	20,831	21,899	+5.1	307	406	+32.2
Liquor laws	23,007	24,206	+5.2	4,900	5,172	+5.6	8,106	8,483	+4.7	2,720	2,881	+5.9
Drunkenness	15,843	15,769	-0.5	324	345	+6.5	3,177	3,312	+4.2	104	116	+11.5
Disorderly conduct	15,515	14,979	-3.5	3,287	3,111	-5.4	5,588	5,293	-5.3	1,562	1,362	-12.8
Vagrancy	160	146	-8.8	5	15	+200.0	53	33	-37.7	8	3	-62.5
All other offenses (except traffic)	179,658	182,800	+1.7	8,654	8,445	-2.4	52,279	54,166	+3.6	3,091	3,138	+1.5
Suspicion	100	147	+47.0	17	18	+5.9	25	29	+16.0	6	4	-33.3
Curfew and loitering law violations	351	428	+21.9	351	428	+21.9	228	171	-25.0	228	171	-25.0
Runaways	1,983	1,983	*	1,983	1,983	*	2,671	2,664	-0.3	2,671	2,664	-0.3

[1] Does not include suspicion.
[2] Violent crimes are offenses of murder and nonnegligent manslaughter, forcible rape, robbery, and aggravated assault. Property crimes are offenses of burglary, larceny-theft, motor vehicle theft, and arson.
* Less than one-tenth of 1 percent.

Table 58. Arrests in Nonmetropolitan Counties, Distribution by Age, 2006

(Number, percent; 1,799 agencies; 2006 estimated population 19,439,450.)

Offense charged	Total all ages	Ages under 15	Ages under 18	Ages 18 and over	Under 10	10-12	13-14	15	16	17	18	19	20
TOTAL	784,411	16,459	69,468	714,943	1,011	3,269	12,179	11,611	17,482	23,916	34,223	36,367	36,060
Total percent distribution[1]	100.0	2.1	8.9	91.1	0.1	0.4	1.6	1.5	2.2	3.0	4.4	4.6	4.6
Murder and nonnegligent manslaughter	626	3	23	603	0	0	3	6	9	5	24	27	37
Forcible rape	1,547	63	212	1,335	1	11	51	31	56	62	84	89	74
Robbery	1,990	23	199	1,791	1	1	21	20	61	95	152	152	136
Aggravated assault	20,373	503	1,874	18,499	20	114	369	305	468	598	703	694	704
Burglary	18,294	1,112	4,309	13,985	56	214	842	796	1,021	1,380	1,588	1,340	1,084
Larceny-theft	29,543	1,370	4,863	24,680	59	337	974	839	1,192	1,462	1,757	1,459	1,387
Motor vehicle theft	5,087	258	1,109	3,978	5	29	224	248	270	333	320	294	258
Arson	970	133	279	691	9	41	83	38	62	46	62	62	41
Violent crime[2]	24,536	592	2,308	22,228	22	126	444	362	594	760	963	962	951
Violent crime percent distribution[1]	100.0	2.4	9.4	90.6	0.1	0.5	1.8	1.5	2.4	3.1	3.9	3.9	3.9
Property crime[2]	53,894	2,873	10,560	43,334	129	621	2,123	1,921	2,545	3,221	3,727	3,155	2,770
Property crime percent distribution	100.0	5.3	19.6	80.4	0.2	1.2	3.9	3.6	4.7	6.0	6.9	5.9	5.1
Other assaults	67,664	2,934	8,843	58,821	143	727	2,064	1,648	2,094	2,167	2,081	2,047	2,100
Forgery and counterfeiting	5,139	12	124	5,015	0	2	10	14	26	72	169	190	200
Fraud	29,475	50	312	29,163	5	8	37	37	81	144	472	716	840
Embezzlement	774	1	24	750	0	1	0	2	9	12	24	19	25
Stolen property; buying, receiving, possessing	5,063	120	600	4,463	6	17	97	105	172	203	313	264	240
Vandalism	12,801	1,405	3,831	8,970	136	368	901	637	895	894	997	692	587
Weapons; carrying, possessing, etc.	7,186	286	899	6,287	30	74	182	158	196	259	350	286	277
Prostitution and commercialized vice	227	0	5	222	0	0	0	0	3	2	7	0	12
Sex offenses (except forcible rape and prostitution)	5,070	361	877	4,193	27	82	252	150	179	187	220	228	200
Drug abuse violations	92,388	810	6,316	86,072	43	88	679	846	1,628	3,032	5,382	5,622	5,383
Gambling	506	3	14	492	0	1	2	0	3	8	18	22	20
Offenses against the family and children	12,678	100	329	12,349	17	24	59	55	78	96	230	231	242
Driving under the influence	150,599	188	2,260	148,339	170	1	17	82	552	1,438	3,497	4,707	5,193
Liquor laws	36,198	750	8,906	27,292	11	36	703	1,299	2,573	4,284	6,270	6,489	5,354
Drunkenness	18,125	39	459	17,666	1	1	37	69	114	237	582	639	646
Disorderly conduct	21,887	1,703	5,021	16,866	77	359	1,267	954	1,183	1,181	998	803	834
Vagrancy	169	5	23	146	0	2	3	4	3	11	5	3	4
All other offenses (except traffic)	234,481	2,587	12,366	222,115	161	486	1,940	1,930	3,037	4,812	7,917	9,285	10,180
Suspicion	187	8	27	160	0	4	4	8	6	5	1	7	2
Curfew and loitering law violations	535	159	535	-	6	30	123	110	155	111	-	-	-
Runaways	4,829	1,473	4,829	-	27	211	1,235	1,220	1,356	780	-	-	-

[1] Because of rounding, the percentages may not add to 100.0.
[2] Violent crimes are offenses of murder and nonnegligent manslaughter, forcible rape, robbery, and aggravated assault. Property crimes are offenses of burglary, larceny-theft, motor vehicle theft, and arson.

Table 58. Arrests in Nonmetropolitan Counties, Distribution by Age, 2006 (*Contd.*)

(Number, percent; 1,799 agencies; 2006 estimated population 19,439,450.)

Offense charged	21	22	23	24	25-29	30-34	35-39	40-44	45-49	50-54	55-59	60-64	65 and over
TOTAL	32,763	30,895	29,378	28,185	117,968	87,649	82,106	76,666	57,881	32,413	16,908	8,118	7,363
Total percent distribution[1]	4.2	3.9	3.7	3.6	15.0	11.2	10.5	9.8	7.4	4.1	2.2	1.0	0.9
Murder and nonnegligent manslaughter	32	22	35	20	98	73	44	55	42	39	23	13	19
Forcible rape	69	55	51	45	197	154	166	137	90	48	35	19	22
Robbery	130	127	98	80	330	183	139	145	69	25	14	5	6
Aggravated assault	719	747	732	697	3,087	2,357	2,180	2,264	1,672	953	477	254	259
Burglary	883	737	672	567	2,301	1,483	1,254	992	618	262	122	48	34
Larceny-theft	1,164	1,086	1,015	905	3,965	3,027	2,925	2,405	1,722	941	484	211	227
Motor vehicle theft	207	173	186	161	681	506	461	351	210	92	40	18	20
Arson	37	34	32	21	97	75	59	57	47	29	21	8	9
Violent crime[2]	950	951	916	842	3,712	2,767	2,529	2,601	1,873	1,065	549	291	306
Violent crime percent distribution[1]	3.9	3.9	3.7	3.4	15.1	11.3	10.3	10.6	7.6	4.3	2.2	1.2	1.2
Property crime[2]	2,291	2,030	1,905	1,654	7,044	5,091	4,699	3,805	2,597	1,324	667	285	290
Property crime percent distribution	4.3	3.8	3.5	3.1	13.1	9.4	8.7	7.1	4.8	2.5	1.2	0.5	0.5
Other assaults	2,147	2,168	2,130	2,045	9,625	8,021	8,007	7,467	5,257	2,752	1,419	761	794
Forgery and counterfeiting	236	198	213	222	1,050	753	638	545	344	147	67	24	19
Fraud	938	923	1,015	1,147	5,190	4,800	4,392	3,541	2,418	1,324	776	367	304
Embezzlement	28	25	13	21	105	108	116	125	71	30	25	9	6
Stolen property; buying, receiving, possessing	246	169	204	190	814	581	504	419	278	127	50	37	27
Vandalism	596	520	376	353	1,420	904	816	695	463	261	139	63	88
Weapons; carrying, possessing, etc.	332	301	283	274	997	665	629	601	555	333	216	92	96
Prostitution and commercialized vice	3	3	7	7	36	27	34	27	26	11	5	5	12
Sex offenses (except forcible rape and prostitution)	173	155	132	146	573	464	474	435	324	223	140	138	168
Drug abuse violations	4,974	4,546	4,211	4,081	15,299	9,610	8,400	7,853	5,880	2,961	1,224	377	269
Gambling	22	26	14	18	68	58	66	54	37	36	17	8	8
Offenses against the family and children	275	329	344	376	2,228	2,272	2,134	1,809	1,069	457	218	67	68
Driving under the influence	6,776	6,575	6,338	5,917	23,541	16,948	16,445	17,289	14,945	9,616	5,472	2,830	2,250
Liquor laws	912	652	528	451	1,610	1,088	990	1,064	842	472	294	161	115
Drunkenness	811	713	698	593	2,549	1,939	1,978	2,271	2,031	1,193	589	236	198
Disorderly conduct	904	727	711	676	2,529	1,855	1,894	1,814	1,430	813	432	197	249
Vagrancy	7	4	8	4	16	20	23	19	14	8	7	3	1
All other offenses (except traffic)	10,138	9,871	9,328	9,160	39,541	29,656	27,309	24,214	17,409	9,250	4,598	2,167	2,092
Suspicion	4	9	4	8	21	22	29	18	18	10	4	0	3
Curfew and loitering law violations	-	-	-	-	-	-	-	-	-	-	-	-	-
Runaways	-	-	-	-	-	-	-	-	-	-	-	-	-

[1] Because of rounding, the percentages may not add to 100.0.
[2] Violent crimes are offenses of murder and nonnegligent manslaughter, forcible rape, robbery, and aggravated assault. Property crimes are offenses of burglary, larceny-theft, motor vehicle theft, and arson.

Table 59. Arrests in Nonmetropolitan Counties of Persons Under 15, 18, 21, and 25 Years of Age, 2006

(Number, percent; 1,799 agencies; 2006 estimated population 19,439,450.)

Offense charged	Total all ages	Number of persons arrested				Percent of total all ages			
		Under 15	Under 18	Under 21	Under 25	Under 15	Under 18	Under 21	Under 25
TOTAL	784,411	16,459	69,468	176,118	297,339	2.1	8.9	22.5	37.9
Murder and nonnegligent manslaughter	626	3	23	111	220	0.5	3.7	17.7	35.1
Forcible rape	1,547	63	212	459	679	4.1	13.7	29.7	43.9
Robbery	1,990	23	199	639	1,074	1.2	10.0	32.1	54.0
Aggravated assault	20,373	503	1,874	3,975	6,870	2.5	9.2	19.5	33.7
Burglary	18,294	1,112	4,309	8,321	11,180	6.1	23.6	45.5	61.1
Larceny-theft	29,543	1,370	4,863	9,466	13,636	4.6	16.5	32.0	46.2
Motor vehicle theft	5,087	258	1,109	1,981	2,708	5.1	21.8	38.9	53.2
Arson	970	133	279	444	568	13.7	28.8	45.8	58.6
Violent crime[1]	24,536	592	2,308	5,184	8,843	2.4	9.4	21.1	36.0
Property crime[1]	53,894	2,873	10,560	20,212	28,092	5.3	19.6	37.5	52.1
Other assaults	67,664	2,934	8,843	15,071	23,561	4.3	13.1	22.3	34.8
Forgery and counterfeiting	5,139	12	124	683	1,552	0.2	2.4	13.3	30.2
Fraud	29,475	50	312	2,340	6,363	0.2	1.1	7.9	21.6
Embezzlement	774	1	24	92	179	0.1	3.1	11.9	23.1
Stolen property; buying, receiving, possessing	5,063	120	600	1,417	2,226	2.4	11.9	28.0	44.0
Vandalism	12,801	1,405	3,831	6,107	7,952	11.0	29.9	47.7	62.1
Weapons; carrying, possessing, etc.	7,186	286	899	1,812	3,002	4.0	12.5	25.2	41.8
Prostitution and commercialized vice	227	0	5	24	44	0.0	2.2	10.6	19.4
Sex offenses (except forcible rape and prostitution)	5,070	361	877	1,525	2,131	7.1	17.3	30.1	42.0
Drug abuse violations	92,388	810	6,316	22,703	40,515	0.9	6.8	24.6	43.9
Gambling	506	3	14	74	154	0.6	2.8	14.6	30.4
Offenses against the family and children	12,678	100	329	1,032	2,356	0.8	2.6	8.1	18.6
Driving under the influence	150,599	188	2,260	15,657	41,263	0.1	1.5	10.4	27.4
Liquor laws	36,198	750	8,906	27,019	29,562	2.1	24.6	74.6	81.7
Drunkenness	18,125	39	459	2,326	5,141	0.2	2.5	12.8	28.4
Disorderly conduct	21,887	1,703	5,021	7,656	10,674	7.8	22.9	35.0	48.8
Vagrancy	169	5	23	35	58	3.0	13.6	20.7	34.3
All other offenses (except traffic)	234,481	2,587	12,366	39,748	78,245	1.1	5.3	17.0	33.4
Suspicion	187	8	27	37	62	4.3	14.4	19.8	33.2
Curfew and loitering law violations	535	159	535	535	535	29.7	100.0	100.0	100.0
Runaways	4,829	1,473	4,829	4,829	4,829	30.5	100.0	100.0	100.0

[1] Violent crimes are offenses of murder and nonnegligent manslaughter, forcible rape, robbery, and aggravated assault. Property crimes are offenses of burglary, larceny-theft, motor vehicle theft, and arson.

Table 60. Arrests in Nonmetropolitan Counties, Distribution by Sex, 2006

(Number, percent; 1,799 agencies; 2006 estimated population 19,439,450.)

Offense charged	Number of persons arrested			Percent male	Percent female	Percent distribution[1]		
	Total	Male	Female			Total	Male	Female
TOTAL	784,411	606,579	177,832	77.3	22.7	100.0	100.0	100.0
Murder and nonnegligent manslaughter	626	549	77	87.7	12.3	0.1	0.1	*
Forcible rape	1,547	1,522	25	98.4	1.6	0.2	0.3	*
Robbery	1,990	1,738	252	87.3	12.7	0.3	0.3	0.1
Aggravated assault	20,373	16,584	3,789	81.4	18.6	2.6	2.7	2.1
Burglary	18,294	15,924	2,370	87.0	13.0	2.3	2.6	1.3
Larceny-theft	29,543	21,023	8,520	71.2	28.8	3.8	3.5	4.8
Motor vehicle theft	5,087	4,135	952	81.3	18.7	0.6	0.7	0.5
Arson	970	810	160	83.5	16.5	0.1	0.1	0.1
Violent crime[2]	24,536	20,393	4,143	83.1	16.9	3.1	3.4	2.3
Property crime[2]	53,894	41,892	12,002	77.7	22.3	6.9	6.9	6.7
Other assaults	67,664	50,989	16,675	75.4	24.6	8.6	8.4	9.4
Forgery and counterfeiting	5,139	2,919	2,220	56.8	43.2	0.7	0.5	1.2
Fraud	29,475	15,154	14,321	51.4	48.6	3.8	2.5	8.1
Embezzlement	774	376	398	48.6	51.4	0.1	0.1	0.2
Stolen property; buying, receiving, possessing	5,063	4,172	891	82.4	17.6	0.6	0.7	0.5
Vandalism	12,801	10,565	2,236	82.5	17.5	1.6	1.7	1.3
Weapons; carrying, possessing, etc.	7,186	6,609	577	92.0	8.0	0.9	1.1	0.3
Prostitution and commercialized vice	227	138	89	60.8	39.2	*	*	0.1
Sex offenses (except forcible rape and prostitution)	5,070	4,779	291	94.3	5.7	0.6	0.8	0.2
Drug abuse violations	92,388	73,128	19,260	79.2	20.8	11.8	12.1	10.8
Gambling	506	421	85	83.2	16.8	0.1	0.1	*
Offenses against the family and children	12,678	10,197	2,481	80.4	19.6	1.6	1.7	1.4
Driving under the influence	150,599	122,696	27,903	81.5	18.5	19.2	20.2	15.7
Liquor laws	36,198	26,522	9,676	73.3	26.7	4.6	4.4	5.4
Drunkenness	18,125	15,029	3,096	82.9	17.1	2.3	2.5	1.7
Disorderly conduct	21,887	16,172	5,715	73.9	26.1	2.8	2.7	3.2
Vagrancy	169	138	31	81.7	18.3	*	*	*
All other offenses (except traffic)	234,481	181,675	52,806	77.5	22.5	29.9	30.0	29.7
Suspicion	187	157	30	84.0	16.0	*	*	*
Curfew and loitering law violations	535	386	149	72.1	27.9	0.1	0.1	0.1
Runaways	4,829	2,072	2,757	42.9	57.1	0.6	0.3	1.6

[1] Because of rounding, the percentages may not add to 100.0.
[2] Violent crimes are offenses of murder and nonnegligent manslaughter, forcible rape, robbery, and aggravated assault. Property crimes are offenses of burglary, larceny-theft, motor vehicle theft, and arson.
* Less than one-tenth of 1 percent.

Table 61. Arrests in Nonmetropolitan Counties, Distribution by Race, 2006

(Number, percent; 1,799 agencies; 2006 estimated population 19,439,450.)

Offense charged	Total arrests					Percent distribution[1]				
	Total	White	Black	American Indian or Alaskan Native	Asian or Pacific Islander	Total	White	Black	American Indian or Alaskan Native	Asian or Pacific Islander
TOTAL	779,872	644,643	107,129	21,056	7,044	100.0	82.7	13.7	2.7	0.9
Murder and nonnegligent manslaughter	622	401	189	29	3	100.0	64.5	30.4	4.7	0.5
Forcible rape	1,536	1,226	258	46	6	100.0	79.8	16.8	3.0	0.4
Robbery	1,988	1,110	801	59	18	100.0	55.8	40.3	3.0	0.9
Aggravated assault	20,312	15,299	3,987	904	122	100.0	75.3	19.6	4.5	0.6
Burglary	18,253	15,106	2,441	592	114	100.0	82.8	13.4	3.2	0.6
Larceny-theft	29,429	24,242	4,137	741	309	100.0	82.4	14.1	2.5	1.0
Motor vehicle theft	5,068	4,247	567	178	76	100.0	83.8	11.2	3.5	1.5
Arson	968	828	104	28	8	100.0	85.5	10.7	2.9	0.8
Violent crime[2]	24,458	18,036	5,235	1,038	149	100.0	73.7	21.4	4.2	0.6
Property crime[2]	53,718	44,423	7,249	1,539	507	100.0	82.7	13.5	2.9	0.9
Other assaults	67,440	53,609	11,153	2,179	499	100.0	79.5	16.5	3.2	0.7
Forgery and counterfeiting	5,117	4,236	795	52	34	100.0	82.8	15.5	1.0	0.7
Fraud	29,364	23,113	5,838	335	78	100.0	78.7	19.9	1.1	0.3
Embezzlement	765	633	111	12	9	100.0	82.7	14.5	1.6	1.2
Stolen property; buying, receiving, possessing	5,047	4,103	817	108	19	100.0	81.3	16.2	2.1	0.4
Vandalism	12,750	10,905	1,329	435	81	100.0	85.5	10.4	3.4	0.6
Weapons; carrying, possessing, etc.	7,171	5,430	1,444	246	51	100.0	75.7	20.1	3.4	0.7
Prostitution and commercialized vice	227	166	37	2	22	100.0	73.1	16.3	0.9	9.7
Sex offenses (except forcible rape and prostitution)	5,048	4,490	427	106	25	100.0	88.9	8.5	2.1	0.5
Drug abuse violations	92,014	74,340	15,422	1,499	753	100.0	80.8	16.8	1.6	0.8
Gambling	506	325	166	6	9	100.0	64.2	32.8	1.2	1.8
Offenses against the family and children	12,576	8,878	2,913	765	20	100.0	70.6	23.2	6.1	0.2
Driving under the influence	149,706	133,764	10,765	3,493	1,684	100.0	89.4	7.2	2.3	1.1
Liquor laws	35,736	33,175	1,344	989	228	100.0	92.8	3.8	2.8	0.6
Drunkenness	18,029	15,982	1,336	662	49	100.0	88.6	7.4	3.7	0.3
Disorderly conduct	21,714	16,957	3,786	878	93	100.0	78.1	17.4	4.0	0.4
Vagrancy	168	124	36	8	0	100.0	73.8	21.4	4.8	0.0
All other offenses (except traffic)	232,784	187,537	36,508	6,536	2,203	100.0	80.6	15.7	2.8	0.9
Suspicion	185	125	22	38	0	100.0	67.6	11.9	20.5	0.0
Curfew and loitering law violations	533	483	18	17	15	100.0	90.6	3.4	3.2	2.8
Runaways	4,816	3,809	378	113	516	100.0	79.1	7.8	2.3	10.7

[1] Because of rounding, the percentages may not add to 100.0.
[2] Violent crimes are offenses of murder and nonnegligent manslaughter, forcible rape, robbery, and aggravated assault. Property crimes are offenses of burglary, larceny-theft, motor vehicle theft, and arson.

Table 61. Arrests in Nonmetropolitan Counties, Distribution by Race, 2006 (*Contd.*)

(Number, percent; 1,799 agencies; 2006 estimated population 19,439,450.)

Offense charged	Arrests under 18					Percent distribution[1]				
	Total	White	Black	American Indian or Alaskan Native	Asian or Pacific Islander	Total	White	Black	American Indian or Alaskan Native	Asian or Pacific Islander
TOTAL..	68,990	56,778	8,839	2,198	1,175	100.0	82.3	12.8	3.2	1.7
Murder and nonnegligent manslaughter......	23	19	4	0	0	100.0	82.6	17.4	0.0	0.0
Forcible rape.................................	209	177	20	12	0	100.0	84.7	9.6	5.7	0.0
Robbery......................................	198	95	95	7	1	100.0	48.0	48.0	3.5	0.5
Aggravated assault..........................	1,866	1,354	414	85	13	100.0	72.6	22.2	4.6	0.7
Burglary.....................................	4,292	3,513	532	191	56	100.0	81.8	12.4	4.5	1.3
Larceny-theft................................	4,823	4,079	551	117	76	100.0	84.6	11.4	2.4	1.6
Motor vehicle theft..........................	1,102	922	118	44	18	100.0	83.7	10.7	4.0	1.6
Arson..	279	251	20	4	4	100.0	90.0	7.2	1.4	1.4
Violent crime[2].............................	2,296	1,645	533	104	14	100.0	71.6	23.2	4.5	0.6
Property crime[2]............................	10,496	8,765	1,221	356	154	100.0	83.5	11.6	3.4	1.5
Other assaults...............................	8,789	6,424	2,046	264	55	100.0	73.1	23.3	3.0	0.6
Forgery and counterfeiting...................	123	99	21	2	1	100.0	80.5	17.1	1.6	0.8
Fraud..	308	266	36	6	0	100.0	86.4	11.7	1.9	0.0
Embezzlement.................................	24	19	4	1	0	100.0	79.2	16.7	4.2	0.0
Stolen property; buying, receiving, possessing..	595	492	86	16	1	100.0	82.7	14.5	2.7	0.2
Vandalism....................................	3,814	3,409	287	98	20	100.0	89.4	7.5	2.6	0.5
Weapons; carrying, possessing, etc.	897	605	238	47	7	100.0	67.4	26.5	5.2	0.8
Prostitution and commercialized vice	5	5	0	0	0	100.0	100.0	0.0	0.0	0.0
Sex offenses (except forcible rape and prostitution)......................................	869	783	65	17	4	100.0	90.1	7.5	2.0	0.5
Drug abuse violations........................	6,294	5,355	678	140	121	100.0	85.1	10.8	2.2	1.9
Gambling.....................................	14	10	4	0	0	100.0	71.4	28.6	0.0	0.0
Offenses against the family and children......	329	291	38	0	0	100.0	88.4	11.6	0.0	0.0
Driving under the influence..................	2,241	2,085	66	62	28	100.0	93.0	2.9	2.8	1.2
Liquor laws..................................	8,812	8,291	152	313	56	100.0	94.1	1.7	3.6	0.6
Drunkenness..................................	457	431	7	17	2	100.0	94.3	1.5	3.7	0.4
Disorderly conduct...........................	5,002	3,236	1,510	236	20	100.0	64.7	30.2	4.7	0.4
Vagrancy.....................................	23	18	4	1	0	100.0	78.3	17.4	4.3	0.0
All other offenses (except traffic)............	12,226	10,233	1,444	388	161	100.0	83.7	11.8	3.2	1.3
Suspicion....................................	27	24	3	0	0	100.0	88.9	11.1	0.0	0.0
Curfew and loitering law violations...........	533	483	18	17	15	100.0	90.6	3.4	3.2	2.8
Runaways.....................................	4,816	3,809	378	113	516	100.0	79.1	7.8	2.3	10.7

[1] Because of rounding, the percentages may not add to 100.0.
[2] Violent crimes are offenses of murder and nonnegligent manslaughter, forcible rape, robbery, and aggravated assault. Property crimes are offenses of burglary, larceny-theft, motor vehicle theft, and arson.

Table 61. Arrests in Nonmetropolitan Counties, Distribution by Race, 2006 (*Contd.*)

(Number, percent; 1,799 agencies; 2006 estimated population 19,439,450.)

Offense charged	Arrests 18 and over					Percent distribution[1]				
	Total	White	Black	American Indian or Alaskan Native	Asian or Pacific Islander	Total	White	Black	American Indian or Alaskan Native	Asian or Pacific Islander
TOTAL	710,882	587,865	98,290	18,858	5,869	100.0	82.7	13.8	2.7	0.8
Murder and nonnegligent manslaughter	599	382	185	29	3	100.0	63.8	30.9	4.8	0.5
Forcible rape	1,327	1,049	238	34	6	100.0	79.1	17.9	2.6	0.5
Robbery	1,790	1,015	706	52	17	100.0	56.7	39.4	2.9	0.9
Aggravated assault	18,446	13,945	3,573	819	109	100.0	75.6	19.4	4.4	0.6
Burglary	13,961	11,593	1,909	401	58	100.0	83.0	13.7	2.9	0.4
Larceny-theft	24,606	20,163	3,586	624	233	100.0	81.9	14.6	2.5	0.9
Motor vehicle theft	3,966	3,325	449	134	58	100.0	83.8	11.3	3.4	1.5
Arson	689	577	84	24	4	100.0	83.7	12.2	3.5	0.6
Violent crime[2]	22,162	16,391	4,702	934	135	100.0	74.0	21.2	4.2	0.6
Property crime[2]	43,222	35,658	6,028	1,183	353	100.0	82.5	13.9	2.7	0.8
Other assaults	58,651	47,185	9,107	1,915	444	100.0	80.5	15.5	3.3	0.8
Forgery and counterfeiting	4,994	4,137	774	50	33	100.0	82.8	15.5	1.0	0.7
Fraud	29,056	22,847	5,802	329	78	100.0	78.6	20.0	1.1	0.3
Embezzlement	741	614	107	11	9	100.0	82.9	14.4	1.5	1.2
Stolen property; buying, receiving, possessing	4,452	3,611	731	92	18	100.0	81.1	16.4	2.1	0.4
Vandalism	8,936	7,496	1,042	337	61	100.0	83.9	11.7	3.8	0.7
Weapons; carrying, possessing, etc.	6,274	4,825	1,206	199	44	100.0	76.9	19.2	3.2	0.7
Prostitution and commercialized vice	222	161	37	2	22	100.0	72.5	16.7	0.9	9.9
Sex offenses (except forcible rape and prostitution)	4,179	3,707	362	89	21	100.0	88.7	8.7	2.1	0.5
Drug abuse violations	85,720	68,985	14,744	1,359	632	100.0	80.5	17.2	1.6	0.7
Gambling	492	315	162	6	9	100.0	64.0	32.9	1.2	1.8
Offenses against the family and children	12,247	8,587	2,875	765	20	100.0	70.1	23.5	6.2	0.2
Driving under the influence	147,465	131,679	10,699	3,431	1,656	100.0	89.3	7.3	2.3	1.1
Liquor laws	26,924	24,884	1,192	676	172	100.0	92.4	4.4	2.5	0.6
Drunkenness	17,572	15,551	1,329	645	47	100.0	88.5	7.6	3.7	0.3
Disorderly conduct	16,712	13,721	2,276	642	73	100.0	82.1	13.6	3.8	0.4
Vagrancy	145	106	32	7	0	100.0	73.1	22.1	4.8	0.0
All other offenses (except traffic)	220,558	177,304	35,064	6,148	2,042	100.0	80.4	15.9	2.8	0.9
Suspicion	158	101	19	38	0	100.0	63.9	12.0	24.1	0.0
Curfew and loitering law violations	-	-	-	-	-	-	-	-	-	-
Runaways	-	-	-	-	-	-	-	-	-	-

[1] Because of rounding, the percentages may not add to 100.0.
[2] Violent crimes are offenses of murder and nonnegligent manslaughter, forcible rape, robbery, and aggravated assault. Property crimes are offenses of burglary, larceny-theft, motor vehicle theft, and arson.

Table 62. Arrest Trends for Suburban Areas,[1] 2005–2006

(Number, percent change; 391 agencies; 2006 estimated population 87,257,110; 2005 estimated population 86,434,011.)

Offense charged	Number of persons arrested								
	Total all ages			Under 18 years of age			18 years of age and over		
	2005	2006	Percent change	2005	2006	Percent change	2005	2006	Percent change
TOTAL[2]	3,584,644	3,618,997	+1.0	542,147	554,333	+2.2	3,042,497	3,064,664	+0.7
Murder and nonnegligent manslaughter	2,660	2,687	+1.0	214	210	-1.9	2,446	2,477	+1.3
Forcible rape	6,037	5,735	-5.0	971	881	-9.3	5,066	4,854	-4.2
Robbery	20,293	22,240	+9.6	4,804	5,836	+21.5	15,489	16,404	+5.9
Aggravated assault	105,248	103,812	-1.4	14,845	14,588	-1.7	90,403	89,224	-1.3
Burglary	72,401	73,330	+1.3	19,554	21,005	+7.4	52,847	52,325	-1.0
Larceny-theft	268,788	254,871	-5.2	68,635	66,281	-3.4	200,153	188,590	-5.8
Motor vehicle theft	30,164	28,350	-6.0	7,054	6,415	-9.1	23,110	21,935	-5.1
Arson	4,454	4,480	+0.6	2,464	2,419	-1.8	1,990	2,061	+3.6
Violent crime[3]	134,238	134,474	+0.2	20,834	21,515	+3.3	113,404	112,959	-0.4
Property crime[3]	375,807	361,031	-3.9	97,707	96,120	-1.6	278,100	264,911	-4.7
Other assaults	318,976	314,189	-1.5	66,975	67,475	+0.7	252,001	246,714	-2.1
Forgery and counterfeiting	28,594	26,472	-7.4	1,125	949	-15.6	27,469	25,523	-7.1
Fraud	107,246	92,494	-13.8	2,245	1,983	-11.7	105,001	90,511	-13.8
Embezzlement	4,921	5,239	+6.5	297	395	+33.0	4,624	4,844	+4.8
Stolen property; buying, receiving, possessing	32,535	32,105	-1.3	5,050	5,367	+6.3	27,485	26,738	-2.7
Vandalism	70,951	76,128	+7.3	28,677	32,092	+11.9	42,274	44,036	+4.2
Weapons; carrying, possessing, etc.	43,400	43,231	-0.4	11,209	11,394	+1.7	32,191	31,837	-1.1
Prostitution and commercialized vice	4,760	4,706	-1.1	93	135	+45.2	4,667	4,571	-2.1
Sex offenses (except forcible rape and prostitution)	20,739	20,375	-1.8	4,444	4,098	-7.8	16,295	16,277	-0.1
Drug abuse violations	422,786	433,234	+2.5	49,626	50,806	+2.4	373,160	382,428	+2.5
Gambling	1,111	1,397	+25.7	130	125	-3.8	981	1,272	+29.7
Offenses against the family and children	46,403	45,853	-1.2	1,739	1,575	-9.4	44,664	44,278	-0.9
Driving under the influence	418,391	432,980	+3.5	5,412	5,648	+4.4	412,979	427,332	+3.5
Liquor laws	157,312	168,970	+7.4	38,418	42,125	+9.6	118,894	126,845	+6.7
Drunkenness	122,106	127,564	+4.5	4,210	5,067	+20.4	117,896	122,497	+3.9
Disorderly conduct	160,384	163,760	+2.1	54,345	55,772	+2.6	106,039	107,988	+1.8
Vagrancy	4,425	4,444	+0.4	529	598	+13.0	3,896	3,846	-1.3
All other offenses (except traffic)	1,064,204	1,083,415	+1.8	103,727	104,158	+0.4	960,477	979,257	+2.0
Suspicion	946	902	-4.7	181	160	-11.6	765	742	-3.0
Curfew and loitering law violations	19,096	20,596	+7.9	19,096	20,596	+7.9	-	-	-
Runaways	26,259	26,340	+0.3	26,259	26,340	+0.3	-	-	-

[1] Suburban area includes law enforcement agencies in cities with less than 50,000 inhabitants and county law enforcement agencies that are within a Metropolitan Statistical Area. Suburban area excludes all metropolitan agencies associated with a principal city.
[2] Does not include suspicion.
[3] Violent crimes are offenses of murder and nonnegligent manslaughter, forcible rape, robbery, and aggravated assault. Property crimes are offenses of burglary, larceny-theft, motor vehicle theft, and arson.

Table 63. Arrest Trends for Suburban Areas,[1] by Age and Sex, 2005–2006

(Number, percent change; 5,391 agencies; 2006 estimated population 87,257,110; 2005 estimated population 86,434,011.)

Offense charged	Male						Female					
	Total			Under 18			Total			Under 18		
	2005	2006	Percent change	2005	2006	Percent change	2005	2006	Percent change	2005	2006	Percent change
TOTAL[2]	2,729,873	2,756,084	+1.0	386,193	397,323	+2.9	854,771	862,913	+1.0	155,954	157,010	+0.7
Murder and nonnegligent manslaughter	2,287	2,342	+2.4	174	200	+14.9	373	345	-7.5	40	10	-75.0
Forcible rape	5,957	5,649	-5.2	949	865	-8.9	80	86	+7.5	22	16	-27.3
Robbery	18,137	19,879	+9.6	4,399	5,355	+21.7	2,156	2,361	+9.5	405	481	+18.8
Aggravated assault	84,597	83,404	-1.4	11,499	11,324	-1.5	20,651	20,408	-1.2	3,346	3,264	-2.5
Burglary	62,387	63,363	+1.6	17,487	18,904	+8.1	10,014	9,967	-0.5	2,067	2,101	+1.6
Larceny-theft	168,180	160,752	-4.4	41,872	40,914	-2.3	100,608	94,119	-6.4	26,763	25,367	-5.2
Motor vehicle theft	24,782	23,209	-6.3	5,707	5,283	-7.4	5,382	5,141	-4.5	1,347	1,132	-16.0
Arson	3,807	3,802	-0.1	2,172	2,132	-1.8	647	678	+4.8	292	287	-1.7
Violent crime[3]	110,978	111,274	+0.3	17,021	17,744	+4.2	23,260	23,200	-0.3	3,813	3,771	-1.1
Property crime[3]	259,156	251,126	-3.1	67,238	67,233	*	116,651	109,905	-5.8	30,469	28,887	-5.2
Other assaults	239,204	234,163	-2.1	45,416	45,361	-0.1	79,772	80,026	+0.3	21,559	22,114	+2.6
Forgery and counterfeiting	17,193	16,191	-5.8	762	663	-13.0	11,401	10,281	-9.8	363	286	-21.2
Fraud	57,049	49,186	-13.8	1,448	1,320	-8.8	50,197	43,308	-13.7	797	663	-16.8
Embezzlement	2,452	2,494	+1.7	187	232	24.1	2,469	2,745	+11.2	110	163	+48.2
Stolen property; buying, receiving, possessing	26,066	25,880	-0.7	4,218	4,489	+6.4	6,469	6,225	-3.8	832	878	+5.5
Vandalism	59,591	64,525	+8.3	24,771	28,086	+13.4	11,360	11,603	+2.1	3,906	4,006	+2.6
Weapons; carrying, possessing, etc.	39,769	39,754	*	9,965	10,186	+2.2	3,631	3,477	-4.2	1,244	1,208	-2.9
Prostitution and commercialized vice	2,271	2,022	-11.0	40	48	+20.0	2,489	2,684	+7.8	53	87	+64.2
Sex offenses (except forcible rape and prostitution)	19,763	19,229	-2.7	4,126	3,758	-8.9	976	1,146	+17.4	318	340	+6.9
Drug abuse violations	339,171	347,594	+2.5	40,308	41,708	+3.5	83,615	85,640	+2.4	9,318	9,098	-2.4
Gambling	879	1,010	+14.9	127	114	-10.2	232	387	+66.8	3	11	+266.7
Offenses against the family and children	37,221	36,926	-0.8	1,055	957	-9.3	9,182	8,927	-2.8	684	618	-9.6
Driving under the influence	337,215	344,895	+2.3	4,233	4,374	+3.3	81,176	88,085	+8.5	1,179	1,274	+8.1
Liquor laws	113,481	120,999	+6.6	24,588	26,820	+9.1	43,831	47,971	+9.4	13,830	15,305	+10.7
Drunkenness	102,250	106,034	+3.7	3,224	3,681	+14.2	19,856	21,530	+8.4	986	1,386	+40.6
Disorderly conduct	118,553	120,683	+1.8	37,572	38,213	+1.7	41,831	43,077	+3.0	16,773	17,559	+4.7
Vagrancy	3,442	3,374	-2.0	406	448	+10.3	983	1,070	+8.9	123	150	+22.0
All other offenses (except traffic)	820,310	833,158	+1.6	75,629	76,321	+0.9	243,894	250,257	+2.6	28,098	27,837	-0.9
Suspicion	752	716	-4.8	129	133	+3.1	194	186	-4.1	52	27	-48.1
Curfew and loitering law violations	12,842	13,873	+8.0	12,842	13,873	+8.0	6,254	6,723	+7.5	6,254	6,723	+7.5
Runaways	11,017	11,694	+6.1	11,017	11,694	+6.1	15,242	14,646	-3.9	15,242	14,646	-3.9

[1] Suburban area includes law enforcement agencies in cities with less than 50,000 inhabitants and county law enforcement agencies that are within a Metropolitan Statistical Area. Suburban area excludes all metropolitan agencies associated with a principal city.
[2] Does not include suspicion.
[3] Violent crimes are offenses of murder and nonnegligent manslaughter, forcible rape, robbery, and aggravated assault. Property crimes are offenses of burglary, larceny-theft, motor vehicle theft, and arson.
* Less than one-tenth of 1 percent.

Table 64. Arrests in Suburban Areas,[1] Distribution by Age, 2006

(Number, percent; 6,122 agencies; 2006 estimated population 94,714,217.)

Offense charged	Total all ages	Ages under 15	Ages under 18	Ages 18 and over	Under 10	10-12	13-14	15	16	17	18	19	20
TOTAL	4,119,968	181,899	635,574	3,484,394	5,352	38,304	138,243	124,585	154,053	175,037	206,985	209,240	194,445
Total percent distribution[2]	100.0	4.4	15.4	84.6	0.1	0.9	3.4	3.0	3.7	4.2	5.0	5.1	4.7
Murder and nonnegligent manslaughter	3,074	16	231	2,843	0	3	13	29	65	121	208	201	175
Forcible rape	6,567	386	1,005	5,562	8	85	293	175	218	226	370	344	302
Robbery	26,620	1,536	7,028	19,592	21	231	1,284	1,455	1,790	2,247	2,455	2,107	1,594
Aggravated assault	117,886	5,357	16,678	101,208	193	1,359	3,805	3,217	3,850	4,254	4,595	4,466	4,350
Burglary	83,110	7,332	23,849	59,261	263	1,447	5,622	4,840	5,750	5,927	6,703	5,271	4,068
Larceny-theft	303,538	25,405	78,942	224,596	734	5,542	19,129	15,870	18,146	19,521	18,812	15,353	12,837
Motor vehicle theft	31,306	1,602	7,293	24,013	8	167	1,427	1,719	1,953	2,019	2,124	1,748	1,457
Arson	5,271	1,481	2,687	2,584	113	457	911	503	412	291	293	228	134
Violent crime[3]	154,147	7,295	24,942	129,205	222	1,678	5,395	4,876	5,923	6,848	7,628	7,118	6,421
Violent crime percent distribution[2]	100.0	4.7	16.2	83.8	0.1	1.1	3.5	3.2	3.8	4.4	4.9	4.6	4.2
Property crime[3]	423,225	35,820	112,771	310,454	1,118	7,613	27,089	22,932	26,261	27,758	27,932	22,600	18,496
Property crime percent distribution[2]	100.0	8.5	26.6	73.4	0.3	1.8	6.4	5.4	6.2	6.6	6.6	5.3	4.4
Other assaults	362,365	29,892	76,248	286,117	986	7,756	21,150	15,246	16,225	14,885	12,400	11,723	11,295
Forgery and counterfeiting	32,418	140	1,128	31,290	12	23	105	141	282	565	1,113	1,383	1,540
Fraud	97,223	311	2,315	94,908	13	46	252	329	623	1,052	2,068	2,833	3,424
Embezzlement	5,931	15	422	5,509	2	2	11	16	131	260	484	442	366
Stolen property; buying, receiving, possessing	37,696	1,513	6,369	31,327	31	236	1,246	1,330	1,607	1,919	2,323	2,074	1,915
Vandalism	86,831	14,457	36,370	50,461	687	3,884	9,886	6,951	7,491	7,471	6,084	4,699	3,746
Weapons; carrying, possessing, etc.	49,206	4,754	12,870	36,336	179	1,245	3,330	2,343	2,738	3,035	3,266	2,897	2,556
Prostitution and commercialized vice	6,275	25	158	6,117	1	5	19	33	38	62	176	192	199
Sex offenses (except forcible rape and prostitution)	23,807	2,303	4,792	19,015	129	618	1,556	861	836	792	975	969	864
Drug abuse violations	493,312	8,629	57,209	436,103	119	900	7,610	9,493	15,843	23,244	33,496	33,333	29,716
Gambling	1,564	26	147	1,417	0	2	24	39	35	47	69	41	70
Offenses against the family and children	50,271	513	1,708	48,563	25	115	373	382	414	399	751	770	935
Driving under the influence	484,907	90	6,523	478,384	37	6	47	228	1,535	4,670	11,667	15,755	17,705
Liquor laws	197,822	4,182	48,971	148,851	52	300	3,830	7,304	14,167	23,318	38,289	38,449	30,124
Drunkenness	143,163	632	5,494	137,669	19	33	580	904	1,366	2,592	5,145	5,187	5,088
Disorderly conduct	196,035	24,806	64,605	131,430	505	5,935	18,366	13,750	13,801	12,248	9,701	8,236	7,282
Vagrancy	6,063	170	700	5,363	3	24	143	137	185	208	298	206	211
All other offenses (except traffic)	1,213,199	30,704	118,141	1,095,058	976	5,638	24,090	23,741	29,315	34,381	43,046	50,265	52,454
Suspicion	987	44	170	817	1	5	38	30	45	51	74	68	38
Curfew and loitering law violations	23,400	6,273	23,400	-	55	893	5,325	5,616	6,754	4,757	-	-	-
Runaways	30,121	9,305	30,121	-	180	1,347	7,778	7,903	8,438	4,475	-	-	-

[1] Suburban area includes law enforcement agencies in cities with less than 50,000 inhabitants and county law enforcement agencies that are within a Metropolitan Statistical Area. Suburban area excludes all metropolitan agencies associated with a principal city.
[2] Because of rounding, the percentages may not add to 100.0.
[3] Violent crimes are offenses of murder and nonnegligent manslaughter, forcible rape, robbery, and aggravated assault. Property crimes are offenses of burglary, larceny-theft, motor vehicle theft, and arson.

Table 64. Arrests in Suburban Areas,[1] Distribution by Age, 2006 *(Contd.)*

(Number, percent; 6,122 agencies; 2006 estimated population 94,714,217.)

Offense charged	21	22	23	24	25-29	30-34	35-39	40-44	45-49	50-54	55-59	60-64	65 and over
TOTAL	173,252	157,686	150,389	142,411	571,523	408,135	386,091	356,937	264,074	141,626	67,770	29,193	24,637
Total percent distribution[2]	4.2	3.8	3.7	3.5	13.9	9.9	9.4	8.7	6.4	3.4	1.6	0.7	0.6
Murder and nonnegligent manslaughter	193	143	140	128	516	313	272	196	152	75	63	30	38
Forcible rape	325	244	234	201	901	653	693	489	372	200	108	58	68
Robbery	1,360	1,038	948	840	3,049	1,874	1,693	1,359	751	336	121	39	28
Aggravated assault	4,514	4,286	4,134	4,146	17,319	12,814	12,332	11,346	8,236	4,521	2,138	1,037	974
Burglary	3,357	2,990	2,626	2,329	9,443	6,355	5,867	4,978	3,079	1,444	489	137	125
Larceny-theft	10,757	9,244	8,677	8,164	33,030	24,712	25,175	23,473	17,043	9,263	4,302	1,930	1,824
Motor vehicle theft	1,391	1,221	1,105	1,045	4,187	3,042	2,646	2,082	1,144	498	199	75	49
Arson	111	100	67	80	324	256	269	257	223	124	60	34	24
Violent crime[3]	6,392	5,711	5,456	5,315	21,785	15,654	14,990	13,390	9,511	5,132	2,430	1,164	1,108
Violent crime percent distribution[2]	4.1	3.7	3.5	3.4	14.1	10.2	9.7	8.7	6.2	3.3	1.6	0.8	0.7
Property crime[3]	15,616	13,555	12,475	11,618	46,984	34,365	33,957	30,790	21,489	11,329	5,050	2,176	2,022
Property crime percent distribution[2]	3.7	3.2	2.9	2.7	11.1	8.1	8.0	7.3	5.1	2.7	1.2	0.5	0.5
Other assaults	12,049	11,332	11,262	11,018	47,538	37,723	37,087	34,262	24,408	12,445	6,202	2,701	2,672
Forgery and counterfeiting	1,379	1,279	1,340	1,329	6,233	4,552	4,126	3,240	2,170	915	404	161	126
Fraud	3,343	3,097	3,527	3,326	16,669	14,927	14,393	11,460	7,603	4,328	2,190	930	790
Embezzlement	347	280	270	203	793	631	584	496	310	153	85	44	21
Stolen property; buying, receiving, possessing	1,699	1,537	1,459	1,385	5,337	3,853	3,543	2,913	1,882	897	312	125	73
Vandalism	3,340	2,751	2,425	2,148	7,509	4,817	4,414	3,682	2,534	1,200	611	257	244
Weapons; carrying, possessing, etc.	2,405	2,113	1,864	1,716	6,241	3,622	2,836	2,555	1,985	1,090	606	306	278
Prostitution and commercialized vice	220	219	226	207	919	833	910	857	558	300	132	82	87
Sex offenses (except forcible rape and prostitution)	806	671	656	626	2,489	2,142	2,278	2,102	1,610	1,140	700	427	560
Drug abuse violations	25,931	22,943	21,201	19,936	74,976	46,862	41,836	38,101	27,406	12,906	5,083	1,564	813
Gambling	40	31	31	33	172	157	153	138	133	113	96	67	73
Offenses against the family and children	1,136	1,228	1,319	1,495	8,298	8,450	8,481	7,503	4,775	2,144	780	302	196
Driving under the influence	24,641	23,881	23,465	22,012	85,067	57,008	51,810	50,726	41,980	26,341	14,504	6,565	5,257
Liquor laws	4,754	3,133	2,486	2,024	6,777	4,519	4,486	4,826	3,997	2,564	1,317	622	484
Drunkenness	7,346	6,429	5,945	5,168	19,571	14,306	14,891	17,242	15,058	8,863	4,395	1,840	1,195
Disorderly conduct	8,523	7,254	6,318	5,613	19,793	12,962	12,760	12,722	9,941	5,406	2,522	1,258	1,139
Vagrancy	170	169	157	173	687	526	742	740	649	369	161	61	44
All other offenses (except traffic)	53,067	50,031	48,464	47,026	193,561	140,150	131,731	119,123	86,013	43,967	20,175	8,537	7,448
Suspicion	48	42	43	40	124	76	83	69	62	24	15	4	7
Curfew and loitering law violations	-	-	-	-	-	-	-	-	-	-	-	-	-
Runaways	-	-	-	-	-	-	-	-	-	-	-	-	-

[1] Suburban area includes law enforcement agencies in cities with less than 50,000 inhabitants and county law enforcement agencies that are within a Metropolitan Statistical Area. Suburban area excludes all metropolitan agencies associated with a principal city.
[2] Because of rounding, the percentages may not add to 100.0.
[3] Violent crimes are offenses of murder and nonnegligent manslaughter, forcible rape, robbery, and aggravated assault. Property crimes are offenses of burglary, larceny-theft, motor vehicle theft, and arson.

Table 65. Arrests in Suburban Areas[1] of Persons Under 15, 18, 21, and 25 Years of Age, 2006

(Number, percent; 6,122 agencies; 2006 estimated population 94,714,217.)

Offense charged	Total all ages	Number of persons arrested				Percent of total all ages			
		Under 15	Under 18	Under 21	Under 25	Under 15	Under 18	Under 21	Under 25
TOTAL	4,119,968	181,899	635,574	1,246,244	1,869,982	4.4	15.4	30.2	45.4
Murder and nonnegligent manslaughter	3,074	16	231	815	1,419	0.5	7.5	26.5	46.2
Forcible rape	6,567	386	1,005	2,021	3,025	5.9	15.3	30.8	46.1
Robbery	26,620	1,536	7,028	13,184	17,370	5.8	26.4	49.5	65.3
Aggravated assault	117,886	5,357	16,678	30,089	47,169	4.5	14.1	25.5	40.0
Burglary	83,110	7,332	23,849	39,891	51,193	8.8	28.7	48.0	61.6
Larceny-theft	303,538	25,405	78,942	125,944	162,786	8.4	26.0	41.5	53.6
Motor vehicle theft	31,306	1,602	7,293	12,622	17,384	5.1	23.3	40.3	55.5
Arson	5,271	1,481	2,687	3,342	3,700	28.1	51.0	63.4	70.2
Violent crime[2]	154,147	7,295	24,942	46,109	68,983	4.7	16.2	29.9	44.8
Property crime[2]	423,225	35,820	112,771	181,799	235,063	8.5	26.6	43.0	55.5
Other assaults	362,365	29,892	76,248	111,666	157,327	8.2	21.0	30.8	43.4
Forgery and counterfeiting	32,418	140	1,128	5,164	10,491	0.4	3.5	15.9	32.4
Fraud	97,223	311	2,315	10,640	23,933	0.3	2.4	10.9	24.6
Embezzlement	5,931	15	422	1,714	2,814	0.3	7.1	28.9	47.4
Stolen property; buying, receiving, possessing	37,696	1,513	6,369	12,681	18,761	4.0	16.9	33.6	49.8
Vandalism	86,831	14,457	36,370	50,899	61,563	16.6	41.9	58.6	70.9
Weapons; carrying, possessing, etc.	49,206	4,754	12,870	21,589	29,687	9.7	26.2	43.9	60.3
Prostitution and commercialized vice	6,275	25	158	725	1,597	0.4	2.5	11.6	25.5
Sex offenses (except forcible rape and prostitution)	23,807	2,303	4,792	7,600	10,359	9.7	20.1	31.9	43.5
Drug abuse violations	493,312	8,629	57,209	153,754	243,765	1.7	11.6	31.2	49.4
Gambling	1,564	26	147	327	462	1.7	9.4	20.9	29.5
Offenses against the family and children	50,271	513	1,708	4,164	9,342	1.0	3.4	8.3	18.6
Driving under the influence	484,907	90	6,523	51,650	145,649	*	1.3	10.7	30.0
Liquor laws	197,822	4,182	48,971	155,833	168,230	2.1	24.8	78.8	85.0
Drunkenness	143,163	632	5,494	20,914	45,802	0.4	3.8	14.6	32.0
Disorderly conduct	196,035	24,806	64,605	89,824	117,532	12.7	33.0	45.8	60.0
Vagrancy	6,063	170	700	1,415	2,084	2.8	11.5	23.3	34.4
All other offenses (except traffic)	1,213,199	30,704	118,141	263,906	462,494	2.5	9.7	21.8	38.1
Suspicion	987	44	170	350	523	4.5	17.2	35.5	53.0
Curfew and loitering law violations	23,400	6,273	23,400	23,400	23,400	26.8	100.0	100.0	100.0
Runaways	30,121	9,305	30,121	30,121	30,121	30.9	100.0	100.0	100.0

[1] Suburban area includes law enforcement agencies in cities with less than 50,000 inhabitants and county law enforcement agencies that are within a Metropolitan Statistical Area. Suburban area excludes all metropolitan agencies associated with a principal city.
[2] Violent crimes are offenses of murder and nonnegligent manslaughter, forcible rape, robbery, and aggravated assault. Property crimes are offenses of burglary, larceny-theft, motor vehicle theft, and arson.
* Less than one-tenth of 1 percent.

Table 66. Arrests in Suburban Areas,[1] Distribution by Sex, 2006

(Number, percent; 6,122 agencies; 2006 estimated population 94,714,217.)

Offense charged	Number of persons arrested			Percent male	Percent female	Percent distribution[2]		
	Total	Male	Female			Total	Male	Female
TOTAL	4,119,968	3,132,510	987,458	76.0	24.0	100.0	100.0	100.0
Murder and nonnegligent manslaughter	3,074	2,683	391	87.3	12.7	0.1	0.1	*
Forcible rape	6,567	6,472	95	98.6	1.4	0.2	0.2	*
Robbery	26,620	23,840	2,780	89.6	10.4	0.6	0.8	0.3
Aggravated assault	117,886	94,379	23,507	80.1	19.9	2.9	3.0	2.4
Burglary	83,110	71,941	11,169	86.6	13.4	2.0	2.3	1.1
Larceny-theft	303,538	189,915	113,623	62.6	37.4	7.4	6.1	11.5
Motor vehicle theft	31,306	25,684	5,622	82.0	18.0	0.8	0.8	0.6
Arson	5,271	4,455	816	84.5	15.5	0.1	0.1	0.1
Violent crime[3]	154,147	127,374	26,773	82.6	17.4	3.7	4.1	2.7
Property crime[3]	423,225	291,995	131,230	69.0	31.0	10.3	9.3	13.3
Other assaults	362,365	269,944	92,421	74.5	25.5	8.8	8.6	9.4
Forgery and counterfeiting	32,418	19,762	12,656	61.0	39.0	0.8	0.6	1.3
Fraud	97,223	52,426	44,797	53.9	46.1	2.4	1.7	4.5
Embezzlement	5,931	2,790	3,141	47.0	53.0	0.1	0.1	0.3
Stolen property; buying, receiving, possessing	37,696	30,422	7,274	80.7	19.3	0.9	1.0	0.7
Vandalism	86,831	73,309	13,522	84.4	15.6	2.1	2.3	1.4
Weapons; carrying, possessing, etc.	49,206	45,232	3,974	91.9	8.1	1.2	1.4	0.4
Prostitution and commercialized vice	6,275	2,392	3,883	38.1	61.9	0.2	0.1	0.4
Sex offenses (except forcible rape and prostitution)	23,807	22,400	1,407	94.1	5.9	0.6	0.7	0.1
Drug abuse violations	493,312	396,315	96,997	80.3	19.7	12.0	12.7	9.8
Gambling	1,564	1,162	402	74.3	25.7	*	*	*
Offenses against the family and children	50,271	40,241	10,030	80.0	20.0	1.2	1.3	1.0
Driving under the influence	484,907	385,800	99,107	79.6	20.4	11.8	12.3	10.0
Liquor laws	197,822	141,545	56,277	71.6	28.4	4.8	4.5	5.7
Drunkenness	143,163	119,198	23,965	83.3	16.7	3.5	3.8	2.4
Disorderly conduct	196,035	144,578	51,457	73.8	26.2	4.8	4.6	5.2
Vagrancy	6,063	4,563	1,500	75.3	24.7	0.1	0.1	0.2
All other offenses (except traffic)	1,213,199	931,133	282,066	76.8	23.2	29.4	29.7	28.6
Suspicion	987	783	204	79.3	20.7	*	*	*
Curfew and loitering law violations	23,400	15,727	7,673	67.2	32.8	0.6	0.5	0.8
Runaways	30,121	13,419	16,702	44.6	55.4	0.7	0.4	1.7

[1] Suburban area includes law enforcement agencies in cities with less than 50,000 inhabitants and county law enforcement agencies that are within a Metropolitan Statistical Area. Suburban area excludes all metropolitan agencies associated with a principal city.
[2] Because of rounding, the percentages may not add to 100.0.
[3] Violent crimes are offenses of murder and nonnegligent manslaughter, forcible rape, robbery, and aggravated assault. Property crimes are offenses of burglary, larceny-theft, motor vehicle theft, and arson.
* Less than one-tenth of 1 percent.

Table 67. Arrests in Suburban Areas,[1] Distribution by Race, 2006

(Number, percent; 6,121 agencies; 2006 estimated population 94,712,647.)

Offense charged	Total arrests					Percent distribution[2]				
	Total	White	Black	American Indian or Alaskan Native	Asian or Pacific Islander	Total	White	Black	American Indian or Alaskan Native	Asian or Pacific Islander
TOTAL	4,105,074	3,119,705	925,822	29,289	30,258	100.0	76.0	22.6	0.7	0.7
Murder and nonnegligent manslaughter	3,073	1,775	1,254	26	18	100.0	57.8	40.8	0.8	0.6
Forcible rape	6,534	4,782	1,656	53	43	100.0	73.2	25.3	0.8	0.7
Robbery	26,578	13,057	13,238	117	166	100.0	49.1	49.8	0.4	0.6
Aggravated assault	117,565	83,484	32,189	921	971	100.0	71.0	27.4	0.8	0.8
Burglary	82,916	62,896	18,944	482	594	100.0	75.9	22.8	0.6	0.7
Larceny-theft	302,288	215,585	81,391	2,205	3,107	100.0	71.3	26.9	0.7	1.0
Motor vehicle theft	31,243	23,258	7,574	179	232	100.0	74.4	24.2	0.6	0.7
Arson	5,261	4,297	886	23	55	100.0	81.7	16.8	0.4	1.0
Violent crime[3]	153,750	103,098	48,337	1,117	1,198	100.0	67.1	31.4	0.7	0.8
Property crime[3]	421,708	306,036	108,795	2,889	3,988	100.0	72.6	25.8	0.7	0.9
Other assaults	361,321	263,017	92,780	2,721	2,803	100.0	72.8	25.7	0.8	0.8
Forgery and counterfeiting	32,325	23,591	8,341	103	290	100.0	73.0	25.8	0.3	0.9
Fraud	96,872	68,071	28,017	270	514	100.0	70.3	28.9	0.3	0.5
Embezzlement	5,907	3,885	1,945	18	59	100.0	65.8	32.9	0.3	1.0
Stolen property; buying, receiving, possessing	37,602	26,500	10,621	207	274	100.0	70.5	28.2	0.6	0.7
Vandalism	86,493	70,887	14,413	592	601	100.0	82.0	16.7	0.7	0.7
Weapons; carrying, possessing, etc.	49,077	32,765	15,589	273	450	100.0	66.8	31.8	0.6	0.9
Prostitution and commercialized vice	6,263	4,056	1,784	25	398	100.0	64.8	28.5	0.4	6.4
Sex offenses (except forcible rape and prostitution)	23,732	18,931	4,434	156	211	100.0	79.8	18.7	0.7	0.9
Drug abuse violations	491,999	365,791	121,184	2,224	2,800	100.0	74.3	24.6	0.5	0.6
Gambling	1,554	942	545	2	65	100.0	60.6	35.1	0.1	4.2
Offenses against the family and children	50,024	33,185	16,214	380	245	100.0	66.3	32.4	0.8	0.5
Driving under the influence	483,197	434,381	41,600	3,306	3,910	100.0	89.9	8.6	0.7	0.8
Liquor laws	196,333	176,212	14,930	2,893	2,298	100.0	89.8	7.6	1.5	1.2
Drunkenness	142,756	127,333	13,537	1,198	688	100.0	89.2	9.5	0.8	0.5
Disorderly conduct	195,112	140,866	51,400	1,386	1,460	100.0	72.2	26.3	0.7	0.7
Vagrancy	6,060	3,860	2,166	11	23	100.0	63.7	35.7	0.2	0.4
All other offenses (except traffic)	1,208,571	874,192	317,758	9,097	7,524	100.0	72.3	26.3	0.8	0.6
Suspicion	987	581	396	1	9	100.0	58.9	40.1	0.1	0.9
Curfew and loitering law violations	23,337	18,407	4,655	90	185	100.0	78.9	19.9	0.4	0.8
Runaways	30,094	23,118	6,381	330	265	100.0	76.8	21.2	1.1	0.9

[1] Suburban area includes law enforcement agencies in cities with less than 50,000 inhabitants and county law enforcement agencies that are within a Metropolitan Statistical Area. Suburban area excludes all metropolitan agencies associated with a principal city.
[2] Because of rounding, the percentages may not add to 100.0.
[3] Violent crimes are offenses of murder and nonnegligent manslaughter, forcible rape, robbery, and aggravated assault. Property crimes are offenses of burglary, larceny-theft, motor vehicle theft, and arson.

Table 67. Arrests in Suburban Areas,[1] Distribution by Race, 2006 (*Contd.*)

(Number, percent; 6,121 agencies; 2006 estimated population 94,712,647.)

Offense charged	Arrests under 18					Percent distribution				
	Total	White	Black	American Indian or Alaskan Native	Asian or Pacific Islander	Total	White	Black	American Indian or Alaskan Native	Asian or Pacific Islander
TOTAL...	633,379	468,105	155,234	4,190	5,850	100.0	73.9	24.5	0.7	0.9
Murder and nonnegligent manslaughter............	231	92	136	3	0	100.0	39.8	58.9	1.3	0.0
Forcible rape	1,001	728	257	10	6	100.0	72.7	25.7	1.0	0.6
Robbery	7,016	2,533	4,413	20	50	100.0	36.1	62.9	0.3	0.7
Aggravated assault	16,629	10,358	6,014	118	139	100.0	62.3	36.2	0.7	0.8
Burglary	23,781	17,379	6,019	167	216	100.0	73.1	25.3	0.7	0.9
Larceny-theft...	78,423	53,824	22,880	571	1,148	100.0	68.6	29.2	0.7	1.5
Motor vehicle theft	7,272	4,830	2,303	54	85	100.0	66.4	31.7	0.7	1.2
Arson..	2,679	2,251	389	8	31	100.0	84.0	14.5	0.3	1.2
Violent crime[3]	24,877	13,711	10,820	151	195	100.0	55.1	43.5	0.6	0.8
Property crime[3]	112,155	78,284	31,591	800	1,480	100.0	69.8	28.2	0.7	1.3
Other assaults..	76,027	48,513	26,514	456	544	100.0	63.8	34.9	0.6	0.7
Forgery and counterfeiting........................	1,118	890	206	9	13	100.0	79.6	18.4	0.8	1.2
Fraud..	2,303	1,618	664	4	17	100.0	70.3	28.8	0.2	0.7
Embezzlement..	422	236	180	0	6	100.0	55.9	42.7	0.0	1.4
Stolen property; buying, receiving, possessing..	6,342	3,981	2,262	34	65	100.0	62.8	35.7	0.5	1.0
Vandalism...	36,239	30,081	5,710	177	271	100.0	83.0	15.8	0.5	0.7
Weapons; carrying, possessing, etc.	12,840	8,725	3,870	74	171	100.0	68.0	30.1	0.6	1.3
Prostitution and commercialized vice	158	82	73	0	3	100.0	51.9	46.2	0.0	1.9
Sex offenses (except forcible rape and prostitution)...	4,770	3,604	1,115	21	30	100.0	75.6	23.4	0.4	0.6
Drug abuse violations...............................	57,035	45,983	10,296	316	440	100.0	80.6	18.1	0.6	0.8
Gambling	147	36	108	0	3	100.0	24.5	73.5	0.0	2.0
Offenses against the family and children............	1,698	1,379	300	11	8	100.0	81.2	17.7	0.6	0.5
Driving under the influence.........................	6,496	6,182	209	54	51	100.0	95.2	3.2	0.8	0.8
Liquor laws...	48,759	45,603	2,084	529	543	100.0	93.5	4.3	1.1	1.1
Drunkenness	5,482	5,065	336	45	36	100.0	92.4	6.1	0.8	0.7
Disorderly conduct	64,475	41,954	21,638	314	569	100.0	65.1	33.6	0.5	0.9
Vagrancy...	700	567	123	3	7	100.0	81.0	17.6	0.4	1.0
All other offenses (except traffic)......................	117,735	90,001	26,016	772	946	100.0	76.4	22.1	0.7	0.8
Suspicion..	170	85	83	0	2	100.0	50.0	48.8	0.0	1.2
Curfew and loitering law violations....................	23,337	18,407	4,655	90	185	100.0	78.9	19.9	0.4	0.8
Runaways..	30,094	23,118	6,381	330	265	100.0	76.8	21.2	1.1	0.9

[1] Suburban area includes law enforcement agencies in cities with less than 50,000 inhabitants and county law enforcement agencies that are within a Metropolitan Statistical Area. Suburban area excludes all metropolitan agencies associated with a principal city.

[2] Because of rounding, the percentages may not add to 100.0.

[3] Violent crimes are offenses of murder and nonnegligent manslaughter, forcible rape, robbery, and aggravated assault. Property crimes are offenses of burglary, larceny-theft, motor vehicle theft, and arson.

Table 67. Arrests in Suburban Areas,[1] Distribution by Race, 2006 (*Contd.*)

(Number, percent; 6,121 agencies; 2006 estimated population 94,712,647.)

Offense charged	Arrests 18 and over					Percent distribution[2]				
	Total	White	Black	American Indian or Alaskan Native	Asian or Pacific Islander	Total	White	Black	American Indian or Alaskan Native	Asian or Pacific Islander
TOTAL................................	3,471,695	2,651,600	770,588	25,099	24,408	100.0	76.4	22.2	0.7	0.7
Murder and nonnegligent manslaughter............	2,842	1,683	1,118	23	18	100.0	59.2	39.3	0.8	0.6
Forcible rape................................	5,533	4,054	1,399	43	37	100.0	73.3	25.3	0.8	0.7
Robbery....................................	19,562	10,524	8,825	97	116	100.0	53.8	45.1	0.5	0.6
Aggravated assault........................	100,936	73,126	26,175	803	832	100.0	72.4	25.9	0.8	0.8
Burglary...................................	59,135	45,517	12,925	315	378	100.0	77.0	21.9	0.5	0.6
Larceny-theft..............................	223,865	161,761	58,511	1,634	1,959	100.0	72.3	26.1	0.7	0.9
Motor vehicle theft........................	23,971	18,428	5,271	125	147	100.0	76.9	22.0	0.5	0.6
Arson.....................................	2,582	2,046	497	15	24	100.0	79.2	19.2	0.6	0.9
Violent crime[3]............................	128,873	89,387	37,517	966	1,003	100.0	69.4	29.1	0.7	0.8
Property crime[3]...........................	309,553	227,752	77,204	2,089	2,508	100.0	73.6	24.9	0.7	0.8
Other assaults.............................	285,294	214,504	66,266	2,265	2,259	100.0	75.2	23.2	0.8	0.8
Forgery and counterfeiting.................	31,207	22,701	8,135	94	277	100.0	72.7	26.1	0.3	0.9
Fraud.....................................	94,569	66,453	27,353	266	497	100.0	70.3	28.9	0.3	0.5
Embezzlement.............................	5,485	3,649	1,765	18	53	100.0	66.5	32.2	0.3	1.0
Stolen property; buying, receiving, possessing..................................	31,260	22,519	8,359	173	209	100.0	72.0	26.7	0.6	0.7
Vandalism.................................	50,254	40,806	8,703	415	330	100.0	81.2	17.3	0.8	0.7
Weapons; carrying, possessing, etc.	36,237	24,040	11,719	199	279	100.0	66.3	32.3	0.5	0.8
Prostitution and commercialized vice	6,105	3,974	1,711	25	395	100.0	65.1	28.0	0.4	6.5
Sex offenses (except forcible rape and prostitution)...............................	18,962	15,327	3,319	135	181	100.0	80.8	17.5	0.7	1.0
Drug abuse violations......................	434,964	319,808	110,888	1,908	2,360	100.0	73.5	25.5	0.4	0.5
Gambling..................................	1,407	906	437	2	62	100.0	64.4	31.1	0.1	4.4
Offenses against the family and children...........	48,326	31,806	15,914	369	237	100.0	65.8	32.9	0.8	0.5
Driving under the influence................	476,701	428,199	41,391	3,252	3,859	100.0	89.8	8.7	0.7	0.8
Liquor laws...............................	147,574	130,609	12,846	2,364	1,755	100.0	88.5	8.7	1.6	1.2
Drunkenness..............................	137,274	122,268	13,201	1,153	652	100.0	89.1	9.6	0.8	0.5
Disorderly conduct........................	130,637	98,912	29,762	1,072	891	100.0	75.7	22.8	0.8	0.7
Vagrancy.................................	5,360	3,293	2,043	8	16	100.0	61.4	38.1	0.1	0.3
All other offenses (except traffic)................	1,090,836	784,191	291,742	8,325	6,578	100.0	71.9	26.7	0.8	0.6
Suspicion.................................	817	496	313	1	7	100.0	60.7	38.3	0.1	0.9
Curfew and loitering law violations....................	-	-	-	-	-	-	-	-	-	-
Runaways.................................	-	-	-	-	-	-	-	-	-	-

[1] Suburban area includes law enforcement agencies in cities with less than 50,000 inhabitants and county law enforcement agencies that are within a Metropolitan Statistical Area. Suburban area excludes all metropolitan agencies associated with a principal city.
[2] Because of rounding, the percentages may not add to 100.0.
[3] Violent crimes are offenses of murder and nonnegligent manslaughter, forcible rape, robbery, and aggravated assault. Property crimes are offenses of burglary, larceny-theft, motor vehicle theft, and arson.

Table 68. Police Disposition of Juvenile Offenders Taken into Custody, 2006

(Number, percent.)

Population group		Total[1]	Handled within depart- ment and released	Referred to juvenile court juris- diction	Referred to welfare agency	Referred to other police agency	Referred to criminal or adult court	Number of agencies	2006 estimated population
TOTAL AGENCIES:	Number	677,346	140,758	469,670	3,639	8,021	55,258	5,314	118,700,928
	Percent[2]	100.0	20.8	69.3	0.5	1.2	8.2		
TOTAL CITIES	Number	577,182	127,939	396,912	2,951	6,469	42,911	3,986	86,098,095
	Percent[2]	100.0	22.2	68.8	0.5	1.1	7.4		
GROUP I (250,000 and over)	Number	153,785	51,833	98,960	655	771	1,566	33	22,004,970
	Percent[2]	100.0	33.7	64.3	0.4	0.5	1.0		
GROUP II (100,000 to 249,999)	Number	82,376	17,843	58,832	455	1,748	3,498	93	13,947,587
	Percent[2]	100.0	21.7	71.4	0.6	2.1	4.2		
GROUP III (50,000 to 99,999).................................	Number	104,091	19,484	75,723	450	1,041	7,393	229	15,568,963
	Percent[2]	100.0	18.7	72.7	0.4	1.0	7.1		
GROUP IV (25,000 to 49,999)...............................	Number	79,611	13,779	56,571	651	1,731	6,879	371	12,869,843
	Percent[2]	100.0	17.3	71.1	0.8	2.2	8.6		
GROUP V (10,000 to 24,999)	Number	85,238	13,529	58,425	300	535	12,449	803	12,781,404
	Percent[2]	100.0	15.9	68.5	0.4	0.6	14.6		
GROUP VI (under 10,000).....................................	Number	72,081	11,471	48,401	440	643	11,126	2,457	8,925,328
	Percent[2]	100.0	15.9	67.1	0.6	0.9	15.4		
METROPOLITAN COUNTIES............................	Number	78,236	9,977	57,923	411	1,263	8,662	657	24,228,021
	Percent[2]	100.0	12.8	74.0	0.5	1.6	11.1		
NONMETROPOLITAN COUNTIES	Number	21,928	2,842	14,835	277	289	3,685	671	8,374,812
	Percent[2]	100.0	13.0	67.7	1.3	1.3	16.8		
SUBURBAN AREA[3]	Number	285,130	48,227	198,068	1,237	3,058	34,540	3,275	57,971,585
	Percent[2]	100.0	16.9	69.5	0.4	1.1	12.1		

[1] Includes all offenses except traffic and neglect cases.
[2] Because of rounding, the percentages may not add to 100.0.
[3] Suburban area includes law enforcement agencies in cities with less than 50,000 inhabitants and county law enforcement agencies that are within a Metropolitan Statistical Area.
   Suburban area excludes all metropolitan agencies associated with a principal city. The agencies associated with suburban areas also appear in other groups within this table.

Table 69. Total Arrests, by State, 2006

(Number.)

State		Total all classes[1]	Violent crime[2]	Property crime[2]	Murder and non-negligent man-slaughter	Forcible rape	Robbery	Aggra-vated assault	Burglary	Larceny-theft	Motor vehicle theft
ALABAMA	Under 18	11,577	580	2,436	18	27	236	299	588	1,704	114
	Total all ages............	189,558	5,925	17,246	347	320	1,610	3,648	3,262	12,820	1,057
ALASKA	Under 18	4,136	176	1,311	2	8	40	126	224	954	110
	Total all ages............	36,994	1,632	4,366	36	60	144	1,392	555	3,383	385
ARIZONA	Under 18	50,744	1,622	9,403	26	27	338	1,231	1,420	6,733	1,062
	Total all ages............	307,695	8,633	35,301	294	208	1,566	6,565	4,629	25,846	4,538
ARKANSAS	Under 18	11,389	515	2,621	6	19	98	392	690	1,833	78
	Total all ages............	113,791	4,720	11,800	130	240	646	3,704	2,610	8,619	485
CALIFORNIA	Under 18	231,735	16,796	44,651	241	224	6,632	9,699	13,473	24,710	5,554
	Total all ages............	1,543,797	123,875	166,417	1,965	2,119	20,343	99,448	52,204	84,265	28,283
COLORADO[4]	Under 18	44,178	1,066	7,625	11	70	218	767	951	6,014	491
	Total all ages............	247,536	7,047	24,194	112	484	1,053	5,398	3,070	18,963	1,886
CONNECTICUT	Under 18	15,185	968	2,710	10	31	271	656	490	1,932	197
	Total all ages............	96,616	4,501	12,178	93	234	978	3,196	1,945	9,207	694
DELAWARE	Under 18	7,448	562	1,381	3	29	193	337	331	943	45
	Total all ages............	39,832	2,563	5,465	19	132	550	1,862	1,083	4,126	167
DISTRICT OF COLUMBIA[4, 5]	Under 18	437	45	28	0	0	32	13	0	18	9
	Total all ages............	5,681	94	59	0	0	53	41	1	42	15
FLORIDA[4, 6]	Under 18	121,173	8,885	32,444	60	264	2,676	5,885	9,019	19,769	3,445
	Total all ages............	1,110,535	50,769	121,160	755	1,960	9,703	38,351	27,188	81,597	11,902
GEORGIA	Under 18	24,368	1,396	4,602	17	27	504	848	1,015	3,083	428
	Total all ages............	234,735	10,295	23,418	252	255	2,002	7,786	3,948	17,305	1,682
HAWAII	Under 18	10,315	245	1,227	3	16	89	137	142	935	133
	Total all ages............	48,018	1,145	3,958	28	89	303	725	421	2,893	613
IDAHO	Under 18	14,339	214	2,708	3	24	26	161	364	2,153	112
	Total all ages............	65,945	1,330	6,060	27	127	110	1,066	904	4,779	278
ILLINOIS[4]	Under 18	33,775	123	5,756	38	7	1,563	1,920	1,053	2,655	2,013
	Total all ages............	191,165	402	23,461	320	14	3,320	5,253	2,988	14,583	5,785
INDIANA	Under 18	27,770	625	5,997	9	35	134	447	808	4,830	311
	Total all ages............	170,293	5,571	21,087	161	153	916	4,341	3,075	16,747	1,112
IOWA	Under 18	19,605	720	4,584	0	30	83	607	782	3,523	187
	Total all ages............	109,230	3,847	11,736	26	107	331	3,383	2,013	9,064	508
KANSAS	Under 18	10,036	332	1,814	5	33	30	264	285	1,391	103
	Total all ages............	70,057	2,177	5,626	47	175	206	1,749	946	4,190	422
KENTUCKY	Under 18	8,746	394	2,223	6	11	206	171	563	1,511	135
	Total all ages............	73,504	2,039	8,443	41	64	807	1,127	1,754	6,342	320
LOUISIANA	Under 18	22,355	1,035	3,764	40	45	188	762	1,032	2,457	250
	Total all ages............	161,316	7,248	17,087	292	306	953	5,697	3,819	12,081	1,078
MAINE	Under 18	7,765	127	1,978	0	22	27	78	457	1,391	95
	Total all ages............	57,351	741	7,001	0	81	186	474	1,376	5,258	291
MARYLAND	Under 18	49,359	3,661	11,868	43	58	1,767	1,793	2,612	7,356	1,567
	Total all ages............	297,530	12,431	34,745	317	400	4,213	7,501	7,389	22,774	4,016
MASSACHUSETTS	Under 18	17,862	2,072	2,872	5	38	556	1,473	732	1,921	168
	Total all ages............	130,219	11,563	15,070	74	303	1,951	9,235	3,191	10,932	856
MICHIGAN	Under 18	44,002	2,450	11,710	31	137	764	1,518	1,895	8,261	1,382
	Total all ages............	324,698	13,929	35,466	209	747	2,680	10,293	6,000	25,085	4,014
MINNESOTA[4]	Under 18			8,959	7		406	795	1,103	7,098	600
	Total all ages............			24,559	90		1,292	4,224	3,344	19,085	1,885
MISSISSIPPI	Under 18	11,802	260	1,931	14	16	139	91	604	1,195	115
	Total all ages............	119,506	2,268	9,857	155	203	642	1,268	2,245	6,981	525
MISSOURI	Under 18	49,659	2,188	10,601	33	96	629	1,430	2,048	7,271	1,066
	Total all ages............	372,182	15,892	42,055	351	737	2,443	12,361	7,129	30,253	4,205
NEBRASKA	Under 18	14,967	184	3,295	3	16	59	106	357	2,757	107
	Total all ages............	88,602	1,575	8,973	44	145	317	1,069	962	7,565	333
NEVADA	Under 18	20,725	590	3,360	9	26	250	305	637	2,403	217
	Total all ages............	163,109	4,895	15,323	159	207	1,659	2,870	2,954	10,025	2,195

Note: Because the number of agencies submitting arrest data varies from year to year, users are cautioned about making direct comparisons between 2006 arrest totals and those published in previous years' editions of Crime in the United States. Further, arrest figures may vary widely from state to state because some Part II crimes are not considered crimes in some states.

[1] Does not include traffic arrests.
[2] Violent crimes are offenses of murder and nonnegligent manslaughter, forcible rape, robbery, and aggravated assault. Property crimes are offenses of burglary, larceny-theft, motor vehicle theft, and arson.
[4] See Appendix I for details.
[5] Includes arrests reported by the Metro Transit Police. This agency has no population associated with it.
[6] The arrest category all other offenses also includes the arrest counts for offenses against the family and children, drunkenness, disorderly conduct, vagrancy, suspicion, curfew and loitering law violations, and runaways.

Table 69. Total Arrests, by State, 2006 (*Contd.*)

(Number.)

State		Arson	Other assaults	Forgery and counter-feiting	Fraud	Embezzle-ment	Stolen property; buying, receiving, possessing	Vandalism	Weapons; carrying, possessing, etc.	Prostitution and com-mercialized vice
ALABAMA	Under 18	30	2,088	24	55	0	220	317	151	2
	Total all ages	107	24,666	1,901	8,524	34	2,232	2,058	1,238	191
ALASKA	Under 18	23	419	3	9	1	2	274	80	2
	Total all ages	43	4,130	122	165	8	16	954	400	192
ARIZONA	Under 18	188	5,041	67	113	46	230	3,481	541	20
	Total all ages	288	24,721	3,122	2,075	294	1,435	11,074	3,703	1,518
ARKANSAS	Under 18	20	1,137	29	27	0	112	362	166	4
	Total all ages	86	8,286	1,278	2,934	8	1,124	1,384	1,429	251
CALIFORNIA	Under 18	914	22,736	327	620	182	3,308	16,864	9,248	558
	Total all ages	1,665	89,196	10,110	10,157	2,269	21,380	34,527	33,547	12,908
COLORADO[4]	Under 18	169	2,451	70	167	13	190	2,006	721	11
	Total all ages	275	15,801	1,699	2,537	192	1,226	6,351	2,388	497
CONNECTICUT	Under 18	91	2,745	16	41	8	79	662	285	3
	Total all ages	332	14,613	645	996	165	606	1,928	1,243	481
DELAWARE	Under 18	62	1,603	9	112	21	116	390	158	0
	Total all ages	89	7,890	588	2,077	227	426	1,149	464	105
DISTRICT OF COLUMBIA[4,5]	Under 18	1	55	0	1	0	2	17	10	0
	Total all ages	1	178	3	1	1	12	29	29	0
FLORIDA[4,6]	Under 18	211	18,573	146	675	148	331	3,513	2,417	66
	Total all ages	473	94,816	4,804	16,240	1,569	2,737	9,880	8,611	5,443
GEORGIA	Under 18	76	2,881	94	168	0	426	520	697	36
	Total all ages	483	16,434	3,555	6,293	127	3,295	2,076	4,380	1,540
HAWAII	Under 18	17	829	11	8	1	17	513	40	5
	Total all ages	31	4,334	222	209	28	127	937	226	428
IDAHO	Under 18	79	1,222	12	33	15	49	522	167	0
	Total all ages	99	5,846	281	511	123	248	1,170	560	7
ILLINOIS[4]	Under 18	35	6,404	11	117	0	19	2,177	1,054	50
	Total all ages	105	27,853	324	1,296	0	88	5,737	4,096	4,736
INDIANA	Under 18	48	3,222	24	67	8	166	1,192	145	4
	Total all ages	153	13,567	1,007	1,867	42	1,004	2,447	1,324	198
IOWA	Under 18	92	2,458	35	64	7	54	1,603	114	3
	Total all ages	151	9,416	748	1,031	63	200	3,278	483	95
KANSAS	Under 18	35	1,323	18	11	20	42	464	130	0
	Total all ages	68	9,728	508	1,358	125	275	1,701	680	212
KENTUCKY	Under 18	14	644	14	31	0	396	290	145	3
	Total all ages	27	3,612	706	1,170	21	1,242	779	661	656
LOUISIANA	Under 18	25	4,215	18	22	5	221	905	313	3
	Total all ages	109	20,364	814	1,974	170	1,607	3,393	1,785	519
MAINE	Under 18	35	949	20	32	1	40	589	53	3
	Total all ages	76	7,100	367	892	48	198	1,732	400	28
MARYLAND	Under 18	333	8,605	64	68	43	21	2,383	1,610	35
	Total all ages	566	29,762	1,207	2,563	348	201	4,444	4,385	1,694
MASSACHUSETTS	Under 18	51	2,058	20	48	7	295	1,040	261	17
	Total all ages	91	15,931	753	1,365	90	1,317	3,231	1,301	823
MICHIGAN	Under 18	172	4,130	61	416	54	624	1,766	1,026	8
	Total all ages	367	28,791	1,261	6,384	1,358	2,464	4,326	5,309	834
MINNESOTA[4]	Under 18	158	4,277	121	241	1	437	2,349	930	35
	Total all ages	245	18,075	1,927	3,786	26	1,992	5,034	2,472	1,200
MISSISSIPPI	Under 18	17	1,757	21	47	21	115	270	239	16
	Total all ages	106	12,565	1,030	2,311	739	907	1,291	1,176	171
MISSOURI	Under 18	216	7,686	119	93	22	530	2,624	817	11
	Total all ages	468	37,720	3,158	4,614	165	3,228	8,093	4,100	1,085
NEBRASKA	Under 18	74	1,850	27	74	6	186	1,057	158	1
	Total all ages	113	8,594	570	1,703	78	1,047	2,783	1,123	233
NEVADA	Under 18	103	2,159	13	82	34	236	1,039	499	49
	Total all ages	149	19,001	999	2,858	452	1,890	2,221	2,445	4,609

Note: Because the number of agencies submitting arrest data varies from year to year, users are cautioned about making direct comparisons between 2006 arrest totals and those published in previous years' editions of Crime in the United States. Further, arrest figures may vary widely from state to state because some Part II crimes are not considered crimes in some states.

[4] See Appendix I for details.

[5] Includes arrests reported by the Metro Transit Police. This agency has no population associated with it.

[6] The arrest category all other offenses also includes the arrest counts for offenses against the family and children, drunkenness, disorderly conduct, vagrancy, suspicion, curfew and loitering law violations, and runaways.

Table 69. Total Arrests, by State, 2006 (Contd.)

(Number.)

State		Sex offenses (except forcible rape and prostitution)	Drug abuse violations	Gambling	Offenses against the family and children	Driving under the influence	Liquor laws	Drunkenness[3]
ALABAMA	Under 18	31	1,082	3	13	120	716	99
	Total all ages	553	16,860	87	975	12,374	5,778	9,371
ALASKA	Under 18	44	254	0	4	63	293	24
	Total all ages	183	1,701	1	345	4,334	1,940	172
ARIZONA	Under 18	253	5,176	3	311	588	5,443	1
	Total all ages	1,505	35,470	23	3,371	35,251	24,317	1
ARKANSAS	Under 18	37	959	1	6	141	228	240
	Total all ages	235	11,154	13	273	9,388	1,723	8,623
CALIFORNIA	Under 18	2,351	21,434	61	3	1,699	5,033	4,190
	Total all ages	15,665	301,406	557	509	197,775	21,533	106,859
COLORADO[4]	Under 18	260	3,578	0	77	539	5,376	89
	Total all ages	1,018	19,513	5	2,976	30,862	16,968	384
CONNECTICUT	Under 18	95	1,304	0	69	80	338	1
	Total all ages	423	12,249	13	1,087	5,105	994	12
DELAWARE	Under 18	50	799	2	9	0	439	14
	Total all ages	177	5,538	13	221	233	2,321	472
DISTRICT OF COLUMBIA[4, 5]	Under 18	1	21	0	0	0	2	0
	Total all ages	2	91	0	0	17	1,397	78
FLORIDA[4, 6]	Under 18	370	14,452	33		388	1,418	
	Total all ages	3,861	168,119	352		55,278	32,137	
GEORGIA	Under 18	341	2,525	23	76	196	713	82
	Total all ages	3,231	33,922	268	2,420	16,615	10,220	3,207
HAWAII	Under 18	56	405	0	0	65	170	0
	Total all ages	305	2,428	21	27	5,059	895	6
IDAHO	Under 18	89	754	0	6	262	1,827	11
	Total all ages	326	5,285	15	446	10,308	5,453	242
ILLINOIS[4]	Under 18	114	8,277	1,030	16	41	387	0
	Total all ages	944	57,495	3,882	424	5,971	1,537	0
INDIANA	Under 18	219	2,031	0	390	212	2,957	372
	Total all ages	1,063	19,633	32	2,059	22,586	11,880	12,522
IOWA	Under 18	78	1,083	0	18	293	1,787	388
	Total all ages	280	8,512	12	931	13,028	8,739	10,013
KANSAS	Under 18	75	862	0	12	245	1,277	2
	Total all ages	285	6,523	0	247	11,249	6,852	238
KENTUCKY	Under 18	32	1,474	0	16	54	111	172
	Total all ages	110	12,192	18	1,203	4,971	1,014	5,543
LOUISIANA	Under 18	132	1,832	17	64	76	316	34
	Total all ages	809	23,506	80	975	8,755	6,945	2,193
MAINE	Under 18	53	629	1	3	172	1,247	16
	Total all ages	278	5,779	9	378	7,704	4,952	78
MARYLAND	Under 18	302	7,366	87	29	283	1,265	0
	Total all ages	1,330	55,466	356	2,267	22,898	6,061	3
MASSACHUSETTS	Under 18	68	2,218	1	92	143	1,049	293
	Total all ages	553	17,729	10	1,356	8,359	4,575	6,827
MICHIGAN	Under 18	347	3,958	14	5	776	5,475	20
	Total all ages	1,203	33,886	160	3,348	44,553	25,263	538
MINNESOTA[4]	Under 18	291	2,928	4	24	677	6,996	0
	Total all ages	1,375	18,186	26	814	26,098	25,700	0
MISSISSIPPI	Under 18	31	994	24	172	129	241	174
	Total all ages	432	16,190	397	4,263	11,250	3,022	7,324
MISSOURI	Under 18	542	4,517	35	105	655	2,842	11
	Total all ages	2,981	44,762	195	5,169	38,859	15,123	108
NEBRASKA	Under 18	104	1,112	0	39	309	2,385	0
	Total all ages	609	10,321	18	1,621	12,726	11,549	0
NEVADA	Under 18	128	1,398	16	14	90	1,689	98
	Total all ages	1,308	13,784	126	1,766	11,060	8,409	189

Note: Because the number of agencies submitting arrest data varies from year to year, users are cautioned about making direct comparisons between 2006 arrest totals and those published in previous years' editions of Crime in the United States. Further, arrest figures may vary widely from state to state because some Part II crimes are not considered crimes in some states.

[3] Drunkenness is not considered a crime in some states; therefore, the figures vary widely from state to state.

[4] See Appendix I for details.

[5] Includes arrests reported by the Metro Transit Police. This agency has no population associated with it.

[6] The arrest category all other offenses also includes the arrest counts for offenses against the family and children, drunkenness, disorderly conduct, vagrancy, suspicion, curfew and loitering law violations, and runaways.

Table 69. Total Arrests, by State, 2006 (*Contd.*)

(Number.)

State		Disorderly conduct	Vagrancy	All other offenses (except traffic)	Suspicion	Curfew and loitering law violations	Runaways	Number of agencies	2006 estimated population
ALABAMA	Under 18	1,569	8	1,603	0	31	429	270	3,691,413
	Total all ages............	4,478	288	74,319	0	31	429		
ALASKA	Under 18	66	0	826	0	0	285	31	641,049
	Total all ages............	913	3	15,131	1	0	285		
ARIZONA	Under 18	3,429	30	5,702	0	3,973	5,271	83	5,893,944
	Total all ages............	17,251	1,128	88,258	0	3,973	5,271		
ARKANSAS	Under 18	947	48	2,460	9	810	530	185	1,943,587
	Total all ages............	3,012	1,608	43,009	199	810	530		
CALIFORNIA	Under 18	12,203	350	44,222	0	19,613	5,286	689	36,291,331
	Total all ages............	17,014	5,198	347,996	0	19,613	5,286		
COLORADO[4]	Under 18	3,727	9	10,012	7	2,579	3,605	187	4,493,272
	Total all ages............	12,023	190	95,458	23	2,579	3,605		
CONNECTICUT	Under 18	2,840	1	2,767	0	137	36	74	2,137,426
	Total all ages............	12,879	23	26,302	0	137	36		
DELAWARE	Under 18	969	0	701	0	112	1	53	853,476
	Total all ages............	2,769	706	6,315	0	112	1		
DISTRICT OF COLUMBIA[4,5]	Under 18	102	0	151	0	2	0	2	
	Total all ages............	248	182	3,258	0	2	0		
FLORIDA[4,6]	Under 18			37,314				591	18,015,015
	Total all ages............			534,759					
GEORGIA	Under 18	2,839	47	5,191	4	535	976	161	3,185,684
	Total all ages............	20,530	835	70,543	20	535	976		
HAWAII	Under 18	65	0	2,103	0	216	4,339	2	1,081,338
	Total all ages............	588	0	22,520	0	216	4,339		
IDAHO	Under 18	579	0	3,407	0	696	1,766	96	1,236,683
	Total all ages............	2,451	7	22,814	0	696	1,766		
ILLINOIS[4]	Under 18	3,520	0	3,953	0	706	20	2	3,011,534
	Total all ages............	21,513	179	30,501	0	706	20		
INDIANA	Under 18	1,803	10	4,160	7	513	3,646	153	3,741,675
	Total all ages............	5,435	40	42,647	123	513	3,646		
IOWA	Under 18	2,280	0	2,671	0	927	438	177	2,479,827
	Total all ages............	5,789	13	29,651	0	927	438		
KANSAS	Under 18	650	0	1,147	0	0	1,612	229	1,783,369
	Total all ages............	3,708	0	16,953	0	0	1,612		
KENTUCKY	Under 18	538	0	1,833	0	216	160	17	984,186
	Total all ages............	1,943	646	26,159	0	216	160		
LOUISIANA	Under 18	4,513	54	3,778	17	497	524	86	2,057,838
	Total all ages............	17,941	294	43,800	36	497	524		
MAINE	Under 18	179	0	1,458	0	74	141	162	1,317,948
	Total all ages............	1,845	0	17,606	0	74	141		
MARYLAND	Under 18	2,386	53	7,952	119	281	878	142	5,571,209
	Total all ages............	6,697	155	108,635	723	281	878		
MASSACHUSETTS	Under 18	1,398	1	3,555	25	19	310	301	5,471,817
	Total all ages............	7,385	16	31,463	173	19	310		
MICHIGAN	Under 18	1,507	0	6,603	0	1,527	1,525	548	9,426,852
	Total all ages............	10,301	563	101,709	0	1,527	1,525		
MINNESOTA[4]	Under 18	4,940	18	6,399	0	4,847	4,247	260	4,610,061
	Total all ages............	13,282	332	37,857	0	4,847	4,247		
MISSISSIPPI	Under 18	2,124	17	2,466	17	475	261	96	1,616,759
	Total all ages............	8,235	71	35,165	106	475	261		
MISSOURI	Under 18	2,982	91	7,925	0	1,914	3,349	548	5,748,820
	Total all ages............	16,123	324	123,165	0	1,914	3,349		
NEBRASKA	Under 18	941	0	2,453	0	379	407	207	1,543,773
	Total all ages............	4,136	42	20,114	1	379	407		
NEVADA	Under 18	843	21	3,309	26	3,381	1,651	35	2,481,554
	Total all ages............	2,876	1,775	62,064	27	3,381	1,651		

Note: Because the number of agencies submitting arrest data varies from year to year, users are cautioned about making direct comparisons between 2006 arrest totals and those published in previous years' editions of Crime in the United States. Further, arrest figures may vary widely from state to state because some Part II crimes are not considered crimes in some states.

[4] See Appendix I for details.

[5] Includes arrests reported by the Metro Transit Police. This agency has no population associated with it.

[6] The arrest category all other offenses also includes the arrest counts for offenses against the family and children, drunkenness, disorderly conduct, vagrancy, suspicion, curfew and loitering law violations, and runaways.

Table 69. Total Arrests, by State, 2006

(Number.)

State		Total all classes[1]	Violent crime[2]	Property crime[2]	Murder and non-negligent man-slaughter	Forcible rape	Robbery	Aggra-vated assault	Burglary	Larceny-theft	Motor vehicle theft
NEW HAMPSHIRE	Under 18	8,314	104	1,025	0	12	24	68	133	819	46
	Total all ages	46,100	592	2,885	8	67	145	372	397	2,298	136
NEW JERSEY	Under 18	60,840	3,402	8,276	29	59	1,655	1,659	1,755	5,888	338
	Total all ages	388,116	14,314	31,288	312	428	4,425	9,149	6,144	23,595	1,094
NEW MEXICO	Under 18	8,466	399	1,504	2	13	50	334	266	1,102	92
	Total all ages	72,114	2,806	5,520	67	99	350	2,290	984	4,039	421
NEW YORK[4]	Under 18	48,209	3,227	11,349	31	91	1,396	1,709	2,749	7,619	794
	Total all ages	345,357	16,095	48,763	298	730	4,300	10,767	8,611	36,906	2,824
NORTH CAROLINA	Under 18	44,691	2,095	9,734	47	78	680	1,290	2,842	6,476	303
	Total all ages	436,676	18,660	53,401	629	702	3,921	13,408	14,874	36,471	1,682
NORTH DAKOTA	Under 18	6,769	42	976	0	4	8	30	127	734	98
	Total all ages	28,597	275	2,256	4	39	25	207	329	1,696	201
OHIO	Under 18	38,509	1,242	6,808	19	98	515	610	1,177	5,010	484
	Total all ages	235,005	6,564	28,912	164	476	2,320	3,604	5,320	21,816	1,495
OKLAHOMA	Under 18	20,192	726	4,265	19	37	170	500	830	2,998	234
	Total all ages	145,171	5,304	13,622	154	261	750	4,139	2,882	9,407	969
OREGON	Under 18	24,723	689	5,926	5	27	188	469	661	4,771	285
	Total all ages	124,612	4,142	22,488	101	263	939	2,839	2,482	17,950	1,767
PENNSYLVANIA	Under 18	106,572	5,546	12,385	39	213	2,082	3,212	2,468	8,199	1,366
	Total all ages	457,514	25,102	52,799	476	1,072	7,367	16,187	9,803	37,691	4,598
RHODE ISLAND	Under 18	4,900	144	901	1	7	37	99	180	638	48
	Total all ages	35,999	697	2,816	13	48	144	492	587	2,035	146
SOUTH CAROLINA	Under 18	23,565	1,469	4,476	22	68	314	1,065	1,261	2,932	211
	Total all ages	187,578	10,311	20,899	282	390	1,609	8,030	4,678	14,984	1,041
SOUTH DAKOTA	Under 18	2,214	11	173	0	1	0	10	30	120	12
	Total all ages	13,677	154	751	1	25	10	118	108	581	48
TENNESSEE	Under 18	35,228	1,699	5,760	35	59	457	1,148	1,362	3,827	475
	Total all ages	285,475	13,340	31,606	326	345	2,885	9,784	5,869	23,027	2,475
TEXAS	Under 18	169,460	4,968	26,895	69	285	1,477	3,137	5,400	19,696	1,482
	Total all ages	1,078,961	33,025	111,837	777	2,131	7,222	22,895	18,328	85,266	7,459
UTAH	Under 18	23,519	297	4,552	1	48	56	192	375	3,917	186
	Total all ages	109,762	1,598	12,313	28	163	355	1,052	1,152	10,568	484
VERMONT	Under 18	1,645	57	325	0	22	0	35	74	211	36
	Total all ages	13,798	386	1,431	6	65	13	302	310	1,007	96
VIRGINIA	Under 18	34,797	1,076	5,699	17	37	425	597	1,108	4,155	238
	Total all ages	276,305	6,908	23,877	228	323	1,856	4,501	3,967	18,492	1,039
WASHINGTON	Under 18	34,902	1,376	9,853	13	122	484	757	1,772	7,254	609
	Total all ages	246,388	7,674	34,948	148	783	1,866	4,877	5,841	26,429	2,294
WEST VIRGINIA	Under 18	1,438	40	243	0	3	8	29	52	160	29
	Total all ages	26,566	882	2,377	18	35	75	754	496	1,636	203
WISCONSIN	Under 18	103,275	1,747	15,191	23	161	585	978	1,785	11,926	1,288
	Total all ages	414,975	8,081	38,521	182	732	1,650	5,517	4,898	30,637	2,554
WYOMING	Under 18	6,682	76	837	1	2	3	70	92	703	35
	Total all ages	38,780	573	2,341	4	25	26	518	315	1,889	121

Note: Because the number of agencies submitting arrest data varies from year to year, users are cautioned about making direct comparisons between 2006 arrest totals and those published in previous years' editions of Crime in the United States. Further, arrest figures may vary widely from state to state because some Part II crimes are not considered crimes in some states.

[1] Does not include traffic arrests.

[2] Violent crimes are offenses of murder and nonnegligent manslaughter, forcible rape, robbery, and aggravated assault. Property crimes are offenses of burglary, larceny-theft, motor vehicle theft, and arson.

[4] See Appendix I for details.

Table 69. Total Arrests, by State, 2006 (*Contd.*)

(Number.)

State		Arson	Other assaults	Forgery and counter-feiting	Fraud	Embezzle-ment	Stolen property; buying, receiving, possessing	Vandalism	Weapons; carrying, possessing, etc.	Prostitution and com-mercialized vice
NEW HAMPSHIRE	Under 18	27	954	14	82	12	101	538	20	0
	Total all ages	54	5,427	210	1,027	35	411	1,350	127	98
NEW JERSEY	Under 18	295	5,132	55	106	7	1,441	3,728	2,039	32
	Total all ages	455	28,048	1,972	4,855	120	5,114	7,660	6,460	2,022
NEW MEXICO	Under 18	44	1,126	15	37	21	72	348	294	3
	Total all ages	76	5,608	295	508	149	753	692	758	333
NEW YORK[4]	Under 18	187	4,920	185	377	2	1,249	4,222	874	22
	Total all ages	422	31,920	4,439	9,354	196	5,884	13,440	4,361	1,765
NORTH CAROLINA	Under 18	113	7,643	62	455	68	783	2,563	1,561	15
	Total all ages	374	53,250	3,182	25,006	1,734	5,757	8,904	7,624	1,414
NORTH DAKOTA	Under 18	17	469	11	29	4	46	386	43	0
	Total all ages	30	1,919	146	1,122	27	123	657	143	2
OHIO	Under 18	137	5,420	52	139	5	717	1,885	603	8
	Total all ages	281	24,083	1,390	3,392	21	3,888	4,327	2,932	951
OKLAHOMA	Under 18	203	1,296	19	74	55	348	522	364	2
	Total all ages	364	9,703	898	2,082	500	2,156	1,323	2,551	450
OREGON	Under 18	209	1,883	44	106	2	62	1,709	272	18
	Total all ages	289	13,202	1,254	1,451	61	678	4,277	1,732	677
PENNSYLVANIA	Under 18	352	8,244	111	343	30	724	5,298	1,775	11
	Total all ages	707	43,568	3,495	10,777	405	3,308	13,383	4,998	2,380
RHODE ISLAND	Under 18	35	623	9	21	7	72	560	132	0
	Total all ages	48	3,941	181	883	174	304	1,323	352	215
SOUTH CAROLINA	Under 18	72	4,511	50	118	31	307	1,142	874	4
	Total all ages	196	22,182	2,423	19,181	470	2,408	3,626	2,658	520
SOUTH DAKOTA	Under 18	11	117	0	14	2	3	71	6	0
	Total all ages	14	1,153	20	537	8	8	189	52	4
TENNESSEE	Under 18	96	5,885	83	177	49	86	1,572	775	20
	Total all ages	235	30,460	3,899	10,309	1,029	893	4,443	3,353	2,142
TEXAS	Under 18	317	22,041	246	340	53	118	5,454	1,846	118
	Total all ages	784	100,697	8,443	15,440	531	758	13,022	14,326	8,403
UTAH	Under 18	74	1,819	40	69	7	131	1,646	360	9
	Total all ages	109	8,401	780	930	22	654	3,326	1,033	512
VERMONT	Under 18	4	247	3	13	0	19	105	7	0
	Total all ages	18	1,406	97	378	40	128	352	9	1
VIRGINIA	Under 18	198	4,667	64	112	119	148	1,597	662	1
	Total all ages	379	32,939	2,199	8,480	1,588	827	4,444	3,711	586
WASHINGTON	Under 18	218	4,999	112	48	16	605	2,258	841	41
	Total all ages	384	30,243	2,435	1,278	183	4,649	6,984	3,593	1,313
WEST VIRGINIA	Under 18	2	198	6	6	1	6	96	9	0
	Total all ages	42	4,032	255	614	64	170	599	248	29
WISCONSIN	Under 18	192	4,069	151	241	29	464	4,421	1,537	24
	Total all ages	432	19,162	2,424	8,300	197	1,324	11,111	5,110	690
WYOMING	Under 18	7	758	3	7	1	14	373	48	1
	Total all ages	16	3,223	135	167	14	102	863	145	6

Note: Because the number of agencies submitting arrest data varies from year to year, users are cautioned about making direct comparisons between 2006 arrest totals and those published in previous years' editions of Crime in the United States. Further, arrest figures may vary widely from state to state because some Part II crimes are not considered crimes in some states.

[4] See Appendix I for details.

Table 69. Total Arrests, by State, 2006 *(Contd.)*

(Number.)

State		Sex offenses (except forcible rape and prostitution)	Drug abuse violations	Gambling	Offenses against the family and children	Driving under the influence	Liquor laws	Drunkenness[3]
NEW HAMPSHIRE	Under 18	42	715	0	7	102	1,211	456
	Total all ages	200	3,228	1	158	4,783	5,376	4,453
NEW JERSEY	Under 18	342	6,526	15	39	367	2,902	0
	Total all ages	1,761	54,168	309	15,307	25,181	8,036	3
NEW MEXICO	Under 18	17	927	6	2	144	620	1
	Total all ages	128	5,775	13	857	8,441	3,716	167
NEW YORK[4]	Under 18	812	6,247	17	372	302	1,203	0
	Total all ages	4,490	61,748	157	2,640	28,696	5,864	0
NORTH CAROLINA	Under 18	145	3,321	13	87	618	1,731	0
	Total all ages	1,347	35,066	593	8,297	50,674	16,408	0
NORTH DAKOTA	Under 18	23	244	0	101	71	1,476	7
	Total all ages	78	1,783	0	186	4,581	6,336	605
OHIO	Under 18	195	2,763	22	761	233	2,274	69
	Total all ages	895	31,368	100	7,541	18,960	11,710	4,138
OKLAHOMA	Under 18	69	1,712	5	36	258	473	748
	Total all ages	737	20,823	49	775	15,936	3,588	22,120
OREGON	Under 18	186	1,812	3	9	156	3,485	0
	Total all ages	1,129	17,352	13	509	14,016	13,434	0
PENNSYLVANIA	Under 18	530	6,432	32	30	584	7,726	342
	Total all ages	2,651	54,412	337	954	46,093	27,319	21,686
RHODE ISLAND	Under 18	23	465	0	38	32	113	7
	Total all ages	103	3,688	15	85	2,118	766	14
SOUTH CAROLINA	Under 18	155	2,988	10	49	82	694	119
	Total all ages	709	28,713	113	876	7,650	8,339	8,033
SOUTH DAKOTA	Under 18	8	71	0	32	84	901	7
	Total all ages	26	640	0	228	3,695	3,670	146
TENNESSEE	Under 18	175	3,305	41	39	199	1,422	428
	Total all ages	769	35,455	264	1,582	23,296	8,737	20,935
TEXAS	Under 18	741	14,702	72	141	1,172	5,489	3,175
	Total all ages	4,359	135,914	428	5,519	88,165	29,348	120,286
UTAH	Under 18	305	1,212	0	110	139	2,759	89
	Total all ages	823	7,653	17	2,105	6,452	10,054	4,134
VERMONT	Under 18	11	165	0	13	42	235	1
	Total all ages	44	1,394	0	359	3,544	770	6
VIRGINIA	Under 18	235	2,591	4	16	159	1,603	196
	Total all ages	981	29,273	102	1,237	21,422	8,855	24,684
WASHINGTON	Under 18	188	2,849	1	20	754	3,987	3
	Total all ages	1,427	29,264	12	614	36,986	13,030	7
WEST VIRGINIA	Under 18	15	172	0	0	28	161	13
	Total all ages	133	4,100	0	61	4,028	1,274	1,063
WISCONSIN	Under 18	1,166	4,932	57	147	754	10,505	1
	Total all ages	3,113	25,329	157	2,448	41,105	42,935	5
WYOMING	Under 18	9	518	0	11	104	1,183	64
	Total all ages	157	3,160	1	256	5,423	4,471	2,002

Note: Because the number of agencies submitting arrest data varies from year to year, users are cautioned about making direct comparisons between 2006 arrest totals and those published in previous years' editions of Crime in the United States. Further, arrest figures may vary widely from state to state because some Part II crimes are not considered crimes in some states.

[3] Drunkenness is not considered a crime in some states; therefore, the figures vary widely from state to state.

[4] See Appendix I for details.

Table 69. Total Arrests, by State, 2006 *(Contd.)*

(Number.)

State		Disorderly conduct	Vagrancy	All other offenses (except traffic)	Suspicion	Curfew and loitering law violations	Runaways	Number of agencies	2006 estimated population
NEW HAMPSHIRE	Under 18	281	5	2,277	0	17	351	122	1,039,150
	Total all ages	1,482	48	13,841	0	17	351		
NEW JERSEY	Under 18	5,357	49	9,685	5	6,322	5,013	539	8,446,877
	Total all ages	21,548	1,635	146,975	5	6,322	5,013		
NEW MEXICO	Under 18	683	0	1,841	2	18	386	40	1,268,388
	Total all ages	2,727	0	32,339	125	18	386		
NEW YORK[4]	Under 18	2,656	91	10,082	0	0	0	628	9,446,127
	Total all ages	16,474	1,599	87,472	0	0	0		
NORTH CAROLINA	Under 18	5,654	25	6,693	0	12	1,413	363	6,749,209
	Total all ages	16,351	503	127,080	0	12	1,413		
NORTH DAKOTA	Under 18	730	0	1,192	0	252	667	69	575,177
	Total all ages	1,751	0	5,688	0	252	667		
OHIO	Under 18	3,437	19	9,210	2	1,764	881	315	5,693,115
	Total all ages	18,146	79	62,940	23	1,764	881		
OKLAHOMA	Under 18	1,112	0	2,843	0	2,228	3,037	276	3,254,461
	Total all ages	3,094	0	34,195	0	2,228	3,037		
OREGON	Under 18	1,312	0	3,013	0	2,160	1,876	132	3,099,031
	Total all ages	6,355	4	17,802	0	2,160	1,876		
PENNSYLVANIA	Under 18	16,840	134	7,638	0	29,734	2,083	841	10,932,970
	Total all ages	57,363	1,041	53,626	0	29,734	2,083		
RHODE ISLAND	Under 18	747	0	923	0	35	48	44	954,017
	Total all ages	3,046	11	15,183	1	35	48		
SOUTH CAROLINA	Under 18	3,056	0	2,946	0	45	439	421	3,877,177
	Total all ages	13,040	734	34,219	0	45	439		
SOUTH DAKOTA	Under 18	105	0	248	0	164	197	73	365,423
	Total all ages	662	1	1,372	0	164	197		
TENNESSEE	Under 18	4,111	0	5,364	0	1,564	2,474	400	4,877,891
	Total all ages	11,245	25	77,655	0	1,564	2,474		
TEXAS	Under 18	23,221	2,178	32,043	7	12,999	11,441	943	22,453,094
	Total all ages	42,913	2,779	318,321	7	12,999	11,441		
UTAH	Under 18	1,948	277	5,552	0	1,944	254	91	2,003,810
	Total all ages	4,619	301	41,837	0	1,944	254		
VERMONT	Under 18	161	0	238	0	2	1	74	520,953
	Total all ages	813	2	2,635	0	2	1		
VIRGINIA	Under 18	1,630	0	6,282	0	2,961	4,975	309	5,895,712
	Total all ages	5,526	134	90,596	0	2,961	4,975		
WASHINGTON	Under 18	678	0	4,276	0	60	1,937	220	5,254,276
	Total all ages	4,931	21	64,789	10	60	1,937		
WEST VIRGINIA	Under 18	22	0	342	0	49	31	180	885,812
	Total all ages	474	6	6,077	0	49	31		
WISCONSIN	Under 18	19,313	189	26,793	0	7,164	4,380	313	5,294,726
	Total all ages	63,761	3,496	126,158	4	7,164	4,380		
WYOMING	Under 18	238	9	1,703	69	359	297	61	502,901
	Total all ages	1,360	16	13,591	118	359	297		

Note: Because the number of agencies submitting arrest data varies from year to year, users are cautioned about making direct comparisons between 2006 arrest totals and those published in previous years' editions of Crime in the United States. Further, arrest figures may vary widely from state to state because some Part II crimes are not considered crimes in some states.

[4] See Appendix I for details.

SECTION V:
LAW ENFORCEMENT PERSONNEL

LAW ENFORCEMENT PERSONNEL

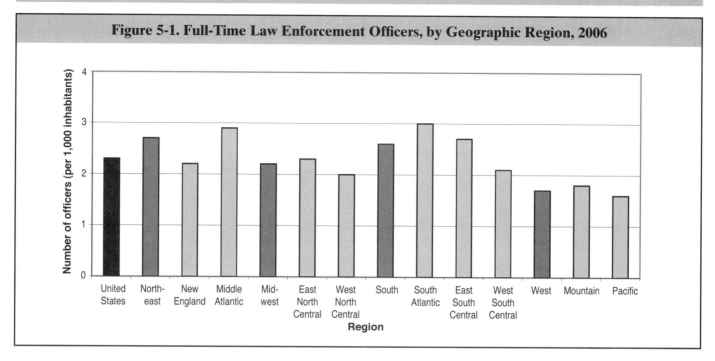

Figure 5-1. Full-Time Law Enforcement Officers, by Geographic Region, 2006

Because of differing service requirements and functions, caution should be used when drawing comparisons between and among the staffing levels of law enforcement agencies. What follows is not intended as recommended or preferred officer strength; the data should only be used as a guide.

Each year, UCR Program staff ask law enforcement agencies across the United States to report the total number of sworn law enforcement officers and civilians employed in their agencies as of October 31. This section of *Crime in the United States* presents those data as the number and rate of law enforcement officers and civilian employees throughout the United States. In 2006, 14,336 state, city, university and college, metropolitan and nonmetropolitan county, and other law enforcement agencies employed 683,396 sworn officers and 303,729 civilians, who provided law enforcement services to more than 283 million people nationwide. (Table 74)

The data in this section are broken down by geographic region and division, population group, state, city, university and college, metropolitan and nonmetropolitan county, and other law enforcement agencies. (Information about geographic regions and divisions and population groups can be found in Appendix III.) UCR Program staff compute the rate of sworn officers and law enforcement employees by taking the number of employees (sworn officers only or in combination with civilians), dividing by the population for which the agency provides law enforcement service, and multiplying by 1,000.

- Tables 70 and 71 present the number and rate of law enforcement personnel per 1,000 inhabitants collectively employed by agencies, broken down by geographic region and division by population group.

- Tables 72 and 73 provide a count of law enforcement agencies by population group, based on the employment rate ranges for sworn officer and civilian employees per 1,000 inhabitants.

- Table 74 provides the number and percentage of male and female sworn officers and civilian employees by population group.

- Table 75 lists the percentage of full-time civilian law enforcement employees by population group.

- Table 76 breaks down by state the number of sworn law enforcement officers and civilians employed by state law enforcement agencies.

- Tables 78 to 80 list the number of law enforcement employees for cities, universities and colleges, and metropolitan and nonmetropolitan counties.

- Table 81 supplies employee data for those law enforcement agencies that serve the nation's transit systems, parks and forests, schools and school districts, hospitals, etc.

The demographic traits and characteristics of a jurisdiction affect its requirements for law enforcement service. For instance, a village between two large cities may require more law enforcement than a community of the same size with no urban center nearby. A town with legal gambling may have different law enforcement needs than a town near a military base. A city largely made up of college students may have different law enforcement needs than a city whose residents are mainly retirees.

Similarly, the functions of law enforcement agencies are diverse. Employees of these agencies patrol local streets and major highways, protect citizens in the nation's smallest towns and largest cities, and conduct investigations on offenses at the local and state level. State police in one area may enforce traffic laws on state highways and interstates; in another area, they may be responsible for investigating violent crimes. Sheriff's departments may collect tax monies, serve as the enforcement authority for local and state courts, administer jail facilities, or carry out some combination of these duties. This has an impact on an agency's staffing levels.

Because of the differing service requirements and functions, care should be taken when drawing comparisons between and among the staffing levels of law enforcement agencies. The data in this section are not intended as recommended or preferred officer strength; they should be used merely as guides. Adequate staffing levels can be determined only after careful study of the conditions that affect the service requirements in a particular jurisdiction.

Rate

The rate of full-time law enforcement employees (civilian and sworn) per 1,000 inhabitants in the nation for 2006 was 3.5; the rate of sworn officers was 2.4 per 1,000. (Table 74) The UCR Program computes these rates by taking the number of employees, dividing by the population of the agency's jurisdiction, and multiplying by 1,000.

Among the nation's four regions, law enforcement agencies in the Northeast had the highest rate of law enforcement employees in 2006, with 3.5 per 1,000 inhabitants. Agencies in the South had 3.4 law enforcement employees per 1,000 inhabitants, followed by the Midwest (2.7) and the West (2.4). (Table 70)

An examination of the 2006 law enforcement employee data by population group showed that the nation's cities had a collective rate of 3.0 law enforcement employees per 1,000 inhabitants. Cities with under 10,000 inhabitants had the highest rate of law enforcement employees, with 4.2 per 1,000 inhabitants. Cities with 25,000 to 49,999 inhabitants and cities with 50,000 to 99,999 inhabitants had the lowest rate of law enforcement employees (2.3 per 1,000 in population). The nation's largest cities, those with 250,000 or more inhabitants, averaged 3.8 law enforcement employees for every 1,000 inhabitants. (Table 70)

Sworn Personnel

The UCR Program defines law enforcement officers as individuals who ordinarily carry a firearm and a badge, have full arrest powers, and are paid from government funds set aside specifically for sworn law enforcement representatives.

An analysis of the 2006 data showed that law enforcement agencies in the cities in the Northeast had the highest rate of sworn officers—2.7 per 1,000 inhabitants, followed by the South (2.6), the Midwest (2.2), and the West (1.7). (Table 71)

By population group in 2006, there were 2.3 sworn officers for each 1,000 resident population in the nation's cities collectively. This rate was unchanged from the 2005 data. Cities with under 10,000 inhabitants had the highest rate at 3.3 sworn officers per 1,000 inhabitants. The nation's largest cities, those with 250,000 or more inhabitants, averaged 2.8 officers per 1,000 inhabitants. (Table 71)

Female employees accounted for 61.6 percent of all full-time civilian law enforcement employees in 2006. Males accounted for 88.2 percent of all full-time sworn law enforcement officers in 2006. In cities collectively, 88.2 percent of sworn officers were male. In metropolitan counties, 86.6 percent of officers were male, and in nonmetropolitan counties, 92.4 percent of officers were male. (Table 74)

Civilian Employees

Civilian employees provide a myriad of services to the nation's law enforcement and criminal justice agencies. Among other duties, they dispatch officers, provide administrative and record-keeping support, and query local, state, and national databases.

In 2006, 30.8 percent of all law enforcement employees in the nation were civilians. In cities, civilians made up 23.2 percent of law enforcement agencies employees. Civilians made up 41.0 percent of law enforcement employees in metropolitan counties and 41.1 percent of law enforcement employees in nonmetropolitan counties. Of the civilians working in law enforcement agencies throughout the nation, 61.6 percent were female and 38.4 percent were male. (Tables 74 and 75)

Table 70. Full-Time Law Enforcement Employees,[1] by Geographic Region and Division by Population Group, 2006

(Number, rate per 1,000 population.)

Geographic region/ division		Total (10,872 cities; population 189,942,258)	Group I (71 cities, 250,000 and over; population 53,957,412)	Group II (181 cities, 100,000 to 249,999; population 27,081,536)	Group III (423 cities, 50,000 to 99,999; population 29,029,089)	Group IV (788 cities, 25,000 to 49,999; population 27,199,664)	Group V (1,818 cities, 10,000 to 24,999; population 28,813,877)
TOTAL	Number of employees	569,149	203,153	66,660	66,017	63,074	69,994
	Average number of employees per 1,000 inhabitants	3.0	3.8	2.5	2.3	2.3	2.4
NORTHEAST	Number of employees	148,986	66,917	10,113	15,565	18,496	19,990
	Average number of employees per 1,000 inhabitants	3.5	6.0	3.3	2.5	2.4	2.2
NEW ENGLAND	Number of employees	33,565	2,625	4,686	5,976	7,017	7,560
	Average number of employees per 1,000 inhabitants	2.6	4.7	3.3	2.4	2.3	2.2
MIDDLE ATLANTIC	Number of employees	115,421	64,292	5,427	9,589	11,479	12,430
	Average number of employees per 1,000 inhabitants	3.8	6.1	3.4	2.6	2.4	2.2
MIDWEST	Number of employees	121,090	36,944	9,410	15,308	15,797	19,636
	Average number of employees per 1,000 inhabitants	2.7	4.0	2.3	2.0	2.1	2.2
EAST NORTH CENTRAL	Number of employees	88,817	29,340	6,021	10,919	12,447	14,377
	Average number of employees per 1,000 inhabitants	2.8	4.2	2.3	2.2	2.1	2.2
WEST NORTH CENTRAL	Number of employees	32,273	7,604	3,389	4,389	3,350	5,259
	Average number of employees per 1,000 inhabitants	2.5	3.4	2.2	1.7	2.0	2.2
SOUTH	Number of employees	187,552	51,229	27,521	20,152	18,584	23,594
	Average number of employees per 1,000 inhabitants	3.4	3.2	2.9	2.8	2.8	3.0
SOUTH ATLANTIC	Number of employees	90,211	21,394	14,651	10,978	9,296	11,348
	Average number of employees per 1,000 inhabitants	3.9	4.3	3.0	3.1	3.0	3.3
EAST SOUTH CENTRAL	Number of employees	33,163	6,677	4,159	2,454	3,795	5,543
	Average number of employees per 1,000 inhabitants	3.5	2.8	3.4	3.0	2.8	3.2
WEST SOUTH CENTRAL	Number of employees	64,178	23,158	8,711	6,720	5,493	6,703
	Average number of employees per 1,000 inhabitants	2.8	2.6	2.4	2.3	2.4	2.6
WEST	Number of employees	111,521	48,063	19,616	14,992	10,197	6,774
	Average number of employees per 1,000 inhabitants	2.4	2.7	1.9	1.9	2.0	2.1
MOUNTAIN	Number of employees	38,704	16,019	6,876	4,093	3,705	2,484
	Average number of employees per 1,000 inhabitants	2.6	2.9	2.1	2.0	2.2	2.4
PACIFIC	Number of employees	72,817	32,044	12,740	10,899	6,492	4,290
	Average number of employees per 1,000 inhabitants	2.3	2.7	1.8	1.8	1.9	2.0

[1] Full-time law enforcement employees include civilians.

Table 70. Full-Time Law Enforcement Employees,[1] by Geographic Region and Division by Population Group, 2006
(Contd.)

(Number, rate per 1,000 population.)

Geographic region/ division		Group VI (7,591 cities, under 10,000; population 23,860,680)	Total city agencies	2006 estimated city population	County[2] (3,464 agencies; population 93,296,402)	Total city and county agencies	2006 estimated total agency population	Suburban area[3] (7,438 agencies; population 121,334,744)
TOTAL	Number of employees	100,251	10,872	189,942,258	417,976	14,336	283,238,660	459,698
	Average number of employees per 1,000 inhabitants	4.2			4.5			3.8
NORTHEAST	Number of employees	17,905	2,343	43,159,649				
	Average number of employees per 1,000 inhabitants	2.9						
NEW ENGLAND	Number of employees	5,701	791	12,770,040				
	Average number of employees per 1,000 inhabitants	3.1						
MIDDLE ATLANTIC	Number of employees	12,204	1,552	30,389,609				
	Average number of employees per 1,000 inhabitants	2.9						
MIDWEST	Number of employees	23,995	3,196	44,589,036				
	Average number of employees per 1,000 inhabitants	3.3						
EAST NORTH CENTRAL	Number of employees	15,713	2,007	31,598,623				
	Average number of employees per 1,000 inhabitants	3.3						
WEST NORTH CENTRAL	Number of employees	8,282	1,189	12,990,413				
	Average number of employees per 1,000 inhabitants	3.1						
SOUTH	Number of employees	46,472	3,989	55,491,842				
	Average number of employees per 1,000 inhabitants	5.9						
SOUTH ATLANTIC	Number of employees	22,544	1,705	22,992,879				
	Average number of employees per 1,000 inhabitants	7.4						
EAST SOUTH CENTRAL	Number of employees	10,535	1,031	9,561,474				
	Average number of employees per 1,000 inhabitants	5.2						
WEST SOUTH CENTRAL	Number of employees	13,393	1,253	22,937,489				
	Average number of employees per 1,000 inhabitants	4.8						
WEST	Number of employees	11,879	1,344	46,701,731				
	Average number of employees per 1,000 inhabitants	4.6						
MOUNTAIN	Number of employees	5,527	577	14,840,930				
	Average number of employees per 1,000 inhabitants	4.3						
PACIFIC	Number of employees	6,352	767	31,860,801				
	Average number of employees per 1,000 inhabitants	5.0						

[1] Full-time law enforcement employees include civilians.
[2] The designation county is a combination of both metropolitan and nonmetropolitan counties.
[3] Suburban area includes law enforcement agencies in cities with less than 50,000 inhabitants and county law enforcement agencies that are within a Metropolitan Statistical Area. Suburban area excludes all metropolitan agencies associated with a principal city. The agencies associated with suburban areas also appear in other groups within this table.

Table 71. Full-Time Law Enforcement Officers, by Geographic Region and Division by Population Group, 2006

(Number, rate per 1,000 population.)

Geographic region/division		Total (10,872 cities; population 189,942,258)	Group I (71 cities, 250,000 and over; population 53,957,412)	Group II (181 cities, 100,000 to 249,999; population 27,081,536)	Group III (423 cities, 50,000 to 99,999; population 29,029,089)	Group IV 788 cities, 25,000 to 49,999; population 27,199,664)	Group V (1,818 cities, 10,000 to 24,999; population 28,813,877)
TOTAL	Number of officers............	436,908	152,315	50,019	50,896	49,616	55,907
	Average number of officers per 1,000 inhabitants	2.3	2.8	1.8	1.8	1.8	1.9
NORTHEAST	Number of officers............	115,984	47,298	8,319	13,052	15,542	16,796
	Average number of officers per 1,000 inhabitants	2.7	4.3	2.8	2.1	2.0	1.9
NEW ENGLAND	Number of officers............	27,609	2,056	3,898	5,122	5,874	6,155
	Average number of officers per 1,000 inhabitants	2.2	3.7	2.7	2.1	1.9	1.8
MIDDLE ATLANTIC	Number of officers............	88,375	45,242	4,421	7,930	9,668	10,641
	Average number of officers per 1,000 inhabitants	2.9	4.3	2.8	2.2	2.0	1.9
MIDWEST	Number of officers............	98,618	31,075	7,619	12,130	12,412	15,703
	Average number of officers per 1,000 inhabitants	2.2	3.4	1.8	1.6	1.6	1.8
EAST NORTH CENTRAL	Number of officers............	73,238	25,516	4,964	8,676	9,757	11,484
	Average number of officers per 1,000 inhabitants	2.3	3.7	1.9	1.7	1.7	1.8
WEST NORTH CENTRAL	Number of officers............	25,380	5,559	2,655	3,454	2,655	4,219
	Average number of officers per 1,000 inhabitants	2.0	2.5	1.8	1.4	1.6	1.7
SOUTH	Number of officers............	143,315	39,702	20,654	15,283	14,400	18,313
	Average number of officers per 1,000 inhabitants	2.6	2.4	2.1	2.1	2.2	2.4
SOUTH ATLANTIC	Number of officers............	68,542	16,005	10,899	8,220	7,313	8,943
	Average number of officers per 1,000 inhabitants	3.0	3.2	2.2	2.3	2.4	2.6
EAST SOUTH CENTRAL	Number of officers............	25,910	5,476	3,077	1,903	2,976	4,277
	Average number of officers per 1,000 inhabitants	2.7	2.3	2.5	2.3	2.2	2.4
WEST SOUTH CENTRAL	Number of officers............	48,863	18,221	6,678	5,160	4,111	5,093
	Average number of officers per 1,000 inhabitants	2.1	2.1	1.9	1.8	1.8	2.0
WEST	Number of officers............	78,991	34,240	13,427	10,431	7,262	5,095
	Average number of officers per 1,000 inhabitants	1.7	2.0	1.3	1.3	1.4	1.6
MOUNTAIN	Number of officers............	26,915	10,731	4,722	2,909	2,625	1,900
	Average number of officers per 1,000 inhabitants	1.8	1.9	1.4	1.4	1.6	1.8
PACIFIC	Number of officers............	52,076	23,509	8,705	7,522	4,637	3,195
	Average number of officers per 1,000 inhabitants	1.6	2.0	1.2	1.3	1.3	1.5

Table 71. Full-Time Law Enforcement Officers, by Geographic Region and Division by Population Group, 2006 *(Contd.)*

(Number, rate per 1,000 population.)

Geographic region/ division		Group VI (7,591 cities, under 10,000; population 23,860,680)	Total city agencies	2006 estimated city population	County[1] (3,464 agencies; population 93,296,402)	Total city and county agencies	2006 estimated total agency population	Suburban area[2] (7,438 agencies; population 121,334,744)
TOTAL	Number of officers..........................	78,155	10,872	189,942,258	246,488	14,336	283,238,660	302,210
	Average number of officers per 1,000 inhabitants	3.3			2.6			2.5
NORTHEAST	Number of officers..........................	14,977	2,343	43,159,649				
	Average number of officers per 1,000 inhabitants	2.5						
NEW ENGLAND	Number of officers..........................	4,504	791	12,770,040				
	Average number of officers per 1,000 inhabitants	2.4						
MIDDLE ATLANTIC	Number of officers..........................	10,473	1,552	30,389,609				
	Average number of officers per 1,000 inhabitants	2.5						
MIDWEST	Number of officers..........................	19,679	3,196	44,589,036				
	Average number of officers per 1,000 inhabitants	2.7						
EAST NORTH CENTRAL	Number of officers..........................	12,841	2,007	31,598,623				
	Average number of officers per 1,000 inhabitants	2.7						
WEST NORTH CENTRAL	Number of officers..........................	6,838	1,189	12,990,413				
	Average number of officers per 1,000 inhabitants	2.6						
SOUTH	Number of officers..........................	34,963	3,989	55,491,842				
	Average number of officers per 1,000 inhabitants	4.4						
SOUTH ATLANTIC	Number of officers..........................	17,162	1,705	22,992,879				
	Average number of officers per 1,000 inhabitants	5.6						
EAST SOUTH CENTRAL	Number of officers..........................	8,201	1,031	9,561,474				
	Average number of officers per 1,000 inhabitants	4.0						
WEST SOUTH CENTRAL	Number of officers..........................	9,600	1,253	22,937,489				
	Average number of officers per 1,000 inhabitants	3.4						
WEST	Number of officers..........................	8,536	1,344	46,701,731				
	Average number of officers per 1,000 inhabitants	3.3						
MOUNTAIN	Number of officers..........................	4,028	577	14,840,930				
	Average number of officers per 1,000 inhabitants	3.1						
PACIFIC	Number of officers..........................	4,508	767	31,860,801				
	Average number of officers per 1,000 inhabitants	3.5						

[1] The designation county is a combination of both metropolitan and nonmetropolitan counties.
[2] Suburban area includes law enforcement agencies in cities with less than 50,000 inhabitants and county law enforcement agencies that are within a Metropolitan Statistical Area. Suburban area excludes all metropolitan agencies associated with a principal city. The agencies associated with suburban areas also appear in other groups within this table.

Table 72. Full-Time Law Enforcement Employees,[1] by Rate Range, 2006

(Number, rate per 1,000 population.)

Rate range		Total cities[2] (9,946 cities; population 189,942,258)	Group I (71 cities, 250,000 and over; population 53,957,412)	Group II (181 cities, 100,000 to 249,999; population 27,081,536)	Group III (423 cities, 50,000 to 99,999; population 29,029,089)	Group IV (788 cities, 25,000 to 49,999; population 27,199,664)	Group V (1,818 cities, 10,000 to 24,999; population 28,813,877)	Group VI (6,665 cities, under 10,000; population 23,860,680)
Total cities	Number	9,946	71	181	423	788	1,818	6,665
	Percent[3]	100.0	100.0	100.0	100.0	100.0	100.0	100.0
.1-.5	Number	81	0	0	1	1	3	76
	Percent	0.8	0.0	0.0	0.2	0.1	0.2	1.1
.6-1.0	Number	400	0	1	4	18	39	338
	Percent	4.0	0.0	0.6	0.9	2.3	2.1	5.1
1.1-1.5	Number	1,077	0	13	49	88	187	740
	Percent	10.8	0.0	7.2	11.6	11.2	10.3	11.1
1.6-2.0	Number	1,920	9	56	142	207	407	1,099
	Percent	19.3	12.7	30.9	33.6	26.3	22.4	16.5
2.1-2.5	Number	1,969	16	45	114	233	470	1,091
	Percent	19.8	22.5	24.9	27.0	29.6	25.9	16.4
2.6-3.0	Number	1,447	21	29	57	119	356	865
	Percent	14.5	29.6	16.0	13.5	15.1	19.6	13.0
3.1-3.5	Number	930	6	18	29	70	172	635
	Percent	9.4	8.5	9.9	6.9	8.9	9.5	9.5
3.6-4.0	Number	620	5	13	12	34	89	467
	Percent	6.2	7.0	7.2	2.8	4.3	4.9	7.0
4.1-4.5	Number	389	5	3	6	11	45	319
	Percent	3.9	7.0	1.7	1.4	1.4	2.5	4.8
4.6-5.0	Number	294	2	3	7	3	27	252
	Percent	3.0	2.8	1.7	1.7	0.4	1.5	3.8
5.1 and over	Number	819	7	0	2	4	23	783
	Percent	8.2	9.9	0.0	0.5	0.5	1.3	11.7

[1] Full-time law enforcement employees include civilians.
[2] The number of agencies used to compile these figures differs from other tables that include data about law enforcement employees because agencies with no resident population are excluded from this table. These agencies include those associated with universities and colleges (see Table 79) and other agencies (see Table 81), as well as some state agencies that have concurrent jurisdiction with other local law enforcement.
[3] Because of rounding, the percentages may not add to 100.0.

Table 73. Full-Time Law Enforcement Officers, by Rate Range, 2006

(Number, rate per 1,000 population.)

Rate range		Total cities[1] (9,946 cities; population 189,942,258)	Group I (71 cities, 250,000 and over; population 53,957,412)	Group II (181 cities, 100,000 to 249,999; population 27,081,536)	Group III (423 cities, 50,000 to 99,999; population 29,029,089)	Group IV (788 cities, 25,000 to 49,999; population 27,199,664)	Group V (1,818 cities, 10,000 to 24,999; population 28,813,877)	Group VI (6,665 cities, under 10,000; population 23,860,680)
Total cities	Number	9,946	71	181	423	788	1,818	6,665
	Percent[2]	100.0	100.0	100.0	100.0	100.0	100.0	100.0
.1-.5	Number	95	0	1	1	1	3	89
	Percent	1.0	0.0	0.6	0.2	0.1	0.2	1.3
.6-1.0	Number	594	1	12	35	47	91	408
	Percent	6.0	1.4	6.6	8.3	6.0	5.0	6.1
1.1-1.5	Number	1,868	12	65	144	231	406	1,010
	Percent	18.8	16.9	35.9	34.0	29.3	22.3	15.2
1.6-2.0	Number	2,610	21	43	139	283	651	1,473
	Percent	26.2	29.6	23.8	32.9	35.9	35.8	22.1
2.1-2.5	Number	1,825	14	35	63	128	385	1,200
	Percent[3]	18.3	19.7	19.3	14.9	16.2	21.2	18.0
2.6-3.0	Number	1,044	9	12	20	71	155	777
	Percent	10.5	12.7	6.6	4.7	9.0	8.5	11.7
3.1-3.5	Number	658	5	12	12	19	82	528
	Percent	6.6	7.0	6.6	2.8	2.4	4.5	7.9
3.6-4.0	Number	357	2	1	6	5	29	314
	Percent	3.6	2.8	0.6	1.4	0.6	1.6	4.7
4.1-4.5	Number	219	2	0	2	1	5	209
	Percent	2.2	2.8	0.0	0.5	0.1	0.3	3.1
4.6-5.0	Number	188	4	0	0	0	6	178
	Percent	1.9	5.6	0.0	0.0	0.0	0.3	2.7
5.1 and over	Number	488	1	0	1	2	5	479
	Percent	4.9	1.4	0.0	0.2	0.3	0.3	7.2

[1] The number of agencies used to compile these figures differs from other tables that include data about law enforcement officers because agencies with no resident population are excluded from this table. These agencies include those associated with universities and colleges (see Table 79) and other agencies (see Table 81), as well as some state agencies that have concurrent jurisdiction with other local law enforcement.
[2] Because of rounding, the percentages may not add to 100.0.

Table 74. Full-Time Law Enforcement Employees, by Population Group, 2006

(Number, percent.)

Population group	Total law enforce-ment employees	Percent law enforcement employees		Total officers	Percent officers		Total civilians	Percent civilians		Number of agencies	2006 estimated population
		Male	Female		Male	Female		Male	Female		
TOTAL AGENCIES:......................	987,125	72.9	27.1	683,396	88.2	11.8	303,729	38.4	61.6	14,336	283,238,660
TOTAL CITIES	569,149	74.8	25.2	436,908	88.2	11.8	132,241	30.6	69.4	10,872	189,942,258
GROUP I (250,000 and over)	203,153	70.4	29.6	152,315	83.0	17.0	50,838	32.5	67.5	71	53,957,412
1,000,000 and over (Group I subset)	111,769	68.7	31.3	82,227	81.7	18.3	29,542	32.5	67.5	10	25,080,811
500,000 to 999,999 (Group I subset)...............	52,047	73.3	26.7	40,490	84.1	15.9	11,557	35.5	64.5	23	15,413,225
250,000 to 499,999 (Group I subset)...............	39,337	71.2	28.8	29,598	85.1	14.9	9,739	29.1	70.9	38	13,463,376
GROUP II (100,000 to 249,999)	66,660	73.0	27.0	50,019	88.3	11.7	16,641	26.9	73.1	181	27,081,536
GROUP III (50,000 to 99,999)........................	66,017	76.1	23.9	50,896	90.6	9.4	15,121	26.9	73.1	423	29,029,089
GROUP IV (25,000 to 49,999)........................	63,074	77.9	22.1	49,616	91.5	8.5	13,458	27.6	72.4	788	27,199,664
GROUP V (10,000 to 24,999)	69,994	79.2	20.8	55,907	92.5	7.5	14,087	26.6	73.4	1,818	28,813,877
GROUP VI (under 10,000)	100,251	79.3	20.7	78,155	91.7	8.3	22,096	35.7	64.3	7,591	23,860,680
METROPOLITAN COUNTIES...................	298,417	69.7	30.3	176,049	86.6	13.4	122,368	45.4	54.6	1,308	65,765,925
NONMETROPOLITAN COUNTIES	119,559	71.7	28.3	70,439	92.4	7.6	49,120	42.0	58.0	2,156	27,530,477
SUBURBAN AREA[1]	459,698	72.9	27.1	302,210	88.7	11.3	157,488	42.6	57.4	7,438	121,334,744

[1] Suburban area includes law enforcement agencies in cities with less than 50,000 inhabitants and county law enforcement agencies that are within a Metropolitan Statistical Area. Suburban area excludes all metropolitan agencies associated with a principal city. The agencies associated with suburban areas also appear in other groups within this table.

Table 75. Full-Time Civilian Law Enforcement Employees, by Population Group, 2006

(Number, percent.)

Population group	Percent civilian employees	Number of agencies	2006 estimated population
TOTAL AGENCIES:..	30.8	14,336	283,238,660
TOTAL CITIES	23.2	10,872	189,942,258
GROUP I (250,000 and over)	25.0	71	53,957,412
1,000,000 and over (Group I subset)......................	26.4	10	25,080,811
500,000 to 999,999 (Group I subset)......................	22.2	23	15,413,225
250,000 to 499,999 (Group I subset)......................	24.8	38	13,463,376
GROUP II (100,000 to 249,999)	25.0	181	27,081,536
GROUP III (50,000 to 99,999)...............................	22.9	423	29,029,089
GROUP IV (25,000 to 49,999)...............................	21.3	788	27,199,664
GROUP V (10,000 to 24,999)	20.1	1,818	28,813,877
GROUP VI (under 10,000)	22.0	7,591	23,860,680
METROPOLITAN COUNTIES..............................	41.0	1,308	65,765,925
NONMETROPOLITAN COUNTIES	41.1	2,156	27,530,477
SUBURBAN AREA[1]..	34.3	7,438	121,334,744

[1] Suburban area includes law enforcement agencies in cities with less than 50,000 inhabitants and county law enforcement agencies that are within a Metropolitan Statistical Area. Suburban area excludes all metropolitan agencies associated with a principal city. The agencies associated with suburban areas also appear in other groups within this table.

Table 76. Full-Time State Law Enforcement Employees, by State, 2006

(Number.)

State	Agency	Total law enforcement employees	Total officers		Total civilians	
			Male	Female	Male	Female
ALABAMA	Department of Public Safety	1,322	660	16	184	462
	Other state agencies	233	180	11	9	33
ALASKA	State Troopers	584	332	18	99	135
	Other state agencies	5	1	0	4	0
ARIZONA	Department of Public Safety	1,993	1,076	72	333	512
ARKANSAS	Other state agencies	48	32	3	7	6
CALIFORNIA	Highway Patrol	9,901	6,170	637	1,388	1,706
	Other state agencies	1,043	725	200	41	77
COLORADO	State Patrol	988	682	44	74	188
	Other state agencies	58	15	2	24	17
CONNECTICUT	State Police	1,737	1,142	80	224	291
	Other state agencies	34	25	1	6	2
DELAWARE	State Police	899	598	72	97	132
	Other state agencies	657	295	99	54	209
FLORIDA	Highway Patrol	2,219	1,493	186	181	359
	Other state agencies	3,226	1,360	175	585	1,106
GEORGIA	Department of Public Safety	927	746	23	92	66
	Other state agencies	1,100	308	71	234	487
IDAHO	State Police	422	258	12	51	101
ILLINOIS	State Police	3,612	1,801	209	669	933
	Other state agencies	396	227	26	92	51
INDIANA	State Police	1,821	1,086	62	271	402
	Other state agencies	8	7	0	0	1
IOWA	Department of Public Safety	947	613	38	124	172
KANSAS	Highway Patrol	833	521	19	103	190
	Other state agencies	506	267	12	130	97
KENTUCKY	State Police	1,765	970	27	388	380
	Other state agencies	537	428	11	49	49
LOUISIANA	State Police	1,630	1,086	47	121	376
	Other state agencies	56	39	4	1	12
MAINE	State Police	510	280	22	99	109
	Other state agencies[1]	50	20	1	20	9
MARYLAND	State Police	2,301	1,377	132	456	336
	Other state agencies	1,718	913	137	307	361
MASSACHUSETTS	State Police	3,064	2,339	197	233	295
	Other state agencies	258	216	28	5	9
MICHIGAN	State Police	2,703	1,566	217	387	533
MINNESOTA	State Patrol	800	501	48	145	106
	Other state agencies	50	10	1	31	8
MISSISSIPPI	Highway Safety Patrol	1,245	537	11	307	390
MISSOURI	State Highway Patrol	2,152	1,005	36	593	518
	Other state agencies[1]	588	514	23	9	42
MONTANA	Highway Patrol	258	204	9	15	30
	Other state agencies	20	17	0	0	3
NEBRASKA	State Patrol	729	458	29	104	138
NEVADA	Highway Patrol	839	436	41	126	236
	Other state agencies	61	33	2	12	14
NEW HAMPSHIRE	State Police	434	258	26	51	99
	Other state agencies	32	20	2	4	6
NEW JERSEY	State Police	4,527	2,923	114	706	784
	Other state agencies	452	343	34	44	31
	Port Authority of New York and New Jersey[2]	929	771	82	20	56
NEW MEXICO	State Police	644	491	21	42	90
NEW YORK	State Police	5,965	4,422	422	483	638
NORTH CAROLINA	Highway Patrol	2,204	1,630	42	295	237
	Other state agencies	1,230	723	166	84	257
NORTH DAKOTA	Highway Patrol	169	119	3	14	33
OHIO	Other state agencies	503	412	26	50	15
OKLAHOMA	Department of Public Safety	1,393	707	14	341	331
	Other state agencies	66	33	3	18	12
OREGON	State Police	915	562	45	99	209
	Other state agencies	51	31	13	0	7
PENNSYLVANIA	State Police	6,192	4,270	199	803	920
	Other state agencies	690	548	60	17	65

Note: Caution should be used when comparing data from one state to that of another. The responsibilities of the various state police, highway patrol, and department of public safety agencies range from full law enforcement duties to only traffic patrol, which can impact both the level of employment for agencies as well as the ratio of sworn officers to civilians employed. Any valid comparison must take these factors and the other identified variables affecting crime into consideration.

[1] The total employee count includes employees from agencies that are not represented in other law enforcement employee tables.
[2] Data reported are the number of law enforcement employees for the state of New Jersey.

Table 76. Full-Time State Law Enforcement Employees, by State, 2006

(Number.)

State	Agency	Total law enforcement employees	Total officers		Total civilians	
			Male	Female	Male	Female
RHODE ISLAND	State Police	269	198	20	33	18
	Other state agencies	43	31	4	7	1
SOUTH CAROLINA	Highway Patrol	1,087	859	33	66	129
	Other state agencies[1]	1,294	825	145	97	227
SOUTH DAKOTA	Highway Patrol	240	158	3	58	21
	Other state agencies	142	39	3	37	63
TENNESSEE	Department of Safety	1,579	809	43	187	540
	Other state agencies	1,063	587	65	126	285
TEXAS	Department of Public Safety	7,912	3,263	202	1,452	2,995
UTAH	Highway Patrol	509	448	24	4	33
	Other state agencies	160	141	11	4	4
VERMONT	State Police	456	286	24	47	99
	Other state agencies	101	83	6	1	11
VIRGINIA	State Police	2,610	1,839	106	202	463
	Other state agencies	508	281	42	77	108
WASHINGTON	State Patrol	2,109	931	82	543	553
WEST VIRGINIA	State Police	1,012	655	18	116	223
	Other state agencies	190	164	1	2	23
WISCONSIN	State Patrol	598	430	60	8	100
	Other state agencies	517	425	54	17	21
WYOMING	Highway Patrol	208	178	8	3	19

Note: Caution should be used when comparing data from one state to that of another. The responsibilities of the various state police, highway patrol, and department of public safety agencies range from full law enforcement duties to only traffic patrol, which can impact both the level of employment for agencies as well as the ratio of sworn officers to civilians employed. Any valid comparison must take these factors and the other identified variables affecting crime into consideration.

Table 77. Full-Time Law Enforcement Employees, by State, 2006

(Number.)

State	Total law enforcement employees	Total officers		Total civilians		Number of agencies	2006 estimated population
		Male	Female	Male	Female		
ALABAMA	15,697	9,580	767	1,952	3,398	358	4,459,997
ALASKA	1,937	1,097	123	237	480	42	669,380
ARIZONA	21,434	10,674	1,258	4,298	5,204	98	6,153,379
ARKANSAS	8,266	4,862	543	1,104	1,757	264	2,809,079
CALIFORNIA	115,912	65,804	9,679	14,602	25,827	460	31,660,392
COLORADO	16,471	9,833	1,465	1,578	3,595	235	4,752,554
CONNECTICUT	9,703	7,166	709	709	1,119	101	3,504,809
DELAWARE	3,085	1,950	297	297	541	53	853,476
DISTRICT OF COLUMBIA	4,880	3,233	963	279	405	3	581,530
FLORIDA	74,051	39,192	6,531	10,355	17,973	450	18,002,234
GEORGIA	30,854	18,995	3,167	2,945	5,747	436	8,663,117
HAWAII	3,654	2,617	279	221	537	4	1,285,498
IDAHO	3,896	2,422	172	248	1,054	107	1,464,850
ILLINOIS	52,055	31,478	5,751	7,021	7,805	757	12,793,900
INDIANA	15,934	9,449	748	2,566	3,171	208	5,570,912
IOWA	7,615	4,667	373	969	1,606	231	2,961,632
KANSAS	10,451	6,469	616	1,343	2,023	327	2,678,243
KENTUCKY	10,194	7,473	555	789	1,377	391	4,106,153
LOUISIANA	18,969	11,983	2,796	1,309	2,881	171	3,792,516
MAINE	2,933	2,076	126	314	417	133	1,321,574
MARYLAND	20,097	13,006	2,042	1,939	3,110	149	5,613,488
MASSACHUSETTS	20,410	15,656	1,376	1,350	2,028	340	6,378,563
MICHIGAN	25,896	16,638	2,590	2,824	3,844	600	9,825,520
MINNESOTA	13,179	7,509	984	1,868	2,818	317	5,030,630
MISSISSIPPI	9,200	5,158	466	1,442	2,134	193	2,507,121
MISSOURI	19,378	12,265	1,319	2,371	3,423	552	5,790,380
MONTANA	2,753	1,567	112	481	593	109	943,628
NEBRASKA	4,774	3,078	375	385	936	156	1,730,689
NEVADA	9,080	4,748	514	1,400	2,418	37	2,495,529
NEW HAMPSHIRE	3,197	2,228	186	229	554	148	1,156,338
NEW JERSEY	36,456	26,561	2,452	2,597	4,846	529	8,444,334
NEW MEXICO	4,731	3,106	315	425	885	75	1,507,980
NEW YORK	86,053	53,597	8,579	7,820	16,057	402	18,719,867
NORTH CAROLINA	30,671	18,917	2,502	3,903	5,349	512	8,851,847
NORTH DAKOTA	1,619	1,080	98	146	295	93	632,973
OHIO	29,607	19,063	2,226	3,290	5,028	563	10,476,045
OKLAHOMA	11,001	6,513	545	1,711	2,232	296	3,579,212
OREGON	7,471	4,173	383	1,110	1,805	171	2,928,366
PENNSYLVANIA	27,811	20,785	2,629	1,685	2,712	783	8,387,382
RHODE ISLAND	3,223	2,380	181	311	351	47	1,067,610
SOUTH CAROLINA	14,332	9,343	1,254	1,348	2,387	365	4,275,140
SOUTH DAKOTA	2,070	1,146	85	364	475	141	775,859
TENNESSEE	24,121	13,587	1,397	4,051	5,086	450	6,034,250
TEXAS	81,462	44,192	5,278	13,736	18,256	981	23,183,189
UTAH	7,502	4,172	323	1,487	1,520	129	2,549,402
VERMONT	1,567	1,072	91	130	274	69	372,588
VIRGINIA	22,872	15,656	2,016	1,447	3,753	280	7,641,879
WASHINGTON	14,420	9,259	1,001	1,374	2,786	246	6,385,798
WEST VIRGINIA	4,208	3,225	108	321	554	339	1,802,755
WISCONSIN	18,111	11,192	1,846	1,802	3,271	370	5,553,640
WYOMING	1,862	1,203	110	117	432	65	511,433

Table 78. Full-Time Law Enforcement Employees, by City, 2006

(Number.)

State	City	Total law enforcement employees	Total officers	Total civilians	State	City	Total law enforcement employees	Total officers	Total civilians
ALABAMA	Abbeville	17	7	10		Dauphin Island	13	9	4
	Adamsville	30	18	12		Decatur	156	133	23
	Addison	3	3	0		Demopolis	22	19	3
	Alabaster	81	64	17		Dora	8	4	4
	Albertville	55	38	17		Dothan	215	143	72
	Alexander City	58	41	17		Double Springs	5	5	0
	Aliceville	12	8	4		Dozier	1	1	0
	Andalusia	37	28	9		East Brewton	8	6	2
	Anniston	114	81	33		Eclectic	9	5	4
	Arab	32	25	7		Elberta	7	6	1
	Ardmore	12	8	4		Enterprise	72	52	20
	Argo	3	3	0		Eufaula	51	33	18
	Ariton	2	2	0		Eutaw	11	10	1
	Ashford	9	5	4		Evergreen	18	13	5
	Ashland	8	4	4		Excel	1	1	0
	Ashville	5	5	0		Fairfield	50	36	14
	Athens	55	43	12		Fairhope	52	30	22
	Atmore	28	24	4		Falkville	4	4	0
	Attalla	26	21	5		Fayette	12	12	0
	Auburn	105	99	6		Florala	12	10	2
	Autaugaville	2	2	0		Florence	118	94	24
	Baker Hill	2	2	0		Foley	58	33	25
	Bay Minette	32	24	8		Fort Payne	40	36	4
	Bayou La Batre	19	14	5		Frisco City	2	2	0
	Bear Creek	3	3	0		Fultondale	18	17	1
	Berry	3	3	0		Gadsden	134	96	38
	Birmingham	1,071	791	280		Gardendale	37	28	9
	Blountsville	7	7	0		Geneva	15	11	4
	Boaz	34	24	10		Georgiana	11	8	3
	Brent	5	5	0		Geraldine	2	2	0
	Brewton	28	22	6		Glencoe	9	6	3
	Bridgeport	10	6	4		Goodwater	7	4	3
	Brighton	13	10	3		Graysville	8	5	3
	Brilliant	3	3	0		Greensboro	7	7	0
	Brookside	2	2	0		Greenville	41	32	9
	Brundidge	12	7	5		Grove Hill	5	5	0
	Butler	6	6	0		Guin	5	5	0
	Calera	32	25	7		Gulf Shores	49	36	13
	Camden	9	8	1		Guntersville	38	31	7
	Carbon Hill	10	5	5		Gurley	4	4	0
	Carrollton	4	3	1		Hackleburg	4	4	0
	Cedar Bluff	4	4	0		Haleyville	17	12	5
	Centre	10	9	1		Hamilton	15	14	1
	Centreville	5	5	0		Hanceville	12	8	4
	Chatom	6	6	0		Harpersville	8	8	0
	Cherokee	4	4	0		Hartford	15	10	5
	Chickasaw	23	23	0		Hartselle	37	29	8
	Childersburg	16	11	5		Hayneville	3	3	0
	Citronelle	13	10	3		Headland	19	12	7
	Clanton	23	22	1		Heflin	13	12	1
	Clayhatchee	1	1	0		Helena	26	21	5
	Clayton	2	2	0		Henagar	9	5	4
	Cleveland	2	2	0		Hillsboro	1	1	0
	Clio	3	3	0		Hobson City	4	2	2
	Coffeeville	1	1	0		Hokes Bluff	9	7	2
	Collinsville	7	3	4		Hollywood	2	2	0
	Columbia	2	2	0		Homewood	110	75	35
	Columbiana	12	8	4		Hoover	213	153	60
	Coosada	3	3	0		Hueytown	34	28	6
	Cordova	9	2	7		Huntsville	475	357	118
	Cottonwood	2	2	0		Ider	5	4	1
	Courtland	4	4	0		Irondale	34	27	7
	Creola	10	6	4		Jackson	21	16	5
	Crossville	3	3	0		Jacksonville	28	24	4
	Cullman	69	49	20		Jasper	69	45	24
	Dadeville	13	12	1		Jemison	10	9	1
	Daleville	24	17	7		Killen	5	5	0
	Daphne	75	45	30		Kimberly	9	5	4

Table 78. Full-Time Law Enforcement Employees, by City, 2006 (*Contd.*)

(Number.)

State	City	Total law enforcement employees	Total officers	Total civilians	State	City	Total law enforcement employees	Total officers	Total civilians
	Kinsey	3	2	1		Prichard	72	48	24
	Lafayette	16	15	1		Ragland	7	4	3
	Lake View	4	4	0		Rainbow City	30	20	10
	Lanett	20	18	2		Rainsville	14	10	4
	Leeds	24	19	5		Ranburne	2	2	0
	Leighton	1	1	0		Red Bay	11	7	4
	Level Plains	3	2	1		Red Level	2	1	1
	Lexington	1	1	0		Reform	5	5	0
	Lincoln	21	16	5		Riverside	4	4	0
	Linden	8	8	0		Roanoke	27	22	5
	Lineville	11	7	4		Robertsdale	26	14	12
	Lipscomb	11	4	7		Rockford	2	1	1
	Littleville	7	5	2		Rogersville	5	5	0
	Livingston	12	8	4		Russellville	29	24	5
	Lockhart	2	1	1		Samson	6	5	1
	Louisville	3	3	0		Saraland	48	37	11
	Loxley	13	8	5		Satsuma	18	14	4
	Madison	85	62	23		Scottsboro	63	44	19
	Maplesville	6	5	1		Section	2	2	0
	Marion	13	7	6		Selma	80	57	23
	McIntosh	5	5	0		Sheffield	33	28	5
	McKenzie	1	1	0		Silas	1	1	0
	Midfield	19	15	4		Silverhill	1	1	0
	Midland City	8	5	3		Skyline	2	1	1
	Millbrook	32	23	9		Slocomb	8	6	2
	Millport	1	1	0		Snead	5	5	0
	Millry	5	3	2		Somerville	4	4	0
	Mobile	662	514	148		Southside	16	11	5
	Montevallo	19	15	4		Spanish Fort	13	12	1
	Montgomery	600	452	148		Springville	10	10	0
	Moody	17	16	1		Steele	2	2	0
	Morris	7	6	1		Stevenson	6	4	2
	Mosses	1	1	0		St. Florian	2	1	1
	Moulton	11	11	0		Sulligent	5	5	0
	Moundville	6	5	1		Sumiton	12	7	5
	Mountain Brook	62	48	14		Summerdale	7	6	1
	Mount Vernon	4	4	0		Sylacauga	49	38	11
	Muscle Shoals	44	35	9		Talladega	56	40	16
	Napier Field	1	1	0		Tallassee	24	18	6
	New Brockton	4	4	0		Tarrant City	28	22	6
	New Hope	6	6	0		Taylor	2	2	0
	New Site	1	1	0		Thomasville	20	15	5
	Newville	11	1	10		Thorsby	5	5	0
	North Courtland	5	4	1		Town Creek	4	4	0
	Northport	76	58	18		Triana	2	2	0
	Notasulga	7	4	3		Trinity	5	5	0
	Oakman	1	1	0		Troy	66	48	18
	Odenville	5	5	0		Trussville	47	36	11
	Ohatchee	6	6	0		Tuscaloosa	326	252	74
	Oneonta	19	18	1		Tuscumbia	26	20	6
	Opelika	107	84	23		Tuskegee	38	25	13
	Opp	28	21	7		Union Springs	20	13	7
	Orange Beach	62	40	22		Uniontown	43	6	37
	Owens Crossroads	2	2	0		Valley Head	3	2	1
	Oxford	61	50	11		Vance	4	4	0
	Ozark	40	34	6		Vernon	7	7	0
	Pelham	80	65	15		Vestavia Hills	63	61	2
	Pell City	33	31	2		Wadley	2	2	0
	Phenix City	97	76	21		Warrior	18	13	5
	Phil Campbell	2	2	0		Weaver	9	6	3
	Pickensville	2	1	1		Wedowee	8	8	0
	Piedmont	16	12	4		West Blocton	1	1	0
	Pinckard	2	2	0		Wetumpka	34	27	7
	Pine Hill	5	5	0		Wilton	1	1	0
	Pleasant Grove	22	17	5		Winfield	11	10	1
	Powell	2	1	1		Woodstock	4	4	0
	Prattville	81	73	8		Woodville	1	1	0
	Priceville	4	4	0		York	10	5	5

Table 78. Full-Time Law Enforcement Employees, by City, 2006 (*Contd.*)

(Number.)

State	City	Total law enforcement employees	Total officers	Total civilians	State	City	Total law enforcement employees	Total officers	Total civilians
ALASKA	Anchorage	536	367	169		Mammoth	9	6	3
	Bethel	20	11	9		Marana	98	74	24
	Bristol Bay Borough....	8	3	5		Mesa	1,321	829	492
	Cordova	9	5	4		Miami	11	7	4
	Craig.............................	11	5	6		Nogales..........................	82	64	18
	Dillingham	19	7	12		Oro Valley.....................	116	87	29
	Emmonak	4	4	0		Page	33	22	11
	Fairbanks	58	42	16		Paradise Valley.............	42	33	9
	Haines	10	6	4		Parker	16	13	3
	Homer	22	15	7		Patagonia	4	4	0
	Hoonah	7	4	3		Payson	44	29	15
	Houston	2	2	0		Peoria	241	166	75
	Juneau	78	46	32		Phoenix	3,829	2,896	933
	Kenai	26	17	9		Pima	4	4	0
	Ketchikan......................	32	21	11		Pinetop-Lakeside	23	15	8
	Klawock	3	3	0		Prescott	110	59	51
	Kodiak	33	18	15		Prescott Valley	70	56	14
	Kotzebue.......................	18	8	10		Quartzsite	15	13	2
	Nome	16	10	6		Safford..........................	24	21	3
	North Pole	11	10	1		Sahuarita	35	30	5
	North Slope Borough ...	66	41	25		San Luis	47	33	14
	Palmer	28	13	15		Scottsdale......................	629	382	247
	Petersburg.....................	14	8	6		Sedona...........................	37	28	9
	Sand Point....................	5	4	1		Show Low	45	30	15
	Seldovia........................	1	1	0		Sierra Vista	81	54	27
	Seward	22	10	12		Snowflake-Taylor	19	12	7
	Sitka.............................	35	19	16		Somerton	27	19	8
	Skagway........................	8	4	4		South Tucson	29	21	8
	Soldotna........................	15	13	2		Springerville	10	7	3
	St. Paul	6	3	3		St. Johns	11	9	2
	Togiak...........................	2	2	0		Superior	12	7	5
	Unalaska	32	15	17		Surprise	133	95	38
	Valdez...........................	20	10	10		Tempe............................	501	323	178
	Wasilla	46	22	24		Thatcher........................	11	10	1
	Whittier	1	1	0		Tolleson	39	29	10
	Wrangell.......................	14	6	8		Tucson	1,376	994	382
ARIZONA	Apache Junction	84	52	32		Wellton	4	4	0
	Avondale.......................	128	79	49		Wickenburg	21	13	8
	Benson	19	11	8		Willcox	14	6	8
	Bisbee	24	15	9		Williams	19	11	8
	Buckeye	66	50	16		Winslow.........................	38	25	13
	Bullhead City	131	80	51		Youngtown....................	15	13	2
	Camp Verde.................	32	20	12		Yuma	235	151	84
	Casa Grande.................	96	67	29	**ARKANSAS**	Alma..............................	16	8	8
	Chandler	459	306	153		Altheimer.......................	1	1	0
	Chino Valley.................	41	28	13		Arkadelphia...................	27	21	6
	Clarkdale	11	9	2		Arkansas City..............	1	1	0
	Clifton	4	2	2		Ashdown........................	12	11	1
	Colorado City...............	6	5	1		Ash Flat	2	2	0
	Coolidge........................	39	29	10		Atkins............................	7	6	1
	Douglas	45	35	10		Augusta	7	7	0
	Eagar	12	9	3		Austin............................	1	1	0
	El Mirage	47	40	7		Bald Knob.....................	8	4	4
	Eloy	51	37	14		Barling...........................	9	9	0
	Flagstaff	148	98	50		Bay................................	4	3	1
	Florence	33	23	10		Bearden.........................	2	2	0
	Fredonia........................	3	3	0		Beebe	14	8	6
	Gilbert...........................	288	191	97		Benton...........................	61	54	7
	Glendale........................	513	370	143		Bentonville	74	49	25
	Globe.............................	33	24	9		Berryville.......................	12	10	2
	Goodyear	95	73	22		Blytheville......................	57	38	19
	Hayden..........................	9	8	1		Bono..............................	3	3	0
	Holbrook	25	16	9		Booneville......................	12	8	4
	Huachuca City..............	12	5	7		Bradford.........................	3	3	0
	Jerome...........................	5	5	0		Brinkley	15	11	4
	Kearny...........................	8	5	3		Bryant............................	35	28	7
	Kingman........................	81	54	27		Bull Shoals	3	3	0
	Lake Havasu City	123	95	28		Cabot.............................	47	35	12

Table 78. Full-Time Law Enforcement Employees, by City, 2006 (*Contd.*)

(Number.)

State	City	Total law enforcement employees	Total officers	Total civilians	State	City	Total law enforcement employees	Total officers	Total civilians
	Caddo Valley	5	4	1		Judsonia	3	2	1
	Camden	33	22	11		Kensett	3	3	0
	Cammack Village	4	3	1		Lake City	4	4	0
	Caraway	3	3	0		Lakeview	2	2	0
	Carlisle	9	5	4		Lake Village	16	9	7
	Cave City	3	3	0		Leachville	4	4	0
	Cave Springs	4	3	1		Lepanto	8	4	4
	Centerton	11	10	1		Lincoln	5	5	0
	Charleston	5	4	1		Little Flock	6	6	0
	Cherokee Village	6	5	1		Little Rock	631	519	112
	Clarendon	4	4	0		Lonoke	18	13	5
	Clarksville	24	17	7		Lowell	21	15	6
	Clinton	8	7	1		Luxora	3	3	0
	Conway	115	95	20		Magnolia	26	21	5
	Corning	11	7	4		Malvern	28	24	4
	Crossett	25	16	9		Marianna	14	9	5
	Danville	6	5	1		Marion	21	19	2
	Dardanelle	13	9	4		Marked Tree	12	8	4
	Decatur	7	7	0		Marmaduke	4	4	0
	De Queen	15	12	3		Marvell	5	2	3
	Dermott	13	7	6		Maumelle	31	24	7
	Des Arc	4	4	0		Mayflower	6	5	1
	De Witt	14	8	6		McCrory	5	5	0
	Diaz	2	2	0		McGehee	22	8	14
	Dierks	3	3	0		McRae	3	1	2
	Dover	4	3	1		Mena	14	13	1
	Dumas	23	11	12		Mineral Springs	3	3	0
	Earle	6	5	1		Monticello	27	22	5
	El Dorado	61	45	16		Morrilton	31	20	11
	Elkins	7	7	0		Mountain Home	34	25	9
	England	10	6	4		Mountain View	8	7	1
	Etowah	1	1	0		Murfreesboro	3	3	0
	Eureka Springs	16	10	6		Nashville	16	15	1
	Fairfield Bay	14	8	6		Newport	23	16	7
	Farmington	10	9	1		North Little Rock	216	187	29
	Fayetteville	181	120	61		Ola	3	3	0
	Flippin	7	7	0		Osceola	36	22	14
	Fordyce	11	6	5		Ozark	10	8	2
	Forrest City	48	38	10		Pangburn	2	2	0
	Fort Smith	208	164	44		Paragould	50	42	8
	Gassville	4	4	0		Paris	13	8	5
	Gentry	10	8	2		Pea Ridge	7	7	0
	Glenwood	3	3	0		Piggott	9	8	1
	Gosnell	8	8	0		Pine Bluff	156	132	24
	Gould	4	4	0		Plainview	2	2	0
	Gravette	8	7	1		Plummerville	4	4	0
	Greenbrier	15	10	5		Pocahontas	14	12	2
	Green Forest	8	6	2		Pottsville	5	5	0
	Greenland	4	4	0		Prairie Grove	9	8	1
	Greenwood	19	18	1		Prescott	9	8	1
	Greers Ferry	3	2	1		Quitman	4	4	0
	Gurdon	4	3	1		Redfield	5	4	1
	Hamburg	6	5	1		Rison	3	3	0
	Hampton	4	4	0		Rockport	9	5	4
	Harrisburg	5	4	1		Rogers	120	84	36
	Harrison	38	28	10		Rose Bud	2	2	0
	Hazen	6	5	1		Russellville	57	49	8
	Heber Springs	21	13	8		Salem	3	3	0
	Helena-West Helena	40	29	11		Searcy	53	39	14
	Hermitage	3	3	0		Sheridan	25	12	13
	Highland	3	3	0		Sherwood	82	57	25
	Hope	37	26	11		Siloam Springs	41	25	16
	Horseshoe Bend	5	5	0		Smackover	4	4	0
	Hot Springs	126	95	31		Springdale	136	100	36
	Hoxie	5	4	1		Star City	5	4	1
	Huntsville	7	6	1		Stuttgart	30	21	9
	Jacksonville	86	74	12		Sulphur Springs	2	2	0
	Jonesboro	140	127	13		Swifton	2	1	1

Table 78. Full-Time Law Enforcement Employees, by City, 2006 *(Contd.)*

(Number.)

State	City	Total law enforcement employees	Total officers	Total civilians	State	City	Total law enforcement employees	Total officers	Total civilians
	Texarkana	118	80	38		City of Angels	10	9	1
	Trumann	22	15	7		Claremont	63	42	21
	Tuckerman	6	5	1		Clayton	13	11	2
	Van Buren	57	43	14		Clearlake	29	24	5
	Vilonia	7	7	0		Cloverdale	22	14	8
	Waldron	10	9	1		Clovis	148	102	46
	Walnut Ridge	9	8	1		Coalinga	27	18	9
	Ward	8	6	2		Colma	26	19	7
	Warren	21	13	8		Colton	100	70	30
	Weiner	1	1	0		Colusa	9	8	1
	West Fork	7	6	1		Concord	212	154	58
	West Memphis	102	82	20		Corcoran	28	19	9
	White Hall	15	13	2		Corning	22	14	8
	Wynne	18	16	2		Corona	259	172	87
CALIFORNIA	Alameda	142	98	44		Coronado	61	41	20
	Albany	37	27	10		Costa Mesa	224	151	73
	Alhambra	126	82	44		Cotati	20	13	7
	Alturas	7	6	1		Covina	84	54	30
	Anaheim	579	410	169		Crescent City	12	11	1
	Anderson	30	20	10		Culver City	154	117	37
	Antioch	154	105	49		Cypress	73	56	17
	Arcadia	96	59	37		Daly City	146	105	41
	Arcata	34	23	11		Davis	91	55	36
	Arroyo Grande	36	27	9		Delano	65	48	17
	Arvin	20	14	6		Del Rey Oaks	6	6	0
	Atascadero	43	28	15		Desert Hot Springs	32	25	7
	Atherton	27	21	6		Dinuba	39	30	9
	Atwater	41	32	9		Dixon	31	25	6
	Auburn	35	24	11		Dos Palos	7	5	2
	Azusa	79	54	25		Downey	160	110	50
	Bakersfield	477	321	156		East Palo Alto	42	34	8
	Baldwin Park	99	70	29		El Cajon	221	141	80
	Banning	61	41	20		El Centro	72	48	24
	Barstow	50	34	16		El Cerrito	47	38	9
	Bear Valley	16	8	8		Elk Grove	181	114	67
	Beaumont	38	27	11		El Monte	228	159	69
	Bell	52	40	12		El Segundo	95	62	33
	Bell Gardens	69	51	18		Emeryville	48	31	17
	Belmont	42	31	11		Escalon	14	11	3
	Belvedere	8	7	1		Escondido	227	163	64
	Benicia	46	32	14		Etna	3	2	1
	Berkeley	289	184	105		Eureka	69	43	26
	Beverly Hills	194	131	63		Exeter	18	16	2
	Bishop	19	13	6		Fairfax	16	11	5
	Blue Lake	7	5	2		Fairfield	188	122	66
	Blythe	39	23	16		Farmersville	15	14	1
	Brawley	40	28	12		Ferndale	4	4	0
	Brea	146	107	39		Firebaugh	15	11	4
	Brentwood	68	54	14		Folsom	116	85	31
	Brisbane	20	17	3		Fontana	244	174	70
	Broadmoor	11	10	1		Fort Bragg	19	14	5
	Buena Park	143	91	52		Fortuna	23	15	8
	Burbank	250	155	95		Foster City	53	36	17
	Burlingame	60	42	18		Fountain Valley	81	63	18
	Calexico	66	46	20		Fowler	10	8	2
	California City	21	15	6		Fremont	291	188	103
	Calipatria	6	6	0		Fresno	1,217	798	419
	Calistoga	14	10	4		Fullerton	223	158	65
	Campbell	64	43	21		Galt	38	27	11
	Capitola	33	21	12		Gardena	96	74	22
	Carlsbad	155	112	43		Garden Grove	229	158	71
	Carmel	16	10	6		Gilroy	99	59	40
	Cathedral City	86	55	31		Glendale	380	257	123
	Ceres	68	46	22		Glendora	101	57	44
	Chico	157	102	55		Gonzales	14	13	1
	Chino	143	95	48		Grass Valley	33	22	11
	Chowchilla	23	16	7		Greenfield	20	16	4
	Chula Vista	356	241	115		Gridley	20	17	3

Table 78. Full-Time Law Enforcement Employees, by City, 2006 (*Contd.*)

(Number.)

State	City	Total law enforcement employees	Total officers	Total civilians	State	City	Total law enforcement employees	Total officers	Total civilians
	Grover Beach	27	18	9		Monterey Park	110	77	33
	Guadalupe	15	12	3		Moraga	12	11	1
	Gustine	13	10	3		Morgan Hill	49	32	17
	Half Moon Bay	23	18	5		Morro Bay	23	17	6
	Hanford	72	53	19		Mountain View	138	93	45
	Hawthorne	141	93	48		Mount Shasta	15	9	6
	Hayward	312	191	121		Murrieta	112	78	34
	Healdsburg	29	18	11		Napa	114	71	43
	Hemet	113	81	32		National City	112	80	32
	Hercules	30	27	3		Nevada City	12	11	1
	Hermosa Beach	63	37	26		Newark	82	57	25
	Hillsborough	34	25	9		Newman	13	11	2
	Hollister	34	29	5		Newport Beach	238	141	97
	Holtville	7	7	0		Novato	72	55	17
	Hughson	7	6	1		Oakdale	36	26	10
	Huntington Beach	355	217	138		Oakland	1,009	688	321
	Huntington Park	102	62	40		Oceanside	286	199	87
	Huron	15	11	4		Ontario	327	225	102
	Imperial	21	18	3		Orange	226	158	68
	Indio	125	79	46		Orland	15	12	3
	Inglewood	269	192	77		Oroville	37	25	12
	Ione	7	6	1		Oxnard	350	232	118
	Irvine	252	163	89		Pacifica	52	39	13
	Irwindale	35	27	8		Pacific Grove	27	20	7
	Isleton	4	4	0		Palm Springs	151	89	62
	Jackson	13	11	2		Palo Alto	149	84	65
	Kensington	11	10	1		Palos Verdes Estates	34	24	10
	Kerman	21	18	3		Paradise	40	26	14
	King City	16	13	3		Parlier	16	13	3
	Kingsburg	20	15	5		Pasadena	367	240	127
	Laguna Beach	80	47	33		Paso Robles	51	38	13
	La Habra	106	70	36		Patterson	18	16	2
	Lakeport	14	12	2		Petaluma	100	74	26
	Lake Shastina	5	4	1		Piedmont	26	18	8
	La Mesa	92	67	25		Pinole	44	28	16
	La Palma	31	24	7		Pismo Beach	33	22	11
	La Verne	68	48	20		Pittsburg	99	72	27
	Lemoore	35	29	6		Placentia	70	53	17
	Lincoln	37	30	7		Placerville	29	18	11
	Lindsay	19	12	7		Pleasant Hill	63	42	21
	Livermore	145	95	50		Pleasanton	118	83	35
	Livingston	29	20	9		Pomona	325	186	139
	Lodi	106	76	30		Porterville	67	46	21
	Lompoc	71	49	22		Port Hueneme	32	25	7
	Long Beach	1,363	901	462		Red Bluff	38	24	14
	Los Alamitos	26	22	4		Redding	169	117	52
	Los Altos	44	30	14		Redlands	166	95	71
	Los Angeles	12,685	9,393	3,292		Redondo Beach	157	104	53
	Los Banos	63	41	22		Redwood City	127	92	35
	Los Gatos	57	42	15		Rialto	124	88	36
	Madera	78	57	21		Richmond	221	153	68
	Mammoth Lakes	26	21	5		Ridgecrest	46	31	15
	Manhattan Beach	87	58	29		Rio Dell	5	5	0
	Manteca	96	70	26		Rio Vista	19	14	5
	Marina	34	26	8		Ripon	38	26	12
	Martinez	54	39	15		Riverbank	22	18	4
	Marysville	35	24	11		Riverside	565	389	176
	Maywood	52	38	14		Rocklin	79	50	29
	Menlo Park	66	47	19		Rohnert Park	106	73	33
	Merced	134	94	40		Roseville	205	132	73
	Millbrae	26	18	8		Ross	8	8	0
	Mill Valley	28	22	6		Sacramento	1,083	663	420
	Milpitas	111	86	25		Salinas	214	161	53
	Modesto	376	266	110		San Anselmo	24	18	6
	Monrovia	79	55	24		San Bernardino	466	308	158
	Montclair	77	55	22		San Bruno	65	48	17
	Montebello	113	77	36		San Carlos	41	30	11
	Monterey	68	47	21		Sand City	11	10	1

Table 78. Full-Time Law Enforcement Employees, by City, 2006 *(Contd.)*

(Number.)

State	City	Total law enforcement employees	Total officers	Total civilians	State	City	Total law enforcement employees	Total officers	Total civilians
	San Diego	2,701	1,911	790		Westmorland	5	5	0
	San Fernando	49	33	16		West Sacramento	108	70	38
	San Francisco	2,541	2,202	339		Wheatland	6	6	0
	San Gabriel	65	52	13		Whittier	164	119	45
	Sanger	39	30	9		Williams	10	8	2
	San Jacinto	40	32	8		Willits	20	13	7
	San Jose	1,749	1,373	376		Willows	9	8	1
	San Leandro	136	93	43		Winters	12	10	2
	San Luis Obispo	83	57	26		Woodlake	15	13	2
	San Marino	30	23	7		Woodland	90	63	27
	San Mateo	153	113	40		Yreka	20	14	6
	San Pablo	70	53	17		Yuba City	94	63	31
	San Rafael	96	69	27	**COLORADO**	Alamosa	30	25	5
	Santa Ana	655	360	295		Arvada	208	130	78
	Santa Barbara	204	138	66		Aspen	36	27	9
	Santa Clara	203	129	74		Ault	6	6	0
	Santa Cruz	115	88	27		Aurora	761	631	130
	Santa Maria	146	106	40		Avon	18	16	2
	Santa Monica	402	204	198		Basalt	11	8	3
	Santa Paula	41	30	11		Bayfield	5	5	0
	Santa Rosa	249	162	87		Berthoud	7	6	1
	Sausalito	23	18	5		Black Hawk	33	21	12
	Scotts Valley	24	17	7		Boulder	258	163	95
	Seal Beach	40	30	10		Breckenridge	27	22	5
	Seaside	56	41	15		Brighton	68	53	15
	Sebastopol	21	14	7		Broomfield	187	102	85
	Selma	47	34	13		Brush	14	12	2
	Shafter	29	21	8		Buena Vista	9	7	2
	Sierra Madre	21	17	4		Burlington	10	9	1
	Signal Hill	47	33	14		Calhan	3	3	0
	Simi Valley	182	121	61		Campo	1	1	0
	Soledad	25	22	3		Canon City	47	34	13
	Sonora	18	14	4		Carbondale	16	13	3
	South Gate	127	86	41		Castle Rock	65	49	16
	South Lake Tahoe	60	38	22		Cedaredge	6	5	1
	South Pasadena	47	34	13		Centennial	62	25	37
	South San Francisco	105	74	31		Center	8	3	5
	Stallion Springs	4	4	0		Central City	7	6	1
	St. Helena	16	12	4		Cherry Hills Village	21	18	3
	Stockton	606	404	202		Collbran	2	2	0
	Suisun City	35	23	12		Colorado Springs	994	681	313
	Sunnyvale	290	219	71		Columbine Valley	6	6	0
	Susanville	19	17	2		Commerce City	97	73	24
	Sutter Creek	7	7	0		Cortez	52	28	24
	Taft	21	11	10		Craig	29	23	6
	Tiburon	17	13	4		Crested Butte	8	6	2
	Torrance	336	240	96		Cripple Creek	24	13	11
	Tracy	121	77	44		Dacono	12	10	2
	Trinidad	2	2	0		De Beque	2	2	0
	Truckee	27	23	4		Del Norte	6	5	1
	Tulare	81	59	22		Delta	20	17	3
	Tulelake	3	3	0		Denver	1,824	1,497	327
	Turlock	98	64	34		Dillon	10	9	1
	Tustin	134	93	41		Durango	61	52	9
	Twin Cities	40	29	11		Eagle	11	9	2
	Ukiah	38	28	10		Eaton	9	8	1
	Union City	112	78	34		Edgewater	17	14	3
	Upland	122	80	42		Elizabeth	6	5	1
	Vacaville	166	101	65		Empire	1	1	0
	Vallejo	189	136	53		Englewood	100	69	31
	Ventura	174	125	49		Erie	21	19	2
	Vernon	70	51	19		Estes Park	25	18	7
	Visalia	172	122	50		Evans	33	30	3
	Walnut Creek	115	78	37		Federal Heights	33	24	9
	Watsonville	87	65	22		Firestone	22	17	5
	Weed	15	8	7		Florence	21	8	13
	West Covina	158	112	46		Fort Collins	246	156	90
	Westminster	144	99	45		Fort Lupton	22	18	4

Table 78. Full-Time Law Enforcement Employees, by City, 2006 (*Contd.*)

(Number.)

State	City	Total law enforcement employees	Total officers	Total civilians	State	City	Total law enforcement employees	Total officers	Total civilians
	Fort Morgan	34	28	6		Parker	75	53	22
	Fountain	51	38	13		Platteville	8	7	1
	Fowler	2	2	0		Pueblo	245	190	55
	Fraser/Winter Park	9	8	1		Rangely	7	3	4
	Frederick	20	18	2		Ridgway	3	3	0
	Frisco	14	13	1		Rifle	22	18	4
	Fruita	15	13	2		Rocky Ford	11	9	2
	Georgetown	3	3	0		Salida	17	15	2
	Gilcrest	3	3	0		Sheridan	34	25	9
	Glendale	35	24	11		Silt	7	6	1
	Glenwood Springs	28	22	6		Silverthorne	17	14	3
	Golden	56	42	14		Simla	2	2	0
	Grand Junction	160	95	65		Snowmass Village	14	10	4
	Greeley	232	132	100		South Fork	3	3	0
	Green Mountain Falls	2	2	0		Springfield	2	2	0
	Greenwood Village	81	62	19		Steamboat Springs	36	24	12
	Gunnison	28	15	13		Sterling	19	16	3
	Haxtun	3	3	0		Stratton	1	1	0
	Hayden	5	5	0		Telluride	15	10	5
	Holyoke	4	4	0		Thornton	178	144	34
	Hotchkiss	3	3	0		Trinidad	30	20	10
	Hugo	3	3	0		Vail	55	25	30
	Idaho Springs	9	7	2		Victor	5	4	1
	Ignacio	8	7	1		Walsenburg	20	11	9
	Johnstown	15	13	2		Walsh	1	1	0
	Kersey	4	4	0		Westminster	254	173	81
	Kiowa	2	2	0		Wheat Ridge	100	70	30
	Kremmling	4	4	0		Wiggins	2	2	0
	Lafayette	49	38	11		Windsor	20	17	3
	La Junta	18	15	3		Woodland Park	28	20	8
	Lakeside	5	5	0		Wray	6	5	1
	Lakewood	396	263	133		Yuma	6	5	1
	Lamar	23	18	5	CONNECTICUT	Ansonia	50	43	7
	La Salle	6	6	0		Avon	39	31	8
	Las Animas	7	6	1		Berlin	51	40	11
	La Veta	4	3	1		Bethel	48	35	13
	Leadville	10	8	2		Bloomfield	60	51	9
	Limon	6	5	1		Branford	62	49	13
	Littleton	93	70	23		Bridgeport	513	410	103
	Lochbuie	6	6	0		Bristol	149	124	25
	Log Lane Village	3	3	0		Brookfield	41	31	10
	Lone Tree	40	37	3		Canton	20	15	5
	Longmont	156	121	35		Cheshire	59	48	11
	Louisville	38	33	5		Clinton	29	26	3
	Loveland	122	85	37		Coventry	16	12	4
	Mancos	3	2	1		Cromwell	34	25	9
	Manitou Springs	16	15	1		Danbury	153	147	6
	Manzanola	1	1	0		Darien	56	50	6
	Meeker	8	6	2		Derby	28	27	1
	Milliken	10	9	1		East Hampton	18	16	2
	Minturn	3	2	1		East Hartford	166	128	38
	Monte Vista	15	11	4		East Haven	51	48	3
	Montrose	52	35	17		Easton	18	15	3
	Monument	16	13	3		East Windsor	31	24	7
	Morrison	3	2	1		Enfield	110	92	18
	Mountain View	6	5	1		Fairfield	114	108	6
	Mount Crested Butte	8	7	1		Farmington	60	44	16
	Nederland	6	5	1		Glastonbury	75	59	16
	New Castle	7	6	1		Granby	20	15	5
	Northglenn	88	64	24		Greenwich	172	147	25
	Oak Creek	2	2	0		Groton	37	29	8
	Olathe	6	5	1		Groton Long Point	10	7	3
	Ouray	5	5	0		Groton Town	69	65	4
	Pagosa Springs	9	8	1		Guilford	47	38	9
	Palisade	8	6	2		Hamden	118	95	23
	Palmer Lake	5	4	1		Hartford	469	410	59
	Paonia	4	4	0		Madison	26	23	3
	Parachute	8	7	1		Manchester	151	119	32

Table 78. Full-Time Law Enforcement Employees, by City, 2006 *(Contd.)*

(Number.)

State	City	Total law enforcement employees	Total officers	Total civilians	State	City	Total law enforcement employees	Total officers	Total civilians
	Meriden	137	124	13		Elsmere	11	10	1
	Middlebury	17	11	6		Felton	4	4	0
	Middletown	107	95	12		Fenwick Island	6	6	0
	Milford	121	105	16		Georgetown	19	18	1
	Monroe	47	36	11		Greenwood	2	1	1
	Naugatuck	67	55	12		Harrington	11	10	1
	New Britain	169	157	12		Laurel	11	10	1
	New Canaan	50	45	5		Lewes	14	13	1
	New Haven	489	406	83		Milford	39	30	9
	Newington	58	45	13		Millsboro	13	12	1
	New London	91	75	16		Milton	10	9	1
	New Milford	64	47	17		Newark	78	62	16
	Newtown	49	43	6		New Castle	19	17	2
	North Branford	28	23	5		Newport	9	9	0
	North Haven	55	46	9		Ocean View	9	8	1
	Norwalk	188	171	17		Rehoboth Beach	27	17	10
	Norwich	97	78	19		Seaford	32	23	9
	Old Saybrook	30	21	9		Selbyville	7	6	1
	Orange	49	38	11		Smyrna	28	21	7
	Plainfield	21	17	4		South Bethany	6	6	0
	Plainville	43	35	8		Wilmington	364	285	79
	Plymouth	21	21	0		Wyoming	4	4	0
	Portland	11	10	1	**DISTRICT OF COLUMBIA**	Washington	4,342	3,799	543
	Putnam	18	14	4	**FLORIDA**	Alachua	29	22	7
	Redding	22	16	6		Altamonte Springs	122	103	19
	Ridgefield	48	42	6		Apalachicola	9	8	1
	Rocky Hill	43	34	9		Apopka	89	79	10
	Seymour	41	39	2		Arcadia	24	20	4
	Shelton	64	54	10		Astatula	4	4	0
	Simsbury	45	35	10		Atlantic Beach	39	28	11
	Southington	79	62	17		Atlantis	16	11	5
	South Windsor	54	41	13		Auburndale	42	30	12
	Stamford	342	284	58		Aventura	108	76	32
	Stonington	48	36	12		Avon Park	39	26	13
	Stratford	107	104	3		Bal Harbour Village	34	26	8
	Suffield	24	19	5		Bartow	68	43	25
	Thomaston	16	13	3		Bay Harbor Island	31	25	6
	Torrington	87	76	11		Belleair	8	6	2
	Trumbull	83	72	11		Belleair Beach	5	5	0
	Vernon	62	48	14		Belleair Bluffs	5	5	0
	Wallingford	92	71	21		Belle Glade	25	19	6
	Waterbury	354	294	60		Belleview	17	15	2
	Waterford	53	46	7		Biscayne Park	12	11	1
	Watertown	49	38	11		Blountstown	12	8	4
	West Hartford	135	116	19		Boca Raton	273	188	85
	West Haven	129	116	13		Bonifay	6	5	1
	Weston	17	16	1		Bowling Green	7	7	0
	Westport	90	70	20		Boynton Beach	210	150	60
	Wethersfield	57	46	11		Bradenton	148	119	29
	Willimantic	46	41	5		Bradenton Beach	10	10	0
	Wilton	47	43	4		Brooksville	30	21	9
	Winchester	28	23	5		Bunnell	11	9	2
	Windsor	62	51	11		Cape Coral	333	209	124
	Windsor Locks	30	24	6		Carrabelle	6	6	0
	Wolcott	33	24	9		Casselberry	85	55	30
	Woodbridge	34	26	8		Cedar Grove	6	5	1
DELAWARE	Bethany Beach	10	10	0		Cedar Key	5	5	0
	Blades	2	2	0		Center Hill	4	4	0
	Bridgeville	7	7	0		Chattahoochee	11	10	1
	Camden	17	15	2		Chiefland	14	11	3
	Cheswold	5	5	0		Chipley	14	13	1
	Clayton	8	8	0		Clearwater	375	255	120
	Dagsboro	2	2	0		Clermont	56	41	15
	Delaware City	4	4	0		Clewiston	28	18	10
	Delmar	13	12	1		Cocoa	89	65	24
	Dewey Beach	8	8	0		Cocoa Beach	50	34	16
	Dover	119	90	29		Coconut Creek	119	81	38
	Ellendale	2	2	0					

Table 78. Full-Time Law Enforcement Employees, by City, 2006 (*Contd.*)

(Number.)

State	City	Total law enforcement employees	Total officers	Total civilians	State	City	Total law enforcement employees	Total officers	Total civilians
	Coleman	2	2	0		Indian Rocks Beach	10	10	0
	Cooper City	72	53	19		Indian Shores	12	11	1
	Coral Gables	258	184	74		Inglis	6	5	1
	Coral Springs	292	197	95		Interlachen	3	3	0
	Cottondale	3	3	0		Jacksonville	2,858	1,690	1,168
	Crescent City	9	8	1		Jacksonville Beach	76	56	20
	Crestview	49	39	10		Jasper	9	8	1
	Cross City	5	5	0		Jennings	1	1	0
	Crystal River	22	19	3		Juno Beach	18	14	4
	Dade City	30	22	8		Jupiter	138	104	34
	Dania	74	65	9		Jupiter Inlet Colony	4	4	0
	Davenport	9	8	1		Jupiter Island	17	13	4
	Davie	231	174	57		Kenneth City	15	13	2
	Daytona Beach Shores	41	31	10		Key Biscayne	39	27	12
	Deerfield Beach	149	120	29		Key Colony Beach	6	6	0
	De Funiak Springs	17	16	1		Key West	127	92	35
	Deland	71	52	19		Kissimmee	195	127	68
	Delray Beach	221	149	72		Lady Lake	41	28	13
	Doral	87	84	3		Lake Alfred	14	9	5
	Dundee	14	9	5		Lake City	55	40	15
	Dunedin	41	40	1		Lake Clarke Shores	11	11	0
	Dunnellon	11	9	2		Lake Hamilton	7	6	1
	Eagle Lake	5	5	0		Lake Helen	8	7	1
	Eatonville	16	14	2		Lakeland	364	235	129
	Edgewater	36	32	4		Lake Mary	52	36	16
	Edgewood	12	11	1		Lake Park	26	24	2
	El Portal	10	10	0		Lake Placid	11	9	2
	Eustis	58	45	13		Lake Wales	61	42	19
	Fellsmere	9	8	1		Lake Worth	117	85	32
	Fernandina Beach	42	34	8		Lantana	37	28	9
	Flagler Beach	19	16	3		Largo	186	134	52
	Florida City	41	29	12		Lauderdale-by-the-Sea	27	25	2
	Fort Lauderdale	678	483	195		Lauderdale Lakes	72	55	17
	Fort Meade	20	13	7		Lauderhill	140	114	26
	Fort Myers	282	194	88		Lawtey	1	1	0
	Fort Pierce	146	111	35		Leesburg	98	72	26
	Fort Walton Beach	64	47	17		Lighthouse Point	38	29	9
	Frostproof	12	8	4		Live Oak	19	16	3
	Fruitland Park	12	11	1		Longboat Key	28	20	8
	Gainesville	350	278	72		Longwood	47	40	7
	Golden Beach	18	17	1		Lynn Haven	43	32	11
	Graceville	9	7	2		Madeira Beach	11	11	0
	Greenacres City	66	46	20		Madison	15	14	1
	Green Cove Springs	28	23	5		Maitland	52	41	11
	Greensboro	1	1	0		Manalapan	15	10	5
	Gretna	1	1	0		Mangonia Park	12	11	1
	Groveland	29	22	7		Marco Island	33	31	2
	Gulf Breeze	27	19	8		Margate	190	118	72
	Gulfport	39	29	10		Marianna	22	15	7
	Gulf Stream	11	11	0		Mascotte	13	12	1
	Haines City	62	44	18		Medley	39	32	7
	Hallandale	121	87	34		Melbourne	221	160	61
	Havana	13	8	5		Melbourne Beach	10	9	1
	Hialeah	472	352	120		Melbourne Village	5	5	0
	Hialeah Gardens	41	31	10		Mexico Beach	7	6	1
	Highland Beach	12	11	1		Miami	1,380	1,058	322
	High Springs	18	13	5		Miami Beach	539	386	153
	Hillsboro Beach	16	12	4		Miami Gardens	162	143	19
	Holly Hill	36	30	6		Miami Lakes	47	46	1
	Hollywood	507	327	180		Miami Shores	42	30	12
	Holmes Beach	20	13	7		Miami Springs	52	41	11
	Homestead	144	106	38		Milton	28	21	7
	Howey-in-the-Hills	6	6	0		Miramar	218	168	50
	Hypoluxo	4	4	0		Monticello	13	9	4
	Indialantic	17	11	6		Mount Dora	48	32	16
	Indian Creek Village	17	11	6		Mulberry	18	14	4
	Indian Harbour Beach	25	18	7		Naples	115	74	41
	Indian River Shores	20	19	1					

Table 78. Full-Time Law Enforcement Employees, by City, 2006 *(Contd.)*

(Number.)

State	City	Total law enforcement employees	Total officers	Total civilians	State	City	Total law enforcement employees	Total officers	Total civilians
	Neptune Beach............	27	18	9		Sneads	8	5	3
	New Port Richey.........	47	36	11		South Bay	9	8	1
	New Smyrna Beach	59	49	10		South Daytona	34	25	9
	Niceville	23	18	5		South Miami	56	49	7
	North Bay Village	34	26	8		South Palm Beach........	8	8	0
	North Lauderdale	67	57	10		South Pasadena	10	10	0
	North Miami..............	163	124	39		Southwest Ranches......	10	10	0
	North Miami Beach.....	156	117	39		Springfield	19	17	2
	North Palm Beach	41	30	11		Starke	27	19	8
	North Port.................	94	74	20		St. Augustine	59	46	13
	North Redington Beach..............	2	2	0		St. Augustine Beach	16	14	2
	Oak Hill	6	6	0		St. Cloud	85	56	29
	Oakland	10	9	1		St. Pete Beach	40	29	11
	Oakland Park	93	83	10		St. Petersburg	733	504	229
	Ocala	243	158	85		Stuart.......................	62	44	18
	Ocean Ridge................	18	13	5		Sunny Isles Beach	63	47	16
	Ocoee.........................	89	66	23		Sunrise.....................	272	170	102
	Okeechobee.................	29	20	9		Surfside	41	28	13
	Oldsmar	16	16	0		Sweetwater	47	21	26
	Opa Locka	41	31	10		Tallahassee.................	490	354	136
	Orange City	26	23	3		Tamarac.....................	88	71	17
	Orange Park	26	21	5		Tampa.......................	1,330	983	347
	Orlando.......................	972	695	277		Tarpon Springs	60	46	14
	Ormond Beach.............	101	70	31		Tavares	31	28	3
	Oviedo........................	76	59	17		Temple Terrace	72	51	21
	Pahokee......................	17	15	2		Tequesta....................	26	19	7
	Palatka	48	39	9		Titusville	127	86	41
	Palm Bay.....................	226	154	72		Treasure Island............	27	20	7
	Palm Beach..................	129	76	53		Trenton.....................	4	3	1
	Palm Beach Gardens	146	110	36		Umatilla	10	9	1
	Palm Beach Shores	16	11	5		Valparaiso	14	10	4
	Palmetto	46	33	13		Venice.......................	68	50	18
	Palmetto Bay	42	39	3		Vero Beach	82	56	26
	Palm Springs...............	50	38	12		Village of Pinecrest......	68	50	18
	Panama City	135	95	40		Virginia Gardens..........	9	7	2
	Panama City Beach	69	54	15		Waldo.......................	7	6	1
	Parker.........................	10	9	1		Wauchula	18	13	5
	Parkland......................	32	29	3		Webster	2	2	0
	Pembroke Park	13	12	1		Welaka......................	1	1	0
	Pembroke Pines	310	243	67		Wellington..................	53	49	4
	Pensacola	204	152	52		West Melbourne...........	39	29	10
	Perry..........................	23	21	2		West Miami.................	19	16	3
	Pinellas Park................	134	100	34		Weston......................	92	61	31
	Plantation....................	281	176	105		West Palm Beach	390	287	103
	Plant City	85	66	19		White Springs..............	4	4	0
	Pompano Beach	300	218	82		Wildwood...................	22	16	6
	Ponce Inlet..................	18	12	6		Williston....................	19	11	8
	Port Orange	97	81	16		Wilton Manors	39	27	12
	Port Richey.................	20	14	6		Windermere................	17	13	4
	Port St. Joe	13	11	2		Winter Garden	66	49	17
	Port St. Lucie...............	293	228	65		Winter Haven	104	72	32
	Quincy........................	36	24	12		Winter Park	112	86	26
	Redington Beaches.......	2	2	0		Winter Springs.............	91	70	21
	Riviera Beach..............	139	99	40		Zephyrhills..................	47	33	14
	Rockledge....................	65	46	19		Zolfo Springs	4	3	1
	Royal Palm Beach	53	49	4	GEORGIA	Acworth....................	46	35	11
	Safety Harbor..............	15	15	0		Adairsville..................	17	14	3
	Sanford.......................	143	120	23		Adel..........................	20	17	3
	Sanibel.......................	34	24	10		Adrian	2	2	0
	Sarasota.....................	259	193	66		Alamo.......................	3	3	0
	Satellite Beach	32	23	9		Albany.......................	215	184	31
	Sea Ranch Lakes..........	11	7	4		Alma.........................	12	10	2
	Sebastian....................	51	38	13		Alpharetta	133	99	34
	Sebring	37	30	7		Americus....................	44	36	8
	Seminole	19	19	0		Aragon	5	4	1
	Sewall's Point..............	6	6	0		Arlington	3	3	0
	Shalimar	4	4	0		Athens-Clarke County......................	281	225	56

Table 78. Full-Time Law Enforcement Employees, by City, 2006 (*Contd.*)

(Number.)

State	City	Total law enforcement employees	Total officers	Total civilians	State	City	Total law enforcement employees	Total officers	Total civilians
	Atlanta	2,182	1,669	513		Eastman	13	12	1
	Attapulgus	1	1	0		East Point	175	121	54
	Auburn	22	16	6		Eatonton	21	15	6
	Austell	31	23	8		Edison	2	2	0
	Avondale Estates	10	10	0		Elberton	20	17	3
	Baldwin	12	8	4		Ellaville	5	5	0
	Ball Ground	3	3	0		Emerson	8	8	0
	Barnesville	18	16	2		Eton	3	3	0
	Bartow	2	1	1		Euharlee	12	11	1
	Barwick	2	1	1		Fairburn	30	27	3
	Baxley	14	12	2		Fairmount	3	3	0
	Blairsville	8	7	1		Fayetteville	47	42	5
	Bloomingdale	14	11	3		Fitzgerald	35	30	5
	Blythe	1	1	0		Folkston	7	6	1
	Bowdon	11	8	3		Forest Park	85	64	21
	Braselton	13	12	1		Forsyth	27	21	6
	Bremen	25	20	5		Fort Gaines	6	6	0
	Brooklet	3	3	0		Fort Oglethorpe	28	26	2
	Broxton	4	4	0		Fort Valley	35	31	4
	Brunswick	74	66	8		Franklin Springs	3	2	1
	Buchanan	10	9	1		Gainesville	121	101	20
	Buena Vista	4	4	0		Garden City	39	34	5
	Byron	19	16	3		Glennville	18	13	5
	Cairo	24	21	3		Gray	12	11	1
	Calhoun	50	44	6		Greensboro	18	14	4
	Camilla	20	16	4		Greenville	7	6	1
	Canton	46	39	7		Griffin	124	96	28
	Carrollton	71	60	11		Grovetown	30	18	12
	Cartersville	57	49	8		Hagan	2	2	0
	Cave Spring	5	5	0		Hahira	7	5	2
	Cedartown	34	32	2		Hamilton	1	1	0
	Centerville	19	16	3		Hapeville	47	34	13
	Chamblee	45	32	13		Harlem	12	7	5
	Chatsworth	17	14	3		Hazlehurst	15	13	2
	Clarkesville	6	5	1		Helen	13	9	4
	Clarkston	20	15	5		Hephzibah	6	6	0
	Claxton	9	8	1		Hiawassee	5	4	1
	Clayton	11	10	1		Hinesville	91	79	12
	Cleveland	12	11	1		Hiram	16	14	2
	Cochran	16	15	1		Hogansville	18	11	7
	College Park	133	108	25		Hoschton	7	6	1
	Colquitt	10	9	1		Ivey	3	3	0
	Columbus	452	349	103		Jasper	15	13	2
	Commerce	28	22	6		Jefferson	27	25	2
	Conyers	58	45	13		Jonesboro	21	18	3
	Coolidge	3	3	0		Kingsland	42	38	4
	Cordele	36	30	6		LaGrange	101	82	19
	Covington	64	54	10		Lake Park	2	2	0
	Crawfordville	1	1	0		Lavonia	14	13	1
	Cumming	21	15	6		Lawrenceville	78	61	17
	Cuthbert	9	5	4		Lenox	2	1	1
	Dallas	19	14	5		Leslie	2	2	0
	Dalton	106	89	17		Locust Grove	22	20	2
	Danielsville	2	2	0		Loganville	28	25	3
	Darien	5	5	0		Lookout Mountain	7	7	0
	Davisboro	2	1	1		Ludowici	10	6	4
	Dawson	20	14	6		Lumber City	4	3	1
	Decatur	49	35	14		Luthersville	4	3	1
	Demorest	5	3	2		Macon	359	272	87
	Dillard	2	2	0		Madison	14	12	2
	Donalsonville	11	9	2		Manchester	27	11	16
	Doraville	61	40	21		Marietta	168	136	32
	Douglas	41	33	8		Marshallville	5	4	1
	Douglasville	92	74	18		Maysville	3	3	0
	Dublin	55	47	8		McDonough	47	42	5
	Duluth	65	54	11		McIntyre	5	5	0
	East Dublin	8	8	0		McRae	7	6	1
	East Ellijay	8	8	0		Meigs	4	4	0

Table 78. Full-Time Law Enforcement Employees, by City, 2006 (*Contd.*)

(Number.)

State	City	Total law enforcement employees	Total officers	Total civilians	State	City	Total law enforcement employees	Total officers	Total civilians
	Metter	11	10	1		Sylvester	22	16	6
	Midville	3	2	1		Tallapoosa	15	14	1
	Milledgeville	61	41	20		Tallulah Falls	2	2	0
	Monroe	44	39	5		Temple	11	11	0
	Monticello	14	12	2		Tennille	8	8	0
	Morrow	36	33	3		Thomaston	29	26	3
	Morven	2	2	0		Thomasville	64	57	7
	Moultrie	47	42	5		Thomson	15	13	2
	Mount Airy	1	1	0		Thunderbolt	10	9	1
	Mount Zion	5	4	1		Tifton	56	46	10
	Nahunta	3	3	0		Trenton	7	7	0
	Nashville	20	16	4		Trion	9	8	1
	Nelson	1	1	0		Tunnel Hill	4	3	1
	Newington	1	1	0		Tybee Island	24	17	7
	Newnan	80	67	13		Tyrone	17	15	2
	Newton	2	2	0		Unadilla	4	4	0
	Nicholls	3	2	1		Union City	61	44	17
	Norcross	41	31	10		Valdosta	139	127	12
	Norman Park	4	3	1		Varnell	5	5	0
	Oakwood	10	8	2		Vidalia	37	28	9
	Oglethorpe	3	2	1		Vienna	7	7	0
	Omega	3	3	0		Villa Rica	40	32	8
	Oxford	3	3	0		Warm Springs	2	1	1
	Palmetto	14	11	3		Warner Robins	139	110	29
	Patterson	2	2	0		Warwick	2	2	0
	Pavo	3	3	0		Watkinsville	7	7	0
	Peachtree City	61	57	4		Waverly Hall	3	3	0
	Pearson	6	5	1		Waycross	62	52	10
	Pelham	10	9	1		Waynesboro	24	18	6
	Pembroke	8	6	2		West Point	17	14	3
	Pendergrass	4	4	0		Willacoochee	3	3	0
	Perry	40	36	4		Winder	48	40	8
	Pine Lake	4	3	1		Winterville	2	2	0
	Pine Mountain	6	6	0		Woodbury	9	6	3
	Pooler	30	25	5		Woodstock	50	41	9
	Porterdale	6	6	0		Wrens	12	7	5
	Port Wentworth	24	21	3		Zebulon	6	6	0
	Poulan	4	4	0	**HAWAII**	Honolulu	2,532	2,053	479
	Powder Springs	37	31	6	**IDAHO**	Aberdeen	8	5	3
	Quitman	19	13	6		American Falls	8	7	1
	Reidsville	9	8	1		Bellevue	5	4	1
	Remerton	7	6	1		Blackfoot	27	24	3
	Richland	3	3	0		Boise	344	268	76
	Richmond Hill	29	23	6		Bonners Ferry	8	8	0
	Rincon	14	12	2		Buhl	10	8	2
	Riverdale	37	33	4		Caldwell	73	58	15
	Roberta	3	3	0		Cascade	6	5	1
	Rome	106	91	15		Challis	1	1	0
	Rossville	11	10	1		Chubbuck	31	19	12
	Roswell	194	129	65		Coeur d'Alene	80	66	14
	Royston	24	20	4		Cottonwood	1	1	0
	Sale City	1	1	0		Emmett	14	13	1
	Sandersville	20	17	3		Filer	5	5	0
	Savannah-Chatham Metropolitan	708	539	169		Fruitland	9	8	1
	Shiloh	2	1	1		Garden City	35	27	8
	Smyrna	118	90	28		Gooding	8	7	1
	Snellville	54	44	10		Grangeville	6	6	0
	Sparks	5	4	1		Hagerman	2	2	0
	Springfield	5	4	1		Hailey	17	15	2
	Statesboro	72	59	13		Heyburn	6	5	1
	Statham	6	6	0		Homedale	5	5	0
	St. Marys	41	37	4		Idaho City	1	1	0
	Stone Mountain	20	19	1		Idaho Falls	126	88	38
	Summerville	19	18	1		Jerome	17	15	2
	Suwanee	38	30	8		Kamiah	2	2	0
	Sycamore	1	1	0		Kellogg	8	7	1
	Sylvania	14	11	3		Ketchum	28	12	16
						Kimberly	7	7	0

Table 78. Full-Time Law Enforcement Employees, by City, 2006 (*Contd.*)

(Number.)

State	City	Total law enforcement employees	Total officers	Total civilians	State	City	Total law enforcement employees	Total officers	Total civilians
	Lewiston	66	44	22		Bedford Park	45	36	9
	McCall	11	9	2		Beecher	9	8	1
	Meridian	82	68	14		Belleville	100	81	19
	Montpelier	6	6	0		Bellwood	42	39	3
	Moscow	41	34	7		Belvidere	46	41	5
	Mountain Home	32	25	7		Benld	4	4	0
	Nampa	150	108	42		Bensenville	41	33	8
	Orofino	6	5	1		Benton	9	8	1
	Osburn	2	2	0		Berkeley	20	16	4
	Parma	4	4	0		Berwyn	120	92	28
	Payette	13	11	2		Bethalto	21	15	6
	Pinehurst	5	2	3		Bloomingdale	63	46	17
	Pocatello	126	89	37		Bloomington	165	126	39
	Ponderay	5	4	1		Blue Island	58	40	18
	Post Falls	54	33	21		Blue Mound	1	1	0
	Preston	7	6	1		Bolingbrook	157	113	44
	Rathdrum	13	11	2		Bourbonnais	27	20	7
	Rexburg	41	34	7		Bradley	41	31	10
	Rigby	8	7	1		Braidwood	25	16	9
	Rupert	16	15	1		Breese	8	7	1
	Salmon	7	6	1		Bridgeport	2	2	0
	Sandpoint	26	21	5		Bridgeview	46	43	3
	Shelley	7	7	0		Brighton	5	3	2
	Soda Springs	8	7	1		Broadview	30	24	6
	Spirit Lake	4	4	0		Brookfield	39	32	7
	St. Anthony	6	6	0		Brooklyn	8	8	0
	St. Maries	5	5	0		Buffalo Grove	82	69	13
	Sun Valley	10	9	1		Bull Valley	3	3	0
	Twin Falls	94	64	30		Bunker Hill	5	3	2
	Weiser	14	12	2		Burbank	69	52	17
	Wendell	6	5	1		Burnham	11	6	5
	Wilder	3	3	0		Burr Ridge	31	27	4
ILLINOIS	Abingdon	3	3	0		Byron	8	7	1
	Addison	91	66	25		Cahokia	46	31	15
	Albany	1	1	0		Cairo	13	8	5
	Albion	3	3	0		Calumet City	120	83	37
	Aledo	7	6	1		Calumet Park	32	25	7
	Algonquin	55	48	7		Cambridge	1	1	0
	Alorton	8	8	0		Camp Point	2	2	0
	Alsip	47	36	11		Canton	32	23	9
	Altamont	5	5	0		Carbondale	75	57	18
	Alton	89	65	24		Carlinville	18	13	5
	Amboy	4	4	0		Carlyle	8	7	1
	Anna	8	8	0		Carmi	11	9	2
	Annawan	1	1	0		Carol Stream	89	65	24
	Antioch	39	26	13		Carpentersville	81	67	14
	Arcola	6	5	1		Carrier Mills	2	2	0
	Argenta	1	1	0		Carrollton	6	6	0
	Arlington Heights	150	113	37		Carterville	7	7	0
	Arthur	4	4	0		Carthage	3	3	0
	Ashland	1	1	0		Cary	34	29	5
	Assumption	1	1	0		Casey	8	7	1
	Athens	3	3	0		Caseyville	14	10	4
	Atkinson	2	2	0		Catlin	1	1	0
	Atlanta	1	1	0		Central City	4	4	0
	Atwood	3	3	0		Centralia	36	27	9
	Auburn	10	6	4		Centreville	13	10	3
	Aurora	360	286	74		Chadwick	1	1	0
	Aviston	1	1	0		Champaign	151	122	29
	Bannockburn	7	7	0		Channahon	22	19	3
	Barrington Hills	27	19	8		Charleston	35	33	2
	Barrington-Inverness	41	34	7		Chatham	19	14	5
	Barry	1	1	0		Chenoa	3	3	0
	Bartlett	66	49	17		Cherry Valley	13	13	0
	Bartonville	16	11	5		Chester	13	10	3
	Batavia	50	43	7		Chicago	14,692	13,624	1,068
	Beardstown	12	8	4		Chicago Heights	115	87	28
	Beckemeyer	1	1	0		Chicago Ridge	35	31	4

Table 78. Full-Time Law Enforcement Employees, by City, 2006 *(Contd.)*

(Number.)

State	City	Total law enforcement employees	Total officers	Total civilians	State	City	Total law enforcement employees	Total officers	Total civilians
	Chillicothe	13	8	5		Fairbury	9	8	1
	Christopher	4	4	0		Fairfield	17	13	4
	Cicero	159	146	13		Fairmont City	9	7	2
	Clarendon Hills	16	15	1		Fairview	1	1	0
	Clinton	14	13	1		Fairview Heights	55	40	15
	Coal City	11	10	1		Farmer City	6	3	3
	Coal Valley	7	6	1		Farmington	5	5	0
	Cobden	3	3	0		Fisher	2	2	0
	Colfax	1	1	0		Flora	16	11	5
	Collinsville	54	39	15		Flossmoor	24	19	5
	Colona	11	9	2		Ford Heights	6	5	1
	Columbia	19	13	6		Forest Park	51	36	15
	Cordova	2	2	0		Forest View	11	8	3
	Cortland	3	3	0		Fox Lake	31	26	5
	Coulterville	2	2	0		Fox River Grove	12	12	0
	Country Club Hills	48	34	14		Frankfort	32	28	4
	Countryside	32	25	7		Franklin Park	54	49	5
	Crest Hill	29	27	2		Freeburg	10	9	1
	Crestwood	3	3	0		Freeport	72	54	18
	Crete	20	18	2		Fulton	8	7	1
	Creve Coeur	7	5	2		Galena	13	10	3
	Crystal Lake	72	60	12		Galesburg	77	50	27
	Cuba	2	2	0		Galva	3	3	0
	Dallas City	2	2	0		Geneseo	20	14	6
	Danvers	1	1	0		Geneva	48	37	11
	Danville	78	61	17		Genoa	10	10	0
	Darien	52	35	17		Georgetown	4	4	0
	Decatur	191	162	29		Germantown	1	1	0
	Deerfield	52	39	13		Gibson City	13	8	5
	De Kalb	73	60	13		Gifford	1	1	0
	De Pue	3	3	0		Gilberts	10	9	1
	De Soto	4	3	1		Gillespie	9	6	3
	Des Plaines	130	102	28		Gilman	2	2	0
	Divernon	2	2	0		Girard	4	4	0
	Dixmoor	15	10	5		Glasford	1	1	0
	Dixon	29	26	3		Glen Carbon	25	18	7
	Dolton	57	41	16		Glencoe	45	35	10
	Downers Grove	113	80	33		Glendale Heights	79	52	27
	Dupo	6	6	0		Glen Ellyn	48	40	8
	Du Quoin	15	11	4		Glenview	104	78	26
	Durand	1	1	0		Glenwood	24	23	1
	Dwight	10	9	1		Golf	4	4	0
	Earlville	3	3	0		Grafton	4	4	0
	East Alton	17	12	5		Granite City	65	55	10
	East Carondelet	1	1	0		Grant Park	5	5	0
	East Dubuque	7	7	0		Granville	2	2	0
	East Dundee	15	14	1		Grayslake	40	34	6
	East Hazel Crest	11	9	2		Grayville	7	3	4
	East Moline	47	36	11		Greenfield	2	2	0
	East Peoria	54	41	13		Greenup	4	4	0
	East St. Louis	85	60	25		Greenville	14	10	4
	Edwardsville	52	37	15		Gurnee	93	65	28
	Effingham	33	21	12		Hamilton	4	4	0
	Elburn	10	9	1		Hampshire	11	11	0
	Eldorado	10	7	3		Hampton	4	4	0
	Elgin	236	182	54		Hanover	1	1	0
	Elizabeth	1	1	0		Hanover Park	73	52	21
	Elk Grove Village	107	94	13		Harrisburg	15	14	1
	Elmhurst	91	69	22		Hartford	5	4	1
	Elmwood	2	2	0		Harvard	24	18	6
	Elmwood Park	41	35	6		Harvey	89	58	31
	El Paso	5	5	0		Harwood Heights	35	26	9
	Elwood	6	6	0		Havana	13	9	4
	Energy	4	4	0		Hawthorn Woods	16	15	1
	Erie	3	3	0		Hazel Crest	30	27	3
	Eureka	6	6	0		Hebron	5	5	0
	Evanston	214	158	56		Henry	4	4	0
	Evergreen Park	70	58	12		Herrin	22	15	7

Table 78. Full-Time Law Enforcement Employees, by City, 2006 (*Contd.*)

(Number.)

State	City	Total law enforcement employees	Total officers	Total civilians	State	City	Total law enforcement employees	Total officers	Total civilians
	Herscher	3	3	0		Loves Park	32	29	3
	Hickory Hills	36	29	7		Lynwood	24	17	7
	Highland	28	20	8		Lyons	33	27	6
	Highland Park	77	57	20		Machesney Park	24	23	1
	Highwood	12	11	1		Mackinaw	1	1	0
	Hillsboro	8	8	0		Macomb	29	26	3
	Hillside	34	26	8		Madison	16	11	5
	Hinckley	3	3	0		Mahomet	7	6	1
	Hinsdale	37	28	9		Manhattan	9	9	0
	Hodgkins	21	19	2		Manito	4	4	0
	Hoffman Estates	119	101	18		Manteno	17	16	1
	Homer	1	1	0		Marengo	20	15	5
	Hometown	5	1	4		Marion	38	27	11
	Homewood	43	38	5		Marissa	5	5	0
	Hoopeston	16	10	6		Markham	46	36	10
	Hopedale	1	1	0		Maroa	4	4	0
	Hopkins Park	2	2	0		Marquette Heights	5	5	0
	Huntley	30	25	5		Marseilles	13	9	4
	Hutsonville	1	1	0		Marshall	11	10	1
	Indian Head Park	11	10	1		Martinsville	2	2	0
	Island Lake	20	14	6		Maryville	16	11	5
	Itasca	34	26	8		Mascoutah	14	13	1
	Jacksonville	49	39	10		Mason City	5	5	0
	Jerome	8	8	0		Matteson	45	35	10
	Jerseyville	22	15	7		Mattoon	53	40	13
	Johnsburg	11	10	1		Maywood	78	56	22
	Johnston City	4	4	0		McCook	21	16	5
	Joliet	372	292	80		McCullom Lake	2	2	0
	Jonesboro	3	3	0		McHenry	60	45	15
	Justice	34	28	6		McLean	1	1	0
	Kankakee	86	71	15		McLeansboro	5	5	0
	Kenilworth	14	11	3		Melrose Park	86	71	15
	Kewanee	30	23	7		Mendota	20	15	5
	Kildeer	26	22	4		Meredosia	2	2	0
	Kincaid	1	1	0		Metamora	5	5	0
	Kirkland	3	3	0		Metropolis	22	17	5
	Knoxville	5	5	0		Midlothian	29	22	7
	Lacon	3	3	0		Milan	18	13	5
	La Grange	38	29	9		Milledgeville	2	2	0
	La Grange Park	28	23	5		Millstadt	7	7	0
	Lake Bluff	23	17	6		Minier	2	2	0
	Lake Forest	62	43	19		Minonk	3	3	0
	Lake in the Hills	55	40	15		Minooka	14	12	2
	Lakemoor	8	8	0		Mokena	33	30	3
	Lake Villa	19	17	2		Moline	107	81	26
	Lakewood	9	8	1		Momence	8	8	0
	Lake Zurich	55	36	19		Monee	12	11	1
	La Moille	1	1	0		Monmouth	28	18	10
	Lanark	2	2	0		Montgomery	26	18	8
	Lansing	87	62	25		Monticello	7	6	1
	La Salle	27	21	6		Morris	36	27	9
	Lebanon	12	12	0		Morrison	6	6	0
	Leland	1	1	0		Morton	29	22	7
	Leland Grove	6	6	0		Morton Grove	59	45	14
	Lemont	33	30	3		Mound City	2	2	0
	Le Roy	5	5	0		Mount Carmel	17	13	4
	Lewistown	4	4	0		Mount Carroll	3	3	0
	Lexington	3	3	0		Mount Morris	5	4	1
	Libertyville	57	41	16		Mount Olive	6	4	2
	Lincoln	25	24	1		Mount Prospect	110	88	22
	Lincolnshire	35	24	11		Mount Pulaski	2	2	0
	Lincolnwood	43	33	10		Mount Sterling	9	5	4
	Lindenhurst	17	15	2		Mount Vernon	59	46	13
	Lisle	57	43	14		Mount Zion	11	9	2
	Litchfield	24	16	8		Moweaqua	2	2	0
	Livingston	1	1	0		Mundelein	70	51	19
	Lockport	45	38	7		Murphysboro	19	13	6
	Lombard	86	72	14		Naperville	296	190	106

Table 78. Full-Time Law Enforcement Employees, by City, 2006 (*Contd.*)

(Number.)

State	City	Total law enforcement employees	Total officers	Total civilians	State	City	Total law enforcement employees	Total officers	Total civilians
	Nashville	8	7	1		Princeton	16	15	1
	Nauvoo	3	3	0		Prophetstown	4	3	1
	Neoga	3	3	0		Prospect Heights	29	26	3
	New Athens	5	5	0		Quincy	90	76	14
	New Baden	5	5	0		Rantoul	40	31	9
	New Lenox	43	39	4		Raymond	1	1	0
	Newman	1	1	0		Red Bud	6	6	0
	Newton	7	6	1		Richmond	4	4	0
	Niles	72	60	12		Richton Park	31	27	4
	Nokomis	5	4	1		Ridge Farm	1	1	0
	Normal	91	78	13		Ridgway	2	2	0
	Norridge	55	39	16		Riverdale	43	32	11
	North Aurora	31	29	2		River Forest	32	29	3
	Northbrook	89	63	26		River Grove	29	23	6
	North Chicago	74	56	18		Riverside	25	19	6
	Northfield	29	19	10		Robbins	19	6	13
	Northlake	53	36	17		Robinson	14	13	1
	North Pekin	3	3	0		Rochelle	28	21	7
	North Riverside	35	26	9		Rochester	8	8	0
	Oak Brook	60	44	16		Rockdale	4	4	0
	Oakbrook Terrace	22	19	3		Rock Falls	25	18	7
	Oak Forest	53	40	13		Rockford	336	304	32
	Oak Lawn	148	103	45		Rock Island	112	84	28
	Oak Park	140	125	15		Rockton	13	12	1
	Oblong	1	1	0		Rolling Meadows	80	54	26
	O'Fallon	61	45	16		Romeoville	84	64	20
	Oglesby	24	10	14		Roodhouse	4	4	0
	Okawville	2	2	0		Roscoe	15	13	2
	Olney	18	13	5		Roselle	52	37	15
	Olympia Fields	20	19	1		Rosemont	94	75	19
	Oregon	10	9	1		Rossville	2	2	0
	Orion	3	3	0		Round Lake	27	21	6
	Orland Hills	14	13	1		Round Lake Beach	50	41	9
	Orland Park	127	97	30		Round Lake Heights	4	4	0
	Oswego	56	48	8		Round Lake Park	13	11	2
	Ottawa	44	34	10		Roxana	6	5	1
	Palatine	136	109	27		Royalton	2	2	0
	Palestine	3	3	0		Rushville	5	5	0
	Palos Heights	27	26	1		Salem	22	14	8
	Palos Hills	35	33	2		Sandwich	19	13	6
	Palos Park	13	12	1		Sauget	16	15	1
	Pana	14	9	5		Sauk Village	32	24	8
	Paris	23	18	5		Savanna	8	8	0
	Park City	12	11	1		Schaumburg	194	130	64
	Park Forest	54	42	12		Schiller Park	38	33	5
	Park Ridge	74	60	14		Seneca	12	4	8
	Pawnee	10	6	4		Sesser	5	4	1
	Paxton	7	7	0		Shawneetown	4	4	0
	Pecatonica	4	4	0		Shelbyville	7	6	1
	Pekin	63	56	7		Sheridan	3	3	0
	Peoria	287	246	41		Sherman	6	6	0
	Peoria Heights	17	12	5		Shiloh	14	14	0
	Peotone	11	10	1		Shorewood	30	26	4
	Peru	28	21	7		Silvis	21	14	7
	Petersburg	5	5	0		Skokie	142	111	31
	Phoenix	3	1	2		Sleepy Hollow	7	6	1
	Pinckneyville	8	7	1		Smithton	5	5	0
	Piper City	1	1	0		Somonauk	3	3	0
	Pittsfield	6	6	0		South Barrington	18	15	3
	Plainfield	70	50	20		South Beloit	16	14	2
	Plano	19	17	2		South Chicago Heights	12	8	4
	Polo	4	4	0		South Elgin	38	29	9
	Pontiac	24	22	2		Southern View	4	4	0
	Pontoon Beach	20	14	6		South Holland	43	41	2
	Port Barrington	1	1	0		South Jacksonville	6	5	1
	Port Byron	2	2	0		South Pekin	2	2	0
	Posen	17	15	2		South Roxana	5	5	0
	Potomac	1	1	0					

Table 78. Full-Time Law Enforcement Employees, by City, 2006 (*Contd.*)

(Number.)

State	City	Total law enforcement employees	Total officers	Total civilians	State	City	Total law enforcement employees	Total officers	Total civilians
	Sparta	18	12	6		Wheeling	89	62	27
	Springfield	314	271	43		White Hall	7	4	3
	Spring Grove	12	10	2		Williamsfield	2	2	0
	Spring Valley	14	11	3		Williamsville	3	3	0
	St. Anne	3	3	0		Willowbrook	29	25	4
	Staunton	9	6	3		Willow Springs	21	16	5
	St. Charles	67	53	14		Wilmette	63	45	18
	Steger	24	17	7		Wilmington	18	12	6
	Sterling	43	30	13		Winchester	2	2	0
	St. Francisville	1	1	0		Winfield	23	21	2
	Stickney	22	16	6		Winnebago	6	6	0
	Stockton	4	4	0		Winnetka	37	28	9
	Stone Park	25	19	6		Winthrop Harbor	16	11	5
	Stonington	1	1	0		Witt	1	1	0
	Streamwood	70	58	12		Wonder Lake	2	1	1
	Streator	31	24	7		Wood Dale	50	33	17
	Sugar Grove	17	16	1		Woodhull	1	1	0
	Sullivan	10	8	2		Woodridge	79	55	24
	Summit	36	31	5		Wood River	25	19	6
	Sumner	2	2	0		Woodstock	51	38	13
	Swansea	27	20	7		Worden	1	1	0
	Sycamore	29	26	3		Worth	25	23	2
	Taylorville	28	22	6		Yates City	2	2	0
	Thomasboro	1	1	0		Yorkville	28	25	3
	Thomson	1	1	0		Zeigler	5	5	0
	Thornton	11	9	2		Zion	63	47	16
	Tilton	3	3	0	**INDIANA**	Albion	6	6	0
	Tinley Park	105	76	29		Alexandria	17	13	4
	Tolono	4	4	0		Anderson	139	117	22
	Tremont	3	3	0		Angola	21	17	4
	Trenton	5	5	0		Attica	6	6	0
	Troy	22	16	6		Auburn	30	23	7
	Tuscola	8	7	1		Bargersville	6	6	0
	University Park	19	16	3		Bedford	41	32	9
	Urbana	67	54	13		Beech Grove	41	30	11
	Valmeyer	2	2	0		Berne	8	7	1
	Vandalia	18	13	5		Bloomington	113	78	35
	Venice	15	11	4		Bluffton	31	20	11
	Vernon Hills	70	48	22		Boonville	15	14	1
	Vienna	4	4	0		Brazil	15	11	4
	Villa Grove	5	4	1		Bremen	16	12	4
	Villa Park	54	39	15		Brownsburg	52	36	16
	Virden	10	6	4		Burns Harbor	5	4	1
	Virginia	1	1	0		Carmel	115	96	19
	Wamac	4	4	0		Cedar Lake	21	16	5
	Warren	4	3	1		Charlestown	21	16	5
	Warrensburg	2	2	0		Chesterfield	7	6	1
	Warrenville	35	29	6		Chesterton	24	19	5
	Warsaw	3	3	0		Clarksville	43	34	9
	Washburn	2	2	0		Clinton	8	6	2
	Washington	27	19	8		Columbia City	20	18	2
	Washington Park	10	7	3		Columbus	85	78	7
	Waterloo	14	14	0		Connersville	33	31	2
	Waterman	2	2	0		Corydon	7	7	0
	Watseka	11	10	1		Crawfordsville	48	31	17
	Wauconda	37	24	13		Crown Point	48	37	11
	Waukegan	219	161	58		Culver	4	4	0
	Wayne	5	5	0		Danville	24	15	9
	Westchester	48	35	13		Decatur	21	17	4
	West Chicago	65	48	17		Delphi	11	7	4
	West City	8	4	4		Dyer	33	26	7
	West Dundee	24	21	3		East Chicago	124	108	16
	Western Springs	28	21	7		Edinburgh	15	10	5
	West Frankfort	15	11	4		Elkhart	141	118	23
	Westmont	56	42	14		Elwood	20	16	4
	West Salem	1	1	0		Evansville	318	287	31
	Westville	3	3	0		Fairmount	9	5	4
	Wheaton	93	70	23		Fishers	82	75	7

Table 78. Full-Time Law Enforcement Employees, by City, 2006 (*Contd.*)

(Number.)

State	City	Total law enforcement employees	Total officers	Total civilians	State	City	Total law enforcement employees	Total officers	Total civilians
	Fort Wayne	456	422	34		Shelbyville	52	41	11
	Frankfort	42	31	11		South Bend	328	257	71
	Franklin	53	37	16		South Whitley	4	4	0
	Garrett	16	12	4		Speedway	39	30	9
	Gary	342	264	78		St. John	22	17	5
	Gas City	15	11	4		Tell City	18	11	7
	Georgetown	4	4	0		Terre Haute	152	129	23
	Goshen	60	55	5		Tipton	14	12	2
	Greencastle	17	14	3		Union City	13	8	5
	Greendale	15	11	4		Vincennes	40	35	5
	Greenfield	46	35	11		Wabash	32	26	6
	Greensburg	27	18	9		Walkerton	12	7	5
	Greenwood	75	52	23		Warsaw	42	35	7
	Griffith	39	31	8		Washington	25	18	7
	Hagerstown	5	5	0		Waterloo	6	6	0
	Hammond	255	201	54		Westfield	38	33	5
	Hartford City	15	13	2		West Lafayette	57	42	15
	Hebron	8	7	1		West Terre Haute	11	10	1
	Highland	49	40	9		Westville	3	3	0
	Hobart	71	55	16		Whiting	25	18	7
	Huntington	46	35	11		Winchester	17	12	5
	Indianapolis	2,434	1,581	853		Winona Lake	5	5	0
	Jasonville	5	5	0	**IOWA**	Adel	9	8	1
	Jasper	28	20	8		Albia	7	6	1
	Kendallville	27	18	9		Algona	16	10	6
	Knox	8	8	0		Altoona	24	22	2
	Kokomo	143	104	39		Ames	71	49	22
	Lafayette	150	115	35		Anamosa	8	7	1
	Lake Station	31	26	5		Ankeny	50	43	7
	La Porte	52	42	10		Atlantic	14	12	2
	Lawrence	60	53	7		Audubon	3	3	0
	Lebanon	30	29	1		Belle Plaine	4	4	0
	Ligonier	10	9	1		Belmond	4	4	0
	Linton	16	11	5		Bettendorf	57	44	13
	Long Beach	6	5	1		Bloomfield	4	4	0
	Loogootee	5	4	1		Boone	18	17	1
	Lowell	18	13	5		Burlington	55	42	13
	Madison	33	25	8		Camanche	6	6	0
	Marion	86	69	17		Carlisle	5	5	0
	Martinsville	29	21	8		Carroll	16	15	1
	Merrillville	66	53	13		Carter Lake	10	9	1
	Michigan City	107	89	18		Cedar Falls	40	38	2
	Mishawaka	130	100	30		Cedar Rapids	223	189	34
	Monticello	17	12	5		Centerville	17	12	5
	Mooresville	27	21	6		Chariton	7	6	1
	Muncie	122	113	9		Charles City	18	12	6
	Munster	50	39	11		Cherokee	8	7	1
	Nappanee	22	15	7		Clarinda	13	9	4
	New Albany	68	65	3		Clarion	7	6	1
	New Castle	38	35	3		Clear Lake	18	13	5
	New Chicago	6	2	4		Clinton	55	46	9
	New Whiteland	11	6	5		Clive	26	23	3
	Noblesville	78	67	11		Coralville	34	30	4
	North Liberty	4	4	0		Council Bluffs	123	106	17
	North Manchester	15	11	4		Cresco	7	7	0
	North Vernon	21	18	3		Creston	16	12	4
	Plainfield	51	45	6		Davenport	205	160	45
	Plymouth	27	22	5		Decorah	19	12	7
	Portage	76	58	18		Denison	17	12	5
	Portland	17	13	4		Des Moines	491	373	118
	Princeton	17	16	1		De Witt	9	9	0
	Rensselaer	14	9	5		Dubuque	96	90	6
	Richmond	86	74	12		Dyersville	10	6	4
	Rushville	18	13	5		Eagle Grove	7	7	0
	Salem	17	12	5		Eldridge	7	7	0
	Schererville	63	49	14		Emmetsburg	7	6	1
	Scottsburg	13	13	0		Estherville	12	12	0
	Seymour	53	38	15		Evansdale	7	6	1

Table 78. Full-Time Law Enforcement Employees, by City, 2006 (*Contd.*)

(Number.)

State	City	Total law enforcement employees	Total officers	Total civilians	State	City	Total law enforcement employees	Total officers	Total civilians
	Fairfield	17	13	4		Urbandale	49	45	4
	Forest City	8	8	0		Vinton	8	8	0
	Fort Dodge	41	36	5		Washington	11	10	1
	Fort Madison	23	18	5		Waterloo	125	115	10
	Garner	5	5	0		Waukee	12	11	1
	Glenwood	10	9	1		Waukon	7	7	0
	Grinnell	16	14	2		Waverly	17	16	1
	Grundy Center	3	3	0		Webster City	17	13	4
	Hampton	11	6	5		West Burlington	11	10	1
	Harlan	9	8	1		West Des Moines	78	63	15
	Hawarden	4	4	0		West Liberty	7	6	1
	Hiawatha	13	12	1		West Union	4	4	0
	Humboldt	5	5	0		Williamsburg	6	6	0
	Independence	15	11	4		Wilton	4	4	0
	Indianola	20	18	2		Windsor Heights	14	13	1
	Iowa City	98	71	27		Winterset	8	8	0
	Iowa Falls	14	10	4	KANSAS	Abilene	16	14	2
	Jefferson	7	7	0		Andover	24	17	7
	Johnston	19	18	1		Anthony	5	5	0
	Keokuk	32	23	9		Arkansas City	34	26	8
	Knoxville	13	11	2		Atchison	25	23	2
	Le Claire	7	6	1		Attica	1	1	0
	Le Mars	16	14	2		Atwood	2	2	0
	Leon	3	3	0		Augusta	31	23	8
	Manchester	13	9	4		Baldwin City	9	8	1
	Maquoketa	17	11	6		Basehor	10	9	1
	Marion	47	38	9		Baxter Springs	15	9	6
	Marshalltown	59	42	17		Bel Aire	12	11	1
	Mason City	51	46	5		Belle Plaine	5	5	0
	Missouri Valley	6	6	0		Belleville	5	5	0
	Monticello	7	6	1		Beloit	9	8	1
	Mount Pleasant	16	14	2		Blue Rapids	1	1	0
	Mount Vernon	6	6	0		Bonner Springs	24	23	1
	Muscatine	40	37	3		Burden	1	1	0
	Nevada	9	8	1		Burlingame	2	2	0
	New Hampton	7	7	0		Burlington	7	7	0
	Newton	30	24	6		Bushton	1	1	0
	North Liberty	6	6	0		Caldwell	4	4	0
	Norwalk	13	11	2		Caney	10	6	4
	Oelwein	15	10	5		Canton	2	2	0
	Ogden	3	3	0		Carbondale	3	3	0
	Onawa	6	6	0		Cawker City	1	1	0
	Orange City	7	7	0		Chanute	24	20	4
	Osage	3	3	0		Chapman	4	4	0
	Osceola	11	10	1		Chase	1	1	0
	Oskaloosa	19	17	2		Cheney	4	4	0
	Ottumwa	42	35	7		Cherokee	1	1	0
	Pella	17	13	4		Cherryvale	4	4	0
	Perry	20	14	6		Chetopa	4	4	0
	Pleasant Hill	15	14	1		Claflin	2	2	0
	Polk City	6	6	0		Clearwater	6	6	0
	Red Oak	13	11	2		Coffeyville	33	26	7
	Rock Rapids	2	2	0		Colby	16	11	5
	Rock Valley	4	4	0		Coldwater	1	1	0
	Sac City	4	4	0		Columbus	11	9	2
	Sergeant Bluff	9	8	1		Colwich	3	3	0
	Sheldon	7	7	0		Concordia	16	10	6
	Shenandoah	8	5	3		Conway Springs	2	2	0
	Sioux Center	7	7	0		Council Grove	6	6	0
	Sioux City	155	125	30		Derby	50	36	14
	Spencer	26	18	8		Dodge City	58	44	14
	Spirit Lake	10	9	1		Eastborough	6	6	0
	St. Ansgar	1	1	0		Edwardsville	17	16	1
	State Center	1	1	0		El Dorado	26	24	2
	Storm Lake	21	17	4		Ellinwood	5	5	0
	Story City	5	5	0		Ellis	5	5	0
	Tama	5	5	0		Ellsworth	6	5	1
	Tipton	6	6	0		Elwood	5	5	0

Table 78. Full-Time Law Enforcement Employees, by City, 2006 (*Contd.*)

(Number.)

State	City	Total law enforcement employees	Total officers	Total civilians	State	City	Total law enforcement employees	Total officers	Total civilians
	Emporia	66	45	21		Meade	3	3	0
	Enterprise	1	1	0		Medicine Lodge	7	6	1
	Erie	2	2	0		Merriam	32	28	4
	Eudora	10	9	1		Minneapolis	5	5	0
	Fairway	11	9	2		Mission	32	30	2
	Florence	2	1	1		Moran	1	1	0
	Fort Scott	23	20	3		Moundridge	3	3	0
	Fredonia	6	5	1		Mount Hope	2	2	0
	Frontenac	9	6	3		Mulvane	17	11	6
	Galena	11	7	4		Neodesha	8	7	1
	Garden City	80	51	29		Newton	36	32	4
	Garden Plain	3	3	0		Nickerson	2	2	0
	Gardner	33	30	3		North Newton	2	2	0
	Garnett	13	9	4		Norwich	1	1	0
	Girard	6	6	0		Oakley	11	6	5
	Goddard	6	6	0		Oberlin	4	4	0
	Goodland	11	10	1		Olathe	202	164	38
	Grandview Plaza	5	5	0		Osage City	6	6	0
	Great Bend	33	29	4		Osawatomie	16	10	6
	Halstead	6	5	1		Osborne	4	4	0
	Harper	3	3	0		Oswego	5	5	0
	Hays	48	31	17		Ottawa	34	27	7
	Haysville	29	22	7		Overbrook	2	2	0
	Herington	7	6	1		Overland Park	294	240	54
	Hesston	7	6	1		Oxford	4	4	0
	Hiawatha	8	7	1		Paola	22	16	6
	Hill City	3	3	0		Park City	21	19	2
	Hillsboro	5	5	0		Parsons	29	23	6
	Hoisington	9	7	2		Perry	1	1	0
	Holcomb	4	3	1		Pittsburg	50	39	11
	Holton	12	8	4		Plainville	5	5	0
	Horton	10	6	4		Pleasanton	2	2	0
	Hugoton	8	7	1		Prairie Village	57	45	12
	Humboldt	6	6	0		Pratt	19	14	5
	Hutchinson	102	69	33		Protection	1	1	0
	Independence	31	22	9		Quinter	1	1	0
	Inman	2	2	0		Richmond	1	1	0
	Iola	23	14	9		Roeland Park	17	15	2
	Junction City	67	49	18		Rolla	1	1	0
	Kansas City	472	357	115		Rose Hill	10	9	1
	Kechi	4	4	0		Rossville	3	3	0
	Kingman	6	6	0		Russell	18	8	10
	Kiowa	2	2	0		Salina	104	75	29
	La Crosse	3	3	0		Scranton	1	1	0
	La Cygne	2	2	0		Sedgwick	2	2	0
	La Harpe	2	2	0		Seneca	6	6	0
	Lake Quivira	3	3	0		Shawnee	110	90	20
	Lansing	16	15	1		Silver Lake	2	2	0
	Larned	12	8	4		Smith Center	3	3	0
	Lawrence	174	139	35		South Hutchinson	9	7	2
	Leavenworth	87	63	24		Spearville	1	1	0
	Leawood	77	57	20		Spring Hill	12	10	2
	Lebo	2	2	0		Stafford	4	4	0
	Lenexa	127	83	44		Sterling	5	5	0
	Le Roy	1	1	0		St. Francis	5	4	1
	Lewis	1	1	0		St. George	1	1	0
	Liberal	48	37	11		St. John	4	4	0
	Lindsborg	7	6	1		St. Marys	5	5	0
	Linn Valley	2	2	0		Stockton	5	5	0
	Little River	1	1	0		Tonganoxie	9	8	1
	Louisburg	9	9	0		Topeka	349	294	55
	Lyndon	3	3	0		Towanda	3	3	0
	Lyons	8	7	1		Udall	3	3	0
	Macksville	1	1	0		Ulysses	12	11	1
	Maize	7	6	1		Valley Falls	2	2	0
	Marion	5	5	0		Victoria	1	1	0
	Marysville	8	7	1		Wa Keeney	5	5	0
	McPherson	34	28	6					

Table 78. Full-Time Law Enforcement Employees, by City, 2006 (*Contd.*)

(Number.)

State	City	Total law enforcement employees	Total officers	Total civilians	State	City	Total law enforcement employees	Total officers	Total civilians
	Wakefield	1	1	0		Dawson Springs	9	5	4
	Walton	1	1	0		Dayton	8	8	0
	Wamego	11	7	4		Earlington	2	2	0
	Wathena	2	2	0		Eddyville	6	6	0
	Waverly	1	1	0		Edgewood	12	12	0
	Wellington	19	16	3		Edmonton	7	7	0
	Wellsville	3	3	0		Elizabethtown	59	43	16
	Westwood	8	7	1		Elkhorn City	3	2	1
	Wichita	830	640	190		Elkton	5	5	0
	Winfield	30	22	8		Elsmere	10	9	1
	Yates Center	3	3	0		Eminence	6	6	0
KENTUCKY	Adairville	1	1	0		Erlanger	44	37	7
	Albany	9	8	1		Eubank	1	1	0
	Alexandria	16	13	3		Evarts	4	4	0
	Allen	1	1	0		Falmouth	8	7	1
	Anchorage	15	10	5		Flatwoods	11	10	1
	Ashland	54	46	8		Fleming-Neon	1	1	0
	Auburn	2	2	0		Flemingsburg	7	7	0
	Audubon Park	8	7	1		Florence	62	58	4
	Augusta	3	3	0		Fort Mitchell	14	13	1
	Barbourville	18	14	4		Fort Thomas	24	23	1
	Bardstown	29	23	6		Fort Wright	12	11	1
	Bardwell	1	1	0		Frankfort	73	68	5
	Beattyville	7	5	2		Franklin	23	22	1
	Beaver Dam	7	7	0		Fulton	13	9	4
	Bellefonte	4	4	0		Gamaliel	1	1	0
	Bellevue	11	10	1		Georgetown	57	50	7
	Benham	4	4	0		Glasgow	48	36	12
	Benton	9	7	2		Glencoe	1	1	0
	Berea	33	26	7		Graymoor-Devondale	3	3	0
	Bloomfield	1	1	0		Grayson	8	8	0
	Booneville	3	3	0		Greensburg	7	7	0
	Bowling Green	134	99	35		Greenup	3	3	0
	Brandenburg	4	4	0		Greenville	9	9	0
	Brodhead	1	1	0		Guthrie	4	4	0
	Brooksville	1	1	0		Hardinsburg	3	3	0
	Brownsville	4	4	0		Harlan	13	10	3
	Burgin	1	1	0		Harrodsburg	25	17	8
	Burkesville	9	5	4		Hartford	6	6	0
	Burnside	5	5	0		Hawesville	1	1	0
	Butler	1	1	0		Hazard	25	20	5
	Cadiz	9	8	1		Henderson	66	58	8
	Calhoun	1	1	0		Hickman	2	2	0
	Calvert City	7	6	1		Highland Heights	10	10	0
	Campbellsburg	1	1	0		Hillview	12	12	0
	Campbellsville	23	21	2		Hindman	2	1	1
	Campton	1	1	0		Hodgenville	7	7	0
	Caneyville	1	1	0		Hopkinsville	80	72	8
	Carlisle	8	4	4		Horse Cave	5	5	0
	Carrollton	9	9	0		Hustonville	1	1	0
	Catlettsburg	8	8	0		Hyden	8	8	0
	Cave City	7	7	0		Independence	29	28	1
	Central City	12	12	0		Indian Hills	10	10	0
	Clarkson	2	2	0		Inez	3	3	0
	Clay	1	1	0		Irvine	6	6	0
	Clay City	2	2	0		Irvington	4	4	0
	Clinton	4	4	0		Jackson	14	12	2
	Cloverport	2	2	0		Jamestown	5	5	0
	Cold Spring	11	11	0		Jeffersontown	59	50	9
	Columbia	10	10	0		Jenkins	6	5	1
	Corbin	29	21	8		Junction City	3	3	0
	Covington	129	106	23		La Center	3	2	1
	Crab Orchard	1	1	0		La Grange	12	12	0
	Crescent Springs	8	8	0		Lakeside Park-Crestview Hills	9	8	1
	Crofton	1	1	0		Lancaster	9	9	0
	Cumberland	6	6	0		Lawrenceburg	24	17	7
	Cynthiana	16	15	1					
	Danville	31	29	2					

Table 78. Full-Time Law Enforcement Employees, by City, 2006 (Contd.)

(Number.)

State	City	Total law enforcement employees	Total officers	Total civilians	State	City	Total law enforcement employees	Total officers	Total civilians
	Lebanon	22	15	7		Russell Springs	9	8	1
	Lebanon Junction	5	5	0		Russellville	26	24	2
	Leitchfield	17	16	1		Sadieville	1	1	0
	Lewisburg	1	1	0		Salyersville	2	2	0
	Lewisport	2	2	0		Science Hill	2	2	0
	Lexington	641	553	88		Scottsville	13	13	0
	Liberty	4	4	0		Sebree	2	2	0
	London	35	32	3		Shelbyville	23	22	1
	Lone Oak	2	2	0		Shepherdsville	21	20	1
	Louisa	8	8	0		Shively	25	20	5
	Louisville Metro	1,408	1,206	202		Silver Grove	1	1	0
	Loyall	1	1	0		Smiths Grove	3	3	0
	Ludlow	11	10	1		Somerset	36	33	3
	Lynch	2	2	0		Southgate	7	7	0
	Lynnview	2	2	0		South Shore	2	2	0
	Madisonville	48	40	8		Springfield	12	8	4
	Manchester	13	13	0		Stamping Ground	1	1	0
	Marion	6	6	0		Stanford	6	6	0
	Martin	3	3	0		Stanton	8	8	0
	Mayfield	32	24	8		St. Matthews	36	30	6
	Maysville	30	22	8		Sturgis	4	4	0
	Middlesboro	28	24	4		Taylor Mill	11	10	1
	Millersburg	1	1	0		Taylorsville	4	4	0
	Monticello	9	9	0		Tompkinsville	10	8	2
	Morehead	29	19	10		Uniontown	2	2	0
	Morganfield	13	8	5		Vanceburg	5	5	0
	Morgantown	4	4	0		Versailles	48	38	10
	Mortons Gap	1	1	0		Villa Hills	9	8	1
	Mount Olivet	1	1	0		Vine Grove	8	8	0
	Mount Sterling	25	23	2		Wallins	1	1	0
	Mount Vernon	8	8	0		Warsaw	6	6	0
	Mount Washington	17	16	1		Wayland	1	1	0
	Muldraugh	3	3	0		West Buechel	8	8	0
	Munfordville	4	4	0		West Liberty	13	6	7
	Murray	38	32	6		West Point	3	3	0
	New Castle	1	1	0		Wheelwright	1	1	0
	New Haven	1	1	0		Whitesburg	6	6	0
	Newport	53	49	4		Wilder	7	7	0
	Nicholasville	60	53	7		Williamsburg	13	12	1
	Nortonville	1	1	0		Williamstown	7	6	1
	Oak Grove	17	13	4		Wilmore	8	7	1
	Olive Hill	6	6	0		Winchester	49	34	15
	Owensboro	129	100	29		Wingo	1	1	0
	Owenton	4	4	0		Worthington	4	4	0
	Owingsville	6	6	0		Wurtland	1	1	0
	Paducah	86	72	14	LOUISIANA	Abbeville	39	37	2
	Paintsville	12	11	1		Addis	7	6	1
	Paris	32	23	9		Alexandria	185	152	33
	Park City	1	1	0		Amite	25	20	5
	Park Hills	5	5	0		Baker	35	34	1
	Pembroke	1	1	0		Baldwin	8	7	1
	Perryville	1	1	0		Ball	7	6	1
	Pewee Valley	1	1	0		Basile	11	7	4
	Pikeville	31	22	9		Bastrop	39	36	3
	Pineville	8	8	0		Baton Rouge	786	699	87
	Pioneer Village	5	5	0		Bernice	4	4	0
	Pippa Passes	1	1	0		Berwick	11	11	0
	Pleasureville	1	1	0		Blanchard	4	4	0
	Powderly	1	1	0		Bogalusa	63	38	25
	Prestonsburg	16	16	0		Bossier City	238	198	40
	Princeton	15	14	1		Brusly	8	7	1
	Prospect	10	9	1		Cheneyville	5	4	1
	Providence	5	5	0		Clinton	8	7	1
	Raceland	5	5	0		Coushatta	5	5	0
	Radcliff	51	38	13		Covington	39	30	9
	Ravenna	2	2	0		Crowley	40	35	5
	Richmond	81	59	22		Delhi	10	6	4
	Russell	12	12	0		Denham Springs	35	27	8

Table 78. Full-Time Law Enforcement Employees, by City, 2006 (Contd.)

(Number.)

State	City	Total law enforcement employees	Total officers	Total civilians	State	City	Total law enforcement employees	Total officers	Total civilians
	De Quincy	14	14	0		Thibodaux	60	51	9
	De Ridder	28	23	5		Tickfaw	7	7	0
	Dixie Inn	2	2	0		Vidalia	24	24	0
	Erath	12	8	4		Vinton	14	11	3
	Farmerville	12	12	0		Vivian	15	10	5
	Folsom	4	3	1		Westlake	21	20	1
	Franklin	24	23	1		West Monroe	81	77	4
	French Settlement	2	2	0		Westwego	41	40	1
	Golden Meadow	5	3	2		Winnfield	23	14	9
	Gonzales	35	35	0		Woodworth	7	5	2
	Grambling	15	10	5		Zachary	40	37	3
	Gramercy	7	7	0	**MAINE**	Ashland	2	2	0
	Gretna	109	85	24		Auburn	50	46	4
	Hammond	102	78	24		Augusta	56	41	15
	Harahan	30	30	0		Baileyville	7	7	0
	Haughton	10	7	3		Bangor	89	71	18
	Homer	10	10	0		Bar Harbor	13	9	4
	Houma	93	75	18		Bath	24	19	5
	Iowa	14	10	4		Belfast	14	12	2
	Jackson	4	4	0		Berwick	12	11	1
	Jeanerette	14	10	4		Bethel	4	4	0
	Jena	7	6	1		Biddeford	64	42	22
	Jennings	35	26	9		Boothbay Harbor	8	7	1
	Jonesboro	15	11	4		Brewer	22	20	2
	Kaplan	15	15	0		Bridgton	12	8	4
	Kenner	222	174	48		Brownville	2	2	0
	Kentwood	9	8	1		Brunswick	48	33	15
	Kinder	18	18	0		Bucksport	11	7	4
	Lafayette	289	228	61		Buxton	15	9	6
	Lake Charles	184	179	5		Calais	12	8	4
	Lake Providence	11	7	4		Camden	15	11	4
	Lecompte	3	3	0		Cape Elizabeth	17	13	4
	Leesville	33	32	1		Caribou	15	14	1
	Mandeville	44	31	13		Carrabassett Valley	1	1	0
	Mansfield	15	11	4		Clinton	3	3	0
	Many	13	11	2		Cumberland	12	11	1
	Marksville	23	18	5		Damariscotta	6	5	1
	McNary	2	1	1		Dexter	6	5	1
	Minden	33	32	1		Dixfield	4	4	0
	Monroe	225	176	49		Dover-Foxcroft	5	5	0
	Morgan City	57	54	3		East Millinocket	4	4	0
	Napoleonville	2	2	0		Eastport	4	4	0
	Natchitoches	61	46	15		Eliot	8	7	1
	Newllano	14	13	1		Ellsworth	19	15	4
	New Orleans	1,644	1,424	220		Fairfield	12	11	1
	New Roads	24	23	1		Falmouth	23	16	7
	Olla	4	4	0		Farmington	15	14	1
	Patterson	18	18	0		Fort Fairfield	4	4	0
	Pearl River	13	9	4		Fort Kent	8	4	4
	Pineville	63	55	8		Freeport	17	12	5
	Plaquemine	35	27	8		Fryeburg	5	5	0
	Pollock	2	2	0		Gardiner	13	11	2
	Ponchatoula	24	20	4		Gorham	23	21	2
	Port Allen	23	19	4		Gouldsboro	2	2	0
	Port Barre	14	8	6		Greenville	4	3	1
	Rayville	9	8	1		Hallowell	4	4	0
	Richwood	17	10	7		Hampden	12	11	1
	Ruston	48	40	8		Holden	2	2	0
	Scott	19	18	1		Houlton	17	12	5
	Shreveport	683	598	85		Jay	11	7	4
	Slidell	103	69	34		Kennebunk	28	20	8
	Sorrento	5	4	1		Kennebunkport	17	12	5
	Springhill	16	15	1		Kittery	27	20	7
	Sterlington	8	8	0		Lewiston	94	80	14
	St. Gabriel	14	8	6		Limestone	3	3	0
	St. Martinville	16	10	6		Lincoln	7	6	1
	Sulphur	65	44	21		Lisbon	21	16	5
	Tallulah	18	18	0		Livermore Falls	10	6	4

Table 78. Full-Time Law Enforcement Employees, by City, 2006 (*Contd.*)

(Number.)

State	City	Total law enforcement employees	Total officers	Total civilians	State	City	Total law enforcement employees	Total officers	Total civilians
	Machias	4	4	0		Capitol Heights	11	9	2
	Madawaska	7	6	1		Centreville	10	9	1
	Madison	8	7	1		Chestertown	13	12	1
	Mechanic Falls	5	5	0		Cheverly	14	12	2
	Mexico	5	5	0		Cottage City	6	5	1
	Milbridge	3	3	0		Crisfield	13	9	4
	Millinocket	9	9	0		Cumberland	51	49	2
	Milo	3	3	0		Delmar	13	12	1
	Monmouth	4	4	0		Denton	12	11	1
	Mount Desert	10	6	4		District Heights	13	10	3
	Newport	6	6	0		Easton	60	46	14
	North Berwick	10	9	1		Edmonston	7	7	0
	Norway	7	6	1		Elkton	44	33	11
	Oakland	10	9	1		Fairmount Heights	2	2	0
	Ogunquit	12	10	2		Federalsburg	9	8	1
	Old Orchard Beach	25	18	7		Forest Heights	8	7	1
	Old Town	15	14	1		Frederick	165	128	37
	Orono	13	13	0		Frostburg	19	15	4
	Oxford	5	4	1		Fruitland	14	13	1
	Paris	8	7	1		Glenarden	7	6	1
	Phippsburg	1	1	0		Greenbelt	65	54	11
	Pittsfield	7	6	1		Greensboro	4	4	0
	Portland	218	165	53		Hagerstown	117	97	20
	Presque Isle	22	19	3		Hampstead	10	8	2
	Rangeley	3	3	0		Hancock	5	4	1
	Richmond	5	5	0		Havre de Grace	38	29	9
	Rockland	22	19	3		Hurlock	10	9	1
	Rockport	7	6	1		Hyattsville	43	33	10
	Rumford	19	14	5		Landover Hills	4	3	1
	Sabattus	8	7	1		La Plata	11	10	1
	Saco	46	34	12		Laurel	68	52	16
	Sanford	53	40	13		Luke	1	1	0
	Scarborough	48	33	15		Manchester	5	5	0
	Searsport	3	3	0		Morningside	7	6	1
	Skowhegan	13	13	0		Mount Rainier	16	14	2
	South Berwick	12	8	4		New Carrollton	10	8	2
	South Portland	65	49	16		North East	8	7	1
	Southwest Harbor	5	5	0		Oakland	7	6	1
	Swan's Island	1	1	0		Ocean City	118	99	19
	Thomaston	5	5	0		Ocean Pines	16	12	4
	Topsham	15	14	1		Oxford	3	3	0
	Van Buren	4	4	0		Perryville	3	2	1
	Veazie	6	6	0		Pocomoke City	21	14	7
	Waldoboro	7	6	1		Port Deposit	2	2	0
	Washburn	2	2	0		Princess Anne	13	12	1
	Waterville	39	30	9		Ridgely	5	5	0
	Wells	31	23	8		Rising Sun	6	5	1
	Westbrook	34	31	3		Riverdale Park	24	18	6
	Wilton	5	5	0		Rock Hall	4	4	0
	Windham	38	27	11		Salisbury	109	83	26
	Winslow	11	9	2		Seat Pleasant	16	14	2
	Winter Harbor	1	1	0		Smithsburg	4	3	1
	Winthrop	12	8	4		Snow Hill	7	6	1
	Wiscasset	5	4	1		St. Michaels	6	5	1
	Yarmouth	20	12	8		Sykesville	7	6	1
	York	38	27	11		Takoma Park	50	36	14
MARYLAND	Aberdeen	52	42	10		Taneytown	12	11	1
	Annapolis	158	115	43		Thurmont	11	10	1
	Baltimore	3,712	2,974	738		University Park	8	8	0
	Baltimore City Sheriff	153	125	28		Upper Marlboro	5	5	0
	Bel Air	41	30	11		Westernport	3	3	0
	Berlin	16	11	5		Westminster	57	43	14
	Berwyn Heights	8	7	1	MASSACHU-SETTS				
	Bladensburg	22	17	5		Abington	30	28	2
	Boonsboro	3	3	0		Acton	42	33	9
	Brunswick	9	7	2		Acushnet	20	18	2
	Cambridge	59	47	12		Adams	20	16	4
						Agawam	60	52	8

Table 78. Full-Time Law Enforcement Employees, by City, 2006 (*Contd.*)

(Number.)

State	City	Total law enforcement employees	Total officers	Total civilians	State	City	Total law enforcement employees	Total officers	Total civilians
	Amesbury	37	31	6		Easthampton	27	26	1
	Amherst	56	49	7		East Longmeadow	22	21	1
	Andover	71	52	19		Easton	34	30	4
	Aquinnah	4	4	0		Edgartown	17	16	1
	Arlington	77	61	16		Egremont	2	2	0
	Ashburnham	13	9	4		Erving	4	4	0
	Ashby	6	6	0		Essex	12	8	4
	Ashfield	2	2	0		Everett	107	97	10
	Ashland	31	27	4		Fairhaven	38	32	6
	Athol	22	16	6		Fall River	300	244	56
	Attleboro	91	78	13		Falmouth	72	64	8
	Auburn	45	35	10		Fitchburg	111	91	20
	Avon	18	15	3		Foxborough	29	26	3
	Ayer	22	17	5		Framingham	123	115	8
	Barnstable	134	115	19		Franklin	57	46	11
	Barre	12	8	4		Freetown	17	17	0
	Becket	2	2	0		Gardner	42	32	10
	Bedford	36	28	8		Georgetown	14	12	2
	Belchertown	21	16	5		Gill	3	3	0
	Bellingham	38	30	8		Gloucester	66	61	5
	Belmont	59	45	14		Goshen	3	2	1
	Berkley	8	7	1		Grafton	23	18	5
	Berlin	11	7	4		Granby	12	10	2
	Beverly	71	68	3		Granville	1	1	0
	Billerica	85	65	20		Great Barrington	14	13	1
	Blackstone	19	16	3		Greenfield	47	35	12
	Bolton	14	9	5		Groton	22	17	5
	Boston	2,625	2,056	569		Groveland	13	8	5
	Bourne	43	38	5		Hadley	15	11	4
	Boxborough	15	10	5		Halifax	15	11	4
	Boxford	15	13	2		Hamilton	15	15	0
	Boylston	12	9	3		Hampden	12	9	3
	Braintree	80	72	8		Hanover	30	28	2
	Brewster	18	15	3		Hanson	26	20	6
	Bridgewater	36	35	1		Hardwick	3	3	0
	Brockton	212	185	27		Harwich	37	31	6
	Brookfield	2	2	0		Hatfield	1	1	0
	Brookline	156	136	20		Haverhill	101	91	10
	Buckland	2	2	0		Hingham	57	47	10
	Burlington	69	61	8		Hinsdale	1	1	0
	Cambridge	300	265	35		Holbrook	19	18	1
	Canton	46	45	1		Holden	26	23	3
	Carlisle	10	10	0		Holland	2	2	0
	Carver	21	18	3		Holliston	23	22	1
	Charlton	23	19	4		Holyoke	138	121	17
	Chatham	25	19	6		Hopedale	16	12	4
	Chelmsford	69	53	16		Hopkinton	25	20	5
	Chelsea	90	84	6		Hubbardston	10	6	4
	Chicopee	128	125	3		Hudson	37	31	6
	Clinton	32	27	5		Hull	33	24	9
	Cohasset	24	18	6		Ipswich	25	24	1
	Concord	42	35	7		Kingston	32	24	8
	Dalton	13	12	1		Lakeville	21	16	5
	Danvers	59	46	13		Lancaster	11	10	1
	Dartmouth	75	60	15		Lanesboro	6	6	0
	Dedham	70	60	10		Lawrence	195	158	37
	Deerfield	7	6	1		Lee	12	11	1
	Dennis	51	41	10		Leicester	22	17	5
	Dighton	10	10	0		Lenox	10	10	0
	Douglas	18	13	5		Leominster	91	75	16
	Dover	16	16	0		Leverett	1	1	0
	Dracut	46	41	5		Lexington	61	47	14
	Dudley	16	12	4		Lincoln	19	13	6
	Dunstable	7	7	0		Littleton	18	13	5
	Duxbury	38	30	8		Longmeadow	33	27	6
	East Bridgewater	26	23	3		Lowell	322	240	82
	East Brookfield	4	4	0		Ludlow	36	31	5
	Eastham	21	15	6		Lunenburg	13	13	0

Table 78. Full-Time Law Enforcement Employees, by City, 2006 (*Contd.*)

(Number.)

State	City	Total law enforcement employees	Total officers	Total civilians	State	City	Total law enforcement employees	Total officers	Total civilians
	Lynn	203	183	20		Princeton	8	5	3
	Lynnfield	24	19	5		Provincetown	25	18	7
	Malden	112	105	7		Quincy	230	200	30
	Manchester-by-the-Sea	18	16	2		Randolph	51	51	0
	Mansfield	43	31	12		Raynham	34	26	8
	Marblehead	38	29	9		Reading	49	39	10
	Marion	14	14	0		Rehoboth	28	23	5
	Marlborough	71	60	11		Revere	105	97	8
	Marshfield	45	42	3		Rochester	10	10	0
	Mashpee	46	38	8		Rockland	41	33	8
	Mattapoisett	18	18	0		Rockport	19	16	3
	Maynard	22	20	2		Rowley	16	14	2
	Medfield	23	18	5		Royalston	1	1	0
	Medford	111	106	5		Russell	1	1	0
	Medway	20	19	1		Rutland	9	8	1
	Melrose	41	40	1		Salem	89	84	5
	Mendon	17	13	4		Salisbury	19	15	4
	Merrimac	11	7	4		Sandwich	35	34	1
	Methuen	105	88	17		Saugus	74	56	18
	Middleboro	44	40	4		Scituate	35	30	5
	Middleton	13	12	1		Seekonk	33	31	2
	Milford	50	45	5		Sharon	31	27	4
	Millbury	24	20	4		Sheffield	6	6	0
	Millis	18	14	4		Shelburne	2	2	0
	Millville	7	4	3		Sherborn	14	14	0
	Milton	62	55	7		Shirley	16	12	4
	Monson	17	12	5		Shrewsbury	57	42	15
	Montague	20	15	5		Somerset	37	31	6
	Monterey	2	2	0		Somerville	153	130	23
	Nahant	13	12	1		Southampton	7	7	0
	Nantucket	39	34	5		Southborough	21	16	5
	Natick	65	53	12		Southbridge	36	34	2
	Needham	56	44	12		South Hadley	33	28	5
	New Bedford	344	292	52		Southwick	20	16	4
	New Braintree	1	1	0		Spencer	21	17	4
	Newbury	14	12	2		Springfield	541	445	96
	Newburyport	33	30	3		Sterling	17	12	5
	Newton	195	152	43		Stockbridge	6	6	0
	Norfolk	18	17	1		Stoneham	42	34	8
	Northampton	63	55	8		Stoughton	59	52	7
	North Adams	30	25	5		Stow	11	11	0
	North Andover	51	38	13		Sturbridge	23	17	6
	North Attleboro	59	47	12		Sudbury	35	29	6
	Northborough	26	20	6		Sunderland	5	5	0
	Northbridge	24	19	5		Sutton	20	15	5
	North Brookfield	6	6	0		Swampscott	36	34	2
	Northfield	4	3	1		Swansea	35	29	6
	North Reading	31	30	1		Taunton	116	112	4
	Norton	29	28	1		Templeton	13	8	5
	Norwell	23	18	5		Tewksbury	60	56	4
	Norwood	73	62	11		Tisbury	13	12	1
	Oak Bluffs	16	14	2		Topsfield	12	10	2
	Oakham	3	3	0		Townsend	18	16	2
	Orange	13	12	1		Truro	17	12	5
	Orleans	27	21	6		Tyngsboro	27	20	7
	Oxford	23	19	4		Upton	18	13	5
	Palmer	25	20	5		Uxbridge	23	18	5
	Paxton	13	9	4		Wakefield	42	41	1
	Peabody	113	97	16		Walpole	45	40	5
	Pembroke	29	27	2		Waltham	180	148	32
	Pepperell	18	17	1		Ware	16	16	0
	Petersham	2	2	0		Wareham	59	48	11
	Phillipston	3	2	1		Warren	12	7	5
	Pittsfield	104	84	20		Watertown	79	68	11
	Plainville	20	15	5		Wayland	30	21	9
	Plymouth	116	100	16		Webster	30	26	4
	Plympton	6	6	0		Wellesley	55	40	15
						Wellfleet	17	13	4

Table 78. Full-Time Law Enforcement Employees, by City, 2006 *(Contd.)*

(Number.)

State	City	Total law enforcement employees	Total officers	Total civilians	State	City	Total law enforcement employees	Total officers	Total civilians
	Wenham	11	10	1		Bridgeport Township	9	8	1
	Westborough	33	26	7		Bridgman	4	4	0
	West Boylston	18	13	5		Brighton	17	15	2
	West Bridgewater	22	21	1		Bronson	5	5	0
	West Brookfield	6	6	0		Brown City	2	2	0
	Westfield	90	79	11		Brownstown Township	52	41	11
	Westford	49	40	9		Buchanan	10	9	1
	Westminster	16	12	4		Buena Vista Township	17	15	2
	West Newbury	14	7	7		Burr Oak	1	1	0
	Weston	31	25	6		Burton	43	38	5
	Westport	33	29	4		Cadillac	19	16	3
	West Springfield	90	81	9		Calumet	1	1	0
	West Tisbury	10	9	1		Cambridge Township	4	3	1
	Westwood	31	25	6		Canton Township	112	76	36
	Weymouth	116	101	15		Capac	3	3	0
	Whately	2	2	0		Carleton	4	3	1
	Whitman	25	24	1		Caro	9	8	1
	Wilbraham	28	27	1		Carrollton Township	8	7	1
	Williamsburg	1	1	0		Carsonville	1	1	0
	Williamstown	14	11	3		Caseville	2	2	0
	Wilmington	48	46	2		Caspian	1	1	0
	Winchendon	17	12	5		Cass City	4	4	0
	Winchester	46	38	8		Cassopolis	5	5	0
	Winthrop	35	33	2		Cedar Springs	7	7	0
	Woburn	80	74	6		Center Line	30	26	4
	Worcester	516	464	52		Central Lake	1	1	0
	Wrentham	18	16	2		Charlevoix	7	7	0
	Yarmouth	69	59	10		Charlotte	19	18	1
MICHIGAN	Adrian	37	33	4		Cheboygan	10	9	1
	Adrian Township	2	2	0		Chelsea	14	10	4
	Albion	30	23	7		Chesterfield Township	64	48	16
	Algonac	9	8	1		Chikaming Township	5	4	1
	Allegan	12	11	1		Chocolay Township	5	4	1
	Allen Park	47	42	5		Clare	9	8	1
	Alma	14	13	1		Clarkston	2	2	0
	Almont	9	9	0		Clawson	18	17	1
	Alpena	20	18	2		Clayton Township	7	5	2
	Ann Arbor	222	155	67		Clay Township	16	12	4
	Argentine Township	8	7	1		Clinton	4	4	0
	Armada	2	2	0		Clinton Township	135	103	32
	Auburn	3	2	1		Clio	7	6	1
	Auburn Hills	69	55	14		Coldwater	19	18	1
	Bad Axe	9	9	0		Coleman	2	2	0
	Bangor	5	5	0		Coloma Township	10	8	2
	Baraga	3	3	0		Colon	3	3	0
	Bath Township	11	10	1		Columbia Township	4	4	0
	Battle Creek	132	113	19		Concord	2	2	0
	Bay City	67	61	6		Constantine	7	6	1
	Beaverton	1	1	0		Corunna	4	3	1
	Belding	10	8	2		Covert Township	6	6	0
	Bellaire	3	3	0		Croswell	6	6	0
	Belleville	12	10	2		Crystal Falls	4	4	0
	Benton Harbor	42	31	11		Davison	11	9	2
	Benton Township	36	25	11		Davison Township	20	18	2
	Berkley	51	35	16		Dearborn	203	191	12
	Berrien Springs-Oronoko Township	8	7	1		Dearborn Heights	109	86	23
	Beverly Hills	29	25	4		Decatur	4	4	0
	Big Rapids	18	17	1		Denmark Township	1	1	0
	Birch Run	6	5	1		Denton Township	4	4	0
	Birmingham	51	35	16		Detroit	3,509	3,164	345
	Blackman Township	29	28	1		Dewitt	7	6	1
	Blissfield	6	6	0		Dewitt Township	15	14	1
	Bloomfield Hills	28	24	4		Douglas	9	8	1
	Bloomfield Township	95	71	24		Dowagiac	16	15	1
	Bloomingdale	1	1	0		Dryden Township	4	4	0
	Boyne City	8	7	1		Durand	6	6	0
	Breckenridge	2	2	0					

Table 78. Full-Time Law Enforcement Employees, by City, 2006 (*Contd.*)

(Number.)

State	City	Total law enforcement employees	Total officers	Total civilians	State	City	Total law enforcement employees	Total officers	Total civilians
	East Grand Rapids	33	30	3		Hesperia	2	2	0
	East Jordan	5	4	1		Hillsdale	17	15	2
	East Lansing	93	63	30		Holland	73	61	12
	Eastpointe	58	53	5		Holly	17	12	5
	East Tawas	7	6	1		Homer	3	3	0
	Eaton Rapids	12	11	1		Houghton	7	7	0
	Edmore	1	1	0		Howard City	3	3	0
	Elk Rapids	5	5	0		Howell	19	17	2
	Elkton	2	2	0		Hudson	11	11	0
	Elsie	2	2	0		Huntington Woods	18	17	1
	Emmett Township	18	16	2		Huron Township	32	24	8
	Erie Township	7	6	1		Imlay City	8	7	1
	Essexville	8	8	0		Inkster	67	57	10
	Evart	3	3	0		Ionia	19	17	2
	Farmington	30	23	7		Iron Mountain	14	14	0
	Farmington Hills	171	120	51		Iron River	8	7	1
	Fenton	21	16	5		Ironwood	14	14	0
	Ferndale	56	48	8		Ishpeming	11	10	1
	Flat Rock	33	27	6		Ishpeming Township	1	1	0
	Flint	287	258	29		Ithaca	4	4	0
	Flint Township	45	38	7		Jackson	90	68	22
	Flushing	14	13	1		Jonesville	5	5	0
	Flushing Township	11	10	1		Kalamazoo	288	236	52
	Forsyth Township	6	5	1		Kalamazoo Township	39	30	9
	Fowlerville	6	6	0		Kalkaska	6	5	1
	Frankenmuth	7	7	0		Keego Harbor	7	6	1
	Frankfort	3	3	0		Kentwood	87	71	16
	Franklin	10	10	0		Kingsford	20	20	0
	Fraser	53	41	12		Kingston	1	1	0
	Fremont	9	8	1		Kinross Township	3	3	0
	Frost Township	1	1	0		Laingsburg	3	3	0
	Fruitport	9	8	1		Lake Angelus	8	4	4
	Garden City	44	35	9		Lake Linden	1	1	0
	Gaylord	13	11	2		Lake Odessa	4	4	0
	Genesee Township	31	27	4		Lake Orion	8	4	4
	Gerrish Township	7	7	0		Lakeview	2	2	0
	Gibraltar	10	9	1		L'anse	4	4	0
	Gladstone	11	10	1		Lansing	335	243	92
	Gladwin	5	5	0		Lansing Township	15	14	1
	Grand Beach	4	4	0		Lapeer	23	20	3
	Grand Blanc	21	18	3		Lapeer Township	1	1	0
	Grand Blanc Township	54	45	9		Lathrup Village	8	8	0
	Grand Haven	36	33	3		Laurium	4	4	0
	Grand Ledge	16	15	1		Lawton	6	6	0
	Grand Rapids	417	332	85		Lennon	1	1	0
	Grandville	30	26	4		Leoni Township	2	1	1
	Grant	1	1	0		Leslie	3	3	0
	Grayling	6	6	0		Lexington	3	3	0
	Green Oak Township	16	14	2		Lincoln Park	62	51	11
	Greenville	20	16	4		Lincoln Township	13	11	2
	Grosse Ile Township	24	17	7		Linden	5	5	0
	Grosse Pointe	27	25	2		Litchfield	4	4	0
	Grosse Pointe Farms	48	34	14		Livonia	180	147	33
	Grosse Pointe Park	50	44	6		Lowell	9	7	2
	Grosse Pointe Shores	20	17	3		Ludington	16	15	1
	Grosse Pointe Woods	45	39	6		Luna Pier	3	3	0
	Hamburg Township	15	14	1		Mackinac Island	10	9	1
	Hampton Township	11	10	1		Mackinaw City	5	5	0
	Hamtramck	41	41	0		Madison Heights	73	59	14
	Hancock	7	7	0		Madison Township	2	2	0
	Harbor Beach	4	4	0		Mancelona	3	3	0
	Harbor Springs	6	5	1		Manistee	15	13	2
	Harper Woods	37	33	4		Manton	1	1	0
	Hart	4	4	0		Marine City	9	8	1
	Hartford	6	6	0		Marion	1	1	0
	Hastings	16	14	2		Marlette	4	4	0
	Hazel Park	42	37	5		Marquette	37	33	4
						Marshall	20	15	5

Table 78. Full-Time Law Enforcement Employees, by City, 2006 (*Contd.*)

(Number.)

State	City	Total law enforcement employees	Total officers	Total civilians	State	City	Total law enforcement employees	Total officers	Total civilians
	Marysville	18	15	3		Plymouth	16	15	1
	Mason	14	13	1		Plymouth Township	45	31	14
	Mattawan	5	5	0		Pontiac	136	113	23
	Mayville	3	3	0		Portage	74	57	17
	Melvindale	24	21	3		Port Austin	1	1	0
	Memphis	2	2	0		Port Huron	71	51	20
	Mendon	2	2	0		Portland	5	5	0
	Menominee	18	16	2		Port Sanilac	1	1	0
	Meridian Township	50	43	7		Potterville	2	2	0
	Metamora Township	6	6	0		Prairieville Township	3	3	0
	Midland	51	48	3		Raisin Township	3	3	0
	Milan	13	10	3		Reading	1	1	0
	Milford	26	19	7		Redford Township	81	67	14
	Millington	1	1	0		Reed City	4	4	0
	Monroe	51	45	6		Reese	2	2	0
	Montague	5	5	0		Richfield Township, Genesee County	11	9	2
	Montrose Township	9	8	1		Richfield Township, Roscommon County	6	6	0
	Morenci	3	3	0		Richland	2	2	0
	Morrice	2	2	0		Richland Township	4	4	0
	Mount Morris	9	8	1		Richmond	12	9	3
	Mount Morris Township	35	32	3		River Rouge	18	15	3
	Mount Pleasant	39	31	8		Riverview	30	28	2
	Mundy Township	22	19	3		Rochester	26	19	7
	Munising	5	5	0		Rockford	12	10	2
	Muskegon	89	79	10		Rockwood	10	9	1
	Muskegon Heights	24	21	3		Rogers City	7	7	0
	Muskegon Township	16	15	1		Romeo	12	8	4
	Napoleon Township	3	3	0		Romulus	73	58	15
	Nashville	2	2	0		Roosevelt Park	7	6	1
	Negaunee	9	8	1		Rose City	1	1	0
	Newaygo	5	4	1		Roseville	92	81	11
	New Baltimore	21	17	4		Royal Oak	101	84	17
	New Buffalo	8	7	1		Saginaw Township	47	43	4
	New Haven	10	9	1		Saline	18	13	5
	Niles	31	21	10		Sandusky	7	6	1
	North Branch	2	2	0		Sault Ste. Marie	27	25	2
	Northfield Township	15	12	3		Schoolcraft	3	3	0
	North Muskegon	7	7	0		Scottville	3	3	0
	Northville	17	16	1		Shelby	3	3	0
	Northville Township	45	32	13		Shelby Township	91	70	21
	Norton Shores	29	27	2		Shepherd	2	2	0
	Norvell Township	2	2	0		Somerset Township	2	2	0
	Norway	5	5	0		Southfield	162	149	13
	Novi	75	65	10		Southgate	48	38	10
	Oakley-Brady	3	3	0		South Haven	24	19	5
	Oak Park	75	65	10		South Lyon	20	18	2
	Onaway	1	1	0		South Rockwood	4	4	0
	Ontwa Township-Edwardsburg	8	7	1		Sparta	7	6	1
	Orchard Lake	9	8	1		Spring Arbor Township	2	2	0
	Oscoda Township	13	12	1		Springfield	16	15	1
	Otsego	7	6	1		Spring Lake-Ferrysburg	10	9	1
	Ovid	3	3	0		Springport Township	1	1	0
	Owosso	23	21	2		St. Charles	3	3	0
	Oxford	16	8	8		St. Clair	11	10	1
	Parchment	3	3	0		St. Clair Shores	101	85	16
	Parma-Sandstone	2	2	0		Sterling Heights	220	163	57
	Paw Paw	11	9	2		St. Ignace	6	6	0
	Pentwater	3	3	0		St. Johns	12	10	2
	Perry	6	6	0		St. Joseph	25	18	7
	Petoskey	21	19	2		St. Joseph Township	13	12	1
	Pigeon	2	2	0		St. Louis	7	6	1
	Pinckney	4	4	0		Stockbridge	2	2	0
	Pinconning	3	3	0		Sturgis	24	19	5
	Pittsfield Township	47	37	10		Sumpter Township	21	14	7
	Plainwell	10	9	1		Suttons Bay	2	2	0
	Pleasant Ridge	6	6	0					

Table 78. Full-Time Law Enforcement Employees, by City, 2006 (*Contd.*)

(Number.)

State	City	Total law enforcement employees	Total officers	Total civilians	State	City	Total law enforcement employees	Total officers	Total civilians
	Swartz Creek	9	8	1		Blooming Prairie	3	3	0
	Sylvan Lake	4	4	0		Bloomington	148	116	32
	Taylor	124	98	26		Blue Earth	6	6	0
	Tecumsehv	15	13	2		Brainerd	33	26	7
	Thomas Township	8	7	1		Breckenridge	6	6	0
	Three Rivers	18	14	4		Brooklyn Center	56	44	12
	Tittabawassee Township	5	5	0		Brooklyn Park	110	85	25
	Traverse City	36	33	3		Browns Valley	2	2	0
	Trenton	42	41	1		Brownton	1	1	0
	Troy	189	135	54		Buffalo	21	17	4
	Tuscarora Township	8	7	1		Burnsville	94	74	20
	Ubly	3	2	1		Caledonia	5	5	0
	Unadilla Township	1	1	0		Cambridge	13	11	2
	Union City	4	4	0		Cannon Falls	7	7	0
	Utica	21	16	5		Centennial Lakes	19	17	2
	Van Buren Township	50	37	13		Champlin	29	25	4
	Vassar	6	6	0		Chaska	24	22	2
	Vernon	4	4	0		Chisholm	12	11	1
	Vicksburg	8	7	1		Cloquet	21	19	2
	Walker	47	38	9		Cold Spring	8	8	0
	Walled Lake	19	14	5		Columbia Heights	29	23	6
	Warren	276	235	41		Coon Rapids	75	64	11
	Waterford Township	97	73	24		Corcoran	7	6	1
	Waterloo Township	3	3	0		Cottage Grove	47	38	9
	Watervliet	3	3	0		Crookston	17	15	2
	Wayland	6	5	1		Crosby	9	8	1
	Wayne	52	41	11		Crystal	36	27	9
	West Bloomfield Township	103	78	25		Dawson	3	3	0
	West Branch	6	5	1		Dayton	6	5	1
	Westland	127	100	27		Deephaven-Woodland	8	7	1
	White Cloud	2	2	0		Detroit Lakes	16	14	2
	Whitehall	8	8	0		Dilworth	7	6	1
	White Lake Township	38	27	11		Duluth	170	143	27
	White Pigeon	4	4	0		Eagan	99	71	28
	Williamston	8	8	0		Eagle Lake	2	2	0
	Wixom	25	21	4		East Grand Forks	23	21	2
	Wolverine Lake	9	8	1		Eden Prairie	91	65	26
	Woodstock Township	1	1	0		Edina	66	50	16
	Wyandotte	48	37	11		Elk River	39	30	9
	Wyoming	116	88	28		Elmore	1	1	0
	Yale	4	4	0		Ely	8	7	1
	Ypsilanti	43	35	8		Eveleth	11	10	1
	Zeeland	10	9	1		Fairmont	20	17	3
	Zilwaukee	2	2	0		Faribault	38	29	9
MINNESOTA	Albany	3	3	0		Farmington	24	21	3
	Albert Lea	39	30	9		Fergus Falls	28	22	6
	Alexandria	22	18	4		Floodwood	3	3	0
	Annandale	5	5	0		Forest Lake	25	22	3
	Anoka	34	27	7		Fridley	45	39	6
	Appleton	4	4	0		Gilbert	5	5	0
	Apple Valley	70	50	20		Glencoe	11	10	1
	Austin	33	30	3		Glenwood	4	4	0
	Avon	3	3	0		Golden Valley	39	29	10
	Babbitt	4	4	0		Goodview	4	4	0
	Baxter	14	13	1		Grand Rapids	21	17	4
	Bayport	5	5	0		Granite Falls	4	4	0
	Becker	6	5	1		Hallock	1	1	0
	Belgrade	2	2	0		Hastings	33	28	5
	Belle Plaine	8	7	1		Hermantown	15	13	2
	Bemidji	32	29	3		Hibbing	31	28	3
	Benson	7	6	1		Hokah	1	1	0
	Big Lake	16	13	3		Hopkins	34	25	9
	Biwabik	3	3	0		Houston	1	1	0
	Blackduck	2	2	0		Hoyt Lakes	5	5	0
	Blaine	64	52	12		Hutchinson	34	23	11
						International Falls	14	13	1
						Inver Grove Heights	37	30	7

Table 78. Full-Time Law Enforcement Employees, by City, 2006 (*Contd.*)

(Number.)

State	City	Total law enforcement employees	Total officers	Total civilians	State	City	Total law enforcement employees	Total officers	Total civilians
	Jackson	8	7	1		Robbinsdale	25	20	5
	Janesville	4	4	0		Rochester	166	117	49
	Jordan	10	8	2		Rogers	12	11	1
	Kasson	9	8	1		Roseau	6	5	1
	Kimball	2	2	0		Rosemount	22	19	3
	La Crescent	8	7	1		Roseville	54	47	7
	Lake City	11	10	1		Sartell	17	15	2
	Lake Crystal	3	3	0		Sauk Centre	8	7	1
	Lakefield	3	3	0		Sauk Rapids	14	12	2
	Lakes Area	13	11	2		Savage	33	28	5
	Lakeville	66	48	18		Shakopee	49	44	5
	Lester Prairie	3	3	0		Silver Bay	5	5	0
	Le Sueur	8	7	1		Silver Lake	2	2	0
	Lewiston	2	2	0		Slayton	4	4	0
	Lino Lakes	29	26	3		Sleepy Eye	6	6	0
	Litchfield	10	9	1		South Lake Minnetonka	17	15	2
	Little Falls	13	11	2		South St. Paul	28	26	2
	Long Prairie	6	6	0		Springfield	4	4	0
	Madison	3	3	0		Spring Grove	2	2	0
	Mankato	61	48	13		Spring Lake Park	13	11	2
	Maple Grove	75	61	14		St. Anthony	22	20	2
	Maplewood	65	51	14		Staples	5	5	0
	Marshall	23	21	2		St. Charles	4	4	0
	Medina	10	9	1		St. Cloud	122	94	28
	Melrose	6	5	1		St. Francis	13	10	3
	Mendota Heights	18	17	1		Stillwater	26	23	3
	Milaca	7	6	1		St. James	8	7	1
	Minneapolis	1,107	818	289		St. Joseph	9	8	1
	Minnetonka	75	56	19		St. Louis Park	68	50	18
	Minnetrista	13	10	3		St. Paul	740	563	177
	Montevideo	11	10	1		St. Paul Park	8	8	0
	Montgomery	6	5	1		St. Peter	19	14	5
	Moorhead	61	50	11		Thief River Falls	18	16	2
	Moose Lake	4	4	0		Tracy	3	3	0
	Mora	7	6	1		Two Harbors	8	7	1
	Morris	10	8	2		Virginia	21	20	1
	Mound	16	13	3		Wabasha	7	6	1
	Mounds View	21	19	2		Wadena	9	8	1
	Mountain Lake	4	4	0		Waite Park	12	10	2
	New Brighton	30	27	3		Warroad	7	6	1
	New Hope	33	27	6		Waseca	15	13	2
	Newport	8	8	0		Wayzata	11	10	1
	New Prague	11	9	2		Wells	4	4	0
	New Richland	2	2	0		West Hennepin	11	9	2
	New Ulm	24	21	3		West St. Paul	28	25	3
	North Branch	12	10	2		Wheaton	4	3	1
	Northfield	28	22	6		White Bear Lake	32	25	7
	North Mankato	13	12	1		Willmar	37	33	4
	North St. Paul	19	17	2		Windom	9	8	1
	Oakdale	40	31	9		Winnebago	6	3	3
	Oak Park Heights	10	9	1		Winona	42	38	4
	Olivia	5	5	0		Winsted	4	4	0
	Orono	23	20	3		Woodbury	64	54	10
	Ortonville	4	4	0		Worthington	32	24	8
	Osakis	3	3	0		Wyoming	7	7	0
	Osseo	5	4	1		Zumbrota	4	4	0
	Owatonna	34	32	2	MISSISSIPPI	Aberdeen	25	20	5
	Park Rapids	10	9	1		Amory	27	20	7
	Paynesville	4	4	0		Baldwyn	11	10	1
	Plainview	6	6	0		Batesville	44	35	9
	Plymouth	82	67	15		Bay St. Louis	29	22	7
	Princeton	11	9	2		Belzoni	18	12	6
	Prior Lake	26	23	3		Biloxi	181	134	47
	Proctor	8	7	1		Booneville	26	22	4
	Ramsey	26	21	5		Brandon	50	34	16
	Red Wing	33	27	6		Brookhaven	37	31	6
	Redwood Falls	12	10	2		Bruce	7	6	1
	Richfield	55	43	12					

Table 78. Full-Time Law Enforcement Employees, by City, 2006 (*Contd.*)

(Number.)

State	City	Total law enforcement employees	Total officers	Total civilians	State	City	Total law enforcement employees	Total officers	Total civilians
	Byhalia	14	9	5		Pass Christian	22	16	6
	Calhoun City	5	5	0		Pearl	67	52	15
	Canton	34	27	7		Pelahatchie	8	6	2
	Charleston	8	8	0		Petal	35	28	7
	Clarksdale	50	37	13		Philadelphia	31	23	8
	Cleveland	55	43	12		Picayune	54	37	17
	Clinton	72	48	24		Pickens	5	5	0
	Coldwater	3	3	0		Poplarville	11	11	0
	Collins	15	11	4		Port Gibson	12	8	4
	Columbia	26	21	5		Purvis	11	8	3
	Columbus	80	70	10		Quitman	7	6	1
	Como	11	7	4		Raymond	6	6	0
	Corinth	50	38	12		Richland	47	36	11
	De Kalb	4	3	1		Ridgeland	82	55	27
	Drew	9	5	4		Ripley	14	13	1
	Durant	7	7	0		Rolling Fork	7	6	1
	Edwards	1	1	0		Rosedale	5	5	0
	Eupora	7	7	0		Ruleville	8	5	3
	Fayette	6	3	3		Sandersville	4	4	0
	Florence	17	11	6		Senatobia	18	15	3
	Flowood	53	42	11		Shaw	9	5	4
	Fulton	11	11	0		Shelby	7	3	4
	Gloster	7	5	2		Southaven	103	83	20
	Greenville	144	103	41		Starkville	53	46	7
	Greenwood	69	54	15		Stonewall	1	1	0
	Grenada	50	45	5		Summit	8	7	1
	Gulfport	241	173	68		Sunflower	2	2	0
	Hattiesburg	164	96	68		Tchula	3	3	0
	Hazlehurst	16	16	0		Terry	9	7	2
	Heidelberg	5	4	1		Tupelo	124	110	14
	Hernando	35	27	8		Tylertown	6	5	1
	Hollandale	10	6	4		Utica	5	4	1
	Holly Springs	24	19	5		Vaiden	6	4	2
	Horn Lake	65	55	10		Verona	5	5	0
	Houston	11	8	3		Vicksburg	94	67	27
	Indianola	35	27	8		Water Valley	9	8	1
	Inverness	6	5	1		Waveland	20	19	1
	Itta Bena	7	4	3		Waynesboro	19	14	5
	Iuka	12	9	3		West Point	30	24	6
	Jackson	647	452	195		Wiggins	19	14	5
	Kosciusko	19	19	0		Winona	12	10	2
	Laurel	88	60	28		Yazoo City	39	23	16
	Leakesville	3	2	1	**MISSOURI**	Adrian	2	2	0
	Leland	24	18	6		Advance	3	3	0
	Lexington	8	7	1		Alton	2	2	0
	Long Beach	45	30	15		Anderson	4	4	0
	Louisville	27	21	6		Appleton City	2	2	0
	Lucedale	17	11	6		Arbyrd	4	4	0
	Madison	66	49	17		Archie	3	3	0
	Magee	18	14	4		Arnold	60	48	12
	Magnolia	6	6	0		Ash Grove	3	3	0
	Marks	6	6	0		Ashland	5	5	0
	McComb	60	34	26		Aurora	22	15	7
	McLain	2	1	1		Ava	10	7	3
	Mendenhall	9	6	3		Ballwin	69	53	16
	Meridian	105	88	17		Bates City	2	2	0
	Moorhead	4	4	0		Battlefield	5	5	0
	Morton	15	10	5		Bella Villa	3	3	0
	Moss Point	40	25	15		Belle	5	3	2
	Mound Bayou	10	7	3		Bellefontaine Neighbors	32	29	3
	Natchez	76	48	28		Bellflower	1	1	0
	New Albany	23	21	2		Bel-Nor	10	9	1
	Newton	14	9	5		Bel-Ridge	16	16	0
	Ocean Springs	49	39	10		Belton	62	43	19
	Okolona	9	9	0		Berkeley	57	45	12
	Olive Branch	60	57	3		Bernie	9	5	4
	Oxford	55	47	8		Bethany	6	6	0
	Pascagoula	84	53	31					

Table 78. Full-Time Law Enforcement Employees, by City, 2006 (*Contd.*)

(Number.)

State	City	Total law enforcement employees	Total officers	Total civilians	State	City	Total law enforcement employees	Total officers	Total civilians
	Beverly Hills	10	8	2		De Soto	20	15	5
	Billings	4	4	0		Des Peres	45	38	7
	Birch Tree	1	1	0		Dexter	24	18	6
	Bismarck	4	4	0		Diamond	3	3	0
	Bland	2	1	1		Dixon	7	5	2
	Bloomfield	3	3	0		Doniphan	12	9	3
	Blue Springs	105	76	29		Drexel	2	2	0
	Bolivar	23	19	4		Duenweg	9	4	5
	Bonne Terre	10	10	0		Duquesne	5	5	0
	Boonville	28	21	7		East Lynne	1	1	0
	Bourbon	9	8	1		East Prairie	12	8	4
	Bowling Green	13	8	5		Edina	4	3	1
	Branson	57	42	15		Edmundson	10	9	1
	Branson West	6	6	0		Eldon	14	12	2
	Braymer	1	1	0		El Dorado Springs	10	7	3
	Breckenridge Hills	15	14	1		Ellington	1	1	0
	Brentwood	32	25	7		Ellisville	21	20	1
	Bridgeton	70	53	17		Elsberry	5	5	0
	Brookfield	18	11	7		Eminence	1	1	0
	Bucklin	1	1	0		Emma	1	1	0
	Buckner	2	2	0		Eureka	27	23	4
	Buffalo	9	8	1		Excelsior Springs	32	22	10
	Bunker	1	1	0		Fair Grove	4	4	0
	Butler	15	9	6		Fair Play	1	1	0
	Byrnes Mill	5	5	0		Farmington	34	25	9
	Cabool	10	6	4		Fayette	8	8	0
	California	6	5	1		Ferguson	60	51	9
	Calverton Park	6	6	0		Festus	38	27	11
	Camdenton	15	12	3		Florissant	105	84	21
	Cameron	25	19	6		Foley	1	1	0
	Campbell	10	4	6		Foristell	7	7	0
	Canton	6	5	1		Forsyth	7	6	1
	Cape Girardeau	89	74	15		Fredericktown	7	7	0
	Cardwell	2	2	0		Freeman	2	1	1
	Carl Junction	17	12	5		Frontenac	27	21	6
	Carrollton	7	7	0		Fulton	32	25	7
	Carterville	5	5	0		Galena	1	1	0
	Carthage	35	28	7		Gallatin	3	3	0
	Caruthersville	19	18	1		Garden City	4	4	0
	Cassville	10	10	0		Gerald	5	5	0
	Centralia	12	7	5		Gideon	2	2	0
	Chaffee	10	6	4		Gladstone	42	42	0
	Charlack	8	8	0		Glasgow	3	3	0
	Charleston	18	13	5		Glendale	15	12	3
	Chesterfield	94	84	10		Goodman	3	2	1
	Chillicothe	22	16	6		Gower	3	3	0
	Clarkton	2	2	0		Grain Valley	22	19	3
	Claycomo	14	10	4		Granby	4	4	0
	Clayton	60	51	9		Grandin	1	1	0
	Cleveland	3	3	0		Grandview	66	53	13
	Clinton	22	20	2		Greenfield	2	2	0
	Cole Camp	3	3	0		Greenwood	9	9	0
	Columbia	180	147	33		Hallsville	3	3	0
	Concordia	6	6	0		Hamilton	4	3	1
	Conway	1	1	0		Hannibal	50	37	13
	Cool Valley	11	10	1		Harrisonville	28	20	8
	Cooter	3	1	2		Hartville	2	2	0
	Corder	3	2	1		Hawk Point	2	2	0
	Cottleville	12	11	1		Hayti	8	7	1
	Country Club Hills	8	8	0		Hayti Heights	2	1	1
	Crane	3	3	0		Hazelwood	78	65	13
	Crestwood	35	29	6		Herculaneum	14	13	1
	Creve Coeur	62	52	10		Hermann	11	7	4
	Crocker	3	3	0		Higginsville	15	9	6
	Crystal City	21	16	5		Highlandville	2	2	0
	Cuba	13	12	1		Hillsboro	8	8	0
	Dellwood	18	17	1		Hillsdale	13	12	1
	Desloge	10	10	0		Holcomb	2	2	0

Table 78. Full-Time Law Enforcement Employees, by City, 2006 (*Contd.*)

(Number.)

State	City	Total law enforcement employees	Total officers	Total civilians	State	City	Total law enforcement employees	Total officers	Total civilians
	Holden	10	8	2		Marble Hill	4	4	0
	Hollister	15	10	5		Marceline	12	6	6
	Holt	2	1	1		Marionville	4	4	0
	Holts Summit	8	7	1		Marquand	1	1	0
	Houston	5	5	0		Marshall	34	23	11
	Humansville	1	1	0		Marshfield	9	9	0
	Huntsville	2	2	0		Marston	1	1	0
	Hurley	1	1	0		Marthasville	1	1	0
	Iberia	3	3	0		Maryland Heights	95	77	18
	Independence	284	194	90		Maryville	27	20	7
	Indian Point	1	1	0		Matthews	1	1	0
	Iron Mountain Lake	2	1	1		Memphis	2	1	1
	Ironton	5	4	1		Merriam Woods	1	1	0
	Jackson	30	22	8		Mexico	35	33	2
	JASCO Metropolitan	5	4	1		Milan	5	5	0
	Jasper	2	2	0		Miller	2	1	1
	Jefferson City	115	85	30		Miner	13	8	5
	Jennings	47	43	4		Moberly	47	33	14
	Jonesburg	1	1	0		Moline Acres	8	8	0
	Joplin	86	76	10		Monett	26	17	9
	Kahoka	3	3	0		Monroe City	8	7	1
	Kansas City	2,045	1,357	688		Montgomery City	6	6	0
	Kearney	14	13	1		Montrose	1	1	0
	Kennett	27	22	5		Morehouse	1	1	0
	Keytesville	1	1	0		Mosby	2	2	0
	Kimberling City	8	6	2		Moscow Mills	8	7	1
	Kimmswick	6	6	0		Mound City	1	1	0
	King City	1	1	0		Mountain Grove	14	10	4
	Kirksville	28	25	3		Mountain View	7	7	0
	Kirkwood	63	53	10		Mount Vernon	9	9	0
	Knob Noster	12	7	5		Napoleon	2	2	0
	Ladue	33	27	6		Neosho	29	26	3
	La Grange	8	7	1		Nevada	28	19	9
	Lake Lotawana	7	6	1		Newburg	1	1	0
	Lake Ozark	14	8	6		New Florence	1	1	0
	Lakeshire	4	4	0		New Haven	5	5	0
	Lake St. Louis	34	28	6		New London	2	2	0
	Lake Tapawingo	1	1	0		New Madrid	8	7	1
	Lake Waukomis	1	1	0		New Melle	2	2	0
	Lake Winnebago	4	4	0		Niangua	1	1	0
	Lamar	12	10	2		Nixa	34	22	12
	La Monte	2	2	0		Noel	5	5	0
	Lanagan	2	2	0		Norborne	1	1	0
	La Plata	3	3	0		Normandy	22	21	1
	Lathrop	4	4	0		North Kansas City	56	39	17
	Laurie	6	6	0		Northmoor	2	2	0
	Lawson	7	6	1		Northwoods	27	18	9
	Leadington	6	5	1		Oak Grove	15	14	1
	Leadwood	4	4	0		Oakview Village	4	4	0
	Lebanon	37	28	9		Odessa	12	11	1
	Lee's Summit	164	114	50		O'Fallon	133	101	32
	Lexington	9	8	1		Olivette	24	23	1
	Liberal	1	1	0		Olympian Village	3	3	0
	Liberty	53	37	16		Orrick	1	1	0
	Licking	4	4	0		Osage Beach	38	24	14
	Lilbourn	3	3	0		Osceola	2	2	0
	Lincoln	3	3	0		Overland	51	41	10
	Linn	4	4	0		Owensville	8	7	1
	Linn Creek	2	2	0		Ozark	35	30	5
	Lockwood	2	2	0		Pacific	25	17	8
	Lone Jack	4	4	0		Pagedale	17	16	1
	Louisiana	14	9	5		Palmyra	10	6	4
	Lowry City	1	1	0		Park Hills	13	11	2
	Macon	14	12	2		Parkville	16	15	1
	Malden	14	12	2		Parma	3	2	1
	Manchester	41	38	3		Peculiar	11	10	1
	Mansfield	4	4	0		Perry	1	1	0
	Maplewood	34	31	3		Perryville	27	25	2

Table 78. Full-Time Law Enforcement Employees, by City, 2006 (*Contd.*)

(Number.)

State	City	Total law enforcement employees	Total officers	Total civilians	State	City	Total law enforcement employees	Total officers	Total civilians
	Pevely	20	14	6		St. Peters	104	85	19
	Piedmont	7	7	0		Strafford	7	7	0
	Pierce City	4	4	0		St. Robert	30	21	9
	Pilot Grove	1	1	0		Sturgeonv	2	2	0
	Pilot Knob	1	1	0		Sugar Creek	21	15	6
	Pine Lawn	22	19	3		Sullivan	25	17	8
	Pineville	10	10	0		Summersville	2	2	0
	Platte City	11	11	0		Sunset Hills	32	25	7
	Platte Woods	2	2	0		Sweet Springs	3	3	0
	Plattsburg	6	6	0		Tarkio	2	2	0
	Pleasant Hill	16	11	5		Thayer	10	8	2
	Pleasant Hope	2	2	0		Theodosia	1	1	0
	Pleasant Valley	10	6	4		Tipton	3	3	0
	Poplar Bluff	54	43	11		Town and Country	46	34	12
	Portageville	13	9	4		Trenton	18	11	7
	Potosi	11	10	1		Troy	27	25	2
	Purdy	1	1	0		Truesdale	1	1	0
	Puxico	3	2	1		Union	20	18	2
	Randolph	2	2	0		Unionville	4	4	0
	Raymore	33	24	9		University City	98	77	21
	Raytown	74	56	18		Uplands Park	10	6	4
	Reeds Spring	2	2	0		Urbana	1	1	0
	Republic	29	19	10		Van Buren	3	3	0
	Rich Hill	3	3	0		Vandalia	7	4	3
	Richland	5	4	1		Velda City	10	10	0
	Richmond	19	13	6		Verona	2	2	0
	Richmond Heights	43	42	1		Versailles	10	10	0
	Risco	1	1	0		Viburnum	1	1	0
	Riverside	24	21	3		Vienna	4	4	0
	Riverview	12	11	1		Vinita Park	12	11	1
	Rockaway Beach	2	2	0		Walnut Grove	2	2	0
	Rock Hill	10	9	1		Wardell	2	2	0
	Rock Port	3	3	0		Warrensburg	30	28	2
	Rogersville	6	6	0		Warrenton	21	18	3
	Rolla	52	30	22		Warsaw	7	7	0
	Salem	19	14	5		Warson Woods	8	7	1
	Salisbury	5	4	1		Washington	31	28	3
	Sarcoxie	5	3	2		Waynesville	9	8	1
	Savannah	6	6	0		Weatherby Lake	3	3	0
	Scott City	16	11	5		Webb City	23	19	4
	Sedalia	57	45	12		Webster Groves	45	42	3
	Seligman	2	1	1		Wellston	13	13	0
	Senath	3	3	0		Wellsville	3	3	0
	Seneca	6	6	0		Wentzville	62	44	18
	Seymour	6	6	0		Weston	4	4	0
	Shelbina	4	4	0		West Plains	29	23	6
	Sheldon	1	1	0		Wheaton	1	1	0
	Shrewsbury	20	18	2		Willard	10	9	1
	Sikeston	76	67	9		Willow Springs	6	5	1
	Silex	1	1	0		Windsor	6	6	0
	Slater	7	4	3		Winfield	5	4	1
	Smithville	15	15	0		Winona	3	3	0
	Southwest City	2	2	0		Wood Heights	2	2	0
	Sparta	3	3	0		Woodson Terrace	20	17	3
	Springfield	413	321	92		Wright City	9	8	1
	St. Ann	50	38	12	**MONTANA**	Baker	3	3	0
	St. Charles	152	110	42		Belgrade	14	11	3
	St. Clair	14	12	2		Billings	165	132	33
	Steele	8	8	0		Boulder	2	2	0
	Steelville	6	6	0		Bozeman	48	43	5
	Ste. Genevieve	12	11	1		Chinook	4	4	0
	St. George	6	5	1		Colstrip	13	6	7
	St. James	7	6	1		Columbia Falls	15	9	6
	St. John	25	23	2		Columbus	5	4	1
	St. Joseph	161	118	43		Conrad	5	5	0
	St. Louis	1,936	1,407	529		Cut Bank	7	5	2
	St. Marys	1	1	0		Dillon	9	8	1
	Stover	3	3	0		East Helena	4	4	0

Table 78. Full-Time Law Enforcement Employees, by City, 2006 (*Contd.*)

(Number.)

State	City	Total law enforcement employees	Total officers	Total civilians	State	City	Total law enforcement employees	Total officers	Total civilians
	Ennis	1	1	0		McCook	19	15	4
	Eureka	3	3	0		Milford	5	5	0
	Fort Benton	4	3	1		Minden	5	5	0
	Glasgow	8	7	1		Mitchell	4	4	0
	Glendive	15	9	6		Nebraska City	13	11	2
	Great Falls	116	80	36		Neligh	3	3	0
	Hamilton	16	14	2		Norfolk	56	36	20
	Havre	27	19	8		North Platte	65	42	23
	Helena	71	50	21		Ogallala	11	10	1
	Hot Springs	1	1	0		Omaha	946	774	172
	Joliet	2	2	0		O'Neill	8	7	1
	Kalispell	35	32	3		Ord	4	4	0
	Laurel	19	12	7		Papillion	40	36	4
	Lewistown	20	14	6		Pierce	3	3	0
	Libby	6	6	0		Plattsmouth	17	15	2
	Livingston	14	13	1		Ralston	13	12	1
	Manhattan	3	3	0		Schuyler	9	7	2
	Miles City	16	15	1		Scottsbluff	37	32	5
	Missoula	122	103	19		Scribner	1	1	0
	Pinesdale	3	3	0		Seward	13	11	2
	Plains	3	3	0		Sidney	15	13	2
	Plentywood	4	3	1		South Sioux City	28	27	1
	Polson	11	10	1		St. Paul	4	4	0
	Poplar	3	3	0		Superior	4	4	0
	Red Lodge	7	7	0		Syracuse	2	2	0
	Ronan City	5	4	1		Tecumseh	3	2	1
	Sidney	10	9	1		Tekamah	2	2	0
	Stevensville	1	1	0		Valentine	6	5	1
	St. Ignatius	2	2	0		Valley	5	5	0
	Thompson Falls	4	4	0		Wahoo	6	6	0
	Three Forks	3	3	0		Wayne	12	7	5
	Troy	3	3	0		West Point	8	7	1
	West Yellowstone	9	5	4		Wilber	4	4	0
	Whitefish	30	22	8		Wymore	3	3	0
	Whitehall	6	3	3		York	19	13	6
	Wolf Point	11	8	3	**NEVADA**	Boulder City	42	33	9
NEBRASKA	Alliance	25	18	7		Carlin	5	4	1
	Ashland	6	5	1		Elko	43	38	5
	Auburn	6	6	0		Fallon	32	19	13
	Aurora	7	7	0		Henderson	472	321	151
	Bayard	3	3	0		Las Vegas Metropolitan Police Department	4,530	2,231	2,299
	Beatrice	32	21	11		Lovelock	7	6	1
	Bellevue	88	82	6		Mesquite	47	34	13
	Blair	17	15	2		North Las Vegas	418	278	140
	Bridgeport	3	3	0		Reno	455	365	90
	Broken Bow	7	6	1		Sparks	162	111	51
	Central City	6	5	1		West Wendover	21	14	7
	Chadron	15	11	4		Winnemucca	20	17	3
	Columbus	52	34	18		Yerington	7	6	1
	Cozad	7	7	0	**NEW HAMPSHIRE**	Alexandria	1	1	0
	Crete	18	11	7		Alstead	2	2	0
	David City	6	5	1		Alton	13	11	2
	Elkhorn	15	14	1		Amherst	18	17	1
	Fairbury	9	8	1		Andover	1	1	0
	Falls City	12	8	4		Antrim	4	4	0
	Fremont	46	38	8		Ashland	6	6	0
	Gering	19	16	3		Auburn	9	7	2
	Gothenburg	10	6	4		Barnstead	5	5	0
	Grand Island	83	74	9		Barrington	10	9	1
	Hastings	51	37	14		Bartlett	4	4	0
	Holdrege	15	10	5		Bedford	39	28	11
	Imperial	4	4	0		Belmont	16	13	3
	Kearney	61	47	14		Bennington	2	2	0
	Kimball	6	5	1		Berlin	30	22	8
	La Vista	35	31	4		Bethlehem	4	4	0
	Lexington	17	15	2					
	Lincoln	409	307	102					
	Madison	4	4	0					

Table 78. Full-Time Law Enforcement Employees, by City, 2006 (*Contd.*)

(Number.)

State	City	Total law enforcement employees	Total officers	Total civilians	State	City	Total law enforcement employees	Total officers	Total civilians
	Boscawen	6	5	1		Milford	29	24	5
	Bow	22	15	7		Milton	8	7	1
	Brentwood	6	6	0		Mont Vernon	3	3	0
	Bristol	10	9	1		Moultonborough	15	11	4
	Campton	6	5	1		Nashua	221	166	55
	Candia	7	6	1		New Boston	6	5	1
	Canterbury	1	1	0		Newbury	3	3	0
	Carroll	4	4	0		New Durham	5	4	1
	Charlestown	8	5	3		Newfields	4	4	0
	Chester	3	2	1		New Hampton	5	5	0
	Claremont	26	21	5		Newington	11	10	1
	Colebrook	5	5	0		New Ipswich	6	5	1
	Concord	100	77	23		New London	12	8	4
	Conway	30	21	9		Newmarket	19	13	6
	Danville	5	4	1		Newport	15	12	3
	Deerfield	9	8	1		Newton	8	5	3
	Deering	2	2	0		Northfield	11	10	1
	Derry	71	59	12		North Hampton	13	12	1
	Dover	68	56	12		Northumberland	4	4	0
	Dublin	4	3	1		Northwood	8	7	1
	Dunbarton	2	2	0		Nottingham	7	6	1
	Durham	21	19	2		Ossipee	9	8	1
	Enfield	7	6	1		Pelham	27	19	8
	Epping	14	13	1		Pembroke	13	11	2
	Epsom	7	6	1		Peterborough	13	11	2
	Exeter	35	25	10		Pittsfield	9	8	1
	Farmington	16	14	2		Plaistow	24	16	8
	Fitzwilliam	3	3	0		Plymouth	15	10	5
	Franconia	3	3	0		Portsmouth	88	66	22
	Franklin	19	13	6		Raymond	23	15	8
	Freedom	2	2	0		Rindge	10	8	2
	Fremont	4	3	1		Rochester	71	53	18
	Gilford	23	17	6		Rollinsford	4	4	0
	Gilmanton	5	4	1		Rye	10	9	1
	Goffstown	41	29	12		Sandown	6	6	0
	Gorham	13	7	6		Sandwich	2	2	0
	Grantham	4	4	0		Seabrook	36	28	8
	Greenland	7	7	0		Somersworth	30	23	7
	Hampstead	7	7	0		Springfield	1	1	0
	Hampton	42	33	9		Strafford	3	3	0
	Hancock	3	3	0		Stratham	11	10	1
	Hanover	33	19	14		Sugar Hill	2	2	0
	Haverhill	8	7	1		Thornton	5	4	1
	Henniker	10	8	2		Tilton	19	17	2
	Hillsborough	18	12	6		Troy	4	4	0
	Hinsdale	7	6	1		Tuftonboro	3	3	0
	Hooksett	35	25	10		Wakefield	8	7	1
	Hopkinton	9	7	2		Walpole	4	3	1
	Hudson	58	44	14		Warner	5	4	1
	Jaffrey	10	9	1		Washington	1	1	0
	Keene	55	40	15		Waterville Valley	6	5	1
	Kingston	10	9	1		Weare	12	11	1
	Laconia	46	35	11		Webster	3	3	0
	Lancaster	8	7	1		Wilton	7	6	1
	Lebanon	49	35	14		Winchester	8	7	1
	Lee	8	7	1		Windham	25	19	6
	Lincoln	11	6	5		Wolfeboro	15	10	5
	Lisbon	4	4	0		Woodstock	5	5	0
	Litchfield	12	10	2	**NEW JERSEY**	Aberdeen Township	39	32	7
	Littleton	15	13	2		Absecon	27	25	2
	Londonderry	76	60	16		Allendale	19	14	5
	Loudon	6	5	1		Allenhurst	13	9	4
	Madison	3	3	0		Allentown	6	6	0
	Manchester	261	200	61		Alpine	12	12	0
	Marlborough	3	3	0		Andover Township	18	12	6
	Meredith	17	13	4		Asbury Park	101	82	19
	Merrimack	43	37	6		Atlantic City	450	317	133
	Middleton	3	3	0		Atlantic Highlands	20	15	5

Table 78. Full-Time Law Enforcement Employees, by City, 2006 (*Contd.*)

(Number.)

State	City	Total law enforcement employees	Total officers	Total civilians	State	City	Total law enforcement employees	Total officers	Total civilians
	Audubon	24	22	2		Cliffside Park	58	48	10
	Avalon	28	19	9		Clifton	188	158	30
	Avon-by-the-Sea	12	12	0		Clinton	10	10	0
	Barnegat Township	49	40	9		Clinton Township	25	23	2
	Barrington	16	15	1		Closter	30	23	7
	Bay Head	9	8	1		Collingswood	41	37	4
	Bayonne	270	227	43		Colts Neck Township	23	22	1
	Beach Haven	12	10	2		Cranbury Township	18	17	1
	Beachwood	20	18	2		Cranford Township	68	51	17
	Bedminster Township	19	17	2		Cresskill	31	25	6
	Belleville	118	111	7		Deal	20	16	4
	Bellmawr	26	24	2		Delanco Township	11	10	1
	Belmar	28	21	7		Delaware Township	8	7	1
	Belvidere	7	6	1		Delran Township	37	32	5
	Bergenfield	55	46	9		Demarest	14	14	0
	Berkeley Heights Township	33	26	7		Denville Township	42	32	10
	Berkeley Township	90	70	20		Deptford Township	76	70	6
	Berlin	19	18	1		Dover	41	34	7
	Berlin Township	21	19	2		Dumont	40	33	7
	Bernards Township	47	38	9		Dunellen	19	15	4
	Bernardsville	24	18	6		Eastampton Township	18	17	1
	Beverly	7	6	1		East Brunswick Township	119	93	26
	Blairstown Township	7	6	1		East Greenwich Township	20	18	2
	Bloomfield	156	138	18		East Hanover Township	41	33	8
	Bloomingdale	17	16	1		East Newark	11	6	5
	Bogota	20	15	5		East Orange	319	266	53
	Boonton	26	22	4		East Rutherford	38	34	4
	Boonton Township	13	13	0		East Windsor Township	62	48	14
	Bordentown	14	12	2		Eatontown	46	35	11
	Bordentown Township	28	22	6		Edgewater	31	29	2
	Bound Brook	27	22	5		Edgewater Park Township	15	14	1
	Bradley Beach	18	15	3		Edison Township	258	204	54
	Branchburg Township	28	26	2		Egg Harbor City	19	13	6
	Brick Township	169	127	42		Egg Harbor Township	122	95	27
	Bridgeton	81	67	14		Elizabeth	491	357	134
	Bridgewater Township	91	77	14		Elk Township	11	11	0
	Brielle	15	15	0		Elmer	1	1	0
	Brigantine	48	37	11		Elmwood Park	48	46	2
	Brooklawn	7	7	0		Emerson	20	18	2
	Buena	15	9	6		Englewood	82	80	2
	Burlington	37	32	5		Englewood Cliffs	24	24	0
	Burlington Township	52	43	9		Englishtown	8	8	0
	Butler	18	17	1		Essex Fells	14	13	1
	Byram Township	16	15	1		Evesham Township	83	75	8
	Caldwell	23	22	1		Ewing Township	96	82	14
	Camden	483	423	60		Fairfield Township	46	39	7
	Cape May	29	22	7		Fair Haven	19	15	4
	Carlstadt	33	31	2		Fair Lawn	73	59	14
	Carney's Point Township	26	20	6		Fairview	34	31	3
	Carteret	73	63	10		Fanwood	22	21	1
	Cedar Grove Township	35	32	3		Far Hills	6	6	0
	Chatham	30	24	6		Flemington	20	16	4
	Chatham Township	31	24	7		Florence Township	31	25	6
	Cherry Hill Township	171	134	37		Florham Park	36	30	6
	Chesilhurst	11	10	1		Fort Lee	126	106	20
	Chester	9	8	1		Franklin	14	13	1
	Chesterfield Township	11	10	1		Franklin Lakes	28	23	5
	Chester Township	17	16	1		Franklin Township, Gloucester County	32	29	3
	Cinnaminson Township	37	32	5		Franklin Township, Hunterdon County	6	6	0
	Clark Township	51	40	11		Franklin Township, Somerset County	137	116	21
	Clayton	21	18	3		Freehold	43	35	8
	Clementon	19	17	2					

Table 78. Full-Time Law Enforcement Employees, by City, 2006 (*Contd.*)

(Number.)

State	City	Total law enforcement employees	Total officers	Total civilians	State	City	Total law enforcement employees	Total officers	Total civilians
	Freehold Township	83	70	13		Kenilworth	31	30	1
	Frenchtown	3	2	1		Keyport	24	18	6
	Galloway Township	85	73	12		Kinnelon	17	16	1
	Garfield	69	61	8		Lacey Township	59	44	15
	Garwood	15	14	1		Lake Como	9	9	0
	Gibbsboro	6	6	0		Lakehurst	10	9	1
	Glassboro	51	45	6		Lakewood Township	160	132	28
	Glen Ridge	33	26	7		Lambertville	13	10	3
	Glen Rock	22	21	1		Laurel Springs	7	7	0
	Gloucester City	33	30	3		Lavallette	17	12	5
	Gloucester Township	128	109	19		Lawnside	12	10	2
	Green Brook Township	28	22	6		Lawrence Township	84	69	15
	Greenwich Township, Gloucester County	23	18	5		Lebanon Township	10	9	1
						Leonia	25	19	6
	Greenwich Township, Warren County	12	11	1		Lincoln Park	30	25	5
	Guttenberg	28	21	7		Linden	145	133	12
	Hackensack	134	112	22		Lindenwold	44	41	3
	Hackettstown	23	21	2		Linwood	24	20	4
	Haddonfield	25	23	2		Little Egg Harbor Township	52	41	11
	Haddon Heights	18	17	1		Little Falls Township	29	23	6
	Haddon Township	32	30	2		Little Ferry	31	28	3
	Haledon	19	16	3		Little Silver	20	15	5
	Hamburg	9	8	1		Livingston Township	85	74	11
	Hamilton Township, Atlantic County	106	79	27		Lodi	51	40	11
						Logan Township	21	20	1
	Hamilton Township, Mercer County	212	182	30		Long Beach Township	51	40	11
	Hammonton	42	33	9		Long Branch	120	99	21
	Hanover Township	38	31	7		Long Hill Township	37	29	8
	Harding Township	16	15	1		Longport	18	13	5
	Hardyston Township	25	19	6		Lopatcong Township	15	14	1
	Harrington Park	12	12	0		Lower Alloways Creek Township	17	12	5
	Harrison	69	50	19		Lower Township	60	45	15
	Harrison Township	17	16	1		Lumberton Township	32	28	4
	Harvey Cedars	9	9	0		Lyndhurst Township	56	49	7
	Hasbrouck Heights	34	32	2		Madison	39	35	4
	Haworth	13	12	1		Magnolia	12	12	0
	Hawthorne	36	31	5		Mahwah Township	64	56	8
	Hazlet Township	54	46	8		Manalapan Township	82	66	16
	Helmetta	3	3	0		Manasquan	23	17	6
	High Bridge	6	6	0		Manchester Township	84	67	17
	Highland Park	35	28	7		Mansfield Township, Burlington County	13	10	3
	Highlands	17	13	4					
	Hightstown	18	13	5		Mansfield Township, Warren County	16	15	1
	Hillsborough Township	68	55	13		Mantoloking	8	7	1
	Hillsdale	23	20	3		Mantua Township	30	28	2
	Hillside Township	81	74	7		Manville	28	22	6
	Hi-Nella	5	5	0		Maple Shade Township	44	35	9
	Hoboken	169	153	16		Maplewood Township	80	66	14
	Ho-Ho-Kus	17	15	2		Margate City	49	38	11
	Holland Township	8	7	1		Marlboro Township	94	74	20
	Holmdel Township	53	43	10		Matawan	22	20	2
	Hopatcong	37	28	9		Maywood	28	24	4
	Hopewell Township	40	32	8		Medford Lakes	10	9	1
	Howell Township	111	94	17		Medford Township	53	43	10
	Independence Township	9	8	1		Mendham	14	12	2
	Interlaken	6	6	0		Mendham Township	18	15	3
	Irvington	220	190	30		Merchantville	15	14	1
	Island Heights	5	5	0		Metuchen	33	28	5
	Jackson Township	117	96	21		Middlesex	33	31	2
	Jamesburg	17	13	4		Middle Township	66	51	15
	Jefferson Township	46	39	7		Middletown Township	129	103	26
	Jersey City	1,071	870	201					
	Keansburg	41	33	8		Midland Park	14	13	1
	Kearny	125	118	7		Millburn Township	64	53	11

Table 78. Full-Time Law Enforcement Employees, by City, 2006 *(Contd.)*

(Number.)

State	City	Total law enforcement employees	Total officers	Total civilians	State	City	Total law enforcement employees	Total officers	Total civilians
	Milltown	19	16	3		Palisades Park	38	31	7
	Millville	93	78	15		Palmyra	18	16	2
	Monmouth Beach	11	10	1		Paramus	113	91	22
	Monroe Township, Gloucester County	80	68	12		Park Ridge	19	18	1
	Monroe Township, Middlesex County	65	48	17		Parsippany-Troy Hills Township	132	107	25
	Montclair	133	108	25		Passaic	222	189	33
	Montgomery Township	43	32	11		Paterson	545	457	88
	Montvale	24	22	2		Paulsboro	22	20	2
	Montville Township	49	42	7		Peapack and Gladstone	10	9	1
	Moonachie	22	19	3		Pemberton	8	7	1
	Moorestown Township	48	38	10		Pemberton Township	65	57	8
	Morris Plains	22	17	5		Pennington	7	6	1
	Morristown	67	59	8		Pennsauken Township	121	93	28
	Morris Township	52	44	8		Penns Grove	22	16	6
	Mountain Lakes	18	14	4		Pennsville Township	26	24	2
	Mountainside	26	21	5		Pequannock Township	35	30	5
	Mount Arlington	14	13	1		Perth Amboy	156	125	31
	Mount Ephraim	14	13	1		Phillipsburg	38	35	3
	Mount Holly Township	28	26	2		Pine Beach	7	6	1
	Mount Laurel Township	85	71	14		Pine Hill	24	22	2
	Mount Olive Township	63	53	10		Pine Valley	4	4	0
	Mullica Township	15	14	1		Piscataway Township	111	92	19
	National Park	7	7	0		Pitman	17	16	1
	Neptune City	21	16	5		Plainfield	186	153	33
	Neptune Township	91	73	18		Plainsboro Township	45	32	13
	Netcong	12	9	3		Pleasantville	72	56	16
	Newark	1,498	1,286	212		Plumsted Township	12	11	1
	New Brunswick	166	137	29		Pohatcong Township	15	14	1
	Newfield	5	5	0		Point Pleasant	41	33	8
	New Hanover Township	4	4	0		Point Pleasant Beach	32	25	7
	New Milford	39	36	3		Pompton Lakes	29	25	4
	New Providence	32	26	6		Princeton	44	34	10
	Newton	32	24	8		Princeton Township	44	35	9
	North Arlington	40	32	8		Prospect Park	17	16	1
	North Bergen Township	139	120	19		Rahway	87	80	7
	North Brunswick Township	102	85	17		Ramsey	39	33	6
	North Caldwell	21	16	5		Randolph Township	49	40	9
	Northfield	23	22	1		Raritan	24	19	5
	North Haledon	23	18	5		Raritan Township	40	37	3
	North Hanover Township	9	9	0		Readington Township	28	26	2
	North Plainfield	52	46	6		Red Bank	45	41	4
	Northvale	15	14	1		Ridgefield	29	27	2
	North Wildwood	38	30	8		Ridgefield Park	39	30	9
	Norwood	14	13	1		Ridgewood	48	44	4
	Nutley Township	79	65	14		Ringwood	28	23	5
	Oakland	29	23	6		Riverdale	21	17	4
	Oaklyn	14	13	1		River Edge	26	22	4
	Ocean City	77	62	15		Riverside Township	15	15	0
	Ocean Gate	7	6	1		Riverton	7	6	1
	Oceanport	20	15	5		River Vale Township	22	20	2
	Ocean Township, Monmouth County	77	62	15		Rochelle Park Township	27	21	6
	Ocean Township, Ocean County	29	19	10		Rockaway	15	14	1
	Ogdensburg	7	7	0		Rockaway Township	68	56	12
	Old Bridge Township	139	104	35		Roseland	32	27	5
	Old Tappan	14	13	1		Roselle	67	56	11
	Oradell	23	22	1		Roselle Park	40	35	5
	Orange	124	104	20		Roxbury Township	55	48	7
	Oxford Township	5	4	1		Rumson	22	17	5
						Runnemede	22	20	2
						Rutherford	49	43	6
						Saddle Brook Township	37	34	3
						Saddle River	21	16	5
						Salem	29	22	7

Table 78. Full-Time Law Enforcement Employees, by City, 2006 *(Contd.)*

(Number.)

State	City	Total law enforcement employees	Total officers	Total civilians	State	City	Total law enforcement employees	Total officers	Total civilians
	Sayreville	105	87	18		Washington Township, Morris County	37	35	2
	Scotch Plains Township	51	44	7		Washington Township, Warren County	14	13	1
	Sea Bright	12	11	1		Watchung	35	28	7
	Sea Girt	16	12	4		Waterford Township	28	25	3
	Sea Isle City	31	24	7		Wayne Township	142	116	26
	Seaside Heights	30	23	7		Weehawken Township	63	58	5
	Seaside Park	20	15	5		Wenonah	6	6	0
	Secaucus	69	60	9		Westampton Township	25	22	3
	Ship Bottom	12	11	1		West Amwell Township	6	5	1
	Shrewsbury	21	16	5		West Caldwell Township	34	29	5
	Somerdale	14	13	1		West Deptford Township	45	40	5
	Somers Point	32	26	6		Westfield	73	59	14
	Somerville	39	32	7		West Long Branch	25	20	5
	South Amboy	35	29	6		West Milford Township	55	48	7
	South Bound Brook	14	13	1		West New York	137	126	11
	South Brunswick Township	107	82	25		West Orange	127	111	16
	South Hackensack Township	18	17	1		West Paterson	31	26	5
	South Harrison Township	5	5	0		Westville	11	10	1
	South Orange	63	55	8		West Wildwood	6	6	0
	South Plainfield	72	55	17		West Windsor Township	56	45	11
	South River	39	31	8		Westwood	30	26	4
	South Toms River	13	12	1		Wharton	23	21	2
	Sparta Township	46	37	9		Wildwood	58	46	12
	Spotswood	23	19	4		Wildwood Crest	30	22	8
	Springfield	47	41	6		Willingboro Township	83	71	12
	Springfield Township	10	9	1		Winfield Township	10	10	0
	Spring Lake	19	14	5		Winslow Township	96	76	20
	Spring Lake Heights	12	12	0		Woodbine	2	2	0
	Stafford Township	81	56	25		Woodbridge Township	250	201	49
	Stanhope	8	7	1		Woodbury	30	27	3
	Stillwater Township	6	5	1		Woodbury Heights	8	7	1
	Stone Harbor	22	15	7		Woodcliff Lake	19	18	1
	Stratford	14	14	0		Wood-Ridge	27	22	5
	Summit	60	51	9		Woodstown	10	9	1
	Surf City	10	10	0		Woolwich Township	18	17	1
	Swedesboro	8	7	1		Wyckoff Township	33	26	7
	Teaneck Township	115	100	15	NEW MEXICO	Alamogordo	121	72	49
	Tenafly	43	38	5		Albuquerque	1,384	972	412
	Tewksbury Township	12	11	1		Angel Fire	6	5	1
	Tinton Falls	42	41	1		Aztec	15	11	4
	Toms River Township	213	165	48		Bayard	6	6	0
	Totowa	30	27	3		Belen	30	20	10
	Trenton	419	359	60		Bernalillo	17	15	2
	Tuckerton	10	10	0		Bloomfield	22	17	5
	Union Beach	20	16	4		Bosque Farms	12	11	1
	Union City	224	175	49		Capitan	3	2	1
	Union Township	189	135	54		Carlsbad	74	54	20
	Upper Saddle River	24	18	6		Clayton	17	6	11
	Ventnor City	51	39	12		Cloudcroft	3	3	0
	Vernon Township	44	34	10		Clovis	83	64	19
	Verona	37	31	6		Cuba	6	5	1
	Vineland	174	149	25		Deming	43	38	5
	Voorhees Township	66	51	15		Estancia	5	3	2
	Waldwick	25	20	5		Eunice	9	5	4
	Wallington	26	24	2		Farmington	155	108	47
	Wall Township	84	71	13		Grants	18	14	4
	Wanaque	28	24	4		Jal	9	5	4
	Warren Township	35	28	7		Las Cruces	242	165	77
	Washington	14	13	1		Las Vegas	53	38	15
	Washington Township, Bergen County	24	24	0					
	Washington Township, Gloucester County	92	85	7					
	Washington Township, Mercer County	36	26	10					

Table 78. Full-Time Law Enforcement Employees, by City, 2006 (Contd.)

(Number.)

State	City	Total law enforcement employees	Total officers	Total civilians	State	City	Total law enforcement employees	Total officers	Total civilians
	Lordsburg	12	9	3		Canajoharie Village	5	5	0
	Los Lunas	37	27	10		Canandaigua	30	26	4
	Lovington	29	20	9		Canastota Village	8	7	1
	Melrose	2	2	0		Canton Village	11	9	2
	Mesilla	8	8	0		Carmel Town	42	34	8
	Milan	12	7	5		Carthage Village	6	6	0
	Questa	3	2	1		Catskill Village	16	15	1
	Rio Rancho	184	119	65		Cayuga Heights Village	7	6	1
	Roswell	109	78	31		Cazenovia Village	5	4	1
	Ruidoso	34	19	15		Centre Island Village	8	8	0
	Ruidoso Downs	17	9	8		Chatham Village	5	4	1
	Santa Clara	8	7	1		Cheektowaga Town	166	125	41
	Santa Rosa	14	7	7		Chester Town	12	12	0
	Silver City	38	33	5		Chester Village	12	11	1
	Socorro	30	21	9		Chittenango Village	7	6	1
	Springer	3	3	0		Cicero Town	12	11	1
	Sunland Park	24	21	3		Clarkstown Town	197	172	25
	Taos	28	21	7		Clayton Village	3	3	0
	Tatum	9	4	5		Clay Town	24	19	5
	Texico	3	3	0		Clifton Springs Village	2	2	0
	Truth or Consequences	17	15	2		Cobleskill Village	11	11	0
	Tucumcari	23	13	10		Coeymans Town	8	5	3
	Tularosa	11	7	4		Cohoes	46	33	13
NEW YORK	Addison Town and Village	2	2	0		Colonie Town	154	109	45
	Akron Village	2	2	0		Cooperstown Village	4	4	0
	Albany	456	338	118		Corning	26	22	4
	Alexandria Bay Village	2	2	0		Cornwall Town	13	9	4
	Alfred Village	6	6	0		Cortland	47	44	3
	Allegany Village	3	2	1		Crawford Town	11	10	1
	Altamont Village	1	1	0		Croton-on-Hudson Village	21	20	1
	Amherst Town	181	149	32		Cuba Town	4	4	0
	Amity Town and Belmont Village	1	1	0		Dansville Village	10	8	2
	Amityville Village	29	26	3		Deerpark Town	4	4	0
	Amsterdam	38	37	1		Delhi Village	4	4	0
	Angola Village	3	3	0		Depew Village	36	29	7
	Arcade Village	6	6	0		Deposit Village	2	2	0
	Ardsley Village	19	19	0		Dewitt Town	39	35	4
	Asharoken Village	3	3	0		Dobbs Ferry Village	29	28	1
	Attica Village	5	5	0		Dryden Village	7	6	1
	Auburn	78	69	9		Dunkirk	37	36	1
	Avon Village	5	5	0		East Aurora-Aurora Town	22	17	5
	Baldwinsville Village	17	14	3		Eastchester Town	59	52	7
	Ballston Spa Village	10	6	4		East Fishkill Town	38	29	9
	Batavia	37	32	5		East Greenbush Town	32	24	8
	Bath Village	15	12	3		East Hampton Town	85	59	26
	Beacon	34	32	2		East Hampton Village	30	26	4
	Bedford Town	50	45	5		East Rochester Village	9	8	1
	Bethlehem Town	61	42	19		East Syracuse Village	12	10	2
	Binghamton	153	143	10		Eden Town	5	4	1
	Blooming Grove Town	17	15	2		Ellenville Village	13	11	2
	Bolivar Village	1	1	0		Ellicott Town	13	12	1
	Boonville Village	3	3	0		Ellicottville	3	3	0
	Briarcliff Manor Village	20	20	0		Elmira	91	78	13
	Brighton Town	47	41	6		Elmira Heights Village	10	10	0
	Brockport Village	12	11	1		Elmira Town	3	3	0
	Bronxville Village	24	21	3		Elmsford Village	18	18	0
	Buchanan Village	6	6	0		Endicott Village	38	34	4
	Buffalo	901	753	148		Evans Town	27	22	5
	Caledonia Village	2	2	0		Fairport Village	11	10	1
	Cambridge Village	4	4	0		Fallsburg Town	25	21	4
	Camden Village	3	3	0		Floral Park Village	45	33	12
	Camillus Town and Village	26	23	3		Florida Village	1	1	0

Table 78. Full-Time Law Enforcement Employees, by City, 2006 (*Contd.*)

(Number.)

State	City	Total law enforcement employees	Total officers	Total civilians	State	City	Total law enforcement employees	Total officers	Total civilians
	Fort Edward Village	5	5	0		Lloyd Harbor Village ...	12	11	1
	Fort Plain Village	4	4	0		Lloyd Town...............	14	11	3
	Frankfort Town	2	2	0		Lockport	51	48	3
	Franklinville Village	2	2	0		Lowville Village	6	6	0
	Fredonia Village	19	15	4		Lynbrook Village	51	45	6
	Freeport Village	107	91	16		Lyons Village	12	10	2
	Fulton City....................	37	35	2		Macedon Town and Village	5	5	0
	Garden City Village.....	66	53	13		Malone Village	14	14	0
	Gates Town..................	37	30	7		Malverne Village..........	22	22	0
	Geddes Town...............	18	16	2		Mamaroneck Town......	41	40	1
	Geneseo Village	8	8	0		Mamaroneck Village ...	52	52	0
	Geneva	41	36	5		Manlius Town	43	36	7
	Glen Cove	54	50	4		Marcellus Village	3	1	2
	Glens Falls	37	31	6		Marlborough Town......	10	8	2
	Glenville Town.............	36	21	15		Massena Village	26	22	4
	Gloversville	33	31	2		Maybrook Village	2	2	0
	Goshen Town	13	12	1		Mechanicville	13	12	1
	Goshen Village.............	19	17	2		Medina Village	12	11	1
	Gouverneur Village	12	8	4		Menands Village	13	10	3
	Granville Village	6	6	0		Middleport Village	3	3	0
	Great Neck Estates Village	15	12	3		Middletown	79	66	13
	Greece Town	99	92	7		Mohawk Village	2	2	0
	Greenburgh Town........	138	119	19		Monroe Village	23	18	5
	Greene Village	2	1	1		Montgomery Town	12	11	1
	Green Island Village ...	3	2	1		Monticello Village	26	24	2
	Greenwood Lake Village	9	6	3		Moriah Town	2	2	0
	Guilderland Town........	52	36	16		Mount Kisco Village....	37	33	4
	Hamburg Town	58	58	0		Mount Morris Village ...	4	4	0
	Hamburg Village...........	16	14	2		Mount Pleasant Town....	56	47	9
	Hamilton Village..........	4	4	0		Mount Vernon..............	210	183	27
	Harriman Village	7	7	0		Newark Village	16	15	1
	Harrison Town	88	79	9		New Berlin Town	1	1	0
	Hastings-on-Hudson Village	21	21	0		Newburgh	113	102	11
	Haverstraw Town........	75	71	4		Newburgh Town............	72	59	13
	Hempstead Village	147	118	29		New Castle Town	46	42	4
	Herkimer Village	22	21	1		New Paltz Town and Village	24	20	4
	Highland Falls Village ...	14	10	4		New Rochelle	248	182	66
	Hoosick Falls Village...	5	3	2		New Windsor Town	56	44	12
	Horseheads Village......	14	11	3		New York	53,473	35,690	17,783
	Hudson Falls Village ...	16	12	4		Niagara Falls.................	155	141	14
	Hunter Town	2	2	0		Niagara Town	7	6	1
	Huntington Bay Village	6	6	0		Niskayuna Town	41	30	11
	Hyde Park Town	18	15	3		Nissequogue Village	3	3	0
	Ilion Village	20	18	2		North Castle Town.......	42	39	3
	Inlet Town....................	2	2	0		North Greenbush Town	20	18	2
	Irondequoit Town........	69	57	12		Northport Village	19	15	4
	Irvington Village	25	23	2		North Syracuse Village	15	13	2
	Jamestown	77	64	13		North Tonawanda	58	48	10
	Johnson City Village ...	42	37	5		Norwich........................	20	19	1
	Kenmore Village	24	24	0		Ocean Beach Village ...	3	3	0
	Kensington Village	6	6	0		Ogdensburg	34	29	5
	Kent Town	26	21	5		Old Brookville Village	51	40	11
	Kings Point Village	25	23	2		Old Westbury Village	30	25	5
	Kirkland Town	7	6	1		Olean............................	40	33	7
	Lackawanna..................	66	46	20		Oneonta City...............	26	26	0
	Lake Placid Village......	18	14	4		Orangetown Town	96	91	5
	Lake Success Village ...	24	21	3		Orchard Park Town	37	32	5
	Lakewood-Busti..........	9	9	0		Ossining Town.............	19	17	2
	Lancaster Town............	62	47	15		Ossining Village	67	58	9
	Larchmont Village	31	28	3		Oswego City	47	42	5
	Le Roy Village	11	8	3		Owego Village	9	8	1
	Lewiston Town and Village	11	10	1		Oxford Village..............	1	1	0
	Liberty Village	19	16	3					
	Liverpool Village	6	5	1					

ate5 ==== CRIME IN THE UNITED STATES (BERNAN PRESS)

Table 78. Full-Time Law Enforcement Employees, by City, 2006 (Contd.)

(Number.)

State	City	Total law enforcement employees	Total officers	Total civilians
	Oyster Bay Cove Village	11	11	0
	Painted Post Village	4	4	0
	Palmyra Village	6	5	1
	Peekskill	75	60	15
	Pelham Manor Village	29	28	1
	Pelham Village	30	27	3
	Penn Yan Village	12	11	1
	Perry Village	7	6	1
	Piermont Village	8	8	0
	Plattsburgh City	59	50	9
	Pleasantville Village	28	26	2
	Port Chester Village	65	62	3
	Port Dickinson Village	5	4	1
	Port Jervis	33	31	2
	Portville Village	1	1	0
	Port Washington	70	63	7
	Potsdam Village	18	14	4
	Poughkeepsie	136	101	35
	Poughkeepsie Town	97	87	10
	Pulaski Village	2	2	0
	Quogue Village	14	14	0
	Ramapo Town	138	114	24
	Rensselaer City	31	25	6
	Riverhead Town	103	82	21
	Rochester	922	725	197
	Rockville Centre Village	60	50	10
	Rome	81	77	4
	Rosendale Town	3	3	0
	Rotterdam Town	64	45	19
	Rouses Point Village	3	3	0
	Rye	44	40	4
	Rye Brook Village	27	26	1
	Sag Harbor Village	12	11	1
	Salamanca	18	18	0
	Sands Point Village	21	21	0
	Saranac Lake Village	14	14	0
	Saratoga Springs	87	71	16
	Saugerties Town	20	15	5
	Saugerties Village	11	11	0
	Scarsdale Village	45	39	6
	Schenectady	198	155	43
	Schodack Town	12	10	2
	Schoharie Village	1	1	0
	Scotia Village	14	13	1
	Seneca Falls Village	18	14	4
	Shandaken Town	4	4	0
	Shawangunk Town	4	4	0
	Sherrill	4	4	0
	Sidney Village	9	9	0
	Silver Creek Village	6	5	1
	Skaneateles Village	5	5	0
	Sleepy Hollow Village	25	25	0
	Sodus Village	1	1	0
	Solvay Village	15	14	1
	Southampton Town	139	100	39
	Southampton Village	48	37	11
	South Glens Falls Village	7	7	0
	South Nyack Village	6	6	0
	Southold Town	73	56	17
	Spring Valley Village	69	61	8
	Stony Point Town	31	30	1
	Suffern Village	31	26	5
	Syracuse	549	485	64
	Tarrytown Village	41	34	7
	Tonawanda	32	27	5
	Tonawanda Town	154	105	49
	Troy	133	117	16
	Tuckahoe Village	29	26	3
	Tuxedo Park Village	5	2	3
	Tuxedo Town	16	13	3
	Ulster Town	30	27	3
	Utica	183	165	18
	Vernon Village	1	1	0
	Vestal Town	41	37	4
	Wallkill Town	43	37	6
	Walton Village	7	6	1
	Wappingers Falls Village	3	2	1
	Warsaw Village	6	6	0
	Warwick Town	41	34	7
	Washingtonville Village	18	16	2
	Waterford Town and Village	13	10	3
	Waterloo Village	8	7	1
	Watertown	63	59	4
	Watervliet	30	26	4
	Watkins Glen Village	4	4	0
	Waverly Village	11	10	1
	Wayland Village	2	2	0
	Webb Town	5	5	0
	Webster Town and Village	39	33	6
	Wellsville Village	15	11	4
	Westfield Village	5	5	0
	Westhampton Beach Village	20	18	2
	West Seneca Town	78	64	14
	Whitehall Village	3	3	0
	White Plains	232	218	14
	Whitesboro Village	8	8	0
	Whitestown Town	5	5	0
	Windham Town	3	3	0
	Woodbury Town	26	22	4
	Woodstock Town	13	10	3
	Yonkers	682	609	73
	Yorktown Town	65	55	10
	Yorkville Village	3	3	0
NORTH CAROLINA	Aberdeen	23	21	2
	Ahoskie	21	16	5
	Albemarle	55	49	6
	Andrews	6	6	0
	Angier	13	12	1
	Apex	57	45	12
	Archdale	28	23	5
	Asheboro	76	70	6
	Asheville	238	193	45
	Atlantic Beach	22	18	4
	Aulander	1	1	0
	Aurora	2	2	0
	Ayden	22	17	5
	Badin	5	5	0
	Bailey	3	3	0
	Bald Head Island	12	11	1
	Banner Elk	9	8	1
	Beaufort	17	16	1
	Beech Mountain	13	9	4
	Belhaven	12	8	4
	Belmont	41	33	8
	Benson	14	13	1
	Bethel	6	6	0

Table 78. Full-Time Law Enforcement Employees, by City, 2006 (*Contd.*)

(Number.)

State	City	Total law enforcement employees	Total officers	Total civilians	State	City	Total law enforcement employees	Total officers	Total civilians
	Beulaville	6	5	1		Elkin	20	16	4
	Biltmore Forest	14	12	2		Elon	15	14	1
	Biscoe	9	8	1		Emerald Isle	21	16	5
	Black Creek	3	3	0		Enfield	6	5	1
	Black Mountain	19	15	4		Erwin	10	9	1
	Bladenboro	6	6	0		Fair Bluff	3	3	0
	Blowing Rock	15	11	4		Fairmont	14	10	4
	Boiling Spring Lakes	8	7	1		Farmville	19	14	5
	Boiling Springs	7	7	0		Fayetteville	497	308	189
	Bolton	1	1	0		Fletcher	14	13	1
	Boone	42	35	7		Forest City	37	31	6
	Boonville	3	3	0		Four Oaks	5	5	0
	Brevard	30	24	6		Foxfire Village	2	2	0
	Broadway	4	4	0		Franklin	17	16	1
	Brookford	1	1	0		Franklinton	11	10	1
	Bryson City	7	7	0		Fremont	3	3	0
	Bunn	2	2	0		Fuquay-Varina	32	27	5
	Burgaw	10	9	1		Garland	2	2	0
	Burlington	150	110	40		Garner	62	56	6
	Burnsville	9	8	1		Garysburg	2	2	0
	Butner	49	42	7		Gaston	2	2	0
	Cameron	1	1	0		Gastonia	175	147	28
	Candor	5	5	0		Gibsonville	15	14	1
	Canton	18	13	5		Glen Alpine	2	2	0
	Cape Carteret	5	5	0		Goldsboro	111	101	10
	Carolina Beach	30	27	3		Graham	36	33	3
	Carrboro	38	36	2		Granite Falls	14	12	2
	Carthage	12	11	1		Granite Quarry	6	6	0
	Cary	184	152	32		Greensboro	664	530	134
	Caswell Beach	4	4	0		Greenville	210	170	40
	Catawba	2	2	0		Grifton	7	7	0
	Chadbourn	9	8	1		Hamlet	21	17	4
	Chapel Hill	131	110	21		Havelock	34	27	7
	Charlotte-Mecklenburg[1]	2,007	1,558	449		Haw River	8	8	0
	Cherryville	23	18	5		Henderson	56	47	9
	China Grove	12	12	0		Hendersonville	48	37	11
	Chocowinity	3	3	0		Hertford	8	7	1
	Claremont	9	8	1		Hickory	134	108	26
	Clayton	43	39	4		Highlands	11	10	1
	Cleveland	4	4	0		High Point	256	222	34
	Clinton	38	35	3		Hillsborough	26	24	2
	Clyde	4	4	0		Holden Beach	9	9	0
	Coats	5	5	0		Holly Ridge	6	6	0
	Columbus	6	6	0		Holly Springs	32	25	7
	Concord	164	139	25		Hope Mills	41	30	11
	Conover	24	21	3		Hot Springs	1	1	0
	Conway	1	1	0		Hudson	12	11	1
	Cooleemee	3	3	0		Huntersville	69	62	7
	Cornelius	55	40	15		Indian Beach	4	4	0
	Cramerton	11	11	0		Jackson	3	1	2
	Creedmoor	17	13	4		Jacksonville	127	103	24
	Dallas	17	13	4		Jefferson	3	3	0
	Davidson	17	16	1		Jonesville	11	10	1
	Denton	6	6	0		Kannapolis	94	72	22
	Dobson	5	5	0		Kenansville	4	4	0
	Drexel	5	5	0		Kenly	9	9	0
	Dunn	49	38	11		Kernersville	82	63	19
	Durham	599	458	141		Kill Devil Hills	29	23	6
	East Bend	2	2	0		King	23	21	2
	East Spencer	5	5	0		Kings Mountain	38	32	6
	Eden	57	47	10		Kingstown	2	2	0
	Edenton	16	14	2		Kinston	86	76	10
	Elizabeth City	54	43	11		Kitty Hawk	19	17	2
	Elizabethtown	15	14	1		Knightdale	21	20	1
						Kure Beach	11	10	1
						La Grange	9	9	0
						Lake Lure	10	9	1
						Lake Royale	5	5	0

[1] The employee data presented in this table for Charlotte-Mecklenburg represent only Charlotte-Mecklenburg Police Department employees and exclude Mecklenburg County Sheriff's Office employees.

Table 78. Full-Time Law Enforcement Employees, by City, 2006 (*Contd.*)

(Number.)

State	City	Total law enforcement employees	Total officers	Total civilians	State	City	Total law enforcement employees	Total officers	Total civilians
	Lake Waccamaw	5	5	0		Pilot Mountain	10	9	1
	Landis	10	9	1		Pinebluff	3	3	0
	Laurel Park	6	6	0		Pinehurst	28	23	5
	Laurinburg	41	35	6		Pine Knoll Shores	10	9	1
	Leland	25	22	3		Pine Level	4	4	0
	Lenoir	71	54	17		Pinetops	7	5	2
	Lexington	76	65	11		Pineville	47	36	11
	Liberty	11	10	1		Pink Hill	1	1	0
	Lilesville	1	1	0		Pittsboro	11	10	1
	Lillington	13	12	1		Plymouth	12	12	0
	Lincolnton	36	31	5		Princeton	4	4	0
	Littleton	3	3	0		Raeford	16	15	1
	Locust	7	6	1		Raleigh	810	691	119
	Longview	15	15	0		Ramseur	7	7	0
	Louisburg	14	13	1		Randleman	13	13	0
	Lowell	8	8	0		Ranlo	7	7	0
	Lumberton	85	75	10		Red Springs	20	16	4
	Madison	13	12	1		Reidsville	53	44	9
	Maggie Valley	10	9	1		Richlands	6	6	0
	Magnolia	2	2	0		Rich Square	2	2	0
	Maiden	15	14	1		River Bend	5	5	0
	Manteo	8	7	1		Roanoke Rapids	45	42	3
	Marion	28	23	5		Robbins	6	6	0
	Marshall	3	3	0		Robersonville	5	5	0
	Mars Hill	5	5	0		Rockingham	39	34	5
	Marshville	8	8	0		Rockwell	4	4	0
	Matthews	63	52	11		Rocky Mount	166	131	35
	Maxton	15	10	5		Rolesville	8	8	0
	Mayodan	16	14	2		Roseboro	5	5	0
	Maysville	2	2	0		Rose Hill	4	4	0
	McAdenville	2	2	0		Rowland	7	6	1
	Mebane	22	19	3		Roxboro	36	32	4
	Middlesex	5	5	0		Rutherfordton	15	15	0
	Mint Hill	29	27	2		Salisbury	104	85	19
	Mocksville	21	19	2		Saluda	4	4	0
	Monroe	82	76	6		Sanford	95	75	20
	Montreat	5	5	0		Scotland Neck	7	5	2
	Mooresville	61	49	12		Seagrove	1	1	0
	Morehead City	47	38	9		Selma	26	22	4
	Morganton	94	63	31		Seven Devils	5	5	0
	Morrisville	30	28	2		Shallotte	12	11	1
	Mount Airy	53	40	13		Sharpsburg	6	6	0
	Mount Gilead	6	5	1		Shelby	87	71	16
	Mount Holly	37	30	7		Siler City	24	19	5
	Mount Olive	16	15	1		Smithfield	35	31	4
	Murfreesboro	15	10	5		Southern Pines	34	26	8
	Murphy	11	7	4		Southern Shores	8	7	1
	Nags Head	24	22	2		Southport	11	10	1
	Nashville	15	14	1		Sparta	6	6	0
	Navassa	3	3	0		Spencer	14	13	1
	New Bern	129	88	41		Spindale	14	14	0
	Newland	5	5	0		Spring Hope	6	6	0
	Newport	9	9	0		Spring Lake	23	18	5
	Newton	43	35	8		Spruce Pine	10	10	0
	Newton Grove	3	3	0		Stallings	20	18	2
	Norlina	5	5	0		Stanfield	4	4	0
	North Topsail Beach	12	11	1		Stanley	14	10	4
	Northwest	2	2	0		Stantonsburg	4	4	0
	North Wilkesboro	27	23	4		Star	4	4	0
	Norwood	7	6	1		Statesville	83	67	16
	Oakboro	4	4	0		Stoneville	5	5	0
	Oak Island	29	24	5		St. Pauls	18	13	5
	Ocean Isle Beach	12	12	0		Sugar Mountain	5	5	0
	Old Fort	6	5	1		Sunset Beach	11	11	0
	Oxford	37	31	6		Surf City	17	16	1
	Parkton	2	2	0		Swansboro	7	7	0
	Pembroke	18	14	4		Sylva	13	12	1
	Pikeville	3	3	0		Tabor City	10	9	1

Table 78. Full-Time Law Enforcement Employees, by City, 2006 (*Contd.*)

(Number.)

State	City	Total law enforcement employees	Total officers	Total civilians	State	City	Total law enforcement employees	Total officers	Total civilians
	Tarboro	34	28	6		Linton	1	1	0
	Taylorsville	11	11	0		Lisbon	3	3	0
	Taylortown	2	2	0		Mandan	36	27	9
	Thomasville	70	62	8		Mayville	3	3	0
	Topsail Beach	8	7	1		Minot	81	60	21
	Trent Woods	4	4	0		Northwood	2	2	0
	Troutman	7	7	0		Oakes	2	2	0
	Troy	10	9	1		Rolla	3	3	0
	Tryon	9	7	2		Rugby	4	4	0
	Valdese	13	12	1		Steele	1	1	0
	Vanceboro	2	2	0		Thompson	1	1	0
	Vass	3	3	0		Valley City	19	13	6
	Wadesboro	25	20	5		Wahpeton	16	14	2
	Wagram	2	2	0		Watford City	4	4	0
	Wake Forest	49	41	8		West Fargo	43	30	13
	Wallace	16	13	3		Williston	30	22	8
	Walnut Cove	6	6	0	OHIO	Ada	11	8	3
	Walnut Creek	2	2	0		Addyston	1	1	0
	Warrenton	6	5	1		Akron	496	453	43
	Warsaw	14	10	4		Alliance	52	39	13
	Washington	42	33	9		Amberley Village	20	16	4
	Waxhaw	13	12	1		Amelia	7	6	1
	Waynesville	36	30	6		Amherst	26	20	6
	Weaverville	14	13	1		Amsterdam	1	1	0
	Weldon	8	6	2		Ansonia	2	2	0
	Wendell	17	15	2		Arcanum	4	4	0
	West Jefferson	7	7	0		Archbold	8	8	0
	Whispering Pines	8	7	1		Ashland	39	30	9
	Whitakers	3	3	0		Ashtabula	35	31	4
	White Lake	5	5	0		Ashville	6	6	0
	Whiteville	23	19	4		Athens	34	26	8
	Wilkesboro	19	17	2		Aurora	32	25	7
	Williamston	20	19	1		Austintown	44	36	8
	Wilmington	299	240	59		Avon	34	27	7
	Wilson	129	108	21		Avon Lake	34	29	5
	Windsor	8	8	0		Bainbridge Township	26	18	8
	Wingate	7	7	0		Baltimore	1	1	0
	Winston-Salem	627	485	142		Barberton	52	40	12
	Winterville	20	19	1		Barnesville	11	7	4
	Winton	1	1	0		Batavia	4	4	0
	Woodfin	11	11	0		Bath Township, Summit County	28	20	8
	Woodland	1	1	0		Bay Village	28	24	4
	Wrightsville Beach	28	23	5		Beachwood	56	43	13
	Yadkinville	12	11	1		Beavercreek	65	48	17
	Yanceyville	6	6	0		Beaver Township	16	12	4
	Youngsville	8	7	1		Bedford	43	33	10
	Zebulon	21	20	1		Bedford Heights	63	32	31
NORTH DAKOTA	Beulah	6	5	1		Bellaire	11	11	0
	Bismarck	114	88	26		Bellbrook	17	12	5
	Bowman	4	3	1		Bellefontaine	30	23	7
	Carrington	4	4	0		Bellevue	18	14	4
	Cavalier	4	4	0		Bellville	5	5	0
	Crosby	2	2	0		Bentleyville Village	5	5	0
	Devils Lake	18	16	2		Bethel	13	12	1
	Dickinson	40	27	13		Bethesda	1	1	0
	Emerado	1	1	0		Bettsville	1	1	0
	Fargo	144	126	18		Beverly	2	2	0
	Fessenden	1	1	0		Bexley	35	28	7
	Grafton	10	9	1		Blanchester	6	6	0
	Grand Forks	94	79	15		Blendon Township	12	11	1
	Harvey	3	3	0		Bluffton	6	6	0
	Hazen	4	4	0		Boardman	79	61	18
	Hillsboro	2	2	0		Bowling Green	57	42	15
	Jamestown	32	28	4		Bradford	2	2	0
	Lamoure	2	2	0		Bratenahl	14	11	3
	Larimore	2	2	0		Brecksville	38	31	7
	Lincoln	2	2	0		Brewster	4	4	0

Table 78. Full-Time Law Enforcement Employees, by City, 2006 (Contd.)

(Number.)

State	City	Total law enforcement employees	Total officers	Total civilians	State	City	Total law enforcement employees	Total officers	Total civilians
	Brimfield Township	13	12	1		Edgerton	4	4	0
	Broadview Heights	44	31	13		Elida	2	1	1
	Brookfield Township	9	8	1		Elyria	131	86	45
	Brooklyn	40	32	8		Englewood	24	19	5
	Brooklyn Heights	17	17	0		Euclid	150	96	54
	Brook Park	55	44	11		Evendale	22	20	2
	Brookville	16	11	5		Fairborn	58	42	16
	Brunswick	54	39	15		Fairfax	9	8	1
	Bryan	26	18	8		Fairfield	80	60	20
	Buckeye Lake	4	4	0		Fairfield Township	16	15	1
	Bucyrus	22	18	4		Fairlawn	33	23	10
	Burton	3	3	0		Fairport Harbor	8	7	1
	Butler Township	16	15	1		Fairview Park	27	26	1
	Cadiz	6	6	0		Fayette	2	2	0
	Cambridge	29	23	6		Findlay	92	73	19
	Canal Fulton	9	8	1		Forest	2	2	0
	Canfield	20	14	6		Forest Park	41	34	7
	Canton	214	176	38		Fort Recovery	1	1	0
	Carey	11	7	4		Fort Shawnee	5	4	1
	Carlisle	8	7	1		Franklin	32	25	7
	Carrollton	8	8	0		Fremont	40	33	7
	Celina	22	16	6		Gahanna	71	57	14
	Centerville	53	40	13		Galion	19	14	5
	Chagrin Falls	19	11	8		Gallipolis	13	12	1
	Champion Township	10	9	1		Garfield Heights	80	61	19
	Chardon	16	10	6		Gates Mills	16	12	4
	Chester Township	14	13	1		Geneva	16	12	4
	Cheviot	10	10	0		Genoa	4	4	0
	Chillicothe	50	44	6		Genoa Township	26	24	2
	Cincinnati	1,335	1,086	249		Georgetown	8	8	0
	Circleville	32	24	8		Germantown	16	11	5
	Clayton	15	15	0		German Township, Montgomery County	5	5	0
	Clearcreek Township	11	11	0		Gibsonburg	4	4	0
	Cleveland	1,962	1,591	371		Girard	16	13	3
	Cleveland Heights	121	109	12		Glendale	7	7	0
	Cleves	3	3	0		Gnadenhutten	2	2	0
	Clinton Township	10	9	1		Golf Manor	10	9	1
	Clyde	18	14	4		Goshen Township, Clermont County	14	13	1
	Coitsville Township	2	2	0		Grandview Heights	20	16	4
	Coldwater	6	6	0		Granville	13	10	3
	Columbiana	16	12	4		Greenfield	12	10	2
	Columbus	2,178	1,829	349		Greenhills	9	8	1
	Conneaut	25	19	6		Greenville	29	22	7
	Copley Township	27	20	7		Greenwich	4	4	0
	Cortland	10	10	0		Grove City	77	59	18
	Covington	6	5	1		Groveport	19	18	1
	Crestline	12	8	4		Hamilton	162	135	27
	Creston	3	2	1		Hamler-Marion Township	1	1	0
	Cridersville	3	3	0		Harrison	24	21	3
	Crooksville	6	5	1		Hartville	7	7	0
	Cuyahoga Falls	116	93	23		Heath	25	18	7
	Dalton	1	1	0		Hebron	7	6	1
	Danville	2	2	0		Hicksville	9	8	1
	Defiance	30	27	3		Highland Heights	29	22	7
	Delaware	64	47	17		Highland Hills	7	7	0
	Delhi Township	32	29	3		Hilliard	67	50	17
	Delphos	18	14	4		Hillsboro	18	16	2
	Delta	6	6	0		Hinckley Township	13	10	3
	Dennison	4	4	0		Holgate	1	1	0
	Deshler	2	2	0		Holland	8	8	0
	Donnelsville	1	1	0		Howland Township	19	18	1
	Dover	22	21	1		Hubbard Township	7	6	1
	Doylestown	7	6	1		Huber Heights	67	50	17
	Dublin	89	67	22		Hudson	36	28	8
	Eastlake	48	34	14		Hunting Valley	10	10	0
	East Liverpool	23	18	5					
	East Palestine	8	6	2					
	Eaton	20	14	6					

Table 78. Full-Time Law Enforcement Employees, by City, 2006 (*Contd.*)

(Number.)

State	City	Total law enforcement employees	Total officers	Total civilians	State	City	Total law enforcement employees	Total officers	Total civilians
	Huron	19	14	5		Mentor	113	81	32
	Independence	49	35	14		Mentor-on-the-Lake	16	11	5
	Indian Hill	25	20	5		Miamisburg	48	39	9
	Ironton	20	15	5		Miami Township	36	34	2
	Jackson	22	17	5		Middleburg Heights	38	31	7
	Jackson Township, Mahoning County	3	3	0		Middlefield	12	8	4
	Jackson Township, Montgomery County	6	6	0		Middletown	116	78	38
	Jackson Township, Stark County	47	39	8		Milford	16	14	2
	Jefferson	6	5	1		Millersburg	11	11	0
	Johnstown	14	10	4		Minerva	14	9	5
	Junction City	1	1	0		Minerva Park	5	5	0
	Kalida	1	1	0		Mingo Junction	10	9	1
	Kelleys Island	1	1	0		Minster	6	6	0
	Kent	54	40	14		Mogadore	8	8	0
	Kenton	16	16	0		Monroe	22	17	5
	Kettering	111	81	30		Monroeville	4	4	0
	Kirtland	14	9	5		Montgomery	24	21	3
	Kirtland Hills	9	8	1		Montpelier	9	8	1
	Lagrange	5	5	0		Montville Township	10	10	0
	Lakemore	6	6	0		Moraine	43	33	10
	Lake Township	15	14	1		Moreland Hills	13	12	1
	Lakewood	109	88	21		Mount Healthy	11	10	1
	Lancaster	82	62	20		Mount Orab	6	6	0
	Lawrence Township	5	5	0		Mount Sterling	9	5	4
	Lebanon	36	27	9		Mount Vernon	28	26	2
	Leipsic	4	4	0		Munroe Falls	8	8	0
	Lexington	13	9	4		Napoleon	22	16	6
	Liberty Township	27	22	5		Nelsonville	8	8	0
	Lima	104	82	22		New Albany	21	15	6
	Lincoln Heights	8	8	0		Newark	100	80	20
	Lisbon	10	6	4		New Boston	12	8	4
	Lithopolis	2	2	0		New Bremen	6	6	0
	Lockland	14	13	1		Newburgh Heights	5	2	3
	Logan	19	17	2		Newcomerstown	12	7	5
	London	19	14	5		New Franklin	16	12	4
	Lorain	125	103	22		New Lebanon	8	8	0
	Lordstown	12	8	4		New Lexington	11	7	4
	Louisville	12	9	3		New Paris	1	1	0
	Loveland	20	18	2		New Philadelphia	26	22	4
	Luckey	1	1	0		Newton Falls	10	7	3
	Lyndhurst	40	31	9		Newtown	6	6	0
	Macedonia	29	22	7		Niles	41	35	6
	Madeira	13	12	1		North Baltimore	6	6	0
	Madison Township, Lake County	19	17	2		North Canton	32	24	8
	Magnolia	2	2	0		North College Hill	15	14	1
	Malvern	1	1	0		Northfield	6	6	0
	Mansfield	130	90	40		North Kingsville	5	5	0
	Maple Heights	48	40	8		North Olmsted	74	57	17
	Mariemont	11	10	1		North Randall	15	13	2
	Marietta	38	30	8		North Ridgeville	46	37	9
	Marion	80	64	16		North Royalton	57	37	20
	Marion Township	2	2	0		Northwood	28	21	7
	Marlboro Township	4	3	1		Norwalk	31	24	7
	Martins Ferry	18	14	4		Norwood	51	50	1
	Marysville	34	29	5		Oak Harbor	8	5	3
	Mason	43	39	4		Oakwood, Montgomery County	37	31	6
	Massillon	49	47	2		Oakwood Village	15	13	2
	Maumee	59	44	15		Oberlin	22	16	6
	Mayfield Heights	46	36	10		Olmsted Falls	16	10	6
	Mayfield Village	24	16	8		Olmsted Township	26	22	4
	McComb	4	4	0		Ontario	21	17	4
	McConnelsville	3	3	0		Oregon	60	47	13
	Mechanicsburg	3	3	0		Orrville	18	14	4
	Medina	46	36	10		Orwell	6	5	1
	Medina Township	10	9	1		Ottawa	8	8	0
						Ottawa Hills	15	11	4
						Owensville	1	1	0

Table 78. Full-Time Law Enforcement Employees, by City, 2006 (*Contd.*)

(Number.)

State	City	Total law enforcement employees	Total officers	Total civilians	State	City	Total law enforcement employees	Total officers	Total civilians
	Oxford	38	25	13		Spencer	3	3	0
	Oxford Township	3	3	0		Spencerville	4	4	0
	Painesville	40	36	4		Springboro	29	23	6
	Parma	128	84	44		Springdale	47	38	9
	Parma Heights	41	34	7		Springfield	140	120	20
	Pataskala	21	20	1		Springfield Township, Hamilton County	56	49	7
	Paulding	5	4	1		Springfield Township, Mahoning County	7	7	0
	Payne	1	1	0		Springfield Township, Summit County	18	16	2
	Peebles	1	1	0		St. Bernard	14	13	1
	Pepper Pike	27	20	7		Steubenville	54	45	9
	Perkins Township	30	24	6		St. Henry	2	2	0
	Perrysburg	39	30	9		St. Marys	19	15	4
	Perry Township, Franklin County	11	10	1		Stow	48	38	10
	Perry Township, Montgomery County	4	4	0		St. Paris	4	4	0
	Perry Township, Stark County	23	18	5		Streetsboro	30	23	7
	Perrysville	2	2	0		Strongsville	97	76	21
	Pickerington	34	24	10		Sycamore	1	1	0
	Pierce Township	15	15	0		Sylvania	40	33	7
	Piqua	40	34	6		Tallmadge	38	27	11
	Plain City	9	9	0		Terrace Park	6	6	0
	Poland Township	13	11	2		Tiffin	42	29	13
	Poland Village	6	6	0		Tipp City	21	18	3
	Pomeroy	11	7	4		Toledo	815	690	125
	Port Clinton	18	13	5		Toronto	10	10	0
	Powell	18	17	1		Trenton	17	13	4
	Ravenna	32	24	8		Trotwood	48	44	4
	Reading	23	19	4		Twinsburg	46	34	12
	Reminderville	8	8	0		Uhrichsville	8	8	0
	Reynoldsburg	65	52	13		Union City	4	4	0
	Richfield	23	17	6		Uniontown	9	7	2
	Richmond Heights	29	22	7		Union Township, Clermont County	68	53	15
	Richwood	6	6	0		Union Township, Licking County	2	2	0
	Rittman	11	8	3		University Heights	34	28	6
	Riverside	34	32	2		Upper Arlington	62	49	13
	Roaming Shores Village	2	2	0		Urbana	22	22	0
	Rockford	2	2	0		Utica	9	4	5
	Roseville	3	3	0		Valley View	20	18	2
	Rossford	14	13	1		Vandalia	40	31	9
	Russell Township	8	7	1		Van Wert	31	23	8
	Russellville	1	1	0		Vermilion	23	18	5
	Sagamore Hills	13	10	3		Wadsworth	38	29	9
	Salem	25	24	1		Waite Hill	5	5	0
	Saline Township	5	5	0		Walbridge	5	4	1
	Sandusky	62	52	10		Walton Hills	20	15	5
	Sebring	11	7	4		Wapakoneta	19	14	5
	Seven Hills	19	18	1		Warren	101	82	19
	Seville	9	8	1		Warrensville Heights	47	36	11
	Shadyside	10	6	4		Warren Township	8	8	0
	Shaker Heights	100	72	28		Washington Court House	27	21	6
	Sharon Township	10	10	0		Waterville Township	5	5	0
	Sharonville	48	38	10		Wauseon	16	14	2
	Shawnee Hills	2	2	0		Waynesburg	1	1	0
	Shawnee Township	14	9	5		Waynesville	4	4	0
	Sheffield Lake	16	12	4		Wellington	8	6	2
	Shelby	19	15	4		Wells Township	12	11	1
	Sidney	52	40	12		Wellsville	7	7	0
	Silverton	13	10	3		West Carrollton	32	25	7
	Smith Township	4	4	0		West Chester Township	105	82	23
	Smithville	3	3	0		Westerville	85	71	14
	Solon	64	46	18		West Jefferson	13	10	3
	Somerset	2	2	0		Westlake	69	51	18
	South Bloomfield	3	3	0		West Liberty	3	3	0
	South Euclid	49	37	12					
	South Russell	9	9	0					
	South Zanesville	3	3	0					

Table 78. Full-Time Law Enforcement Employees, by City, 2006 (*Contd.*)

(Number.)

State	City	Total law enforcement employees	Total officers	Total civilians	State	City	Total law enforcement employees	Total officers	Total civilians
	Whitehall	51	42	9		Duncan	49	42	7
	Wickliffe	40	31	9		Durant	43	32	11
	Willard	16	13	3		Edmond	141	112	29
	Williamsburg	5	5	0		Elk City	37	25	12
	Willoughby	59	44	15		El Reno	33	23	10
	Willoughby Hills	25	18	7		Enid	108	91	17
	Willowick	35	25	10		Eufaula	14	11	3
	Wilmington	26	24	2		Fairfax	5	2	3
	Wintersville	9	8	1		Fairview	7	4	3
	Woodlawn	16	15	1		Fort Gibson	16	11	5
	Woodsfield	6	6	0		Frederick	17	9	8
	Woodville	5	5	0		Geary	9	5	4
	Wooster	43	38	5		Glenpool	21	14	7
	Wyoming	19	16	3		Goodwell	3	3	0
	Xenia	69	45	24		Grove	25	18	7
	Youngstown	217	178	39		Guthrie	24	19	5
	Zanesville	90	55	35		Guymon	25	17	8
OKLAHOMA	Achille	5	3	2		Harrah	11	11	0
	Ada	40	34	6		Hartshorne	5	5	0
	Agra	1	1	0		Haskell	6	6	0
	Altus	58	39	19		Healdton	8	4	4
	Alva	10	9	1		Heavener	12	8	4
	Anadarko	16	11	5		Henryetta	17	12	5
	Antlers	10	6	4		Hinton	4	4	0
	Apache	3	3	0		Hobart	13	7	6
	Ardmore	56	48	8		Holdenville	11	8	3
	Arkoma	7	3	4		Hollis	9	5	4
	Atoka	15	14	1		Hominy	11	6	5
	Bartlesville	75	50	25		Hooker	4	4	0
	Beaver	2	2	0		Hugo	18	12	6
	Beggs	6	3	3		Hulbert	4	3	1
	Bethany	35	28	7		Hydro	2	2	0
	Bixby	33	23	10		Idabel	24	18	6
	Blackwell	22	15	7		Jay	11	6	5
	Blanchard	18	14	4		Jenks	20	14	6
	Boise City	3	3	0		Jones	5	5	0
	Boley	1	1	0		Kingfisher	10	8	2
	Bristow	14	9	5		Kingston	7	7	0
	Broken Arrow	171	123	48		Konawa	6	5	1
	Broken Bow	18	13	5		Krebs	6	6	0
	Caddo	3	3	0		Lawton	214	159	55
	Calera	10	9	1		Lexington	11	6	5
	Carnegie	8	4	4		Lindsay	11	7	4
	Catoosa	17	16	1		Locust Grove	10	6	4
	Chandler	15	8	7		Lone Grove	9	6	3
	Checotah	13	11	2		Luther	5	5	0
	Chelsea	9	6	3		Madill	13	11	2
	Cherokee	3	3	0		Mangum	10	6	4
	Chickasha	37	27	10		Mannford	11	8	3
	Choctaw	16	14	2		Marietta	5	4	1
	Chouteau	8	7	1		Marlow	13	10	3
	Claremore	52	37	15		Maysville	5	4	1
	Clayton	6	3	3		McAlester	59	46	13
	Cleveland	6	6	0		McLoud	11	6	5
	Clinton	24	14	10		Meeker	4	4	0
	Coalgate	6	6	0		Miami	43	31	12
	Colbert	5	5	0		Midwest City	117	93	24
	Collinsville	14	9	5		Minco	4	4	0
	Comanche	4	4	0		Moore	75	69	6
	Cordell	9	6	3		Mooreland	2	2	0
	Coweta	19	13	6		Morris	4	4	0
	Crescent	7	4	3		Mountain View	3	3	0
	Cushing	22	15	7		Muldrow	8	8	0
	Davenport	2	2	0		Muskogee	111	89	22
	Davis	14	10	4		Mustang	26	19	7
	Del City	39	30	9		Newcastle	20	14	6
	Dewey	10	8	2		Newkirk	8	6	2
	Drumright	5	5	0		Nichols Hills	17	13	4

Table 78. Full-Time Law Enforcement Employees, by City, 2006 (*Contd.*)

(Number.)

State	City	Total law enforcement employees	Total officers	Total civilians	State	City	Total law enforcement employees	Total officers	Total civilians
	Nicoma Park	6	5	1		Wetumka	5	5	0
	Noble	14	10	4		Wewoka	11	8	3
	Norman	181	129	52		Wilburton	7	6	1
	Nowata	8	6	2		Wilson	5	3	2
	Oilton	4	4	0		Woodward	33	24	9
	Okemah	11	7	4		Wright City	2	2	0
	Oklahoma City	1,233	994	239		Wynnewood	5	4	1
	Okmulgee	28	27	1		Yale	7	7	0
	Oologah	4	4	0		Yukon	50	34	16
	Owasso	56	40	16	**OREGON**	Albany	92	62	30
	Pauls Valley	20	14	6		Amity	2	2	0
	Pawhuska	13	7	6		Ashland	38	30	8
	Pawnee	6	6	0		Astoria	25	16	9
	Perkins	6	6	0		Athena	2	2	0
	Perry	18	10	8		Aumsville	5	4	1
	Piedmont	11	9	2		Aurora	2	2	0
	Pocola	8	5	3		Baker City	17	15	2
	Ponca City	62	50	12		Bandon	8	7	1
	Porum	2	2	0		Banks	3	3	0
	Poteau	34	27	7		Beaverton	149	120	29
	Prague	9	6	3		Bend	105	81	24
	Pryor	25	19	6		Black Butte	7	6	1
	Purcell	18	18	0		Boardman	8	7	1
	Ringling	1	1	0		Brookings	20	13	7
	Roland	14	9	5		Burns	4	4	0
	Rush Springs	3	3	0		Canby	30	25	5
	Sallisaw	31	21	10		Cannon Beach	9	8	1
	Sand Springs	43	30	13		Carlton	3	3	0
	Sapulpa	58	46	12		Central Point	28	23	5
	Sayre	10	6	4		Clatskanie	6	5	1
	Seiling	2	2	0		Coburg	6	5	1
	Seminole	15	12	3		Condon	2	1	1
	Shawnee	71	49	22		Coos Bay	32	22	10
	Skiatook	19	14	5		Coquille	7	6	1
	Snyder	3	3	0		Cornelius	13	13	0
	Spencer	9	7	2		Corvallis	71	48	23
	Spiro	3	3	0		Cottage Grove	24	17	7
	Stigler	13	8	5		Culver	1	1	0
	Stillwater	107	72	35		Dallas	20	19	1
	Stilwell	20	13	7		Eagle Point	15	13	2
	Stratford	3	3	0		Elgin	3	3	0
	Stringtown	7	6	1		Enterprise	4	4	0
	Stroud	14	9	5		Eugene	292	178	114
	Sulphur	15	11	4		Fairview	13	12	1
	Tahlequah	42	28	14		Florence	23	15	8
	Talihina	10	5	5		Forest Grove	30	28	2
	Tecumseh	16	11	5		Gearhart	3	3	0
	Texhoma	2	2	0		Gervais	4	4	0
	The Village	27	21	6		Gladstone	18	16	2
	Tishomingo	7	6	1		Gold Beach	5	4	1
	Tonkawa	11	8	3		Grants Pass	67	42	25
	Tulsa	952	816	136		Gresham	159	119	40
	Tushka	3	3	0		Hermiston	34	23	11
	Tuttle	15	10	5		Hillsboro	150	115	35
	Valliant	7	4	3		Hines	3	3	0
	Vian	4	4	0		Hood River	17	15	2
	Vinita	21	16	5		Hubbard	6	5	1
	Wagoner	18	13	5		Independence	15	13	2
	Walters	4	4	0		Jacksonville	5	4	1
	Warner	3	3	0		John Day	9	4	5
	Warr Acres	26	21	5		Junction City	14	9	5
	Watonga	11	8	3		Keizer	48	40	8
	Waukomis	3	3	0		King City	5	5	0
	Waurika	2	2	0		Klamath Falls	45	40	5
	Waynoka	4	4	0		La Grande	33	18	15
	Weatherford	31	20	11		Lake Oswego	70	40	30
	Weleetka	9	3	6		Lakeview	6	6	0
	Westville	11	7	4		Lebanon	34	22	12

Table 78. Full-Time Law Enforcement Employees, by City, 2006 (*Contd.*)

(Number.)

State	City	Total law enforcement employees	Total officers	Total civilians	State	City	Total law enforcement employees	Total officers	Total civilians
	Lincoln City	26	18	8		Albion	1	1	0
	Madras	10	9	1		Aldan	4	4	0
	Malin	1	1	0		Aliquippa	18	18	0
	Manzanita	3	3	0		Allegheny Township, Blair County	5	5	0
	McMinnville	39	32	7		Allegheny Township, Westmoreland County	9	8	1
	Medford	151	98	53		Allentown	277	191	86
	Milton-Freewater	17	11	6		Altoona	74	66	8
	Milwaukie	37	33	4		Ambler	14	12	2
	Molalla	15	12	3		Ambridge	12	12	0
	Monmouth	14	12	2		Amity Township	14	13	1
	Mount Angel	7	6	1		Arnold	12	11	1
	Myrtle Creek	10	8	2		Ashland	5	5	0
	Myrtle Point	6	6	0		Ashley	2	2	0
	Newberg-Dundee	41	28	13		Aspinwall	7	6	1
	Newport	23	19	4		Aston Township	18	16	2
	North Bend	24	17	7		Athens	7	6	1
	North Plains	2	2	0		Athens Township	10	9	1
	Nyssa	7	7	0		Auburn	1	1	0
	Oakridge	11	6	5		Avalon	6	6	0
	Ontario	29	22	7		Baldwin Township	5	5	0
	Oregon City	40	33	7		Bally	2	2	0
	Pendleton	26	23	3		Bangor	10	9	1
	Philomath	9	8	1		Barrett Township	6	6	0
	Phoenix	8	6	2		Beaver	10	8	2
	Pilot Rock	2	2	0		Beaver Falls	19	18	1
	Prairie City	1	1	0		Bedford	5	5	0
	Prineville	28	17	11		Bedminster Township	6	5	1
	Rainier	7	6	1		Bell Acres	4	4	0
	Redmond	48	33	15		Bellefonte	11	9	2
	Reedsport	15	10	5		Bellevue	16	13	3
	Rockaway Beach	2	2	0		Bellwood	2	2	0
	Rogue River	6	5	1		Bensalem Township	100	77	23
	Roseburg	39	35	4		Berks-Lehigh Regional	27	26	1
	Salem	290	185	105		Bern Township	13	13	0
	Sandy	13	11	2		Berwick	14	13	1
	Scappoose	10	9	1		Bessemer	1	1	0
	Seaside	27	20	7		Bethel Park	44	38	6
	Shady Cove	4	3	1		Bethel Township, Berks County	2	2	0
	Sherwood	25	22	3		Bethlehem Township	36	34	2
	Silverton	16	15	1		Biglerville	2	2	0
	Springfield	109	71	38		Birdsboro	8	7	1
	Stanfield	4	4	0		Birmingham Township	4	4	0
	Stayton	18	15	3		Blairsville	6	6	0
	St. Helens	19	17	2		Blair Township	4	4	0
	Sunriver	12	11	1		Blakely	3	3	0
	Sutherlin	15	13	2		Blawnox	4	4	0
	Sweet Home	22	15	7		Bloomsburg Town	19	15	4
	Talent	10	8	2		Boyertown	8	7	1
	The Dalles	21	19	2		Brackenridge	4	4	0
	Tigard	80	64	16		Braddock Hills	1	1	0
	Tillamook	13	10	3		Bradford	22	22	0
	Toledo	13	8	5		Bradford Township	5	5	0
	Troutdale	25	21	4		Brandywine Regional	17	16	1
	Tualatin	44	36	8		Brecknock Township, Berks County	6	6	0
	Turner	3	3	0		Brentwood	17	15	2
	Umatilla	11	9	2		Bridgeport	10	9	1
	Vernonia	5	5	0		Bridgeville	10	9	1
	Warrenton	9	8	1		Bridgewater	2	2	0
	West Linn	33	27	6		Brighton Township	6	6	0
	Weston	1	1	0		Bristol	15	13	2
	Winston	8	7	1		Bristol Township	81	69	12
	Woodburn	40	31	9		Brockway	2	2	0
	Yamhill	2	2	0					
PENNSYL–VANIA	Abington Township	116	91	25					
	Adams Township, Butler County	5	5	0					
	Akron	4	4	0					

Table 78. Full-Time Law Enforcement Employees, by City, 2006 (*Contd.*)

(Number.)

State	City	Total law enforcement employees	Total officers	Total civilians	State	City	Total law enforcement employees	Total officers	Total civilians
	Brookhaven	9	8	1		Conshohocken..............	21	19	2
	Brookville	6	5	1		Coopersburg.................	6	6	0
	Brownsville	3	3	0		Coplay	4	4	0
	Bryn Athyn..................	5	5	0		Coraopolis	12	9	3
	Buckingham Township......................	23	21	2		Cornwall......................	9	8	1
	Buffalo Township.........	5	5	0		Corry	16	12	4
	Burgettstown	1	1	0		Covington Township......	2	2	0
	Bushkill Township	12	10	2		Cranberry Township....	27	24	3
	Butler	23	22	1		Cresson........................	1	1	0
	Butler Township, Butler County.............	23	21	2		Cresson Township........	2	2	0
	Butler Township, Luzerne County	10	9	1		Croyle Township	1	1	0
	California	8	7	1		Cumberland Township, Adams County	6	6	0
	Caln Township.............	22	20	2		Cumru Township..........	29	26	3
	Cambria Township.......	4	4	0		Curwensville	4	4	0
	Cambridge Springs	3	3	0		Dale	2	2	0
	Camp Hill	11	10	1		Dallas	4	4	0
	Canton........................	3	3	0		Dallas Township..........	7	7	0
	Carbondale	15	15	0		Danville......................	8	7	1
	Carlisle	37	32	5		Decatur Township........	1	1	0
	Carnegie	15	13	2		Delmont	4	4	0
	Carrolltown	1	1	0		Derry Township, Dauphin County	44	37	7
	Carroll Township, Washington County	3	3	0		Dickson City...............	7	7	0
	Carroll Township, York County	11	11	0		Donegal Township.......	2	2	0
	Carroll Valley	5	4	1		Dormont	16	15	1
	Castle Shannon	13	12	1		Downingtown	19	16	3
	Catawissa	3	3	0		Doylestown	21	16	5
	Center Township..........	26	26	0		Doylestown Township......................	23	21	2
	Centerville	2	2	0		Dublin Borough	2	2	0
	Central Berks Regional......................	13	12	1		Du Bois	13	13	0
	Chalfont	7	6	1		Duboistown	1	1	0
	Chambersburg..............	34	31	3		Duncannon	2	2	0
	Charleroi.....................	8	6	2		Dunmore......................	17	17	0
	Chartiers Township......	11	11	0		Duquesne	15	14	1
	Cheltenham Township....................	95	84	11		East Bangor	1	1	0
	Chester	106	96	10		East Berlin	1	1	0
	Chester Township	10	9	1		East Bethlehem Township......................	1	1	0
	Cheswick.....................	3	3	0		East Buffalo Township......................	8	8	0
	Chippewa Township	8	7	1		East Cocalico Township......................	25	23	2
	Christiana....................	8	7	1		East Conemaugh..........	2	2	0
	Churchill	10	10	0		East Coventry Township......................	8	7	1
	Clairton	13	13	0		East Earl Township	7	7	0
	Claysville....................	2	2	0		Eastern Adams Regional......................	9	9	0
	Clearfield	7	7	0		East Fallowfield Township......................	8	7	1
	Cleona	4	4	0		East Franklin Township......................	42	40	2
	Clifton Heights............	9	8	1		East Hempfield Township......................	32	28	4
	Coaldale	4	4	0		East Lampeter Township......................	43	39	4
	Coal Township.............	13	12	1		East McKeesport	2	2	0
	Cochranton	1	1	0		East Norriton Township......................	30	27	3
	Colebrookdale District	10	9	1		East Pennsboro Township......................	20	19	1
	Collegeville.................	9	8	1		East Pikeland Township......................	9	8	1
	Collier Township..........	16	15	1		Easttown Township	15	14	1
	Collingdale..................	10	8	2		East Vincent Township......................	7	7	0
	Colonial Regional........	24	22	2		East Washington	1	1	0
	Columbia	23	20	3		East Whiteland Township......................	21	19	2
	Colwyn	3	3	0		Ebensburg....................	4	4	0
	Conemaugh Township, Cambria County..........	2	2	0					
	Conewago Township ...	8	7	1					
	Conewango Township ...	4	4	0					
	Conneaut Lake Regional......................	3	3	0					
	Connellsville	19	18	1					

Table 78. Full-Time Law Enforcement Employees, by City, 2006 (*Contd.*)

(Number.)

State	City	Total law enforcement employees	Total officers	Total civilians	State	City	Total law enforcement employees	Total officers	Total civilians
	Economy	13	12	1		Hastings	1	1	0
	Eddystone	10	9	1		Hatboro	18	14	4
	Edgewood	12	10	2		Hatfield Township	30	25	5
	Edgeworth	6	4	2		Haverford Township	85	69	16
	Edinboro	9	8	1		Hazleton	33	30	3
	Edwardsville	4	4	0		Heidelberg	3	3	0
	Elizabethtown	18	16	2		Heidelberg Township, Berks County	1	1	0
	Elizabeth Township	16	15	1		Hellam Township	11	10	1
	Emlenton Borough	1	1	0		Hellertown	11	10	1
	Emmaus	18	17	1		Hemlock Township	6	6	0
	Emporium	2	2	0		Hempfield Township, Mercer County	7	6	1
	Emsworth	11	10	1		Highspire	6	6	0
	Ephrata	35	31	4		Hilltown Township	22	19	3
	Erie	201	173	28		Hollidaysburg	11	8	3
	Etna	6	5	1		Homestead	11	11	0
	Evans City	2	2	0		Honesdale	9	9	0
	Everett	4	4	0		Hooversville	1	1	0
	Exeter	5	4	1		Horsham Township	49	40	9
	Exeter Township, Berks County	34	32	2		Huntingdon	12	12	0
	Fairview Township, Luzerne County	5	5	0		Independence Township, Beaver County	4	4	0
	Fairview Township, York County	18	16	2		Indiana	27	20	7
	Falls Township, Bucks County	60	52	8		Indiana Township	10	10	0
	Fawn Township	3	3	0		Industry	1	1	0
	Ferguson Township	18	16	2		Ingram	4	4	0
	Ferndale	1	1	0		Irwin	5	5	0
	Findlay Township	23	16	7		Jackson Township, Butler County	6	6	0
	Fleetwood	6	6	0		Jackson Township, Cambria County	2	2	0
	Folcroft	9	9	0		Jackson Township, Luzerne County	4	4	0
	Ford City	3	3	0		Jeannette	17	14	3
	Forest City	2	2	0		Jefferson Hills Borough	15	14	1
	Forest Hills	12	11	1		Jenkins Township	2	2	0
	Forks Township	19	18	1		Jenkintown	11	10	1
	Forty Fort	2	2	0		Jermyn	1	1	0
	Foster Township	5	5	0		Jersey Shore	8	7	1
	Fountain Hill	9	9	0		Johnstown	56	49	7
	Fox Chapel	10	10	0		Kane	5	5	0
	Frackville	6	6	0		Kennedy Township	15	11	4
	Franconia Township	13	12	1		Kidder Township	8	8	0
	Franklin Park	10	9	1		Kingston	25	20	5
	Franklin Township, Carbon County	4	4	0		Kingston Township	12	11	1
	Freeport	2	2	0		Kiskiminetas Township	1	1	0
	Gallitzin	1	1	0		Kline Township	1	1	0
	Gettysburg	16	14	2		Knox	3	3	0
	Gilpin Township	1	1	0		Koppel	1	1	0
	Girard	4	4	0		Kutztown	11	10	1
	Glenolden	10	9	1		Laflin Borough	3	3	0
	Granville Township	8	7	1		Lake City	3	3	0
	Greencastle	2	2	0		Lancaster	197	175	22
	Greenfield Township, Blair County	3	3	0		Lancaster Township, Butler County	2	2	0
	Greensburg	37	27	10		Lansdale	26	20	6
	Green Tree	12	11	1		Larksville	4	4	0
	Greenwood Township	1	1	0		Latimore-York Springs Regional	1	1	0
	Grove City	10	9	1		Laureldale	5	5	0
	Hamburg	8	7	1		Lawrence Township	10	9	1
	Hamiltonban Township	1	1	0		Lebanon	54	47	7
	Hampden Township	22	22	0		Leechburg	2	2	0
	Hanover	22	20	2		Leetsdale	3	3	0
	Hanover Township, Luzerne County	17	16	1		Leet Township	10	5	5
	Harmar Township	8	8	0		Lehighton	8	7	1
	Harmony Township	4	4	0					
	Harrisburg	230	179	51					
	Harrison Township	18	14	4					

Table 78. Full-Time Law Enforcement Employees, by City, 2006 (*Contd.*)

(Number.)

State	City	Total law enforcement employees	Total officers	Total civilians	State	City	Total law enforcement employees	Total officers	Total civilians
	Lehigh Township, Northampton County ...	12	11	1		Mifflin County Regional	27	25	2
	Lehman Township	2	2	0		Mifflin Township	4	4	0
	Lewisburg	8	8	0		Milford	2	2	0
	Limerick Township	17	16	1		Millcreek Township	77	58	19
	Lincoln	1	1	0		Millersburg	4	4	0
	Lititz	16	13	3		Millersville	14	12	2
	Littlestown	8	7	1		Millvale	4	4	0
	Locust Township	5	5	0		Millville	1	1	0
	Logan Township	18	16	2		Milton	10	9	1
	Lower Burrell	16	16	0		Minersville	5	5	0
	Lower Gwynedd Township	19	18	1		Mohnton	3	3	0
	Lower Heidelberg Township	8	7	1		Monaca	7	7	0
	Lower Makefield Township	35	31	4		Monessen	12	12	0
	Lower Merion Township	157	139	18		Monroeville	54	50	4
	Lower Moreland Township	27	22	5		Montgomery Township	42	33	9
	Lower Paxton Township	60	54	6		Montrose	1	1	0
	Lower Pottsgrove Township	16	14	2		Moon Township	36	30	6
	Lower Providence Township	32	28	4		Moore Township	9	8	1
	Lower Salford Township	21	19	2		Moosic	9	9	0
	Lower Saucon Township	16	14	2		Morris-Cooper Regional	1	1	0
	Lower Southampton Township	33	30	3		Morrisville	12	11	1
	Lower Swatara Township	11	10	1		Morton	5	4	1
	Lower Windsor Township	11	10	1		Moscow	3	3	0
	Luzerne Township	1	1	0		Mount Carmel	10	9	1
	Madison Township	1	1	0		Mount Gretna Borough	9	8	1
	Mahoning Township, Carbon County	5	5	0		Mount Joy	13	12	1
	Mahoning Township, Montour County	7	6	1		Mount Oliver	6	6	0
	Malvern	5	4	1		Mount Union	4	4	0
	Manheim	8	7	1		Muhlenberg Township	33	30	3
	Manheim Township	69	51	18		Munhall	25	21	4
	Mansfield	5	5	0		Murrysville	26	21	5
	Marion Township	1	1	0		Nanticoke	13	12	1
	Marlborough Township	4	4	0		Narberth	7	7	0
	Marple Township	38	33	5		Neshannock Township	7	7	0
	Martinsburg	2	2	0		Nether Providence Township	18	16	2
	Masontown	5	5	0		Neville Township	11	10	1
	Mayfield	1	1	0		Newberry Township	18	16	2
	McAdoo	1	1	0		New Bethlehem	1	1	0
	McCandless	29	27	2		New Britain	5	4	1
	McDonald Borough	2	2	0		New Britain Township	13	11	2
	McKeesport	53	50	3		New Cumberland	9	8	1
	McKees Rocks	10	9	1		New Gardern Township	12	11	1
	McSherrystown	5	5	0		New Hanover Township	11	10	1
	Meadville	26	22	4		New Holland	14	13	1
	Mechanicsburg	16	15	1		New Hope	11	9	2
	Media	24	16	8		Newport	2	2	0
	Mercer	4	4	0		Newport Township	1	1	0
	Mercersburg	2	2	0		New Sewickley Township	11	10	1
	Meyersdale	1	1	0		Newtown	4	4	0
	Middletown	16	15	1		Newtown Township, Bucks County	32	28	4
	Middletown Township	60	53	7		Newtown Township, Delaware County	18	16	2
	Midland	5	5	0		Newville	2	2	0
	Mifflinburg	8	7	1		New Wilmington	4	4	0
						Norristown	79	66	13
						Northampton	14	12	2
						Northampton Township	47	41	6
						North Apollo	1	1	0

Table 78. Full-Time Law Enforcement Employees, by City, 2006 *(Contd.)*

(Number.)

State	City	Total law enforcement employees	Total officers	Total civilians	State	City	Total law enforcement employees	Total officers	Total civilians
	North Catasauqua........	5	5	0		Pittsburgh.....................	910	848	62
	North Cornwall Township.....................	10	9	1		Pittston	10	10	0
	North Coventry Township.....................	13	12	1		Plainfield Township	13	12	1
	North East	8	7	1		Plains Township	16	15	1
	Northeastern Regional.....................	11	10	1		Pleasant Hills...............	19	17	2
	Northern Berks Regional.....................	15	14	1		Plum	37	30	7
	Northern Cambria Borough	5	5	0		Plumstead Township....	17	15	2
	Northern Regional.......	30	28	2		Plymouth Township, Montgomery County ...	55	46	9
	Northern York Regional.....................	50	46	4		Pocono Mountain Regional.....................	34	29	5
	North Fayette Township.....................	24	19	5		Pocono Township........	16	16	0
	North Franklin Township.....................	8	8	0		Point Township	5	5	0
	North Huntingdon Township.....................	34	28	6		Portage	2	2	0
	North Lebanon Township.....................	10	9	1		Port Allegany	3	3	0
	North Londonderry Township.....................	9	8	1		Pottstown	57	43	14
	North Middleton Township.....................	9	8	1		Pottsville	28	27	1
	North Strabane Township.....................	20	19	1		Prospect Park	9	9	0
	Northumberland	5	5	0		Punxsutawney	11	8	3
	North Versailles Township.....................	22	19	3		Pymatuning Township.....................	4	4	0
	North Wales.................	5	4	1		Quakertown..................	23	15	8
	Northwest Lancaster County Regional.........	16	15	1		Radnor Township	57	47	10
	Northwest Lawrence County Regional..........	2	2	0		Rankin..........................	1	1	0
	Norwood	7	7	0		Reading.........................	233	206	27
	Oakmont.......................	7	7	0		Reynoldsville	2	2	0
	O'Hara Township	14	13	1		Rice Township..............	4	4	0
	Ohio Township	11	10	1		Richland Township, Bucks County	11	10	1
	Ohioville	2	2	0		Richland Township, Cambria County..........	20	19	1
	Oil City........................	23	18	5		Ridgway........................	5	4	1
	Old Forge.....................	2	2	0		Ridley Park..................	14	10	4
	Old Lycoming Township.....................	11	10	1		Ridley Township	37	32	5
	Olyphant.......................	5	5	0		Riverside	3	3	0
	Orwigsburg	4	4	0		Roaring Brook Township.....................	2	2	0
	Oxford..........................	12	11	1		Roaring Spring............	2	2	0
	Paint Township............	5	4	1		Robesonia	2	2	0
	Palmerton	9	8	1		Robeson Township	6	5	1
	Palmyra	10	9	1		Robinson Township, Allegheny County........	26	21	5
	Parkesburg...................	10	9	1		Robinson Township, Washington County	2	2	0
	Patterson Area	4	4	0		Rochester......................	11	9	2
	Patton	2	2	0		Rochester Township	4	4	0
	Patton Township	19	17	2		Rockledge	5	5	0
	Paxtang........................	3	3	0		Roseto	2	1	1
	Pen Argyl.....................	5	5	0		Rosslyn Farms..............	2	2	0
	Penn Hills	58	53	5		Ross Township	43	43	0
	Pennridge Regional	23	15	8		Rostraver Township	15	14	1
	Penn Township, Butler County..............	4	3	1		Rush Township.............	3	3	0
	Penn Township, Lancaster County........	8	8	0		Sadsbury Township......	2	2	0
	Penn Township, Westmoreland County......................	22	20	2		Salisbury Township......	14	12	2
	Penn Township, York County	24	22	2		Sandy Township	9	8	1
	Perkasie........................	19	17	2		Saxton...........................	1	1	0
	Peters Township..........	23	21	2		Sayre.............................	14	14	0
	Philadelphia.................	7,510	6,665	845		Schuylkill Haven..........	7	7	0
	Phoenixville	26	24	2		Schuylkill Township, Chester County	11	10	1
						Scottdalev	7	7	0
						Scott Township, Columbia County........	6	6	0
						Scott Township, Lackawanna County....	5	5	0
						Scranton........................	170	150	20
						Selinsgrove...................	6	5	1
						Seven Springs	7	6	1
						Seward...........................	1	1	0
						Sewickley	13	12	1

Table 78. Full-Time Law Enforcement Employees, by City, 2006 (Contd.)

(Number.)

State	City	Total law enforcement employees	Total officers	Total civilians	State	City	Total law enforcement employees	Total officers	Total civilians
	Sewickley Heights........	6	2	4		State College	77	65	12
	Shaler Township..........	27	26	1		St. Clair Boro	7	7	0
	Shamokin	13	13	0		St. Marys City..............	13	12	1
	Shamokin Dam	3	3	0		Steelton	9	8	1
	Sharon Hill	8	7	1		Stewartstown	6	5	1
	Sharpsburg	5	5	0		Stonycreek Township ...	2	2	0
	Sharpsville	6	5	1		Stowe Township	5	4	1
	Shenandoah	8	7	1		Strasburg......................	4	4	0
	Shenango Township, Lawrence County........	6	6	0		Stroud Area Regional ...	58	53	5
	Shillington..................	8	8	0		Sugarcreek	6	6	0
	Shippensburg...............	11	10	1		Sugarloaf Township, Luzerne County	4	4	0
	Shippingport	2	2	0		Summerhill Township....	2	2	0
	Shiremanstown.............	2	2	0		Summit Hill	3	3	0
	Shohola Township........	1	1	0		Sunbury........................	15	12	3
	Silver Lake Township	2	2	0		Susquehanna Township, Cambria County........................	1	1	0
	Silver Spring Township......................	13	12	1		Susquehanna Township, Dauphin County........................	42	40	2
	Sinking Spring	5	5	0		Swarthmore	9	9	0
	Slatington....................	6	6	0		Swatara Township........	42	40	2
	Slippery Rock..............	3	3	0		Swissvale	14	14	0
	Smethport	2	2	0		Swoyersville	7	7	0
	Solebury Township	15	13	2		Tamaqua	10	8	2
	South Abington Township......................	12	10	2		Tarentum......................	10	7	3
	South Beaver Township......................	4	4	0		Telford..........................	8	7	1
	South Buffalo ownship	2	2	0		Tidioute	1	1	0
	South Centre Township......................	4	4	0		Tinicum Township, Bucks County	5	5	0
	Southern Regional, Lancaster County.........	9	9	0		Tinicum Township, Delaware County.........	16	15	1
	Southern Regional, York County	12	11	1		Titusville	16	16	0
	South Fayette Township......................	18	17	1		Towamencin Township......................	34	22	12
	South Fork	1	1	0		Towanda........................	8	7	1
	South Greensburg........	2	2	0		Trafford	2	2	0
	South Heidelberg Township......................	6	6	0		Trainer..........................	6	6	0
	South Lebanon Township......................	8	7	1		Tredyffrin Township	60	51	9
	South Londonderry Township......................	6	6	0		Troy	3	3	0
	South Park Township....	17	16	1		Tullytown	6	4	2
	South Pymatuning Township......................	2	2	0		Tunkhannock Township, Wyoming County.........................	4	4	0
	South Waverly	3	3	0		Union City	2	2	0
	Southwestern Regional......................	15	14	1		Uniontown....................	18	18	0
	Southwest Greensburg..................	2	2	0		Union Township, Lawrence County........	2	2	0
	Southwest Regional.....	3	2	1		Upland	1	1	0
	South Whitehall Township......................	38	35	3		Upper Chichester Township......................	24	22	2
	South Williamsport......	8	7	1		Upper Darby Township......................	134	124	10
	Spring City	4	3	1		Upper Dublin Township......................	45	40	5
	Springdale	2	2	0		Upper Makefield Township......................	17	15	2
	Springettsbury Township......................	33	30	3		Upper Merion Township......................	83	62	21
	Springfield Township, Bucks County	4	4	0		Upper Moreland Township......................	50	40	10
	Springfield Township, Delaware County.........	41	35	6		Upper Nazareth Township......................	4	3	1
	Springfield Township, Montgomery County ...	31	30	1		Upper Perkiomen	9	8	1
	Spring Garden Township......................	19	17	2		Upper Pottsgrove Township......................	12	11	1
	Spring Township, Berks County......................	27	26	1		Upper Providence Township, Delaware County........................	13	12	1
	Spring Township, Centre County...........	7	6	1		Upper Providence Township, Montgomery County ...	23	21	2

Table 78. Full-Time Law Enforcement Employees, by City, 2006 (*Contd.*)

(Number.)

State	City	Total law enforcement employees	Total officers	Total civilians	State	City	Total law enforcement employees	Total officers	Total civilians
	Upper Saucon Township	19	18	1		West Shore Regional	11	9	2
	Upper Southampton Township	24	21	3		Westtown-East Goshen Regional	34	32	2
	Upper St. Clair Township	33	28	5		West View	12	8	4
	Upper Uwchlan Township	10	10	0		West Whiteland Township	30	28	2
	Uwchlan Township	25	23	2		West Wyoming	2	2	0
	Vandergrift	8	8	0		West York	7	7	0
	Vernon Township	3	3	0		Whitehall	25	20	5
	Verona	3	3	0		Whitehall Township	58	49	9
	Walnutport	4	4	0		White Haven Borough	2	2	0
	Warminster Township	52	46	6		White Township	2	2	0
	Warren	20	15	5		Whitpain Township	36	29	7
	Warrington Township	31	28	3		Wilkes-Barre	86	80	6
	Warwick Township, Bucks County	21	19	2		Wilkes-Barre Township	18	16	2
	Warwick Township, Lancaster County	18	16	2		Wilkinsburg	27	24	3
	Washington, Washington County	31	29	2		Wilkins Township	12	12	0
	Washington Township, Fayette County	3	3	0		Williamsport	55	51	4
	Washington Township, Franklin County	15	14	1		Willistown Township	18	16	2
	Washington Township, Northampton County	3	3	0		Windber	3	2	1
	Washington Township, Westmoreland County	7	7	0		Wyoming	5	5	0
	Watsontown	5	5	0		Wyomissing	27	22	5
	Waynesboro	21	19	2		Yardley	3	3	0
	Waynesburg	9	8	1		Yeadon	16	14	2
	Weatherly	4	4	0		York Area Regional	52	47	5
	Wellsboro	7	7	0		Youngsville	2	2	0
	Wernersville	2	2	0		Zelienople	10	9	1
	Wesleyville	11	10	1	**RHODE ISLAND**	Barrington	31	24	7
	West Brandywine Township	8	7	1		Bristol	52	41	11
	West Conshohocken	9	8	1		Burrillville	35	25	10
	West Cornwall Township	9	8	1		Central Falls	52	42	10
	West Earl Township	6	6	0		Charlestown	26	21	5
	West Fallowfield Township	1	1	0		Coventry	71	59	12
	Westfall Township	6	6	0		Cranston	187	152	35
	Westfield	2	2	0		Cumberland	61	49	12
	West Goshen Township	30	25	5		East Greenwich	42	33	9
	West Hempfield Township	21	19	2		East Providence	123	103	20
	West Hills Regional	12	11	1		Foster	11	7	4
	West Kittanning	1	1	0		Glocester	23	16	7
	West Lampeter Township	15	14	1		Hopkinton	21	16	5
	West Lebanon Township	10	9	1		Jamestown	19	14	5
	West Manchester Township	29	26	3		Johnston	95	77	18
	West Manheim Township	7	7	0		Lincoln	42	34	8
	West Mifflin	38	33	5		Little Compton	14	10	4
	West Norriton Township	32	27	5		Middletown	38	34	4
	West Pikeland Township	4	4	0		Narragansett	53	41	12
	West Pike Run	1	1	0		Newport	101	79	22
	West Pittston	3	3	0		New Shoreham	9	4	5
	West Pottsgrove Township	9	8	1		North Kingstown	51	44	7
	West Reading	14	12	2		North Providence	92	71	21
	West Sadsbury Township	4	3	1		North Smithfield	28	22	6
						Pawtucket	185	153	32
						Portsmouth	33	32	1
						Providence	579	480	99
						Richmond	17	12	5
						Scituate	24	17	7
						Smithfield	54	41	13
						South Kingstown	73	55	18
						Tiverton	40	28	12
						Warren	27	22	5
						Warwick	225	177	48
						Westerly	62	50	12
						West Greenwich	17	11	6
						West Warwick	73	60	13
						Woonsocket	115	100	15

Table 78. Full-Time Law Enforcement Employees, by City, 2006 (*Contd.*)

(Number.)

State	City	Total law enforcement employees	Total officers	Total civilians	State	City	Total law enforcement employees	Total officers	Total civilians
SOUTH CAROLINA	Abbeville	23	21	2		Greenwood	53	45	8
	Aiken	119	81	38		Greer	67	54	13
	Allendale	8	7	1		Hanahan	36	29	7
	Anderson	122	87	35		Hardeeville	15	13	2
	Atlantic Beach	4	4	0		Harleyville	3	3	0
	Aynor	6	5	1		Hartsville	32	29	3
	Bamberg	12	10	2		Hemingway	4	3	1
	Barnwell	18	16	2		Holly Hill	8	8	0
	Batesburg-Leesville	25	20	5		Honea Path	14	14	0
	Beaufort	52	47	5		Inman	7	7	0
	Belton	14	13	1		Irmo	24	22	2
	Bennettsville	36	33	3		Isle of Palms	29	19	10
	Bethune	1	1	0		Iva	6	5	1
	Bishopville	12	11	1		Jackson	4	4	0
	Blacksburg	15	14	1		Jamestown	2	1	1
	Blackville	8	6	2		Johnsonville	5	4	1
	Bluffton	32	30	2		Johnston	8	8	0
	Bowman	2	2	0		Jonesville	6	6	0
	Branchville	5	4	1		Kingstree	20	18	2
	Brunson	4	3	1		Lake City	29	21	8
	Burnettown	2	2	0		Lake View	4	4	0
	Calhoun Falls	9	8	1		Lamar	3	3	0
	Camden	30	26	4		Lancaster	44	33	11
	Campobello	7	7	0		Landrum	17	16	1
	Cayce	74	61	13		Latta	8	8	0
	Central	10	10	0		Laurens	34	27	7
	Chapin	5	5	0		Lexington	39	34	5
	Charleston	503	367	136		Liberty	15	10	5
	Cheraw	30	24	6		Lynchburg	4	4	0
	Chesnee	5	5	0		Marion	25	21	4
	Chester	33	27	6		Mauldin	48	37	11
	Chesterfield	6	4	2		McBee	3	2	1
	Clemson	35	26	9		McColl	7	7	0
	Clinton	32	26	6		Moncks Corner	26	23	3
	Clio	5	4	1		Mount Pleasant	171	130	41
	Clover	17	13	4		Mullins	17	15	2
	Columbia	368	328	40		Myrtle Beach	242	184	58
	Conway	60	45	15		Newberry	32	28	4
	Cottageville	4	4	0		New Ellenton	6	6	0
	Coward	1	1	0		Ninety Six	4	4	0
	Cowpens	6	6	0		North	3	3	0
	Darlington	29	26	3		North Augusta	66	49	17
	Denmark	9	7	2		North Charleston	366	285	81
	Dillon	29	24	5		North Myrtle Beach	107	101	6
	Due West	5	5	0		Norway	14	2	12
	Duncan	13	13	0		Orangeburg	92	70	22
	Easley	49	38	11		Pacolet	5	5	0
	Edgefield	9	9	0		Pageland	15	10	5
	Edisto Beach	7	6	1		Pamplico	5	5	0
	Ehrhardt	4	4	0		Pawleys Island	4	3	1
	Elgin	4	4	0		Pelion	3	3	0
	Elloree	4	3	1		Pickens	15	13	2
	Estill	8	6	2		Pine Ridge	2	1	1
	Eutawville	4	3	1		Prosperity	5	4	1
	Fairfax	8	7	1		Ridgeland	14	13	1
	Florence	121	100	21		Ridgeville	2	1	1
	Folly Beach	19	13	6		Rock Hill	158	117	41
	Forest Acres	32	26	6		Salem	1	1	0
	Fort Lawn	5	4	1		Salley	1	1	0
	Fort Mill	30	24	6		Saluda	11	10	1
	Fountain Inn	28	21	7		Santee	14	9	5
	Gaffney	42	38	4		Scranton	2	2	0
	Georgetown	44	35	9		Seneca	41	30	11
	Goose Creek	75	57	18		Simpsonville	48	38	10
	Great Falls	5	4	1		Society Hill	5	5	0
	Greeleyville	2	2	0		South Congaree	7	7	0
	Greenville	228	185	43		Spartanburg	140	120	20
						Springdale	9	9	0

Table 78. Full-Time Law Enforcement Employees, by City, 2006 (*Contd.*)

(Number.)

State	City	Total law enforcement employees	Total officers	Total civilians	State	City	Total law enforcement employees	Total officers	Total civilians
	Springfield	1	1	0		Martin	6	5	1
	St. Matthews	8	7	1		McIntosh	1	1	0
	Sullivans Island	9	8	1		Menno	1	1	0
	Summerton	11	10	1		Milbank	5	5	0
	Summerville	91	70	21		Miller	4	4	0
	Sumter	150	108	42		Mitchell	30	22	8
	Surfside Beach	25	17	8		Mobridge	13	7	6
	Swansea	7	7	0		Murdo	1	1	0
	Tega Cay	20	15	5		New Effington	1	1	0
	Timmonsville	7	7	0		North Sioux City	8	6	2
	Travelers Rest	21	15	6		Parkston	2	2	0
	Turbeville	3	3	0		Philip	2	2	0
	Union	32	29	3		Pierre	34	23	11
	Vance	1	1	0		Platte	1	1	0
	Wagener	3	3	0		Rapid City	127	101	26
	Walhalla	15	14	1		Rosholt	1	1	0
	Walterboro	29	20	9		Scotland	1	1	0
	Ware Shoals	8	7	1		Selby	1	1	0
	Wellford	4	4	0		Sioux Falls	252	216	36
	West Columbia	61	49	12		Sisseton	8	8	0
	Westminster	10	10	0		Spearfish	25	18	7
	West Pelzer	3	3	0		Springfield	2	2	0
	West Union	1	1	0		Sturgis	18	15	3
	Whitmire	4	4	0		Tea	4	4	0
	Williston	9	8	1		Tripp	1	1	0
	Winnsboro	27	27	0		Tyndall	2	2	0
	Woodruff	13	11	2		Vermillion	16	15	1
	Yemassee	6	6	0		Viborg	1	1	0
	York	36	30	6		Wagner	3	3	0
						Watertown	46	32	14
SOUTH DAKOTA	Aberdeen	50	42	8		Waubay	1	1	0
	Alcester	2	2	0		Webster	5	5	0
	Armour	1	1	0		Whitewood	2	2	0
	Avon	1	1	0		Winner	31	6	25
	Belle Fourche	9	8	1		Yankton	46	27	19
	Beresford	8	4	4	**TENNESSEE**	Adamsville	10	6	4
	Box Elder	9	7	2		Alamo	3	3	0
	Brandon	12	11	1		Alcoa	44	37	7
	Brookings	34	26	8		Alexandria	2	2	0
	Burke	1	1	0		Algood	11	11	0
	Canton	5	5	0		Ardmore	11	7	4
	Centerville	1	1	0		Ashland City	14	13	1
	Chamberlain	5	5	0		Athens	33	31	2
	Clark	2	2	0		Atoka	12	11	1
	Colman	1	1	0		Baileyton	2	2	0
	Corsica	1	1	0		Bartlett	117	90	27
	Deadwood	14	11	3		Baxter	4	4	0
	Eagle Butte	2	2	0		Bean Station	7	7	0
	Elk Point	4	4	0		Belle Meade	19	16	3
	Estelline	1	1	0		Bells	5	5	0
	Eureka	2	2	0		Benton	8	7	1
	Faith	2	1	1		Berry Hill	17	13	4
	Flandreau	7	7	0		Bethel Springs	3	2	1
	Freeman	2	2	0		Big Sandy	2	2	0
	Gettysburg	2	2	0		Blaine	4	4	0
	Gregory	3	3	0		Bluff City	10	10	0
	Groton	3	3	0		Bolivar	25	20	5
	Highmore	1	1	0		Bradford	3	3	0
	Hot Springs	9	7	2		Brentwood	68	54	14
	Huron	28	22	6		Brighton	5	4	1
	Jefferson	2	2	0		Bristol	93	68	25
	Kadoka	1	1	0		Brownsville	38	33	5
	Kimball	1	1	0		Bruceton	4	4	0
	Lead	6	5	1		Burns	2	2	0
	Lemmon	4	4	0		Calhoun	2	2	0
	Lennox	4	4	0		Camden	18	13	5
	Leola	2	2	0		Carthage	11	7	4
	Madison	11	10	1		Caryville	6	6	0

Table 78. Full-Time Law Enforcement Employees, by City, 2006 (Contd.)

(Number.)

State	City	Total law enforcement employees	Total officers	Total civilians	State	City	Total law enforcement employees	Total officers	Total civilians
	Celina	6	4	2		Henning	2	1	1
	Centerville	19	13	6		Henry	1	1	0
	Chapel Hill	5	5	0		Hohenwald	14	13	1
	Charleston	2	2	0		Hollow Rock	2	2	0
	Chattanooga	600	429	171		Hornbeak	1	1	0
	Church Hill	9	8	1		Humboldt	32	26	6
	Clarksville	290	237	53		Huntingdon	16	12	4
	Cleveland	104	92	12		Huntland	4	4	0
	Clifton	6	6	0		Jacksboro	4	4	0
	Clinton	30	28	2		Jackson	221	179	42
	Collegedale	23	22	1		Jamestown	9	9	0
	Collierville	127	87	40		Jasper	8	8	0
	Collinwood	4	4	0		Jefferson City	21	19	2
	Columbia	91	82	9		Jellico	11	8	3
	Cookeville	94	72	22		Johnson City	171	145	26
	Coopertown	8	8	0		Jonesborough	20	15	5
	Copperhill	1	1	0		Kenton	5	5	0
	Covington	31	30	1		Kimball	10	9	1
	Cowan	6	6	0		Kingsport	147	103	44
	Cross Plains	3	3	0		Kingston	13	12	1
	Crossville	43	39	4		Kingston Springs	6	5	1
	Crump	2	2	0		Knoxville	476	359	117
	Cumberland City	3	3	0		Lafayette	21	14	7
	Cumberland Gap	1	1	0		La Follette	29	22	7
	Dandridge	11	10	1		La Grange	1	1	0
	Dayton	18	16	2		Lake City	10	7	3
	Decatur	5	5	0		Lakewood	4	4	0
	Decaturville	1	1	0		La Vergne	60	43	17
	Decherd	11	10	1		Lawrenceburg	40	34	6
	Dickson	48	43	5		Lebanon	85	68	17
	Dover	5	5	0		Lenoir City	20	19	1
	Dresden	9	8	1		Lewisburg	37	28	9
	Dunlap	12	11	1		Lexington	30	25	5
	Dyer	6	6	0		Livingston	22	16	6
	Dyersburg	65	54	11		Lookout Mountain	21	16	5
	Eagleville	2	1	1		Loretto	3	3	0
	East Ridge	44	34	10		Loudon	15	14	1
	Elizabethton	42	38	4		Lynnville	1	1	0
	Elkton	2	2	0		Madisonville	16	14	2
	Englewood	6	6	0		Manchester	35	30	5
	Erin	6	5	1		Martin	35	27	8
	Erwin	11	11	0		Maryville	57	48	9
	Estill Springs	6	5	1		Mason	6	5	1
	Ethridge	2	1	1		Maynardville	4	4	0
	Etowah	14	10	4		McEwen	4	3	1
	Fairview	17	16	1		McKenzie	21	16	5
	Fayetteville	25	23	2		McMinnville	40	36	4
	Franklin	143	119	24		Medina	10	10	0
	Friendship	1	1	0		Memphis	2,440	1,990	450
	Gainesboro	4	4	0		Middleton	3	3	0
	Gallatin	74	56	18		Milan	32	26	6
	Gallaway	7	7	0		Millersville	17	12	5
	Gates	2	2	0		Millington	46	36	10
	Gatlinburg	50	43	7		Minor Hill	2	1	1
	Germantown	99	79	20		Monteagle	11	4	7
	Gibson	2	2	0		Monterey	8	8	0
	Gleason	6	5	1		Morristown	85	79	6
	Goodlettsville	50	36	14		Moscow	4	4	0
	Gordonsville	5	5	0		Mountain City	9	9	0
	Grand Junction	1	1	0		Mount Carmel	8	8	0
	Graysville	5	4	1		Mount Juliet	48	37	11
	Greenbrier	13	12	1		Mount Pleasant	13	12	1
	Greeneville	47	45	2		Munford	13	12	1
	Greenfield	8	7	1		Murfreesboro	219	174	45
	Halls	9	9	0		Nashville	1,526	1,213	313
	Harriman	22	20	2		Newbern	20	13	7
	Henderson	15	14	1		New Hope	1	1	0
	Hendersonville	92	71	21		New Johnsonville	5	5	0

Table 78. Full-Time Law Enforcement Employees, by City, 2006 (*Contd.*)

(Number.)

State	City	Total law enforcement employees	Total officers	Total civilians	State	City	Total law enforcement employees	Total officers	Total civilians
	New Market	2	3	0		Tusculum	2	2	0
	Newport	32	29	3		Union City	44	36	8
	New Tazewell	11	11	0		Vonore	12	11	1
	Niota	3	3	0		Wartburg	3	3	0
	Nolensville	6	6	0		Wartrace	1	1	0
	Norris	7	7	0		Watertown	7	4	3
	Oakland	15	13	2		Waverly	13	12	1
	Oak Ridge	72	60	12		Waynesboro	9	9	0
	Obion	4	4	0		Westmoreland	10	5	5
	Oliver Springs	15	11	4		White Bluff	3	3	0
	Oneida	19	14	5		White House	27	18	9
	Paris	35	25	10		White Pine	9	8	1
	Parsons	6	6	0		Whiteville	8	8	0
	Petersburg	2	2	0		Whitwell	8	5	3
	Pigeon Forge	64	52	12		Winchester	24	23	1
	Pikeville	3	3	0		Winfield	3	3	0
	Piperton	8	7	1		Woodbury	9	8	1
	Pittman Center	1	1	0	**TEXAS**	Abernathy	4	4	0
	Pleasant View	4	4	0		Abilene	249	186	63
	Portland	31	25	6		Addison	76	55	21
	Powells Crossroads	2	2	0		Alamo	34	24	10
	Pulaski	28	25	3		Alamo Heights	32	20	12
	Puryear	2	2	0		Alice	48	39	9
	Red Bank	24	22	2		Allen	132	98	34
	Red Boiling Springs	5	5	0		Alpine	17	10	7
	Ridgely	6	5	1		Alto	4	4	0
	Ridgetop	6	6	0		Alvarado	19	13	6
	Ripley	31	25	6		Alvin	70	45	25
	Rockwood	15	14	1		Amarillo	386	295	91
	Rogersville	15	14	1		Andrews	21	15	6
	Rossville	4	4	0		Angleton	48	37	11
	Rutherford	4	4	0		Anna	7	7	0
	Rutledge	6	4	2		Anson	3	3	0
	Savannah	27	16	11		Anthony	12	11	1
	Scotts Hill	2	2	0		Anton	1	1	0
	Selmer	18	16	2		Aransas Pass	27	19	8
	Sevierville	59	47	12		Arcola	7	6	1
	Sewanee	13	8	5		Argyle	8	8	0
	Sharon	3	3	0		Arlington	738	559	179
	Shelbyville	49	39	10		Arp	4	4	0
	Signal Mountain	14	13	1		Athens	35	26	9
	Smithville	10	9	1		Atlanta	19	15	4
	Smyrna	98	70	28		Austin	1,946	1,373	573
	Sneedville	1	1	0		Azle	30	20	10
	Soddy-Daisy	28	23	5		Baird	2	2	0
	Somerville	9	8	1		Balch Springs	47	32	15
	South Carthage	4	4	0		Balcones Heights	22	17	5
	South Fulton	7	5	2		Ballinger	8	6	2
	South Pittsburg	7	7	0		Bangs	4	4	0
	Sparta	16	15	1		Bartlett	3	3	0
	Spencer	2	2	0		Bastrop	23	20	3
	Spring City	6	6	0		Bay City	45	33	12
	Springfield	53	38	15		Bayou Vista	5	5	0
	Spring Hill	45	32	13		Baytown	184	127	57
	St. Joseph	1	1	0		Beaumont	318	252	66
	Surgoinsville	3	3	0		Bedford	119	77	42
	Sweetwater	20	18	2		Beeville	23	18	5
	Tazewell	6	6	0		Bellaire	55	42	13
	Tellico Plains	4	4	0		Bellmead	23	16	7
	Tiptonville	7	7	0		Bellville	12	11	1
	Toone	1	1	0		Belton	37	28	9
	Townsend	3	3	0		Benbrook	47	36	11
	Tracy City	4	4	0		Bertram	3	3	0
	Trenton	25	17	8		Beverly Hills	12	7	5
	Trezevant	1	1	0		Big Sandy	6	5	1
	Trimble	2	2	0		Big Spring	57	37	20
	Troy	4	4	0		Bishop	8	4	4
	Tullahoma	40	35	5		Blanco	4	4	0

Table 78. Full-Time Law Enforcement Employees, by City, 2006 *(Contd.)*

(Number.)

State	City	Total law enforcement employees	Total officers	Total civilians	State	City	Total law enforcement employees	Total officers	Total civilians
	Bloomburg	1	1	0		Corinth	29	28	1
	Blue Mound	12	7	5		Corpus Christi	636	439	197
	Boerne	38	24	14		Corrigan	9	6	3
	Bogata	3	3	0		Corsicana	53	40	13
	Bonham	26	18	8		Cottonwood Shores	2	2	0
	Borger	36	26	10		Crane	11	7	4
	Bovina	2	2	0		Crockett	17	15	2
	Bowie	19	14	5		Crowell	1	1	0
	Brady	16	9	7		Crowley	31	23	8
	Brazoria	9	5	4		Crystal City	15	10	5
	Breckenridge	17	12	5		Cuero	14	13	1
	Bremond	1	1	0		Cuney	3	1	2
	Brenham	30	27	3		Daingerfield	7	6	1
	Bridge City	18	13	5		Dalhart	16	13	3
	Bridgeport	22	14	8		Dallas	3,610	3,043	567
	Brookshire	13	9	4		Dalworthington Gardens	16	11	5
	Brookside Village	5	5	0		Danbury	3	3	0
	Brownfield	24	17	7		Dayton	21	15	6
	Brownsville	306	232	74		Decatur	24	18	6
	Brownwood	54	34	20		Deer Park	72	51	21
	Bruceville-Eddy	4	4	0		De Kalb	6	6	0
	Bryan	161	118	43		De Leon	4	4	0
	Bullard	6	5	1		Del Rio	90	66	24
	Bulverde	10	10	0		Denison	55	45	10
	Burkburnett	23	18	5		Denton	205	148	57
	Burleson	65	49	16		Denver City	13	8	5
	Burnet	14	13	1		DeSoto	80	68	12
	Caddo Mills	2	2	0		Devine	11	9	2
	Caldwell	10	9	1		Diboll	19	13	6
	Calvert	4	4	0		Dickinson	39	31	8
	Cameron	14	9	5		Dilley	6	5	1
	Caney City	1	1	0		Dimmitt	9	7	2
	Canton	19	14	5		Donna	33	22	11
	Canyon	22	19	3		Double Oak	6	6	0
	Carrollton	217	157	60		Driscoll	3	2	1
	Carthage	21	14	7		Dublin	7	6	1
	Castle Hills	26	20	6		Dumas	28	24	4
	Castroville	11	9	2		Duncanville	69	57	12
	Cedar Hill	75	59	16		Eagle Lake	9	8	1
	Cedar Park	80	57	23		Early	8	7	1
	Celina	7	7	0		Earth	2	2	0
	Center	23	15	8		Eastland	11	9	2
	Childress	14	9	5		East Mountain	1	1	0
	Chillicothe	2	2	0		Edcouch	13	9	4
	Cibolo	18	16	2		Eden	4	4	0
	Cisco	8	6	2		Edgewood	4	4	0
	Clarksville	7	7	0		Edinburg	137	100	37
	Cleburne	67	51	16		Edna	11	9	2
	Cleveland	31	21	10		El Campo	33	24	9
	Clifton	7	6	1		Electra	12	7	5
	Clint	5	5	0		Elgin	22	17	5
	Clute	34	25	9		El Paso	1,444	1,098	346
	Clyde	8	7	1		Elsa	18	12	6
	Cockrell Hill	19	14	5		Ennis	39	34	5
	Coffee City	2	2	0		Euless	117	79	38
	Coleman	15	9	6		Everman	17	12	5
	College Station	147	101	46		Fairfield	10	10	0
	Colleyville	43	33	10		Fair Oaks Ranch	13	13	0
	Collinsville	2	2	0		Falfurrias	12	11	1
	Colorado City	12	6	6		Farmers Branch	100	70	30
	Columbus	10	9	1		Farmersville	7	7	0
	Comanche	6	5	1		Ferris	12	8	4
	Combes	6	6	0		Flatonia	4	4	0
	Commerce	22	17	5		Florence	3	3	0
	Conroe	128	96	32		Floresville	15	14	1
	Converse	32	29	3		Flower Mound	99	66	33
	Coppell	69	54	15		Floydada	7	7	0
	Copperas Cove	63	43	20					

Table 78. Full-Time Law Enforcement Employees, by City, 2006 (*Contd.*)

(Number.)

State	City	Total law enforcement employees	Total officers	Total civilians	State	City	Total law enforcement employees	Total officers	Total civilians
	Forest Hill	29	25	4		Hollywood Park	11	10	1
	Forney	26	16	10		Hondo	20	18	2
	Fort Stockton	28	21	7		Hooks	5	5	0
	Fort Worth	1,733	1,368	365		Horizon City	13	12	1
	Frankston	4	3	1		Horseshoe Bay	14	13	1
	Fredericksburg	29	25	4		Houston	6,223	4,781	1,442
	Freeport	34	24	10		Howe	7	7	0
	Freer	11	5	6		Hubbard	4	4	0
	Friendswood	68	51	17		Hudson	6	5	1
	Friona	10	6	4		Hudson Oaks	12	12	0
	Frisco	142	98	44		Humble	75	57	18
	Gainesville	50	38	12		Huntsville	55	48	7
	Galena Park	23	18	5		Hurst	115	71	44
	Galveston	193	143	50		Hutchins	21	16	5
	Ganado	4	3	1		Hutto	17	14	3
	Garland	460	329	131		Idalou	3	3	0
	Gatesville	22	16	6		Ingleside	22	15	7
	Georgetown	80	59	21		Ingram	6	5	1
	Giddings	19	13	6		Iowa Park	18	11	7
	Gilmer	20	17	3		Irving	457	323	134
	Gladewater	21	15	6		Italy	5	4	1
	Glenn Heights	18	13	5		Itasca	6	6	0
	Godley	4	4	0		Jacinto City	25	19	6
	Gonzales	24	17	7		Jacksboro	14	9	5
	Gorman	3	3	0		Jacksonville	33	23	10
	Graham	21	19	2		Jasper	31	22	9
	Granbury	32	26	6		Jefferson	8	7	1
	Grand Prairie	302	205	97		Jersey Village	35	25	10
	Grand Saline	7	7	0		Johnson City	4	4	0
	Granger	3	3	0		Jones Creek	4	4	0
	Granite Shoals	16	8	8		Jonestown	8	7	1
	Grapeland	3	2	1		Joshua	14	13	1
	Grapevine	128	91	37		Jourdanton	8	8	0
	Greenville	68	48	20		Junction	5	5	0
	Gregory	3	3	0		Karnes City	7	6	1
	Groesbeck	8	8	0		Katy	60	43	17
	Groves	20	19	1		Kaufman	23	17	6
	Gruver	2	2	0		Keene	15	11	4
	Gun Barrel City	21	16	5		Keller	71	49	22
	Hale Center	3	3	0		Kemah	25	20	5
	Hallettsville	7	6	1		Kemp	6	6	0
	Hallsville	4	4	0		Kempner	1	1	0
	Haltom City	94	71	23		Kenedy	9	6	3
	Hamlin	8	4	4		Kennedale	26	20	6
	Harker Heights	50	37	13		Kermit	17	10	7
	Harlingen	146	115	31		Kerrville	64	48	16
	Hart	2	2	0		Kilgore	40	31	9
	Haskell	4	4	0		Killeen	232	177	55
	Hawk Cove	1	1	0		Kingsville	64	49	15
	Hawkins	5	5	0		Kirby	16	12	4
	Hawley	3	2	1		Kirbyville	6	6	0
	Hearne	18	11	7		Knox City	1	1	0
	Heath	15	14	1		Kountze	7	6	1
	Hedwig Village	22	17	5		Kress	1	1	0
	Helotes	17	15	2		Kyle	28	19	9
	Hemphill	3	3	0		Lacy-Lakeview	21	13	8
	Hempstead	17	15	2		La Feria	16	12	4
	Henderson	41	34	7		Lago Vista	20	13	7
	Hereford	28	22	6		La Grange	8	8	0
	Hewitt	30	22	8		Laguna Vista	6	6	0
	Hickory Creek	11	11	0		Lake Dallas	20	12	8
	Hidalgo	49	35	14		Lake Jackson	58	43	15
	Highland Park	66	53	13		Lakeside	4	4	0
	Highland Village	32	25	7		Lakeview	16	12	4
	Hill Country Village	10	10	0		Lakeway	32	25	7
	Hillsboro	29	20	9		Lake Worth	33	25	8
	Hitchcock	13	9	4		La Marque	38	28	10
	Holliday	3	3	0		Lamesa	21	15	6

Table 78. Full-Time Law Enforcement Employees, by City, 2006 (*Contd.*)

(Number.)

State	City	Total law enforcement employees	Total officers	Total civilians	State	City	Total law enforcement employees	Total officers	Total civilians
	Lampasas	24	16	8		Muleshoe	12	7	5
	Lancaster	65	50	15		Munday	1	1	0
	Laredo.........................	480	399	81		Murphy.........................	28	20	8
	La Vernia	4	4	0		Mustang Ridge	3	3	0
	Lavon	6	5	1		Nacogdoches	74	57	17
	League City	122	89	33		Nash........................	8	8	0
	Leander......................	36	25	11		Nassau Bay	14	13	1
	Leon Valley.................	29	21	8		Navasota	25	17	8
	Levelland	32	22	10		Nederland	32	21	11
	Lewisville	180	131	49		Needville	5	5	0
	Lexington....................	4	4	0		New Boston	13	9	4
	Liberty.....................	17	10	7		New Braunfels..............	103	83	20
	Lindale	17	13	4		New Deal	3	2	1
	Linden	6	5	1		Nocona.......................	9	6	3
	Little Elm....................	33	28	5		Nolanville...................	8	8	0
	Littlefield	20	13	7		Northlake	7	7	0
	Live Oak	43	29	14		North Richland Hills ...	156	109	47
	Livingston	21	15	6		Oak Ridge...................	4	2	2
	Llano	10	8	2		Oak Ridge North	17	17	0
	Lockhart......................	33	24	9		Odessa	210	152	58
	Lockney	3	3	0		O'Donnell...................	1	1	0
	Lone Star	7	6	1		Olmos Park	12	12	0
	Longview	172	151	21		Olney.........................	9	5	4
	Lorena	7	6	1		Oltonv	3	3	0
	Lorenzo......................	2	2	0		Onalaska	6	6	0
	Los Fresnos..................	19	14	5		Orange	56	42	14
	Lubbock	487	368	119		Orange Grove	6	5	1
	Lufkin	95	73	22		Overton	8	5	3
	Luling	25	15	10		Ovilla	10	9	1
	Lumberton	17	15	2		Oyster Creek	9	6	3
	Lytle...........................	5	5	0		Paducah......................	6	1	5
	Madisonville	11	9	2		Palacios	15	11	4
	Magnolia	10	9	1		Palestine	39	31	8
	Malakoff.....................	5	5	0		Palmer	9	8	1
	Manor	15	13	2		Pampa........................	37	25	12
	Mansfield	173	75	98		Panhandle	3	3	0
	Manvel	14	7	7		Pantego	17	12	5
	Marble Falls................	35	23	12		Paris..........................	82	62	20
	Marfa	3	3	0		Parker	7	7	0
	Marion	4	3	1		Pasadena	334	256	78
	Marshall	69	52	17		Pearland	127	100	27
	Marshall Creek............	1	1	0		Pearsall......................	13	11	2
	Mart	3	3	0		Pecos.........................	40	17	23
	Martindale	5	5	0		Pelican Bay	4	4	0
	Mathis........................	13	7	6		Penitas	11	6	5
	McAllen	393	261	132		Perryton	14	8	6
	McGregor	18	11	7		Pflugerville..................	66	51	15
	McKinney	161	129	32		Pharr..........................	150	109	41
	Meadows Place............	16	15	1		Pilot Point	9	9	0
	Melissa	9	8	1		Pinehurst....................	10	6	4
	Memorial Villages........	39	32	7		Pineland	2	2	0
	Memphis	4	3	1		Pittsburg.....................	11	10	1
	Mercedes.....................	35	28	7		Plainview.....................	40	32	8
	Meridian......................	3	2	1		Plano..........................	483	333	150
	Merkel	4	4	0		Pleasanton	23	17	6
	Mesquite	292	220	72		Point Comfort	1	1	0
	Mexia..........................	29	18	11		Ponder........................	2	2	0
	Midland.......................	207	158	49		Port Aransas................	22	14	8
	Midlothian	35	26	9		Port Arthur..................	139	108	31
	Milford	5	5	0		Port Isabel..................	24	19	5
	Mineola	14	12	2		Portland	32	21	11
	Mineral Wells	35	28	7		Port Lavaca	25	19	6
	Mission	157	115	42		Port Neches	21	18	3
	Missouri City	100	73	27		Poteet	6	6	0
	Monahans	16	10	6		Pottsboro	6	6	0
	Mont Belvieu...............	15	10	5		Premont	5	5	0
	Morgans Point Resort....	8	7	1		Primera	7	6	1
	Mount Pleasant	35	25	10		Princeton.....................	12	11	1

Table 78. Full-Time Law Enforcement Employees, by City, 2006 (*Contd.*)

(Number.)

State	City	Total law enforcement employees	Total officers	Total civilians	State	City	Total law enforcement employees	Total officers	Total civilians
	Progreso	11	9	2		Sinton	11	10	1
	Prosper	8	7	1		Slaton	16	10	6
	Queen City	5	5	0		Smithville	12	9	3
	Quinlan	3	3	0		Snyder	20	18	2
	Quitman	6	6	0		Socorro	31	21	10
	Ranger	5	5	0		Somerset	2	2	0
	Ransom Canyon	3	3	0		Somerville	5	5	0
	Red Oak	32	22	10		Sonora	5	3	2
	Refugio	11	8	3		Sour Lake	6	5	1
	Reno	5	4	1		South Houston	36	27	9
	Richardson	231	142	89		South Padre Island	34	25	9
	Richland Hills	25	19	6		Southside Place	11	7	4
	Richmond	42	33	9		Spearman	4	4	0
	Richwood	7	6	1		Springtown	15	11	4
	Riesel	3	3	0		Spring Valley	21	16	5
	Rio Grande City	30	23	7		Spur	1	1	0
	River Oaks	24	18	6		Stafford	50	37	13
	Roanoke	33	23	10		Stanton	5	5	0
	Robinson	25	17	8		Stephenville	45	33	12
	Robstown	28	21	7		Stratford	3	3	0
	Rockdale	16	11	5		Sugar Land	176	126	50
	Rockport	24	22	2		Sulphur Springs	40	31	9
	Rockwall	78	61	17		Sunset Valley	10	10	0
	Rollingwood	6	6	0		Surfside Beach	6	5	1
	Roma	32	24	8		Sweeny	6	6	0
	Roman Forest	6	6	0		Sweetwater	27	22	5
	Ropesville	1	1	0		Taft	7	7	0
	Roscoe	1	1	0		Tahoka	4	4	0
	Rosebud	3	3	0		Tatum	5	4	1
	Rose City	2	1	1		Taylor	37	27	10
	Rosenberg	76	60	16		Teague	6	5	1
	Round Rock	173	126	47		Temple	155	130	25
	Rowlett	102	72	30		Terrell	49	34	15
	Royse City	15	13	2		Terrell Hills	12	12	0
	Runaway Bay	3	3	0		Texarkana	104	92	12
	Rusk	13	11	2		Texas City	106	84	22
	Sabinal	3	3	0		The Colony	67	46	21
	Sachse	37	24	13		Thorndale	2	2	0
	Saginaw	35	30	5		Thrall	3	3	0
	Salado	4	4	0		Three Rivers	7	6	1
	San Angelo	176	150	26		Tioga	1	1	0
	San Antonio	2,516	1,993	523		Tolar	1	1	0
	San Augustine	7	6	1		Tomball	49	38	11
	San Benito	46	44	2		Tool	9	7	2
	San Diego	5	4	1		Trinity	10	6	4
	Sanger	14	13	1		Trophy Club	13	12	1
	San Juan	49	39	10		Troup	7	6	1
	San Marcos	111	79	32		Tulia	11	6	5
	San Saba	5	4	1		Tye	4	4	0
	Sansom Park Village	15	11	4		Tyler	227	178	49
	Santa Anna	3	3	0		Universal City	37	27	10
	Santa Fe	24	18	6		University Park	50	37	13
	Santa Rosa	4	4	0		Uvalde	41	30	11
	Seabrook	36	30	6		Valley View	1	1	0
	Seadrift	2	2	0		Van	6	6	0
	Seagoville	28	20	8		Van Alstyne	13	9	4
	Seagraves	4	3	1		Vernon	29	22	7
	Sealy	16	13	3		Victoria	140	104	36
	Seguin	61	45	16		Vidor	29	22	7
	Selma	22	20	2		Waco	326	228	98
	Seminole	12	11	1		Waelder	4	4	0
	Seven Points	10	6	4		Wake Village	7	6	1
	Seymour	10	7	3		Waller	9	8	1
	Shallowater	5	5	0		Wallis	2	2	0
	Shamrock	10	3	7		Watauga	49	35	14
	Shavano Park	14	13	1		Waxahachie	61	47	14
	Shenandoah	25	23	2		Weatherford	71	53	18
	Sherman	81	57	24		Webster	59	44	15

Table 78. Full-Time Law Enforcement Employees, by City, 2006 (*Contd.*)

(Number.)

State	City	Total law enforcement employees	Total officers	Total civilians	State	City	Total law enforcement employees	Total officers	Total civilians
	Weimar	7	6	1		Midvale	50	44	6
	Wells	2	1	1		Minersville	1	1	0
	Weslaco	95	66	29		Moab	16	12	4
	West	6	6	0		Monticello	5	4	1
	West Columbia	14	7	7		Moroni	1	1	0
	West Lake Hills	19	13	6		Mount Pleasant	5	5	0
	West Orange	10	9	1		Murray	89	70	19
	Westover Hills	13	11	2		Naples	7	6	1
	West Tawakoni	7	7	0		Nephi	11	9	2
	West University Place	32	22	10		North Ogden	19	16	3
	Westworth	17	11	6		North Park	11	9	2
	Wharton	33	24	9		North Salt Lake	16	14	2
	Whitehouse	23	15	8		Ogden	157	127	30
	White Oak	17	13	4		Orem	120	88	32
	Whitesboro	11	7	4		Park City	37	28	9
	White Settlement	44	30	14		Parowan	3	3	0
	Whitney	13	7	6		Payson	18	17	1
	Wichita Falls	259	169	90		Perry	6	6	0
	Willis	15	13	2		Pleasant Grove/Lindon	40	32	8
	Willow Park	10	9	1		Pleasant View	8	7	1
	Wills Point	10	9	1		Price	18	16	2
	Wilmer	17	12	5		Provo	146	93	53
	Windcrest	22	15	7		Richfield	15	13	2
	Wink	1	1	0		Riverdale	22	18	4
	Winnsboro	13	9	4		Roosevelt	11	10	1
	Winters	4	4	0		Roy	45	39	6
	Wolfforth	9	8	1		Salem	8	7	1
	Woodville	8	7	1		Salina	5	4	1
	Woodway	34	25	9		Salt Lake City	598	401	197
	Wortham	2	2	0		Sandy	145	114	31
	Wylie	40	37	3		Santaquin/Genola	8	8	0
	Yoakum	17	10	7		Smithfield	8	7	1
	Yorktown	3	3	0		South Jordan	50	44	6
UTAH	Alpine/Highland	19	17	2		South Ogden	29	24	5
	Alta	8	4	4		South Salt Lake	88	62	26
	American Fork	37	32	5		Spanish Fork	27	25	2
	Big Water	1	1	0		Springville	32	24	8
	Blanding	6	5	1		St. George	121	93	28
	Bountiful	48	34	14		Stockton	1	1	0
	Brian Head	5	5	0		Sunset	9	8	1
	Brigham City	29	24	5		Syracuse	19	17	2
	Cedar City	41	34	7		Taylorsville City	61	55	6
	Centerville	19	16	3		Tooele	32	27	5
	Clearfield	44	31	13		Tremonton	10	9	1
	Clinton	16	15	1		Vernal	22	19	3
	Draper	38	31	7		Washington	19	16	3
	East Carbon	3	3	0		Wellington	4	4	0
	Ephraim	5	5	0		Wendover	5	4	1
	Fairview	1	1	0		West Bountiful	10	9	1
	Farmington	15	12	3		West Jordan	127	92	35
	Garland	4	4	0		West Valley	223	177	46
	Grantsville	12	9	3		Willard	2	2	0
	Gunnison	2	2	0		Woods Cross	13	11	2
	Harrisville	9	8	1	VERMONT	Barre	24	17	7
	Heber	16	14	2		Barre Town	9	8	1
	Helper	6	6	0		Bellows Falls	12	8	4
	Hildale	6	5	1		Bennington	32	25	7
	Hurricane	19	14	5		Berlin	9	8	1
	Ivins	8	7	1		Brandon	8	7	1
	Kamas	2	2	0		Brattleboro	44	28	16
	Kanab	9	7	2		Bristol	3	3	0
	Kaysville	21	19	2		Burlington	127	96	31
	La Verkin	5	4	1		Castleton	3	3	0
	Layton	98	71	27		Chester	5	4	1
	Lehi	33	30	3		Colchester	33	26	7
	Logan	90	58	32		Dover	5	4	1
	Mantua	1	1	0		Essex	33	27	6
	Mapleton	8	7	1					

Table 78. Full-Time Law Enforcement Employees, by City, 2006 (*Contd.*)

(Number.)

State	City	Total law enforcement employees	Total officers	Total civilians	State	City	Total law enforcement employees	Total officers	Total civilians
	Fair Haven	3	3	0		Colonial Beach	16	11	5
	Hardwick	8	7	1		Colonial Heights	48	44	4
	Hartford	28	20	8		Courtland	3	1	2
	Hinesburg	3	3	0		Covington	27	16	11
	Ludlow	9	5	4		Crewe	5	5	0
	Lyndonville	1	1	0		Culpeper	49	41	8
	Manchester	12	8	4		Damascus	6	6	0
	Middlebury	15	13	2		Danville	136	126	10
	Milton	15	14	1		Dayton	7	7	0
	Montpelier	23	15	8		Dublin	10	9	1
	Morristown	10	10	0		Dumfries	17	15	2
	Newport	12	10	2		Edinburg	1	1	0
	Northfield	8	7	1		Elkton	8	7	1
	Norwich	6	5	1		Emporia	35	26	9
	Randolph	6	6	0		Exmore	7	7	0
	Richmond	5	5	0		Fairfax City	79	63	16
	Rutland	50	41	9		Falls Church	40	29	11
	Shelburne	17	11	6		Farmville	39	26	13
	South Burlington	45	37	8		Franklin	37	25	12
	Springfield	21	16	5		Fredericksburg	91	66	25
	St. Albans	26	18	8		Fries	1	1	0
	St. Johnsbury	16	11	5		Front Royal	45	36	9
	Stowe	15	12	3		Galax	39	24	15
	Swanton	5	4	1		Gate City	6	6	0
	Thetford	2	2	0		Glade Spring	1	1	0
	Vergennes	4	4	0		Glasgow	1	1	0
	Vernon	4	3	1		Glen Lyn	1	1	0
	Waterbury	4	4	0		Gordonsville	6	6	0
	Weathersfield	1	1	0		Gretna	4	4	0
	Williston	17	15	2		Grottoes	4	4	0
	Wilmington	6	5	1		Grundy	6	6	0
	Windsor	10	7	3		Halifax	5	5	0
	Winhall	7	6	1		Hampton	395	284	111
	Winooski	23	16	7		Harrisonburg	93	79	14
	Woodstock	6	5	1		Haymarket	6	5	1
VIRGINIA	Abingdon	24	22	2		Haysi	2	2	0
	Alexandria	449	322	127		Herndon	70	56	14
	Altavista	11	11	0		Hillsville	12	11	1
	Amherst	5	5	0		Honaker	3	2	1
	Appalachia	5	5	0		Hopewell	63	49	14
	Ashland	24	22	2		Hurt	2	2	0
	Bedford	31	27	4		Independence	2	2	0
	Berryville	10	9	1		Jonesville	3	3	0
	Big Stone Gap	18	16	2		Kenbridge	9	8	1
	Blacksburg	73	57	16		Kilmarnock	4	4	0
	Blackstone	15	11	4		La Crosse	2	2	0
	Bluefield	21	16	5		Lawrenceville	5	5	0
	Boykins	1	1	0		Lebanon	12	11	1
	Bridgewater	9	9	0		Leesburg	83	65	18
	Bristol	74	54	20		Lexington	17	15	2
	Broadway	4	4	0		Louisa	5	5	0
	Brookneal	2	2	0		Luray	13	11	2
	Buena Vista	15	14	1		Lynchburg	230	159	71
	Burkeville	1	1	0		Manassas	115	89	26
	Cape Charles	5	5	0		Manassas Park	37	28	9
	Cedar Bluff	3	3	0		Marion	21	19	2
	Charlottesville	138	113	25		Martinsville	59	53	6
	Chase City	11	10	1		McKenney	1	1	0
	Chatham	4	4	0		Middleburg	4	4	0
	Chesapeake	519	343	176		Middletown	2	2	0
	Chilhowie	6	6	0		Mount Jackson	4	4	0
	Chincoteague	14	10	4		Narrows	4	4	0
	Christiansburg	61	46	15		New Market	4	4	0
	Clarksville	9	8	1		Newport News	534	392	142
	Clifton Forge	16	10	6		Norfolk	844	729	115
	Clinchco	2	2	0		Norton	22	16	6
	Clintwood	3	3	0		Occoquan	1	1	0
	Coeburn	8	7	1		Onancock	4	4	0

Table 78. Full-Time Law Enforcement Employees, by City, 2006 (*Contd.*)

(Number.)

State	City	Total law enforcement employees	Total officers	Total civilians	State	City	Total law enforcement employees	Total officers	Total civilians
	Onley	3	3	0		Brier	10	8	2
	Orange	17	15	2		Buckley	9	9	0
	Parksley	3	3	0		Burien	46	39	7
	Pearisburg	8	7	1		Burlington	29	23	6
	Pembroke	2	2	0		Camas	30	25	5
	Pennington Gap	6	6	0		Castle Rock	6	5	1
	Petersburg	142	98	44		Centralia	36	30	6
	Pocahontas	1	1	0		Chehalis	19	15	4
	Poquoson	26	21	5		Cheney	18	13	5
	Portsmouth	352	248	104		Chewelah	6	5	1
	Pound	4	4	0		Clarkston	14	13	1
	Pulaski	33	25	8		Cle Elum	9	7	2
	Purcellville	14	13	1		Clyde Hill	8	7	1
	Quantico	3	2	1		Colfax	6	6	0
	Radford	46	33	13		College Place	14	12	2
	Rich Creek	1	1	0		Colton	1	1	0
	Richlands	22	17	5		Colville	13	11	2
	Richmond	923	690	233		Connell	7	7	0
	Roanoke	311	258	53		Cosmopolis	6	5	1
	Rocky Mount	16	14	2		Coulee City	1	1	0
	Rural Retreat	1	1	0		Coulee Dam	7	7	0
	Salem	85	62	23		Coupeville	5	5	0
	Saltville	6	5	1		Covington	13	12	1
	Shenandoah	4	4	0		Des Moines	47	37	10
	Smithfield	26	21	5		Dupont	11	10	1
	South Boston	28	26	2		Duvall	14	13	1
	South Hill	22	20	2		East Wenatchee	21	18	3
	Stanley	3	3	0		Eatonville	7	6	1
	Staunton	67	52	15		Edgewood	8	8	0
	Stephens City	3	3	0		Edmonds	64	53	11
	St. Paul	4	4	0		Ellensburg	32	23	9
	Strasburg	19	17	2		Elma	8	7	1
	Suffolk	216	160	56		Enumclaw	28	16	12
	Tappahannock	12	11	1		Ephrata	16	13	3
	Tazewell	12	11	1		Everett	217	180	37
	Timberville	3	3	0		Everson	6	6	0
	Victoria	6	5	1		Federal Way	147	116	31
	Vienna	52	41	11		Ferndale	19	16	3
	Vinton	33	23	10		Fife	43	27	16
	Virginia Beach	955	800	155		Fircrest	11	10	1
	Warrenton	20	18	2		Forks	15	7	8
	Warsaw	3	3	0		Garfield	1	1	0
	Waverly	12	7	5		Gig Harbor	18	16	2
	Waynesboro	58	50	8		Goldendale	10	9	1
	Weber City	4	4	0		Grand Coulee	7	7	0
	West Point	10	9	1		Grandview	24	18	6
	Williamsburg	50	34	16		Granger	9	7	2
	Winchester	85	72	13		Granite Falls	7	6	1
	Wise	14	13	1		Hoquiam	20	18	2
	Woodstock	17	16	1		Issaquah	45	31	14
	Wytheville	40	25	15		Kalama	5	5	0
WASHINGTON	Aberdeen	50	37	13		Kelso	32	28	4
	Airway Heights	13	12	1		Kenmore	15	14	1
	Algona	7	6	1		Kennewick	109	90	19
	Anacortes	33	25	8		Kent	173	125	48
	Arlington	31	26	5		Kettle Falls	4	3	1
	Asotin	3	3	0		Kirkland	106	68	38
	Auburn	113	83	30		Kittitas	3	3	0
	Bainbridge Island	26	21	5		La Center	10	9	1
	Battle Ground	31	25	6		Lacey	60	48	12
	Bellevue	275	167	108		Lake Forest Park	25	21	4
	Bellingham	158	109	49		Lake Stevens	19	16	3
	Black Diamond	10	10	0		Lakewood	122	101	21
	Blaine	17	13	4		Langley	4	4	0
	Bonney Lake	32	28	4		Liberty Lake	8	8	0
	Bothell	80	54	26		Long Beach	7	6	1
	Bremerton	76	57	19		Longview	64	52	12
	Brewster	8	6	2		Lynden	18	14	4

Table 78. Full-Time Law Enforcement Employees, by City, 2006 (*Contd.*)

(Number.)

State	City	Total law enforcement employees	Total officers	Total civilians	State	City	Total law enforcement employees	Total officers	Total civilians
	Lynnwood	97	67	30		Soap Lake	4	4	0
	Mabton	2	2	0		South Bend	4	3	1
	Malden	1	1	0		Spokane	385	278	107
	Maple Valley	12	11	1		Spokane Valley	101	100	1
	Marysville	68	44	24		Springdale	1	1	0
	Mattawa	2	2	0		Stanwood	13	11	2
	McCleary	3	3	0		Steilacoom	11	10	1
	Medical Lake	8	7	1		Sultan	9	8	1
	Medina	11	9	2		Sumas	6	6	0
	Mercer Island	35	31	4		Sumner	31	17	14
	Mill Creek	29	19	10		Sunnyside	40	24	16
	Milton	12	11	1		Tacoma	404	357	47
	Monroe	42	30	12		Tenino	6	6	0
	Montesano	10	8	2		Tieton	2	2	0
	Morton	3	2	1		Toledo	2	2	0
	Moses Lake	36	29	7		Tonasket	5	4	1
	Mountlake Terrace	41	31	10		Toppenish	24	17	7
	Mount Vernon	57	45	12		Tukwila	83	67	16
	Moxee	3	3	0		Tumwater	30	25	5
	Mukilteo	26	22	4		Union Gap	21	16	5
	Napavine	4	3	1		University Place	25	24	1
	Newcastle	7	7	0		Vader	1	1	0
	Normandy Park	15	13	2		Vancouver	225	193	32
	North Bend	5	5	0		Walla Walla	74	44	30
	North Bonneville	1	1	0		Wapato	23	13	10
	Oakesdale	1	1	0		Warden	5	4	1
	Oak Harbor	42	29	13		Washougal	20	18	2
	Ocean Shores	16	14	2		Wenatchee	51	40	11
	Odessa	2	2	0		Westport	9	7	2
	Olympia	96	68	28		West Richland	17	14	3
	Omak	14	12	2		White Salmon	6	6	0
	Oroville	7	5	2		Wilbur	2	2	0
	Orting	10	9	1		Winlock	2	2	0
	Othello	20	14	6		Winthrop	2	2	0
	Pacific	9	7	2		Woodinville	11	10	1
	Palouse	2	2	0		Woodland	11	9	2
	Pasco	71	60	11		Yakima	171	126	45
	Pe Ell	1	1	0		Yelm	14	12	2
	Port Angeles	58	31	27		Zillah	8	7	1
	Port Orchard	21	19	2	**WEST**				
	Port Townsend	17	14	3	**VIRGINIA**	Alderson	1	1	0
	Poulsbo	20	17	3		Anawalt	2	1	1
	Prosser	18	11	7		Anmoore	2	2	0
	Pullman	39	28	11		Ansted	1	1	0
	Puyallup	75	55	20		Athens	1	1	0
	Quincy	12	10	2		Barboursville	19	17	2
	Raymond	7	6	1		Barrackville	2	2	0
	Reardan	1	1	0		Beckley	61	44	17
	Redmond	106	74	32		Belington	2	2	0
	Renton	132	92	40		Belle	4	4	0
	Republic	3	3	0		Berkeley Springs	3	3	0
	Richland	62	52	10		Bethlehem	6	5	1
	Ridgefield	5	4	1		Bluefield	31	22	9
	Ritzville	4	4	0		Bradshaw	3	3	0
	Rosalia	1	1	0		Bramwell	2	2	0
	Roy	3	3	0		Bridgeport	24	22	2
	Royal City	3	3	0		Buckhannon	8	7	1
	Ruston	3	3	0		Burnsville	1	1	0
	Sammamish	24	23	1		Cameron	2	2	0
	SeaTac	51	42	9		Capon Bridge	1	1	0
	Seattle	1,746	1,276	470		Cedar Grove	2	2	0
	Sedro Woolley	20	15	5		Ceredo	9	6	3
	Selah	15	13	2		Chapmanville	4	4	0
	Sequim	20	18	2		Charleston	211	183	28
	Shelton	35	19	16		Charles Town	19	16	3
	Shoreline	57	49	8		Chesapeake	2	2	0
	Snohomish	24	20	4		Chester	5	5	0
	Snoqualmie	14	12	2		Clarksburg	41	36	5

Table 78. Full-Time Law Enforcement Employees, by City, 2006 (*Contd.*)

(Number.)

State	City	Total law enforcement employees	Total officers	Total civilians	State	City	Total law enforcement employees	Total officers	Total civilians
	Clendenin	3	3	0		Oak Hill	14	12	2
	Danville	3	3	0		Oceana	5	5	0
	Delbarton	2	2	0		Paden City	4	3	1
	Dunbar	16	13	3		Parkersburg	76	63	13
	East Bank	3	3	0		Paw Paw	2	1	1
	Eleanor	1	1	0		Pennsboro	1	1	0
	Elkins	13	10	3		Petersburg	1	1	0
	Fairmont	40	34	6		Peterstown	1	1	0
	Fairview	1	1	0		Philippi	6	6	0
	Farmington	1	1	0		Piedmont	1	1	0
	Fayetteville	11	9	2		Pineville	3	3	0
	Follansbee	8	8	0		Point Pleasant	11	10	1
	Fort Gay	2	2	0		Pratt	5	4	1
	Gary	1	1	0		Princeton	21	17	4
	Gassaway	1	1	0		Ranson	14	13	1
	Gauley Bridge	5	4	1		Ravenswood	10	9	1
	Gilbert	5	4	1		Reedsville	2	1	1
	Glasgow	3	3	0		Richwood	5	5	0
	Glen Dale	8	5	3		Ridgeley	1	1	0
	Glenville	4	3	1		Ripley	10	9	1
	Grafton	8	7	1		Romney	4	3	1
	Grantsville	1	1	0		Ronceverte	5	4	1
	Grant Town	1	1	0		Salem	3	3	0
	Granville	7	6	1		Shepherdstown	7	5	2
	Handley	1	1	0		Shinnston	6	6	0
	Harpers Ferry/Bolivar	4	3	1		Sistersville	4	4	0
	Harrisville	2	2	0		Smithers	8	7	1
	Henderson	3	1	2		Sophia	4	4	0
	Hinton	7	6	1		South Charleston	32	28	4
	Huntington	92	86	6		Spencer	7	6	1
	Hurricane	14	12	2		St. Albans	24	20	4
	Iaeger	1	1	0		Star City	5	5	0
	Kenova	13	9	4		St. Marys	4	4	0
	Kermit	2	2	0		Stonewood	3	3	0
	Keyser	12	8	4		Summersville	15	13	2
	Keystone	2	2	0		Sutton	2	1	1
	Kimball	1	1	0		Sylvester	2	2	0
	Kingwood	4	4	0		Terra Alta	1	1	0
	Lewisburg	13	11	2		Vienna	21	17	4
	Logan	14	8	6		Wardensville	2	1	1
	Lumberport	2	2	0		Wayne	3	1	2
	Mabscott	6	5	1		Weirton	39	36	3
	Madison	5	4	1		Welch	8	7	1
	Man	4	4	0		Wellsburg	7	6	1
	Mannington	4	4	0		West Logan	1	1	0
	Marlinton	1	1	0		Weston	8	7	1
	Marmet	5	5	0		Westover	9	9	0
	Martinsburg	49	40	9		West Union	1	1	0
	Mason	7	6	1		Wheeling	82	80	2
	Masontown	1	1	0		White Sulphur Springs	8	7	1
	Matewan	1	1	0		Whitesville	1	1	0
	Matoaka	1	1	0		Williamson	9	8	1
	McMechen	2	2	0		Williamstown	6	5	1
	Milton	6	5	1		Winfield	4	4	0
	Mitchell Heights	1	1	0	**WISCONSIN**	Albany	3	3	0
	Monongah	1	1	0		Algoma	6	6	0
	Montgomery	7	6	1		Altoona	12	11	1
	Moorefield	6	6	0		Amery	7	6	1
	Morgantown	63	54	9		Antigo	16	14	2
	Moundsville	18	17	1		Appleton	131	103	28
	Mount Hope	6	5	1		Arcadia	5	5	0
	Mullens	5	5	0		Ashland	20	19	1
	New Cumberland	3	3	0		Ashwaubenon	58	47	11
	New Haven	8	6	2		Bangor	2	2	0
	New Martinsville	12	10	2		Baraboo	25	20	5
	Nitro	17	16	1		Barron	7	7	0
	Northfork	3	3	0		Bayfield	4	4	0
	Nutter Fort	6	6	0					

Table 78. Full-Time Law Enforcement Employees, by City, 2006 (*Contd.*)

(Number.)

State	City	Total law enforcement employees	Total officers	Total civilians	State	City	Total law enforcement employees	Total officers	Total civilians
	Bayside	21	14	7		Fond du Lac	76	71	5
	Beaver Dam	39	29	10		Fontana	6	5	1
	Belleville	4	4	0		Fort Atkinson	27	20	7
	Beloit	96	77	19		Fox Lake	4	3	1
	Beloit Town	11	10	1		Fox Point	17	16	1
	Berlin	13	12	1		Fox Valley	29	26	3
	Black River Falls	8	7	1		Franklin	75	57	18
	Blair	3	3	0		Frederic	1	1	0
	Bloomer	8	7	1		Geneva Town	8	6	2
	Bloomfield	6	6	0		Genoa City	5	4	1
	Boscobel	6	6	0		Germantown	42	31	11
	Brillion	9	8	1		Glendale	46	42	4
	Brodhead	12	8	4		Grafton	28	20	8
	Brookfield	81	62	19		Grand Chute	30	26	4
	Brookfield Township	11	11	0		Grand Rapids	6	4	2
	Brown Deer	31	28	3		Grantsburg	3	3	0
	Burlington	27	21	6		Green Bay	222	182	40
	Burlington Town	9	9	0		Greendale	36	28	8
	Butler	8	7	1		Greenfield	76	54	22
	Caledonia	42	34	8		Green Lake	4	4	0
	Campbellsport	2	2	0		Hales Corners	21	17	4
	Campbell Township	5	5	0		Hartford	35	25	10
	Cedarburg	29	20	9		Hartland	18	16	2
	Chenequa	9	8	1		Hayward	8	7	1
	Chetek	5	4	1		Hazel Green	2	2	0
	Chilton	6	6	0		Hillsboro	2	2	0
	Chippewa Falls	32	24	8		Hobart-Lawrence	3	2	1
	Cleveland	9	9	0		Holmen	9	8	1
	Clinton	4	4	0		Horicon	11	9	2
	Clintonville	15	11	4		Hortonville	5	5	0
	Colby-Abbotsford	7	6	1		Hudson	23	20	3
	Columbus	24	11	13		Hurley	6	6	0
	Combined Locks	5	5	0		Independence	2	2	0
	Cornell	3	3	0		Iron Ridge	1	1	0
	Cottage Grove	11	10	1		Jackson	12	11	1
	Crandon	3	2	1		Janesville	115	103	12
	Cross Plains	6	5	1		Jefferson	17	14	3
	Cuba City	5	4	1		Juneau	5	4	1
	Cudahy	41	29	12		Kaukauna	26	24	2
	Cumberland	5	5	0		Kenosha	197	186	11
	Dane	2	1	1		Kewaskum	7	7	0
	Darien	6	5	1		Kewaunee	6	6	0
	Darlington	4	4	0		Kiel	8	7	1
	Deerfield	3	3	0		Kohler	8	7	1
	DeForest	16	13	3		La Crosse	113	93	20
	Delafield	16	14	2		Ladysmith	10	9	1
	Delavan	23	17	6		Lake Delton	17	16	1
	Delavan Town	8	7	1		Lake Geneva	28	20	8
	Denmark	2	2	0		Lake Hallie	6	5	1
	De Pere	40	33	7		Lake Mills	13	11	2
	Dodgeville	10	9	1		Lancaster	7	6	1
	Durand	4	4	0		Lodi	6	5	1
	Eagle River	5	5	0		Luxemburg	2	2	0
	East Troy	8	7	1		Madison	479	388	91
	Eau Claire	110	99	11		Manitowoc	70	64	6
	Edgar	1	1	0		Maple Bluff	5	5	0
	Edgerton	11	10	1		Marathon City	2	2	0
	Eleva	1	1	0		Marinette	29	24	5
	Elkhart Lake	3	3	0		Marion	3	3	0
	Elkhorn	19	16	3		Markesan	4	4	0
	Elk Mound	2	2	0		Marshall Village	10	8	2
	Ellsworth	7	6	1		Marshfield	47	39	8
	Elm Grove	25	17	8		Mauston	8	7	1
	Elroy	4	4	0		Mayville	12	10	2
	Evansville	7	6	1		McFarland	13	11	2
	Everest	29	25	4		Medford	10	9	1
	Fennimore	5	5	0		Menasha	33	26	7
	Fitchburg	49	39	10		Menomonee Falls	66	56	10

Table 78. Full-Time Law Enforcement Employees, by City, 2006 (*Contd.*)

(Number.)

State	City	Total law enforcement employees	Total officers	Total civilians	State	City	Total law enforcement employees	Total officers	Total civilians
	Menomonie	35	28	7		Shawano	21	19	2
	Mequon	44	36	8		Sheboygan	112	87	25
	Merrill	21	18	3		Sheboygan Falls	15	13	2
	Middleton	40	32	8		Shorewood	31	25	6
	Milton	9	8	1		Shorewood Hills	8	6	2
	Milwaukee	2,415	1,951	464		Silver Lake	5	4	1
	Mineral Point	6	6	0		Siren	3	3	0
	Minocqua	13	9	4		Slinger	9	8	1
	Mishicot	2	1	1		Somerset	6	5	1
	Mondovi	4	4	0		South Milwaukee	37	31	6
	Monona	24	19	5		Sparta	19	17	2
	Monroe	35	26	9		Spencer	2	2	0
	Mosinee	7	6	1		Spooner	7	6	1
	Mount Horeb	12	10	2		Spring Green	4	3	1
	Mount Pleasant	48	37	11		Stanley	4	4	0
	Mukwonago	21	14	7		St. Croix Falls	5	4	1
	Muskego	46	36	10		Stevens Point	57	44	13
	Neenah	45	36	9		St. Francis	24	19	5
	Neillsville	7	6	1		Stoughton	26	20	6
	New Berlin	90	71	19		Strum	2	2	0
	New Glarus	5	5	0		Sturgeon Bay	22	21	1
	New Holstein	8	7	1		Sturtevant	10	8	2
	New Lisbon	4	4	0		Summit	8	8	0
	New London	20	16	4		Sun Prairie	70	45	25
	New Richmond	14	12	2		Superior	58	52	6
	Niagara	5	5	0		Theresa	2	2	0
	North Fond du Lac	13	11	2		Thiensville	8	7	1
	North Hudson	6	5	1		Three Lakes	5	4	1
	Oak Creek	80	58	22		Tomah	20	18	2
	Oconomowoc	28	22	6		Tomahawk	8	7	1
	Oconomowoc Town	13	11	2		Town of East Troy	6	5	1
	Oconto	8	8	0		Town of Madison	20	18	2
	Oconto Falls	5	5	0		Town of Menasha	25	21	4
	Omro	6	5	1		Trempealeau	2	2	0
	Onalaska	30	28	2		Twin Lakes	19	13	6
	Oregon	17	15	2		Two Rivers	29	25	4
	Osceola	6	5	1		Valders	1	1	0
	Oshkosh	114	96	18		Verona	17	16	1
	Osseo	4	4	0		Viroqua	10	8	2
	Palmyra	5	5	0		Walworth	7	6	1
	Park Falls	8	7	1		Washburn	5	5	0
	Pepin	1	1	0		Waterloo	9	8	1
	Peshtigo	7	6	1		Watertown	51	37	14
	Pewaukee	28	26	2		Waukesha	145	110	35
	Pewaukee Village	19	17	2		Waunakee	18	16	2
	Phillips	6	5	1		Waupaca	16	14	2
	Platteville	26	20	6		Waupun	20	18	2
	Pleasant Prairie	27	25	2		Wausau	71	65	6
	Plover	21	18	3		Wautoma	6	5	1
	Plymouth	18	17	1		Wauwatosa	115	89	26
	Portage	30	22	8		West Allis	157	133	24
	Port Washington	24	19	5		West Bend	72	53	19
	Poynette	5	5	0		Westby	2	2	0
	Prairie du Chien	21	15	6		West Milwaukee	20	17	3
	Prescott	9	8	1		West Salem	5	4	1
	Princeton	2	2	0		Whitefish Bay	28	24	4
	Pulaski	6	6	0		Whitehall	4	4	0
	Racine	260	197	63		Whitewater	33	23	10
	Reedsburg	24	17	7		Williams Bay	8	7	1
	Rhinelander	18	15	3		Winneconne	6	5	1
	Rice Lake	22	21	1		Wisconsin Dells	18	12	6
	Richland Center	13	11	2		Wisconsin Rapids	47	37	10
	Ripon	19	14	5		Woodruff	6	5	1
	River Falls	22	20	2	**WYOMING**	Afton	5	5	0
	River Hills	12	12	0		Baggs	3	2	1
	Rothschild	9	7	2		Basin	3	3	0
	Sauk Prairie	15	13	2		Buffalo	18	10	8
	Saukville	13	11	2		Casper	133	91	42

Table 78. Full-Time Law Enforcement Employees, by City, 2006 (*Contd.*)

(Number.)

State	City	Total law enforcement employees	Total officers	Total civilians
	Cheyenne	121	96	25
	Cody	20	19	1
	Diamondville	4	3	1
	Douglas	26	16	10
	Evanston	33	27	6
	Evansville	10	8	2
	Gillette	72	47	25
	Glenrock	10	7	3
	Green River	38	29	9
	Guernsey	3	3	0
	Hanna	6	1	5
	Jackson	27	21	6
	Kemmerer	9	8	1
	La Barge	1	1	0
	Lander	21	20	1
	Laramie	77	47	30
	Lovell	9	6	3
	Lusk	4	4	0
	Lyman	6	5	1
	Mills	11	10	1
	Moorcroft	5	4	1
	Newcastle	15	7	8
	Pine Bluffs	6	2	4
	Powell	22	15	7
	Rawlins	31	19	12
	Riverton	31	23	8
	Rock Springs	66	44	22
	Saratoga	9	4	5
	Sheridan	46	26	20
	Sundance	4	4	0
	Thermopolis	13	7	6
	Torrington	21	15	6
	Wheatland	10	9	1
	Worland	9	8	1

Table 79. Full-Time Law Enforcement Employees, by State by University and College, 2006

(Number.)

State	University/College	Campus	Total law enforcement employees	Total officers	Total civilians
ALABAMA	Alabama A&M University		35	17	18
	Alabama State University		33	24	9
	Auburn University	Montgomery	18	11	7
	Calhoun Community College		7	5	2
	George C. Wallace State Community College		4	3	1
	Jacksonville State University		16	12	4
	Troy University		12	10	2
	University of Alabama:	Birmingham	124	61	63
		Huntsville	16	12	4
		Tuscaloosa	63	54	9
	University of Montevallo		14	9	5
	University of North Alabama		15	13	2
	University of South Alabama		45	25	20
	University of West Alabama		9	6	3
ALASKA	University of Alaska:	Anchorage	19	13	6
		Fairbanks	17	10	7
ARIZONA	Arizona State University	Main Campus	102	58	44
	Arizona Western College		13	7	6
	Central Arizona College		10	7	3
	Northern Arizona University		25	17	8
	Pima Community College		32	25	7
	University of Arizona		86	51	35
	Yavapai College		9	8	1
ARKANSAS	Arkansas State University:	Beebe	4	3	1
		Jonesboro	21	17	4
	Arkansas Tech University		11	9	2
	Henderson State University		7	6	1
	Northwest Arkansas Community College		8	4	4
	Southern Arkansas University		5	5	0
	University of Arkansas:	Fayetteville	34	27	7
		Little Rock	38	26	12
		Medical Sciences	47	40	7
		Monticello	7	6	1
		Pine Bluff	17	13	4
	University of Central Arkansas		30	24	6
CALIFORNIA	Allan Hancock College		20	6	14
	California State Polytechnic University:	Pomona	32	20	12
		San Luis Obispo	30	15	15
	California State University:	Bakersfield	15	11	4
		Channel Islands	19	14	5
		Chico	28	17	11
		Dominguez Hills	18	14	4
		East Bay	28	14	14
		Fresno	26	17	9
		Fullerton	31	22	9
		Long Beach	32	24	8
		Los Angeles	33	17	16
		Monterey Bay	16	14	2
		Northridge	35	20	15
		Sacramento	26	20	6
		San Bernardino	24	15	9
		San Jose	73	29	44
		San Marcos	21	13	8
		Stanislaus	22	11	11
	College of the Sequoias		6	5	1
	Contra Costa Community College		31	21	10
	Cuesta College		7	6	1
	El Camino College		21	15	6
	Foothill-De Anza College		20	11	9
	Fresno Community College		17	13	4
	Humboldt State University		21	10	11
	Marin Community College		6	5	1
	Pasadena Community College		12	6	6
	Riverside Community College		21	16	5
	San Bernardino Community College		18	14	4
	San Diego State University		43	24	19
	San Francisco State University		49	27	22
	San Jose/Evergreen Community College		13	6	7

Table 79. Full-Time Law Enforcement Employees, by State by University and College, 2006 (*Contd.*)

(Number.)

State	University/College	Campus	Total law enforcement employees	Total officers	Total civilians
	Santa Rosa Junior College		24	12	12
	Solano Community College		7	6	1
	Sonoma State University		21	13	8
	University of California:	Berkeley	132	73	59
		Davis	67	41	26
		Hastings College of Law	12	12	0
		Irvine	39	25	14
		Lawrence-Livermore Laboratory	9	1	8
		Los Angeles	92	55	37
		Merced	15	8	7
		Riverside	32	24	8
		San Diego	56	30	26
		San Francisco	98	35	63
		Santa Barbara	43	26	17
		Santa Cruz	43	16	27
	Ventura County Community College		17	17	0
	West Valley-Mission College		13	9	4
COLORADO	Adams State College		6	4	2
	Arapahoe Community College		10	7	3
	Auraria Higher Education Center		35	20	15
	Colorado School of Mines		8	7	1
	Colorado State University:	Fort Collins	58	29	29
		Pueblo	2	2	0
	Fort Lewis College		9	7	2
	Pikes Peak Community College		18	16	2
	Red Rocks Community College		1	1	0
	University of Colorado:	Boulder	52	36	16
		Colorado Springs	24	13	11
		Health Sciences Center	11	8	3
		Health Sciences Center, Fitzsimon Campus	45	16	29
	University of Northern Colorado		19	12	7
CONNECTICUT	Central Connecticut State University		27	20	7
	Eastern Connecticut State University		25	19	6
	Southern Connecticut State University		33	26	7
	University of Connecticut:	Health Center	20	14	6
		Storrs, Avery Point, and Hartford	90	71	19
	Western Connecticut State University		30	19	11
	Yale University		89	74	15
DELAWARE	Delaware State University		31	12	19
	University of Delaware		75	41	34
FLORIDA	Florida A&M University		36	27	9
	Florida Atlantic University		47	35	12
	Florida Gulf Coast University		21	13	8
	Florida International University		55	36	19
	Florida State University:	Panama City	4	3	1
		Tallahassee	76	56	20
	New College of Florida		20	13	7
	Pensacola Junior College		16	12	4
	Santa Fe Community College		21	15	6
	Tallahassee Community College		21	9	12
	University of Central Florida		93	55	38
	University of Florida		129	84	45
	University of North Florida		36	27	9
	University of South Florida:	St. Petersburg	16	9	7
		Tampa	53	39	14
	University of West Florida		28	20	8
GEORGIA	Abraham Baldwin Agricultural College		12	11	1
	Albany State University		21	14	7
	Armstrong Atlantic State University		10	6	4
	Augusta State University		23	17	6
	Berry College		16	10	6
	Clark Atlanta University		43	16	27
	Clayton College and State University		18	11	7
	Coastal Georgia Community College		9	9	0
	Columbus State University		28	23	5
	Dalton State College		9	8	1
	Emory University		55	38	17

Table 79. Full-Time Law Enforcement Employees, by State by University and College, 2006 *(Contd.)*

(Number.)

State	University/College	Campus	Total law enforcement employees	Total officers	Total civilians
	Georgia College and State University		15	11	4
	Georgia Institute of Technology		83	62	21
	Georgia Perimeter College		58	18	40
	Georgia Southern University		31	26	5
	Georgia State University		102	61	41
	Gordon College		9	8	1
	Kennesaw State University		68	25	43
	Medical College of Georgia		45	34	11
	Mercer University		33	24	9
	Middle Georgia College		12	11	1
	Morehouse College		39	16	23
	Morris-Brown College		5	2	3
	North Georgia College		9	7	2
	Piedmont College		2	2	0
	Savannah State University		29	14	15
	Southern Polytechnic State University		19	14	5
	South Georgia College		4	4	0
	University of Georgia		93	70	23
	University of West Georgia		27	20	7
	Valdosta State University		35	26	9
	Wesleyan College		4	4	0
	Young Harris College		2	2	0
ILLINOIS	Black Hawk College		9	8	1
	Chicago State University		32	22	10
	College of DuPage		20	15	5
	College of Lake County		20	12	8
	Eastern Illinois University		24	21	3
	Governors State University		10	8	2
	Illinois State University		27	22	5
	John A. Logan College		7	6	1
	Joliet Junior College		19	10	9
	Loyola University of Chicago		50	29	21
	Moraine Valley Community College		15	10	5
	Morton College		7	3	4
	Northeastern Illinois University		23	18	5
	Northern Illinois University		69	45	24
	Northwestern University:	Chicago	18	14	4
		Evanston	41	27	14
	Oakton Community College		10	9	1
	Parkland College		17	12	5
	Rock Valley College		14	12	2
	Southern Illinois University:	Carbondale	47	36	11
		Edwardsville	39	31	8
		School of Medicine	14	2	12
	South Suburban College		13	8	5
	Triton College		16	11	5
	University of Illinois:	Chicago	126	75	51
		Springfield	19	13	6
		Urbana	69	54	15
	Waubonsee College		2	2	0
	Western Illinois University		33	27	6
	William Rainey Harper College		16	11	5
INDIANA	Ball State University		30	23	7
	Indiana State University		30	22	8
	Indiana University:	Bloomington	50	42	8
		Gary	15	11	4
		Indianapolis	49	32	17
		New Albany	9	8	1
	Marian College		7	5	2
	Purdue University		50	39	11
IOWA	Iowa State University		37	31	6
	University of Iowa		54	31	23
	University of Northern Iowa		24	18	6
KANSAS	Emporia State University		10	9	1
	Fort Hays State University		11	9	2
	Kansas City Community College		11	10	1
	Kansas State University		37	23	14
	Pittsburg State University		16	13	3

Table 79. Full-Time Law Enforcement Employees, by State by University and College, 2006 (*Contd.*)

(Number.)

State	University/College	Campus	Total law enforcement employees	Total officers	Total civilians
	University of Kansas:	Main Campus	45	26	19
		Medical Center	58	29	29
	Washburn University		18	13	5
	Wichita State University		32	22	10
KENTUCKY	Eastern Kentucky University		38	25	13
	Kentucky State University		12	9	3
	Morehead State University		27	16	11
	Murray State University		23	15	8
	Northern Kentucky University		21	15	6
	University of Kentucky		54	44	10
	University of Louisville		63	29	34
	Western Kentucky University		36	26	10
LOUISIANA	Grambling State University		24	13	11
	Louisiana State University:	Baton Rouge	63	61	2
		Health Sciences Center, Shreveport	59	39	20
		Shreveport	9	9	0
	McNeese State University		16	7	9
	Nicholls State University		14	9	5
	Northwestern State University		16	14	2
	Southeastern Louisiana University		33	23	10
	Southern University and A&M College:	Baton Rouge	38	23	15
		New Orleans	9	8	1
		Shreveport	11	10	1
	Tulane University		51	37	14
	University of Louisiana	Monroe	28	21	7
MAINE	University of Maine:	Farmington	5	4	1
		Orono	32	19	13
	University of Southern Maine		27	15	12
MARYLAND	Bowie State University		26	12	14
	Coppin State University		17	15	2
	Frostburg State University		18	14	4
	Morgan State University		41	35	6
	Salisbury University		19	15	4
	St. Mary's College		15	2	13
	Towson University		65	40	25
	University of Baltimore		37	12	25
	University of Maryland:	Baltimore City	142	56	86
		Baltimore County	36	25	11
		College Park	120	89	31
		Eastern Shore	11	9	2
MASSACHUSETTS	Assumption College		20	13	7
	Bentley College		35	24	11
	Boston College		62	45	17
	Boston University		59	51	8
	Brandeis University		22	18	4
	Bridgewater State College		24	20	4
	Bristol Community College		7	5	2
	Clark University		14	12	2
	Dean College		13	8	5
	Emerson College		14	13	1
	Fitchburg State College		16	14	2
	Framingham State College		17	13	4
	Harvard University		94	71	23
	Holyoke Community College		12	12	0
	Lasell College		14	14	0
	Massachusetts College of Art		8	8	0
	Massachusetts College of Liberal Arts		11	8	3
	Massachusetts Institute of Technology		59	56	3
	Massasoit Community College		13	11	2
	Merrimack College		16	10	6
	Mount Holyoke College		22	14	8
	Northeastern University		78	54	24
	North Shore Community College		21	19	2
	Quinsigamond Community College		12	12	0
	Salem State College		26	23	3
	Springfield College		32	14	18
	Tufts University	Medford	65	43	22
	University of Massachusetts:	Amherst	76	60	16

Table 79. Full-Time Law Enforcement Employees, by State by University and College, 2006 *(Contd.)*

(Number.)

State	University/College	Campus	Total law enforcement employees	Total officers	Total civilians
		Dartmouth	42	23	19
		Harbor Campus, Boston	35	27	8
		Medical Center, Worcester	28	20	8
	Wellesley College..		16	11	5
	Western New England College		24	15	9
	Westfield State College		16	14	2
MICHIGAN	Central Michigan University..........................		31	21	10
	Delta College		7	5	2
	Eastern Michigan University..........................		29	23	6
	Ferris State University		18	13	5
	Grand Rapids Community College		14	11	3
	Grand Valley State University		19	15	4
	Lansing Community College...........................		18	15	3
	Macomb Community College		36	29	7
	Michigan State University		104	67	37
	Michigan Technological University................		12	9	3
	Mott Community College		2	2	0
	Northern Michigan University.......................		25	21	4
	Oakland Community College		26	25	1
	Oakland University		25	20	5
	Saginaw Valley State University		9	7	2
	University of Michigan:.................................	Ann Arbor	98	55	43
		Dearborn	19	3	16
		Flint	18	5	13
	Western Michigan University.........................		59	28	31
MINNESOTA	University of Minnesota:	Duluth	11	10	1
		Morris	6	3	3
		Twin Cities	64	45	19
MISSISSIPPI	Coahoma Community College..........................		6	5	1
	Itawamba Community College		10	9	1
	Jackson State University................................		61	31	30
	Mississippi State University..........................		34	27	7
	University of Mississippi:	Medical Center	81	57	24
		Oxford	38	21	17
MISSOURI	Central Missouri State University		21	17	4
	Lincoln University..		12	10	2
	Missouri Western State University................		12	9	3
	Northwest Missouri State University		10	10	0
	Southeast Missouri State University		23	17	6
	St. Louis Community College	Meramec	12	9	3
	Truman State University................................		10	9	1
	University of Missouri:.................................	Columbia	46	31	15
		Kansas City	37	21	16
		Rolla	23	11	12
		St. Louis	24	20	4
	Washington University..................................		37	26	11
MONTANA	Montana State University..............................		26	13	13
	University of Montana		20	13	7
NEBRASKA	University of Nebraska:	Kearney	7	7	0
		Lincoln	36	29	7
NEVADA	Truckee Meadows Community College............		11	6	5
	University of Nevada:	Las Vegas	51	35	16
		Reno	32	26	6
NEW JERSEY	Brookdale Community College		19	12	7
	Essex County College		63	17	46
	Kean University of New Jersey......................		47	28	19
	Middlesex County College		16	11	5
	Monmouth University....................................		35	20	15
	Montclair State University............................		42	27	15
	New Jersey Institute of Technology		65	30	35
	Richard Stockton College.............................		25	19	6
	Rowan University..		45	10	35
	Rutgers University:.......................................	Camden	36	18	18
		Newark	34	25	9
		New Brunswick	86	50	36
	Stevens Institute of Technology....................		23	12	11
	The College of New Jersey............................		25	19	6
	University of Medicine and Dentistry:...........	Camden	18	17	1

Table 79. Full-Time Law Enforcement Employees, by State by University and College, 2006 (*Contd.*)

(Number.)

State	University/College	Campus	Total law enforcement employees	Total officers	Total civilians
		Newark	147	48	99
		Piscataway	34	27	7
	William Paterson University		37	25	12
NEW MEXICO	Eastern New Mexico University		9	8	1
	New Mexico State University		29	17	12
	University of New Mexico		52	30	22
NEW YORK	Cornell University		53	39	14
	State University of New York:	Buffalo	66	60	6
		Downstate Medical Center	116	30	86
		Stony Brook	136	55	81
		Upstate Medical Center	75	12	63
	State University of New York Agricultural and Technical College:	Alfred	17	12	5
		Canton	12	11	1
		Farmingdale	21	16	5
	State University of New York College:	Cortland	21	18	3
		Environmental Science and Forestry	12	10	2
		Fredonia	16	15	1
		New Paltz	26	23	3
		Optometry	13	4	9
		Plattsburgh	22	15	7
NORTH CAROLINA	Appalachian State University		30	18	12
	Beaufort County Community College		2	2	0
	Belmont Abbey College		7	7	0
	Davidson College		9	8	1
	Duke University		121	46	75
	East Carolina University		69	51	18
	Elizabeth City State University		14	9	5
	Elon University		12	11	1
	Fayetteville State University		24	15	9
	North Carolina Agricultural and Technical State University		44	24	20
	North Carolina Central University		32	17	15
	North Carolina School of the Arts		14	13	1
	North Carolina State University	Raleigh	59	47	12
	Queens University		8	4	4
	Saint Augustine's College		23	5	18
	University of North Carolina:	Asheville	20	11	9
		Chapel Hill	77	48	29
		Charlotte	34	25	9
		Greensboro	48	31	17
		Pembroke	16	13	3
		Wilmington	32	23	9
	Wake Forest University		45	19	26
	Western Carolina University		17	12	5
	Winston-Salem State University		24	16	8
NORTH DAKOTA	North Dakota State College of Science		3	3	0
	North Dakota State University		14	9	5
	University of North Dakota		15	12	3
OHIO	Bowling Green State University		28	21	7
	Cleveland State University		30	21	9
	Columbus State Community College		31	17	14
	Cuyahoga Community College		34	28	6
	Kent State University		33	26	7
	Lakeland Community College		14	10	4
	Marietta College		9	7	2
	Miami University		40	28	12
	Muskingum College		6	5	1
	Ohio State University		62	46	16
	Ohio University		26	20	6
	Sinclair Community College		26	22	4
	University of Akron		38	32	6
	University of Cincinnati		118	61	57
	University of Toledo		38	29	9
	Wright State University		21	13	8
	Youngstown State University		26	21	5
OKLAHOMA	Cameron University		10	10	0
	East Central University		5	5	0

Table 79. Full-Time Law Enforcement Employees, by State by University and College, 2006 (*Contd.*)

(Number.)

State	University/College	Campus	Total law enforcement employees	Total officers	Total civilians
	Murray State College		2	2	0
	Northeastern Oklahoma A&M College		9	7	2
	Northeastern State University		17	16	1
	Oklahoma State University:	Main Campus	35	28	7
		Okmulgee	6	5	1
		Tulsa	6	4	2
	Rogers State University		4	4	0
	Seminole State College		4	3	1
	Southeastern Oklahoma State University		8	7	1
	Southwestern Oklahoma State University		7	5	2
	Tulsa Community College		16	10	6
	University of Central Oklahoma		20	16	4
	University of Oklahoma:	Health Sciences Center	51	42	9
		Norman	60	29	31
PENNSYLVANIA	California University		15	13	2
	Cheyney University		14	13	1
	Dickinson College		14	9	5
	East Stroudsburg University		17	14	3
	Edinboro University		15	14	1
	Elizabethtown College		16	11	5
	Indiana University		30	22	8
	Kutztown University		24	17	7
	Lehigh University		30	20	10
	Lock Haven University		11	10	1
	Mansfield University		11	11	0
	Millersville University		22	14	8
	Moravian College		12	7	5
	Pennsylvania State University:	Altoona	8	7	1
		Beaver	5	5	0
		Behrend	10	6	4
		Berks	8	7	1
		Harrisburg	9	7	2
		Hazelton	4	3	1
		McKeesport	5	5	0
		Mont Alto	4	4	0
		University Park	65	43	22
	Shippensburg University		19	17	2
	Slippery Rock University		16	14	2
	University of Pittsburgh:	Bradford	6	5	1
		Pittsburgh	122	68	54
	West Chester University		35	19	16
RHODE ISLAND	Brown University		64	27	37
	University of Rhode Island		46	25	21
SOUTH CAROLINA	Aiken Technical College		10	2	8
	Benedict College		25	19	6
	Bob Jones University		4	4	0
	Clemson University		45	28	17
	Coastal Carolina University		58	19	39
	College of Charleston		56	31	25
	Columbia College		11	8	3
	Denmark Technical College		5	5	0
	Erskine College		2	2	0
	Francis Marion University		12	11	1
	Lander University		11	9	2
	Medical University of South Carolina		71	47	24
	Midlands Technical College		6	6	0
	Presbyterian College		8	7	1
	South Carolina State University		34	19	15
	Spartanburg Methodist College		4	4	0
	The Citadel		14	13	1
	Trident Technical College		22	20	2
	University of South Carolina:	Aiken	7	7	0
		Columbia	72	47	25
		Upstate	9	8	1
	Winthrop University		22	15	7
SOUTH DAKOTA	South Dakota State University		18	12	6
TENNESSEE	Austin Peay State University		22	12	10
	Christian Brothers University		15	7	8

Table 79. Full-Time Law Enforcement Employees, by State by University and College, 2006 (*Contd.*)

(Number.)

State	University/College	Campus	Total law enforcement employees	Total officers	Total civilians
	East Tennessee State University		25	18	7
	Middle Tennessee State University		35	28	7
	Northeast State Technical Community College		5	5	0
	Southwest Tennessee Community College		31	27	4
	Tennessee State University		48	33	15
	Tennessee Technological University		22	15	7
	University of Memphis		34	29	5
	University of Tennessee:	Chattanooga	20	14	6
		Knoxville	77	50	27
		Martin	14	11	3
		Memphis	36	23	13
	Vanderbilt University		92	68	24
	Volunteer State Community College		5	4	1
	Walters State Community College		8	8	0
TEXAS	Abilene Christian University		10	9	1
	Alvin Community College		11	9	2
	Amarillo College		16	14	2
	Angelo State University		15	11	4
	Austin College		8	7	1
	Baylor Health Care System		139	52	87
	Baylor University	Waco	29	24	5
	Central Texas College		9	6	3
	College of the Mainland		7	6	1
	Eastfield College		10	9	1
	El Paso Community College		42	34	8
	Grayson County College		4	3	1
	Hardin-Simmons University		6	5	1
	Houston Baptist University		13	11	2
	Lamar University	Beaumont	31	17	14
	Laredo Community College		22	21	1
	McLennan Community College		14	6	8
	Midwestern State University		14	9	5
	Mountain View College		15	15	0
	North Lake College		16	15	1
	Paris Junior College		3	3	0
	Prairie View A&M University		36	24	12
	Rice University		43	27	16
	Richland College		11	10	1
	Southern Methodist University		33	23	10
	South Plains College		3	3	0
	Southwestern University		7	6	1
	Stephen F. Austin State University		38	21	17
	St. Mary's University		15	12	3
	St. Thomas University		10	1	9
	Sul Ross State University		9	7	2
	Tarleton State University		13	11	2
	Texas A&M International University		21	14	7
	Texas A&M University:	College Station	113	55	58
		Commerce	25	15	10
		Corpus Christi	25	16	9
		Galveston	8	7	1
		Kingsville	16	10	6
	Texas Christian University		34	21	13
	Texas Southern University		60	39	21
	Texas State Technical College:	Harlingen	12	9	3
		Marshall	4	4	0
		Waco	14	12	2
	Texas State University	San Marcos	71	30	41
	Texas Technological University	Lubbock	70	45	25
	Texas Woman's University		35	16	19
	Trinity University		25	14	11
	Tyler Junior College		11	4	7
	University of Houston:	Central Campus	56	40	16
		Clearlake	22	11	11
		Downtown Campus	28	17	11
	University of Mary Hardin-Baylor		8	8	0
	University of North Texas:	Denton	73	41	32
		Health Science Center	23	10	13

Table 79. Full-Time Law Enforcement Employees, by State by University and College, 2006 (*Contd.*)

(Number.)

State	University/College	Campus	Total law enforcement employees	Total officers	Total civilians
	University of Texas:	Arlington	80	29	51
		Austin	132	58	74
		Brownsville	35	14	21
		Dallas	40	18	22
		El Paso	50	22	28
		Health Science Center, San Antonio	96	32	64
		Health Science Center, Tyler	23	5	18
		Medical Branch	90	42	48
		Pan American	33	12	21
		Permian Basin	13	7	6
		San Antonio	85	40	45
		Southwestern Medical School	137	44	93
		Tyler	15	8	7
	Western Texas College		2	2	0
	West Texas A&M University		14	10	4
UTAH	Brigham Young University		40	29	11
	College of Eastern Utah		1	1	0
	Southern Utah University		5	4	1
	University of Utah		92	28	64
	Utah State University		17	11	6
	Utah Valley State College		9	7	2
	Weber State University		10	9	1
VERMONT	University of Vermont		36	22	14
VIRGINIA	Christopher Newport University		20	15	5
	College of William and Mary		23	18	5
	Emory and Henry College		4	2	2
	Ferrum College		7	7	0
	George Mason University		61	45	16
	Hampton University		35	18	17
	James Madison University		32	25	7
	J. Sargeant Reynolds Community College		12	6	6
	Longwood College		21	13	8
	Mary Washington College		17	10	7
	Norfolk State University		53	28	25
	Northern Virginia Community College		34	34	0
	Old Dominion University		54	42	12
	Radford University		25	19	6
	Thomas Nelson Community College		16	10	6
	University of Richmond		31	16	15
	University of Virginia		115	54	61
	University of Virginia	College at Wise	9	8	1
	Virginia Commonwealth University		173	76	97
	Virginia Military Institute		7	7	0
	Virginia Polytechnic Institute and State University		52	36	16
	Virginia State University		30	14	16
	Virginia Western Community College		6	6	0
WASHINGTON	Central Washington University		14	13	1
	Eastern Washington University		12	11	1
	Evergreen State College		15	10	5
	University of Washington		55	42	13
	Washington State University:	Pullman	19	16	3
		Vancouver	3	2	1
	Western Washington University		19	13	6
WEST VIRGINIA	Bluefield State College		1	1	0
	Concord University		8	7	1
	Fairmont State University		5	3	2
	Glenville State College		2	2	0
	Marshall University		22	21	1
	Potomac State College		6	6	0
	Shepherd University		9	8	1
	West Liberty State College		4	4	0
	West Virginia State University		11	9	2
	West Virginia Tech		5	5	0
	West Virginia University		57	49	8
WISCONSIN	University of Wisconsin:	Eau Claire	12	10	2
		Green Bay	12	5	7
		La Crosse	9	7	2

Table 79. Full-Time Law Enforcement Employees, by State by University and College, 2006 (*Contd.*)

(Number.)

State	University/College	Campus	Total law enforcement employees	Total officers	Total civilians
		Madison	105	63	42
		Milwaukee	39	28	11
		Oshkosh	12	10	2
		Parkside	18	16	2
		Platteville	9	7	2
		Stevens Point	8	3	5
		Stout	10	9	1
		Superior	8	1	7
		Whitewater	10	9	1
WYOMING	Sheridan College...		3	2	1
	University of Wyoming		18	12	6

Table 80. Full-time Law Enforcement Employees, by Metropolitan and Nonmetropolitan County, 2006

(Number.)

State	County	Total law enforcement employees	Total officers	Total civilians	State	County	Total law enforcement employees	Total officers	Total civilians
ALABAMA–						Pinal	444	186	258
Metropolitan Counties	Autauga	59	22	37		Yavapai	354	115	239
	Bibb	13	12	1		Yuma	311	66	245
	Blount	73	42	31	**ARIZONA–**				
	Calhoun	45	39	6	**Nonmetropolitan Counties**	Apache	68	30	38
	Chilton	52	25	27		Cochise	195	87	108
	Colbert	50	31	19		Gila	136	44	92
	Elmore	77	31	46		Graham	59	22	37
	Etowah	153	59	94		Greenlee	27	12	15
	Geneva	23	11	12		La Paz	91	35	56
	Greene	26	10	16		Navajo	126	45	81
	Hale	7	5	2		Santa Cruz	79	40	39
	Henry	14	10	4	**ARKANSAS–**				
	Houston	79	49	30	**Metropolitan Counties**	Benton	179	86	93
	Jefferson	700	542	158		Cleveland	12	7	5
	Lauderdale	39	30	9		Craighead	40	28	12
	Lawrence	41	20	21		Crawford	54	23	31
	Lee	132	58	74		Crittenden	151	35	116
	Limestone	44	33	11		Faulkner	143	46	97
	Lowndes	41	14	27		Franklin	17	9	8
	Madison	282	102	180		Garland	117	41	76
	Mobile	437	151	286		Grant	12	10	2
	Montgomery	163	123	40		Jefferson	49	43	6
	Morgan	157	50	107		Lincoln	22	9	13
	Russell	87	29	58		Lonoke	39	21	18
	Shelby	182	105	77		Madison	16	9	7
	St. Clair	76	36	40		Miller	66	26	40
	Tuscaloosa	193	91	102		Perry	15	6	9
	Walker	79	65	14		Poinsett	40	12	28
ALABAMA–						Pulaski	440	320	120
Nonmetropolitan Counties	Baldwin	223	78	145		Saline	78	42	36
	Barbour	15	13	2		Sebastian	135	30	105
	Bullock	21	6	15		Washington	259	113	146
	Butler	16	4	12	**ARKANSAS–**				
	Chambers	46	18	28	**Nonmetropolitan Counties**	Arkansas	47	12	35
	Cherokee	48	17	31		Ashley	40	14	26
	Choctaw	15	7	8		Baxter	49	31	18
	Clarke	19	15	4		Boone	38	22	16
	Clay	27	8	19		Bradley	5	4	1
	Cleburne	24	9	15		Calhoun	12	6	6
	Coosa	19	8	11		Carroll	31	16	15
	Covington	49	22	27		Chicot	8	6	2
	Crenshaw	8	7	1		Clark	14	8	6
	Cullman	123	73	50		Clay	23	8	15
	Dale	17	11	6		Cleburne	32	20	12
	Dallas	49	24	25		Columbia	25	13	12
	De Kalb	82	34	48		Conway	32	15	17
	Escambia	53	18	35		Cross	36	16	20
	Fayette	16	10	6		Dallas	28	6	22
	Jackson	73	30	43		Desha	8	8	0
	Lamar	17	7	10		Drew	27	10	17
	Macon	32	14	18		Fulton	11	5	6
	Marengo	29	12	17		Greene	42	12	30
	Marshall	41	35	6		Hempstead	20	13	7
	Monroe	56	20	36		Hot Spring	23	20	3
	Perry	14	7	7		Howard	21	10	11
	Pickens	21	7	14		Independence	74	47	27
	Pike	30	16	14		Izard	23	11	12
	Randolph	31	12	19		Jackson	21	12	9
	Sumter	6	4	2		Johnson	34	13	21
	Talladega	97	40	57		Lafayette	16	7	9
	Tallapoosa	56	24	32		Lawrence	21	12	9
	Washington	13	7	6		Lee	7	5	2
	Winston	24	10	14		Little River	22	8	14
ARIZONA–						Logan	25	12	13
Metropolitan Counties	Coconino	249	64	185		Marion	21	11	10
	Maricopa	3,302	736	2,566		Mississippi	82	25	57
	Mohave	234	85	149		Monroe	11	5	6
	Pima	1,338	496	842		Montgomery	15	7	8

Table 80. Full-time Law Enforcement Employees, by Metropolitan and Nonmetropolitan County, 2006 (*Contd.*)

(Number.)

State	County	Total law enforcement employees	Total officers	Total civilians	State	County	Total law enforcement employees	Total officers	Total civilians
	Nevada	16	6	10		Lassen	91	70	21
	Newton	11	7	4		Mariposa	71	57	14
	Ouachita	29	16	13		Mendocino	171	129	42
	Phillips	35	15	20		Modoc	25	22	3
	Pike	15	8	7		Mono	43	26	17
	Polk	23	11	12		Nevada	186	70	116
	Pope	88	32	56		Plumas	70	35	35
	Prairie	16	7	9		Sierra	15	11	4
	Randolph	11	11	0		Siskiyou	131	99	32
	Scott	15	8	7		Tehama	104	75	29
	Searcy	13	7	6		Trinity	38	18	20
	Sevier	22	11	11		Tuolumne	132	65	67
	Sharp	20	10	10	**COLORADO–**				
	St. Francis	29	11	18	**Metropolitan Counties**	Adams	498	348	150
	Stone	19	8	11		Arapahoe	573	396	177
	Union	57	27	30		Boulder	318	202	116
	Van Buren	28	13	15		Clear Creek	60	27	33
	White	77	33	44		Douglas	417	272	145
	Woodruff	13	6	7		Elbert	36	33	3
	Yell	26	14	12		El Paso	584	416	168
CALIFORNIA–						Gilpin	38	25	13
Metropolitan Counties	Alameda	1,535	935	600		Jefferson	751	533	218
	Butte	269	108	161		Larimer	398	170	228
	Contra Costa	1,032	711	321		Mesa	206	156	50
	El Dorado	368	192	176		Park	76	31	45
	Fresno	1,126	489	637		Pueblo	278	135	143
	Imperial	256	174	82		Teller	87	57	30
	Kern	1,099	480	619		Weld	255	75	180
	Kings	208	86	122	**COLORADO–**				
	Los Angeles	14,340	8,459	5,881	**Nonmetropolitan Counties**	Alamosa	35	22	13
	Madera	107	76	31		Archuleta	45	14	31
	Marin	305	199	106		Baca	11	4	7
	Merced	238	189	49		Bent	7	6	1
	Monterey	418	312	106		Chaffee	41	18	23
	Napa	122	88	34		Cheyenne	10	6	4
	Orange	3,396	1,695	1,701		Conejos	20	7	13
	Placer	424	207	217		Costilla	14	8	6
	Riverside	3,342	1,818	1,524		Crowley	9	6	3
	Sacramento	2,003	1,392	611		Custer	18	7	11
	San Benito	65	30	35		Delta	56	25	31
	San Bernardino	3,246	1,761	1,485		Dolores	7	5	2
	San Diego	3,679	2,112	1,567		Eagle	83	67	16
	San Francisco	930	790	140		Fremont	70	31	39
	San Joaquin	717	289	428		Garfield	110	38	72
	San Luis Obispo	354	150	204		Grand	49	20	29
	San Mateo	640	442	198		Gunnison	26	12	14
	Santa Barbara	667	314	353		Hinsdale	5	4	1
	Santa Clara	683	487	196		Huerfano	20	8	12
	Santa Cruz	298	134	164		Jackson	8	4	4
	Shasta	194	106	88		Kiowa	5	4	1
	Solano	450	110	340		Kit Carson	19	6	13
	Sonoma	672	289	383		Lake	17	9	8
	Stanislaus	592	467	125		La Plata	114	86	28
	Sutter	125	98	27		Las Animas	37	13	24
	Tulare	694	499	195		Lincoln	19	5	14
	Ventura	1,216	733	483		Logan	47	19	28
	Yolo	252	91	161		Mineral	7	4	3
	Yuba	170	129	41		Moffat	37	18	19
CALIFORNIA–						Montezuma	56	48	8
Nonmetropolitan Counties	Alpine	16	12	4		Montrose	100	47	53
	Amador	91	45	46		Morgan	58	43	15
	Calaveras	101	56	45		Otero	22	20	2
	Colusa	57	29	28		Ouray	8	8	0
	Del Norte	58	29	29		Phillips	3	3	0
	Glenn	68	28	40		Pitkin	39	22	17
	Humboldt	223	171	52		Prowers	32	10	22
	Inyo	70	51	19		Rio Blanco	24	13	11
	Lake	143	56	87		Rio Grande	24	6	18

Table 80. Full-time Law Enforcement Employees, by Metropolitan and Nonmetropolitan County, 2006 (Contd.)

(Number.)

State	County	Total law enforcement employees	Total officers	Total civilians	State	County	Total law enforcement employees	Total officers	Total civilians
	Routt	42	24	18		Madison	32	28	4
	Saguache	18	8	10		Monroe	515	225	290
	San Juan	4	3	1		Okeechobee	198	89	109
	San Miguel	37	33	4		Putnam	224	123	101
	Sedgwick	8	5	3		Sumter	194	142	52
	Summit	74	55	19		Suwannee	99	55	44
	Washington	49	14	35		Taylor	46	30	16
	Yuma	16	7	9		Union	12	10	2
DELAWARE–	New Castle County Police					Walton	243	199	44
Metropolitan Counties	Department	480	364	116		Washington	71	32	39
FLORIDA–					**GEORGIA–**	Augusta-			
Metropolitan Counties	Alachua	761	260	501	**Metropolitan Counties**	Richmond	687	484	203
	Baker	48	40	8		Barrow	153	108	45
	Bay	266	201	65		Bartow	225	179	46
	Brevard	623	425	198		Bibb	290	251	39
	Broward	3,172	1,538	1,634		Brantley	23	16	7
	Charlotte	551	274	277		Brooks	40	18	22
	Clay	529	261	268		Bryan	57	36	21
	Collier	1,277	642	635		Butts	60	38	22
	Escambia	767	387	380		Carroll	194	113	81
	Flagler	150	104	46		Catoosa	131	68	63
	Gadsden	81	52	29		Chattahoochee	10	4	6
	Gilchrist	55	26	29		Cherokee	356	309	47
	Hernando	359	235	124		Clarke	138	113	25
	Hillsborough	3,319	1,187	2,132		Clayton County Police			
	Indian River	469	198	271		Department	315	278	37
	Jefferson	41	19	22		Cobb	617	405	212
	Lake	656	300	356		Cobb County Police			
	Lee	902	567	335		Department	711	569	142
	Leon	369	266	103		Columbia	314	199	115
	Manatee	1,004	647	357		Coweta	192	123	69
	Marion	880	359	521		Crawford	32	14	18
	Martin	521	267	254		Dade	43	25	18
	Miami-Dade	4,551	3,139	1,412		Dawson	98	58	40
	Nassau	230	106	124		DeKalb	762	582	180
	Okaloosa	369	259	110		DeKalb County Police			
	Orange	1,954	1,305	649		Department	1,410	938	472
	Osceola	510	345	165		Dougherty	256	109	147
	Palm Beach	2,960	1,958	1,002		Dougherty County Police			
	Pasco	1,026	532	494		Department	52	44	8
	Pinellas	1,277	793	484		Douglas	313	199	114
	Polk	1,446	563	883		Effingham	105	65	40
	Santa Rosa	405	195	210		Fayette	217	135	82
	Sarasota	943	421	522		Floyd	141	75	66
	Seminole	982	380	602		Floyd County Police			
	St. Johns	547	260	287		Department	79	74	5
	St. Lucie	595	273	322		Forsyth	289	245	44
	Volusia	734	454	280		Fulton	872	729	143
	Wakulla	94	55	39		Fulton County Police			
FLORIDA–						Department	277	248	29
Nonmetropolitan Counties	Bradford	70	22	48		Glynn	141	55	86
	Calhoun	25	18	7		Glynn County Police			
	Citrus	322	208	114		Department	119	112	7
	Columbia	193	86	107		Gwinnett County Police			
	DeSoto	107	49	58		Department	869	624	245
	Dixie	54	24	30		Hall	372	324	48
	Franklin	88	44	44		Haralson	62	34	28
	Glades	41	28	13		Harris	59	43	16
	Gulf	45	30	15		Heard	33	15	18
	Hamilton	58	18	40		Henry County Police	228	193	35
	Hardee	88	44	44		Department			
	Hendry	98	62	36		Houston	316	120	196
	Highlands	287	118	169		Jasper	35	20	15
	Holmes	43	21	22		Jones	66	35	31
	Jackson	72	53	19		Lamar	55	26	29
	Lafayette	11	10	1		Lanier	17	11	6
	Levy	155	73	82		Lee	74	37	37
	Liberty	13	12	1					

Table 80. Full-time Law Enforcement Employees, by Metropolitan and Nonmetropolitan County, 2006 (*Contd.*)

(Number.)

State	County	Total law enforcement employees	Total officers	Total civilians	State	County	Total law enforcement employees	Total officers	Total civilians
	Liberty	114	61	53		Sumter	92	75	17
	Long	16	15	1		Talbot	14	8	6
	Lowndes	207	172	35		Tattnall	32	15	17
	McIntosh	55	30	25		Taylor	19	19	0
	Meriwether	45	31	14		Tift	109	56	53
	Monroe	106	54	52		Toombs	89	25	64
	Murray	63	35	28		Towns	19	17	2
	Newton	210	110	100		Treutlen	19	11	8
	Oconee	64	41	23		Troup	118	71	47
	Oglethorpe	27	17	10		Turner	16	14	2
	Paulding	183	153	30		Upson	73	33	40
	Pickens	65	36	29		Ware	122	40	82
	Rockdale	200	184	16		Warren	4	4	0
	Spalding	173	90	83		Washington	34	19	15
	Twiggs	41	19	22		Wayne	49	26	23
	Walker	101	68	33		Webster	5	4	1
	Whitfield	188	157	31		White	57	36	21
	Worth	32	21	11		Wilkes	31	13	18
GEORGIA–						Wilkinson	22	13	9
Nonmetropolitan Counties	Appling	46	14	32	**HAWAII–** **Nonmetropolitan Counties**	Hawaii Police Department	523	391	132
	Atkinson	13	6	7		Kauai Police Department	176	131	45
	Baldwin	93	52	41		Maui Police Department	423	321	102
	Banks	49	29	20	**IDAHO–**				
	Ben Hill	51	25	26	**Metropolitan Counties**	Ada	339	145	194
	Berrien	32	14	18		Bannock	71	41	30
	Bleckley	26	13	13		Boise	15	9	6
	Bulloch	86	46	40		Bonneville	81	55	26
	Candler	18	7	11		Canyon	143	79	64
	Charlton	25	16	9		Franklin	12	9	3
	Chattooga	47	47	0		Gem	23	13	10
	Clay	9	3	6		Jefferson	28	18	10
	Clinch	14	12	2		Kootenai	134	73	61
	Colquitt	95	52	43		Nez Perce	36	23	13
	Cook	48	15	33		Owyhee	19	11	8
	Crisp	67	48	19		Power	18	10	8
	Dodge	21	18	3	**IDAHO–**				
	Dooly	63	20	43	**Nonmetropolitan Counties**	Adams	14	10	4
	Elbert	57	41	16		Bear Lake	12	5	7
	Emanuel	30	15	15		Benewah	16	8	8
	Glascock	4	3	1		Bingham	51	31	20
	Gordon	86	55	31		Blaine	32	19	13
	Grady	39	14	25		Bonner	57	36	21
	Greene	57	38	19		Boundary	18	10	8
	Habersham	56	29	27		Butte	10	4	6
	Hancock	35	24	11		Camas	5	3	2
	Hart	39	23	16		Caribou	14	8	6
	Irwin	18	11	7		Cassia	51	32	19
	Jackson	110	68	42		Clark	7	3	4
	Jeff Davis	34	15	19		Clearwater	26	18	8
	Jefferson	41	39	2		Custer	14	7	7
	Jenkins	8	4	4		Elmore	39	22	17
	Johnson	14	6	8		Fremont	24	16	8
	Laurens	103	58	45		Gooding	18	11	7
	Miller	23	12	11		Idaho	31	22	9
	Mitchell	41	32	9		Jerome	21	15	6
	Peach	59	27	32		Latah	38	26	12
	Polk	74	25	49		Lemhi	6	5	1
	Polk County Police Department	40	37	3		Lewis	11	6	5
	Pulaski	27	12	15		Lincoln	7	6	1
	Putnam	57	30	27		Madison	32	20	12
	Rabun	46	44	2		Minidoka	25	16	9
	Randolph	18	10	8		Oneida	13	7	6
	Schley	6	3	3		Payette	33	16	17
	Screven	21	19	2		Shoshone	31	17	14
	Seminole	21	12	9		Teton	17	9	8
	Stephens	51	33	18		Twin Falls	62	42	20
	Stewart	11	5	6					

Table 80. Full-time Law Enforcement Employees, by Metropolitan and Nonmetropolitan County, 2006 (*Contd.*)

(Number.)

State	County	Total law enforcement employees	Total officers	Total civilians	State	County	Total law enforcement employees	Total officers	Total civilians
	Valley	27	13	14		Jasper	19	9	10
	Washington	17	10	7		Jefferson	63	24	39
ILLINOIS–						Jo Daviess	36	18	18
Metropolitan Counties	Bond	19	11	8		Johnson	12	7	5
	Boone	91	35	56		Knox	52	49	3
	Calhoun	4	4	0		La Salle	107	48	59
	Champaign	148	124	24		Lawrence	16	7	9
	Clinton	38	16	22		Lee	40	32	8
	Cook	6,807	2,503	4,304		Livingston	62	30	32
	De Kalb	93	41	52		Logan	27	20	7
	Du Page	546	430	116		Marion	31	12	19
	Ford	22	7	15		Mason	21	9	12
	Grundy	60	29	31		Massac	28	12	16
	Henry	74	23	51		McDonough	25	13	12
	Jersey	26	13	13		Montgomery	25	13	12
	Kane	139	96	43		Morgan	41	15	26
	Kankakee	193	67	126		Moultrie	19	10	9
	Kendall	103	95	8		Ogle	65	47	18
	Lake	468	182	286		Perry	30	12	18
	Macon	156	49	107		Pike	25	10	15
	Macoupin	52	47	5		Pope	3	3	0
	Madison	172	81	91		Pulaski	15	10	5
	Marshall	16	7	9		Putnam	11	6	5
	McHenry	367	101	266		Randolph	25	12	13
	McLean	115	50	65		Richland	19	7	12
	Menard	16	8	8		Saline	47	10	37
	Mercer	28	11	17		Schuyler	10	5	5
	Monroe	29	14	15		Scott	7	3	4
	Peoria	190	62	128		Shelby	31	11	20
	Piatt	33	10	23		Stephenson	70	27	43
	Rock Island	156	65	91		Union	15	8	7
	Sangamon	231	76	155		Wabash	8	3	5
	Stark	11	4	7		Warren	21	11	10
	St. Clair	178	163	15		Washington	21	6	15
	Tazewell	104	41	63		Wayne	21	11	10
	Vermilion	84	34	50		White	26	7	19
	Will	520	270	250		Whiteside	51	24	27
	Winnebago	332	106	226		Williamson	66	35	31
	Woodford	41	38	3	**INDIANA–**				
ILLINOIS–					**Metropolitan Counties**	Allen	342	124	218
Nonmetropolitan Counties	Adams	60	27	33		Bartholomew	77	37	40
	Alexander	7	7	0		Brown	39	13	26
	Brown	7	6	1		Carroll	29	13	16
	Bureau	34	20	14		Clark	113	33	80
	Carroll	22	9	13		Delaware	108	48	60
	Cass	8	7	1		Elkhart	193	66	127
	Christian	35	17	18		Floyd	84	27	57
	Clark	10	9	1		Franklin	12	10	2
	Clay	15	8	7		Gibson	42	17	25
	Coles	45	25	20		Greene	37	13	24
	Crawford	19	9	10		Hancock	78	39	39
	Cumberland	18	7	11		Harrison	62	21	41
	De Witt	39	15	24		Hendricks	103	46	57
	Douglas	30	10	20		Howard	105	35	70
	Edgar	19	8	11		Jasper	45	20	25
	Edwards	6	3	3		Johnson	111	88	23
	Effingham	45	19	26		Lake	478	170	308
	Fayette	42	10	32		La Porte	150	57	93
	Franklin	39	16	23		Madison	102	51	51
	Fulton	43	22	21		Monroe	93	30	63
	Gallatin	2	2	0		Morgan	70	23	47
	Greene	14	6	8		Newton	43	15	28
	Hamilton	7	3	4		Ohio	9	9	0
	Hancock	24	9	15		Porter	144	121	23
	Hardin	7	4	3		Posey	13	12	1
	Henderson	14	8	6		Putnam	34	15	19
	Iroquois	31	18	13		Shelby	82	26	56
	Jackson	72	25	47		St. Joseph	287	119	168

Table 80. Full-time Law Enforcement Employees, by Metropolitan and Nonmetropolitan County, 2006 (*Contd.*)

(Number.)

State	County	Total law enforcement employees	Total officers	Total civilians	State	County	Total law enforcement employees	Total officers	Total civilians
	Tippecanoe	147	46	101		Calhoun	11	6	5
	Tipton	19	11	8		Carroll	15	9	6
	Vanderburgh	252	105	147		Cass	14	7	7
	Vermillion	24	8	16		Cedar	36	11	25
	Warrick	79	37	42		Cerro Gordo	64	19	45
	Wells	40	15	25		Cherokee	17	6	11
INDIANA–						Chickasaw	13	8	5
Nonmetropolitan Counties	Blackford	26	8	18		Clarke	17	5	12
	Clinton	65	16	49		Clay	17	10	7
	Crawford	15	7	8		Clayton	25	12	13
	Daviess	58	16	42		Clinton	39	22	17
	Fayette	13	11	2		Crawford	12	10	2
	Fulton	21	10	11		Davis	11	5	6
	Grant	141	45	96		Decatur	11	6	5
	Henry	61	29	32		Delaware	16	10	6
	Huntington	40	14	26		Des Moines	48	21	27
	Jackson	51	14	37		Dickinson	17	8	9
	Jefferson	18	12	6		Emmet	17	8	9
	Knox	30	13	17		Fayette	33	9	24
	Kosciusko	83	36	47		Floyd	17	10	7
	LaGrange	49	17	32		Franklin	11	8	3
	Lawrence	63	26	37		Fremont	18	7	11
	Marshall	52	21	31		Greene	14	7	7
	Martin	15	7	8		Hamilton	28	9	19
	Miami	33	15	18		Hancock	10	8	2
	Noble	68	20	48		Hardin	27	10	17
	Pike	25	9	16		Henry	25	11	14
	Randolph	48	15	33		Howard	14	7	7
	Ripley	25	11	14		Humboldt	12	9	3
	Spencer	43	12	31		Ida	16	9	7
	Starke	27	12	15		Iowa	20	11	9
	Steuben	61	21	40		Jackson	14	9	5
	Union	12	7	5		Jasper	45	14	31
	Wabash	34	14	20		Jefferson	29	8	21
	Warren	20	7	13		Keokuk	8	4	4
	Wayne	110	68	42		Kossuth	25	9	16
	White	35	13	22		Lee	31	15	16
IOWA–						Louisa	21	9	12
Metropolitan Counties	Benton	27	12	15		Lucas	13	5	8
	Black Hawk	135	101	34		Lyon	25	12	13
	Bremer	28	12	16		Mahaska	25	9	16
	Dallas	39	15	24		Marion	27	12	15
	Dubuque	72	64	8		Mitchell	15	6	9
	Grundy	16	12	4		Monona	18	8	10
	Guthrie	11	5	6		Monroe	13	5	8
	Harrison	24	8	16		Muscatine	23	23	0
	Johnson	89	60	29		O'Brien	30	11	19
	Jones	23	10	13		Osceola	13	8	5
	Linn	167	108	59		Page	15	8	7
	Madison	15	7	8		Palo Alto	15	8	7
	Mills	20	11	9		Plymouth	27	10	17
	Polk	352	152	200		Pocahontas	13	8	5
	Pottawattamie	155	47	108		Poweshiek	19	12	7
	Scott	160	41	119		Ringgold	9	5	4
	Story	81	31	50		Sac	18	6	12
	Warren	34	23	11		Shelby	13	7	6
	Washington	27	16	11		Sioux	33	12	21
	Woodbury	112	32	80		Tama	21	12	9
IOWA–						Taylor	10	6	4
Nonmetropolitan Counties	Adair	8	6	2		Union	11	5	6
	Adams	9	4	5		Van Buren	11	5	6
	Allamakee	14	8	6		Wapello	40	10	30
	Appanoose	14	7	7		Wayne	10	5	5
	Audubon	8	4	4		Webster	20	16	4
	Boone	27	10	17		Winnebago	13	5	8
	Buchanan	26	13	13		Winneshiek	23	10	13
	Buena Vista	23	9	14		Worth	17	7	10
	Butler	18	10	8					

Table 80. Full-time Law Enforcement Employees, by Metropolitan and Nonmetropolitan County, 2006 (*Contd.*)

(Number.)

State	County	Total law enforcement employees	Total officers	Total civilians	State	County	Total law enforcement employees	Total officers	Total civilians
KANSAS–	Wright	19	7	12		Meade	17	5	12
Metropolitan Counties						Mitchell	14	8	6
	Butler	52	48	4		Montgomery	32	21	11
	Doniphan	11	5	6		Morris	13	7	6
	Douglas	129	80	49		Morton	9	5	4
	Franklin	53	27	26		Nemaha	18	8	10
	Harvey	32	14	18		Neosho	29	13	16
	Jackson	26	16	10		Ness	12	6	6
	Jefferson	41	22	19		Norton	10	5	5
	Johnson	576	459	117		Osborne	14	9	5
	Leavenworth	97	48	49		Ottawa	9	5	4
	Linn	20	10	10		Phillips	14	9	5
	Miami	41	28	13		Pottawatomie	35	24	11
	Osage	43	23	20		Pratt	15	8	7
	Sedgwick	509	174	335		Rawlins	5	3	2
	Shawnee	150	111	39		Republic	11	6	5
	Sumner	32	18	14		Rice	6	5	1
	Wabaunsee	17	6	11		Riley County Police Department	173	98	75
	Wyandotte	182	105	77		Rooks	6	5	1
KANSAS–	Allen	26	8	18		Rush	9	4	5
Nonmetropolitan Counties	Anderson	14	7	7		Russell	18	9	9
	Atchison	25	9	16		Saline	96	42	54
	Barber	9	4	5		Scott	4	3	1
	Barton	22	19	3		Seward	37	11	26
	Bourbon	24	6	18		Sheridan	7	3	4
	Chase	10	5	5		Sherman	11	5	6
	Chautauqua	9	3	6		Smith	5	5	0
	Cherokee	49	17	32		Stafford	9	4	5
	Cheyenne	4	3	1		Stanton	13	5	8
	Clark	10	5	5		Stevens	18	9	9
	Clay	16	6	10		Trego	3	3	0
	Cloud	13	7	6		Wallace	2	2	0
	Coffey	31	13	18		Washington	6	6	0
	Comanche	3	3	0		Wichita	9	4	5
	Cowley	39	22	17		Wilson	27	11	16
	Crawford	70	34	36		Woodson	11	7	4
	Decatur	2	2	0	**KENTUCKY–**	Boone	137	128	9
	Dickinson	28	15	13	**Metropolitan Counties**	Bourbon	6	5	1
	Edwards	8	4	4		Boyd	23	20	3
	Elk	9	3	6		Boyd County Police Department	4	4	0
	Ellis	27	17	10		Bracken	3	2	1
	Ellsworth	16	8	8		Bullitt	38	34	4
	Finney	96	39	57		Campbell	13	9	4
	Ford	55	26	29		Campbell County Police Department	32	31	1
	Geary	64	23	41		Christian	17	15	2
	Gove	5	4	1		Christian County Police Department	8	7	1
	Graham	7	3	4		Clark	12	10	2
	Grant	15	5	10		Daviess	52	38	14
	Gray	13	6	7		Edmonson	6	4	2
	Greeley	6	3	3		Fayette	70	36	34
	Greenwood	22	11	11		Gallatin	6	6	0
	Hamilton	12	6	6		Gallatin County Police Department	1	1	0
	Harper	17	5	12		Grant	19	17	2
	Haskell	18	13	5		Greenup	13	12	1
	Hodgeman	7	3	4		Hancock	6	5	1
	Jewell	9	5	4		Hardin	37	33	4
	Kearny	18	10	8		Henderson	22	18	4
	Kingman	17	7	10		Henry	5	5	0
	Kiowa	13	6	7		Jefferson	281	235	46
	Labette	35	17	18		Jessamine	26	20	6
	Lane	9	5	4		Kenton	35	28	7
	Lincoln	13	8	5					
	Logan	4	3	1					
	Lyon	39	26	13					
	Marion	10	8	2					
	Marshall	16	7	9					
	McPherson	35	16	19					

Table 80. Full-time Law Enforcement Employees, by Metropolitan and Nonmetropolitan County, 2006 (*Contd.*)

(Number.)

State	County	Total law enforcement employees	Total officers	Total civilians	State	County	Total law enforcement employees	Total officers	Total civilians
	Kenton County Police Department	62	36	26		Lyon	5	5	0
	Larue	5	4	1		Madison	17	16	1
	McLean	9	7	2		Marion	7	5	2
	Meade	10	8	2		Marshall	20	17	3
	Nelson	28	22	6		Martin	7	5	2
	Oldham	18	16	2		Mason	11	9	2
	Oldham County Police Department	35	32	3		McCracken	30	28	2
						McCreary	8	4	4
	Pendleton	7	6	1		Menifee	7	6	1
	Scott	34	32	2		Mercer	10	9	1
	Shelby	23	22	1		Metcalfe	4	3	1
	Spencer	7	6	1		Monroe	6	5	1
	Trigg	5	5	0		Montgomery	18	16	2
	Trimble	4	3	1		Morgan	5	3	2
	Warren	66	45	21		Muhlenberg	11	11	0
	Webster	7	5	2		Nicholas	4	2	2
	Woodford	7	7	0		Ohio	20	17	3
KENTUCKY–						Owen	7	5	2
Nonmetropolitan Counties	Adair	10	8	2		Owsley	5	4	1
	Allen	13	11	2		Perry	21	14	7
	Anderson	14	13	1		Powell	7	5	2
	Ballard	11	11	0		Pulaski	36	28	8
	Barren	14	12	2		Robertson	1	1	0
	Bath	4	3	1		Rockcastle	7	5	2
	Bell	19	9	10		Rowan	13	10	3
	Boyle	17	16	1		Russell	8	7	1
	Breathitt	3	2	1		Simpson	13	11	2
	Breckinridge	8	6	2		Taylor	12	10	2
	Butler	4	3	1		Todd	2	1	1
	Caldwell	8	6	2		Union	9	8	1
	Calloway	23	18	5		Washington	5	5	0
	Carlisle	3	3	0		Wayne	12	9	3
	Carroll	5	4	1		Whitley	9	7	2
	Carter	11	9	2		Wolfe	3	2	1
	Casey	6	6	0	**LOUISIANA–**				
	Clay	6	4	2	**Metropolitan Counties**	Ascension	237	205	32
	Clinton	6	5	1		Bossier	325	288	37
	Crittenden	4	3	1		Caddo	613	409	204
	Cumberland	5	4	1		Calcasieu	766	622	144
	Elliott	4	3	1		Cameron	65	58	7
	Estill	3	2	1		De Soto	84	72	12
	Fleming	9	9	0		East Baton Rouge	795	648	147
	Floyd	14	7	7		East Feliciana	63	63	0
	Fulton	5	4	1		Grant	66	24	42
	Garrard	7	7	0		Iberville	134	76	58
	Graves	15	11	4		Jefferson	1,289	854	435
	Grayson	6	4	2		Lafourche	279	203	76
	Green	4	4	0		Livingston	192	192	0
	Harlan	15	12	3		Ouachita	341	341	0
	Harrison	9	9	0		Plaquemines	173	172	1
	Hart	4	4	0		Pointe Coupee	84	84	0
	Hickman	3	3	0		Rapides	481	362	119
	Hopkins	24	17	7		St. Bernard	192	168	24
	Jackson	5	3	2		St. Charles	339	245	94
	Johnson	13	9	4		St. Helena	44	16	28
	Knott	9	6	3		St. John the Baptist	218	186	32
	Knox	12	10	2		St. Martin	156	109	47
	Laurel	26	26	0		St. Tammany	607	468	139
	Lawrence	7	5	2		Terrebonne	274	274	0
	Lee	3	2	1		Union	43	30	13
	Leslie	9	6	3		West Baton Rouge	156	40	116
	Letcher	14	5	9		West Feliciana	77	53	24
	Lewis	6	4	2	**LOUISIANA–**				
	Lincoln	8	7	1	**Nonmetropolitan Counties**	Acadia	114	114	0
	Livingston	7	7	0		Allen	46	23	23
	Logan	20	20	0		Assumption	73	41	32
						Beauregard	67	50	17

Table 80. Full-time Law Enforcement Employees, by Metropolitan and Nonmetropolitan County, 2006 (*Contd.*)

(Number.)

State	County	Total law enforcement employees	Total officers	Total civilians	State	County	Total law enforcement employees	Total officers	Total civilians
	Bienville	47	42	5	MARYLAND– Nonmetropolitan Counties	Wicomico	101	80	21
	Caldwell	28	28	0		Caroline	30	27	3
	Catahoula	98	16	82					
	Claiborne	33	27	6		Dorchester	38	34	4
	East Carroll	213	181	32		Garrett	53	30	23
	Jackson	37	37	0		Kent	21	18	3
	Jefferson Davis	46	33	13		St. Mary's	231	128	103
	La Salle	37	15	22		Talbot	18	16	2
	Lincoln	58	34	24		Worcester	52	45	7
	Madison	67	67	0	MICHIGAN– Metropolitan Counties	Bay	83	38	45
	Morehouse	146	37	109					
	Natchitoches	61	59	2		Berrien	168	72	96
	Red River	39	39	0		Calhoun	169	70	99
	Richland	127	113	14		Cass	70	35	35
	Sabine	68	68	0		Clinton	59	25	34
	St. James	98	56	42		Eaton	129	72	57
	St. Mary	155	125	30		Genesee	272	115	157
	Tensas	150	29	121		Ingham	210	120	90
	Vermilion	120	59	61		Ionia	50	20	30
	Vernon	138	42	96		Jackson	137	52	85
	West Carroll	19	16	3		Kalamazoo	207	160	47
	Winn	28	28	0		Kent	557	211	346
MAINE– Metropolitan Counties	Androscoggin	25	16	9		Lapeer	82	46	36
						Livingston	131	74	57
	Cumberland	54	50	4		Macomb	504	251	253
	Penobscot	28	24	4		Monroe	200	97	103
	Sagadahoc	21	19	2		Muskegon	115	37	78
	York	29	25	4		Newaygo	59	26	33
MAINE– Nonmetropolitan Counties	Aroostook	21	15	6		Oakland	1,039	858	181
	Franklin	26	15	11		Ottawa	219	125	94
	Hancock	18	16	2		St. Clair	170	67	103
	Kennebec	31	21	10		Van Buren	102	49	53
	Knox	20	19	1		Washtenaw	160	130	30
	Lincoln	32	21	11		Wayne	1,206	982	224
	Oxford	17	16	1	MICHIGAN– Nonmetropolitan Counties	Alcona	24	15	9
	Piscataquis	17	7	10					
	Somerset	17	15	2		Alger	13	10	3
	Waldo	18	16	2		Allegan	101	56	45
	Washington	22	12	10		Alpena	27	13	14
MARYLAND– Metropolitan Counties	Allegany	22	20	2		Antrim	45	18	27
	Anne Arundel	85	63	22		Arenac	18	10	8
	Anne Arundel County Police Department	857	644	213		Baraga	13	6	7
						Benzie	41	13	28
	Baltimore County	86	71	15		Branch	50	26	24
	Baltimore County Police Department	2,173	1,826	347		Charlevoix	24	18	6
						Cheboygan	34	16	18
	Calvert	112	96	16		Chippewa	33	16	17
	Carroll	93	67	26		Clare	22	18	4
	Cecil	91	73	18		Crawford	27	15	12
	Charles	415	262	153		Delta	30	16	14
	Frederick	223	165	58		Dickinson	14	13	1
	Harford	313	264	49		Emmet	46	24	22
	Howard	58	36	22		Gladwin	39	17	22
	Howard County Police Department	531	380	151		Gogebic	19	13	6
						Grand Traverse	126	66	60
	Montgomery	157	130	27		Gratiot	35	19	16
	Montgomery County Police Department	1,651	1,211	440		Hillsdale	45	29	16
						Houghton	18	18	0
	Prince George's	332	234	98		Huron	37	22	15
	Prince George's County Police Department	1,629	1,394	235		Iosco	26	8	18
						Iron	21	9	12
	Queen Anne's	50	47	3		Isabella	52	25	27
	Somerset	23	20	3		Kalkaska	36	19	17
	Washington	208	81	127		Keweenaw	6	6	0
						Lake	67	15	52
						Leelanau	20	19	1
						Lenawee	105	46	59
						Luce	4	3	1

Table 80. Full-time Law Enforcement Employees, by Metropolitan and Nonmetropolitan County, 2006 (*Contd.*)

(Number.)

State	County	Total law enforcement employees	Total officers	Total civilians	State	County	Total law enforcement employees	Total officers	Total civilians
	Mackinac	18	7	11		Kandiyohi	110	34	76
	Manistee	29	13	16		Kittson	10	5	5
	Marquette	47	23	24		Koochiching	16	9	7
	Mason	39	20	19		Lac Qui Parle	9	5	4
	Mecosta	48	24	24		Lake	29	16	13
	Menominee	13	13	0		Lake of the Woods	9	5	4
	Midland	60	37	23		Le Sueur	28	15	13
	Missaukee	27	12	15		Lincoln	11	4	7
	Montcalm	59	27	32		Lyon	35	13	22
	Montmorency	26	11	15		Mahnomen	19	11	8
	Ogemaw	26	16	10		Marshall	18	13	5
	Ontonagon	12	12	0		Martin	29	10	19
	Osceola	38	20	18		McLeod	58	25	33
	Oscoda	17	11	6		Meeker	38	15	23
	Otsego	24	11	13		Mille Lacs	62	22	40
	Presque Isle	26	14	12		Morrison	51	16	35
	Roscommon	44	28	16		Mower	48	20	28
	Sanilac	30	26	4		Murray	11	7	4
	Schoolcraft	12	5	7		Nicollet	26	11	15
	Shiawassee	65	33	32		Nobles	32	10	22
	St. Joseph	53	25	28		Norman	7	4	3
	Tuscola	46	30	16		Otter Tail	79	33	46
	Wexford	51	25	26		Pennington	32	7	25
MINNESOTA–						Pine	55	27	28
Metropolitan Counties	Anoka	222	113	109		Pipestone	22	12	10
	Benton	69	25	44		Pope	13	7	6
	Carlton	44	23	21		Red Lake	10	6	4
	Carver	149	84	65		Redwood	25	12	13
	Chisago	78	37	41		Renville	17	11	6
	Clay	58	28	30		Rice	51	23	28
	Dakota	169	76	93		Rock	16	11	5
	Dodge	30	21	9		Roseau	18	10	8
	Hennepin	784	325	459		Sibley	23	11	12
	Houston	25	12	13		Steele	24	17	7
	Isanti	58	19	39		Stevens	11	5	6
	Olmsted	139	52	87		Swift	13	6	7
	Polk	29	24	5		Todd	31	14	17
	Ramsey	402	253	149		Traverse	6	3	3
	Scott	123	35	88		Wadena	18	7	11
	Sherburne	211	60	151		Waseca	27	12	15
	Stearns	159	58	101		Watonwan	19	8	11
	St. Louis	246	104	142		Wilkin	16	6	10
	Wabasha	32	17	15		Winona	59	19	40
	Washington	231	90	141		Yellow Medicine	20	7	13
	Wright	195	124	71	**MISSISSIPPI–**	Copiah	46	17	29
MINNESOTA–					**Metropolitan Counties**				
Nonmetropolitan Counties	Aitkin	48	18	30		Desoto	201	162	39
	Becker	57	22	35		Hancock	44	40	4
	Beltrami	68	27	41		Harrison	304	135	169
	Big Stone	7	4	3		Hinds	431	114	317
	Blue Earth	62	23	39		Madison	122	48	74
	Brown	37	10	27		Marshall	47	26	21
	Cass	60	35	25		Perry	16	11	5
	Chippewa	19	9	10		Rankin	158	76	82
	Clearwater	17	7	10		Simpson	36	16	20
	Cook	17	12	5		Stone	20	17	3
	Cottonwood	18	7	11		Tate	18	16	2
	Crow Wing	114	45	69		Tunica	143	71	72
	Douglas	72	23	49	**MISSISSIPPI–**	Adams	56	32	24
	Faribault	21	8	13	**Nonmetropolitan Counties**				
	Fillmore	30	18	12		Attala	12	7	5
	Freeborn	52	21	31		Benton	15	6	9
	Goodhue	103	39	64		Bolivar	101	18	83
	Grant	11	6	5		Chickasaw	23	14	9
	Hubbard	37	13	24		Choctaw	5	5	0
	Itasca	70	59	11		Claiborne	22	8	14
	Jackson	18	7	11		Clay	30	10	20
	Kanabec	28	12	16		Coahoma	18	13	5

Table 80. Full-time Law Enforcement Employees, by Metropolitan and Nonmetropolitan County, 2006 (Contd.)

(Number.)

State	County	Total law enforcement employees	Total officers	Total civilians
	Covington	15	9	6
	Franklin	7	3	4
	Greene	12	5	7
	Humphreys	15	8	7
	Issaquena	5	3	2
	Itawamba	21	11	10
	Jefferson	18	10	8
	Kemper	16	6	10
	Lauderdale	135	55	80
	Lee	128	43	85
	Leflore	21	15	6
	Lincoln	43	20	23
	Lowndes	49	41	8
	Marion	36	25	11
	Monroe	40	16	24
	Montgomery	7	6	1
	Neshoba	17	16	1
	Newton	18	9	9
	Noxubee	10	8	2
	Oktibbeha	25	22	3
	Panola	59	20	39
	Pearl River	111	40	71
	Pike	44	26	18
	Pontotoc	33	22	11
	Prentiss	30	13	17
	Quitman	10	7	3
	Scott	24	16	8
	Sharkey	13	6	7
	Smith	14	8	6
	Sunflower	38	11	27
	Tallahatchie	24	10	14
	Tippah	24	9	15
	Tishomingo	24	12	12
	Union	36	26	10
	Walthall	17	8	9
	Warren	67	41	26
	Washington	54	30	24
	Wayne	20	9	11
	Webster	9	6	3
	Wilkinson	17	8	9
	Winston	7	6	1
	Yalobusha	13	9	4
	Yazoo	11	9	2
MISSOURI– Metropolitan Counties	Andrew	17	12	5
	Bates	31	11	20
	Boone	135	59	76
	Buchanan	102	74	28
	Caldwell	44	9	35
	Callaway	24	22	2
	Cass	86	68	18
	Christian	71	49	22
	Clay	182	109	73
	Clinton	21	15	6
	Cole	49	42	7
	Dallas	21	16	5
	De Kalb	9	5	4
	Franklin	114	95	19
	Greene	242	108	134
	Howard	8	7	1
	Jackson	129	90	39
	Jasper	144	92	52
	Jefferson	222	150	72
	Lafayette	31	27	4
	Lincoln	101	60	41
	McDonald	27	20	7
	Moniteau	8	5	3
	Newton	64	37	27

State	County	Total law enforcement employees	Total officers	Total civilians
	Osage	12	9	3
	Platte	119	84	35
	Polk	32	19	13
	Ray	39	12	27
	St. Charles	213	150	63
	St. Louis County Police Department	951	715	236
	Warren	56	33	23
	Washington	37	24	13
	Webster	29	18	11
MISSOURI– Nonmetropolitan Counties	Adair	27	12	15
	Atchison	8	3	5
	Audrain	39	28	11
	Barry	37	21	16
	Barton	15	7	8
	Benton	14	14	0
	Bollinger	12	7	5
	Butler	43	17	26
	Camden	49	37	12
	Cape Girardeau	62	38	24
	Carroll	13	7	6
	Carter	8	3	5
	Cedar	20	14	6
	Chariton	12	9	3
	Clark	21	8	13
	Cooper	11	10	1
	Crawford	37	23	14
	Dade	11	6	5
	Daviess	5	4	1
	Dent	18	12	6
	Douglas	9	5	4
	Dunklin	23	9	14
	Gasconade	12	11	1
	Gentry	6	6	0
	Grundy	9	4	5
	Harrison	12	5	7
	Henry	24	16	8
	Hickory	13	8	5
	Holt	11	5	6
	Howell	38	28	10
	Iron	13	8	5
	Johnson	43	34	9
	Knox	5	2	3
	Laclede	19	18	1
	Lawrence	31	21	10
	Lewis	10	5	5
	Linn	5	4	1
	Livingston	17	9	8
	Macon	15	12	3
	Madison	11	9	2
	Maries	11	7	4
	Marion	38	16	22
	Mercer	8	3	5
	Miller	18	14	4
	Mississippi	14	10	4
	Monroe	9	9	0
	Montgomery	14	13	1
	Morgan	46	23	23
	New Madrid	26	13	13
	Nodaway	12	10	2
	Oregon	10	6	4
	Ozark	17	8	9
	Pemiscot	44	17	27
	Perry	29	15	14
	Pettis	46	28	18
	Phelps	59	26	33
	Pike	28	10	18

Table 80. Full-time Law Enforcement Employees, by Metropolitan and Nonmetropolitan County, 2006 (*Contd.*)

(Number.)

State	County	Total law enforcement employees	Total officers	Total civilians	State	County	Total law enforcement employees	Total officers	Total civilians
	Pulaski	30	17	13		Roosevelt	12	10	2
	Putnam	4	3	1		Rosebud	24	13	11
	Ralls	6	5	1		Sanders	21	11	10
	Randolph	35	21	14		Sheridan	7	4	3
	Reynolds	14	13	1		Silver Bow	95	42	53
	Ripley	9	7	2		Stillwater	7	5	2
	Saline	29	17	12		Sweet Grass	6	6	0
	Schuyler	8	3	5		Teton	9	9	0
	Scotland	6	3	3		Toole	19	11	8
	Scott	38	21	17		Treasure	2	2	0
	Shannon	7	3	4		Valley	16	7	9
	Shelby	11	6	5		Wheatland	12	5	7
	St. Clair	59	19	40		Wibaux	3	3	0
	Ste. Genevieve	49	36	13	**NEBRASKA–** **Metropolitan Counties**	Cass	70	42	28
	Stoddard	21	11	10		Dixon	11	6	5
	Stone	53	42	11		Douglas	197	134	63
	Sullivan	5	4	1		Lancaster	94	73	21
	Taney	72	39	33		Sarpy	191	130	61
	Texas	14	8	6		Saunders	22	10	12
	Vernon	22	9	13		Seward	22	12	10
	Wayne	12	5	7		Washington	48	24	24
	Worth	2	1	1	**NEBRASKA–** **Nonmetropolitan Counties**	Antelope	11	6	5
	Wright	13	6	7		Arthur	1	1	0
MONTANA– **Metropolitan Counties**	Carbon	12	8	4		Blaine	1	1	0
	Cascade	129	34	95		Boone	11	4	7
	Missoula	162	49	113		Box Butte	6	6	0
	Yellowstone	158	53	105		Boyd	3	3	0
MONTANA– **Nonmetropolitan Counties**	Beaverhead	8	6	2		Brown	10	6	4
	Big Horn	27	12	15		Buffalo	38	23	15
	Blaine	11	10	1		Burt	10	5	5
	Broadwater	26	13	13		Butler	21	7	14
	Carter	3	3	0		Cedar	4	4	0
	Chouteau	18	9	9		Chase	8	4	4
	Custer	7	6	1		Cherry	10	5	5
	Daniels	5	3	2		Cheyenne	9	8	1
	Dawson	59	6	53		Clay	7	4	3
	Deer Lodge	17	16	1		Colfax	9	7	2
	Fallon	3	3	0		Cuming	6	5	1
	Fergus	23	9	14		Custer	6	5	1
	Flathead	112	49	63		Dawes	10	3	7
	Gallatin	81	45	36		Dawson	39	16	23
	Garfield	4	3	1		Deuel	4	3	1
	Glacier	16	12	4		Dodge	25	16	9
	Golden Valley	2	2	0		Dundy	8	4	4
	Granite	9	5	4		Fillmore	12	7	5
	Hill	27	13	14		Franklin	7	3	4
	Jefferson	21	11	10		Frontier	8	5	3
	Judith Basin	5	5	0		Furnas	14	9	5
	Lake	51	21	30		Gage	23	11	12
	Lewis and Clark	68	40	28		Garden	9	4	5
	Liberty	10	4	6		Garfield	2	2	0
	Lincoln	23	19	4		Gosper	4	3	1
	Madison	15	9	6		Greeley	4	3	1
	McCone	4	4	0		Hall	36	28	8
	Meagher	4	4	0		Hamilton	16	8	8
	Mineral	20	8	12		Harlan	8	4	4
	Musselshell	7	6	1		Hayes	2	2	0
	Park	15	13	2		Hitchcock	7	4	3
	Petroleum	1	1	0		Holt	4	3	1
	Phillips	10	6	4		Hooker	1	1	0
	Pondera	15	8	7		Howard	12	6	6
	Powder River	8	3	5		Jefferson	8	7	1
	Powell	16	10	6		Johnson	8	4	4
	Prairie	3	3	0		Kearney	12	7	5
	Ravalli	60	28	32		Keith	15	8	7
	Richland	13	7	6		Keya Paha	1	1	0

Table 80. Full-time Law Enforcement Employees, by Metropolitan and Nonmetropolitan County, 2006 (*Contd.*)

(Number.)

State	County	Total law enforcement employees	Total officers	Total civilians	State	County	Total law enforcement employees	Total officers	Total civilians
	Kimball	9	3	6		Gloucester	87	76	11
	Knox	11	5	6		Hudson	279	197	82
	Lincoln	42	22	20		Hunterdon	31	26	5
	Logan	2	2	0		Mercer	165	128	37
	Madison	18	15	3		Middlesex	226	186	40
	McPherson	1	1	0		Monmouth	660	460	200
	Merrick	11	6	5		Morris	343	267	76
	Morrill	8	3	5		Ocean	232	128	104
	Nance	9	5	4		Passaic	859	688	171
	Nemaha	5	5	0		Salem	153	133	20
	Nuckolls	7	4	3		Somerset	225	183	42
	Otoe	21	12	9		Sussex	143	118	25
	Pawnee	4	3	1		Union	215	169	46
	Perkins	8	4	4		Warren	23	19	4
	Pierce	8	4	4	**NEW MEXICO– Metropolitan Counties**	Bernalillo	316	246	70
	Platte	61	18	43		Sandoval	50	44	6
	Polk	10	6	4		San Juan	110	87	23
	Red Willow	8	6	2		Torrance	11	9	2
	Richardson	11	6	5	**NEW MEXICO– Nonmetropolitan Counties**	Catron	10	6	4
	Rock	8	3	5		Chaves	50	38	12
	Saline	11	11	0		Cibola	14	11	3
	Scotts Bluff	26	18	8		Colfax	12	9	3
	Sheridan	7	6	1		Curry	14	11	3
	Sherman	6	5	1		Eddy	56	42	14
	Stanton	8	7	1		Grant	74	37	37
	Thayer	10	7	3		Luna	32	29	3
	Thomas	1	1	0		McKinley	42	34	8
	Thurston	15	11	4		Mora	10	7	3
	Valley	6	3	3		Otero	44	32	12
	Wayne	5	4	1		Quay	8	7	1
	Webster	10	7	3		Rio Arriba	29	23	6
	Wheeler	1	1	0		Roosevelt	14	10	4
	York	22	9	13		Sierra	15	13	2
NEVADA– Metropolitan Counties	Carson City	139	94	45		Socorro	12	10	2
	Storey	22	16	6		Taos	22	16	6
	Washoe	773	418	355		Union	3	2	1
NEVADA– Nonmetropolitan Counties	Churchill	48	39	9	**NEW YORK– Metropolitan Counties**	Albany	154	114	40
	Douglas	122	104	18		Broome	73	54	19
	Elko	69	55	14		Chemung	50	43	7
	Esmeralda	15	11	4		Dutchess	131	111	20
	Eureka	18	12	6		Erie	178	138	40
	Humboldt	39	27	12		Livingston	62	44	18
	Lander	29	19	10		Madison	39	32	7
	Lincoln	27	15	12		Monroe	320	270	50
	Lyon	110	77	33		Nassau	3,450	2,622	828
	Mineral	20	16	4		Niagara	137	106	31
	Nye	143	102	41		Oneida	107	89	18
	Pershing	20	12	8		Onondaga	274	234	40
	White Pine	26	20	6		Ontario	108	71	37
NEW HAMPSHIRE– Metropolitan Counties	Rockingham	57	26	31		Orange	113	101	12
NEW HAMPSHIRE– Nonmetropolitan Counties	Carroll	25	13	12		Orleans	41	27	14
	Cheshire	19	10	9		Oswego	70	63	7
	Merrimack	27	16	11		Putnam	108	90	18
NEW JERSEY–Metro-politan Counties	Atlantic	123	93	30		Rensselaer	36	31	5
	Bergen	531	457	74		Rockland	84	76	8
	Bergen County Police Department	178	94	84		Saratoga	138	102	36
	Burlington	91	73	18		Schenectady	20	14	6
	Camden	174	151	23		Schoharie	27	15	12
	Cape May	137	121	16		Suffolk	400	262	138
	Cumberland	60	52	8		Suffolk County Police Department	3,338	2,725	613
	Essex	469	391	78		Tioga	56	37	19
	Essex County Police Department	31	31	0		Tompkins	46	40	6
						Ulster	69	59	10
						Warren	107	72	35

Table 80. Full-time Law Enforcement Employees, by Metropolitan and Nonmetropolitan County, 2006 (*Contd.*)

(Number.)

State	County	Total law enforcement employees	Total officers	Total civilians
	Washington	39	33	6
	Wayne	63	51	12
	Westchester Public Safety	321	252	69
NEW YORK– **Nonmetropolitan Counties**	Allegany	46	32	14
	Cattaraugus	77	56	21
	Chautauqua	120	77	43
	Chenango	29	24	5
	Clinton	36	21	15
	Columbia	51	42	9
	Cortland	49	32	17
	Delaware	23	14	9
	Essex	25	22	3
	Franklin	7	3	4
	Fulton	50	32	18
	Genesee	74	48	26
	Jefferson	47	38	9
	Lewis	23	14	9
	Montgomery	34	22	12
	Schuyler	23	20	3
	Seneca	45	28	17
	Steuben	55	44	11
	St. Lawrence	40	35	5
	Sullivan	47	37	10
	Wyoming	40	29	11
	Yates	40	21	19
NORTH CAROLINA– **Metropolitan Counties**	Alamance	204	104	100
	Alexander	44	31	13
	Anson	54	28	26
	Brunswick	139	100	39
	Buncombe	325	228	97
	Burke	105	82	23
	Cabarrus	176	170	6
	Caldwell	105	67	38
	Catawba	118	108	10
	Chatham	88	70	18
	Cumberland	503	260	243
	Currituck	86	54	32
	Davie	63	34	29
	Durham	405	158	247
	Edgecombe	128	51	77
	Forsyth	523	207	316
	Franklin	93	46	47
	Gaston[1]	203	114	89
	Gaston County Police Department[1]	206	127	79
	Greene	41	25	16
	Guilford	510	247	263
	Haywood	84	45	39
	Henderson	166	127	39
	Hoke	74	48	26
	Johnston	177	99	78
	Madison	29	19	10
	Mecklenburg[2]	1,085	279	806
	Nash	125	73	52
	New Hanover	363	265	98
	Onslow	144	99	45
	Orange	135	91	44
	Pender	76	44	32
	Person	79	42	37
	Pitt	255	117	138

State	County	Total law enforcement employees	Total officers	Total civilians
	Randolph	212	154	58
	Rockingham	133	90	43
	Stokes	60	40	20
	Union	221	161	60
	Wake	760	345	415
	Wayne	148	82	66
	Yadkin	57	34	23
NORTH CAROLINA– **Nonmetropolitan Counties**	Alleghany	27	11	16
	Ashe	38	20	18
	Avery	29	21	8
	Beaufort	71	43	28
	Bertie	30	22	8
	Bladen	77	48	29
	Camden	17	16	1
	Carteret	83	39	44
	Caswell	39	26	13
	Cherokee	44	23	21
	Chowan	37	18	19
	Clay	17	13	4
	Cleveland	120	78	42
	Columbus	102	62	40
	Craven	115	59	56
	Dare	137	59	78
	Davidson	179	121	58
	Duplin	81	62	19
	Gates	11	10	1
	Graham	19	11	8
	Granville	79	40	39
	Halifax	73	49	24
	Harnett	156	100	56
	Hertford	55	21	34
	Hyde	16	11	5
	Iredell	208	151	57
	Jackson	63	42	21
	Jones	14	8	6
	Lee	69	38	31
	Lenoir	92	55	37
	Lincoln	148	76	72
	Macon	60	41	19
	Martin	30	27	3
	McDowell	62	43	19
	Mitchell	16	14	2
	Montgomery	42	29	13
	Moore	110	71	39
	Northampton	55	18	37
	Pamlico	34	11	23
	Pasquotank	42	38	4
	Perquimans	13	11	2
	Polk	43	26	17
	Richmond	77	52	25
	Robeson	224	114	110
	Rowan	153	107	46
	Rutherford	104	66	38
	Sampson	100	69	31
	Scotland	54	30	24
	Stanly	67	44	23
	Surry	92	69	23
	Swain	16	15	1
	Transylvania	56	45	11
	Tyrrell	13	7	6
	Vance	88	45	43
	Warren	48	23	25
	Washington	37	17	20
	Watauga	70	36	34
	Wilkes	111	69	42
	Wilson	120	71	49
	Yancey	25	15	10

[1] The employee data are listed separately for both Gaston County and Gaston County Police Department, North Carolina. However, Gaston County reports its crime figures combined with those of the Gaston County Police Department; they can be found in Table 10 under Gaston County Police Department.

[2] The employee data presented in this table for Mecklenburg represent only Mecklenburg County Sheriff's Office employees and exclude Charlotte-Mecklenburg Police Department employees.

Table 80. Full-time Law Enforcement Employees, by Metropolitan and Nonmetropolitan County, 2006 (*Contd.*)

(Number.)

State	County	Total law enforcement employees	Total officers	Total civilians
NORTH DAKOTA– **Metropolitan Counties**	Burleigh	71	39	32
	Cass	125	67	58
	Grand Forks	33	27	6
	Morton	33	20	13
NORTH DAKOTA– **Nonmetropolitan Counties**	Adams	4	4	0
	Barnes	7	6	1
	Benson	4	4	0
	Billings	4	4	0
	Bottineau	12	8	4
	Bowman	3	3	0
	Burke	4	4	0
	Cavalier	11	5	6
	Dickey	6	5	1
	Divide	3	3	0
	Dunn	4	3	1
	Eddy	5	5	0
	Emmons	4	3	1
	Foster	4	3	1
	Golden Valley	5	4	1
	Grant	3	3	0
	Griggs	4	4	0
	Hettinger	3	3	0
	Kidder	3	2	1
	Lamoure	5	4	1
	Logan	4	2	2
	McHenry	8	7	1
	McIntosh	3	3	0
	McKenzie	10	5	5
	McLean	27	19	8
	Mercer	26	13	13
	Mountrail	12	7	5
	Nelson	5	4	1
	Oliver	4	3	1
	Pembina	14	8	6
	Pierce	7	3	4
	Ramsey	7	6	1
	Ransom	5	4	1
	Renville	5	5	0
	Richland	25	16	9
	Rolette	18	9	9
	Sargent	4	3	1
	Sheridan	2	2	0
	Sioux	1	1	0
	Slope	1	1	0
	Stark	13	10	3
	Steele	4	3	1
	Stutsman	10	8	2
	Towner	3	2	1
	Traill	10	5	5
	Walsh	18	11	7
	Ward	43	21	22
	Wells	3	3	0
	Williams	28	17	11
OHIO– **Metropolitan Counties**	Allen	159	74	85
	Belmont	62	51	11
	Brown	30	29	1
	Butler	317	164	153
	Carroll	20	18	2
	Clark	156	128	28
	Clermont	198	86	112
	Cuyahoga	1,028	165	863
	Delaware	180	81	99
	Erie	75	37	38
	Fairfield	123	92	31
	Franklin	847	631	216

State	County	Total law enforcement employees	Total officers	Total civilians
	Fulton	31	19	12
	Geauga	116	50	66
	Greene	151	107	44
	Hamilton	1,068	355	713
	Jefferson	45	37	8
	Lake	216	56	160
	Licking	189	132	57
	Madison	35	31	4
	Mahoning	220	205	15
	Medina	173	76	97
	Miami	131	48	83
	Montgomery	443	222	221
	Morrow	62	33	29
	Ottawa	54	53	1
	Portage	129	54	75
	Preble	22	18	4
	Richland	111	51	60
	Stark	247	135	112
	Summit	487	391	96
	Trumbull	110	40	70
	Warren	173	93	80
	Washington	81	44	37
OHIO– **Nonmetropolitan Counties**	Adams	34	19	15
	Ashland	61	38	23
	Ashtabula	82	42	40
	Auglaize	55	21	34
	Champaign	25	23	2
	Clinton	68	37	31
	Columbiana	26	22	4
	Coshocton	56	45	11
	Crawford	39	25	14
	Darke	67	40	27
	Defiance	36	21	15
	Fayette	38	27	11
	Gallia	26	20	6
	Guernsey	21	21	0
	Hancock	86	36	50
	Hardin	25	22	3
	Harrison	19	15	4
	Henry	23	23	0
	Highland	56	56	0
	Hocking	23	18	5
	Holmes	49	35	14
	Huron	68	25	43
	Knox	73	55	18
	Logan	105	42	63
	Marion	40	29	11
	Meigs	12	11	1
	Monroe	20	17	3
	Morgan	16	11	5
	Muskingum	117	80	37
	Noble	16	5	11
	Perry	16	12	4
	Pike	17	12	5
	Putnam	55	31	24
	Sandusky	63	41	22
	Scioto	81	50	31
	Seneca	79	33	46
	Shelby	67	33	34
	Tuscarawas	97	31	66
	Van Wert	26	20	6
	Vinton	15	11	4
	Wayne	86	72	14
	Williams	26	22	4
OKLAHOMA– **Metropolitan Counties**	Canadian	52	27	25
	Cleveland	96	43	53

Table 80. Full-time Law Enforcement Employees, by Metropolitan and Nonmetropolitan County, 2006 *(Contd.)*

(Number.)

State	County	Total law enforcement employees	Total officers	Total civilians	State	County	Total law enforcement employees	Total officers	Total civilians
	Comanche	33	28	5		Seminole	21	13	8
	Creek	65	30	35		Stephens	32	8	24
	Grady	19	14	5		Texas	40	11	29
	Le Flore	15	10	5		Tillman	11	5	6
	Lincoln	31	9	22		Washington	19	16	3
	Logan	26	13	13		Washita	16	7	9
	McClain	23	12	11		Woods	6	5	1
	Oklahoma	709	169	540		Woodward	22	8	14
	Okmulgee	13	11	2	**OREGON–**				
	Osage	44	39	5	**Metropolitan Counties**	Benton	52	29	23
	Pawnee	17	15	2		Columbia	15	12	3
	Rogers	64	22	42		Deschutes	173	72	101
	Sequoyah	18	11	7		Jackson	166	119	47
	Tulsa	504	184	320		Lane	380	74	306
	Wagoner	45	16	29		Marion	326	88	238
OKLAHOMA–						Multnomah	126	93	33
Nonmetropolitan Counties	Adair	31	9	22		Polk	65	24	41
	Alfalfa	9	4	5		Washington	482	212	270
	Atoka	11	6	5		Yamhill	96	45	51
	Beaver	13	7	6	**OREGON–**				
	Beckham	28	10	18	**Nonmetropolitan Counties**	Baker	24	10	14
	Blaine	17	7	10		Clatsop	53	25	28
	Bryan	15	13	2		Coos	125	37	88
	Caddo	31	16	15		Crook	17	13	4
	Carter	58	19	39		Curry	41	19	22
	Cherokee	19	16	3		Douglas	150	71	79
	Choctaw	15	6	9		Gilliam	6	5	1
	Cimarron	8	4	4		Grant	17	5	12
	Coal	6	5	1		Harney	11	5	6
	Cotton	10	4	6		Hood River	34	18	16
	Craig	28	10	18		Jefferson	21	11	10
	Custer	25	10	15		Josephine	88	34	54
	Delaware	44	28	16		Klamath	38	32	6
	Dewey	11	4	7		Lake	8	7	1
	Ellis	14	4	10		Lincoln	84	29	55
	Garfield	43	17	26		Linn	140	69	71
	Garvin	22	10	12		Malheur	50	19	31
	Grant	11	5	6		Morrow	27	15	12
	Greer	6	2	4		Sherman	6	5	1
	Harmon	3	3	0		Tillamook	52	27	25
	Harper	10	6	4		Umatilla	19	15	4
	Haskell	17	8	9		Union	25	11	14
	Hughes	14	9	5		Wallowa	12	7	5
	Jackson	36	11	25		Wasco	20	17	3
	Jefferson	14	6	8		Wheeler	14	5	9
	Johnston	24	7	17	**PENNSYLVANIA–**				
	Kay	30	12	18	**Metropolitan Counties**	Allegheny	199	158	41
	Kingfisher	14	7	7		Allegheny County Police Department	286	218	68
	Kiowa	13	5	8		Beaver	29	23	6
	Latimer	10	4	6		Centre	16	14	2
	Love	19	6	13		Cumberland	27	23	4
	Major	10	4	6		Pike	19	15	4
	Marshall	16	5	11		York	105	94	11
	Mayes	40	18	22	**PENNSYLVANIA–**				
	McCurtain	24	20	4	**Nonmetropolitan Counties**	Adams	9	8	1
	McIntosh	20	12	8		Bradford	11	9	2
	Murray	8	5	3		Clarion	10	7	3
	Muskogee	35	33	2		Elk	6	5	1
	Noble	10	5	5		Franklin	17	14	3
	Nowata	23	10	13		Greene	8	7	1
	Okfuskee	16	7	9		Jefferson	4	3	1
	Ottawa	35	15	20		Snyder	4	4	0
	Payne	57	26	31	**SOUTH CAROLINA–**				
	Pittsburg	33	20	13	**Metropolitan Counties**	Aiken	146	112	34
	Pontotoc	18	12	6		Anderson	284	186	98
	Pottawatomie	23	17	6		Berkeley	188	124	64
	Pushmataha	19	7	12		Calhoun	24	22	2
	Roger Mills	14	9	5					

Table 80. Full-time Law Enforcement Employees, by Metropolitan and Nonmetropolitan County, 2006 (*Contd.*)

(Number.)

State	County	Total law enforcement employees	Total officers	Total civilians	State	County	Total law enforcement employees	Total officers	Total civilians
	Charleston	675	250	425		Custer	11	11	0
	Darlington	69	62	7		Davison	25	6	19
	Dorchester	178	95	83		Day	6	3	3
	Edgefield	58	29	29		Deuel	8	4	4
	Fairfield	50	43	7		Dewey	3	2	1
	Florence	229	117	112		Douglas	2	2	0
	Greenville	445	357	88		Edmunds	6	4	2
	Horry	220	40	180		Fall River	14	4	10
	Horry County Police Department	277	250	27		Faulk	9	3	6
	Kershaw	71	59	12		Grant	8	3	5
	Laurens	115	57	58		Gregory	4	3	1
	Lexington	352	220	132		Haakon	2	2	0
	Pickens	129	91	38		Hamlin	4	4	0
	Richland	499	461	38		Hand	3	2	1
	Saluda	55	18	37		Hanson	2	2	0
	Spartanburg	318	289	29		Harding	3	2	1
	Sumter	125	115	10		Hughes	23	6	17
	York	186	153	33		Hutchinson	3	3	0
SOUTH CAROLINA–						Hyde	1	1	0
Nonmetropolitan Counties	Abbeville	49	27	22		Jackson	2	2	0
	Allendale	14	12	2		Jerauld	3	3	0
	Bamberg	14	11	3		Jones	2	2	0
	Barnwell	43	26	17		Kingsbury	5	4	1
	Beaufort	214	193	21		Lake	10	5	5
	Cherokee	93	45	48		Lawrence	45	15	30
	Chester	76	43	33		Lyman	5	4	1
	Chesterfield	67	44	23		Marshall	11	6	5
	Clarendon	43	34	9		McPherson	1	1	0
	Colleton	127	61	66		Mellette	5	4	1
	Dillon	80	33	47		Miner	4	3	1
	Georgetown	89	74	15		Moody	9	4	5
	Greenwood	112	69	43		Perkins	4	3	1
	Hampton	26	20	6		Potter	2	1	1
	Jasper	35	30	5		Roberts	11	4	7
	Lancaster	114	70	44		Sanborn	3	2	1
	Lee	29	25	4		Shannon	1	1	0
	Marion	43	37	6		Spink	13	8	5
	Marlboro	28	24	4		Stanley	6	5	1
	McCormick	28	14	14		Sully	3	3	0
	Newberry	93	48	45		Todd	1	1	0
	Oconee	128	79	49		Tripp	7	6	1
	Orangeburg	97	76	21		Walworth	10	2	8
	Union	51	28	23		Yankton	10	9	1
	Williamsburg	66	32	34		Ziebach	2	2	0
SOUTH DAKOTA–					**TENNESSEE–**				
Metropolitan Counties	Lincoln	15	14	1	**Metropolitan Counties**	Anderson	122	38	84
	McCook	7	6	1		Blount	301	256	45
	Meade	50	17	33		Bradley	212	97	115
	Minnehaha	191	62	129		Cannon	24	12	12
	Pennington	181	63	118		Carter	82	42	40
	Turner	7	6	1		Cheatham	67	32	35
	Union	21	7	14		Chester	25	11	14
SOUTH DAKOTA–						Dickson	120	50	70
Nonmetropolitan Counties	Aurora	4	3	1		Fayette	56	33	23
	Beadle	19	7	12		Grainger	36	14	22
	Bennett	6	4	2		Hamblen	68	32	36
	Bon Homme	9	3	6		Hamilton	362	138	224
	Brookings	20	11	9		Hartsville-Trousdale	31	14	17
	Brown	46	15	31		Hawkins	58	39	19
	Brule	11	4	7		Hickman	35	22	13
	Buffalo	1	1	0		Jefferson	64	37	27
	Butte	14	5	9		Knox	1,021	476	545
	Campbell	2	2	0		Loudon	60	39	21
	Charles Mix	12	4	8		Macon	48	22	26
	Clark	4	2	2		Madison	211	57	154
	Clay	10	7	3		Marion	47	19	28
	Codington	10	7	3		Montgomery	287	70	217
	Corson	3	2	1					

Table 80. Full-time Law Enforcement Employees, by Metropolitan and Nonmetropolitan County, 2006 (*Contd.*)

(Number.)

State	County	Total law enforcement employees	Total officers	Total civilians
	Polk	34	17	17
	Robertson	101	38	63
	Rutherford	384	173	211
	Sequatchie	35	16	19
	Shelby	1,970	504	1,466
	Smith	41	15	26
	Stewart	36	16	20
	Sullivan	226	100	126
	Sumner	217	60	157
	Tipton	69	38	31
	Unicoi	42	20	22
	Union	32	18	14
	Washington	187	86	101
	Williamson	202	103	99
	Wilson	154	79	75
TENNESSEE– **Nonmetropolitan Counties**	Bedford	81	27	54
	Benton	40	18	22
	Bledsoe	17	12	5
	Campbell	55	25	30
	Carroll	35	18	17
	Claiborne	73	21	52
	Clay	17	10	7
	Cocke	50	32	18
	Coffee	72	39	33
	Crockett	28	11	17
	Cumberland	90	44	46
	Decatur	15	10	5
	DeKalb	32	11	21
	Dyer	66	24	42
	Fentress	31	12	19
	Franklin	56	29	27
	Gibson	62	25	37
	Giles	50	22	28
	Greene	146	52	94
	Grundy	22	14	8
	Hancock	39	10	29
	Hardeman	41	22	19
	Hardin	24	15	9
	Haywood	37	16	21
	Henderson	36	24	12
	Henry	58	28	30
	Houston	23	10	13
	Humphreys	27	16	11
	Jackson	20	10	10
	Johnson	38	15	23
	Lake	20	9	11
	Lauderdale	61	16	45
	Lawrence	58	43	15
	Lewis	28	14	14
	Lincoln	55	22	33
	Marshall	46	20	26
	Maury	129	70	59
	McMinn	66	34	32
	McNairy	37	16	21
	Meigs	26	7	19
	Monroe	63	27	36
	Moore	24	12	12
	Morgan	51	17	34
	Obion	54	26	28
	Overton	53	23	30
	Perry	31	14	17
	Pickett	16	10	6
	Putnam	119	55	64
	Rhea	52	28	24
	Roane	51	29	22
	Scott	46	24	22
	Sevier	137	82	55

State	County	Total law enforcement employees	Total officers	Total civilians
	Van Buren	11	6	5
	Warren	80	38	42
	Wayne	30	12	18
	Weakley	40	20	20
	White	59	25	34
TEXAS– **Metropolitan Counties**	Aransas	61	22	39
	Archer	10	7	3
	Armstrong	5	2	3
	Atascosa	70	27	43
	Austin	47	28	19
	Bandera	47	27	20
	Bastrop	136	54	82
	Bell	249	90	159
	Bexar	1,717	489	1,228
	Bowie	44	39	5
	Brazoria	314	156	158
	Brazos	197	109	88
	Burleson	31	14	17
	Caldwell	75	25	50
	Calhoun	58	24	34
	Callahan	11	6	5
	Cameron	395	100	295
	Carson	13	6	7
	Chambers	83	36	47
	Clay	19	10	9
	Collin	445	128	317
	Comal	220	108	112
	Coryell	58	21	37
	Crosby	15	5	10
	Dallas	1,830	448	1,382
	Delta	15	8	7
	Denton	545	139	406
	Ector	187	89	98
	Ellis	201	77	124
	El Paso	1,035	246	789
	Fort Bend	563	370	193
	Galveston	403	233	170
	Goliad	27	12	15
	Grayson	132	56	76
	Gregg	200	89	111
	Guadalupe	196	62	134
	Hardin	58	29	29
	Harris	3,473	2,400	1,073
	Hays	241	108	133
	Hidalgo	698	245	453
	Hunt	122	34	88
	Irion	8	4	4
	Jefferson	358	146	212
	Johnson	251	116	135
	Jones	18	8	10
	Kaufman	220	81	139
	Kendall	58	35	23
	Lampasas	33	20	13
	Liberty	60	43	17
	Lubbock	270	113	157
	McLennan	292	95	197
	Medina	64	25	39
	Midland	180	82	98
	Montgomery	556	320	236
	Nueces	318	81	237
	Orange	130	60	70
	Parker	127	71	56
	Potter	204	98	106
	Randall	148	72	76
	Robertson	27	11	16
	Rockwall	102	32	70
	Rusk	66	38	28

Table 80. Full-time Law Enforcement Employees, by Metropolitan and Nonmetropolitan County, 2006 (*Contd.*)

(Number.)

State	County	Total law enforcement employees	Total officers	Total civilians	State	County	Total law enforcement employees	Total officers	Total civilians
	San Jacinto	38	17	21		Gonzales	44	16	28
	San Patricio	85	42	43		Gray	41	14	27
	Tarrant	1,344	491	853		Grimes	54	24	30
	Taylor	172	71	101		Hale	67	16	51
	Tom Green	162	59	103		Hall	9	3	6
	Travis	1,387	753	634		Hamilton	25	14	11
	Victoria	165	80	85		Hansford	8	4	4
	Waller	59	33	26		Hardeman	14	9	5
	Wichita	170	39	131		Harrison	87	49	38
	Williamson	459	189	270		Hartley	4	4	0
	Wilson	68	24	44		Haskell	7	3	4
	Wise	102	45	57		Hemphill	15	8	7
						Henderson	124	72	52
TEXAS– Nonmetropolitan Counties	Anderson	79	32	47		Hill	66	30	36
	Andrews	32	14	18		Hockley	21	10	11
	Angelina	116	45	71		Hood	115	37	78
	Bailey	18	4	14		Hopkins	54	26	28
	Baylor	6	2	4		Houston	36	22	14
	Bee	52	21	31		Howard	30	13	17
	Blanco	16	9	7		Hudspeth	36	16	20
	Borden	3	2	1		Hutchinson	31	11	20
	Bosque	38	18	20		Jack	34	11	23
	Brewster	18	10	8		Jackson	30	13	17
	Briscoe	3	2	1		Jasper	43	15	28
	Brooks	156	11	145		Jeff Davis	3	3	0
	Brown	64	24	40		Jim Hogg	41	21	20
	Burnet	74	44	30		Jim Wells	59	27	32
	Camp	17	6	11		Karnes	18	9	9
	Cass	42	18	24		Kenedy	17	12	5
	Castro	16	6	10		Kent	5	2	3
	Cherokee	62	26	36		Kerr	97	46	51
	Childress	12	4	8		Kimble	13	9	4
	Cochran	13	7	6		King	2	2	0
	Coke	6	5	1		Kinney	15	6	9
	Coleman	11	5	6		Kleberg	45	18	27
	Collingsworth	11	5	6		Knox	8	4	4
	Colorado	41	18	23		Lamar	76	25	51
	Comanche	33	12	21		Lamb	26	9	17
	Concho	11	5	6		La Salle	30	11	19
	Cooke	72	20	52		Lavaca	27	12	15
	Cottle	2	1	1		Lee	15	9	6
	Crane	11	7	4		Leon	39	20	19
	Crockett	18	13	5		Limestone	52	18	34
	Culberson	15	8	7		Lipscomb	10	5	5
	Dallam	26	5	21		Live Oak	26	11	15
	Dawson	17	6	11		Llano	47	25	22
	Deaf Smith	35	12	23		Loving	3	2	1
	Dewitt	24	9	15		Lynn	21	6	15
	Dickens	6	2	4		Madison	23	8	15
	Dimmit	26	9	17		Marion	15	14	1
	Donley	9	6	3		Martin	9	4	5
	Duval	35	18	17		Mason	9	5	4
	Eastland	26	8	18		Matagorda	70	42	28
	Edwards	10	4	6		Maverick	92	41	51
	Erath	50	23	27		McCulloch	12	7	5
	Falls	15	8	7		McMullen	3	2	1
	Fannin	40	17	23		Menard	9	5	4
	Fayette	39	19	20		Milam	46	13	33
	Fisher	9	5	4		Mills	8	5	3
	Floyd	7	3	4		Mitchell	10	5	5
	Foard	3	2	1		Montague	23	10	13
	Franklin	16	8	8		Moore	47	16	31
	Freestone	39	16	23		Morris	23	8	15
	Frio	21	13	8		Motley	1	1	0
	Gaines	24	11	13		Nacogdoches	94	39	55
	Garza	15	9	6		Navarro	108	42	66
	Gillespie	30	18	12		Newton	19	10	9
	Glasscock	6	3	3		Nolan	23	11	12

Table 80. Full-time Law Enforcement Employees, by Metropolitan and Nonmetropolitan County, 2006 (*Contd.*)
(Number.)

State	County	Total law enforcement employees	Total officers	Total civilians
	Ochiltree	17	8	9
	Oldham	10	5	5
	Palo Pinto	51	23	28
	Panola	41	24	17
	Parmer	18	6	12
	Polk	81	47	34
	Presidio	29	6	23
	Rains	22	9	13
	Reagan	19	6	13
	Real	9	3	6
	Red River	34	14	20
	Reeves	438	18	420
	Refugio	35	9	26
	Roberts	6	5	1
	Runnels	21	6	15
	Sabine	18	8	10
	San Augustine	13	5	8
	San Saba	9	4	5
	Schleicher	11	5	6
	Scurry	23	10	13
	Shackelford	14	5	9
	Shelby	29	13	16
	Sherman	9	4	5
	Somervell	41	19	22
	Starr	89	31	58
	Stephens	11	6	5
	Sterling	4	4	0
	Stonewall	7	2	5
	Sutton	14	6	8
	Swisher	10	6	4
	Terrell	10	5	5
	Terry	39	9	30
	Throckmorton	6	6	0
	Titus	55	23	32
	Trinity	13	7	6
	Tyler	30	23	7
	Upton	21	11	10
	Uvalde	29	14	15
	Val Verde	53	34	19
	Van Zandt	72	24	48
	Walker	67	31	36
	Ward	27	12	15
	Washington	54	28	26
	Wharton	70	41	29
	Wheeler	12	7	5
	Wilbarger	18	7	11
	Willacy	36	13	23
	Winkler	28	11	17
	Wood	64	25	39
	Yoakum	20	9	11
	Young	39	14	25
	Zapata	118	44	74
UTAH– Metropolitan Counties	Cache	142	111	31
	Davis	228	99	129
	Juab	24	22	2
	Morgan	13	11	2
	Salt Lake	1,179	330	849
	Summit	95	46	49
	Tooele	83	30	53
	Utah	357	128	229
	Washington	151	48	103
	Weber	379	120	259
UTAH– Nonmetropolitan Counties	Beaver	56	14	42
	Box Elder	82	27	55
	Carbon	40	18	22
	Daggett	28	9	19

State	County	Total law enforcement employees	Total officers	Total civilians
	Duchesne	51	17	34
	Emery	41	26	15
	Garfield	28	6	22
	Grand	30	14	16
	Iron	80	32	48
	Kane	24	11	13
	Millard	48	39	9
	Piute	3	3	0
	Rich	10	4	6
	San Juan	35	16	19
	Sanpete	24	19	5
	Sevier	62	28	34
	Uintah	49	19	30
	Wasatch	40	19	21
	Wayne	5	5	0
VERMONT– Metropolitan Counties	Chittenden	14	12	2
	Franklin	24	15	9
	Grand Isle	3	2	1
VERMONT– Nonmetropolitan Counties	Addison	17	10	7
	Bennington	17	12	5
	Caledonia	5	3	2
	Essex	3	2	1
	Lamoille	21	10	11
	Orange	4	2	2
	Orleans	7	5	2
	Rutland	22	18	4
	Washington	11	9	2
	Windham	26	20	6
	Windsor	10	8	2
VIRGINIA– Metropolitan Counties	Albemarle County Police Department	136	113	23
	Amelia	20	12	8
	Amherst	69	63	6
	Appomattox	32	29	3
	Arlington County Police Department	450	365	85
	Bedford	73	71	2
	Botetourt	83	66	17
	Campbell	57	54	3
	Caroline	57	40	17
	Charles City	17	10	7
	Chesterfield County Police Department	565	463	102
	Clarke	29	17	12
	Craig	12	7	5
	Cumberland	23	16	7
	Dinwiddie	46	38	8
	Fairfax County Police Department	1,676	1,409	267
	Fauquier	117	101	16
	Fluvanna	39	25	14
	Franklin	92	74	18
	Frederick	112	103	9
	Giles	34	24	10
	Gloucester	93	75	18
	Goochland	35	27	8
	Greene	40	24	16
	Hanover	208	189	19
	Henrico County Police Department	712	524	188
	Isle of Wight	44	37	7
	James City County Police Department	82	77	5

Table 80. Full-time Law Enforcement Employees, by Metropolitan and Nonmetropolitan County, 2006 (*Contd.*)

(Number.)

State	County	Total law enforcement employees	Total officers	Total civilians	State	County	Total law enforcement employees	Total officers	Total civilians
	King and Queen.....	16	9	7		Southampton.........	80	65	15
	King William	33	21	12		Tazewell	52	45	7
	Loudoun................	498	406	92		Westmoreland	29	20	9
	Louisa....................	58	45	13		Wise........................	63	60	3
	Mathews.................	19	12	7		Wythe......................	46	39	7
	Montgomery..........	123	108	15	WASHINGTON– Metropolitan Counties	Asotin....................	15	10	5
	Nelson	21	16	5		Benton...................	66	54	12
	New Kent..............	37	27	10		Chelan	71	61	10
	Pittsylvania	123	67	56		Clark......................	217	142	75
	Powhatan	47	33	14		Cowlitz	57	43	14
	Prince George County Police Department	66	51	15		Douglas	34	28	6
						Franklin.................	25	23	2
	Prince William County Police Department	607	491	116		King......................	1,022	658	364
	Pulaski....................	51	41	10		Kitsap....................	164	128	36
	Roanoke County Police Department	164	120	44		Pierce....................	335	278	57
						Skagit....................	107	56	51
	Rockingham	166	55	111		Skamania	23	20	3
	Scott......................	26	24	2		Snohomish	323	261	62
	Spotsylvania...........	173	138	35		Spokane	191	138	53
	Stafford	186	133	53		Thurston................	113	88	25
	Surry.....................	21	12	9		Whatcom................	96	78	18
	Sussex....................	41	36	5		Yakima	106	68	38
	Warren...................	93	42	51	WASHINGTON– Nonmetropolitan Counties	Adams	21	18	3
	Washington	74	55	19		Clallam..................	42	32	10
	York.......................	101	95	6		Columbia	13	8	5
VIRGINIA– Nonmetropolitan Counties	Accomack	67	60	7		Ferry......................	20	10	10
	Alleghany...............	59	43	16		Garfield..................	12	7	5
	Augusta..................	79	68	11		Grant.....................	62	48	14
	Bath	18	18	0		Grays Harbor	73	40	33
	Bland	17	10	7		Island.....................	46	39	7
	Brunswick	47	35	12		Jefferson................	49	21	28
	Buchanan	40	30	10		Kittitas	36	29	7
	Buckingham............	25	18	7		Klickitat	48	19	29
	Carroll	35	29	6		Lewis	59	42	17
	Charlotte	36	33	3		Lincoln	29	17	12
	Culpeper	94	78	16		Mason....................	59	45	14
	Dickenson..............	21	19	2		Okanogan	37	32	5
	Essex......................	19	19	0		Pacific	22	19	3
	Floyd......................	27	17	10		Pend Oreille	34	17	17
	Grayson..................	24	18	6		San Juan................	31	18	13
	Greensville.............	33	24	9		Stevens	33	29	4
	Halifax...................	43	35	8		Wahkiakum............	10	9	1
	Henry	129	115	14		Walla Walla............	31	26	5
	Highland	12	7	5		Whitman	21	17	4
	King George	45	30	15	WEST VIRGINIA– Metropolitan Counties	Berkeley................	83	57	26
	Lancaster	30	26	4		Boone	23	20	3
	Lee	39	38	1		Brooke	31	17	14
	Lunenburg	19	12	7		Cabell....................	56	40	16
	Madison	29	17	12		Clay.......................	6	5	1
	Mecklenburg	51	49	2		Hampshire	13	11	2
	Middlesex...............	22	16	6		Hancock	30	27	3
	Northampton..........	52	42	10		Jefferson................	32	26	6
	Northumberland	26	17	9		Kanawha	122	94	28
	Nottoway	21	13	8		Lincoln	7	7	0
	Orange	44	34	10		Marshall	26	23	3
	Page	63	56	7		Mineral	12	9	3
	Patrick	45	31	14		Monongalia............	51	32	19
	Prince Edward........	27	27	0		Morgan..................	11	10	1
	Rappahannock	25	24	1		Ohio......................	29	28	1
	Richmond	20	11	9		Pleasants	7	6	1
	Rockbridge	38	30	8		Preston	21	15	6
	Russell	52	33	19		Putnam..................	41	34	7
	Shenandoah	70	61	9		Wayne....................	21	18	3
	Smyth	41	41	0		Wirt.......................	2	2	0
						Wood	69	35	34

Table 80. Full-time Law Enforcement Employees, by Metropolitan and Nonmetropolitan County, 2006 (*Contd.*)

(Number.)

State	County	Total law enforcement employees	Total officers	Total civilians	State	County	Total law enforcement employees	Total officers	Total civilians
WEST VIRGINIA– **Nonmetropolitan Counties**	Barbour	6	5	1		Clark	70	65	5
	Braxton	9	8	1		Crawford	25	24	1
	Calhoun	5	3	2		Dodge	165	51	114
	Doddridge	5	5	0		Door	61	46	15
	Fayette	35	30	5		Dunn	22	20	2
	Gilmer	5	5	0		Florence	18	10	8
	Grant	6	6	0		Forest	37	35	2
	Greenbrier	31	25	6		Grant	47	25	22
	Hardy	10	9	1		Green	52	31	21
	Harrison	40	38	2		Green Lake	40	18	22
	Jackson	21	15	6		Iron	19	11	8
	Lewis	15	13	2		Jackson	43	20	23
	Logan	29	19	10		Jefferson	125	98	27
	Marion	36	25	11		Juneau	53	42	11
	Mason	23	16	7		Lafayette	27	15	12
	McDowell	16	14	2		Langlade	41	16	25
	Mercer	33	29	4		Lincoln	55	27	28
	Mingo	20	18	2		Manitowoc	98	52	46
	Monroe	7	7	0		Marinette	61	28	33
	Nicholas	28	24	4		Marquette	42	42	0
	Pendleton	6	3	3		Menominee	11	9	2
	Pocahontas	12	7	5		Monroe	44	41	3
	Raleigh	62	48	14		Oneida	86	38	48
	Randolph	9	7	2		Pepin	18	17	1
	Ritchie	9	7	2		Polk	75	28	47
	Roane	8	7	1		Portage	87	43	44
	Summers	7	6	1		Price	22	20	2
	Taylor	10	7	3		Richland	20	18	2
	Tucker	4	4	0		Rusk	31	27	4
	Tyler	6	5	1		Sauk	146	108	38
	Upshur	12	10	2		Sawyer	34	26	8
	Webster	5	5	0		Shawano	57	39	18
	Wetzel	9	9	0		Taylor	43	22	21
	Wyoming	20	19	1		Trempealeau	49	23	26
WISCONSIN– **Metropolitan Counties**	Brown	316	144	172		Vernon	39	25	14
	Calumet	45	24	21		Vilas	70	34	36
	Chippewa	69	55	14		Walworth	218	83	135
	Columbia	90	41	49		Washburn	32	15	17
	Dane	516	424	92		Waupaca	124	106	18
	Douglas	85	29	56		Waushara	64	25	39
	Eau Claire	96	54	42		Wood	76	42	34
	Fond du Lac	115	54	61	**WYOMING–** **Metropolitan Counties**	Laramie	62	46	16
	Iowa	40	28	12		Natrona	52	43	9
	Kenosha	310	104	206	**WYOMING–** **Nonmetropolitan Counties**	Albany	21	16	5
	Kewaunee	40	36	4		Big Horn	20	11	9
	La Crosse	102	41	61		Campbell	59	43	16
	Marathon	170	64	106		Carbon	34	18	16
	Milwaukee	912	533	379		Converse	19	12	7
	Oconto	64	26	38		Crook	13	6	7
	Outagamie	196	76	120		Fremont	34	29	5
	Ozaukee	93	72	21		Goshen	16	9	7
	Pierce	53	51	2		Hot Springs	13	9	4
	Racine	257	169	88		Johnson	13	12	1
	Rock	178	87	91		Lincoln	39	16	23
	Sheboygan	174	77	97		Niobrara	14	4	10
	St. Croix	85	78	7		Park	52	19	33
	Washington	166	66	100		Platte	10	7	3
	Waukesha	332	144	188		Sheridan	25	19	6
	Winnebago	189	126	63		Sublette	37	32	5
WISCONSIN– **Nonmetropolitan Counties**	Adams	53	53	0		Sweetwater	40	28	12
	Ashland	28	17	11		Teton	41	20	21
	Barron	65	47	18		Uinta	36	23	13
	Bayfield	40	21	19		Washakie	10	8	2
	Buffalo	21	10	11		Weston	15	7	8
	Burnett	57	35	22					

Table 81. Full-Time Law Enforcement Employees, by State and Other Agencies, 2006

(Number.)

State	State/Other Agency	Unit/Office	Total law enforcement employees	Total officers	Total civilians
ALABAMA– **State Agencies**	Alabama Alcoholic Beverage Control Board..		117	97	20
	Alabama Conservation Department Marine Police....................................		80	67	13
	Alabama Department of Mental Health		5	4	1
	Alabama Public Service Commission Enforcement Division...................		7	7	0
	State Capitol Police		24	16	8
ALABAMA– **Other Agencies**	24th Judicial Circuit Drug and Violent Crime Task Force		4	3	1
	City of Montgomery, Housing Authority Investigative Unit		3	3	0
	Huntsville International Airport		24	17	7
	Marshall County Drug Enforcement Unit		6	5	1
ALASKA– **State Agencies**	Alcohol Beverage Control Board..		5	1	4
ALASKA– **Other Agencies**	Anchorage International Airport		57	54	3
	Fairbanks International Airport		17	16	1
ARKANSAS– **State Agencies**	Camp Robinson		26	16	10
	State Capitol Police		22	19	3
CALIFORNIA– **State Agencies**	Atascadero State Hospital..		135	122	13
	California State Fair		8	4	4
	Department of Parks and Recreation	Capital	797	703	94
	Napa State Hospital		94	88	6
	Sonoma Developmental Center		9	8	1
CALIFORNIA– **Other Agencies**	East Bay Regional Parks	Alameda County	79	57	22
	Fontana Unified School District		22	14	8
	Grant Joint Union High School		27	21	6
	Monterey Peninsula Airport		7	6	1
	Port of San Diego Harbor		164	136	28
	San Bernardino Unified School District		77	24	53
	San Francisco Bay Area Rapid Transit	Contra Costa County	269	176	93
	Stockton Unified School District		21	15	6
COLORADO– **State Agencies**	Colorado Mental Health Institute		58	17	41
COLORADO– **Other Agencies**	Two Rivers Drug Enforcement Team		7	7	0
CONNECTICUT–State **Agencies**	State Capitol Police		34	26	8
DELAWARE– **State Agencies**	Attorney General:	Kent County	63	37	26
		New Castle County	281	147	134
		Sussex County	46	23	23
	Division of Alcohol and Tobacco Enforcement		18	14	4
	Environmental Control..		13	12	1
	Fish and Wildlife		34	29	5
	Office of Narcotics and Dangerous Drugs..		4	4	0
	Park Rangers		22	22	0
	River and Bay Authority		63	49	14
	State Capitol Police		61	38	23
	State Fire Marshal		52	19	33
DELAWARE– **Other Agencies**	Drug Enforcement Administration..	Wilmington Resident Office	11	8	3
	Wilmington Fire Department..		12	12	0
DISTRICT OF COLUMBIA– **Other Agencies**	Metro Transit Police..		515	374	141
	National Zoological Park..		23	23	0
FLORIDA–State Agencies	Capitol Police		84	60	24
	Department of Environmental Protection, Division of Law Enforcement:..	Alachua County	6	6	0
		Bay County	9	9	0
		Brevard County	5	5	0
		Broward County	4	4	0
		Citrus County	1	1	0
		Collier County	1	1	0
		Columbia County	1	1	0
		Duval County	11	8	3
		Franklin County	1	1	0
		Hernando County	1	1	0
		Hillsborough County	13	8	5
		Jackson County	1	1	0

Table 81. Full-Time Law Enforcement Employees, by State and Other Agencies, 2006 (*Contd.*)

(Number.)

State	State/Other Agency	Unit/Office	Total law enforcement employees	Total officers	Total civilians
		Lake County	1	1	0
		Lee County	7	6	1
		Leon County	43	14	29
		Levy County	2	2	0
		Manatee County	2	2	0
		Marion County	2	2	0
		Martin County	3	3	0
		Miami-Dade County	10	10	0
		Monroe County	8	7	1
		Nassau County	1	1	0
		Okaloosa County	1	1	0
		Orange County	12	9	3
		Palm Beach County	7	5	2
		Pinellas County	2	2	0
		Polk County	1	1	0
		Sarasota County	1	1	0
		Seminole County	3	3	0
		St. Johns County	1	1	0
		Volusia County	5	5	0
		Walton County	2	2	0
	Department of Insurance:...	Broward County	23	18	5
		Duval County	10	8	2
		Escambia County	7	5	2
		Hillsborough County	20	16	4
		Lee County	5	4	1
		Miami-Dade County	25	19	6
		Orange County	15	12	3
		Palm Beach County	21	17	4
	Department of Law Enforcement:	Duval County, Jacksonville	153	44	109
		Escambia County, Pensacola	77	23	54
		Hillsborough County, Tampa	205	58	147
		Lee County, Fort Myers	73	29	44
		Leon County, Tallahassee	977	167	810
		Miami-Dade County, Miami	180	101	79
		Orange County, Orlando	210	60	150
	Florida Game Commission...		835	670	165
	State Fire Marshal		116	90	26
	State Treasurer's Office..	Division of Insurance Fraud	22	10	12
FLORIDA–Other Agencies	Duval County Schools..		26	11	15
	Florida School for the Deaf and Blind..		20	10	10
	Fort Lauderdale Airport..		144	93	51
	Jacksonville Airport Authority		44	33	11
	Lee County Port Authority		64	40	24
	Melbourne International Airport		12	11	1
	Miami-Dade County Public Schools		250	208	42
	Miccosukee Tribal..		72	51	21
	Palm Beach County School District		243	162	81
	Port Everglades..		170	65	105
	Sarasota-Bradenton International Airport		13	13	0
	Seminole Tribal..		185	137	48
	St. Petersburg-Clearwater International Airport		7	7	0
	Tampa International Airport		144	61	83
	Volusia County Beach Management		68	64	4
GEORGIA–State Agencies	Georgia Bureau of Investigation	Headquarters	807	262	545
	Georgia Department of Transportation..	Office of Investigation	3	3	0
	Georgia Public Safety Training Center		162	24	138
	Georgia World Congress...		35	34	1
	Ports Authority	Savannah	93	56	37
GEORGIA–Other Agencies	Augusta Board of Education		46	43	3
	Cherokee County Marshal		14	7	7
	Cobb County Board of Education...		39	37	2
	Fayette County Marshal		10	10	0

Table 81. Full-Time Law Enforcement Employees, by State and Other Agencies, 2006 (Contd.)

(Number.)

State	State/Other Agency	Unit/Office	Total law enforcement employees	Total officers	Total civilians
	Forsyth County Fire Investigation Unit		2	2	0
	Fulton County Marshal		65	58	7
	Gwinnett County Public Schools		24	20	4
	Macon County Schools		4	4	0
	Metropolitan Atlanta Rapid Transit Authority		331	287	44
	Muscogee City Marshal		15	14	1
	Pickens County Board of Education		4	4	0
	Richmond County Marshal		35	31	4
	Stone Mountain Park		26	22	4
ILLINOIS–State Agencies	Illinois Commerce Commission		15	8	7
	Illinois Department of Natural Resources		164	148	16
	Secretary of State Police	District 3	217	97	120
ILLINOIS–Other Agencies	Burlington Northern Santa Fe Railroad		22	19	3
	Capitol Airport Authority		4	4	0
	Chicago Fire Department	Arson Investigations	15	4	11
	Cook County Forest Preserve		88	83	5
	Crystal Lake Park District		3	3	0
	CSX Transportation		24	24	0
	Decatur Park District		5	5	0
	Du Page County Forest Preserve		29	25	4
	Elgin, Joliet and Eastern Railway		5	5	0
	John H. Stroger Hospital		63	57	6
	Lake County Forest Preserve		19	17	2
	Norfolk Southern Railway		50	49	1
	Pekin Park District		1	1	0
	Rockford Park District		19	18	1
	Springfield Park District		2	2	0
	Will County Forest Preserve		15	14	1
INDIANA–State Agencies	Northern Indiana Commuter Transportation District		8	7	1
INDIANA–Other Agencies	St. Joseph County Airport Authority		17	17	0
KANSAS–State Agencies	Kansas Alcoholic Beverage Control		33	20	13
	Kansas Bureau of Investigation		268	81	187
	Kansas Department of Wildlife and Parks		166	165	1
	Kansas Lottery Security Division		9	5	4
	Securities Office	Investigation Section	30	8	22
KANSAS–Other Agencies	Blue Valley School District		6	6	0
	Iowa Tribal		10	10	0
	Johnson County Park		18	17	1
	Kickapoo Tribal		12	7	5
	Metropolitan Topeka Airport Authority		23	18	5
	Sac and Fox Tribal		7	6	1
	Shawnee Mission Public Schools		11	11	0
	Topeka Fire Department	Arson Investigations	3	3	0
	Unified School District:	Auburn-Washburn	5	1	4
		Goddard	6	4	2
		Maize	3	3	0
		Topeka	17	16	1
	Wyandotte County Parks and Recreation		13	13	0
KENTUCKY–State Agencies	Alcohol Beverage Control		40	36	4
	Fish and Wildlife Enforcement		166	157	9
	Kentucky Horse Park		8	8	0
	Motor Vehicle Enforcement		241	162	79
	Park Security		67	67	0
	South Central Kentucky Drug Task Force	Treatment and Education	2	1	1
	Unlawful Narcotics Investigation		13	8	5
KENTUCKY–Other Agencies	Barren County Drug Task Force		2	1	1
	Buffalo Trace-Gateway Narcotics Task Force		3	3	0
	Cincinnati-Northern Kentucky International Airport		66	51	15
	Clark County School System		2	2	0
	Fayette County Schools		31	27	4
	FIVCO Area Drug Task Force		5	4	1
	Greater Hardin County Narcotics Task Force		11	10	1
	Jefferson County Board of Education		28	20	8
	Lake Cumberland Area Drug Enforcement Task Force		10	9	1
	Land Between the Lakes		4	3	1
	Lexington Bluegrass Airport		28	20	8
	Louisville Regional Airport Authority		29	20	9

Table 81. Full-Time Law Enforcement Employees, by State and Other Agencies, 2006 (*Contd.*)

(Number.)

State	State/Other Agency	Unit/Office	Total law enforcement employees	Total officers	Total civilians
	McCracken County Public Schools		4	4	0
	Nicholas County Schools		1	1	0
	Northern Kentucky Narcotics Enforcement Unit		3	2	1
	Pennyrile Narcotics Task Force		13	11	2
LOUISIANA–State Agencies	Department of Public Safety	State Capitol Detail	53	41	12
	Tensas Basin Levee District		3	2	1
MARYLAND–State Agencies	Comptroller of the Treasury	Field Enforcement Division	88	26	62
	Department of Public Safety and Correctional Services	Internal Investigations Unit	22	18	4
	General Services:	Annapolis, Anne Arundel County	80	39	41
		Baltimore City	110	43	67
	Natural Resources Police		519	284	235
	Rosewood		6	6	0
	Springfield Hospital		13	4	9
	State Fire Marshal		74	43	31
	Transit Administration		207	146	61
	Transportation Authority		599	441	158
MARYLAND–Other Agencies	Maryland-National Capital Park Police:	Montgomery County	109	84	25
		Prince George's County	106	79	27
MASSACHUSETTS– State Agencies	Massachusetts Bay Transportation Authority	Suffolk County	258	244	14
MICHIGAN–Other Agencies	Bishop International Airport		7	7	0
	Huron-Clinton Metropolitan Authority		37	36	1
	Wayne County Airport		132	119	13
MINNESOTA–State Agencies	Capitol Security	St. Paul	50	11	39
MINNESOTA– Other Agencies	Minneapolis-St. Paul International Airport		125	84	41
	Three Rivers Park District		38	21	17
MISSOURI–State Agencies	Capitol Police		38	31	7
MISSOURI–Other Agencies	Clay County Park Authority		7	7	0
	Jackson County Park Rangers		21	19	2
	Lambert-St. Louis International Airport		101	86	15
	St. Charles County Park Rangers		10	10	0
	St. Peters Ranger Division		5	5	0
MONTANA–State Agencies	Gambling Investigations Bureau		20	17	3
NEVADA–State Agencies	Taxicab Authority		61	35	26
NEVADA–Other Agencies	Clark County School District		166	134	32
	Washoe County School District		39	35	4
NEW HAMPSHIRE– State Agencies	Liquor Commission		32	22	10
NEW JERSEY–State Agencies	Department of Human Services		145	132	13
	Human Services	Woodland Township	5	5	0
	Hunterdon Development Center		9	9	0
	New Jersey Transit Police		266	205	61
	Palisades Interstate Parkway		27	26	1
NEW JERSEY– Other Agencies	Park Police:	Camden County	22	21	1
		Morris County	33	32	1
		Union County	364	325	39
	Prosecutor:	Atlantic County	173	75	98
		Bergen County	246	113	133
		Burlington County	152	88	64
		Camden County	248	168	80
		Cape May County	71	29	42
		Cumberland County	95	30	65
		Essex County	282	156	126
		Gloucester County	95	33	62
		Hudson County	228	104	124
		Hunterdon County	51	19	32
		Mercer County	168	107	61
		Middlesex County	195	130	65
		Monmouth County	279	76	203
		Morris County	155	71	84
		Ocean County	159	72	87
		Passaic County	221	89	132
		Salem County	21	17	4
		Somerset County	114	56	58

Table 81. Full-Time Law Enforcement Employees, by State and Other Agencies, 2006 *(Contd.)*

(Number.)

State	State/Other Agency	Unit/Office	Total law enforcement employees	Total officers	Total civilians
		Sussex County	52	31	21
		Union County	250	80	170
		Warren County	63	22	41
NEW MEXICO– **Other Agencies**	Acoma Tribal		19	13	6
	Santa Clara Tribal		17	10	7
	Zuni Tribal		25	14	11
NEW YORK–Other Agencies	CSX Transportation	Albany County	6	6	0
	New York City Metropolitan Transportation Authority		818	748	70
	Norfolk Southern Railway	Erie County	3	3	0
	Suffolk County Parks		40	37	3
NORTH CAROLINA– **State Agencies**	Department of Human Resources		10	6	4
	Department of Wildlife		221	199	22
	Division of Alcohol Law Enforcement		136	114	22
	North Carolina Arboretum		4	4	0
	North Carolina State Bureau of Investigation		559	336	223
	State Capitol Police		74	57	17
	State Fairgrounds		1	1	0
	State Park Rangers:	Carolina Beach	6	4	2
		Cliffs of the Neuse	6	5	1
		Crowders Mountain	8	5	3
		Dismal Swamp	4	3	1
		Elk Knob	2	2	0
		Eno River	9	4	5
		Falls Lake Recreation Area	23	21	2
		Fort Fisher	4	3	1
		Fort Macon	5	4	1
		Goose Creek	3	3	0
		Gorges	4	3	1
		Hammocks Beach	7	5	2
		Hanging Rock	8	6	2
		Jockey's Ridge	7	5	2
		Jones Lake	8	5	3
		Jordan Lake Recreation Area	17	13	4
		Kerr Lake	12	12	0
		Lake James	4	3	1
		Lake Norman	7	4	3
		Lake Waccamaw	3	2	1
		Lumber River	6	5	1
		Medoc Mountain	4	2	2
		Merchants Millpond	5	4	1
		Morrow Mountain	7	5	2
		Mt. Mitchell	5	4	1
		New River-Mount Jefferson	10	8	2
		Pettigrew	4	4	0
		Pilot Mountain	4	4	0
		Raven Rock	4	2	2
		Singletary Lake Group Camp	1	1	0
		South Mountains	8	6	2
		Stone Mountain	9	7	2
		Weymouth Woods Sandhills Preserve	6	3	3
		William B. Umstead	5	5	0
NORTH CAROLINA– **Other Agencies**	Asheville Regional Airport		17	16	1
	Caswell Center Hospital		4	4	0
	Cherokee Tribal		46	42	4
	Durham County Alcohol Beverage Control Law Enforcement Office		2	2	0
	Nash County Alcohol Beverage Control Enforcement		2	2	0
	Piedmont Triad International Airport		27	17	10
	Raleigh-Durham International Airport		30	28	2
	Triad Alcohol Beverage Control Law Enforcement		7	6	1
	Wilmington International Airport		14	10	4
OHIO–State Agencies	Ohio Department of Natural Resources		503	438	65
OHIO–Other Agencies	Cleveland Metropolitan Park District		78	68	10

Table 81. Full-Time Law Enforcement Employees, by State and Other Agencies, 2006 (*Contd.*)

(Number.)

State	State/Other Agency	Unit/Office	Total law enforcement employees	Total officers	Total civilians
	Greater Cleveland Regional Transit Authority....................................		114	101	13
	Hamilton County Park District..		37	34	3
	Johnny Appleseed Metropolitan Park District................................		9	9	0
	Lake Metroparks..		14	12	2
	Port Columbus International Airport..		59	41	18
	Robinson Memorial Hospital...		11	5	6
	Toledo-Lucas County Port Authority..		11	11	0
OKLAHOMA–State Agencies	Wood County Park District..		4	4	0
OKLAHOMA– Other Agencies	Capitol Park Police...		66	36	30
	Jenks Public Schools...		8	6	2
	Madill Public Schools..		1	1	0
	McAlester Public Schools...		3	3	0
	Norman Public Schools...		4	4	0
OREGON–State Agencies	Putnam City Campus..		11	8	3
	Liquor Commission:..	Benton County	1	1	0
		Clatsop County	1	1	0
		Coos County	1	1	0
		Douglas County	1	1	0
		Jackson County	7	6	1
		Klamath County	1	1	0
		Lane County	5	4	1
		Lincoln County	1	1	0
		Marion County	6	5	1
		Multnomah County	24	20	4
		Umatilla County	2	2	0
OREGON–Other Agencies		Washington County	1	1	0
PENNSYLVANIA– State Agencies	Port of Portland		67	52	15
	Bureau of Forestry:	Centre County	1	1	0
		Lackawanna County	1	1	0
	Bureau of Narcotics:..	Berks County	15	14	1
		Blair County	18	15	3
		Bucks County	15	14	1
		Carbon County	15	14	1
		Centre County	18	15	3
		Chester County	31	31	0
		Clearfield County	18	15	3
		Clinton County	18	15	3
		Delaware County	31	31	0
		Erie County	13	11	2
		Huntingdon County	18	15	3
		Juniata County	18	15	3
		Lehigh County	15	14	1
		Luzerne County	21	15	6
		Lycoming County	18	15	3
		Mifflin County	18	15	3
		Monroe County	15	14	1
		Montgomery County	15	14	1
		Montour County	18	15	3
		Northampton County	15	14	1
		Northumberland County	18	15	3
		Philadelphia County	31	31	0
		Potter County	18	15	3
		Schuylkill County	15	14	1
		Snyder County	18	15	3
		Tioga County	18	15	3
		Union County	18	15	3
		Westmoreland County	31	23	8
	Department of Environmental Resources		14	7	7
	State Capitol Police..		141	132	9
PENNSYLVANIA– Other Agencies	State Park Police..	Pymatuning	3	3	0
	Allegheny County Port Authority		68	45	23
	County Detective:	Berks County	34	34	0
		Butler County	4	4	0
		Dauphin County	16	13	3
		Lebanon County	6	6	0

Table 81. Full-Time Law Enforcement Employees, by State and Other Agencies, 2006 (*Contd.*)

(Number.)

State	State/Other Agency	Unit/Office	Total law enforcement employees	Total officers	Total civilians
		Lehigh County	13	12	1
		Westmoreland County	58	15	43
		York County	12	11	1
	Delaware County District Attorney..	Criminal Investigation Division	34	30	4
	Harrisburg International Airport		19	14	5
	Tyrone Area School District		1	1	0
	Westmoreland County Park		22	22	0
RHODE ISLAND– **State Agencies**	Department of Environmental Management...		43	35	8
SOUTH CAROLINA– **State Agencies**	Bureau of Protective Services		71	67	4
	Department of Mental Health		97	60	37
	Department of Natural Resources:	Abbeville County	3	3	0
		Aiken County	6	6	0
		Allendale County	3	3	0
		Anderson County	4	4	0
		Bamberg County	3	3	0
		Barnwell County	3	3	0
		Beaufort County	8	8	0
		Berkeley County	9	9	0
		Calhoun County	3	3	0
		Charleston County	28	24	4
		Cherokee County	3	3	0
		Chester County	3	3	0
		Chesterfield County	2	2	0
		Clarendon County	7	7	0
		Colleton County	5	5	0
		Darlington County	3	3	0
		Dillon County	2	2	0
		Dorchester County	7	7	0
		Edgefield County	3	3	0
		Fairfield County	4	4	0
		Florence County	7	5	2
		Georgetown County	10	10	0
		Greenville County	4	4	0
		Greenwood County	4	4	0
		Hampton County	4	4	0
		Horry County	7	7	0
		Jasper County	3	3	0
		Kershaw County	5	5	0
		Lancaster County	3	3	0
		Laurens County	6	6	0
		Lee County	2	2	0
		Lexington County	6	6	0
		Marion County	3	3	0
		Marlboro County	3	3	0
		McCormick County	5	5	0
		Newberry County	5	5	0
		Oconee County	6	6	0
		Orangeburg County	5	5	0
		Pickens County	9	7	2
		Richland County	30	21	9
		Saluda County	3	3	0
		Spartanburg County	3	3	0
		Sumter County	5	5	0
		Union County	4	4	0
		Williamsburg County	6	6	0
		York County	5	5	0
	Employment Security Commission		3	3	0
	Forestry Commission:	Bamberg County	1	1	0
		Beaufort County	1	1	0
		Berkeley County	1	1	0
		Charleston County	1	1	0
		Chesterfield County	5	5	0
		Clarendon County	1	1	0
		Colleton County	2	2	0
		Darlington County	1	1	0

Table 81. Full-Time Law Enforcement Employees, by State and Other Agencies, 2006 (*Contd.*)

(Number.)

State	State/Other Agency	Unit/Office	Total law enforcement employees	Total officers	Total civilians
		Fairfield County	1	1	0
		Florence County	1	1	0
		Georgetown County	1	1	0
		Greenville County	1	1	0
		Hampton County	1	1	0
		Horry County	2	2	0
		Kershaw County	3	3	0
		Lexington County	2	2	0
		Oconee County	1	1	0
		Orangeburg County	2	2	0
		Pickens County	3	3	0
		Sumter County	2	2	0
		Williamsburg County	2	2	0
		York County	1	1	0
	South Carolina School for the Deaf and Blind		1	1	0
	State Museum		4	3	1
	State Ports Authority		80	40	40
	State Transport Police:	Abbeville County	11	11	0
		Aiken County	42	28	14
		Allendale County	10	10	0
		Anderson County	15	12	3
		Berkeley County	23	20	3
		Cherokee County	9	9	0
		Darlington County	14	14	0
SOUTH CAROLINA–	United States Department of Energy	Savannah River Plant	59	47	12
Other Agencies	Charleston County Aviation Authority		36	25	11
	Columbia Metropolitan Airport		24	20	4
	Greenville-Spartanburg International Airport		21	16	5
	Whitten Center		3	3	0
SOUTH DAKOTA–					
State Agencies	Division of Criminal Investigation		142	42	100
TENNESSEE–State Agencies	Alcoholic Beverage Commission		60	36	24
	State Fire Marshal		31	26	5
	State Park Rangers:	Bicentennial Capitol Mall	6	6	0
		Big Hill Pond	2	2	0
		Big Ridge	4	4	0
		Bledsoe Creek	5	2	3
		Booker T. Washington	3	3	0
		Burgess Falls Natural Area	4	2	2
		Cedars of Lebanon	4	4	0
		Chickasaw	4	4	0
		Cove Lake	13	4	9
		Cumberland Mountain	4	4	0
		Cumberland Trail	5	5	0
		David Crockett	4	4	0
		David Crockett Birthplace	3	3	0
		Dunbar Cave Natural Area	2	2	0
		Edgar Evins	4	4	0
		Fall Creek Falls	8	8	0
		Fort Loudon State Historic Park	4	4	0
		Fort Pillow State Historic Park	1	1	0
		Frozen Head Natural Area	6	3	3
		Harpeth Scenic Rivers	3	3	0
		Harrison Bay	5	5	0
		Henry Horton	8	4	4
		Hiwassee/Ocoee State Scenic Rivers	5	5	0
		Indian Mountain	1	1	0
		Johnsonville State Historic Park	3	1	2
		Long Hunter	4	4	0

Table 81. Full-Time Law Enforcement Employees, by State and Other Agencies, 2006 *(Contd.)*

(Number.)

State	State/Other Agency	Unit/Office	Total law enforcement employees	Total officers	Total civilians
		Meeman-Shelby Forest	6	6	0
		Montgomery Bell	7	7	0
		Mousetail Landing	2	2	0
		Natchez Trace	5	5	0
		Nathan Bedford Forrest	3	3	0
		Norris Dam	4	4	0
		Old Stone Fort State Archaeological Area	3	3	0
		Panther Creek	3	3	0
		Paris Landing	5	5	0
		Pickett	4	4	0
		Pickwick Landing	5	5	0
		Pinson Mounds State Archaeological Park	2	2	0
		Radnor Lake Natural Area	6	6	0
		Red Clay State Historic Park	5	2	3
		Reelfoot Lake	4	4	0
		Roan Mountain	4	4	0
		Rock Island	4	4	0
		Sgt. Alvin C. York	2	2	0
		South Cumberland Recreation Area	6	6	0
		Standing Stone	4	4	0
		Sycamore Shoals State Historic Park	1	1	0
		Tim's Ford	4	4	0
		T.O. Fuller	3	3	0
		Warrior's Path	5	5	0
	TennCare Office of Inspector General		61	16	45
	Tennessee Bureau of Investigation		460	178	282
	Tennessee Department of Revenue	Special Investigations Unit	51	29	22
	Wildlife Resources Agency:	Region 1	42	41	1
		Region 2	60	56	4
		Region 3	41	40	1
		Region 4	45	44	1
TENNESSEE–Other Agencies	Chattanooga Metropolitan Airport		10	10	0
	Dickson Parks and Recreation		3	2	1
	Drug Task Force:	3rd Judicial District	7	6	1
		4th Judicial District	2	1	1
		5th Judicial District	9	7	2
		8th Judicial District	2	2	0
		9th Judicial District	1	1	0
		10th Judicial District	10	8	2
		12th Judicial District	2	2	0
		13th Judicial District	5	4	1
		14th Judicial District	2	2	0
		17th Judicial District	5	4	1
		18th Judicial District	8	7	1
		19th Judicial District	6	5	1
		21st Judicial District	12	10	2
		22nd Judicial District	3	3	0
		23rd Judicial District	11	9	2
		24th Judicial District	7	6	1
		31st Judicial District	1	1	0
	Knoxville Metropolitan Airport		46	27	19
	Memphis International Airport		62	51	11
	Metropolitan Board of Parks and Recreation	Nashville-Davidson	26	25	1
	Nashville International Airport		83	67	16
	Smyrna/Rutherford County Airport Authority		4	4	0
	Tri-Cities Regional Airport		17	16	1
	West Tennessee Violent Crime Task Force		7	6	1
	Amarillo International Airport		15	15	0
	Cameron County Park Rangers		10	10	0
	Dallas-Fort Worth International Airport		296	167	129
TEXAS–Other Agencies	Hospital District:	Dallas County	82	54	28

Table 81. Full-Time Law Enforcement Employees, by State and Other Agencies, 2006 (*Contd.*)

(Number.)

State	State/Other Agency	Unit/Office	Total law enforcement employees	Total officers	Total civilians
		Tarrant County	49	32	17
	Independent School District:	Aldine	46	38	8
		Alvin	19	16	3
		Angleton	5	4	1
		Austin	94	65	29
		Bay City	8	7	1
		Cedar Hill	15	7	8
		Conroe	59	44	15
		Corpus Christi	54	32	22
		East Central	9	8	1
		Ector County	25	23	2
		El Paso	43	35	8
		Fort Bend	54	44	10
		Hempstead	2	2	0
		Humble	24	19	5
		Judson	20	18	2
		Katy	42	33	9
		Kaufman	5	4	1
		Killeen	11	11	0
		Klein	45	31	14
		Laredo	114	26	88
		Mexia	3	3	0
		Midland	22	7	15
		North East	41	35	6
		Pasadena	40	33	7
		Raymondville	4	4	0
		Spring	35	33	2
		Spring Branch	38	29	9
		Taft	2	2	0
		Tyler	11	10	1
		United	134	35	99
UTAH–State Agencies	Parks and Recreation		85	84	1
	Wildlife Resources		75	68	7
UTAH–Other Agencies	Granite School District		28	16	12
	Utah County Attorney Investigations Division		7	5	2
VERMONT–State Agencies	Attorney General		4	4	0
	Department of Liquor Control	Division of Enforcement and Licensing	23	17	6
	Department of Motor Vehicles		32	28	4
	Fish and Wildlife Department...............................	Law Enforcement Division	42	40	2
VIRGINIA–State Agencies	Alcoholic Beverage Control Commission		169	125	44
	Department of Conservation and Recreation............		232	104	128
	Southside Virginia Training Center		21	18	3
	Virginia State Capitol...		86	76	10
VIRGINIA–Other Agencies	Chesapeake Bay Bridge-Tunnel		80	43	37
	Norfolk Airport Authority		42	35	7
	Port Authority..	Norfolk	85	78	7
	Reagan National Airport......................................		253	186	67
	Richmond International Airport		45	32	13
WASHINGTON–Other Agencies	Colville Tribal...		40	27	13
	Lummi Tribal..		19	17	2
	Nisqually Tribal...		14	11	3
	Nooksack Tribal..		7	6	1
	Port of Seattle		126	101	25
	Skokomish Tribal...		11	9	2
	Swinomish Tribal...		13	11	2
WEST VIRGINIA– State Agencies	Capitol Protective Services..................................		25	20	5
	Department of Natural Resources:	Barbour County	1	1	0
		Berkeley County	3	3	0
		Boone County	1	1	0
		Braxton County	4	4	0
		Brooke County	1	1	0
		Calhoun County	2	2	0
		Clay County	2	2	0
		Doddridge County	1	1	0
		Fayette County	2	2	0

Table 81. Full-Time Law Enforcement Employees, by State and Other Agencies, 2006 (*Contd.*)

(Number.)

State	State/Other Agency	Unit/Office	Total law enforcement employees	Total officers	Total civilians
		Gilmer County	1	1	0
		Grant County	2	2	0
		Greenbrier County	2	2	0
		Hampshire County	4	3	1
		Hancock County	1	1	0
		Hardy County	2	2	0
		Harrison County	3	3	0
		Jackson County	2	2	0
		Jefferson County	1	1	0
		Kanawha County	13	9	4
		Lewis County	2	2	0
		Lincoln County	1	1	0
		Logan County	2	2	0
		Marion County	5	4	1
		Marshall County	2	2	0
		Mason County	1	1	0
		McDowell County	2	2	0
		Mercer County	2	2	0
		Mineral County	2	2	0
		Mingo County	1	1	0
		Monongalia County	1	1	0
		Monroe County	1	1	0
		Morgan County	1	1	0
		Nicholas County	2	2	0
		Ohio County	1	1	0
		Pendleton County	2	2	0
		Pleasants County	1	1	0
		Pocahontas County	3	3	0
		Preston County	4	4	0
		Putnam County	6	5	1
		Raleigh County	6	6	0
		Randolph County	4	3	1
		Ritchie County	1	1	0
		Summers County	4	3	1
		Taylor County	1	1	0
		Tucker County	2	2	0
		Tyler County	1	1	0
		Upshur County	3	3	0
		Wayne County	2	2	0
		Webster County	1	1	0
		Wetzel County	1	1	0
		Wirt County	1	1	0
		Wood County	6	5	1
		Wyoming County	2	2	0
	State Fire Marshal	Kanawha County	40	30	10
WEST VIRGINIA– Other Agencies	Central West Virginia Drug Task Force		28	24	4
	Kanawha County Parks and Recreation		6	6	0
WISCONSIN–State Agencies	Capitol Police		53	41	12
	Department of Natural Resources		464	438	26
WISCONSIN–Other Agencies	Lac du Flambeau Tribal		12	10	2
	Menominee Tribal		25	22	3
	Oneida Tribal		29	20	9
PUERTO RICO AND OTHER OUTLYING AREAS	Guam		380	319	61
	Puerto Rico		19,158	17,430	1,728
FEDERAL AGENCY	National Institutes of Health		108	86	22

APPENDIXES

APPENDIX I—METHODOLOGY

Submitting Uniform Crime Reporting (UCR) Program data to the Federal Bureau of Investigation (FBI) is a collective effort on the part of city, county, state, tribal, and federal law enforcement agencies to present a nationwide view of crime. Law enforcement agencies in 46 states and the District of Columbia voluntarily contribute crime data to the UCR Program through their respective state UCR programs. For those states that do not have a state program, local agencies submit crime statistics directly to the FBI. The state UCR Programs function as liaisons between local agencies and the FBI. Many states have mandatory reporting requirements, and many state programs collect data beyond the scope of the UCR Program to address crime problems specific to their particular jurisdictions. In most cases, state programs also provide direct and frequent service to participating law enforcement agencies, make information readily available for statewide use, and help streamline the national program's operations.

The criteria that have been established for state programs ensure consistency and comparability in the data submitted to the national program, and also ensure regular and timely reporting. These criteria include the following: (1) The state program must conform to the national program's standards, definitions, and required information. (2) The state criminal justice agency must have a proven, effective, statewide program, and must have instituted acceptable quality control procedures. (3) The state crime reporting must cover a percentage of the population at least equal to that covered by the national program through direct reporting. (4) The state program must have adequate field staff assigned to conduct audits and to assist contributing agencies in record-keeping practices and crime-reporting procedures. (5) The state program must provide the FBI with all of the detailed data regularly collected by the FBI from individual agencies that report to the state program in the form of duplicate returns, computer printouts, and/or appropriate electronic media. (6) The state program must have the proven capability (tested over a period of time) to supply all the statistical data required in time to meet the publication deadlines of the national program.

The FBI, in order to fulfill its responsibilities in connection with the UCR Program, continues to edit and review individual agency reports for completeness and quality. National program staff members directly contact individual contributors within the state, when necessary, in connection with crime-reporting matters; staff members also coordinate such contact with the UCR Program. Upon request, they conduct training programs within the state on law enforcement record-keeping and crime-reporting procedures. The FBI conducts an audit of each state's UCR data collection procedures once every three years, in accordance with audit standards established by the federal government. Should circumstances develop in which the state program does not comply with the aforementioned requirements, the national program may institute a direct collection of Uniform Crime Reports from law enforcement agencies within the state.

Reporting Procedures

Based on records of all reports of crime received from victims, officers who discover infractions, and other sources, law enforcement agencies tabulate the number of Part I offenses brought to their attention and submit these data to the FBI every month, either directly or through their state UCR program. Part I offenses include murder, and non-negligent manslaughter, forcible rape, robbery, aggravated assault, burglary, larceny-theft, motor vehicle theft, and arson. See Appendix II for definitions of these offenses.

Law enforcement's monthly submission to the FBI includes other important information. When, through investigation, an agency determines that complaints of crimes are unfounded or false, it eliminates that offense from its crime tally through an entry on the monthly report. The report also provides the total number of actual Part I offenses, the number of offenses cleared, and the number of clearances that involve only offenders under 18 years of age. (Law enforcement can clear crimes in one of two ways: by the arrest of at least one person who is charged and turned over to the court for prosecution, or by exceptional means, in which when some element beyond law enforcement's control precludes the arrest of a known offender.) Law enforcement agencies also submit monthly to the FBI the value of property stolen and recovered in connection with the offenses and detailed information pertaining to criminal homicide and arson. In addition, the FBI collects supplementary information about offenses, such as the locations of robberies, time of day of burglaries, and other analyses about the offenses.

The expanded homicide data (details about murders such as the age, sex, and race of both the victim and the offender, the weapon used in the homicide, the circumstances surrounding the offense, and the relationship of the victim to the offender) includes the UCR Program's *Supplementary Homicide Reports* (SHRs). SHRs provide information regarding the ages, sexes, and races of murder victims and offenders; the types of weapons used in murders; the victim-to-offender relationships; and the circumstances surrounding the incidents. Law enforcement agencies are asked to complete an SHR for each murder reported to the UCR Program. The UCR Program's expanded homicide data also provide information about jusitifable homicide (the killing of a felon by either a police officer in the line of duty or a private citizen). For more information, see <http://www.fbi.gov/ucr/cius2006/offenses/expanded_information/homicide.html>.

Expanded arson data include details about the types of structures involved in arsons and arson rates per population group. For more information, see <http://www.fbi.gov/ucr/cius2006/offenses/expanded_information/data/arsontable_01.html> and <http://www.fbi.gov/ucr/cius2006/offenses/expanded_information/data/arsontable_02.html>.

The UCR Program also requires law enforcement agencies to report data regarding law enforcement employees. In addition to reporting monthly data on law enforcement officers killed or assaulted, agencies report anually on the number of full-time sworn and civilian law enforcement personnel employed as of October 31 of the reporting year.

At the end of each quarter, law enforcement agencies report summarized data on hate crimes (specific offenses that were motivated by an offender's bias against the perceived race, religion, ethnic origin, sexual orientation, or physical or mental disability). Those agencies participating in the UCR Program's National Incident-Base Reporting System (NIBRS) submit data on hate crimes monthly.

Editing Procedures

The UCR Program thoroughly examines each report it receives for arithmetical accuracy and for deviations in crime data from month to month and from present to past years that may indicate errors. UCR staff members compare an agency's monthly reports with its previous submissions and with reports from similar agencies to identify any unusual fluctuations in the agency's crime count. Large variations in crime levels may indicate modified records procedures, incomplete reporting, or changes in the jurisdiction's geopolitical structure.

Data reliability is a high priority of the national UCR program, which brings any deviations or arithmetical adjustments to the attention of state UCR programs and other submitting agencies. Typically, staff members study the monthly reports to evaluate periodic trends prepared for individual reporting units. Any significant increase or decrease becomes the subject of a special inquiry. Changes in crime reporting procedures or annexations that affect an agency's jurisdiction can influence the level of reported crime. When this occurs, the UCR Program excludes the figures for specific crime categories or totals (if necessary) from the trend tabulations.

To assist contributors in complying with UCR standards, the UCR Program provides training seminars and instructional materials on crime reporting procedures. Throughout the country, the national program maintains liaison with state programs and law enforcement personnel and holds training sessions to explain the purpose of the program, the rules of uniform classification and scoring, and the methods of assembling the information for reporting. When an individual agency has specific problems in compiling its crime statistics and its remedial efforts are unsuccessful, personnel from the FBI's Criminal Justice Information Services Division may visit the contributor to aid in resolving the difficulties.

The final responsibility for data submissions rests with the individual contributing law enforcement agency. Although every effort is made to ensure the validity of the data, accuracy of the statistics depends primarily on the adherence of each contributor to the established standards of reporting.

Population Estimation

The FBI calculated 2006 state growth rates using revised 2005 state/national population estimates and 2006 provisional state/national population estimates provided by the U.S. Census Bureau. The FBI then estimated population figures for city and county jurisdictions by applying the 2006 state growth rate to the updated 2005 Census Bureau data.

Crime Trends

Trend statistics offer the data user an additional perspective from which to study crime by showing fluctuations from year to year. Percent change tabulations in this publication are computed only for the reporting agencies that provided comparable data for the periods under consideration. The program excludes all figures from the trend calculations, except those received for common months from common agencies. Also excluded are unusual fluctuations that the program determines are the result of variables such as improved records procedures, annexations, etc.

Caution to Users

Data users should exercise care in making any direct comparison between data in this publication and those in prior issues of *Crime in the United States*. Because of differing levels of participation from year to year and reporting problems that require the UCR Program to estimate crime counts for certain contributors, the data are not comparable from year to year.

2006 Arrest Data

Because of changes in state or local agency reporting practices (updates of the National Incident-Based Reporting System), data are not comparable to previous years' data for Colorado (Denver). Limited arrest data were received from Illinois (Chicago and Rockford only). However, the Illinois State UCR Program's guidelines for reporting forcible rape arrest counts do not comply with the national UCR Program's guidelines, i.e., Illinois data include arrests made for forcible rapes of male victims. Therefore, Illinois figures for forcible rape include only the forcible rape offenses from Rockford, submitted via NIBRS, that had female victims. Because the Minnesota State UCR Program's guidelines for reporting forcible rape arrest counts do not comply with the national UCR Program's guidelines, i.e., Minnesota data include arrests made for forcible rapes of male victims, Minnesota figures for forcible rape, the violent crime total, and the total of all classes are not published. For 2006, only arrest totals (with no age or gender breakdowns) are available for Florida. No 2006 arrest data were received from the District of Columbia's Metropolitan Police Department; the only agency (Metro Transit Police) in the District of Columbia for which 12 months of arrest data were received has no attributable population. No 2006 arrest data were received from Montana. However, arrest totals for this state were estimated by the national UCR Program and were included in Table 29 "Estimated Number of Arrests, United States, 2006." No 2006 arrest data were received from the New York City Police Department. However, arrest totals for this area were estimated by the national UCR Program and were included in Table 29 "Estimated Number of Arrests, United States, 2006."

Offense Estimation

Tables 1 through 5 and Table 7 of this publication contain statistics for the entire United States. Because not all law enforcement agencies provide data for complete reporting periods, the UCR Program includes estimated crime numbers in these presentations. The program estimates offenses that occur within three types of areas: metropolitan statistical areas (MSAs), cities outside MSAs, and nonmetropolitan counties. The national program computes estimates by using the known crime figures of similar areas within a state and assigning the same proportion of crime volumes to nonreporting agencies or agencies with missing data. The estimation process considers the following: population size of agency; type of jurisdiction, e.g., police department versus sheriff's office; and geographic location.

Various circumstances require the national program to estimate offense totals for certain states. For example, some states do not provide forcible rape figures in accordance with UCR guidelines, or reporting problems at the state level that resulted in no usable data.

APPENDIX II—DEFINITIONS

The Uniform Crime Reporting (UCR) Program divides offense into two groups. Contributing agencies submit information on the number of Part I offenses known to law enforcement; those offenses cleared by arrest or exceptional means; and the age, sex, and race of persons arrested for each of these offenses. Contributors provide only arrest data for Part II offenses.

Part I offenses include murder, and nonnegligent manslaughter, forcible rape, robbery, aggravated assault, burglary, larceny-theft, motor vehicle theft, and arson.

Violent crime is composed of four offenses: murder and nonnegligent manslaughter, forcible rape, robbery, and aggravated assault. According to the UCR Program's definition, violent crimes involve force or threat of force.

Criminal homicide—a.) Murder and nonnegligent manslaughter: the willful (nonnegligent) killing of one human being by another. Deaths caused by negligence, attempts to kill, assaults to kill, suicides, and accidental deaths are excluded. The program classifies justifiable homicides separately and limits the definition to (1) the killing of a felon by a law enforcement officer in the line of duty; or (2) the killing of a felon, during the commission of a felony, by a private citizen. b.) Manslaughter by negligence: the killing of another person through gross negligence. Traffic fatalities are excluded.

Forcible rape—The carnal knowledge of a female forcibly and against her will. Assaults and attempts to commit rape by force or threat of force are also included. Statutory rape (no force used–female victim is under the age of consent) and other sex offenses are excluded. Sexual attacks on males are counted as aggravated assaults or sex offenses, depending on the circumstances and the extent of any injuries.

Robbery—The taking or attempted taking of anything of value from the care, custody, or control of a person or persons by force or threat of force or violence and/or by putting the victim in fear.

Aggravated assault—An unlawful attack by one person upon another for the purpose of inflicting severe or aggravated bodily injury. This type of assault usually is accompanied by the use of a weapon or by means likely to produce death or great bodily harm. Attempted aggravated assaults that involve the display of–or threat to use–a gun, knife, or other weapon is included in this crime category because serious personal injury would likely result if the assault were completed. When aggravated assault and larceny-theft occur together, the offense falls under the category of robbery. Simple assaults are excluded.

Property crime includes the offenses of burglary, larceny-theft, motor vehicle theft, and arson. The object of the theft-type offenses is the taking of money or property, but there is no force or threat of force against the victims. The property crime category includes arson because the offense involves the destruction of property; however, arson victims may be subjected to force.

Burglary (breaking or entering)—The unlawful entry of a structure to commit a felony or a theft. The use of force to gain entry need not have occurred. The Program has three subclassifications for burglary: forcible entry, unlawful entry where no force is used, and attempted forcible entry. The UCR definition of "structure" includes, for example, apartment, barn, house trailer or houseboat when used as a permanent dwelling, office, railroad car (but not automobile), stable, and vessel (i.e., ship).

Larceny-theft (except motor vehicle theft)—The unlawful taking, carrying, leading, or riding away of property from the possession or constructive possession of another. Examples are thefts of bicycles or automobile accessories, shoplifting, pocket-picking, or the stealing of any property or article that is not taken by force and violence or by fraud. Attempted larcenies are included. Embezzlement, confidence games, forgery, worthless checks, and the like, are excluded.

Motor vehicle theft—The theft or attempted theft of a motor vehicle. It includes the stealing of automobiles, trucks, buses, motorcycles, snowmobiles, and the like. The taking of a motor vehicle for temporary use by persons having lawful access is excluded from this definition. A motor vehicle is self-propelled and runs on land surface and not on rails. Motorboats, construction equipment, airplanes, and farming equipment are specifically excluded from this category.

Arson—Any willful or malicious burning or attempt to burn, with or without intent to defraud, a dwelling house, public building, motor vehicle, aircraft, personal property of another, and the like. Limited data are available for arson because of limited participation and varying collection procedures by local law enforcement agencies. Arson statistics are included in trend, clearance, and arrest tables throughout *Crime in the United States*, but they are not included in any estimated volume data.

In addition to reporting Part I offenses, law enforcement agencies provide the UCR Program with monthly data on persons arrested for all crimes except traffic violations. These arrest data include the age, sex, and race of arrestees for both Part I and Part II offenses. **Part II** offenses encompass all crimes, except traffic violations, that are not classified as Part I offenses, including:

Other assaults (simple)—Assaults and attempted assaults which are not of an aggravated nature and do not result in serious injury to the victim.

Forgery and counterfeiting—The altering, copying, or imitating of something, without authority or right, with the intent to deceive or defraud by passing the copy or thing altered or imitated as that which is original or genuine; or the selling, buying, or possession of an altered, copied, or imitated thing with the intent to deceive or defraud. Attempts are included.

Fraud—The intentional perversion of the truth for the purpose of inducing another person or other entity in reliance upon it to part with something of value or to surrender a legal right. Fraudulent conversion and obtaining of money or property by false pretenses. Confidence games and bad checks, except forgeries and counterfeiting, are included.

Embezzlement—The unlawful misappropriation or misapplication by an offender to his/her own use or purpose of money, property, or some other thing of value entrusted to his/her care, custody, or control.

Stolen property; buying, receiving, possessing—Buying, receiving, possessing, selling, concealing, or transporting any property with the knowledge that it has been unlawfully taken, as by burglary, embezzlement, fraud, larceny, robbery, etc. Attempts are included.

Vandalism—To willfully or maliciously destroy, injure, disfigure, or deface any public or private property, real or personal, without the consent of the owner or person having custody or control by cutting, tearing, breaking, marking, painting, drawing, covering with filth, or any other such means as may be specified by local law. Attempts are included.

Weapons; carrying, possessing, etc.—The violation of laws or ordinances prohibiting the manufacture, sale, purchase, transportation, possession, concealment, or use of firearms, cutting instruments, explosives, incendiary devices, or other deadly weapons. Attempts are included.

Prostitution and commercialized vice—The unlawful promotion of or participation in sexual activities for profit, including attempts.

Sex offenses (except forcible rape, prostitution, and commercialized vice)—Statutory rape, offenses against chastity, common decency, morals, and the like. Attempts are included.

Drug abuse violations—The violation of laws prohibiting the production, distribution, and/or use of certain controlled substances. The unlawful cultivation, manufacture, distribution, sale, purchase, use, possession, transportation, or importation of any controlled drug or narcotic substance. Arrests for violations of state and local laws, specifically those relating to the unlawful possession, sale, use, growing, manufacturing, and making of narcotic drugs. The following drug categories are specified: opium or cocaine and their derivatives (morphine, heroin, codeine); marijuana; synthetic narcotics/manufactured narcotics that can cause true addiction (demerol, methadone); and dangerous nonnarcotic drugs (barbiturates, benzedrine).

Gambling—To unlawfully bet or wager money or something else of value; assist, promote, or operate a game of chance for money or some other stake; possess or transmit wagering information; manufacture, sell, purchase, possess, or transport gambling equipment, devices, or goods; or tamper with the outcome of a sporting event or contest to gain a gambling advantage.

Offenses against the family and children—Unlawful nonviolent acts by a family member (or legal guardian) that threaten the physical, mental, or economic well-being or morals of another family member and that are not classifiable as other offenses, such as assault or sex offenses. Attempts are included.

Driving under the influence—Driving or operating a motor vehicle or common carrier while mentally or physically impaired as the result of consuming an alcoholic beverage or using a drug or narcotic.

Liquor laws—The violation of state or local laws or ordinances prohibiting the manufacture, sale, purchase, transportation, possession, or use of alcoholic beverages, not including driving under the influence and drunkenness. Federal violations are excluded.

Drunkenness—To drink alcoholic beverages to the extent that one's mental faculties and physical coordination are substantially impaired. Excludes driving under the influence.

Disorderly conduct—Any behavior that tends to disturb the public peace or decorum, scandalize the community, or shock the public sense of morality.

Vagrancy—The violation of a court order, regulation, ordinance, or law requiring the withdrawal of persons from the streets or other specified areas; prohibiting persons from remaining in an area or place in an idle or aimless manner; or prohibiting persons from going from place to place without visible means of support.

All other offenses—All violations of state or local laws not specifically identified as Part I or Part II offenses, except traffic violations.

Suspicion—Arrested for no specific offense and released without formal charges being placed.

Curfew and loitering laws (persons under 18 years of age)—Violations by juveniles of local curfew or loitering ordinances.

Runaways (persons under 18 years of age)—Limited to juveniles taken into protective custody under the provisions of local statutes.

APPENDIX III—GEOGRAPHIC AREA DEFINITIONS

The UCR Program collects crime data and supplemental information that make it possible to generate a variety of statistical compilations, including data presented by reporting areas. These statistics allow data users to analyze local crime data in conjunction with those for areas of similar geographic location or population size. The reporting areas that the UCR Program uses in its data breakdowns include community types, population groups, and regions and divisions. For community types, the UCR Program considers proximity to metropolitan areas using the designations created by the U.S. Office of Management and Budget (OMB). (Generally, sheriffs, county police, and state police report crimes within counties but outside of cities; local police report crimes within city limits.) The number of inhabitants living in a locale (based on the U.S. Census Bureau's figures) determines the population group into which the program places it. For its geographic breakdowns, the UCR Program divides the United States into regions, divisions, and states.

The 2006 state growth rates are calculated using revised 2005 state/national population estimates and 2006 provisional state/national population estimates provided by the U.S. Census Bureau. The population figures for city and county jurisdictions were estimated by applying the 2006 state growth rate to the updated 2005 U.S. Census Bureau data.

Regions and Divisions

The map below illustrates the four regions of the United States, along with their nine subdivisions as established by the Census Bureau. The UCR Program uses this widely recognized geographic organization when compiling the nation's crime data. The regions and divisions are as follows:

Northeast

New England—Connecticut, Maine, Massachusetts, New Hampshire, Rhode Island, and Vermont

Middle Atlantic—New York, New Jersey, and Pennsylvania

Midwest

East North Central—Illinois, Indiana, Michigan, Ohio, and Wisconsin

West North Central—Iowa, Kansas, Minnesota, Missouri, Nebraska, North Dakota, and South Dakota

South

South Atlantic—Delaware, District of Columbia, Florida, Georgia, Maryland, North Carolina, South Carolina, Virginia, and West Virginia

East South Central—Alabama, Kentucky, Mississippi, and Tennessee

West South Central—Arkansas, Louisiana, Oklahoma, and Texas

West

Mountain—Arizona, Colorado, Idaho, Montana, Nevada, New Mexico, Utah, and Wyoming

Pacific—Alaska, California, Hawaii, Oregon, and Washington

Community Types

To assist data users who wish to analyze and present uniform statistical data about metropolitan areas, the UCR Program uses reporting units that represent major population centers. The program compiles data for the following three types of communities:

Metropolitan statistical areas (MSAs)—Each MSA contains a principal city or urbanized area with a population of at least 50,000 inhabitants. MSAs include the principal city, the county in which the city is located, and other adjacent counties that have a high degree of economic and social integration with the principal city and county (as defined by the OMB), which is measured through commuting. In the UCR Program, counties within an MSA are considered metropolitan counties. In addition, MSAs may cross state boundaries.

In 2006, approximately 83.1 percent of the Nation's population lived in MSAs. Some presentations in this publication refer to Metropolitan Divisions, which are subdivisions of an MSA that consists of a core with "a population of at least 2.5 million persons. A Metropolitan Division consists of one or more main/secondary counties that represent an employment center or centers, plus adjacent counties associated with the main county or counties through commuting ties," (Federal Register 65 [249]). Also, some tables reference suburban areas, which are subdivisions of MSAs that exclude the principal cities but include all the remaining cities (those having fewer than 50,000 inhabitants) and the unincorporated areas of the MSAs.

Because the elements that comprise MSAs, particularly the geographic compositions, are subject to change, the UCR Program discourages data users from making year-to-year comparisons of MSA data.

Cities Outside MSAs—Ordinarily, cities outside MSAs are incorporated areas. In 2006, cities outside MSAs made up 6.7 percent of the Nation's population.

Nonmetropolitan Counties Outside MSAs—Most nonmetropolitan counties are composed of unincorporated areas. In 2006, 10.2 percent of the population resided in nonmetropolitan counties.

Metropolitan and nonmetropolitan community types are further illustrated in the following table:

Metropolitan	Nonmetropolitan
Principal cities (50,000+ inhabitants) Suburban cities	Cities outside metropolitan areas
Metropolitan counties	Nonmetropolitan counties

Population Groups

The UCR Program uses the following population group designations:

Population Group	Political Label	Population Range
I	City	250,000 or more
II	City	100,000 to 249,999
III	City	50,000 to 99,999
IV	City	25,000 to 49,999
V	City	10,000 to 24,999
VI	City[1]	Fewer than 10,000
VIII (Nonmetropolitan county)	County[2]	N/A
IX (Metropolitan county)	County[2]	N/A

[1]Includes universities and colleges to which no population is attributed.
[2]Includes state police agencies to which no population is attributed.

Individual law enforcement agencies are the source of UCR data. The number of agencies included in each population group may vary from year to year because of population growth, geopolitical consolidation, municipal incorporation, etc. In noncensus years, the UCR Program estimates population figures for individual jurisdictions. (A more comprehensive explanation of population estimations can be found in Appendix I.)

The categories below show the number of agencies contributing to the UCR Program within each population group for 2006:

Population Group	Number of Agencies	Population Covered
I	72	54,499,586
II	189	28,264,509
III	457	31,365,930
IV	838	28,871,906
V	1,907	30,219,162
VI[1]	8,895	26,297,537
VIII (Nonmetropolitan county)[2]	3,009	30,572,430
IX (Metropolitan county)[2]	2,156	69,307,424
Total	17,523	299,398,484

[1]Includes universities and colleges to which no population is attributed.
[2]Includes state police to which no population is attributed.

APPENDIX IV—THE NATION'S TWO CRIME MEASURES

The Department of Justice administers two statistical programs to measure the magnitude, nature, and impact of crime in the nation: the Uniform Crime Reporting (UCR) Program and the National Crime Victimization Survey (NCVS). Each of these programs produces valuable information about aspects of the nation's crime problem. Because the UCR and NCVS programs are conducted for different purposes, use different methods, and focus on somewhat different aspects of crime, the information they produce together provides a more comprehensive panorama of the nation's crime problem than either could produce alone.

Uniform Crime Reporting (UCR) Program

The UCR Program, administered by the Federal Bureau of Investigation (FBI), was created in 1929 and collects information on the following crimes reported to law enforcement authorities: murder and nonnegligent manslaughter, forcible rape, robbery, aggravated assault, burglary, larceny-theft, motor vehicle theft, and arson. Law enforcement agencies also report arrest data for 21 additional crime categories.

The UCR Program compiles data from monthly law enforcement reports and from individual crime incident records transmitted directly to the FBI or to centralized state agencies that report to the FBI. The program thoroughly examines each report it receives for reasonableness, accuracy, and deviations that may indicate errors. Large variations in crime levels may indicate modified records procedures, incomplete reporting, or changes in a jurisdiction's boundaries. To identify any unusual fluctuations in an agency's crime counts, the program compares monthly reports to previous submissions of the agency and to those for similar agencies.

The FBI annually publishes its findings in a preliminary release in the spring of the following calendar year, followed by a detailed annual report, *Crime in the United States*, issued in the fall. (The printed copy of *Crime in the United States* is now published by Bernan Press.) In addition to crime counts and trends, this report includes data on crimes cleared, persons arrested (age, sex, and race), law enforcement personnel (including the number of sworn officers killed or assaulted), and the characteristics of homicides (including age, sex, and race of victims and offenders; victim-offender relationships; weapons used; and circumstances surrounding the homicides). Other periodic reports are also available from the UCR Program.

The state and local law enforcement agencies participating in the UCR Program are continually converting to the more comprehensive and detailed National Incident-Based Reporting System (NIBRS). The NIBRS provides detailed information about each criminal incident in 22 broad categories of offenses.

The UCR Program presents crime counts for the nation as a whole, as well as for regions, states, counties, cities, towns, tribal law enforcement areas, and colleges and universities. This allows for studies among neighboring jurisdictions and among those with similar populations and other common characteristics.

National Crime Victimization Survey

The NCVS, conducted by the Bureau of Justice Statistics (BJS), began in 1973. It provides a detailed picture of crime incidents, victims, and trends. After a substantial period of research, the BJS completed an intensive methodological redesign of the survey in 1993. It conducted this redesign to improve the questions used to uncover crime, update the survey methods, and broaden the scope of crimes measured. The redesigned survey collects detailed information on the frequency and nature of the crimes of rape, sexual assault, personal robbery, aggravated and simple assault, household burglary, theft, and motor vehicle theft. It does not measure homicide or commercial crimes (such as burglaries of stores).

Twice a year, Census Bureau personnel interview household members in a nationally representative sample of approximately 43,000 households (about 76,000 people). Approximately 150,000 interviews of individuals 12 years of age and over are conducted annually. Households stay in the sample for 3 years, and new households rotate into the sample on an ongoing basis.

The NCVS collects information on crimes suffered by individuals and households, whether or not those crimes were reported to law enforcement. It estimates the proportion of each crime type reported to law enforcement, and it summarizes the reasons that victims give for reporting or not reporting.

The survey provides information about victims (age, sex, race, ethnicity, marital status, income, and educational level); offenders (sex, race, approximate age, and victim-offender relationship); and crimes (time and place of occurrence, use of weapons, nature of injury, and economic consequences). Questions also cover victims' experiences with the criminal justice system, self-protective measures used by victims, and possible substance abuse by offenders. Supplements are added to the survey periodically to obtain detailed information on specific topics, such as school crime.

The BJS published the first data from the redesigned NCVS in a June 1995 bulletin. The publication of NCVS data includes *Criminal Victimization in the United States*, an annual report that covers the broad range of detailed information collected by the NCVS. The bureau also publishes detailed reports on topics such as crime against women, urban crime, and gun use in crime. The National Archive of Criminal Justice Data at the University of Michigan archives the NCVS data files to help researchers perform independent analyses.

Comparing the UCR Program and the NCVS

Because the BJS designed the NCVS to complement the UCR Program, the two programs share many similarities. As much as their different collection methods permit, the two measure the same subset of serious crimes with the same definitions. Both programs cover rape, robbery, aggravated assault, burglary, theft, and motor vehicle theft; both define rape, robbery, theft, and motor vehicle theft virtually identically. (Although rape is defined analogously, the UCR Program measures the crime against women only, and the NCVS measures it against both sexes.)

There are also significant differences between the two programs. First, the two programs were created to serve different purposes. The UCR Program's primary objective is to provide a reliable set of criminal justice statistics for law enforcement administration, operation, and management. The BJS established the NCVS to provide previously unavailable information about crime (including crime not reported to police), victims, and offenders.

Second, the two programs measure an overlapping but nonidentical set of crimes. The NCVS includes crimes both reported and not reported to law enforcement. The NCVS excludes—but the UCR Program includes—homicide, arson, commercial crimes, and crimes committed against children under 12 years of age. The UCR Program captures crimes reported to law enforcement but collects only arrest data for simple assaults and sexual assaults other than forcible rape.

Third, because of methodology, the NCVS and UCR have different definitions of some crimes. For example, the UCR defines burglary as the unlawful entry or attempted entry of a structure to commit a felony or theft. The NCVS, not wanting to ask victims to ascertain offender motives, defines burglary as the entry or attempted entry of a residence by a person who had no right to be there.

Fourth, for property crimes (burglary, theft, and motor vehicle theft), the two programs calculate crime rates using different bases. The UCR Program rates for these crimes are per capita (number of crimes per 100,000 persons), whereas the NCVS rates for these crimes are per household (number of crimes per 1,000 households). Because the number of households may not grow at the same annual rate as the total population, trend data for rates of property crimes measured by the two programs may not be comparable.

In addition, some differences in the data from the two programs may result from sampling variation in the NCVS and from estimating for nonresponsiveness in the UCR Program. The BJS derives the NCVS estimates from interviewing a sample and are, therefore, subject to a margin of error. The bureau uses rigorous statistical methods to calculate confidence intervals around all survey estimates, and describes trend data in the NCVS reports as genuine only if there is at least a 90-percent certainty that the measured changes are not the result of sampling variation. The UCR Program bases its data on the actual counts of offenses reported by law enforcement agencies. In some circumstances, the UCR Program estimates its data for nonparticipating agencies or those reporting partial data.

Apparent discrepancies between statistics from the two programs can usually be accounted for by their definitional and procedural differences, or resolved by comparing NCVS sampling variations (confidence intervals) of crimes said to have been reported to police with UCR Program statistics.

For most types of crimes measured by both the UCR Program and the NCVS, analysts familiar with the programs can exclude those aspects of crime not common to both from analysis. Resulting long-term trend lines can be brought into close concordance. The impact of such adjustments is most striking for robbery, burglary, and motor vehicle theft, whose definitions most closely coincide.

With robbery, the BJS bases the NCVS victimization rates on only those robberies reported to the police. It is also possible to remove UCR Program robberies of commercial establishments, such as gas stations, convenience stores, and banks, from analysis. When users compare the resulting NCVS police-reported robbery rates and the UCR Program noncommercial robbery rates, the results reveal closely corresponding long-term trends.

Conclusion

Each program has unique strengths. The UCR Program provides a measure of the number of crimes reported to law enforcement agencies throughout the country. The program's Supplementary Homicide Reports provide the most reliable, timely data on the extent and nature of homicides in the nation. The NCVS is the primary source of information on the characteristics of criminal victimization and on the number and types of crimes not reported to law enforcement authorities.

By understanding the strengths and limitations of each program, it is possible to use the UCR Program and NCVS to achieve a greater understanding of crime trends and the nature of crime in the United States. For example, changes in police procedures, shifting attitudes towards crime and police, and other societal changes can affect the extent to which people report and law enforcement agencies record crime. NCVS and UCR Program data can be used in concert to explore why trends in reported and police-recorded crime may differ.

INDEX

INDEX